2004

2004

ART OF THE FIRST CITIES

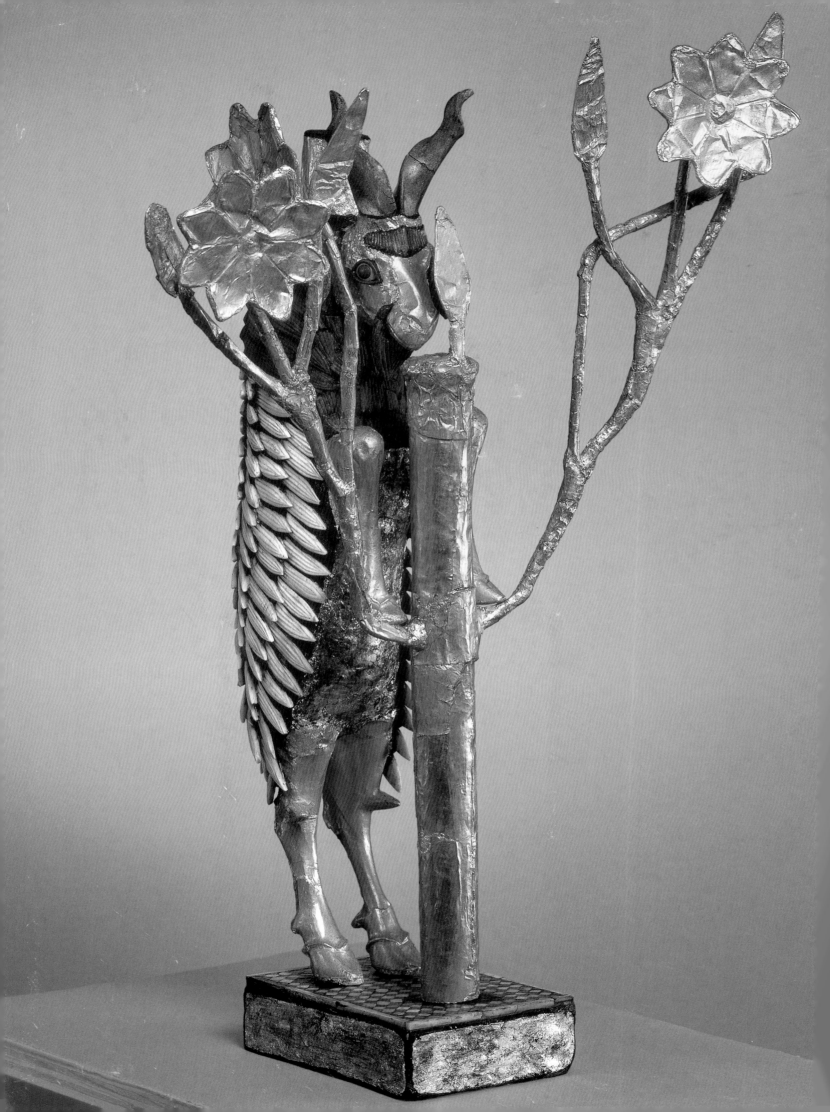

ART OF THE FIRST CITIES

The Third Millennium B.C. from the Mediterranean to the Indus

EDITED BY JOAN ARUZ

WITH RONALD WALLENFELS

The Metropolitan Museum of Art, New York

Yale University Press, New Haven and London

This volume has been published in conjunction with the exhibition "Art of the First Cities: The Third Millennium B.C. from the Mediterranean to the Indus," held at The Metropolitan Museum of Art, New York, from May 8 to August 17, 2003.

The exhibition is made possible by Dorothy and Lewis B. Cullman.

Additional support has been provided by The Hagop Kevorkian Fund.

This publication is made possible in part by The Hagop Kevorkian Fund.

Additional support has been provided by The Adelaide Milton de Groot Fund, in memory of the de Groot and Hawley families.

An indemnity has been granted by the Federal Council on the Arts and the Humanities.

Published by The Metropolitan Museum of Art, New York

John P. O'Neill, Editor in Chief
Carol Fuerstein and Ellyn Childs Allison, Editors
Bruce Campbell, Designer
Peter Antony and Douglas J. Malicki, Production
Jane S. Tai, Editorial Coordinator
Robert Weisberg, Desktop Publishing
Jean Wagner, Bibliographer

Translations from French by Jane Marie Todd, from German by Russell M. Stockman, and from Russian by Marian Schwartz

New photography of works in the Metropolitan Museum collection by Paul Lachenauer, The Photograph Studio, The Metropolitan Museum of Art.

Typeset in Diotima and Bembo
Printed on 130 gsm Lumisilk
Separations by Professional Graphics, Inc., Rockford, Illinois
Printed and bound by CS Graphics PTE, LTD, Singapore

Sources for the epigraphs in this catalogue are as follows: p. 9, The Electronic Text Corpus of Sumerian Literature 1998–, http://www-etcsl.orient.ox.ac.uk/section1/tr174.htm, accessed 2/13/02; p. 58, Cooper 1986, p. 63; p. 89, The Electronic Text Corpus of Sumerian Literature 1998–, http://www-etcsl.orient.ox.ac.uk/section2/tr211.htm, accessed 2/19/02; p. 93, George 1999, p. 203; p. 133, Pettinato 1986, p. 400; p. 148, George 1999, p. 203; p. 187, Frayne 1993, pp. 113–14; p. 237, Krebernik 1992, p. 110; p. 415, Edzard 1997, p. 78; p. 449, translated by Piotr Michalowski (see the entry for number 336 in this catalogue); p. 485, George 1999, pp. 91–92. See the bibliography for full citations.

Jacket/cover illustration: Detail, "Standard of Ur," cat. no. 52
Frontispiece: Rearing goat with a flowering plant, cat. no. 71

Maps by Anandaroop Roy

Library of Congress Cataloging-in-Publication Data
Art of the first cities : the third millennium B.C. from the Mediterranean to the Indus.
    p.   cm.
   Catalog of an exhibition being held at the Metropolitan Museum of Art from May 8 to Aug. 17, 2003.
   Includes bibliographical references and index.
   ISBN 1-58839-043-8 (hc.) — ISBN 1-58839-044-6 (pbk.) —
ISBN 0-300-09883-9 (Yale)
   1. Art, Ancient — Exhibitions. 2. Cities and towns, Ancient — Exhibitions.
I. Metropolitan Museum of Art (New York, N.Y.)

N5330.A68 2003
711'.4'0930747471— dc21   2003044482

CONTENTS

Director's Foreword

Philippe de Montebello   vii

Acknowledgments

Mahrukh Tarapor   ix

Acknowledgments

Joan Aruz   xiii

Contributors to the Catalogue   xvi

Lenders to the Exhibition   xviii

Chronology   xx

Map   xxii

Note to the Reader   xxiv

ART OF THE FIRST CITIES: THE THIRD MILLENNIUM B.C. FROM THE MEDITERRANEAN TO THE INDUS

Joan Aruz   3

CITIES OF THE SOUTH

URUK AND THE FORMATION OF THE CITY

Hans J. Nissen   11

ART OF THE EARLY CITY-STATES

Donald P. Hansen   21

The Proto-Elamite Period

Holly Pittman   42

Fara

Joachim Marzahn   56

Excavations in the Diyala Region

Karen L. Wilson   58

Stone Sculpture Production

Jean-François de Lapérouse   62

Nippur

Jean M. Evans   66

Tello (Ancient Girsu)

Béatrice André-Salvini   68

Metalworking Techniques

Jean-François de Lapérouse   79

Al Ubaid

Paul Collins   84

Kish

Paul Collins   89

THE ROYAL TOMBS OF UR

Julian Reade   93

The Tomb of Puabi

Paul Collins   108

The Great Death Pit at Ur

Julian Reade   120

CITIES OF THE NORTH

MARI AND THE SYRO-MESOPOTAMIAN WORLD

Jean-Claude Margueron   135

The Treasure of Ur from Mari

Nadja Cholidis   139

EBLA AND THE EARLY URBANIZATION OF SYRIA

Paolo Matthiae   165

Tell Umm el-Marra

Glenn M. Schwartz   179

Tell Banat

Anne Porter and Thomas McClellan   184

THE FIRST GREAT EMPIRE

ART OF THE AKKADIAN DYNASTY

Donald P. Hansen   189

Lost-Wax Casting

Jean-François de Lapérouse   210

Tell Mozan (Ancient Urkesh)

Giorgio Buccellati and
Marilyn Kelly-Buccellati   224

Tell Brak in the Akkadian Period

Jean M. Evans   228

FROM THE MEDITERRANEAN TO THE INDUS

ART AND INTERCONNECTIONS
IN THE THIRD MILLENNIUM B.C.
Joan Aruz 239

EGYPT AND THE NEAR EAST IN
THE THIRD MILLENNIUM B.C.
James P. Allen 251

THE AEGEAN AND WESTERN
ANATOLIA: SOCIAL FORMS
AND CULTURAL RELATIONSHIPS
Claus Reinholdt 255

*The Early Bronze Age Jewelry Hoard
from Kolonna, Aigina*
Claus Reinholdt 260

Troy
Eleni Drakaki 262

*Poliochni and the Civilization of the
Northeastern Aegean*
Lena Papazoglou-Manioudaki 270

THE CENTRAL ANATOLIAN
PLATEAU: THE TOMBS OF
ALACA HÖYÜK
Oscar White Muscarella 277

THE NORTH CAUCASUS
Elena Izbitser 289

The Maikop (Oshad) Kurgan
Yuri Piotrovsky 290

Novosvobodnaya
Yuri Piotrovsky 297

Susa: Beyond the Zagros Mountains
Paul Collins 298

THE GULF: DILMUN AND MAGAN
D. T. Potts 307

Copper Alloys and Metal Sources
Jean-François de Lapérouse 310

Tell Abraq
Paul Collins 313

The Island of Tarut
Paul Collins 323

"Intercultural Style" Carved Chlorite Objects
Joan Aruz 325

PATHWAYS ACROSS EURASIA
Maurizio Tosi and C. C. Lamberg-Karlovsky 347

Altyn-depe
Yuri Piotrovsky 355

Gonur-depe
Elisabetta Valtz Fino 366

THE INDUS CIVILIZATION
Jonathan Mark Kenoyer 377

Baluchistan
Paul Collins 381

Cities of the Indus Valley
Paul Collins 385

Beads of the Indus Valley
Jonathan Mark Kenoyer 395

THE DYNASTIES OF LAGASH AND UR

APPROACHING THE DIVINE:
MESOPOTAMIAN ART AT THE END
OF THE THIRD MILLENNIUM B.C.
Jean M. Evans 417

*The Rediscovery of Gudea Statuary in the
Hellenistic Period*
Béatrice André-Salvini 424

LITERATURE AND LEGACY

THE EARLIEST SCHOLASTIC
TRADITION
Piotr Michalowski 450

URUK AND THE WORLD OF GILGAMESH
Beate Salje 479

THE MESOPOTAMIAN LEGACY:
ORIGINS OF THE GENESIS
TRADITION
Ira Spar 485

*Appendix: Problems of Third-Millennium-B.C.
Chronology*
Julian Reade 496

Bibliography 499

Index 524

Photograph Credits 540

DIRECTOR'S FOREWORD

The roots of our own civilization lie in developments that took place more than six thousand years ago in the distant lands of western Asia. The region known to ancient authors as Mesopotamia—the "land between the rivers" of the Tigris and Euphrates—was home to one of the world's great early civilizations, thriving at the eastern end of the so-called Fertile Crescent, which stretched westward toward Egypt. In this harsh landscape arose the first cities, property of the gods, who granted kings the power to bring prosperity to the people. The need to administer and embellish the important institutions of the city—the temple and the palace—occasioned such significant inventions as writing, the creation of monumental architecture, and the flowering of the arts in the service of gods and rulers. The extraordinary innovations effected in Mesopotamia had a profound impact on surrounding cultures in Anatolia, Syria-Levant, Iran, and the Gulf. The desire for rare and precious materials—such as lapis lazuli, carnelian, diorite, gold, silver, and ivory—encouraged long-distance trade and cultural exchanges across Iran, Central and South Asia, the Gulf, and the Arabian Sea.

"Art of the First Cities: The Third Millennium B.C. from the Mediterranean to the Indus" explores the supreme artistic achievements of this seminal period in world history in the Mesopotamian heartland and across the vast expanse of Asia. The exhibition begins with the extraordinary developments of the late fourth millennium B.C. in the first important city, Uruk, where writing was invented and monumental architecture and art flourished. During the succeeding Early Dynastic, Akkadian, and Ur III periods of the third millennium B.C., rival city-states and, for a short time, the first empire emerged in Mesopotamia. Kings glorified their rule by building temples to their gods and leading their armies in battle, celebrating their achievements with ritual banquets—all portrayed on finely carved monumental steles and smaller reliefs. Divine support was maintained by dedicating exceptional objects to the gods. These include statues of rulers depicted as worshipers with clasped hands. Other elite personages—among them singers, scribes, courtiers, and priests—were represented in a similar fashion, in statues that have been found in temples throughout Mesopotamia and Syria, especially at the site of Mari in the middle Euphrates region. The first true palaces were built at sites such as Ebla in western Syria. These buildings were decorated with images of battle and housed archives and raw materials documenting an extensive trade network. Kings, queens, and religious leaders were buried, along with their servants, in the Royal Cemetery at Ur, their tombs arrayed with spectacular jewelry, musical instruments, gaming boards, and animal sculpture, all created from gold, silver, lapis lazuli, carnelian, and other precious materials.

Diplomatic, trading, and military activities brought Mesopotamia into contact with other regions and civilizations, which had their own vibrant artistic traditions. Our exhibition presents masterpieces of these other cultures as well as jewelry and finely carved vessels that share a corpus of forms and imagery with Mesopotamia, demonstrating not only the breadth but also the depth of intercultural exchange along the vast trading network that stretched between the Mediterranean and the Indus.

"Art of the First Cities" stands as a testimony to the birth and first development of some of mankind's greatest achievements. From our own perspective at the threshold of a new third millennium, this exhibition takes on greater meaning, bringing together as it does works of art from museums and collections in many countries. It celebrates mankind's common achievements as well as its great diversity.

We wish to extend our profound gratitude to authorities in the numerous institutions around the world that have expressed their support of this exhibition by granting loans of many of their greatest masterpieces, some of which have never before traveled. We greatly appreciate the exceptional contributions of various countries through which flow the great Tigris, Euphrates, Oxus, and Indus Rivers. Lying along and beyond the Fertile Crescent, modern Syria, Turkey, Bahrain, Kuwait, Saudi Arabia, Sharjah (UAE), Turkmenistan, Uzbekistan, and Pakistan are linked culturally and historically to the ancient lands of Sumer, Akkad, Anatolia, Dilmun, Magan, and Meluhha. We are also grateful to museums in Greece and Russia for the loan of exceptional treasures from the Aegean islands and the north Caucasus, respectively. The nineteenth- and early-twentieth-century practice of dividing finds among institutions participating in archaeological explorations has ensured that large numbers of Mesopotamian works of art are included in European and American collections. Thanks to the generosity of The British Museum in London, the Musée du Louvre in Paris, the Vorderasiatisches Museum in Berlin, the University of Pennsylvania Museum of Archaeology and Anthropology in Philadelphia, and the Oriental Institute of the University of Chicago, the Mesopotamian core of the exhibition has been enriched by critical loans of immense beauty and significance, more than compensating for our inability to borrow objects from Iraqi institutions, which results from the present international situation. The pieces we are able to show include the famous "Standard of Ur" from the Royal Cemetery at Ur, which captures the essence of Mesopotamian kingship; the magnificent statue of Gudea depicted as architect with plan; the exquisite cylinder seal of an Akkadian royal scribe; and the sensitively carved head of a ram from Uruk. Private collectors, prominent among them Georges Antaki, George Ortiz, Jonathan and Jeannette Rosen, and Shelby White and Leon Levy, have also provided important works of Near Eastern and Central Asian art, and we are deeply grateful to these individuals.

People in many countries have helped us with their contributions to this exhibition, and they are mentioned in acknowledgments by Mahrukh Tarapor and by Joan Aruz that follow. Here, however, I wish to single out and thank Mahrukh Tarapor, Associate Director for Exhibitions, who over the past few years has devoted tireless efforts to the realization of this exhibition and is the person most responsible for its success. Traveling frequently to Saudi Arabia and the Gulf countries,

as well as to Syria and Turkey, she has exhibited exceptional fortitude and diplomatic skill, thereby not only ensuring the loan of major works but also enhancing the spirit of cooperation with institutions and collectors in the Middle East. Joan Aruz, Curator in Charge of the Department of Ancient Near Eastern Art, initiated this innovative project, selecting works of art with the goal of presenting the artistic achievements of the earliest Near Eastern cities within their cultural contexts. She also conceived the format of the exhibition and catalogue, coordinating the efforts of the more than fifty leading scholars in the fields of ancient Near Eastern, Aegean, Central Asian, and Harappan art history and archaeology who collaborated on this volume.

An undertaking of this scope cannot be presented without major financial support. The Museum extends its sincere gratitude to Dorothy and Lewis B. Cullman for their exceptional generosity toward this project. In addition, we are indebted to The Hagop Kevorkian Fund for its critical contribution to the exhibition and the accompanying catalogue. We likewise recognize The Adelaide Milton de Groot Fund, in memory of the de Groot and Hawley families, for its support of the exhibition catalogue and are thankful for the kind assistance provided by the Federal Council on the Arts and the Humanities. In addition, we would like to extend gratitude to Trustee Patti Cadby Birch for her generous offer to assist the Metropolitan Museum in bringing to New York special colleagues from the Middle East for the opening of the exhibition.

Philippe de Montebello
Director
The Metropolitan Museum of Art

As of this writing, I must indicate that the loans from Syria are not assured. Throughout the years of preparation of this exhibition, the authorities in Syria have been supportive of the project and given us every indication that the loans would be approved. We have just learned, to our dismay, that at this late date, the Council of Antiquities has decided not to participate

in the Metropolitan's exhibition. We will continue our dialogue with the appropriate authorities in Syria in the hopes of persuading them to reverse this unfortunate decision and of convincing them that this is an especially opportune moment to proclaim and record their country's vital role in the birth and development of our civilization.

ACKNOWLEDGMENTS

As this catalogue goes to press, we face a world disturbed to a degree rarely seen by this generation, a world most particularly vulnerable precisely in those regions "from the Mediterranean to the Indus" that constitute the critical core of our exhibition. First and foremost, therefore, it is to friends and colleagues in that part of the world that I would like to express my own appreciation and the special thanks of the Metropolitan Museum. Our gratitude is extended for their unwavering support of this project even as the world of realpolitik draws threateningly closer to their own lives and concerns, as well as for the warmth and hospitality with which I and other members of the Museum staff were always received. Should political realities prove stronger than cultural aspirations and force withdrawals of objects from the exhibition, or even the cancellation of the exhibition, our thanks to all those listed below stand firm.

Three individuals in particular need to be singled out, not only for their early unconditional advocacy of this endeavor but also, above all, for their belief and conviction that, against all odds, the common language of culture *must* prevail. The extraordinary gesture of Sheikh Nasser Sabah al-Ahmad al-Sabah of Kuwait, who entrusted to us in the traumatic days following the events of September 11, 2001, his priceless exhibition "'Treasury of the World': Jeweled Arts of India in the Age of the Mughals" brought much-needed joy and beauty to an appreciative New York public and most especially gave the Museum the confidence to move forward with the preparations for the present exhibition. At the same time, Sheikha Hussah Sabah al-Salem al-Sabah's introductions, offered with utmost kindness and trust, opened many doors for us in the Gulf states and facilitated loans that might not normally have been available. Her beautiful homes in Kuwait and Damascus provided magical respites from the long and sometimes arduous efforts attendant upon all major international exhibitions. Through an introduction provided by Sheikh Nasser and Sheikha Hussah, in Syria we were privileged to meet and be guided by Georges Antaki, always with the greatest sensitivity and resourcefulness. Himself a discerning and generous lender to many exhibitions, Mr. Antaki took an early and enlightened interest in this undertaking. His deep knowledge and appreciation of Syria's art and history and his abiding desire to share his country's rich cultural heritage with an international audience were especially inspiring. For the many kindnesses shown to us during our frequent visits to Aleppo and for the hospitality offered to us in his extraordinary home—which evokes the old world charm of his cosmopolitan city during its heyday—we extend to him our sincerest thanks.

Among colleagues of long standing, particular mention must be made of Alpay Pasinli, former Director of the Istanbul Archaeological Museum and since 1999 General Director of Monuments and Museums, Ministry of Culture, Ankara. His early intellectual endorsement of the exhibition and his sound advice as it progressed through its various phases have proved invaluable to us. We acknowledge with deep gratitude the many insights he gave us into his beloved city of Istanbul, as well as the warm hospitality we have received from Oğuz Aydemir, Ministry Adviser, and Erol Sağmanli, President of Urart.

Our efforts in Saudi Arabia were greatly facilitated by Faisal bin Abdelrahman bin Muaammar, Deputy of the National Guard for Education and Cultural Affairs and General Supervisor, King Abdulaziz Public Library, Riyadh. It has been an immense pleasure to work with Sa'ad A. al-Rashid, Deputy Minister of Antiquities and Museums, who has been supportive of our efforts from the very beginning, as well as with Abdullah S. al-Saud, Director General of Museums, and Abdul Aziz A. Al Shaikh, Director, National Museum, Riyadh, who have been the most generous and forthcoming of colleagues. We extend our thanks, in addition, to Majeed Khan, Adviser, Deputy Ministry of Antiquities and Museums, Khalifah Al-Khalifah, and Ali Al-Hammad. Our sincere appreciation is also expressed to Abdulrheem i Hobrom, who assisted us during the long hours spent photographing objects for the catalogue and packing them. It was a privilege and an honor to meet Her Royal Highness Princess Adela bint Abdullah bin Abdulaziz, Chairman, Consultative Committee, National Museum, Riyadh, and Her Royal Highness Princess Haifa bint Mansour bin Bandar bin Abdulaziz, and we acknowledge with gratitude their kind and gracious hospitality. A special word of thanks is also offered to Sheikh Rifaat Sheikh El-Ard for his generous loans over the years to the Metropolitan Museum's Department of Arms and Armor and Department of Islamic Art and for his friendship and ready assistance to us in Riyadh.

In Bahrain, the Metropolitan Museum would like to thank Sheikha Mai Bint Mohammed Bin Ebrahim Al-Khalifa, Assistant Undersecretary for Culture and National Heritage, Ministry of Information, Culture, and National Heritage, and Khalid Mohammed Al-Sendi, Acting Director of Archaeology and Heritage, Ministry of Information, Culture, and National Heritage, whose professionalism and expertise proved indispensable. The loans from Sharjah were facilitated by Issam Bin Saqer Al-Qasimi, Chairman, Department of Culture and Information; Abdullah Mohamed Al Owais, Director General, Department of Culture and Information; Ali Al Marri, Director, Sharjah Archaeological Museum; and Sabah Abboud Jasim, Directorate of Antiquities, Department of Culture and Information. In Kuwait, acknowledgment is due to Mohammad Ghanem Al-Rumaihi, former Secretary General, National Council for Culture, Arts, and Letters, and his successor, Bader Abdul Wahab al-Refai, for their help in the process of securing loans.

As I write, the loans from Syria still hang in the balance. Negotiations continue but, whatever the outcome, great efforts have been made there on our behalf, and we thank His Excellency Prime Minister Mohammad Mostafa Miro for his early support of the exhibition. Minister of Culture Najwa Kassab Hassan has also been at all times an enlightened friend and colleague. In his former capacity as Director General of Antiquities and Museums, Abdal Razzaq Moaz followed our project for many years, and we appreciate his continuing interest as Vice Minister of Culture. We also thank The Honorable Theodore H. Kattouf, United States Ambassador to Syria, for his encouragement and Elizabeth Dibble, Counselor for Press and Cultural Affairs, for her sincere and energetic commitment to our cause. We are equally grateful to The Honorable Edward P. Djerejian, former United States Ambassador to Syria and now Director, James A. Baker III Institute for Public Policy of Rice University, Houston, who used his good offices to advance our objectives.

In Greece, Minister of Culture Evangelos Venizelos kindly extended support for the exhibition, and we appreciate as well the efforts of Lina Mendoni, Secretary General, Ministry of Culture, in expediting the loan process. And in spite of having the entire renovation of the National Archaeological Museum in Athens on his hands, Director Nikolaos Kaltsas always found time in his busy schedule to confer with us.

Other individuals have befriended both me and this project at various critical junctures and cannot go unmentioned: Metropolitan Museum Trustee Patti Cadby Birch; Mikhail Piotrovsky, Director, State Hermitage Museum, St. Petersburg; John Curtis, Keeper, Department of the Ancient Near East, The British Museum, London; Ute Collinet, Secrétaire Général, Réunion des Musées Nationaux, Paris; Brahim Alaoui, Chef du Département Musée–Expositions, Institut du Monde Arabe, Paris; Navina Haidar, Assistant Curator, Department of Islamic Art, The Metropolitan Museum of Art, New York; Salman Haidar and Martand Singh, both of New Delhi; and Raju Singh, Ventours International Travel, Bombay. Contributing to our ever-expanding network of indebtedness, a chance introduction by Cristina Macaya of Madrid led to a meeting in Bombay with Sir Ronald Grierson and opened doors in London to Lord Powell of Bayswater and philanthropist Wafic Said. For all their efforts on our behalf the Metropolitan Museum offers heartfelt thanks. Finally, Salam (Sue) Kaoukji, curator at the Dar al-Athar al-Islamiyyah, Kuwait, has been a constant and comforting source of encouragement, humor, and discretion, and I have benefited greatly from her perceptive knowledge of parts of the world very new to me.

For some of the international aspects of this undertaking, we have been fortunate in securing the assistance of Congressman Eliot L. Engel; Congresswoman Carolyn B. Maloney; and Tim Goeglein, Special Assistant to the President of the United States and Deputy Director of Public Liaison. At the Metropolitan, the efforts of Harold Holzer, Vice President for Communications and Marketing; Thomas P. Schuler, Associate Manager and Assistant to the President for Government Affairs; and our valued consultant Todd Howe of Whiteman Osterman and Hanna Government Solutions have been critical in enlisting the support of these officials.

We would also like to acknowledge the great talent and artistry of Munnu Kasliwal of Gem Palace, Jaipur, India. In an exciting collaboration with the Museum overseen by Sally Pearson, Vice President and General Manager of Merchandise and Retail, and Valerie Troyansky, General Manager, Product Development, and working closely with Joanne Lyman, Manager, Jewelry Reproduction, utilizing materials and techniques that date from the third millennium, Munnu has handcrafted an innovative selection of jewelry and decorative objects to accompany the exhibition.

At the Metropolitan, many colleagues have contributed significantly in various capacities toward the realization of this exhibition, and I add my voice to that of Joan Aruz in thanking them. But political uncertainties have thrust on this project more than the usual number of vicissitudes, making overwhelming demands on three individuals in particular. To them my professional debt is tremendous; personally it is incalculable. Franz Schmidt, Manager for Special Projects, often summoned to travel with me at very short notice, has been a stoic and resourceful colleague who has handled crises, both big and small, with exceptional versatility. It is not too much to say that he is now as beloved in the many countries in which we have worked together as he is at the Museum. Martha Deese, Senior Assistant for Exhibitions, working in close tandem with the Department of Ancient Near Eastern Art, has been, for the rest of the Museum, the pivotal administrative center of the exhibition. Every aspect of the project has been subjected to, and improved by, her rigorous and intelligent scrutiny. Ably assisted by Alexandra Klein, Assistant for Exhibitions, she maintained the smooth running of the Exhibitions Office, effecting a near seamless transition during my many absences from the Museum during the lengthy process of loan negotiations, and it gives me special pleasure to acknowledge here her always forthcoming and indispensable efforts. In the final analysis, however, it is usually to a single vision and commitment that any project owes its successful realization. That vision and that commitment, rocklike in their steadfastness, have been provided by Philippe de Montebello, Director. His absolute confidence in the transcending power of the language of art has been a source of inspiration for everyone involved in this exhibition—not only the Museum's staff but also the many lenders across the world who at an uncertain moment in time have parted with their treasures because they share his conviction.

Mahrukh Tarapor
Associate Director for Exhibitions

ACKNOWLEDGMENTS

"Art of the First Cities: The Third Millennium B.C. from the Mediterranean to the Indus" is a project of vast scope, as the exhibition's title reveals. Fifty-four lenders in many countries have supported the undertaking in the form of loans to the exhibition, and more than fifty authors have made contributions to the catalogue. We are profoundly grateful to all of them for their commitment, as well as to many others who have shared ideas regarding the formulation of the exhibition and advised on the choice of loans and the means of securing them. First and foremost, we thank Philippe de Montebello, Director of The Metropolitan Museum of Art, for his vision and his belief in the significance and broad implications of the presentation. His steadfast support throughout many difficult moments over the last few years has been a precious resource. Mahrukh Tarapor, Associate Director for Exhibitions, tirelessly pursued loans, frequently in the most problematic of circumstances. Donald P. Hansen, Craig Hugh Smyth Professor of Fine Arts, Institute of Fine Arts, New York University—whose understanding of third-millennium-B.C. Mesopotamian art and archaeology is unparalleled—generously offered both his time and his expertise. His two outstanding essays, one on the Early Dynastic period and the other on the Akkadian period, are major contributions to the catalogue. These efforts, along with those of many others, have helped us create a vehicle for demonstrating the magnificent artistic and intellectual legacy of the world's first cities.

We wish to extend special thanks to the following colleagues for providing curatorial and other scholarly assistance at different stages of the project: AUSTRALIA, D. T. Potts, Professor of Middle Eastern Archaeology, University of Sydney. BAHRAIN, Khalid Mohammed Al-Sendi, Acting Director of Archaeology and Heritage, Ministry of Information, Culture, and National Heritage. ENGLAND, John Curtis, Keeper, Christopher Walker, Deputy Keeper, Dominique Collon, Assistant Keeper, and Julian Reade, Department of the Ancient Near East, The British Museum, London; P. R. S. Moorey, Vice-Gerent, Wolfson College, Oxford. FRANCE, Annie Caubet, Conservateur générale, chargé du Département des Antiquités Orientales, Musée du Louvre, Paris, and members of her staff, particularly Béatrice André-Salvini, Françoise Demange, and Agnès Benoit, Curators; Professor Jean-Claude Margueron, Director, French Archaeological Mission at Mari, Syria, and Directeur d'Études, École Pratique des Hautes Études, Paris. GERMANY, Beate Salje, Director, Vorderasiatisches Museum, Berlin, and members of her staff, particularly Joachim Marzahn and Lutz Martin, Curators, Nadja Cholidis, Research Fellow, and Raphaela Heitmann, Fellow; Almut Hoffman, Scientific Coordinator, Museum für Vor- und Frühgeschichte, Berlin. GREECE, Nicoletta Divari-Valakou, Director of Prehistoric and Classical Antiquities, Ministry of Culture; Nikolaos Kaltsas, Director, Lena Papazoglou-Manioudaki, Curator in Charge, Prehistoric Collection, Eleni Tsivilika, Curator of the Prehistoric Collection, National Archaeological Museum, Athens; Maria Andreadaki-Vlasaki, Acting Director, Eleni S. Banou, Curator, Archaeological Museum, Heraklion. ITALY, Paolo Matthiae, Director, Italian Archaeological Expedition at Ebla, Syria, and Professor of Archaeology and Art History of the Ancient Near East, University "La Sapienza," Rome; Maurizio Tosi, Chair Professor of Paleoethnology, University of Bologna. JAPAN, Mihoko Koyama, Founder, Shinji Shumeikai; Hiroko Koyama, Chairman of the Board of the Shumei Culture Foundation; Hajime Inagaki, Curator, Head of Research, Miho Museum. KUWAIT, Bader Abdul Wahab al-Refai, Secretary General, National Council for Culture, Arts, and Letters; Mohammad Ghanem Al-Rumaihi, former Secretary General; Shihab Al-Shihab, Director, Department of Antiquities and Museums, Kuwait National Museum; Sultan al-Duwaish, Head of Department of Excavations, Department of Antiquities and Museums. PAKISTAN, Department of Archaeology and Museums, Ministry of Minorities, Culture, Sports, Tourism, and Youth Affairs; Jonathan Mark Kenoyer, Professor of Anthropology, University of Wisconsin, Madison, who played a major role in coordinating the loans from museums in Pakistan, as well as bringing jewelry reproductions to New York during the exhibition. RUSSIA, Mikhail Piotrovsky, Director, and Yuri Piotrovsky, Curator, Department of Archaeology, The State Hermitage Museum, St. Petersburg; Vadim Alekshin, Deputy Director, Institute of the History of Material Culture of the Russian Academy of Sciences, St. Petersburg; A. N. Abregov, National Museum of the Republic of Adygeya. SAUDI ARABIA, Sa'ad A. al-Rashid, Deputy Minister of Antiquities and Museums; Abdullah S. al-Saud, Director General of Museums; and Abdul Aziz A. Al Shaikh, Director, National Museum, Riyadh. SHARJAH, UNITED ARAB EMIRATES, Sabah Abboud

Jasim, Directorate of Antiquities, Department of Culture and Information. SWITZERLAND, George Ortiz, for generously lending his bull-man statue, for arranging new photography, and for his contribution to the catalogue; Werner Rutishauser, Curator, Sammlung Ebnöther, Museum zu Allerheiligen, Schaffhausen; Professor Hans Peter Isler, Director, Archäologisches Institut, Zurich University. SYRIA, Georges Antaki; Abdal Razzaq Moaz, Vice Minister of Culture, and colleagues in the Department of Antiquities and Museums; Tammam Fakouch, Director General of Antiquities and Museums, Ministry of Culture; and Rabab Sha'ar. TURKEY, Alpay Pasinli, General Director of Monuments and Museums; Aykut Özet, Deputy General Director of Monuments and Museums, assisted by Nilüfer Ertan, Director, Cultural Activities Bureau; Halil Özek, Director, Istanbul Archaeological Museum; Zeynep Kiziltan, Curator, Eski Şark Museum, Istanbul; Emel Yurttagül, Deputy Director, Ankara Museum of Anatolian Civilizations, for their generosity in providing loans of Anatolian material from Troy and Alaca Höyük and of major Mesopotamian objects that came into Turkish collections during the period of the Ottoman Empire. TURKMENISTAN, Mukhammed A. Mamedov, Chief of Memorials Protection and Restoration Department, Turkmenistan Ministry of Culture; Ovezmuhammet Mametnurov, Director, National Museum of Turkmenistan Named After Saparmurat Turkmenbashi, Ashgabat, for his support of the first foreign loan of materials from that museum; Viktor Sarianidi, Director of Excavations, Gonur Depe. UZBEKISTAN, Deputy Prime Minister Hamidullah Karamatov and Professor Bekhzad Yuldadshev, Uzbekistan Academy of Sciences, Tashkent. UNITED STATES: Rita Freed, Curator, and Joan Cummins, Assistant Curator, Museum of Fine Arts, Boston; Douglas G. Schultz, Director, Albright-Knox Art Gallery, Buffalo; C. C. Lamberg-Karlovsky, Professor of Archaeology, Peabody Museum, Harvard University, Cambridge; Karen L. Wilson, Director of the Oriental Institute Museum of The University of Chicago; Glenn Markoe, Curator, Cincinnati Art Museum; Elsie Peck, Curator of Ancient Art, Detroit Institute of Arts; Marc F. Wilson, Director, Nelson-Atkins Museum of Art, Kansas City; Benjamin R. Foster, Curator, and Ulla Kasten, Museum Editor, Yale Babylonian Collection, New Haven; Laurel Kendall, Curator of Asian Ethnographic Collections, and Paul Beelitz, Director of Collections and Archives, Division of Anthropology, American Museum of Natural History, New York; James F. Romano, Curator, Department of Egyptian Art, Brooklyn Museum of Art, who coordinated the special loan from Robin B. Martin, to whom we are most grateful; Charles E. Pierce Jr., Director, and Sidney Babcock, Associate Curator of Seals and Tablets, Pierpont Morgan Library, New York; John M. Lundquist, Chief Librarian, Oriental Division, and Roseann Panebienco, Registrar, The New York Public Library; Ralph P. Minasian, President of The Hagop Kevorkian Fund, New York, for his unflagging encouragement and continuing support; Richard L. Zettler, Curator in Charge, Holly Pittman, Professor, Department of the History of Art, Shannon White, Assistant Keeper, and Fredrik Hiebert, Assistant Professor of Anthropology, University of Pennsylvania and the Museum of Archaeology and Anthropology, Philadelphia; Louise Virgin, Curator of Asian Art, Worcester Art Museum; Jeannette and Jonathan P. Rosen; Shelby White and Leon Levy.

Many members of the staff of the Metropolitan Museum have been engaged for a number of years in the preparation of this complex exhibition. Ronald Wallenfels, Associate Curator, worked closely with me in editing the catalogue, providing wise counsel. Jean M. Evans, Curatorial Assistant, wrote a major essay and numerous entries for the catalogue, and did a heroic job in coordinating the catalogue illustrations and layout with the Editorial Department; Paul Collins, Research Associate, wrote many entries, did research on the chronology, and worked on educational projects related to the exhibition, including a web feature. Both assisted with editing the catalogue and with the preparation of maps and exhibition labels, as well as providing countless illustrated loan lists. Melanie J. Hatz played a major role in designing the exhibition and coordinating the installation. Special thanks go to Elena Izbitser, Library Associate, for her assistance in communicating with Russian colleagues and in securing their contributions and illustrations. Prudence O. Harper, Curator Emerita, provided advice and encouragement at the outset of the project.

In addition, assistance in the preparation of both the catalogue and the exhibition was given by Elisabetta Valtz Fino, Oscar White Muscarella, Ira Spar, Jean-François de Lapérouse, Shoki Goodarzi, Cynthia Wilder, Beth Tedesco, Shawn Osborne, Eleni Drakaki, Melissa Eppihimer, Alice A. Petty, Sarah Scott, Sarah Davis, Karsten Boyer, David Ghezelbash, Victoria Vanzandt-Southwell, and Nanette Kelekian. We are grateful to Martha Deese, Alexandra Klein, and Sian Wetherill in the Exhibitions Office; Doralynn Pines in the Director's Office; Linda M. Sylling in Facilities Management; Rebecca Noonan in the Counsel's Office; Emily Kernan Rafferty, Senior Vice President for External Affairs; and Christine Scornavacca in Development. We would also like to voice our appreciation for the brilliant work of designers Michael Batista, Barbara Weiss, and Zack Zanolli; gratitude also goes to the exhibition-label editor Pamela Barr; installers Alexandra Walcott, Jeffrey Perhacs, and Fred Sager; educators Stella Paul, Teresa Russo, and Elizabeth Hammer-Munemura; and Chief Registrar Herbert M. Moskowitz, who had the complex task of coordinating the packing and transport of loans from many distant lands. Acknowledgment is due also to Paul Lachenaeur of The Photograph Studio of the Museum for his new photography of works in the Metropolitan's collection. Very special thanks for their uncompromising commitment, patience, and extraordinary skill in working on the catalogue go to John P. O'Neill, Editor in Chief and General Manager of Publications; Gwen Roginsky, Associate General Manager of Publications; Carol Fuerstein and Ellyn Childs Allison, Senior Editors, as well as to editors Sharon Herson, Kathleen Howard, Ruth Kozodoy, Ellen Shultz, Fronia Simpson, and Dale Tucker, who assisted them; Jane S. Tai, Editorial Coordinator; Bruce Campbell, Designer; Robert Weisberg, Desktop Publishing Manager; and Jean Wagner, Bibliographer. Gratitude is also due to Peter Antony and Douglas J. Malicki, who produced and oversaw the printing of the catalogue. Bruce White provided beautiful photographs of loan objects from the Louvre in Paris, Turkey, Saudi Arabia, Bahrain, Kuwait, and Sharjah (UAE), and Abdel Anwar Ghafour skillfully photographed the loan objects from Syrian institutions with assistance from Samer Abdel Ghafour, who facilitated photography in Syria. All of the efforts of the people acknowledged have helped us to reveal the cultures of the remote past, which stood at the beginning of the urban revolution.

Joan Aruz
Curator in Charge
Department of Ancient Near Eastern Art

CONTRIBUTORS TO THE CATALOGUE

JPA   James P. Allen
Curator, Department of Egyptian Art, The Metropolitan Museum of Art, New York

BA-S   Béatrice André-Salvini
Curator, Département des Antiquités Orientales, Musée du Louvre, Paris

JA   Joan Aruz
Curator in Charge, Department of Ancient Near Eastern Art, The Metropolitan Museum of Art, New York

SB   Sidney Babcock
Associate Curator of Seals and Tablets, The Pierpont Morgan Library, New York

ESB   Eleni S. Banou
Curator, Archaeological Museum, Heraklion

AB   Agnès Benoit
Curator, Département des Antiquités Orientales, Musée du Louvre, Paris

GB   Giorgio Buccellati
Professor Emeritus, Department of Near Eastern Languages, University of California, Los Angeles

JVC   Jeanny Vorys Canby
Research Associate, University of Pennsylvania Museum of Archaeology and Anthropology, Philadelphia

NC   Nadja Cholidis
Research Fellow, Vorderasiatisches Museum, Berlin

PC   Paul Collins
Research Associate, Department of Ancient Near Eastern Art, The Metropolitan Museum of Art, New York

SC   Sarah Collins
Assistant Keeper, Department of the Ancient Near East, The British Museum, London

FD   Françoise Demange
Curator, Département des Antiquités Orientales, Musée du Louvre, Paris

ED   Eleni Drakaki
Hagop Kevorkian Curatorial Fellow, Department of Ancient Near Eastern Art, The Metropolitan Museum of Art, New York

SD   Sally Dunham
Independent scholar

JME   Jean M. Evans
Curatorial Assistant, Department of Ancient Near Eastern Art, The Metropolitan Museum of Art, New York

PF   Pelio Fronzaroli
Director, Department of Linguistics, Università degli Studi, Florence

SG   Shoki Goodarzi
Lecturer, Department of Art, State University of New York at Stony Brook

DPH   Donald P. Hansen
Craig Hugh Smyth Professor of Fine Arts, Institute of Fine Arts, New York University

MJH   Melanie J. Hatz
Gallery Supervisor, Department of Ancient Near Eastern Art, The Metropolitan Museum of Art, New York

RH   Raphaela Heitmann
Fellow, Vorderasiatisches Museum, Berlin

EI   Elena Izbitser
Library Associate, Thomas J. Watson Library, The Metropolitan Museum of Art, New York

MK-B   Marilyn Kelly-Buccellati
Professor of Art History, Department of Art, University of California, Los Angeles

JMK   Jonathan Mark Kenoyer
Professor of Anthropology, University of Wisconsin, Madison

CCL-K C. C. Lamberg-Karlovsky
Stephen Philips Professor of Archaeology, Peabody Museum, Harvard University, Cambridge, Massachusetts

J-FL   Jean-François de Lapérouse
Associate Conservator, Department of Objects Conservation, The Metropolitan Museum of Art, New York

J-CM   Jean-Claude Margueron
Director, French Archaeological Mission at Mari, Syria, and Directeur d'Études, École Pratique des Hautes Études, Paris

LM   Lutz Martin
Curator, Vorderasiatisches Museum, Berlin

JM   Joachim Marzahn
Curator, Vorderasiatisches Museum, Berlin

PMa   Paolo Matthiae
Director, Italian Archaeological Expedition at Ebla, Syria, and
Professor of Archaeology and Art History of the Ancient Near
East, University "La Sapienza," Rome

TM   Thomas McClellan
Independent scholar

PM   Piotr Michalowski
George G. Cameron Professor of Ancient Near Eastern
Languages and Civilizations, Department of Near Eastern
Studies, University of Michigan, Ann Arbor

OWM   Oscar White Muscarella
Senior Research Fellow, Department of Ancient Near Eastern
Art, The Metropolitan Museum of Art, New York

HJN   Hans J. Nissen
Professor Emeritus, Seminar für Vorderasiatische
Altertumskunde, Freie Universität, Berlin

GO   George Ortiz
Independent scholar

LP-M   Lena Papazoglou-Manioudaki
Curator in Charge, Prehistoric Collection, National
Archaeological Museum, Athens

EP   Elsie Peck
Curator, Detroit Institute of Arts

AAP   Alice A. Petty
The Jane and Morgan Whitney Fellow, Department of Ancient
Near Eastern Art, The Metropolitan Museum of Art, New York

YP   Yuri Piotrovsky
Curator, Department of Archaeology, The State Hermitage
Museum, St. Petersburg

HP   Holly Pittman
College for Women Class of 1963 Endowed Professor in the
Humanities, Department of the History of Art, University of
Pennsylvania, Philadelphia

AP   Anne Porter
Visiting Research Fellow, The Institute for the Transregional
Study of the Contemporary Middle East, North Africa, and
Central Asia, Princeton University

DTP   D. T. Potts
Edwin Cuthbert Hall Professor of Middle Eastern
Archaeology, Department of Archaeology, University of
Sydney

JR   Julian Reade
Department of the Ancient Near East, The British Museum,
London

CR   Claus Reinholdt
Assistant, Institut für Klassische Archäologie, Paris Lodron-
Universität Salzburg

BS   Beate Salje
Director, Vorderasiatisches Museum, Berlin

GMS   Glenn M. Schwartz
Whiting Professor of Archaeology, Department of Near
Eastern Studies, Johns Hopkins University, Baltimore

IS   Ira Spar
Professor of History and Ancient Studies, Ramapo College of
New Jersey, Mahwah

MT   Maurizio Tosi
Chair Professor of Paleoethnology, University of Bologna

ET   Eleni Tsivilika
Curator of the Prehistoric Collection, National Archaeological
Museum, Athens

EVF   Elisabetta Valtz Fino
Associate Curator, Department of Ancient Near Eastern Art,
The Metropolitan Museum of Art, New York

RW   Ronald Wallenfels
Associate Curator, Department of Ancient Near Eastern Art,
The Metropolitan Museum of Art, New York

KLW   Karen L. Wilson
Director of the Oriental Institute Museum of The University
of Chicago

LENDERS TO THE EXHIBITION

The numbers in the following list refer to works in the catalogue.

BAHRAIN
Manama, Bahrain National Museum   205, 206, 207, 208, 220a, 220b, 239, 301e

ENGLAND
London, Trustees of The British Museum   9, 16a, 29, 33, 34, 35, 44a, 52, 53, 55a, 56, 60a, 66, 67a, 70b, 72, 73, 74, 75, 76, 132, 138, 139, 143, 147, 148, 150, 163c, 227, 229, 301a, 301b, 315, 319
Oxford, Visitors of the Ashmolean Museum   10c, 48, 49, 50, 51, 160, 330

FRANCE
Paris, Musée du Louvre, Département des Antiquités Orientales   30, 37, 127, 129, 135, 137, 153a, 164, 199, 200, 201, 202, 203, 204, 228, 241, 244, 248, 261, 273, 287b, 289b, 292b, 301c, 301d, 303, 304, 307, 310, 313, 314, 316

GERMANY
Berlin, Staatliche Museen zu Berlin, Museum für Vor- und Frühgeschichte   178b
Berlin, Staatliche Museen zu Berlin, Vorderasiatisches Museum   1, 2, 3, 4, 5, 12, 23, 27, 36, 42, 233, 308, 311, 321

GREECE
Aigina, Archaeological Museum of Aigina   165, 166
Athens, National Archaeological Museum   168, 171, 172, 174, 175, 176, 177, 178a, 179
Heraklion, Archaeological Museum   162

JAPAN
Shiga Prefecture, Miho Museum   253, 255, 257
Shiga Prefecture, The Shinji Shumeikai   235

KUWAIT
Al-Kuwait, National Council for Culture, Arts, and Letters, Kuwait National Museum   217, 218, 219, 220c, 220d, 220e, 220f, 220g, 221, 240

PAKISTAN
Harappa, Harappa Museum, Courtesy of the Department of Archaeology and Museums, Ministry of Minorities, Culture, Sports, Tourism, and Youth Affairs, Government of Pakistan 295b, 300b
Islamabad, Islamabad Museum, Courtesy of the Department of Archaeology and Museums, Ministry of Minorities, Culture, Sports, Tourism, and Youth Affairs, Government of Pakistan   268b, 293, 294, 296, 299
Karachi, Exploration Branch, Courtesy of the Department of Archaeology and Museums, Ministry of Minorities, Culture, Sports, Tourism, and Youth Affairs, Government of Pakistan 274, 302a
Karachi, National Museum of Pakistan, Courtesy of the Department of Archaeology and Museums, Ministry of Minorities, Culture, Sports, Tourism, and Youth Affairs, Government of Pakistan   267, 268a, 269, 270, 271, 272a, 275a, 277, 278, 286, 287a, 295a, 297, 300a
Lahore, Lahore Museum, Courtesy of the Department of Archaeology and Museums, Ministry of Minorities, Culture, Sports, Tourism, and Youth Affairs, Government of Pakistan 298, 300d
Mohenjo-daro, Mohenjo-daro Museum, Courtesy of the Department of Archaeology and Museums, Ministry of Minorities, Culture, Sports, Tourism, and Youth Affairs, Government of Pakistan   272b, 275b, 279, 280, 281, 282, 285, 288, 300c, 302b

RUSSIA
Maikop, National Museum of the Republic of Adygeya   197
St. Petersburg, Institute of the History of Material Culture of the Russian Academy of Sciences   251
St. Petersburg, The State Hermitage Museum   191, 192, 193, 194, 195, 196, 198, 250, 252

SAUDI ARABIA
Riyadh, National Museum   222, 223, 224, 225a

SWITZERLAND
Schaffhausen, Museum zu Allerheiligen, Sammlung Ebnöther 262

Zurich, Archäologische Sammlung der Universität
Zürich 8

SYRIA
Aleppo, National Museum   6, 7, 88, 89c, 93, 96, 97, 107, 109a,
109b, 111, 112, 113, 114, 116, 117, 118, 119, 120, 121, 122, 123,
124, 125, 126, 161, 178c, 232, 326a
Damascus, National Museum   25, 81, 82, 83, 84, 85, 86, 87,
89a, 89b, 90, 91a, 92, 94, 95, 100, 102, 103, 104, 105, 151, 231
Deir ez-Zor, Museum of Deir ez-Zor   91b, 98, 99, 106, 152,
154, 155, 156, 157a, 158, 159, 163a
Idlib, Idlib Museum   108, 109c, 109d, 110, 115, 322, 323, 324,
325, 326b, 326c, 327, 328

TURKEY
Ankara, Ankara Museum of Anatolian Civilizations   173c,
181, 182, 183, 184, 185, 186, 187a, 188, 189, 190
Istanbul, Eski Şark Museum   26, 39, 130, 234
Istanbul, Istanbul Archaeological Museum   167, 169b, 170a,
173a
Kayseri, Kayseri Archaeological Museum   180
Samsun, Samsun Museum   170b
Urfa, Urfa Museum   163b

TURKMENISTAN
Ashgabat, The National Museum of Turkmenistan Named
After Saparmurat Turkmenbashi   237, 249, 258, 259a, 260,
263, 265, 266

UNITED ARAB EMIRATES
Sharjah, Sharjah Archaeological Museum   209, 210, 211, 212,
213, 214, 215, 216

UNITED STATES
Brooklyn, Brooklyn Museum of Art   14, 15a

Boston, Museum of Fine Arts   131, 276, 283, 284, 289a, 290a,
292a
Buffalo, Albright-Knox Art Gallery   15b
Cambridge, Peabody Museum, Harvard University   242,
243
Chicago, Oriental Institute of The University of Chicago
16b, 17, 32, 230, 309
Cincinnati, Cincinnati Art Museum   19
Detroit, Detroit Institute of Arts   306
Kansas City, The Nelson-Atkins Museum of Arts   312a
Philadelphia, University of Pennsylvania Museum of
Archaeology and Anthropology   21, 22, 24c, 24d, 31, 41, 43,
44b, 45, 46, 47, 54, 55b, 57, 58, 59, 60b, 60c, 61, 62, 63, 64, 65, 67b,
68, 69, 70a, 71, 77, 78, 79, 80, 128, 169a, 173b, 238, 247a, 247b,
247c, 247d, 290b, 291, 317, 329, 331, 332, 333, 334, 335, 336, 337,
338, 339, 341
New Haven, Yale Babylonian Collection   10a, 10b
New York, American Museum of Natural History   245, 246,
247e
New York, The Metropolitan Museum of Art   11, 13, 20, 24a,
28, 38, 40, 136, 144, 145, 149, 153b, 187b, 225b, 259b, 264, 305,
307, 318b, 320
New York, The Pierpont Morgan Library   140, 141, 142, 146,
312b, 318a, 340
Worcester, Massachusetts, Worcester Art Museum   24b

UZBEKISTAN
Tashkent, Historical Museum of Uzbekistan   236

PRIVATE COLLECTIONS
Georges Antaki Collection, London   101
George Ortiz Collection   18
Jeannette and Jonathan Rosen   133, 134, 157b
Mrs. Constantine Sidamon-Eristoff   226
Shelby White and Leon Levy   254, 256

CHRONOLOGY

Year (BCE)	Egypt	Aegean	Anatolia		Syria		Mesopotamia
3300	Predynastic						
3200							Late Uruk
3100					■ Habuba Kabira		
3000							Jamdat Nasr
2900	Archaic	Early Bronze I	Troy I	Early Bronze I	Mari City I	Early Bronze I–II	
2800							Early Dynastic 1
2700							
2600		Poliochni Red Period	Troy II	Early Bronze II		Early Bronze III	Early Dynastic II
2500		Early Bronze II					Early Dynastic IIIA
2400	Old Kingdom	Poliochni Yellow Period			Mari City II	Early Bronze IVA (Mardikh IIb1)	Early Dynastic IIIB
2300			Troy III				Akkadian — ○ Sargon, ○ Rimush, ○ Manishtushu, ○ Naram-Sin, ○ Shar-kali-sharri
2200				Early Bronze III ■ Alaca Höyük ■ Horoztepe	Mari City III	Early Bronze IVB	Guti / Lagash — ○ Ur-Ba'u, ○ Gudea, ○ Ur-Ningirsu / Ur III — ○ Ur-Namma, ○ Shulgi, ○ Amar-Su'ena, ○ Shu-Sin, ○ Ibbi-Sin
2100	First Intermediate	Early Bronze III					
2000			Troy IV				

KEY: ■ Site ○ Ruler

Western Iran (Susa)	Eastern Iran	Gulf/Arabia	Caucasus	Western Central Asia	Baluchistan	Indus Valley	
							3300
Susa II				Namazga III	Mehrgarh V		3200
							3100
			Maikop Culture				3000
Susa III Proto-Elamite					Mehrgarh VI	Early Harappan	2900
				Namazga IV			2800
					Mehrgarh VII		2700
							2600
Susa IV							2500
	Yahya IVB	Umm an-Nar		Namazga V	Kulli	Harappan	2400
							2300
							2200
○ Puzur-Inshushinak				Namazga VI BMAC			2100
							2000

XXI

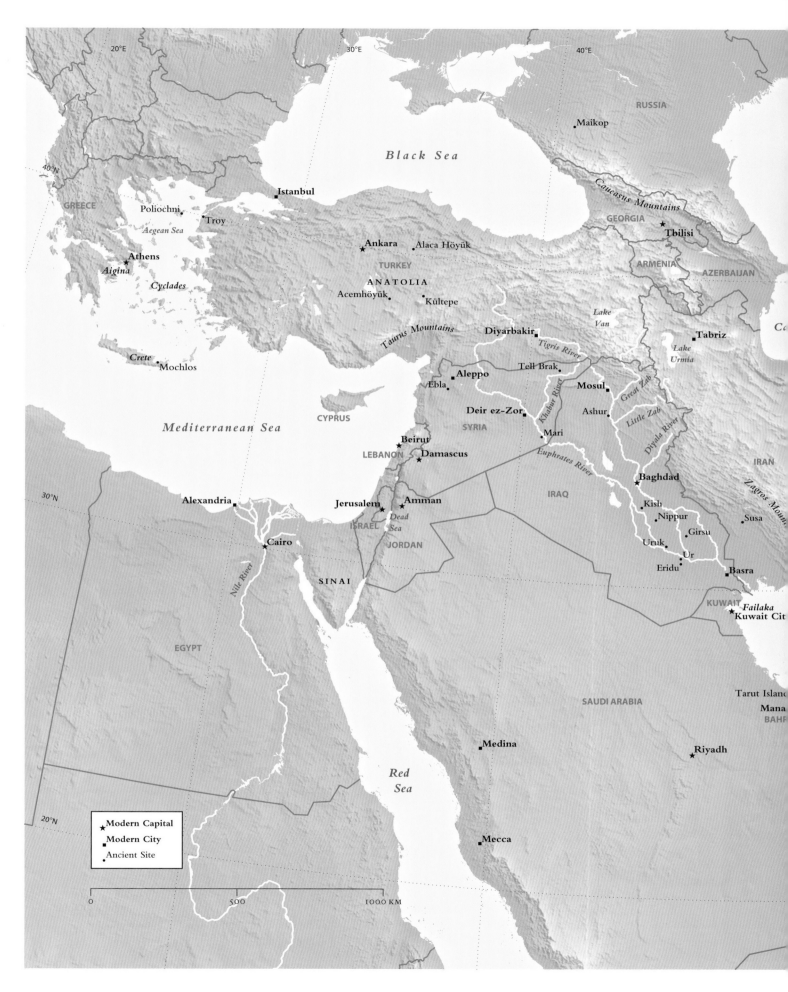

Black Sea

Mediterranean Sea

Red Sea

RUSSIA

Maikop

Caucasus Mountains

GEORGIA

Tbilisi

ARMENIA

AZERBAIJAN

Istanbul

Poliochni

Troy

Aegean Sea

Athens

Aigina

Cyclades

Ankara

Alaca Höyük

TURKEY

ANATOLIA

Acemhöyük

Kültepe

Taurus Mountains

Lake Van

Diyarbakir

Tigris River

Tabriz

Lake Urmia

Ca

Crete

Mochlos

CYPRUS

Ebla

Aleppo

Tell Brak

Mosul

Khabur River

Ashur

Great Zab

Little Zab

Deir ez-Zor

SYRIA

Mari

Diyala River

IRAN

Zagros Moun

Beirut

Damascus

LEBANON

Euphrates River

Baghdad

IRAQ

Alexandria

Jerusalem

Amman

ISRAEL

Dead Sea

JORDAN

Kish

Nippur

Susa

Girsu

Cairo

Nile River

Uruk

Eridu

Ur

Basra

SINAI

KUWAIT

Failaka

Kuwait Cit

EGYPT

SAUDI ARABIA

Tarut Island

Mana

BAHR

Medina

Riyadh

Red Sea

Mecca

★ Modern Capital
■ Modern City
• Ancient Site

0   500   1000 KM

20°E

30°E

40°E

40°N

30°N

20°N

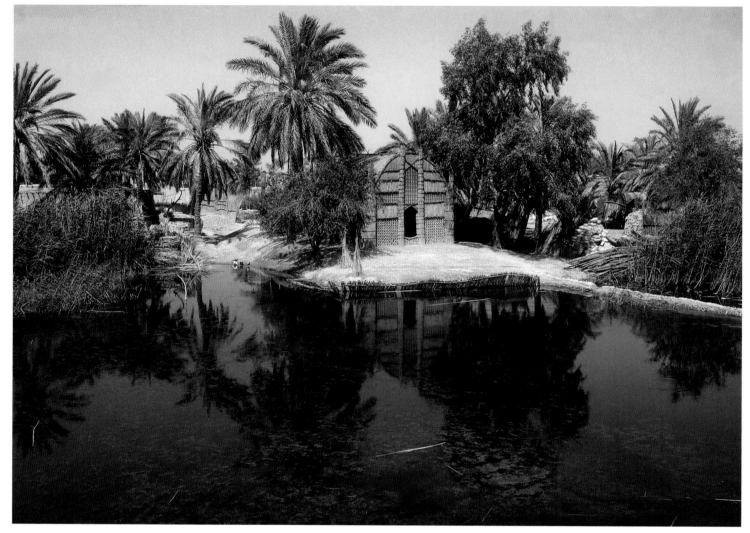

A modern house made from reeds in the Shobaish marshes of southern Iraq. Known as *mudhif*, such structures are part of a building tradition represented in art of the Late Uruk period (ca. 3300–3000 B.C.; see cat. no. 10c)

ART OF THE FIRST CITIES

NOTE TO THE READER

Because both the languages and the writing systems of the ancient Near East are imperfectly understood, scholars do not entirely agree on their transcription. Further, there is no agreement on the transcription of the region's modern languages. In this catalogue names are generally spelled according to commonly used transcriptions.

In quotations of transcribed material, interpolations are given in roman type in parentheses, restorations are in roman type in brackets, and uncertain translations are in italics.

Most dates provided in this volume are approximate. Years given for individuals represent dates of known activity or, in the case of rulers, regnal years.

The dates employed by the authors of this catalogue have sometimes been at variance within and between specific regions. In order to provide a consistent chronology, all dates have been adjusted in accordance with the assessment of relative and absolute chronology by Julian Reade in the appendix to this volume.

Both the identifications of materials and the dimensions provided for objects are based on information supplied by the authors or the lending institutions. The materials are often named on the basis of educated assumptions or conventions and may be revised by future scientific analysis. Where no dimensions are given, the data were not available at press time.

The exact nature and materials of the garments worn by the divine and human figures depicted on the objects in this catalogue are uncertain. Therefore, no clear terminology has been developed to describe them. We have adopted the term "skirt" or "kilt" to signify either a wrapped or sewn garment covering the lower part of the body. Garments worn by divinities and some other personages that are marked by horizontal rows or flounces of vertically hatched or wavy lines suggesting fleece are termed "tufted."

Cylinder seals are illustrated together with their modern impressions. "Left" and "right" in the catalogue entries describe the images as seen in the impression, not in the intaglio.

Unsigned entries are by the staff of the Department of Ancient Near Eastern Art at the Metropolitan Museum.

Certain objects included in the catalogue may not be available for exhibition.

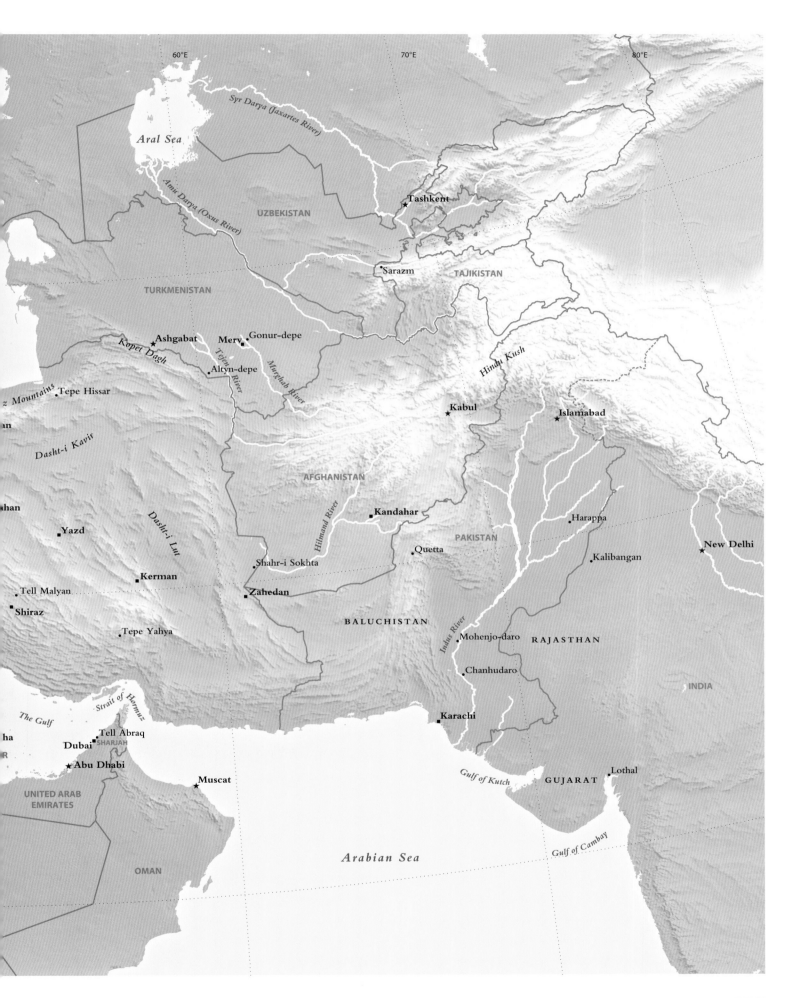

Aral Sea

Syr Darya (Jaxartes River)

Amu Darya (Oxus River)

UZBEKISTAN

★ Tashkent

• Sarazm

TURKMENISTAN

TAJIKISTAN

Kopet Dagh ★ Ashgabat • Merv • Gonur-depe

Tejen River • Altyn-depe

Murghab River

Hindu Kush

z Mountains • Tepe Hissar

Dasht-i Kavir

★ Kabul ★ Islamabad

an

AFGHANISTAN

• Yazd

Dasht-i Lut

Hilmand River

• Kandahar

Harappa

PAKISTAN

• Quetta

New Delhi ★

• Kalibangan

■ Kerman

• Tepe Yahya

■ Zahedan

• Shahr-i Sokhta

• Tell Malyan

■ Shiraz

BALUCHISTAN

Indus River

RAJASTHAN

• Mohenjo-daro

INDIA

• Chanhudaro

The Gulf

Strait of Hormuz

■ Tell Abraq

ha

• Dubai SHARJAH

★ Abu Dhabi

★ Karachi

UNITED ARAB
EMIRATES

★ Muscat

Gulf of Kutch GUJARAT • Lothal

Gulf of Cambay

OMAN

Arabian Sea

ART OF THE FIRST CITIES: THE THIRD MILLENNIUM B.C. FROM THE MEDITERRANEAN TO THE INDUS

JOAN ARUZ

Having crossed the threshold of a new millennium to stand, as we do, in the midst of perhaps the most intensely urban environment in the world, one often feels disassociated from the ancient past and the great civilizations to which it gave rise. However, in exploring the first instances in which early cultures coalesced first into cities and then into states, one becomes acutely aware of the ancient foundations upon which all succeeding societies were built. The rich and varied artistic traditions that are the focus of this exhibition highlight both a common element and a great diversity in the approach to basic questions regarding the nature of man and his vision of the world. Such issues have been at the heart of philosophies of history. As Karl Jaspers comments,

> The unity of mankind is impressively evident in the fact that similar basic traits of religion, forms of thought, implements, and social forms recur all over the earth. The simplicity of man is great despite his diversity. . . . Precisely through observation of the common element, however, does that which is divergent become clear.[1]

In his exploration of the reasons for the study of history, Jaspers also speaks of great leaps forward that characterize humanity's advancement through time:

> In history, that which is unrepeatable and irreplaceable comes to light in unique creations, break-throughs and realisations . . . these creative steps . . . are like revelations from some other source than the mere course of happenings . . . they lay the foundations of the humanity that comes after. From them man acquires his knowledge and volition, his prototypes and anti-types, his criteria, his thought-patterns and his symbols, his inner world.

Although remote in time and place, the urban revolution represented by the formation of the cities of southern Mesopotamia must be looked upon as one of humanity's defining moments. These complex centers of civilization, which arose toward the end of the fourth millennium B.C. in the fertile plains bordered by the Tigris and Euphrates Rivers, stimulated great inventions, such as writing, and witnessed a flowering of artistic expression. Much of this art demonstrated devotion to the gods and celebrated the power of kings. Political and economic mechanisms were elaborated to procure, manufacture, secure, and control the flow of materials and goods that sustained and embellished society. Partly as a result of these advances in Mesopotamia, other major civilizations developed along the great maritime and land routes that connected them to one another. Some of the more exotic cultures and places, such as Dilmun and Aratta, achieved mythical status.

This exhibition attempts to portray some of the extraordinary developments in the cities of the Near Eastern heartland as well as their impact on and stimuli deriving from the contemporary civilizations to the east and west. In such an endeavor, however, we can at best glimpse only those aspects of the third-millennium-B.C. world that have been largely reconstructed from the materials recovered by archaeologists in the temples, palaces, and tombs of its social elite. With our knowledge of the era enhanced by analyses of surviving cuneiform documents and using interpretations derived from the disciplines of art history, anthropology, political science, history, and economics, we hope to gain some perspective about the major artistic and cultural achievements as well as the enduring legacy of this earliest urban environment.

THE SETTING

The Greek historian Herodotos, writing in the sixth century B.C., marveled at the fertility of Babylonia, the richest grain-bearing country in the world, and its enormous crops of wheat, millet, and sesame that grew to unbelievable size.[2] This land—known in the third millennium B.C. as Sumer and Akkad and later named after the city of Babylon—encompasses the southern part of a diverse landscape that is referred to in later Greek sources as Mesopotamia, or "the land between the rivers," the Tigris and the Euphrates. It comprises the eastern tip of the Fertile Crescent of popular literature. Mesopotamia's fertility, however, is not the natural state of this southern alluvial plain, where the first cities were founded. On the contrary, the bounty praised by Herodotos was the work of men, who invented irrigation agriculture to overcome an adverse climate characterized by unpredictable rainfall and damaging floods.[3] This is a motif that is expressed throughout Sumerian literature.[4]

Although the term "Mesopotamia" is often used by scholars to indicate the area roughly covered by modern Iraq, the entire region that falls between the Tigris and Euphrates Rivers may be referred to by this term or as "Greater Mesopotamia." It extends from the mountains and fertile plains of eastern Turkey and the barren plateau of the Jazira in eastern Syria and northern Iraq to the lowland alluvial plains that reach beyond the Tigris into Elam, in southwestern Iran. In the south, the plains give way to the vast marshlands in the delta at the head of the Gulf. Other areas under the cultural hegemony of Sumer or Akkad are also sometimes referred to as being part of Mesopotamia.

Geography was one of the determining factors that promoted technological and cultural advancement in the southern Mesopotamian alluvium. The flat plains and river channels promoted unification and communication. Approximately 1,800 miles east of the mouth of the Tigris, the Harappan civilization arose in another large alluvial plain, formed by the Indus River system. The Indus River is slightly longer than the Euphrates; it, too, traverses many lands, flowing from the northern mountains of Tibet to the marshy delta south of

Karachi at its mouth on the Arabian Sea. Bringing fertility to the dry Punjab and Sindh plains, the Indus created an enormous agricultural area that supported cities such as Mohenjo-daro and Harappa.[5]

Another great water system, comprising the Amu Darya (Oxus River) and Syr Darya (Jaxartes River), flows through Central Asia but provided no access to the maritime routes from the Gulf to the Arabian Sea. Rather, these rivers flow into inland basins and watered the oasis towns that arose along the precursors of the Silk Road. Mountain ranges in Central Asia as well as in eastern Iran appear to have acted as additional barriers to the intense communication that elsewhere encouraged the formation of unified centers of civilization.[6]

THE PEOPLES

During the third millennium B.C. diverse populations inhabited the vast areas stretching from the Mediterranean Sea to the Indus River and from Central Asia to the Gulf. In attempting to identify them, we are guided by the survival of several distinct languages, writing systems, and references in texts associated with specific sites and cultural complexes. Perhaps the most intriguing of these peoples are those who dwelt in the cities and countryside of Sumer, concentrated in the lower part of southern Mesopotamia. They had probably inhabited the region long before the advent of cities, and there is little evidence to support either a major break in continuity of development or a great migration from areas to the north or east, as some scholars have argued. In their own language, Sumerian, they call themselves *sag giga,* or "black-headed ones." Sumerian and later Near Eastern tradition attributes the introduction of Sumerian civilization to the gods, who granted authority to kings: in the era before the Great Flood, seven sages, who were attendants of the god Enki and ministers to rulers, brought forth architecture, poetry, and the other arts and crafts of civilization.[7]

There were Semitic-speaking peoples in Greater Mesopotamia—to the north and northwest of Sumer—during the early third millennium B.C. With the foundation of the Akkadian dynasty by Sargon of Akkad (ca. 2300–2245 B.C.), they established a political center in southern Mesopotamia. The Akkadian kings created the world's first empire, which at the height of its power united an area that included not only the entirety of Mesopotamia but also parts of western Syria and Anatolia, Iran, the Caucasus, and Arabia.[8] The still-undiscovered capital city of Agade is presumed to have been located near the confluence of the Tigris and Diyala Rivers, close to the modern city of Baghdad. Akkadian, perhaps the earliest attested Semitic language, was introduced into Sumer and written in the cuneiform writing system used originally for Sumerian.

Numerous other languages were spoken by the many peoples in the surrounding regions. Shulgi, king of Ur (ca. 2079–2032 B.C.), claimed to be able to give verdicts in five of the languages of his realm. Cuneiform inscriptions from the third millennium B.C. attest to the existence of additional Semitic languages, including Amorite and Eblaite, as well as lesser-known languages such as Hurrian and Elamite. Some languages, such as that of the Guti peoples, are unknown.

One undeciphered language that draws a great deal of attention is Harappan, named after the major Indus Valley city of Harappa. Unlike the cuneiform script adopted for Sumerian and Akkadian, which was largely written on clay, the Harappan, or Indus, script is composed of signs familiar from short inscriptions above animal representations on numerous Harappan stone seals. It has been suggested that this language may belong to the native Dravidian family. The script disappeared in the beginning of the second millennium B.C.[9]

THE TIME FRAME

Two primary systems are employed to establish a relative chronology for the third millennium B.C. in the Near East. Both are based largely on the interpretation of archaeological data and the development of a typology of artifacts. The first emphasizes human technological achievements in the mastery of materials, using terminology derived from ancient literary references to legendary ages of gold, silver, bronze, and iron. In this system, the term "Early Bronze Age" corresponds roughly to the third millennium B.C. As with many descriptions of ancient cultures, the period is subdivided into an early, middle, and late phase, designated as I, II, and III.

The second system utilizes terms that refer to developments in Mesopotamian history and government. Early Dynastic I, II, and III, for example, designate the period of Sumerian city-states. The Akkadian period that followed was a time of conquest and empire. Lagash II and Ur III—names of dominant city-states—indicate the succeeding phase, during which Mesopotamian cities were unified into a bureaucratic state. "Neo-Sumerian" describes this last era of the third millennium B.C., emphasizing that its art and culture reflect in some ways those of the period before Sargon, the first ruler of the Akkadian dynasty.

The sequences within both systems provide frameworks to which scholars have attempted to affix specific or "absolute" dates. This is a complicated task, fraught with uncertainty, and a universally accepted chronology remains to be established for the entire ancient Near East. The *Royal Canon* of Ptolemy, the second-century-A.D. Alexandrian astronomer, presents us with a chronology of Babylonian kings dating back to the era of Nabonassar in 747 B.C. Ptolemy based his *Canon* on the dates of Babylonian astronomical observations that had been converted into Egyptian 365-day calendrical years.[10] Near Eastern royal annals and chronicles, along with lists of annually appointed state officials *(limmu),* allow us to extend the Ptolemaic chronology back to the accession of the Assyrian king Adad-nirari II in 911 B.C. For "absolute" dates prior to that time, however, surviving documents—including those providing synchronisms with Egypt—offer no certainty. Although scientific dating methods such as carbon 14, dendrochronology, thermoluminescence, and archaeoastronomy provide a narrower range of dates that helps to confirm the relative sequence, they lack the accuracy required to fix events of the third and second millennia B.C. absolutely to specific years with any certainty. Issues of chronology, very much at the center of present scholarly debate, are discussed by Julian Reade in an appendix to this volume. The chronology adopted for this catalogue reflects his consideration of the most recent archaeological and scientific data.[11]

ART OF THE CITY AND ITS INSTITUTIONS

The great civilizations of the third millennium B.C.—Mesopotamian, Egyptian, and Harappan—shared many characteristic features of urban life. From their earliest beginnings, however, essential differences in art and culture set them apart. As Henri Frankfort, discussing Mesopotamia and Egypt, recognized long ago:

> . . . the purpose of their writing, the contents of their representations, the functions of their monumental buildings and the structure of their new societies differed completely. What we observe is not merely the establishment of civilized life, but the emergence, concretely, of the distinctive "forms" of . . . civilization.[12]

The distinctly Mesopotamian form of civilization—which affected the development of the Near East from Anatolia and Syria to Iran, the Gulf, and, to some extent, even Central Asia—

crystallized with the advent of the city-state. Consisting of a capital city and surrounded by villages, the city-state proliferated in the southern Mesopotamian plain during the third millennium B.C. According to the official ideology expounded by rulers and court poets, city-states were the property of the gods, who invested the king with the power to bring prosperity and harmony to the land. These earthly rulers, like shepherds, protected and nurtured their flock, the people.

The nature of Mesopotamian institutions is captured to some extent in texts describing the practical functions of the temple and palace, which controlled most of the economic and political life of the city. The distinctive style of Mesopotamian civilization, however, is further illuminated by the arts, which reveal the awesome majesty of the temple as the house of the god; the impressive wealth of the palace as the residence of the king; and the important role of the cemetery as the eternal dwelling place of the social elite.

The basic characteristics of the artistic style that came to define the art of the Near East were already established by the third millennium B.C. in Mesopotamia (see "Art of the Early City-States," by Donald P. Hansen, in this catalogue). An interest in reproducing the human form is manifest in numerous sculptures in the round that were created as suppliants in stone and placed in the inner sanctuaries of temples as sacred objects. These votive images were not replicas of individual donors, however. Already at this early stage in the history of art, we are introduced to the notion of combining naturalism with abstraction to yield idealized figures suggesting inner qualities as well as outward appearances. Their frontality, the combination of modeling and geometric forms to capture the essence of facial features and musculature, as well as their garments and hairstyles had a lasting impact on art in the following millennia.

Relief sculpture demonstrates the ability of early Near Eastern artists to master a variety of postures, including the body in profile (see fig. 61). Artistic devices were developed both to represent figures in space and to project Mesopotamian ideals. A conceptual art evolved in which multiple views were combined in the rendering of single images, producing conventions that persisted in the Near East long after its encounter with the Classical Greek world. Human figures, for example, display frontal or profile heads combined with frontal torsos and profile legs; animals—with the exception of the frontally displayed bird of prey—were generally rendered in profile, often with frontal horns. Although some postures exhibit movement, adherence to a real or imaginary groundline generally restricts the depiction of motion and remains a

point of contrast with the dynamic art that developed in Aegean and later Greek art.

One of the primary aims of Mesopotamian art was to capture the relationship between the terrestrial and divine realms. The major divinities are represented in human form but come to be distinguished from humans by their horned crowns, tufted fleecy or flounced garments, as well as specific attributes and animals that symbolize their presence. Combinations of human and animal features create images of supernatural creatures: four-legged ones, such as human-headed bisons (traditionally referred to as human-headed bulls) and lions, and two-legged ones, such as bison-men (bull-men), which can be found throughout ancient art.

Compositional schemes, such as registers, were introduced to indicate different levels, depths, and realities (see figs. 9, 10; cat. no. 52). Great size expresses the power of both god and the divine king, as exemplified in the monumental stele of the Akkadian ruler Naram-Sin. Wearing the divine horned crown, Naram-Sin not only ascends toward the stars, which are the symbols of the gods, but is also represented as larger than life (fig. 59).

As the earthly representatives of the gods, rulers are depicted in battle, hunt, and ritual ceremonies, including banqueting scenes and processions with divine offerings. These are predominant themes in ancient Near Eastern art, expressing a desire to control destructive forces and maintain order and prosperity. The narrative of military conquest is at first illustrated by orderly rows of figures (cat. no. 52); in later periods we get actual glimpses of battle (cat. no. 129; fig. 59), including specific visual references such as landscape, garments, and hairstyles. War in the divine realm is revealed through scenes of combating gods (cat. no. 144). Man's domination of the wild beasts that threaten his flocks is expressed in the hunt and the "contest scene," one of the most characteristic motifs engraved on cylinder seals from the Early Dynastic and Akkadian periods (see cat. nos. 55, 146, 203). Composed of interwoven or distinct antithetic groups of so-called masters of animals or pairs of combatants, including heroes and bull- or bison-men, the resulting imagery conveys more the universal theme of restoring the balance of nature rather than any ephemeral act of violence. From this tradition the lion and the bull emerge as the most potent animal symbols of power and fertility and are adopted throughout the ancient world (see "Art of the Early City-States," by Donald P. Hansen, in this catalogue).

Mesopotamian sculptural styles and iconography of divine and human rule were transmitted to diverse sites such as Mari and Ebla in northern Syria as well as to Iran and as far as Arabia (see cat. no. 222). Local schools arose, each with distinctive regional interpretations of Sumerian art. Although circumstances permit us to present only a few representative examples from southwestern Iran (cat. nos. 199, 200), we focus attention on perhaps the finest sculptural workshops, which furnished the temples at Mari with superb creations (cat. nos. 88–93). Mari and Ebla also provide us with early palaces that appear to reflect a centralized political system, one perhaps more characteristic of northern than southern Mesopotamia during the mid-third millennium B.C. Divisions between north and south, as well as between temple and palace, are expressed visually in the arrangement of the exhibition.

In more distant regions, the Mesopotamian stylistic imprint is less in evidence, and depictions of contest and banquet scenes take on a peculiar local character (cat. nos. 257, 300b, c). In the distinctive art of the Indus Valley region—characterized by small but very accomplished images that display a high degree of naturalism, particularly in the modeling of animal forms—the only hints of Near Eastern stimuli are evident in a few iconographic themes. The phenomenon of "intercultural" or "international" style is introduced on portable objects, such as vessels and seals, in which stylistic and iconographic elements from different traditions were synthesized, reflecting on a small scale the cross-fertilization of cultures.

The life of the royal court in the third millennium B.C. is difficult to evoke from the few sculptures and the more numerous shell and stone inlays found among the remains of palaces. Rather, texts, like those found in the extensive archive at Ebla, along with masses of precious materials, such as lapis lazuli from the courtyard of the Ebla palace, serve to highlight the level of royal wealth, perhaps best illustrated in elite graves and hoards. This milieu—the highest levels of society—is thus necessarily our focus. The world of the common individual and family, although documented by cuneiform writings and architectural remains, cannot be properly displayed. Only a few rare finds indicating certain professions and creations in less "noble" materials, such as clay, provide us with hints about this elusive aspect of Mesopotamian society as revealed in the arts.

ART AND INTERCONNECTIONS: BEYOND GREATER MESOPOTAMIA

In contrast to the arts of Mesopotamia, those of Egypt glorified the pharaoh, who was the embodiment of divine power. Despite visible contacts with the Levant and the suggestion of allusions to Egyptian royal conquest imagery in Akkadian art, it remains difficult to assess the Nilotic contribution to Mesopotamian artistic style.[13] Although we have clear evidence that Near Eastern elements were present in Predynastic Egypt, the Nile Valley appears to have developed independently and remained remote, largely removed from the cultural exchange that accompanied the flow of goods from east to west. Its brilliant flowering during the third millennium B.C. thus lies beyond the scope of this exhibition.

The farther distant Indus Valley region, however, seems to have interacted more intimately with the Near East in the third millennium B.C., maintaining merchant enclaves in Central Asia and perhaps even in Mesopotamia itself. Yet the structures that define and reflect this civilization are quite different. There is no evidence of monumental temples and palaces or large-scale sculpture in the Harappan world. Rather, the focus seems to have been on private housing, public works, and urban infrastructure, with an emphasis on a sanitary and abundant water supply. Lacking a deciphered language, we can glimpse this enigmatic civilization only through a few small sculptures of important personages; large quantities of terracotta figurines; stone seals and impressed clay tablets depicting myth, ritual, and divine imagery; and hoards of impressive jewelry made of gold, silver, and carnelian and other semiprecious stones. Representative objects have been selected for the exhibition to demonstrate both the unique nature of Harappan civilization and its interaction with the west.

The arts of the intervening regions of eastern Iran and western Central Asia reflect, in the words of Maurizio Tosi, "the vast and diversified tapestry of peoples and languages organized in independent polities but culturally unified by . . . an exchange economy."[14] Many of the same factors present in these exotic lands of fabled wealth and access to resources—alluded to in Mesopotamian texts as sources of precious stone to adorn their temples and palaces—would later lead to the creation of the legendary Silk Road. The so-called trans-Elamite culture of Iran and the Bactria-Margiana Archaeological Complex of the Oxus region in western Central Asia produced impressive metalwork with elaborate figural imagery, small sculptures of male and female figures, stamp and cylinder seals, as well as stone vessels, demonstrating the impact of Mesopotamia on locally developed artistic traditions.

At the other end of the exchange network were the cultures that emerged along the Mediterranean littoral. Finds in the residences and tombs of Early Bronze Age sites on the Greek mainland as well as on the islands of the Cyclades, the eastern Aegean, and Early Minoan Crete suggest contacts with both western Anatolia and Syria. Perhaps as expected, there are links with sites such as Troy, where the fabled "Treasure of Priam" was uncovered by Heinrich Schliemann—one of many hoards found in the Early Bronze Age city that he originally misdated to the era of the Trojan War. Such connections extended through central Anatolia and northern Syria, which shared distinctive pendant and bead forms (see "Art and Interconnections in the Third Millennium B.C.," by Joan Aruz, in this catalogue). More astonishing, however, is the discovery in a tomb on the Aegean island of Aigina of an etched carnelian bead (cat. no. 166a), an object type never before found west of the sites of Ur and Kish in Mesopotamia. Other beads in the tomb—particularly flat, disk-shaped examples, a widespread type—further illuminate this extensive network of interconnections.

It encompassed much of Asia west from the Indus and extended into the Caucasus and the Aegean, consisting of many routes along which jewelry and other precious objects were traded, imitated, and adapted.

Evidence of cultural enrichment is manifest in the transfer of materials, object types, stylistic elements, and iconography. Indeed, our understanding of the ancient attitude to foreign contacts relies heavily on artistic representations and texts. The rulers and gods of Mesopotamia required riches that could only be supplied from abroad, necessitating encounters with exotic worlds. Yet the Mesopotamian view of the foreign is made quite evident in images of subjugated mountain peoples (see cat. no. 133) and in literary allusions.[15] Beyond Sumer, "the great country with a culture of nobility," simply meant beyond civilization.[16]

1. Jaspers 1953, pp. 247–67, cited in Meyerhoff 1959, pp. 335–36.
2. Herodotos, *The Histories,* 1.193.
3. Postgate 1992, pp. 3ff.; Pollock 1999, pp. 29–34.
4. Jacobsen 1987a, pp. 235ff.
5. Harappan culture also spread southward to sites near the Arabian Sea coast, such as Dholavira in the Rann of Kutch and Lothal near the Gulf of Cambay, as well as into the desert area of Rajasthan.
6. Postgate 1992, p. 3.
7. Hallo and Simpson 1971, pp. 28–29.
8. Steinkeller 1998, p. 89.
9. Kenoyer 1998, pp. 77–79.
10. Depuydt 1995, pp. 97ff.
11. For a summary of recent debate over the relative merits of the High, Middle, and Low Chronologies, see Åström 1987. The "New Chronology"

of Gasche et al. 1998, which dates Hammurabi from 1696 to 1654 B.C., has occasioned considerable controversy; see *Just in Time* 2000. For a reevaluation of the royal graves at Ur in light of the New Chronology, see Reade 2001. Malcolm Wiener (forthcoming) has recently reviewed issues of absolute chronology in connection with the dating of the eruption at Thera.
12. Frankfort 1956, p. 50.
13. See Hansen 2002, p. 109, n. 72.
14. See "Pathways across Eurasia," by Maurizio Tosi and C. C. Lamberg-Karlovsky, in this catalogue.
15. Hansen 2002, pp. 100–101.
16. Alster 1973, p. 103; see also Electronic Text Corpus of Sumerian Literature, king Shulgi on the future of Sumerian literature: "foreign lands where the sons of Sumer are not known, where people do not have the use of paved roads, where they have no access to the written word."

CITIES OF THE SOUTH

Let them build many cities . . . let them lay the bricks of many cities in pure places, let them establish places of divination in pure places, and . . . I (Enki, god of fresh waters,) will establish well-being there.

The Sumerian Flood Story

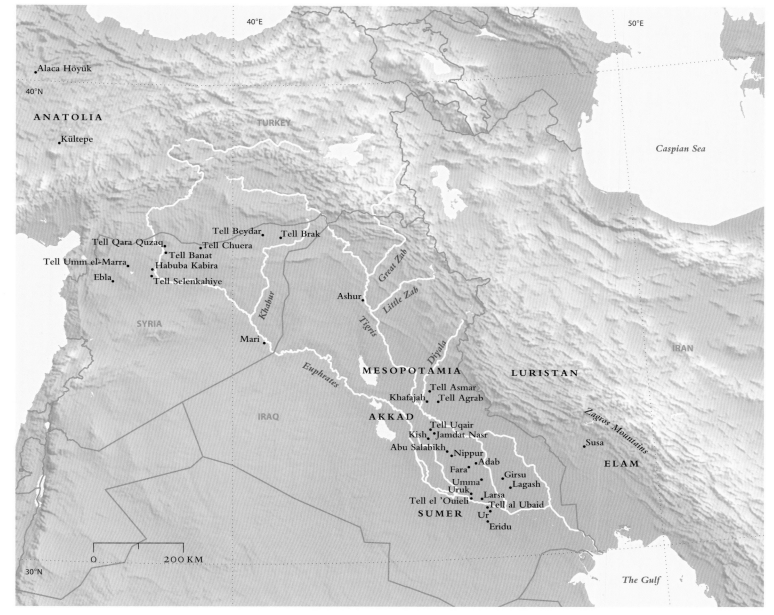

Fig. 2. Map of the Near East during the Late Uruk and Early Dynastic periods, showing the sites mentioned in this section.

URUK AND THE FORMATION OF THE CITY

HANS J. NISSEN

Mesopotamia occupies a special place among the world's first civilizations. It appears to be not only the oldest, having produced the first cities, but also one of the most enduring, lasting for more than three thousand years. Mesopotamian civilization emerged during the fourth millennium B.C. within the wide alluvial plain formed by the Euphrates and Tigris Rivers between modern Baghdad and the head of the Gulf.

The creation of the city is one of the most significant legacies of ancient Mesopotamia. Cities emerged after millennia of continuous settlement on the level of villages and small towns over large areas that extended from the mountainous realms toward the great central plains. Eventually, increasing dependence on agriculture and experience in food production enabled settlements to occupy ever larger areas. The move onto the southern Mesopotamian plain marks the culmination of this pattern, surprising in a region where human survival would appear to be difficult. The climatic conditions, with hot summers and cold winters and extremely little precipitation but an abundance of surface water in the form of rivers and swamps, had created a narrow range of usable plants and animals. Permanent survival was possible only by employing artificial irrigation. In addition, a similarly narrow spectrum of utilizable material for housing and implements was available, requiring organized ways of securing further resources from abroad. These developments indicate a level of organization that implies the existence of a set of rules as a guiding principle for societal institutions. More than other well-known criteria—the appearance of city walls, the specialization of labor, the emergence of writing and administration—these principles define urban life.

Living in larger communities obviously offers a number of advantages: specialization of labor and acquisition of specialized goods, physical and material security, and, not least, entertainment. However, it is undeniable that living together in closer quarters confined by a city wall provoked a rise in number and intensity of conflicts for which solutions had to be found. As towns of three to four thousand inhabitants became cities of thirty to forty thousand, it became necessary to create institutions that not only monitored a host of new rules but also had at their disposal sanctions to enforce these rules.

URUK

The site of Uruk (present-day Warka) will serve here as the archetype for explaining both the layout and the internal organization of the first cities. Uruk was especially suited for archaeological exploration because large areas within the central city had been left undisturbed for a long while after the early urban phase. In addition, a part of the surrounding area had become desert after the fourth century A.D. Consequently, traces of all older settlement periods could be found undisturbed on the surface, allowing not only study of the extent of settlement over various periods but also, in particular, the evaluation of the relations between Uruk and the hinterland.

Scientific excavation of the site was begun in 1912 by the Deutsche Orientgesellschaft Expedition and revived in 1928. Almost from the outset there were found clay tablets with archaic, partly pictographic signs recognized immediately as forerunners of the cuneiform writing system. However, even more fascinating than these tablets to the archaeologists—all historians of architecture by training—were the structures. Based on their work, we can now give a detailed picture of that early phase—Archaic Level IV, dating to about 3200 B.C.

The urban character of the city is suggested by its exceptional size of 250 hectares, or 0.96 square miles. Deducting about

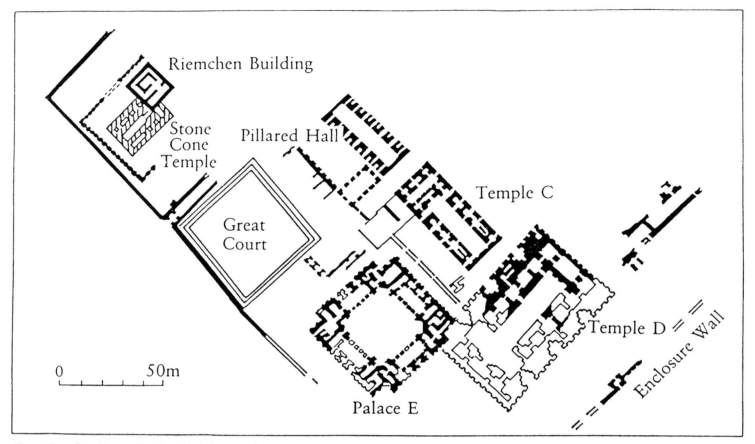

Fig. 3. Plan of the E-anna Precinct, Uruk. Late Uruk, ca. 3300–3000 B.C.

50 hectares for public space, we get an area that once may have accommodated up to forty thousand people—taking as our rule of thumb about two hundred people living on one hundred by one hundred meters of settled area. The central area was marked by two public spaces where the god of heaven, An, and the city goddess of Uruk, Inanna, the lady of heaven, to judge by later sources, had their temples. The layouts of the areas differ in crucial respects. The Anu District is centered around a high terrace with a temple (the White Temple) on top and seems to have served an exclusively religious function. The layout of the eastern district, known as E-anna, "the temple of heaven," on the other hand, displays a multitude of buildings of various sizes and arrangements, suggesting that a number of different functions were performed there. It is surrounded by a wall of its own. Surprisingly there is no unequivocal hint of a religious element in the architecture of this area. Likewise, the written sources point to Uruk's being ruled by a set of officials without appar-

ent cultic affiliation—although, supposedly, in these early periods everything had a religious aspect.

THE ARCHITECTURE

The architectural complex of the period about 3200 B.C. is not the result of deliberate planning but of a long sequence of rebuilding. Only three large structures around a plaza bordered by a large water basin on one side may present a planned ensemble.

The primary feature of these large buildings is a long hall. One seems to have been covered by a barrel vault eight meters wide supported on the sides by massive buttresses. The other buildings presumably had flat roofs accessible by stairways. In one case, Building C, the long hall was flanked on both sides by rows of small rooms, while a scaled-down replica of the plan of the main building was added to a short side at a ninety-degree angle. Another building, E, had four such halls around a square courtyard. In all cases, an essential feature seems to have been the free access of light and air to the halls through numerous doorways and other openings. The walls, like those of other buildings, were adorned with colored cone mosaics (see cat. no. 5; fig. 4). We may assume that these buildings served for the gathering of large or small groups of people, for cultic or other purposes. We think of a passage in the Epic of Gilgamesh, which refers to an assembly of the city elders opposing the king, and we are even tempted to locate the city government here.

WRITING AND SEALS

In preparation for a complete restructuring of the central area of the city in Uruk period III (about 3000 B.C.), perhaps as a result of a major shift in the city administration and/or cult, the walls of all buildings within E-anna Level IV were demolished down to a few courses of bricks. The interstices were carefully filled with the demolition material so as to form a huge platform that served as the ground level for the new structures. Since the Level IV buildings had been cleaned out before they were razed, no remains of the original furnishings were found. All the objects recovered from E-anna were found in layers of rubbish used to fill pits and depressions, such as the water basin, up to the level of the platform. This discarded material contained thousands of clay tablets and tablet fragments and broken impressed clay sealings originally used to secure containers and doors. In all likelihood, the date of some of this material, especially the oldest written documents, corresponds with that of the buildings of Level IV.

The main reason we cannot read these early texts is the fact that writing initially was nothing more than a means, more comprehensive than those employed before, of recording the details of economic transactions. Seals and clay counters (small clay artifacts in geometric shapes that represented numbers or quantities) had been used since the sixth millennium. In order to reconstruct specific transactions, seals were relied upon to identify the participants, and tokens, or counters, identified the amounts and numbers of the commodities involved. Shortly before the appearance of script, attempts were made to expand the range of information to be recorded by using sealed clay balls impressed by cylinder seals *and* containing counters, but only writing offered the possibility of noting all items deemed necessary. Yet even the writing system was predicated on common knowledge, since only abbreviated pieces of the total body of information were written down. Obviously, writing represented

an answer to the urgent needs of the economic administration and not a desire to write religious, historical, or literary texts. Thus, there was no incentive to render the spoken language. In fact, this need was felt only six hundred to seven hundred years later, when the system was reorganized to allow for the full representation of language.

THE ADMINISTRATIVE TEXTS

Of the approximately fifteen hundred clay tablets and fragments that can be ascribed to the time of Level IVa (the last phase of Level IV), all except a few pieces contain information pertaining to a central economic administration, which seems to have had its seat in E-anna. Apparently, much of the economy was based on a system of gathering and redistribution of goods handled in large complexes. Accordingly, large quantities of goods were collected in central storerooms and then redistributed to consumers, particularly to administrative personnel and other employees. Many administrators and controllers were responsible for the process. Such complexes acted as mostly self-sufficient units or large households, perhaps comparable to the later *oikos* of ancient Greece.

Unfortunately, the administrators seem to have been interested only in calculating the actual contents of the storerooms by deducting the disbursements from the aggregate intake. This systemic restriction prevents us from knowing anything about the origin and final destination of goods. Though the area surrounding Uruk must certainly have contributed heavily to the provisioning of the city, there is no evidence for this found in the texts.

THE LEXICAL LISTS

The few nonadministrative texts recovered mentioned lists of signs or sign combinations that belong to the same semantic family, such as names of trees, animals, and places. One of these lists requires special attention because it enumerates titles and functions in a hierarchical order.

This text begins with a rare sign combination that is translated as "king" in a dictionary composed two thousand years later. The next entries combine the sign for something like "leader" with a specification for the area of responsibility. Thus we find "the leader of law," "the leader of the city," "the leader of the plough," "the leader of barley," and "the leader of the labor force"—a list reading like the modern directory of a city government. Elsewhere in the list groups of two or three lines indicate internal ranking within a given area of responsibility or professions. Principles of both vertical and horizontal structuring suggest that we are dealing with a very complex, highly stratified society.

THE LANGUAGE

The presence of written material fosters the hope that we might be able to identify the language used by the scribes. But, as stated above, the early script was not designed to render language but to serve as a notational system for administrative data. Thus, the notes could be read in every language of the world. Consequently, the tablets offer no clue to the nature of the population of Uruk in the early urban phase, though later evidence shows that it is highly likely that the Sumerians were at least the strongest element.

THE SEAL IMPRESSIONS

The same layers of debris that yielded the tablets contained thousands of broken sealings—lumps of clay bearing impressions of cylinder seals on one side. This was a new form of seal introduced in the Uruk period that was rolled rather than stamped. On the other side of these clay lumps are negative imprints of objects ranging from clay vessels to door fasteners to which the clay had originally been attached. Applying a seal increased security, as the seal identified the person responsible for the closure of the container or door. Like writing, seals undoubtedly were part of the economic system.

Cylinder seals bear easily recognizable images of a wider range of elaborate themes and variations than the earlier stamp seals with their limited surfaces. These variations allowed more and more people to be equipped with individual seal patterns. Thus, we can assume that cylinder seals developed as a response to an increase in the numbers of people involved in economic transactions. Unfortunately, the themes displayed on the cylinders do not help us to gain more information about Uruk's administration or the types of goods referred to, as they tend to depict such general subjects as religious processions and rituals, the protection of herds, and mythical creatures.

RELIGION AND ART

We know regrettably little about religion and cult in Uruk in this period. Most of the buildings formerly thought to be temples are now considered to have served a range of purposes beyond religious functions, while the remaining ones, among them the White Temple, lack features, such as a central niche, that define the later temple. Thus, reference to later traditions does not help us. Depictions of stylized temple facades on cylinder seals do, however, shed some light on details in the exteriors of the architecture, much as the upper register of the so-called Uruk Vase (figs. 9, 10) reveals something of their interiors by depicting a representative inventory stored within the building. Any hope that seal images and large-scale art might help us further is shattered, on the one hand, by the small size and the nonspecific nature of seal representations and, on the other, by the fact that nearly all examples of large-scale art serve the purpose of glorifying the ruler. A bridge to religious concepts can only be found by assuming that the ruler himself was a religious figure.

URUK BEFORE 3000 B.C.

Based on our knowledge of the city's size and population, we can conclude that at the end of the Uruk period, that is, about 3000 B.C., Uruk had reached a mature stage of development and was a major center governed by economic, social, religious, and political rules that remained vital for centuries to come. Uruk must have been an economic and political center of power, entertaining relations with its immediate as well as outlying neighbors. Its structures cannot have grown overnight but must have taken some time to develop. But how much time?

Unfortunately, information about the Middle and the earlier part of the Late Uruk periods is very scarce and is even less satisfactory for the Early Uruk period, since these levels have not been reached by archaeologists in either Uruk or any other place on a sufficient scale. We can only be relatively certain that writing emerged sometime during Level IV (about 3200 B.C.), while monumental buildings, large-scale art, cylinder seals, and the economic, social, and political structures discussed above certainly emerged in the Middle and early Late Uruk periods, perhaps as early as about 3500 B.C.

Except for a sequence of pottery representing the Early Uruk period, there is little evidence available to help us. During the archaeological survey of the hinterland of the city of Uruk, approximately 110 settlements of the Late Uruk period, which undoubtedly served as the support system for the central city of Uruk, were located. However, only 10 settlements, which were widely spaced and did not appear to represent a closed system of relations, could be detected for the Early Uruk period. Neither Uruk, which at that time probably was no more than twin villages on either side of a ford of the Euphrates—perhaps Kulaba on the western and Uruk on the eastern bank—nor any other site could have been a central place with urban potential. We can only conclude that the urban features mentioned above must have developed within the Late Uruk period, probably in its initial phase, to be more specific.

URUK AFTER THE URUK PERIOD

Though it remains difficult to interpret the numerous written documents from the time of Level III, or Jamdat Nasr in archaeological terminology (about 3000 B.C.), they reveal enough to allow us to see that the major lines of political and economic administration remained the same as before or at least very similar to those of Level IV. Yet significant changes altered the picture of the city of Uruk itself.

The main changes were connected with a totally new concept for the central areas. The White Temple of the former western center was engulfed within a huge terrace extending from the former temple terrace to the western corner of E-anna. Nothing is known about its intended purpose, as nearly the entire terrace is now occupied by the massive Bit Resh temple complex of Seleucid times (third century B.C.). E-anna, for the first time, was furnished with a visible architectural center in the form of a terrace of moderate height, probably serving as the base of a temple. Although the line of the temenos wall and the extent of the area remained the same, the huge platform created by razing the buildings of Level IVa was now used as a foundation for a totally different array of buildings and installations, mostly on a much smaller scale. Since they either fell victim to later building activities or were exposed to severe weather conditions over a long period of time, the traces remain largely incomprehensible. Only the remains of a monumental gate point to the existence of some major complex.

We fail to recognize the purpose of the changes and have only a feeling that they were the expression of a comprehensive internal reshuffling. Though the focus on a single central building as opposed to the former array of magnificent structures sometimes is taken as a sign of simplification, we certainly cannot interpret these changes in terms of decline, especially in light of what followed.

THE THIRD MILLENNIUM B.C.

Despite the lack of information about the E-anna District, we can assert that Uruk must have seen one of its most prosperous periods during the early third millennium B.C. Hardly any buildings survive from the beginning of the Early Dynastic period (ED I, about 2900 B.C.) in E-anna. This was primarily because the lower subterranean part of an extensive structure of unknown function (the so-called pisé building) of the later Early Dynastic period had been dug well into the levels of the Uruk period, destroying earlier architecture. The pisé building gives us some evidence that construction continued in E-anna, as did frequent rebuilding and enlargements of the central terrace.

The main information we have concerns the city in general. Not only was the city wall, still visible today, constructed during this time, but a study has also revealed that almost the entire area within the wall, amounting to the largest extension of Uruk in its long history, had been in use. The built-up area must have been even larger, because the entire northeast sector outside the wall is covered by a thick layer of ED I pottery up to five kilometers beyond the wall. Although we still lack good information, there are a number of hints that we should take aspects of the Epic of Gilgamesh more literally as the tale of the king of Uruk who built the city wall (see "Uruk and the World of Gilgamesh," by Beate Salje, in this catalogue).

There is even less information regarding the rest of the third millennium. Only the surface surveys of the city and the hinterland can shed some light on possible reasons for this situation. These surveys tell us that the line of the city wall was retained but that both the built-up area within the city and the number of settlements in the countryside shrank considerably, probably following a shift in the main course of the Euphrates River. Despite its former importance, in particular as the primary cult city of the goddess Inanna, Uruk is hardly ever mentioned in the numerous historic inscriptions that began to appear in the later part of the Early Dynastic period, which are full of reports on the changing relations among the principal cities of southern Mesopotamia. And again, we hardly find it mentioned during the time of the central state of the Dynasty of Akkad. Only toward the end of the third millennium did Utuhengal of Uruk succeed in expelling the Gutians, probably mountain tribes whose home was in the Zagros range to the east. When his brother Ur-Namma was able to re-create a central state following the Akkadian example (see "Approaching the Divine," by Jean M. Evans, in this catalogue), encompassing all of southern Mesopotamia, the new capital, however, was Ur, not Uruk.

In summary, a change in settlement opportunities and an opening of the southern Mesopotamian flood plain during the first half of the fourth millennium B.C. led to a massive and probably rapid occupation of the area after about 3500 B.C. This created a previously unheard-of population density. The fertility of the soil enabled the area of land necessary to feed a village to decrease, thus allowing settlements to move closer together.

The closer living quarters resulted in new conflicts calling for comprehensive solutions. Among several possibilities for creating an urban social structure, Mesopotamia, from the beginning, chose centralization, including the principles of central storage and redistribution. New forceful instruments of control were developed, as witnessed by the use of cylinder seals and particularly writing. The growth of settlements on a new scale also called for new structures of power and political leadership. We get a glimpse of the extent of the challenges by looking at the sophisticated list of titles and the impressive imagery created to glorify the ruler.

In the end, our admiration concerns not only the achievement of mastering such a host of problems within a relatively short period of time but also the fact that, almost from scratch, solutions were found that were powerful as well as flexible enough to answer the many new challenges of the centuries to come.

I

Head of a sheep

Red sandstone
H. 9 cm (3½ in.); W. 11.5 cm (4½ in.); L. 15.5 cm
(6⅛ in.)
Mesopotamia, Uruk (modern Warka), E-anna
Precinct, Sammelfund of Level III in Pa XVI 2
Late Uruk–Jamdat Nasr, ca. 3300–2900 B.C.
Staatliche Museen zu Berlin, Vorderasiatisches
Museum VA 11026

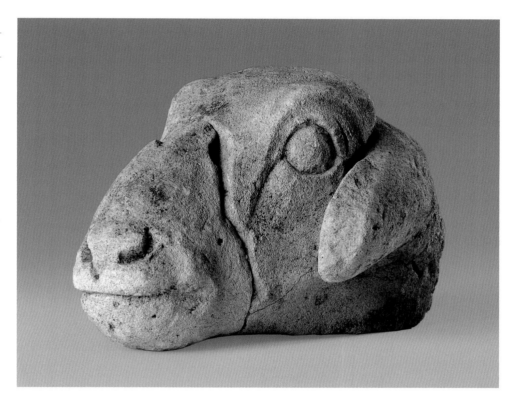

This quite realistically modeled sheep's head is one of the most impressive examples of sculpture in the Uruk period and demonstrates the high degree of artistry sometimes achieved. The horns are missing. The left ear stands free of the head; the right one has been broken off. The head was presumably part of an almost lifesize statue, for the underside is hollowed out and traces of plaster were found in the cavity, suggesting that the head was affixed to the body with dowels.

The piece belongs to the *Sammelfund,* a hoard found in the E-anna Precinct.[1] Along with other finds from the offering courtyard in E-anna, it indicates that animal sculptures played a role in religious practice. LM

1. Between what may have been a monumental court with a gateway and a raised terrace lay a long, narrow room where a mass of small objects known as the "*Kleinfunde* hoard" or *Sammelfund* (collection of objects) was discovered. The objects may represent temple furnishings and include the famous Uruk Vase (figs. 9, 10). The relationship of this room to the other buildings is not clear, but it certainly dates to the late phase of Level III (Jamdat Nasr period–Early Dynastic I).

2a, b

Recumbent animals

Mesopotamia, Uruk (modern Warka), E-anna
Precinct, Sammelfund of Level III in Pa XVI 2
Late Uruk–Jamdat Nasr, ca. 3300–2900 B.C.

a. Bituminous limestone and silver
H. 10.1 cm (4 in.); L. 9.7 cm (3⅞ in.)
Staatliche Museen zu Berlin, Vorderasiatisches
Museum VA 11025

b. Limestone and lapis lazuli
H. 2.6 cm (1 in.); L. 5.2 cm (2 in.)
Staatliche Museen zu Berlin, Vorderasiatisches
Museum VA 14536

Many of the artifacts discovered in Uruk Level III in or outside rooms 240 and 241, square Pa XVI 2, display considerable artistry and exquisite craftsmanship; among them are a large number of animal figures, including representations of sheep, goats, cattle, lions, gazelles, fish, and birds.

The figures were apparently votive offerings to the goddess Inanna to ensure her continuing goodwill. The artifacts in these rooms suggest that they could have served as storerooms for temple equipment that was

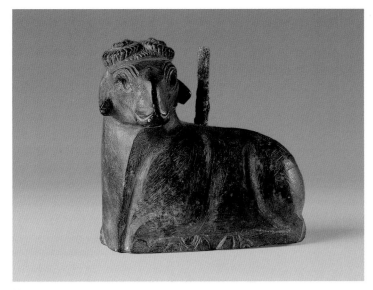

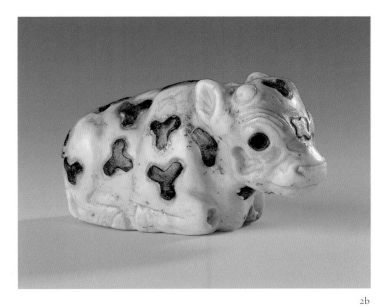

2a

2b

currently in use or that had been replaced by new votive gifts.

The sculpture of a recumbent ram (cat. no. 2a) is notable for the exquisite engraving of the coiled horns and the head. The silver pin projecting from its back supported an ornament, perhaps some symbol wrought in a precious metal. The small calf (cat. no. 2b) is a composite piece; its clover-shaped inlays of lapis lazuli may have been intended to suggest the animal's spots. Animal figures were also worn as amulets or used as handles on cylinder seals (see cat. no. 10c).   LM

3

String of beads

Lapis lazuli, gypsum, and shell
L. 44 cm (17⅜ in.)
Mesopotamia, Uruk (modern Warka), E-anna
Precinct, Sammelfund of Level III in Pa XVI 2
Late Uruk–Jamdat Nasr, ca. 3300–2900 B.C.
Staatliche Museen zu Berlin, Vorderasiatisches
Museum VA 11094

During excavations in the southern Mesopotamian city of Uruk, thousands of small ornamental beads were discovered in the E-anna temple precinct. They were part of a hoard that also included numerous precious vessels, animal figures (see cat. nos. 1, 2), seals, and seal impressions. The arrangement of this necklace is modern, strung to show a group of the beads to good advantage. It is also possible that beads were sewn onto articles of clothing.

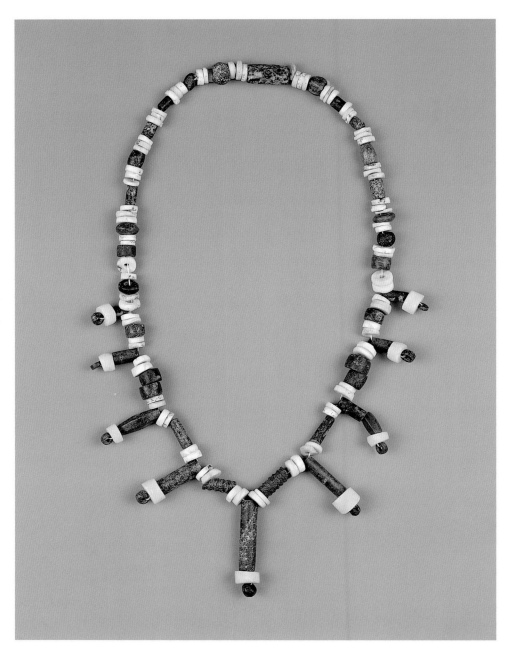

Many of the materials of the beads in this find are foreign to the alluvial plain of southern Mesopotamia and would have had to be imported from distant lands. Trading ties extended to the mountainous regions of Afghanistan, where some ancient lapis lazuli mines have been rediscovered.

The shortage of raw material in the Uruk area is mentioned in the Sumerian epic Enmerkar and the Lord of Aratta (see cat. no. 336). Enmerkar, the legendary king of Uruk, tries to trade grain for precious stones, gold, and silver needed to adorn the temples to the goddess Inanna in Uruk and Eridu. Only after long and heated negotiations involving threats and the solving of complicated riddles does the lord of Aratta agree to furnish the desired goods.

From imported raw materials, beads of many shapes and with all kinds of decoration were created in local Mesopotamian workshops. One such workshop in Uruk contained beads in various stages of completion along with the requisite flint tools.

It was not just human beings who adorned themselves with strings of precious beads. The goddess Inanna was fond of them, too. A song that describes how she makes herself beautiful relates that after she had bathed, rubbed herself with fragrant oils, put on a regal garment, applied eye makeup, and straightened her hair, she adorned herself with precious jewelry:

> Rings of gold I put on my hands,
> Little stone beads I hung around my neck,
> Straightened their counterbalance on the
> nape of my neck.

RH

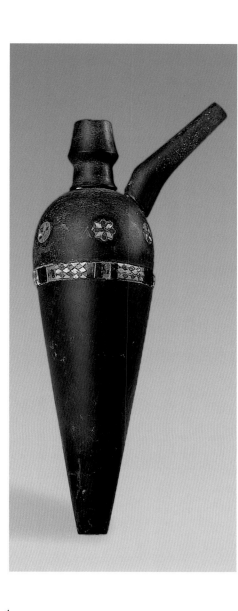

4

Spouted vessel with inlaid bands

Bituminous limestone and calcite
H. 21.5 cm (8½ in.); Diam. 6.3 cm (2½ in.)
Mesopotamia, Uruk (modern Warka), E-anna
Precinct, Sammelfund of Level III/I7 in Oe V13
Late Uruk–Jamdat Nasr, ca. 3300–2900 B.C.
Staatliche Museen zu Berlin, Vorderasiatisches
Museum VA 11055

Spouted vessels made of stone are usually composite pieces consisting of a hemispherical top with a narrow mouth joined to a conical bottom. Wire cramps made of copper-alloy encircle the top and bottom, and the spout is attached in the area of the shoulder. Bitumen or some sort of adhesive seals the joint between the two sections. Circling the junction is generally an intarsia band composed of small chips of colored stones and mollusk shells in a pattern that might include lozenges, rosettes, stars, circles, and half-moons. While the body of the vessel is frequently made of dark gray bituminous limestone, the neck opening and spout are a stone of a different color. Spouted bottles, the majority of which came to light in the E-anna shrine, could have been used in religious rites for libations or drink offerings.

Although the spout and neck of this bottle were not found together with the body of the vessel, they fitted exactly into the opening of the lower part, making it possible to reconstruct the vessel.   LM

5

Cone mosaic panel

Fired clay
H. 13 cm (5⅛ in.); L. 85.8 cm (33¾ in.); Thickness
10.5 cm (4⅛ in.); L. of cones approx. 10 cm (4 in.)
Mesopotamia, Uruk (modern Warka)
Late Uruk–Jamdat Nasr, ca. 3300–2900 B.C.
Staatliche Museen zu Berlin, Vorderasiatisches
Museum VA 16119

The technique of ornamenting facades with cone mosaics was known as early as the middle of the fourth millennium B.C., and by the end of the millennium such work had became a characteristic feature of monumental cultic and palatial architecture in the E-anna Precinct (see fig. 4).

6

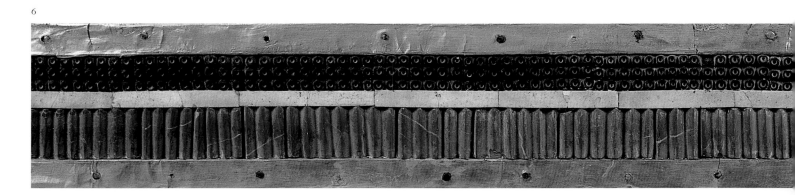

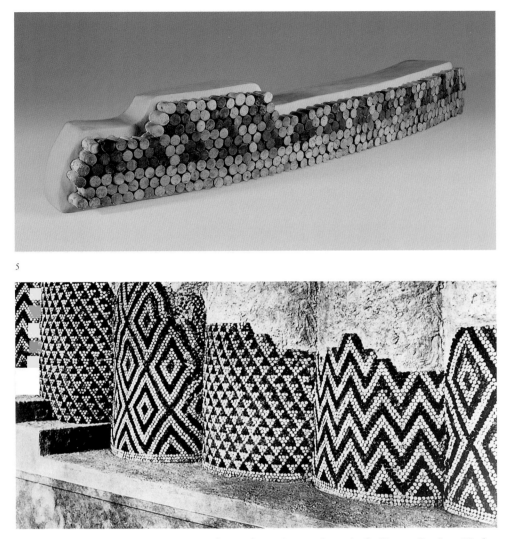

5

Fig. 4. Reconstructed clay cone-mosaic columns decorating a staircase in the E-anna Precinct, Uruk. Late Uruk, ca. 3300–3000 B.C. Staatliche Museen zu Berlin, Vorderasiatisches Museum.

To create the ornamentation, cones of baked clay or gypsum about 10 centimeters long were pressed into a wall coated with a thick layer of wet plaster, arranged together tightly. The cones were usually painted black, red, or white on their tops, but larger, unpainted clay or stone cones were sometimes used as well. The decorative patterns produced consist of lozenges, triangles, and zigzag bands. These designs were apparently based on wickerwork and textile patterns. In the mosaic fragment shown here, the dominant design is a pattern of stacked black triangles.

This type of work was not solely decorative. The sheathing of mud-brick outer walls and pillars with mosaics made of harder materials helped to minimize weathering from wind and water.

Facades adorned with cone mosaics are found beyond Uruk in the Late Uruk period. They were common in southern Mesopotamian cities such as Ur and Eridu, as well as in Habuba Kabira on the central Euphrates.

LM

6

Frieze from a temple altar

Blue limestone, white marble, green shale, gold foil, and silver
H. 12.3 cm (4⅞ in.); L. 119 cm (46⅞ in.)
Syria, Tell Brak, Eye Temple, G.564
Late Uruk, ca. 3300–3000 B.C.
National Museum, Aleppo, Syria 10100

During the Late Uruk period people from southern Mesopotamia established colonies in the north, bringing with them their architectural, artistic, and administrative traditions. By this time Tell Brak was already a site of some importance, with major buildings and a long history of contact with the south.[1] One temple there, known as the Eye Temple following the discovery at a lower level of hundreds of figurines with pronounced eyes, was rebuilt during the Late Uruk period and employed southern decorative forms such as cone mosaics.[2]

This unique frieze from an altar in the Eye Temple consists of a band of gold foil at the top and bottom, an upper band of blue limestone decorated with hollowed circles in high relief, a central band consisting of strips of white marble, and a lower band of corrugated strips of green shale. The gold foil elements are folded in half, bent over at right angles to the depth of twenty millimeters, the depth of the frieze when it was mounted on wood that has since decayed. Nails, with stems of silver and heads of gold foil, attach the gold bands, into which they are hammered at irregular intervals. The different-colored stone bands

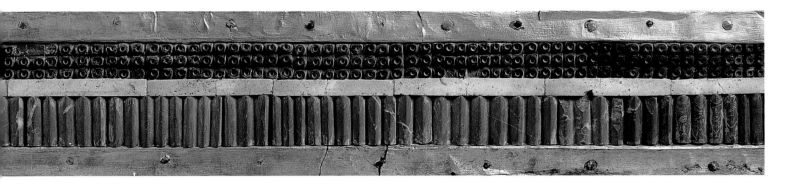

are formed from rectangular pieces that are perforated at the back to allow thin copper wire to be threaded through them and attached to the original wood backing. A similar technique was used later on columns from Tell al Ubaid (see cat. no. 44).

The frieze decorated a pedestal made of small mud bricks that stood at the center of the south wall of the long sanctuary of the temple. Diagnostic pottery dates the level of the pedestal to the Late Uruk period. The pedestal originally was embellished with three panels of frieze—one at the top of each side—beneath which it was decorated with white lime plaster. It has been suggested that the frieze depicts a type of facade, common on temples and public buildings in the Late Uruk period, on which the plain wall made of mud brick was relieved by niches and mosaic decoration.[3]

PC

1. Oates and Oates 1994.
2. Mallowan 1947, pp. 93–95, pls. 3, 4.
3. Heinrich 1982.

7

Spouted ring-shaped vessel

Fired clay
H. 45 cm (17¾ in.); Diam. 33 cm (13 in.)
Syria, Tell Qannas, TK74/1204
Late Uruk, ca. 3300–3000 B.C.
National Museum, Aleppo, Syria 12358

Southern Mesopotamian colonies established during the Late Uruk period took the form of small enclaves in local settlements or of entire new cities. Among the latter, the most extensively excavated is the site of Habuba Kabira on the Euphrates River. Southern styles of pottery, found at sites such as Habuba, were largely mass-produced on a fast wheel in a limited repertoire of shapes, with little or no decoration; vessels found in elite monumental buildings, however, are often very exotic. Examples made of stone tend to imitate ceramic shapes but frequently are highly decorated (see cat. no. 4); similarly, fired clay vessels from such contexts can be unusual.

This unique vessel comes from Habuba Kabira's administrative and religious area (known today as Tell Qannas). A band of clay was fashioned into a tube, its ends joined to form a loop. Holes were made in the top for

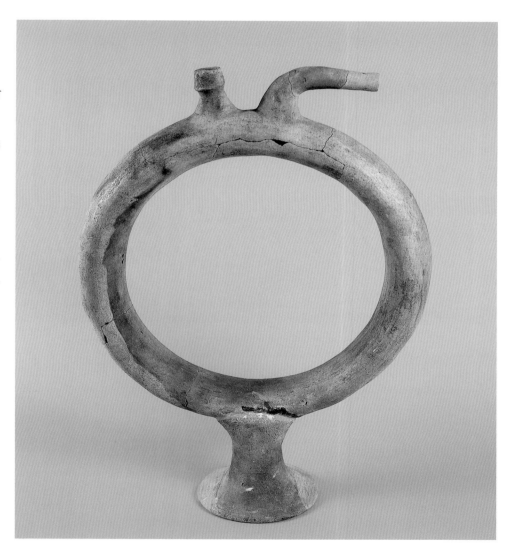

two spouts, perhaps one for filling and a bent spout for pouring. A large foot was attached to the vessel, enabling it to stand. The association of this vessel with monumental buildings, which may have had ritual significance, suggests that it possibly was used for libations. There appears to have been a high degree of specialization in the southern communities,[1]

and potters figure among other specialists on the Late Uruk professions list from Uruk.[2]

PC

1. Wright and Johnson 1975; D. Potts 1997, p. 153.
2. Nissen 1986, p. 329. See also "The Earliest Scholastic Tradition," by Piotr Michalowski, in this catalogue.

ART OF THE EARLY CITY-STATES

DONALD P. HANSEN

tudents of ancient Near Eastern culture have generally used the term "Early Dynastic period" to designate the approximately five hundred and fifty years or more of Mesopotamian history following the Jamdat Nasr age. These years are generally divided into Early Dynastic I, Early Dynastic II, and Early Dynastic IIIA and IIIB. The enormous complications surrounding the chronology of the period are discussed in the appendix "Problems of Third-Millennium-B.C. Chronology," by Julian Reade, in this catalogue.

During the third millennium the Mesopotamian region, known in later times as Babylonia, was divided into Sumer and Akkad, the former located in the extreme south of the alluvium and the latter in the more northerly area. In Sumer a number of city-states emerged as territories consisting of one or more major cities surrounded by smaller outlying towns and villages. The territorial limits of such states as Ur, Uruk, Umma, and Lagash were often insecure, bringing the ruler, or *ensi,* of one city into conflict with the leader of another, and skirmishes and open war sometimes ensued. Control of the northern part of the southern alluvium seems to have centered around the great city of Kish, whose rulers may at times have also exerted a degree of authority in the south.[1] Akshak, located on the Tigris; Mari, in the middle Euphrates region; and Ebla, in northeastern Syria, were also major contending powers during this period. Because of the Mesopotamian propensity for record keeping, for the latter part of the period at least, we know the names of the dynasts of some of the states, among them Ur, Kish, and Uruk. This knowledge comes not only from the Sumerian King List (cat. no. 330), which is historical as well as quasi-mythological, but also from a series of historical written documents inscribed on stone monuments and on clay tablets.

Sometimes during the process of determining archaeological periods when documentation is relatively scarce, finding ways to discuss salient aspects of cultural development involves focusing on small changes that may take on larger meaning. In the case of the city-states of Sumer, for example, the Early Dynastic period is partly defined by a peculiar form of the all-pervasive building material, mud brick. Prior to the Early Dynastic period, during the Uruk and Jamdat Nasr cultural phases, the mud constituting the brick was formed into a rectangular shape similar to that of our present-day baked brick. Subsequently, this type was rather rapidly replaced by a brick of an entirely different form. The new brick was flat on the bottom and curved on the top; consequently it was called by archaeologists the "plano-convex" brick. The best way to build a wall with such ungainly bricks was to stand them on an end or side with each course slanting, like books on a shelf, in the opposite direction from the course below. This produced a herringbone pattern, which was no longer visible when the building was completed and the exterior surfaces of the wall were covered with mud plaster. Nevertheless, the brick type is so singular that it has been theorized that the new manner of building was not one inherent to mud-brick construction but must have been developed outside of southern Mesopotamia proper, say in a region where houses were built with river stones and pebbles—which would have inspired the plano-convex form. Such a dramatic change in building technique, a change not yet fully understood, has led some scholars to postulate that the arrival of the new brick was synonymous with the arrival of the Sumerians.[2] Most scholars, however, point out that the archaeological continuity of the successive early phases of settlement in the alluvium suggests that the Sumerians were probably among the first inhabitants.[3]

Archaeological excavations in Mesopotamia began in the middle of the nineteenth century and have continued up to the present day, interrupted only by modern wars. A great deal has been learned about the early Sumerians from these excavations, yet we still lack adequate knowledge for an understanding of many aspects of Sumerian culture. We are aided somewhat by comprehensible textual materials dating to the last quarter of the third millennium, but these scarcely provide us with enough information to fathom the real nature of Sumerian lore and concerns we see reflected in the world of their visual arts. Consequently, we are dependent upon the testimony of the arts themselves, textual evidence from later periods in Mesopotamia, and what we might glean from comparative studies of other cultures. Admittedly, all such approaches are fraught with difficulty.

Based on these approaches and speaking in very general terms, it is possible to posit that during the third millennium in Sumer much of life was focused on the temples of the gods. Individual deities owned their own cities and territories. For example, Inanna, a complex goddess of many aspects including both love and war, owned Uruk; Nanna, the moon god, possessed Ur; and Ningirsu, a fertility god as well as a warrior god, retained Lagash. The temple in which the gods were worshiped, called *e*, or "house," was more than a single building that contained the main shrine. It was actually composed of a number of buildings that served various cultic functions and included orchards and agricultural fields as well as herds of animals that provided sustenance for the gods and for the personnel needed to maintain the huge divine estates or manors. Even though much archaeological research has focused on the excavation of temples, we still do not have the physical evidence for the complete building complex of any major divinity. For example, we have only the core—the main sanctuary area—of the Early Dynastic great temple of Inanna at the holy city of Nippur. And the primary sanctuary of Ningirsu remains to be discovered at Lagash, where we know at present only parts of the complex— namely, a building where some of the god's food was prepared and another erected solely to house his brewery. So vast were these manors that the labor of a sizable portion of the population in early Sumer apparently was devoted to their maintenance.[4]

In addition to fishermen, farmers, and bakers who provided food for the temple, and many other varieties of workers concerned with its upkeep, artists and craftsmen were included among the estate personnel. Their production of fine objects as well as works of art provided the appropriate furnishings for the performance of the cultic ritual and also additional objects, generally and conveniently called votive, that were dedicated to the gods by individuals from certain classes of society. Other works of art, often similar to those found in temples, were made for the express purpose of accompanying the deceased on the journey

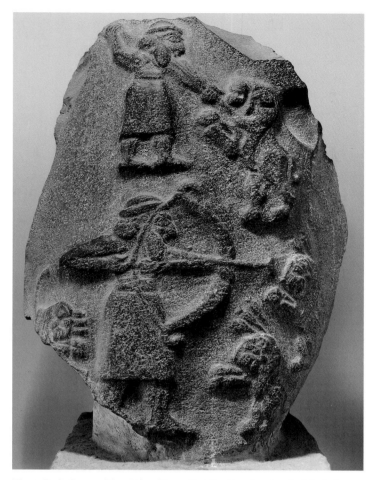

Fig. 5. Relief-carved basalt boulder called the lion-hunt stele. Uruk, Late Uruk, ca. 3300–3000 B.C. Iraq Museum, Baghdad, IM 23477.

in the afterlife. Indeed, almost all the art from ancient Sumer in our museums and collections was created for the worship of the gods and to heighten the human relationship with the numinous presence. Even monuments of state were conceived within a framework that encompassed the divine realm.

The Sumerians of the third millennium inherited some of the means for the artistic expression of their societal values from the complex visual and conceptual vocabulary that had developed in the great city of Uruk before the onset of the Early Dynastic period. This inherited iconographic system included the definition of the ruler as celebrated and eminent warrior, as masterful hunter, and as the supreme priest who mediates and effectuates the man-god relationship, a link that encompasses all aspects of life. These specific ruler virtues persisted throughout the millennia of Mesopotamian history. Only the ruler's role as consummate builder and architect, an important aspect of royal service noted first in the art of the Early Dynastic period, seems to be missing from the visual evidence of the Uruk and Jamdat Nasr periods, although this may be due to the vagaries of excavation.

The monument that best shows the ruler as hunter is the famous lion-hunt stele from Uruk (fig. 5). The lion hunt is a motif that was interpreted throughout the history of Mesopotamia and informs the royal iconography of numerous other Near Eastern and Mediterranean regions.[5] Typically for the Uruk and Jamdat Nasr periods (see cat. no. 8), the ruler shown on the Uruk stele is dressed only in a skirt with a broad belt or sash at the waist. Often this skirt is shown with a pattern of crossed lines as if the garment were made of net (see cat. nos. 10a, b). The stele portrays the ruler shooting arrows at lions in the lower part of a rather free-form composition, and in the upper part of the roughly hewn boulder his figure is repeated; here, however, he is holding a spear, which he thrusts at another lion. The repetition of a figure shown performing two different actions within a single composition is the essence of continuous narration, an art form fully developed throughout later Mesopotamian art and one of Mesopotamia's great contributions to the history of world art.

The equally important theme of the hunt of the wild bull is seen on a Late Uruk cylinder seal in the British Museum (fig. 6). The ruler, wearing a net skirt, again shoots with bow and arrow, but in this instance at four bulls that fill the space before the hunter. Each bull is depicted with remarkable dexterity, posed in a different dynamic position, including a notable one effected by the bull in the lower register of the design: what amounts to a flying gallop, a carriage later exploited in the Aegean region and Egypt. That this hunt scene, like most artistic expression of the period, was conceived within a religious context is indicated by a small gatepost with a streamer, the symbol of the goddess Inanna, interjected between the hunter and the bearer who stands behind him. Thus the hunt is carried out either for the goddess or under her command. The bull and the lion in early art of this kind probably are meant to denote certain vital and raw powers of nature.[6] Indeed, in later literature the potency of the gods and even the king is sometimes described metaphorically with reference to the lion and the wild bull. The

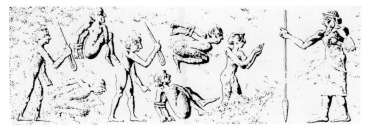

Fig. 7. Composite drawing of impressions on clay from a cylinder seal depicting a "priest-king" as warrior. Seal: Uruk, Late Uruk, ca. 3300–3000 B.C. Staatliche Museen zu Berlin, Vorderasiatisches Museum, VA 10744.

ruler's ability to bring order out of chaos, to master the elemental forces of nature, to be part of, partake of, and have control of the essential cycle of death in life and life in death—as symbolized by the pursuit and conquest of these beasts—was an imperative part of rulership. Seen in this light, the hunt is in essence a ritual.

There is no major or large-scale work of art from the Uruk period that preserves the representation of the ruler as warrior; however, there are probably reflections of such compositions in a number of impressions made on clay by cylinder seals. In one of these, an impression excavated at Uruk (fig. 7), the ruler is shown holding before him his spear with the head turned down, perhaps a negative gesture. His warriors, who hold smaller spears, are situated before him, as are bound nude enemies with bended knees. The nudity that helps define the conquered enemy underscores the captives' helplessness and deprives them of identity. Nudity employed with similar intent is a recurring motif with many variations in Near Eastern and Egyptian art in this and other periods: thus, in a roughly contemporary sealing from Susa, an Elamite city in present-day southwestern Iran, for example, the ruler figure, who stands before a temple placed on an elaborate platform that introduces the divine presence into the scene, also destroys nude enemies with his bow and arrows (fig. 8). Yet the meaning of nude figures in other types of compositions is difficult to ascertain. For reasons yet to be understood, warriors, attendants, and workers are also often shown nude.

It is on the basis of many representations in the art of the period that we can posit that an important function of the ruler, in present-day writings often called the "priest-king," was to act as intermediary between man and the gods.[7] He enjoyed the responsibility of assuring the favorable action of the gods in providing the necessities of life and in effecting the continuation and proliferation of the procreation of plant and animal, as well as human, life. This aspect of the ruler is probably best expressed

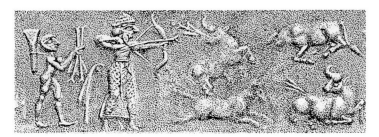

Fig. 6. Drawing of a modern impression from a limestone cylinder seal depicting a bull hunt. Seal: Mesopotamia, Late Uruk, ca. 3300–3000 B.C. British Museum, London, BM 131440.

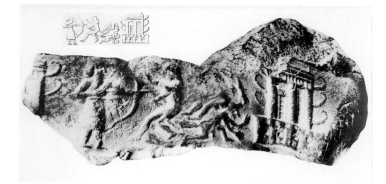

Fig. 8. Drawing of an impression on clay from a cylinder seal depicting a "priest-king" fighting enemies before a horned building. Seal: Susa, Late Uruk, ca. 3300–3000 B.C. Musée du Louvre, Paris, Sb 2125.

in the monumental stone cult vase from the precinct of the goddess Inanna in Uruk (figs. 9, 10).[8] The outer surface of the vase is divided into a series of registers showing waters, grains, male and female animals, and nude men carrying baskets of foodstuffs. Each register represents one component necessary for the fecundity of life in Sumer brought about by the union of Inanna and her consort, Dumuzi, who greet each other before the goddess's storehouse shown behind the female figure in the uppermost band. The male figure is mostly destroyed, but a portion of his foot and net skirt are preserved. Inanna may be represented by her priestess, Dumuzi may appear in the guise of the ruler. The fusion of the world of the gods and that of the humans was so complete at the end of the fourth millennium, when the vase was produced, that depictions of figures lack indicators of divinity. The portrayal is the same whether the main figures are meant as Inanna and Dumuzi or her priestess and the priest-king, for in the cult performance they are one and the same.[9]

The priest-king is shown playing his part in the sacred marriage with the goddess and often in other roles as well on cylinder seals. On a seal in the Yale Babylonian Collection, New Haven (cat. no. 10b), he feeds the temple flocks of both horned and hornless animals, which probably represent, respectively, male and female creatures. On another seal in the same collection (cat. no. 10a) both the priest-king and an attendant stand before a temple whose facade is composed of a variety of patterns, in all likelihood derived from reed construction. A gigantic string of beads is presented by the attendant to the deity, and the ruler proffers a feline lacking the lower parts of its legs. They have been removed purposefully in order to serve a different ritual function. The find of feline forelegs that had been built into the so-called Anu ziggurat, in another precinct at Uruk, suggests an aspect of what that ritual might have been.[10]

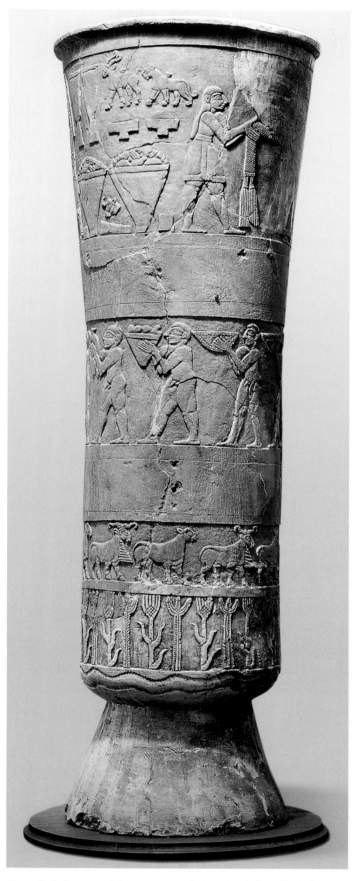

Fig. 9. Relief-carved alabaster vessel called the Uruk Vase. Uruk, Late Uruk, ca. 3300–3000 B.C. Iraq Museum, Baghdad, IM 19606.

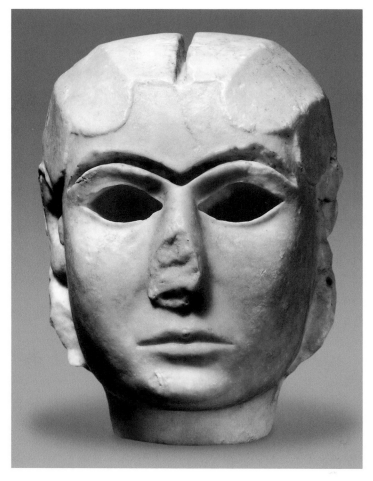

Fig. 10. Drawing of the Uruk Vase (fig. 9).

Remarkable works of art were created in Uruk for the E-anna, the temple of Inanna (figs. 11a, b). Most impressive is a woman's head carved in limestone that originally was part of a composite image (fig. 11a). The head is flat on the back, and presumably was made this way so that it could be attached to a smooth surface, but it is not known how the sculpture was used. The eyes are now lost and would originally have been made of shell, bitumen, and perhaps even lapis lazuli, creating a piercing gaze. Her hair, seen now in simple waves, was most likely covered with gold that may have been chased with series of parallel lines suggesting fine strands of hair. No matter how the head was finished, it is clear that the final effect would have been intensely coloristic with sharp contrasts of tone. The accents of bright color provided by the inlaid elements would have contrasted strongly with the extraordinary sensitivity of the carving of the cheeks, chin, and particularly the mouth. Indeed, the sculpture marks a new view of the world that emerged in the Late Uruk period, a view that conceived this feminine goddess or priestess in realistic terms. The realism of the head denotes a humanization

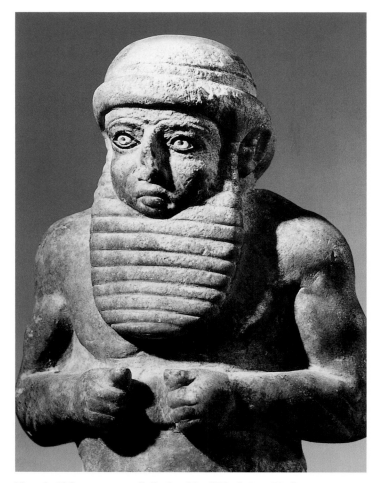

Fig. 11a. Alabaster head of a woman. Uruk, Late Uruk, ca. 3300–3000 B.C. Iraq Museum, Baghdad, IM 45434.

Fig. 11b. Alabaster statue of a "priest-king." Uruk, Late Uruk, ca. 3300–3000 B.C. Iraq Museum, Baghdad, IM 61986.

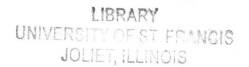

of the divine and stands at the opposite end of a spectrum of idol-like feminine images extending back into Neolithic times. The immediate predecessors of the Uruk head are female terracottas of the Late Ubaid period that have dowel bodies and serpentlike heads totally at odds with the Late Uruk concept of the feminine principle.[11] Unfortunately, we know nothing about the more than five-hundred-year history of sculpture represented by the Early and Middle Uruk phases; however, an image as sophisticated as the Uruk head suggests that a long sculptural tradition and many intermediaries stand between it and the terracottas of the Late Ubaid period.

The same realistic approach seen in the head, albeit an idealized one, also extended to animal sculptures. A prime example is a sandstone ewe's head from Uruk (cat. no. 1). The care manifested in the carving and a mastery of the medium allowed the sculptor to suggest a sense of the structure of the creature's head and to individualize it with its floppy ear, soft fold of flesh over the eye, and smooth lips that differentiate the piece from any earlier animal sculpture. Like the Uruk woman's head, this one must derive from a temple context, though its specific use can only be conjectured.

Obviously, not all sculptures of the time were of the same quality or style as the female head and the ewe. Others were executed more simply, with greater emphasis on linear accents or even with heightened abstract forms. The nude male figure now in Zurich (cat. no. 8) is one such example of variant style. The forms are simple, and the lower part of the body is carried out in severe blocky shapes. The subject's full hair bound with a fillet and his full rounded beard suggest that the piece was meant to represent the priest-king, although this is by no means certain. Nor can we be certain about the place of this image in the history of the sculpture of the period. Since so much of the material preserved for us from excavations comes from secondary or even tertiary archaeological deposits, it is difficult to judge whether differences in style are due to chronological development and thus separated in time, or whether different styles might well be contemporary or even regional. Sometimes we are too ready to assume that art in the ancient Near East developed along lines similar to those of ancient Greece, for it is just as likely that what we differentiate as "styles" existed not necessarily sequentially but simultaneously.

During the Uruk and Jamdat Nasr periods the region of Elam in southwest Iran, with its major cites of Susa and Anshan, was closely allied culturally with Sumer. In fact, in many instances the pottery of one region is scarcely distinguishable from that of the other. In archaeological terminology this time span in Elam is called Susa II and III, and the latter is also known as Proto-Elamite. Late in the Proto-Elamite age, which may well have overlapped with the Early Dynastic I period of Sumer, the representation of animals performing as humans was favored in both sculpture and cylinder seals; that is, animals assume human poses and carry out activities usually reserved for the human species. One of the finest sculptures of this type is a sexually ambivalent lion carved in crystalline limestone or magnesite that is truly monumental, even though it is only 8.8 centimeters high (cat. no. 14). The lion stands on its hind legs, its muscular body twisted and its enlarged paws or hands clasped before its chest. Its shoulders and upper arms are inflated and explode with energy. Originally the lower legs were fashioned from another material such as silver or even gold, and a colorful long tail was inserted into several drill holes on the back of the sculpture. Images of an entire figure of this kind are preserved in imaginative compositions on Proto-Elamite seal impressions, where the female (?) feline is contrasted with a powerful bull that also assumes a pose more appropriate to a human than a bovine (fig. 12). A sculpture of a kneeling bull in the present exhibition (cat. no. 13) is another outstanding example of an animal with human characteristics and of the use of rich materials for a small work that assumes monumental proportions. Crafted of many pieces of silver fused together, it is a remarkable embodiment of early metalwork. Totally human body parts such as arms and shoulders are reinterpreted using the haunches and legs of the bull; the amalgamation is so complete that an explanation of these features in either human or animal terms is equally satisfactory. The kneeling pose was particularly favored in Elam and was employed for both deities and humans as well as for animals of this type. These Elamite sculptures, whose significance is difficult to interpret, mark the beginning of a long tradition that would appear repeatedly throughout the history of art, surviving even today in the ever-popular cartoons of the cinema and children's books.

The artistic legacy of the Uruk, Jamdat Nasr, and Proto-Elamite periods was great, and its lineage can be discerned often in the various arts and crafts of the city-states of the succeeding Early Dynastic age. The archaeological record, however, is sometimes spotty, and a complete picture or history of Sumerian artistic achievements of the Early Dynastic period cannot yet be fully presented. Once thought to be a rather short transitional moment between two more substantial stages of Sumerian culture, Early Dynastic I—the period in which plano-convex bricks first came to be used consistently—is now known to be an important and rich phase in its own right. Cylinder seal impressions from such cities as Fara and Nippur,

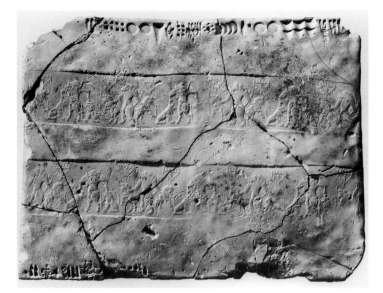

Fig. 12. Clay tablet with cylinder-seal impressions of dominating animals. Susa, Proto-Elamite, ca. 3000–2800 B.C. Musée du Louvre, Paris, Sb 2801.

and particularly from the so-called Seal Impression Strata (SIS) at Ur, provide an index of the themes and details of the iconography prevalent during Early Dynastic I (see cat. no. 22).[12] Old themes that characterized Uruk and Jamdat Nasr glyptic such as the animal file, attacking animals, and the temple facade survive; but a host of new subjects is introduced—among them a hero contending and fighting with animals or a new creature, half human and half bull/bison—and for the first time seal designs incorporate the names of cities (see cat. no. 21). Based on seal impressions from these ancient sites, it can be ascertained that common stylistic features include a predilection for horizontal compositions in animal attack groups, a tendency to form patterns of closely interlocked animal and human body parts, and a propensity for employing violently distorted animal poses.[13] These sealings constitute the link between the Protoliterate Uruk ages and the subsequent period, when comprehensible historical documents first appear.

A few sculptures in the exhibition probably belong to Early Dynastic I. One (cat. no. 17) is a figurine from the Shara temple of Tell Agrab, a site in the Diyala region not far from the juncture of the Tigris and Diyala Rivers in central Mesopotamia. This small piece represents a bearded nude man kneeling on one knee. His arms are raised, and his hands support a large vessel that rests upon his head. The shape of the vessel, which is quite distinctive, clearly dates the sculpture to Early Dynastic I, as it is a pottery type known from this period in the Diyala region as well as Nippur. Although the figurine was heavily restored in modern times, the essentials of the forms are cor-

rect.[14] The sense of movement implied in the man's bended knees parallels that conveyed in the seal-impression designs of Early Dynastic I.

On the basis of their stylistic affinities with this figurine, we can suggest that certain other works, such as the large sculpture of a bull-man in the Ortiz collection (cat. no. 18), may also date to Early Dynastic I. Indeed, the approaches to the definition of form in the bull-man and the kneeling figure are rather similar. Furthermore, the bull-man continues a tradition of the Uruk and Jamdat Nasr periods in that it is a composite sculpture: the lower legs, horns, ears, and other body parts were made from a variety of materials and affixed to the stone body. This is a technique more in keeping with early sculptures such as the Proto-Elamite lion figure in the present exhibition (cat. no. 14) and a magnificent stylistically related bull from Uruk now in the Iraq Museum, Baghdad (fig. 13), than with Early Dynastic II and III pieces.

Considerably more is known about Sumerian art of Early Dynastic II and III than about that of Early Dynastic I. In these later periods, as before, much of the art was created to serve the gods in their temples. In contrast to the dearth of information about temple decoration in Early Dynastic I, the archaeological record of succeeding periods provides some details. The main temple shrines were usually raised on platforms so that they stood out impressively from the surrounding city architecture, visually expressing the union of heaven and earth provided by the temple. Because the temples were constructed of mud brick and were continuously rebuilt one atop the other, no entire building facade is preserved. We can, however, assume that many facades were lavishly decorated with freestanding sculptures and figures in relief made of metal and stone. Paintings on the mud-plastered wall surfaces probably also helped to set off the temple from its drab, earth-colored surroundings.[15] Fortunately, we have

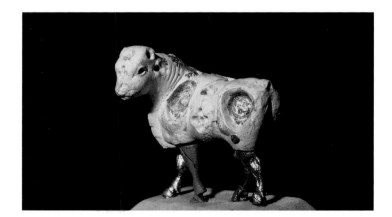

Fig. 13. Limestone and silver figure of a bull. Uruk, Late Uruk, ca. 3300–3000 B.C. Iraq Museum, Baghdad, IM 22472.

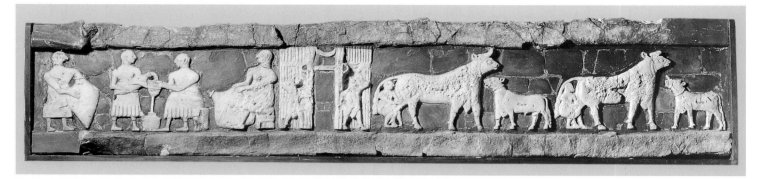

Fig. 14. Limestone, bituminous stone, and copper-alloy temple frieze with a milking scene. Tell al Ubaid, Early Dynastic IIIA, ca. 2550–2400 B.C. Iraq Museum, Baghdad, IM 513.

remains of one temple dedicated to the goddess Ninhursanga (fig. 14; see also fig. 29), an early mother goddess, at Tell al Ubaid, a city close to Ur, that give us some idea of its exterior decoration. A'anepada, the second king of the First Dynasty of Ur, perhaps built it, for his name appears on a stone foundation tablet found out of context but close to the temple. The concept of fertility and continuous procreation that underlay the religious notions of the Protoliterate age still governed much of the iconography of the Early Dynastic period and was treated here. The choice of this theme was particularly apt in the case of a temple to the mother goddess. It was elaborated, for example, in part of a frieze that stretched across the front of the building, which consists of a line of cattle made of limestone—apparently cows—moving to the right (cat. no. 46a). Another section of the frieze (fig. 14) has at its center a reed hut or bier from which newborn calves emerge; its doorway, marked by the gatepost symbols of Inanna, thereby introduces an additional aspect of fertility. To the right of the reed structure cows being milked by tiny male workers placed behind them and beneath their tails face to the right. Other young calves stand before their mothers. To the left of the bier workers dressed in short, fringed skirts and holding jars and a funnel are engaged in preparing milk products. Either above or below this frieze was a row of copper-alloy bulls fashioned in the round (see cat. no. 43). They stand with their heads turned out toward a viewer situated in front of the building. The limestone frieze as a whole represents the aspect of Ninhursanga concerned with the female power over birth, animals, and milk, while the copper animals represent the male principle as manifested through the bull, the prime progenitor.

The temples of the Early Dynastic age were very different from those of other historical eras.[16] Their interiors were in marked contrast to anything that we might know from our own experience. On entering a Gothic cathedral, for example, we leave the sensually chaotic mundane world and walk into a totally spiritual ambience. The spatial magnitude, the upward thrust of the architectural members, the optimistic roseate diffused light of the stained glass that illuminates yet partially obscures are but a few of the qualities that produce a deep sense of awe and an aura of otherworldliness that permit a communication with the divine. Even though the worshiper is not physically in contact with the most sacred high altar, a divine presence is materialized and he or she can receive the awaited and needed blessings. None of these elements was present in the Early Dynastic temples.

Moreover, these temples do not conform to any regular pattern, and we can therefore deduce that there was no all-pervasive plan that guided temple building throughout Sumer. In some instances the orderly tripartite architectural scheme that usually governed temple construction in Greater Mesopotamia during Uruk and Jamdat Nasr times continued and was modified during the various rebuildings of the shrines carried out in the Early Dynastic period. In other cases, the form of the main shrine may have developed out of non-temple architecture, for the most part following the plan of a building that existed before the temple dedicated to a specific divinity was erected. One general rule was observed: the doorway to the main shrine room, which was rectangular, was placed at the end of one long wall, so that someone entering had to turn ninety degrees to face the main altar, which was set against a short wall at the opposite end of the shrine. Many rooms of this "house" of the god were filled with mud-brick furniture in the form of other altars and offering tables and included, as well, places for building fires and stations for pouring liquids. Such a building obviously needed to be properly maintained. Maintenance of mud-brick architecture, in general, meant adding new coats of mud plaster to the walls, floors, and roofs from time to time to keep the building dry. In the Sumerian temple, however, the addition of mud plasters, renewed at least annually, was more than simple upkeep. It became part of a ritual of purification that included the replastering of all the temple furniture as well as of the walls. Oftentimes splashes of white paint or whitewash were cast onto the walls during this ritual. The altars, tables, benches, and other protuberances grew to such great size that they became like free-form sculptures so dense that movement within the holiest of rooms, the cella, became virtually impossible. Certainly the shrine could not have been open to everyone—not even to all the temple personnel—and, in fact, access was probably limited to only a few who served the god's own special needs.

It is perhaps for this very reason that during the Early Dynastic period a special type of sculpture—often called a worshiper statue or a votive figure—became popular (see cat. nos. 24–26, 28, 29, 88–93). These statues, which were images that literally embodied the essence of the worshiper, were dedicated to the god and stood on benches or offering tables before the divine presence inside the cella. Some are inscribed with simple dedications giving the name of the god and the profession and name of the donor. In these statues the worshiper is normally shown with hands clasped and held at the waist, a purposive gesture signifying prayer and expressing a readiness to communicate with the god. Hence, the dedicant's spirit was eternally present even though the physical living body was absent. Once the statue was offered and became part of the temple, it could not be disposed of profanely. Instead groups of statues, perhaps after the donor died, were either buried beneath floors in the cella (see fig. 25) or other temple rooms, or placed within the offering tables, or else they were used as building materials within cult installations. What was important was not precisely where they were put when discarded but rather that they were kept within the temple. This need to retain the sculptures relates to the requisites imposed in certain later Near Eastern religions. In medieval Islam, for instance, in the great mosque in Sana'a, Qu'rans that were no longer in use were literally buried within the rafters of the attic. Here and elsewhere fragments of Qu'ran pages could not simply be disposed of but were stuck into crevices in mosque walls and were eventually plastered over. Judaism demands that written documents that might contain the name of God in one form or another be disposed of in a hallowed place, the genizah, the most famous being the genizah of the synagogue of Fustat in Cairo. Thus, the Sumerian attitude toward votive objects in the Early Dynastic period is part of a long tradition in the treatment of sacred objects that reaches into our own times.[17]

The votive statues, of various sizes and usually carved in gypsum or limestone, represent both men and women. The men generally wear either a tasseled skirt distinguished by an allover pattern resembling tufts of fleece or a plain skirt with a fringe at the bottom. They are nude above the waist. Some wear their hair and beard long, others are bald. In contrast, women wear a long robe or wraparound that leaves the right shoulder bare and often display elaborately complex coiffures. Certain statues retain evidence of having been painted. Sometimes pigment can be observed in the fine incisions of the hair patterns, indicating that the hair, at least, was painted black. How much other paint may have been used for details of dress or even for skin color is not known.

All of these votive figures are frontal, and their style ranges from highly abstract, with sharp sculptural transitions between different parts of the body, to relatively naturalistic, with a softer integration of forms (see cat. nos. 24a–d). One of the finest of the naturalistic type was excavated in the Nintu temple at Khafajah, a city located in the Diyala region of central Mesopotamia (cat. no. 24d). It was found in a stratum dated to Early Dynastic II in the chronological scheme proposed by the excavators for the Diyala region, indicating that the naturalistic style was fully developed in that part of the Early Dynastic age. Moreover, as more abstract objects were also discovered in that stratum, we can conclude that the two approaches coexisted for a considerable time, just as both styles appeared concurrently in the Protoliterate period of Uruk and Jamdat Nasr.[18]

A large headless statue of diorite found at Ur and now preserved in the Iraq Museum, Baghdad (fig. 15), is a typical votive figure in that the donor is nude from the waist up and wears only a fleece skirt with a tassel, albeit a particularly large one, attached at the back. It is atypical in that it is a statue of a ruler, or *ensi,* representing, as it does, Enmetena of Lagash, who reigned during the period of Early Dynastic IIIB. The piece is important for a variety of reasons. First, it is one of the earliest Mesopotamian statues made of diorite, thus beginning the tradition, favored in later periods, of using that hard stone brought from Oman for royal statues. Significantly, diorite is a stone of great density suitable to last for eternity and one that can be polished to a high sheen. The figure of Enmetena is also important because it is inscribed with a long text offering a dedication that includes a special name for the statue itself: in the statement of a name, the concept becomes a reality. This statue was simply called "Enlil (the god) loves Enmetena,"[19] though in later periods the names of the statues often became more complex (see cat. nos. 304–308). Third, the long inscription on the Enmetena statue goes beyond a simple dedication to record a land transaction, in which respect it is like a great many early

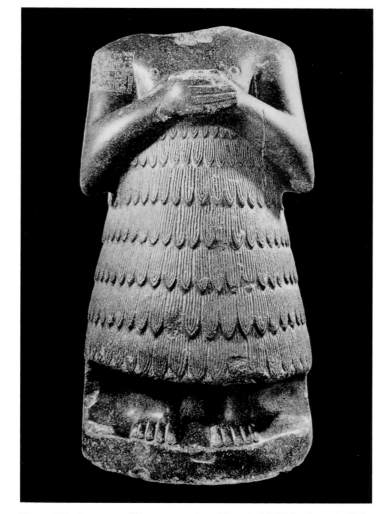

Fig. 15. Diorite statue of Enmetena, ruler of Lagash. Ur, Early Dynastic IIIB, ca. 2400–2250 B.C. Iraq Museum, Baghdad, IM 5.

inscribed monuments, such as catalogue number 20, that are concerned with dealings of this kind.[20] The Enmetena inscription involves a transaction between the ruler and the temple, suggesting that the statue was created in honor of this donation. This is an idea that might be carried a step further to suggest that the votive figurines were dedicated in the temple by elite members of society in relation to gifts made, for example, for temple maintenance or rituals. To draw a modern analogy, this act may have resembled one effected for the waqf of a mosque, dedications made usually but not necessarily in the form of monies or grants of land for the institution's upkeep, namely renovations, repairs, and repainting.

Statues were not the only works of art dedicated in a temple. Plain or carved stone vessels with images in relief (see cat. nos. 94, 231), wall plaques with a variety of scenes in relief (see cat. nos. 30–33), and even weapons (see cat. no. 35) could be inscribed and dedicated. Unfortunately, only part of an inscription and an incomplete figure remain on what once was a

magnificent basalt vessel of unknown provenance now in Berlin (cat. no. 36). Enmetena dedicated it to a divinity whose name is not preserved in the inscription. The figure that is still partially visible is probably Nisaba, one of several goddesses associated with agricultural abundance.[21] Either additional deities or the dedicant and attendants along with symbols would have completed the composition on the lost part of the vase. Nisaba is a goddess of grain and other forms of vegetation. Appropriately, six curving plant stems surmounted by buds emanate from her shoulders, plant fronds are secured within her crown, and she holds in her right hand the date cluster, fruit of the pollinated palm. But unlike Inanna, who, according to the conventions of the Protoliterate period, bore no special marking to announce divinity, the figure on the Berlin vessel, as is always the case with godhead in the Early Dynastic age, is distinguished by a horned crown, which in this instance surmounts a most luxuriant head of hair with long curls falling down over her shoulders and onto her breasts. Perhaps the superabundant hair, often associated with sex and power, that dominates the image was also meant to emphasize the idea of fertility. The frontal image of the head, a view reserved for the representation of gods and heroes, commands attention. It causes the viewer's eye to stop, focus on the figure's accentuated eyes and brows, and absorb the nature of the goddess.

That relief plaques made of various types of stones (see cat. nos. 30–33) were also dedicated to the gods by individual worshipers is indicated by inscriptions on several examples.[22] Such reliefs were affixed to the temple walls by means of clay or stone nails inserted though a hole in the center of the plaque. The nailheads either were semispherical or were carved in the form of animal heads. Usually the plaques were divided into registers, and scenes of numerous different kinds were selected to fill each register. The scenes might include, for example, a combat between a hero and lion (cat. no. 200), the pouring of libations before a god as well as before a temple (cat. no. 33), or even the presentation of an empty chariot drawn by equids (cat. no. 31). The most favored theme, however, was the banquet.[23] A good example appears in the top register of a plaque from Khafajah, ancient Tutub, in the Diyala region (cat. no. 32). Two facing seated banqueters hold forth drinking cups as if they were about to partake of the liquid within them, which is probably beer. The male, on the right, and the female, on the left, are joined by several attendants. In the second register figures carry foodstuffs and an animal, and in the bottom register, likely accompanying the banquet, is a musician playing a lyre facing another figure who is either dancing or singing. Undoubtedly banquets were held to celebrate a variety of occasions; the content of the three registers of this plaque, however, suggests that the celebration shown here is metaphoric, probably concerned with agricultural productivity and fecundity. This interpretation is underscored by the fact that the male figure holds in his left hand an object that resembles the male date spathe and the female holds in her right hand the fruit in the form of a date cluster.

Not only temple personnel and other members of Sumerian society but also the *ensi* dedicated relief plaques in the temple. Most famous among the latter examples is a relief of Ur-Nanshe, a ruler of the state of Lagash in the Early Dynastic IIIA period (fig. 16). Here the important role of the ruler as temple builder is venerated. Ur-Nanshe is shown carrying on his head a basket with earth for the first or archetypal brick for the E-ninnu temple of the god Ningirsu in Girsu, or modern Tello, one of the cities of the state of Lagash, and also seated and drinking in commemoration of the event. An inscription states that " Ur-Nanshe . . . built the temple of Nanshe, built the Abzubandu."[24] In addition to the two images of Ur-Nanshe, representatives of his family—his sons and perhaps a daughter—are also portrayed and are identified by means of names carved on their skirts. As such, this so-called family relief is one of the first Sumerian works in which the secondary figures are distinguished by inscriptions, marking a step in the evolution of more complex forms of narrative clarification. In a smaller version of a family relief from Girsu (cat. no. 30) Ur-Nanshe is shown bald, beardless, and clothed only in a fleece skirt like his descendant Enmetena in the statue in the round from Ur (fig. 15). The inscription on the little Ur-Nanshe plaque identifies the *ensi,* repeats the dedication to Ningirsu, and also labels the smaller figures as his sons.

The divine command to build temples was taken most seriously by the Mesopotamian rulers. As we know from later texts, temple building was complex and involved intricate rituals. The gods revealed the plan for the building, and it was necessary to secure the embedded foundations in place by nails or cones, indicators of possession. Often the image of the ruler or his personal god served this purpose. One such image (cat. no. 27) represents the bearded Lugalkisalsi, a ruler of Uruk and Ur during the Early Dynastic IIIB period. This statue was originally placed within the foundations of the temple of Namma, a mother goddess and mother of the god Enki. Lugalkisalsi's hands are clasped in front of his chest, the usual gesture for eternal prayer. Lacking any indication of legs or dress, the lower part of the king's body is in the form of a cone, thereby literally pinning

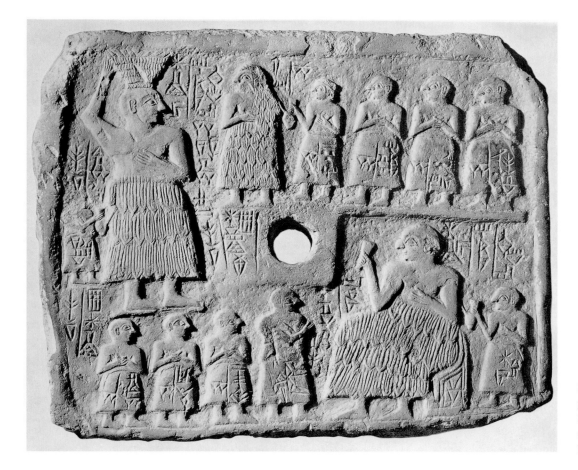

Fig. 16. Limestone relief-carved plaque of Ur-Nanshe, ruler of Lagash. Girsu, Early Dynastic IIIA, ca. 2550–2400 B.C. Musée du Louvre, Paris, AO 2344.

down the temple foundations. The lower conical body also provides a place for the inscription that gives the name and titles of Lugalkisalsi and the dedication to Namma, a mother goddess here titled consort of the god An.

In addition to the many fine votive objects fabricated in Early Dynastic Sumer,[25] other ritual items were used in the temples. Popular were ornately decorated vessels fashioned from ostrich eggshells as well as replicas thereof in both gold and silver. Almost identical eggshell containers were placed in graves to accompany the dead. Similar to an example found in the temple of Inanna at Nippur are two containers from graves of the famed cemetery of Ur excavated by Sir Leonard Woolley (cat. no. 70; see "The Royal Tombs of Ur," by Julian Reade, in this catalogue). Among the burials in this cemetery are those of the rulers of Ur, many dating to Early Dynastic IIIA. But the cemetery included hundreds of graves and continued to be used in later periods. Some tombs were large and held not only a member of the royal family but also a great number of attendants, including harpists, singers, soldiers, and drivers and grooms for the oxen or asses that pulled chariots and sledges.[26] Tomb PG 1237, the Great Death Pit (see "The Great Death Pit at Ur," by Julian Reade, in this catalogue), contained the bodies of seventy-four attendants. Often the retainers had small cups of either stone, metal, or clay that presumably held the poison they seem to have drunk voluntarily; their bodies were laid out as if they had died calmly. Scholars do not agree on the interpretation of these burials. Although there are many examples of retainers dying with their master from various times and parts of the world, all of Mesopotamian history finds graves with rulers and attendants only in Sumer in the Early Dynastic period. Whether the bodies are those of a king or queen and retainers who died in order to serve in the afterlife, whether they died carrying out a particular cult ritual associated with the moon god Nanna, the owner of Ur, or whether their presence is yet to be explained by some totally different rationale is still to be determined.[27]

Our knowledge of Sumerian art of the third millennium would be somewhat meager without the materials excavated in the Ur cemetery. Some of the finest works of art of the Early Dynastic period were included among the remarkably rich finds from several of the tombs. We are indebted to the genius of Woolley for having the excavation skills to dig these tombs and to successfully remove so many fragile objects from the earth.[28]

The exhibition includes a fine lion head, one of a pair in silver found in the front section of the tomb of the queen Puabi (cat. no. 64). It is not clear how the heads were used: they could have been attached to furniture, although no early examples of furniture with embellishments survive to substantiate this hypothesis. Either cast or moulded over a core, this head is amazingly expressive and represents the continuation of the more naturalistic stylistic tendencies perceived in Protoliterate sculpture. Keen observation and the ability to translate this scrutiny into a work of art that seizes the essence of the particular animal form and transmits a sense of leonine grandeur and fearsomeness are achievements associated with some of the master sculptors of this age. A wonderful copper-alloy head of a markhor goat (cat. no. 41), apparently found not at the Ur cemetery but at Fara, also reveals the sculptor's ability to crystallize the essence of the animal type and at the same time displays a self-conscious bravura in the handling of the abstract forms of the spiraling horns.

Among the most famous sculptures from the cemetery are a pair of goats from the Great Death Pit, one now at the University of Pennsylvania Museum of Archaeology and Anthropology, Philadelphia (cat. no. 71), the other now housed in the British Museum, London. An attachment originally affixed to the cylinder that emerges from each head indicates that the goats must have constituted the lower part of some kind of stand. Unlike sculpture of the Uruk and Jamdat Nasr periods in which parts of the anatomy made of precious and semi-precious materials were added to a body carved in stone, these goats are formed entirely of pieces of gold, silver, lapis lazuli, copper, shell, and red limestone attached with bitumen to a core partially made of wood. The eye of the viewer is immediately struck by shimmering contrasts in texture and color of the burnished light-colored shell body fleece, the deep blue matte lapis of the horns and the brow and neck fleece, and the brilliance of the scintillating gold face and legs. The male goat[29] stands erect with his forelegs supported by the branches of a tall plant covered with gold.[30] Emerging from the branches are buds and rosettes, the latter often considered to be symbols of the goddess Inanna. Though goats do stand on branches of trees and nibble at their leaves, the stance is also one assumed by the male animal for sexual engagement. Indeed, this image projects one of the great concerns of the Sumerians, that is, the need for fertility in the world of both plants and animals, a fecundity realized through the powers of the goddess. The idea that sustenance depends on the intimate link between flora and fauna was reinforced visually by the tying of the animal to the tree by a silver wire when the sculpture was first constructed.

Sumerian artists particularly loved the contrasting colors of the materials used in the sculptures of the goats, and they embellished other objects with many of these substances. These pieces included complicated figurative mosaic panels, the most impressive of which is perhaps the so-called Standard of Ur from Grave 779 (cat. no. 52). The end pieces of this box-shaped object are in the form of truncated triangles, so that the entire object is wider at the bottom than at the top. Although called a standard by the excavator, its function is unknown. The long sides are divided into three registers separated by bands of geometric pattern, and each side is devoted to portraying a different but crucial aspect of Sumerian kingship. On one side the ruler is shown in his role as priest and mediator between man and his gods, in which capacity he is responsible for the fertility of the land and the sustenance of his people. Bald and dressed only in a fleece skirt—exactly like the prayerful king Enmetena of Lagash (fig. 15)—the ruler is the largest figure in the register. Although a small piece of shell showing an object in his left hand is missing, we can assume he probably held the male date spathe, as did the male banqueter in the plaque from Khafajah (cat. no. 32). Musicians and cupbearers join him, as do a file of other figures probably best interpreted as a row of men seated in a partial circle before him. The lower registers display the bountifulness of the land as represented by bovines, caprids, and fish brought by Sumerians, shown bald, as well as by people of different aspect whose homeland is perhaps a region other than Ur and who carry produce in backpacks and in bags on their shoulders. The other side portrays the king as warrior. Standing in the middle of the top register, he is again the tallest figure; in fact, his head even projects into the upper border. Holding his spear before him, he faces to the right and surveys nude captives pushed forward toward him by some of his soldiers. Behind him other soldiers and attendants accompany his four-wheeled chariot hauled by four equids. The chariot is drawn in a composite view, the body shown in profile, the front en face, with a large quiver attached to the far side. In the second register helmeted soldiers wearing protective capes advance to the right toward other soldiers dispatching or leading away nude captives; and in the bottom register the king's chariotry moves with increasing speed from left to right while trampling underfoot enemies, degraded in their nudity and spewing blood from gashes in chest and thigh. Pulling each chariot are four equids, their number indicated by the repetition of the basic body outlines. The animals are controlled simply by nose rings with reins leading back through terrets, or rein rings, to the charioteer. The representations on the standard show that the terrets were attached by their brackets to the chariot shaft rather than to a backpad as was usual in later harnessing. Often in Sumerian art an object

of special interest or significance is greatly enlarged in relation to the size of other parts of the composition, and here it is the terrets that are enormous. Composed of only two loops, they are plain in comparison with the magnificent example from the sledge of queen Puabi (cat. no. 66), with its rings and lower bracket of silver. Surmounting the rings is a small sculpture in the round made of electrum that depicts an equid in motion, a very convincing portrayal of precisely the type of animal that pulled the royal sledge.

In terms of objects and materials, Puabi's grave was one of the richest from the Ur cemetery. Some of the precious materials and jewelry were probably placed in the grave so that in the journey through the netherworld the deceased had a supply of gifts to tender to the denizens encountered there. Puabi's own jewelry and garments were sumptuous and apparently included a beaded cape made from hundreds of carnelian, agate, lapis lazuli, silver, and gold beads (cat. no. 62). Whether she wore this cape in life as she did in death is not known. If she did, the glistening effect of such a beaded garment would have been spectacular if not awesome. It is not possible to determine at present the exact meaning of individual stones and jewels, but certainly the Sumerians thought that they could be miraculous—an idea afforded by a reference in the Epic of Gilgamesh to a tree in the garden of sunrise with fruits of jewels. Trees bedecked with jewels continued to appear in later Near Eastern traditions. Examples are the ebullient trees in the mosaic decoration of the Dome of the Rock, which apparently reflect the earlier decorations of the Temple of Solomon.[31]

Puabi's own headdress was particularly complicated. Atop and surrounding a very full head of hair, probably a wig, were a series of gold, carnelian, and lapis lazuli wreaths as well as many wrappings of gold bands or ribbons (cat. no. 61). Attached to some of the circlets were gold leaves in imitation of poplar and willow leaves.[32] Poplar and willow trees existed in Sumer, but these gold leaves probably were not intended primarily as specific naturalistic references; rather they likely had a more symbolic meaning associated with the Sumerian emphasis on plant life celebrated in both art and religious rites.

Accompanying the rituals was music. Representations of a variety of instruments appear in a number of works in this exhibition (cat. nos. 32, 52, 60 b, c, 91, 102) Thanks to Woolley's ingenuity, the remains of many real instruments including harps, lyres, sistra, cymbals, and drums were found in the graves of the Ur cemetery. Particularly impressive is the large lyre from Grave 789 (cat. no. 58), thought to belong to the ruler Meskalamdug.[33] This lyre and another in the British Museum were found resting on the heads of elaborately attired women lying in the tomb against one wall, who were perhaps the very musicians who played the instruments and intoned the chants in the burial rites. The bull head that adorns the front of this large lyre was badly crushed in the earth, and Woolley reconstructed it based on animal heads from other lyres and from the way the individual pieces lay in the ground. The head is formed of gold sheet affixed to an original wood core. An ingenious combination of naturalistic elements and abstract shapes handled rather simply imparts the essence of this bovine creature. A vitality is conveyed by the eyes of contrasting lapis lazuli and shell, which bulge slightly from the smooth golden surface, broken by a series of arching raised bands surmounting them. More lapis was used for the horn tips, for the curls of hair on the forehead, and, most spectacularly, for the twelve grand curling locks of beard hair formed from many pieces of the stone set into a silver background. The head is a fitting enhancement to this large lyre, the other decoration of which was a front panel originally attached to the wood sound box. The trapezoid-shaped panel was composed of shell plaques fitted together to make up four registers. Each plaque, bounded by a border of small shell pieces, had scenes displaying figures raised in relief against a background filled with black bitumen. Details of the figures were picked out in black. The lower three panels visually describe a banquet whose participants are not human but rather animals acting as if they are human. Included are a hyena butcher, a cup-bearing lion, an ass lyre player, and perhaps a dancing bear. They are all part of a vivid scene undoubtedly composed to express the idea of the funeral banquet necessary to ensure the deceased's passage in the underworld. Overseeing the banquet in the top panel is a hero figure grasping two human-headed bison. As a symbol of control of nature's forces, this triad assures the efficacy of the banquet meal.

The original source for such imagery is probably to be found in Elamite art, since during the Proto-Elamite period in southwestern Iran sculptures in the round as well as scenes on cylinder seals depicted animals performing human tasks. This iconography appealed to the Sumerians, who used the animal banquet as early as Early Dynastic I on a cylinder-seal impression from the Seal Impression Strata at Ur (fig. 17). Although, at present, only this seal impression, the panels from the lyre, and a few other examples showing the animal-acting-as-human theme are known, the subject must have been used more extensively in Sumerian iconography.[34]

Following the Proto-Elamite period, the art of Elam was, in its turn, strongly influenced by the art of Early Dynastic Sumer

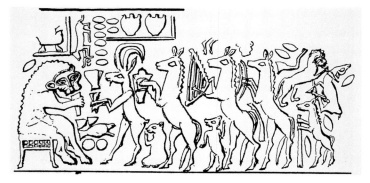

Fig. 17. Composite drawing of impressions on clay from a cylinder seal depicting a banquet with animals. Seal: Ur, Early Dynastic II, ca. 2650–2550 B.C.

(see cat. nos. 199, 200), and it is sometimes difficult to locate in which of the two areas a given object of this era was made. Indeed, art in most of Greater Mesopotamia, including the north of Iraq as well as northern and western Syria, received and adapted to greater and lesser degrees Sumerian stylistic traits and iconography. Each region treated these stimuli differently, often grafting the elements onto the contemporary local art styles and producing regional variations of the same theme.

One city and region of extreme importance in Greater Mesopotamia was Mari on the middle Euphrates, located in what is today Syria, close to the border of Iraq. Mari was strategically situated between Sumer and Akkad in the south and Syria in the north and it continued to be a historically significant city through the first half of the second millennium B.C. The population of Mari was Semitic and worshiped such deities as Ishtar, the Semitic form of Inanna, and Ninni-zaza. Their temples, like numerous Sumerian temples in the south and in the Diyala region in the east, were filled with votive statues. Although ultimately derived from Sumerian prototypes, many of the sculptures are executed in a style developed at Mari and distinguishable from other Early Dynastic works. An example is a statue of a ruler named Ishqi-Mari (cat. no. 88), who called himself *ensi* of the great god Enlil, which was found in the temple of Ishtar. The subject has a full beard and voluminous hair elaborately dressed, with a distinctive chignon at the back of the head. Strands of hair of the chignon are interwoven into a complex pattern, and a large braid encircles Ishqi-Mari's head. This treatment is based on the hairstyle of earlier Sumerian kings, as exemplified by the so-called gold helmet of Meskalamdug, the ruler buried in one of the Royal Cemetery graves at Ur (fig. 18). Meskalamdug's gold head-covering has a similar chignon and a large encircling braid holding the hair in place. Perhaps in the Early Dynastic period this braid replaced the fillet—a detail with clear symbolic significance—that binds the hair of earlier rulers in Uruk and Jamdat Nasr representations (see cat. no. 8). The garments of Ishqi-Mari also recall those seen in southern Mesopotamian works. Like his Lagashite counterpart, Eannatum on the Stele of the Vultures (fig. 52), Ishqi-Mari wears a fleece garment that covers one shoulder. Nevertheless, certain details distinguish the sculpture of Ishqi-Mari from works of the south. In contrast to Enmetena (fig. 15), for example, and like the subjects in many other Mari sculptures, Ishqi-Mari has feet carved fully in the round, and he stands with one foot forward. His gesture with one hand grasping the wrist is rare in works of this time, but in later periods of Mesopotamian art it often occurs in representations of lesser gods. In this early statue, however, it is not clear whether the gesture has the same meaning as the clasped-hands gesture of prayer usually found on votive statues in Sumer and also at Mari itself.

Several votive statues from Mari are included in the exhibition (cat. nos. 88–93). They reveal a number of characteristics in addition to those exemplified by the statue of Ishqi-Mari that help define the distinct style or school of Mari: a careful consideration of body proportions, the manner in which sculptural forms are treated, and details of dress, such as a special treatment of the beard. Based on these works and the others excavated and preserved thus far, it is apparent that the Mari statues generally are of a higher artistic quality than their southern counterparts in terms of their sculptors' particularly fine dexterity in handing stone and in contrasting formal shapes and patterns,

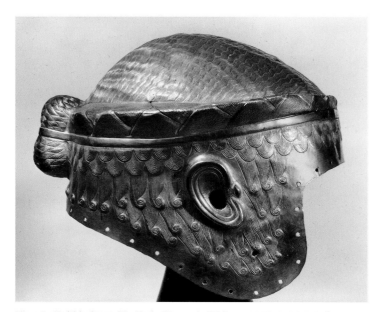

Fig. 18. Gold helmet. Ur, Early Dynastic III A, ca. 2550–2400 B.C. Iraq Museum, Baghdad, IM 8269.

oftentimes bordering on a mannerism (see cat. no. 91). Therefore, the relatively small size and, more important, the somewhat ungainly appearance of the royal statue of Ishqi-Mari is especially surprising.

The artists of Mari shared the Sumerian love of creating figurative panels with cutout pieces of shell set into a background of another material. Unfortunately, no large-scale panels from Mari are preserved, and reconstructions of the extant pieces are purely conjectural.[35] Small panels showing equids (cat. no. 100), a musician (cat. no. 102), a butchering scene (cat. no. 96), and a warrior with a nude bound prisoner (cat. no. 97) indicate that in both Mari and the south artists enjoyed similar themes and compositions. One highly imaginative, incised stone plaque only fourteen centimeters high (cat. no. 99), however, exhibits the technical skill, dexterity of execution, and play of forms that typify the work of a Mari artist and set it apart from that of his Sumerian counterparts. A soldier carrying a spear supports a huge shield apparently made of reeds and protects an archer who shoots into the air toward a nude enemy, already dead and spread out in the field. Amusing to us are the deftly drawn long, pointed medieval-style shoes of the soldiers.

On display in the exhibition are items found buried in the Early Dynastic palace of Mari in a hoard that included figurines and jewelry of copper alloy, ivory, gold, silver, lapis lazuli, and carnelian (cat. nos. 81–87). Neither why nor how this rich hoard came to be buried is understood. Some of the jewelry is much like that from the same period found in various other parts of Greater Mesopotamia, but one bead (cat. no. 84) is unique among material executed thus far. It is a large, twelve-centimeter-long, faceted lapis lazuli bead with a Sumerian inscription indicating that it must have come from the south, most likely from Ur. Its importance lies in the fact that it bears the name of Mesanepada, the first king of the First Dynasty of Ur, thereby providing a chronological link between Mari and Ur. The inscription further states that Mesanepada is the son of Meskalamdug and therefore fixes in place two kings from the Royal Cemetery whose names do not appear in the Sumerian King List.[36]

The copper-alloy and ivory figurines suggest that the hoard was composed of objects originally collected from different places, for they represent sculpture styles far removed from that of the Sumer of the unique lapis lazuli bead. A case in point is the nude copper-alloy figurine with the small horns projecting from the top of the head (cat. no. 82), which probably indicate that what is commonly called a goddess is represented. In comparison with her enormous spreading hips her waist is almost wasplike. Her breasts, although small, are well rounded and originally had shell or lapis lazuli inserts for the nipples. Her head, with huge eyes and pointed chin, is held high. The style accords more comfortably with a basic aesthetic that underlies much of north Syrian or perhaps even north Mesopotamian sculpture than with one derived from the Sumerian south.[37]

The city of Ebla, modern Tell Mardikh, and its kingdom were located in today's northwestern Syria, not far south of Aleppo. Important through many periods of Syrian history, it has become particularly famous because of the tablet archives found there in Palace G of Level IIB1 (see cat. nos. 322–328), a palace probably destroyed by Sargon, the first king of the Akkadian dynasty. If Sargon is indeed responsible, the archaeological remains discovered in the ransacked palace must date to Early Dynastic IIIB.

The contacts between the kingdom of Ebla and the kingdom of Mari were particularly strong, and it is probably via Mari that the elements of Early Dynastic Sumerian art found in the art of Ebla were transmitted.[38] Among the pieces from Ebla that are fairly close to Sumerian prototypes is a small limestone figure from the palace of a recumbent calf with head turned to the side and one raised front leg (cat. no. 113). Precisely that same traditional Sumerian pose is found in a tiny gold, steatite, and wood figurine made in Ebla of a *kusarikkum,* the bearded human-headed bison (cat. no. 111). The figurine might lack the skillful execution usually associated with the best efforts of Sumerian craftsmen, but it nevertheless has an appeal thanks to the inherent attractiveness of its gold and steatite materials.

Cutout figurative pieces assembled into panels like those favored at Mari and Sumer decorated the Ebla palace. At Ebla, however, limestone replaced the usual shell of the cutouts made in the south. The artists of Ebla borrowed from Sumer not only mosaic technique but also the theme of the eagle with outstretched legs and talons grasping human-headed bison. In one limestone inlay that typifies an approach developed at Ebla, the bison is flat and raised only slightly from the stone background, and details are defined by incised lines drawn in a pronounced geometric style (cat. no. 115b). Other limestone inlays from Ebla

informed by this idiosyncratic manner include several examples that originally constituted panels illustrating the prowess of the Eblaite warriors who dispatch enemies or else hold forth severed heads (see cat. nos. 115c–f). Another hallmark of the Ebla style in evidence here is an absence of a rational relationship in size between different elements of the composition; the enemy heads, for example, are gigantic in comparison with the head of the warrior who holds them.

Quite different is the style of the sculpture in the round or partially in the round found in the palace. One of several examples of wood sculpture in the round that have been preserved is a figure holding an axe (fig. 47). The man is heavily bearded and, like Ishqi-Mari of Mari, wears a long fleece garment covering most of his body. The carving is accomplished and remarkably naturalistic, with fine details accorded the definition of the individual tufts of fleece. The high quality suggests that the figure represents an Eblaite ruler, but whether or not this is so is difficult to determine. Also of remarkable quality are carved wigs composed of multiple pieces of steatite (cat. nos. 109a, b), which probably adorned statues in the round assembled from several parts made of different materials. Extraordinary attention has been given to the definition of individual strands of hair, producing striking, richly textured surfaces.

We must wonder how this Eblaite school of subtle sculpture came into being. A clue is offered by evidence of Egyptian contact at the time of the Ebla palace as demonstrated by part of an alabaster jar lid inscribed with the name of Pharaoh Pepi I (cat. no. 161) found at the site. Moreover, during the subsequent Middle Bronze Age of the early second millennium, some of the art produced at Ebla is marked by an obvious overlay of Egyptian style and motifs.[39] Indeed, throughout the ancient Mediterranean world in the course of many periods of history, Egypt was regarded as a land of highly developed civilization and refined taste. Thus it is quite possible that the Eblaite culture was receptive to Egyptian ideals and that its school of sculpture was inspired by Egyptian prototypes. In any case, this Ebla school may well have been an element in the complicated fabric of influences that formed the classic art of Akkad.

1. For the history of the period, see Steinkeller 1992b, pp. 724ff.

2. See most recently Englund 1998, p. 81. For a discussion of the plano-convex brick, see Delougaz 1933, and Nissen 1988, pp. 92–93.

3. J. Oates 1979, pp. 19–23; D. Potts 1997, pp. 43–55.

4. The literature on the temple is vast. See, for example, Postgate 1992, pp. 109–36, and Van de Mieroop 1997.

5. The earliest representation of the lion hunt seems to be a painting on a vase from Arpachiyah dating to the Halaf period of the sixth millennium B.C. (Breniquet 1992, p. 72, fig. 1b). There is no way to know whether the hunter represents a ruler, clan chief, priest, or shaman. The style, iconography, and composition fit comfortably within the Neolithic painting traditions.

6. It is of interest that even as late as the first millennium B.C., the Assyrian kings were shown in combat with both the bull and the lion. See, for example, the reliefs of Ashurnasirpal II, Budge 1914, pl. 42.

7. For the term "priest-king," see Michalowski 1997, p. 100, and Steinkeller 1999, pp. 104–5.

8. The vase, more than a meter in height, was found in pieces in Level III (Jamdat Nasr) of the E-anna Precinct. The fact that the vase was repaired in antiquity suggests that it was created a considerable length of time before it was buried. It most likely dates to Level IV, or the Late Uruk period.

9. For an analysis of the vase, see Bahrani 2002. For the sacred marriage, see Cooper 1993, and Steinkeller 1999.

10. Heinrich 1937, p. 81.

11. For examples, see Woolley 1955, pls. 20–22, and Huot 1983, pls. A:3, A:3,4.

12. For Fara, see Martin 1988; for Nippur, see Hansen 1971; for Ur, see Legrain 1936 and Zettler 1989.

13. For examples, see Legrain 1936.

14. For the figurine before restoration, see Frankfort 1943, pl. 34.

15. Only a few painting fragments from the temples of the Early Dynastic period at Nippur are preserved. However, paintings were undoubtedly used extensively in temple architecture of this time span, just as they had been in the temple of Tell Uqair in the Uruk and Jamdat Nasr periods (Lloyd and Safar 1943, pls. 10–12).

16. See examples in Heinrich 1982.

17. The ideas presented here are primarily based on considerations of the architecture and sculpture of the Early Dynastic Inanna temple at Nippur. Lectures on the subject were given by the present author in Washington, D.C., and New York City in 1996 and 1997. Recently H. Crawford (2002) has made suggestions along similar lines.

18. Frankfort 1943, pp. 4–7.

19. Cooper 1986, p. 63.

20. For other examples, see Gelb, Steinkeller, and Whiting 1991.

21. For the early Sumerian pantheon, see Steinkeller 1999, pp. 113ff. Maxwell-Hyslop (1992, p. 80) suggests that the goddess might be Baba (Ba'u).

22. Hansen 1963; Boese 1971.

23. Selz 1983.

24. Cooper 1986, pp. 22–23.

25. For a catalogue of votive objects, see Braun-Holzinger 1991.

26. For a full discussion of the Royal Cemetery with extensive bibliography, see Zettler and Horne 1998.

27. See, for example, Sürenhagen 2002.

28. See Zettler and Horne 1998, pp. 9–19.

29. The gold genitals on the silver underbody of the goat in the British Museum are preserved. The silver of the underbody of the goat exhibited here as catalogue number 71 was completely eroded. When new silver was fitted to the body during restoration, the genitals were omitted.

30. Originally the rosettes probably all faced forward. The present positions are as found in the earth.

31. Soucek 1976, pp. 93ff.

32. Miller 2000.

33. Reade 2001, p. 18, table 1. Reade also suggests (p. 21) that Mesanepada might be the occupant of Tomb PG 789.

34. For other examples, see Amiet 1980, pl. 99.

35. For the reconstructed scenes, see Parrot 1962, fig. 11; Dolce 1978, pl. 37.

36. Accepted here is the inscription reconstruction of Boese 1978.

37. Hansen 2000, p. 262.

38. For relations between Mari and Ebla, see Michalowski 1985.

39. See, for example, Scandone Matthiae 1991.

8

Standing nude "priest-king"

Limestone
H. 25 cm (9⅞ in.)
Mesopotamia
Late Uruk, ca. 3300–3000 B.C.
Archäologische Sammlung der Universität Zürich,
Switzerland Inv. 1942

A strict adherence to symmetry and a cursory indication of detail characterize this statue of a nude man, who stands with legs together and hands clenched against the chest. The feet and legs are a solid block articulated by an incised line that extends to the genitalia and is aligned with the vertical division of the thorax. The massive feet serve as the statue's base, and the toes, like the fingers, are summarily indicated by parallel incised lines. A fillet binds the hair, which falls to the nape of the neck. The beard is shaped like a disk; the area around the mouth is clean shaven. The cheeks are carved with some fullness, but other features of the head are noticeably flat and geometric. This is pronounced, especially in profile, where the convergence of the fillet, hair, beard, and ear appears as interlocking shapes. Although carved in high relief with an indication of muscula-ture, the arms are pressed tightly against the body in a constricting posture that preserves the blocklike form of the figure when seen from the front.[1] In profile the bent legs relieve the abstract massiveness of the figure.

Two statues of nude men in the Musée du Louvre are almost identical to this one.[2] All three figures are carved from limestone and are roughly of the same dimensions, although the Louvre examples are less carefully worked.[3] Their nudity is probably connected with a rit-ual activity. Nude men appear carrying objects toward an elaborate temple facade on Late Uruk cylinder seals, and on the contemporary Uruk Vase (figs. 9, 10), nude men are depicted in procession carrying produce.[4]

The abstraction embodied here coexisted in the art of Uruk together with the realism that is a hallmark of the Late Uruk period.[5] For example, a fragmentary statue also from Uruk of a "priest-king" emphasizes his powerful mus-culature and accurate proportions (fig. 11b); nevertheless, he also has fillet-bound hair, a disk-shaped beard, and hands clenched against the chest with the thumbs up. These dual modes of sculptural representation persisted through-out the third millennium B.C.[6]   JME

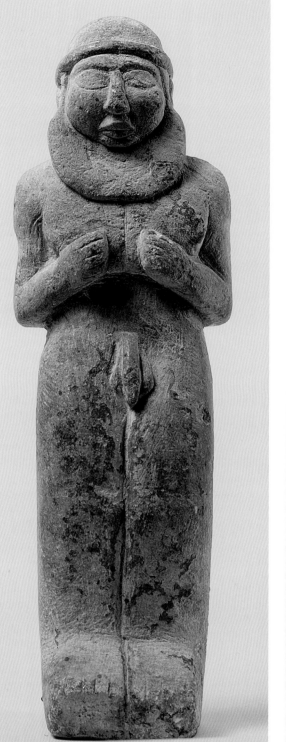

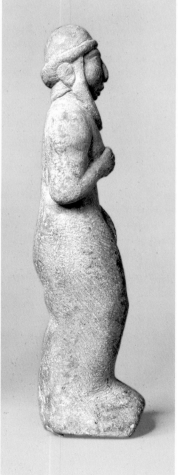

1. Müller 1976, p. 9.
2. Moortgat 1969, pls. 6, 7.
3. Müller 1976, p. 16.
4. For the cylinder seals, see Amiet 1980, pls. 13bis and 120. In the succeeding Early Dynastic period, nude men pouring libations before a seated deity appear on relief plaques (see cat. no. 33). Bahrani (2001, p. 55) observes that nude men "always appear in action: they are not represented in a frontal iso-lated composition as are the females."
5. An alabaster nude female figure from Uruk is simi-lar to the three nude male figures in its blocklike, constricted form and linear articulation, and in the curved profile of the legs (Hansen 1975a, pl. 1).
6. Porada et al. 1992, p. 105.

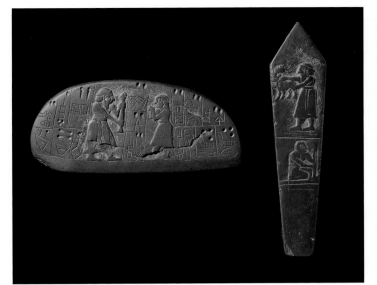

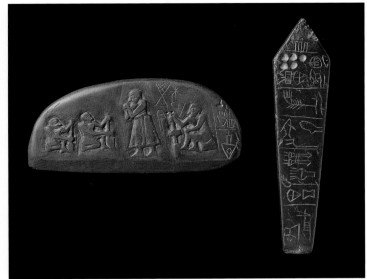

9

9

9

"Blau" monuments

Proto-cuneiform inscription
Schist (phyllite)
Scraper: H. 7.6 cm (3 in.); W. 16 cm (6¼ in.)
Chisel: H. 17.9 cm (7 in.); W. 4.1 cm (1⅝ in.)
Mesopotamia
Jamdat Nasr, ca. 3000–2900 B.C.
Trustees of The British Museum, London BM 86260,
86261

These two objects, known at least since 1886, were named after their first recorded owner, Dr. A. Blau, who was described as a merchant in Mesopotamia formerly in the Turkish medical service.[1] The objects were said to have been found near Warka (Uruk). Initially their authenticity was questioned, but this was prior to a later phase of excavations at Uruk that revealed clay tablets inscribed in archaic pictographic script and other objects with stylistically similar motifs; it is now agreed that the pieces are authentic. They appear to form a pair, and the stylistic and epigraphic similarities between them indicate that they were probably fashioned at the same time and by the same person.[2] Although their purpose and interpretation are not fully understood, it has been suggested that in shape they mimic two craftsman's tools, a chisel and a pottery scraper.[3] The inscriptions indicate that the objects record a transaction in which land was exchanged for a variety of goods, among them wool, silver, goats, and beer. The imagery has therefore been interpreted as a representation of the people involved in the transaction,

including the buyer and the seller, and of the preparation of food for a feast to confirm the contract.[4] However, the bearded figure wearing a headband and a skirt of a netlike material (indicated by the incised crisscross pattern) is of a type found on other objects of this period. Since it appears in both religious and secular contexts, the figure is generally referred to as the "priest-king."[5]   SC

1. Ward 1886, p. 46; Ward 1888, p. 39.
2. Gelb, Steinkeller, and Whiting 1991, p. 40.
3. Mallowan 1965, p. 66; Hiroyuki 1991, pp. 21–24.
4. Gelb, Steinkeller, and Whiting 1991, pp. 41–42.
5. Collon 1995, pp. 48–51.

10a–c

Cylinder seals with humans and animals

Mesopotamia
Late Uruk–Jamdat Nasr, ca. 3300–2900 B.C.

a. Marble
H. 3.5 cm (1⅜ in.); Diam. 2.9 cm (1⅛ in.)
Yale Babylonian Collection, New Haven NCBS 669

b. Marble
H. 6.3 cm (2½ in.); Diam. 3.7 cm (1½ in.)
Yale Babylonian Collection, New Haven NBC 2579

c. Magnetite and copper
H. 8.5 cm (3⅜ in.); Diam. 4.8 cm (1⅞ in.)
Visitors of the Ashmolean Museum, Oxford
AN 1964.744

Although we cannot be certain if the ingenious invention of cylinder seals was made in the southern Mesopotamian city of Uruk, many impressions of engraved glyptic imagery have been found there, together with the earliest examples of pictographic writing.[1] After their simultaneous invention, cylinder seals and cuneiform script became material hallmarks of Mesopotamian culture. They were used in a virtually unbroken sequence for more than three thousand years. Cylinder seals fell out of use during the last centuries B.C., whereas cuneiform lingered into the first centuries A.D. Throughout three millennia cylinder seals were used not only within the administrative spheres of economic and official power but also as markers of institutional or personal identity and as gifts to gods from royalty or other human supplicants.

Early cylinder seals—exemplified by catalogue number 10c—were often large. One scholar has suggested that they were made from the cores of stone vessels.[2] The size of this example projects a miniature monumentality that is enhanced through the addition of a copper terminal, expertly shaped as a recumbent ram.

During the Uruk period, cylinder seals and their ancient impressions on administrative documents and locking devices are our richest source for a wide range of meaningful subject matter. In particular, these three seals are superb examples of one of several themes that were considered worthy of representation in both the administrative and the monumental arts. As discussed in the introduction to this catalogue, one of the greatest concerns of early

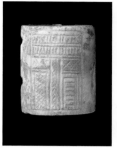

10a

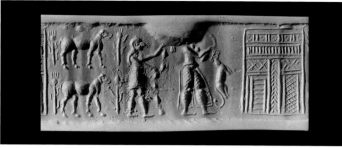

Impression from catalogue number 10a.

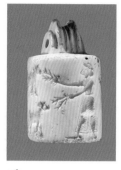

10b

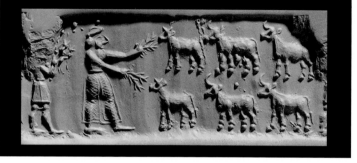

Impression from catalogue number 10b.

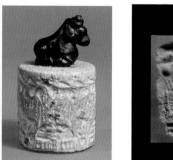

10c

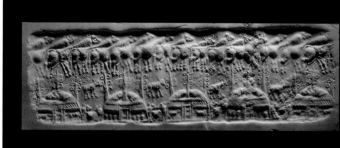

Impression from catalogue number 10c.

Near Eastern urban dwellers was the stable and continuous production of goods. In this early society all causation was believed to be determined by the gods, whose care and feeding was the responsibility of the paramount figure of Uruk society—the so-called priest-king. On one of these seals (cat. no. 10b) a priest-king, assisted by his acolyte, feeds the flocks amid symbols for domestic crops; on another (cat. no. 10a) the same actors bring votive offerings to a sacred structure, its facade enlivened by geometric patterns created by the stone and clay cone-mosaics that decorated public structures.

One of the most striking features of the Uruk period is the highly refined, idealized naturalism of the figural arts. Furthermore, this naturalism seems to reflect quite literally the details of actual events. For example, the

string of beads carried by the acolyte is like those found in great abundance in temple deposits of the period (see cat. no. 3). For another, the forepaws of felines have been found associated with temple architecture (see "Art of the Early City-States," by Donald P. Hansen, in this catalogue), giving authenticity to the remarkable depiction of a dismembered-feline offering carried by the priest-king in catalogue number 10a.

This naturalism, however, is not composed according to modern pictorial rules for rendering three-dimensional space. Rather each element is treated as a separate entity in what appears to be a succession of participants in a social transaction. The overriding purpose of the image was to convey with absolute clarity the identity of the actors and the nature of the relationship among them. If we compare this

with the intense physical interaction that was achieved toward the end of the millennium in the arts of Akkad, it is obvious that entirely different concerns underpinned the visual message of the arts of the Uruk period.

Catalogue number 10c, a magnificent seal, depicts in two registers a vital process, the procreation of the herd. In the upper register bovines walk to the right. This is one of the rare examples of overlapping in the arts of the Uruk period, and it certainly was intentionally used to capture the impression of unlimited numbers. Additionally the overlapping creates the impression that the animals are indeed moving and twisting their bodies. This same impression is captured in a carved open bowl (cat. no. 12) of the Uruk period by a file of bulls that turn their heads out toward the viewer. On the lower register of the present seal the theme of animal abundance is continued through the repetition of four reed enclosures that served as birthing places for the young animals. The identity of the god responsible for them may be indicated by a pole with three pairs of rings emerging from the top of the hut. In a similar manner the important by-product of birthing—the production of milk—is signified by the jars placed inside the huts.   HP

1. For further information on Mesopotamian cylinder seals, see Amiet 1980.
2. Porada 1983, p. 476.

11

Administrative tablet with seal impressions

Proto-cuneiform inscription
Clay
H. 5.3 cm (2⅛ in.); W. 4.8 cm (1⅞ in.); Thickness 3.8 cm (1½ in.)
Mesopotamia
Jamdat Nasr, ca. 3000–2900 B.C.
The Metropolitan Museum of Art, New York; Purchase, Raymond and Beverly Sackler Gift, 1988 1988.433.1

This tablet, which probably documents grain distribution from a large temple, has been impressed five times by a cylinder seal depicting the so-called priest-king (see "Art of the Early City-States," by Donald P. Hansen, in this catalogue). The "priest-king" is recognizable by his prominent nose, seen in profile, by his hair pulled back into a chignon under a cap

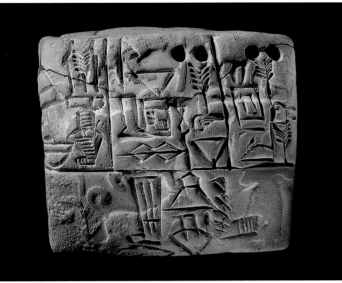
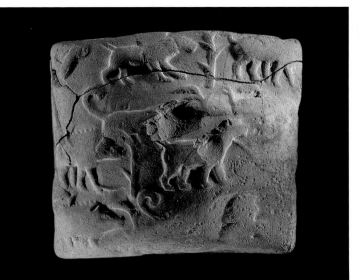

11

with rolled brim, and by his clothing, a belted garment that extends to midcalf. His head, however, is only preserved in one area on the reverse of the tablet (where the expected beard is hard to discern), whereas his body is visible in the three other rollings of the seal on the edges (see figs. 19a, b for a composite drawing and individual drawings of the obverse and reverse impressions).

The cylinder-seal impression appears to depict a hunting scene; the personage, who holds two dogs on leashes, is shown with a two-register series of boars and lions in a landscape that seems to evoke the reed marshes of southern Mesopotamia.[1] A better-preserved priest-king holds a staff in a very similar scene impressed on a numerical tablet from Level IVA at Uruk.[2] He may have been in a boat, accompanied by his hounds, hunting wild boar in the marshlands.[3] Other depictions of the priest-king show him with a bow and arrow, as on the famous lion-hunt stele from Uruk (fig. no. 5).[4] In some cases he

wears a net skirt and shoots at bulls and sheep.[5] It has been suggested that this imagery refers to the role of the ruler, who in many instances is also shown dominating and feeding animals, as the good shepherd who protects flocks from wild predators. According to Denise Schmandt-Besserat, tablets bearing the priest-king's image have been found in areas of Uruk with bureaucratic paraphernalia.[6]

As demonstrated by this tablet, an administrative system in which information was recorded both by writing and by impressing seals was in effect in the early Mesopotamian cities. Seal imagery may have confirmed status and authority and conveyed actual information about the activity recorded, and the act of sealing proved that the seal owner-user was responsible for or a witness to a transaction.[7] Unlike writing, however, seal images are seldom clearly visible, often partially obliterated by inscribed signs and incompletely rolled, without preserving the original composition.[8]

JA

1. The leashed dogs are a rare feature; see Amiet 1980, pl. 40:610 (with a nude hunter).
2. Englund 1994, seal 16: pl. 139, p. 52:W9656ec-ee. See also Boehmer 1999, pp. 51–52, fig. 49.
3. For other scenes of hunting and combat on Uruk tablet impressions, see Strommenger 1964, p. 388; Amiet 1980, pl. 10; Strommenger 1980, p. 62, fig. 55; and Englund 1994, seal 7: pl. 131, p. 36.
4. Amiet 1980, pl. 40:611.
5. Englund 1994, seal 17:38, pl. 140:W 7883. See also Mallowan 1964, p. 66, pl. 8; Heinrich 1936, p. 29, pl. 17b. Schmandt-Besserat (1993, p. 209) argues that he wears different garments on different occasions.
6. Schmandt-Besserat 1993, p. 210.
7. Nissen, Damerow, and Englund 1993, p. 17.
8. On the Metropolitan Museum example, the main personage is positioned in front of the animals in one of the two incomplete rollings of the seal on the obverse (fig. 19b, left), where the inscription is cut into the seal impression as well as on one tablet edge. On the reverse (fig. 19b, right), where the imagery is most completely preserved and there is no writing, the seal was rolled more than once, preserving only the figure's head, in the lower right corner. His full body is depicted faintly on two edges, but the head is not preserved. Another sealing on a tablet edge shows portions of the animal scene.

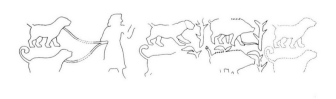

a

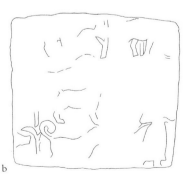
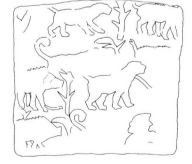

b

Fig. 19. Reconstruction of a cylinder-seal impression (a) based on sealings (b) on an administrative tablet (cat. no. 11).

12

Bowl with bulls in relief

Chlorite
H. 5.9 cm (2⅜ in.); Diam. 7.7 cm (3 in.)
Mesopotamia
Late Uruk–Jamdat Nasr, ca. 3300–2900 B.C.
Staatliche Museen zu Berlin, Vorderasiatisches
Museum VA 10113

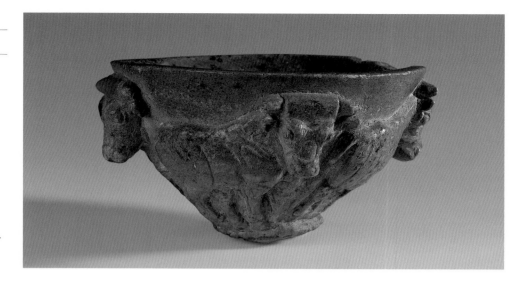

Among material from the end of the Uruk period and the following Early Dynastic period, stone vessels are, after cylinder seals, the most important sources of pictorial information. Depictions are drawn from an idealized worldview, however, and are not always easy to understand. Vessels of this type were frequently found in palaces or religious structures, which suggests that they had a special function in such settings.

The considerable work involved in creating stone vessels and the fact that the stone was imported gave them great value. While fragile ceramic vessels had to be continually replaced and therefore were likely to reflect changes in taste by displaying new shapes or types of decoration, stone vessels tended to be produced in a limited range of shapes and to be used for generations. For that reason it is often difficult to date them very precisely.

The small bowl with relief decoration shown here is a masterly work that attests to the great skill attained by creators of stone vessels about the beginning of the third millennium B.C. The bodies of the animals are carved in low relief, but their heads face outward and are fully three-dimensional. The motif of a row of cattle may be a precursor of the bands of animal and human figures that reached full development in the later Early Dynastic period.   LM

The Proto-Elamite Period

The region in southwestern Iran known as Elam in antiquity and Khuzistan today lies between the alluvial floodplain of Mesopotamia and the highlands of Iran, a prime location from which to control various routes to the rich natural resources found farther east. The artistic production in Elam, best known from excavations at the site of Susa, reflects the shifting influence of Mesopotamia and of the Iranian Plateau. Thus, objects of the late fourth millennium B.C. from Susa are so similar to those of the first Mesopotamian cities that they are usually described as Late Uruk in style (see fig. 8). About 3000 B.C., however, as the region slipped out of the Mesopotamian cultural sphere, Susa produced the earliest writing in Iran (see fig. 12). While the identity of the inhabitants of Susa is unknown, it is likely that they were linguistically distinct from the people of Uruk and lived in smaller communities that rarely reached urban proportions. Since the Elamite language is documented in the region of southwestern Iran during the later part of the third millennium B.C., these people are usually referred to as the Proto-Elamites.

Excavation has demonstrated that the Proto-Elamites extended their presence for a brief period south to ancient Anshan (Tell Malyan), later a highland Elamite capital; as far east as the modern border between Iran and Pakistan; and as far north as Afghanistan (see "Pathways across Eurasia," by Maurizio Tosi and C. C. Lamberg-Karlovsky, in this catalogue).

HP

13

Kneeling bull holding a vessel

Silver
H. 16.3 cm (6⅜ in.); W. 6.3 cm (2½ in.); Thickness
10.8 cm (4¼ in.)
Iran
Proto-Elamite, ca. 3000–2800 B.C.
The Metropolitan Museum of Art, New York;
Purchase, Joseph Pulitzer Bequest, 1966 66.173

The subject of animals engaged in human activities held particular meaning for the people living in the mountains and the lowlands to the east of Uruk at the turn of the third millennium B.C.

While animals consistently replace humans as actors in the cylinder-seal compositions of the Proto-Elamites (fig. 20), only a few three-dimensional sculptures of this type are known. This remarkable figure of a bull wearing a patterned garment and offering a spouted vessel held between its raised forelegs is one of the finest, fashioned from many pieces of hammered silver.[1] The function of these small sculptures is unclear. The bull contains several pebbles, suggesting that it may have served as a noisemaker.   HP

1. For a study of the silver bull, see Hansen 1970b.

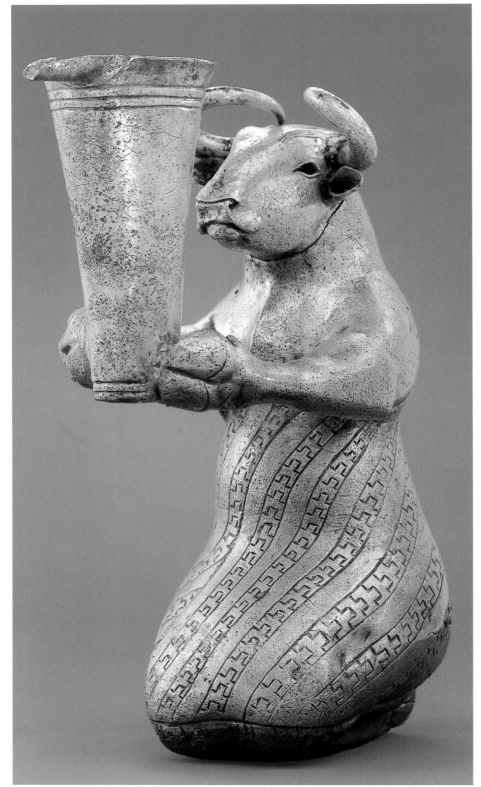

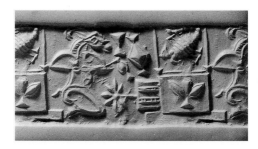

Fig. 20. Modern impression from a black stone cylinder seal depicting a kneeling caprid. Seal: Iran, Proto-Elamite, ca. 3000–2800 B.C. The Metropolitan Museum of Art, New York, Anonymous Loan L.1992.11.1.

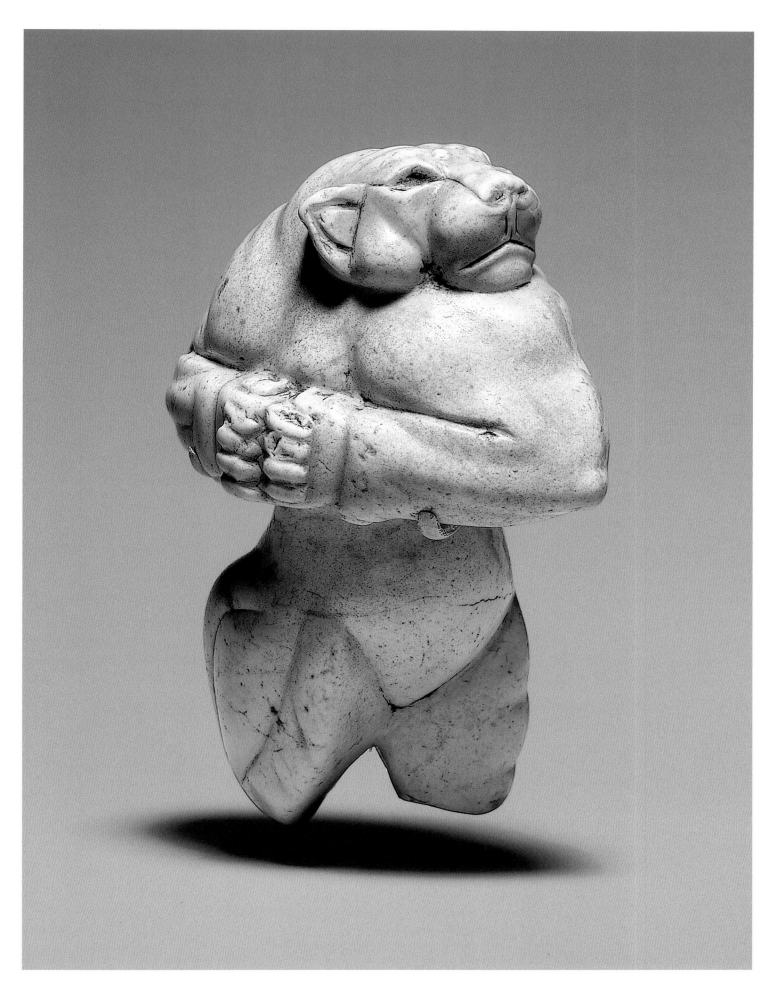

14

Standing lioness demon

Magnesite or crystalline limestone
H. 8.8 cm (3½ in.); W. 6.2 cm (2½ in.)
Iran
Proto-Elamite, ca. 3000–2800 B.C.
On loan to the Brooklyn Museum of Art L.48.7.9,
Collection of Robin B. Martin

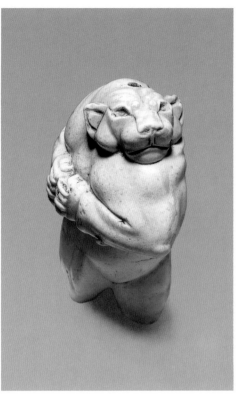
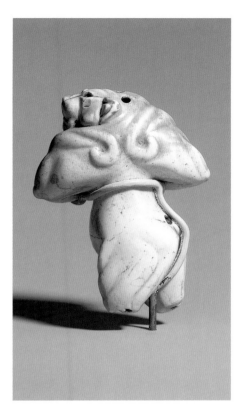

Like the kneeling bull in the Metropolitan Museum (cat. no. 13), this distinctive sculpture can be identified with certainty as Proto-Elamite on the basis of comparison with seal impressions on tablets inscribed with Proto-Elamite script from the site of Susa (fig. 21).[1] It shows a remarkably powerful depiction of a demonic female feline standing on long legs while pressing clenched front paws together in the center of a massive chest. More obviously than the silver bull, this figure is conceived frontally, with its head turned to be seen in strict profile. Neither of these figures captures the torsion of three-dimensional movement so convincingly as the sculptural masterworks of the neighboring Sumerians (see fig. 13).[2]

The idealized naturalism of the silver bull is here replaced by a sophisticated abstraction of bodily forms into curved, volumetric masses that evoke powerful muscles held in absolute tension. These forms are compacted with an almost explosive pressure that gives the small lioness demon a monumentality that could be sustained at a much greater scale. Indeed, it is possible to imagine that there originally existed much larger two- or three-dimensional renderings of this conception of a fundamental force of nature.

While the stark white of the stone appeals to today's tastes, this figure originally was

probably quite colorful. From its tail must have emerged long streamers of perhaps shimmering gold ribbon, and its lower hind legs were certainly constructed of precious metal, either gold or silver. On the back of the head of the feline four holes are drilled through. While they may also have accommodated streamers, their principal purpose was to hold a thong that allowed the powerful token to be suspended, probably from the neck of a powerful leader. Most comparable Proto-Elamite sculptures have loops or holes for suspension.[3] It is possible to imagine that they were worn as potent symbols of association or of rank within the Proto-Elamite communities.

Similar sculptures carved of identical material have been found as far north as the site of Tell Asmar, in the Diyala River valley.[4] They are a strong indication that during the early part of the third millennium numerous highland cultures were in close and continuous association with people of both lowland Sumer and lowland Khuzistan.

HP

1. For a study of the lioness demon, see Porada 1950.
2. For another example, see Hansen 1975a, fig. 14b.
3. On the suspension of Proto-Elamite figures, see Aruz 2002, pp. 1–4.
4. Behm-Blancke 1979, p. 79, no. 102.

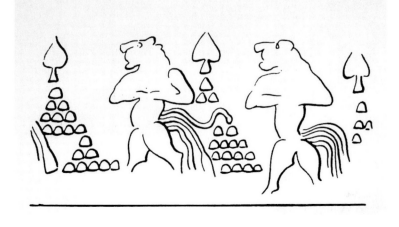

Fig. 21. Drawing of a seal impression on clay depicting a striding lion. Seal: Susa, Proto-Elamite, ca. 3000–2800 B.C. Musée du Louvre, Paris, AS 235.

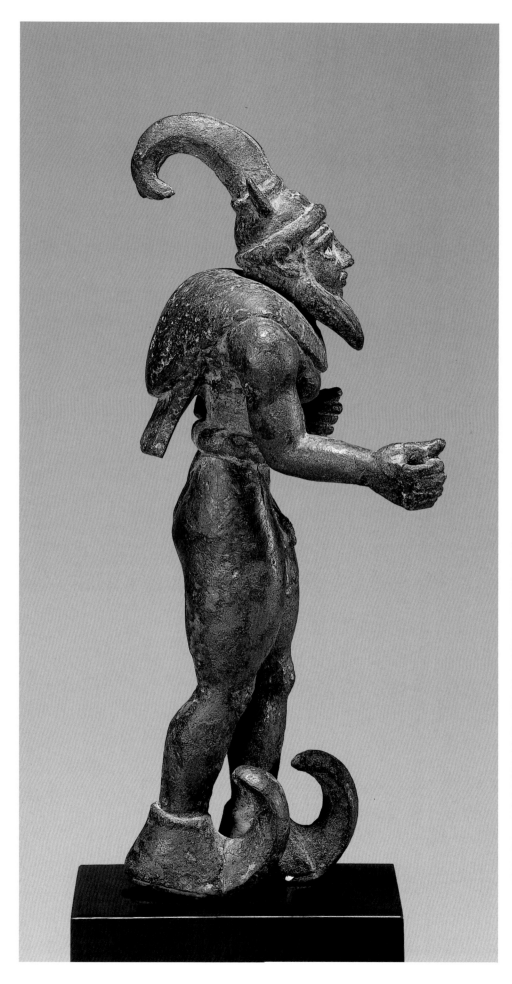

Striding horned demons

Arsenical copper
Iran
Proto-Elamite, ca. 3000–2800 B.C.

a. H. 17.2 cm (6¾ in.); W. 5.7 cm (2¼ in.)
On loan to the Brooklyn Museum of Art L.51.6,
Collection of Robin B. Martin

b. H. 17.5 cm (6⅞ in.); W. 5.4 cm (2⅛ in.)
Albright-Knox Art Gallery, Buffalo; General Purchase
Funds, 1950 1950.8

The figure of a hero who descends from the mountains bearing the mighty horns of an ibex and protected by the body of a vulture with wings outspread has a long history that begins before 5000 B.C.[1] These two powerful three-dimensional renderings of the horned hero probably date late in the life of the image in the Near East, whereas the close association between raptor and ruler continued in Egypt into the Old Kingdom in pharaonic portraiture.

The fact that both of these identical arsenical-copper statuettes exist today is extremely fortuitous. Their existence confirms

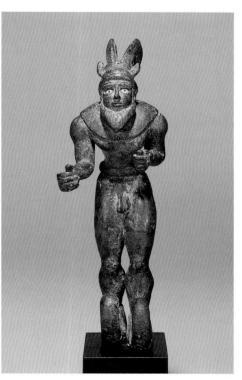

the importance of pairs (see entry for cat. no. 71), something that is suggested by archaic and later texts and by the relief arts of the Uruk period.[2] Sadly, both of these pieces come from the antiquities market, and therefore their point of final deposition cannot be known. It is possible, however, to argue the date and place of their manufacture, if only in hypothetical and formal terms. The most compelling feature of these objects is that their iconography and their style meld two distinct traditions that can be reconstructed through evidence from controlled excavations.

The image of the horned demon is repeatedly seen in the archaeological assemblages of sites in the northern regions of Iran, Iraq, and eastern Turkey beginning in the late Neolithic period.[3] It is not one that is strongly associated with Sumer, in the heartland of Mesopotamia, although, interestingly, one of the earliest examples was found in Level 3 of Tell el 'Ouieli, in southern Sumer.[4] All of the later images of this powerful, "shamanic" hero are known from the highland that defines the fertile crescent running from Susa through Luristan across the Jazira and onto the eastern Anatolian plateau.

Affirming the highland character of the image is its virtual absence from the repertory

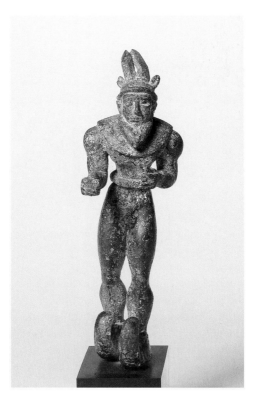

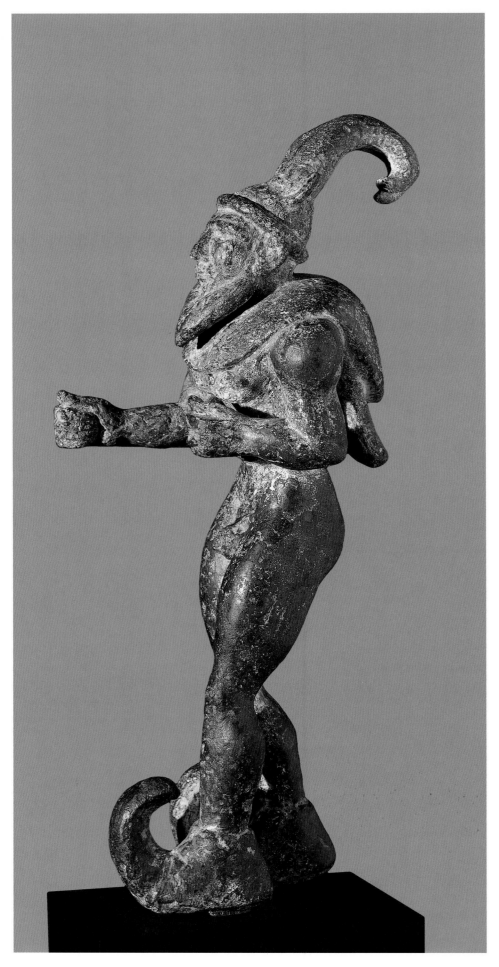

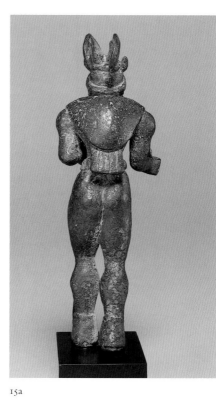

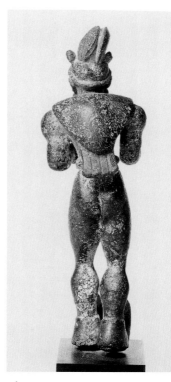

15a   15b

of the Uruk heartland; however, a lowland influence is obvious when one considers the style in which these two superb sculptures are rendered. The bodies as well as details of the beard and belt are closely paralleled among the numerous examples of sculpture formed through highly naturalistic volumes that we know best from the E-anna Precinct of Uruk (see figs. 11a, b).

The largest number of objects of this type in metal come not from the lowland sites of Uruk or Susa, but from farther to the northeast, in sites along the Diyala River valley and in the Zagros Mountains.[5] It is not impossible to imagine that the present pieces were part of a hoard of small-scale sculptures deposited intentionally in an early-third-millennium sacred space. Such caches are well known in third-millennium Mesopotamia. In particular these heroic figures would be perfectly at home with small sculptures like the Proto-Elamite lioness demon (cat. no. 14).

If it is correct to identify these figures as late Proto-Elamite, they must represent a continuation of the power of shamanistic ideas closely associated with a tribal way of life that was obsolete in the urban centers of southern Sumer. Indeed, there are representations of

this figure on cylinder seals of the Diyala River region and pottery from Susa, suggesting that such ideas retained their potency into the middle of the Early Dynastic period.[6]

HP

Technical remarks

The example from the Martin collection (cat. no. 15a) was briefly examined from a technical standpoint.[7] Under magnification, the surface revealed a layered structure of corrosion products consisting of what appear to be thick deposits of reddish brown cuprite overlaid with green copper carbonates. X-radiography indicated that this figure was cast solid and that the metal has a rather high degree of evenly dispersed porosity. This may account for the extensive pitting found in the corrosion layers and was most likely visible on the surface to some extent after casting. Neither the x-radiographs nor viewing under UV light revealed any areas of damage or restoration other than minor areas of consolidation associated with the pitting. Qualitative analysis of several areas of the surface by x-ray fluorescence spectroscopy indicated that the alloy consists mainly of copper, with minor amounts of arsenic and nickel. Based on the

use of arsenical copper, a general attribution to the third millennium B.C. is likely, although a more precise dating within this period cannot be given.   J–FL

1. Pittman 2000.
2. Bahrani 2002.
3. Pittman 2001b.
4. Von Wickede 1990, no. 227.
5. For examples of such metalwork, see Frankfort 1939 and Frankfort 1943.
6. For an example from the Diyala, see Frankfort 1955b, pl. 6; for one from Susa, see Amiet 1966, p. 146, fig. A.
7. See the brief discussion of these figures in Moorey 1982, p. 24.

16a, b

Vessels with nude heroes and animals in relief

Jamdat Nasr–Early Dynastic I, ca. 3000–2650 B.C.

a. Limestone
H. 12.7 cm (5 in.); W. 7.9 cm (3⅛ in.)
Mesopotamia
Trustees of The British Museum, London   BM 118465

b. Gypsum (?)
H. 15.2 cm (6 in.); W. 12.6 cm (5 in.)
Mesopotamia, Tell Agrab, Shara temple
The Oriental Institute of the University of Chicago   A 17948

The limestone vessel fragment from the British Museum (cat. no. 16a) epitomizes the extraordinary quality of the sculpture of the Jamdat Nasr–Early Dynastic I period.[1] It is carved on either side with a bearded figure of a man shown frontally, nude except for a double-strand belt; they have no mustaches, their hair is parted in the center, and they bear a central dot above the eyebrows. One of the figures wears his hair in curls and with each arm holds a bull around the neck. On the back of each bull perches a large bird. The other figure holds the rumps of the bulls; no curls are visible in his hair, and it may be that the birds are meant to hide them. The meaning of this image is unclear, but it is generally identified as the *lahmu*, or Hairy One, a spirit of the rivers, who masters wild animals and takes care of domesticated herds with his water.[2] The piece is unprovenanced, having been bought on the market in 1927.[3]

A very similar figure decorates the stone vessel or vessel support now in the Oriental Institute, University of Chicago (cat. no. 16b). The frontal male figure, nude except for a

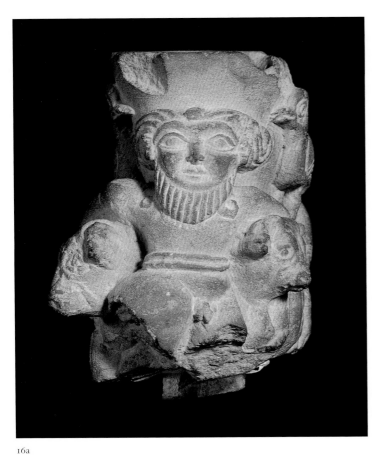

16a

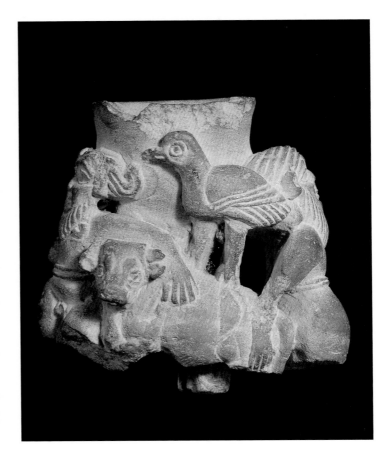

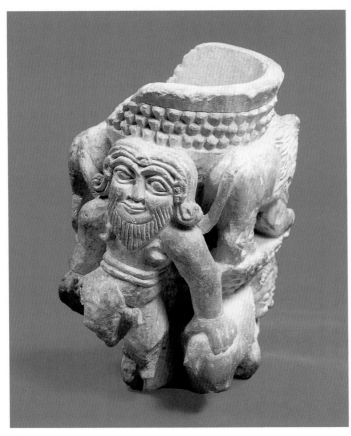

16b

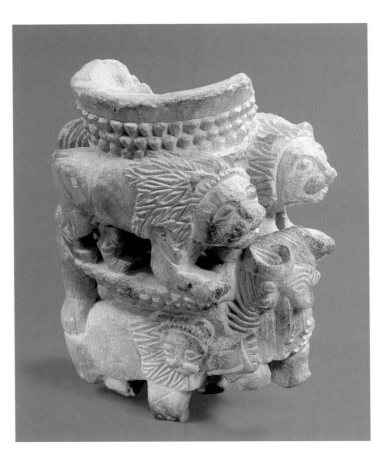

double-strand belt, acting as master of the animals, grasps the rumps of two lions in his hands. The curling tails of two additional lions are tucked under his arms. All four felines menace a bearded bull on the side of the vessel opposite the man. Around the neck of the vessel are stylized mountains. The container was found in 1936 during the Oriental Institute excavations of the Shara temple at Tell Agrab.[4] It was discovered above a level dated to Early Dynastic II.

These two elaborate objects are closely related to an open-worked stand that was also found in the Shara temple.[5] Although the animals and the hero on the Tell Agrab example are less finely modeled than the figures on the British Museum vessel, the composition of the elements suggests a close connection among the three pieces. Unlike the British Museum container, however, the examples discovered in the Shara temple are from secure contexts. Although they were discovered in a temple of the Early Dynastic period, Henri Frankfort suggested that the Shara finds were "almost certainly heirlooms from an earlier temple."[6]

The nude, belted hero of the British Museum and Tell Agrab vessels also appears on cylinder seal impressions of the Late Uruk period. He is regularly depicted, often in association with the bull-man, in Early Dynastic and Akkadian art.   PC/KLW

1. E.g., Collon 1995, p. 53, fig. 36.
2. Wiggermann 1992, pp. 174–79.
3. Hall 1927–28.
4. Delougaz and Lloyd 1942, pp. 242–47.
5. Ibid., p. 242.
6. Frankfort 1936a.

17

Kneeling man holding a vessel

Gypsum and red pigment
H. 11.4 cm (4½ in.); W. 5.4 cm (2⅛ in.); Thickness 5.7 cm (2¼ in.)
Mesopotamia, Tell Agrab, Shara temple
Early Dynastic I, ca. 2900–2650 B.C.
The Oriental Institute of the University of Chicago A 18067

This kneeling man is nude except for a double belt around his waist and three beaded armlets, which retain traces of red pigment, encircling his right upper arm.[1] Two long locks on his otherwise shaven skull hang down in front of his ears and flank his full beard. His eyebrows and eyes were originally inlaid. He raises his arms and hands to balance a large carinated vessel that rests on his head. The forearms and legs of the figure are restored, but enough of the latter remains to show that his position, with the right leg bent under his body and the left leg raised, is correct. The position of both the arms and legs wonderfully evokes the strain with which he balances the vessel on his head as he prepares to rise to his feet: an indication of both moment and movement that is extraordinarily rare in Mesopotamian art.

The figure resembles two pieces—one in the Iraq Museum, Baghdad, and one in a private collection—that represent bull-men (see cat. no. 18),[2] although our figure is undeniably human in form. He is dated to the first Early Dynastic period by the shape of the vessel he carries, which is characteristic of Inanna temple

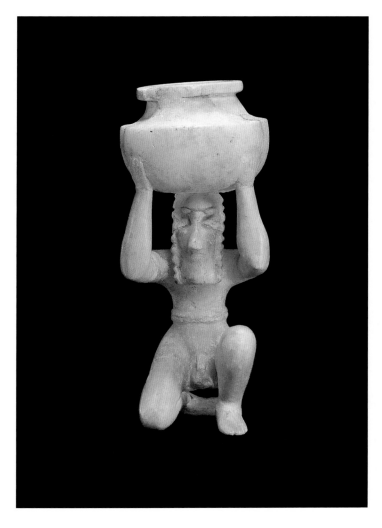

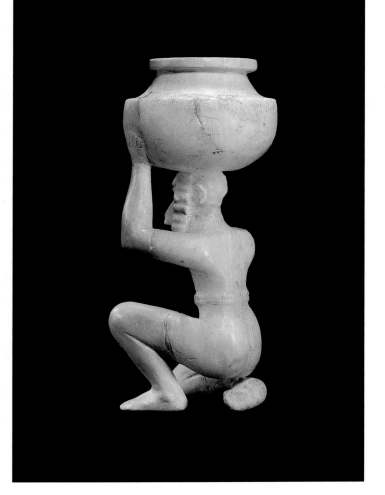

Levels X and IX at Nippur and Early Dynastic
I levels in the Diyala region.[3]

KLW

1. Frankfort 1943, no. 269, pls. 33, 34.
2. Lloyd 1946, pp. 1–5; Frankfort 1943, no. 206,
pl. 115; Hansen in Orthmann 1975, no. 16.
3. Wilson 1986, p. 63, fig. 11:2.

18

Bull-man

Alabaster
H. 34.8 cm (13¾ in.)
Umma (modern Jokha)[1]
Early Dynastic I, ca. 2900–2650 B.C.[2]
George Ortiz Collection

The statue was carved from translucent
alabaster, with details made of different materials, possibly shell, lapis lazuli, gold, silver, or

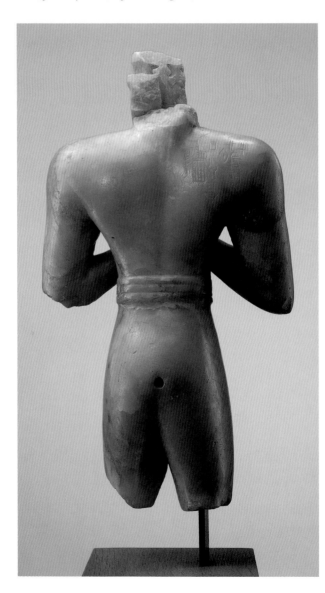

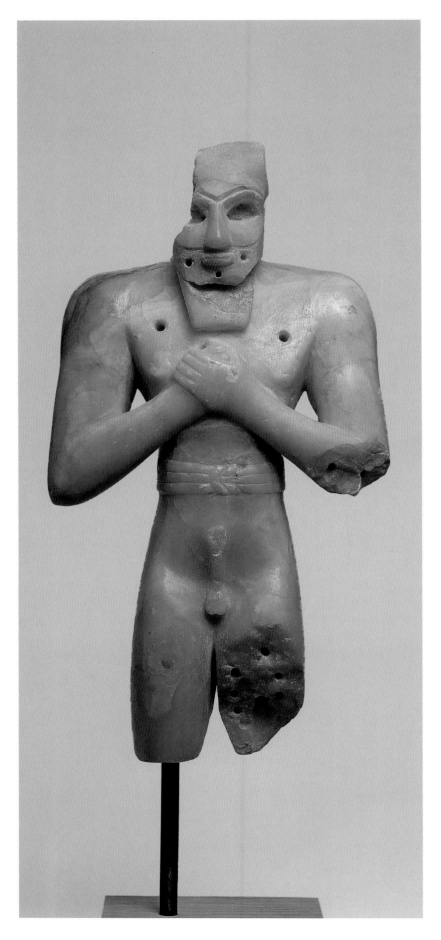

copper. Various drilled holes remain for the insertion of horns, tail, and lower legs; those in the beard suggest that originally the hair was possibly accentuated by metal sheet, and the two in the chest probably served also for affixing or inlaying. The eyes and eyebrows would have been inlaid. The use of composite materials belongs to a tradition that began in the Late Uruk period, though this figure is later in date (see cat. nos. 2b, 14; fig. 13).[3]

The inscription behind the right shoulder of this figure is generally accepted as: "For Enlil. Pabilgagi, king of Umma," a major Sumerian city best known today for the war with its neighbor and rival Lagash (see figs. 52, 53).[4]

The statue represents a nude bull-man, a mythological figure, and has a companion piece in the Iraq Museum in Baghdad.[5] They are the only two known examples of Mesopotamian bull-men in the round. More commonly, the bull-man, often ithyphallic, appears on seals with heroes and in animal combat scenes (see cat. no. 146). Both statues are carved from a particularly fine green-yellow alabaster with rust-colored veins. The example in Baghdad is slightly smaller (27.5 centimeters). However, the workmanship of the sex, nose, and mouth, the similarity of the three-tiered belt, the way the stone is carved to reveal veining across the shoulders, their polish, and general appearance suggest that they are not only from the same major workshop but in all likelihood by the same hand.

These bull-men are related to a group of copper statues of nude males functioning as stands. The vertical hole in the head of the present statue suggests that it served as a cult object, perhaps also as a stand. With clasped hands in a dedicatory gesture, this figure is undoubtedly a temple furnishing. The kneeling figure holding a vessel on its head from the Shara temple at Tell Agrab (cat. no. 17) belongs to the same tradition.   GO

1. For the discovery of the figure at Umma (present-day Jokha) with its companion piece around 1930, and a complete history, see Ortiz 1996.
2. The author of this entry has adopted the earlier ED attribution of Donald P. Hansen, reviewing his later dating for the bull-man and the contemporary smaller piece in Baghdad; see ibid.
3. Information relayed by Donald P. Hansen.
4. Cooper 1986, pp. 91–92.
5. This figure and its pendant were a chance find and found together. This example entered a private collection, and its companion piece, the Iraq Museum in Baghdad. Confusion as to the ownership and location of these figures has led to erroneous information being given in scholarly publications; see Ortiz 1996.

19

Kneeling nude man with serpents

Alabaster
H. 31 cm (12¼ in.)
Mesopotamia
Early Dynastic I–II, ca. 2900–2550 B.C.
Cincinnati Art Museum; Mary Hanna Fund 1957.33

Two serpents bind the arms of this beautifully carved and naturalistic nude kneeling figure.[1] Two more encircle the man's legs with their tails. From a ring around his neck hang two fish. The man's broad face is framed by his shoulder-length hair. A separate raised ridge marks each eyebrow, and the eyes are represented as rounded projections with traces of an upper lid. The lips sink slightly into the cheeks and curve forward in the middle. His beard, which covers the lower part of his face, is made up of horizontal ridges over which runs a zigzag pattern that also marks the hair and occasionally appears on Early Dynastic sculptures.[2] The curls of the beard are separated from the face by a slightly raised zigzag band that forms a point below the chin.

The meaning of this figure is debatable; nude male figures are often included in the generic category of *lahmum* (see cat. no. 16), a water spirit, but there is no evidence that this

example should be counted among that group. The date of this piece is also questionable. Snakes grasped by horned demons appear on stamp seals of the early fourth millennium B.C., while the bound and kneeling posture of the man is first found in the Late Uruk period, on seal impressions (see fig. 7) and in several crudely made stone figures of bearded men.[3] However, the legs of the latter are differentiated by a groove rather than modeled, as they are here, which helps to date the figure to Early Dynastic I or II. Humans are shown with snakes on seals beginning in the mid-fourth millennium B.C., but, unlike this man, they usually grasp them at the mouth. A nude hero grasping snakes appears on cylinder seals from the Late Uruk period that parallel seal designs showing him holding door bolts. Indeed, inscriptions make it clear that serpents guarded temple doors.[4] In these representations snakes never dominate humans as they do here. The imagery of this figure is largely unparalleled—a similar headless sculpture exists in Baghdad[5]—and remains unexplained.   PC

1. Porada 1992.
2. Frankfort 1939, pl. 13:31.
3. Becker 1993, nos. 945–51 (for stone figures).
4. Edzard 1987, p. 83, xxvi 24.
5. Porada 1992, pl. 75, figs. 6, 7.

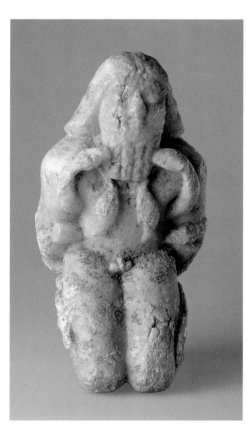

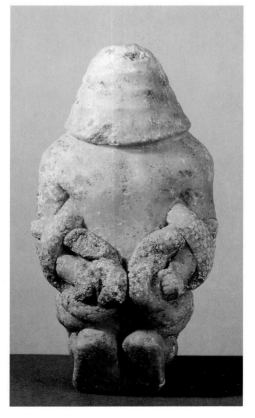

Stele of Ushumgal

Cuneiform inscription
Gypsum
H. 22.4 cm (8⅞ in.); W. at base 14.7 cm (5¾ in.)
Mesopotamia
Early Dynastic I, ca. 2900–2650 B.C.
The Metropolitan Museum of Art, New York,
Purchase, Funds from various donors, 1958 58.29

The cuneiform inscription on this stele records a land transaction involving three houses as well as fields and livestock.[1] A scene wrapping around the sides of the stele shows a meeting that takes place before an elaborate architectural facade, across which the two largest figures face one another (fig. 22). The primary figure in the scene is a bearded man, who is identified in the cuneiform text written across his long, fringed skirt as "Ushumgal the *pab-shesh* priest." Ushumgal also wears a garment draped over the left shoulder, and he clasps his hands at the chest with the thumbs up. Set into the building near the doorway may be the *kag*, a cone or peg driven into a wall to signify the transfer of property.

Facing this figure from one short side of the stele is a woman of the same size who wears a garment draped over her left shoulder and holds a vessel. The writing on the garment identifies her as "the daughter of Ushumgal." A second woman, represented at about half the scale of Ushumgal's daughter, appears behind her, and behind Ushumgal the field is divided into two registers filled with smaller male figures. All three of these men are depicted clasping their hands on their chest and with their skirts looped up.

Because of the difficulty in reading the text (due to the archaic form of the script and to the way it is fitted in the available space) it is not clear whether the transaction is one of buying, selling, or granting. It has been suggested that the stone either records the donation of an estate made by Ushumgal on behalf of his daughter or is a record of the real estate owned by a temple household, whose chief administrator was Ushumgal.[2]   JME

1. For the translation, see Gelb, Steinkeller, and Whiting 1991, pp. 43–48.
2. See ibid., p. 43, for relevant bibliography.

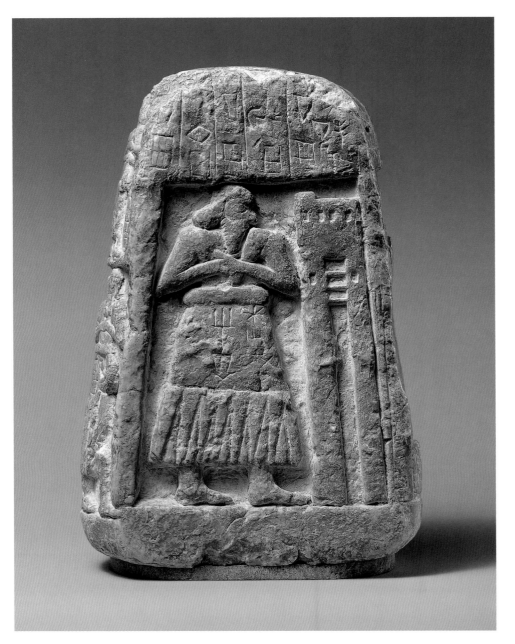

Fig. 22. Drawing of the Stele of Ushumgal (cat. no. 20).

Sealing with impression of City Seal

Cuneiform inscription
Clay
Sealing: H. 11 cm (4⅜ in.); W. 6.3 cm (2½ in.);
Thickness 6.2 cm (2½ in.)
Mesopotamia, Ur, SIS4, U.14896a
Early Dynastic I, ca. 2900–2650 B.C.
University of Pennsylvania Museum of Archaeology
and Anthropology, Philadelphia 31-16-604

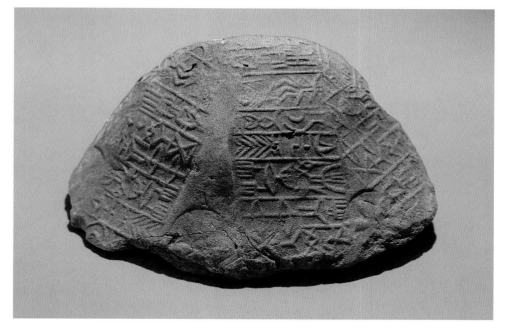

This impression is one of a large group excavated from levels below the Royal Cemetery
at Ur known as the Seal Impression Strata, or
SIS (see cat. no. 22). A complete rolling of a
cylinder seal is preserved in which the symbols are arranged in thirteen boxes in two
registers. It is unclear what the sealing had
secured.[1] Such impressions are known as
"City Seal impressions" since they appear to
bear proto-cuneiform symbols representing
names of cities; there is, however, considerable
doubt as to the identification of all the signs or
sign combinations as ancient city names, which
is the case with this impression. Nonetheless,
the symbols are perhaps the earliest evidence
for the transformation of the cuneiform script
into art. It was recognized that some of the
impressions bore signs that constituted ideograms for cities, including Kesh, Adab, Ur, and
Larsa.[2] Similar impressions are known from
Jamdat Nasr, Uruk, and Susa.[3] Such city lists
may be found on archaic tablets from Uruk
(see "The Earliest Scholastic Tradition," by
Piotr Michalowski, in this catalogue) as well as
on later tablets—for example, on those from
Fara (see cat no. 321). The variable sequences
of city names and groupings on the impressions may reflect intercity cooperation, perhaps
based on military and defensive concerns, as
Thorkild Jacobsen postulated in his so-called
Kengir League.[4] It is likely, however, that any
such collaboration would have been underpinned by political, economic, and religious
interactions. Indeed, the fact that nearly one-
fourth of the Ur sealings, including this one,
are also sealed with a stamp or the butt end
of a cylinder seal depicting a rosette, the symbol of the goddess Inanna, has suggested to
Piotr Steinkeller the existence of a religious
league of city-states.[5]   PC

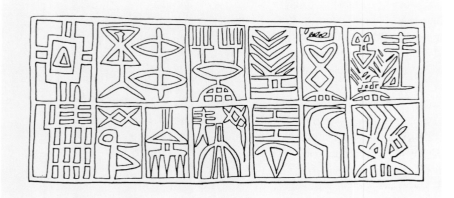

Fig. 23. Drawing of a City Seal impression (cat. no. 21).

1. R. Matthews 1993, p. 73, nos. 114, 114a.
2. Burrows 1930, p. 342.
3. R. Matthews 1993, pp. 33–34.
4. Jacobsen 1957, p. 109.
5. Steinkeller 2002a, pp. 249–57; Steinkeller 2002b,
p. 29.

22

Sealing with impressions of men, snakes, and rosettes

Clay
Diam. of seal (reconstructed) 1.9 cm (¾ in.)
Mesopotamia, Ur, SIS4–5, U.18402
Early Dynastic I, ca. 2900–2650 B.C.
University of Pennsylvania Museum of Archaeology and Anthropology, Philadelphia 33-35-344

In the Early Dynastic period, the carvings on cylinder seals of scenes of contests between humans or with animals sometimes were developed into more elaborate patterns. One-third of the design of this impression is composed of a pair of twisting snakes.[1] At the top, one snake head is shown facing right, while, at the bottom, a second head is facing left as the snake bites the wrist of a nude man, who is depicted upside down with his legs outstretched. He catches the foot of another nude man who is upright and faces left, his back arched to accommodate the man turned on end. The second man grasps the right foot of the first, and the two figures, balancing each other, appear to revolve around a central point. Such swirling, interlocking compositions of either animals or human figures continue as elements of some contest scenes on seals through the Early Dynastic period.[2] The wrist of the upright man, in turn, is being grasped by the left hand of a third man, wearing a hitched-up skirt, who holds a weapon in his right hand with which he pierces the arm of the second nude figure. Between these two men is the upper torso of a small figure with raised arms. The image of a man "punishing" a nude figure may relate to similar scenes on Late Uruk period seal impressions (see fig. 7). Impressions of a stamp seal across the main scene, possibly made by the butt end of the cylinder, are of an eight-petaled rosette, a symbol of Inanna, which may indicate that the sealing functioned as an administrative device in the service of her cult (see entry for cat. no. 21).   PC

1. Twisting snakes are known on seals of the Uruk period (Boehmer 1999, pl. 89), and snakes (Heinrich 1931, pl. 28b) and similar geometric designs (see cat. no. 23) are depicted on Early Dynastic clay tablets from Fara.
2. See, for example, Heinrich 1931, pls. 43:l, 45:l.

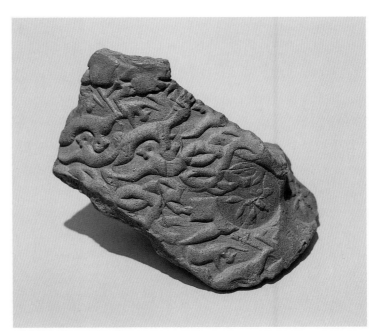

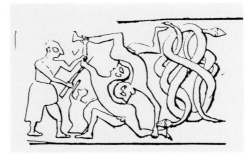

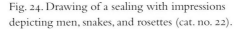

Fig. 24. Drawing of a sealing with impressions depicting men, snakes, and rosettes (cat. no. 22).

Fara

Excavations at Fara, in ancient times the city of Shuruppak, were conducted for a few months in 1902 and 1903 by the Deutsche Orientgesellschaft. This offshoot of the nearby Babylon dig was undertaken mainly to unearth cuneiform tablets, which Berlin's language scholars were eager to have. Since there was little time available and Fara's mound of ruins was quite large, the director of the expedition, Walter Andrae, chose a method already used at Babylon and cut more than twenty trial trenches, each roughly ten meters wide, through the hill. He was confident that this procedure would yield finds of sufficient richness to both satisfy expectations in Berlin and provide some knowledge of the ancient settlement's structure.

Shuruppak is documented beginning in roughly 2800 B.C. and was regarded as a major city until the end of the third millennium. However, its layout could not be ascertained from the excavation. A very few structures were exposed; they appeared to be dwellings, although they contained a few burials and included some archival rooms. Later digs conducted by the University of Pennsylvania in 1931 discovered little more. Thus we still know virtually nothing about this important Mesopotamian city, even though, according to mythic tradition, it was the home of the Babylonian Noah—the hero Uta-napishti, familiar from the Gilgamesh epic (see "Uruk and the World of Gilgamesh," by Beate Salje, in this catalogue).

Fortunately, the more than one thousand cuneiform tablets found during these excavations provide some glimpse of Shuruppak's importance. Hundreds of administrative documents, now in museums in Berlin, Istanbul, and Philadelphia,[1] demonstrate that in the middle of the third millennium B.C. the city had a centralized agricultural administration with a significant number of employees overseeing work in the economy's farming sector and readying its products for trade. In addition, large quantities of so-called school texts—practice exercises and texts for study—were found. They are evidence of the highly developed training received by scribes, who were taught skills required in the religious sphere and in dealing with administration, the economy, and the legal system. The early interest in language and literature revealed in these texts testifies to the high cultural level of at least a portion of the population.

JM

1. Staatliche Museen zu Berlin, Vorderasiatisches Museum; Eski Şark Museum, Istanbul; University of Pennsylvania Museum of Archaeology and Anthropology, Philadelphia.

23

Cuneiform tablet with a word list and an incised bull

Cuneiform inscription
Fired clay
H. 21 cm (8¼ in.); W. 20 cm (7⅞ in.)
Mesopotamia, Shuruppak (modern Fara)
Early Dynastic IIIA, ca. 2550–2400 B.C.
Staatliche Museen zu Berlin, Vorderasiatisches Museum VA 9128

This tablet is a superb example of a so-called school text, or tablet used in the training of scribes.[1] On the obverse are seven columns containing a list of Sumerian homophones, words that sounded roughly the same. They probably represent a dictation exercise made up of sounds especially difficult to distinguish. Translation would be pointless, since it was the vocalization that mattered; some examples from columns 4 and 5 are *shu-ib, bu-ib, bi-ib, bi-ib-ku-a, bi-ib-ka, hur-ib, hum-ib*. The tablet's reverse has a slightly convex surface. On it, beneath a small inscription panel, are two incised drawings distinguished by a very skillful use of line. There is no recognizable connection between them and the word list on the obverse, yet the fine quality of the drawings and their artful placement within the allotted space suggest that they were not mere scribbling.

The larger of the images shows a spirited bull with an elongated back and raised foreleg, his head turned toward the rear. The outline of his slender neck is traced with delicate hatching up as far as the horn. The animal seems to be nibbling on a leaf or branch of a highly stylized tree. This motif, variants of which appear on seals, vessels, and votive tablets, can be traced back to early Sumerian times.[2] The second drawing, a star-shaped ornament, has irregular hatching in the center. It may well represent four intertwined serpents, a subject given a less abstract rendition on another Fara tablet.[3]

Sadly, the findspot of the Fara tablets, located in trench sections Id and Ie, provides no clues about their use or their creators. Ernst Heinrich concluded from the layers of ash and rubble recorded in this area, the absence of any indication of housing, and the way the finds—including jar stoppers, clay

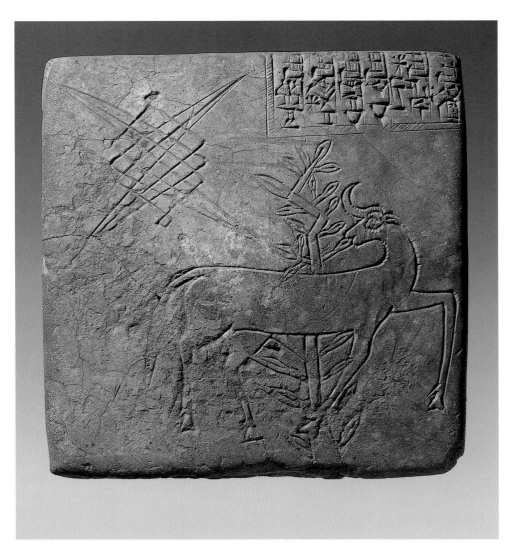

indication that the writing exercises and trial drawings on these tablets were made by the same hand. Specific techniques and their application within a prescribed space had to be practiced before the student moved on to working in more expensive materials, such as shell, ivory, or stone.[7] Since apprentice tablets are relatively rare, it can be assumed that in most cases they were routinely scrapped at the end of an exercise.

JM/NC

1. Deimel 1923, no. 77 (editions: Jestin 1955 and M. Lambert 1953: 84–85).
2. Amiet 1961, pls. 9, 22–25; Boese 1971, pls. 3:AS3, 5:CT2, 7:CS1; Orthmann 1975, fig. 71a.
3. Heinrich 1931, pl. 28b. The relatively widespread motif is also found on seals: Amiet 1961, pls. 14bisH, 51.712, 95.1247–51.
4. Heinrich 1931, pp. 61–69, pls. 27–33.
5. Ibid., pls. 29:a, e, i, 30:g.
6. Hilprecht 1903, p. 59, fig. 41.
7. Orthmann 1975, figs. 80b, 95a, 95c; Christian 1940, pls. 277, 278.

bullae, and simple clay and stone objects—were jumbled together that the area may have been a dump.[4] The tablet fragments carry drawings of animals, men, and hybrid beasts, and half of them appear to have been baked. If they were deliberately fired to harden them (rather than being baked accidentally), they must have been considered important enough to merit permanence.

Some of the tablets show obvious signs of correction, either erased lines or redrawn outlines. They support the view that this group of school texts consists of "apprentice tablets," or tablets on which students copied their teacher's work.[5]

Clay tablets with simple inscribed drawings also known from Nippur[6] could be a further

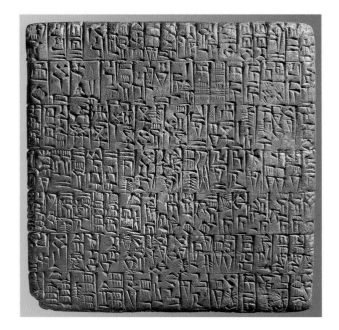

TEMPLE

At that time, Enmetena fashioned his statue, named it "Enmetena
Whom Enlil Loves," and set it up before Enlil in the temple.
Inscription of Enmetena, ruler of Lagash, on a stone statue from Ur

Excavations in the Diyala Region

*In the late 1920s large quantities of unusual, extremely high qual-
ity objects began to appear in antiquities dealers' shops in
Baghdad. They were said to come from illicit excavations in the
desert east of the Diyala River, just north of its confluence with
the Tigris. In 1929 the Oriental Institute of the University of
Chicago obtained a concession to excavate in the area. The Iraq
Expedition worked from 1930 to 1937, and two additional short
campaigns were undertaken in 1937 and 1938 under the joint aus-
pices of the University of Pennsylvania Museum of Archaeology
and Anthropology, Philadelphia, and the American Schools of
Oriental Research, Boston.*

*The Oriental Institute conducted extensive horizontal and ver-
tical excavations on four mounds: Khafajah, Tell Asmar (ancient
Eshnunna), Tell Agrab, and Ishchali. The expedition uncovered
temples, palaces, administrative buildings, and private houses ranging in date from about 3100 to 1750 B.C. The work of the Oriental
Institute, which included archaeological surveys and regional studies, was in many ways innovative for its time and provided a
wealth of information that was—and still is—basic to the study
of early Mesopotamian civilization.*

*Perhaps the greatest contribution of the Oriental Institute's work
in the Diyala region was the information it provided on what
came to be called the Early Dynastic period in Mesopotamia. At*

*the sites of Khafajah and Tell Asmar, six parallel series of stratified
remains were excavated that connected the earliest remains at those
sites with the age of the Akkadian king Sargon (ca. 2300–2245
B.C.). Using changes in material culture—architecture, ceramics,
sculpture, cylinder seals—that could be traced over time, the excavators were able to divide these remains into three periods and to
further subdivide those periods into phases. The process of estab-
lishing this chronology can be traced in the Iraq Expedition's preliminary reports[1] and was brought to full fruition in the impressive
series of final publications.[2] Although subsequent decades have witnessed extensive fine-tuning of this chronology, the periodization
developed as a result of the Oriental Institute excavations in the
Diyala region continues to serve as the basic organizational framework for similar materials uncovered at other sites in the Greater
Mesopotamian area. The final publications also continue to serve
as indispensable tools for the study of Mesopotamian material culture of the late fourth through early second millennium B.C.*

KLW

1. Frankfort, Jacobsen, and Preusser 1932; Frankfort 1933; Frankfort 1934a;
Frankfort 1935b; Frankfort 1936b.
2. Frankfort 1939; Frankfort, Lloyd, and Jacobsen 1940; Delougaz 1940;
Delougaz and Lloyd 1942; Frankfort 1943; Delougaz 1952; Frankfort
1955b; Delougaz, Hill, and Lloyd 1967; Hill, Jacobsen, and Delougaz 1990.

24a–d

Standing male figures with clasped hands

a. Gypsum, shell, black limestone, and bitumen
H. 29.5 cm (11⅝ in.)
*Mesopotamia, Eshnunna (modern Tell Asmar), Abu
temple hoard, As. 33:414*
Early Dynastic I–II, ca. 2900–2550 B.C.
*The Metropolitan Museum of Art, New York; Fletcher
Fund, 1940 40.156*

b. Gypsum
H. 37 cm (14⅝ in.)
*Mesopotamia, Khafajah, Nintu temple, Level V, hoard
beneath floor, Kh. VIII 263*
Early Dynastic II, ca. 2650–2550 B.C.
Worcester Art Museum, Massachusetts 1937.91

c. Gypsum
H. 30 cm (11¾ in.)
*Mesopotamia, Khafajah, Nintu temple, Level V, hoard
beneath floor, Kh. VIII 272*
Early Dynastic II, ca. 2650–2550 B.C.
*University of Pennsylvania Museum of Archaeology
and Anthropology, Philadelphia 37-15-31*

d. Gypsum
H. 23 cm (9 in.)
*Mesopotamia, Khafajah, Nintu temple, Level VI,
Kh. VIII 45*
Early Dynastic II, ca. 2650–2550 B.C.
*University of Pennsylvania Museum of Archaeology
and Anthropology, Philadelphia 37-15-28*

The four statues illustrated here represent the
wide stylistic range that exists among the
hundreds of Early Dynastic dedicatory statues
found at the sites of Tell Asmar, Khafajah,
and Tell Agrab in the Diyala region of
Mesopotamia.

During the 1933–34 excavation season at
Tell Asmar, a hoard of twelve statues was discovered in the Abu temple, buried below the
floor in an oblong cavity beside the altar of
one of the sanctuaries (fig. 25).[1] The hoard
contained the first monumental statues excavated from an ancient Near Eastern site, and
despite subsequent finds, they have remained
the definitive examples of the abstract style of
Early Dynastic sculpture. Catalogue number
24a, a standing male figure from the hoard, is
rigidly frontal, with enormous shoulders that
give the arms a square appearance and contrast with the triangular shape created by the
taper of the torso to the waist. The cone-
shaped skirt has a single row of long fringe at
the hem. The prominent eyes are inlaid with

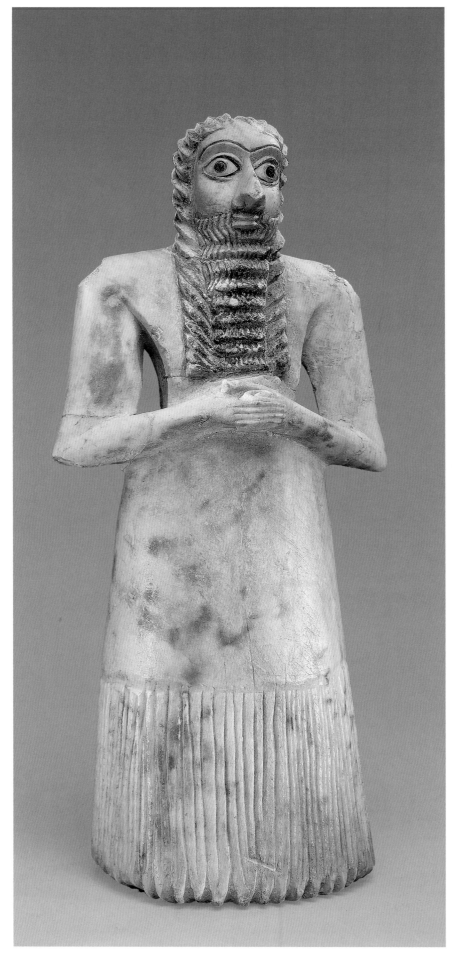

24a

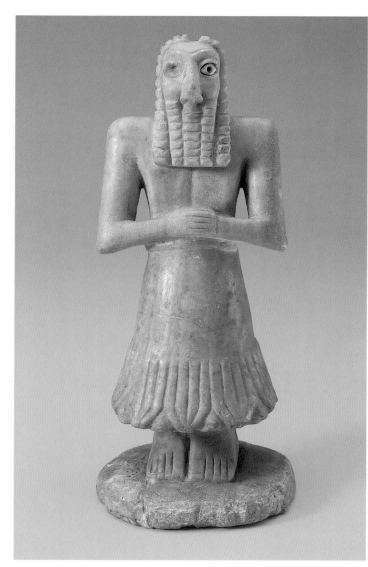

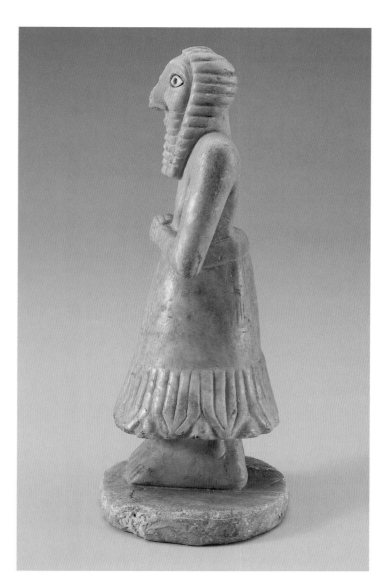

24b

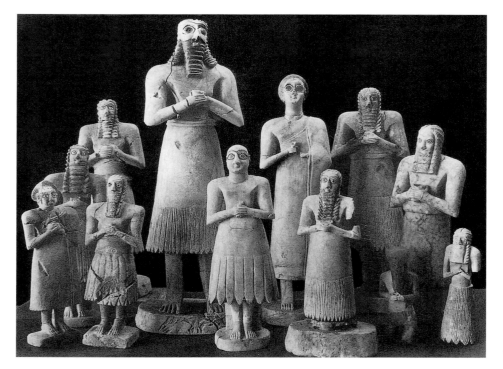

Fig. 25. Hoard of dedicatory statues. Abu temple,
Tell Asmar, Early Dynastic I–II, ca. 2900–2550 B.C.

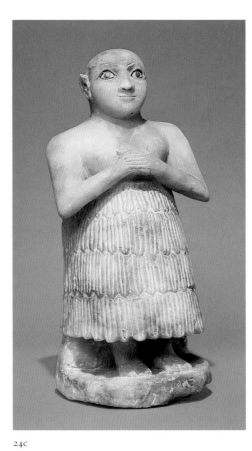

24c

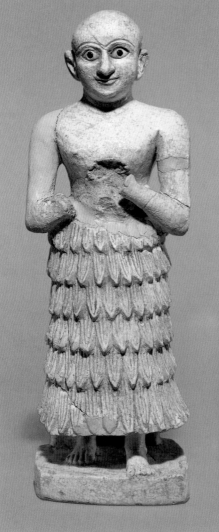

24d

neck is thick and short; and the cranium is unnaturally flat.

A male figure found in a later level of the Nintu temple, Nintu VI (cat. no. 24d), is perhaps the finest Early Dynastic statue from the Diyala region, on a par with the best sculpture of the period, from the site of Mari (see cat. nos. 88–93). Reflecting a greater interest in the relationship between anatomical details, the upper body is better proportioned, the shoulders are less exaggerated, and the upper arms are set closer to the body. Rings of flesh are carved at the neck, and the figure has a double chin. The deep-set eyes and aquiline nose are more softly articulated. The flat, ridgelike lips of the earlier figures are replaced by a delicate curve suggesting a smile. The proportional relationship between the face and the beautifully modeled skull, which is rounded but not perfectly circular, is accurate. The figure steps forward with the left foot, and the tufts of the skirt are carved in higher relief than those of the second figure from Nintu V, breaking up the conical form of the skirt.

The foundations of the Nintu VI temple were partially set over the hole dug for the Nintu V hoard, indicating that the hoard was buried before the construction of the new temple and that the Nintu VI statue was clearly later in date. Both levels of the temple, however, belong to the Early Dynastic II period. The excavator's argument that sculpture developed throughout the entire Early Dynastic period from an abstract to a realistic style therefore had to be revised since the Nintu VI figure shows that the realistic style was already fully developed in the Early Dynastic II period.[3]   JME

1. Delougaz and Lloyd 1942, pp. 189–90.
2. Ibid., pp. 92–95.
3. Frankfort 1943, pp. 6–7; Frankfort 1970, p. 56.

shell and black limestone; the single, arching brow was also originally inlaid. The hair is divided into two symmetrical sections that fall on either side of a rectangular beard, and both hair and beard show traces of their original bitumen coloring.

Standing male figures (cat. nos. 24b, c) were discovered among a hoard of statues stacked one upon the other beneath the floor of the Nintu V temple at Khafajah.[2] Like the Tell Asmar example, the first is carved in an abstract style. Set on a socle with no back support, the feet are carved as a single massive block with a deep line indicating their separation. The smooth, conelike skirt is carved so that the fringe appears to flip up at the bottom. In profile the figure is very flat, and the nose, beard, upper arms, and skirt are a series of sharp, slanted surfaces. The hands, with fingers indicated by three incised lines, are clasped at the waist. Seen from the front, the

upper body is a square, its sides defined by the vertical upper arms and the horizontal shoulders and forearms; the hair is articulated as a gridlike pattern, and the beard is rectangular.

When the famous hoard in the Abu temple at Tell Asmar was published in 1939, the excavator argued that the abstract sculptural style appeared at the beginning of the Early Dynastic period and gradually evolved into the more realistic style found in contexts later in date. Statues that exhibit traits of both styles, such as catalogue number 24c, were defined as transitional and dated accordingly. The clasped hands of this figure are set higher on the body so that the torso is less square in form, and the skirt is articulated with tiers of tufts, which break up the smooth surface; tufted skirts of this type remained the norm until the end of the Early Dynastic period. Still, the statue is compact and stocky, with a short waist and broad, bulky shoulders; the

Stone Sculpture Production

Most stone sculpture in Early Dynastic Mesopotamia was carved from relatively soft, calcium-based minerals such as limestone, calcite, and gypsum rock that were most likely obtained from outcrops in the desert to the west and along the banks of the upper Euphrates River. As no workshop has yet been excavated, evidence of sculpting methods must be deduced from examinations of recovered objects.[1] Unfinished votive statuettes excavated at Tell Asmar suggest that Mesopotamian sculptors did not begin by carefully drawing figures on the stone blocks within a grid system, as known from Egyptian examples. Instead, features were crudely indicated on the uncarved stone, and outlines were roughed out on four sides with stone tools and copper-alloy chisels before the edges were removed. Polishing in selected areas was achieved with mineral abrasives. Eyes were either hollowed out for inlaying or carved and painted. Paint, which rarely survives in more than trace amounts, may have been used to indicate hair and other features. Shell and dark stones such as lapis lazuli or steatite were used both for inlays and for parts of composite statues, for example, the intricately carved fragments recovered at Ebla (see cat. no. 109). Repairs to stone sculptures were made by drilling across break lines and inserting dowels, a joining method that may also have been used to construct new statues.

Beginning in the Akkadian period, a preference for dark igneous-metamorphic rocks, commonly identified as diorite, is evidenced in royal statuary; soft, light-colored stones remained in use for private votive pieces. Diorite, referred to as "esi-stone from Magan" in inscriptions of both Naram-Sin and Gudea of Lagash, was obtained primarily in the Gulf region from sources in present-day Oman or in Iran. The considerable expense required to obtain and transport these stones as well as the difficulty of sculpting in such hard, durable minerals presumably added to their prestige.

J-FL

1. For a detailed overview and further reference on stoneworking, see Moorey 1994, pp. 21–73.

25

Standing male figure with clasped hands

Alabaster
H. 17 cm (6¾ in.); W. 5.8 cm (2¼ in.)
Syria, Tell Chuera, Kleiner Antentempel, T.CH.63109
Early Dynastic III (?), ca. 2550–2250 B.C.
National Museum, Damascus, Syria   1699

Only a few complete statues could be reconstructed from the hundreds of fragments of Early Dynastic sculpture excavated at Tell Chuera, a site in northern Syria near the Turkish border. The fragments were found in the debris that filled the rooms adjacent to a temple located in the center of the site, called by the German excavators the Kleiner (Smaller) Antentempel, and in the cella of the temple itself. Some characteristics of the Tell Chuera statues, such as the broad shoulders, fringed skirts, and enormous eyes, invite comparison with sculpture from the Diyala region of Mesopotamia (see cat. no. 24).[1]

This male figure standing with his hands clasped together in front of his body wears a knee-length, belted skirt with a single row of long, looped fringe at the hem. The arms are

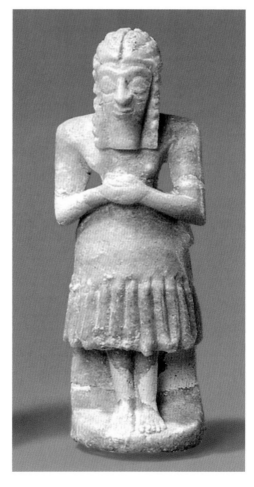

thin, and deep shoulder joints create a triangular space between the chest and arms. The waist is slender, and the spine is articulated with a deep line. Partially restored, the feet and legs are finely carved in high relief against the back support and socle; relieved of their supportive function, the legs are carved in realistic proportion to the body. The long, wavy hair is parted to the base of the neck and falls forward on the shoulders, and the beard is rectangular and unarticulated.

Because of the similarities between the Tell Chuera statues and those of the Diyala region the Kleiner Antentempel has been dated to the Early Dynastic II period.[2] Although crude in execution, the Tell Chuera statues, however, have slimmer, more delicate proportions than their counterparts from the Diyala;[3] moreover, a date at the end of the Early Dynastic III period has been suggested for the assemblage from Tell Chuera on the basis of other artifacts such as pottery and cylinder sealings.[4] One explanation for the discrepancy in style is that the statues reflect a cultural time lag, exemplifying an earlier style still in production in the provinces late in the Early Dynastic period.[5] Another possibility is that this style of sculpture was produced throughout the Early Dynastic period and displays regional variations such as that illustrated here.   JME

1. Braun-Holzinger 1977, p. 42.
2. Moortgat 1965, pp. 36–37; Orthmann 1990a, p. 11.
3. Moortgat 1965, pp. 23ff.; Braun-Holzinger 1977, p. 77.
4. Schwartz and Weiss 1992, p. 241; D. Matthews 1997b, pp. 42–43.
5. Mallowan 1966, p. 93; Winter 1984, p. 112.

26

Standing figure of Lugaldalu

Cuneiform inscription in Sumerian
Limestone
H. 78 cm (30¾ in.)
Mesopotamia, Adab (modern Bismaya)
Early Dynastic III, ca. 2550–2250 B.C.
Eski Şark Museum, Istanbul 3235

The inscription on the right shoulder of this figure states: "For the E-sar. Lugaldalu, king of Adab."[1] The name of this king of Adab is

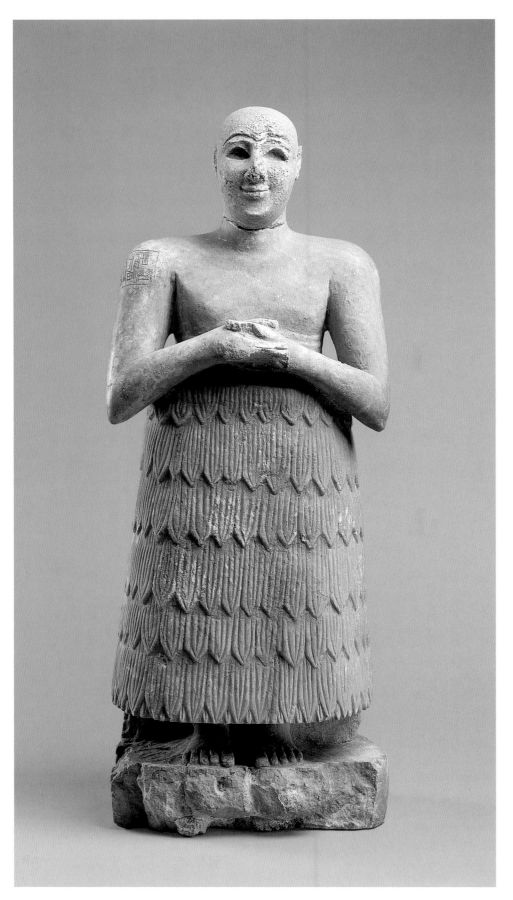

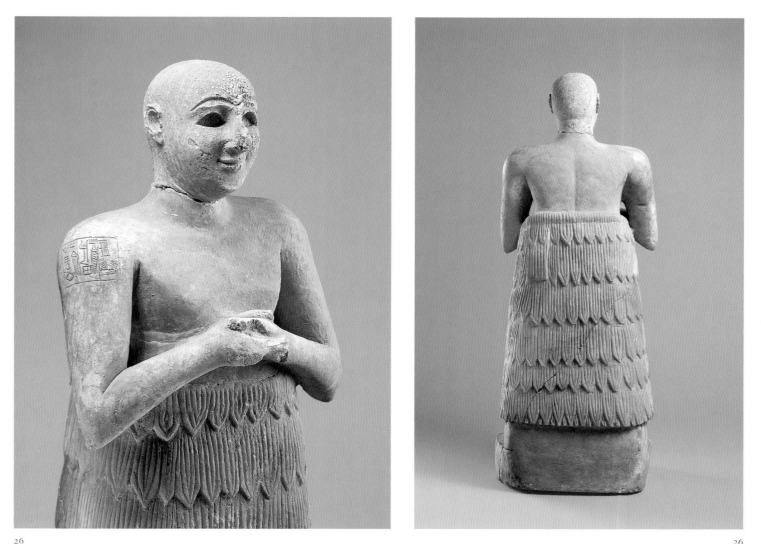

known only from his statue, which is dedicated to the E-sar temple; it is unusual that the deity is not named in the inscription. Unlike at Mari, where the high status of Ishqi-Mari is expressed by his tufted garment, which covers his left shoulder and arm, and elaborate hairstyle (see cat. no. 88), Lugaldalu is depicted in the standard guise of a dedicatory figure, clasping his hands in front of his chest and wearing a tufted skirt. Enmetena, an Early Dynastic ruler of Lagash, is similarly portrayed (fig. 15). Although the tufted skirt was sometimes used in Early Dynastic relief carving and inlay to distinguish important individuals (see cat. no. 52), by the end of the period it was common in dedicatory sculpture. For example, we know from inscribed sculpture at Mari that men of various offices and professions wore the tufted skirt (see cat. nos. 89b, 91a).   JME

1. Cooper 1986, p. 17.

27

Foundation figure of Lugalkisalsi

Cuneiform inscription in Sumerian
Limestone
H. 24.5 cm (9⅝ in.)
Mesopotamia
Early Dynastic IIIB, ca. 2400–2250 B.C.
Staatliche Museen zu Berlin, Vorderasiatisches
Museum VA 4855

By the beginning of the Early Dynastic period in Mesopotamia it was customary to equip important public buildings with a deposit of objects carrying inscriptions. An inscription served not only to commemorate the builders but also to magically protect the structures and was placed in some hidden spot in the course of an elaborate ritual. Such an inscribed object is an invaluable find, for it generally provides information on the builder's name and the function of the structure and consequently

makes it possible to determine the building's age. Foundation deposits also served as historical records even in antiquity. There is repeated documentation of such objects being carefully tended even after a building's later reconstruction; it was standard practice for the rebuilder to replace older inscriptions along with the ritual deposit of his own documents.

The number and form of such records varied in accordance with the structure's importance. As a rule, the building materials themselves—the bricks—already bore their own inscriptions, either written or stamped. Deposited objects were often made of valuable imported materials, and certain types of stone and metals were especially favored. A number of the shapes of foundation deposits developed from the early shapes of bricks and of the metal clamps that secured them (which might also carry inscriptions), and the shapes of cuneiform tablets and of stone or metal documents also served as models. It was not unusual for inscriptions on large bricks or stones to be reflected in the texts on the surfaces of figures, which were usually smaller; sometimes the latter reproduced only an abbreviated form of the text.

One special type of foundation object is a figurine in the form of a man at prayer, a genre familiar from votive statuettes found in temples (see cat. no. 24). The figure shown here, which dates to about the twenty-fourth century B.C., has hands folded in prayer, but in all other respects it takes the form of the traditional ritual foundation peg: a compact upper body atop a tapering base.[1] In this example the depiction of the face is unusually detailed, and the stylized treatment of the hair and beard is striking. The lower body is in the form of a clay nail and is encircled by a single-column cuneiform inscription in which king Lugalkisalsi (or Lugalgiparesi) of Uruk and Ur dedicates a gift to the goddess Namma. The inscription reads:

> For (the goddess) Namma,
> wife of (the god) An,
> Lugalkisalsi,
> king of Uruk
> and king of Ur
> erected
> this temple of Namma.

JM

1. See Ellis 1968.

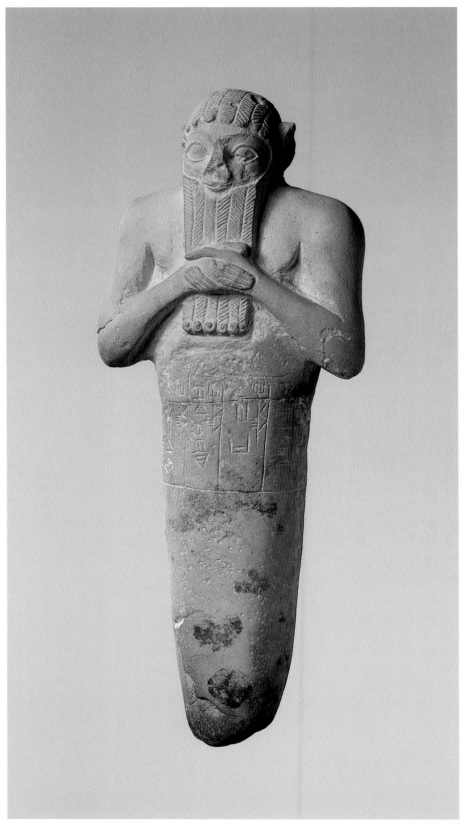

27

Nippur

As the home of Enlil, the supreme Sumerian deity, Nippur was the great holy city of southern Mesopotamia. According to myth, it was at Nippur that Enlil drove his pickaxe into the earth and man emerged. The temple of Enlil (E-kur) dominated the city, but there were also temples for many other deities, including Inanna. Excavations in the area of the goddess's temple are of great importance, since they have provided the longest continuous archaeological sequence that exists for Mesopotamia, with more than twenty building levels dating back to the Middle Uruk period. In existence by Early Dynastic I, the temple itself was thereafter continuously rebuilt until the Parthian period, some three thousand years later.

The most spectacular finds were made in Level VII of the Inanna temple. This level was divided by the excavators into an earlier (B) and a later (A) phase, since the temple was rebuilt and altered several times. By Level VIIB, it had acquired five steps that led up to the northern entrance, which had a porch and a recessed doorway flanked by towers (see fig. 26). At the end of a series of small rooms, a large porticoed court with circular mud-brick columns gave access to a unique double cella, one unit of which was freestanding and separated from its surroundings by a corridor. Hundreds of cult objects were discovered in the temple: statues, stone bowls and plaques, inlays, furniture attachments, and other fragmentary temple items, found either in hoards or scattered throughout the building.   JME

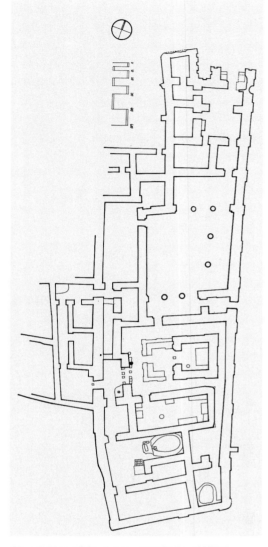

Fig. 26. Plan of the Inanna temple, Level VIIB, Nippur. Early Dynastic IIIA, ca. 2550–2400 B.C.

28

Standing female figure with clasped hands

Limestone, shell, and lapis lazuli
H. 24.9 cm (9¾ in.)
Mesopotamia, Nippur, Inanna temple, Level VIIB, 7N183
Early Dynastic IIIA, ca. 2550–2400 B.C.
The Metropolitan Museum of Art, New York; Rogers Fund, 1962 62.70.2

This statue of a standing woman with her hands clasped in front of her chest was found in the plasterings of a mud-brick bench located in one of the cellas of the Inanna temple. Her garment is draped over the left shoulder and falls in folds indicated by two incised lines along the border of the otherwise smooth fabric. The underside of the skirt is slightly convex,

giving the hem a sharp edge. The feet are carved in high relief against the back support, and the toes and ankles are clearly indicated. The wavy hair is held in place by two plain bands, and curly locks hang down on either side of the face. The best-preserved statues at Nippur are those that were buried within the temple furniture, like the example here. Such

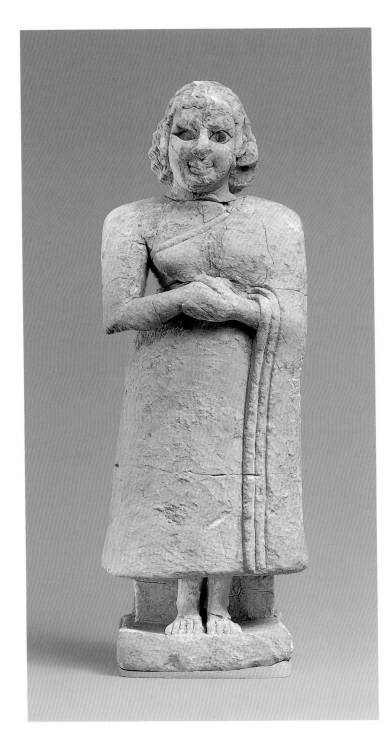 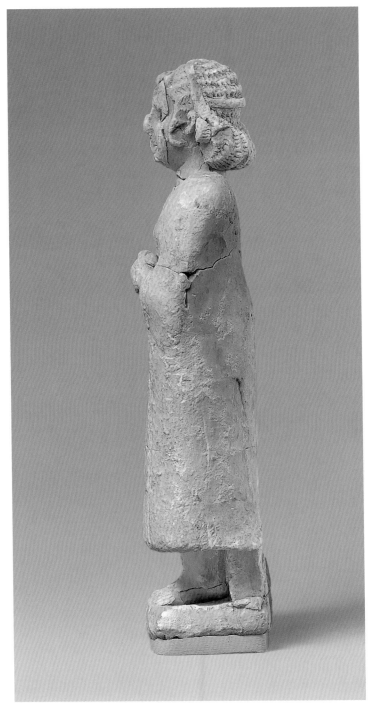

deliberate burials suggest that temple offerings
and equipment remained sacred even when
no longer in use.   JME

1. For a summary of the excavations of the Inanna
temple, see Gibson, Hansen, and Zettler 2001,
pp. 551–57.

Tello (Ancient Girsu)

The site of Tello in southern Mesopotamia is located about three hundred kilometers southeast of Baghdad on the left bank of the Shatt el Hai, a canal that connects the Tigris to the Euphrates midway along the present-day course of both rivers. Tello covers the ruins of the ancient city of Girsu, which was the capital of the Sumerian state of Lagash probably from the beginning of that city's first dynasty, in the Early Dynastic III period. The site includes several hills, or tells; at the north Tell A ("Tell du Palais," or Palace Tell) rises fifteen meters above the plain. The mounds of Tello cover a surface area of about 250 acres, but overall the site measures only 3 by 4 kilometers. A canal to the east once connected Girsu with the two other principal cities of the state of Lagash: the city of Lagash (modern Al-Hiba) and Nina (modern Zurghul), both farther south.

Excavations at Tello by French archaeologists began in 1877, after local people reported the discovery of inscribed statues. The excavations revealed the existence of a Sumerian culture. In all, twenty archaeological campaigns were carried out between 1877 and 1933,[1] by which time the site had been largely plundered. The pre- and protohistorical periods were attested by two deep soundings at Tell K and East Tell ("Tell de l'Est"), primarily by Henri de Genouillac. They revealed pottery from the Ubaid period. This material was connected to tombs as well as objects from the Uruk and Jamdat Nasr periods found at Tell K by Genouillac, who exhumed seals, copper works, bone artifacts, tools, pottery, and stone vessels.

No constructions at Tello dating to the Uruk and Jamdat Nasr periods have been identified, and little is known about the beginnings of Early Dynastic I and II periods. At Tell K, Ernest de Sarzec discovered installations he designated as the "Construction Inférieure" dating from the end of Early Dynastic II or the beginning of Early Dynastic III. That structure was probably a temple, given its foundation deposits of copper peg-figurines. The sanctuary, altered before being destroyed by phase III builders, probably belonged to Ningirsu, tutelary god of the state of Lagash. Ningirsu's name appears on a small limestone bas-relief known as the Figure aux Plumes, recognizable as a representation of the ruler (see fig. 27). Other objects from that period now in the Louvre were collected with no precise context. These include a colossal copper spear adorned with an engraved rearing lion and a

mace-head dedicated to Ningirsu by Mesalim, the king of Kish, who was the arbiter of the conflict between Lagash and its rival city-state Umma, at the beginning of the Early Dynastic III period. The mace-head is decorated with a lion-headed eagle, emblem of Lagash, representing the storm cloud associated with Ningirsu, with rearing lions in its clutches. Two rulers of Lagash are known from that early period: Lugalsha-engur and Enhegal.

Significant archaeological and epigraphic finds dating to the Early Dynastic III period were extracted from Tell K or found reused over the entire site. The nine sovereigns of the First Dynasty of Lagash left royal inscriptions that reported on their official construction and irrigation projects and gave accounts of their military feats. The first ruler, Ur-Nanshe (about 2450 B.C.), evoked in his votive inscriptions (see fig. 16) the power of his state, which extended its commercial relations as far as Dilmun (modern Bahrain and the Arabian coast). The Dilmun fleet brought to

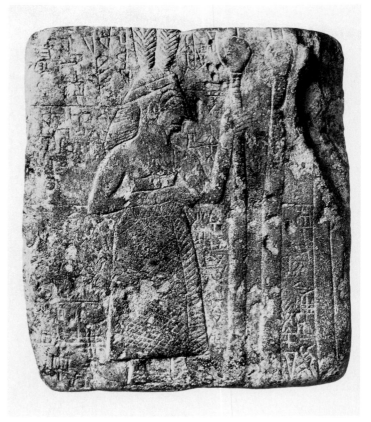

Fig. 27. Limestone relief-carved plaque called the *Figure aux Plumes*. Girsu, Early Dynastic I, ca. 2900–2650 B.C. Musée du Louvre, Paris, AO 221.

Lagash exotic wood destined to embellish the temple of Ningirsu, which was rebuilt at Tell K. It is the partially excavated structure called the "Maison des Fruits" by the excavator Ernest de Sarzec. Perforated stone plaques decorated with bas-reliefs commemorate the construction of the temple and other royal activities (see cat. no. 30), such as the wars Ur-Nanshe waged against his neighbors. The conflict with Umma, involving a border skirmish, lasted for several generations. It began when Mesalim, king of Kish, delimited the boundary between the two states with a stele, which the treacherous prince of Umma then moved. Ur-Nanshe's grandson, Eannatum, erected the Stele of the Vultures (see figs. 52, 53) to commemorate his victory over Umma. On one face of the stele the king goes to battle in a chariot; on the other, the defeated enemies are caught in Ningirsu's net.

Inscriptions attest that Ur-Nanshe challenged other powers, including Mari and Elam, and that his successors continued his policies of restoration and construction. A statue of diorite (fig. 15) has come down to us from Enmetena, the great-grandson of Ur-Nanshe; found in Ur, it was erected in the temple of Enlil. Inscribed clay cones are an exceptional source of information about the age-old conflict between Umma and Lagash, as Enmetena acted as a historian, summarizing its origins. He also established a policy of alliance, or "fraternity," with the kings of Uruk, Larsa, and Badtibira.

One indication of the wealth of the temple of Ningirsu is a large silver vase, engraved with the emblem of Lagash, fashioned by Enmetena for the god's table service. Texts from the temple of the goddess Ba'u show the economic operations of the major temples of Girsu: the arrival and departure of cereals, oil, wool, clothing, and cattle, and the organization of religious festivals. The last prince of the Early Dynastic III period, Urukagina, was a social and religious reformer. Girsu was taken over by Lugalzagezi of Umma in the late twenty-fourth century B.C., just before the conquest of Sumer by Sargon of Akkad.

Although excavations at Tello yielded few objects from the Akkadian period, it appears Girsu served as a regional seat of government. After an interregnum caused by conflict with the Guti barbarians, the state of Lagash and its capital rapidly recovered their fortune under the sovereignty of the Second Dynasty of Lagash, whose most glorious representative was Gudea (see cat. nos. 304–306). Under his reign the city reached its maximum size, and the temple of Ningirsu was sumptuously rebuilt at Tell A. Gudea was an indefatigable builder and the patron of an inspired and prolific literary circle as well as art workshops, whose finest products were statues depicting him. Many were made of diorite imported via reopened commercial routes. Shortly thereafter, during the apogee of the Third Dynasty of Ur and the subsequent loss of Girsu's independence, the city remained active but declined somewhat in importance. That gradual decline continued after the Isin-Larsa and Old Babylonian periods. The site was virtually unoccupied when, in the second century B.C., a Seleucid prince breathed new life into Girsu by building his palace at Tell A, reusing what remained of Gudea's structures.   BA-S

1. Eleven campaigns (1877–1900) were conducted by Ernest de Sarzec, the French consul to Basra, who had difficulty distinguishing between the mud-brick constructions and what was simply landfill, hindering any understanding of the monuments discovered; four campaigns were by Commander Gaston Cros (between 1903 and 1909); three by Henri de Genouillac (1929–31); and two by André Parrot (1931–33). The main publications are Sarzec and Heuzey 1884–1912; Cros 1910–14; Genouillac 1934–36; and Parrot 1948. See also Falkenstein and Opificius 1957–71, pp. 385–401.

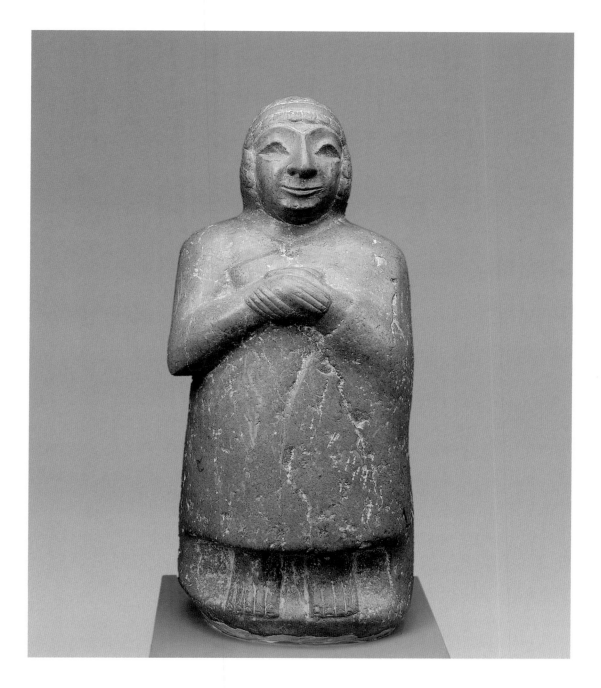

29

Standing female figure with clasped hands

Limestone
H. 30 cm (11¼ in.)
Mesopotamia
Early Dynastic IIIA, ca. 2550–2400 B.C.
Trustees of The British Museum, London BM 90929

Although the face of this woman is carved in fine detail, the body is bulky and compact. A faint diagonal ridge summarily indicates the upper border of the garment, which passes

over the left shoulder and leaves the right arm free. The back of the garment is not differentiated from the socle. The feet are carved flat against the base, and the toes are elongated and show carefully articulated toenails. The hair is a long rectangular mass of incised lines. Secured in place by a headband, it frames the face in a scalloped pattern. The sharply carved facial features have parallels with relief sculpture from the city-state of Lagash (see cat. nos. 30, 35). The eyes, which were originally inlaid, are large and almond-

shaped, and the chin and nose are pronounced. The shape of the body recalls the block of stone from which the statue was carved and in this respect is similar to an inscribed statue of a seated male figure from Tello dated to the Early Dynastic IIIA period.[1]   JME

1. Moortgat 1969, pl. 108. For the dating of the statue from Tello, see Bauer 1987–90, p. 172, and Gelb, Steinkeller, and Whiting 1991, p. 72.

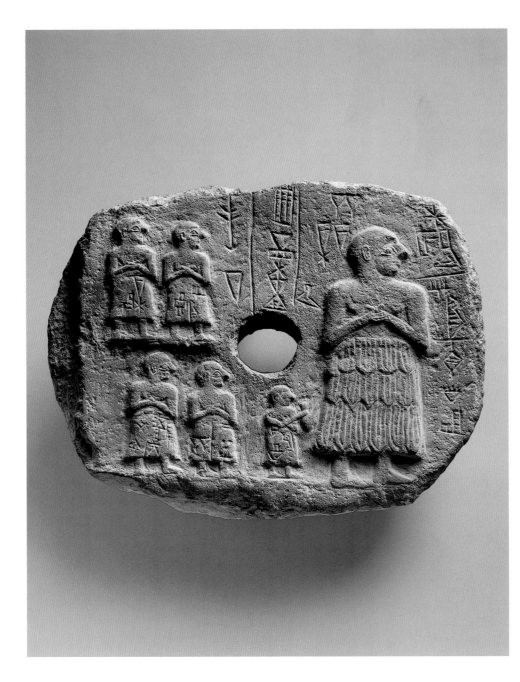

To the left of the perforation are four men of equal size dressed in smooth skirts. Like the king, they clasp their hands at their chests, a gesture of worship similar to one found on numerous contemporary votive statues that were placed in temples. The smallest figure, directly behind the king, is Anita the cupbearer, who holds a long-necked vase used for libations. Behind Anita on the lower register—on the same ground line as the king—stands Akurgal, whose status as the son and successor to Ur-Nanshe is specified in the inscription. Immediately above Akurgal is Lugalezen, designated only by name, but whom other inscriptions mention as another of the ruler's sons. The names of the other figures, Gula and Barasagnudi, do not appear on other inscriptions from that reign, but they, too, are probably royal siblings or high officials in the king's entourage.

This relief commemorates the construction by Ur-Nanshe of a temple dedicated to Ningirsu, tutelary god of Lagash. Oversight of the construction of temples for the city's protective deities was one of the sovereign's foremost duties. This religious function is illustrated by three other votive reliefs of the same type also found in Tello. The most elaborate of these (fig. 16)[2] depicts the king surrounded by his family and members of his court; he carries on his head, like a simple mason, a basket of the first bricks to be used to build the temple. He is then shown presiding over the ritual banquet celebrating the event. In the inscription on this other plaque, Ur-Nanshe boasts that he "had ships of Dilmun transport timber from foreign lands."[3]

FD

1. For further reference, see Sarzec and Heuzey 1884–1912, vol. 2, p. 171, pl. 2bis; Parrot 1948, p. 91, pl. 5b; Boese 1971, pp. 198–99; and Amiet 1977a, fig. 326. This plaque was also exhibited in Tokyo 1991, no. 1.
2. Musée du Louvre, Département des Antiquités Orientales, inv. AO2344; Amiet 1977a, p. 368, fig. 324.
3. Cooper 1986, p. 23.

30

Wall plaque of Ur-Nanshe and family

Cuneiform inscription in Sumerian
Limestone
H. 23 cm (9 in.); W. 29 cm (11⅜ in.); Thickness 7 cm (2¾ in.)
Mesopotamia, Girsu (modern Tello)
Early Dynastic IIIA, ca. 2550–2400 B.C.
Musée du Louvre, Département des Antiquités Orientales, Paris AO 2345

This plaque, perforated through the center, was intended to be affixed to the wall with a peg.[1] Six male figures are represented on it in low relief. Inscriptions engraved on their clothing and on the background of the plaque provide captions for the scene and identify each of the figures, the largest of whom is Ur-Nanshe, *ensi* (ruler) of Lagash. He was a powerful ruler who in about 2450 B.C. founded the First Dynasty of Lagash, which dominated that Sumerian city-state for 150 years. His large size and the careful articulation of his skirt as three rows of tufts distinguish him from the other figures and indicate his importance.

31

Fragment of a wall plaque with a chariot scene

Limestone
H. 13 cm (5⅛ in.); W. 27 cm (10⅝ in.)
Mesopotamia, Ur, U.8557
Early Dynastic II, ca. 2650–2550 B.C.
University of Pennsylvania Museum of Archaeology
and Anthropology, Philadelphia CBS 17086

This fragment of a votive plaque, found in the area of the royal tombs at Ur, shows a two-wheeled chariot drawn by onagers (wild asses) and escorted by three men.[1] A spotted material that may be leopard skin is draped over the high back of the chariot.[2] A team of four is suggested by a common overlapping device, also seen, for example, on the so-called Standard of Ur (cat. no. 52). A quiver attached to the chariot extends beyond the top of the scene into the next, and the figures fill the register so tightly that their heads touch its upper border, as if they had been wedged into the compositional space. The scene is carved in low relief with sharp edges and very little modeling.

The men wear short, belted skirts that hang in long tufts from the waist. A plain, triangular area at the front of each skirt may indicate a fold or a pouch hanging from the waist.[3] The long hair of the only completely preserved figure is rendered in a series of parallel striations, and the beard is smooth and rectangular. In these characteristics as well as in the pointed nose, bulky shoulders, and proportionally small hands, the figure is similar to dedicatory sculpture traditionally dated to Early Dynastic I–II (see entry for cat. no. 24).

Votive plaques are usually perforated in the center, but this one also has holes at the corners, probably to better secure its attachment to a wall. A chariot scene is commonly depicted in the bottom register of such plaques.[4] The scene displayed here closely resembles one that fills the bottom register of a fragmentary plaque from Khafajah. Its preserved parts suggest that there may have been similar banqueting scenes on the missing registers of this fragment.[5]

JME

1. Woolley 1934, pp. 376–77.
2. Strommenger 1971, pp. 42–43. Soldiers are shown wearing leopard skins in plaques from Mari and Ur.
3. Woolley 1934, pp. 376–77; Pelzel 1973, pp. 42–43.
4. Compare with Boese 1971, AG 2 (Shara temple, Tell Agrab), CS 1, CS 4 (Sin temple, Khafajah).
5. The Ur and Khafajah plaques were first compared in a preliminary excavation report for Khafajah; see Frankfort, Jacobsen, and Preusser 1932, pp. 95–98. For the Khafajah plaque, see Hansen 1975b, fig. 82.

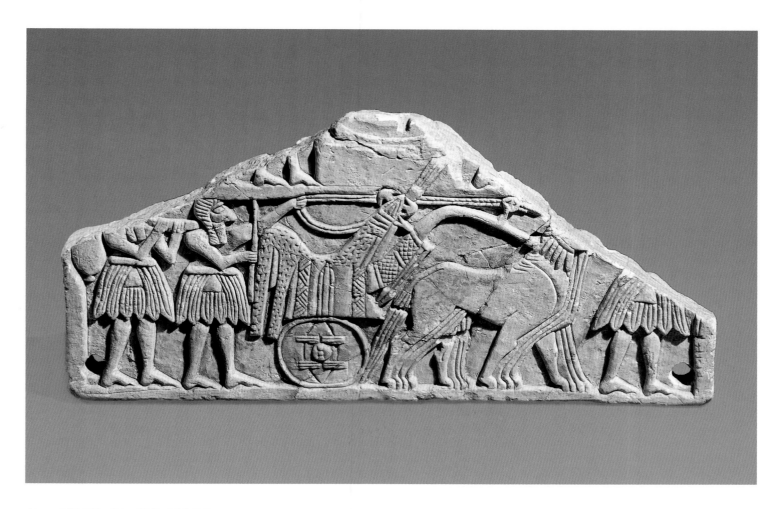

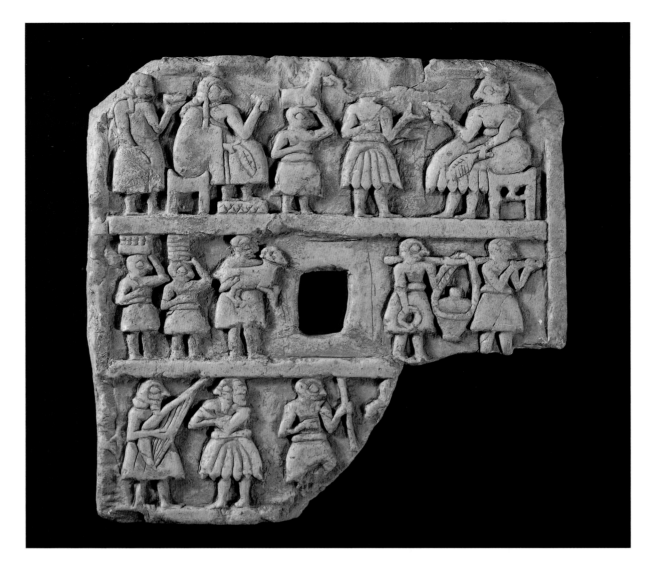

32

Wall plaque with banqueters and musicians

Limestone
H. 20 cm (7⅞ in.); W. 20 cm (7⅞ in.); Thickness
3.8 cm (1½ in.)
Mesopotamia, Khafajah, Sin temple, Level IX
Early Dynastic IIIA, ca. 2550–2400 B.C.
The Oriental Institute of the University of
Chicago A 12417

This plaque is framed and divided into three registers by undecorated relief bands.[1] In the upper register a man and a woman hold small bowls or cups in their upraised hands and grasp what may be leaves or clusters of flowers in their laps. The woman, left, is seated on a plain stool and has a decorated footrest beneath her feet. A female attendant standing behind her holds a vessel in her upraised left hand and an unidentifiable object in her damaged right hand. A small male figure in front of the seated woman carries on his head a reclining animal and follows a taller man, whose head is now missing. This figure reaches toward the cup held by the banqueting man. In the central register, interrupted by a rectangular perforation, five men facing right bring food and drink. The first two carry on their shoulders a large vessel suspended on a rope slung over a pole. The next man carries a goat; the third and fourth bear on their heads what appear to be provisions. All the men in the top two registers are clean shaven.

The bottom register is completed by a piece now in the Iraq Museum, Baghdad.[2] On the left are two men with long hair and beards; one plays a harp, and the other, his arms crossed, sings or dances. A clean-shaven man to the right holds a staff and watches as two men, both with long hair and beards, and nude except for a heavy belt and codpiece, box or wrestle. An inscription on the stone between them appears to say "son of . . . ."

Plaques such as this one formed part of a door-locking mechanism in ancient Mesopotamian temples.[3] Inscribed examples dedicated by kings commemorate royal activities, such as the construction of temples and the importing of precious materials. Uninscribed plaques like this one most often depict banqueting and other related scenes. They may have been dedicated by individuals who participated in or sponsored a temple festival or celebration. The leaves or flowers grasped by the individuals shown on this plaque suggest a celebration associated with the fertility of the plant world.   KLW

1. Frankfort 1939, no. 185, pl. 105.
2. Strommenger 1964, pl. 46 (below).
3. Hansen 1963, pp. 145–66; Zettler 1987b, pp. 210–14.

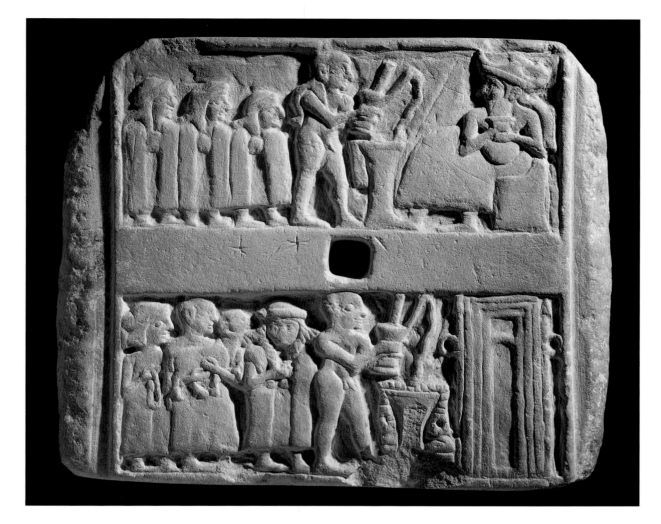

33

Wall plaque with libation scenes

Limestone
H. 22.9 cm (9 in.); W. 26 cm (10¼ in.)
Mesopotamia, Ur, gipar, U.6831
Early Dynastic III, ca. 2550–2250 B.C.
Trustees of The British Museum, London BM 118561

This Early Dynastic votive plaque was found in a late level of the *gipar*, the residence and administrative center of the *entu*-priestess of the moon god Nanna at Ur.[1] The daughters of royalty often held this prestigious position; the earliest known *entu*-priestess of Ur was Enheduanna, daughter of the Akkadian ruler Sargon. Both the frontal figure in the lower register of this plaque and the figure on a limestone disk from Ur thought to be Enheduanna herself (cat. no. 128) wear a rolled-brim headdress and are preceded by a libating figure.[2] The similarities between this carved plaque and the Enheduanna disk have

been cited to suggest that the office of *entu*-priestess existed at the end of the Early Dynastic period.[3]

Both registers of this plaque depict scenes of libation. In the lower register the scene is set before a temple facade decorated with niches and flanked by looped gateposts, which first appear in the art of the Late Uruk period as a conventional way to indicate a temple (see fig. 10). Three figures stand behind a clean-shaven, nude man who pours liquid from a spouted vessel into a stand.[4] The woman immediately behind him is depicted frontally with her hands clasped. Behind her is a clean-shaven man who carries an animal, probably intended for sacrifice. The last figure can be identified by its dress as a woman, but she carries an unidentifiable object.[5] In the upper register a long-haired, nude man pours a libation before a seated figure, bearded and also with long hair, identifiable as a deity by

his horned headdress. Three smaller female figures appear behind the libation bearer; they have identical hairstyles, cloaks, and wide-brimmed headgear.

The upper register of the Ur plaque is similar to relief-carved plaques from Tello and Nippur, in that they all depict a nude male figure with a spouted vessel who stands before a seated deity wearing a horned headdress.[6] The plaques all date to the end of the Early Dynastic period and as such are significant because they bear some of the earliest representations of anthropomorphic deities.

Frontality is associated primarily with goddesses in the late Early Dynastic period (see cat. no. 36), but the convention is used on this plaque to indicate the importance of the female figure in the lower register.[7] With her hands clasped in a gesture commonly seen in dedicatory statues, this personage may be the donor of the plaque. If she is also an

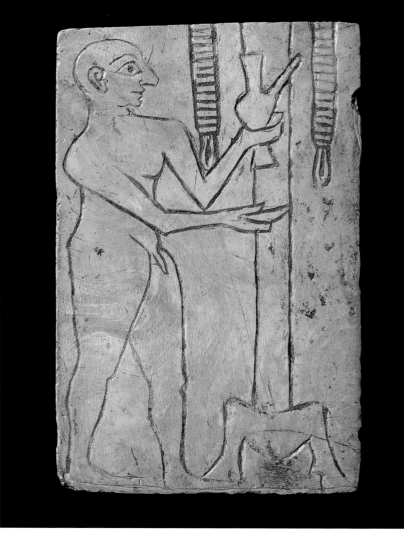

34

-priestess, then her position within the scene, like that of Enheduanna, indicates that the overseeing of libations was one duty of the *entu*-priestess.[8]   JME

1. Woolley 1955, p. 173.
2. The headdress has been identified with the *aga*, which was worn by priestesses and is first referred to in a hymn of Enheduanna; Winter 1987b, p. 192.
3. Woolley 1955, p. 46; Winter 1987b, pp. 195–96. Textual evidence also indicates that the office may predate Enheduanna's tenure; Winter 1987b, p. 201, esp. n. 44. For the Early Dynastic remains of the *gipar*, see Woolley 1926, p. 366, and Weadock 1975, pp. 105–6. The *entu*-priestess served as the human wife of the god Nanna; the figure of Enheduanna is referred to as "wife of Nanna" in an inscription on her disk.
4. The loops on the stand may represent handles, although later analogies would suggest date-palm vegetation; Woolley 1955, p. 45. For a similar representation, see Boese 1971, plaque N11.
5. Asher-Greve (1985, p. 88) suggests she carries a necklace.

6. Boese 1971, plaques N8, N9, T10; UK1 may be the fragment of a similar scene. Similar compositions also appear on seals (Amiet 1980, nos. 1357, 1358) and in inlay (see cat. no. 34).
7. For goddesses represented frontally, see Moortgat 1969, fig. 114; Hansen 1975b, figs. 84a, 87a, 95b; and Amiet 1980, no. 1357.
8. Some scholars suggest that since the *entu*-priestess herself does not offer libations, she was relegated to an auxiliary status, possibly because of her gender; see Asher-Greve 1985, p. 89, and Winter 1987b, pp. 192–93. On the earlier Uruk Vase a clean-shaven, nude male figure bearing bounty for the temple stands between deity and ruler (see figs. 9, 10). The role of the ruler on the Uruk Vase as overseer and his position behind the nude figure are analogous to those of the women seen in the upper register of this plaque, suggesting that the act of overseeing does not indicate diminished status and could instead signify the opposite. Bahrani (2001, p. 115) suggests that the overseeing of libations could itself be an important act.

34

Plaque with a libation scene

Shell
H. 7.5 cm (3 in.); W. 4.6 cm (1¾ in.)
Mesopotamia, Ur, U. 7900
Early Dynastic III, ca. 2550–2250 B.C.
Trustees of The British Museum, London
BM 120850

Leonard Woolley found this large plaque when he excavated the cemetery at Ur.[1] It was lying loose in the surface soil, and what it was originally attached to is unknown. The incised image of a man seems to represent a priest, since the figure is clean shaven and nude, as was typical for purification. Similar figures appear on Early Dynastic votive plaques from Ur (see cat. no. 33). The man pours a libation before a post supported on bull's legs. It is likely that the scene continued on another plaque above it, since the two ribbons hanging from the top of the image may have been attached to the post. The date of carving has been deduced from its style. The shell itself probably came from the Gulf.   PC

1. Woolley 1934, p. 525, pl. 102.

35

Mace-head dedicated for the life of Enannatum

Cuneiform inscription in Sumerian
Limestone
H. 12.7 cm (5 in.); Diam. 11.2 cm (4⅜ in.)
Mesopotamia
Early Dynastic IIIB, ca. 2400–2250 B.C.
Trustees of The British Museum, London BM 23287

The inscription radiating outward from the hole at the top of this pear-shaped mace-head states, "For Ningirsu of E-ninnu, the workman of Enannatum, ruler of Lagash, Barakisumun, the *sukkal,* dedicated this for the life of Enannatum, his master."[1] The mace-head was dedicated for either Enannatum I or Enannatum II, both of whom were rulers of Lagash in the Early Dynastic IIIB period. Three figures encircle the body of the mace-head and advance toward the Imdugud, a lion-headed eagle represented here in an emblematic composition, grasping the tails of

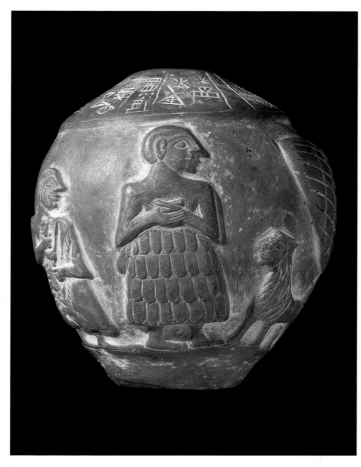

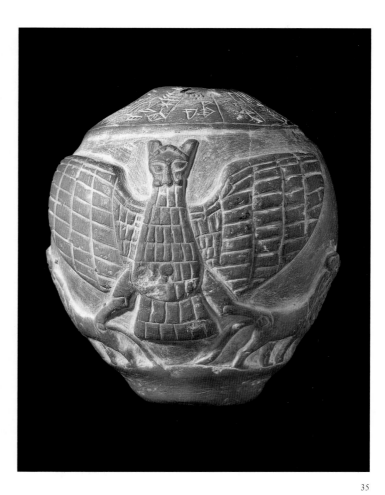

35

35

antithetical lions with its talons.[2] The figure nearest the Imdugud is distinguished by his large size and his skirt, which is tufted and has a tassel at the back. The two figures who follow him are represented in a smaller scale. Both are clean shaven and wear a plain skirt and a fringed cloth, which is draped over the shoulder as in depictions of soldiers (cat. no. 52). The first and smaller figure carries a spouted libation vessel (comparable to cat. no. 33), and the second holds a large staff in his clasped hands.

The Imdugud is generally associated with the god Ningirsu, who is the recipient of this mace-head.[3] The circle in the center of its body is characteristic of representations of the bird in the late Early Dynastic III period; the style of the figures, especially their faces, is more specifically characteristic of art from the city-state of Lagash (see cat. no. 30).[4] All three humans have the same large, pointed nose and exaggerated, stylized ear; the strong articulation of their jawline, brow, and base of the cranium produces a helmetlike effect.[5]

Although votive plaques and other relief carvings from Tello typically have labels that identify the figures depicted on them, the names of the figures are not inscribed on this mace-head.[6] The larger figure here, who clasps his hands in a traditional dedicatory pose, may be the ruler Enannatum, but more likely he is the dedicant, Barakisumun, since in relief carving the dedicant is either the largest figure in a composition or distinguished from the others by posture or costume.[7] The large size of the staff contrasts, moreover, with the scale of the smaller figure who carries it. One explanation for this discrepancy is that the staff belongs to the larger figure, which would further support his identification as the *sukkal* Barakisumun since the staff is identified with his office.[8]   JME

1. Cooper 1986, p. 54.
2. For another example in which a dedicant is shown approaching the Imdugud, see Hansen 1978, p. 83, figs. 26, 27; Hansen 1992, p. 209. The Plaque of Dudu from Tello shows the dedicant in the same register as the Imdugud, but he turns away from the emblem; see Moortgat 1969, fig. 117.
3. For the association of the Imdugud with Ningirsu, see the Stele of the Vultures (figs. 52, 53).

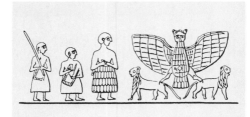

Fig. 28. Drawing of a mace-head dedicated for the life of Enannatum (cat. no. 35).

4. A similar circle is found in a representation of the Imdugud on the Vase of Enmetena of Lagash, from Tello; Hansen 1978, p. 81; Moortgat 1969, fig. 113. For the style of Lagash, see Hansen 1975b, p. 189, figs. 87b, 90, 91.
5. Frankfort 1935a, p. 106. A double line indicates the helmets of the soldiers from Lagash; Moortgat 1969, fig. 119.
6. For examples of labels from Tello, see Braun-Holzinger 1991, pp. 308ff.
7. For identification of the large figure as the ruler, see Hall 1928, pp. 27–28, and Braun-Holzinger 1991, p. 36.
8. For the office of *sukkal*, see Wiggermann 1985–86, esp. pp. 7–22.

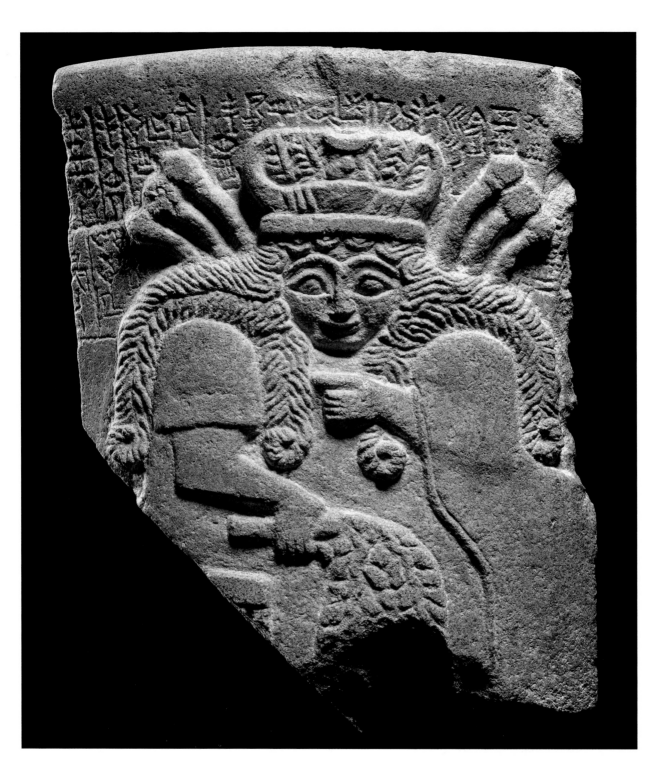

36

Vessel fragment with an image of a goddess

Cuneiform inscription in Sumerian
Diabase
H. 25.1 cm (9⅞ in.); W. 18.6 cm (7⅜ in.)
Original diam. approx. 40 cm (15¾ in.)
Mesopotamia
Early Dynastic IIIB, ca. 2400–2250 B.C.
Staatliche Museen zu Berlin, Vorderasiatisches
Museum VA 7248

Stone vessels with relief designs and inscriptions were part of the furnishings of both sacred and secular buildings in the third millennium B.C. and attest to the advanced stone-cutting skills of their makers. The vessels were used both in religious practices and as imposing luxury goods; a specific example's function can often be determined from its

inscription or the context in which it was found.

The fragment shown here, apparently from a cup, carries the image of a goddess in low relief and part of the inscription that filled the neck area of the vessel. The depiction employs an unusual mixed perspective: while the head and upper torso appear en face, the goddess's right side is seen in profile. As a result she appears stocky and clumsy, as do, for example, isolated figures on relief plaques from Tello and Ur (cat. no. 33). The deity, identified as such by the horns on her crown, wears a short garment beneath a cloak draped over her left shoulder. Her horned crown is adorned with feathers and a kind of mask. Her hair, woven into four braids, falls down across her shoulders, from which sprout six stalks that perhaps support poppy-seed capsules. In her right hand the goddess holds a cluster of dates.

Unfortunately, the inscription on this fragment fails to identify the goddess. However, the inscription is similar in type to building inscriptions composed by Enmetena of Lagash celebrating his construction of a brewery for Ningirsu, patron god of Lagash.

The cluster of dates and the poppy pods—the figure's attributes—show that she is a vegetation deity; she may be the grain goddess Nisaba.   LM

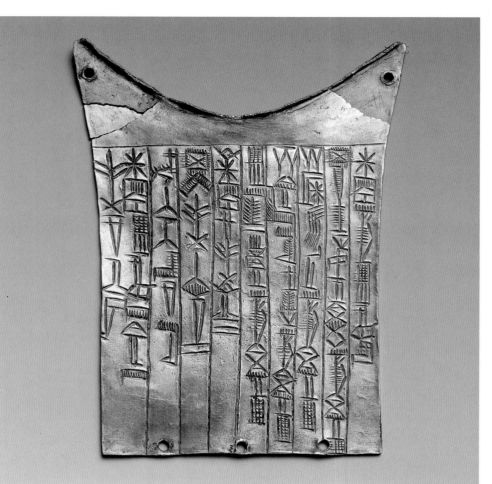

37

Plaque dedicated by a queen of Umma

Cuneiform inscription in Sumerian
Gold
H. 10.5 cm (4⅛ in.); W. 8.5 cm (3⅜ in.)
Mesopotamia, possibly Umma (modern Jokha)
Early Dynastic III, ca. 2550–2250 B.C.
Musée du Louvre, Département des Antiquités
Orientales, Paris AO 19225, AO 25037b, c

The upper part of this plaque is crescent-shaped and has a thin, hammered edge.[1] The sides are slightly curved, becoming narrower toward the bottom. The surface has five perforations—two in the corners at the top and three at the bottom of the tablet—which made it possible to affix the plaque to a wood support with gold nails. It has been suggested that the plaque was actually a votive beard intended to be attached to the chin of a statue;[2] however, the way the fasteners are arranged leads us to interpret this object as either plating used to decorate the statue of a deity[3] or, more likely, an ornament to be applied to a piece of furniture. The plaque is flat on the back and may have covered part of the pedestal or throne mentioned in the inscription, perhaps as a decorative element on one of the panels. The curve along the top would thus have accommodated a projection formed by moulding.[4]

Because of plundering and reuses, the plaque is one of only a few surviving fragments from the relics and ornaments of a large sanctuary from the Early Dynastic III period. The inscription, a dedication by queen Bara'irnun of Umma, reads:

> For (the god) Shara, lord of the E-mah: when Bara'irnun—wife of Gishakidu, king of Umma, daughter of Urluma, king of Umma, granddaughter of Enakale, king of Umma, daughter-in-law of Il, king of Umma—had made Shara resplendent and had built him a holy dais/throne, for her life, to Shara, in the E-mah, she offered (this ornament).

The plaque thus provides the first mention of the temple of Shara, the tutelary god of Umma, which is often named in the literature as among the major sanctuaries of the land of Sumer. It is interesting on a historical level because four generations of Umma kings are mentioned, with queen Bara'irnun connecting the two royal branches issuing from Enakale. These sovereigns are known mostly through the accounts of their Lagash enemies, with whom they shared a disputed border that was the object of a war lasting several generations.

BA-S

1. For further reference, see Thureau-Dangin 1937, pp. 177–82; Sollberger and Kupper 1971, pp. 83–84, ID 5a; André 1982, p. 86, no. 44; Steible 1982, pp. 268–69, Giššakidu 1; Cooper 1986, pp. 93–94, Umma 6; Braun-Holzinger 1991, p. 378, varia 9; André-Salvini 2003.
2. See Sollberger and Kupper 1971.
3. A breastplate has been suggested, but no removable element of that sort is known from this period in Mesopotamia. The breastplates on the statues of Bactria—carved in stone, detachable from the statue, and gold-plated (personal communication of P. Amiet)—date to a later time (ca. 2000 B.C.).
4. Such curved, overhanging moulding could have been the seat of a chair. Similar iconographic representations are found in glyptic and on votive plaques depicting seated figures. The so-called architectural elements depicted on chlorite vases from the Early Dynastic period display fitted elements with similar forms.

Metalworking Techniques

The first half of the third millennium B.C. witnessed an extraordinary florescence of metalworking in the urban centers of the ancient Near East. During this period most of the metal fabrication techniques known in the ancient world were either developed or refined. Casting, using either carved stone moulds (see cat. nos. 163, 164) or the lost-wax process (see "Lost-Wax Casting," by Jean-François de Lapérouse, in this catalogue), produced both solid and carefully modeled objects. Worked metal sheet was employed in the manufacture of vessels and tools as well as to clad wood- or bitumen-core sculptures (see cat. no. 43). In addition to mechanical joins, metal sections were joined using soft lead-tin solders and harder, copper-based solders. Both cast and wrought objects were often decorated with inlaid colored stones or chasing, which involves lightly hammering metal tools against a surface to produce lines, dots, and other simple shapes that could be repeated and combined into patterns.

Some of the most delicate work from the period involved the creation of gold-alloy jewelry, richly represented by finds from the Royal Cemetery at Ur. In addition to masterly working and casting of gold alloys, this jewelry exhibits a remarkable expertise in joining techniques. In some cases localized heat may have been carefully applied to cause diffusion bonding between surfaces. Ground copper salts mixed with an organic binder may also have been used to tack elements together and to form a solder when heated, the copper acting to lower the melting point of the surrounding gold. Such evidence of soldering is rarely visible and is a testament to the skills of Sumerian goldsmiths. Another indication of metallurgical expertise is the fact that depletion gilding, a technique in which a gold-alloy surface is artificially enriched by the removal of baser metals, appears to have been used in the production of chisels found in Puabi's tomb at Ur (PG 800).[1]　　　　J-FL

1. La Niece 1995, pp. 41–47.

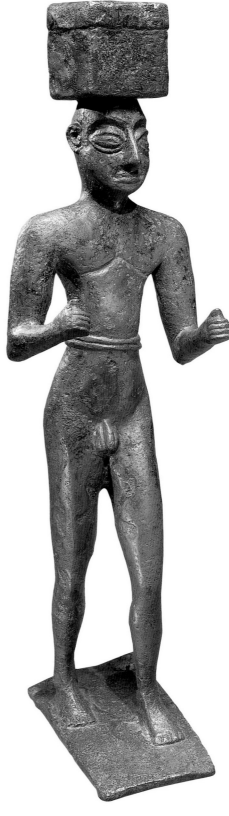

38

Striding male figure with a box on his head

Copper alloy
H. 37.8 cm (14⅞ in.); W. 12.3 cm (4⅞ in.); Thickness 9.7 cm (3⅞ in.)
Mesopotamia
Early Dynastic II, ca. 2650–2550 B.C.
The Metropolitan Museum of Art, New York; Harris Brisbane Dick Fund, 1955 55.142

This statuette depicts a clean-shaven male figure wearing only a belt. He strides forward with bent arms and clenched fists while balancing on his head what appears to be a square box. This figure may relate to rituals accompanying the construction or provisioning of a temple. In Mesopotamia, religious personnel were traditionally depicted nude and clean shaven, as seen, for example, in the fourth register of the Uruk Vase (see fig. 10). In addition, imagery on cylinder seals, such as one from the Treasure of Ur, from Mari (see cat. no. 87c), shows figures in a sacred context bearing what appear to be packaged offerings. The belt on this figure implies that the weight of the box or its contents necessitated additional support around his waist.[1] Some have argued that the figure, given its size and the fact that it was cast in metal, may have served as a foundation deposit. However, as the archaeological context is not known, any assessments of the figure's original meaning and function remain speculative.[2]

The full potential of lost-wax metal casting is exploited in the figure, from the complete articulation of the limbs to the offset placement of the legs, which helps to convey a sense of motion. Both features rarely appear in contemporary stone sculpture. Close parallels to this elongated figural style can be found in several bearded and nude statuettes on metal stands with open-worked bases that were excavated in the Diyala region and dated to Early Dynastic II and III. In technique and style these small statuettes point to the development of extraordinary, large-scale metal sculptures of the human figure in the late Early Dynastic and Akkadian periods that are attested only by fragments found at Tell Agrab and Bassetki (see fig. 58).[3]

Similar to a figure on a stand now preserved in the Oriental Institute of the University of Chicago, this statuette was cast solid using arsenical copper.[4] The absence of a core and insufficient venting of the mould during casting resulted in a significant amount of porosity, particularly in the area of the abdomen, as revealed by X-radiographs. Fortunately this porosity caused no visible flaws on the surface. The ground plane on which the figure stands was intentionally slanted, and the angle has been increased by physical damage that also resulted in cracks across both ankles.   J–FL

1. Ribbed belts normally appear in depictions of nude heroes and wrestlers, but these figures are never clean-shaven.
2. For a discussion and full bibliography, see Muscarella 1988a, pp. 323–27.
3. For the Tell Agrab fragments, see Frankfort 1943, pl. 61, and Braun-Holzinger 1984, nos. 54, 56. For the Bassetki figure, see al-Fouadi 1976, pp. 63–77.
4. For the composition of this figure, see Muscarella 1988a, p. 327, n. 1.

39

Foundation peg with tablet of Enmetena

Cuneiform inscription in Sumerian
Copper alloy and alabaster
H. of peg 35 cm (13¾ in.)
Mesopotamia, Girsu (modern Tello)
Early Dynastic IIIB, ca. 2400–2250 B.C.
Eski Şark Museum, Istanbul 1521, 1531

In southern Mesopotamia at the site of Tello, ancient Girsu, excavations revealed almost forty examples of the earliest known anthropomorphic figurines deposited in the foundations of buildings.[1] They are dated to Early Dynastic II or IIIA (ca. 2650–2400 B.C.). Each takes the form of a long-haired, clean-shaven man with a bare torso, whose hands are clasped before his chest. The lower half of the figure tapers into a thick peg. This feature served to pin the figure upright—symbolically—into the earth or into a brick or tablet, usually placed in a brick box in the foundations of a temple. At a later date Ur-Nanshe (ruled ca. 2450 B.C.) constructed a temple at Tello over the level at which the earlier pegs had been placed, and incorporated similar figurines into the foundations of his building. Some of Ur-Nanshe's examples are of stone, some are inscribed with the ruler's name, and some were associated with an inscribed stone tablet. The basic torso-peg form, now with a sharper peg, continued to be manufactured for at least two generations. To date, examples have been excavated in Mesopotamia at Tello, Al-Hiba (the ancient city of Lagash), Uruk, and Bismaya (ancient Adab).

Ancient texts demonstrate that one of the duties of Mesopotamian kings was to build temples for their gods. Inscriptions refer to laying down a temple's foundations, marking off its boundaries, and driving in foundation pegs. The pegs were a record of a ruler's piety, intended primarily for the gods but also for posterity, as represented by future rulers who might restore the mud-brick buildings. Either the king or his personal deity could be depicted on the pegs, perpetually praying before the god.[2] For example, nine peg figures excavated at Al-Hiba, dating to Early Dynastic IIIB, have a pair of small horns on their heads indicating their divinity. They were recovered standing upright in bricks, accompanied by an inscribed tablet. Inscriptions on both the statues and the tablets record that these figurers represent Shulutul, the personal deity of Enannatum I, so that he

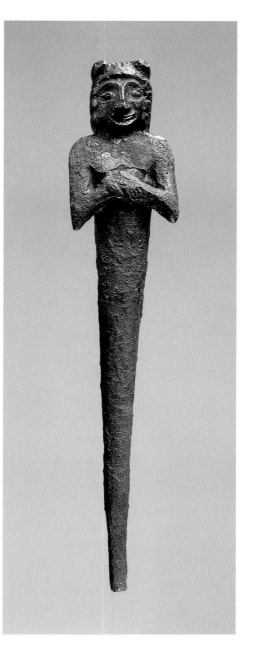

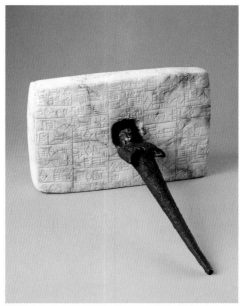

"might pray forever to Inanna . . . for the well being of Enannatum."[3]

Only one form of foundation peg dates to the Akkadian period (or perhaps slightly later). It is exemplified by the upper bodies of two lions, each with its paws covering a tray that held a stone tablet (preserved only on the example in the Musée du Louvre, Paris), set above a thick peg (cat. nos. 153a, b). The text states that a temple was built for a deity by Tishatal of Urkesh (modern Mozan, in north-western Syria) and that various deities protect it.[4] While the form of the Urkesh pieces is unique, they suggest that the tradition of foundation pegs had spread beyond Mesopotamia.[5]

Although foundation pegs of the Akkadian era are unknown from Mesopotamia itself, perhaps because so few sites of this period have been explored, their use is attested under the succeeding dynasties. Foundation figures were once again evident in Tello during the reign of Ur-Ba'u and of Gudea, when a unique form of peg appeared that depicts a kneeling deity (see cat. nos. 312a, b). Under Gudea the traditional peg figurine was further modified. Instead of the upper torso of a man with his hands clasped at his chest in prayer, the peg was now fashioned as a full-bodied human figure who holds with both hands a basket on his head. In addition a peg exists surmounted by a bovine standing among vegetation (cat no. 315); however, apart from examples of foundation pegs with a reclining bovine known from the time of Gudea and of Shulgi, the image of a man with a basket on his head functioned as the only form for the next three hundred years (see cat. nos. 318a, b).

Five foundation pegs of Enmetena I, a successor of Enannatum I, were recovered from below the pavement of a building at Tello, and a half-dozen others are known from the antiquities market.[6] Each peg is the same as the one seen here: the image of a beardless man with a bare, shortened torso, arms tightly held to the body and hands clasped, surmounts a relatively long tang. The head of each excavated example was set into an alabaster tablet. In form they are exactly the same as the pegs of Enmetena's predecessor, Enannatum I.   OWM

1. For discussion and history of early and later building-foundation deposits, see Ellis 1968; Rashid 1957–71; Schlossman 1976; Rashid 1983; Zettler 1987a; and Muscarella 1988a, pp. 303–13. The chronological relationship between metal pegs joined to a bifurcated metal plate and those of the human form remains unclear: see Ellis 1968, p. 72; Dunham

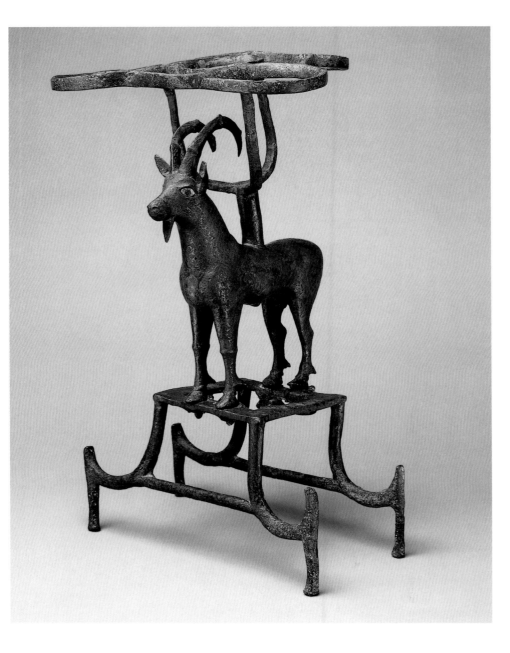

1986, p. 38; and Muscarella 1988a, p. 304.
2. For discussion of a number of issues raised here, see Ellis 1968, pp. 79–91, 145–50; Dunham 1986, pp. 49–64; Zettler 1987a, pp. 32–37; and Muscarella 1988a, pp. 310–12 and notes. See also note 3 below.
3. Hansen 1980–83, p. 425; for the inscription, see Hansen 1970a, pp. 247–48; see also Rashid 1983, p. 8, pl. 5. Van Driel (1973, p. 70) and Kobayashi (1988) argue that the Al-Hiba figures cannot be identified with a personal deity, for they represent the king himself; Suter (2000, p. 62, n. 104) agrees with them. Shulutul is mentioned also as the personal god of Enmetena; see Cooper 1986, p. 60.
4. Muscarella 1988a, pp. 374–77; Rashid 1983, pp. 15–16, nos. 78, 79.
5. The lion form may be related in an ideological manner to that of an Early Dynastic (possibly ED IIIB) foundation figure excavated at Bismaya. It is in the form of a reclining lion attached to a long, thin peg; see Banks 1912, p. 237; Rashid 1957–71, table 1, col. 4; and Rashid 1983, p. 13.
6. Ellis 1968, p. 53; Rashid 1983, pp. 9–10, nos. 59–69.

40

Vessel stand with ibex support

Arsenical copper, shell, and lapis lazuli
H. 40 cm (15¾ in.); W. at base 23.8 cm (9⅜ in.)
Mesopotamia
Early Dynastic II–III, ca. 2650–2250 B.C.
The Metropolitan Museum of Art, New York; Rogers Fund, 1974 1974.190

Excavated finds attest to the use of elaborate stands in sacred contexts during the Early Dynastic period. Three anthropomorphic stands were recovered from the Temple Oval at Khafajah, and parts of another stand were excavated in the Shara temple at Tell Agrab.[1] In addition, imagery on a cylinder seal in the Vorderasiatisches Museum, Berlin (fig. 37), depicts what appears to be a table or tray that is placed before a deity and supported by posts rising from the back of a cervid: a form reminiscent of this stand.

The ibex figure on this example is supported by a rectangular open-worked base with distinctive upturned struts above each foot. The ibex is attached to the base by tangs under each hoof that, at least in the case of the rear legs, were secured in place by casting on additional metal. The upper framework, which consists of three large rings with a smaller one in the center, may have been used to hold cylindrical vessels. This framework is held aloft by three arms extending up from a post that goes through the back of the animal figure.[2]

The head and body of the ibex were cast separately using the lost-wax method. The head, which may be solid, is attached to the body by a tongue-and-groove join secured by a pin inserted through the neck. The seam between both sections is visible just behind the ears. X-radiographs indicate that the body is hollow and has core supports in the shoulders and haunches.[3] The white inlay of the ibex's left eye has been replaced with wax, but the right eye is inlaid with what appears to be original shell. Both eyes also have lapis lazuli pupils, the age of which is undetermined.

As this stand was not obtained from a controlled excavation, its place of manufacture and the context from which it was recovered are not known. However, stylistic similarities with the anthropomorphic stands noted above—particularly in the design of the base as well as the smooth contours and elongated modeling of the ibex's body—suggest that this example may be ascribed to the same period and region. The thinness of both structural elements and freestanding features (such as the ibex's legs, ears, horns, and beard) as seen in these stands and the figure of a man with a box on his head (see cat. no. 38) demonstrates the skill of Early Dynastic craftsmen in using cast metal to produce functional objects that are highly graceful in design and proportions.   J–FL

1. For the Khafajah stands, see Frankfort 1939, pls. 38–103, 181, and Frankfort 1943, pl. 95. See also Braun-Holzinger 1984, pp. 20–23.
2. A complete description and bibliography of this object is found in Muscarella 1988a, pp. 333–36.
3. Analysis of a sample taken from the right hoof indicated the following composition: 94 percent copper, 2.6 percent arsenic, 0.9 percent zinc, 0.2 percent lead, 0.2 percent tin. See ibid., p. 12, for description of the analytical technique.

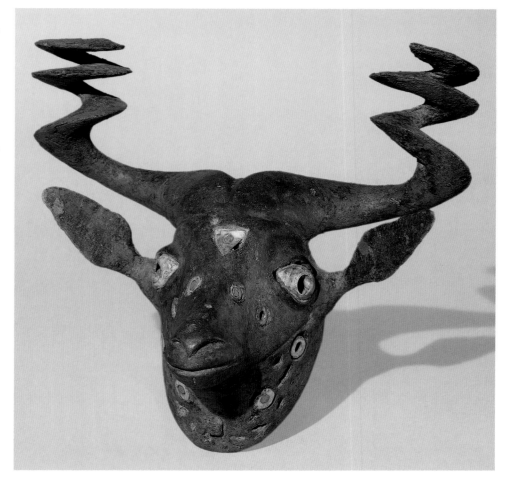

41

Head of a markhor goat

Copper alloy, shell, and red stone
L. 23 cm (9 in.); W. 22.3 cm (8¾ in.); H. 10 cm (4 in.)
Mesopotamia
Early Dynastic III, ca. 2550–2250 B.C.
University of Pennsylvania Museum of Archaeology and Anthropology, Philadelphia 29-20-3

The elegantly stylized corkscrew horns on this head demonstrate the dramatic modeling effects permitted by lost-wax casting. This head is the larger of a pair said to come from Shuruppak.[1] Both heads were hollow-cast and are open at the back of the neck. A pin was inserted vertically near the opening at the back of each head; these pins, which are partially preserved, were probably used to secure the heads to mounts that are now lost. Given the rather substantial weight of the heads, it is unlikely that they were attached to a readily portable object.[2]

The surface is decorated with inlays set into openings that extend through the metal wall. The shell inlays in the eyes were drilled to accommodate pupils that are lost. Shell, inset with a ring of red stone, is laid into a triangular opening on the forehead; circular and oblong inlays of the same materials decorate the muzzle and the neck. The embellishment of animal figures with multicolored inlays derives from a tradition going back to at least the Late Uruk period (see cat. no. 2b) and reflects a long-standing Sumerian interest in the interplay of color and texture (which is somewhat obscured in this example by the corrosion of the copper alloy).[3] Although the exact significance of the triangular and circular inlays on this head is not known, both elements emphasize the numinous character of the animal portrayed.

    J–FL

1. For further reference, see Braun-Holzinger 1984, p. 33.
2. Frankfort, however, suggested that the companion head might have been attached to an instrument. See Frankfort 1970, p. 63.
3. For earlier examples of inlaid animal figures, see Behm-Blancke 1979.

42

Head of a bull

Copper alloy and bone
H. 20.7 cm (8⅛ in.); W. 18.7 cm (7⅜ in.)
Mesopotamia
Early Dynastic III, ca. 2550–2250 B.C.
Staatliche Museen zu Berlin, Vorderasiatisches
Museum VA 3142

The bull's head shown here is one of the most impressive examples of three-dimensional sculpture of the third millennium B.C. and at the same time is an important example of

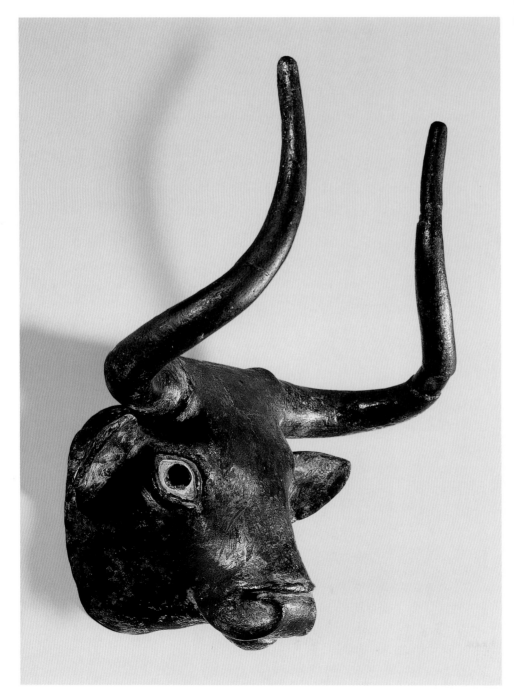

copper-alloy smelting and casting techniques in that era. The bull's rather thickset head is crowned by horns curving upward. Prominent shell-like ears, nostrils in the form of volutes, and an emphatically high brow all demonstrate the ornamental stylization of natural forms that reached a particularly high level in the art of the Early Dynastic period.

The head, executed of high-quality copper alloy in the lost-wax technique, is composed of several separate pieces. The ears and horns were presumably cast onto the head. Traces of bone inlay are preserved in one of the eye sockets.[1] The assembly out of individual pieces

of this and other metal animal heads found in various southern Mesopotamian sites (among them Ur, Tell Agrab, Tello, and Tell al Ubaid) suggests that they were produced serially—"mass-produced."

Animal protomes in gold, silver, and copper excavated from the royal graves at Ur were identified as decorative elements of lyres and harps (see cat. nos. 58, 65); a soundbox in the form of an abstract animal body was generally complemented by a more or less realistic bull's head.[2] Such musical instruments with bull's heads are represented in stone sculpture, in reliefs, and in inlay work (see cat. no. 52). In Sumerian literature the bellowing of a bull is described as a pleasant sound.[3] The bull-shaped lyre symbolizes the powerful voice of this beast—in Mesopotamian mythology and religion considered the embodiment of strength and fertility.

Although the use of animal protomes as embellishments for furniture is known in later times, there are no documented examples of it, even in pictorial representations, from the third millennium B.C. Therefore the bull's head seen here was presumably, like the examples from Ur, part of an instrument.

LM

1. From conversation with G. Jendritzki, Berlin.
2. Rashid 1984, pp. 28ff.
3. Braun-Holzinger 1984, p. 29, n. 98.

Al Ubaid

Al Ubaid is the modern name of a small tell six kilometers west of Ur. The site was excavated by H. R. Hall in the spring of 1919, followed by Leonard Woolley in 1923 and 1924, and Pinhas Delougaz and Seton Lloyd in 1937. Evidence suggests that the site dates to the sixth millennium B.C. Indeed, during the period from 5000 to 4000 B.C. much of Mesopotamia shared a common culture, characterized by a distinctive type of pottery called Ubaid after this site, where the evidence for it was first found. The main structure that was uncovered was a large temple complex dating from Early Dynastic III to Ur III. Although the temple itself does not survive, it was set in an oval enclosure, similar to examples at Khafajah and Lagash (Al-Hiba), and originally stood on a large mud-brick platform (33 by 26 meters). The date of the founding of the temple is unknown. The only stage of the building that has been excavated is a reconstruction by A'anepada, son of Mesanepada, from the First Dynasty of Ur (ca. 2400 B.C.). Decorative elements from the temple were found at the base of the platform; they had been either stuffed into the masonry during the reconstruction or piled up at the foot of the platform for later use, or had fallen from the front of the temple's decayed facade. This collection of artifacts gives us a unique insight into temple decoration of the third millennium B.C.   PC

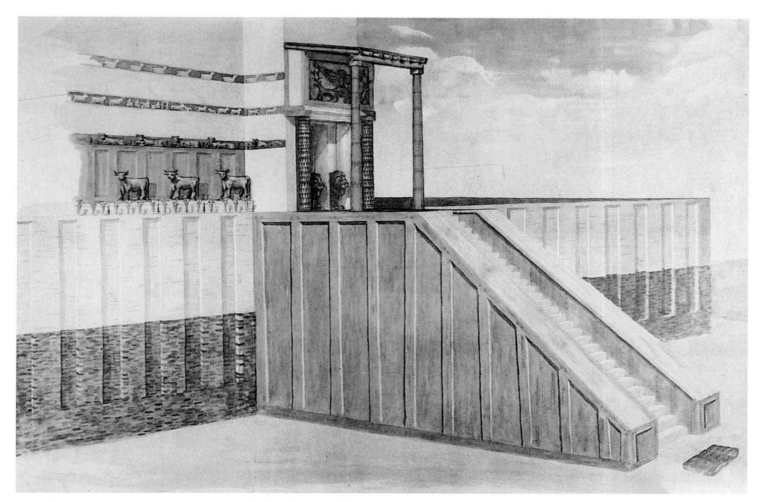

Fig. 29. Reconstructed temple facade, Tell al Ubaid. Early Dynastic III A, ca. 2550–2400 B.C.

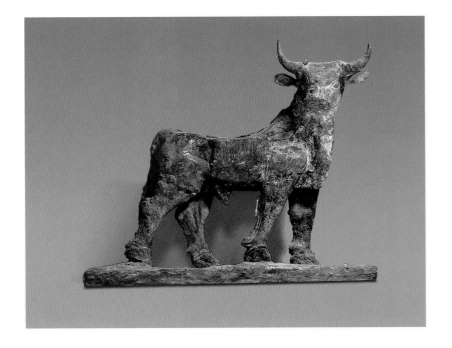

43

Standing bull

Copper alloy, wood, and bitumen
L. 85 cm (33½ in.); H. 71.2 cm (28 in.); W. 27.9 cm
(11 in.)
Mesopotamia, Tell al Ubaid, Ninhursanga temple
Early Dynastic IIIB, ca. 2400–2250 B.C.
University of Pennsylvania Museum of Archaeology
and Anthropology, Philadelphia B15886

This freestanding bull figure is one of at
least four that formed part of the decorative
program of the temple at Tell al Ubaid dedicated to Ninhursanga, which was restored by
A'anepada, a king of the First Dynasty of Ur,
in about 2400 B.C. This group, discovered by
Leonard Woolley during the excavation season
of 1923–24, was found to the west of a ramp
leading to a later temple. Although these bulls

were flattened and in extremely poor condition, Woolley, by dint of his careful excavation
and consolidation methods,[1] was able to preserve two examples. Because the head of this
bull was missing and the left front leg was
damaged beyond repair, they were replaced
with plaster replicas cast after the other bull,
now in the British Museum.

The construction of these bulls began with a
body carved of wood, to which the head, legs,
and tail were attached by mortise-and-tenon
joinery. Once the wood was covered with a thin
layer of bitumen, worked copper-alloy sheets
were nailed in place, beginning with the
appendages and the head, with its separately
made ears and horns. The legs were fashioned

from sheets rolled into tubes and hammered
into shape. This process required frequent
annealing of the copper in order to restore malleability to the metal and reflects the mastery of
Early Dynastic craftsmen in working metal
sheet. After assembly, the final working and
chasing were done on the metal surface, which
was supported by the pliable bitumen layer.

Given the paucity of excavated temple
decoration from this period, it is difficult to
assess to what degree the decoration of the
Ninhursanga temple represented an innovation in technique. It is clear, nevertheless, that
the use of metal-covered wood forms allowed
for themes already known from earlier flat- or
low-relief representations to expand into three
dimensions on a truly impressive scale. This is
particularly evident in a reconstructed panel
from this temple, now in the British Museum,
in which the head of a lion-headed eagle and
the antlers of flanking stags proceed over and
beyond the border of the panel to create a
dramatic and awe-inspiring effect (see fig. 30).

J–FL

1. For a description of the discovery and treatment
of these bull figures, see Hall and Woolley 1927,
pp. 84–86. For a bibliography, see Braun-Holzinger
1984, p. 27.

44a, b

Mosaic columns

Shell, pink limestone, and black shale
Mesopotamia, Tell al Ubaid, Ninhursanga temple
Early Dynastic IIIB, ca. 2400–2250 B.C.

a. H. 115 cm (45¼ in.); Diam. 33 cm (13 in.)
Trustees of The British Museum, London BM 115328

b. H. 173 cm (68⅛ in.); Diam. 33 cm (13 in.)
University of Pennsylvania Museum of Archaeology
and Anthropology, Philadelphia B15887

These inlaid columns were among the material found at the foot of the platform at Tell al
Ubaid.[1] It is possible that they had been set up
on either side of the entrance to the temple.
They were formed from palm logs covered
with a coating of bitumen about one centimeter thick. Against this coating were pressed
tesserae of mother-of-pearl, pink limestone,
and black shale. A copper wire was passed
through a loop at the back of each tessera; the
ends of the wires were twisted into a ring and
sunk into the bitumen to attach the tessera.

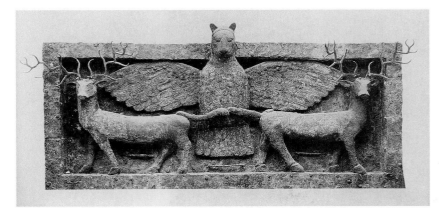

Fig. 30. Copper-alloy relief of a lion-headed eagle grasping two stags. Tell al Ubaid,
Early Dynastic III A, ca. 2550–2400 B.C. British Museum, London, BM 114308.

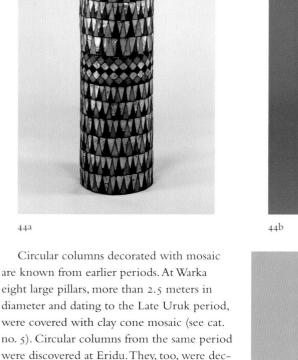

44a

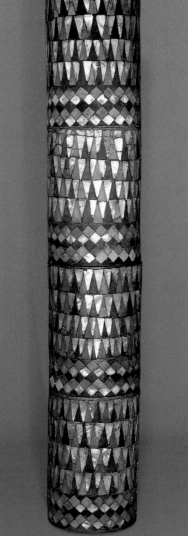

44b

45a–c

Wall nails inlaid with rosettes

Clay
L. 25–37 cm (9⅞–14⅝ in.)
Mesopotamia, Tell al Ubaid, Ninhursanga temple
Early Dynastic IIIB, ca. 2400–2250 B.C.
University of Pennsylvania Museum of Archaeology
and Anthropology, Philadelphia B15795, B15796,
B15888

These clay flowers were found on the west side
of the stairs of the platform upon which the
temple at Tell al Ubaid stood, where more than
fifty complete or nearly complete examples of
the kind were discovered.[1] They are assumed
to have been part of the decoration of the
temple wall: the long stems were inserted into
the wall, and the flowers would have appeared
in relief against the wall face. Every stem has
near its point a small hole that was drilled
through the clay before baking, and under
each calyx a horizontal nick is cut in the clay.
In some examples a copper wire was found in
the hole. The excavator Leonard Woolley suggested that the nick might have been made to
prevent a string or wire looped around the
tapering stem from slipping down. If this were
so, he argued, two strings or wires were used
for each rosette: one passed through the hole
and one wound around the top of the stem
and the ends attached to an upright or a staple
in the wall. In this reconstruction (fig. 29) the
point of the stem rested on the ground and
the flower stood upright with its head in the

Circular columns decorated with mosaic
are known from earlier periods. At Warka
eight large pillars, more than 2.5 meters in
diameter and dating to the Late Uruk period,
were covered with clay cone mosaic (see cat.
no. 5). Circular columns from the same period
were discovered at Eridu. They, too, were decorated with cone mosaic, but some of the
heads were covered in copper plating.[2]

PC

1. Hall and Woolley 1927, pp. 17, 40, 100–103,
pls. 4:5, 20.
2. Safar, Mustafa, and Lloyd 1981, p. 240, fig. 118.

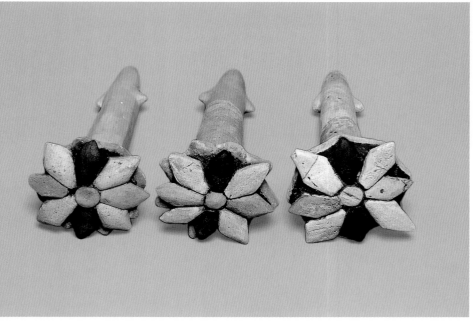

air; the small knobs on many of the stems were buds, according to Woolley.

Similar rosettes are known from the Late Uruk period Eye Temple at Tell Brak, attesting to a long tradition of similar temple decoration. The rosettes from the Eye Temple are composed of eight petals of white marble and black shale, with a centerpiece of pink limestone. As they were found lying flat on the ground adjacent to a fallen strip of cone mosaic, it is assumed that these flowers were part of wall inlay decoration.[2]   PC

1. Hall and Woolley 1927, p. 118, pl. 30.1.
2. Mallowan 1947, p. 95, pl. 5.

46a, b

Friezes with inlays of cows and birds

Limestone, shell, copper, and shale
Mesopotamia, Tell al Ubaid, Ninhursanga temple
Early Dynastic IIIB, ca. 2400–2250 B.C.

a. Frieze of cows: H. 22 cm (8⅝ in.); L. 85 cm (33½ in.)
University of Pennsylvania Museum of Archaeology and Anthropology, Philadelphia   B15880

b. Each bird, set within modern copper border: H. 13 cm (5⅛ in.); L. 18 cm (7⅛ in.)
University of Pennsylvania Museum of Archaeology and Anthropology, Philadelphia   B15883

These two friezes display white figures against mosaic backgrounds of black shale framed by copper borders. The six shell cows in the first frieze are depicted advancing to the right. Their bodies are made in one piece, with the heads and legs carved separately; the parts were assembled when they were fixed into the bitumen backing of the panel. Though all the animals conform to one general type, they show many variations in detail. The modeling of the bodies is in very delicate relief. The strength of the beasts is emphasized through schematization of the muscles, characteristic of the Early Dynastic period, wherein the sharp incised lines that mark muscle and tendon stand in purposeful contrast to the softly graded contours of the flesh. The heads are in profile, showing only one ear, horn, and eye, which is full and round. The muzzle is short, with full nostrils, and the dewlap is heavy and pointed. The long, wavy hair of the tail brushes against one hind leg (with which it is carved in one piece) and reaches to the ground. When the panel was found, it was bent and buckled with nearly all the upper border broken away, and the two end bulls were detached from their setting. The mosaic was subsequently attached to a fresh background and missing parts were restored.[1]

The three limestone birds inlaid against their background form a frieze similar to but distinct from that of the cows. The birds, seen in profile and facing to the right, are of an uncertain genus; the heads are rather like those of doves, but the attitude, which makes them appear to be swimming, especially as the feet are not shown, is that of ducks. They are silhouettes, with the only internal detail being the incised eye and the modeled outline of the wing of each bird. The birds were discovered lying in a row, about five centimeters apart from one another, along with some black shale tesserae from the background. All the heads were broken off. The mosaic was restored with some new black background to form a complete panel with a modern copper border.[2]

The friezes were found in more or less complete panel sections together with numerous scattered figures and fragments that must have made up an ensemble. We can deduce that the subject of the ensemble was pastoral, as the extant remains include a depiction of figures milking cattle and storing milk (fig. 14),[3] and scenes with mythological animals as well as rows of bulls and birds advancing in files. These motifs from a temple context continue a tradition found in the imagery of Late Uruk seals showing sacred herds and temple estates and may be related to ideas of fertility, which would have been appropriate in decoration for a temple of the mother goddess Ninhursanga. The technique of inlay was widely used in the Early Dynastic period. These friezes, which may have fallen from the facade of the temple (see cat. no. 44), are,

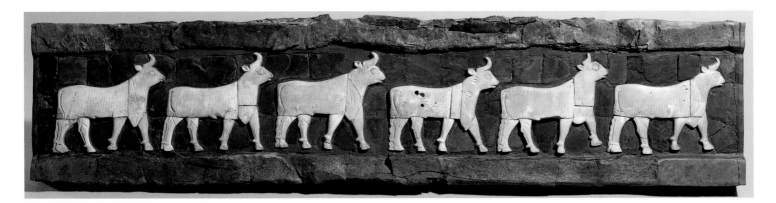

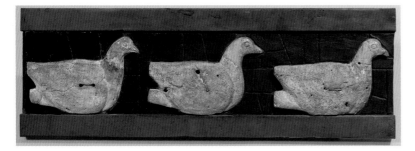

however, unusual for the Early Dynastic period in that inlaid wall decoration was generally an internal feature of buildings of that time, for example, at Kish, Ebla, and Mari.

PC

1. Hall and Woolley 1927, p. 94. The friezes were divided among the British Museum, London, the Iraq Museum, Baghdad, and the University of Pennsylvania Museum of Archaeology and Anthropology, Philadelphia.
2. Ibid, pp. 98–99.
3. Strommenger 1964, p. 398, no. 78.

47

Plaque with a lion-headed eagle and human-headed bull or bison

Limestone
H. 14 cm (5½ in.); W. 14 cm (5½ in.)
Mesopotamia, Tell al Ubaid, Ninhursanga temple
Early Dynastic IIIB, ca. 2400–2250 B.C.
University of Pennsylvania Museum of Archaeology and Anthropology, Philadelphia B15606

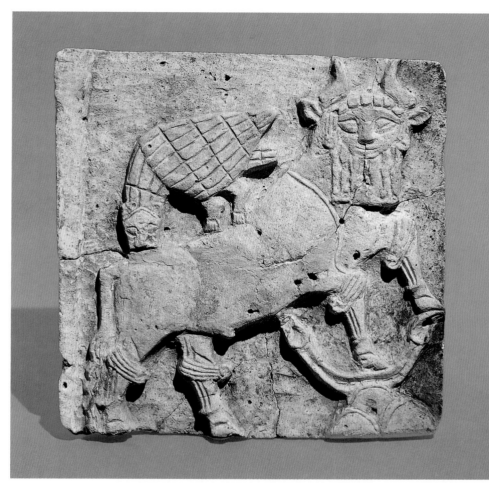

This relief-carved plaque depicts a human-headed bison with forelegs resting on stylized vegetation, which sprouts in a single curving arc from a mountain motif.[1] The horns of the bison curve inward; he is bearded and large curls frame his face. The stylization of both the shoulder and the inward-curling tufts on the fetlocks are characteristic of the late Early Dynastic IIIB period.[2] A lion-headed eagle, thought to represent the Imdugud bird, stands on the back of the bison, biting into its hindquarters. The eagle's folded wings are indicated with gridlike incised lines recalling the eagle on the Enannatum mace-head (cat. no. 35).

The Imdugud bird is more commonly depicted in the Early Dynastic period in an emblematic composition, with wings outstretched above two animals that form an antithetical pair and are grasped in the talons of the bird (see cat. nos. 35, 81, 115; fig. 29). This attacking Imdugud appears almost exclusively at the end of the Early Dynastic period; it is found on incised shell plaques, inlay (see cat. no. 52), and cylinder seals with combat scenes.[3] In later texts the bird is associated with the sun god Shamash and the human-headed bison, probably the *kusarikkum*, whose distant home is a mountain with vegetation.

When this plaque was excavated, traces of black pigment were visible on the background. The plaque, therefore, would have looked like inlaid friezes from Tell al Ubaid, whose figures were set into a dark mosaic background. The plaque was found lying against an inlaid frieze of cows similar to catalogue number 46 and according to the excavators may have been part of the temple-facade decoration.[4]

JME

1. The mountain motif appears in the Late Uruk period (Amiet 1980, pl. 10). For the mountain motif with vegetation, see Frankfort 1955b, pl. 10; Amiet 1980, pls. 32, 34, 35; Woolley 1934, pl. 100.
2. Both features are found on the Vase of Enmetena of Lagash, from Tello, which dates to the Early Dynastic B period (Moortgat 1969, pl. 113).

3. For inlay, see Dolce 1978, U7, T8, T26; Hall and Woolley 1927, p. 98, pl. 37 (TO. 376), and p. 96, pl. 37 (TO. 319). The composition also appears on cylinder seals carved with combat scenes (Amiet 1980, nos. 1076, 1260, 1268–72, 1274). The Imdugud shown attacking anything other than human-headed bison is rare (Amiet 1980, no. 1062 and possibly no. 1121).
4. Hall and Woolley 1927, pp. 88, 96–97. The remains of a copper border similar to that on the inlaid friezes were also found with the plaque that was detached from the border (ibid., p. 96).

PALACE

After the flood had swept over the land and kingship had (once again) descended from the heavens, the (seat of) kingship was in (the city of) Kish.

The Sumerian King List

Kish

For Mesopotamians, the city of Kish represented kingship, and during the Early Dynastic III period a number of Sumerian rulers held the title "King of Kish." It is possible that the prestige of Kish derived from an earlier period when the city dominated Sumer. Indeed, according to tradition, it was from Kish that Sargon left for Akkad to found his empire, and he, too, adopted the title of King of Kish to express his widespread authority. The Sumerian King List emphasizes the importance of Kish by claiming the city as the place where kingship was first lowered from heaven after the Flood.

Kish lies on a (now dry) branch of the Euphrates, fifteen kilometers east of Babylon. It is composed of a series of substantial mounds, or tells, established on an east-west strip of land nearly five kilometers in length and more than one and a half kilometers in width. A deep trench, known as the Y sounding, dug on one of these mounds (Tell Ingharra) revealed that the site dates to the Jamdat Nasr period. Above this earliest level was an Early Dynastic I settlement, and above and partially sunk into both these levels was a cemetery rich with burial goods. One group of graves contained chariots or carts perhaps drawn by both bovines and donkeys. At least four burials with sacrificial victims indicate that the royal graves at Ur were not unique in this respect.

The most impressive building from the Early Dynastic period is Palace A, which takes its name from the tell that contained its ruins. Only two of its structures have been located, and they extend along the sides of an open space. A majestic staircase served as the entrance to the northern building, and a four-columned portico formed the facade of the second. Fragments of inlay from friezes found in the palace reflect the widespread use of such decoration in both palaces and temples thoughout Mesopotamia and Syria. Although the date of the palace is debated, a tablet found in one room is from the beginning of Early Dynastic IIIA; before the end of that period the palace had been abandoned. Some 150 graves from Cemetery A, in the palace area, have been excavated. Another monumental structure, probably of the same date as the palace, is the so-called Plano-Convex Building, some fifteen hundred meters to the north.

PC

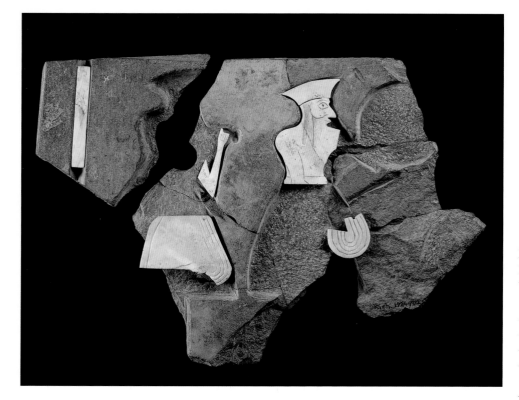

that Palace A may have had earlier phases to which the inlays belonged.[4]   PC

1. Frankfort 1970, pp. 51–52, fig. 46.
2. Heinrich 1936, pls. 17, 18.
3. Hansen 1963, pl. 5. Figures with skirts tucked up at the waist can be depicted as heroes in combat with animals or as warriors driving bound prisoners before them.
4. Dolce 1978, pp. 73–77.

48

Frieze with inlays of warriors

Slate and white limestone
H. 24 cm (9½ in.); W. 27 cm (10⅝ in.)
Mesopotamia, Kish, Palace A, room 61
Early Dynastic II, ca. 2650–2550 B.C.
Visitors of the Ashmolean Museum, Oxford
AN 1924.702

The ground of this substantial inlaid frieze from Kish is made up of irregular pieces of slate cut to fit together. Shallow depressions have been hollowed out of the slate and filled with pieces of shaped white limestone. A similar technique is known to have been used at Nippur, although farther north, for example at Mari, it does not seem to have been employed. The frieze displays fragments of two figures advancing to the right with a rectangular piece of inlay behind them serving as a border. Most of the details on the inlay are drawn in fine incised lines, but the stone is cut deeper to portray larger forms, such as the beard and hair of the man at the right. These larger elements were apparently filled with bituminous black paint.

The man on the right is nude above the waist. His torso is shown frontally, and his right arm is held across the left side of it. The head is in profile and has a pointed nose and pouting lips like those found on sculpture dating to late Early Dynastic II.[1] The single eye is shown frontally with the eyebrow. A long lock of hair hangs down on the left of his face to the bottom of the beard, which is long and narrow. The style of hair is comparable to that seen on a votive sculpture from the Diyala (cat. no. 24). The dress of the figure is distinctive. The flat cap was represented often throughout the Early Dynastic period and is sometimes worn by figures on late Protoliterate seals.[2] Men wearing such caps appear on shell and stone inlays from Mari (see cat. no. 103) and are sometimes portrayed with a long skirt with the front tucked up at the waist, for example on a late Early Dynastic I votive plaque from Nippur and on the Ushumgal stele (cat. no. 20).[3] The figure at the right in this frieze wears his skirt in this fashion: a piece of inlay separate from his body is incised with four folded-back lines that represent the tucked-up pleated cloth. The surviving inlays of the figure on the left represent a skirt with a pleated section hanging down the front and a foot.

Although this frieze comes from Palace A of Early Dynastic III (see cat. no. 49), its inlays have been dated to Early Dynastic II. This suggests

49

Inlay of a bound prisoner

White limestone
Head: H. 3.1 cm (1¼ in.); W. 3.5 cm (1⅜ in.)
Body: H. 10.2 cm (4 in.); W. 5.1 cm (2 in.)
Mesopotamia, Kish, Palace A, room 61
Early Dynastic II, ca. 2650–2550 B.C.
Visitors of the Ashmolean Museum, Oxford
AN 1924.727a, b

This inlay fragment represents a slender, nude, bound male prisoner facing left. His head is in profile and dominated by a large frontal eye with an eyebrow formed by a shallow incision. The pupil is drilled and may originally have contained an inlay of lapis lazuli like those known from similar examples. A very prominent sharp nose sits above pouting lips. A deep cutting of the stone describes the shape of the jaw and the hair at the back of the head. A now-missing piece of inlay probably completed the representation of the hair. A rectangular hollow, also deeply cut, depicts a lock of hair falling from the corner of the jaw. A broader hollow to the left of the first one forms a beard that is the same length as the hair. The head and body are made of separate pieces of stone, and the beard and hair are cut across the join. The upper body is shown frontally. A shallow incised line delineates the figure's back and the upper part of the left arm, which is held away from the body. The left wrist and hand are held against the buttock and tied to the right hand by two twisted ropes. Around the prisoner's waist is a double rope belt.

Similar bound prisoners are depicted on a large slate and limestone frieze from Palace A at Kish that is now in Baghdad.[1] They also appear on inlays from Ur and Mari, where, however, they are roped at the elbows (see cat. nos. 52, 97). The present figure was probably part of a large slate and limestone frieze found

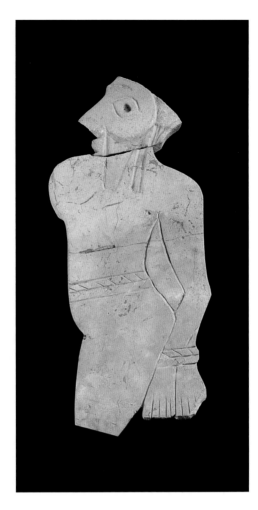

in the same room of Palace A that housed friezes of warriors (see entry for cat. no. 48). The present inlay has been dated to an Early Dynastic II phase of the building.[2]

PC

1. Dolce 1978, pl. 9:K28.
2. Ibid., pp. 73–77.

50

Inlay of a female musician

Shell
H. 5.6 cm (2¼ in.); W. 5.6 cm (2¼ in.)
Mesopotamia, Kish, Palace A, room 61
Early Dynastic II, ca. 2650–2550 B.C.
Visitors of the Ashmolean Museum, Oxford
AN 1924.712

The shell is deeply cut to represent the hair of this female figure. A fillet tied at the back into a knot binds the top of her head, which is in profile facing right. A shallowly incised large, full eye with an eyebrow dominates the face. The pupil is drilled, perhaps for inlay. Smaller drill holes run across the brow and down around the ear. The nose is missing, and the lips—like those seen on the Ushumgal stele (cat. no. 20)—are full, pursed, and open above a small chin and a heavy throat. A line of drill holes represents a necklace. The body is shown frontally with the arms bent at the elbows. Slender hands with long thumbs each hold a curved object of the kind held by women shown in other inlay pieces of the same period from Kish.[1] The arrangement of this inlay within the larger scene to which it belonged is unknown because it was found lying on a floor in Palace A in Kish, where it had fallen from a wall.

Presumably the curved object is a musical instrument. In nine graves of Cemetery A at Kish (see "Kish," by Paul Collins, in this catalogue), Ernest J. H. Mackay found curved strips of thin copper, which in every case except one occurred in pairs.[2] At Ur lying beside the remains of a lyre in a royal tomb were two curved copper strips; one end was cut off squarely, the other was bulbous and had a nail driven through the metal atop it. Along one side of each there were traces of wood.[3] Similar objects are depicted on a gold cylinder seal from another grave at Ur (PG 1054).[4] These are associated with musicians: a seated figure on the seal plays a lyre, behind which are three standing figures: one, with joined hands, seems to be dancing, and the other two hold curved objects. These objects may, therefore, have been castanets, long clappers of metal mounted on wood.

PC

1. Dolce 1978, pl. 8:K5, K7.
2. Mackay 1929, p. 160, pl. 61.
3. Woolley 1934, pp. 126–28.
4. Ibid., p. 127, pl. 193.

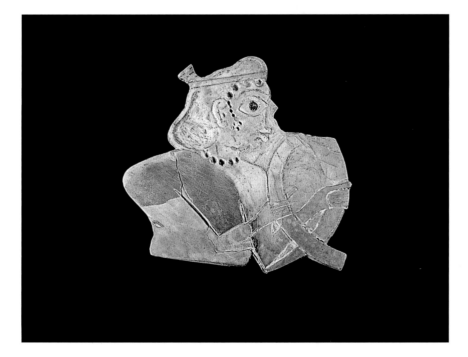

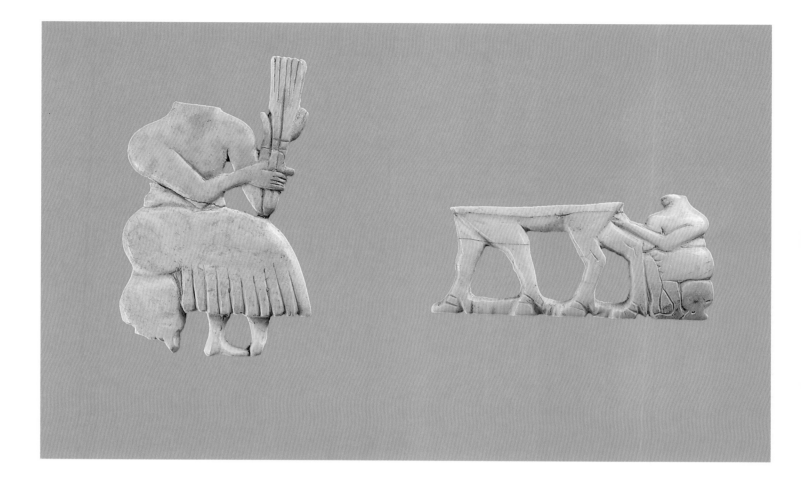

51a, b

Inlays from a milking scene

Shell
a. H. 5 cm (2 in.); W. 2.3 cm (⅞ in.)
b. H. 3.5 cm (1⅜ in.); W. 5 cm (2 in.)
Mesopotamia, Kish, Palace A, room 61
Early Dynastic II, ca. 2650–2550 B.C.
Visitors of the Ashmolean Museum, Oxford
AN 1924.705, 706

The original arrangement and context of these inlays are unknown, as they were found lying loose on the floor along the northern wall of a room in Palace A at Kish.[1] Nevertheless, it is apparent that the fragments represent elements in a scene of milking and dairy production of a type well known from cylinder seals and particularly inlaid friezes from Tell al Ubaid (see fig. 14) of the Early Dynastic period. One fragment shows only a seated headless male figure milking a cow, of which only the lower

section and legs survive. The man wears a plain fringed skirt that reaches to the knee. The spaces between the cow's legs have been cut away except for a groundline at its hoofs. The other fragment consists of a headless male sitting on a rounded stool. He wears a plain fringed skirt falling to the ankles and holds in both hands bunched, sprouting stalks.

PC

1. Mackay 1929, p. 123, pl. 36:3.

TOMB

O (Gilgamesh), I made your destiny a destiny of kingship, but I did not make it [a destiny] of eternal life . . . be not sick at heart, be not in despair, be not heart-stricken! The bane of mankind is thus come, I have told you, what (was fixed) when your navel-cord was cut is thus come . . .

The Death of Gilgamesh

THE ROYAL TOMBS OF UR

JULIAN READE

The ruins of Ur lie in the desert of southern Iraq, abandoned since the Euphrates River changed its course away from the city more than two thousand years ago. The ziggurat (temple-tower) of the moon god still dominates the site, and early archaeologists who dug into the surface of the mounds recovered graves, fragmentary walls, and bricks inscribed with the names of obscure kings. It was recognized that Ur was a place where much might still be learned about the Sumerians, the people who inhabited the region long before Babylon was famous. When Leonard Woolley began work there in 1922, however, on behalf of the British Museum and the University of Pennsylvania Museum of Archaeology and Anthropology, and began to find pieces of fine gold jewelry enhanced with lapis lazuli and carnelian, he had no idea how old they might be. Experts suggested they might have been made during the Persian Empire, about the fifth century B.C. He waited until 1926 before returning to the "gold trench," to be rewarded over his next four seasons by the discovery of the so-called royal tombs (fig. 31), whose marvelous treasures and macabre death pits have continued ever since to amaze and puzzle both the archaeological world and the general public.[1]

The royal tombs were part of a large cemetery, which was used during at least three centuries in the second half of the third millennium B.C. Most of the graves were individual burials—rich and poor, male and female—which had repeatedly cut into one another, but about sixteen Woolley treated as exceptional because the shafts had included a built burial

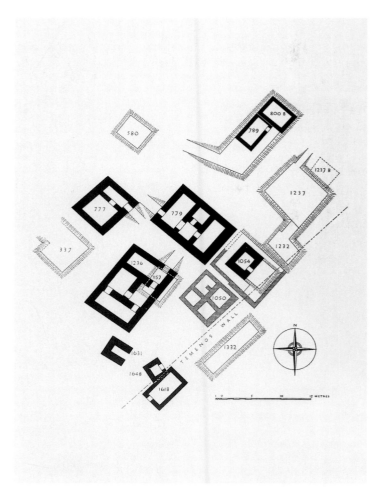

Fig. 31. Detail of the cemetery at Ur, showing the sixteen tombs designated "royal" by the excavator. Early Dynastic III A, ca. 2550–2400 B.C.

93

chamber rather than a mere coffin or mat and because they contained more than one body, in some cases as many as seventy or eighty. These are the tombs that Woolley entitled royal. Some of the bodies had clearly been deposited in the course of elaborate rituals, in which many people died at the same time, whereas in other tombs the bodies were scattered here and there. Many of the burial chambers had been robbed for their gold in antiquity, but the robbers had worked secretly or unsystematically. So there was plenty left for Woolley to find, especially outside the chambers.

These royal tombs all date to the Early Dynastic III period, about 2400 B.C., and contain broadly the same kinds of objects. The materials used for jewelry and other fine things testify to the craftsmanship, wealth, and international contacts of Ur at this time. Gold, silver, and copper all had to be imported, probably overland from Iran or by sea through the Gulf. Lapis lazuli, which is abundant in the tombs, came from Afghanistan, and carnelian may have come from the Indus region. How long a time the tombs span is unknown, but it seems unlikely to be much more than a century, possibly less. The disposition of some of the tombs relative to one another, and various changes in the pottery and other objects, have made it possible to suggest the approximate order in which they were built.[2]

The earliest and indeed the largest of the burial structures was a vaulted stone building, PG 1236. This contained four

rooms and several bodies, inside and out. The next, PG 779, was very similar to it, and PG 777, with two rooms, was roughly contemporary with PG 779. Finds suggested that the principal persons buried in PG 1236 and PG 779 were men, and the one in PG 777 a woman. PG 1054, which had a single stone chamber with the body of a woman and four other people, and a complicated sequence of deposits and several burials above it, is probably not much later than PG 779. PG 789 and PG 800, male and female, respectively, each with a single stone chamber, may be slightly later, and provide the earliest evidence for "death pits" containing a really substantial number of bodies, including soldiers and musicians, that must have been buried together (see fig. 32). The Great Death Pit was PG 1237, an enigmatic tomb, which may be dated broadly in the same phase as PG 789 and PG 800 (see "The Great Death Pit at Ur," by Julian Reade, in this catalogue). PG 1050, a woman's tomb with mud-brick chambers, also incorporated a death pit; its relative date is arguable. PG 1157, a death pit with fifty-eight poorly equipped bodies, was vertically above PG 1236 and must belong toward the end of the sequence.

The resulting sequence also represents a rational evolution, with the stone tomb chambers diminishing in size until replaced by chambers of mud brick, with a rise and subsequent diminution in the quantity of gold buried, and with an increase in the number of bodies in a single tomb. It has recently been proposed, however, that the royal tombs did not

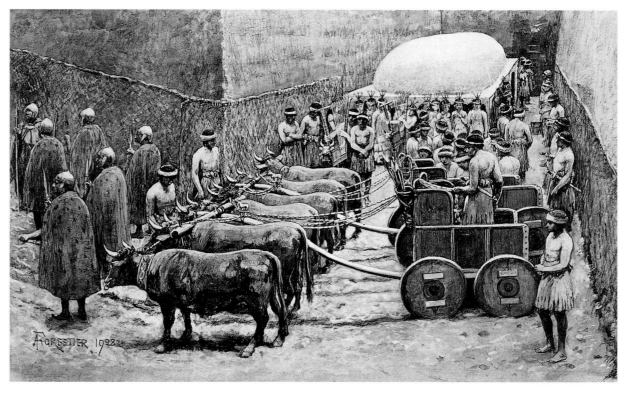

Fig. 32. Reconstructed scene in Tomb PG 789, Ur, before the death of the royal retainers. Early Dynastic III A, ca. 2550–2400 B.C.

belong to single individuals at all, and that instead the tombs remained open or available over a significant period, as was happening at about the same time in Syria.[3] If so, the various bodies that Woolley found scattered had been disturbed or rearranged in antiquity by people returning to the tombs on successive occasions. It seems difficult to believe, however, that the PG 1237 death pit was anything other than what Woolley deduced, a simultaneous mass burial of many people. This must argue in favor of Woolley's interpretation of the other death pits. Similarly, each of the earliest stone chamber-tombs—PG 1236, PG 779, and PG 777—produced in its inner chamber an item of outstanding quality suitable for an individual of very high status: an exceptional cylinder seal, the Standard of Ur (cat. no. 52), and an exceptional headdress, respectively. While it may be questioned whether PG 1050 and PG 1054 are indeed single tombs rather than two or three tombs superimposed, the Syrian evidence is hardly strong enough to invalidate Woolley's essential conclusion that each tomb was built and kept for one principal occupant.

If so, the finds in the tombs represent a grander version of those found in ordinary Sumerian graves. The deceased required personal possessions, provisions for his or her journey to the underworld, and possibly gifts for the gods of the underworld. A Sumerian text describes the purchase of appropriate goods for a temple official; they included food, jewelry, and a chariot.[4] The epic story of the death of the ancient hero Gilgamesh is no less apposite, because he took with him to the tomb, apparently, his wife, his child (perhaps a mistake for "the mother of his child"), his favorite concubine, his minstrel, cupbearer, barber, courtiers, and retainers.[5] Between them, these descriptions account for all the kinds of things found in the royal tombs of Ur.

It seems that in making a tomb a shaft was first dug, ten meters or more deep and of comparable length and width. The entrance was through a ramp on one side. At the bottom a tomb chamber was constructed; sometimes an open space was left in front of it. Then the body of the dead person was brought with appropriate ceremony and laid on a bed or in a coffin inside the tomb chamber. Since the preparations will have taken a considerable time, it is possible that the corpse had sometimes been artificially preserved by smoking, which would account for Woolley's observation that some of the bodies buried at Ur seemed to have been scorched. The tomb chamber was filled with appropriate treasures, including sometimes a model boat that may have been intended for use in traveling to the underworld. Personal attendants, alive or dead,

remained in the tomb chamber with the deceased. Then the door was blocked.

For the next act, Woolley's own dramatic account, based on the remains of PG 789 (fig. 32) and PG 800, which were relatively well preserved, is still much the most satisfactory so far offered:

> Now down the sloping passage comes a procession of people, the members of the court, soldiers, men-servants, and women, the latter in all their finery of brightly colored garments and head-dresses of lapis lazuli and silver and gold, and with them musicians bearing harps or lyres, cymbals, and sistra; they take up their positions in the farther part of the pit, and then there are driven or backed down the slope the chariots drawn by oxen or by asses, the drivers in the cars, the grooms holding the heads of the draught animals, and these too are marshaled in the pit. Each man or woman brought a little cup of clay or stone or metal, the only equipment required for the rite that was to follow. Some kind of service there must have been at the bottom of the shaft, at least it is evident that the musicians played on to the last, and then each drank from the cup; either they brought the potion with them or they found it prepared for them on the spot—in PG 1237 there was in the middle of the pit a great copper pot into which they could have dipped—and they composed themselves for death. Then someone came down and killed the animals and perhaps arranged the drugged bodies, and when that was done earth was flung from above on to them, and the filling-in of the grave-shaft was begun.[6]

The filling in of the shaft was itself a complicated matter, with any number of funeral offerings at different levels. At the top, at ground level, there may have been structures where the customary offerings to the dead could later be made. No trace of these remained, however, and eventually the entire area was covered by rubbish heaps.

This leaves the question of who was buried in the tombs. Woolley always thought that they were kings and queens of Ur, and inscribed seals from PG 1050 and PG 1054 do mention the names of kings. The evidence was not overwhelming, however, and immediately after the discovery some scholars favored alternative theories, especially that the tombs with their unprecedented sacrifices were related to a sacred marriage cult, in which individuals personified the gods and by their deaths ensured the fertility of the land. Woolley himself refuted this by various arguments[7]—among others the observation that any such sacrifice should have been an annual affair—and the theory might never have been put forward had the story of the death of Gilgamesh already been familiar to scholars.

A more sophisticated objection was raised by Roger Moorey.[8] He emphasized that one unusually rich Ur tomb, PG 755, which Woolley did not classify as royal because it had only one occupant, contained vessels inscribed with the name of Meskalamdug, and that this was probably the grave of the king of the same name. Pointing to the large number of complexities in the evidence and the likelihood that some of the people buried in the royal tombs were associated with the moon god, Moorey maintained that not enough was known for the tombs to be accepted as royal.

A contrasting view much closer to Woolley's has been taken by this author,[9] who has attempted to name the principal occupants of the royal tombs, correlating the archaeological record with political events and with the kings or "priest-kings" who are thought to have ruled Ur. The argument is that the sets of evidence—the tombs, stratigraphy, and texts—fit each other reasonably well, and that the occupant of PG 755 was a prince, the son of Meskalamdug. The full list of proposed tomb occupants is given in Table 1.

Table 1. *Proposed occupants of the royal tombs at Ur (in chronological order)*

Tomb number	Occupant
1236	A'Imdugud, king
779	Ur-Pabilsag, king, son of A'Imdugud
777	queen, wife of Ur-Pabilsag
755	son of Meskalamdug, king, and Ninbanda, queen
1054	Ninbanda, queen, wife 1 of Meskalamdug, king
1130	widow of the occupant of PG 755
789	Meskalamdug, king, son of Ur-Pabilsag
800	Puabi, queen, wife 2 of Meskalamdug, king
1050	Ashusikildingir, queen, wife of Akalamdug
1332	Akalamdug, king, son of Meskalamdug
337	queen, wife 2 of Akalamdug
1232/1237	Mesanepada, king, [grand?]son of Meskalamdug
55	queen, wife of A'anepada
580	A'anepada, king, son of Mesanepada
1157	Meskiagnuna, king, son of Mesanepada

It is suggested that the introduction of massive death pits at Ur should be associated with the novel status of Meskalamdug, king of Ur, as additionally king of Kish, paramount ruler of all the Sumerians. It was he who started the practice of interment with many soldiers and an entire choir of women accompanying him and subsequently his widow Puabi to the other world. The practice could have been a conscious allusion to the obsequies of the great early king Gilgamesh, as recorded in tradition. The foundation of Meskalamdug's power was Ur's position at the head of the Gulf with a substantial degree of control over the metals and other goods from the trade routes linking Mesopotamia with Iran, the Indus Valley, and beyond.

If this is correct, then Woolley may have been right in proposing that "the members of the king's court who went down with music into his grave did so more or less voluntarily, that it was a privilege rather than a doom pronounced on them. . . . [They] were translated to a higher sphere of service."[10] Whoever the occupants of the royal tombs really were, and whatever they thought of their fate, the very fact that these discussions continue so long after the excavations finished is a wonderful tribute to the quality of the objects found by Woolley and to his skills as an archaeologist and writer.

1. Woolley 1934 remains the prime publication on the tombs, outstanding for the speed, intelligence, and thoroughness with which it was completed. Woolley accompanied his scholarly work with many popular books, which are listed in his biography, Winstone 1990, p. 297. Zettler and Horne 1998 is a well-illustrated publication of the Ur material in the University of Pennsylvania Museum, Philadelphia.
2. Nissen 1966; Pollock 1985.
3. Sürenhagen 2002.
4. Gelb, Steinkeller, and Whiting 1991, pp. 99–103; Foxvog 1980.
5. Foster, Frayne, and Beckman 2001, pp. 152–53.
6. Woolley 1934, p. 35.
7. Ibid., pp. 38–41.
8. Moorey 1977.
9. Reade 2001, pp. 17–24.
10. Woolley 1934, p. 42.

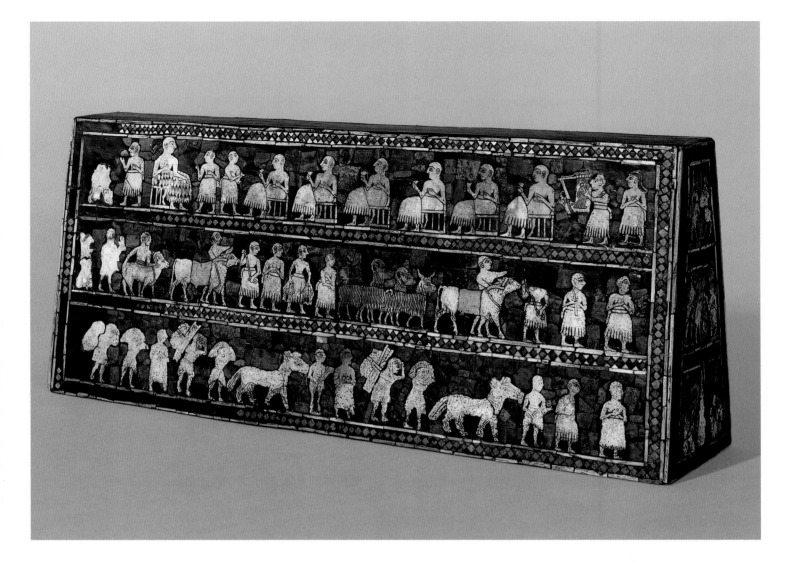

52

"Standard of Ur"

Shell, lapis lazuli, and red limestone
H. 20 cm (7⅞ in.); L. 47 cm (18½ in.)
Mesopotamia, Ur, PG 779, U.11164
Early Dynastic IIIA, ca. 2550–2400 B.C.
Trustees of The British Museum, London BM 121201

The two rectangular side panels and truncated triangular ends of this originally wood box represent one of the most important objects from the Royal Cemetery at Ur. The decayed remains of the box were found in the death pit of a grave, lying close to the shoulder of a man. Leonard Woolley believed this man may have held the object on a pole, and so he called it a "standard." The appellation remains associated with the box panels, even though there is no real evidence to support Woolley's assumption. The side panels and ends of the box (which are modern reconstructions) were covered with three registers of both figurative and geometric mosaics that originally were probably set into bitumen.

One side panel depicts aspects of a battle and its aftermath. The most important person, probably the ruler, is shown in the center of the top register, his status indicated by the fact that he is the tallest figure in the scene. Behind him, to the left on the panel, is his chariot, drawn by four onagers, or wild asses, and before him, to the right, are nude, bound prisoners presented by a few of his soldiers. In the second register a phalanx of almost identical armed soldiers is contrasted with soldiers in a variety of poses dispatching enemies and leading off prisoners. The king's chariotry is depicted in the lowest register. Each four-wheeled chariot carries a charioteer and a warrior and is drawn by four onagers, indi-cated by the lines that parallel the tails, heads, and legs of the nearest animals. The more rapidly moving chariots all show a nude, dead enemy lying beneath the legs of the asses.

The other side panel presents a completely different theme. A banquet with distinct religious overtones is depicted in the upper register. Toward the left, the principal banqueter is joined by six other participants, all of whom hold cups in their right hands. Three standing attendants administer to the banqueters, who enjoy the accompaniment of the lyre played by the musician at the right and perhaps also the words or song of the rightmost figure with long hair. The main figure is distinguished from the others, who are intended to be seen as seated before him in either a straight line or a partial circle, by his larger size and by his tufted skirt. It seems reasonable

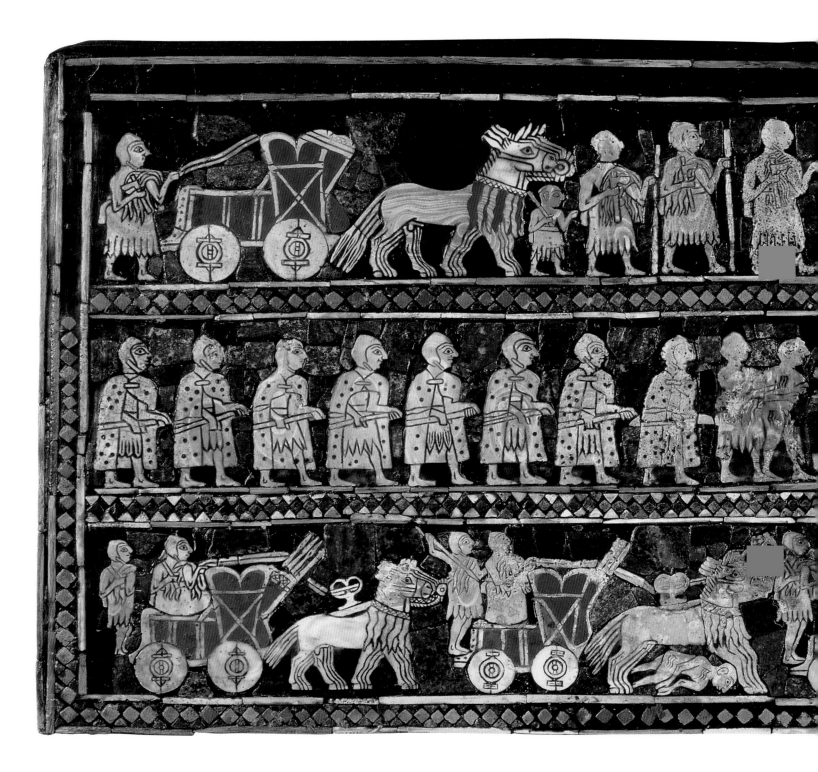

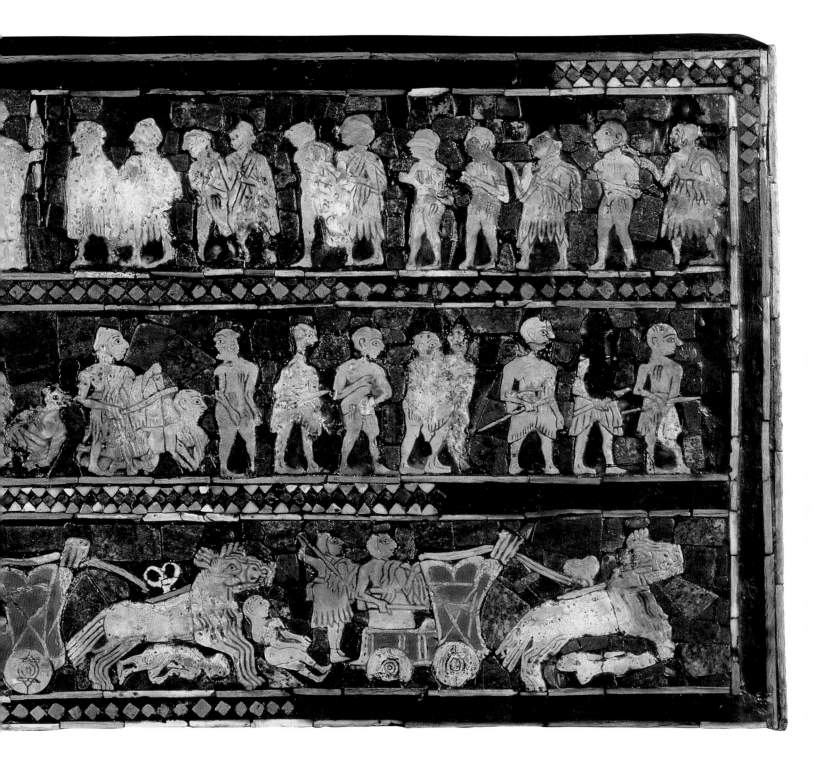

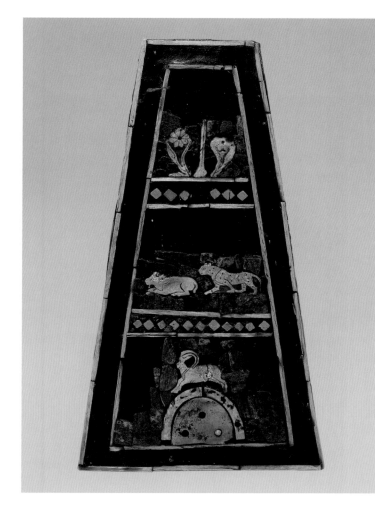

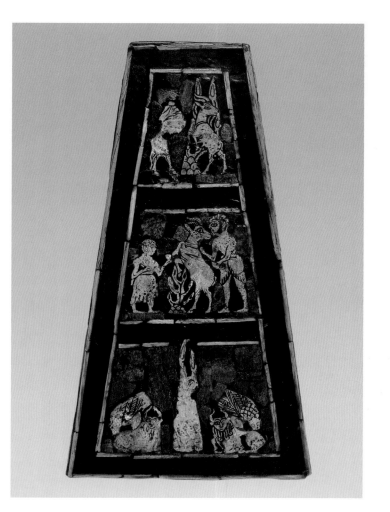

to assume that this figure represents the same ruler depicted on the other side panel. The second register introduces the bountifulness of the land. Bald Sumerians dressed in full, fringed skirts lead bulls and other animals or carry fish. A male figure standing behind the bull at the left of the register has a beard and a full head of black hair (shell colored by bitumen)

topped by a scalloped headdress. His skirt is short, and his belt differs from the belts on the other figures to the right. The implication is that he is leading the procession from the bottom register. In that register some figures carry produce in bags on their shoulders, others carry heavy backpacks supported by headbands, and still others lead asses by ropes attached to

nose rings. Their dress and coiffure indicate that they perhaps come from areas north of Sumer. Thus the Standard of Ur encompasses the two aspects of Sumerian kingship, the military leader and the bountiful mediator between humans and gods.[1]   DPH

1. Hansen 1998, pp. 45–47.

53a, b

Game board and fourteen gaming pieces

Mesopotamia, Ur
Early Dynastic IIIA, ca. 2550–2400 B.C.

a. Shell, red limestone, and lapis lazuli
L. 30.1 cm (11⅞ in.); W. 11 cm (4⅜ in.); Thickness
2.4 cm (1 in.)
PG 513, U.9000
Trustees of The British Museum, London BM
120834

b. Black shale, shell, and lapis lazuli
Diam. of each 2.2 cm (⅞ in.)
PG 341
Trustees of The British Museum, London BM 1928-
10-9, 379a-n

This board for the so-called game of twenty squares is one of several with similar layouts found by Leonard Woolley in the Royal Cemetery at Ur.[1] The wood components had decayed, but the inlays of shell, red limestone, and lapis lazuli survived in their original positions so that the board could be restored in its correct shape and configuration. The board has twenty squares made of shell: five squares are decorated with flower rosettes, five with eyelike shapes, and five with circled dots. The remaining five squares bear various designs made up of five dots. According to information in later cuneiform texts, two players competed to race their pieces from one end of the board to another. Pieces were allowed on the board at the beginning of the game determined by throws of dice.[2]

The gaming pieces for this particular board do not survive. However, sets of gaming pieces of inlaid shale and shell associated with other boards were excavated at Ur. The set of seven roundels of black shale inlaid with five dots of white shell and seven shell roundels inlaid with five lapis lazuli dots seen here was found in a nonroyal grave at Ur.[3] These lay in a row, the colors alternating, as if they had been carefully arranged in a box; presumably this receptacle was a hollow gaming board made of plain wood that had disintegrated, leaving no trace. Stick- and tetrahedral-shaped dice were also found in graves at Ur.

Examples of the game of twenty squares date from about 3000 B.C. to the first millennium A.D. and were found dispersed from the eastern Mediterranean and Egypt to India. A version of the Mesopotamian game survived within the Jewish community at Cochin, south India, until modern times.

PC

1. Woolley 1934, p. 276, pl. 95.
2. Finkel 1992, pp. 154–55.
3. Woolley 1934, pp. 278–79, 536, pl. 95.

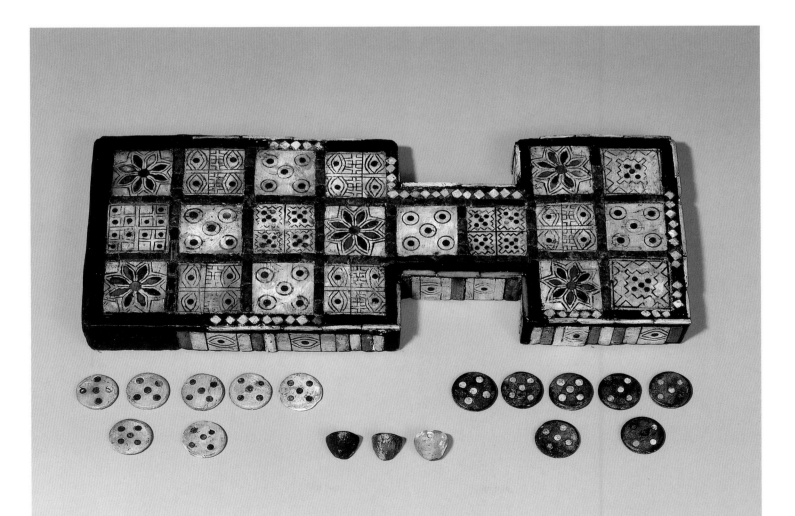

54

Dagger

Gold, with wood restoration
L. (restored) 33 cm (13 in.)
Mesopotamia, Ur, PG 1054, U.11513
Early Dynastic IIIA, ca. 2550–2400 B.C.
University of Pennsylvania Museum of Archaeology
and Anthropology, Philadelphia 30-12-550

Of all the royal graves at Ur, the one numbered PG 1054 best illustrates the ritual of burial. The shaft leading down to the stone-built tomb had been filled with successive layers of soil brought from different locations as well as with a variety of vessels containing food offerings. A chamber of mud bricks in the upper part of the shaft contained human burials. On the floor of this chamber was an outline of white powder, indicating the remains of a decayed wood box.[1] Inside was this magnificent dagger and another similar to it, now in the Iraq Museum, Baghdad, along with a cylinder seal with an inscription of the king Meskalamdug (see cat. no. 55a).

Metal tools and weapons were manufactured either by hammering or, more commonly, by casting. On the double-edged gold blade of this dagger, ribs from casting are visible. Decoration of such tools and weapons was limited primarily to the now-decomposed shafts. On this dagger, small gold nails in the hilt guard and at the end of the wood pommel (restored for display) imitate granulation.[2] Both its material and its association with a royal cylinder seal indicate that this was an elite weapon.   PC

1. See Woolley 1934, pp. 97–99.
2. Weber and Zettler in Zettler and Horne 1998, p. 164.

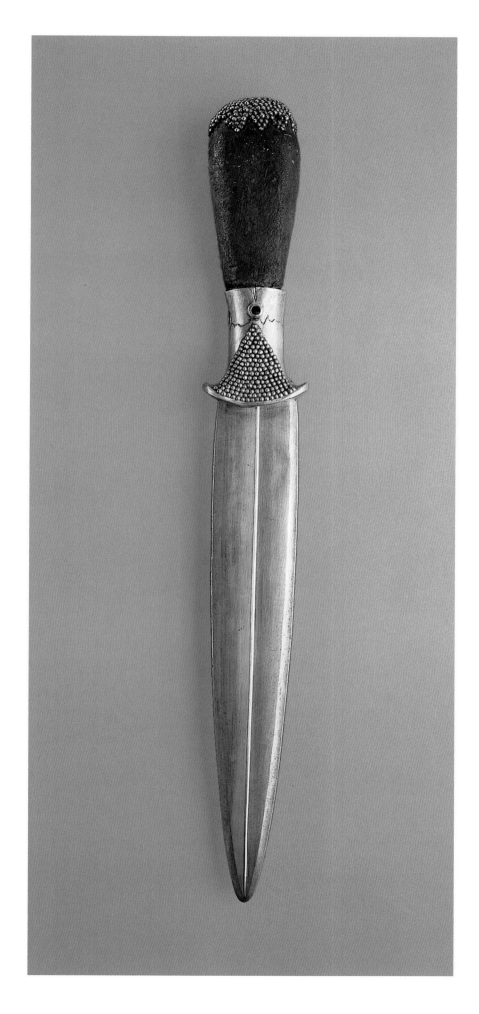

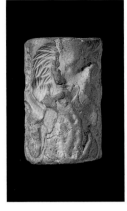

55a

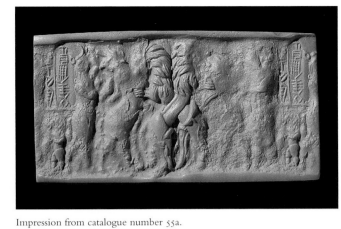

Impression from catalogue number 55a.

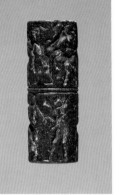

55b

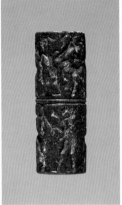

Impression from catalogue number 55b.

55a, b

Cylinder seals with royal names

Cuneiform inscriptions in Sumerian
Mesopotamia, Ur
Early Dynastic IIIA, ca. 2550–2400 B.C.

a. Shell and lapis lazuli
H. 4.9 cm (1⅞ in.); Diam. 3 cm (1⅛ in.)
Above PG 1054, U.11751
Trustees of The British Museum, London BM 122536

b. Lapis lazuli
H. 4.1 cm (1⅝ in.); Diam. 1.3 cm (½ in.)
Found loose in the soil, U.8981
University of Pennsylvania Museum of Archaeology
and Anthropology, Philadelphia B16852

These two royal seals depict different styles of contests between heroes and animals. Such scenes first appeared on cylinder seals in the late fourth millennium B.C., and by the middle of the third millennium B.C. the combatants, which might also include mythological opponents, had assumed heroic status. The first seal is badly decayed, but certain elements can be identified, such as a lion facing right crossing in front of another lion; both their manes are represented as tufts. The lion at the rear, whose head is damaged, is viewed from above, facing left and biting the neck of an animal that stands on its hind legs and arches its neck to the left; the animal is being held by a figure, possibly a nude hero, farther to the left. An inscription behind the hero bears the name Meskalamdug with the title *lugal* (king). The ends of the seal are inlaid with pierced disks of lapis lazuli. The seal was found in a box along with two gold daggers (see cat. no. 54) inside a mud-brick construction with human burials in the shaft leading to one of the royal graves.

The second seal was found loose in the soil above the royal graves. Like the seal of Meskalamdug, it consists of combat scenes but in two registers. In the upper register, the hero protects two rampant bovids that are being attacked on each side by lions but, unlike the lower register, which contains five combatants, as is typical of seals from this period, the figures do not overlap. The inscription cites Ninbanda, described as the "wife of Mesanepada," a king of Ur, who ruled after Meskalamdug.

PC

56

Helmet on a crushed skull

Bone and copper alloy
L. 38.1 cm (15 in.)
Mesopotamia, Ur, PG 789, U.10825
Early Dynastic IIIA, ca. 2550–2400 B.C.
Trustees of The British Museum, London BM 121414

This skull comes from the so-called King's Grave in the Royal Cemetery at Ur. Although the stone tomb of this pit had been plundered in antiquity and there was no evidence of the occupant, Leonard Woolley suggested that it belonged to a king. His interpretation rested on the fact that the tomb chamber lay alongside that of Puabi (see "The Tomb of Puabi," by Paul Collins, in this catalogue). Woolley theorized that the queen had wanted to be buried near her husband, a king of Ur who had died before her. Unlike her tomb chamber, the death pit of the King's Grave contained an enormous array of artifacts. The bodies of six soldiers wearing copper helmets, of which this is one, and carrying spears were found lying at the foot of the ramp that descended to the floor of the large burial pit, more than eight meters below what is the modern surface. The helmets were broken and crushed flat by the weight of the soil that had been thrown back into the grave during the burial. The soldiers presumably were intended to be guardians of the tomb for eternity; if this were so, they failed in their duty because the central tomb had been robbed in antiquity. The soldiers' helmets closely resemble those worn by the figures on the Standard of Ur (cat. no. 52).

PC

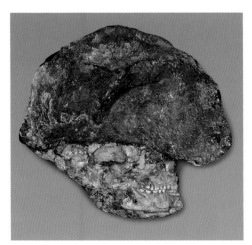

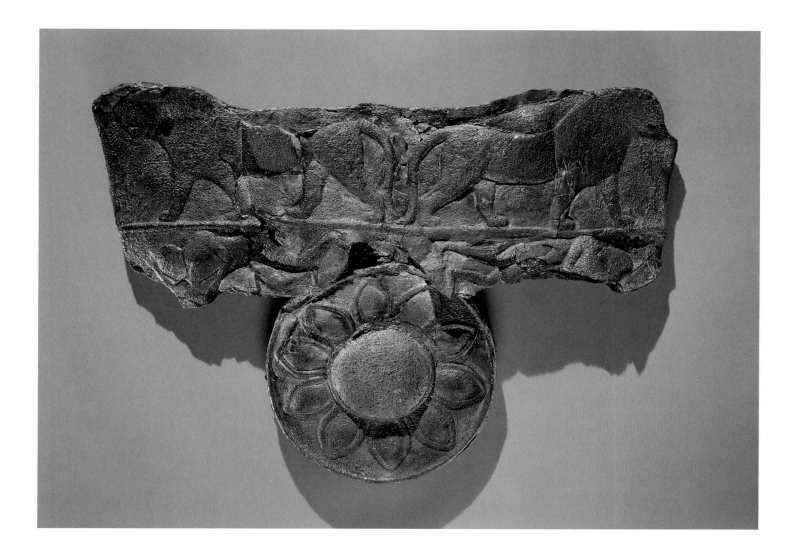

57

Plaque with addorsed lions trampling enemies

Copper alloy
H. 31 cm (12¼ in.); W. 45 cm (17¾ in.)
Mesopotamia, Ur, PG 789, King's Grave, U.10475
Early Dynastic IIIA, ca. 2550–2400 B.C.
University of Pennsylvania Museum of Archaeology
and Anthropology, Philadelphia B17066

This copper-alloy relief came from the death pit floor of the King's Grave, one of the more important tombs in the Royal Cemetery at Ur. Although fragmentary, a panel with registers and a ten-petaled rosette with a boss in the center are preserved; it is not clear if the rosette was originally meant for the position seen here. In the upper register are two addorsed striding lions, and in the lower register appear two enemies, nude, shaven, and lying facedown. Because the relief was found with spears and was originally affixed to a wood backing, the excavator thought it might be part of a shield.

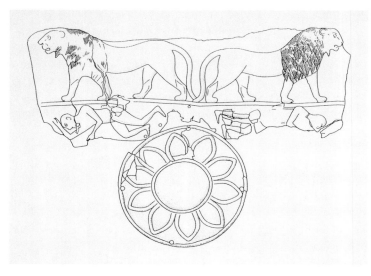

Fig. 33. Drawing of a plaque with addorsed lions trampling enemies (cat. no. 57).

Aspects of the style and iconography of this relief set it apart from other art of the Royal Cemetery and may be due to foreign influence. In particular the association of the lions and the nude fallen enemies, each with one arm stretched over his face, suggests that

the Sumerian artist was aware of examples of Egyptian art in which the pharaoh as lion tramples on his enemies. Interpreted in terms of Sumerian ideas, however, the lion probably symbolizes a deity such as the warlike goddess Inanna, who is conventionally associated with this animal, rather than the king. Similarly, the lion may be associated with the warrior god Ningirsu, whose emblem is the Imdugud, a lion-headed eagle.[1]   DPH

1. Hansen 1998, pp. 67–68.

58

"Great Lyre" with bull's head and inlaid front panel

Gold, silver, lapis lazuli, shell, bitumen, and wood
H. of head 35.6 cm (14 in.); H. of plaque 33 cm
(13 in.); max. L. of lyre 140 cm (55⅛ in.); H. of
upright back arm 117 cm (46⅛ in.)
Mesopotamia, Ur, PG 789, King's Grave, U.10556
Early Dynastic IIIA, ca. 2550–2400 B.C.
University of Pennsylvania Museum of Archaeology
and Anthropology, Philadelphia B17694

Lying against the northwest wall of the death pit of Tomb PG 789 at Ur was this magnificent lyre, the bottom of which rested on the heads of three bodies.[1] On the basis of the types of jewelry on the bodies beneath this lyre and beneath a second one in the pit (now in the British Museum), the bodies were identified as women. They had the most elaborate head-dresses of all the women discovered in the grave, and they may have been musicians and singers who took part in a celebration of the death ritual. The consistency of the lyres' placement on top of the bodies indicates that they were probably put there after the cele-brants died.

Although the wood elements of the lyre had perished, the splendid bull's head was reconstructed based both on the relationship among the various parts as they were found and on other bull's heads excavated from the cemetery (for example, cat. no. 65). Most of the head and horns of the bull are of sheet gold over the original wood core. The eye-balls are made of shell and the pupils and eye-lids of lapis lazuli, which was also used for the tufts of hair on the forehead and for the tips of the horns. The luxurious beard of twelve locks ending in curls is formed from pieces of lapis lazuli set into a silver backing with a raised edge.

The sound box and the arms of the lyre were of undecorated wood, but the front of the sound box was embellished with shell in one of the most intriguing and skillfully exe-cuted Sumerian compositions known. The

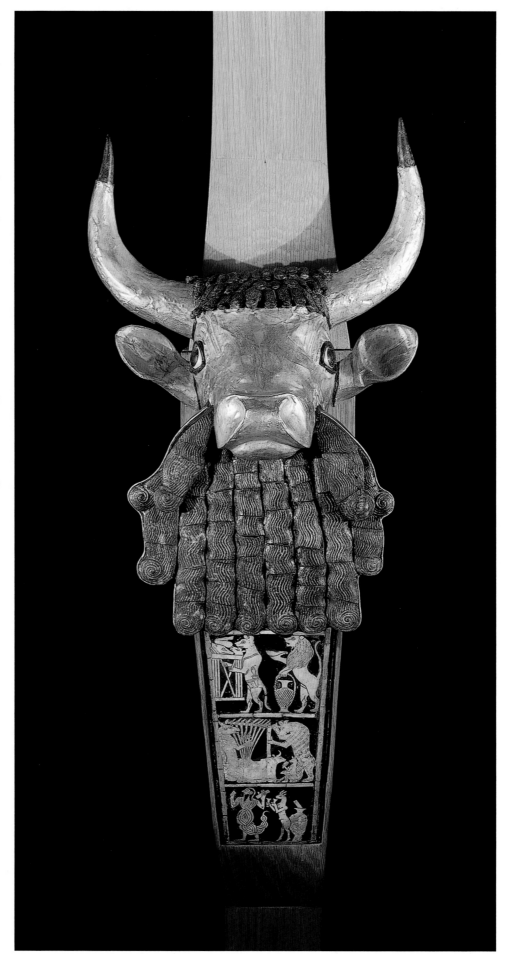

decoration is made up of four registers, each a shell plaque, whose background was cut away and filled with bitumen. In the top register a nude male grasps two human-headed bulls. The man is bearded, which in this instance probably denotes his semidivine status, and he has three large locks of hair on either side of his head. The concept of the intertwined hero and human-headed bulls is not fully understood today, but here the image is related to or represents the deceased. The figures stand physically above and spiritually over the three lower panels, which depict the funerary banquet celebrated in the netherworld or in preparation for the crossing into the netherworld.

This banquet stands apart from others (for example, cat. no. 59) in that the celebrants are depicted as animals, but ones who are performing their tasks as though they are human. In the second register a canine animal, probably a hyena in the role of a butcher, stands on his rear legs. In his human hands he carries a table piled with animal parts, and he wears a dagger (similar to cat. no. 54) stuck in his belt. Behind him a lion walks upright holding a pouring vessel (similar to cat. no. 69) in his right hand and a large jar in his left.

The third register shows an animal orchestra accompanying the banquet. A seated ass plucks an eight-stringed lyre decorated with a bull's head much like the actual lyre. A standing bear helps support the lyre, grasping its front upright arm and crosspiece. A small animal, perhaps a fox, sits on the bear's right foot. The small animal holds a sistrum in his right hand and rests his left hand on an object lying across his knees, perhaps a tablet containing the text of a song performed at this special banquet.

In the bottom register a scorpion-man stands in profile holding a cylindrical object in his left hand. The scorpion-man is a creature associated with the mountains of sunrise and sunset, distant lands of wild animals and demons, a place passed by the dead.[2] Here he stands in front of a rampant gazelle with human shoulders, arms, and hands, who carries two tumblers similar in shape to those actually found in Puabi's tomb (cat. no. 67b). Presumably the vessels have been filled from the large pottery container behind the gazelle.

Such depictions of animals behaving like humans are rare in the art of early Sumer. An elaborate singular early example is found on a seal impression (fig. 17), also from Ur. The ultimate source for an iconography based on the concept of animals acting as humans is

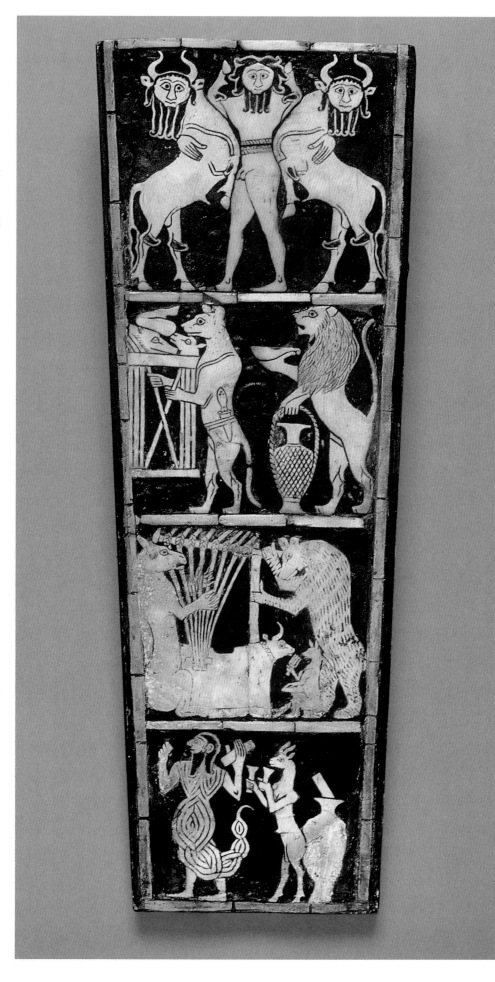

Proto-Elamite Iran (see cat. no. 13), and the adaptation of an originally Iranian type of imagery adds a profound new dimension to this royal Sumerian burial. This lyre was meant to accompany liturgical chants, its sounds associated with those of the divine bull and its decorated sound box providing a glimpse of the underworld banquet.[3]

DPH

1. Woolley 1934, p. 280. A second lyre lay on the head of another body farther along one of the walls.
2. For example, Wiggermann 1995, pp. 79–83.
3. Hansen 1998, pp. 53–57.

59

Inlaid panel from front of a lyre

Lapis lazuli and shell
H. 19 cm (7½ in.); W. 7 cm (2¾ in.)
Mesopotamia, Ur, PG 1332, U.12435
Early Dynastic IIIA, ca. 2550–2400 B.C.
University of Pennsylvania Museum of Archaeology and Anthropology, Philadelphia 30-12-484

These small mosaic plaques were found with a copper-alloy head of a bull; together they formed the decorative front of a lyre. Its sound box and upper frame were made of wood that had disintegrated in the soil. The original lyre would have been a smaller version of the Great Lyre (cat. no. 58) and probably resembled lyres shown carried by musicians on relief plaques and seals.

This group of plaques depicts four human figures in an Early Dynastic banquet scene. All the participants are male. The main character is probably the banqueter seated on a stool—bald and nude from the waist up—who has three attendants standing before him in a line or a row. He wears an ankle-length fleecy, tufted garment about the waist. In his raised right hand he holds a cup; in his lowered left hand he grasps an object that, based on other banquet representations, is probably a plant form. The partially bald attendant standing before the seated figure holds his right arm up with the hand partially open; his left hand is tucked into his armpit. The other two atten-

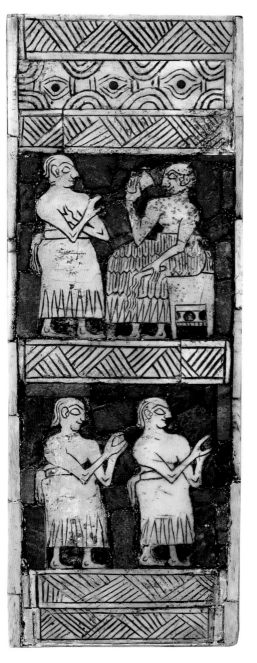

dants extend their joined hands before them, and the one in the rear holds an unidentifiable object. The bottom of the panel is incomplete; it is possible that it originally mirrored the top of the panel, with a border of engraved "eye" motifs set between two shell pieces incised with a woven pattern. The significance of the "eye" is unknown.[1]

DPH

1. Hansen 1998, p. 59.

The Tomb of Puabi

Only one of the royal tombs at Ur survived largely intact. The excavator, Leonard Woolley, uncovered an earth ramp leading down about five meters into a pit approximately twelve by four meters (fig. 34). On the ramp, as if guarding the entrance to the grave, lay the bodies of five men with copper-alloy daggers. At the foot of the ramp were the decayed remains of a vehicle, possibly a sledge, with the bones of two oxen and four men. A fifth body lay near the corner of the entrance. In the middle of the pit were the remains of a wood chest decorated with lapis lazuli and shell inlay, against which rested the body of a man. Other bodies lay near the northeast corner of the grave. At the southern end of the death pit the bodies of ten women wearing elaborate headdresses were positioned in two facing rows. Associated with some of these attendants were musical instruments, including a harp and a lyre. Woolley found traces of reed matting covering the artifacts and bodies that presumably were intended to prevent soil from touching them when the grave was filled in. A tomb chamber built of stone was located to the northeast; its floor was nearly two meters below the level of the death pit. There appeared to be no doorway in its walls, so it is assumed that access was through the roof. Inside the tomb were four bodies. Clearly the most important was that of a woman just under five feet tall and about forty years old at the time of her death. Her body was adorned with beads of gold, silver, lapis lazuli, carnelian, and agate as well as other pieces of elaborate jewelry and cylinder seals. One of these had an inscription that identifies the wearer as Puabi, the queen (see entry for cat. no. 60).

PC

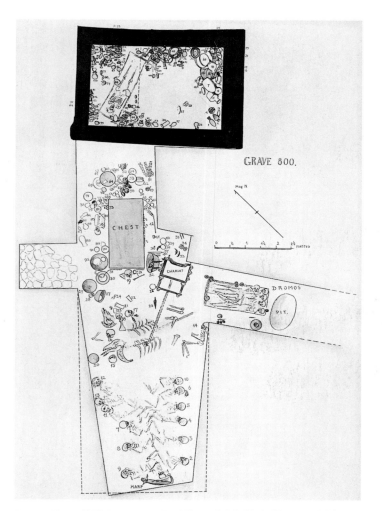

Fig. 34. Plan of PG 800, queen Puabi's tomb, Ur. Early Dynastic IIIA, ca. 2550–2400 B.C.

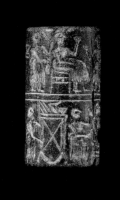

60a

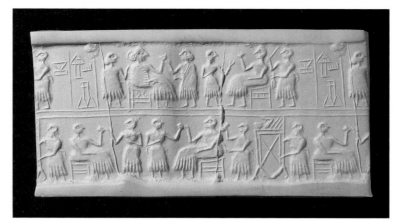

Impression from catalogue number 60a.

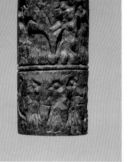

60b

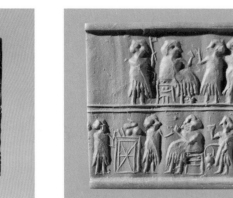

Impression from catalogue number 60b.

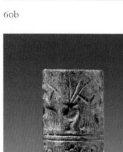

60c

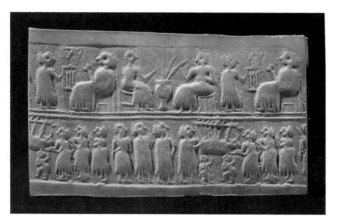

Impression from catalogue number 60c.

60a–c

Cylinder seals with banquet scenes

Cuneiform inscriptions in Sumerian
Lapis lazuli
Mesopotamia, Ur
Early Dynastic IIIA, ca. 2550–2400 B.C.

a. H. 4.9 cm (1⅞ in.); Diam. 2.5 cm (1 in.)
PG 800, Puabi's Tomb, U.10939
Trustees of The British Museum, London BM 121544

b. H. 4 cm (1⅝ in.); Diam. 2 cm (¾ in.)
PG 800, Puabi's Tomb, U.108722

University of Pennsylvania Museum of Archaeology
and Anthropology, Philadelphia B16728

c. H. 4.5 cm (1¾ in.); Diam. 1.5 cm (⁹⁄₁₆ in.)
PG 1237, Great Death Pit, U.12374
University of Pennsylvania Museum of Archaeology
and Anthropology, Philadelphia 30-12-2

One of the two main themes of Early
Dynastic cylinder seals, many of which are
made of lapis lazuli, is the banquet scene,

usually executed in a more linear and imprecise
style than the other main theme—contests
between animals and human figures (see cat.
no. 55). Banquet scenes, which represented
ceremonies, also occur on contemporary stone
plaques (see cat. no. 32), and music appears to
have been an integral part of these events. The
banquet-scene seals from the Royal Cemetery
may have been associated exclusively with
women.[1] The first two seals seen here (cat.
nos. 60a, b) together with a third in the British

Museum were found in the Royal Cemetery close to the body of queen Puabi. In the top register is a woman with her hair in a bun, seated in a chair and facing right, and clad in a fringed garment that covers her right arm. She raises a cup in her left hand, helped by one of two female servants standing on either side of her. Facing the woman is a seated man, also raising a cup but attended by male servants, one of whom lifts a stick, perhaps to strike a bell held in his other hand. The two-line inscription reads *nin* ("queen") *Pu-abi*. In the lower register, all the participants are male. Two seated figures are attended by four servants, one of whom stands behind a tall table laden with a vessel and a haunch of meat.

The second seal depicts a banquet apparently attended only by women, all of whom wear long, fringed robes. In the upper register, two celebrants sit on folding stools facing each other and raising conical cups. Each is attended by a servant with one hand raised. At the far left, another servant holds a square fan. In the lower register, a single female figure sits on a stool facing a heavily laden table. A woman helps her lift a cup while a second holds a handled jar and raises a cup. Another individual holding a four-stringed lyre is accompanied by figures who clap cymbals and perhaps sing (see the top register of the banquet scene on the Standard of Ur [cat. no. 52]).

The third seal, which comes from the so-called Great Death Pit, was found near three lyres, one of which was decorated with a large bull's head. This double-register seal is finely carved with an inscribed name, *Dumu-kisal*. There are three seated figures, two facing each other and drinking through tubes from a large vessel, and another raising a cup before a standing individual. The lower register contains a scene of music-making and dancing. Two women precede a man carrying a staff over his shoulder. The group faces a woman playing a lyre decorated with the head of a bull (see cat. no. 58); below the instrument, two small figures are dancing. Facing the performers are three female figures who appear to be clapping.   PC

1. Moorey 1977, pp. 24–40.

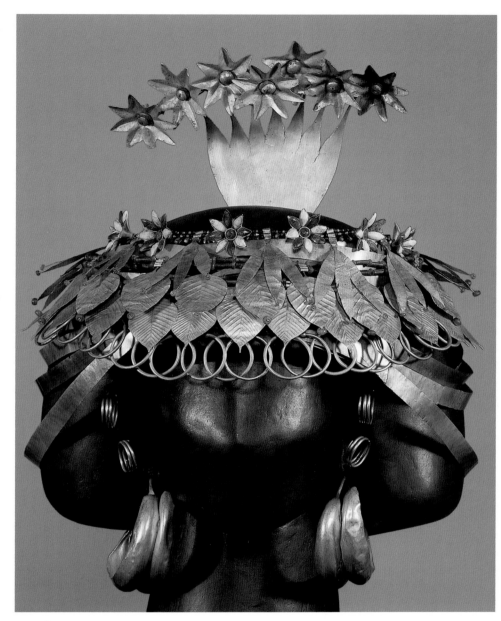

61a–e, front

61a–e

Puabi's headdress

Mesopotamia, Ur, PG 800, Puabi's Tomb
Early Dynastic IIIA, ca. 2550–2400 B.C.

a. Comb
Gold, lapis lazuli, and carnelian
H. 36 cm (14⅛ in.)
U. 10937
University of Pennsylvania Museum of Archaeology
and Anthropology, Philadelphia   B16693

b. Hair rings
Gold
Diam. 2.7 cm (1⅛ in.)
U. 10890
University of Pennsylvania Museum of Archaeology
and Anthropology, Philadelphia   B16992a,b

c. Wreaths
Gold, lapis lazuli, and carnelian
U. 10935a, U. 10936
University of Pennsylvania Museum of Archaeology
and Anthropology, Philadelphia   B17709–11

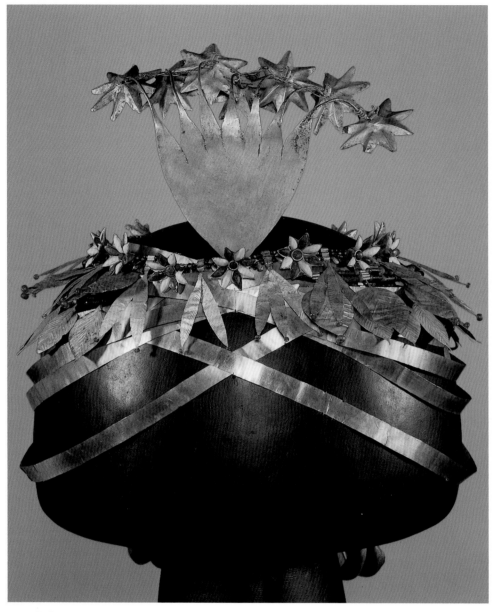

imagery. Two types of leaves, willow and beech, are arranged on top of circles and bands of gold. Small rosettes, their petals filled in with blue or white paste in an alternating pattern, emerge from the pile of leaves. Crowning the whole ensemble is a magnificent comb from which six larger rosettes emerge, each having blue and white petals. From the queen's ears dangled enormous earrings of double-crescent form. Correctly interpreting the symbolism of the headdress will someday enrich our understanding of Sumerian beliefs. Certainly at the most general level it involves fertility, fecundity, and the female procreative potential.

That Puabi, whose name is Akkadian, was a queen of the Sumerian Meskalamdug dynasty is suggested by the title *nin* that qualifies her name on her seal.[1] But that the eleven or more women interred with her are Sumerian or Akkadian is not certain. They are no doubt her entourage, taken into the afterlife along with their lady. It has been suggested that these individuals were musicians and attendants who may have come from farther to the east, along with the precious materials in Puabi's crown—carnelian beads from the Indus Valley and lapis lazuli from the Chagai Hills of Pakistani Baluchistan or from Badakhshan, in modern Afghanistan (see entry for cat. no. 278b).[2]

HP

1. Reade 2001; see also "The Royal Tombs of Ur," by Julian Reade, in this catalogue.
2. Pittman 1998, pp. 89–92; Kenoyer 1998; see also "Art and Interconnections in the Third Millennium B.C.," by Joan Aruz, in this catalogue.

61a–e, back

d. Hair ribbon
Gold
U.10934
University of Pennsylvania Museum of Archaeology and Anthropology, Philadelphia B17711a

e. Earrings
Gold
Diam. 11 cm (4⅜ in.)
U.10933
University of Pennsylvania Museum of Archaeology and Anthropology, Philadelphia B17712a,b

Across human cultures the most elaborate markers of identity are often carried on the head of important individuals. The headdress of queen Puabi of Ur epitomizes this type of badge. The numerous female servants found buried with her wore less-elaborate versions. Puabi's crown consists of layers of gold ornaments arranged over a wig or other hair covering. The present arrangement is the one that Leonard Woolley observed as he carefully removed it from Puabi's skull. The overall impression is one of brilliant gold floral

62a–h

Puabi's beaded cape and jewelry

Mesopotamia, Ur, PG 800, Puabi's Tomb
Early Dynastic IIIA, ca. 2550–2400 B.C.

a. Pins
Gold and lapis lazuli
1. L. 21.1 cm (8¼ in.)
U.10940
2. L. 16 cm (6¼ in.)
PG 1064, U.11553
University of Pennsylvania Museum of Archaeology and Anthropology, Philadelphia B16729, 30-12-552

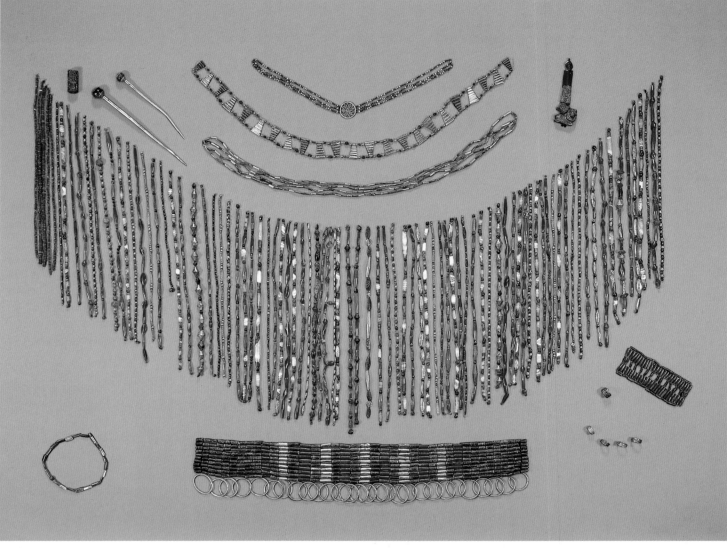

62a–h

b. String of beads with rosette
Gold and lapis lazuli
L. 43 cm (16⅞ in.)
U.10982
University of Pennsylvania Museum of Archaeology
and Anthropology, Philadelphia B16694

c. Beads and amulet
Lapis lazuli and carnelian
L. 12.3 cm (4⅞ in.)
U.10985
University of Pennsylvania Museum of Archaeology
and Anthropology, Philadelphia B16726

d. Choker, string of beads, and beaded cape
Gold, silver, carnelian, agate, and lapis lazuli
University of Pennsylvania Museum of Archaeology
and Anthropology, Philadelphia 83-7-1

e. Garter
Gold, lapis lazuli, and carnelian
L. 38 cm (15 in.)

U.10979
University of Pennsylvania Museum of Archaeology
and Anthropology, Philadelphia B16783

f. Belt
Gold, silver, lapis lazuli, and carnelian
U.10867
University of Pennsylvania Museum of Archaeology
and Anthropology, Philadelphia B17063

g. Finger rings
Gold
Diam. 2–2.2 cm (¾–⅞ in.)
U.10877a–d, U.10878
University of Pennsylvania Museum of Archaeology
and Anthropology, Philadelphia B16717–21

h. Cuff
Lapis lazuli and carnelian
L. 14.5 cm (5¼ in.)
University of Pennsylvania Museum of Archaeology
and Anthropology, Philadelphia B17292

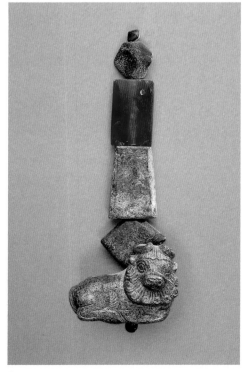

62c

Fig. 35. Excavator's restoration of queen Puabi's cape. Ur, Early Dynastic IIIA, ca. 2550–2400 B.C.

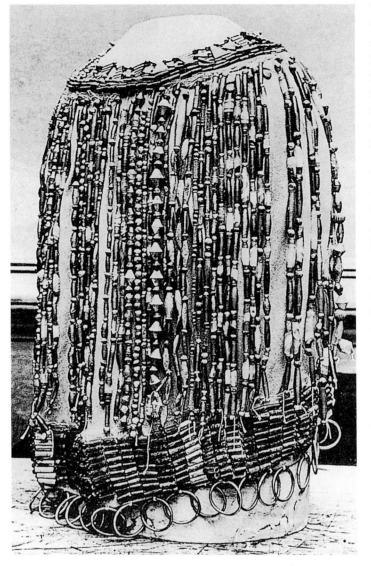

The principal body in tomb chamber PG 800 was that of a woman just under five feet tall and roughly forty years of age at the time of her death.[1] She lay on a bier that was positioned askew across the northwestern end of the chamber (see fig. 34). Her body was elaborately adorned. Three cylinder seals were found with her (see cat. nos. 60a, b); one (cat. no. 60a) identified her as Puabi, the queen.

Between Puabi's neck and waist, Leonard Woolley found some fifty strands of beads completely surrounding the upper body, forming what he described as a cape of beads. Across the body at the level of the waist ran a broad belt of beads in ten rows of alternating colors—gold, carnelian, and lapis lazuli—from which gold rings were suspended. At the top of the cape, groups of triangular beads formed a choker, which Woolley thought had been attached to the cape.

Puabi also wore a necklace of three strands of round gold and lapis lazuli beads with an open-worked gold rosette in the middle, ten gold rings, and a gold pin. Around her right knee was a garter of flat rectangular beads with one carnelian ball.[2]   HP

1. Keith in Woolley 1934, pp. 400–402.
2. Pittman 1998, p. 94.

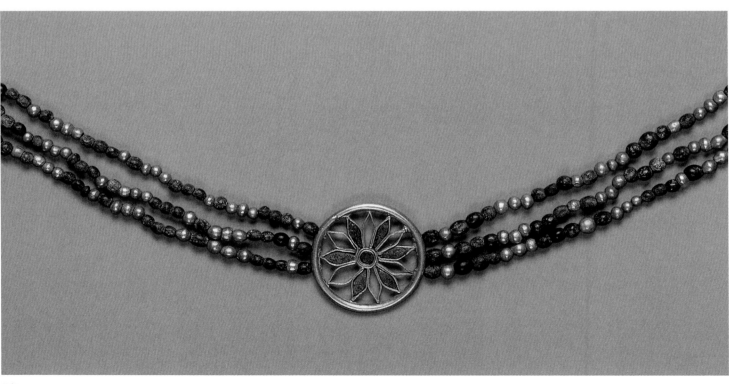

62b

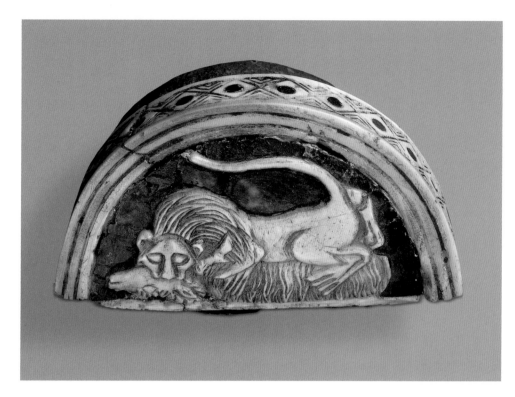

pointing upward while its tufted body hair points downward, forms a groundline for the semicircle preserved here. The contour of the lion's rear haunch, its erect curved tail, and especially its full mane reflect the external curve of the lid.[2]   DPH

1. Woolley 1934, p. 81.
2. Hansen 1998, p. 66.

64

Head of a lion

Silver, lapis lazuli, and shell
H. 11 cm (4⅜ in.); W. 12 cm (4¾ in.)
Mesopotamia, Ur, PG 800, dromos of Puabi's Tomb, U. 10465
Early Dynastic IIIA, ca. 2550–2400 B.C.
University of Pennsylvania Museum of Archaeology and Anthropology, Philadelphia B17064

This silver lion head is one of a pair discovered near the remains of a wood box thought by Leonard Woolley, the excavator, to be a wardrobe chest. Since the lion heads were originally attached to a wood object, he suggested the heads were protomes that had adorned the arms of a chair.[1] The lion was

63

Cosmetic box lid inlaid with a lion attacking a caprid

Silver, lapis lazuli, and shell
H. 3.5 cm (1⅜ in.); Diam. across lid 6.4 cm (2½ in.)
Mesopotamia, Ur, PG 800, Puabi's Tomb, U. 10436
Early Dynastic IIIA, ca. 2550–2400 B.C.
University of Pennsylvania Museum of Archaeology and Anthropology, Philadelphia B16744a

This carved lid of lapis lazuli and shell belonged to a silver box; both were found among the objects close to a wood chest in the death pit associated with PG 800, the tomb of Puabi.[1] Although cosmetic containers were usually either actual shells or imitations of them in gold or silver (see cat. nos. 290b, 291a, b), Leonard Woolley thought this object was used for holding the queen's cosmetics.

The lid represents the finest example of shell carving in the Royal Cemetery at Ur. Carved from a single piece of shell, the lid is set with another piece of shell, a rendering in relief of a lion attacking a caprid. A mosaic background of lapis lazuli surrounds the lion relief. Although the carving style is exemplary of the best Early Dynastic III art, the imaginative composition is unique. The completed lid probably consisted of two semicircular sections, and the supine caprid, its visible legs

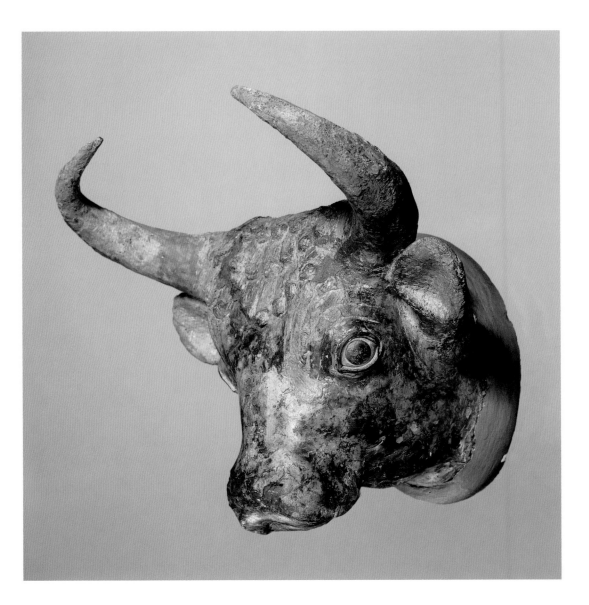

prominent in Sumerian iconography and most often appears in contest scenes (for example, cat. no. 55). In the representation here, the locks of hair suggest a real mane and indicate that a lion, rather than a lioness, is depicted. The sculptural forms are simple, yet the head is boldly executed and is a particularly expressive image of leonine power. The nose is prominently defined, and in the soft flesh of the upper lip incised striations enhance the suggestion of a snarl. The slanted, deeply inset eyes command the viewer's attention and, coupled with the shadows of the nose and mouth, give this lion head an intensity of expression rare in early Mesopotamian art.[2]

DPH

1. Woolley 1934, pp. 81–82, pls. 40, 41.
2. Hansen 1998, pp. 50–52.

65

Head of a bull

Silver, lapis lazuli, and shell
H. 16.5 cm (6½ in.); W. 15.5 cm (6⅛ in.)
Mesopotamia, Ur, PG 800, Puabi's Tomb chamber,
U. 10916
Early Dynastic IIIA, ca. 2550–2400 B.C.
University of Pennsylvania Museum of Archaeology
and Anthropology, Philadelphia B17065

A remarkable example of hollow-cast metal sculpture (see "Lost-Wax Casting," by Jean-François de Lapérouse, in this catalogue) and one of the few examples that can be dated as early as the middle of the third millennium B.C., this silver head of a bull has inlaid eyes of lapis lazuli and shell. Leonard Woolley, the excavator, thought that originally it must have been attached to the wood sound box of a lyre, which did not survive.[1] Like the silver lion head also from the tomb of Puabi (cat. no. 64), this representation exhibits a masterly blend of naturalistic forms and abstract shapes. The treatment of the eye area is an excellent example of this achievement: to emphasize the vitality of the eyes, several bands follow the curvature of the upper eyelids; the eyes themselves bulge slightly in a naturalistic manner and impart to the sculpture a sense of presence. These elements, along with projecting ears, curving horns, and strong muzzle, convincingly convey the essence of a bull.[2]

DPH

1. Woolley 1934, p. 564.
2. Hansen 1998, pp. 52–53.

66

Rein ring with an onager

Electrum and silver
H. 13.5 cm (5⅜ in.); W. 10 cm (4 in.)
Mesopotamia, Ur, PG 800, Puabi's Tomb, U.10439
Early Dynastic IIIA, ca. 2550–2400 B.C.
Trustees of The British Museum, London   BM 121348

This rein ring is one of several found in the Royal Cemetery at Ur.[1] The two rings and the pin beneath them are made of silver. Fixed to the top of the rings by means of casting is an image of a donkey or a wild ass made of electrum (a natural alloy of gold and silver). The rein ring was discovered bent at right angles, and with two of the donkey's legs snapped off, lying among the bones of two oxen. Originally, it would have been attached to a wood pole (now decayed) situated between the animals and extending to the front of a chariot or, as reconstructed by Leonard Woolley, a sledge. The reins were threaded through the rings and affixed to collars worn by the oxen. Donkeys also were used to pull vehicles, as depicted on the Standard of Ur (cat. no. 52), where the reins are shown threaded through undecorated rings.

PC

1. Woolley 1934, p. 556.

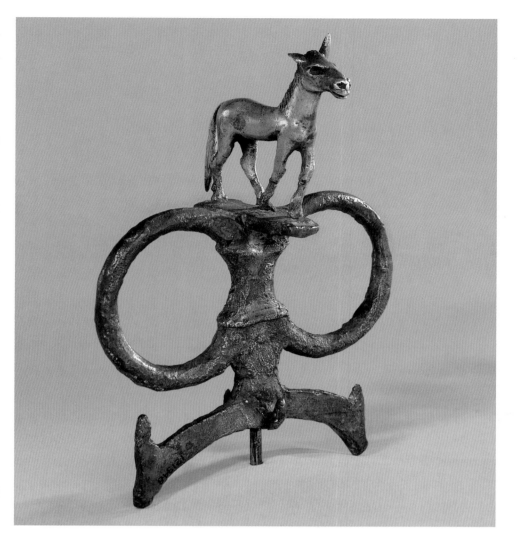

67a, b

Spouted cup and tumbler

Mesopotamia, Ur, PG 800, Puabi's Tomb
Early Dynastic IIIA, ca. 2550–2400 B.C.

a. Gold
H. 12.4 cm (4⅞ in.)
U.10454
Trustees of The British Museum, London   BM 121346

b. Electrum
H. 15.2 cm (6 in.)
U.10453
University of Pennsylvania Museum of Archaeology and Anthropology, Philadelphia   B17691

A magnificent gold cup (cat. no. 67a) was one of four vessels found on the floor of the pit of the Queen's Grave in the Royal Cemetery at Ur.[1] It stands on a small foot and when viewed from above is biconvex in shape. The sides are

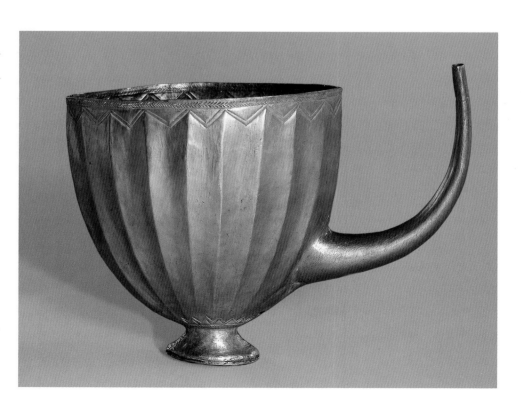

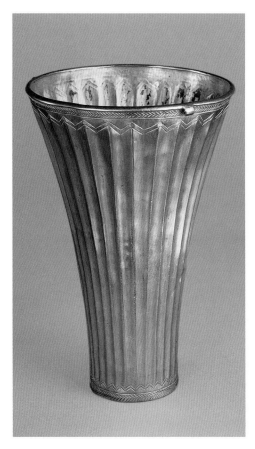

fluted; circling the top and bottom are hammered herringbone and double zigzag patterns. The tubular spout was hard-soldered to the main body of the cup. The excavator suggested that the spout rises too high to be effective for pouring and would rather have been used for sipping the contents of the vessel.[2]

Also recovered from the floor of the Queen's Grave was a fluted tumbler made of electrum, a naturally occurring alloy of gold and silver (cat. no. 67b).[3] Here, too, there are herringbone and zigzag patterns around the rim and the base. On the rim is a small loop for the attachment of a wire or string handle, perhaps for suspension.[4] The bottom of the cup carries an eight-petaled rosette decoration on a background of concentric circles. Vessels of similar shape are depicted on the Great Lyre from Ur (cat. no. 58), in the bottom register of the plaque on the front of the sound box.

Although gold is used extensively in vessels, jewelry, and weapons found in the Royal Cemetery, the source of the metal is difficult to identify. There are no gold deposits in Mesopotamia, and later Sumerian literary texts suggest that gold reached the area from a number of places. These include the mythical city of Aratta and a mythical land of gold

known as Harallu, both thought to refer to locations in Iran. Supplies also came from Anatolia and by way of the Gulf.[5]

PC

1. Woolley 1934, pp. 82, 557.
2. Ibid., p. 82.
3. Weber and Zettler 1998, pp. 126–27, 133.
4. Woolley 1934, p. 557.
5. Moorey 1985, pp. 73–74.

68

Spouted cup

Lapis lazuli
H. 6.7 cm (2⅝ in.); Diam. 10.5 cm (4⅛ in.)
Mesopotamia, Ur, PG 800, Puabi's Tomb, U.10517
Early Dynastic IIIA, ca. 2550–2400 B.C.
University of Pennsylvania Museum of Archaeology and Anthropology, Philadelphia B17167

Crafted of lapis lazuli, this slightly asymmetrical cup has a trough-shaped spout, a ring base, and a gently rounded, protruding lip. It was discovered near the decayed remains of a wood chest in the death pit associated with the tomb of queen Puabi (PG 800),[1] along with a semicircular cosmetic box lid (cat. no. 63). Vessels made of semiprecious stones such as lapis lazuli are referred to in incantations against disease known from copies dating to the early second millennium B.C.[2]

Both the material and the form of this artifact point to significant contact between southern Mesopotamia and Central Asia in the third millennium. In the late Early Dynastic period, the source of this rare and beautiful deep blue stone was the area now known as Badakhshan province in northeastern Afghanistan.[3] Lapis lazuli was traded in raw blocks,[4] then worked into objects in local or regional workshops.[5] In shape this vessel is closely related to a class of spouted steatite cups attributed to late-third-millennium contexts in western Central Asia.[6] Thus the cup may have been imported as a finished object, or it may be local work imitating a Central Asian form.

1. Woolley 1934, p. 81.
2. Zettler 1998b, p. 151.
3. Bowersox and Chamberlin 1995, pp. 37–61.
4. Like those recovered in Palace G at Ebla, Syria (see cat. no. 116).
5. Pinnock 1986, pp. 221–22.
6. Zettler 1998b, p. 151.

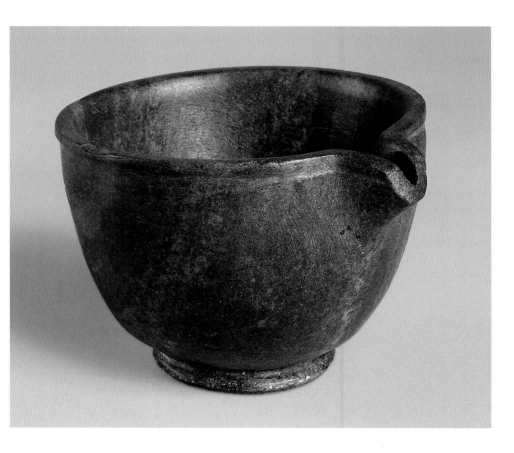

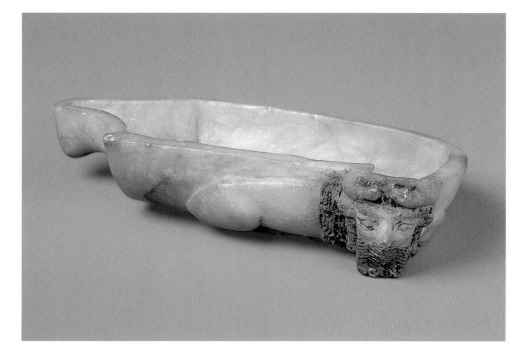

70b

Ostrich egg with inlaid attachments

Ostrich eggshell and bitumen
H. 15.2 cm (6 in.)
Mesopotamia, Ur
Early Dynastic IIIA, ca. 2550–2400 B.C.
Trustees of The British Museum, London
BM 123556

The use of ostrich eggshells as containers is known as early as the Predynastic period in Egypt, where they are found in tombs either whole or with one end cut off to form a vessel. Some are decorated on the surface with a painted or incised design. Although there is evidence for the early appearance of the ostrich in northern Syria, the oldest preserved eggshell containers in southern Mesopotamia come from Early Dynastic IIIA archaeological contexts. Most examples of the fragile eggshells from the Ur tombs were found broken into myriad fragments. Sumerian craftsmen were fond not only of using natural materials such as egg or conch shells for vessels but also of crafting imitations in gold, silver, or copper. Seen here is an example in gold (cat. no. 70a) and another made from an actual ostrich eggshell (cat. no. 70b). Like many objects of this period, the shells were decorated with mosaic patterns of shell, lapis lazuli, and sometimes red limestone, set into a bitumen base. Both the rim and the base of the gold example are decorated with typical mosaics, but the raised foot of catalogue number 70b is unique, if it is indeed correctly restored.

How such vessels were used is not well understood. Since these particular examples were found in Ur graves, they could have held substances to be consumed by the dead in the afterlife, perhaps in a funerary banquet.[1] They could also have been used in rituals performed at the time of the burial. Ritual seems more likely, since several eggshells were found in nonfunerary contexts. Examples have been excavated in the Ishtarat temple at Mari, the temple of Inanna at Nippur, and a monumental building of uncertain use at Kish.[2]

DPH

1. For an example in a Syrian burial, see "Tell Banat," by Anne Porter and Thomas McClellan, in this catalogue.
2. For further discussion of this subject and bibliography, see Hansen 1998, pp. 70–72.

69

Pouring vessel with human-headed bull or bison in relief

Calcite
L. 15 cm (5⅞ in.); W. 8.5 cm (3⅜ in.)
Mesopotamia, Ur, PG 871, in filling above floor,
U. 10746
Early Dynastic IIIB–Akkadian, ca. 2400–2159 B.C.
University of Pennsylvania Museum of Archaeology
and Anthropology, Philadelphia   B17087

This vessel belongs to a class of stone bowls with shapes imitating half shells (see cat. nos. 290b, 291b).[1] Most likely these types of vessels were used for pouring, either liquids that accompanied the dead as drink or funerary libations. A similarly shaped vessel is carried by the lion on the shell plaque on the front of the lyre from Tomb PG 789 (cat. no. 58). The body of a bison is carved on the side of the bowl. The left front leg is bent at the knee, and the other legs are drawn up beneath and directly to the side of the body; the tail follows the contour of the rear haunch. The two right legs are carved in such high relief that they appear almost in the round. The head, with the ears and horns of a bison, is carved in the round and faces outward, perpendicular to the body. The face is human and bearded, with two long curls of hair framing the sides of the face, and a mass of curls covering both the neck and chest. All of the hair was originally painted black, probably using bitumen, and much of the color remains.

Leonard Woolley assigned the grave in which this vessel was found to a group of burials he called "Second Dynasty," which are now dated primarily to the Akkadian period.[2] Although the vessel was found in the filling above the grave gifts and is thus not securely dated, the style of the sculpture, with its deeply set and finely articulated eyes, for example, and its precisely modeled cheeks, connotes a date late in Early Dynastic IIIB or early in the Akkadian period.[3]

DPH

1. Woolley 1934, p. 561.
2. Ibid., p. 377.
3. Hansen 1998, pp. 68–69.

70a

Inlaid vessel in the form of an ostrich egg

Gold, lapis lazuli, red limestone, shell, and bitumen
H. 14.6 cm (5¾ in.); Diam. 13 cm (5⅛ in.)
Mesopotamia, Ur, PG 779, U. 11154
Early Dynastic IIIA, ca. 2550–2400 B.C.
University of Pennsylvania Museum of Archaeology
and Anthropology, Philadelphia   B16692

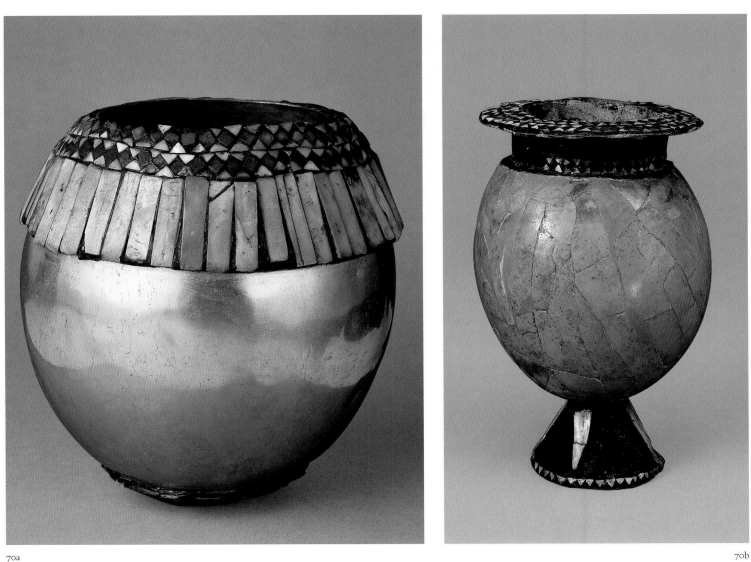

70a

70b

The Great Death Pit at Ur

The Great Death Pit, PG 1237, was probably part of a royal tomb that contained a chamber built of stone, but the latter had been almost totally destroyed when Leonard Woolley found it. All that was left of the chamber were a few stones and some exceptionally fine beads of gold, lapis lazuli, and carnelian. Another part of the same tomb may have been represented by PG 1232, which contained the remains of a vehicle, animal skeletons, and vessels for food. The death pit was a square open space in which were laid out the bodies of six armed men and sixty-eight people thought to be women or young girls (fig. 36).[1]

Prominent among the finds in the pit were the lyres. Two of them had oblong sound boxes and were elaborately decorated with inlay; both of these had bull's heads, one in gold and one in silver. Another lyre, with a rounded sound box, was overlaid with silver and decorated with the figure of a stag. A pair of copper-alloy stags had probably belonged to another musical instrument. It seems likely that the women, whose bodies mostly lay in four rows occupying half the pit, had been singing to the music as they died.[2]

During the excavation the Great Death Pit is said to have glistened with gold, as many of the women were adorned like the three whose jewelry is discussed here as catalogue numbers 72–74. The presence of beads made of gold foil wrapped around a core of baser material indicates that gold was already valuable. At Ur it was often alloyed with silver or copper, but the Sumerians were adept at enhancing the appearance of the metal by depletion gilding, which involves leaching out impurities from the surface and then burnishing it vigorously.[3] The numerous similarities in the jewelry worn by different people in the pit suggest that much of it may have been manufactured at the same time, perhaps even for the burial ceremony itself.

JR

1. Woolley 1934, pp. 107–11, 113–24. Reade (2001, p. 18) has suggested that this was the grave of the king Mesanepada.
2. Barnett 1969.
3. La Niece 1995.

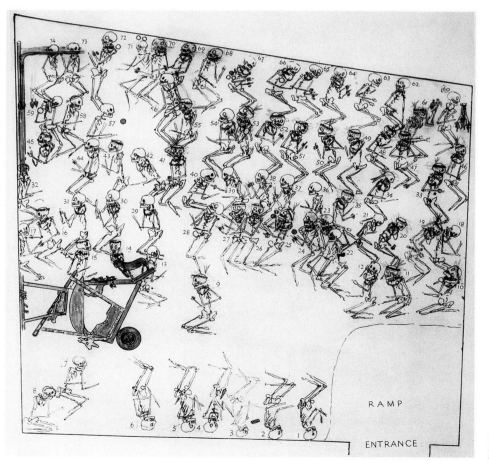

Fig. 36. Plan of PG 1237, the Great Death Pit, Ur. Early Dynastic IIIA, ca. 2550–2400 B.C.

Rearing goat with a flowering plant

*Gold, silver, lapis lazuli, copper alloy, shell,
red limestone, and bitumen
H. 42.6 cm (16¾ in.)
Mesopotamia, Ur, PG 1237, Great Death Pit,
U.12357
Early Dynastic IIIA, ca. 2550–2400 B.C.
University of Pennsylvania Museum of Archaeology
and Anthropology, Philadelphia 30-12-702*

This sculpture and its counterpart in the British
Museum are two of the most famous objects
from the Royal Cemetery at Ur.[1] They have
frequently been referred to as "ram caught in
a thicket" because the imagery in Genesis
22:13 seems to describe them. The sculpture,
however, is actually of a goat rearing on his
hind legs up against a flowering plant.[2] The
Conservation Department of the University
of Pennsylvania Museum of Archaeology and
Anthropology recently cleaned and reconstructed this example; one fundamental change
is that the front hooves of the goat now rest
on the branches of the plant rather than hang
in the air.

This small sculpture is composed of
strongly contrasting elements of gold, silver,
lapis lazuli, and white shell. The highly colored
effect was cherished by Sumerian artists for
the sublime works they created for temples or
elite burials. The goat's horns, beard, eyebrows,
pupils, and eyelids are all crafted of lapis lazuli,
as are the locks of hair on the forehead and
the fleece of the chest and shoulders. The
remaining fleece, like the whites of the eyes, is
made of shell. The face of the goat is of gold
modeled over a wood core, and the ears are
copper; the underside of the body is silver.
The wood base has silver panels set into the
sides and a mosaic surface of shell, red limestone, and lapis lazuli. The stalk of the
flowering plant, made of gold modeled over a
wood core, is set into the base and crowned
with a solitary leaf. A branch extends from
either side of the stalk, and these branches
divide into four smaller shoots, ending in two
leaves and two rosettes on each side.

This statue was not intended as freestanding
sculpture but rather constituted the base of an
object whose upper element was not preserved.
The missing part was originally attached to
the gold-covered cylinder that projects from
the back of the goat's neck. The base probably
supported a small tray or tabletop similar to

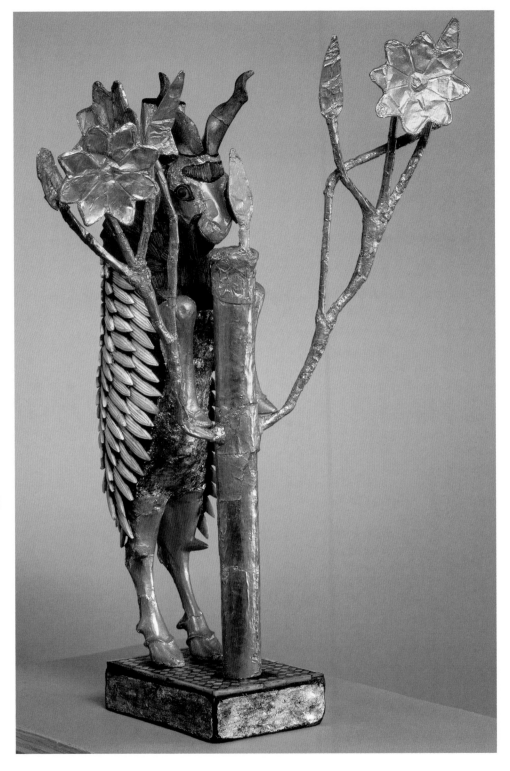

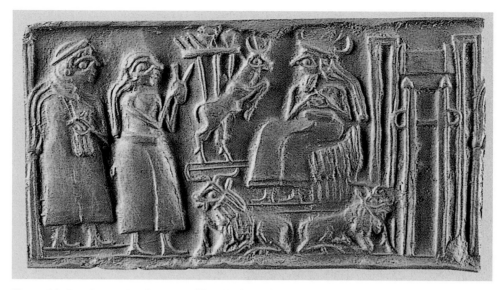

Fig. 37. Modern impression from a marble cylinder seal showing a ram supporting a small tabletop or tray. Seal: Mesopotamia, Early Dynastic III, ca. 2550–2250 B.C. Staatliche Museen zu Berlin, Vorderasiatisches Museum, VA 3878.

the representation of such a piece of furniture shown on a roughly contemporary cylinder seal (fig. 37).[3]

The combination of goat and floral branching tree is one of the most substantive and engaging images from the third millennium. It encapsulates in a highly symbolic manner the basic Sumerian concerns with plant fecundity and animal fertility. Further, the plant combines the rosette, often seen as a symbol of the goddess Inanna, with a shape that on this plant does not function as a leaf. The leaf shape may represent a flower on the end of a branch or twig, or perhaps a stylized bud that will become the rosette, or a simple fruit, the consequence of a fertilized floral spadix.[4]

DPH

1. See Collon 1995, p. 66, no. 49.
2. Although the gender of the goat is not apparent on this example because the underside is badly corroded, the British Museum example preserves the penis sheath and gold-covered testicles; it seems reasonable to assume that the present piece also represents a male.
3. Zettler and Horne 1998, p. 62, fig. 43. Rather than a piece of furniture, Winter (2000, p. 796) has proposed that the object before the seated divinity may also be considered a lyre, such as those found in some of the cemetery graves. This interpretation seems doubtful, since the five elements—two triangular forms and three slashes—situated above the top horizontal line are identical to the offerings (vessels, bread?) seen on top of tables on other seals from the cemetery. See, for example, Woolley 1934, pl. 193:21.
4. Winter (2000, p. 795) interestingly takes this a step further and suggests the possibility that the underlying meaning concerns the divine couple Inanna and Dumuzi-Tammuz.

72a–g

Finds associated with Body 51

Mesopotamia, Ur, PG 1237, Great Death Pit, U.12406
Early Dynastic IIIA, ca. 2550–2400 B.C.

a. Hair ribbons
Gold
1. L. 162 cm (63¾ in.); W. 0.8–0.9 cm (⁵⁄₁₆ –³⁄₈ in.); Thickness 0.01–0.02 cm (<¹⁄₁₆ in.); Weight 31.7 g
2. L. 52 cm (20½ in.); W. 0.75–0.8 cm (⁵⁄₁₆ in.); Thickness 0.01–0.02 cm (<¹⁄₁₆ in.); Weight 11.3 g
3. L. 35 cm (13⅞ in.); W. 0.7–0.75 cm (¼–⁵⁄₁₆ in.); Thickness 0.01–0.02 cm (<¹⁄₁₆ in.); Weight 8.1 g
Trustees of The British Museum, London BM 122339

b. Double-lobed crescent earrings
Gold
1. H. 9.1 cm (3⅝ in.); Diam. 5.8 cm (2¼ in.); Thickness 0.3 cm (⅛ in.); Weight 43.2 g
2. H. 5.8 cm (2¼ in.); Diam. 5 cm (2 in.); Thickness 0.15–0.2 cm (¹⁄₁₆ in.); Weight 20.6 g
Trustees of The British Museum, London BM 122340, 122341

c. Beaded cuff
Gold, lapis lazuli, and carnelian
L. 8.5 cm (3⅜ in.); W. 4.7 cm (1⅞ in.); Thickness 0.4–0.6 cm (³⁄₁₆–¼ in.)
Trustees of The British Museum, London BM 122342

d. Collar
Gold and lapis lazuli
L. 22 cm (8⅝ in.); W. 2.5–2.9 cm (1–1⅛ in.); Thickness 0.5 cm (³⁄₁₆ in.)
Trustees of The British Museum, London BM 122343

e. Leaf headdress
Gold, lapis lazuli, and carnelian
L. 26.5 cm (10⅜ in.); W. 5.3 cm (2⅛ in.)
Trustees of The British Museum, London BM 122344

f. Strings of beads
Gold, silver, and lapis lazuli
1. L. 95 cm (37⅜ in.)
2. L. 58 cm (22⅞ in.)
Trustees of The British Museum, London BM 122345, 122346

g. Toggle pin
Gold, silver, and lapis lazuli
L. 14.7 cm (5¾ in.)
Trustees of The British Museum, London BM 122347

The hair ribbons on the bodies buried in the royal tombs (see cat. no. 72a) were usually found broken, as on this occasion. Each ribbon was originally looped over at its ends. A string could have been passed through the loops to secure the ribbon in position. Alternatively Leonard Woolley suggested that the ribbons may sometimes have been secured by short pins, examples of which were found on the heads of the dead women, although never inside the loops of ribbons.[1] The arrangement of ribbons was particularly well preserved on the head of queen Puabi in Tomb PG 800 (cat. no. 61), and Woolley described it in detail: "The ribbon is wound round the head in such a way that the strands cross each other a little way back from the forehead and form festoons on either side which hang one below the other; at the back of the head the strands cross each other again, most of them between the skull and the chignon, though it is possible that one or two were taken round to confine the chignon also. . . . As the diameter [of the coiffure] was no less than 0.38 m it was evident that the queen wore her hair so full that it must have been dressed over pads."[2] The hair of Body 51 was presumably arranged in a simpler version of the same fashion. Many of the other bodies in PG 1237 had hair ribbons of gold or silver. One of them, Body 56, had a silver hair ribbon that was found coiled up near the waist rather than worn on the head, as if she had forgotten to put it on; it was "precisely like the tape bought in a modern shop, wound in a coil with the end passed over to keep it in place."[3] Many of the gold ribbons had a reddish tinge at the time of excavation; this was turned yellow by heat during laboratory treatment.[4]

The first, slightly damaged earring (cat. no. 72b,1) is typical of those from the royal tombs. It has been made from two pieces of

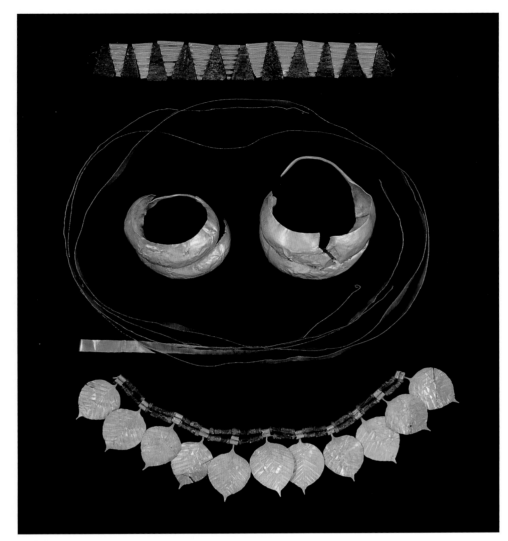

72a,b,d,e

lapis lazuli cylinders framed on each side by one carnelian cylinder, with one gold cylinder in the center and one at each end. The gold beads are foil folded over a core of some other material.

Woolley specifies that "in the case of two or three bodies in the Great Death Pit (PG 1237), a stray fragment of cloth was preserved under a cup or bowl, a thick but closely woven fabric the dust of which still preserved a bright ochrous red colour. Very many of these bodies had round their wrists beads of gold, carnelian, and lapis lazuli which had not been strung together as loose bracelets but had been sewn on to the edges of the sleeves of a garment; it would appear that these women wore red jackets with fairly tight sleeves reaching to the wrist."[7] Many bodies were recorded as having only one cuff; Woolley also noted, however, that it was particularly difficult to know to which body a cuff belonged,[8] so they may really have come in pairs rather than singly. Bodies 50 and 52, on either side of Body 51, were both recorded as having one cuff each.

The neck ornament (cat. no. 72d) consists of eleven triangular beads of lapis lazuli (one broken) and ten of gold, alternating, with the gold pointing upward. Each gold triangle is made from a diamond-shaped and corrugated piece of sheet metal that has been folded back on itself to create seven horizontal tubes; one of the two pointed ends has then been looped back over the other to keep the two sides together, and the loop has been fused into position, as have some of the junctions between the tubes. The surface of the lapis lazuli triangles is corrugated, making it look as if they, too, have seven horizontal perforations, but in fact there are only three perforations through the stones, so that the collar was held together by three rather than seven threads. The range of sizes represented by the triangles suggests that the collar was put together briskly, with the pieces picked up one after another from a large heap.

Collars like these are too short to have fully encircled the neck. They may have been worn as separate items like chokers, extended by cloth straps around the back, or they may have been attached to jackets.

The headdress (cat. no. 72e) consists of eleven gold leaf-pendants hanging with points downward from a double row of beads; in each row, between each pendant, there are two lapis lazuli cylinders flanked by single carnelian

gold, each shaped like a hollow crescent or open boat with raised ends. The crescents were made from sheet gold, and an irregular line across one of them shows where two sheets were hammered together. The crescents were shaped over a bitumen core. Traces of bitumen sometimes survive inside the earrings, and sometimes there is so much bitumen that it must have added considerably to the weight and ensured that the earring hung down properly. Since excavated bitumen is dry and crumbles easily, it is possible that all such earrings once had bitumen filling. The two crescents are fused together along one edge, and the end of one crescent is drawn out as a loop of wire, which arches over toward a tubular hole at the opposite end of the other crescent.

Woolley identified these objects as earrings because they were regularly found in pairs beside the skull, and later smaller earrings of crescent shape are well known. He suggested

that the pin could have passed through the lobe of the ear.[5] He also suggested, however, that part of their weight might have been taken by a lock of hair. If we may judge by the exceptional pair, catalogue number 73b, which are otherwise similarly crescentic in appearance but which do not have pins that could have been passed through the earlobe, they were earrings in appearance rather than reality. One possibility is that they hung beside the ear but were attached to a headdress.

The second earring (cat. no. 72b,2), also slightly damaged, is of the same type as the first but is smaller and lighter, so the two are not a true pair. Woolley remarked that it was sometimes hard to determine exactly to which body in PG 1237 "some of the more outlying objects" belonged.[6] So it is unclear whether or not Body 51 really had a matching set of earrings.

Now laid flat, the cuff (cat. no. 72c) consists of nine similar strands of thirteen beads. Each strand comprises two sets of three adjacent rings, so that there are altogether forty beads of each type. The leaves and their stalks are cut from sheet gold, and each leaf is engraved with nine or ten slanting veins on either side of a central line. The stalk is about 0.1 centimeter thick where it meets the leaf, but widens to 0.5 or 0.6 centimeters as it extends upward, where it is twisted over to form a double loop through which the two strings pass. The leaves are slightly crumpled, and some are torn.

Headdresses like these could have been worn alone or attached to caps. They are not long enough to have encircled the head completely. Sometimes several were worn, one above the other.[9] They will have overhung the eyes, unless the hair was dressed very high. The leaves overlap slightly and must have rustled as the wearer moved. They are probably stylized leaves of the poplar, a common Iraqi tree, rather than beech as supposed by Woolley.[10]

The longer of the two strings of beads (cat. no. 72f,1) consists of 109 biconical beads of lapis lazuli, 19 of silver, and one barrel-shaped bead of slightly crushed gold foil over a core, which is probably bitumen. This is mounted at the center of the string, framed by alternating silver beads and the larger lapis lazuli ones, with the remaining smaller lapis lazuli beads on either side. This order, like that of the beads on most other Ur necklaces, is at least partly reconstructed. Beads were found loose and jumbled in the soil, as the threads that once held them together had perished, and the original arrangements were often hard to record accurately. Many beads were probably attached to clothing rather than strung in necklaces. For Body 51, Woolley refers to a single "necklace of gold, silver, and lapis double conoids,"[11] which must have included the shorter string (cat. no. 72f,2) too. The original restringing always seems to have been done at Ur, however, and represents the excavators' assessment of the available evidence.

The shorter string consists of ninety-seven biconical beads of lapis lazuli, strung with the larger ones toward the center. The three gold beads, made of foil over what may be a copper core, are central but separate, with eighteen lapis lazuli beads between each of them.

The head of the toggle pin (cat. no. 72g) is a roughly spherical lapis lazuli bead, segmented like a pumpkin by thirty-one light incisions. It is capped by a circular piece of thin gold, pierced where the perforation emerges through the bead, and there was probably another such cap on the side into which the top of the shaft fitted, so that only a thin band of lapis

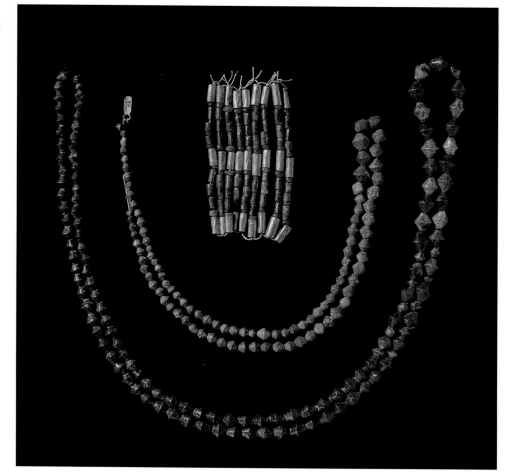

72c,f,1,2

lazuli was visible. A hole about 0.15 centimeter in diameter perforates the circular shaft about 1 centimeter from the head.

Toggle pins like this, with the distinctive hole in the shaft, have generally been found near the left shoulder of a body and were used to fasten clothes. A string passing through the shaft enabled the pin to function as a fastener, but it was sometimes also used for the attachment of the owner's personal seal or amulets.

In addition to catalogue numbers 72a,g, Body 51 also possessed some silver hair-rings, a necklace of small natural shells, two silver finger-rings, some shells containing green paint or cosmetic, and a small stone bowl.

JR

1. Woolley 1934, p. 240.
2. Ibid., p. 86.
3. Ibid., p. 121.
4. Plenderleith 1934, p. 298.
5. Woolley 1934, p. 241.
6. Ibid., p. 120.
7. Ibid., p. 239.
8. Ibid., pp. 120–21.
9. Ibid., pp. 84–87.
10. Miller 2000, pp. 149–51.
11. Woolley 1934, p. 119.

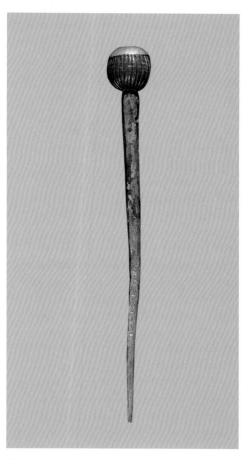

72g

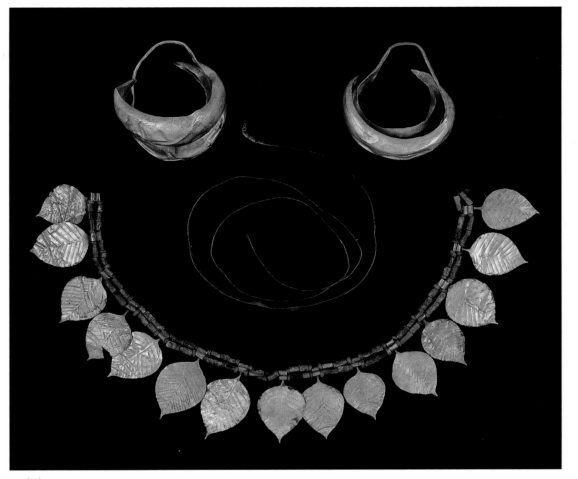

73a,b,d

73a–e

Finds associated with Body 54

Mesopotamia, Ur, PG 1237, Great Death Pit,
U.12416
Early Dynastic IIIA, ca. 2550–2400 B.C.

a. Hair ribbon
Gold
L. 85 cm (33½ in.); W. 0.7–0.85 cm (¼–5/16 in.);
Thickness 0.01–0.02 cm (<1/16 in.)
Trustees of The British Museum, London BM 122357

b. Double-lobed crescent earrings
Gold
1. H. 8.7 cm (3⅜ in.); Diam. 5.8 cm (2¼ in.);
Thickness 0.3 cm (⅛ in.); Weight 33 g
2. H. 8.6 cm (3⅜ in.); Diam. 4.3 cm (1¾ in.);
Thickness 0.3 cm (⅛ in.); Weight 33.2 g
Trustees of The British Museum, London
BM 122358, 122359

c. String of beads
Gold and lapis lazuli
L. 67 cm (26⅜ in.)

Gold beads: L. 0.6–1.1 cm (¼–7/16 in.); Diam. 0.5–
0.8 cm (3/16–5/16 in.)
Lapis lazuli beads: L. 0.7–1.1 cm (¼–7/16 in.);
Diam. 0.7–1 cm (¼–7/16 in.)
Trustees of The British Museum, London BM 122360

d. Leaf headdress
Gold, lapis lazuli, and carnelian
Overall L. 43.5 cm (17⅛ in.); H. of gold leaves 4.9–
6.1 cm (1⅞–2⅜ in.); W. 2.9–3.5 cm (1⅛–1⅜ in.);
Thickness 0.1–0.2 cm (1/16 in.)
Trustees of The British Museum, London BM 122361

e. Toggle pin
Copper alloy and lapis lazuli
Extant L. 5.8 cm (2¼ in.); max. Diam. 0.7 cm (¼ in.)
Trustees of The British Museum, London BM 122362

For a general description of the hair ribbons found with the bodies in PG 1237, see catalogue number 72a. This ribbon (cat. no. 73a) retains one unbroken end, with its original double loop.

The first earring (cat. no. 73b,1) is complete. The second (cat. no. 73b,2), its companion

piece, is complete but slightly squashed. The pair were made from hammered sheet metal like catalogue number 72b, but in a single piece: the two crescents that constitute each ornament are not originally separate pieces fused together along an edge but are directly connected by the arching loop that joins the end of one crescent to the opposite end of the other. So neither loop could have passed through an earlobe.

In the necklace (cat. no. 73c) there are fifty-four biconical beads of lapis lazuli and twenty-five of gold foil over a core. Woolley describes, among the finds with this body, a "necklace of three rows of gold and lapis double conoids."[1] They have been reconstructed as a single strand, which consists of alternating groups of three gold beads and six lapis lazuli ones, with groups of two gold and three lapis lazuli beads at either end.

The arrangement of leaves and beads in the headdress (cat. no. 73d) is much the same as that of catalogue number 72e. There are fifteen gold leaf-pendants pointing downward; they are slightly crumpled, and one is torn. The

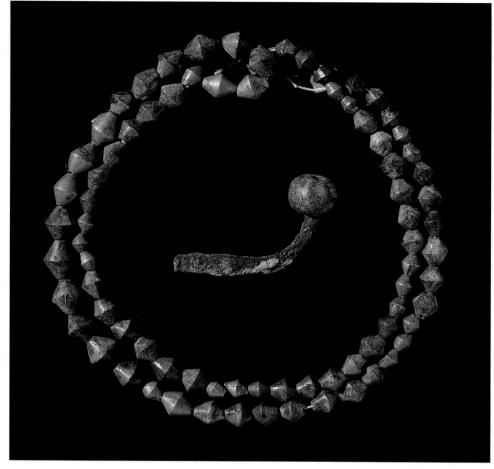

73c,e

number of veins on the leaves ranges from nine to fourteen. There are fifty-six carnelian rings, but sixty-four lapis lazuli cylinders, as there are three cylinders rather than two between some of the pendants, and an extra pair of cylinders at one end.

For a general description of the toggle pins found with the bodies in PG 1237, see catalogue number 72g. The shaft of this example (cat. no. 73e), which is deliberately bent, was round in section but square at the point where it is perforated. The corroded state of this pin, which would have been thinner, is typical of copper objects from Ur, of which the original surfaces are often irrecoverable.   JR

1. Woolley 1934, p. 119.

Mesopotamia, Ur, PG 1237, Great Death Pit, U.12424
Early Dynastic IIIA, ca. 2550–2400 B.C.

a. Hair ribbons
Gold
1. L. 63 cm (24¾ in.); W. 0.8–0.85 cm (⁵⁄₁₆ in.); Thickness 0.01–0.02 cm (<¹⁄₁₆ in.)
2. L. 54 cm (21¼ in.); W. 0.85 cm (⁵⁄₁₆ in.); Thickness 0.01–0.02 cm (<¹⁄₁₆ in.)
3. L. 43.5 cm (17⅛ in.); W. 0.5–1 cm (³⁄₁₆–⅜ in.); Thickness 0.02–0.03 cm (<¹⁄₁₆ in.)
4. L. 34.5 cm (13⅝ in.); W. 0.8–0.85 cm (⁵⁄₁₆ in.); Thickness 0.01–0.02 cm (<¹⁄₁₆ in.)
Trustees of The British Museum, London BM 122388

b. Double-lobed crescent earrings
Gold
1. H. 6.8 cm (2⅝ in.); Diam. 3.8 cm (1½ in.); Thickness 0.2–0.3 cm (¹⁄₁₆–⅛ in.); Weight 19.4 g
2. H. 6.2 cm (2½ in.); Diam. 3.2 cm (1¼ in.); Thickness 0.3 cm (⅛ in.); Weight 19.3 g
Trustees of The British Museum, London
BM 122389, 122390

c. Leaf headdress
Gold, lapis lazuli, and carnelian
Overall L. 23 cm (9 in.); W. 2.4–2.9 cm (1–1⅛ in.); Thickness 0.5 cm (³⁄₁₆ in.)
Trustees of The British Museum, London BM 122391

d. Collar
Gold and lapis lazuli
Overall L. 23 cm (9 in.); W. 2.4–2.9 cm (1–1⅛ in.); Thickness 0.5 cm (³⁄₁₆ in.)
Trustees of The British Museum, London BM 122392

e. Necklace or ornament
Silver and lapis lazuli
Overall L. 25 cm (9⅞ in.); W. 2.5 cm (1 in.)
Trustees of The British Museum, London BM 122393

f. Strings of beads
Lapis lazuli
1. Overall L. 39 cm (15⅜ in.); L. of beads 0.4–0.7 cm (³⁄₁₆–¼ in.); Diam. of beads 0.5–0.7 cm (³⁄₁₆–¼ in.)
2. Overall L. 22 cm (8⅝ in.); L. of beads 1.7–2 cm (¹¹⁄₁₆–¾ in.); Diam. of beads 0.7–0.9 cm (¼–⅜ in.)
Trustees of The British Museum, London
BM 122394, 122395

g. Toggle pin
Silver and lapis lazuli
L. 16.3 cm (6⅜ in.); Diam. of head 1–1.5 cm (⅜–⁹⁄₁₆ in.); Diam. of shaft 0.15–0.5 cm (¹⁄₁₆–³⁄₁₆ in.)
Trustees of The British Museum, London BM 122396

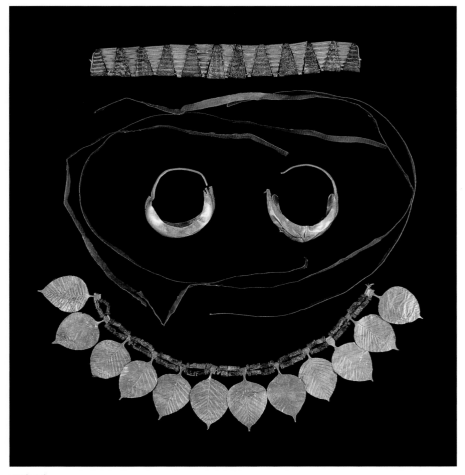

74a,b,c,d

mounted in four strands, on each of which the silver beads are in two sets of 3, with 6 lapis lazuli beads between them and with 12 (in one place eleven) lapis lazuli beads at either end. The larger lapis lazuli beads are toward the center. It seems possible, given the arrangement, that some of the beads were attached as an ornament on the woman's clothing rather than forming a necklace.

The first string (cat. no. 74f,1) has seventy-one biconical beads. The second (cat. no. 74f,2) has only twelve. Both sets probably belonged with catalogue number 74e.

For a general discussion of the toggle pins found with the bodies in PG 1237, see catalogue number 72g. The head of this one (cat. no. 74g) is a spheroid bead of lapis lazuli, into which the end of the shaft fits. As with catalogue number 73e, the shaft is deliberately bent. It is round in section except near the perforation, inside which there remains a trace of thread.   JR

1. Woolley 1934, p. 119.

These ribbons (cat. no. 74a) would have been worn like the ones described in catalogue number 72a. The third one found with Body 55 is more substantial than all the others, leaving open the question whether some of the women in the tomb indeed had ribbons of different qualities in their hair or whether there was some confusion during or after the excavation.

This pair of earrings (cat. no. 74b) are the same type as catalogue number 72b. The first is slightly crumpled and damaged, but the other is complete.

The arrangement of leaves and beads (cat. no. 74c) is the same as that on the headdress of Body 51 (cat. no. 72e). The twelve leaves, which are slightly crumpled and split, have between seven and fifteen veins.

The collar (cat. no. 74d) resembles catalogue number 72d but consists of twelve triangular beads of lapis lazuli and eleven of gold.

Woolley recorded, for this body, "a necklace of silver and lapis double conoids,"[1] which must also have included catalogue number 74f. Catalogue number 74e consists of 119 (perhaps once 120) biconical beads of lapis lazuli, and twenty-four of silver. They are

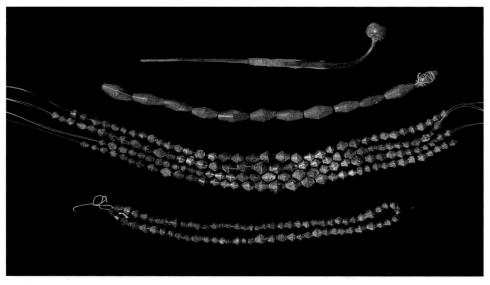

74e,f,1,2,g

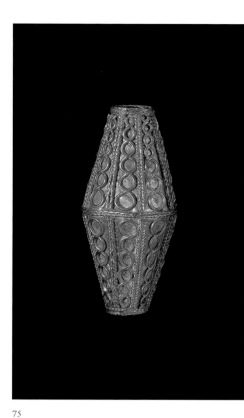

75

which the bead may originally have lain had been ruined in antiquity by plunderers and that much of the material in it had been disturbed.

Most of the known goldwork from Mesopotamia is concentrated in the royal graves at Ur. There are only few techniques of metalworking known to the ancient world not represented in these graves.   PC

1. Moorey 1985, p. 88.
2. Woolley 1934, p. 53, pl. 138.

76

Child's diadem with roundels

Gold, lapis lazuli, and carnelian
Diam. of disks: 4.7 cm (1⅞ in.); 4.1 cm (1⅝ in.);
4.6 cm (1¾ in.)
Mesopotamia, Ur, PG 1133, U.11806–7
Early Dynastic IIIA, ca. 2550–2400 B.C.
Trustees of The British Museum, London BM 122206–8

Two of the three gold disk ornaments seen here, which originally were part of a diadem, are formed from rings separated by finely bent strips of gold, as are their central rosettes. The other disk consists of four concentric gold rings inlaid with lapis lazuli and carnelian. All three appear to have been attached to a chain made up of sets of four long, biconical beads of gold, lapis lazuli, and carnelian. Leonard Woolley discovered the diadem in one of the simpler graves in the cemetery at Ur.[1] A small wood coffin containing the badly preserved bones of a very young child lay at the bottom of a shaft; the diadem was around the child's head. Bowls made of silver, copper, calcite, and limestone also were found, along with a wood scepter overlaid with gold and mosaic and two copper imitations of cockleshells. This evidence provides one of the few instances of the existence in the cemetery of a richly furnished child's grave.   PC

1. Woolley 1934, pp. 167–68, pls. 133, 138.

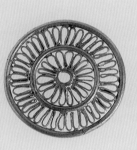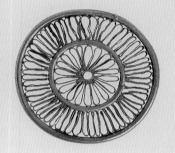

76

75

Bead with filligree and cloisons

Gold
L. 3.3 cm (1¼ in.); Diam. 1.4 cm (⁹⁄₁₆ in.)
Mesopotamia, Ur, PG 580, U.9779
Early Dynastic IIIA, ca. 2550–2400 B.C.
Trustees of The British Museum, London BM 121427

This beautiful gold bead, formed from two joined cones, is elaborately decorated with appliqué filigree work and circular cloisons once filled with lapis lazuli. All the lapis is now missing, but a tiny splinter of the material remained in one cloison when the bead was found, indicating its original presence. Beads like this one were generally sweated, that is, the filigree was attached to the background by the carefully controlled use of heat without the medium of solder. The cones were joined with a solder (either a thin strip of the gold of the bead or an alloy richer in silver and consequently with a lower melting point than gold).[1] This bead was found beneath the floor level of a royal grave at Ur but may have filtered down from grave level into the loose soil below.[2] The excavator, Leonard Woolley, suggested that the grave in

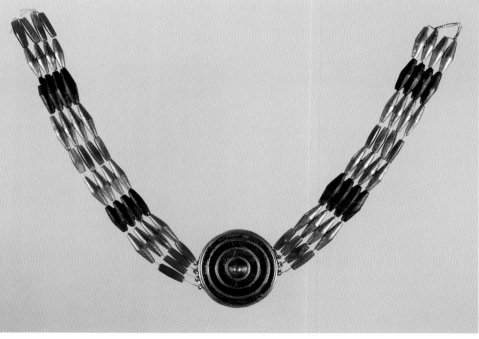

76

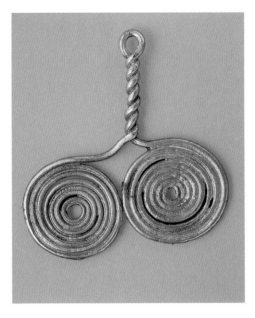

77

Double-spiral pendant

Gold
H. 2.5 cm (1 in.)
Mesopotamia, Ur, PG 1133, U.11808
Early Dynastic IIIA, ca. 2550–2400 B.C.
University of Pennsylvania Museum of Archaeology
and Anthropology, Philadelphia 30-12-560

The gold wire that forms this large pendant
found in the cemetery at Ur (see cat. no. 76) is
shaped into a double spiral. Although the excavation report does not indicate the position of
the pendant,[1] its placement in a very young
child's grave perhaps reflects the use of such
spiral ornaments as amulets by pregnant women
(see entry for cat. no. 246 and note 7). Pins and
pendants with similar double spirals are known
from sites in Anatolia, Iran, Central Asia, and
the Indus Valley, suggesting that the transmission
of artistic motifs (both their forms and their
meaning) occurred along the trade routes that
linked the region.   PC

1. Woolley 1934, p. 574.

78

String of beads with quadruple-spiral pendant

Gold, carnelian, and lapis lazuli
L. 14.5 cm (5¾ in.)
Mesopotamia, Ur, sixth expedition
Early Dynastic IIIA, ca. 2550–2400 B.C.
University of Pennsylvania Museum of Archaeology
and Anthropology, Philadelphia B17650

These beads were found at Ur loose in the
soil. Because they had originally been strung
using organic material that had disintegrated,
it is not certain if they were ever associated.
They attest to the importance of long-distance
trade in precious materials in the third millennium B.C. The lapis lazuli, for example, would
have originated in the Badakhshan region of
Afghanistan, and the carnelian would have
reached Mesopotamia from sources in Iran or,
more likely, the Indus Valley. Dominating this
collection is a pendant made of two pieces of
gold wire twisted around each other to form a
vertical center. The ends of the wire are coiled
into four separate cones, and the resulting

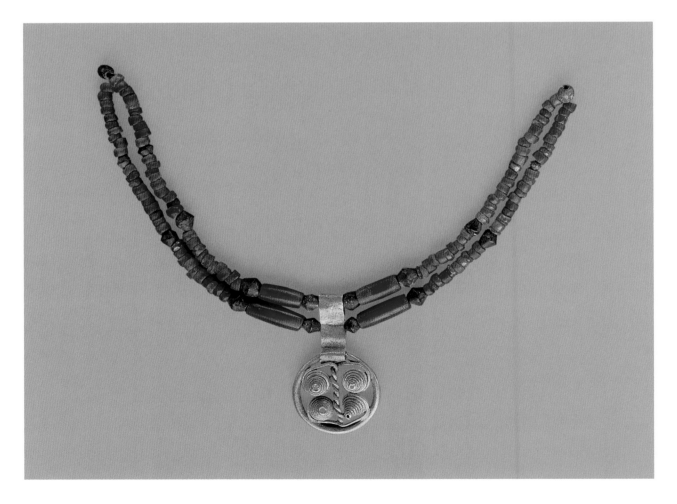

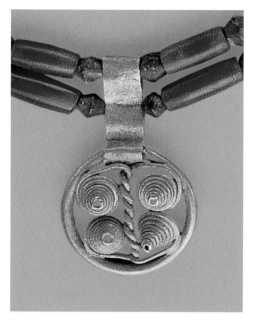

quadruple spiral is fixed into a circle of gold. A number of similar pendants were discovered in the Royal Cemetery. On more elaborate examples, the gold circle is decorated with lapis lazuli beads.[1] Coiled gold wire was also used at Ur to form individual cone-shaped beads and double-spiral pendants (see cat. no. 77). Although made using a different technique, such coiled pendants may be related to the tradition of quadruple- and double-spiral beads found widely outside of southern Mesopotamia (see "Art and Interconnections in the Third Millennium B.C.," by Joan Aruz, in this catalogue).   PC

1. Zettler and Horne 1998, p. 111, no. 67.

Detail, cat. no. 78.

79a, b

Strings of etched carnelian and other beads

Gold, carnelian, and lapis lazuli
Mesopotamia, Ur
Early Dynastic IIIA, ca. 2550–2400 B.C.

a. L. 14 cm (5½ in.)
PG 453, U.8931b
University of Pennsylvania Museum of Archaeology and Anthropology, Philadelphia   B16799

b. L. 10.5 cm (4⅛ in.)
Seventh expedition
University of Pennsylvania Museum of Archaeology and Anthropology, Philadelphia   30-12-573

These beads, like those in catalogue number 78, indicate the importance of long-distance

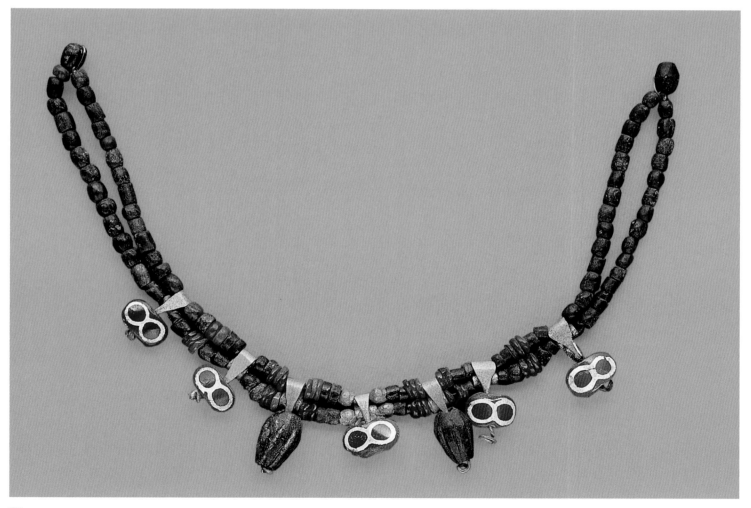

79a

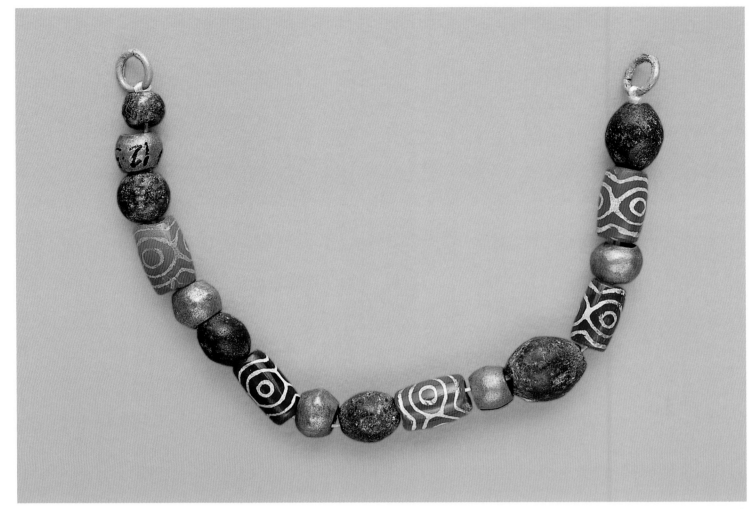

connections in the trade of precious materials in the third millennium B.C. The lapis lazuli would have originated in the Badakhshan region of Afghanistan, and the gold could have reached Mesopotamia from a number of areas since there were ancient sources in Iran, Anatolia, and even as far away as Egypt.

The etched carnelian beads further demonstrate the extent of this trade. A tradition of decorating beads by etching originated in the Indus Valley, although it appears to have been adopted and developed in other places (see "Beads of the Indus Valley," by Jonathan Mark Kenoyer, and "Art and Interconnections in the Third Millennium B.C.," by Joan Aruz, in this catalogue). Julian Reade identifies nine basic groups of etched beads excavated at Ur.[1] Within these groups are approximately forty-six different designs. Exact counts for each design type are difficult to make, however, as individual types of beads were not always recorded by excavators. Only six types of Indus beads duplicate Mesopotamian types. Many barrel-shaped beads, for example, such as those decorated with double concentric circles framed by curving lines, as seen in the second necklace (cat. no. 79b), are known from Ur, and this design is certainly close to that used on some beads found in the Indus Valley. Nonetheless, the five carnelian beads with a figure-eight design in the first necklace (cat. no. 79a) are the only ones in this group that can be positively identified, by virtue of their design, as imports from the Indus Valley.

PC

1. Reade 1979.

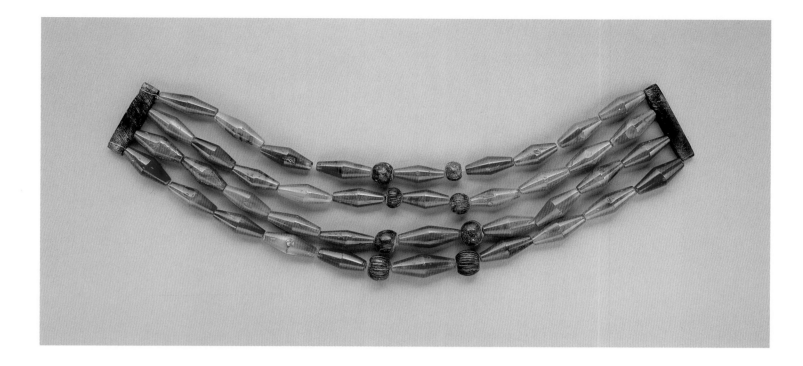

80

Strings of beads

Carnelian, lapis lazuli, and shale
L. 43 cm (16⅞ in.)
Mesopotamia, Ur, PG 55, U.8011
Early Dynastic IIIA, ca. 2550–2400 B.C.
University of Pennsylvania Museum of Archaeology
and Anthropology, Philadelphia B16811

In the remains of a very disturbed but rich grave, Leonard Woolley found a mass of beads crafted in gold, lapis lazuli, carnelian, and shell. Unfortunately the bones in the grave had disintegrated, and accompanying objects, including these beads, were in disorder, piled together in one area. It appeared to Woolley that the tomb, which may have been a royal one, had been robbed. The remaining contents, like the goods found in the other royal tombs at Ur, clearly demonstrate the commercial and/or diplomatic links between southern Mesopotamia and the Indus Valley civilization.

The carnelian beads on this string are double conoids, like those on the belt from Mohenjo-daro, although slightly smaller (see cat. no. 279). Woolley found them arranged in four parallel strings (he does not refer to the shale spacers as part of this group).[1] In addition there are two gold double conoids that apparently alternated with lapis balls, four of which are ribbed. Although the order of the beads is not certain, they would have made a very heavy necklace, which suggests that— like those from the Indus Valley—the beads were worn as a belt.   PC

1. Woolley 1934, pp. 148–49, 527.

For additional objects from Ur, see catalogue numbers 290b, 291a, b.

CITIES OF THE NORTH

The friendship of Ebla is not good, better to establish good
friendship with Mari.

Letter from the ruler of Adu found at Ebla

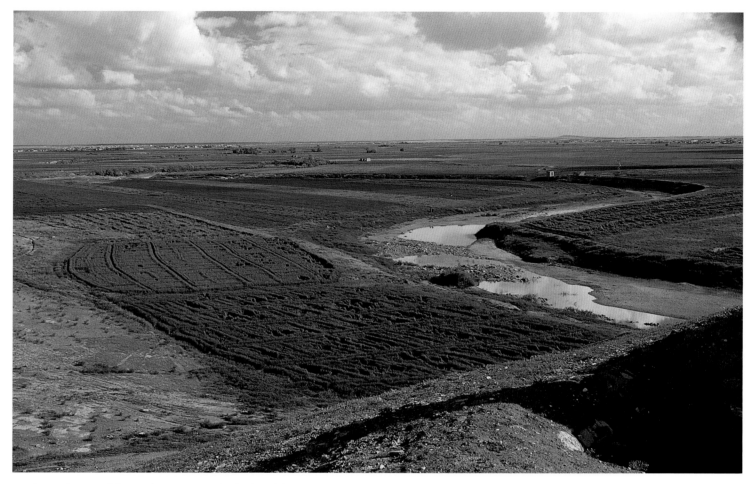

A minor tributary of the Euphrates crosses the Syrian plain.

MARI AND THE
SYRO-MESOPOTAMIAN WORLD

JEAN-CLAUDE MARGUERON

After thirty-seven excavation campaigns conducted between 1933 and 2001 at Tell Hariri, the ancient city of Mari, the site stands as the foremost source for understanding the third millennium B.C. in the northern Syro-Mesopotamian region. The city, constructed on the Euphrates River at the midpoint of its long journey across the Syrian plateau, is located at the junction of three major regions: Mesopotamia, with Iran and the Gulf as its backdrop; northern Syria, encompassing the Khabur basin and the foothills of the Taurus Mountains, which were deeply rooted in the Anatolian world; and western Syria, which established the connection to the major north-south route between Anatolia and the Levant and provided access to the Mediterranean world. This position on a major communications axis, which drew from the entire Mesopotamian basin, secured Mari a preeminent role in the developing economic relations that gave birth to the urban age.

MARI: GEOGRAPHICAL ENVIRONMENT AND TOPOGRAPHY

Excavations have shown that Mari was founded about 2900 B.C. and built on virgin soil according to a circular plan about 1,920 meters in diameter.

The geographical environment was largely unfavorable for the establishment and development of a city: it consisted of an arid or semiarid expanse on either side of a narrow valley, partially covered with an infertile crust. The arable region was limited to the major riverbed and the most recent (Holocene) terrace, which could not provide adequately for the needs of a dense population. Rainfall was insufficient and poorly distributed through the year—fourteen centimeters at Mari's elevation (natural farming methods require twenty-four and a half)—and river levels were marked by extreme annual variations and

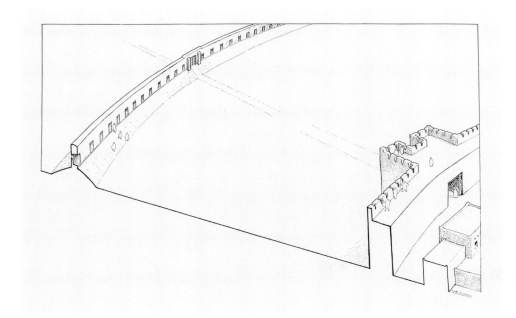

Fig. 38. Reconstruction of the outer embankment, interior rampart, and gate of City II, Mari. Early Dynastic III, ca. 2550–2250 B.C.

dangerous spring flooding. The founders of the city, aware of these difficulties, sought to manage the region as a whole. They established the city on the terrace a few kilometers from the river, surrounding it with a dike to protect it from floods and connecting it to the river by a diversion canal. They also set up an irrigation network with a large canal on the west bank, where the cultivable terrace was at its fullest extent.

But why did they undertake such a task? The creation of Mari was the result of the desire of a political power to secure control of the river traffic that united Syria and Mesopotamia and to assure the safety of the city's system for supplying metallurgical products, which were undoubtedly the basis of its wealth. Proof of this is provided, first, in the number of metalworking furnaces and workshop installations uncovered in the most ancient layers of the city, and, second, by the navigation canal—121 kilometers long—built between dams in the valley, and partly dug into the plateau, connecting the Khabur to the Euphrates at Abu Kemal.

Mari was thus the fruit of a new and dynamic way of thinking linked to the emergence of cities: a way of thinking that integrated the city into its geographical environment and made the kingdom a complex organism that managed its economic life within the framework of the activities of the Syro-Mesopotamian world.

The territorial core of the kingdom integrated the area formed by that portion of the valley included between two natural choke points: one to the north formed by the confluence of the Khabur with the Euphrates, assuring it a secure place at the foot of the Taurus Mountains via the river's rich cereal plain; the other to the south in the area formed by the cliffs of Baghouz near Abu Kemal.

THE FOUNDING OF MARI AND CITY I (EARLY DYNASTIC I AND II, CA. 2900 – 2550 B.C.)

From City I, which is buried deep in the ground and hence difficult to reach, excavations have unearthed a defense system composed of a circular embankment that protected it from floods and an inner rampart 6.7 meters thick that provided defense against enemies. One of the gates of the city has been uncovered. The road system is known only from a single street beginning at the center of the upper city and ending at the gate. Two districts have been studied: they were largely devoted to artisanal activities—smelting, dyeing, pottery making. A few residential houses have been identified, but temples and palaces are still unknown to us, which no doubt explains why we have few art objects with which to characterize this period.

A long interval of abandonment, probably beginning toward the end of Early Dynastic II (or the very start of ED III), marked the conclusion of that first period of Mari's history. The reasons for this eclipse are not known.

THE REFOUNDING OF MARI AND CITY II (EARLY DYNASTIC III AND THE AKKADIAN DYNASTY, CA. 2450 – 2200 B.C.)

In about 2450 B.C., that is, during Early Dynastic III, after the period of Mari's abandonment, an undoubtedly new population arrived. Upon the leveled ruins of City I, these people rebuilt the city following highly developed techniques and new principles, the origins of which have not been clearly identified at any known site in Mesopotamia or Syria. There is persuasive evidence of a true urbanism, not only in the layout of the defensive system but also in the structure of the new city, with its political, religious, and economic sectors and its living quarters. Before any construction began, a system of roads was planned and set in place, ensuring the rapid elimination of rainwater, either through drainage along the wide streets descending from the center of the tell or through absorption via a substrate of gravel beneath the transverse streets.

City II lasted three centuries, straddling Early Dynastic III and the Akkadian dynasty. It was closely connected to sites in Syria (Ebla and Emar) and Mesopotamia (Kish and Ur, in particular). And it was destroyed by Naram-Sin, the ruler of the Akkadian dynasty—the first dynasty to unite Mesopotamia—during his great conquest of the western and northern regions of the empire. Of the three cities of Mari, City II is the most completely known. The outer embankment was made higher, and it was surmounted by a first wall of defense, relatively light but sufficient for the protection of archers placed on the front line. The interior rampart was rebuilt at its original location, as was, in all probability, the identified gate (fig. 38). The road system was composed of large radial streets starting in the upper city and connected so that the network resembled a spider's web. The residential areas contain several houses that have yielded evidence of everyday life.

The royal palace (fig. 39) was built in the heart of the upper city and has a peculiarity unique to Mesopotamia, in that it is both a palace and a temple. The excavation is far from complete, but it has been possible to identify four successive architectural phases covering the entire period. Only two small

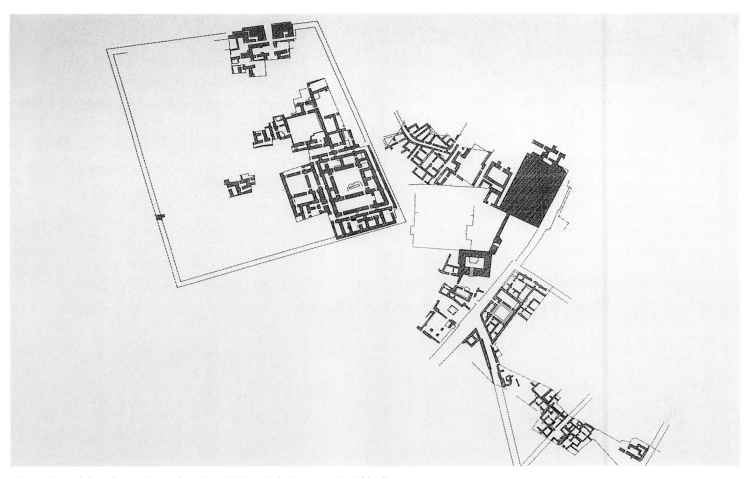

Fig. 39. Plan of the palace and temples, City II, Mari, Early Dynastic III–Akkadian, ca. 2550–2159 B.C.

sectors of the building from the two early phases (P-3 and P-2) are known; for the final phases (P-1 and P-0), dating from the Akkadian period, only the eastern half is known. The eastern section includes a temple, the largest in the city, called the Enceinte Sacrée (Sacred Enclosure); the area of the palace gate; a pillared throne room; a great hall with three double wood pillars leading to the temple; and units that are difficult to define. This structure is undoubtedly the most monumental of any palace from the period yet to be unearthed; it is also among the most innovative in its architectural techniques.

Six temples from City II have been unearthed: two are incomplete or unimportant (the Shamash and Ishtarat temples); the mound known as the *massif rouge* is the oldest temple-tower known; and the other three—the Ishtar, Ninni-zaza (fig. 40), and Ninhursanga temples—are, along with the Enceinte Sacrée, perfectly representative of the sacred architecture of Mari. In each there is a large covered hall where offerings were made

and which provided access to the room where the god was enthroned. In the Ninhursanga and Ishtar temples this room was very compact in form; in the Enceinte Sacrée and Ninni-zaza temples it was very elongated. These halls sometimes reached remarkable dimensions, about sixteen meters to a side for the Enceinte Sacrée, for example. The hall in the Ninni-zaza temple was equipped with a baetyl, an oblong aniconic stone, standing in its center. In various locations of the Ninni-zaza temple, worshipers dedicated statuettes to the deity that depicted themselves in the attitude of prayer or adoration. The baetyl and the temple-tower may be of Syrian origin, whereas the other features appear more Mesopotamian, though no precise model has been proposed.

These temples, burned down by the king Naram-Sin, housed significant religious materials. In addition to famous statuettes, such as those of the king Ishqi-Mari (formerly read as Lamgi-Mari; cat. no. 88), the superintendent Ebih-Il, and the

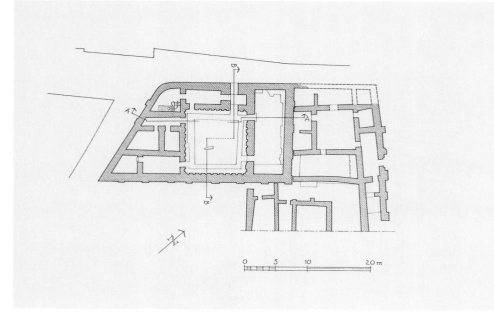

inger Ur-Nanshe (cat. no. 91), there were remains of mosaic panels (see cat. nos. 96, 100, 102, 104); stone vases, some of them sculpted (see cat. nos. 94, 231, 232); exotic and costly shells; copper-alloy tools and receptacles; and various objects made of precious metals.

THE RECONSTRUCTION OF MARI AND CITY III (SHAKKANAKKU AND AMORITE PERIODS, CA. 2200 – 1750 B.C.)

The general reconstruction that resulted in City III, following the destruction inflicted by Naram-Sin, can be attributed to the new dynasty of the Shakkanakku (literally, "governor," the title used by Mari kings of the period). Palaces and temples, large residences, and private houses were erected on the leveled ruins of City II. New principles presided over the architectural organization, but the structure of the city still followed that of City II.

It was under the Shakkanakku that Mari shone for the last time; the city declined markedly under the ensuing Amorite dynasty (mainly during the reigns of Iahdun-Lim and Zimri-Lim) and under the brief domination of the Assyrian king Samsi-Addu (Shamshi-Adad), who united north Mesopotamia under his rule. Mari's fate was sealed with its seizure and by the fire set by another Amorite king, Hammurabi of Babylon, in

about 1750 B.C. Owing to that destruction thousands of cuneiform clay tablets were preserved in the ruins, and it is because of them that the life of the kingdom under the Amorite dynasty is the best known.

THE SIGNIFICANCE OF MARI

Mari's preeminent importance lies in the fact that it represents an example of a city dating from the beginning of the urban age. In addition, Mari occupied a central position between the northern mountains and the alluvial plains of the southern Mesopotamian region, which it used to its advantage in controlling trade and securing its power. As a result, any political or economic event affecting the surrounding regions had repercussions for Mari. Hence this city midway along the Euphrates reveals much about the Syro-Mesopotamian world as a whole. The decline or disappearance of urban activity in Mari was the sign of a grave crisis in one or another of these regions. Conversely, Mari prospered only during periods of intense activity and economic wealth in each of these regions.

The study of Mari itself, from its founding in the early third millennium B.C. to its end in the beginning of the second millennium B.C., then, allows us to define the evolution and history of the Near East.

The Treasure of Ur from Mari

The legend of the Treasure of Ur goes back to April 17, 1965, when, by the weak light of a petroleum lamp, André Parrot and his coworkers at Mari began to sift through their findings.[1] A few days before, beneath the floor in Court XXVII of the so-called pre-Sargonic palace, the excavators had discovered a container that they at first took to be a funerary jar (fig. 41). Only after removing the lid, which consisted of two small bowls, and catching a glimpse of what was inside did they realize that this unremarkable jar contained a treasure. In the two days that were spent unpacking the vessel, the excavators counted more than one hundred separate objects—a spectacular pendant; beads of lapis lazuli, carnelian, and gold; amulets, bracelets, and pins; seals made of shell; and copper-alloy and ivory statuettes (cat. nos. 81–87). These were all catalogued in their subsequent publication in fifty-two numbered entries.

The precious contents, the findspot inside a palace, and the particular circumstances of the find have given rise to much speculation regarding the provenance, ownership, and time of the deposit.[2] The primary focus of nearly all the discussion has been the "Mesanepada bead" (cat. no. 84), whose inscription has been translated in various ways, leading to conflicting interpretations. The first person to work on the inscription, Georges Dossin, understood the hoard as a gift from king Mesanepada of Ur to his counterpart in Mari.[3] Wolfram von Soden considered it more probable that the king of Mari had collected the objects as a gift for Mesanepada but had somehow been prevented from sending them.[4] Both theories rested on the assumption that the pieces in the Treasure of Ur constitute a coherent group of objects and thus were produced either in Mari or in Ur. Subsequent stylistic consideration of individual pieces and of comparable examples from northern Mesopotamia, the middle Euphrates region, and the Diyala territory, however, has led scholars to view the find as a more complex collection.[5] In this new interpretation, the carefully buried hoard was made up of some objects produced in Mari itself and some from other centers.

The find continues to raise more questions than it answers. How, for example, did a bead with an inscription naming the king of Ur find its way to Mari? Was it possibly donated to a deity there, or was it, like the later agate bead of the Kassite king Kurigalzu, taken as booty?[6] How does the group of fourteen cylinder seals fit in? If one compares them with the seals from the

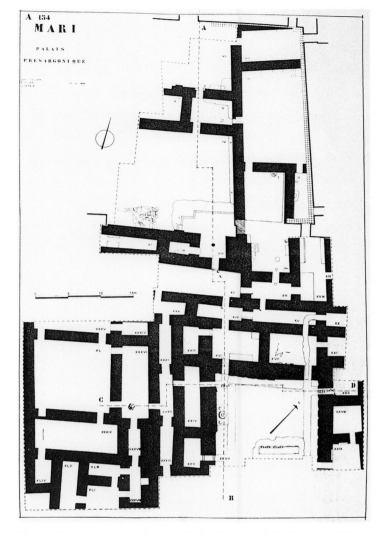

Fig. 41. Plan of the palace, Mari, with the findspot of the Treasure of Ur indicated. Early Dynastic III, ca. 2550–2250 B.C.

vase à la cachette (cat. nos. 203, 204), a hoard from Susa, the similarities in material and style are quite striking.[7] Who commissioned these seals without ever using them,[8] and how did they find their way into the collection? Were the contents of the jar perhaps remainders from the inventory of a temple associated with the location of the find? Closer investigation of Court XXVII, including previous structures on the spot, led researchers to conclude that there had indeed been a palace temple, with a cult chamber and cella, immediately to the south of the court.

The excavation of a level revealing destruction could explain the circumstances of the deposit itself: it is conceivable that these most valuable objects were buried, safely hidden in a jar, in expectation of an enemy attack, and that not only was the jar never discovered but also its owner never returned to retrieve it. Perhaps, however, the hoard was buried as part of some religious rite wholly unrelated to subsequent events.

Although the circumstances of the find and the objects themselves were carefully documented and analyzed, none of these questions can be definitively answered. Perhaps the fascination that the Treasure of Ur holds even today owes something to this wide range of interpretations. The historical value of the Mesanepada bead remains undisputed. At the time of its discovery, its mention of the king of Ur provided the first link between Mari and southern Mesopotamia (see "Problems of Third-Millennium-B.C. Chronology," by Julian Reade, in this catalogue). NC

1. Parrot 1968b, pp. 11–13.
2. Moortgat and Moortgat-Correns 1974, pp. 155–67.
3. Dossin 1968, pp. 53–59.
4. Von Soden 1971, cols. 141–44.
5. Moortgat and Moortgat-Correns 1974, pp. 155–67.
6. The Kassite bead was among a group of objects discovered in the sacred area of the Acropole at Susa; the findspot indicates that they were part of a dedication, very probably to the Elamite god Inshushinak. The inscription on the bead reads, "To Ishtaran, Kurigalzu has dedicated (this)." If the Kassite king Kurigalzu had deposited the bead, one would not expect to find on it the name of Ishtaran, a local deity from Der. It is more likely that the bead's precious material attracted Shutruk-Nahhunte (ca. 1190–1155 B.C.) when he plundered Mesopotamian cities in the twelfth century B.C. and brought the spoils back to Elam. Tallon in Harper, Aruz, and Tallon 1992, p. 153.
7. Aruz in Harper, Aruz, and Tallon 1992, pp. 108–10.
8. The seals show no sign of use. Kohlmeyer 1985, p. 133.

81

Lion-headed eagle pendant

Lapis lazuli, gold, bitumen, and copper alloy
H. 12.8 cm (5 in.); W. 11.9 cm (4⅝ in.); Thickness 1 cm (⅜ in.)
Syria, Mari, Palace, Court XXVII, "Treasure of Ur," M.4405
Early Dynastic IIIB, ca. 2400–2250 B.C.
National Museum, Damascus, Syria 2399

The lion-headed eagle, which combines the qualities of two fearsome predators, is first seen on a seal from the Late Uruk period.[1] Over the course of the Early Dynastic period it took on a largely standardized appearance, with spread wings, wide tail feathers, and the head en face.[2] Despite this fixed form, stylistic differences are found in the configuration of the feathers or the modeling that permit more precise dating within this period.

In the past, scholars very often equated the lion-headed eagle with the mythical bird Imdugud (Akkadian Anzu) because of certain images and the cuneiform inscription on Gudea's Cylinder A; however, this identification creates several problems.[3] Ronald Wallenfels[4] has suggested that Anzu may also be associated with a winged dragon with water flowing from its mouth (see, for example, cat. no. 142).

This pendant from the Treasure of Ur, executed in hammered gold and lapis lazuli, is distinguished by its extraordinarily fine and detailed workmanship. The head and the tail feathers, affixed to the body with copper wire, are of sheet gold over a core of bitumen. The body with its outspread wings was cut from a piece of lapis lazuli and decorated with a fine network of incised lines in a herringbone and lozenge pattern. The very slender legs,

also incised on the lapis lazuli, are spread to the sides. The back was polished but otherwise unornamented. The head, with upright ears and closed muzzle, bends slightly forward. The relatively large eye sockets were filled with bitumen; if there were inlays, they have not survived.[5] The nose is fully three-dimensional, with delicate prickings and lines indicating whiskers. A wide ruff extends up to the ears. Two small rosettes above the eyes were impressed with a punch.

Similar pendants have been found at Tell Asmar and Tell Brak (see cat. no. 158c).[6] The size and placement of two drilled holes in this lion-headed eagle from Mari indicate that it was affixed to a chain, as are comparable examples from Ur.[7] The pendant, like similar pieces, may have served as an apotropaic amulet. Its very high quality workmanship suggests that it was commissioned or owned by a royal patron. NC

1. Orthmann 1975, fig. 125b.
2. Fuhr-Jaeppelt 1972.
3. Hruška 1975; Braun-Holzinger 1987–90, p. 96; Annus 2001.
4. Personal communication.
5. See Woolley 1934, pl. 124.
6. Frankfort 1934a, figs. 28, 29; R. Matthews 1994, figs. 7–9.
7. Woolley 1934, pls. 140, 142.

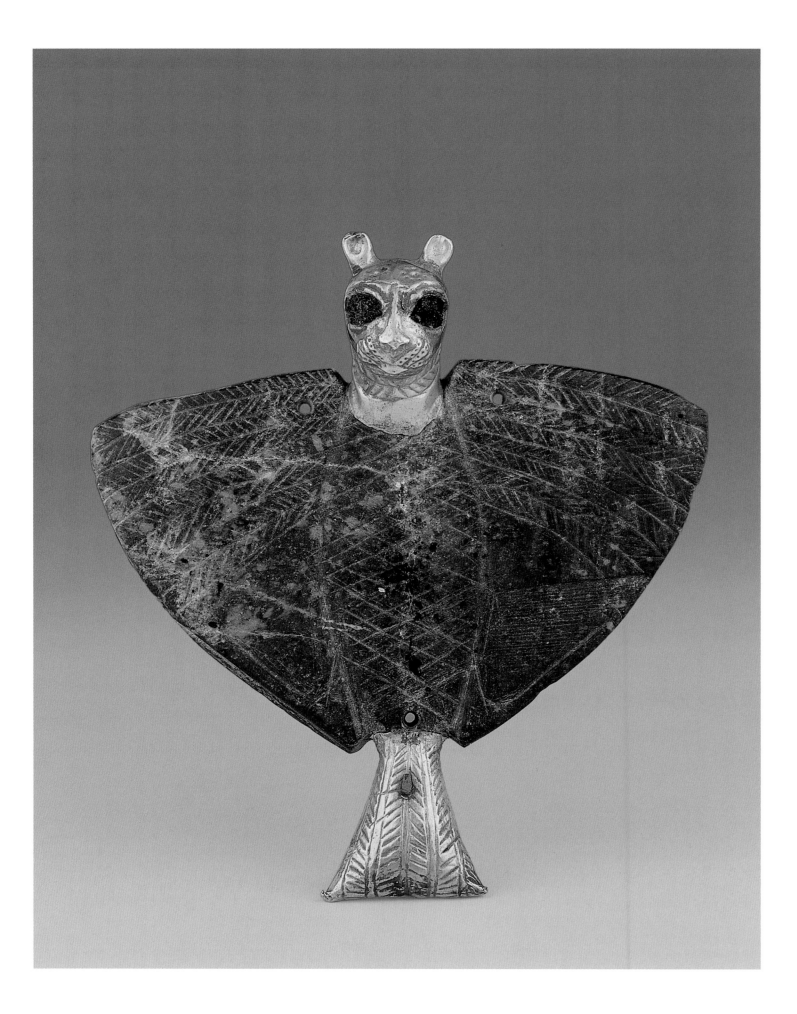

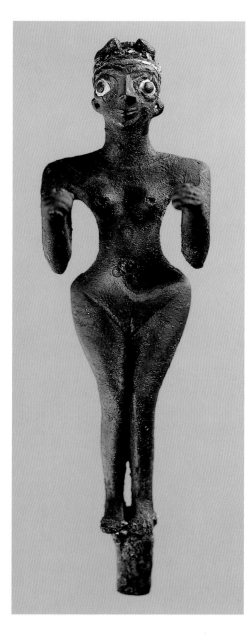

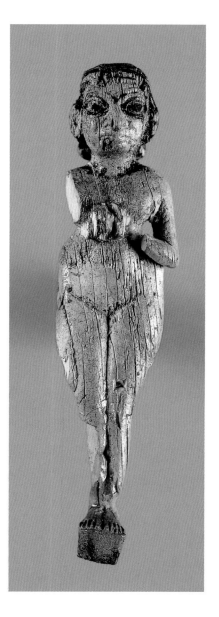

The figure is distinguished by delicate modeling and its suggestion of movement. The large, thick-rimmed eyes, with shell inlays and lapis lazuli pupils, give lively expression to the face. The wedge-shaped nose protrudes sharply in profile; two simple loops stand for the ears. With its turned-up corners, the little mouth seems to present a gentle smile. The silver-plated hair, parted in the middle, is rolled into a bun at the back that is secured by a narrow gold band. Gold inlays were used to indicate the delicately curving eyebrows. On the head is a pair of horns. The strikingly broad shoulders balance the projecting hips. The small breasts are naturalistically rounded. Nipples, navel, groin, vulva, and the cleft between the buttocks were carefully modeled, and some details were inlaid. The depressions above the buttocks were inlaid with lapis lazuli. The elbows are held away from the body, and the arms, with balled fists, point upward at an angle. The slender legs, modestly kept together, are slightly separated above the ankles. Both the techniques employed and the specific stylistic details place the piece in the late Early Dynastic period.   NC

1. Braun-Holzinger 1984, pp. 13–14.

83

Standing nude female figure

Ivory, shell, and black paste
H. 8.4 cm (3¼ in.); W. 2.2 cm (⅞ in.)
Syria, Mari, Palace, Court XXVII, "Treasure of Ur,"
M.4404
Early Dynastic IIIB, ca. 2400–2250 B.C.
National Museum, Damascus, Syria 2424

Despite breaks on one side of this small ivory figure, the sensitive execution of both the nude body and the head is apparent. The contrasting colors provided by the inlaid eyes and eyebrows and blackened hair give the face a lively expression. The heavy shock of hair beneath a narrow band is shaped into a square bun and pinned up at the neck. Unlike the copper-alloy figure in the Treasure of Ur (cat. no. 82), this sculpture has narrow shoulders and a very high waist. The lower arms are raised and the hands placed beneath the breasts. Particular significance appears to have been accorded the buttocks, which are amply rounded and take up two-thirds of the upper body. The legs stand together; the feet, with delicately rendered toes, are supported by a

small base. A short black chain adorns the neck, with a small section hanging down from the clasp in back. It is clear that the figure was intended to be seen not only from the front but from the side and back as well.

The closest parallels in terms of material, modeling, hairstyle, and the position of the hands are provided by a small number of ivory figures from the Ishtar temple in Ashur. They came to light in Layer G, pointing to a date in the late Early Dynastic and Akkadian periods.[1] The face of the Mari figure also shows a certain similarity to that of the statuette of a female supplicant from Ur that dates to the late Early Dynastic period.[2] Two comparable pieces in copper alloy were purchased on the art market and their provenance is uncertain.[3]

Whether this figure and a second small one from the Treasure of Ur that is in poorer

82

Standing nude goddess with horned headdress

Copper alloy, gold, silver, lapis lazuli, shell, and bitumen
H. 11.3 cm (4½ in.); W. 3.2 cm (1¼ in.); Thickness 3 cm (1⅛ in.)
Syria, Mari, Palace, Court XXVII, "Treasure of Ur,"
M.4403
Early Dynastic IIIB, ca. 2400–2250 B.C.
National Museum, Damascus, Syria 2366

The small metal figure, unique in the Treasure of Ur, depicts a nude goddess with raised arms. The short rod that projects from the feet suggests that the statuette was originally mounted on a base, although the rod could merely be the remains of a plug that was not ground off after casting.[1]

condition were carved at Mari or in Mesopotamia cannot yet be determined. Given the figure's size, it may have been carved from a hippopotamus tooth, but since more precise analysis of the material has not been undertaken, this is mere speculation. Written sources from the second millennium B.C. tell us that Egyptian pharaohs went as far as Syria to trap elephants. The Syrian elephant, a smaller relative of the Indian (or Asian) elephant, could thus have been hunted from Mari. However, ivory imports from the Indus Valley cannot be ruled out.[4]

Unfortunately, the situation of this find tells us nothing about the original use of the figure and others like it; we do know, however, that they were considered so precious that their owner deposited them, together with seals and beads, in the Treasure of Ur.

NC

1. Andrae 1922, pl. 29.
2. Orthmann 1975, fig. 4.
3. Braun-Holzinger 1984, nos. 38, 39, pl. 6.
4. Becker 1994, pp. 169–81.

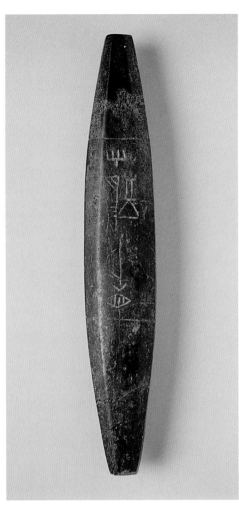

84

Bead naming Mesanepada

Cuneiform inscription in Sumerian
Lapis lazuli
L. 11.8 cm (4⅝ in.); W. 1.9 cm (¾ in.)
Syria, Mari, Palace, Court XXVII, "Treasure of Ur,"
M.4439
Early Dynastic IIIB, ca. 2400–2250 B.C.
National Museum, Damascus, Syria 2409

Ornamental beads with writing are known since the Early Dynastic period. Some have votive inscriptions and others simply carry names. Characteristic of the former is the Sumerian verb form *mu-na-ru,* meaning "consecrated," often in combination with "for his/her life." This eight-faceted, elongated bead from Mari bears a votive inscription that names Mesanepada, king of Ur, as donor. The entire bead survives, with only two breaks on one end. The text consists of seven lines running one beneath the other, parallel to the drilled hole. Because a few syllables are no longer legible, various widely differing translations have been proposed, and contested, since Georges Dossin first published the piece.[1] Votive inscriptions generally follow a strictly

fixed formula, which is taken into account in the following translation:

> For [. . .],
> Mesanepada,
> king of Ur,
> the son
> of Meskalamdug,
> king of Kish,
> has consecrated (this bead).[2]

The first line might end with the name of a goddess, for beads were very often dedicated to a female deity.[3] The Sumerian King List names Mesanepada as the founder of the First Dynasty of Ur, and the length of his reign is given as a legendary eighty or one hundred years.[4] By naming his father, Mesanepada proves his legitimacy as successor to the throne. Both rulers bore the title "king of Kish," which had been adopted by Mesopotamian rulers to evoke the mythological origins of kingship at Kish. The name "Mes-ane-pada" is translated "young man

called by (the god) An."[5] An ancient seal impression from Ur associated with Mesanepada also survives.[6]

Signs of use suggest that the bead was worn for a long time before it was deposited, along with the other objects in the Treasure of Ur, beneath the palace floor. It could have been strung on a chain or suspended from a pin.[7] Possibly a protective amulet or talisman, it would have been meant to ward off evil. Naming the owner's favorite deity was helpful, but the expensive material and blue color were also considered to have magical properties.[8]

NC

1. Dossin 1968, pp. 53–59; Boese 1978, pp. 6–33.
2. Braun-Holzinger 1991, p. 365.
3. Ibid., p. 360.
4. Edzard 1980–83, pp. 77–84.
5. Edzard 1972, pp. 10–14.
6. Woolley 1934, p. 313, pl. 207, no. 214 (U. 13607).
7. Parrot 1962, pl. 12:3; Woolley 1934, pl. 143.
8. Mayer-Opificius 1986, pp. 27–30.

85a–c

Strings of beads

Syria, Mari, Palace, Court XXVII, "Treasure of Ur"
Early Dynastic IIIB, ca. 2400–2250 B.C.

a. Lapis lazuli and carnelian
M.4430, M.4432
National Museum, Damascus, Syria 2407

b. Lapis lazuli and carnelian
M.4431, M.4433, M.4434, M.4436, M.4437
National Museum, Damascus, Syria 2408

c. Gold and lapis lazuli
Weight 24.6 g
M.4407
National Museum, Damascus, Syria 2406

Included in the Treasure of Ur were seventy individual beads made of gold and semi-precious stones; after their discovery they were strung together in modern reconstructions of necklaces and a bracelet. Only the reconstruction of the bracelet can be considered relatively accurate, on the basis of information about the position of its beads in the vessel where they were found.

Necklaces and bracelets made up of many small pieces are rarely found in their original forms, since the string holding them together

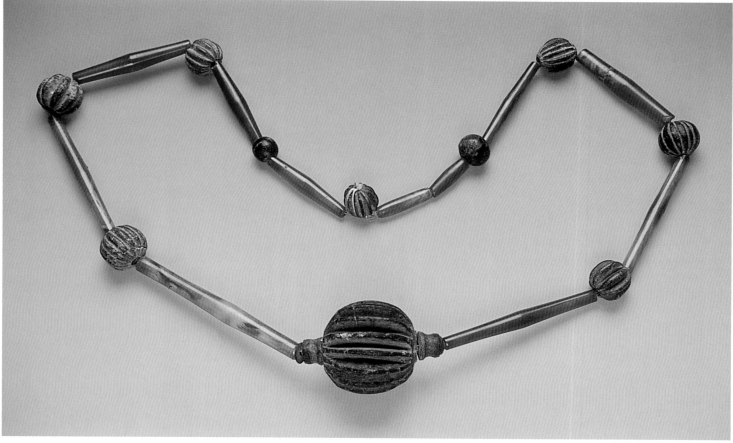

85a

is less durable than the other components and usually has decayed. In his investigation of the royal graves in Ur, Leonard Woolley discovered necklaces and head ornaments that were made up of tiny pieces in situ—that is, in their original placement—and on their original strings. He had the discovery carefully documented so that each piece could be placed in its proper position during later restoration (cat. nos. 72a–g).[1] His observations have been very helpful as well in the reconstruction of the two necklaces from Mari, for not only are these beads from the same period as those in the Ur graves, they are also similar in style.[2]

All three ornaments catalogued here have a single bead in the center, from which the others extend outward in a largely symmetrical

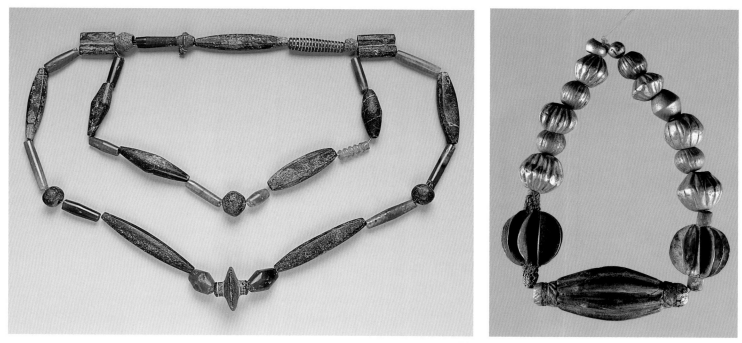

85b

85c

arrangement. Most of the beads are made of lapis lazuli or carnelian. The only ones of gold are in the bracelet. The shapes of the beads are not determined by their material, since there are ribbed spheres with attached rings made both of gold (cat. no. 85c) and of lapis lazuli (cat. no. 85a). There are also beads of simpler shapes, such as biconicals with and without facets, tubes, spheres, ribbed spheres, and beads shaped like dates. The large necklace (cat. no. 85b), made up of thirty-two beads, includes two spacers, so it could hang properly if combined with other strands.[3]

The prosperity of the southern Mesopotamian city-states is mirrored in their trading contacts with centers of the Harappan culture, the most probable source of many of these beads. Established along the Indus, these centers profited from the demand for lapis lazuli and carnelian. From them finished products such as etched carnelian beads found their way into Mesopotamia, Iran, and the Gulf (see cat. nos. 79, 201, 208, 209), although unworked chips were traded as well.

However, faceted carnelian beads, so far discovered only in Mesopotamia, could have been produced locally.[4] Some of the beads from the Treasure of Ur could have been produced in Ur itself, to judge from the Mesanepada bead (cat. no. 84). The finds from Grave JN 4 at Ur suggest as much, for the excavators tell us that they included a bead-cutter's tools and raw materials.[5]   NC

1. Woolley 1934, pls. 131–35, 140, 144.
2. Parrot 1956, p. 27, n. 27; Maxwell-Hyslop 1971, pp. 8–10.
3. Spacers with as many as twelve holes were found at Uruk; Limper 1988, p. 29.
4. Kenoyer 1998, p. 97. The production of long, biconical carnelian beads involved a number of steps, of which drilling presented the greatest risk of damage. Ibid., pp. 160–62.
5. Woolley 1934, pp. 206–7; and for a general discussion of beads from Ur, see ibid., pp. 366–75.

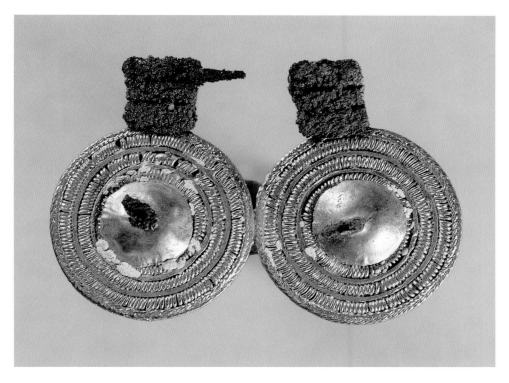

86

Pendant with two roundels

Gold, silver, and lapis lazuli
H. 2.6 cm (1 in.); W. 3.9 cm (1½ in.)
Syria, Mari, Palace, Court XXVII, "Treasure of Ur,"
M.4408
Early Dynastic IIIB, ca. 2400–2250 B.C.
National Museum, Damascus, Syria 2428

This pendant made up of contrasting materials found at Mari is distinguished by its elaborate technique. It consists of two gold disks fused together side by side. On the front of each a bead is set in the center of four concentric patterned bands. According to the excavators' description, each bead was mounted on a piece of lapis lazuli. On the back of the pendant, two hollow-boss hemispheres, also encircled by four concentric patterned bands, ornament the centers of the disks. The pendant hung by two silver loops connected by a slender wire.

Composite disk pendants were also found at Ur and at other sites. Three larger, single-disk pendants of silver that are similar in style, although more delicately worked and without separate loops for hanging, are known from Ur, Tell Asmar, and Uruk.[2] A much less well preserved example from Ur, which according to the find description must originally have been made of two attached disks, was among the grave goods in Grave PG 55.[3] The decoration in its center consisted of seven smaller bosses, a type also documented on two separate ornamental disks from Mari found in an Early Dynastic III grave.[4] The example from Ur not only had the same form as the pendant seen here but also employed a similar type of suspension loop. The parallels suggest the possibility that the pendant from the Treasure of Ur was, in fact, produced at Ur.   NC

1. Woolley 1934, pls. 133, 135.
2. Ibid., pl. 219; Frankfort 1934a, fig. 29; Lenzen 1965, pl. 13.
3. Woolley 1934, p. 527, pl. 219 (U. 8007).
4. Jean-Marie 1999, pp. 132–33, pl. 45; for the dating of this grave, see also Lebeau 1990, pp. 349ff.

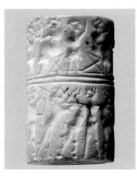

87a

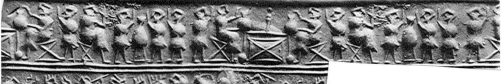

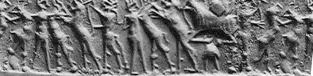

Impression from catalogue number 87a.

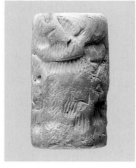

87b

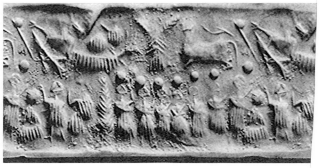

Impression from catalogue number 87b.

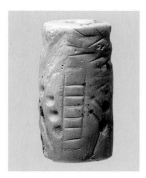

87c

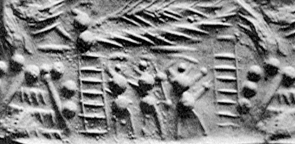

Impression from catalogue number 87c.

87a–c

Cylinder seals with ritual and ceremonial scenes

Shell
Syria, Mari, Palace, Court XXVII, "Treasure of Ur"
Early Dynastic IIIB, ca. 2400–2250 B.C.

a. H. 5.1 cm (2 in.); Diam. 2.8 cm (1⅛ in.)
M.4440
National Museum, Damascus, Syria 2410

b. H. 4 cm (1⅝ in.); Diam. 2 cm (¾ in.)
M.4442
National Museum, Damascus, Syria 2412

c. H. 3.2 cm (1¼ in.); Diam. 1.6 cm (⅝ in.)
M.4451
National Museum, Damascus, Syria 2423

Included in the Treasure of Ur were fourteen cylinder seals made of shell and constituting a group that is uniform in style and subject matter.[1] The largest (cat. no. 87a) presents a scene in two registers separated by an incised horizontal line. The upper frieze shows two people seated on folding stools and positioned symmetrically facing a rectangular banquet table. Each reaches upward with both arms toward a rather large vessel, either a jar without handles or a beaker. At the center of the table stands a staff made of three spheres, one atop the other. This object may be a scale, as André Parrot has suggested, or perhaps some kind of emblem or weapon, since banqueting scenes often represent victory celebrations.

Two smaller figures stand behind the stools, with one or both hands held to their faces. A second group includes a seated man facing a trio of smaller men who stand before a round-bottomed vessel placed on a stand.

The lower frieze contains three scenes. The largest group is a contest scene; it shows, in a heraldic arrangement, a nude hero with his hair standing on end, holding two rampant goats. These look back over their shoulders at two rampant menacing lions, each restrained by a bull-man. A smaller group consists of only three figures: a second hero, also nude and with upright hair, defends a deer that is threatened by a rampant lion. The third scene leaves behind the theme of fighting animals to depict a servant who is half obscured by a disproportionately large recumbent goat, probably a sacrificial animal. This scene could belong with the subject matter of the top register.

The human figures are simply rendered, their faces and bodies all similarly shaped. The seated figures are distinguished from the standing ones only by their larger size. This type of perspective of relative importance is particularly evident on the Standard of Ur (cat. no. 52). The fighting animals, which symbolize a struggle between opposing parties, suggest that the banquet scene can be interpreted as a victory feast.

The second seal (cat. no. 87b) depicts a male deity in a boat in the upper register and the building of a ziggurat in the lower one. The stern of the boat is surmounted by an animal head. Better-preserved examples of the subject show that frequently the prow was fused with the upper torso of an anthropomorphic deity holding a punting pole.[2] On the Mari seal this section is unclear, but here too the prow may take such a form. The god and boat subject, which often appears with other recurring motifs—a bird, a human-headed lion, a vessel,

a plough—may be associated with to a myth centered on the sun god Utu.[3] Behind the boat on this seal are an eagle with outstretched wings and a recumbent quadruped with what is perhaps a plough above its rump.

Not only the lower register of the seal but also the scene on the last seal (cat. no. 87c) focus on the building of a ziggurat. Each shows a group of men, some of whom raise one hand to help balance a round object on their heads. The object in question, by analogy with images on late Early Dynastic votive plaques from Girsu (cat. no. 30; fig. 16) or with later foundation figures (see cat. no. 318), could be a basket filled with clay or bricks.[4] The seal depictions would document the transport of building material to a stepped tower, in one case accompanied by a seated person with an attendant (?) (cat. no. 87b), in the other flanked by two ladders (cat. no. 87c).

The remaining seals from the Treasure of Ur present variations on the contest scene, the banquet scene, and the building of a ziggurat. The images were all executed with a drill and a graving tool. Although the rendition is rather simple, it takes up important themes of

Early Dynastic seal carving. The closest comparable works are mainly from Kish and Tell Asmar;[5] nonetheless, these seals could have been carved at Mari itself. However, motifs such as the banquet and the contest scene are also common on seals and ancient seal impressions from southern Mesopotamia.[6]

Seashells and snail shells are not very hard and for that reason were not commonly employed by seal-cutters in Mesopotamia, except in the early period.[7] Their principal use was in beads and inlay work. One characteristic that recommended shell as a material for seals was the natural hole through the center, which made it easy to string the seal like a pendant.   NC

1. Moortgat and Moortgat-Correns 1974, pp. 158–67.
2. Orthmann 1975, figs. 131c,f.
3. Amiet 1961, pls. 106–9.
4. Orthmann 1975, figs. 65, 85.
5. Amiet 1961, nos. 1441–48.
6. Collon 1987, p. 27.
7. In general, see Gensheimer 1984, pp. 65–73, and Kenoyer 1984, pp. 46–63. For a shell seal in the *vase à la cachette* at Susa, see cat. no. 204.

MARI SCULPTURE

Men, as many as are given names, their statues have been fashioned
since days of old, and stationed in chapels in the temples of the gods:
how their names are pronounced will never be forgotten!

The Death of Gilgamesh

88

Standing figure of Ishqi-Mari (formerly read Lamgi-Mari)

Cuneiform inscription in an early Semitic dialect
Gypsum
H. 27.7 cm (10⅞ in.); W. 10.3 cm (4 in.); Thickness
11.5 cm (4½ in.)
Syria, Mari, Ishtar temple, Level a, room 20, M.174
Early Dynastic IIIB, ca. 2400–2250 B.C.
National Museum, Aleppo, Syria 10406

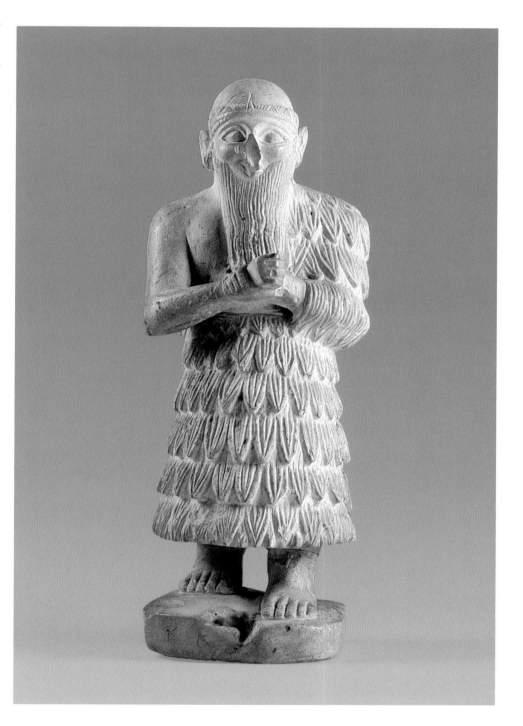

The inscription on this statue, which was
found in the uppermost level of the Ishtar
temple at Mari, begins on the right arm and
continues across the back: "Ishqi-Mari, king of
Mari, the great *ensi* of Enlil, dedicated his
statue to Inanna."[1] Its quality and diminutive
stature do not immediately suggest royal patronage, yet Ishqi-Mari is singular in pose, gesture,
and costume. The ruler steps forward with his
left foot, and because the sculptor dispensed
with the usual support behind the legs, the feet
are massive in order to provide a solid base for
the statue. The heavy, tufted garment covers
the left shoulder and arm, leaving the right
side bare, and has a massive tassel at the back.
The beard begins at the ear in a scalloped
design, falling behind the hands and ending in
curls, and the hairstyle is carefully articulated
as a series of patterns. Ishqi-Mari's long hair is
parted in the middle and rendered in striations
similar to those of the beard. A braid of hatched
triangles encircles the head, and the hair is
bound at the back in a chignon secured by a
double band. Across the forehead, a narrow,
plain band lies underneath the braid, beneath
which a fringe of hair protrudes. Rows of curls
appear below the braid at the back.

This statue of Ishqi-Mari does not resemble
the dedicatory statues of southern Mesopotamian rulers, who wear the tufted skirt and

clasp their hands in front of the chest (see cat. no. 26; fig. 15).[2] At the end of the Early Dynastic period, both the garment and the chignon worn by Ishqi-Mari are of a type found in depictions of rulers in battle (see fig. 52) and of seated deities.[3] The gesture of grasping the clenched right wrist with the left hand is rare. A similar sense of iconographic daring and a more explicit connotation of deification, rather than the subtle allusions expressed here, are characteristic of royal images in the subsequent Akkadian period. In the inscription, Ishqi-Mari refers to himself as "chief *ensi* of Enlil," a title that appears in the epithets of the Early Dynastic IIIB rulers of Lagash as well as in those of Lugalzagezi and Sargon.[4]

JME

1. Cooper 1986, p. 89. For the king's name, formerly read Lamgi-Mari, see ibid., and Krebernik 1984, p. 164.
2. The two other excavated Early Dynastic statues of rulers are those of Lugaldalu, ruler of Adab (cat. no. 26), and Enmetena, ruler of Lagash (Braun-Holzinger 1977, pls. 26e, f, 27d, e).
3. Amiet 1976a, pp. 9–10; Braun-Holzinger 1977, pp. 53–54.
4. Hallo 1957, pp. 47–48.

89a–c

Standing male figures with clasped hands

Gypsum
Syria, Mari, Ninni-zaza temple, room 13, Court XII
Early Dynastic III, ca. 2550–2250 B.C.

a. H. 53.8 cm (21⅛ in.); W. 21 cm (8¼ in.); Thickness 18 cm (7⅛ in.)
M.2076, M.2319, M.2369
National Museum, Damascus, Syria 2076

b. Cuneiform inscription in an early Semitic dialect
H. 104 cm (41 in.); W. 22 cm (8⅝ in.); Thickness 20.5 cm (8⅛ in.)
M.2270, M.2271, M.2307, M.2318, M.2793, M.2855
National Museum, Damascus, Syria 7916

c. H. 54 cm (21¼ in.); W. 20 cm (7⅞ in.); Thickness 23 cm (9 in.)
M.2317, M.2367
National Museum, Aleppo, Syria 7902

The sculpture from Mari has been cited for its vitality, naturalism, and elegance, qualities that are attributed to its careful modeling and slender proportions.[1] Most Mari sculpture is consistent in iconography and style, but the finest

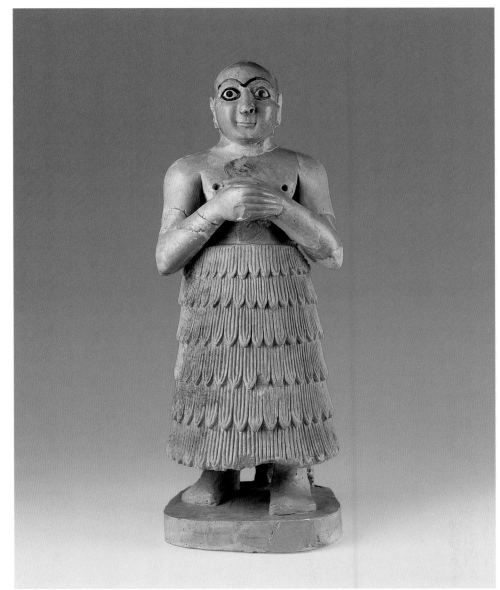

89a

examples are anomalous in pose, gesture, and costume (see cat. nos. 88, 91). The most common type of votive image from the site is a male figure standing with his hands clasped at his chest and wearing a long, tufted skirt. Mari figures typically stand with the left foot forward, a pose that provides a solid base for the statue so that only a minimal stone support behind the legs is needed. A long skirt falls almost to the feet and is usually composed of six rows of tufts, each carved as two loops, one inside the other. The skirt projects out at the waist and has a tassel at the back, either in the middle of the body or on the left side. The arms are held at the sides, and the elbows, at least, are carved free from the body. The upper arms and shoulders are rounded. The facial features themselves are idealized or standardized so that little variation exists from one countenance to the next. Only the lower part

of the face and the inlaid left eye of the first statue (cat. no. 89a) are original.[2] In spite of the heavy restoration, it remains one of the finest statues from Mari. The nose is prominent and carefully carved with the nostrils hollowed out. The cheeks are puffy, and the lips are raised ridges slightly upturned at the corners. Creases run from the nose to the chin.

The second statue (cat no. 87b), inscribed "Ipum-Sar, the exalted scribe," is stiffer and less carefully modeled than the first example.[3] The massive upper arms and shoulders also lack the more delicate proportions common to other Mari statues—perhaps because of the figure's remarkable size. At a little over a meter in height, it is one of the largest surviving Early Dynastic statues.

Many of the details in the rendering of the third figure (cat. no. 89c) are not typical of

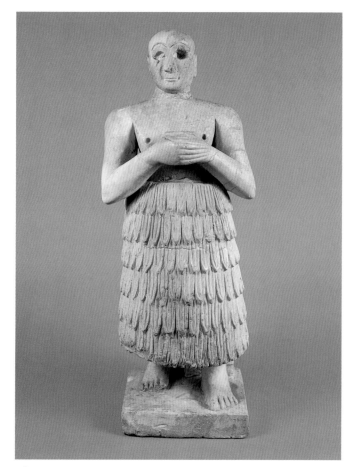

89b

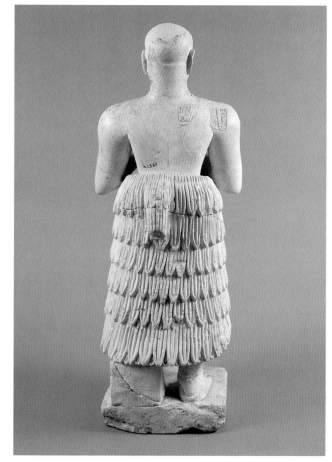

89b

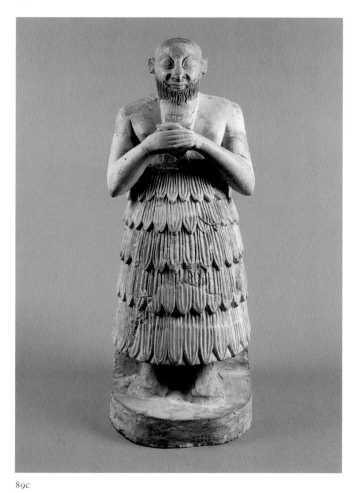

89c

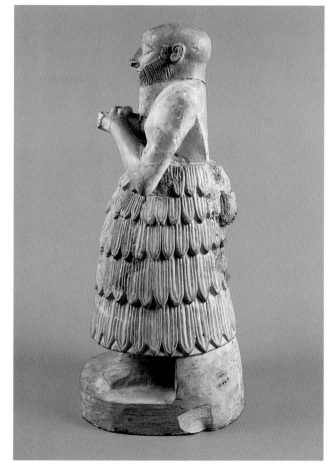

89c

Mari sculpture; struck by this, the excavator dubbed it "the Bedouin," although nothing would indicate that this is indeed a representation of a desert Arab.[4] The large, almond-shaped eyes are sculpted in relief. They must have been painted rather than inlaid, for they still retain faint traces of black coloring, which would have indicated the pupils. The front of the bald head is flat, and the ears protrude. The beard, which is reconstructed at the bottom, is rendered in wavy strands, as are the curls at the ears. The hands are oversized. The excavator noted that there was red coloring on the chest of this figure when it was found, but none of it remains, although some of the black pigment of the beard is still present.

JME

1. Porada 1961, p. 162. Other descriptions of Mari sculpture can be found in Hansen 1975a, nos. 3:24, 26, 30; Spycket 1981, pp. 86–99; Braun-Holzinger 1977, pp. 51ff.
2. Parrot 1967, pp. 59–60.
3. For the inscription, see ibid., p. 315.
4. See ibid., pp. 58–59.

90

Standing male figure

Pink breccia
H. 41 cm (16⅛ in.); W. 16 cm (6¼ in.)
Syria, Mari, Ninni-zaza temple, room 13, M.2347, M.2454
Early Dynastic III, ca. 2550–2250 B.C.
National Museum, Damascus, Syria 2074

The projection in the socle of this standing figure has been drilled to form a circular depression.[1] Although the face of the sculpture is fragmentary, its features are subtly rendered and lack the stylization common in Mari sculpture (see cat. nos. 89a–c). The eyes are carved, not inlaid, and the rims are raised ridges. The eyebrows are softly indicated in relief. Egyptian influence has been suggested for the unusual coiffure, which shows the hair tucked behind the ears and falling forward on the shoulders.[2]

The cubical form of the lower body is emphasized by the division of the skirt into four sections. A row of elongated tufts falls from the waist, around which a second length

of material with a scalloped edge is wrapped. On the sides, the tufts are layered, and the skirt projects out at the back. There are a few other examples of this rare type of skirt, in inlay and in relief carving (see cat. no. 103b). The many iconographic variations in Mari sculpture as a whole indicate that there was a greater freedom to experiment there than at other cities.

JME

1. Moortgat (1968) and Mayer-Opificius (1988) conclude that a cult of the dead existed in the temples of Ishtarat and Ninni-zaza and that libations were made before the statues there. Although it is possible that the circular depression on the base of this statue was designed to hold liquid offerings, the presence of a hole drilled in the bottom of the hollow argues against such an interpretation. Since the figure wears a distinctive type of skirt seen on a staff bearer depicted on an inlay from Mari (cat. no. 103b), perhaps a more likely explanation is that the figure originally held a staff, which was fitted in the depression.
2. Parrot 1967, p. 100.

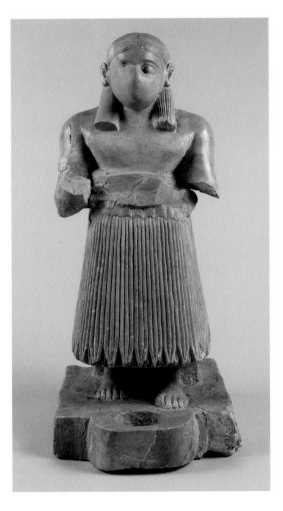

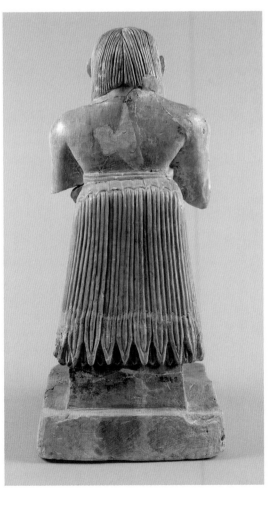

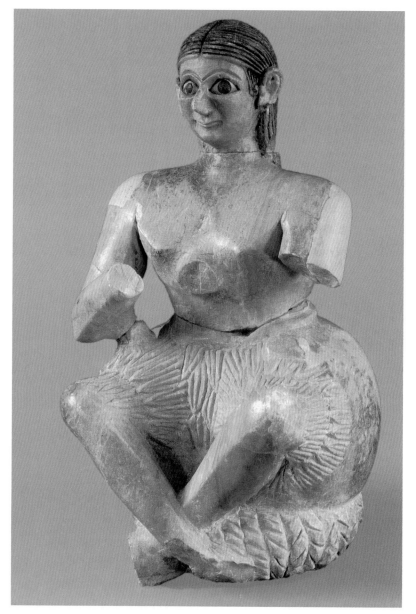

91a

91a, b

Seated figure and torso fragment of the singer Ur-Nanshe

Gypsum
Syria, Mari, Ninni-zaza temple, room 13
Early Dynastic III, ca. 2550–2250 B.C.

a. Statue
Cuneiform inscription in an early Semitic dialect
H. 26 cm (10¼ in.); W. 11.6 cm (4⅝ in.)
M.2416, M.2365
National Museum, Damascus, Syria 2071

b. Fragment
Cuneiform inscription in an early Semitic dialect
H. 12.5 cm (4⅞ in.); W. 16 cm (6¼ in.); Thickness
9.3 cm (3⅝ in.)
M.2272, M.2376, M.2384
Museum of Deir ez-Zor, Syria 21077

The statue of the singer Ur-Nanshe (cat. no. 91a) is a masterpiece of Mari sculpture and one of the great works of art from the third millennium B.C. The inscription on the fragmentary upper body of a second sculpture (cat. no. 91b), which shows a figure holding what is left of a stringed instrument, probably a lyre, helps complete the partially preserved inscription on the shoulder of the first: "For Iplul-Il, king of Mari, Ur-Nanshe the master musician dedicated his statue to INANNA-ZA.ZA (Ninni-zaza)."[1] Ur-Nanshe's posture and unique garment are both executed with a freedom of form that is a hallmark of the art of Mari. In the more complete statue, Ur-Nanshe is seated on a round, woven cushion;

his crossed legs emerge from his tufted, knee-length skirt and are shown in extremely high relief. The tufts are restricted to the front of the skirt, a rendering that has no known parallels, and highlights the sculptor's achievement in depicting the singer's posture. The statue must have been all the more impressive when complete, for the feet were surely represented in the round. The shell and lapis lazuli inlays of the eyes are preserved, and the long hair, parted in the middle, still retains some of its black coloring.

The name Ur-Nanshe is the only Sumerian personal name attested at Early Dynastic Mari, perhaps suggesting the geographic expanse over which singers and musicians may have traveled

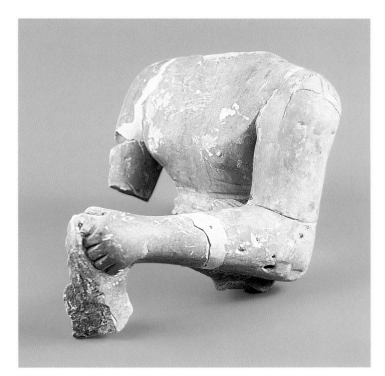

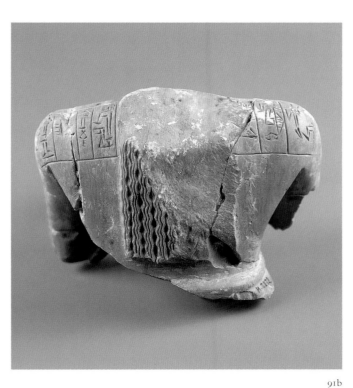

in the Early Dynastic period. The archives of the city of Ebla, for example, list groups of singers and musicians from Mari who were sent to Ebla, a journey of some 350 kilometers.

JME

1. Cooper 1986, p. 89. For a different reading of the inscription, see Boese 1996, in which a persuasive argument is offered against the identification of this figure as Ur-Nanshe.

92a, b

Female figures wearing tall headdresses

Gypsum
Syria, Mari
Early Dynastic III, ca. 2550–2250 B.C.

a. H. 23 cm (9 in.); W. 14 cm (5½ in.); Thickness 34 cm (13⅜ in.)
Ninni-zaza temple, room 13, M.2308, M.2368, M.2383
National Museum, Damascus, Syria 2072

b. H. 25.8 cm (10⅛ in.); W. 6.9 cm (2¾ in.); Thickness 5 cm (2 in.)
Ishtar temple, Level a, M.172
National Museum, Damascus, Syria 10103

The tall, bulbous headdress worn by some of the women who appear in sculpture and inlay from Mari, including these two statues, was

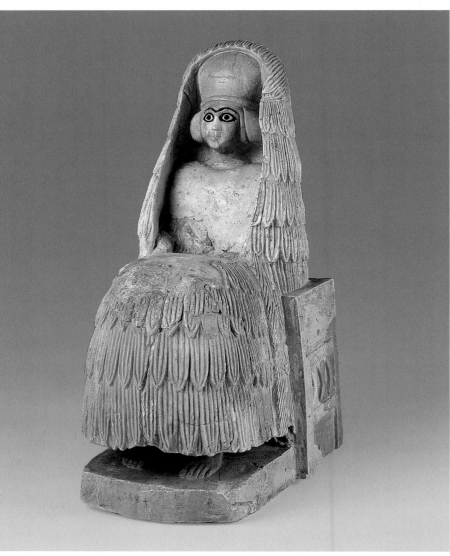

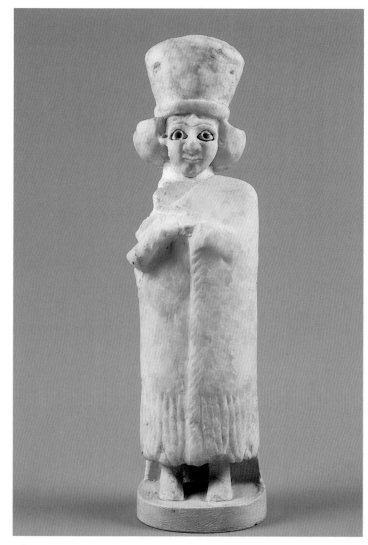

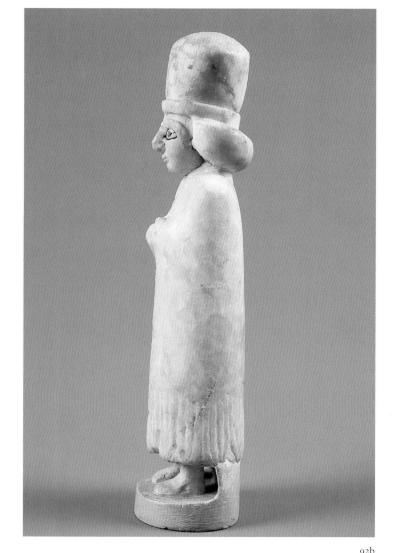

92b

92b

dubbed a *polos* by the excavator. A large piece of tufted fabric is draped over the *polos* of the seated figure (cat. no. 92a). Her upper body and the cube-shaped seat have been heavily restored.[1] Her hair is smooth and gathered at the sides, except around the face, where it is braided. The seat is decorated with a spindle-shaped pattern bordered at the top and bottom by a band of chevrons.

The hair framing the face of the standing woman (cat. no. 92b) was originally inlaid, and her ears are pierced for jewelry; such adornment is typical of sculpture from the Ishtar temple, although unusual outside of Mari.[2] The hairstyle is similar to that worn by the seated figure here, although it is swept out to a point on either side. The smooth garment has a single row of tufts along the hem and a fringed border; it is draped over the left shoulder, leaving the right shoulder and arm free.

Since they wear a unique headdress, women with the *polos* have been referred to as

goddesses, priestesses, and even queens, but the evidence is scant for any of these interpretations.[3] The specific association of the *polos* headdress with priestesses, for example, rests on the evidence of fragmentary inlays from the Dagan temple at Mari. One depicts a woman with a *polos* who is thought to be participating in a cultic scene, since she holds a vessel that the excavator associated with libations.[4] Another inlay fragment from the Dagan temple shows two women who may wear the *polos* flanking an unidentifiable piece of furniture with bull's feet, which some suggest had a cultic significance.[5]

On the inlay from the Dagan temple, women with the *polos* are generally shown with more jewelry than women who do not wear the headdress: they are depicted wearing pins and beads as well as cylinder seals. Such a wealth of adornment, to which the *polos* surely contributes, may reflect status, occasion, or simply fashion.[6]   JME

1. The original appearance of the woman's upper body is suggested by the figure of a seated woman with a *polos* from the Ishtar temple at Mari; Parrot 1956, pl. 37.

2. For example, a female statue from Ur also has inlay, still intact, framing the face (Hansen 1975a, pl. 4); pierced ears and inlaid hair appear on sculpture from Tell Agrab (Frankfort 1943, no. 287).

3. Parrot 1967, p. 97; Strommenger 1971, p. 44; Asher-Greve 1985, pp. 78–79, 81–82. The *polos* may later have come to be associated with goddesses, but a statue of the goddess Narundi, now dated to the Ur III period (Harper, Aruz, and Tallon 1992, no. 55), shows a horned headdress, indicating that, as in the Early Dynastic period, the latter was still the preferred headdress for female divinities. Other reasons for the association of the *polos* with goddesses include the elaborate seats and the high quality of the carving. The seats, however, are not unique to statues of women wearing the *polos*. For example, the decoration of the seat illustrated here (cat. no. 92a) is similar to that on the bench where the couple from Mari sit (cat. no. 93), and the pattern is also be found on inlay from Mari; Parrot 1956, p. 103, fig. 65; Parrot 1967, pl. 60.

4. Parrot 1962, pl. 11, no. 4. The excavator assembled the fragmentary inlay from the Dagan temple into a

panel that shows this type of vessel being used to receive libations, but the reconstruction is entirely modern; ibid., figs. 11, 12.

5. Ibid., fig. 13; Asher-Greve 1985, p. 95. A parallel for the bull's-leg furniture is found at Tell Asmar; Boese 1971, plaque AS4. The fragmentary inlay from the Dagan temple shows women whose heads are missing; probably only one of them wore the *polos* because her cloak is secured with a double pin, whereas other women depicted in inlay without the *polos* have single pins; Parrot 1962, pl. 11.

6. The only two female heads found in the Ninni-zaza temple at Mari show the *polos* (Parrot 1967, pp. 96–99), but female heads without the *polos* were found in the Ishtar temple (Parrot 1956, pp. 84–93). The latter have inlaid hair and pierced ears like statues of women with the *polos*; therefore, although women depicted in inlay with a *polos* wear more jewelry than women who do not, the same distinction cannot be made in sculpture, since females typically have inlaid hair and pierced ears.

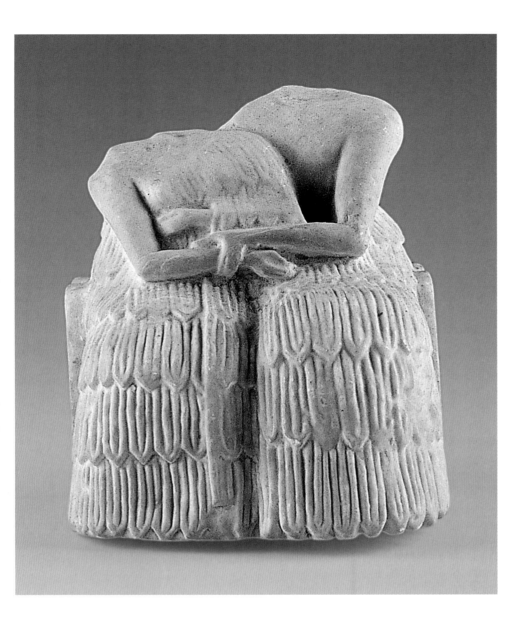

93

Seated couple

Gypsum
H. 12.8 cm (5 in.); W. 9.5 cm (3¾ in.); Thickness 8.5 cm (3⅜ in.)
Syria, Mari, Ishtar temple, Level a, room 17, M.303
Early Dynastic III, ca. 2550–2250 B.C.
National Museum, Aleppo, Syria 10104

This statue from Mari depicts a man and a woman seated together on a bench; the heads of the figures are broken off, and their upper bodies are very worn. The man's tufted skirt is belted at the waist, and his companion's tufted garment drapes over her left shoulder and has a smooth band along the border. Holes drilled into the base of the statue indicate where the feet, carved separately, were once attached and show that the statue was originally mounted on a base. Another drill hole indicates that the head of the woman was also attached separately.

The upper edge of the bench has a scalloped decoration, and the back is embellished with a row of drilled holes framed by bands of chevrons. Although the woman's left arm and the unnatural bend of the man's hand as he grasps her wrist are somewhat awkward in execution, the slightly turned torso of the man breaks the strict frontality that usually governs dedicatory figures. The seated couple is a type of dedicatory sculpture also known at Khafajah and Nippur.[1]   JME

1. See Frankfort 1939, pls. 68, 69 (Khafajah), and Hansen 1975a, fig. 20 (Nippur).

94

Vessel dedicated for Iku-Shamagan

Cuneiform inscription in an early Semitic dialect
Steatite
H. 19 cm (7½ in.); Diam. 22 cm (8⅝ in.)
Syria, Mari, Ishtarat temple, room 6, M.2241
Early Dynastic III, ca. 2550–2250 B.C.
National Museum, Damascus, Syria 2055

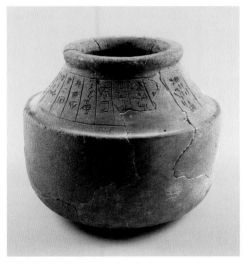

Along with sculpture, stone vessels are among the objects most commonly dedicated in temples. This small restored vessel slopes from its rounded rim to a sharp ridge that marks the transition from neck to body; the base is slightly rounded. A layer of bitumen coats the interior, suggesting that the vessel held liquid. The carefully carved inscription on the neck reads: "For Iku-Shamagan, [king] of Ma[ri], Shuwed[a] the cup-bearer, son of . . . the merchant, dedicated (this vessel) to the river-god and Ishtarat."[1] The name of Iku-Shamagan is also known from two inscribed statues found in the Ninni-zaza temple at Mari.[2] Dedications to a pair of deities are rare. The reference to the river god is among the first known to this deity, whose importance at Mari continued into the second millennium B.C.[3]   JME

1. Cooper 1986, p. 87.
2. Parrot 1967, pp. 309–10.
3. W. Lambert 1985, p. 535.

95

Bull fitting

Diorite and shell
H. 5.8 cm (2¼ in.); W. 4.8 cm (1⅞ in.); L. 13.6 cm (5⅜ in.)
Syria, Mari, Ishtarat temple, room 4, M.2274
Early Dynastic III, ca. 2550–2250 B.C.
National Museum, Damascus, Syria 2057

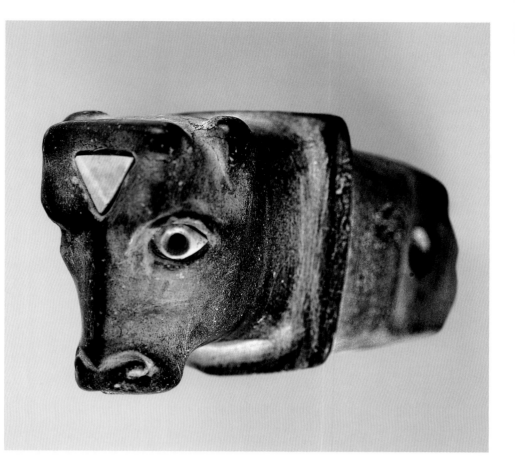

The head and neck of this bull are carved at one end of a single piece of stone. The neck terminates in a thin square block that divides it from the wedge-shaped remainder of the stone. A hole is drilled through the width of the wedgelike part of the stone, which may have been used for a dowel that secured the sculpture to a wood support. The animal's head is slightly bowed; the realistically modeled face looks forward. The strong neck is indicated by two creases behind the ears, which are shown as rounded projections. A straight line forms the bridge of the nose, accentuating the triangularity of the face. The finely modeled snout has flaring nostrils. A piece of drilled shell is inlaid to form the left eye (the inlay of the right eye is missing). Inlaid into the flat front of the animal's head is a triangular piece of shell that is similar to the inserts of various materials on the copper-alloy head of a bull from the Royal Cemetery at Ur, on a goat's head from Nippur (cat. no. 41), and on a piece from farther afield, a standard at Alaca Höyük.[1] The application of such inserts belongs to a long tradition in southern Mesopotamia that went back some five hundred years to works of art created in the Uruk and Jamdat Nasr periods. The triangle probably had a specific meaning beyond its use as decorative detail.   PC

1. Woolley 1934, pp. 125–26 (bull); Koşay 1951, pl. 139 (standard).

96

Inlaid panel with an animal sacrifice scene

Ivory, shell, red limestone, schist; modern frame
H. 21.5 cm (8½ in.); W. 30 cm (11¼ in.)
Syria, Mari, Shamash temple and temple to the northeast of massif rouge
Early Dynastic III, ca. 2550–2250 B.C.
National Museum, Aleppo, Syria 1922

During the 1950s, elements of this frieze were excavated from a number of different locations at Mari and were brought together to suggest a type of frieze that was a popular form of decoration during the Early Dynastic period in Mesopotamia. The arrangement of the ancient inlay pieces is therefore a modern creation.[1] Rectangles, triangles, and diamond-shaped pieces of shell, red limestone, and schist have been set against a modern black mosaic background, bordered at the top and bottom by a modern wood frame. On the left is a large, standing male figure, whose upper torso was discovered in a temple to the northeast of the *massif rouge*.[2] He faces right, his shaved head in profile and his body shown frontally; he is nude above his waist, which is marked by a belt. His hands are held together over his chest in the manner of a votive sculpture. The upper torsos of the two smaller standing figures facing left, together with the most interesting part of the frieze, the slaughter or sacrifice of a goat, were discovered in the Shamash temple.[3] The scene of butchery depicts two males grasping the legs of a goat lying on its back. The figure on the right places his left knee on the throat of the goat, while the man on the left sits on the ground with his left leg bent and his right leg extended, pushing against the animal. A flap of the man's tufted skirt hangs down his back.

This is one of three comparable inlays found in the Shamash temple. Whether the scene represented involves butchery or ritual

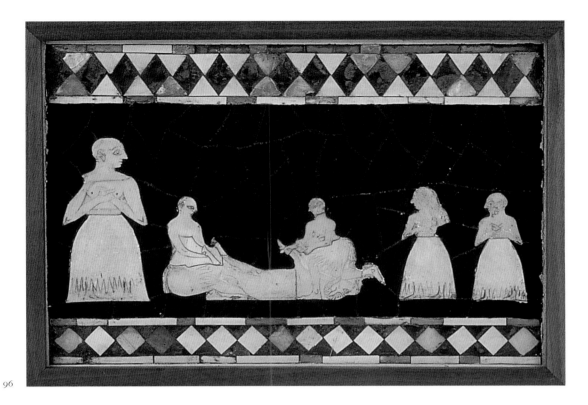

96

slaughter, perhaps related to the temple in which they were found, is unclear. PC

1. Not all of the inlay pieces in the present arrangement appear to have been recorded by the excavator; see Parrot 1952, p. 195, pl. 20:1, and Parrot 1954, p. 163, pl. 18:1–2.
2. Parrot 1952, p. 195, pl. 20.1; Dolce 1978, p. 145, pl. 38.
3. Parrot 1954, p. 163, pl. 18:1–2; Dolce 1978, pp. 142–43, pls. 36, 40.

97

Inlaid frieze of a soldier and prisoner

Shell and schist
H. 13 cm (5⅛ in.); W. 14 cm (5½ in.)
Syria, Mari, Palace, PP1, corridor 49, room 52,
M.4785, M.4793
Early Dynastic III, ca. 2550–2250 B.C.
National Museum, Aleppo, Syria 1968

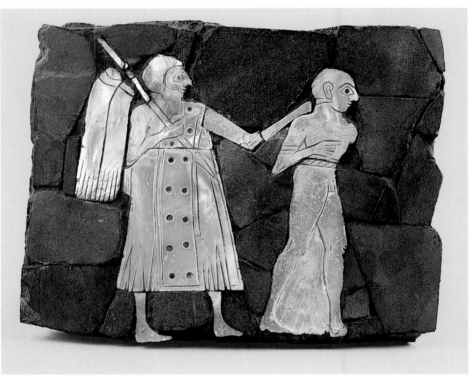

97

Against a background of dark schist, shell inlays depict a soldier using his left hand to hold a nude male prisoner by the right shoulder. The prisoner's arms are bound above the elbow and tied to his torso by a rope; the space between his legs has not been cut away. The soldier is bearded and wears a tight-fitting helmet and an ankle-length skirt with a long, fringed hem. Over his right shoulder he carries a spear with its point down and forward, and from the end of which hangs a double pennant. Suspended from his left shoulder, across his body, is a broad sash with a border and a double row of drill holes that may represent leopard skin or studded leather; it resembles examples worn by figures on the mace-head of Enannatum (cat. no. 35) and on the plaque depicting an archer from Mari (cat. no. 99).

Along with many other similar plaques found at Mari, this would have been part of a mosaic composed of several panels.[1] The image should not be seen as narrating a specific event but rather as expressing the idea of victory through the symbolism of a captured enemy. PC

1. Parrot 1969, p. 202, figs. 11, 12, pl. 15.

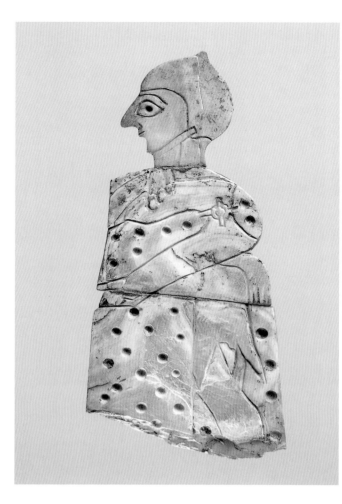

apparent indication of a beard with three curls at the neck on the lower section suggests that the two pieces may not belong together. A wide cloak decorated with drill holes that perhaps represent a spotted leopard's skin (see cat. no. 97) is fastened over the soldier's left shoulder with a circular pin with four radiating elements. The unclothed left arm is positioned across his body. Under the cloak he wears a plain skirt with wide tufts at the hem. One leg is indicated. The lower part of the inlay is missing.   PC

99

Incised plaque with a battle scene

Limestone
H. 14.3 cm (5⅝ in.); W. 10 cm (4 in.); Thickness
1.4 cm (⁹⁄₁₆ in.)
Syria, Mari, Palace, room 46
Early Dynastic III, ca. 2550–2250 B.C.
Museum of Deir ez-Zor, Syria   11233

This incised stone plaque, discovered in the sacred area of the Royal Palace at Mari,[1] is a rare depiction from the Early Dynastic period

98

Inlay of a soldier

Shell
H. 9.5 cm (3¾ in.); W. 4.3 cm (1¾ in.)
Syria, Mari, TH82-260A
Early Dynastic IIIA, ca. 2550–2400 B.C.
Museum of Deir ez-Zor, Syria   3746

This inlay originally would have formed part of a frieze, probably depicting soldiers with a parade of prisoners, as is known from similar examples at Mari and elsewhere (see cat. nos. 48, 97). The soldier wears a tight-fitting helmet, possibly of leather, with a pointed tip, held on by a strap under the chin, like the headgear worn by the soldiers on the Standard of Ur (cat. no. 52). His large eye and eyebrow are shown frontally. He has a prominent nose and a small mouth, typical of inlay works and votive sculpture of the Early Dynastic period. The head and body are made from separate pieces of shell, the figure is beardless, and the

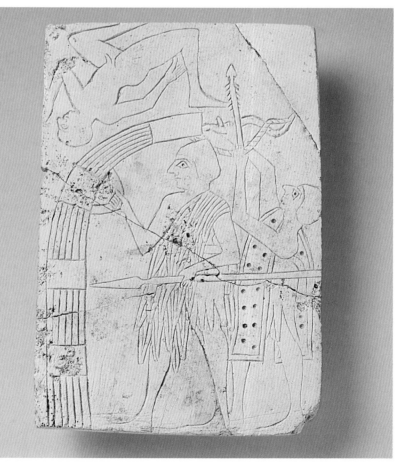

of foot soldiers engaged in combat. Surviving scenes of war show a phalanx of marching soldiers with shields and spears (see cat. no. 52; fig. 52). Here, however, with his right hand, a standing soldier holds the hoop handle of a large, arched shield, possibly made of bound reeds, while in his left hand he grasps a spear, its point forward. He wears a helmet and a knee-length skirt with long, tufted fringe; a tufted sash thrown over his left shoulder hangs down below the knees. Behind the soldier and partially obscured by him stands a second man dressed in a similar fashion except that his sash has a border and is decorated with spots, perhaps to indicate leopard skin. He looks upward as he pulls back the string of a bow with his left hand, in which he also holds an arrow with the feathering close to its head. Although images of hunters and warriors using bows and arrows are known from the Late Uruk period (see figs. 5, 6, 8), these weapons were rarely depicted during the Early Dynastic period. Above the soldiers, a nude, shaved man is falling backward, his lack of clothing probably a sign that he is dead.

PC

1. Parrot 1971, p. 269, pl. 14.4. For an interpretation of the room as sacred, see "Mari and the Syro-Mesopotamian World," by Jean-Claude Margueron, in this catalogue.

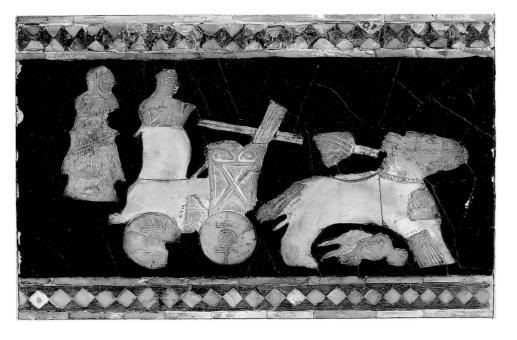

100a, b

Inlay of onager heads in a reconstructed chariot scene

Shell
Panel (reconstructed): H. 17 cm (6¾ in.); W. 25.5 cm (10 in.)
Syria, Mari, Ninni-zaza temple, room 13
Early Dynastic III, ca. 2550–2250 B.C.
National Museum, Damascus, Syria 1917

a. Head: H. 3.2 cm (1¼ in.); W. 4.3 cm (1¼ in.)
M.2467

b. Head: H. 2.8 cm (1⅛ in.); W. 1.5 cm (⁹⁄₁₆ in.)
M.2468

Images of equids are not uncommon in Early Dynastic inlays. These shell examples from Mari were set in a decorative frieze and have been assembled here to suggest a scene of warfare, with the animals pulling chariots as on the Standard of Ur (see cat. no. 52). Typically, the double outline and four ears indicate two animals side by side on each inlay.

The bridles are depicted as twisted rope. The ears are laid back, and the manes are indicated by upright tufts of hair. The Mesopotamian war chariot was steered using reins that passed through a ring carried on the onager's back (see cat. no. 66) and was attached to a ring in its nose. Here, the ropes from the nose rings are drawn under the onagers' heads and, presumably, exit between the animals. The rope around each animal's neck would have

been tied to a pole secured on the front of the chariot.

Equids such as donkeys or onagers were also used as pack animals (see cat. no. 323b), and they remained the most important beasts of burden even after horses were introduced into Mesopotamia from the Central Asian steppes at the end of the third millennium B.C.

PC

101

Cylinder seal with a chariot scene

Stone
H. 4.9 cm (1⅞ in.); Diam. 2 cm (¾ in.)
Syria
Early Dynastic III, ca. 2550–2250 B.C.
Georges Antaki Collection, London

The motif and iconography displayed by this seal evoke the Early Dynastic glyptics of Tell Beydar and Tell Brak.[1] The seal presents two scenes divided into registers by a chain of crescents.

The top register shows a contest scene[2] depicting a hero en face, interspersed with animals and mythical creatures. This motif may suggest a "battle drama, in which a primeval contest for world order against the forces of chaos [is] re-fought and re-won."[3] The bottom

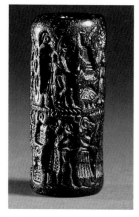

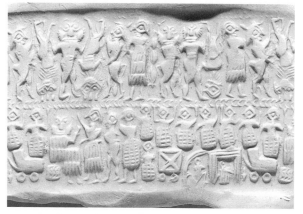

101

Impression from catalogue number 101.

register features a complex composition of cultic and/or military[4] significance. The central figure is a seated deity[5] wearing a tufted robe, body in profile and enlarged head shown en face. To the right stands a bound and nude prisoner flanked by two standing figures in skirts. The rest of this scene is divided horizontally into two parts. Below is a four-wheeled wagon, followed by a stylized architectural shape housing a clothed figure with raised arms. Extending from this structure is a half-arched roof or enclosed area within which a seemingly nude person kneels. This kneeling figure may be a prisoner or a hero in the act of worship.[6] Finally, there is a wagon with a diagonal, cross-shaped decoration, pushed by a figure with a block-shaped lower body wearing a checkered-pattern garment. Above there is a procession of seven figures with the same block-shaped lower body and checkered-pattern garment.[7]

This cylinder seal has been enlarged at one end and reused as the mouthpiece for a pipe.[8]

AAP

1. For Tell Beydar, see Jans and Bretschneider 1998, p. 158; see also Bretschneider and Dietrich 1995, pp. 28–40. For Tell Brak, see Matthews, Matthews, and McDonald 1994, pp. 189, fig. 1, 193.
2. Collon 1986, p. 37.
3. Regarding cultic meaning, see Hansen 1998, p. 50, citing Jacobsen 1976, p. 14. For military significance, Amiet 1963, p. 73, and Amiet 1980, pp. 167–69.
4. Jans and Bretschneider 1998, p. 164.
5. Collon 1987, p. 165; Jans and Bretschneider 1998, p. 164.
6. For the prisoner, see Börker-Klähn 1982, figs. 18, 20, 31, 33. For the hero, Jans and Bretschneider 1998, p. 164.
7. Jans and Bretschneider 1998, pp. 170–71.
8. Collon 1987, p. 165.

102

Inlay of a musician with a bull's-head lyre

Shell
H. 3.8 cm (1½ in.); W. 2.5 cm (1 in.)
Syria, Mari, Ninni-zaza temple, room 13, M.2459
Early Dynastic III, ca. 2550–2250 B.C.
National Museum, Damascus, Syria 2100

Musicians, often included in banquet scenes, were favorite subjects for inlay decoration. The head of this male lyre player is missing. His body faces right, and deeply incised parallel lines decorate his long skirt, which is gathered at the back. His right hand plucks at the strings of a lyre. The instrument is decorated with a bull's head similar to those depicted on the Standard of Ur and on lyres discovered in the royal graves at Ur (see cat. nos. 52, 58).

PC

103a, b

Inlays of men holding walking sticks

Syria, Mari, Palace
Early Dynastic III, ca. 2550–2250 B.C.

a. Stone
H. 7.7 cm (3 in.); W. 6.6 cm (2⅝ in.)
M.4694
National Museum, Damascus, Syria 2501

b. Stone and lapis lazuli
H. 11.2 cm (6¼ in.); W. 6.1 cm (2⅜ in.); Thickness 2.3 cm (⅞ in.)
M.4465
National Museum, Damascus, Syria 2382

The man in the first fragment faces right, and his head is shown in profile. There is more modeling than in many inlays from Mari, perhaps because the material used is a soft stone that made such treatment possible. The flat cap

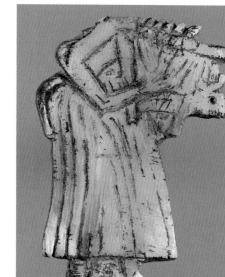

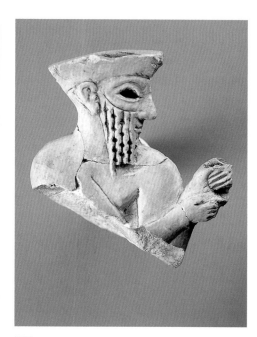

103a

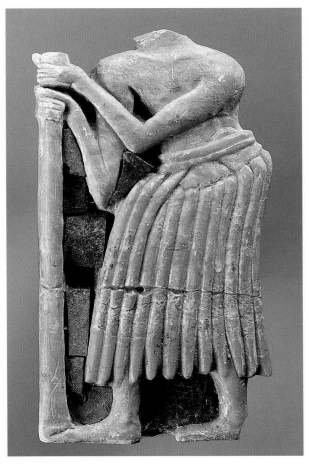

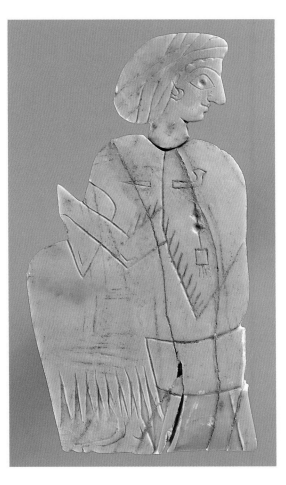

103b

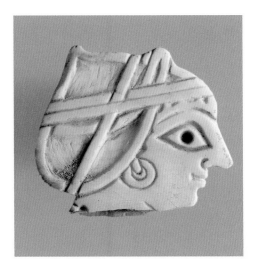

the man wears is not uncommon in the art of the Early Dynastic period—for example, it is often represented on stone inlays from Kish (see cat. no. 48)—and sometimes appears on figures on Jamdat Nasr period seals.[1] His eye was probably inlaid and appears to be in profile thanks to the deep cutting of the eyebrow, its rounded shape close to the nose, and the full cheek. A beard curves from the top of the ear to the side of the nose. The strands of the beard, which fall to the top of the chest, are separated by drill holes, as in dedicatory sculpture from Early Dynastic Mari. The man has outstretched arms in which a vertical bore appears, indicating that he originally held a staff or a standard like some figures depicted in Early Dynastic shell inlays. Only the front surface of this figure is carefully worked; toward the back it narrows and shows traces of cutting and carving tools, since this area would have been covered by other pieces of inlay.

A staff is held in a similar manner by the headless man in the second inlay. He is shown nude above the waist and wears a long pleated skirt. The stick he holds in both hands rests on the front of his foot. Three pleats of the skirt fall from the front of a double belt and over other

pleats that fall from a scalloped border below the belt. A similar form of dress is depicted on a dedicatory sculpture of the Early Dynastic III period from Mari (cat. no. 90). The background behind the figure is formed by pieces of lapis lazuli.   PC

1. Heinrich 1936, pls. 17, 18.

104a

Inlay of a woman wearing a cylinder seal

Shell
Body: H. 7.3 cm (2⅞ in.); W. 4.9 cm (1⅞ in.)
Head: H. 2.8 cm (1⅛ in.)
Syria, Mari, Dagan temple, room 10, M.3575, M.3576
Early Dynastic III, ca. 2550–2250 B.C.
National Museum, Damascus, Syria 1271, 1272

104b

Inlay of a woman's head

Shell
H. 2 cm (¾ in.); W. 2.1 cm (¹³⁄₁₆ in.)
Syria, Mari, Ninni-zaza temple, surface find, M.2765

Early Dynastic III, ca. 2550–2250 B.C.
National Museum, Damascus, Syria 2137

The first shell inlay (cat. no. 104a) depicts a woman with her head in profile facing right. Her turban is formed from strips indicated by shallow, incised lines; comparable headdresses are worn by figures on votive sculpture from Nippur and from the Diyala region.[1] The excavator has assembled the head with an inlay representing a woman's body facing left. She wears a fringed robe, joined across the chest by a single, bent pin, in contrast to inlays from Mari of women wearing a *polos*-type headdress and two bent pins.[2] A string of beads and possibly a cylinder seal are suspended from the pin. Her arms are uncovered, and the hands, now missing, were held together pointing upward. She sits on a stool with two straight legs. The woman's activity is unclear but may be related to weaving. The excavator associated this woman and similar examples with inlays showing women wearing *polos*-type headdresses and men with shaved heads. He thus interpreted these pieces as part of a mosaic panel depicting a temple ritual.[3] However, the inlays were found scattered and their relationship is questionable.

In the second inlay (104b) a piece of shell has been cut to represent a woman's head in profile facing right. Her incised eye is shown frontally, under a long eyebrow. She wears a turban, the outline of which is delineated by bands. Deeper cutting between the lines of the headdress possibly was intended to hold inlays. The earlobe with its hoop earring protrudes from under the turban. Her chin is small but broad.   PC

1. See, for example, Strommenger 1964, nos. 61, 108.
2. Parrot 1962, pls. 11.4, 12.3.
3. Ibid., pp. 163–68, pl. 11.

105

Human face for a composite figure

White marble, shell, and lapis lazuli
H. 3.5 cm (1⅜ in.)
Syria, Mari, massif rouge, M.4462
Early Dynastic III, ca. 2550–2250 B.C.
National Museum, Damascus, Syria   2374

Figures assembled from different colored materials were popular in the Late Uruk and Early Dynastic periods. Of this example only the face is preserved. The eyes are outlined with lapis lazuli and inlaid with shell and a lapis lazuli pupil; the right eyebrow and the left pupil are lost. The modeling around the nose and thin, dimpled mouth is very fine. A double chin and fleshy cheeks emphasize the naturalistic approach, a feature of many figures from Mari and Ebla, which may have influenced the art of the Akkadian period. The upper part of

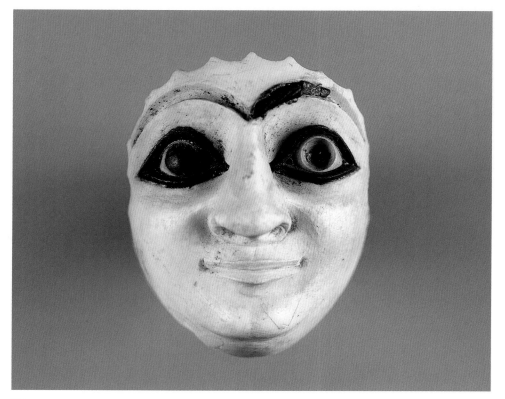

105

the face ends in a serrated edge, where the hair might have been attached. Wigs for similar figures are known from Ebla (see cat. nos. 109a, b). Composite sculptures are also known from southern Mesopotamia: a large female head of limestone and various animal figurines made of both metal and stone of the late fourth millennium B.C. (see figs. 11a, 13) come from Uruk;[1] and an Early Dynastic female statuette of translucent green stone with a gold foil face and lapis lazuli inlay was found at Nippur (fig. 42).[2]   PC

1. Strommenger 1964, nos. 30, 31.
2. Orthmann 1975, pl. 2.

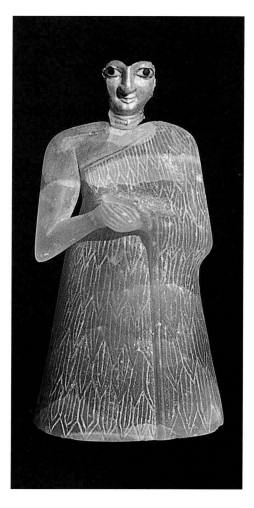

Fig. 42. Greenstone and gold standing female figure with clasped hands. Nippur, Early Dynastic IIIA, ca. 2550–2400 B.C. Iraq Museum, Baghdad, IM 96190.

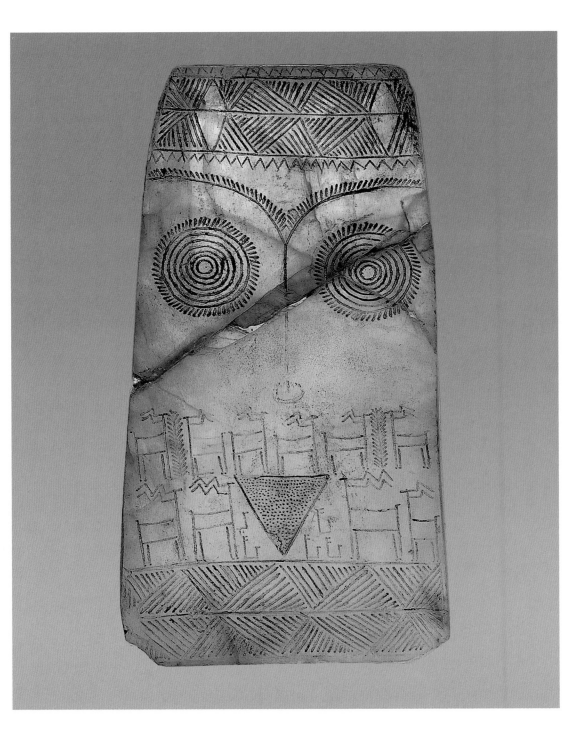

106

Incised slab with an abstract female figure and animals

Alabaster
H. 35.3 cm (13⅞ in.); W. 18.5 cm (7¼ in.); Thickness 1.6 cm (⅝ in.)
Syria, Mari, TH97, 154
Early Bronze Age, early third millennium B.C.
Museum of Deir ez-Zor, Syria 19088

Under an altar dedicated to the goddess Ninhursanga dating to about 2300 B.C., a pit containing fifty objects was discovered. They included this unique stele, which may have been used in the cult and which the excavator considered to be one of the oldest finds in the pit.[1] On one side the stele shows elements of a female body arranged in a facelike design that calls to mind René Magritte's painting *The Rape*.[2] Across the top between parallel zigzag lines are two bands of triangles, all but four of which are hatched. Two large eyes that can be read as breasts, formed from concentric circles, are incised below eyebrows that join in the center as the single line of the nose. A circle suggests the end of the nose or a navel. Above and on either side of a schematic triangle of the mouth or pubic triangle are stylized birds and ibex flanking plants. Two bands of hatched triangles like those at the top of the stele form the groundline for four of the ibex.

Similar schematic representations of the female form are found only on stone figurines from the Levant, the Aegean area, and western Anatolia (see cat. no. 180).   PC

1. Fortin 1999, p. 284.
2. Mundy 2001, p. 279, fig. 269.

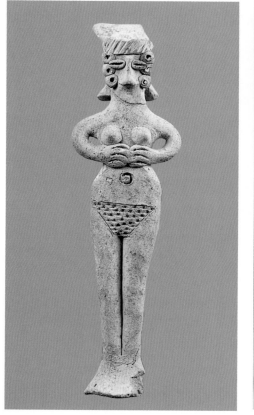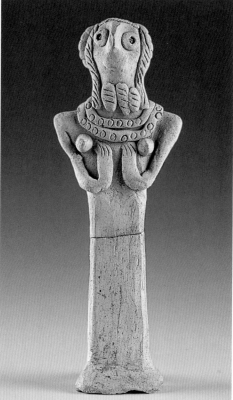

107a, b

Standing nude female figures

Terracotta
Early Bronze Age, late 3rd millennium B.C.

a. H. 14.2 cm (5⅝ in.); W. 4 cm (1⅝ in.)
Syria, Mari, Ishtar temple, H.50
National Museum, Aleppo, Syria 7970

b. H. 16 cm (6¼ in.); W. 5.5 cm (2⅛ in.)
Syria, Tell Selenkahiye, SLK.72.233
National Museum, Aleppo, Syria 9092

Third-millennium Syrian figurines display a variety of stylistic characteristics. These examples, from Mari and Selenkahiye, depict female figures with clearly indicated breasts. Flared at the base, they stand independently. On both figures the eyes are the most pronounced facial feature; the mouth is absent.

Recovered from the Ishtar temple,[1] the Mari figurine (cat. no. 107a) has bent arms, with hands resting on the upper midriff. The figure is nude, and the pubic triangle and navel are indicated with incised lines. It has coffee-bean-shaped eyes and wears a headdress over perforated, plaited hair.

The Selenkahiye figurine (cat. no. 107b) is one of a group of three found buried in a pit underneath the floor in an Early Bronze Age house.[2] The arms are bent, with hands resting on the chest. Because the pubic triangle is not indicated, the figure appears to be clothed. The eyes are open wide and punctured in the center. There are two coils decorated with incised circles draping across the chest and over the shoulders and three small loaf-shaped ornaments

on the neck. The hair is modeled into face-framing plaits that rest on the shoulders.

Clay figurines appeared throughout the ancient Near East as early as the Neolithic period and were crafted and used for millennia thereafter. These enigmatic objects may represent the mother goddess, another major deity, or household gods.[3] They may have been used as fertility talismans, erotic emblems, trinkets or playthings, protective amulets to safeguard the home, or vehicles of apotropaic or sympathetic magic.[4]   AAP

1. Parrot 1956, p. 36
2. Van Loon 1973, p. 148.
3. For the mother goddess, see Dales 1960, p. 250, and Parrot 1956, p. 13; for another deity, Pritchard 1943, p. 87; and, for household gods, Van Loon 1973, p. 148.
4. For fertility gods, Pritchard 1943, p. 87; erotic emblems, Caquot 1969, p. 61; trinkets or playthings, Genouillac 1934–36, vol. 2, p. 38, and Woolley 1955, p. 249; protective amulets, Margueron 1976, pp. 207, 220; magic vehicles, Badre 1980, pp. 156–57, and Voigt 1983, p. 195.

EBLA AND THE EARLY URBANIZATION OF SYRIA

PAOLO MATTHIAE

In the regions around the great alluvial plain of Mesopotamia and western Syria urbanization took place rapidly during the centuries immediately before the middle of the third millennium B.C. Within a few decades urban centers arose, comparable in size to the cities of southern Mesopotamia but with economic organization, social structures, and ideological beliefs that were certainly different.[1] The most important and best-documented site of this period of emergent urbanization in Syria (which followed the first wave of urbanization in southern Mesopotamia and Susiana) is Ebla. Located at what is today Tell Mardikh, sixty kilometers south of Aleppo, Ebla was a great city, which by about 2400 B.C. already covered about twenty-four acres (fig. 43). The "La Sapienza" Branch of the University of Rome started an ongoing program of exploration at the site in 1964.[2]

Only lesser, partially explored architectural remains—in the southern area of the acropolis, in Sector G South, and in Area CC—testify to the earliest stages of urban development at Ebla, during Early Bronze Age (EB) III (ca. 2700–2400 B.C.).[3] The monumental ruins of the Royal Palace, in Area G in the southwestern area of the acropolis, date just after the end of the period, about 2400–2250 B.C., during EB IVA, the so-called Mature Early Syrian period. Also from this era date the well-preserved structures of Building P4 in Area P South and some sectors of the massive fortified wall of the town, brought to light in Area AA. Articulated and multifunctional, Building P4 was devoted to storage, workshops, and food production. It may have been a dependency of the Royal Palace (Palace G), but more probably it was part of a large sacred area that may have antedated the goddess Ishtar's Middle Bronze Age sanctuary (MB I–II,

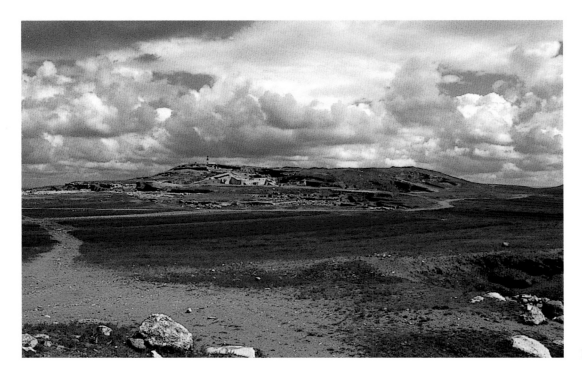

Fig. 43. Tell Mardikh (ancient Ebla).

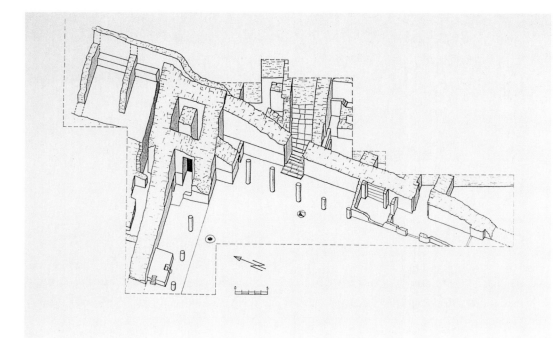

Fig. 44. Axiometric plan of the excavated area of Palace G, Ebla. Early Bronze IVA, Mardikh IIb 1, ca. 2350–2250 B.C.

ca. 2000–1600 B.C.).[4] Made of mud brick, the town wall, discovered below the large Northern Fort of the MB II age (ca. 1800–1600 B.C.), was more than six meters thick.[5]

The Royal Palace, a large complex of units perhaps including cult buildings, was probably the building called Saza in the texts. It has been excavated only in two important peripheral sectors, the Administrative Quarter and the Southern Quarter (an area of nearly 2,500 square meters) because major superimpositions partially destroyed and partially overlie the rest (fig. 44). The two excavated quarters are located below the southwest slope of the acropolis and above the lower town; since they were not covered by later buildings, they are particularly well preserved, rising to a height of seven meters.[6]

West of the Administrative Quarter lay the Audience Court, a large quadrangle bordered by porches and measuring nearly thirty-five by sixty meters. There was a small suite of rooms below the porch of the Audience Court and a larger unit around an inner court of the Administrative Quarter of the palace, beyond which lay the throne room, eleven by sixteen meters in area. Three gates opened into the Audience Court, which is preserved largely in the northeast sector. In addition to the monumental gateway, on the east side, and an independent entrance to the Administrative Quarter, a ceremonial staircase opened at the end of the north side. Reserved for the king, this was a magnificent passage in a tower with a four-ramp staircase; its steps were decorated with wood planks inlaid with shell

flowers. Via the ceremonial staircase the kings of Early Syrian Ebla could proceed directly from their private apartments at the top of the Royal Palace to the throne, which was placed on a dais in the middle of the northern facade of the court.[7]

The most important artistic works in the palace were probably in the inner court of the Administrative Quarter, where the remains of numerous wood panels decorated with the figures of officials in high-relief limestone inlay were found. They were covered with gold leaf and decorated further with skirts, turbans, and belts of applied limestone (see cat. no. 110); these were the only parts left after the city was sacked.[8] In the same court a pile of unworked lapis lazuli blocks was discovered. Imported from Afghanistan (see cat. no. 116), they were probably awaiting shipment to other countries, perhaps Egypt.[9] In this regard, it is interesting to note that Egyptian bowls and goblets of diorite and alabaster were also discovered in the court; they had been produced during the Fourth, Fifth, and Sixth Dynasties, under direct pharaonic control. Among these vessels, many of which had been severely damaged during the sack of the Royal Palace, about 2250 B.C., there is a diorite bowl carved in hieroglyphs with the name of King Khafre of the Fourth Dynasty, who built the second pyramid at Giza, and an Egyptian-alabaster jar lid with the cartouche of Pepi I (cat. no. 161), the third king of the Sixth Dynasty of the Old Kingdom.[10]

The most sensational discoveries made in the Royal Palace took place in 1975. More than seventeen thousand complete and fragmentary cuneiform documents from the state archives were brought to light in three rooms of the Audience Court and Administrative Quarter. The so-called Great Archive (L.2769), which contained more than fifteen thousand documents, was found below the porch near the entrance to the Administrative Quarter (fig. 45). The so-called Small Archive (L.2761), with fewer than one thousand texts and fragments, was discovered below the porch opposite the monumental gateway. The Trapezoidal Archive (L.2864) was located on the north side of the inner court of the Administrative Quarter.[11] In the Great Archive the tablets were placed vertically on wood shelves in two rows, in orderly horizontal lines, like the files in a modern archive; in the Small Archive they were placed on suspended shelves; and in the Trapezoidal Archive they were arranged on benches (see fig. 46), probably enclosed in wood chests. The documents that were found in a complete state number slightly fewer than two thousand; after examining the fragments we calculated that the three archives must have held about five thousand texts at the time of the destruction of the town.[12]

The texts in the state archives included a great variety of administrative documents. Some were financial, for the most part registering the receipt of silver and gold by the palace from the elite of the town or disbursements to individuals of goods produced by the palace, mainly textiles and objects of bronze, silver, and gold (see cat. nos. 323, 324).[13] Of great interest are the numerous lists of offerings to the deities of Ebla made monthly by the king, queen, princes, officials, high dignitaries, and even foreign visitors. From these texts one can gain an extraordinarily complete picture of the religious pantheon of Early Syrian Ebla.[14] A few very important texts include messages from officials

to the king, royal orders to officials, court verdicts, and treaties between towns on commercial and legal matters (see cat. no. 326c). A very limited number of tablets preserve literary texts of great significance, from works of magic to hymns of praise. Among the latter, a hymn to the sun god Shamash is the most ancient extant literary text in a Semitic language (cat. no. 328).[15] Also worth mentioning here are several special texts, one recording the long ritual of dynastic marriage and another the coronation of the king—the latter kept in three redactions, one for each king documented in the state archives.[16]

One group of texts of exceptional importance—preserved on the upper shelf on the north side of the Great Archive—includes the numerous Sumerian and bilingual Sumerian-Eblaite lexical lists (cat. nos. 322a, b). The Sumerian lexicons are quite numerous and frequently well preserved. They include lists of words for the professions, fish, and birds, but are copies of well-documented lexical works of lower Mesopotamia. The bilingual texts have an extraordinary philological and historical importance because they are the most ancient vocabularies in existence. In four different redactions, in fact, on the basis of one of the canonical Sumerian lists, the Eblaite scribes added the Eblaite translation of the Sumerian words. As a result we have more than 1,500 correspondences between Sumerian and Eblaite; however, some of the words are quite rare and not easy to identify in either language.[17]

Arguably the state archives of Early Syrian Ebla are the most important archaeological discovery of the second half of the twentieth century. This proposition is supported by four considerations. First, they suggested something unexpected: that Mesopotamian cuneiform writing had been widely adopted in Syria during the third millennium B.C. Second, in their huge size the archives are comparable to the great bibliographical finds of the nineteenth century, such as those at Nineveh, Lagash, Nippur, Hattusha, Ugarit, and Mari. Third, unlike the typical archives in ancient Mesopotamia, which are always quite specialized, Ebla's did not belong to a great temple organization; rather, they documented the activity of a great city of the twenty-fourth century B.C. Fourth, this library, like the one at Ugarit, which was excavated in the first half of the twentieth century, revealed an unexpected very ancient Semitic language, Eblaite, which with Old Akkadian is one of the two most ancient written Semitic languages.

It is not surprising, therefore, that two great scholars of the twentieth century expressed the importance of the discoveries at Ebla in the following ways. I. J. Gelb, Assyriologist of the

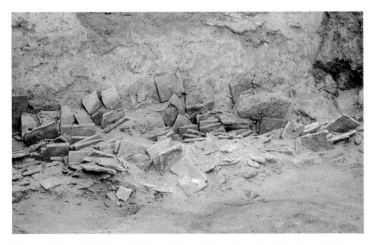

Fig. 45. Palace G, Ebla, with the tablets of the Great Archive (L.2769) in situ. Early Bronze IVA, Mardikh IIb 1, ca. 2350–2250 B.C.

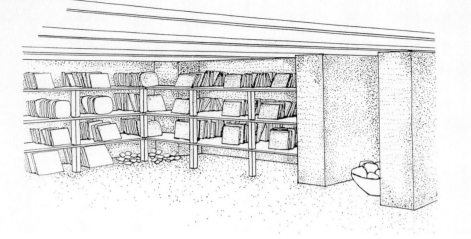

Fig. 46. Reconstruction of the Great Archive (L.2769), Palace G, Ebla. Early Bronze IVA, Mardikh IIb 1, ca. 2350–2250 B.C.

Oriental Institute, Chicago, maintained that the Italian excavators had discovered at Ebla a new culture, a new history, and a new language. And in 1979, on the occasion of the fiftieth anniversary of the discovery of Ugarit, Claude Schaeffer, of the Collège de France and the excavator at Ugarit, maintained that Ebla is like Ugarit but one millennium older.

After Ebla was destroyed, the victory inscription by the most famous king of ancient Mesopotamia, Sargon of Akkad, preserved the memory of the event. In it, Sargon recalls that during his famous expedition against the Upper Country (Upper Syria), he conquered and destroyed three towns: Mari, Yarmuti, and Ebla.[18] This statement by the founder of the Akkadian dynasty corresponds well with the archaeological and epigraphic evidence from Ebla and suggests that a similar statement by Sargon's grandson Naram-Sin should be understood to refer not to the latter's victory over Ebla and Armanum, but to his conquest of Armanum alone. This new town had gained power in the Ebla region, taking advantage precisely of the political void created by Sargon's destruction of Early Syrian Ebla.[19]

Ebla did not disappear after it was sacked by Sargon, however. It was rebuilt shortly thereafter, only to be destroyed again about 2000 B.C. A second reconstruction of the city at the beginning of the second millennium B.C. initiated a new and splendid era, whose history predated and complemented that of the powerful dynasty of Yarim-Lim I at Aleppo, as celebrated by Hammurabi of Babylon himself.[20] When, shortly before the fall of Babylon in about 1500 B.C., Ebla and Aleppo were attacked by Hittites and Hurrians, led by the great Old Hittite king Mursilis I, and burned to the ground, contemporaries certainly felt they had lived through memorable events.

In order to memorialize the final destruction of Ebla, an unknown Hurrian poet composed the Song of Liberation, an epic that was recently discovered in fragments, in the original Hurrian version, and also in a Hittite translation, in the capital of the Hittite empire, Boğazköy, ancient Hattusha.[21] Though incompletely preserved, this extraordinary poetic composition is highly significant. Through the historical-mythical representation of events, it throws light on the circumstances of the final destruction of Ebla. Furthermore, this song of the demise of this great Near Eastern city presents singular resemblances to the way in which Homer, in the *Iliad,* sang of the events of the siege of Troy.[22]

1. Weiss 1986.
2. Matthiae 1995, pp. 36–65.
3. Matthiae 2000, pp. 572–76.
4. Matthiae 1993, pp. 613–48; Marchetti and Nigro 1995–96, pp. 9–36.
5. Matthiae 2000, pp. 580–81, 584–87.
6. Matthiae 1995, pp. 73–76.
7. Ibid., pp. 66–94.
8. Matthiae, Pinnock, and Scandone Matthiae 1995, pp. 272–84, 298–329.
9. Pinnock 1988.
10. Scandone Matthiae 1982, pp. 125–30.
11. Matthiae 1986, pp. 53–71.
12. Archi 1986, pp. 72–86.
13. Archi 1988.
14. Pomponio and Xella 1997.
15. Edzard 1984; Krebernik 1984; Fronzaroli 1992.
16. Fronzaroli 1993.
17. Pettinato 1982; Archi 1992, pp. 1–39.
18. Frayne 1993, pp. 29–31.
19. Ibid., pp. 132–35; Matthiae 1995, pp. 241–50.
20. Matthiae 1995, pp. 133–220.
21. Neu 1996.
22. Matthiae forthcoming.

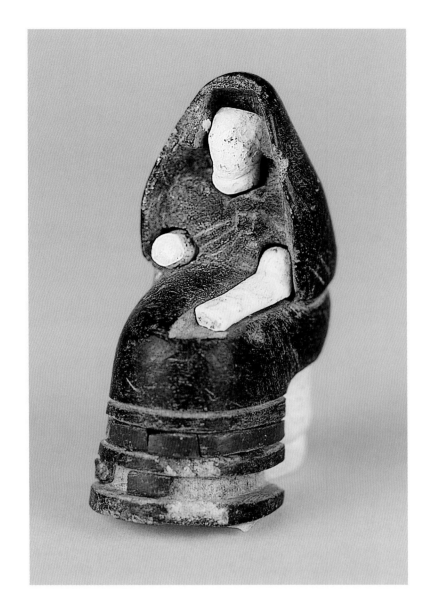

1. Matthiae, Pinnock, and Scandone Matthiae 1995, p. 317.
2. Matthiae 1977, p. 45.
3. Parrot 1967, pl. 48; Matthiae 1984, pp. 44–45.

(see cat. no. 110). Although part of a long sculptural tradition in Mesopotamia—beginning in the fourth millennium (see fig. 13)—this figure can perhaps be more closely linked to composite statues found in western Central Asia (see cat. no. 259).   AAP

109a–d

Headdresses for composite statues

a. Steatite
H. 11.5 cm (4½ in.); W. 15 cm (5⅞ in.)
Syria, Ebla (modern Tell Mardikh), Palace G,
Administrative Quarter, rooms L.2862 and L.2913,
TM.77.G.200a–d, 157, 180; TM.78.G.300a, b
Early Bronze Age, Mardikh IIb 1, ca. 2350–2250 B.C.
National Museum, Aleppo, Syria 10787

b. Steatite
H. 28.5 cm (11¼ in.); W. 14 cm (5½ in.)
Syria, Ebla (modern Tell Mardikh), Palace G,
Administrative Quarter, rooms L.2862 and L.2913,
TM.76.G.433a–c; TM.77.G.116, 115, 184a–c;
TM.78.G.178
Early Bronze Age, Mardikh IIb 1, ca. 2350–2250 B.C.
National Museum, Aleppo, Syria 10590

c. Limestone
H. 2.2 cm (⅞ in.); W. 2.9 cm (1⅛ in.); Thickness
2.9 cm (1⅛ in.)
Syria, Ebla (modern Tell Mardikh), Palace G, room
L.2890, TM.89.G.268
Early Bronze Age, Mardikh IIb 1, ca. 2350–2250 B.C.
Idlib Museum, Syria 8151

d. Limestone
H. 3.4 cm (1⅜ in.); W. 1.9 cm (¾ in.)
Syria, Tell Banat, Tomb 7, Chamber F, TB.197.95
Early Bronze Age, mid-to-late 3rd millennium B.C.
Idlib Museum, Syria

Third-millennium officials most likely wore ornate wigs for festive, sacred, and ceremonial occasions,[1] the hairstyle of the wig probably being specific to the function for which it was worn.[2] Hairstyle (cat. nos. 88, 267), hair ornamentation, and certain headdresses (see cat. nos. 61, 92, 128, 278) were markers of identity that could indicate age, ethnicity, status, profession, or even duties within a given office, and artisans of the ancient world frequently

108

Composite figure of a seated veiled woman

Steatite, limestone, and jasper
H. 5.3 cm (2⅛ in.); W. 2.2 cm (⅞ in.)
Syria, Ebla (modern Tell Mardikh), Palace G,
Southern Quarter, room L.3600, TM.83.G.400
Early Bronze Age, Mardikh IIb 1, ca. 2350–2250 B.C.
Idlib Museum, Syria 3209

Probably produced locally in the Ebla palace workshop,[1] this rare example of a miniature composite sculpture depicts a seated woman wearing a veil over her head. The veil, which drapes against her shoulders and across her back, may represent a typical element of dress worn by women of status in ancient Syria. Evidence recorded in the Ebla archives reveals that the mothers, daughters, and sisters of major dignitaries and landholders could hold prestigious priestly offices.[2]

This veiled figure is dressed in a long garment crafted in steatite, the hem inlaid with two decorative jasper bands. The head and arms are made of limestone, which was burned during the destruction of the palace at Ebla about 2250 B.C. The left arm is bent at the elbow. The chair on which the figure was seated is missing; its original presence is witnessed by the two cylindrical holes on the back of the statue indicating how the piece was assembled.

The statue is similar in form to one recovered from a pre-Sargonic temple at Mari[3] depicting a veiled, seated woman wearing a tufted garment (cat. no. 92a). Other pieces of composite sculpture were found in Palace G

utilized these features to convey information about the figures they created.[3] Indeed, stone wigs have been found that display a range of elaborate coiffures, their variety imbued with significance now largely lost to us.[4]

The four stone headdresses seen here crowned composite statues (made up of different materials) that were either miniature or nearly lifesize. All were excavated in locales associated with elite, if not royal, personages: three were found in the destruction levels of Palace G at Ebla (Tell Mardikh) and one in a rich tomb excavated at Tell Banat (Tomb 7). The fact that the objects were found in both palatial and burial contexts attests to the variety of functions composite statuary may have served. Although thus far no contemporary stone wigs have been excavated in Mesopotamia proper,[5] separate headdresses are thought to have been attached to figural sculpture from at least the Late Uruk period (fig. 11a).[6] In later periods, notably during the Third Dynasty of Ur, inscribed stone wigs were themselves dedicated in temples as votive objects.[7]

Of the three stone wigs from Ebla exhibited here, two (cat. nos. 109a, b) were found together, their fragments scattered on the floor of the inner court of the Administrative Quarter of Palace G.[8] Both are made of a dark gray-green steatite, which, along with lapis lazuli, was exclusively used on Eblaite composite statues to represent hair (see cat. no. 111). The carving itself is remarkably well defined, giving the steatite a rich texture reminiscent of the surfaces of vessels carved in the "Intercultural Style" (see "Art and Interconnections in the Third Millennium B.C.," by Joan Aruz, in this catalogue). While the hairstyles are strikingly different, the two wigs were similarly constructed and would have been affixed to nearly lifesize heads by the same technique. Each wig is made up of concave plaques with drilled holes on the inside that allowed them to be attached with metal or wood pegs to the core of the head, which was most probably of wood.[9] The faces of the composite statues would have been separate elements made of stone and perhaps precious materials (see cat. no. 105 for an example in miniature).

Catalogue number 109a is the more elaborate of the two wigs and is complete except for the top portion, which may have been surmounted by an additional headdress of a more precious material.[10] At what is believed to be the front of the wig, eight thick, wavy locks fall from high on the head. They are carved in

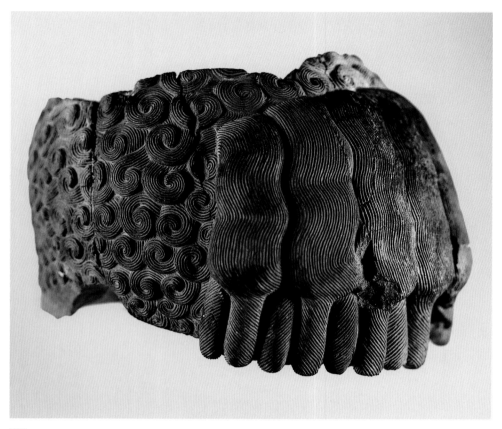

109a

high relief and end in two rows of short plaits. Incised lines indicate the waves of the hair as well as the direction of the hair within the plaits. The remaining part of the wig is covered with tightly twisted curls coiling upward both clockwise and counterclockwise and becoming progressively smaller toward the nape of the neck, where thin vertical incised lines represent a straightening of the hair.[11]

Catalogue number 109b, a simpler wig assembled from ten parts, is characterized by long rows of wavy loose tresses separated from one another by deep vertical grooves. Shallower incisions within the tresses indicate individual strands of hair. The tresses begin at the edges of the face and extend back over the top of the head or back over the ear; they divide well beyond the nape of the neck and fall onto the shoulders in individual curls rendered in three dimensions. The ends would have been fastened directly to the back of the statue.

The large dimensions, elaborate hairstyles, and contiguous findspots of the two wigs have led to the tentative interpretation that they belong to images of a royal couple (cat. no. 109a belonging to the king)[12] set up in the Administrative Quarter of the palace to celebrate important individuals.[13] While the wigs

must indeed have been a marker of high status, it is difficult to determine whether they necessarily indicated royalty, since no contemporary images of Eblaite rulers with either coiffure are known. Certain Mesopotamian hairstyles seem to retain their meanings in Syria, at least at Mari, where, for example, the statue of Ishqi-Mari (cat. no. 88) displays the royal chignon typical of Mesopotamian kingship, and the singer Ur-Nanshe (cat. no. 91a) wears his hair long in a fashion similar to that of singers depicted on the so-called Standard of Ur (cat. no. 52). Catalogue number 109b resembles the hairstyle worn by these singers, but whether or not connotations of this kind can be read from the Ebla wigs remains unclear, leaving the identification of both the figures and their genders ambiguous. No other parts of the composite statues to which these wigs were affixed have been found.

Catalogue number 109c, a miniature wig made for a much smaller composite statue, has also been interpreted as a royal headdress, since similar turbans are worn by prominent men depicted on furniture plaques (fig. 47) and sealings found within Palace G.[14] It represents a woolen cap made of tufts of fleece pulled tightly over the round of the head and encircled

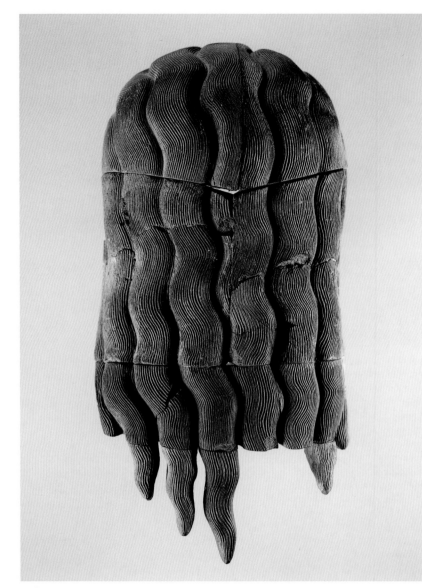

109b

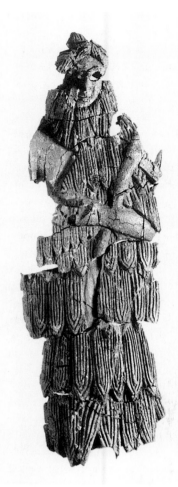

Fig. 47. Wood and shell furniture fragment depicting a male figure holding an axe. Ebla, Early Bronze IVA, Mardikh IIb 1, ca. 2350–2250 B.C. National Museum, Damascus, Syria, TM.74.G.1000.

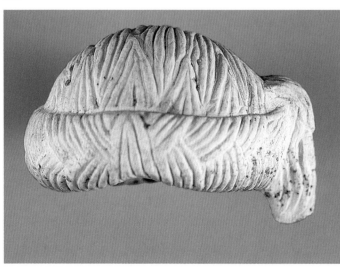

109c

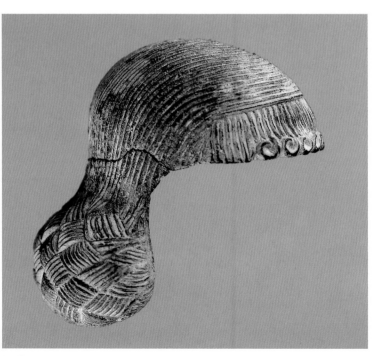

109d

by a braided brim finishing in a short tassel, which falls to one side. Limestone was favored by Eblaite artisans as a medium in which to render the color and texture of wool, as is also apparent with the skirts of composite figures (see cat. no. 110). The cap is slightly elevated in front and is concave on the underside; it may have formed part of a composite panel made up of elements in varying levels of relief.[15] Other miniature stone turbans similar to the one represented here have been found in Palace G.[16]

Similar in scale but from an entirely different context is the miniature stone wig from Tell Banat (cat. no. 109d), where it was found among the rich grave goods of Tomb 7 (see "Tell Banat," by Anne Porter and Thomas McClellan, in this catalogue). It, too, is carved in the round. Short vertical incisions in front indicate a band of straight hair that would have fallen down onto the forehead, while the rest of the hair is pulled back and elaborately tied in a braided fashion represented by a complex pattern of incised squares. The hair is everywhere incised with thin wavy lines to indicate individual strands. No other pieces that could be attributed to the same statue were found within the tomb, although several other inlay elements (such as sets of clay eyes and eyebrows) recovered from the same chamber indicate that the tomb originally held a number of composite statues, which probably were removed when it was disturbed.

MJH

composite female statuette from Nippur (fig. 42), which presumably had a separate headdress attached to the gold-and-inlay face.
7. See Braun-Holzinger 1991, pp. 373–74; Wiseman 1960, p. 168 and pl. 22b.
8. Matthiae 1980c, his nos. A and B, figs. 1–5; see also Matthiae 1980b, figs. 4, 5; Matthiae 1984, pls. 45, 46; Matthiae 1995, nos. 63, 64. Fragments of a third, nearly lifesize wig were found in the Audience Court, on the steps of the monumental doorway; Matthiae 1980c, no. C.
9. For interior views of the wigs and a detailed description of their manufacture, see Matthiae 1980c.
10. Matthiae 1995, p. 298.
11. This is the reconstruction favored by the excavator (Matthiae 1980c, p. 263, figs. 9, 10). However, thick plaits like those seen here usually decorate the back of the head in other miniature examples; see Matthiae 1980c, fig. 17, and Pinnock 1990, fig. 4d.
12. Matthiae 1980c, p. 268. The excavator proposed that the wigs might belong to busts or "portrait" heads rather than complete statues. The identification of cat. no. 109b as female is based on contemporary glyptic evidence from Palace G that shows female figures with long hair; however, an untied coiffure is not necessarily a marker of gender since Early Dynastic statuary, reliefs, and seals often represent both males and females with long hair.
13. Matthiae 1980c, p. 268.
14. Matthiae 1980a, p. 88, fig. 14.
15. The excavator bases this assumption on other pieces found near the turban: wood and gold elements believed to have constituted a frame, and smaller, less fully modeled wigs of steatite and lapis lazuli that conceivably were affixed to figures standing in profile facing a central, frontal figure wearing the woolen cap. See Matthiae 1995, p. 300, and Matthiae 1984, pl. 44.
16. See Weiss 1985, no. 74; Pinnock 1992, pp. 15–16.

1. Jacobsen 1987b, p. 3; Moorey 1996, p. 233.
2. Moorey 1996, pp. 233–36.
3. Robins 1999. For a study of Mesopotamian hairstyles, see Spycket 1954 and Spycket 1955.
4. Various steatite and lapis lazuli wigs have been found at Ebla; see Matthiae 1984, pls. 44–46, and Pinnock 1990, fig. 4a–d. Recently a steatite wig was excavated as far away as Harappa in the Indus Valley (Meadow 2002). It is thought to have been imported from Bactria-Margiana, where it would have crowned a steatite and alabaster composite figure (like this catalogue's no. 259) in the late third or early second millennium; see Amiet 1988c, p. 200.
5. An unprovenanced stone wig now in the British Museum, London (see Moorey 1996) resembles the gold "wig" of Meskalamdug (fig. 18 in this catalogue); stone wigs do not otherwise appear in Mesopotamia before the Ur III period (Spycket 1981, p. 251, pl. 174:a, b). Fragments of hair from composite statues have been excavated at Ashur (Harper et al. 1995, p. 34, nos. 7–9), but these have been dated tentatively to the first millennium B.C.
6. See "Art of the Early City-States," by Donald P. Hansen, in this catalogue. See also the Early Dynastic

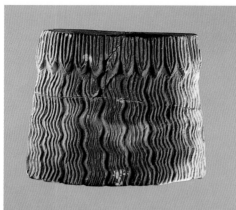

110

Skirt fragment for a composite figure

Limestone
H. 4.2 cm (1⅝ in.); W. 5.3 cm (2⅛ in.)
Syria, Ebla (modern Tell Mardikh), Palace G, Administrative Quarter, room L.2913, TM.77.G.612
Early Bronze Age, Mardikh IIb 1, ca. 2350–2250 B.C.
Idlib Museum, Syria 3117

This object was part of a small sculpture made from stone and possibly metal parts fitted together. This form of composite statue was popular in Early Dynastic Mesopotamia but is also found as far east as Central Asia (see cat. no. 259). The carving is of a skirt with a line of tufts hanging from the top, which is similar to the fleece garments worn by figures on inlays

and on relief sculpture of this period from Syria and southern Mesopotamia and thought to represent the skins of sheep and goats. The body of the skirt is decorated with vertical patterns formed by bands of five parallel wavy lines separated by a deeper incision.

Other examples of composite sculpture were found in Palace G at Ebla, all depicting elements of clothing or wigs (see cat. nos. 109a–c), which might suggest that the body parts were made from precious or perishable materials. The exception is the figure of a cloaked woman from Ebla whose arm and face are made of limestone (cat. no. 108), and which may be more closely linked to the composite sculpture tradition found in Central Asia.

PC

III

Recumbent human-headed bull or bison

Gold, steatite, and wood
H. 4 cm (1⅝ in.); W. 1.8 cm (¹¹⁄₁₆ in.); L. 5 cm (2 in.);
Weight 23.2 g
Syria, Ebla (modern Tell Mardikh), Palace G, Administrative Quarter, room L.2764, TM.76.G.850
Early Bronze Age, Mardikh IIb 1, ca. 2350–2250 B.C.
National Museum, Aleppo, Syria 10782

With the head turned at right angles to the body, this small but exquisite human-faced bison, or *kusarikkum* (see entry for cat. no. 157), can be linked to the art of the Late Uruk and Proto-Elamite worlds (see fig. 13). In addition, the construction of the figurine, which is made of steatite and gold foil over a wood core, connects it with the art of Early Dynastic I (see cat. no. 18) and the later, widespread, composite

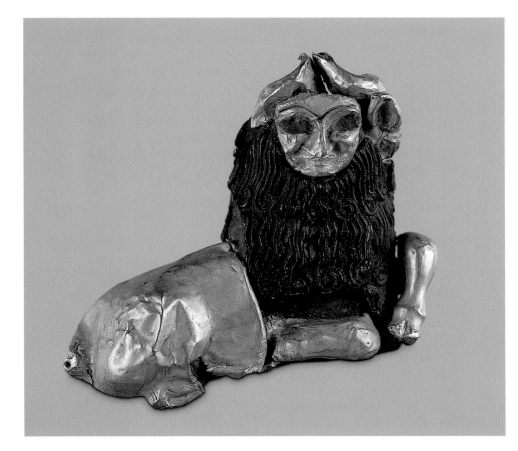

frequently are represented on chlorite vessels, struggling with snakes; often, their spots are inlaid (see cat. nos. 232, 233). PC

1. Van Buren 1939, pp. 10–12; *Chicago Assyrian Dictionary*, N/2, pp. 234–35, s.v. nimru A.
2. See, for example, Dolce 1978, no. T8, and Woolley 1934, pl. 104.

tradition (see cat. no. 259). This statuette was found at Ebla in Palace G. The creature is lying down facing right, with two of the three visible legs tucked under the body. The front left leg, however, has the same twisted, bent knee as does the sculpture from the site of Tell Brak (cat. no. 157a),[1] and the creature's tail passes in similar fashion behind its rear leg and appears on the flank. The large eyes were probably originally inlaid beneath the eyebrows that join above a prominent nose. The full and luxurious beard, which is formed from a single piece of steatite, consists of twelve locks ending in two rows of curls. The use of gold for the body and head may be explained by the connection between the *kusarikkum* and the sun god. Ebla's links with Egypt (see entry for cat. no. 161) provided access to one of the principal sources of the metal. The small size of the object suggests that it served as an amulet. PC

1. A similar posture is adopted by a human-headed bison on one of the side panels of the Standard of Ur, where the beast is shown under attack by a lion-headed eagle (see entry for cat. no. 52).

112

Upright leopard

Limestone
H. 7.1 cm (2¾ in.); W. 2.4 cm (1 in.); Thickness 1.5 cm (⁹⁄₁₆ in.)
Syria, Ebla (modern Tell Mardikh), Palace G, Administrative Quarter, room L.2913, TM.77.G.260
Early Bronze Age, Mardikh IIb 1, ca. 2350–2250 B.C.
National Museum, Aleppo, Syria 10584

This animal, identified as a leopard (in Akkadian, a *nimrum*), was native to Mesopotamia and to Syria in antiquity.[1] The present example combines elements of both inlay and sculpture. The body, in profile, is carved from a flat piece of limestone. The left hind leg is straight, while the right leg is bent, with the tail curling in between. The line of the tail gives the leopard a sinuous look, emphasizing the curve of its back. The interstices are deeply cut. A human hand incised on the leopard's right shoulder suggests that the animal was part of a combat scene, as found on inlays and cylinder seals, where it is associated with bull-men and "flame-haired" heroes.[2] The three-dimensional head, with its prominent, rounded ears, is turned to the right, and the whiskers are indicated by incisions. Leopards

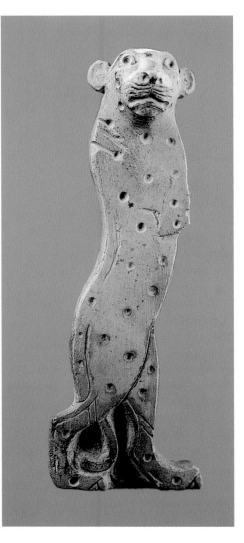

113

Recumbent calf

Limestone
H. 3.4 cm (1⅜ in.); W. 2.4 cm (1 in.); L. 4.4 cm
(1¾ in.)
Syria, Ebla (modern Tell Mardikh), Palace G,
Administrative Quarter, room L.2913, TM.78.G.200
Early Bronze Age, Mardikh IIb 1, ca. 2350–2250 B.C.
National Museum, Aleppo, Syria 10583

The body of this calf lies on the ground with
the left foreleg bent in the typical position of
an animal about to stand. The raised head is
slightly outstretched and turned to the right.
The eyes are incised and display drilled pupils
that may have been inlaid. Short, thin, curving

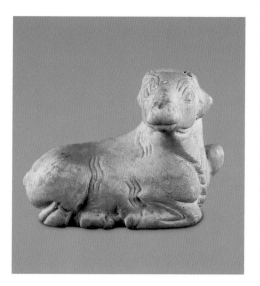

incised lines mark the eyebrows, mouth, chest,
and legs, while a pattern of three parallel waves
is shown on the neck and bend of the legs.
The chest displays five V-shaped lines. The
figure may have been affixed to another object
by means of dowels fitted into two cylindrical
holes in the base.

The sculpture is dependent on traditions
found in the animal forms of Late Uruk and
Jamdat Nasr period art (see cat. no. 2). Typical
features of the earlier style in evidence here are
the legs held below the body, the twisting of
the head, the strong form of the neck, and the
arched eyebrows. However, the foreleg bent
upward is more characteristic of sculpture of the
Early Dynastic period (see cat. nos. 111, 157a).
Moreover, the emphasis on naturalism seen here
and in other animal figures from Ebla (for
example, a similar but broken figure of a bull
that was found in the same place as this calf)
connects this piece with Akkadian art of the
succeeding period.   PC

114

Inlaid open-work furniture panel

Wood and shell
H. 22–40 cm (8⅝–15¾ in.); L. 41–60 cm (16⅛–
23⅜ in.); Thickness 2.5–3.5 cm (1–1⅜ in.)
Syria, Ebla (modern Tell Mardikh), Palace G, room
L.2601
Early Bronze Age, Mardikh IIb 1, ca. 2350–2250 B.C.
National Museum, Aleppo, Syria 12352

Among the extraordinary finds from Palace G
at Ebla are the numerous fragments of wood
found in one of the two long rooms in the
northwest wing of the palace, where the fire
that ultimately destroyed the building left
elaborately carved wood friezes carbonized
but in a remarkable state of preservation. This
wood panel inlaid with shell is part of a group
of fragments found in the south end of this
room, near the east wall. The group is thought
to be from a piece of furniture, perhaps a chair;
the fragment here would then have been a side
panel. The upper border is a rounded moulding, below which is carved an open-worked
register decorated with shell inlay. A file of
animals—an almost completely preserved bull,
a lion, and another quadruped—faces right.
An additional register with an animal file,
facing left, probably appeared at the bottom
of the panel.

The rosette motif on the haunches of the
lion and the bull, although reminiscent of
inlay on sculpture in the round during the
Late Uruk period (see fig. 13), has no known
parallels in Early Dynastic Mesopotamia. The
open-worked section and the animal registers
are, however, separated from one another by a

band of geometric inlay similar to the bands
that originally framed registers of the limestone inlay, also from Ebla (cat. no. 115).
Furthermore, the lion's mane and the hair of
the animal in front of the lion are similar to
the tufts of hair carved on the stone elements
of composite sculpture (see cat. no. 111). Such
similarities suggest that wood and stone sculpture shared a similar aesthetic at Ebla.

JME

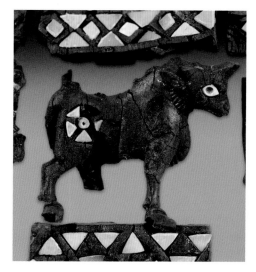

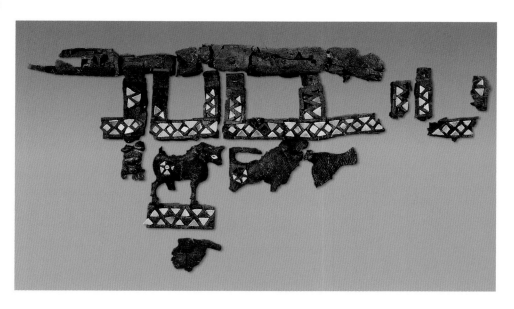

115a–f

Inlays of warriors, a lion-headed bird, and human-headed bulls or bisons

Limestone
Syria, Ebla (modern Tell Mardikh), Palace G, room
L.4436
Early Bronze Age, Mardikh IIb 1, ca. 2350–2250 B.C.

a. H. 13.8 cm (5⅜ in.); W. 9.6 cm (3¾ in.); Thickness
0.7 cm (¼ in.)
TM.88.G.308
Idlib Museum, Syria 3294

b. H. 11.6 cm (4⅝ in.); W. 12.8 cm (5 in.); Thickness
0.6 cm (¼ in.)
TM.88.G.281
Idlib Museum, Syria 3280

c. H. 14 cm (5½ in.); W. 10 cm (4 in.); Thickness
0.7 cm (¼ in.)
TM.88.G.451a, b
Idlib Museum, Syria 3297

d. H. 14.6 cm (5¾ in.); W. 7.5 cm (3 in.); Thickness
0.8 cm (⁵⁄₁₆ in.)

TM.88.G.300, 301
Idlib Museum, Syria 3292

e. H. 13.6 cm (5⅜ in.); W. 9.3 cm (3⅝ in.); Thickness
0.7 cm (¼ in.)
TM.88.G.191
Idlib Museum, Syria 3245

f. H. 10.5 cm (4⅛ in.); W. 11.9 cm (4⅝ in.); Thickness
0.8 cm (⁵⁄₁₆ in.)
TM.88.G.244
Idlib Museum, Syria 3269

These six inlays are among more than thirty related examples excavated in the western area of the Royal Palace at Ebla.[1] They appear to have been fixed to a plank (or planks) of wood that the excavator believes would originally have been displayed vertically.[2] At some point the wood was laid down into a floor, spanning at least two entrances to a room. The inlays were turned facedown in the ground, their imagery hidden, and were still in place at the time of the destruction of the palace. It was possible to reconstruct the original arrangement of the inlays in one of the furrows formed in the soil by the decayed wood. They

were placed in twelve horizontal registers, each separated by a double line of triangular tesserae. The images alternated, with a register of soldiers followed by one with lion-headed eagles and human-headed bulls. The inlays are all made of a very fine limestone and are homogeneous not only in their material but also in their technique and style. Every inlay represents a complete subject. Only in the lower part of each inlay, where animal or human legs are depicted, is the background included. Internal details are not carved as deeply as the backgrounds. The imagery can be compared with that of similar scenes of victory parades depicted on inlays from Ur and Mari (see cat. nos. 52, 97). The combination of military activity with mythological images recalls the Stele of the Vultures from Tello (figs. 52, 53).

Catalogue number 115a preserves part of a scene depicting a lion-headed eagle grasping a human-headed bison (*kusarikkum*). The missing element would have shown a second human-headed bison in mirror image. The lion-headed eagle, often identified as the Imdugud or Anzu creature, appears frequently in Early Dynastic imagery in both Mesopotamia and Syria, as here, associated with warfare and related to a victorious king (see cat. no. 35). The lion's mouth hangs open above its feathered chest, and, typically, a double circle indicates its navel. The creature's talons grasp the human-headed bison, its head turned to face the viewer.

This human-headed bison (cat. no. 115b),[3] faces right but turns its head toward the viewer. A long, curled beard frames its face, and tufts of hair are depicted at the top of its legs. The bison originally would have formed a heraldic group with a second *kusarikkum* and the lion-headed eagle, whose left talon is incised across the body of this creature, grasping both of them (see cat no. 115a). The human-headed bison sometimes also is shown in the grip of a belted heroic figure (cat. no. 58).

The soldier in catalogue number 115c wears a distinctive helmet on which two parallel lines distinguish the small knob on the top, in contrast to the usual pointed helmets worn by soldiers that are held in place with a strap under the chin (see cat. no. 98).[4] The band that curves around the front of the helmet is the same as those seen on helmets worn by figures on inlays and sculpture from Mari and sites in southern Mesopotamia.[5] On these last examples, the figures are depicted with their hair gathered in a double bun that protrudes from the back of the helmet; the

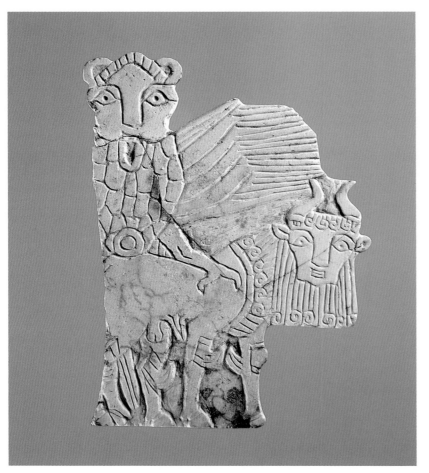

115a

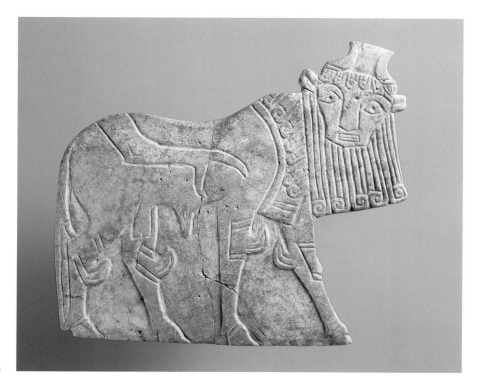

115b

knob on the present inlay may represent this same feature. This might indicate that the figure represents a ruler or important personage—a suggestion supported by his knee-length spotted cloak, perhaps made of leopard skin, which is worn over his left shoulder like the fleece garment of king Ishqi-Mari (cat. no. 88). In his left hand, which emerges from under the cloak, the soldier holds a spear with which he pierces the jaw of a man. The victim is bound around the waist by a double rope, and his legs, which appear to be bent behind him, are grasped by the soldier's right hand. The prisoner, in turn, grips the front leg of the soldier.

Catalogue number 115d is one of a series of inlays from the Royal Palace showing soldiers in profile carrying severed heads. Here the soldier, facing left and wearing a knee-length skirt with a tufted hem, holds an exaggeratedly large severed head by the hair with

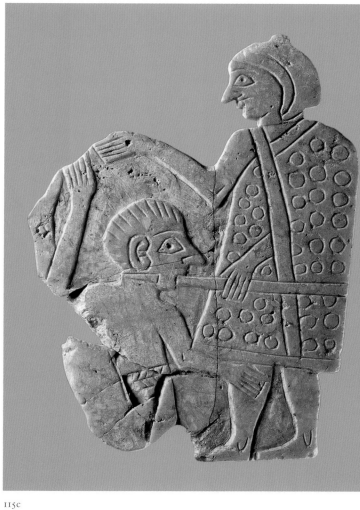

115c

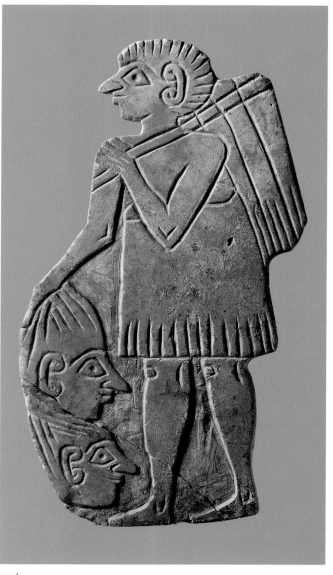

115d

his right hand; a second oversize head is seen below the first one. With his left hand the soldier supports a pole resting on his shoulder from which hangs a pennant with fringes or perhaps a folded battle net, used to entangle and disable the enemy.

In catalogue number 115e a soldier, in profile, uses his left hand to grip a pole slung over his shoulder from which a pennant or folded battle net composed of four strips is suspended. He strides toward the left, holding in his right hand the right leg of a nude man depicted upside down. The victim reaches behind the soldier's front leg to grasp his rear ankle.

In catalogue number 115f a headless figure wearing a skirt with a tufted hem grips a man's elbow with his left hand and, with the dagger in his right hand, attempts to stab the man in the eye. The victim grasps the dagger, with its distinctive crescent-shaped pommel and ridged blade, with his left hand, while he secures the legs of his attacker with his right arm. The victim is lying on his back, his body hidden behind his attacker, but his legs are visible, raised and bent at the knee.

PC

1. Matthiae 1989a.
2. Ibid., pp. 36–37.
3. Wiggermann 1992, pp. 174–81.
4. See, for example, Matthiae 1995, p. 274, no. 20.
5. For examples from Mari, see Dolce 1978, pl. 33:M349; see also cat. no. 88. For examples from Ur, see ibid., pl. 33:U191; for those from Tello (ancient Girsu), see fig. 52.

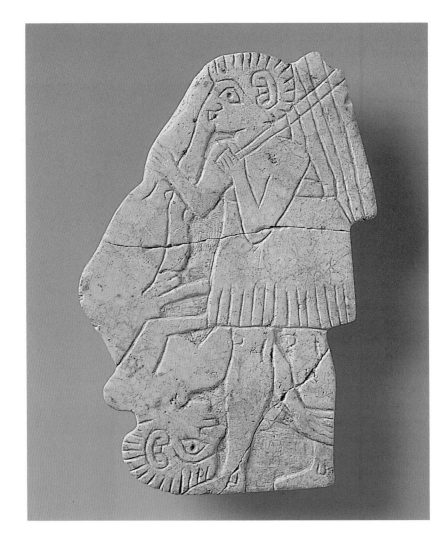

115e

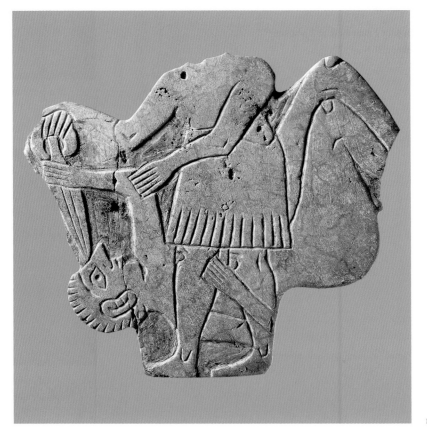

115f

Umm el-Marra tomb were probably members of this select group. The tomb, found with its contents intact in the summer excavation season of 2000, was a freestanding one-room mausoleum located at a high point in the center of the site (fig. 48). Three layers of bodies were interred in what appear to be wood coffins lined with textiles. Side by side in the top layer were two individuals in their late teens (one female, the other probably female but with ambiguous skeletal remains), each with a baby at the knee (fig. 50). Ornaments of precious materials such as gold, silver, and lapis lazuli adorned these individuals (fig. 49). In the middle layer were two adult men with more modest accoutrements of bronze and silver, and a baby off to the side. The lowest layer contained only one adult (whose sex is indeterminate) and a few silver items. The contrast between the rich furnishing of the female burials in the top layer and the modest objects with the men below is striking but difficult to explain. Given the conspicuous character of the mausoleum, it is possible that the veneration of elite ancestors may have been an important practice—as has been suggested in connection with sites on the Euphrates such as Tell Banat.   GMS

1. Excavations at the roughly sixty-acre site were initiated by a Belgian team in the 1970s and have been conducted since 1994 by a joint expedition of Johns Hopkins University and the University of Amsterdam directed by Glenn M. Schwartz and Hans Curvers. The Hopkins–Amsterdam project investigates problems of urban origins, collapse, and regeneration in early west Syrian complex societies. For further reference, see Matthiae 1979b; Tefnin 1981–82; Curvers and Schwartz 1997; Peltenburg 1999; Schwartz et al. 2000; and Schwartz, Curvers, and Stuart 2000.

117

Wild goat pendant

Lapis lazuli
H. 1.8 cm (¾ in.); L. 2.4 cm (1 in.); Weight 4.8 g
Syria, Tuba (?) (modern Tell Umm el-Marra),
Skeleton A, Tomb 1, UMM00B006
Early Bronze Age, ca. 2300 B.C.
National Museum, Aleppo, Syria 11693

The sculptor of this tiny figurine expressed the caprid nature of the subject in simple but elegant volumes. The dominant feature is the pair of horns, which make an arc from the top of the head to halfway down the back, where they join the torso, thus forming a loop by which the object could be hung on a string or chain. The face has a blunt muzzle, below which hangs a clearly marked beard. The eyes, which are large for the head, are surrounded by an emphatic incised line that makes them stand out even more noticeably. The oval ears extend up the sides of the horns. Incised lines make clear the division between neck and shoulder and between the torso and the hindquarters. The short legs bend under the body, suggesting that the animal is lying down. A short tail is indicated in relief.[1]

This pendant was found between the jaw and the top of the right humerus of Skeleton A in the "royal" tomb at Tell Umm el-Marra. A barrel-shaped lapis lazuli bead was found under the pendant, and a cylinder seal, a pierced shell, and a badly preserved iron object lay nearby. Perhaps these objects were on a string around the neck of the deceased.

While this tiny figure is a unique piece, it clearly reflects the tradition of making beads, pendants, and amulets in the shape of animals during the third millennium in Syria and Mesopotamia. Many of these pieces are carved in lapis lazuli, gold, or a combination of the two media, and many have been found at large urban sites such as Ur, Mari, and Tell Brak. The most common motifs are bearded recumbent bulls and lion-headed eagles with wings widespread, but individual finds suggest an originally larger repertoire than what has been discovered so far. At Ur, queen Puabi's jewelry included pairs of recumbent rams, deer, and what are perhaps antelopes, as well as bulls. In Grave PG 755 at Ur, Leonard Woolley found a small recumbent ram of lapis lazuli behind the body in the coffin, along with a lapis lazuli frog and beads of lapis lazuli and gold.[2] At Mari, the Treasure of Ur (see "The Treasure of Ur from Mari," by Nadja Cholidis, in this catalogue) included small lapis lazuli figures of a recumbent ram, two hedgehoglike animals, and three simplified kneeling women.[3] At Tell Brak a unique lapis lazuli pendant depicting a long-haired woman was found in a ritual deposit.[4] As with

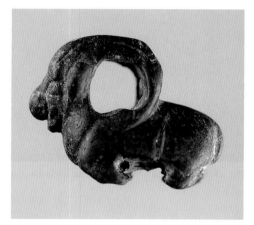

the present pendant, the appearance of the subject is constructed through simple volumes delineated by clearly incised lines. In both cases, part of the message was conveyed by the material, lapis lazuli, a stone available in the third millennium only to the most elite members of Near Eastern society.   SD

1. Wild bezoar goats *(Capra aegagrus)* and Nubian ibex *(Capra nubiana)* both have magnificently long, curving horns and a beard, and this pendant may represent either species. For pictures, see Ligabue and Salvatori 1988, p. 82 *(Capra aegagrus),* and Uerpmann 1987, p. 119 *(Capra nubiana).* The Nubian ibex, the only species of ibex indigenous to the Near East, is not attested in faunal remains from archaeological

sites north of the Dead Sea, however, whereas the wild goat *(Capra aegagrus)*, which ranges today from the Taurus Mountains in Turkey to Pakistani Baluchistan, is archaeologically attested as far south as Beidha in Jordan. For this reason the Umm el-Marra pendant is likely to represent a wild bezoar goat. Uerpmann (1987, pp. 113–21) notes that the wild goat must have been a common animal in antiquity; cf. Gilbert 1995, pp. 163–69.

2. The small ram measures 2.9 by 2.2 centimeters. It is illustrated in Woolley 1934, p. 552, pl. 142 (U.1009). The frog (U.1008) is illustrated in the same plate. For the identification of Grave PG 755 as the tomb of Meskalamdug's son, see "The Royal Tombs of Ur," by Julian Reade, in this catalogue.

3. Parrot 1968, pp. 29–30, pl. 16:1.

4. The pendant measures 2.1 centimeters in length. McDonald 2001, p. 228, fig. 242.

118

Pendant with a filigree guilloche pattern

Gold
H. 2.6 cm (1 in.); W. 1.2 cm (½ in.); Thickness 0.3 cm (⅛ in.); Weight 2.6 g
Chain: L. 1.1 cm (⁷⁄₁₆ in.)
Syria, Tuba (?) (modern Tell Umm el-Marra), Tomb 1, UMM00M032
Early Bronze Age, ca. 2300 B.C.
National Museum, Aleppo, Syria 11674

Both faces of this delicate triangular pendant are decorated with eight rows of guilloches framed by pairs of thin wires. The wires in each pair twist in opposite directions, and the effect is that of a braided frame between each guilloche. The same double-wire decoration runs around the perimeter of the pendant on both sides. The short chain is made of rings of gold wire, each bent in half, threaded through the previous loop, and then bent back on itself.[1]

Two gold beads from Grave PG 580 in the Royal Cemetery of Ur offer the closest known comparisons to this lovely filigree work. One is a biconical bead with panels of guilloches framed by twisted wires. The circular cloisons formed by the guilloches were originally filled with pieces of lapis lazuli (see cat. no. 75). The other bead is made of four biconical beads soldered together, each of which is decorated with guilloches in compartments framed by pairs of wires that twist in opposite directions.[2] Another object with filigree work from the same grave is a sheathed gold dagger, which was found attached to the remains of a silver-covered

leather belt. The sheath has intricate decoration that includes the guilloche motif as well as other patterns.[3]

Further examples of filigree decoration with twisted wires have been found in mid-to-late third-millennium-B.C. contexts at sites in Syria and Anatolia. The Treasure of Ur from Mari, in Syria, included a pendant of two gold disks whose outer border was composed of two gold wires twisted clockwise and counterclockwise (cat. no. 86).[4] At Tell Brak, in northeastern Syria, a hoard of jewelry contained eleven circle pendants made of four concentric coils of gold wire, alternately plain and twisted.[5] Another example of twisted wires in filigree work occurs on a circular gold pendant found in a grave at Kültepe, Anatolia.[6] On the gold pendant from Tomb 7 at Tell Banat, in Syria, twisted wires form a diamond-shaped ornament (cat. no. 126).

Like its filigree work, the chain of the Tell Umm el-Marra pendant is made in a fashion that seems to have been common in the Near East in the mid-to-late third millennium B.C. Examples have been found at Ur, Kish, Tell Brak, and Troy.[7]   SD

1. For the findspot of this pendant, see the entry for cat. no. 119.

2. Woolley 1934, p. 371, pl. 146, no. U.9657;

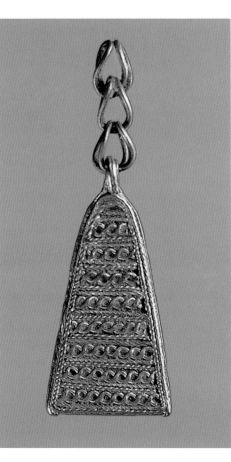

Quarantelli 1985, p. 313, no. 81.

3. Woolley 1934, p. 51, pl. 151, no. U.9361; Strommenger 1964, pl. 16. A gold toilet set that was also attached to the belt has a gold case with similar decoration; however, Woolley (1934, p. 51, pl. 151) says this decoration was not applied filigree but had instead been cast with the case.

4. Parrot 1968, p. 28, pl. 15.

5. Mallowan 1947, pp. 177–78, pl. 35; cf. also pl. 36, no. 11; Maxwell-Hyslop 1971, p. 15.

6. See also T. Özgüç 1986, p. 42, figs. 3–36.

7. For those found at Ur, see Zettler and Horne 1998, pp. 96 no. 35, 101 no. 43, 105 no. 52. The links on these chains from Ur are very closely attached and give the effect of being braided. For those found at Kish, see Mackay 1929, p. 182, pl. 43, no. 2304; cf. Oates, Oates, and McDonald 2001, p. 244. For those found at Tell Brak, see ibid., fig. 265. For those found at Troy, see Tolstikov and Treister 1996, nos. 10, 11.

119

Bead with flanges

Gold
L. 2.8 cm (1⅛ in.); Diam. 2.2 cm (⅞ in.); Weight 10.2 g
Syria, Tuba (?) (modern Tell Umm el-Marra), Tomb 1, UMM00M033
Early Bronze Age, ca. 2300 B.C.
National Museum, Aleppo, Syria 11672

This heavy gold bead (weighing 10 grams) has seven flat, triangular flanges projecting from a hollow tube about 0.45 centimeters in diameter. Originally the bead had eight flanges, but one has broken off. At each end of the tube a double row of wire spirals has been soldered. This bead and a gold filigree pendant (cat. no. 118) were found together in the "royal" tomb at Tell Umm el-Marra behind the skull of Skeleton A and beneath the cervical vertebrae, in a position suggesting they were on a cord around the woman's neck.

Multiple-flanged beads of third-millennium date are rare at sites in the ancient Near East. The only others found to date in Syria are two examples in the Treasure of Ur from Mari (cat. no. 85c). They differ from this bead in that the flanges are hemispherical rather than triangular, and only one of them has wire spirals at the ends.[1] Gold pins with a multiple-flanged head were found in the royal graves of Alaca Höyük, also dating from about 2300 B.C. (see cat. no. 185).[2] Smaller gold beads (0.50–0.80 centimeters in diameter and in length), with three, four, or five flanges but without a collar on the ends, were also found in these

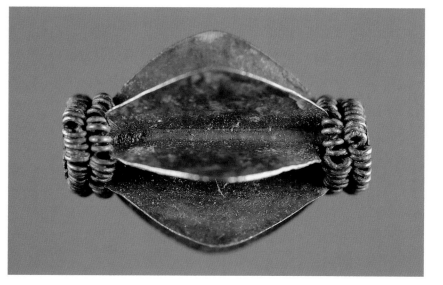

119

graves.[3] Several larger four-flanged gold beads (diameter 1.8 centimeters) were discovered in an Akkadian grave at Ur.[4] In the published photograph these appear to have a small cylindrical collar at one end. While the differences among these beads from Anatolia, Syria, and Mesopotamia suggest different places of manufacture, perhaps all these beads can be understood as different expressions of the same idea, that of elaborating a flat bead with a tubular midrib into a bead with multiple flanges around a central tube.[5]   SD

1. Parrot 1968, pp. 27–28, pls. B–3, 14–1. Parrot says that the arrangement of the beads as a bracelet in the published photograph is a conjectural reconstruction.
2. Cat. no. 185; see Arik 1937, pl. 167 (A1.240, Tomb B). Another example is illustrated in Akurgal 1962, pl. 19, bottom (Grave A).
3. For multiple-flanged gold beads from Alaca Höyük, see Arik 1937, pl. 181 (A1.319–52, A1.872–76); Koşay 1951, pl. 134, middle row (Tomb H), and p. 169, pl. 200, bottom row (A1.d./17 [should read A1.d./15], fifty-two beads from Tomb L); Akurgal 1962, pl. 19, middle row (Grave A).
4. Maxwell-Hyslop 1971, p. 26, pl. 20.
5. For flat beads with a tubular midrib, see catalogue numbers 120, 158d, 159, 211.

120

Flat beads with a tubular midrib

Silver
Each bead: L. 10.1 cm (4 in.); W. 7.8 cm (3⅛ in.);
Thickness 0.95 cm (⅜ in.); Weight 50–52 g
Syria, Tuba (?) (modern Tell Umm el-Marra), Tomb 1,
UMM00M015
Early Bronze Age, ca. 2300 B.C.
National Museum, Aleppo, Syria 11679.1–2

These two large silver beads from the "royal" tomb at Tell Umm el-Marra have a flat triangular wing on either side of a hollow central midrib that was presumably used for stringing. Smaller beads of lozenge or disk shape in gold and silver have been found in third-millennium contexts at Ur (Mesopotamia), Tell Brak (Syria), Troy (Anatolia), and Tell Abraq (the Gulf).[1] Whereas these smaller beads are easily understood as parts of necklaces, bracelets, or other articles of personal adornment, the Tell Umm el-Marra lozenges seem awkward owing to their large size. They were found lying on top of one another behind but near the shoulder of Skeleton A (the young woman buried in the uppermost level of the northern part of the tomb). Their position suggests that the deceased was not wearing them at the time. Near them was a silver disk—6 centimeters in diameter, with a central hole 1.3 centimeters in diameter—which was perhaps part of the same piece of jewelry as the lozenges. Support for this idea comes from a partially preserved mosaic panel discovered in Syria, at Mari, in 1961.[2] Among the preserved figures on this panel are twelve women. While they all appear to wear long robes with a fringed cape over the shoulders, their headdresses and jewelry differ in certain details. Some women wear what looks like a low turban with soft bands wrapped around it, or a kind of flat "bonnet" (see cat. no. 104).[3] These women's capes are always fastened with a single toggle pin—positioned vertically with its head up or horizontally—from which hang two lozenge-shaped beads and then a rectangular object, which is probably a cylinder seal.[4] In the lower left corner of a reconstructed panel, these women seem to be engaged in spinning

yarn.[5] Other women wear a high round hat, and their capes are fastened with two long, crossed pins with the pinheads down and the points up.[6] These women wear a string of three lozenge-shaped beads, below which is a circular disk and then a cylinder seal. The string of beads is not suspended from the crossed pins but seems to hang from something under the cape. Since these women appear to be engaged in ritual actions—one carries a footed vessel and the others follow her—their distinctive headdresses and jewelry probably indicate their particular role in the scene. This suggests that the juxtaposition of lozenges and disk in the jewelry of Skeleton A has a specific meaning.[7] The large size of the Tell Umm el-Marra beads may reflect a regional tradition, may indicate that Skeleton A had higher status in her community than the Mari women, or may be connected with the specific ceremonial times at which they were worn. A cylinder seal was found in front of the head of Skeleton A. It thus may have been strung on a necklace along with several other items found near it; however, this does not rule out the possibility that it may have sometimes been worn in the manner seen on the Mari panel.[8]   SD

1. For examples found at Ur, see Woolley 1934, pp. 366 fig. 10, 368 fig. 76, type 19. Maxwell-Hyslop (1971, p. 10, pls. 6a, 17a) says that while only a few examples occur at Ur in the Early Dynastic graves, they become more common in the Akkadian and Ur III periods. Cf. Nissen 1966, p. 82, pl. 21, type 19k,l,m. For examples at Tell Brak, see cat. nos. 158d, 159; see also Mallowan 1947, pp. 176–77, pl. 33:14. For examples

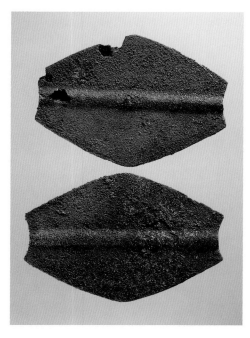

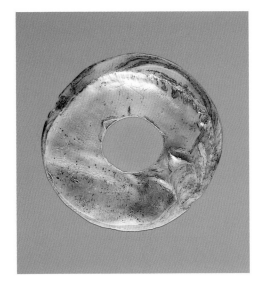

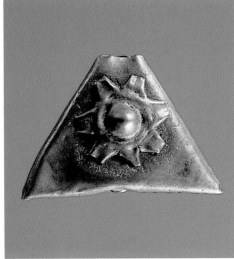

at Troy, see Tolistikov and Treister 1996, p. 42, no. 11. And for examples from Tell Abraq, see in cat. no. 211. Flat metal beads with a raised midrib were widespread in the second half of the third millennium B.C. They may be disk-shaped, rectangular, or lozenge-shaped. They are found at various sites from Anatolia to the Indus Valley. (See cat. nos. 167, 168d, 197, 280. Woolley (1934, p. 368) said they were made by soldering two disks together and hammering them over a wire to make the hollow midrib. Maxwell-Hyslop noted that a jewelry mould from the Ishtarat temple at Mari has a form for making disk beads; Maxwell-Hyslop 1971, p. 10, n. 1; Parrot 1967, p. 198, figs. 245, 246.
2. Parrot 1962, p. 164, fig. 11. This panel comes from excavations in the area north of the Ur III–Old Babylonian temple of Dagan, where a building was revealed that Parrot interpreted as part of a still earlier temple of Dagan and its dependencies; Parrot 1962, pp. 151–79; Parrot 1964, pp. 3–16. This interpretation has been doubted by Tunca (1984, p. 206) and Margueron (1985, pp. 494–96), who both note that none of the published information supports such an identification.
3. Parrot 1962, pl. 11:1–2.
4. Collon 2001, p. 17.
5. Parrot 1962, p. 164, pl. 11:1, fig. 11.
6. Ibid., pls. 11, 12, fig. 11.
7. Although the published pieces of the inlaid panel from Mari all show women wearing three lozenge-shaped beads, Parrot mentions that he found a large fragment from another area of the site that shows the same assortment of jewelry, but including only two lozenge-shaped beads; ibid., p. 168.
8. The registration number of the cylinder seal in the excavation records is UMM00G001.

121a, b

Disk ornament and triangular pendant with a star motif

Syria, Tuba (?) (modern Tell Umm el-Marra), Tomb 1 Early Bronze Age, ca. 2300 B.C.

a. Shell
Diam. 4.4 cm (1¾ in.); Thickness 0.3 cm (⅛ in.); Diam. of hole 1.4 cm (9⁄16 in.)
UMM00I024
National Museum, Aleppo, Syria 11691

b. Gold
H. 1.8 cm (¾ in.); W. 2.5 cm (1 in.); Thickness 0.7 cm (¼ in.); Weight 2.5 g
UMM00M017
National Museum, Aleppo, Syria 11673

Near the bodies interred in the "royal" tomb at Tell Umm el-Marra were found groups of jewelry pieces. A gold circle lay behind the skull of Skeleton D, a young, probably female individual buried along the south side of the tomb, opposite Skeleton A. Close by were a gold headband, one gold and two silver bracelets, and one copper-alloy and two silver pins. Below the headband was the gold triangular pendant (cat. no. 121b). The shell disk (cat. no. 121a) was in the southwest corner of the tomb, to the west of the skull of Skeleton C, a man buried below Skeleton D. Near it were several pieces of silver headbands and a silver disk with a rosette design. Groups of jewelry pieces have also been found placed near the dead at Alaca Höyük (Anatolia) and at Ur.[1] In connection with these Ur finds,

Steve Tinney has suggested that some of the jewelry and other precious items were meant for the deceased to offer to the gods of the underworld, since this custom is mentioned in certain Mesopotamian literary texts.[2] This purpose, however, may not apply to the jewelry found in northern Syria or Anatolia because contemporary and later texts from these areas reveal different ideas.[3]

The gold triangle found near Skeleton D is a hollow pendant made of sheet gold, to one face of which a star ornament is soldered. It has a hole at the apex and one directly opposite, in the base. Since it was found below the headband, possibly it was fastened to the gold circle and the headband in some way. The star has a large, round, convex center surrounded by seven flat, short points. The same star design can be seen in a much more elaborate silver pendant found in an Akkadian-period context at Tell Brak.[4]

The shell disk has no holes for attachment, and if worn, it must have been tied through the central hole. Two similar disks were found in an Early Bronze Age grave near the village of Hammam on the Euphrates, near the mouth of the Sajur River.[5] Recent excavations at Tell Qara Quzak, on the bank opposite Hammam, revealed many such shell disks in a hoard of beads and pendants buried in a jar under the floor of a third-millennium building.[6] Shells were highly valued in the ancient Near East for objects of personal adornment and for ritual objects, and they were imported from as far away as the Indian Ocean (see cat. nos. 289b, 291a).[7] In two graves of the Early Dynastic period at Khafajah (Mesopotamia) were found shell rings and disks like this one that had been attached to a gray backing, perhaps leather, to form a belt around the hips of the deceased.[8]

SD

1. For such groups at Alaca Höyük, see Arik 1937, pp. 61–62 (Tomb B.M.); for those at Ur, see Woolley 1934, pp. 152–53 (Grave PG 689), 156–58 (Grave PG 755).
2. Tinney 1998a, p. 28.
3. See Xella 1995 (Syria) and Haas 1995 (Anatolia).
4. Oates, Oates, and McDonald 2001, p. 390 fig. 387, p. 579 fig. 481, no. 138.
5. Woolley 1914, pp. 90–91, pl. 21a.
6. Pereiro 1999, p. 121, fig. 4b.
7. Gensheimer 1984.
8. Frankfort 1936b, pp. 49–50, fig. 41; cf. Delougaz, Hill, and Lloyd 1967, pp. 104–5, pl. 58c (Grave 107).

Tell Banat

Tell Banat, located on about sixty acres of land on the east bank of the Euphrates River in Syria, dates to the mid-to-late third millennium B.C. During that time it contained extensive manufacturing, administrative, and mortuary facilities. The unusual burial structures found there are of particular note, for they indicate complex social relationships beyond simple class divisions that no doubt included the pastoralists utilizing the steppe to the east of the settlement as well as the farmers of the river valley.[1] These structures include a large earthen funerary mound outside the city, one inside the city beneath the first public buildings of the mid-third millennium B.C., and an elaborate stone-built sepulchre of five chambers constructed in conjunction with those buildings—Tomb 7—in which all the objects described and illustrated below were found. Although the architecture of Tomb 7 is unique, many of the objects it contained have parallels in the cultural remains of southern Mesopotamia, Anatolia, and the Aegean. Decorated ostrich eggs, alabaster vessels, and a variety of inlaid objects are only some of the materials that reflect these international connections. In one richly furnished chamber was found the negative impression of a disintegrated wood coffin that contained a single articulated skeleton. Wood coffins are known from the Royal Cemetery of Ur, and the archaeologist Heinrich Schliemann said he found part of the treasures at Troy in a "wooden chest."[2] While, no doubt, the tomb's furnishings included the personal possessions of the deceased as well as gifts made by mourners, the specialized nature of some of the objects suggests that they may have been used in mortuary rituals performed at burial and in subsequent commemoration of the dead.[3]   AP/TM

1. Porter 2002.
2. On Ur, see Woolley 1934; on Troy, see Easton 1984, p. 147.
3. Winter 1999b.

122

Bowl with triangle cutouts for inlays

Stone
H. 2.9 cm (1⅛ in.); Diam. of rim 8.4 cm (3¼ in.);
Diam. of base 3.1 cm (1¼ in.)
Syria, Tell Banat, Tomb 7, TB193.95, ART1261
Early Bronze Age, mid-to-late 3rd millennium B.C.
National Museum, Aleppo, Syria   12354

This shallow stone bowl was decorated on its flat rim with three rings of precisely cut triangles pointing toward the basin. On the exterior is a row of isosceles triangles with their apexes just below the rim, bordered by two rows of smaller triangles in opposing pairs, leaving diamond-shaped interstices. The triangular recesses were no doubt cut to hold inlay; although a large number of inlay pieces were found throughout the room where the bowl lay, none could be associated with it. A common decorative technique, inlay was applied to several pieces of wood furniture and small objects found in the tomb.

AP/TM

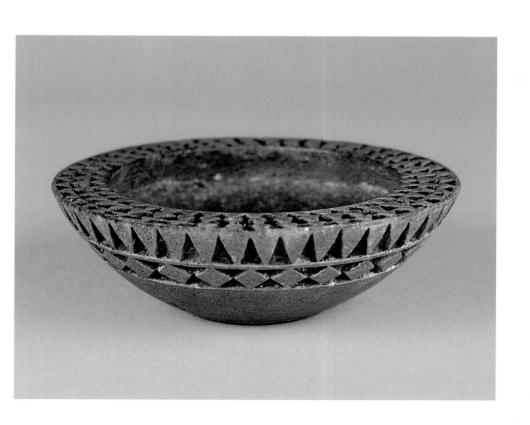

123a–e

Beads and pendants

Gold
Syria, Tell Banat, Tomb 7, TB192.95
Early Bronze Age, mid-to-late 3rd millennium B.C.

a. L. 0.5 cm (³⁄₁₆ in.); W. 0.6 cm (¼ in.); Thickness
0.2 cm (¹⁄₁₆ in.); Weight 0.4 g
National Museum, Aleppo, Syria 11561

b. L. 1.6 cm (⅝ in.); W. 0.5 cm (³⁄₁₆ in.); Thickness
0.4 cm (³⁄₁₆ in.); Weight 0.9 g
National Museum, Aleppo, Syria 11564

c. L. 1.5 cm (⁹⁄₁₆ in.); W. 1 cm (⅜ in.); Thickness
0.2 cm (¹⁄₁₆ in.); Weight 0.7 g
National Museum, Aleppo, Syria 11565

d. L. 1.9 cm (¾ in.); W. 0.8 cm (⁵⁄₁₆ in.); Thickness
0.2 cm (¹⁄₁₆ in.); Weight 0.4 g
National Museum, Aleppo, Syria 11566

e. L. 0.7 cm (¼ in.); W. 0.4 cm (³⁄₁₆ in.); Thickness
0.4 cm (³⁄₁₆ in.); Weight 0.8 g
National Museum, Aleppo, Syria 11568

Scattered over the skeleton in the coffin found in Tomb 7 at Tell Banat were hundreds of carnelian, gypsum, and polished black stone beads and more than twenty-five types of gold beads, many with parallels at Troy.[1] The types include quadruple-spiral, pumpkin-shaped, and rilled beads, scallop shells, and bell and biconical forms, as well as a range of tiny rings cut from long tubular beads. The tubes were formed from sheets wrapped around a mandrel-and-block and then fused. One barrel-shaped bead was decorated with bezels in which gold shot had been placed. There are also six-collared beads that may have received inlay, and pieces with double hemispherical dapping or bosses and end loops; these latter two types are similar to examples found at Alaca Höyük, in Anatolia.[2] Mushroom-shaped pendants cut from sheet metal and with loop-in-loop chain (above right) are similar to "idol-shaped" pendants from diadems and earrings found at Troy and Poliochni (see cat. no. 174). The perforated gold bars were probably for decorative attachment, although they have also been interpreted as the by-product of bead manufacture.[3]   AP/TM

1. Tolstikov and Treister 1996.
2. Koşay 1951, pls. 186, 206.
3. Tolstikov and Treister 1996, p. 115, no. 124.

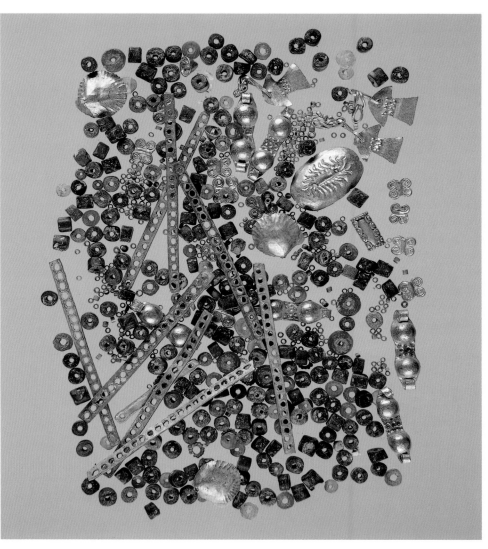

123a–e, 124, 125

124

Bead

Lapis lazuli and gold
L. 0.92 cm (⅜ in.); Diam. of base 1.3 cm (½ in.)
Syria, Tell Banat, Tomb 7, Chamber F, TB201.95
Early Bronze Age, mid-to-late 3rd millennium B.C.
National Museum, Aleppo, Syria

This fluted, hemispherical bead topped with a small gold cap was one of a group of enigmatic miniature objects made of low-grade lapis lazuli found in Tomb 7. The other similar pieces consisted of fluted sticks, broken off at twenty millimeters and twelve millimeters respectively, and both three millimeters thick; and half of a convex annular band; a small triangle twelve millimeters by twenty-two millimeters in size; and a plain, uncapped hemispherical bead. All of these pieces were neatly placed beside one another.   AP/TM

125

Pin with a bird head

Copper alloy
L. 16.7 (6⅝ in.)
Syria, Tell Banat, Tomb 7, TB198.95
Early Bronze Age, mid-to-late 3rd millennium B.C.
National Museum, Aleppo, Syria

Perched on the head of a straight copper-alloy pin with a pierced shaft is the figure of a bird. It was found in a wall niche beside an unguent vessel made from an ostrich egg in which a stone spout inlaid with lapis lazuli and shell had been inserted.

AP/TM

Pendant with an applied lozenge

Gold
H. 1.9 cm (¾ in.); W. 3.3 cm (1¼ in.)
Syria, Tell Banat, Tomb 7, TB191.95
Early Bronze Age, mid-to-late 3rd millennium B.C.
National Museum, Aleppo, Syria

This gold pendant was found among the fragmentary remains of a disarticulated individual placed on the floor of Tomb 7 in a chamber parallel to that in which the coffin was found. Weighing 8.66 grams, the gold pendant is pierced for stringing through a pumpkin-shaped ornament attached to the body. On the base of the pendant there are fifteen bosses formed in the casting process. The chased shoulders are complemented by a circle-and-punctate design stamped twenty-one times on the reverse and nineteen on the obverse, where the design is interrupted by the applied lozenge. The lozenge is formed by two rows of twisted gold wire, probably cut from thin sheets.   AP/TM

For another object excavated at Tell Banat, see catalogue number 109d.

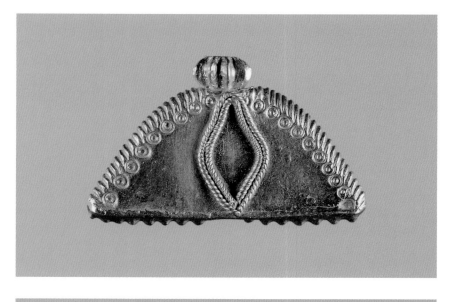

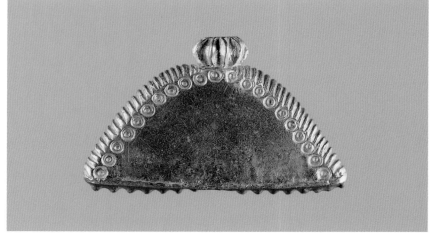

THE FIRST
GREAT EMPIRE

When the four regions together revolted against him, Naram-Sin, the mighty, king of Agade, through the love which the goddess Ishtar showed him . . . was victorious in nine battles in one year. . . . (Then the citizens of) his city requested from . . . (the gods) . . . that (he) be the god of their city and they built within Agade a temple to him.

Inscription of Naram-Sin, king of Agade, on a copper-alloy statue from Bassetki

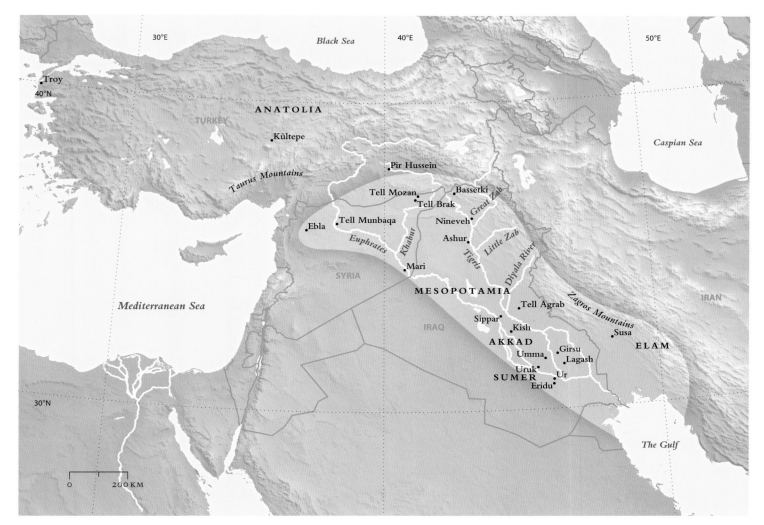

Fig. 51. Map of the Near East during the Akkadian period, showing the empire at its greatest extent and the sites mentioned in this section.

ART OF THE AKKADIAN DYNASTY

DONALD P. HANSEN

Later tradition credits the foundation of the Akkadian dynasty (ca. 2300–2159 B.C.) to Sargon, who had formerly held the influential position of cupbearer to a king of Kish at a time when Kish was a particularly important and powerful city in the northern part of lower Mesopotamia.[1] Usurping power and assuming for himself the title of king, Sargon became the first ruler of a new dynasty. He set about constructing his capital city of Agade, probably located not far from modern-day Baghdad. Sargon established the beginnings of an empire that at its greatest extent under later kings would reach as far as Anatolia in the north, inner Iran in the east, Arabia in the south, and the Mediterranean in the west.

Although many scholars have tried to locate Agade, none have succeeded,[2] and the site of the city remains a mystery. Without knowledge of the capital on which Sargon and the later kings focused their attention and royal patronage, our understanding of Akkadian art is limited and consequently somewhat skewed. Not much architecture has been excavated in the heart of the kingdom in southern Mesopotamia, and thus to gain any idea of the scale and magnificence of Akkadian monumental buildings we are dependent on a few remains in the far reaches of the empire.[3] We lack the richness of excavated material of the type that contributed to our understanding of the Early Dynastic period; instead, we must rely on chance finds of works of art attributable to the Akkadian period that have been excavated at a few widely separated sites. Other objects without provenances are in museums and private collections and unless inscribed must be attributed to the period stylistically. Curiously, for much of the important material we are indebted to a single Elamite king, Shutruk-Nahhunte, who in the twelfth century B.C. seized major Akkadian monuments as booty and carried them off to his own capital, Susa, in present-day Iran, where they were excavated by a French archaeological expedition.[4] From these

various sources, enough of a picture emerges to indicate that the Akkadian period was an era of profound artistic creativity, reaching one of the peaks of artistic achievement in the history of Mesopotamian art—and even in the history of world art.

The Sumerian King List states that Sargon ruled some fifty-six years, but there is little definitive information available about the chronology of his reign. At some point he campaigned and conquered in the north and west, reaching as far as Ebla. At another time he incorporated Sumer into an Akkadian kingdom. We know that at least the early part of his reign coincided with that of the rulers of Early Dynastic IIIB in Sumer.[5] It is therefore not surprising to find that the art Sargon commissioned to proclaim his emerging state reflected many of the qualities and ideals of art produced for Early Dynastic rulers in such centers as Ur and Lagash.

Fragmentary stone relief sculptures of the early Akkadian period all celebrate wars waged by the kings. This theme had also been used in Sumer in the Early Dynastic period, as is evidenced by the stele of Eannatum of Lagash, probably a contemporary of Mesanepada of Ur, that was found at Tello (the ancient city of Girsu, in Lagash; figs. 52, 53). The relief, organized in registers, shows on one side a series of depictions of Eannatum dressed in a fleeced garment (compare that of king Ishqi-Mari of Mari, cat. no. 88). In the upper register Eannatum holds a battle-axe as he advances at the head of a phalanx of soldiers with overlapping shields forming a large rectangular protective mass. The soldiers proceed to the right treading on the prone naked bodies of the enemy, who are soldiers of the neighboring state of Umma. In the next register Eannatum advances to the right in his chariot, holding a long spear aloft in his left hand. Behind him march two rows of warriors from Lagash, one overlapping the other, with raised spears supported on their shoulders. While much of this stele is lost, it is clear

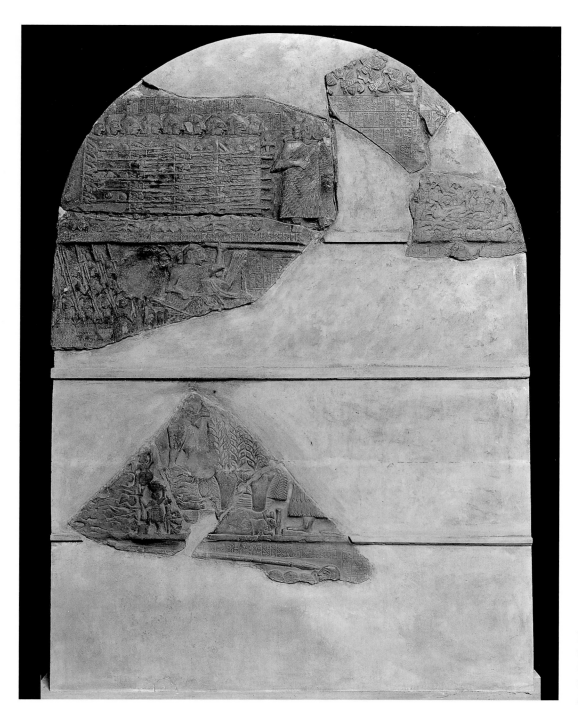

Fig. 52. Battle scenes carved on the limestone Stele of the Vultures. Girsu, Early Dynastic IIIA, ca. 2550–2400 B.C. Musée du Louvre, Paris, AO 50.

from what remains that this side displayed the might and prowess of Eannatum as manifest in different phases of the battle, including its aftermath. The engagement is also described in the text that fills the background.[6] Although the text and the relief scenes tell the same story, they relate them in different ways: in addition to employing two quite dissimilar means of expression, the visual and the textual accounts apparently rely on two separate narrative traditions. The text is certainly not a literal description of the scene that engages the viewer.

The stele was undoubtedly a freestanding monument in a court or major room of the temple of Ningirsu in Girsu, and like most monumental steles in Mesopotamia it was sculpted on both sides. While one side depicted the terrestrial victory of Eannatum over the warriors of Umma, the opposite side illustrated the same battle from a totally different perspective, that is, as waged in the world of the gods. What happens on earth is only a reflection of the divine will, and here Ningirsu, the special god of Lagash, is shown triumphant. He stands tall, filling a large portion of the stele surface, and holds a symbol, the lion-headed eagle grasping addorsed lions in its talons atop a net filled with the defeated enemies. By this dedication of the stele's two sides to different interpretations of the same event, the

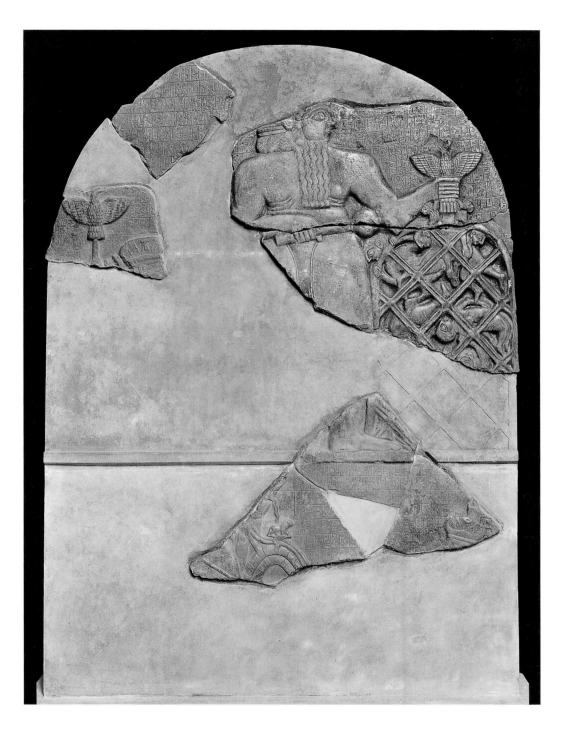

Fig. 53. The god Ningirsu carved on the limestone Stele of the Vultures (see fig. 52).

earthly and godly realms are kept separate and yet at the same time are intimately related.

Sargon's monuments, even in their badly damaged state, show clear indebtedness to Sumerian victory steles.[7] An example is a stele of Sargon, found at Susa and now in the Musée du Louvre, Paris, made of diorite from Oman, the preferred material for royal sculpture in the Akkadian period (fig. 54). The composition adheres to a strict register system. In the lower register Sargon appears, identified by his name inscribed in front of his head and looking much like a Sumerian king. He is dressed in a fleece garment covering his right shoulder and wears a beard and a headdress with the same style of royal chignon as that sported by Ishqi-Mari (cat. no. 88), Meskalamdug (fig. 18), and Eannatum (fig. 52). His soldiers line up behind him. In the upper register, bound nude prisoners, their bodies overlapping slightly, march to the left, while a group of Akkadian soldiers are probably dispatching an enemy, shown down on one knee. Details of representation suggest that another fragment also in the Louvre (cat. no. 127) either is part of the same stele or derives from the same workshop. Here, too, the upper register shows standing soldiers juxtaposed with debased enemies kneeling on one knee. In the lower register an Akkadian soldier, clothed

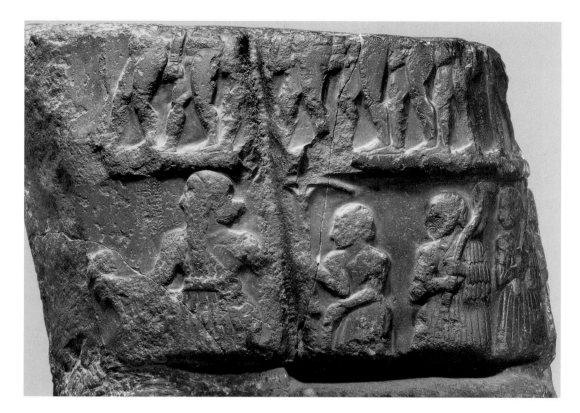

Fig. 54. Diorite fragment of a stele of Sargon found at Susa. Akkadian, ca. 2300–2245 B.C. Musée du Louvre, Paris, Sb 1.

somewhat differently from the soldiers behind Sargon, hurries along two nude enemies whose wrists are bound behind their backs. On the preserved fragments no text is included except the name of Sargon.

New in Akkadian sculpture is the endeavor to provide visual indicators to elucidate the narrative. Nude bound prisoners, deprived of power and any ability to act, are clearly set apart from the Akkadian soldiers. In their nudity they no longer appear even as soldiers, members of a group that chose to confront Sargon. Yet in order for the viewer to comprehend the campaign the prisoners must be identified, and therefore we see a distinctive hairstyle on the figure best preserved. He wears a series of clearly defined locks of hair, an attribute that would have geographically placed the scene of the battle for the sophisticated viewer.

The carving of the relief is high, with a particular emphasis on rounding the edges of corporeal forms of the soldiers and prisoners. Although the evident interest in delineating musculature (particularly apparent at the knees) suggests close observation, the conventions adopted by the artist do not approach anatomical correctness. The bodies stand out clearly against a neutral background, yet any narrative relationship between the figures is established solely by their physical presence next to one another or by the overlapping of body parts. Even though the general organization of the stele and certain aspects of its iconography derive from the art of the Sumerian city-states, the style is quite different from that of the Early Dynastic reliefs discussed above. Using only the material preserved for us at present, it is not easy to account for these changes. One wonders, for example, whether in the latter part of Early Dynastic III there may have been a recognizable school of sculpture in the region of Kish with a distinctive style that formed the basis for the style of Sargon's sculptors. Since Akkad was established first in the northern part of southern Mesopotamia, it is only reasonable to assume that Akkadian art emerged from the artistic practices of that very region.

Another fragmentary stele found at Susa (fig. 55) is similar in style and iconography to the one just described. Here the motif of a net encasing nude enemies, which Ningirsu holds on Eannatum's stele, is taken up by Sargon's sculptor. The figure grasping the net—perhaps Sargon, perhaps a god[8]—wields a mace as Ningirsu does and resoundingly smashes the head of a ruler particularized by his long strands of hair. To the right of the net is the goddess Ishtar, the Akkadian form of the Sumerian goddess Inanna. Ishtar was both the goddess of war and the goddess of Agade, the deity who granted kingship to the Akkadian kings. She is seated and facing to the left, and originally her weapons of war emanated from her shoulders. The style of carving on this fragment is much like that of the Sargon stele catalogue number 127. The head smasher and the goddess are related by the theme of war and victory celebrated on the monument; yet visually they are isolated entities, part of a string of paratactic

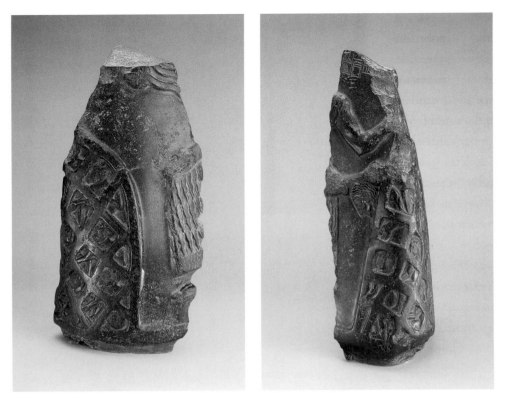

Fig. 55. Diorite fragment of a victory stele, probably of Sargon, found at Susa. Akkadian, ca. 2300–2245 B.C. Musée du Louvre, Paris, Sb 2.

Fig. 56. Diorite statue of Manishtushu found at Susa. Akkadian, ca. 2235–2221 B.C. Musée du Louvre, Paris, Sb 9099.

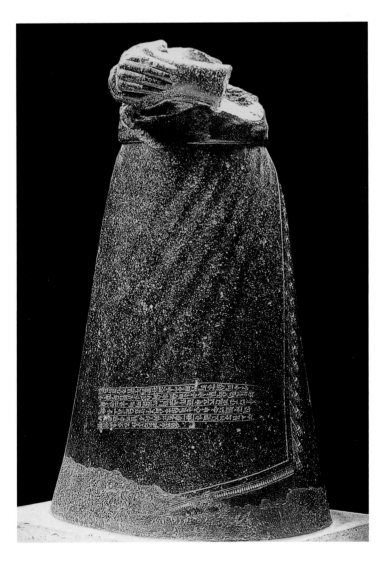

iconic images that originally signified different aspects of the battle.

A portion of another victory stele was found at Tello (cat. no. 129a). The stylistic tendencies seen in the steles of Sargon are here more pronounced, suggesting that this sculpture was created during the reign of one of Sargon's heirs, perhaps his son Rimush.[9] Organization of the visual elements is still governed by a register system, yet there is decidedly more space between the figures than on the earlier steles. Overlapping body parts are abandoned as a device, and more variations exist in the scale of the soldiers and enemies. Rounding and articulation of the body parts are more developed than before, and pronounced, convincing gestures engage the viewer and enliven the dead space of the background.

Several examples of sculpture in the round of Manishtushu, the successor of Rimush, were also found at Susa. While they are all badly damaged and fragmentary, one statue made of diorite, a standing image of the king with his hands clasped, is preserved from the waist down (fig. 56). On the front of the skirt is a long inscription of Shutruk-Nahhunte informing the reader that the statue was taken from the capital city of Agade. The frontal image with hands together in a prayerful gesture continues the tradition established in Early Dynastic III. The hands, executed with extraordinary detail and skill, project out farther from the body than do hands of earlier votive statues. Not enough of the statue is preserved to determine whether or not the upper part of the king's body was clothed or whether the torso was bare—

like that of the Early Dynastic ruler Enmetena (fig. 15). The sculptural treatment of the voluminous skirt of Manishtushu introduces elements quite new to Mesopotamian sculpture. One of these is the manner in which the fringes of the garment are suggested by the use of small, tightly controlled and organized repetitive patterns that contrast strikingly with the smooth polished surface of the diorite. Another aspect of this particular statue is the indication of a series of slightly raised folds in the garment caused by tucking the cloth overlap up into the waistband. Not only does this convey the sense of a soft cloth such as wool, it also interjects a subtle play of light and shadow on the surface of the stone. Such sculptural treatments demonstrate the considerable skill of the Akkadian sculptors in handling the very hard diorite, but beyond this dexterity they show a heightened awareness of formal elements and the self-conscious introduction of aesthetic formal qualities. These refinements characterize the "classic" art of the Akkadians, which we associate with Manishtushu's successors, Naram-Sin and Shar-kali-sharri. Undoubtedly, the art of Manishtushu's reign begins this classic phase.[10]

If the reign of Sargon actually overlapped that of the late Early Dynastic rulers, as the evidence seems to indicate, then the appearance of the classic Akkadian style with Manishtushu was not far removed in time from some of the best works of the Early Dynastic period, not only in southern Mesopotamia proper but also at Mari and even at Ebla to the west. It has been noted elsewhere that the art of these Syrian cities, although frequently based on Sumerian prototypes, is often composed with a special emphasis on studied formal elements far more developed than is usually the case with Sumerian art. It may well be that the western contacts of the newly formed Akkadian Empire provided a catalyst or stimulus that was adopted and transformed, helping to bring about the changes that underlay this classic phase of Akkad.

Although the head of the Manishtushu statue is lost, it probably looked much like a magnificent, hollow-cast copper-alloy head found at the Assyrian city of Nineveh in northern Iraq and now in the Iraq Museum, Baghdad (fig. 57). Unfortunately, the eyes of this head do not survive; they were probably made of shell or ivory with lapis lazuli pupils. When first found, the work was thought to represent Sargon.[11] Although it is not possible to be definite, the superb head clearly belongs to the classic phase of Akkadian art, and many scholars believe it to be part of a statue of Naram-Sin, although it could portray Manishtushu or even Shar-kali-sharri. The head epitomizes physical ideals of Akkadian kingship, stressing as it does by means of the beard and elaborate hairstyle the heroic, masculine importance of hair. It displays the

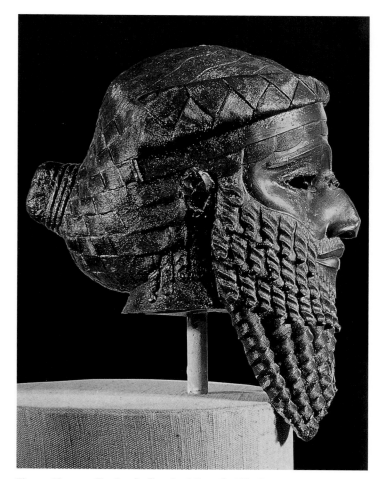

Fig. 57. Copper-alloy head of a ruler. Nineveh, Akkadian, ca. 2300–2159 B.C. Iraq Museum, Baghdad, IM 11331.

perfect blend of varied patterns of beard and hair that set off the lips, nose, and eyes of the ruler, a combination that imbues the king with a real sense of serene, yet powerful and all-knowing majesty. Treated in a more complex fashion than previously, the coiffure incorporates the Sumerian signifiers of royalty—a plaited braid encircling the head and a plaited chignon at the back of the head—that have been noted on the Early Dynastic golden helmet of Meskalamdug (fig. 18) and the headdress of Ishqi-Mari (cat. no. 88). In the case of the copper-alloy head, an added fillet placed just under the braid apparently surrounds the head and recalls the fillet of the much earlier "priest-king" from Uruk (cat. no. 8).

With today's means of rapid photographic reproduction, we are constantly beset and plagued by ruler images, be they royal or simply elected officials, no matter what part of the world we enter. Like present-day leaders, the Akkadian kings also wanted to have their likenesses seen throughout their realm. Although we do not know how this was accomplished, it seems reasonable to assume that there were workshops under royal patronage in many of the major cities capable of producing the desired reliefs and sculptures in the round. This copper-alloy head was found in the north, at Nineveh, but may have been sent there from the capital. On the other hand, a fragmentary stone head from Girsu in Lagash (cat. no. 137) probably came from a workshop in that city. It is a diorite counterpart to the copper-alloy head, save for the fact that its eyes were not inlays but instead were carved into the stone fabric. Despite its badly damaged state, the head still manages to impress us with a sense of Akkadian majesty.

Given the metallurgical skill of the Akkadian artists, it is likely that an accomplished copper-alloy head of a ruler long in the collection of The Metropolitan Museum of Art (cat. no. 136) dates to the time of the Akkadian Empire or at least close to it. Certainly this image is derived from the Akkadian ruler type, even though the exact hair patterns and the details of the coiffure differ from that model. Since there is no known provenance, one can only surmise either that it represents the king and was made for display in one of the more distant parts of the empire, or that it portrays a local ruler or governor, perhaps from a region to the east in Iran.[12]

During the course of road construction near the town of Bassetki in Iraq, close to the border between Iraq and Turkey—thus, from the northern part of the Akkadian Empire—a bulldozer uncovered a copper-alloy sculpture now in the Iraq Museum, Baghdad (fig. 58). This half-lifesized, hollow-cast sculpture not only is important as a work of art but also is significant for the content of an inscription carved on its circular

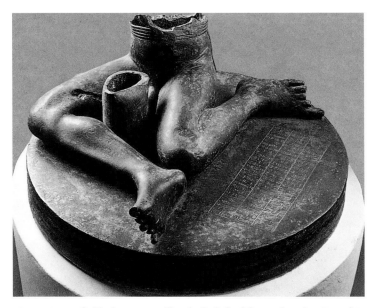

Fig. 58. Lower half of a copper-alloy nude, belted figure found at Bassetki. Akkadian, ca. 2300–2159 B.C. Iraq Museum, Baghdad, IM 77823.

base. Only the lower half of a male figure seated on the base is preserved. He is nude except for a belt with two small tassels, an iconographic detail indicating that the statue represents the nude bearded hero, usually shown with long locks of hair, similar to the hero on the top panel of the lyre from the Royal Cemetery of Ur (cat. no. 58). A socket on the base between the legs suggests that the hero originally held a standard, which would have fitted into the socket. An Akkadian cylinder seal in the Metropolitan Museum (cat. no. 145) shows this same hero, repeated four times, holding a gatepost standard. His head is frontal, but his body, shown in profile, rests on one knee. Perhaps this two-dimensional rendering of the hero's position is meant to suggest the complicated seated posture of the figure in the copper-alloy sculpture. The sensitive shaping of lower body, legs, and curling toes is the work of a master sculptor; surely, then, other great examples of Akkadian art are lost to us forever, or in some cases perhaps yet to be discovered.

The inscription indicates that the sculpture was created for Naram-Sin, the mightiest of the Akkadian rulers. It is particularly important, for it is the only preserved text to mention that during the course of his reign Naram-Sin became divine.[13] The text states that the people of Agade erected a temple in their city for the worship of Naram-Sin, whose name, thereafter, was always written with a divine determinative. Steles were made for him, and like those of Sargon and Rimush they continued to celebrate the king's victories and the expansion of the empire. But they had important new features; now that the king was accepted into the world of the gods, a new rhetoric needed to be developed that could combine the transitory, temporal ruler with the concept of the god incarnate on earth. This need found eloquent expression on a stele of Naram-Sin that originally stood in the Mesopotamian city of Sippar. Like steles of his predecessors, it was carried away by the same Shutruk-Nahhunte to Susa, where it was subsequently discovered.

The Sippar stele (fig. 59) represents Naram-Sin's battle with the Lullubi, a people dwelling in the eastern Zagros Mountains. In contrast to the stele of Rimush (cat. no. 129), here a composition employing a register system has been totally abandoned. The actual battle scene, coupled with an icon of the king triumphant, is set within a unified landscape setting, with the human figures of Akkadian soldiers and Lullubi enemy organized around a series of ascending diagonals. The focus of the composition is Naram-Sin, who appears as god-hero-king, his divinity signaled by his horned helmet, his heroic magnificence suggested by the perfection of his body, and his role as gallant king and warrior intimated by his stance with one foot slightly

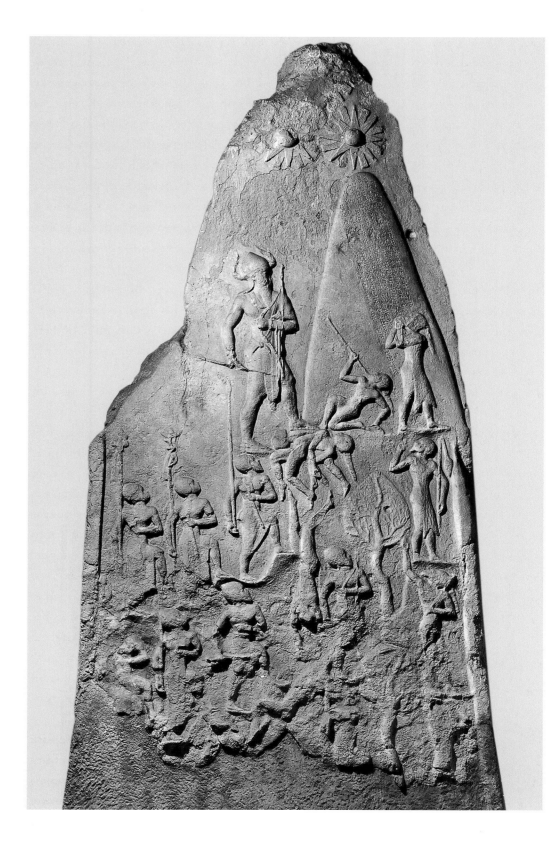

Fig. 59. Limestone stele of Naram-Sin, originally set up at Sippar but found at Susa. Akkadian, ca. 2220–2184 B.C. Musée du Louvre, Paris, Sb 4.

raised, crushing the broken bodies of the defeated enemy. Because Naram-Sin was now considered both god and king, it was no longer necessary to separate the terrestrial and divine worlds and relegate them to different sides of the stele, as had been done earlier in the depiction of Eannatum's battle with the soldiers of Umma (figs. 52, 53). Now one landscape representation fuses both worlds and even includes the great gods, emblazoned as star symbols situated at the top of the stele above the mountain peak. The text—unfortunately fragmentary—situates the battle, and the peculiarities of dress and hairstyle visually identify the mountaineers to the initiated viewers. Furthermore, a new element of specificity is introduced by the inclusion not of generic trees but rather of carefully depicted trees from the very region in which the battle took place, an added component important for narrative clarification.[14] The convincing corporeality of the soldiers and their naturalistic gestures are only two of the factors that help generate the sense of a unified and active space that intensifies for the viewer the impact of the god-king triumphant.

A fragmentary mould now in a private collection illustrates on a small scale another aspect of the complex iconography developed for expressing Naram-Sin's new role as god, king, and possessor of a vast empire (cat. no. 133).[15] The original shape of the limestone mould was similar to that of a rounded stone bowl or a hollowed-out hemisphere. The interior was carved with a scene in reverse, or intaglio, so that when a malleable material—undoubtedly gold—was pressed into the mould, an object was produced in the form of a boss with a series of scenes in relief. There is no indication of how this boss was used. Clearly the work of a most accomplished cylinder-seal carver, the completed object must have contained some nine individual vignettes surrounding a major circular central image.

The one scene that is preserved shows Ishtar, the goddess of Akkad as well as of war, seated on her lion throne atop a temple platform that perhaps signifies her own temple Ulmash in Agade. As in many of the images of Ishtar, her lower body is depicted in profile and her upper body is shown frontally, with her head en face and fully engaging the viewer's attention. Even though Naram-Sin is a lesser god, he is now entitled to sit opposite Ishtar, whereas a human, even the king, was normally required to stand before the enthroned deity. Naram-Sin holds a ring to which ropes are attached. Ishtar assists him by grasping his wrist with one hand and guiding the ropes that pass behind her with the other hand. The ropes are attached to the nose rings not only of two rulers or chieftains standing on images of their own particular cities but also of two mountain gods, who emerge from a mountain range and present bowls containing tribute to Ishtar and Naram-Sin. The scene indicates not only that, through Ishtar, Naram-Sin has conquered one mountainous area—to either the east or the north of Agade—and incorporated it into his domain, but also that he controls and administers that region by the goddess's benevolence. Forever lost to us, the other scenes surrounding the center must have used different iconographies to indicate other parts of the empire stretching out from Agade in four directions. Each region would have been identifiable by appropriate signifiers associated with other chieftains and gods. Thus, the boss was essentially a world map of Naram-Sin's empire as seen from its center, Agade.

A huge corpus of Akkadian cylinder seals is preserved; most of them are rich in both iconography and style. Some seals are carved with a dexterity and bravura equaling that of the stone mould. A serpentine seal in the Musée du Louvre (cat. no. 135) stands out as a perfect embodiment of the developed classic style. Its inscription states that it belonged to Ibni-sharrum, who held the important position of scribe under Shar-kali-sharri, successor of Naram-Sin. The main theme of the seal carving concerns the waters of life, suggested not only by the river—an undulating band flanked by overlapping scallops indicating mountains or earth—at the bottom of the seal but also by heroes and water buffaloes placed above the river. The strong aesthetic appeal of the seal, with its highly formal scheme and the decorative interlocking of its pictorial elements, almost overrides its meaning for the modern viewer. The heroes, who are similar to the hero of the Bassetki sculpture (fig. 58), kneel on one knee and hold forth vessels from which the waters of life flow. Two water buffaloes with upraised heads, their sweeping horns supporting the rectangular box containing the inscription, drink from these very waters. The seal-cutter has carved the heroes and animals in high relief and has paid great attention to their mass and strength by emphasizing the musculature. Without approaching anatomical accuracy, the abstractions used to indicate the muscles and structure of the body effectively imbue the heroes and animals with a sense of life and reality.

A chalcedony seal in the British Museum is carved in much the same style (cat. no. 147). It belonged to one Shakullum, also a high official who held the title of scribe, with the inscription that names him being in this case relegated to the side. The composition of this seal is built around the "sacred" tree or plant of life shown in the center. On either side of the plant form, the now-familiar heroic figure contends with a lion standing erect, leg and paw outstretched. The hero struggles to keep in control the elemental animal forces of nature, here symbolized by the lion. The master carver, employing conventions for showing the structure of bodies, similar to those used in the Ibni-sharrum seal, managed to suggest convincingly the tension and torsion of this combat between hero and lion. A variation of this same idea is shown in a seal in the Pierpont Morgan Library (cat. no. 146). On this seal, a central tree is flanked on one side by a bull- or bison-man grasping a lion and on the other side by the hero controlling a bull.

The rich repertory of motifs in the glyptic of the Akkadian period is executed in a variety of styles and with varying degrees of competency. In addition to contest scenes, the presentation of a worshiper to a deity continues as an important theme (e.g., cat. no. 141). Particularly popular are scenes with a battle among the gods. This subject may stand alone on the cylinder (cat. no. 144) or be in combination with another scene, such as that of a presentation (cat. no. 143). Interestingly, the battle among the successive cycles or generations of gods is a theme found in several ancient cultures. Different gods, for instance the weather god (cat. no. 142), are shown in full regalia. Many scholars believe that certain Akkadian seals depict scenes from myths; the human figure astride an eagle on some seals (cat. no. 148, for example) is often interpreted as the shepherd Etana borne to heaven by an eagle (see cat. no. 340).[16] However, other correspondences have proven more difficult to establish.

The accomplishments of the Akkadian artists are impressive. Although these are based in large part on the art of their Sumerian predecessors and contemporaries, the Akkadians introduced new iconographies and new interpretations generated by different stimuli, including their Semitic background and their contacts with new peoples encountered in their expanding empire. Artistic expression attained a height not to be reached again in later Mesopotamian art. Even though we do not know the capital city of Agade, enough works of its art are preserved to give a glimpse of their importance and brilliance. The Akkadian achievements and traditions they represent were so impressive that later peoples in Mesopotamia were inspired to emulate them.

1. See Steinkeller 1992b.
2. On the location of Agade, see the bibliography in Liverani 1993, p. 272.
3. See, for example, the so-called palace of Naram-Sin excavated by Mallowan at Tell Brak (Mallowan 1947) and other buildings excavated by David and Joan Oates, also at Tell Brak (Oates, Oates, and McDonald 2001).
4. See Harper, Aruz, and Tallon 1992, pp. 159ff.
5. See Gibson and McMahon 1995; Gibson and McMahon 1997; and D. Matthews 1997.
6. For the text, see Cooper 1983b and Cooper 1986; for a study of the relationship between text and image on the stele, see Winter 1985.
7. For a detailed description and discussion of Sargon's monuments, see Nigro 1998a and Nigro 1998b.
8. For the fragmentary inscription, see Frayne 1993, p. 310.
9. A detailed study of this monument dated to Rimush is presented by Foster 1985.
10. For an introduction to Akkadian art, see Amiet 1976a.
11. Mallowan 1936, p. 104.
12. On the question of Akkadian influence in the east, see Pittman 1984.
13. For the inscription, see Frayne 1993, pp. 113–14.
14. For this important observation and a study of the landscape, see Winter 1999c.
15. For a detailed study of the mould, see Hansen 2002.
16. See, most recently, Steinkeller 1992a.

Fragment of a Mesopotamian victory stele

Olivine-gabbro
H. 46.2 cm (18¼ in.); W. 35 cm (13¾ in.)
Iran, Susa, Acropole
Akkadian, reign of Sargon, ca. 2300–2245 B.C.
Musée du Louvre, Département des Antiquités
Orientales, Paris Sb 3

Sargon inaugurated an official art in which royal victory, the favorite theme, was illustrated on steles executed as a series in the royal workshops. These monuments, shaped like large, slightly pyramidal blocks, were placed in the temples of principal cities of the Akkadian Empire. None has come down to us intact, but the Musée du Louvre, Paris, houses several fragments found at Susa, where they were taken as war booty in the twelfth century B.C. (figs. 54, 55).

On the lower register of this fragment, which shows a procession of enemies captured in combat, only two prisoners are visible.[1] Nude and divested of weapons, they have their hands bound behind their backs. Their hair, which is pulled into tufts at the tops of their skulls, indicates they are foreigners. The Akkadian soldier pushing them forward has a very different hairstyle: a bowl cut. He is dressed in a midlength skirt, and his torso is protected by a broad crossed sash, probably cut from thick cloth, which functioned as a breastplate. Weapons of the type he carries on his shoulder—composed of a curved blade attached to a handle—have been found in the royal tombs at Ur. The upper register of the fragment, which is in very poor condition, evokes the battle. The legs of one figure, who falls over backward as he is pierced by a spear, can be distinguished.

The iconography of the scenes, as represented in superposed registers, is a stylistic convention of the Early Dynastic period (cat. no. 52); however, the elegance of line, the vitality of the modeling, and the care taken in rendering the sculptural beauty of the nude bodies attest to the new trend toward realism that was characteristic of the Akkadian period. The quality of the relief obtained from the olivine-gabbro, a very hard volcanic stone, demonstrates the technical virtuosity of the artists working in the Akkadian royal workshops. Since their use was part of a royal tradition that continued throughout the history of

Mesopotamia, such stones were imported from great distances, which further enhanced their prestige.   FD

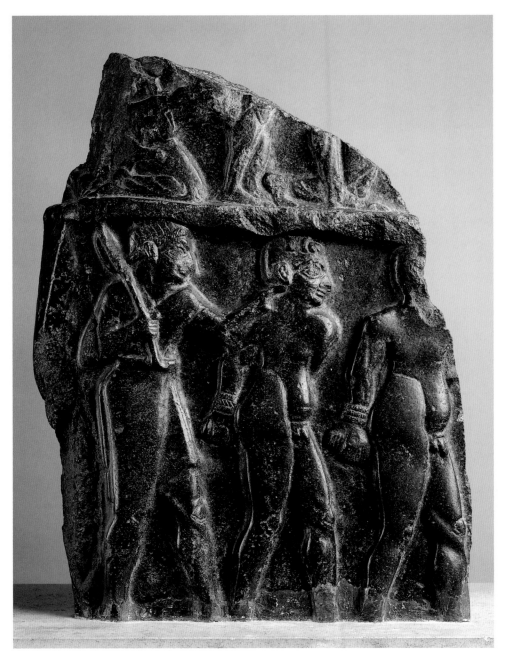

1. For further reference, see Jéquier 1905, p. 22, pl. I-b; Barrelet 1959, p. 28, fig. 2; and Amiet 1976a, p. 11, fig. 6.

Disk of Enheduanna, daughter of Sargon

Cuneiform inscription in Sumerian
Alabaster
Diam. 25.6 cm (10⅛ in.); Thickness 7.1 cm (2¾ in.)
Mesopotamia, Ur, gipar, U.6612
Akkadian, ca. 2300–2184 B.C.
University of Pennsylvania Museum of Archaeology
and Anthropology, Philadelphia CBS 16665

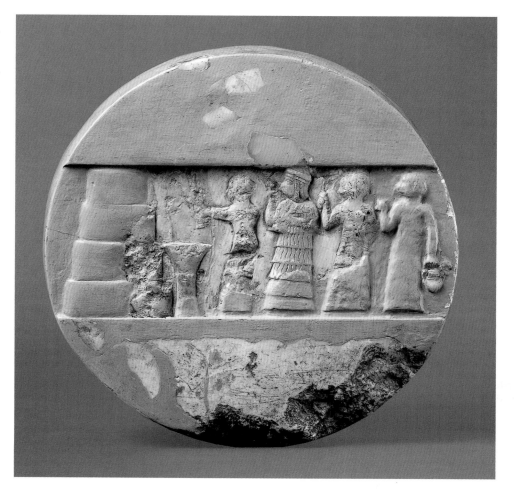

Found in the excavations at Ur was a heavily damaged votive disc dedicated by Enheduanna, the daughter of Sargon.[1] The disk is carved on one side with a horizontal band of figural relief and inscribed on the other: "Enheduanna, *zirru*-priestess, wife of the god Nanna, daughter of Sargon, [king] of the world, in [the temple of the goddess Inan]na-ZA.ZA in [U]r, made a [soc]le (and) named it: 'dais, table of (the god) An.'"[2] Enheduanna, a figure known to us from historical, archaeological, and literary sources,[3] was strategically appointed sometime during her father's reign to the prestigious office of *entu*-priestess of the moon god Nanna at Ur[4] and continued in that capacity into the reign of her nephew, Naram-Sin.[5] As the *entu*-priestess, Enheduanna was believed to have been chosen by divination to act as the embodiment of the goddess Ningal, the divine consort of Nanna, and to maintain the god's cult on Ningal's behalf.[6]

Several literary works that have been ascribed to Enheduanna's authorship[7] further illuminate her role as *entu*-priestess and allude to the existence of an earlier *gipar,* an all-encompassing temple structure at Ur known archaeologically from later levels.[8] The Sumerian word *gipar* may originally have meant "storehouse," but it came to refer to the residence and administrative center of the *entu*-priestess, which included the temple of the goddess Ningal as well as storerooms and operative areas associated with the divine cult. This inscribed alabaster disk was found defaced in the fill of the Isin-Larsa levels of the *gipar* (fig. 60),[9] having survived intact at least into the second millennium B.C., when a complete Old Babylonian tablet copy of the inscription was made.[10]

The pictorial relief appears within a single register, resembling impressions made from cylinder seals.[11] It contains four figures and depicts a ritual enacted by a nude male priest, who pours a libation from a spouted vessel

into a widely flaring vase or plant stand. According to the modern reconstruction, the scene takes place before a four-tiered altar or temple tower.[12] Whatever the specific interpretation of this element, it can generally be

read as an emblem denoting a sacred space. Behind the priest stands a dominant female figure seen in profile, identified as Enheduanna on the basis of her central position in the scene, her larger scale, and her apparent role

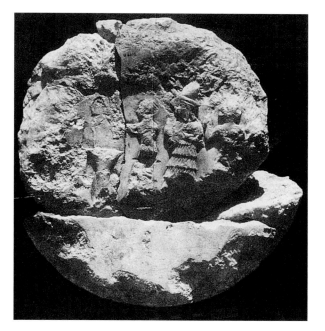

Fig. 60. Disk of Enheduanna (cat. no. 128) before restoration.

as overseer of the cultic ritual. She wears a long tufted garment and rolled-brim cap *(aga)*, a special headdress associated with the office of *entu*-priestess,[13] beneath which plaits of her hair are visible. Two male attendants, one holding what seems to be a fly whisk and the other a loop-handled vessel,[14] follow Enheduanna and visually balance the composition. Enheduanna raises her right hand in a gesture of greeting, sanctioning the ritual taking place before her and indirectly implying the divine approval of the Akkad dynasty commanded by her father, brothers, and ultimately nephew, all of whom ruled during her tenure as *entu*-priestess.

MJH

1. Woolley 1926, pp. 376–77, pl. 54b; Woolley 1955, pp. 49, 172, pl. 41d.
2. Gadd and Legrain 1928, fig. 23; Frayne 1993, pp. 35–36. See also Westenholz 1989, pp. 541–44, for reading of the title *zirru*.
3. The bibliography is extensive; see Frayne 1993, pp. 35–36. In addition to the disk, two seals and one sealing that belonged to servants of Enheduanna were found at Ur; see ibid., pp. 38–40, for references.
4. The position of *entu*-priestess was reserved for women of royalty and primarily daughters of the king; this practice lasted into the second millennium. The office is believed to predate Enheduanna (Winter 1987b), but thus far she remains the first woman known to bear the title "*entu*-priestess." See ibid., p. 200, for suggested appointment during Sargon's reign.
5. Hallo and Van Dijk 1968, p. 2, n. 6. At some point (perhaps on Enheduanna's death?) Naram-Sin appointed his own daughter Enmenanna to be high priestess at Ur. Other daughters of Naram-Sin were also in the service of various temples as *entu*-priestesses; see Buccellati and Kelly-Buccellati 2002, pp. 16–17, n. 3.
6. For functions within the cult, see Westenholz 1989. For the additional function of diviner, see Hallo 1976, p. 30.
7. If this attribution is correct, Enheduanna would be the first attested author of either gender. See note 3 above for her literary works; for opposition to this attribution of authorship, see Civil 1980, p. 229.
8. No remains have been found of the Akkadian *gipar;* rather, the building is known primarily from archaeological remains of the Ur III period and later. For an overview of the *gipar*, see Weadock 1975. For Enheduanna's mention of the *gipar*, see Hallo and Van Dijk 1968, p. 28, l. 66.
9. Specifically, the disk was found at the northeast end of the passageway between blocks A and B (*gipar* proper) and C (the more public area, perhaps the temple of Ningal); see the plan in Weadock 1975, pl. 26. See also Winter 1987b, n. 15. Whether the disk was intentionally defaced, as proposed by the excavator (Woolley 1955, p. 49), is debatable, since neither the priestess's face nor her name had been completely erased (McHale-Moore 2000, p. 70).
10. See Frayne 1993, p. 35.
11. Winter 1987b, p. 190.
12. There is evidence for only the lower stages; see ibid., p. 192, n. 17. For Early Dynastic seals showing a tiered structure, see numbers 87b, c in this catalogue; Amiet 1980, nos. 1441–64, 1482, 1484; and Winter 1987b, p. 193, n. 24.
13. Hallo and Van Dijk 1968, pp. 2, 29, l. 107; Winter 1987b, p. 126; Renger 1967, pp. 126–27.
14. All that was preserved of the fourth figure is the left hand and the vessel; the rest is restored.

129a, b

Stele fragments with combat scenes and inscriptions attributed to Rimush

Cuneiform inscription in Sumerian
Limestone
Mesopotamia, Girsu (modern Tello), Telloh K
Akkadian, reign of Rimush, ca. 2244–2236 B.C.

a. Sculpted fragment: H. 34 cm (13⅜ in.); W. 28 cm (11 in.)
Musée du Louvre, Département des Antiquités Orientales, Paris AO 2678

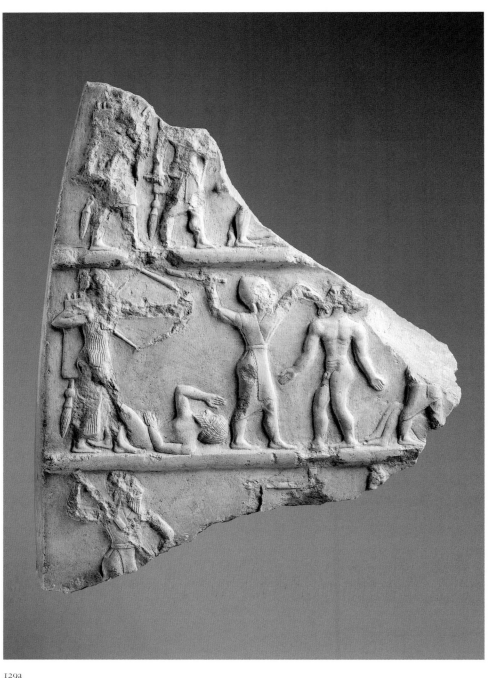

129a

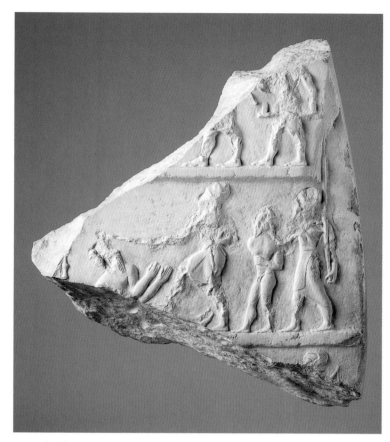

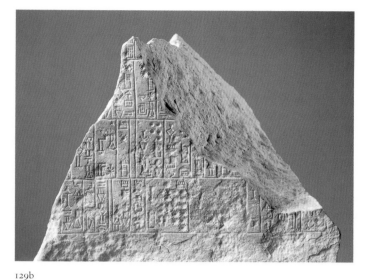

129a, other face   129b

b. Inscribed fragment: H. 28 cm (11 in.); W. 28.5 cm (11¼ in.)
Musée du Louvre, Département des Antiquités Orientales, Paris AO 2679

Sculpted on both faces, this slab (cat. no. 129a) formed part of the rounded top of a stele that was probably inscribed over much of its surface.[1] Two other fragments, both bearing inscriptions, likely come from the same monument: one (cat. no. 129b) was found by Ernest de Sarzec in Tello (ancient Girsu) along with the sculpted fragment; a second was acquired before 1915 by the Yale Babylonian Collection, New Haven, and has been linked to the two fragments in the Louvre by Benjamin R. Foster.[2]

The sculpted motifs illustrate a royal victory, a predominant theme in Akkadian art. On the damaged upper register the legs of three archers are discernible. On their backs they carry quivers, each adorned with one long tassel. Underneath, they are paired off in battle. The first figure arches his bow while trampling an enemy. He wears a tufted garment, an indication that he is of high rank, possibly the king himself.[3] Next to him is an Akkadian warrior dressed in a midlength

skirt with his torso protected by a broad sash; he wears the narrow leather helmet characteristic of Akkadian soldiers after Sargon's reign. He is preparing to finish off an enemy who is shown surrendering with knees bent and hands open, an attitude similar to that of the vanquished gods in glyptic from that period (see cat. no. 144). On the other face, two soldiers, one of them armed with an axe, march forward; underneath, a soldier carrying a spear drives before him an enemy whose arms are bound; farther along, another warrior strikes a defeated enemy who lies on the ground with his hands raised, begging for mercy.

Although the superposed registers are traditional, the airy composition, with its regular rhythm marked by alternating standing figures and figures on the ground, sets it apart from the dense arrangements on steles from the reign of Sargon (see fig. 54). The more slender canon of silhouettes and the careful detail, which results in a less powerful but more refined relief, point to a date for this stele after the reign of the first Akkadian king.[4]

Although the two inscribed fragments do not join, reading them together has made it possible to gain a clearer understanding of the text, which mentions lists of properties in the

region of Lagash, associated with either proper names or the titles of individuals, during the reign of an Akkadian king. Benjamin Foster, relying on a reading of the text, the shape of certain cuneiform signs, and the theme and style of the relief, argues that this victory stele should be attributed to Rimush, whose name he restores on the Yale fragment.[5] The monument would therefore commemorate the repression of the uprising of the chief Sumerian cities, including Lagash, shortly after Rimush acceded to the throne. The "bowl" hairstyle of the prostrate enemies suggests that they are Sumerians, not foreigners (see entry for cat. no. 127), and the lands mentioned would thus be properties granted by the king to his supporters after the victory.

FD

1. For further reference, see Sarzec and Heuzey 1884–1912, vol. 2, pp. 198–202, pl. 5bis; Parrot 1948, pp. 133–34; Amiet 1976a; and Foster 1985, pp. 15–30.
2. The Yale Babylonian Collection fragment is YBC2409; see Foster 1985, pp. 15–30.
3. Amiet 1976a, p. 26.
4. Foster 1985, n. 2; Amiet 1976a, p. 27.
5. "I restore here Rimush with considerable reserve"; Foster 1985, p. 21.

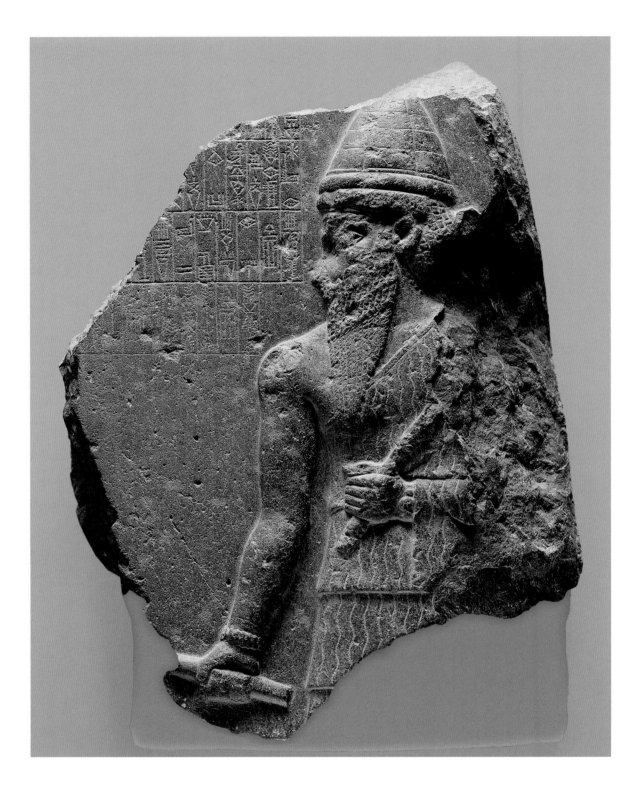

130

Stele fragment naming Naram-Sin

Cuneiform inscription in Old Akkadian
Basalt
H. 57 cm (22½ in.); W. 42 cm (16½ in.); Thickness
20 cm (7⅞ in.)
Anatolia, Pir Hussein
Akkadian, reign of Naram-Sin, ca. 2220–2184 B.C.
Eski Şark Museum, Istanbul 1027

This fragment of a stele commemorating a
military victory of Naram-Sin was found in
eastern Anatolia. It is not clear how it came to
be found in the Diyarbakir region; nor is it
known where the stele was initially erected
and where originally carved. The fact that the
material is basalt suggests that it was probably
sculpted in a major Akkadian center within
the northern part of the empire.

Unfortunately, only one fragment of the
original stele is preserved, so that both the
inscription and the royal figure are incomplete.
Nevertheless, it is possible to reconstruct in the
inscription the name of Naram-Sin, probably
originally written with the divine determinative, and to establish that a burial mound is
mentioned, indicating that the stele celebrates
a victory.[1] The god Ea is referred to in the

text, and at the end is a reference to the goddess Ishtar, along with a curse upon anyone who should destroy the inscription.

Naram-Sin stands facing to the left.[2] He wears a tufted garment that covers his left shoulder, leaving the right shoulder bare. On each wrist is a heavy bracelet, and in each hand he holds the handle of a weapon (the heads are broken away). Much of his face is covered by a long, elaborately styled beard, which resembles the beards on the Akkadian sculptures in the round seen in figure 57 and catalogue number 137. The hair on the back of the head is plaited, and it is reasonable to assume that on the original unbroken stele, a bound chignon was formed from the interwoven tresses. The king wears a conical cap with a raised bottom edge that is decorated with both horizontal and vertical incised lines. Although the shape of this cap is perplexing, it clearly is not the horned crown associated with divinities, as seen on the Sippar stele of Naram-Sin (fig. 59) or on the limestone mould (cat. no. 133). A conical cap is worn by certain heroes on Akkadian cylinder seals, and it has been noted that it resembles the military cap of Ebla, suggesting that Naram-Sin assumed this crown after his northern conquests.[3] This is a unique representation of Naram-Sin that contains both royal and divine signifiers.[4]

DPH

1. Frayne (1993, pp. 128–29) corrects the interpretation of Börker-Klähn (1982, pp. 133–34).
2. For a reasonable reconstruction of the stele, see Bänder 1995, pl. 57.
3. See the seals cited in Collon 1982, p. 32; for Ebla, see Matthiae 1980a, p. 47.
4. The details of this image of Naram-Sin are fully discussed in Bänder 1995, pp. 156–59.

the decoration of the stele was arranged in registers (for a similar organization of a stele, see cat. no. 129). The style depends in part upon earlier models of scenes of conquerors and captives (see cat. no. 48), but the typical Akkadian approach featuring more vivid and detailed modeling of anatomy is also present. The bearded warrior facing left in profile escorts a captive; of the latter figure only the bound arms survive. The warrior's right arm rests on the left shoulder of the captive. This captive may have been similar to the prisoners in one of the Baghdad fragments, which depicts a line of nude prisoners, with arms bound behind their backs and with heads in neck stocks.[1] The striations on the warrior's helmet may be meant to show that it is formed from bands of metal (see entry for cat. no. 130). His left hand grasps the handle of a battle-axe, the blade of which rests upon his left shoulder. He wears a long, broad, fringed sash draped over his shoulders and extending over the front of a long fringed garment.

Above the warrior is the only surviving portion of another register, which displays the lower front of the skirt and the lower legs of a warrior who holds a lance in front of him. In contrast to the figure below him and on the other fragments, this warrior faces to the right.

Fragments of an alabaster steles discovered at Susa[2] and Eridu (cat. no. 132) may come from the same workshop as this example.

PC

1. McKeon 1970, p. 226, pls. 4–6. The prisoners in one of the Baghdad fragments wear various hairstyles, which may represent different conquered areas or peoples. Indeed, the other Baghdad fragment (fig. 61) shows Anatolian-style vessels being carried by soldiers.
2. Amiet 1965, p. 243. The fragments in Baghdad were discovered about 1954 and were said to have come from the region around the modern town of Nasiriya, southern Iraq.

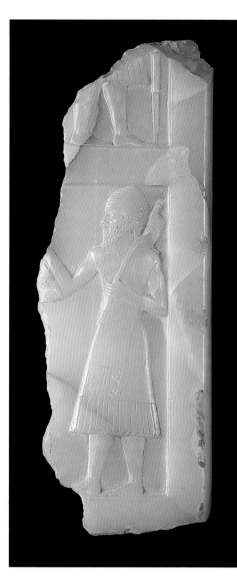

131

Stele fragment with a warrior

Alabaster
H. 35 cm (13¾ in.); W. 11.5 cm (4½ in.)
Mesopotamia
Akkadian, ca. 2220–2159 B.C.
Museum of Fine Arts, Boston; Gift of the Guide Foundation and Mrs. Hilary Barrat-Brown
MFA 66.893

This stele fragment contains the best-preserved figure of an Akkadian warrior that survives. Two other fragments (fig. 61) as well as the rectangular borders of this piece show that

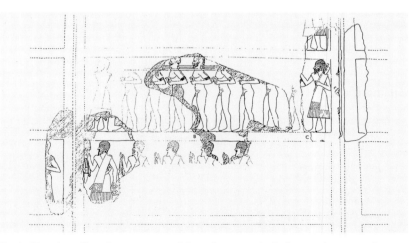

Fig. 61. Drawing of a stele reconstructed from fragments, including catalogue number 131.

132a, b

Stele fragments with male and female figures

Alabaster
a. H. 9.5 cm (3¾ in.)
b. H. 6 cm (2⅜ in.)
Mesopotamia, Eridu (modern Abu Shahrein)
Akkadian, ca. 2220–2159 B.C.
Trustees of The British Museum, London BM 114259,
BM 114260

Akkadian sculpture is famous for the exceptionally high quality of the carving. Although these two fragments cannot be shown to have belonged to the same monument, they share the same material and style.[1] The larger piece depicts a standing figure. Only part of the chest, the left forearm and hand, and the upper part and elbow of the right arm are visible. Since the chest appears to be unclothed it is likely that the figure is male. He holds an unidentifiable, double, tubelike object, which tapers down to a band near the bottom, in his very finely modeled hand. At the left elbow is a rounded projection, below which the line of the skirt is indicated alongside the break.

The smaller fragment is believed to depict a woman,[2] wearing a multiple-strand choker, as found on carvings from Girsu;[3] a vertical division toward the back of the choker probably represents the clasp. A double band extends from the bottom corners of the choker and meets on the chest, the longer end reaching as far as the left breast. The necklace is similar to those worn by male figures on an Akkadian monument from Susa.[4]

These fragments are comparable in material and in style to the so-called Nasiriya Stele (cat. no. 131), of which they may have been a part. However, it is equally possible that they belong to separate monuments if, as suggested by Pierre Amiet, Akkadian steles were mass-produced for display in different cities of the Akkadian Empire.[5]   PC

1. Reade 1981, pp. 9–11, pl. 56.
2. Ibid., p. 9.
3. Strommenger 1967, pl. 129.
4. Amiet 1976a, pls. 21, 22.
5. Amiet 1965, p. 243.

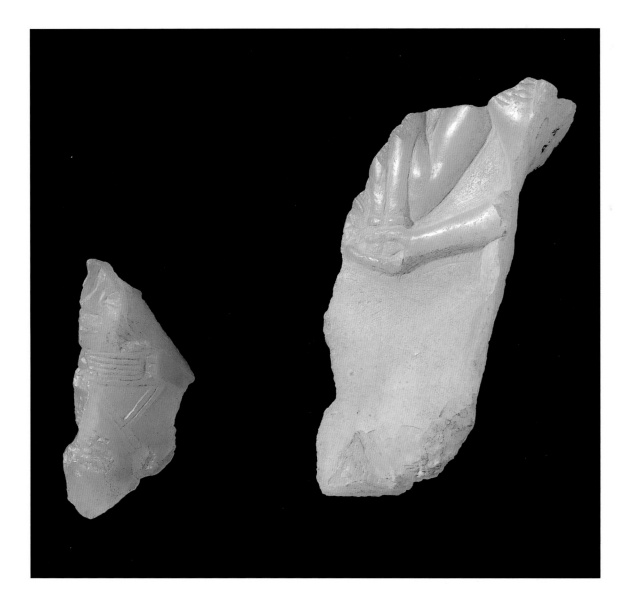

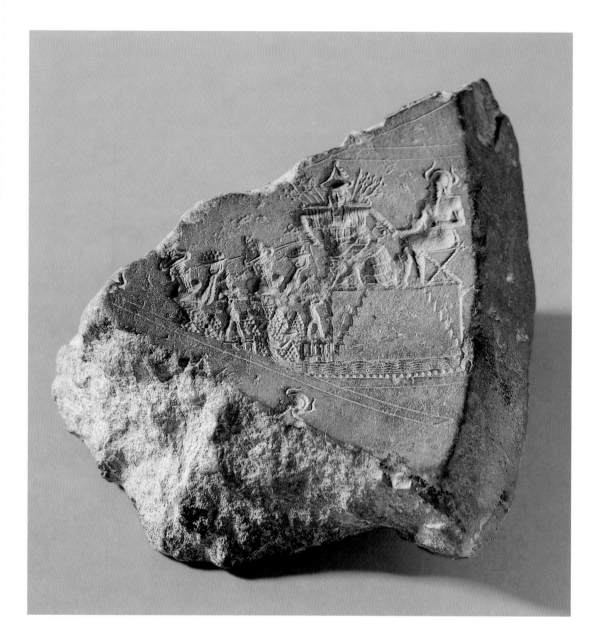

133

Mould fragment with a deified ruler and the goddess Ishtar

Limestone
H. 11 cm (4⅜ in.); W. 13.5 cm (5⅜ in.); external
Diam. approx. 31 cm (12¼ in.); internal Diam.
approx. 26 cm (10¼ in.)
Mesopotamia
Akkadian, reign of Naram-Sin (?), ca. 2220–2184 B.C.
Jeannette and Jonathan Rosen

This fragment of a mould, which may have been used in the making of a shield, illustrates the complex iconography developed to express the Akkadian king Naram-Sin's new role as god, king, and possessor of a vast empire.[1] The interior is carved with a scene in reverse so that a malleable material (undoubtedly gold),

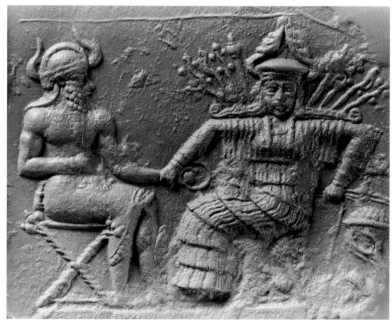

Detail, impression from catalogue number 133.

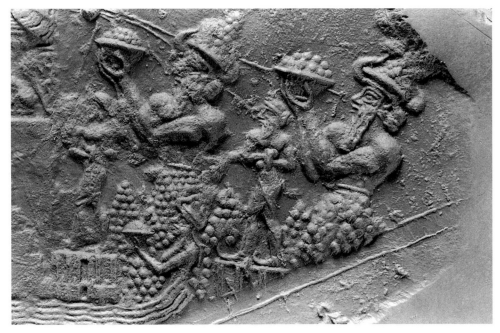

Detail, impression from catalogue number 133.

pressed into the mould, produced an object in the form of a boss with a series of scenes in relief. The preserved scene shows the goddess Ishtar and most likely king Naram-Sin seated opposite each other atop a rectangular platform or tower. Ishtar is represented in her warlike aspect, seated on her lion throne and with weapons emerging from her shoulders. With her right hand the goddess grasps the left wrist of Naram-Sin, whose horned crown clearly indicates his divine status, and with her left hand she holds four ropes bound to the noses of prisoners both mortal and divine, defeated enemies of the Akkadian king. The nose ropes pass behind Ishtar and attach to a large ring held by Naram-Sin. This extraordinary work of art, a powerful visual expression of the divine kingship of Naram-Sin and the divine sponsorship of his empire, is also one of the very few creations of royal Akkadian patronage to survive.   DPH

1. For a complete study of the mould fragment, see Hansen 2002 and "Art of the Akkadian Dynasty," by Donald P. Hansen, in this catalogue.

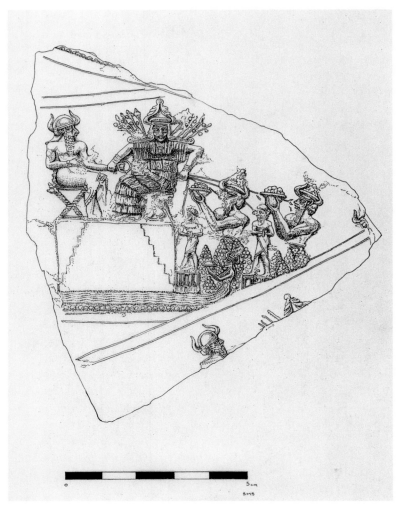

Fig. 62. Drawing of an impression from catalogue number 133.

134

Jar sealing with a contest scene and an inscription of Naram-Sin

Cuneiform inscription in Old Akkadian
Clay
L. 8.3 cm (3¼ in.); H. 6.4 cm (2½ in.); Thickness
2.9 cm (1⅛ in.)
Mesopotamia
Akkadian, reign of Naram-Sin, ca. 2220–2184 B.C.
Jeannette and Jonathan Rosen

In order to secure the contents of a jar, a piece of cloth or skin was often placed over the opening and bound in place by several turns of string around the cloth overlap on the neck. The string turnings were then covered with a soft lump of clay, over which a cylinder seal was rolled several times in different directions. The seal impression probably indicated institutional control; the sealing had to be broken to remove the contents of the jar.

This jar sealing has string impressions on the back and a number of rollings of a seal on the front. Although no one rolling is complete, the combination of several impressions makes it possible to reconstruct the entire design of the seal (fig. 63). This particular sealing is important because it is dated to the

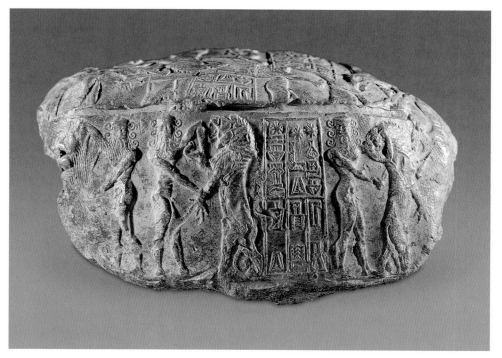

134

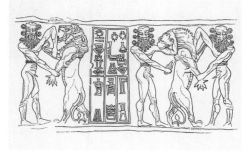

Fig. 63. Drawing of impression from catalogue number 134.

time of Naram-Sin's reign, and the seal belonged to a high official of the court. The king's name, written with the divine determinative, fills the first two lines of the inscription, which reads, "Naram-Sin, god of Akkad, Urab, scribe, is his servant."[1]

The seal design is a contest scene showing heroes struggling with various animals, an extremely popular theme in the Akkadian period.[2] (Another fine example is a seal in the Pierpont Morgan Library, number 146 in this catalogue.) Several basic figural groupings were employed in such compositions; this seal includes a three-figure group coupled with one of two figures.[3] It is not clear whether the inscription was conceived of as central to the entire seal design or was used as a terminal

element bordering the fighting groups. In the three-figure contest, two heroes with large sidelocks of hair and only wearing three-strand belts combat a lion that stands erect, its head turned back. Both heroes grasp the lion, and the one on the left plunges a dagger into the shoulder of the breast. In the group composed of two elements, the lion faces the hero, who grasps its forelegs. The device of the enlarged paw with outstretched claws, indicating the agony of the defeated lion, is one that continues into later Mesopotamian art.

The pattern of small, parallel, raised ridges on the surface of the sealing is formed by fingerprints of the seal roller. The deep impression extending through part of the sealing was probably produced by a metal (?) cap fitted to one end of the seal.   DPH

1. ᵈna-ra-am-ᵈEN.ZU
   DINGIR a-kà-dè.KI
   ur-ab
   DUB.SAR
   IR₁₁-sú
This formula is found on other seals of Naram-Sin's officials. See, e.g., the seal of the scribe Urda; Frayne 1993, p. 173. There is a group of such sealings from Tello with the name Naram-Sin and the title "god of Agade"; ibid., pp. 169ff. For photographs and drawings, see Boehmer 1964, pp. 47–51.
2. See Boehmer 1965.
3. For similar compositions, see ibid., nos. 137 (Berlin), 199 (British Museum).

135

Cylinder seal of Ibni-sharrum, a scribe of Shar-kali-sharri

Cuneiform inscription in Old Akkadian
Serpentine
H. 3.9 cm (1½ in.); Diam. 2.6 cm (1 in.)
Mesopotamia
Akkadian, reign of Shar-kali-sharri, ca. 2183–2159 B.C.
Musée du Louvre, Département des Antiquités Orientales, Paris AO 22303

This seal, which belonged to Ibni-sharrum, the scribe of king Shar-kali-sharri, is one of the finest examples of the perfection achieved by Akkadian-period engravers.[1] Two nude heroes with long curls are represented kneeling on one knee. In a strictly symmetrical composition, each of them holds a vase from which water gushes forth—a symbol of fertility and abundance—and two water buffaloes are shown drinking from them. Underneath, a river winds its way between mountains, represented here in a conventional manner by a motif of two lines of scales. The text panel containing the inscription is supported on the backs of the water buffaloes. It reads: *Shar-ka-li-shar-ri / shar / A-ga-de*(ki) / *Ib-ni-sharrum / dub-sar / warad-su,* "Shar-kali-sharri, king of Akkad, Ibni-sharrum, the scribe, (is) his servant."

Water buffaloes, animals emblematic of Akkadian glyptic, were exotic creatures and were probably kept in zoos. The first representations of them appeared during Sargon's

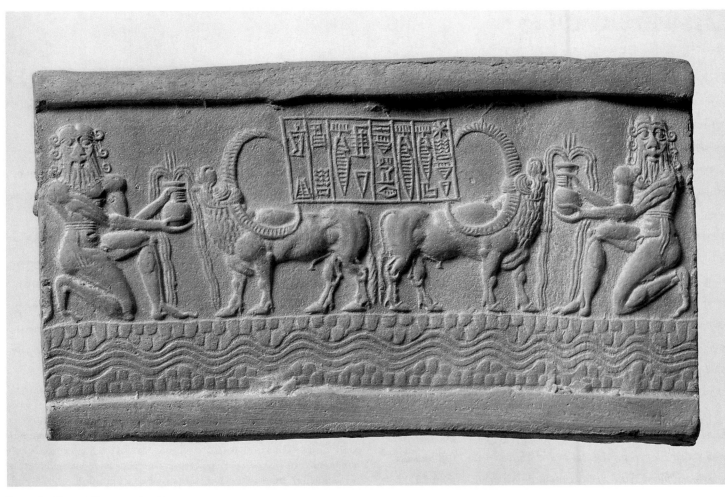

Impression from catalogue number 135.

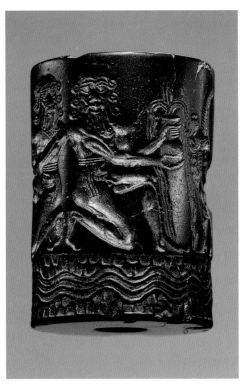

reign and evidence the relations that existed between the Akkadian Empire and the region of Meluhha in the Indus Valley, where they originated. They do not seem to have been acclimatized to Mesopotamia in the late third millennium B.C., however, because there is no further evidence of their existence there until much later, during the Sasanian period.[2] The engraver carefully detailed their powerful musculature and spectacular horns, which are depicted here, as they are on Indus seals (see cat. no. 297), as viewed from above. The equilibrium of the composition, based on horizontal and vertical lines, confers on this

minuscule bas-relief a monumentality characteristic of the late Akkadian-period style. Seals of such high quality were the monopoly of relatives of the royal family or of high officials and probably came from a workshop where production was reserved for the elite.[3]

FD

1. For further reference, see de Clercq and Ménant 1888, no. 46; Frankfort 1939, pl. 17c; Boehmer 1965, no. 724, fig. 232; Amiet 1976a; and Collon 1987, no. 529. This seal was also exhibited in *Bas-reliefs imaginaires*; Amiet 1973, no. 231.
2. Boehmer 1974, pp. 1–19.
3. Zettler 1977, pp. 33–39.

135

Lost-Wax Casting

The development of lost-wax casting in the ancient Near East during the fourth and third millennia B.C. represents one of the most impressive accomplishments in the history of technology. Lost-wax casting begins with the sculpting of a model in wax that is covered—or invested—with clay and fired, causing the wax to melt out through channels provided in the investment. During casting, these channels provide access for the molten metal to enter the mould, and they allow for the escape of gases that could impede its flow. In order to reduce the amount of metal required as well as the risk of casting flaws, the model can be fashioned over a core of refractory clay. This core is held in place after the removal of the wax and during the casting pour by metal supports inserted through the investment and into the core. Once the metal has cooled and solidified, the investment is broken away and the core supports, if present, are removed down to the surrounding surface.

Very ambitious lost-wax castings were produced during the Akkadian period, including the lifesize head of a ruler (cat. no. 136), the so-called Sargon head excavated at Nineveh (fig. 57), and the fragmentary figure with an inscription of Naram-Sin found at Bassetki (fig. 58) that originally may have weighed more than 200 kilograms. Along with metal sculpture fragments recovered at Tell Agrab, these works represent the earliest hollow-cast large-scale sculptures known from the ancient world.[1]

The alloy used to create these three sculptures consisted of more than 98 percent copper and contained no tin or lead to facilitate the casting process.[2] While the use of this rather intractable casting alloy may have been dictated by available supplies, it should be noted that a considerable amount of postcasting work was done on the surface in order to add details through chasing and to remove casting flaws and imperfections. This work would have been easier to perform on a soft copper surface rather than on bronze before the appearance of iron-alloy tools.

J-FL

1. The earliest hollow-cast statues from Egypt are dated to the Middle Kingdom. See Taylor, Craddock, and Shearman 1998, p. 10.
2. For a discussion of the composition of the head of a ruler and the Nineveh head, see the entry for catalogue number 136, note 2. According to the analysis cited in al-Fouadi 1976, p. 66, the Bassetki statue has a composition of 98.2 percent copper with 0.80 percent arsenic and 0.32 percent nickel along with minor amounts of iron and cobalt.

136

Head of a ruler

Copper alloy
H. 34.3 cm (13½ in.); W. 21.3 cm (8⅜ in.); Thickness 21.3 cm (8⅜ in.)
Iran (?)
Akkadian (?), late 3rd millennium B.C.
The Metropolitan Museum of Art, New York; Rogers Fund, 1947 47.100.80

This sculpture is an extraordinary example of the fusion of artistic skill and innovative technology found in the highest quality metalwork of the ancient Near East. Whether or not it is a true portrait, this head possesses a strikingly lifelike presence that is enhanced by specifically modeled features, including a broad nose, deeply set eyes, and prominent ears. Details such as the curls of the full beard, the intricate patterning of the closely knit hair, and the interwoven band circling the top of the head are rendered in a meticulous but understated manner that does not distract from the confident gaze of the face. The eye sockets, now empty, were probably inlaid with shell or stone. Although the head was thought to be virtually solid, recent examination by computer tomography revealed that it once contained a core held in place by metal supports and thus may be among the earliest known examples of lifesize hollow casting.

As this sculpture was not obtained from a controlled excavation, no reliable information exists concerning the location of its interment. Based on a purported Iranian provenance as well as the perceived ethnicity of the facial features and hair treatment, the head has most often been attributed to the Elamite cultural sphere, although the proposed date of production has varied widely. Compelling stylistic similarities with the so-called Sargon copper-alloy head found at Nineveh (see fig. 57), which has been more securely dated to the Akkadian period, have been noted.[1] This connection is further supported by the discovery of technical similarities between both sculptures.

In addition to the fact that both the Nineveh and Metropolitan heads are of comparable size, both were hollow cast using a copper alloy of similar composition that contains very low amounts of arsenic, nickel, and

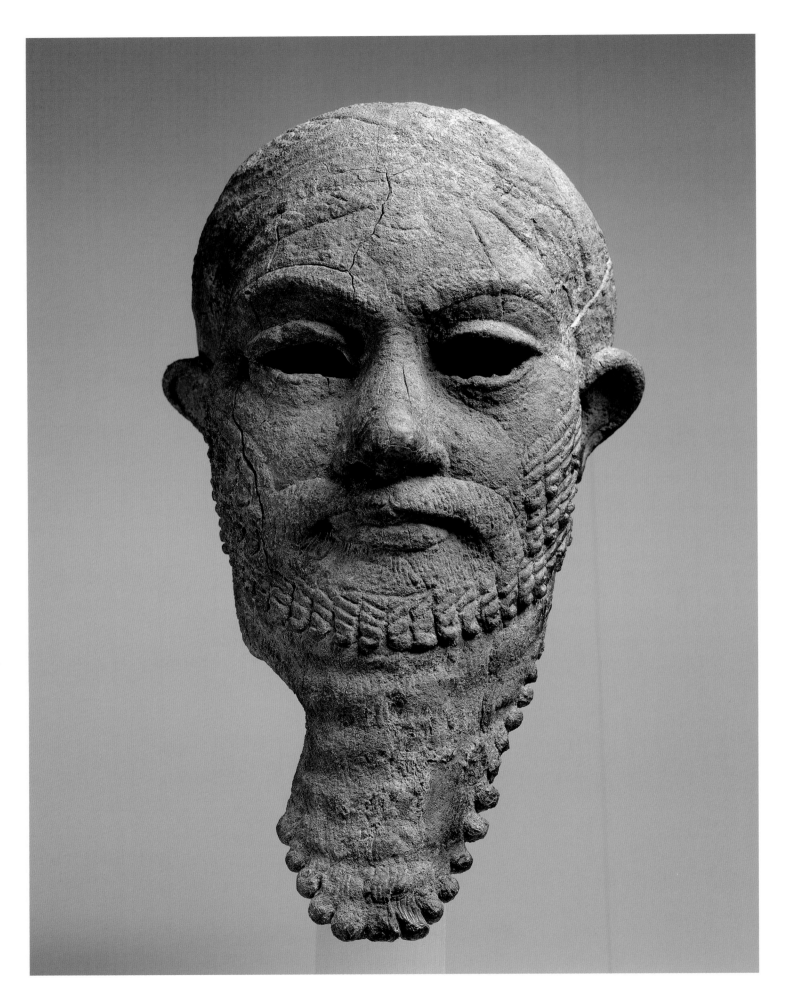

other metals: a considerable achievement considering the difficulty of casting this material.[2] Each head has a plate across the neck that incorporates a square peg originally set into a body or other mount, which may have been made of a different material. There is also evidence that the ears of both heads were made separately. In the Nineveh head, premade ears were joined by a metal plate that ran vertically across the head. The core was then built up around this plate. Although a similar feature is not present in the Metropolitan head, porosity in the metal wall where the ears connect to the head, as seen in the tomography images, suggests that premade ears may have been set into the wax model before its investment.[3]

At the same time, the Metropolitan head has suffered numerous casting flaws that are not found in the example from Nineveh. These flaws may be attributable to an insufficient venting of the mould during casting and to the considerable thickness of its metal walls. X-radiographs reveal irregularly shaped voids in the area of the beard that appear to have been caused by trapped gases. These gases may have impeded the flow of metal, causing the gap on the right side of the beard as well as the elongated hole below the jawline on the same side. Additional flaws include the network of deep cracks on the left side of the head, which may have formed when the metal surface cooled and contracted considerably faster than the large interior volume of the thick metal walls.[4] That the Nineveh head does not suffer similar flaws may be due to the fact that its core more closely follows the contours of the surface, enabling a swift and even flow of metal during casting.

Whether or not the flaws found in the Metropolitan head are indicative of an earlier date relative to the Nineveh head cannot be determined at this time. Until more is known of the development of casting technology in this period, the evidence can only support a rather broad attribution to the late third millennium B.C. Further insight into the cultural affiliation, social position, and possible identity of the subject awaits the evidence of future archaeological discovery.　　　　J-FL

1. Diakonoff (1947) was the first to discern a formal parallel with the Nineveh head based on a systematic analysis. See discussion and bibliography of proposed provenances in Muscarella 1988a, pp. 368–74. See also Harper, Aruz, and Tallon 1992, pp. 175–76, no. 113.
2. For composition and technical information concerning the Nineveh head, see Strommenger 1986, pp. 114–15. In a group of five samples taken from this

head, the percentage of arsenic and nickel, which were the main secondary elements, ranged from 0.21 to 0.77 percent arsenic and 0.05 to 0.26 percent nickel. At least two samples have been taken from the Metropolitan head for compositional analysis. Although the analyses were performed by different techniques and are not directly comparable, it is interesting to note that the sample taken from the dowel was found to contain considerably more arsenic (3.3 percent) than a sample taken from the head, which was found to have 0.69 percent arsenic and 0.28 percent nickel.
3. It is possible that other factors may account for the details seen in the tomography images. In any case, the large size and outward curve of the ears on the Metropolitan head noted by Muscarella (1988a, p. 368) and the attention to the ears during production evidenced by the Nineveh head suggest the symbolic importance of endowing these heads with auditory faculties as if they were animate. The intentional mutilation of the eyes and the removal of the ears from the Nineveh head at a much later period may have been intended to deny them the use of sight and hearing. See Nylander 1980, pp. 329–33.
4. These cracks may have been less noticeable before their subsequent enlargement by corrosion.

137

Fragment of a head of a ruler

Diorite
H. 17 cm (6¾ in.); W. 12 cm (4¾ in.); Thickness 15 cm (5⅞ in.)
Mesopotamia, Girsu (modern Tello)
Akkadian, ca. 2240–2159 B.C.
Musée du Louvre, Département des Antiquités Orientales, Paris AO 14

Although the entire upper portion of this male head is missing, it remains a work of very high quality.[1] The head belonged to a relatively large statue, about half lifesize. The general shape of the face, which is thin with high, marked cheekbones, is still perceptible. The almond-shaped eyes, of which only the lower eyelids survive, are rimmed. A copious beard rendered as rows of carefully engraved long curls, the conventional manner for the Akkadian period, frames a finely carved, full-lipped mouth. Directly around the mouth, the beard is indicated by flat, tonguelike strands of hair similar to those depicted on a contemporaneous copper-alloy royal head found at Nineveh (fig. 57). Little curls of hair arranged in layers on the back of the neck are also visible on both sculptures.

Despite its mutilations, this head, found at Tello, creates the same impression of grandeur as the Nineveh masterpiece and another

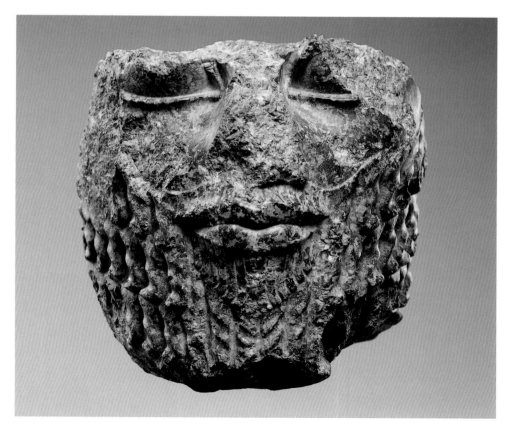

copper-alloy head attributed to Iran (cat. no. 136). The rarity and prestige attributed to diorite, an extremely hard stone that had to be imported from a great distance, confirm the royal character of the figure, although it is not possible to specify which king of Akkad is depicted. Sargon[2] and Naram-Sin have both been suggested as the subjects of the Nineveh head; the quality and the delicate execution of the Tello head argue in favor of a date subsequent to Sargon's reign.[3]   FD

1. For further reference, see Sarzec and Heuzey 1884–1912, vol. 2, pp. 47–48, pl. 21:1; Parrot 1948, p. 136; Amiet 1976a; and Spycket 1981, p. 148, pl. 98.
2. Mallowan 1936, p. 104.
3. Amiet 1976a, p. 33.

138

Fragments of a head of a ruler (?)

Diorite
H. 22.8 cm (9 in.)
Mesopotamia, Ur
Akkadian, ca. 2300–2159 B.C.
Trustees of The British Museum, London
BM 114197, BM 114198

This diorite head, of which only the back section and part of the left side of the face remain, reflects the continued attention paid by Akkadian artisans to portraying detailed hairstyles—something previously evidenced in the large corpus of Early Dynastic sculpture (see cat. nos. 24a, b, 25, 28, 29, 88, 109). Found in two fragments in the 1919 British Museum excavations at Ur,[1] the piece shows an elaborate coiffure defined by a braided band encircling the front three-quarters of the head. The rest of the hair is pulled back into a complex interwoven pattern, revealing a heavily modeled ear.

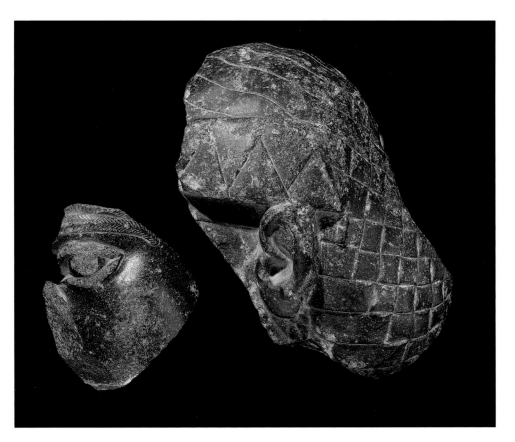

The head bears a remarkable similarity to the copper-alloy head found at Nineveh and thought to portray Naram-Sin (fig. 57),[2] although this example is cruder in execution and lacks the distinctive royal chignon (see "Art of the Akkadian Dynasty," by Donald P. Hansen, in this catalogue). The care lavished on the hair and face and the use of diorite, a stone imported from Oman and used primarily for Akkadian royal statuary, reflect the high if not royal status probably enjoyed by this faceless official.

MJH

1. Hall 1919, pp. 25–27, fig. 7; Hall 1923, p. 186, pl. 37, no. 3; Hall 1928, p. 31, pl. 8, no. 8.
2. Spycket 1981, pp. 147–48, fig. 48.

139

Cylinder seal with Mesopotamian deities

Cuneiform inscription
Greenstone
H. 3.9 cm (1½ in.); Diam. 2.6 cm (1 in.)
Mesopotamia
Akkadian, ca. 2200–2159 B.C.
Trustees of The British Museum, London BM 89115

This is one of the many high-quality greenstone seals made during the Akkadian Empire.[1] The figures can be identified as gods by their pointed headdresses with multiple horns. The figure with streams of water and fish flowing

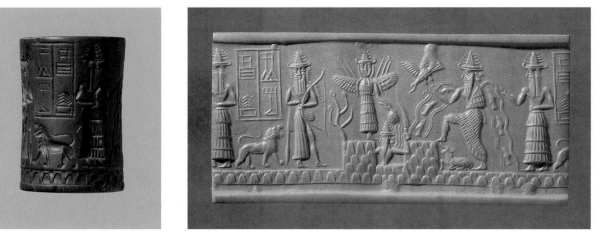

139

Impression from catalogue number 139.

from his shoulders, and who places his right foot on a scaly mountain, is Ea, god of sweet water and of wisdom, called Enki by the Sumerians. His hair is worn in a triple bun, and he stretches out his right hand toward a bird; a couchant bull lies between his legs. Ea's vizier, Usmu, who has two faces, stands behind him with his right hand raised. On the mountain at left, beside a small tree, is Ishtar, the goddess of fertility (indicated by the cluster of dates) and of war (symbolized by the weapons rising from her shoulders); she is depicted frontally, standing on one leg, with her hair falling on each side of her face, and winged. The deities all wear flounced robes. The sun god Shamash (known to the Sumerians as Utu), who has rays issuing from his shoulders, uses a serrated blade to cut his way through the mountains so that he can rise at dawn. The figure, shown full face, with his long hair curling down his left side, wearing a hiked-up striated robe, and armed with a bow and quiver with a long tassel attached, has not been identified with certainty but may represent a hunting god like Nuska. Behind him, a roaring lion paces to the right. The male figures are all bearded. The scales of the mountains continue around the lower part of the seal and form a groundline for the figures. A two-line inscription above the lion identifies the seal's owner as Adda, a scribe.[2]   PC

1. Collon 1982, p. 92, no. 190.
2. The inscription reads, *ad-da dub-sar.*

140

Cylinder seal with sun god

Black serpentine
H. 4.1 cm (1⅝ in.); Diam. 2.8 cm (1⅛ in.)
Mesopotamia
Akkadian, ca. 2220–2159 B.C.
The Pierpont Morgan Library, New York 178

The sun god Shamash is the most frequently represented mythological figure on Akkadian seals. He is identified by a serrated blade, the *shasharum* saw, which is his emblem, and usually by rays emanating from his shoulders (see "Art of the Early City-States," by Donald P. Hansen, in this catalogue). The impression of this seal shows Shamash rising at dawn between the eastern mountains. He thrusts his saw upward with his right hand and places his right foot on a mountain. At either side, a divine attendant opens the wings of the gates of heaven to reveal Shamash in majesty. At the far left, a god, carrying a mace that is visible behind his body, observes the proceedings. In some versions of this scene, lions occupy the top and bottom of the gate wings,[1] perhaps to add the concept of sound to that of movement, their roar meant to suggest the thunder in heaven made by the opening of the massive portal.   SB

1. Boehmer 1965, pl. 35, no. 420.

141

Cylinder seal with water god seated in enclosure

Cuneiform inscription
Black serpentine with calcite vein
H. 3 cm (1⅛ in.); Diam. 1.9 cm (¾ in.)
Mesopotamia
Akkadian, ca. 2220–2159 B.C.
The Pierpont Morgan Library, New York 202

The water god Ea, often depicted on Akkadian cylinder seals, is identified by the vase that he holds close to his chest and from which two streams of water flow. On this seal, Ea is shown enthroned in an enclosure representing his home, which was thought to be at the bottom of the freshwater ocean below the earth, or *apsu*. Based on other representations on seals,[1] it is likely that the enclosure is made of water. At each corner of the structure the watercourse makes a loop.

Standing before Ea is his divine vizier, who has two faces and thus can look forward and backward simultaneously. On either side of Ea and his vizier stand nude, bearded heroes, each holding a gatepost of the water god's abode. These heroic figures are taller than the others, and with their frontal, masklike faces and muscled bodies, together with the symmetry of the design created by their opposed stances and their hands firmly grasping the gateposts, they present an image of permanence and protection. At the left (in the impression), a male worshiper approaches the sanctuary, raising his left hand to his face in a gesture of recognition and humility toward the god. The vizier looks back at the worshiper with one

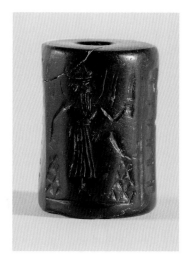

140

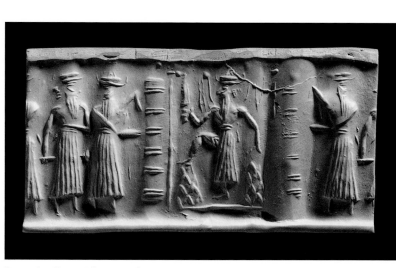

Impression from catalogue number 140.

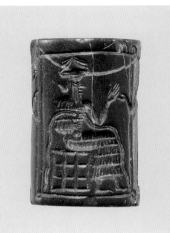

141

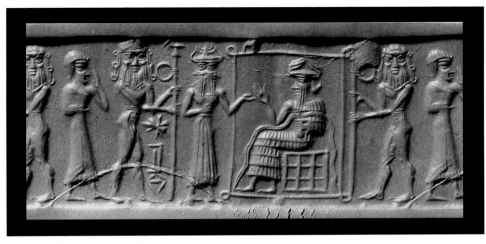

Impression from catalogue number 141.

face and with the other looks ahead toward Ea, while gesturing with his left hand as he presents the worshiper to the enthroned god.

SB

1. Porada 1960, pp. 116–23.

142

Cylinder seal with storm god in a chariot pulled by a lion-griffin

Shell
H. 3.4 cm (1⅜ in.); Diam. 2 cm (¾ in.)
Mesopotamia
Akkadian, ca. 2220–2159 B.C.
The Pierpont Morgan Library, New York 220

Among the more dramatic scenes created by Akkadian artists to glorify the gods are those depicting the storm or weather god. On this seal, the storm god is shown in a chariot being pulled by a lion-griffin with the head, body, and

forepaws of a lion, and the wings, tail feathers, and taloned hind legs of a bird of prey. Standing on the monster's back between its wings is a nude goddess wearing a horned crown and holding bundles of rain. At the left, a worshiper pours a libation from a spouted vessel over an altar, in homage to the gods. The storm god, holding a rein in one hand, controls the lion-griffin, bowing its head as it roars and spews forth fire or lightning. With his other hand, the storm god raises a whip high behind him, as if to spur the beast onward.

As a motif, the griffin has a long history in the Near East, making its first appearance in the Uruk period.[1] By combining various parts of different animals, the artists of this region devised a more impressive and threatening supernatural creature. The image of the lion-griffin on this magnificent seal certainly evokes the raging storm itself as it makes its steady, inevitable progress through the land.

SB

1. See Porada 1993b, p. 570.

143

Cylinder seal with vegetation deities

Cuneiform inscription
Greenstone
H. 3.5 cm (1⅜ in.); Diam. 2.1 cm (¹³⁄₁₆ in.)
Mesopotamia
Akkadian, ca. 2220–2159 B.C.
Trustees of The British Museum, London BM 89802

This Akkadian cylinder seal combines a presentation scene with a battle of the gods; similar combinations of subjects are known on other seals of this period (see cat no. 156). On this example, an enthroned goddess facing left (in the modern impression) wears a fringed garment and with her left hand holds a branch across her lap, while lifting two more branches in her right hand. Like all the other divine figures in the scene, she wears a multi-horned headdress. Approaching her from the left are two bearded gods. The first wears a striated robe, has branches sprouting from his shoulders, and holds a branch in his left hand;

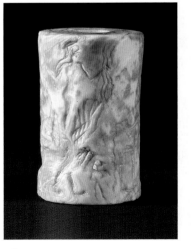

142

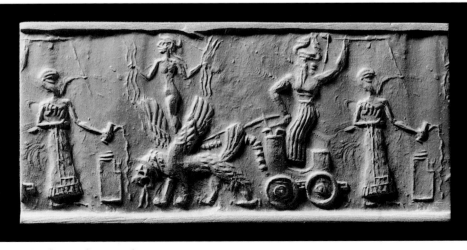

Impression from catalogue number 142.

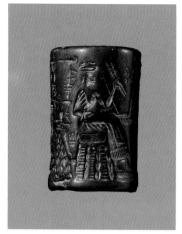

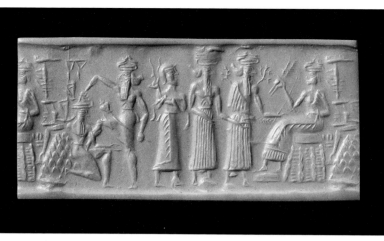

143

Impression from catalogue number 143.

the deity following him wears a striated skirt. Behind the gods stands a worshiper dressed in an ankle-length fringed skirt and carrying an antelope in his arms. A separate scene depicts a scaly mountain in front of which kneels a bearded god facing right and wearing only a loincloth and a different variety of horned headdress. Another bearded god, who wears a skirt and holds a mace in his left hand, grasps this headdress while placing his right foot on his opponent's stomach. Above the mountain is a short inscription, which names the owner as Lugalkase, son of Sheshshesh.[1] Contrary to usual practice, the cuneiform signs are cut in the correct order on the seal itself, so that the impressions produced appear in mirror image. It is possible that an earlier inscription was erased, as often happened with high quality seals of the Akkadian period, and that the new inscription was cut incorrectly.   PC

1. Collon 1982, no. 210.

144

Cylinder seal with battle of the gods

Lapis lazuli
H. 2.8 cm (1⅛ in.); Diam. 1.7 cm (¹¹⁄₁₆ in.)
Mesopotamia, Kish
Akkadian, ca. 2220–2159 B.C.
The Metropolitan Museum of Art, New York;
Anonymous Loan L.1992.23.4

This lapis lazuli seal, excavated at Kish (Tell Ingharra),[1] is an exceptionally fine example of the mature Akkadian style. Executed with great attention to detail, it shows a battle among several gods, identified as deities by their horned headdresses. Three of the standing gods appear to be conquerors. One, wearing a long skirt partially tucked up at the waist to allow easy leg movement, smashes his mace on the head of an enemy god fallen before him, who raises his right hand to ward off the blow. Above the head and raised arm of the vanquished god are three incised horizontal lines probably intended to set off the space above for an inscription

that was never carved. To the right, a second standing god, also wearing the tucked-up skirt and carrying a dagger at his waist, triumphantly places his foot on a second fallen enemy, who looks up toward his attacker and like the first victim raises his right arm and hand over his head. The attacking deity grasps the arm of yet another enemy god with his right hand and seizes the god's horned crown with his left. This embattled god also holds one arm aloft. His lower body disappears behind the second defeated god, as does the lower body of another smaller god to the right. Next to this complex group stand two more gods similarly dressed in long skirts. One raises his mace and grasps the crown of the other, who stretches out his hands in a supplicatory gesture while dropping his own mace in defeat.

The theme of a battle among the gods was particularly popular in the seal-cutter's art of the Akkadian period. There are a few earlier antecedents, and the motif persisted into later

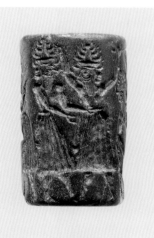

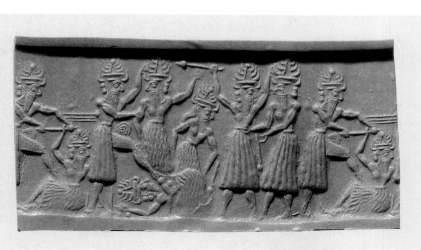

144

Impression from catalogue number 144.

periods.[2] Since later texts provide no assistance in interpreting the specifics of the depicted scenes, it has not been possible to associate the theme with a particular myth. One might surmise that the difference between the skirts of the gods with raised legs and the more intricate skirts of their enemies is significant, yet the two contending gods on the right are dressed identically to each other.

In several world mythologies, battles between the successive generations of gods appear at the ends of cycles of creation. At the beginning of the later Creation Epic of Mesopotamia, for example, it is necessary for Tiamat and her brood to be defeated. Nonetheless, any real understanding of this iconography is difficult to acquire.   DPH

1. Watelin and Langdon 1934, pl. 34:3.
2. For a history of the motif, see Boehmer 1971, pp. 49–59.

145

Cylinder seal with kneeling nude heroes

Cuneiform inscription
Red jasper
H. 2.8 cm (1⅛ in.); Diam. 1.6 cm (⅝ in.)
Mesopotamia
Akkadian, ca. 2220–2159 B.C.
The Metropolitan Museum of Art, New York;
Anonymous Loan L.1992.23.5

Four representations of a nude, bearded hero with six sidelocks of hair appear on this jasper cylinder seal. Each wears only a three-strand belt with a tassel, a customary appendage to the heroic belt, which is lightly incised on his

rump and thus difficult to discern.[1] In all cases the hero kneels on one knee and with both hands holds up a gatepost standard in front of his raised leg. This is probably the same standard that was held by the hero of the roughly contemporary Bassetki copper-alloy statue (fig. 58). Two vertical lines of inscription, one placed before a hero and another placed behind a second hero, give the owner's name as Shatpum, son of Shallum, but do not provide an official title. Placed vertically in the field, a serpent appears behind one hero. In the spaces between the tops of the standards are four symbols including a sun disk, a lunar crescent, a fish, and a vase with flowing streams of water.

The nude hero is often shown with this very explicit type of gatepost, which perhaps is the emblem of a specific god or group of deities. On an Early Dynastic cylinder seal in the British Museum the hero holds two gateposts; or, he may be shown holding the gatepost in a scene associated with a major god. In an Akkadian seal in the Pierpont Morgan Library collection (cat. no. 141), for example, two heroes with gateposts flank a shrine in which Enki or Ea, the god of sweet waters and wisdom, sits enthroned, holding a vase with flowing streams in one hand.[2] The flowing vase, a symbol of abundance, was probably known as the emblem *hegallum*.[3] The heroes with gateposts, the flowing vase, and the fish (wisdom) suggest that the iconography of this seal is somehow connected with the god Ea. It is difficult to be precise, however, because the meaning of individual symbols could change in different contexts. On an Akkadian seal from the Royal Cemetery of Ur, for instance, a bull-man holding the same gatepost faces a contest scene in which two very different hero types contend with crossed

human-faced bisons, or *kusarikku*, often associated with Shamash, the sun god.[4] In any case, the sun, moon, vase, and fish are undoubtedly astral or planetary symbols—the vase with streams and the fish are forerunners of what in much later times become zodiacal signs.

DPH

1. Wiggermann (1992) suggested on the basis of later texts that the hero with long sidelocks is the *lahmum*, or Hairy One. But since his thesis has been effectively disputed in Ellis 1995, the *lahmum* identification is not used in this catalogue.
2. Both this seal and the one in the British Museum are reproduced in Porada 1987, pp. 284, 285.
3. *Chicago Assyrian Dictionary*, Ḫ, pp. 167–69, s.v. *ḫegallu*.
4. Woolley 1934, pl. 208:232.

146

Cylinder seal with a hero combating a buffalo and a bull-man combating a lion

Green-black serpentine
H. 3.6 cm (1⅜ in.); Diam. 2.5 cm (1 in.)
Mesopotamia
Akkadian, ca. 2220–2159 B.C.
The Pierpont Morgan Library, New York 159

The scene on this seal, finely carved in a mature Akkadian style, shows two pairs of fighting figures flanking a central element. At the left (in the impression), the nude, bearded hero grapples with a water buffalo, while, at the right, a bull-man wrestles with a lion; between them is a tree on a mountain. The hero is the tallest figure in the scene: his masklike visage, which is depicted frontally, becomes the main focus of the scene, emphasizing his power and importance.

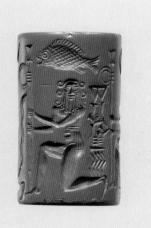

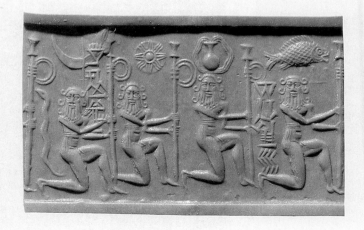

145

Impression from catalogue number 145.

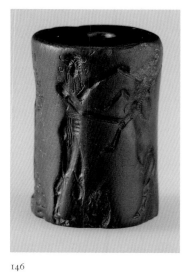

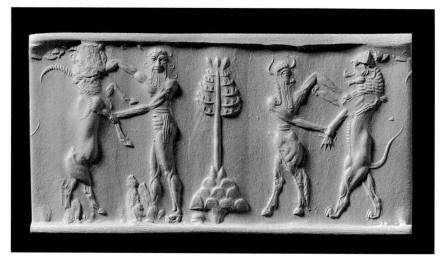

146

Impression from catalogue number 146.

The lion is shown with its head thrown back in profile, its mouth wide open, and its sharp teeth exposed, roaring in anger at being dominated. The claws on the lion's paw, which is firmly grasped at its wrist by the bull-man, are extended but splayed and ineffectual.

In the preceding Early Dynastic III period, contest scenes were carved mostly as friezes of interconnected figures, with the emphasis on the continuity of the struggle expressed through the design itself (see cat. no. 55). In Akkadian examples, the friezes are broken up into more formal groups of two or sometimes three contesting figures (see entry for cat. no. 134). Now emphasized are power and dominance. The combination of extraordinary attention to naturalistic details, such as the musculature of the arms of the hero and of the bull-man, with stylistic invention, as in the angularity of the gesturing arms, creates a visual tension that is one of the most original achievements of the Akkadian artists.   SB

147

Cylinder seal with a hero combating a lion

Cuneiform inscription
Chalcedony
H. 3.6 cm (1⅜ in.); Diam. 2.3 cm (⅞ in.)
Mesopotamia
Akkadian, ca. 2220–2159 B.C.
Trustees of The British Museum, London BM 89147

The theme of contests of strength among animals, heroes, and, later, bull-men was developed on cylinder seals from the Late Uruk period. By the time of the Akkadian Empire, the contest had split into two antithetical groups of well-matched opponents. This beautifully cut seal, typical of the Akkadian style in its emphasis on musculature and modeling, depicts a bearded hero (full face), nude except for a belt, the end of which hangs across his thigh. He kneels on one knee and wrestles

with a lion. With one arm around the lion's neck, the hero pulls the animal back, while he grabs its tail by reaching around its body with his other arm. The mirror image of this scene originally was included to balance a two-line inscription. The inscription, however, has been erased, and the lines, which once framed the cuneiform signs, have been transformed into three fronds. A surviving five-line inscription identifies the seal's owner as Shakullum, a servant of Puzur-Shullat, priest of the city of Duram.[1] Puzur-Shullat's name and title also occur on a copper-alloy bowl from Tell Munbaqa, Syria, suggesting the wide extent of the Akkadian Empire.[2]   PC

1. Collon 1982, p. 63, no. 114.
2. Steinkeller 1984, pp. 83–84.

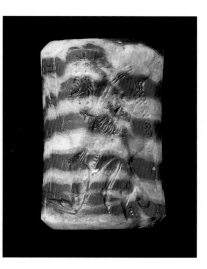

147

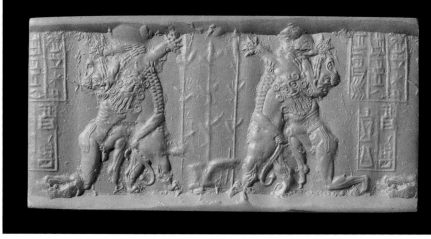

Impression from catalogue number 147.

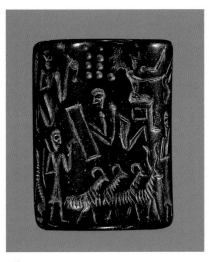

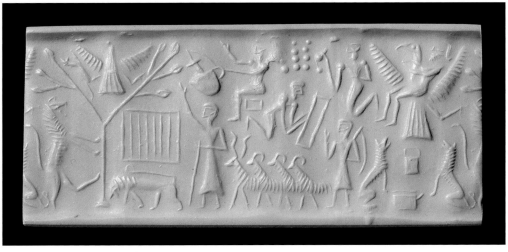

148

Impression from catalogue number 148.

148

Cylinder seal with the myth of Etana (?)

Serpentine
H. 3.8 cm (1½ in.); Diam. 2.8 cm (1⅛ in.)
Mesopotamia
Akkadian, ca. 2220–2159 B.C.
Trustees of The British Museum, London BM 129480

Rarely can Mesopotamian myths be equated with artistic representations. However, the story of Etana, known from cuneiform texts dating as early as the Old Babylonian period (see cat. no. 340), may be illustrated on Akkadian seals.[1] Here a lion facing right stands on its hind legs beside a tree, while a second lion paces to the left. In the branches an eagle with outspread wings holds an animal. Two shepherds with their flock, a goat and three sheep, face left and raise their right arms. The shepherd in the front wears a skirt and has a staff in his left hand, while the one in the rear, also wearing a skirt, holds a flail over his

left shoulder. They may be leading the flock toward a square hatched area, perhaps a barn. Above the shepherds, a seated figure facing left holds a large pot by the handle and raises his right arm; behind him a kneeling figure faces right, before a rectangular shape. Farther right, a kneeling figure facing left may be pouring the contents of a pot into the ten drill holes in front of him.[2] Two seated dogs facing each other look up at the eagle on whose back Etana is seated. Between the dogs are a bucket and a rectangular object. Although, according to the surviving version of the myth, Etana rescued an eagle from a pit where it had been thrown by a serpent, in the story depicted on this seal the eagle is associated with lions instead of snakes.   PC

1. Haul 2000, pp. 40–44.
2. Possibly indicating cheese moulds; see Collon 1982, pp. 78–79, no. 151.

149

Cylinder seal with ibex in a landscape

Cuneiform inscription
Chert
H. 2.8 cm (1⅛ in.); Diam. 1.8 cm (¾ in.)
Mesopotamia
Akkadian, ca. 2220–2159 B.C.
The Metropolitan Museum of Art, New York; Bequest of W. Gedney Beatty, 1941 41.160.192

A few components—animals, a human, trees, and hills or mountains—are combined into two basic groupings on this seal belonging to Balu-ili, a cupbearer. The composition continues an earlier Mesopotamian design scheme in which antithetical elements are symmetrically arranged on either side of a central axis (see fig. 110). In this case, one central motif is a group of three trees and a second is a hunter and his prey. The hunter, perhaps Balu-ili himself, holds a weapon in one hand and with the other grasps the horn of a mouflon or ibex. A two-line inscription giving the name and title

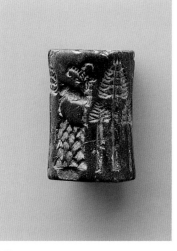

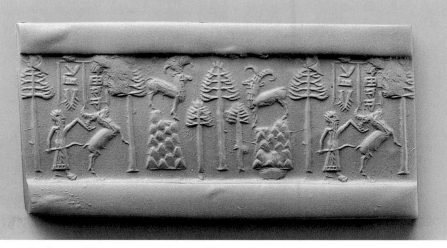

149

Impression from catalogue number 149.

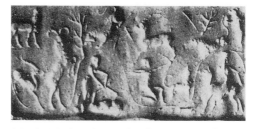

Fig. 64. Modern impression from a serpentine cylinder seal depicting a landscape setting. Seal: Akkadian, ca. 2300–2159 B.C. Musées Royaux d'Art et d'Histoire, Brussels, o. 452.

of the owner fills the area above the hunter, and two tall trees flank this central group. The tree to the right of the mouflon also serves to connect to the other group, which has a similar tall tree as its central axis. This tree is bordered by two smaller trees, which in turn are flanked by two mountains atop which stand mouflons. Although the compositional device is simple, the overall design is skillfully worked out to be continuous and unbroken—an excellent scheme for a cylinder seal, which can be rolled to any length.

Trees and mountains, although elements of landscape, are here combined with geometric regularity.[1] They are much like the paratactic images of the early stele of Sargon (fig. 55) and lack the quality of a unified landscape that finds its most fully developed expression in the Naram-Sin stele originally from Sippar (fig. 59). Some seal designs show greater complexity, attempting to situate a scene in a landscape setting. One example is a seal in Brussels (fig. 64), on which animals and humans are organized around an undulating line suggestive of a hilly landscape. This type of composition is not inherent to cylinder seal design and probably was inspired by large-scale works in another medium, such as painting.   DPH

1. For a study of landscape in Akkadian art, see Kantor 1966 and Amiet 1976a.

150

Cylinder seal with hunters

Cuneiform inscription in Old Akkadian (?)
Diorite
H. 3.3 cm (1¼ in.); Diam. 2.1 cm (¹³⁄₁₆ in.)
Mesopotamia
Akkadian, ca. 2220–2159 B.C.
Trustees of The British Museum, London   BM 89137

This fine Akkadian seal, which shows the concern, typical of the period, for modeling and musculature, depicts seven figures moving toward the left. The first figure has a short beard, his hair is in a bun, and he wears a short skirt and shoes with upturned toes; he carries a quiver with a tassel attached and a bow over his left shoulder, and he holds an arrow in his right hand. Behind him is a man with short curly hair and a beard, dressed in a striated robe; he holds a stick in his clasped hands. Both men turn to focus their attention on the middle figure, who also has a short curly beard but is distinguished by his hair, which is gathered in a bun under a flat cap, and by a flounced robe worn over the left shoulder (see the earlier royal figure of Ishqi-Mari, cat. no. 88), against which he holds an axe. Behind him is a figure in a fringed robe, with a completely shaven

head, who holds an object in his left hand. The fifth figure, dressed like the second one, holds an axe in the crook of his left arm and a sling in his right hand. Finally, two small, beardless figures are depicted, wearing short skirts. The five-line inscription, set above three horizontal lines, identifies the seal's owner as the scribe Kalki, servant of Ubil-Eshtar, brother of the king. The central figure may be Ubil-Eshtar, on a tour of inspection rather than on a hunting expedition.[1] His scribe, probably Kalki, is shown behind him, bearing a tablet, while servants carry the personal effects of the official: a stool and a net at the end of a crook.   PC

1. Collon 1982, pp. 73–74, no. 141.

151

Cylinder seal with a seated deity and vegetation deities

Shell with copper alloy caps
H. 4 cm (1⅝ in.); H. with caps 6.1 cm (2⅜ in.);
Diam. 2.8 cm (1⅛ in.)
Syria, Mari, Temples Anonymes, M.2734
Akkadian, ca. 2220–2159 B.C.
National Museum, Damascus, Syria   2184

Shell was a common material used for seals at Mari (see cat. no. 87). The imagery on this shell seal, with copper caps still intact at either end, is more elaborate than that of any other known Akkadian cylinder seal from the site of Mari. In the center of the image a bearded

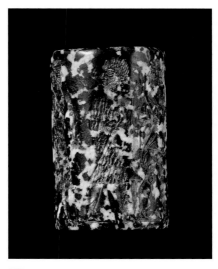

150

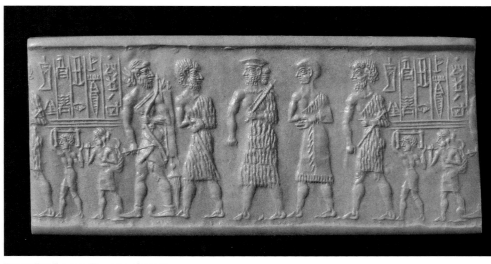

Impression from catalogue number 150.

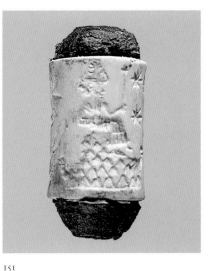

151

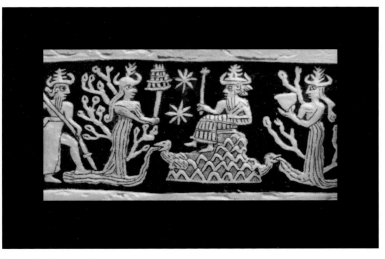

Impression from catalogue number 151.

god wearing a tufted skirt and horned head-dress is seated on a mountain motif. His hair is bound into a chignon, and he holds a mace in his right hand. Animals with elongated necks appear on either side of the mountain and spout streams of water, from which two long-haired female goddesses emerge; both god-desses make gestures of offering to the seated god, one with a vessel and the other with a stand or vegetation, suggesting they are dependent on him for their fecundity. They are identified as vegetation goddesses by the branches that grow from their bodies and adorn their horned headdresses.

Two stars fill the space in front of the seated god. Although sometimes interpreted as the name of the sky god Anu, the stars are more likely compositional elements and the deity is a water god.[1] Another bearded god with his hair bound into a chignon and who wears a horned headdress approaches one of the goddesses. His left leg is raised, and he holds a spear toward the goddess in a unique pose probably related to the battle of the gods motif (see entry for cat. no. 144). Although the seal belongs to the southern Mesopotamian tradition of Akkadian cylinder seals, some ele-ments of the scene are rendered in a local idiom. In particular, the depiction of deities rising from the water is characteristic of Mari (see cat. no. 133).[2]   JME

1. Amiet 1960, p. 219.
2. Ibid., pp. 215–17, figs. 1–3.

152

Lobed crescent earrings

Gold
H. 4 cm (1⅝ in.); W. 1 cm (⅜ in.)
Syria, Mari
Akkadian, ca. 2300–2159 B.C.
Museum of Deir ez-Zor, Syria 13145–47, 13155–60

The simple yet elegant form of the six double-crescent earrings in this group found at Mari appears to have been widely admired during the Akkadian period. Examples of this type have been found at Tell Brak and in Sargonic period graves at Ur, where two or three were linked together like a chain.[1] This group also contains two unpaired earrings with pouch-like lobes that are comparable to examples

found at Ashur, Ur, and Tell Brak, as well as at Kültepe in central Anatolia.[2] Similar lobed earrings from Mari have been found in graves that have been dated to the Shakkanakku period.[3] In general form and construction, this lobed type may derive from large earrings from the Royal Cemetery at Ur that consist of separately made lobes of gold or silver joined side by side.[4]

The widespread diffusion of these two types of crescent earrings attests to the long-distance passage of goods and possibly craftsmen in the mid-to-late third millennium B.C. Imported goods found in archaeological excavations at Kültepe, for example, indicate contact between central Anatolia and southern Mesopotamia during the Akkadian period.[5] Sites such as Mari, Tell Brak, and Ashur were well situated

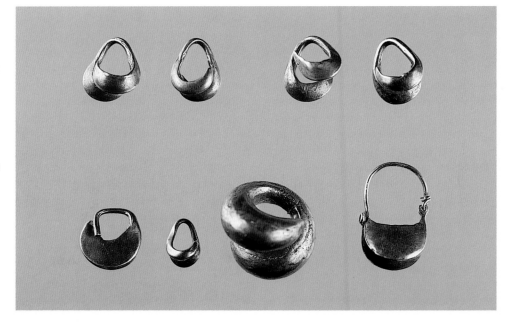

to serve as pivotal links in the exchange network between southern Mesopotamia and the areas to the north.

J–FL

1. For an example from Tell Brak, see Mallowan 1947, p. 71. For an example from Ur, see Maxwell-Hyslop 1971, pp. 23–24.
2. See the discussion by Benzel concerning this type of earring in Harper et al. 1995, pp. 55–57. As noted there, the lobes of the Ashur earrings were made separately. Whether or not this is also the case with Mari earrings is not known, as they have not been examined by this author.
3. For Mari Tombs 809 and 1048, see Marylou 1999, pls. 149, 218.
4. Zettler and Horne 1998, p. 107.
5. Maxwell-Hyslop 1971, pp. 47–48.

153a, b

Foundation pegs

Cuneiform inscriptions in Hurrian
Syria, possibly from Urkesh (modern Tell Mozan)
Akkadian, ca. 2300–2159 B.C.

a. Lion with an inscribed plate and a stone tablet mentioning Urkesh
Copper alloy and limestone
Lion: H. 12.2 cm (4¾ in.); W. 8.5 cm (3⅜ in.)
Tablet: W. 9 cm (3½ in.); L. 10 cm (4 in.)
Musée du Louvre, Département des Antiquités Orientales, Paris; Gift of the Société des Amis du Louvre, 1948 AO 19937, AO 19938

b. Lion with an inscribed plate mentioning Urkesh
Copper alloy
H. 11.7 cm (4⅝ in.); W. 7.9 cm (3⅛ in.)
The Metropolitan Museum of Art, New York; Purchase, Joseph Pulitzer Bequest, 1948 48.180

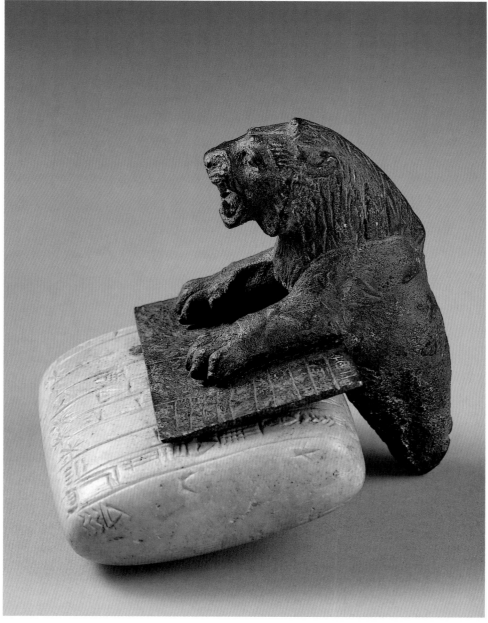

153a

In the first example (cat. no. 153a), a lion places its front paws on an inscribed copper plate. Only the upper half of the lion is shown; its mouth is open, and its hindquarters end in a thick peg. The cuneiform text, composed in the Hurrian language, is repeated on the stone tablet beneath the copper plate: "Tishatal, ruler *(endan)* of Urkesh, has built a temple for the god Nergal. This temple, may the god Lubadag protect it. For the one who would destroy [it], may Lubadag destroy [him]; may his god not listen to his prayer. May the Lady of Nagar, Shimiga (the sun god), and the storm god [curse ten thousand times] the one who would destroy it."[1]

The Hurrians, whose language was neither Semitic nor Indo-European, appear in written Mesopotamian sources beginning about 2400 B.C. They seem to have occupied the piedmont region of the Taurus and Zagros Mountains, a vast area bordering the Mesopotamian plain to the north and east and extending between the upper courses of the Tigris and Euphrates Rivers. Their country was called Subir in Sumerian, Subartu in Akkadian. The tablets placed under the claws of the lion of Urkesh apparently bear the oldest known Hurrian text. The Hurrians were in close contact with Mesopotamian culture, from which they adopted the custom of depositing foundation documents in their constructions. The combination of the large feline with the tablets in a homogenous whole, however, is an original application of the conventional iconography and layout of the foundation deposit as developed by Sumerian rulers in southern Mesopotamia (see cat. nos. 27, 39).

The image of the lion as a guardian animal is well attested throughout the history of Mesopotamia and the surrounding regions. It is depicted here roaring to frighten off the enemy and to protect the dedicatory inscription of the sanctuary. A virtually identical figurine (cat. no. 153b) is housed at the Metropolitan Museum. These twin foundation pegs were

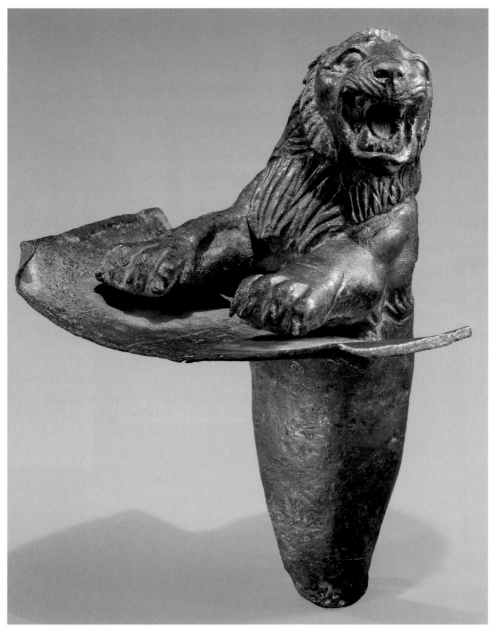

153b

almost identical peg, with an accompanying inscribed stone tablet, now in the collection of the Louvre. If a similar stone tablet accompanied the Metropolitan's peg, it is now lost.[3]

While it is probable that they served as foundation deposits for a temple at Urkesh, neither was obtained from controlled excavations. As noted above, the lions represented on the pegs most likely served an apotropaic function, protecting the pegs from displacement and, by extension, preserving the integrity of the temple in which they were placed. While this leonine form is unique in the corpus of known foundation pegs, it is difficult to discern in this figure a distinctive style that can be ascribed specifically to the Hurrians.[4] The Hurrians appear to have assimilated rapidly to the prevailing Akkadian cultural milieu, and a full understanding of their stylistic contribution to the art of the late third millennium B.C. has yet to be elucidated.

The Metropolitan peg, despite its modest scale, evidences in its fabrication some interesting technical features. The peg was hollow cast using an arsenical copper alloy containing less than 2 percent arsenic.[5] During casting the core was supported by at least three metal supports, visible in X-radiographs. While the presence of a core enabled an economical use of metal, its primary function may have been to provide a quick distribution of metal in order to reduce the possibility of casting flaws, particularly in the projecting limbs. The inscribed plaque appears to have been made separately and attached to the wax model of the peg before it was invested and cast.

J-FL

1. Parrot and Nougayrol 1948, pp. 1–20; Amiet 1976b, pp. 42ff., 132, fig. 64; Whiting 1976, pp. 173–82; Muscarella 1988b, pp. 93–99; Frayne 1997, pp. 463–64; Buccellati 1998, pp. 28–29; Salvini 1998, pp. 106–8; Wilhelm 1998, pp. 117–43 (and bibliography); André-Salvini 2000, pp. 69–71.
2. See Buccellati and Kelly-Buccellati 1995, pp. 65–70; and Buccellati and Kelly-Buccellati 1995–96, pp. 1–36.
3. For a complete discussion and bibliography, see Muscarella 1988a, pp. 374–77.
4. Ibid., pp. 376–77.
5. Ibid., p. 377, n. 2.

deposited in the earth—probably in brick enclosures during the construction of the temple—and were intended to preserve the name of the builder prince and to guarantee the stability and timelessness of the temple of Nergal in the city-state of Urkesh. The political and religious center of the Hurrian region in the first centuries of its history, Urkesh was recently identified as the site of Tell Mozan in the Khabur basin, in the Syrian Jazira (see "Tell Mozan [Ancient Urkesh]," by Giorgio Buccellatti and Marilyn Kelly-Buccellatti, in this catalogue).[2]

Nergal, god of the underworld, was the object of especial veneration by the ancient Hurrian rulers. Lubadag is an ethnic deity who in the second millennium B.C. is found, under the name of Nubadig, as far away as Ugarit on the Mediterranean coast. The great gods invoked in the curse, which was intended to reinforce the dissuasive and threatening role of the peg figurine, are major deities in the Hurrian pantheon.

BA-S

The top half of the Metropolitan's peg consists of the forepart of a snarling lion with forelegs outstretched over an inscribed plaque. Although the inscription on the plaque is largely lost to corrosion, enough remains to show that it most likely duplicates an inscription found on the

Tell Brak in the Akkadian Period

Extensive excavations at the site of Tell Brak (probably ancient Nagar), in the Khabur region of Syria, have provided some of the most important information for any third-millennium-B.C. city in northern Mesopotamia, especially during the Akkadian period (about 2300–2159 B.C.). Texts and seal impressions suggest that Akkadian authority over the entire Khabur region was based at Tell Brak, the empire's most powerful northern administrative center. The first substantial archaeological evidence of this authority is from the reign of Naram-Sin (ca. 2220–2184 B.C.), whose name is stamped on the bricks of the monumental, fortified administrative building that was excavated at the site in the 1940s. Recent excavations of other monumental building complexes on the site (Areas FS and SS) have yielded additional evidence for the Akkadian presence in Syria as well as one of the most significant collections of third-millennium-B.C. glyptic.

Area FS, possibly a caravanserai situated near what was likely the north gate of the city, included a temple with its own courtyard. Bullae discovered here suggest that the building was dedicated to the god Shakkan, patron of animals of the countryside. This identification is reinforced by the discovery of gazelle horns in the temple's antecella and of eight donkeys ritually deposited in an adjoining building. Area SS contained a massive structure that included administrative and domestic quarters and another temple consisting of a cella, an antecella, and an adjacent courtyard. The buildings of both areas were abandoned and had been deliberately filled in with soil into which objects were placed, perhaps as part of a ritual offering.

JME

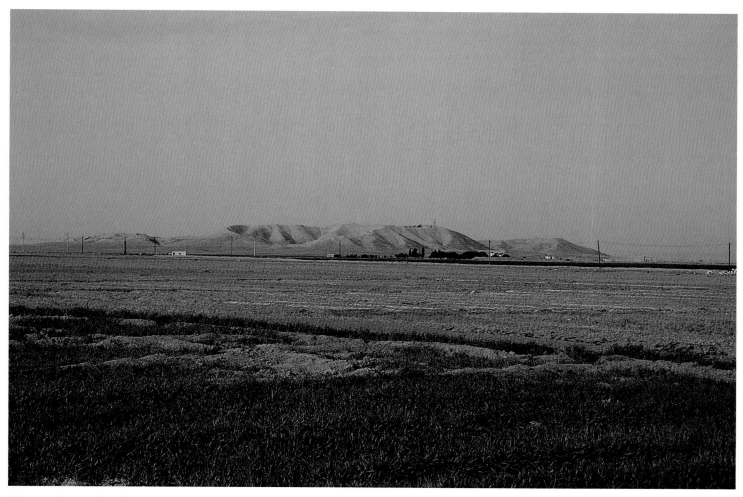

The extensive remains of ancient Nagar (modern Tell Brak).

156

Sealing with a cylinder seal impression depicting a battle of the gods

Cuneiform inscription
Clay
Impression of seal: H. 8.6 cm (3⅜ in.); W. 6.7 cm
(2⅝ in.); Thickness 3.8 cm (1½ in.)
Syria, Nagar (modern Tell Brak), Area SS, TB10014a, b;
TB10015a, b; TB11026
Akkadian, ca. 2300–2159 B.C.
Museum of Deir ez-Zor, Syria 11762

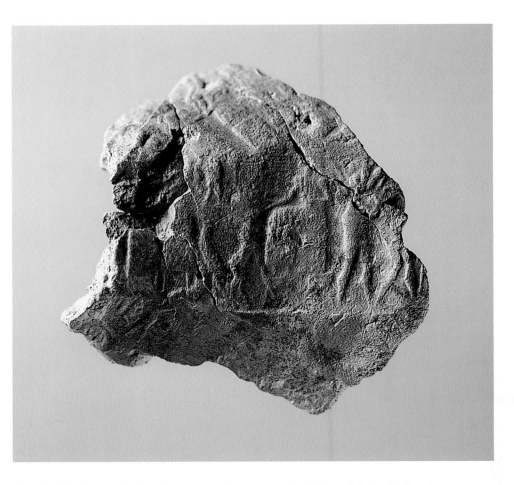

The cylinder seals and seal impressions found at Tell Brak in northeastern Syria form the most important corpus of Akkadian seal imagery outside of southern Mesopotamia. Among the many seal impressions recovered from Area SS, more than twenty fragmentary impressions from the same inscribed cylinder seal, which itself was never found, were recovered from the fill and from deposits directly on the floors.[1] The cylinder seal was called the Scribe's Seal by the excavators, since the first case of the inscription bears the word "scribe" *(dub-sar)* and the second case contains a personal name.[2] The fragmentary impressions have been combined to reconstruct the imagery that was carved on the cylinder seal itself (fig. 69), which is remarkable for its unusual subject matter and the quality of its carving.

The main scene shows two seated male figures wearing tufted garments and facing each other. Decorated differently, their stools are set on the backs of paired, antithetical animals, on which the seated figures also rest

their feet. Each extends a hand to a rampant quadruped, and the one on the left also holds a cup. Two figures approach the seated pair. One wears a long robe with fringe along the edge and the bottom. The other, who can be identified as a god by his horned headdress, is clad in a hitched-up skirt and holds what is probably an axe. Subsidiary to the principal

scene is a battle of the gods, showing a sun god and a defeated deity who holds a broken mace (see entry for cat. no. 144).

While the seated figure on the right wears the horned headdress of divinity, the figure on the left does not and thus offers a rare example of a human allowed to sit in the presence of a deity (see cat. no. 133). The closed composition,

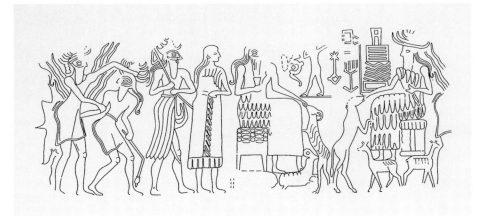

Fig. 69. Reconstruction of a seal impression based on fragments, including catalogue number 156.

in which this person is seated with his back to the approaching deity, is also unusual. It has been suggested that the human is the Akkadian king Manishtushu, since his stool resembles the seat in one of the ruler's surviving statues.[4]

JME

1. See Oates, Oates, and McDonald 2001, pp. 73–98, for a summary of the Area SS investigation.
2. Ibid., p. 137.
3. Felli 2001, pp. 144–45, figs. 182, 183.
4. Ibid., p. 148; see also D. Matthews (1997, pp. 140–41), who argues for an earlier date.

157a

Recumbent human-headed bull or bison

Limestone, shell, and bitumen
H. 28.2 cm (11⅛ in.); L. 41.5 cm (16⅜ in.); W. 16.5 cm (6½ in.)
Syria, Nagar (modern Tell Brak), Area SS, TB11001
Akkadian, ca. 2300–2159 B.C.
Museum of Deir ez-Zor, Syria   11754

157b

Cylinder seal with a sun god and a human-headed bull or bison

Dark serpentine
H. 4.1 cm (1⅝ in.); Diam. 2.4 cm (1 in.)
Mesopotamia
Akkadian, ca. 2300–2159 B.C.
Jeannette and Jonathan Rosen

The reclining bison (cat. no. 157a) was excavated at Tell Brak—probably ancient Nagar, a major city located in the Khabur region of northern Syria. It was found in a monumental Akkadian building that had been abandoned and intentionally filled with earth at the end of the Akkadian period. Since the sculpture was found in this fill, it cannot date later than the Akkadian period, although it could have been made somewhat earlier than the time of its burial. The iconography of a reclining human-headed bison with one leg bent at the knee as if the animal were rising is based on earlier Sumerian prototypes, and the awkward-seeming placement of the bent leg follows a Sumerian tradition.[1] This Sumerian iconography reached Nagar via the other Syrian cities of Mari and Ebla or directly from Sumer itself. The style, however, is decidedly un-Sumerian. Rather, the approach to sculptural form is basically geometric without any sense of the structure of the animal's body. Although there

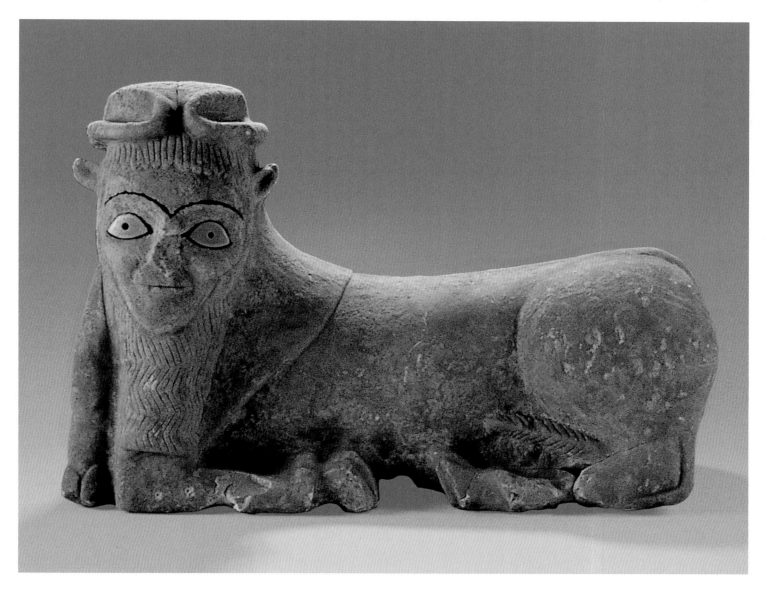

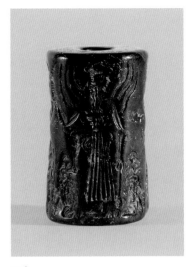

157b

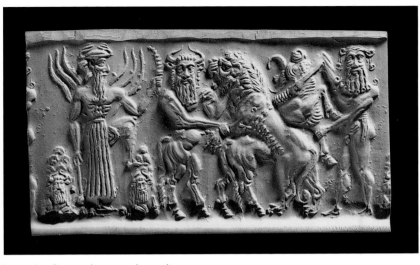

Impression from catalogue number 157b.

are certain antecedents, this sculpture is particularly important, for it marks the beginning of a distinctive Syrian style or approach to sculptural form that was to last for many centuries in such centers as Alalakh or Guzanna (Tell Halaf).

The same composite animal was also found at Ebla in Palace G (see cat. no. 111). Since this city was most likely destroyed by Sargon, the tiny figurine made of steatite and gold foil over a wood core must date to the late Early Dynastic III period in terms of southern chronology. The execution is somewhat crude, but the contrasting gold and steatite are visually engaging. This human-headed bison has the same twisted, bent knee as the Nagar sculpture.

This type of mythological creature was known in antiquity as the *kusarikkum* in Akkadian, or *gud-alim* in Sumerian,[2] and was associated with the sun god. It figures on a seal in classic Akkadian style in the Rosen collection (cat. no. 157b). The seal shows two contests, a hero struggling with a water buffalo and a human-headed bison engaging a lion. Next to this interlocked group of four figures is the sun god, Shamash, identified by the sun rays emanating from his shoulders and by his emblem, the *shasharum* saw, held in his upraised left hand. He grasps a mace in his lowered right hand. On another seal (cat. no. 140), attendant figures open the gates of the sunrise to reveal Shamash rising between mountains and again holding the saw. On the Rosen seal, Shamash, one leg raised in ascendant posture, rises from the eastern mountains, indicated by the usual scalloped motif, but in this case the mountains are supported by two *kusarikkum*—each with one foreleg bent, and Shamash actually places

his raised foot on the head of one of them. Here, the *kusarikku* are physically linked with the eastern sunrise. DPH

1. For a detailed study of the Tell Brak sculpture, see Hansen 2001.
2. Steinkeller 1992a, pp. 259ff.; Wiggermann 1992, pp. 174–79.

158a–e

Hoard

Syria, Nagar (modern Tell Brak), Area HS
Akkadian, ca. 2300–2159 B.C.

a. Pendant with crossed lions
Gold
H. 4.9 cm (1⅞ in.); W. 6.2 cm (2½ in.); Thickness 0.5 cm (³⁄₁₆ in.); Weight 5.5 g
TB15070
Museum of Deir ez-Zor, Syria 13245

b. Double bull's or bison's head pendant
Lapis lazuli
H. 2.6 cm (1 in.); W. 1.9 cm (¾ in.); Thickness 0.9 cm (⅜ in.)
TB15068
Museum of Deir ez-Zor, Syria 13244

c. Lion-headed eagle pendant
Lapis lazuli, gold, frit, and silver
H. 4.2 cm (1⅝ in.); W. 5.4 cm (2⅛ in.); Thickness 1.6 cm (⅝ in.); Weight 22.8 g
TB15071
Museum of Deir ez-Zor, Syria 13246

d. String of beads
Red jasper, gold, and carnelian
Weight 10.2 g
TB15063, TB15067
Museum of Deir ez-Zor, Syria 13243

e. Horse pendant
Silver
H. 2 cm (¾ in.); L. 3 cm (1⅛ in.); W. 0.5 cm (³⁄₁₆ in.); Weight 3.9 g
TB15075
Museum of Deir ez-Zor, Syria 13250

This collection of objects is from a hoard buried in a room of an Akkadian-period building at Tell Brak. In this room a large white stone covered a pit into which two containers had been set: one was a small bowl that lay over the mouth of a larger jar, which contained these precious items and other material. The mouth of the jar had been closed with clay bearing an impression of a cylinder seal. Inside the jar was another clay sealing with a seal impression, indicating that the objects were originally deposited in a container of perishable material that has disintegrated.

Silver items form the bulk of the hoard and probably represent the portable wealth of its owner, which he buried for safekeeping. It includes silver in the form of ingots, folded sheets, circular and spiral lengths, and small decorated scrap items. Spiral silver rings are known to have served as an early form of currency, and the small copper rings that also appear in the hoard may have served the same purpose.

A particularly beautiful object from the find is the carved lapis lazuli lion-headed eagle

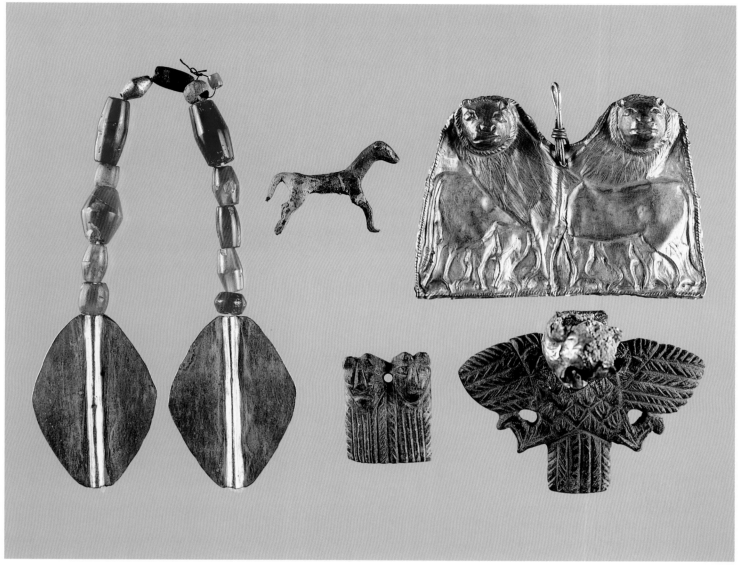

158a–e

(cat. no. 158a). The head is made from a gold-sheet mask covering a core of frit. The eagle is attached to a silver hook, which is threaded through a hole in the lapis and forms a silver hanger at the back of the piece.[1] The sheet-gold plaque or pendant with a gold-wire suspension loop (cat. no. 158c) is unique. It depicts two crossed lions in relief with incised decoration, which is particularly fine on the manes. The lions' feet are represented as eagles' claws. Other unusual pieces include a small silver figurine of a horse (cat. no. 158e), an incised pendant of dark red jasper, two gold leaf-shaped

flat beads with tubular midribs, and eleven carnelian beads (cat. no. 158d). In addition to the lion-headed eagle, there are two other carved lapis lazuli pieces: a small pendant with incised detail and a pendant depicting a double bull (cat. no. 158b).

Although it predates the HS material, the Treasure of Ur from Mari (see cat. nos. 81–87) includes items that provide good parallels for objects in this hoard. It has been suggested that the more finely finished objects, such as the lion-headed eagle, were manufactured in southern Mesopotamia during Early Dynastic

times. According to this theory, they were perhaps brought to Tell Brak later as personal possessions of southern Mesopotamians who went north to work in the Akkadian imperial administration. The circumstances that led to the burial of the hoard are unknown.[2]

PC

1. A late Akkadian hoard from Tell Asmar in the Diyala region included three Imdugud figures, one with a lapis body and silver wings, head, and tail, the other two with lapis wings and silver torsos, heads, and tails. See R. Matthews 1994, p. 296.
2. R. Matthews 1994; R. Matthews, Matthews, and McDonald 1994.

String of beads

Silver and gold
Each quadruple-spiral bead: L. 1.1 cm (⁷⁄₁₆ in.);
W. 1.2 cm (½ in.); Thickness 0.2 cm (¹⁄₁₆ in.)
Double-spiral bead: L. 1.2 cm (½ in.); W. 0.7 cm
(¼ in.); Thickness 0.2 cm (¹⁄₁₆ in.)
Flat disk bead: L. 1 cm (³⁄₈ in.); W. 0.95 cm (³⁄₈ in.);
Thickness 0.2 cm (¹⁄₁₆ in.)
Syria, Nagar (modern Tell Brak), FS hoard 1957,
TB15073
Akkadian, ca. 2300–2159 B.C.
Museum of Deir ez-Zor, Syria 13248

Various metalwork deposits were found in the southwest corner of a temple building at Tell Brak. The objects had been placed within the earth fill of the building after it had been abandoned, perhaps as part of a ritual closure. The beads in this reconstructed necklace were among a group of silver and copper-alloy objects found there that had been contained in a cloth or leather bag.[1] They include three quadruple-spiral beads, made by joining two of this type with spiral ends, and one half-bead with spiral. Two of the quadruple beads have spirals formed from heavy round wire; the other is made of flat sheet. Quadruple-spiral beads are distributed widely, from the Aegean to the Indus Valley; however, the majority are made of gold, not silver, as are these examples (see "Art and Interconnections in the Third Millennium B.C.," by Joan Aruz, in this catalogue).

The manufacturing technique used for beads at Ashur[2] and Troy (see cat. no. 170a) is identical with that used at Tell Brak. In contrast, another type of bead from both Tell Brak[3] and Tell Selenkahiye has spirals formed of wire soldered to the exterior of the central tube, and a silver bead from Eskiyapar has spirals formed in one piece from lengths of metal drawn out of a central tube. Flat beads with tubular midribs are often, as seen here, associated with quadruple-spiral beads. These beads were formed by hammering two pieces of sheet metal on either side of a tube made of rolled sheet, a more elaborate method than that used at other sites. The other beads in this necklace are barrel-like and smaller cylindrical types.

PC

1. McDonald, Curtis, and Maxwell-Hyslop in Oates, Oates, and McDonald 2001, pp. 133–234, 245–46.
2. Harper et al. 1995, p. 50.
3. Maxwell-Hyslop 1971, p. 31, fig. 22.

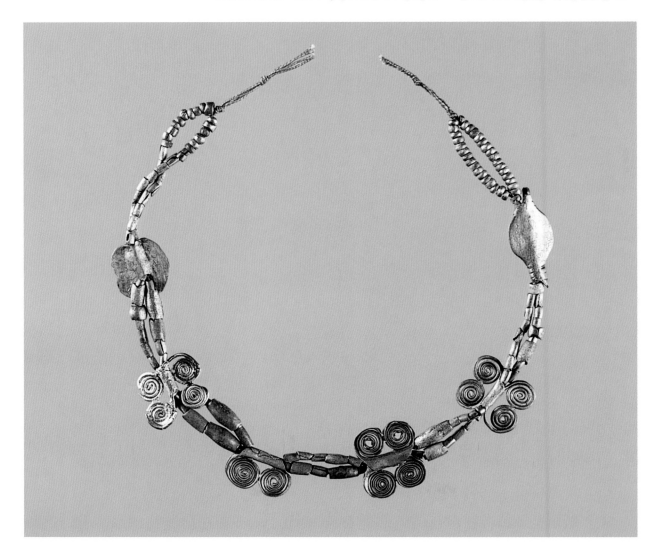

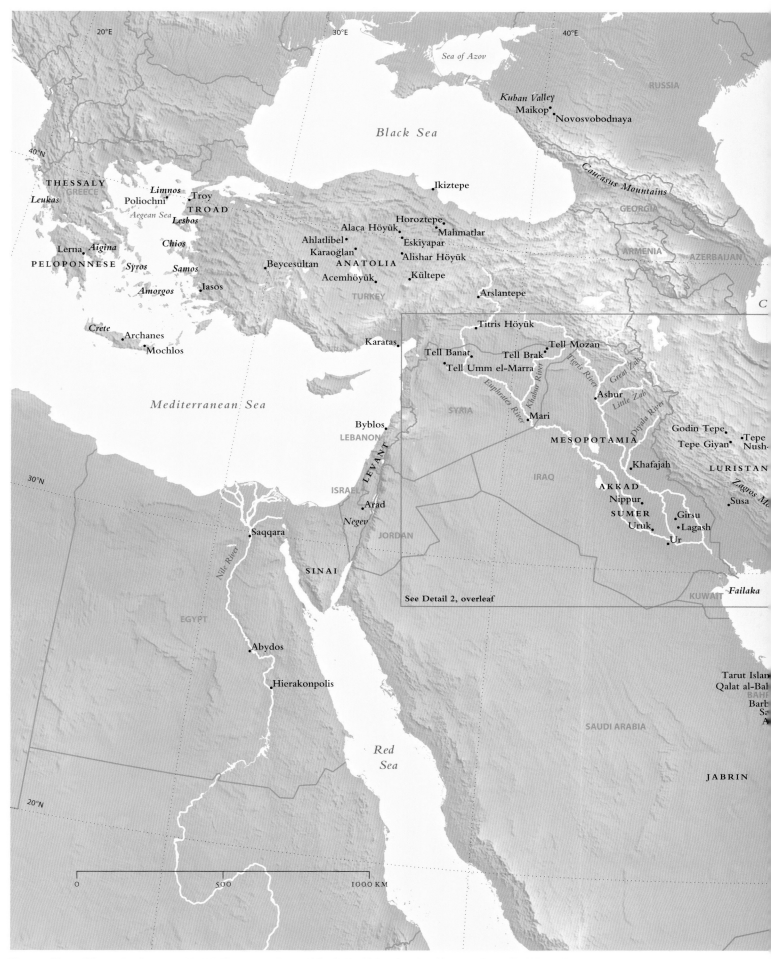

Fig. 70a. Map of the region between the Mediterranean Sea and the Indus Valley, showing sites mentioned in this section.

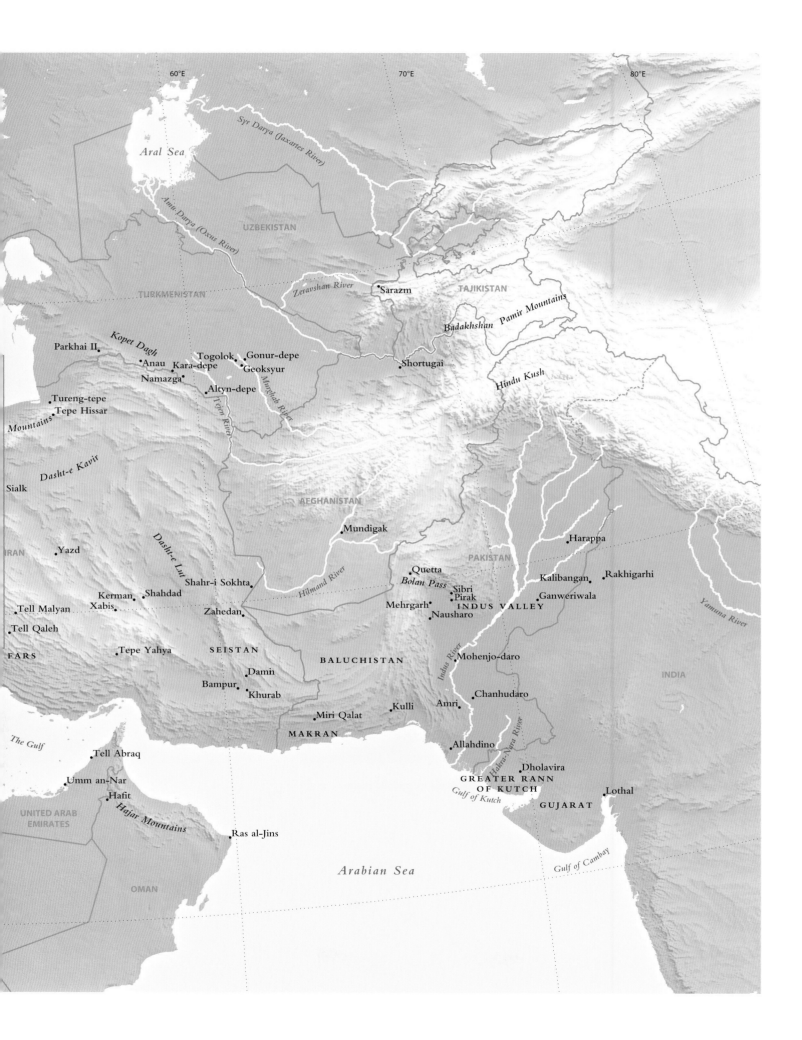

Aral Sea

Syr Darya (Jaxartes River)

Amu Darya (Oxus River)

UZBEKISTAN

TURKMENISTAN

Zeravshan River

• Sarazm

TAJIKISTAN

Badakhshan *Pamir Mountains*

Parkhai II •

Kopet Dagh

• Togolok • Gonur-depe

• Shortugai

• Anau   Kara-depe   Geoksyur •

Munghab River

• Namazga

• Altyn-depe

Hindu Kush

Tejen River

• Tureng-tepe

• Tepe Hissar

Mountains

Dasht-e Kavir

Sialk •

AFGHANISTAN

• Mundigak

• Yazd

Dasht-e Lut

Hilmand River

• Harappa

PAKISTAN

• Shahr-i Sokhta

• Quetta

• Kerman • Shahdad

Bolan Pass

• Kalibangan   • Rakhigarhi

• Tell Malyan • Xabis

• Zahedan

• Sibri

• Ganweriwala

• Mehrgarh

Pirak

Yamuna River

IRAN

• Tell Qaleh

• Nausharo

INDUS VALLEY

FARS

• Tepe Yahya

SEISTAN

• Damin

BALUCHISTAN

Indus River

• Mohenjo-daro

INDIA

• Bampur

• Khurab

• Kulli

• Amri

• Chanhudaro

The Gulf

• Miri Qalat

MAKRAN

• Allahdino

Hakra-Nara River

• Tell Abraq

• Dholavira

• Umm an-Nar

GREATER RANN

OF KUTCH

• Lothal

• Hafit

Gulf of Kutch

GUJARAT

Hajar Mountains

UNITED ARAB

EMIRATES

• Ras al-Jins

Gulf of Cambay

Arabian Sea

OMAN

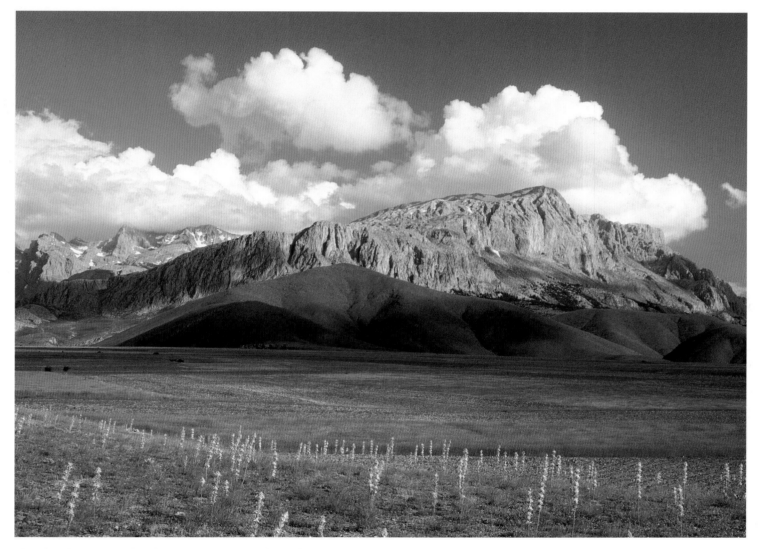

The Ali Dağ, a range within the Taurus Mountains of Anatolia.

ART AND INTERCONNECTIONS IN THE THIRD MILLENNIUM B.C.

JOAN ARUZ

Mesopotamian literary and historical sources allude to warfare and trade in distant and exotic lands, undertaken with an interest in obtaining precious and unusual materials. While some regions are only referred to in connection with specific materials—Magan, for example (which has been identified with the Oman Peninsula), and Meluhha (identified with the Indus Valley)—others are accorded near-mythical status. These include Aratta, "in the mountains where the sun rises," with its fabulous wealth in precious stones and metals, and Dilmun (in the Gulf), a pristine land filled with riches traded from over the seas (see cat. nos. 336, 337).[1] Some kings, such as Enmerkar of Uruk and, later, Sargon of Akkad, are celebrated for opening trade (and tribute) routes, both to the east and to the west. Sargon, in the text called "King of Battle," undertakes a campaign on behalf of his merchants residing in Purushkanda (identified with Acemhöyük, in central Anatolia).[2]

Mary Helms has written about the significance of acquired goods and ideas and the role of the traveler-trader in traditional societies: "Acquisitional acts . . . become dynamic expressions of the quality of the acquirer's association with [the] powerful (foreign) domain." "Long distance traveler/traders . . . obtaining intangible or tangible expressions" of this power, also attain "honor and prestige." For the ruler as accumulator of society's prosperity, "the act of acquisition in itself becomes a mark of exceptionality, exclusivity, ability to control, and allows the cultivation of a kingly image."[3] Marc Van de Mieroop notes that in Mesopotamia during the mid-third millennium B.C. a social elite that gained status by displaying its wealth in its houses and tombs (and, one might add, also probably as votive offerings to the gods in temples) created an impetus to acquire precious and rare objects and materials. Along with gift exchange, booty, and tribute, the aim of the early long-distance traders appears to have been largely to acquire these symbols of power, status, and devotion rather than to sustain the Mesopotamian population.[4]

Although the specific nature of the acquisition of luxury goods and the choices of objects may be too complex for us to fully understand—particularly since specific materials developed religious and magical associations—we know that they became available with the establishment of maritime and land routes to the foreign sources and production centers. The result was an intercultural exchange among distinct civilizations that extended both to the west and to the east of Mesopotamia. The interaction, which in many cases must have been indirect, can

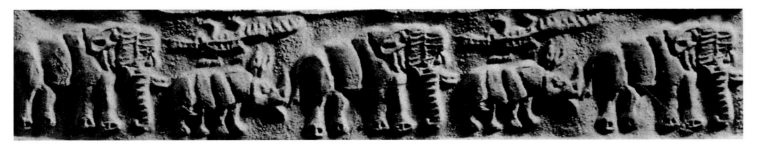

Fig. 71a. Modern impression from a glazed-steatite cylinder seal depicting a rhinoceros, an elephant, and a gharial. Seal: Tell Asmar, late 3rd millennium B.C. Iraq Museum, Baghdad, 14674.

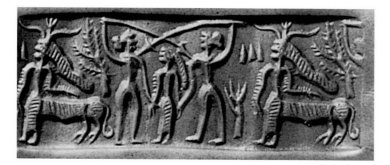

Fig. 71b. Modern impression from a stone cylinder seal. Seal: Indus Valley, Kalibangan, Harappan, ca. 2600–1900 B.C. Archaeological Survey of India, Purana Qila, New Delhi, 68.1.177.

only be glimpsed through isolated textual references and surviving works of art.

Art historical analysis of the formal, stylistic, and iconographic properties of particular groups of elite objects of exotic material and forms—created for the temple, palace, and tomb—helps to illuminate these cultural exchanges. It identifies the defining character of the art of individual civilizations and attempts to determine whether individual pieces were imported from abroad or altered in some aspect of appearance as a response to an acquaintance with the work of foreign craftsmen.

During the third millennium B.C. three great urban civilizations—Egyptian, Mesopotamian, and Harappan—developed independently along the Nile, the Tigris and Euphrates, and the Indus Rivers, demonstrating only marginal effects from contacts with one another. Egypt appears to have remained the most pristine, having only isolated and indirect contacts with the Mesopotamian world. Its impact on cultural developments in the Near East is most clearly documented by imported goods and by objects exhibiting Egyptian-looking features concentrated mostly at sites near the Mediterranean coast (see, however, "Art of the Early City-States," by Donald P. Hansen, in this catalogue). Among the rich finds from the administrative sector of the royal

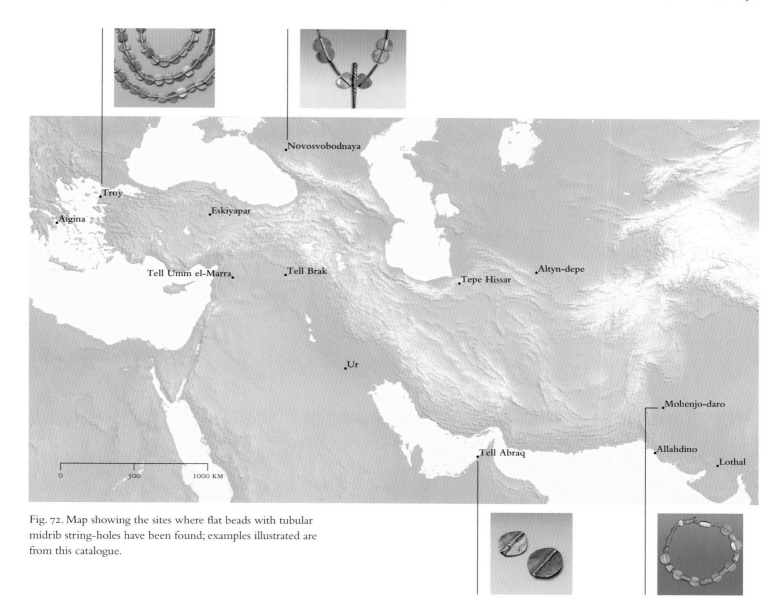

Fig. 72. Map showing the sites where flat beads with tubular midrib string-holes have been found; examples illustrated are from this catalogue.

palace at Ebla, in northwestern Syria, was a hoard of pharaonic gifts, including Egyptian diorite and alabaster vases inscribed with the names of the Fourth and Sixth Dynasty pharaohs Khafre and Pepi I (see cat. no. 161). Communications between Egypt and Ebla may have traveled indirectly through coastal cities of the Levant, such as Byblos, where gifts were made to the Egyptian temple there during Pepi's reign (ca. 2289–2255 B.C.).[5] Pepi was a contemporary of the Akkadian ruler (identified by Paolo Matthiae as Sargon rather than Naram-Sin) thought to be responsible for the destruction of the royal residence at Ebla about 2250 B.C. Excavation of Indus Valley sites has yielded imports from Central Asia but not from Mesopotamia, although some Harappan artistic imagery suggests Near Eastern stimuli. The ports and goods of the Indus region, however, were the main objective in the exchange network that developed along the sea and land routes connecting West, Central, and South Asia.

While certain raw materials and artifacts demonstrate the entire geographic breadth of intercultural exchange, others were confined to eastern or western parts of the vast network of cultural centers. The evidence includes not only jewelry made of gold, silver, and precious stones but also elaborately carved chlorite and plain alabaster vessels;[6] stone sculpture either imported or demonstrating foreign features;[7] cosmetic implements and bangles made of shell (see cat. nos. 287b, 289b);[8] ivory tusks and artifacts (see cat. no. 212);[9] wood and reeds;[10] pottery (see cat. no. 216); board games;[11] utilitarian items such as weights (see cat. no. 292b);[12] and live animals such as monkeys.[13] We focus on a few in this essay.

LAPIS LAZULI AND CARNELIAN JEWELRY

Objects of gold, silver, lapis lazuli, carnelian, and other precious materials appear in profusion in the ancient Near East. In addition

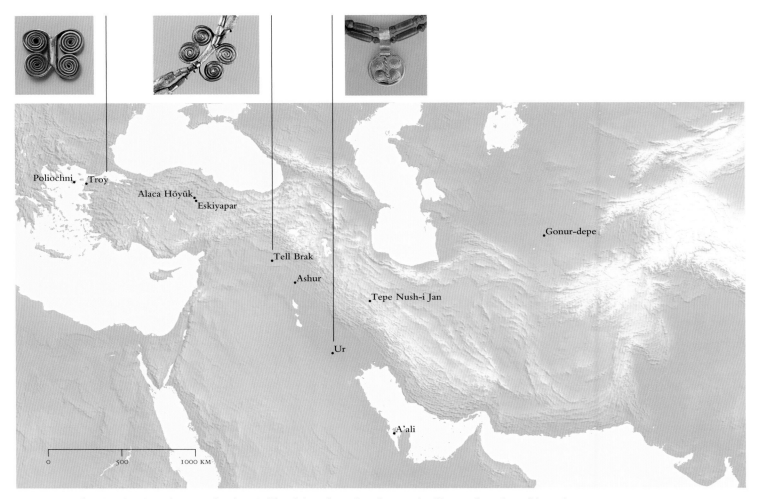

Fig. 73. Map showing the sites where quadruple-spiral beads have been found; examples illustrated are from this catalogue.

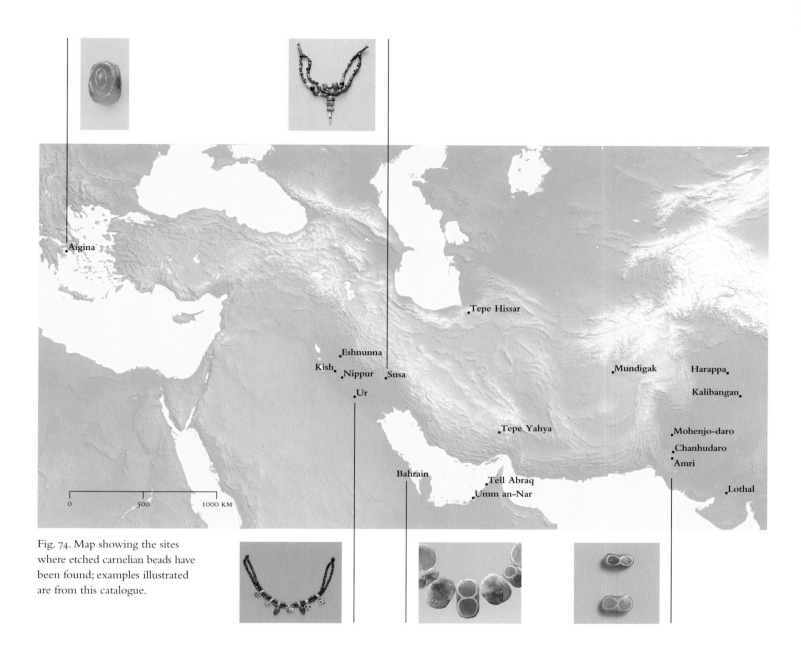

Fig. 74. Map showing the sites where etched carnelian beads have been found; examples illustrated are from this catalogue.

to enhancing the owner's status, the materials themselves appear to have been charged with religious significance, used in temple rituals and to decorate temple altars and divine images, as well as—according to the texts—worn as personal adornment by the gods.[14] Appropriate for gift exchange, booty, and tribute, these luxuries were deposited in temple and palace treasuries.[15] In elite burials, the dead were bedecked in jewelry that, perhaps as in some traditional Asian societies, may have been a means of enhancing the body itself as a divine offering.

Lapis lazuli, legendary for its procurement from distant eastern mountains, accorded the divine attribute "gleaming splendor," worn by the goddess Inanna/Ishtar, and offered as gifts to the gods, was perhaps the most prestigious precious stone used in early Mesopotamia.[16] We imagine that the amuletic value of its color—ideally, deep blue with golden "starry" flecks—was paramount, along with its rarity and exotic associations. The raw

material was mined at Sar-i Sang in the Badakhshan mountains of modern northern Afghanistan.[17] It circulated widely during the third millennium, throughout western Central Asia, Iran, Mesopotamia, Syria, and the Mediterranean region. Enormous quantities of the raw stone found in the palace of Ebla may have been destined in part for Egypt (see cat. no. 116).[18] Although major installations for working lapis lazuli have been identified not very far from sources of the raw material, at Shahr-i Sokhta (see "Pathways across Eurasia," by Maurizio Tosi and C. C. Lamberg-Karlovsky, in this catalogue), comparatively few objects made of lapis have been found in Iran.[19] Similarly, the stone was not frequently used in the Harappan world in its flourishing period, despite textual associations of Meluhha with lapis lazuli and the possibility that Harappan traders at the site of Shortugai, on the Oxus River, were involved in the trade.[20] This may indicate that the amuletic and aesthetic value of lapis was not appreciated universally.[21] The same seems to hold true for the greener stone turquoise, which very rarely appears in Mesopotamia (it is absent, for example, from the Royal Cemetery at Ur) and is more common in Iran and Central Asia (see cat. nos. 247, 249).[22]

By contrast, carnelian, a hard stone that achieves a brilliant red color when heated, appears to have been valued second to lapis lazuli both in Mesopotamian and in Harappan society.[23] Not as rare as the blue stone, carnelian was extensively worked in the area of the Gulf of Cambay in India, and both the raw material and certain very characteristic bead types appear to have been exported from the Indus Valley to the Near East. Ancient texts mention Meluhha as a source of the material.[24]

Although cuneiform documents do not elaborate on carnelian as a material appropriate for the gods, deposits of the unworked stone have been found along with lapis lazuli in the foundations of Mesopotamian temples.[25] Otherwise it was used largely to create beads and amulets, and unlike lapis lazuli, this hard-to-engrave variety of quartz was not utilized to produce royal or elite cylinder seals during the third millennium B.C.

Perhaps the most spectacular objects made of carnelian are the long biconical "barrel-cylinder" beads, some more than five inches in length, crafted in the Indus Valley into spectacular pieces of jewelry found at many Harappan sites (see cat. no. 279).[26] Imported long carnelian beads were also used for jewelry in the Near East; they are found, notably, in the Ur Royal Cemetery and in tombs at Kish and Tello. One bead from Susa bears a Sumerian dedicatory inscription to the goddess Ningal by the king Shulgi of Ur.[27] As shorter carnelian beads and one lapis lazuli bead of the same form were found in Mesopotamia, and since hard stones were worked in the region at the time, it is probable that some less ambitious examples were in fact made locally. Leonard Woolley, the excavator of Ur, points to the existence of a bead maker's grave in the Akkadian cemetery there.[28]

The Near Eastern appreciation of Harappan beadworking also extended to carnelian beads etched with white (and, rarely, black) geometric patterns; these imports have been found along with the long biconical beads.[29] Etched carnelian beads, relatively small, were produced in a variety of shapes and designs. They were distributed over a vast area extending from the Indus to the Gulf and the Mediterranean (the only example found west of Ur and Kish was recently discovered on the island of Aigina; see cat. no. 166a; fig. 74) and along land routes from Baluchistan to Iran and Central Asia.[30] Among the types carried to the west were cylindrical, barrel, ovoid, lentoid, and cushion shapes, bearing designs featuring concentric and tangent circles, circles

within lozenge or arc patterns, and series of chevrons. It is of particular interest that some etched carnelian bead patterns are typically Near Eastern and were not popular in the Indus region. These include the guilloche design on beads found in Mesopotamia and at Susa (see cat. no. 201) as well as a stepped pattern on beads from Susa, Kish, and Ur, the last also bearing a Mesopotamian sun symbol.[31] The stepped form is characteristic of designs used both in Iran and western Central Asia, appearing in wall paintings, pottery, and metalwork and used as a bead shape (see cat. nos. 247, 248, 251–254). The iconographic evidence, along with the observation that the largest collection of etched carnelian beads was in fact found not in the Indus Valley but rather at the site of Ur (some with uncharacteristic patterns), may suggest that a local workshop—possibly in the hands of foreign craftsmen—supplemented the supply of imported etched as well as long biconical beads.[32]

GOLD AND SILVER JEWELRY

Jonathan Mark Kenoyer makes the suggestion (see cat. no 278b), based on the similarity between gold and silver floral headdresses at Ur and diadems shown on Harappan terracottas, that some of the servants buried in the tombs at Ur may have come to Mesopotamia from the Indus Valley. The facts that a gold floral ornament was also worn by queen Puabi and that in both her grave and another there were belts made of biconical carnelian beads (cat. nos. 62, 80) may rather reflect the predilection of the Ur elite for Indus jewelry and fashion, including Harappan belts (see cat. no. 279).

Other gold jewelry elements in the Near East point toward connections not only farther east but also with the west.[33] One particular bead type made of gold and silver, a flat disk with a tubular midrib string-hole, appears to have been distributed, and probably manufactured as well, at sites along the same routes as the etched carnelian beads (see fig. 72). Such beads were found at many Indus sites, including the port of Lothal, at Altyn-depe in Turkmenistan, at Tepe Hissar in Iran, in the Royal Cemetery at Ur, at Eskiyapar and Troy in Anatolia, and on Aigina in the Aegean.[34]

Another widely distributed, distinctive, and valuable gold or silver bead type in the third millennium B.C.—found in hoards and burials and often associated with flat beads—is in the shape of a quadruple spiral (see fig. 73). The early form of this bead (known as Type A) was made by hammering and pulling four wires from a one-piece tube or by overlapping two half tubes with spiral ends.[35] The quadruple spiral may have had ritual significance in the Near East, as it is depicted before a deity on

73. For the cylinder seal, see During Caspers 1994a, p. 94. The attachment of a complete human body to the belly and hindquarters of a feline is rare in the West, before its use for sphinxes on a Mycenaean krater from Enkomi on Cyprus; see Demisch 1977, p. 71, fig. 198. The composite creature is also found on Harappan stamp seals; see During Caspers 1984, p. 364 pls. 151, 152. See Amiet 1986, p. 299, fig. 8, for an East Iranian parallel. See During Caspers 1993–95 on the use of cylinder seals in the Indus region.

74. During Caspers 1984, p. 367.

75. Sarianidi 1998b, p. 297:1634; Winkelmann 1995. See Aruz 1995b, pp. 16ff., for a discussion of this theme in the Aegean and the Near East.

76. See During Caspers 1994a, pp. 93–98. During Caspers (1982, pp. 342–43) suggests they may have been produced for a Sumerian merchant abroad and that the Tell Asmar seal (fig. 71a) may have been cut by a Meluhhan in Mesopotamia.

77. During Caspers 1994a, p. 92; Masson 1981b.

78. For one example, see Winkelmann 2001. Another is in the Metropolitan Museum. Lent by the Schoyen Collection (L.1999.75); it depicts an archer shooting at a boar, with an attacking (leonine) dog below and with signs in the field.

79. Beyer 1989, p. 113 fig. 3 (the Mari seal); During Caspers 1994a, p. 103, pl. 1:c,d (the Harappa example).

80. Baghestani 1997, p. 184 fig. 27:64, 67–69.

81. A kilted horned figure with snakes on a Metropolitan Museum seal (David L. Klein, Jr., Memorial Foundation, Inc., and Lester Wolfe [by exchange] Gifts, 1984, 1984.4) may also have a bovine ear and bull's head (see Pittman 1984, p. 57, no. 26b), like the kilted figure on a door-sealing from Susa (see Harper, Aruz, and Tallon 1992, p. 6, fig. 6).

82. Discussed in Winkelmann 1993.

83. Ravn 1960, pp. 97–98, no. 118; Aruz 1984.

84. Aruz 1986, p. 166 n. 7.

85. Aruz 1999a, pp. 11–13.

86. Aruz 1994, p. 215, fig. 11.

87. Lamberg-Karlovsky 1993, p. 289.

88. Possehl 1996, p. 140.

EGYPT AND THE NEAR EAST IN THE THIRD MILLENNIUM B.C.

JAMES P. ALLEN

In keeping with the ancient Egyptians' view of their country as the privileged center of the universe, Egyptian textual and pictorial records portray a relationship between Egypt and its eastern neighbors that is almost uniformly antagonistic. The archaeological record, however, reveals a much more pragmatic reality.

The birth of pharaonic civilization itself, shortly before the beginning of the third millennium B.C., was marked by the appearance of new motifs in art and architecture that had direct antecedents in archaic Susa and the Uruk culture of Mesopotamia. Evidence of direct trade exists in Mesopotamian cylinder seals found in Egypt and in the use of silver imported from Anatolia. These commodities were probably acquired through contact with the Uruk–Jamdat Nasr culture in northern Syria rather than directly from Mesopotamia itself.

Mesopotamian motifs and objects disappeared from the Egyptian archaeological record in the middle of the First Dynasty, contemporary with Early Bronze Age II. By this time tombs at Abydos, in Upper Egypt, were being equipped with pottery from elsewhere in the Near East and with Lebanese cedar. Sites from the same era in the Negev and other areas of the southern Levant have produced Egyptian pottery, in some cases inscribed with the names of Egyptian kings. Such contacts extended to the city of Arad, in the northeastern Negev, and were made possible through a trade route that ran from the eastern Delta through the northern Sinai. After the fall of Arad, at the end of Early Bronze Age II (Egypt's Second Dynasty), this land route seems to have been abandoned in favor of maritime trade with the seaport of Byblos.

Lebanese cedar in tombs of the First Dynasty probably attests to Egyptian trade with Byblos from the beginning of the pharaonic period. From the reign of Khasekhemui (Second Dynasty, ca. 2650 B.C.) onward, Egyptian kings sent regular trading missions by sea to Byblos, primarily for cedar. The names of several pharaohs of the Old Kingdom (Third through Sixth Dynasty, ca. 2600–2250 B.C.) are preserved on objects discovered at Byblos, presented there either as votives or as royal gifts. Similar inscribed objects have been found at Ebla (see cat. no. 161), but direct contact with this Syrian kingdom is less certain.

Egyptian inscriptions throughout the third millennium B.C. mention frequent military campaigns in the Sinai and the southern Levant. These seem to have been intended primarily to protect Egyptian commercial interests from the predations of nomads, both along the land route used between about 3000 and 2700 B.C., that is, through most of the Archaic Period (First Dynasty through Second Dynasty), and in the Egyptian turquoise and copper mines of the Sinai. Such campaigns were more numerous toward the end of the Old Kingdom, probably reflecting the contemporary dissolution of urban culture in the Levant and Syria.

The end of the third millennium corresponds to Egypt's First Intermediate Period (ca. 2250–2050 B.C.). This was a time of weakened central rule and internal turmoil in Egypt, and contemporary records for Egypt's relations with the Near East during this period are lacking. Literary texts from the early Middle Kingdom (ca. 2000–1900 B.C.), however, reflect incursions of nomadic populations from the east into Egypt's Delta. Though largely regulated by pharaohs of the Middle Kingdom, these migrations continued into the middle of the second millennium, eventually resulting in Asian control of northern Egypt.

Standing nude female figure with folded arms

Lapis lazuli
H. 8.9 cm (3½ in.); W. 2.5 cm (1 in.); Thickness
1.8 cm (¾ in.)
Egypt, Hierakonpolis
Archaic Period, ca. 2900 B.C.
Visitors of the Ashmolean Museum, Oxford E.1057,
E.1057a

This figurine depicts a nude female standing with her hands on her stomach. The breasts are small and placed low in relation to the wide shoulders. The pubic triangle is indicated by dots. Her legs are straight and separated by a line. There are no feet, and it is possible that the figurine never had them but was fitted to another object at the bottom of the legs. The subject appears much more naturalistic in the side view, which reveals rounded buttocks and slightly indicated knees, than from the front. The head and body, which were made (and found) separately, are held together by means of a peg.[1] The eyes are hollowed out for inlays. The most distinctive feature is the stylization of the hair, which represents tight little curls close to the head.

The piece is significant because of its material, lapis lazuli. Two varieties of the stone, which would have been imported to Egypt from Afghanistan, are used. The body is made from a mottled type, while the head is carved from the rarer, deep blue kind. The juxtaposition was either deliberate or the result of an accident that required a replacement head or body. It has been suggested that the figurine was made not in Egypt but in an area close to the Afghan lapis mines.[2] However, the distinctive gesture of the hands, with the right laid over the left rather than clasped or held apart as on other ancient Near Eastern nude female figures, and the stylization of the hair are characteristic of contemporary art made in Egypt.

PC

1. Quibell and Green 1902, p. 38; Garstang 1906, p. 135.
2. Porada 1980.

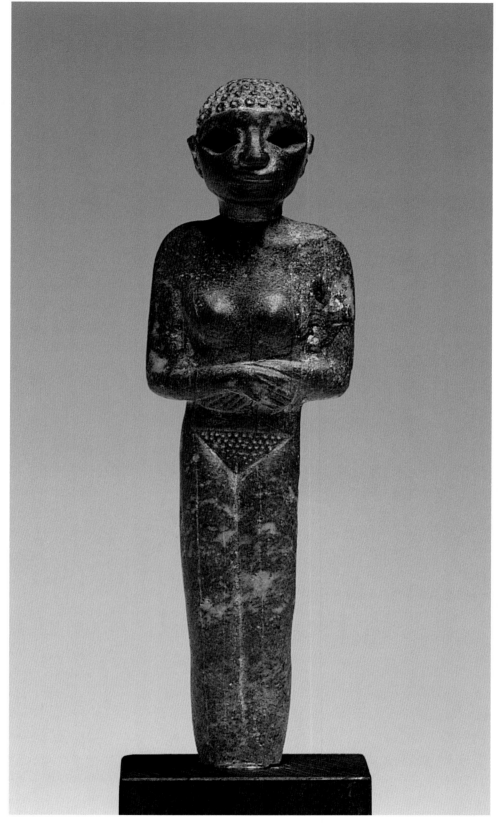

Fragment of an Egyptian jar lid naming Pepi I

Egyptian hieroglyphic inscription
Calcite
Diam. 16.4 cm (6½ in.); Thickness 0.9 cm (⅜ in.)
Syria, Ebla (modern Tell Mardikh), Palace G,
TM.77.G.600
Old Kingdom, reign of Pepi I, ca. 2289–2255 B.C.
National Museum, Aleppo, Syria   10588

The excavation of Palace G at Ebla, Syria, revealed a number of fragmentary stone vessels of Egyptian origin, including this inscribed piece made of Egyptian alabaster (calcite).[1] It was apparently damaged in a fire, perhaps during the destruction of the palace at the end of the Mardikh IIb1 period (ca. 2250 B.C.). When complete, it was the circular lid to a jar designed to hold perfumed ointment. A complete example nearly identical in size, material, and inscription was found in the Egyptian necropolis of Saqqara, south of modern Cairo.[2] On the basis of that parallel, the text on the Ebla fragment can be restored as the royal names of the pharaoh Pepi I within a cartouche: "[The Horus Belov]ed of the Two Lands, the King of Upper and Lower Egypt and son of Hathor, mistress of Dendera, Pep[i, given life, stability, and dominion]." Pepi I, who ruled in the first half of Egypt's Sixth Dynasty, from about 2289 to 2255 B.C., was a contemporary of Ebla's last king, Ibbi-Zikir. Objects from his reign have been found on the Levantine coast, at Byblos, where they were probably presented as royal gifts.[3] This lid and the jar to which it once belonged were most likely part of a similar gift, which either made its way to Ebla through trade relations with Byblos or was presented to Ibbi-Zikir directly on behalf of Pepi I. The goddess Hathor, mentioned in the inscription, had her chief temple at Dendera, in southern Egypt, but she was also considered the patron goddess of the lands to the east of Egypt.

JPA

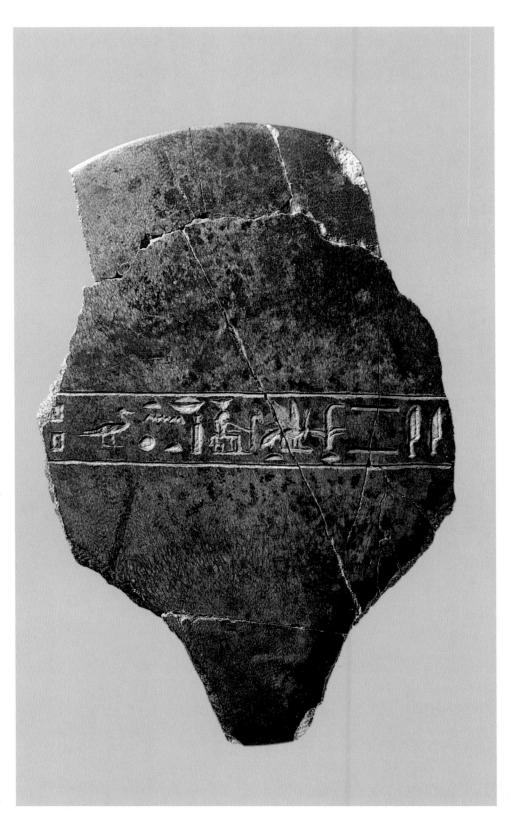

1. This piece was previously published in Eaton-Krauss 1985, p. 170; Scandone Matthiae (1978) 1982; and Scandone Matthiae 1979, pp. 33–44. Another complete example from the same reign is at the Metropolitan Museum (MMA 27.2.2A–8), whose accompanying jar has also survived. The inscription on the lid uses the throne name of Pepi I ("The Horus Beloved of the Two Lands, the King of Upper and Lower Egypt Meryre, given life"), and the text on the jar itself mentions the king's first jubilee, celebrated in his thirtieth regnal year (ca. 2260 B.C.).
2. Firth and Gunn 1926, vol. 1, p. 30, vol. 2, pl. 13A.
3. Helck 1971, p. 21 n. 64.

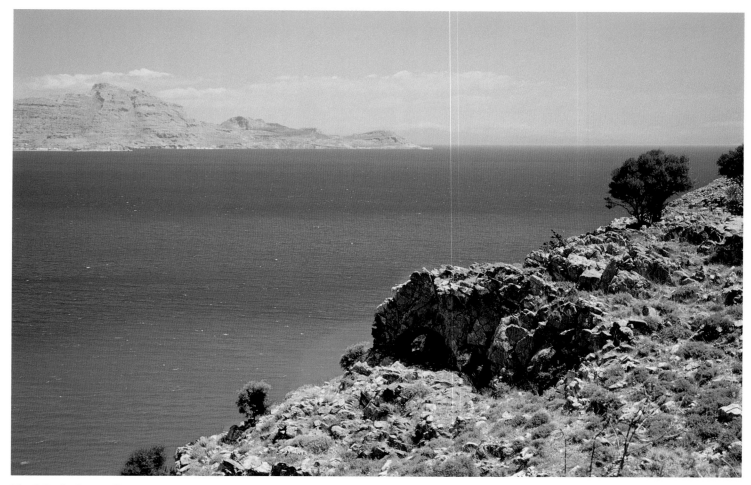

Islands in the Aegean Sea.

THE AEGEAN AND WESTERN ANATOLIA: SOCIAL FORMS AND CULTURAL RELATIONSHIPS

CLAUS REINHOLDT

The Early Bronze Age, particularly the second half of the third millennium B.C., was a period of increasing exchange between the prehistoric peoples of the Aegean and Anatolia. Sparked by the Aegean search for metals and technological skills, these seafaring contacts inevitably led to cultural and artistic influences between east and west, with the islands of the northeastern Aegean and the Cyclades acting as stepping-stones between the Greek mainland and western Anatolia. During the late third millennium, a small scale "migration" of Anatolians of either a hostile or commercial nature is believed to have taken place. Some scholars suggest this migration also operated as an external catalyst for the impressive social developments in Greece that led to a transition from loosely organized farmsteads and village settlements to more centralized social structures.[1] The apex of these developments occurred in what for Greece was the late phase of Early Helladic II; for the northeastern Aegean the Poliochni Red to Yellow Periods; and for western Anatolia the end of Early Bronze II to Early Bronze III (late Troy II–III).

In the field of sculpture, general similarities have been noted between examples of figurines from Anatolia (Troy) and the "folded arm" marble figurines from the Cyclades, which represent one of the major achievements in Cycladic sculpture. With regard to metalworking, although nearly all Early Bronze Age Aegean copper alloys are arsenical, a significant number of objects from sites on the island of Syros (specifically Kastri) were made of tin-bronze. Analyses of the objects have concluded that both the copper and the type and technology of the alloy are of Anatolian, and specifically Trojan, origin. Furthermore, the typology of many of these objects recalls Anatolian (Trojan) prototypes.[2] A number of hoards of jewelry made of precious metals and semiprecious stones discovered across a broad geographical area—from south-central Greece (Aigina, Thyreatis) to the northeastern Aegean (Poliochni); northwestern Anatolia (Troy) to central Anatolia (Alaca Höyük, Eskiyapar, Kültepe); and Syria

and Mesopotamia (Tell Brak, Ur)—are also characterized by great similarities both in date and typology. Even gold finds from tombs of the Pre-Palatial cemetery of Mochlos, Crete, are considered comparable.

Anatolian influences are also strong in regard to the introduction in the Aegean of distinctive wheel-made, red- and black-burnished ceramic forms such as the one-handled tankard, the two-handled cup, and the *depas amphikypellon*,[3] which clearly derive from western Anatolian prototypes. These forms were among the most characteristic of the Kastri/Lefkandi I group,[4] which spread throughout the central Aegean and along the central part of the eastern coast of the Greek mainland (Cyclades, Euboia, coastal Thessaly, Boiotia, eastern Attika, and Aigina). The important site of Limantepe on the western Anatolian coast, a settlement with massive fortifications and monumental architecture, has yielded pottery comparable to the Anatolian-looking examples of the Kastri/Lefkandi I group and can thus be considered as another potential source of influence.

The innovations in ceramic forms represented by the Kastri/Lefkandi I group were immediately preceded by, and partly contemporary with, a significant innovation of architecture in Early Bronze Age Greece: the appearance of a building form termed the "corridor house."[5] A number of scholars have strongly argued that the corridor house was a development indigenous to Greece; however, the general similarities with the contemporary monumental, freestanding, axial buildings (megara) of Anatolia—especially of Troy II (ca. 2600/2550–2250 B.C.)—should be taken into account.

Although the exact function of the corridor house is debatable, it is nevertheless associated with a new, more centralized form of government for localities on the Greek mainland. This is supported by the discovery of a great cache of impressed clay sealings from the House of Tiles at Lerna, in the Peloponnese, which is by all accounts the most monumental and sophisticated in plan of the corridor houses. The cache presents us with indications that Anatolian stimuli were at work in the development of seals and sealing systems in Early Bronze Age Greece.[6] Thus over the course of the third millennium B.C., the Greek mainland, the Cyclades, the eastern Aegean, and western Asia Minor all played crucial roles in an extremely complex process that transformed the Aegean region into a zone of energetic interaction.

1. See Heath Wiencke 1989, pp. 495–509.
2. For these analyses, see Stos-Gale, Gale, and Gilmore 1984, pp. 23–43. Early tin-bronze objects were discovered at other Greek sites, such as Leukas (an island in western Greece), Manika (on the island of Euboia), and Aghios Kosmas in Attika. It is possible that they are roughly contemporary with the ones from Syros. See Heath Wiencke 1989, p. 508 n. 77.
3. The term *depas amphikypellon* designates a tall, narrow tubular vessel with two prominent handles (see cat. no. 178).
4. The group is named after the two major sites where this pottery was discovered: Kastri, on Syros, and Lefkandi, on Euboia.
5. A corridor house is a rectangular, freestanding building composed of a linear series of square or rectangular halls flanked lengthwise by corridors, which often serve as stairwells leading up to a second story. According to Heath Wiencke and Rutter, the appearance of the Kastri/Lefkandi I group was simultaneous with the appearance of corridor houses. Consequently, Heath Wiencke argues that the presence of Anatolians in the Aegean, materially manifested in the Kastri/Lefkandi I group, might have helped to catalyze the social developments that led to the erection of the corridor houses.
6. See Aruz 1994.

162

Standing nude female figure with folded arms

Bone or ivory
H. 8.5 cm (3⅜ in.); W. 2.2 cm (⅞ in.); Thickness 0.9 cm (⅜ in.)
Aegean, Archanes, Crete, cemetery of Fourni, Tholos Tomb Γ
Early Bronze Age, second half of the 3rd millennium B.C.
Archaeological Museum, Heraklion, Crete, Greece HM O-E 440

This figure of a nude female resembles statuettes of the Cycladic type, particularly those in the Spedos group, in such characteristics as the folded arms above the abdomen, the plastically rendered nose, and the lyre-shaped head, which is tilted slightly backward. However, it departs from the type in other ways. The pubic triangle is rendered with several small depressions, in a style rather akin to figurines from Anatolia, and the material is not the standard Cycladic marble, but ivory or bone, both of which were commonly used in the Pre-Palatial period on Crete for manufacturing seals and jewelry. They were very rarely used for sculpture during the Early Bronze Age in the Aegean region.

Female figurines with folded arms suggest pregnancy, and as these sculptures come mostly from graves, it appears that they either played some part in the burial rites (protecting women in life and in the afterlife?) or portray fertility goddesses.

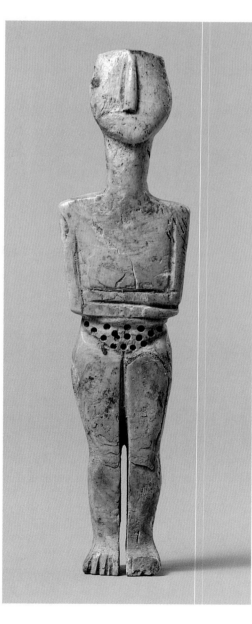

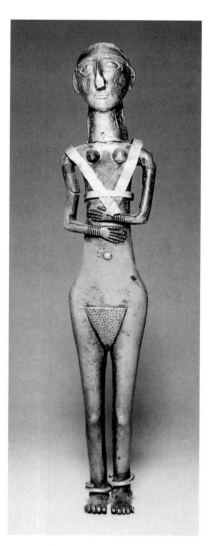

Fig. 75. Silver and gold female figure. Hasanoğlan, Early Bronze Age, ca. 2500–2200 B.C. Museum of Anatolian Civilizations, Ankara, 13922.

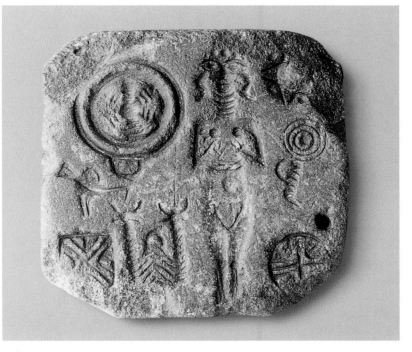

163a

163b

The present figurine was found in Tholos Tomb Γ along with imported Cycladic marble figurines, indicating Crete's close contact with the Cyclades during the Early Bronze Age. The Cycladic type of the present figurine is indisputable, yet its stylistic affinities with counterparts from Anatolia (especially from Hasanoğlan; see fig. 75) cannot rule out the possibility that its Cretan craftsman was familiar with Anatolian artistic trends.[1]   ESB

1. Sakellarakis 1972, pp. 327–51; Höckman 1976, pp. 159–67; Sakellarakis 1977, pp. 93–115; Barber 1987; Sakellarakis 1997, p. 704, fig. 813.

163c

163a

Standing nude female figure with folded arms

Lead
H. 6.3 cm (2½ in.); W. 2 cm (¾ in.); Thickness 0.4 cm (³⁄₁₆ in.)
Syria, Nagar (modern Tell Brak), TB7018
Early Bronze Age, late 3rd millennium B.C.
Museum of Deir ez-Zor, Syria 4590

163b

Mould for jewelry, seals, and amulets

Black stone
H. and W. 7.5 cm (3 in.)
Anatolia, Titris Höyük, house
Early Bronze Age, late 3rd millennium B.C.
Urfa Museum, Turkey TH 60632

163c

Mould for jewelry, seals, and amulets

Stone
H. 9 cm (3½ in.); W. 5.7 cm (2¼ in.)
Mesopotamia, Sippar
Early Bronze Age, late 3rd millennium B.C.
Trustees of The British Museum, London BM 91902

Stone moulds provide good evidence for the mass production of both metal jewelry and stamp seals during the third millennium B.C. These moulds are carved with shallow depres-

sions in various shapes and often also have holes for the dowels that originally attached them to an uncarved cover slab, which kept the molten metal (probably lead) that formed these objects from spilling over. While many early moulds have no provenance, one was recently excavated in the courtyard of a large house at Titris Höyük (cat. no. 163b) in the Tigris area of eastern Anatolia.[1] Others are believed to come from western Anatolia (see cat. no. 164). Four stone moulds have been discovered in Mesopotamia, three in the Ishtar temple at Ashur. Another was one of the numerous antiquities sent back to England by Hormuzd Rassam from his excavations at Sippar (cat. no. 163c).[2] Despite the wide geographic distribution of the moulds, they are quite uniform in their range of imagery. While some of the negative forms look exclusively Anatolian, others resemble artifacts from both Syria and Mesopotamia. Jeanny Vorys Canby's explanation for this mixture of types is that itinerant smiths who made and sold trinkets must have been responding to local preferences.[3]

The most impressive and commonly represented image in the moulds is that of a nude female with prominent, high breasts, a concentric circle to indicate the navel, and a large, patterned pubic triangle. She has long hair and horizontal neck rings and may wear bracelets and a girdle. Her forearms are pulled in toward the belly, and the thighs curve inward, with knees and calves held together. Lead figures made from such moulds have been found at Troy and Tell Brak (see cat. no. 163a).[4] These figurines are considered to be inexpensive votives, imitating larger images of a nude divinity, such as a statuette in silver and gold said to come from Hasanoğlan in central Anatolia (fig. 75).

The form for a bull-shaped pendant in the Sippar mould resembles copper-alloy figures found at Alaca Höyük and Horoztepe in central Anatolia (see cat. no. 188), but another pendant form—a stylized rendering of the joined foreparts of addorsed bulls—seems more at home in eastern Syria and Mesopotamia. There are lapis lazuli versions of this type from Tell Brak (see cat. no. 158b) and the Royal Cemetery at Ur. Gold amulets or pendants depicting addorsed and merged bulls, lions, and caprids have an even wider distribution, in Mesopotamia, eastern Syria (cat. no. 158a), the Gulf (cat. no. 210b), and the east Aegean.[5]

Nonfigural pendants exist in the shape of Anatolian ewers (cat. no. 187) and roundels with radiating designs, probably in imitation of fine gold and silver jewelry of the kind found at Ur, Tell Brak, and Mari (see cat. no. 86).[6] The circular and square stamp-seal forms with hatched and angle-filled cross motifs, seen here in the moulds from Sippar (cat. no. 163c) and Titriş Höyük (cat. no. 163b), must have been used to create Anatolian stamp seals in copper alloy or their imitations in lead.[7]

JA

1. Matney, Algaze, and Pittman 1997, pp. 64, 68–69.
2. Andrae 1922, p. 84: 122, 125, pl. 29, pl. 55:a, b; Walker and Collon 1980, p. 104:74. For an example from Tell Brak in eastern Syria, see Bonatz, Kühne, and Mahmoud 1998, p. 74, no. 68.
3. Canby 1965, pp. 52ff.
4. Emre 1971.
5. Woolley 1934, pl. 142:U.10943, U.11232, U.17776; see also During Caspers 1996, pp. 50–51, pl. 3, in which the possibility of Central Asian influence on this type is raised. For the east Aegean, see Mendone 1997, p. 122.
6. Woolley 1934, pl. 138:U.11806; Bonatz, Kühne, and Mahmoud 1998, p. 69, no. 2.
7. Evans (1895, p. 132, fig. 137) reported a (modern or ancient) lead fragment with two angle-filled cross designs, one inscribed in a circle, the other in a square, said to come from near Heraklion, Crete. The fragment came to light with an Anatolian-style lead figurine in the form of a nude female. While the "seal" designs closely resemble those on a mould now in the Musée du Louvre, Paris (cat. no. 164), the figurine appears somewhat different.

164

Mould for jewelry, seals, and amulets

Serpentine
H. 9.1 cm (3⅝ in.); W. 11.6 cm (4⅝ in.); D. 2.1 cm (¹³⁄₁₆ in.)
Anatolia, possibly Akhisar-Thyatira region
Early Bronze Age, late 3rd millennium B.C.
Musée du Louvre, Département des Antiquités Orientales, Paris AO 26063

This plaque has nine different engraved motifs and is one of two valves of a mould used in the manufacture of jewels and amulets (see cat. nos. 163a, b, c). A second, smooth valve, which attached to the plaque by small pegs that fit into its two holes, completed the mould. Molten metal could then be poured into it, filling the nine different engraved motifs. Moulds of this type, as well as the lead amulets they produced (see cat. no. 163a),[1] have been discovered at many sites in Anatolia, northern Syria, and Mesopotamia.[2]

The maximum possible number of objects was assembled within this plaque's small surface area. At the top a square and circle decorated with geometric lines constitute the faces of two seals. Below them are three pendants: the largest, at right, depicts a crudely stylized lion; another, on the left is composed of a hatched

rectangle surmounted by two vertical bars, each terminating in a cluster of four small rods. The latter is an extremely stylized version of the amulets in the shape of two-headed bulls that were well known in the Sumerian world. The circular pendant beneath it, composed of six rods radiating from a small central lump, is also derived from Mesopotamian prototypes in precious metal, as evidenced in the tombs of the Royal Cemetery at Ur.

In the lower part of the mould two female figurines are shown full-face. The one on the left is nude except for several necklace strands and has only three fingers on each of her hands, which are joined at the waist. Her pubic region is represented by a triangle filled with a stipple motif, her navel by a dotted circle. Her hairstyle consists of a series of globules on top of the head with two long twisted plaits falling onto her shoulders. The second figure, which has the same silhouette as the first, is dressed in a short tunic. Both figures have large round heads with enormous eyes and are similar to a lead figurine discovered in Troy.[3] These similarities allow us to posit a date close to the end of the third millennium B.C. for this type of mould.[4]

The inexpensive production of amulets evidenced by this example shows that purely Mesopotamian motifs had penetrated even the popular culture of Anatolia. This mould also provides further proof of the ties that existed between the two regions at the time. The amulets depicted here, interpreted in the local style, had no doubt lost their profound significance, but they nevertheless retained a prophylactic value and coexisted with the female figurines of the local Anatolian tradition, which also probably played a protective role.

FD

1. Lead has a very low melting point (327.4 degrees Celsius) and is therefore easy to work with.
2. See Canby 1965, pp. 42–61; and Emre 1971.
3. See figurine of a nude female in lead, Troy II (Canby 1965, pl. 10c; Emre 1971, pl. 1.1). It is also similar to a figurine acquired by The Metropolitan Museum of Art (Rogers Fund 1966, 66.12).
4. Canby 1965, p. 49, n. 66.

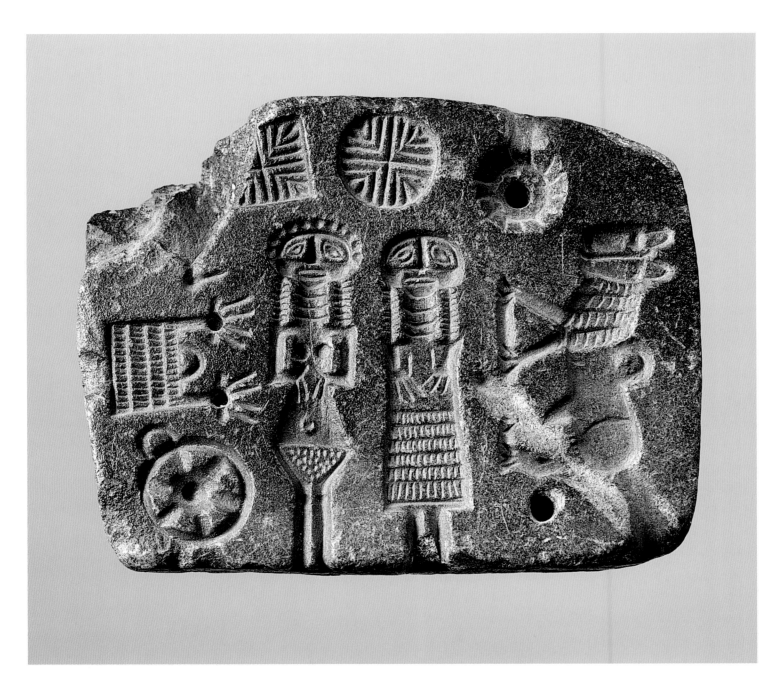

The Early Bronze Age Jewelry Hoard from Kolonna, Aigina

In the summer of 2000, in the course of excavations conducted by the University of Salzburg at Kolonna, on the Greek island of Aigina, a small jewelry hoard was brought to light. The find presents new evidence that the island, in the Saronic Gulf across from Piraeus, was an important place during the third millennium B.C. The hoard was found buried under the floor in a house of Early Bronze Age III (Early Helladic III). It consisted of trinkets made of precious materials—among them gold, silver, carnelian, rock crystal, and dentalium shell—stored in a small, nestlike bundle. The principal items are long bent pins with rolled-head ends, bangles, and disk pendants decorated with dots in repoussé. In the center of the bundle was an assortment of beads that had been threaded on a thin silver wire to make a small necklace. These show a remarkable variety of types and materials, especially the gold and silver beads, which are in the shape of disks, rings, and double axes. A number of carnelian beads and a larger quantity of small ring-beads made of dentalium are also part of the necklace.

The hoard is obviously a collection of reused material. The disk- and ring-shaped beads appear to have originally belonged to larger pieces of jewelry. The components of the hoard are older than the time of its deposit; they date to Early Bronze Age II. One striking carnelian bead is ornamented with white concentric circles in an etched technique well known from sites in Mesopotamia and the Indus Valley. The jewelry hoard proves that the island of Aigina should be grouped with other centers in the Aegean area and western Asia that are characterized by an accumulation of wealth, as representatives of what could be called an "Early Gold Age" during the third millennium B.C.[1]

To date, this extraordinary concentration of trinkets made of precious materials is unique in Early Bronze Age Greece. Apart from the well-known hoards from the Near East–Aegean area, including the Troad (see cat. nos. 167–176), only the Thyreatis Hoard in the Antikensammlung, Berlin, which has close typological and chronological affinities to the material from Aigina, exemplifies similar high standards of craftsmanship and the use of elaborate jewelry-working techniques.[2]

The Austrian excavations on Kolonna hill have drawn a picture of an impressive and well-fortified settlement on Aigina during the period of the corridor houses (a phase of Early Helladic II characterized by the appearance of this large building type at several sites, such as Lerna, Aigina, and Thebes). Aigina's fortifications merit comparison with the walls of Troy.[3] The hoard makes clear not only that Aigina played an important role in the Aegean but also that it acted as a gateway to western Asia during the third millennium B.C.

CR

1. Bass 1985.
2. Reinholdt 1993. The hoard is thought to be from Thyreatis, in Kynouria in the Peloponnese.
3. Walter and Felten 1981.

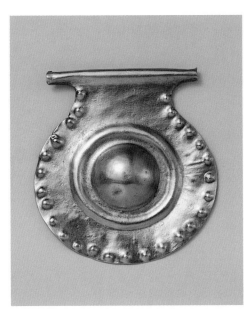

165

Disk pendant with a horizontal string tube

Gold
H. 4.4 cm (1¾ in.); W. 4 cm (1⅝ in.); Thickness
0.3 cm (⅛ in.)
Aegean, Aigina, house, hoard
Early Bronze Age, second half of the 3rd
millennium B.C.
Archaeological Museum of Aigina, Greece MA 6579

This pendant with a central boss, a surrounding ring, and a border of small embossed dots is one of a group of gold and silver disk pendants from the hoard found on the hill of Kolonna at Aigina. A most unusual piece of Early Bronze Age Aegean jewelry, it clearly differs in both technique and decoration from late Neolithic and Chalcolithic disk pendants ("idol pendants") of the Balkan Peninsula and the Aegean region. While the disk's ornamentation displays stylistic affinities with known Anatolian examples of this jewelry type of the Early Bronze Age, the way the suspension device has been formed by turning back the metal and rolling it into a tube has no parallels among disk pendants and pendant rings from the Balkans, the Aegean, or Anatolia. The closed threading channel thus created is set off from the pendant proper by its absence of decoration; the design recalls the visually pleasing pairing of elongated hollow beads with a disk-shaped pendant first encountered in Early Dynastic Mesopotamia. The simple forerunners of this threading technique had already appeared

there during the Late Uruk–Jamdat Nasr period, before the full development of the type attained in Early Dynastic III. Finds from Tell Brak and other sites suggest that the disk-shaped pendant with threading tube was part of the standard repertoire of Mesopotamia's jewelry industry and was exported as far as Anatolia or possibly even the central Aegean.

The ornamentation of the Aigina disk pendant follows a basic decorative pattern found in Early Bronze Age jewelry of the northeast Aegean and northwest Anatolia. Thus the piece is a kind of hybrid, combining a technique typical of Mesopotamian jewelry production with the decorative vocabulary of the northeast Aegean. Surprisingly, however, disk pendants of this type are not represented in the great precious-metal hoards from the Troad and the northeast Aegean. In any event, this disk pendant from the Aigina hoard is one more spectacular representative of the "Early Gold Age" that extended west from Mesopotamia, across Anatolia, and into the central Aegean in the third millennium B.C.   CR

166a, b

Carnelian beads

a. L. 0.6 cm (¼ in.); Diam. 1 cm (⅜ in.); Diam. of
string channel 0.2 cm (1/16 in.)
b. L. 1.4 cm (9/16 in.); Diam. 0.8 cm (5/16 in.); Diam.
of string channel 0.2 cm (1/16 in.)
Aegean, Aigina, house, hoard
Early Bronze Age, second half of the 3rd
millennium B.C.
Archaeological Museum of Aigina, Greece MA 6602,
MA 6603

These two carnelian beads from Aigina clearly demonstrate that the site was the most westerly known settlement on an extensive trade

network linking the Aegean to the Indus Valley and Central Asia. Although carnelian sources were numerous, the most important were in the region of Gujarat and the western Indus Valley. The tradition of decorating beads with an etched technique had originated there, although it appears to have been adopted, often with the use of new designs, in other places (see "Beads of the Indus Valley," by Jonathan Mark Kenoyer, and "Art and Interconnections in the Third Millennium B.C.," by Joan Aruz, in this catalogue). Indeed, the first bead (cat. no. 166a) is decorated with three groups of two concentric circles, a design particularly well known from Kish in Mesopotamia, suggesting that it may have been etched there.[1] Because the string sides of the bead have been recut, which probably removed part of the white pattern, it is possible that the bead was imported from Mesopotamia and adapted for use in local jewelry. The second, undecorated bead (cat. no. 166b) has an oblong barrel shape vaguely reminiscent of Indus long biconical beads (see cat. no. 279). The string channel was drilled from both ends, one of which is broken.

PC

1. Reade 1979, nos. A3, C3.

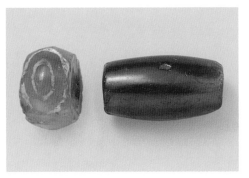

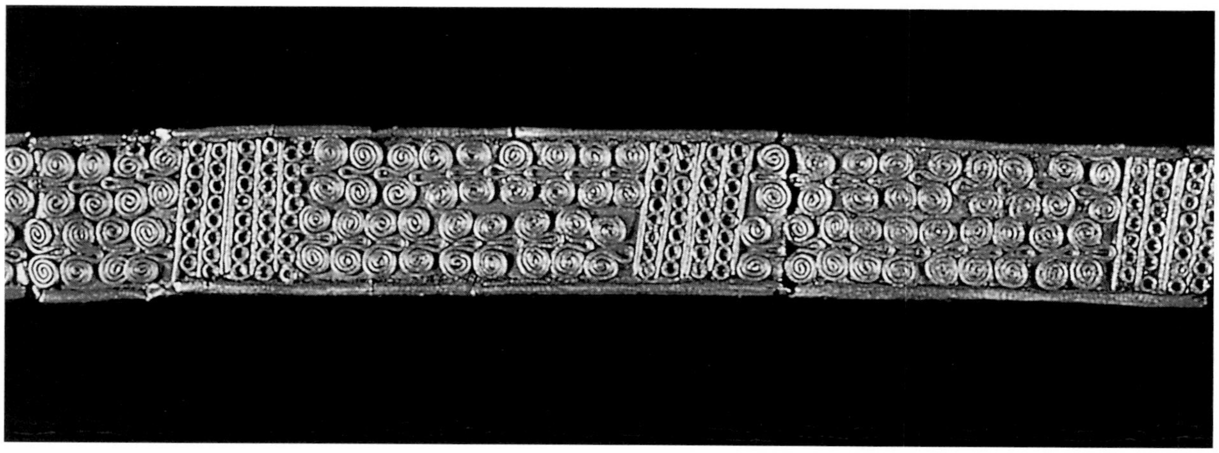

Fig. 76. Gold bracelet with double spirals. Troy, Early Bronze Age, ca. 2500–2300 B.C., Istanbul Archaeological Museum, 645.

Troy

Troy in northwestern Anatolia is one of the most famous sites in the Western world largely through its association with Homer's epic the Iliad. Located in a fertile region, it presumably had easier access to the sea in antiquity, when the shoreline was significantly closer. Two main phases of the site date to the third millennium B.C. Troy I, established about 3000 B.C., includes a fortification wall enclosing freestanding mud-brick houses on stone foundations as well as two examples of a megaron: a long, rectangular building with a vestibule and main hall. Troy II follows with no cultural break. It had greatly expanded fortifications, and the town as a whole must have covered an area of some two hectares. Two impressive gateways, one of them approached by a magnificent stone-paved ramp, gave access to the settlement. By far the most impressive feature of Troy II is a series of five parallel monumental megara set within a separate enclosure in the citadel, a fortified acropolis within the town itself.

The prosperity of Troy II is confirmed by the discovery of impressive hoards of jewelry, tools, and vessels made of gold, silver, and copper alloy (see fig. 76). When Heinrich Schliemann excavated the site, he mistakenly assumed from this wealth that he had discovered the city sacked by the Greeks in the Iliad. The treasures were recovered from different parts of the citadel; the most famous—Treasure A, or "Priam's Treasure"—was discovered below one of the main gateways. The hoards evidence an extensive trade network between Troy and other sites in Anatolia, the Cyclades, and the Greek mainland. The jewelry is comparable to finds from Mochlos on Crete, Poliochni on Limnos, and Alaca Höyük and Eskiyapar in central Anatolia. During the Troy II phase, pottery production had been revolutionized by the introduction of the fast potter's wheel, which led to the creation of new shapes, such as face pots and the legendary, widely distributed depas amphikypellon (two-handled cup). Troy II ended with a massive conflagration about 2300 B.C. and was followed by Troy III, a more impoverished phase of the site's history, with the remains of fortification walls and houses grouped together in blocks but very few freestanding structures or metal finds. Troy III was destroyed about 2100 B.C. for reasons that remain unclear. The new fortified city of Troy IV covered an area of 17,000 square meters. It was designed with a different orientation from that of its predecessor, Troy III, with new forms of residential blocks fronting the streets. Troy IV was destroyed at the end of the third millennium B.C.

ED

Strings of beads

Gold
Diam. of beads: 0.42–0.67 cm (³⁄₁₆–¹⁄₄ in.)
Anatolia, Troy, Level IIg, room 253
Early Bronze Age, ca. 2500–2300 B.C.
Istanbul Archaeological Museum 5554

The extraordinarily rich collection of jewelry recovered by Heinrich Schliemann from Treasure A at Troy included an estimated 8,700 gold-alloy beads. Additional beads, including those in this necklace, were discovered during the Blegen excavations of the 1930s, which clarified the stratigraphy of the site.[1] Among Troy bead types, the flat bead with tubular midrib—the only type in this necklace—is of particular interest in terms of cultural interconnections. Similar beads in both gold and silver alloys have been found in graves at Ur dated to the Early Dynastic through Ur III periods,[2] as well as in the Indus Valley to the east (see cat. no. 280) and on the island of Aigina to the west (see "Art and Interconnections in the Third Millennium B.C.," by Joan Aruz, in this catalogue).

It appears that these beads were formed of two disks, each hammered over a wire running through the center, aligned, and beaten or soldered together leaving a central tube for stringing.[3] It is interesting that a steatite mould found in Early Dynastic levels at Mari included a form for casting this type of bead.[4]

J-FL

1. Blegen et al. 1950–58, vol. 1, p. 367.
2. Maxwell-Hyslop 1971, p. 10.
3. This method of manufacture was also proposed for the Ur beads by Maxwell-Hyslop (ibid., p. 10). The beads of catalogue number 167 do not appear to have been metallurgically examined.
4. Parrot 1967, p. 198, figs. 245, 246. For the importance of portable stone moulds in the widespread transmission of jewelry designs, see Canby 1965.

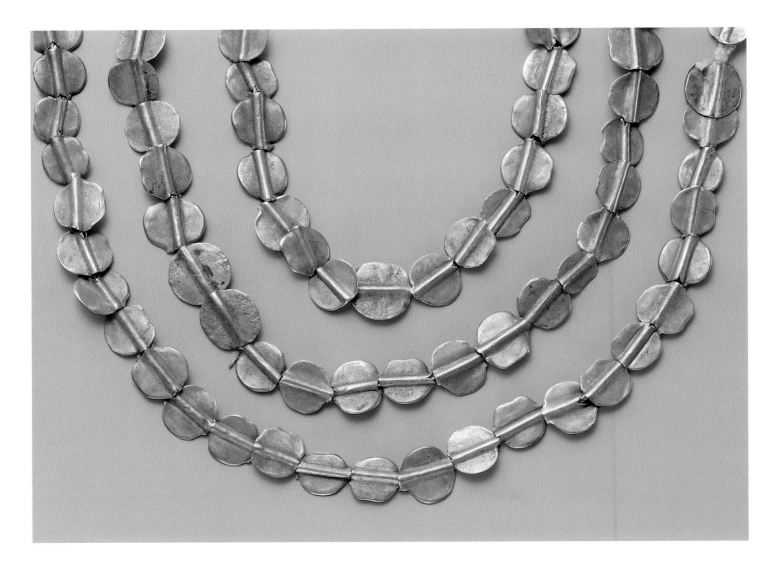

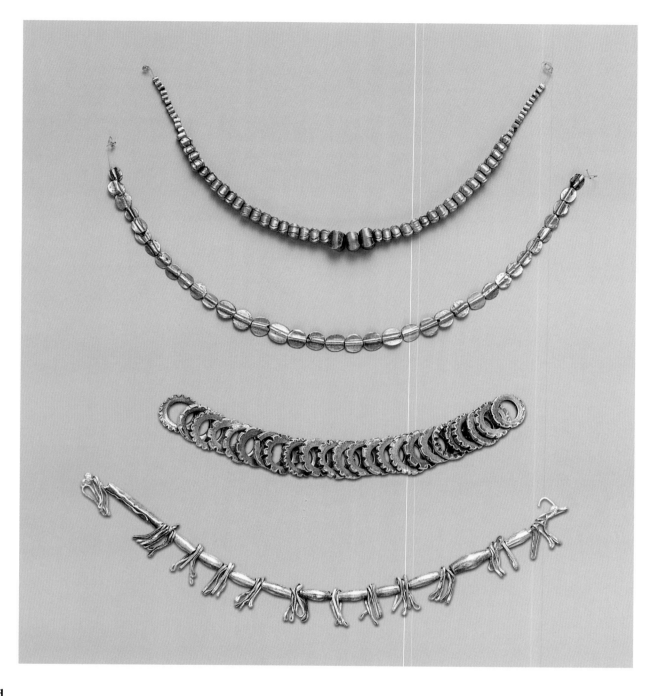

168a–d

Strings of beads

Gold
Anatolia, Troy, Level IIg (?)
Early Bronze Age, ca. 2500–2300 B.C.
National Archaeological Museum, Athens 4331

These necklaces consist of beads of various shapes and sizes: discoid, with a transverse tubular perforation; rectangular, with convex sides and a double vertical incision at the edges (the three central beads and the twenty-three tiny ones have no incisions); serrated wheel; and tubular and flattened loop-shaped, made of fine wire that is rectangular in section.[1]

Similarly shaped beads were found in the great and small treasures of Troy IIg. The arrangements of the beads in these necklaces have been made according to the shapes of the individual beads, since there is no record of the original appearance of the necklaces. Beads of the same or similar shape are also known from Poliochni, as well as from Karataş, in Lycia.[2]

ET

1. Information in this entry is based on Schliemann 1885, p. 579, nos. 776, 778, 785, 788, p. 627, no. 960; Demakopoulou 1990, p. 152, no. 8; Tolstikov and Treister 1996, p. 80, nos. 78–80, p. 108, no. 120.
2. Bernabò-Brea 1976, pl. 252, nos. 14, 21, 247c, 248c, d, e; Mellink 1969, p. 323, pl. 74, fig. 15.

169a, b

Pins

Gold
Anatolia
Early Bronze Age, ca. 2500–2300 B.C.

a. Pin with a spiral-decorated rectangular head and vessels
L. 7.7 cm (3 in.)
University of Pennsylvania Museum of Archaeology
and Anthropology, Philadelphia   UM 66-66-1

b. Pin with four spirals
L. 6.6 cm (2⅝ in.)
Troy, Level IIg
Istanbul Archaeological Museum   685 M

The head of the pin in the University of Pennsylvania Museum of Archaeology and Anthropology (cat. no. 169a) features a rectangular gold-alloy[1] plate decorated with four vertical rows of S-shaped spirals separated by vertical bands. The flattened end of the pin is wrapped around the center of this plate from front to back. Rectangular wire crosspieces terminating in upturned spirals frame the top and bottom of the pinhead. The vertical bands, including the flattened section of the pin in the center as well as the two lower crosspiece sections, are decorated with crisscrossed incisions. Affixed to the top of the upper crosspiece are six miniature biconical jugs with long necks and flat rims that have suffered deformation and losses.[2] Although the origin of this pin is not known, it is typologically related to a pin found at Poliochni and is very similar to one found in Treasure O at Troy.[3] The ornamental use of miniature jugs may also reflect an influence from the Cyclades and mainland Greece.[4]

The pin from Troy (cat. no. 169b) represents the most elaborate example of a related type, which features what appears to be a similarly shaped pot framed by upturned spirals. Its head is decorated with two sets of double spirals separated by a metal sphere with a horizontal seam that represents the body of the pot. The neck of the vessel is indicated by coiled wire, the rim by a flat disk affixed to the end of the shaft.[5]

Although the joins on these pins have not been fully investigated, it is clear that soldering of some form was used. It is thought that joining techniques such as soldering and welding were developed in Mesopotamia in the middle of the third millennium B.C. before spreading west.[6] This work required a careful application of heat, particularly when several elements were to be joined to the same object.

J–FL

1. The color of this pin suggests the presence of silver, but its composition has not been analyzed. During his excavations at Troy, Heinrich Schliemann found lumps and bars of gold alloys that presumably represent the metal used to make the jewelry found at the site. Analysis of one of these bars conducted at that time indicated a composition of 65.10 percent gold and 33.42 percent silver, with minor amounts of lead, copper, and iron. See Schliemann 1881, p. 496. The question whether or not this alloy, known as electrum, was naturally or artificially produced cannot be answered conclusively at this time.
2. For further description, see Bass 1966, p. 29, and Bass 1970, p. 335. It should be noted that this pin was purchased and lacks a known archaeological history.
3. For a description of the pin from Troy and a bibliography of comparative material, see Tolstikov and Treister 1996, pp. 182–83. Also see Maxwell-Hyslop 1971, pp. 55–56.
4. Bass 1966, p. 29.
5. As this pin could not be examined, the description of its construction is taken from Schliemann 1881, pp. 488–89, no. 849.
6. See Tolstikov and Treister 1996, p. 232, and Moorey 1994, pp. 229–31.

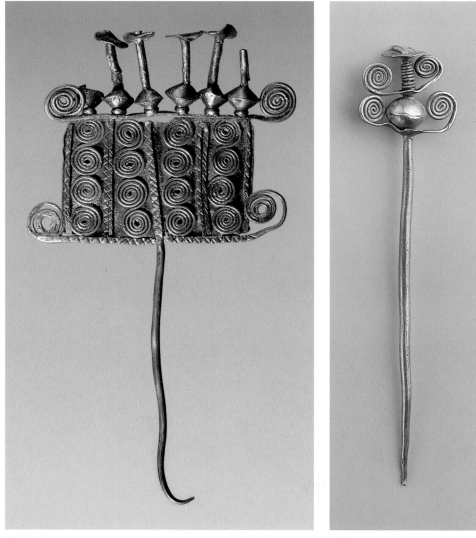

169a

169b

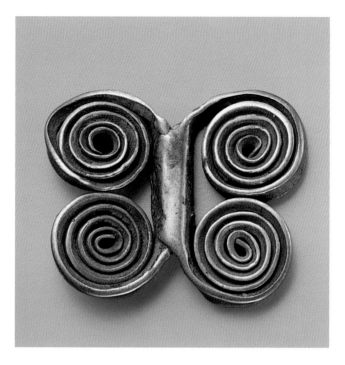

170a

Quadruple-spiral beads

Gold
1. L. 1.8 cm (¾ in.); W. 1.9 cm (¾ in.)
2. L. 1.7 cm (¹¹⁄₁₆ in.); W. 2 cm (¹³⁄₁₆ in.)
Anatolia, Troy, Level II, Treasure D
Early Bronze Age, ca. 2500–2300 B.C.
Istanbul Archaeological Museum 689a, b

170b

Quadruple-spiral plaques

Copper alloy
1. H. 11.4 cm (4 ½ in.); W. 9.3 cm (3 ⅝ in.)
2. H. 9.5 cm (3 ¾ in.); W. 8.8 cm (3 ½ in.)
Anatolia, Ikiztepe, Mound 1, Trench D: destroyed
burial, Grave 106
Early Bronze Age, late 3rd millennium B.C.
Samsun Museum, Turkey 18-2-1978 (I/75-9),
7-39-1985 (I/80-496)

Quadruple spirals—consisting of four spiral coils emerging from a central stem—were usually beads and pendants fashioned of gold and silver, probably intended to be strung or suspended from necklaces with additional beads in other materials and shapes. Ornaments of spiral form first appear in the mid-third millennium B.C. in the Royal Cemetery at Ur as encircled, closely coiled gold wires creating three-dimensional spirals; the spirals were attached to a flat gold suspension loop (see cat. no. 78). These southern Mesopotamian

jewelry elements, however, appear to be unique. They seem quite apart from the phenomenon of a widespread distribution of another very distinctive form of quadruple-spiral bead found in late-third-millennium contexts farther north and west. Occurrences of the latter bead type at sites such as

Poliochni, Troy, Eskiyapar, Alaca Höyük, and Tell Brak (cat. no. 159), and in a mixed third-to early-second-millennium context at Ashur—thought to be the grave of an Old Assyrian merchant—outline a trade route extending from the Aegean to Mesopotamia.[1] These gold and silver beads are composed of either a

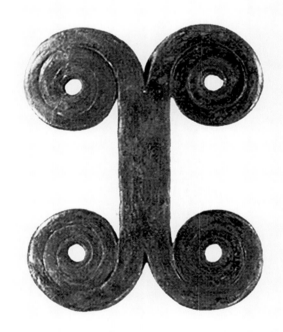 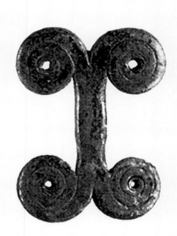

single flattened tube pulled out at its four ends into coiling wires or two double spirals folded around each other, such as catalogue number 170a, found in Treasure D at Troy.[2]

A symbolic significance for the quadruple spiral is suggested by its presence and prominent size on seals and sealings; in one case a quadruple spiral is placed before a seated figure, possibly a divinity.[3] The discovery of a number of arsenical copper quadruple-spiral plaques at two sites in Anatolia (see cat. no. 170b) may also point to some ritual connotation for this pattern. The plaques are flat and consist of coils emerging from a long central stem, the only visible means of attachment being the holes in the spiral coils. A large number of these plaques, measuring from about six to twelve centimeters in height, were discovered in the EB III cemetery at Ikiztepe in north central Anatolia, close to the Black Sea coast. The Ikiztepe graves were rich in metal-work, including jewelry, weapons, and tools. Each plaque apparently comes from a separate grave; they were positioned close to or on the skeleton near the ears, arms, or chest—perhaps the reason some have suggested they were belt buckles.[4] Although most are plain, one spiral bears the impression of a textile in which it was originally wrapped; another is distinguished by chevron incisions on the central stem; and a third has a thicker stem with rayed concentric circles in the coils.[5]

It is quite extraordinary and difficult to explain that a very similar plaque was discovered in a context at the eastern Anatolian site of Arslantepe that dates much earlier than the Ikiztepe finds. This quadruple spiral, which measures 11 to 11.5 centimeters in height, was found along with bundles of arsenical copper swords and spearheads of northern Caucasian affinity.[6] It comes from a building rather than a burial. The structure can be dated to Arslantepe Level VIA, contemporary with the Late Uruk–Jamdat Nasr period in southern Mesopotamia (ca. 3000 B.C.), when the first images of quadruple spirals appear on Near Eastern seals and sealings, including examples at Arslantepe, the Amuq, Tell Brak, and Susa.

JA

1. A single gold example in one piece was found in one of the impressive mounds at A'li on Bahrain. In western Central Asia a lapis lazuli bead of a quadruple-spiral form was discovered at the site of Gonur-depe; see Rossi-Osmida 2002, p. 118, no. 14.
2. For methods of manufacture, see Maxwell-Hyslop 1989, p. 218; Oates, Oates, and McDonald 2001, p. 245; Aruz 1995a, p. 50, fig. 14; and Wartke 1995, p. 52, no. 27.
3. Mallowan 1947, p. 15, pl. 19; see also Maxwell-Hyslop 1989, pp. 215ff.
4. Alkim 1983, p. 35.
5. Bilgi 1990, pp. 163ff., 218, fig. 19:440, 445; Bilgi 1985, pp. 34, 72ff., 95, fig. 18:277.
6. Maxwell-Hyslop 1989, p. 216; Palmieri 1981, pp. 107 fig. 3:5, 110.

171

Pair of lobed crescent earrings

Gold
Each earring: H. 2.1 cm (¹³⁄₁₆ in.); max. W. 1.1 cm (⁷⁄₁₆ in.); Weight 4.5 g
Anatolia, Troy, Level IIg, Treasure A, "Treasure of Priam"
Early Bronze Age, ca. 2500–2300 B.C.
National Archaeological Museum, Athens 4333

Each earring consists of a semicircular body that widens at the center, formed of six cylindrical wires soldered together, terminating at the top in a hook. Two transverse rows of tiny gold cones decorate each surface at midpoint. There are three cones below each hook, and additional cones form a triangle at the bottom as well.

The earrings, which have also been identified as hair rings, are among the items in Treasure A, which Heinrich Schliemann called the Treasure of Priam, found in the "burnt layer" of Troy IIg.[1] They are exquisite examples of the art and technique of jewelry making developed at Troy. Similar items, displaying the same fine technique and also decorated with rows of granulation or with appliquéd bosses, are found in the treasure from Poliochni on Limnos and the Eskiyapar Treasure from central Anatolia.[2]

ET

1. Schliemann 1874, pl. 196, nos. 3558, 3568, and pl. 208; H. Schmidt 1902, p. 235, nos. 5913–28.
2. Özgüç and Temizer 1993, p. 615, pl. 107.

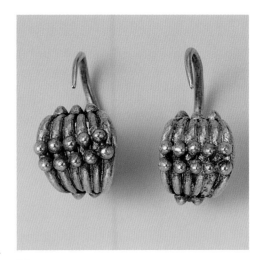

171

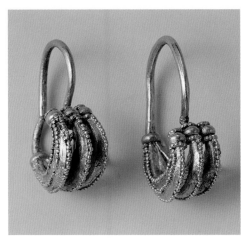

172

172

Pair of lobed crescent earrings

Gold
Each earring: H. 2.9 cm (1⅛ in.); W. 1.6 cm (⅝ in.); Weight 10.5 g
Anatolia, Troy, Level IIg (?)
Early Bronze Age, ca. 2500–2300 B.C.
National Archaeological Museum, Athens 4332

Each earring has a crescent-shaped body and a hook formed at one end of a cylindrical wire (one of the hooks has been repaired). The bodies consist of three lobes soldered together: the curved, external surface of each lobe is decorated with vertical rows of granulation and terminates in a spherical bead outlined above and below with granulated or serrated discoid beads.

The earrings, which are excellent examples of the goldsmiths' work of the period, probably belong to one of the smaller treasures of

Troy IIg. Particularly noteworthy is the extremely fine granulation, which indicates the degree of perfection achieved in this technique at an early date in the region. This type of fine granulation was not known in the Early Dynastic period in Mesopotamia.[1]   ET

1. For further reference, see Dörpfeld 1902, p. 334; Demakopoulou 1990, p. 150, no. 6; and Maxwell-Hyslop 1971, p. 49, fig. 33.

173a–c

Pairs of basket earrings

Gold or electrum
Anatolia

a. 1. H. 2 cm (¾ in.); W. 1.7 cm (¹¹/₁₆ in.)
   2. H. 2.4 cm (1 in.); W. 1.8 cm (¹¹/₁₆ in.)
Early Bronze Age, ca. 2500–2300 B.C.
Troy, Level II, Treasure F
Istanbul Archaeological Museum 679 A/M, 679 B/M

b. 1. L. 12.7 cm (5 in.)
   2. L. 12 cm (4¾ in.)
Early Bronze Age, ca. 2500–2300 B.C.
University of Pennsylvania Museum of Archaeology and Anthropology, Philadelphia UM 66-6-11a, b

c. Each earring: H. 2.8 cm (1⅛ in.); W. 2.7 cm (1⅛ in.)
Eskiyapar, found in Pit 2 below Level II
Early Bronze Age, second half of the 3rd millennium B.C.
Ankara Museum of Anatolian Civilizations, Turkey 109-484-68, 109-485-68

This group of basket earrings attests to the widespread expertise in gold-working techniques, including granulation, that appears in the latter half of the third millennium B.C.[1] The first pair (cat. no. 173a) is among the small group of jewelry excavated at Troy that has remained in Turkey. Heinrich Schliemann discovered these earrings in a clay goblet that also contained an additional pair of earrings and sixteen gold-alloy bars.[2] According to his description, the baskets of these earrings are formed out of a total of forty wires soldered together on either side of a vertically incised plate that tapers to form the earring proper. The exterior sides are decorated with four rows of rosettes. The outer of the two parallel plates soldered along the bottom of both baskets is decorated with a row of eighteen beads soldered into a groove between two strips. Affixed to each of these plates are eight jump rings made of double wire. These jump rings would have held elaborate pendants, now lost.

The original appearance of these earrings can be reconstructed by examining complete examples from Troy Level IIg now in the Pushkin State Museum of Fine Arts, Moscow,[3] and a similar pair, excavated at Poliochni (cat. no. 174). Perhaps the most elaborate example of this type is the pair now in Philadelphia (cat. no. 173b).[4] The baskets of these earrings consist of looped wires soldered together on either side of a flattened section of the hook, which is decorated with cross-hatching. Along the top outer edge of the baskets, one earring (1) has a double row of granulation; the other (2) features two rows of five disks, with one grain affixed to each disk. Two parallel suspension plates are attached along the bottom of each basket. Short loop-in-loop chains terminating with a single leaf are suspended from the five rings attached to the frontal plates. Five longer chains hang from perforations in the rear suspension plates. These chains carry several leaves along their lengths and terminate in idol-shaped pendants. In order to keep the longer chains aligned correctly, two horizontal metal strips were attached across the chains in both earrings. In general these earrings are in excellent condition, although one (2) has lost three of its "idol" pendants.[5]

Catalogue number 173c comes from a hoard of jewelry excavated at the site of an Early Bronze Age urban center at Eskiyapar in central Anatolia.[6] The baskets of these earrings or hair ornaments comprise two pairs of looped and soldered wire separated by two flat, incised bands. The exterior sides are decorated with two horizontal rows of rosettes consisting of conical spheres set onto flat disks.[7] These objects do not have a central hook; instead, holes were made at the ends of the hoops for some form of attachment.

Compared with other jewelry in this group, the workmanship of the Eskiyapar earrings is less accomplished and may represent provincial manufacture. Regardless of where they were produced, these items—along with other pieces from Eskiyapar—bear witness to the existence of overland trade routes linking central Anatolia with the western coast and the Aegean. The flow of both goods and expertise along these routes played an important role in the cultural development of Anatolia in succeeding centuries.

J–FL

1. Although it is generally thought, based on examples found at the Royal Cemetery at Ur, that the technique of granulation first appeared in Sumer, its exact origin remains unknown. Innovative techniques were possibly first developed at centers closer to the sources of gold than Mesopotamia, which had to import precious metals. See Lilyquist 1993, p. 33.
2. For the composition of these bars, which may be representative of the metal used to make the earrings, see entry for cat. no. 169, note 1. For a description of the discovery and construction of these earrings, see Schliemann 1881, pp. 495–96.
3. Especially those examples from Treasure A; see Tolstikov and Treister 1996, pp. 48–53.
4. These earrings were purchased and lack a known archaeological history. They warrant a full metallographic examination to further confirm their authenticity. Although it has been assumed that the earrings were made of electrum, an alloy of gold and silver, they have not been analyzed. See Bass 1970, p. 335.
5. For a full description, see Bass 1966, pp. 32–33; see also Bass 1970, p. 335.
6. Özgüç and Temizer 1993, p. 615.
7. According to a description by Bingöl (1999, p. 86), the spheres are soldered onto "fine disks that were held together with fine gold wire."

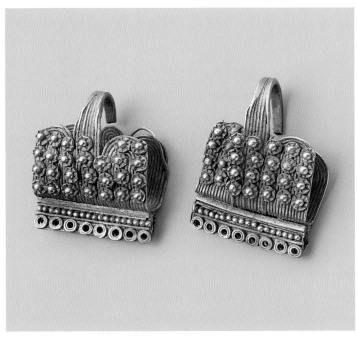

173a, front

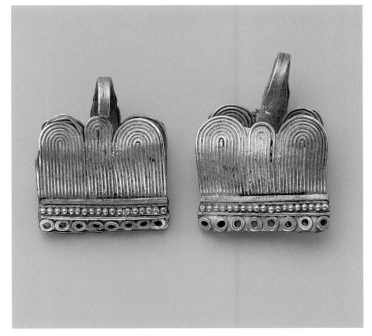

173a, back

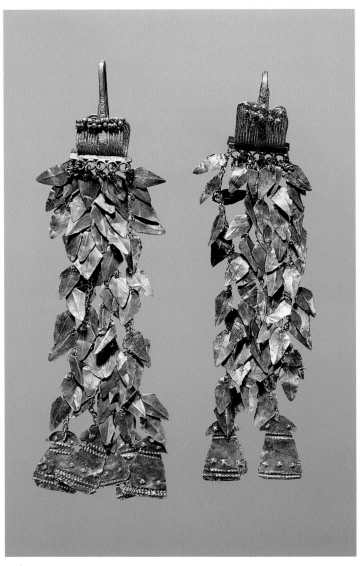

173b

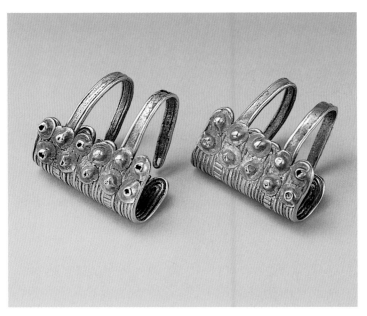

173c

Poliochni and the Civilization of the Northeastern Aegean

The founding of Poliochni, on the east coast of the island of Limnos, took place about 3500 B.C., at the end of the Neolithic period. The location of the settlement close to the Dardanelles, the strait that connects the Aegean to the metal-rich regions bordering the Black Sea, was crucial to the rise of Poliochni as a leading metalworking center about the middle of the third millennium B.C.[1] The impact of the new technology on the way of life in the region gave birth to the Greek legend that the workshop of Hephaistos, the god of fire and the divine smith of the Olympian gods, was situated on Limnos.

The general layout of the successive settlements at Poliochni reveals a high level of spatial organization, with a network of cobbled streets and paved squares, public wells, and a drainage system. The construction of large public buildings and the use of seals provide additional evidence of a central administration and a controlled economy. A hoard of gold and silver jewelry (the so-called Poliochni Treasure), weighing 425 grams, was found in a small jug hidden in a pithos in a building dating to the Yellow Period (ca. 2450–2200 B.C.). The hoard bears witness to the accumulation of wealth and the existence of social stratification at the site. At the same time agriculture and animal husbandry remained the basis of the economy, and the weaving industry flourished. Considerable specialization of labor was another characteristic of the era, and it led to greater technical accomplishments and to mass production.

Poliochni, on Limnos, and Troy, in western Anatolia (Asia Minor), were the foremost proto-urban settlements in the area during the Yellow Period and Troy IIg. Their cultural ties were forged by their geographic proximity. The gold jewelry and other metal artifacts known as the Trojan Treasures date from this time and attest to the widespread cultural and economic exchanges extending from the cities of Mesopotamia to the settlements of central Anatolia (Alaca Höyük and Eskiyapar) and the Caucasus (Maikop). Pottery and figurines are additional common elements at the sites of Troy and Poliochni.

The islands of the northeastern Aegean—such as densely populated Limnos (Poliochni, Myrina, Koukonisi), Lesbos (Thermi), Samos (Heraion), and Chios (Emporio)—and the Troad in northwestern Asia Minor formed an Early Bronze Age cultural group (see fig. 70a). The newly excavated site at Palamari on Skyros was situated on the sea route to the Cyclades, the cradle of an indigenous culture that maintained ties with such sites in western Anatolia as Iasos. The final stages of the Early Bronze Age in the Cyclades (for example, at Kastri on Syros) witnessed the importation of artifacts from the northeastern Aegean as well as the further spread of metallurgy. At the same time, elements of the northeastern Aegean culture have been found on the Greek mainland, notably, the gold and silver jewelry from the Peloponnese (the Thyreatis Hoard) and on the islands of Aigina and Leukas, and the pottery from Thebes and Orchomenos in Boiotia.

LP-M

1. For more information on Poliochni during the Early Bronze Age, see Bernabò-Brea 1964; Bernabò-Brea 1976; Doumas and La Rosa 1997; and La Rosa 1997.

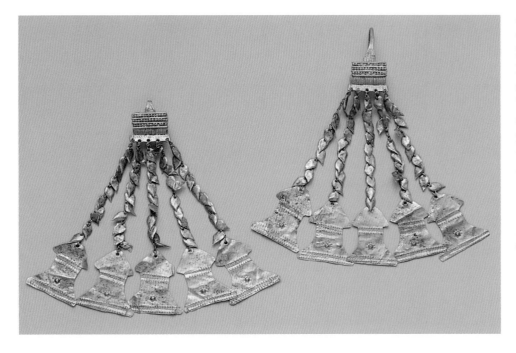

circular in section, soldered together and bent to form a hoop, and terminating in a simple hook for fastening to the ear. This particular kind of ornament, also referred to as a hair ring, is very common among the treasures from the "burnt layer" of Troy IIg—in the same simple form or decorated with rows of studs. Some parallels are to be found as well in treasures unearthed at Eskiyapar, near Alaca Höyük, in central Anatolia.[2]   LP-M

1. Bernabò-Brea 1976, pp. 287–88, pl. 246; Cultraro 1999, pp. 41–52.
2. Özgüç and Temizer 1993, p. 614, figs. 5, 6, pl. 107; see also Tolstikov and Treister 1996, nos. 17–45, 104–13, and Cultraro 1999, pp. 41–52.

174

Pair of basket earrings with dangling pendants

Gold
L. 6.7–7.8 cm (2⅝–3⅛ in.); W. 1.1 cm (⁷⁄₁₆ in.)
Aegean, Limnos, Poliochni, room 643, "Poliochni Treasure"
Early Bronze Age, Yellow Period, ca. 2450–2200 B.C.
National Archaeological Museum, Athens 7159

These earrings are examples of the basket-shaped type.[1] The body of each earring is richly decorated with three rows of granules on the front and arched wires on the back. Five chains covered with leaf-shaped ornaments of sheet metal and terminating in cut-out pendants in the form of stylized figures decorated with rows of dots in the repoussé technique are suspended from the body of each of the earrings. They are fastened to the ears by means of plain gold-wire hooks.

This is the best preserved of the two pairs of similar earrings dating from the Yellow Period at Poliochni. Outstanding pieces of jewelry, they attest to the use of advanced metalworking techniques, such as granulation and filigree, during the Early Bronze Age and find exact parallels in the earrings from the treasures of Troy IIg, testifying to the interconnections between the two settlements. It is interesting that the treasures from Eskiyapar, in central Anatolia, have yielded two pairs of basket-shaped earrings (see cat. no. 173c); however, they lack the pendants characteristic of those from Troy and Poliochni.   LP-M

1. Maxwell-Hyslop 1971, p. 60, pl. 41; Bernabò-Brea 1976, p. 286, pls. 241, 242; and Demakopoulou 1998, no 8. See also Özgüç and Temizer 1993, p. 614, figs. 1–4, pl. 106, and Tolstikov and Treister 1996, nos 14, 15, 155.

175

Pair of crescent earrings

Gold
a. H. 1.6 cm (⅝ in.); W. 1.6 cm (⅝ in.)
b. H. 2 cm (¾ in.); W. 1.6 cm (⅝ in.)
Aegean, Limnos, Poliochni, room 643, "Poliochni Treasure"
Early Bronze Age, Yellow Period, ca. 2450–2200 B.C.
National Archaeological Museum, Athens 7161

These earrings belong to the so-called shell type.[1] Each is made out of six solid-gold wires,

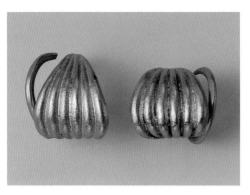

176

Pair of earrings with poppy pendants

Gold
a. H. 3 cm (1⅛ in.); W. 2.1 cm (¹³⁄₁₆ in.)
b. H. 3.1 cm (1¼ in.); W. 2.2 cm (⅞ in.)
Aegean, Limnos, Poliochni, room 643, "Poliochni Treasure"
Early Bronze Age, Yellow Period, ca. 2450–2200 B.C.
National Archaeological Museum, Athens 7186

These earrings consist of two distinct parts, a circular ring of solid-gold wire and the main body in the form of a poppy.[1] The poppy has an oval, hollow capsule, pierced by eight stamens; the tip of each stamen is enhanced by circular wire to represent pollen, while, at the other end of the capsule, the stamens terminate in loosely bent wires. The rings, used for fastening the earrings to the ears, are made of thin wire that is flattened and pierced by the stamens at the point of attachment to the base of each capsule.

This is a unique earring type, paralleled only by the three similar earrings from Poliochni (there are five in all). These are considered the earliest images of the poppy in the Aegean region, where the plant (genus *Papaver*) remains native both to Anatolia and to the islands.

Analogous images of poppies occurred later, in Mycenaean Greece and in Hittite Anatolia, where the use of their seeds as a seasoning and the analgesic properties of the poppy seem to have been known at that time. A gold signet ring from Mycenae (fifteenth

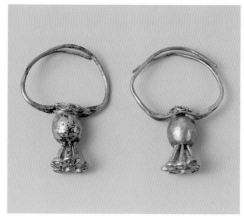

176

century B.C.) with a ritual scene shows, beneath a tree, a seated female deity who receives offerings of poppies and lilies from her female attendants. A large clay figure from Crete of a goddess (twelfth century B.C.) with full-blown poppies on her head also can be mentioned in this context.[2]   LP-M

1. Bernabò-Brea 1976, p. 287, pl. 245c; Branigan 1974, p. 46, Type III, pl. 23.
2. Corpus der minoischen und mykenischen Siegel 1964, no. 17. See also Tzedakis and Martlew 1999, pp. 268–71.

177

Loop-handled stamp cylinder seal with humans and animals

Ivory
H. 4.5 cm (1¾ in.); Diam. 1.7–1.8 cm (¹¹⁄₁₆ in.)
Aegean, Limnos, Poliochni, Megaron 605
Early Bronze Age, Yellow Period, ca. 2450–2200 B.C.
National Archaeological Museum, Athens 7243

Seals are often so distinctive that they can readily be associated with specific cultural areas. The adoption and adaptation of seal forms as well as their designs are often markers of intercultural contacts. Whereas in many areas, such as Mesopotamia, Syria, and Iran, there was a change in seal use from the stamp to the cylinder seal, in other regions, such as the Aegean and Anatolia, the stamp seal remained predominant. It seems significant, therefore, that at the site of Poliochni, in the northeast Aegean, in addition to the expected stamp seals, a cylinder seal, the present example, was found.[1] Made of ivory, with a loop handle (now broken off), and

engraved on the cylinder for rolling and on the base for stamping, it is of a type that had appeared in the Amuq region of Syro-Cilicia and at Byblos on the Levantine coast by the beginning of the third millennium B.C. The form was transmitted both north and west, with isolated examples found at Troy and Alishar Höyük in Anatolia, in the Cyclades, and at Archanes, on Crete.[2] The Poliochni seal, bearing imagery derived from the Near East and executed in a style related both to Levantine and to Anatolian carving, reflects the coming together of the various traditions.

Depicted in a three-register composition is a profusion of figures executed in an abstract, linear manner. The flat background is typically Near Eastern,[3] as are the adaptations of Early Dynastic–period contest scenes, in which heroes and bull-men interact with lions, bulls, and other horned animals in rampant and crossing postures. Yet, though the crossing lions and horned animals on the Poliochni seal evoke Mesopotamian imagery, the theme and arrangement of its figures are quite different. Here, in addition to the pairs of animals attacking one another, we see pairs of humans in violent combat, one often knifing the other from behind. Humans and animals do not appear to interact.

Edith Porada drew attention to the close parallels for this style of rendering animals in the corpus of seal impressions from Hama, in western Syria, where, for example, figures

similar to the two striding lions in the top register of this seal are depicted on an uncluttered field.[4] Other features of the Poliochni seal design appear to be closer to an Anatolian tradition, as we see on examining some seals of the beginning of the second millennium from central Anatolia. The stamp-cylinder seal from Alishar displays figures even further reduced toward linear patterning. Flat, attenuated animals are arrayed in various orientations over the seal field on Anatolian-style glyptic from Kültepe, Level II. They include crouching monkeys like the image on the lower register of the Poliochni piece.[5] This adds further weight to the evidence for connections between the north Aegean island of Limnos and its close neighbors to the east, connections also clearly illustrated by the remarkable gold jewelry from the site (see cat. nos. 174–176).
                                                                                            JA

1. Mendone 1997, pp. 16–17; Bernabò-Brea 1957, pp. 193ff.; Porada 1976, pp. 300ff.
2. Aruz 1999a, pp. 11ff. Sealings at Ur, in southern Mesopotamia, probably also provide evidence for the use of stamp-cylinder seals; see Legrain 1936, p. 8, and number 22 in this catalogue.
3. Contrast an Aegean version from Archanes, illustrated in Aruz 1999a, pl. 3G.
4. Porada 1976, pp. 300ff.; Ingholt 1940, pl. 14. The Hama corpus also provides parallels for an Early Syrian seal, a rare import to Mochlos; see Aruz 1984.
5. N. Özgüç 1965, pl. xx:60.

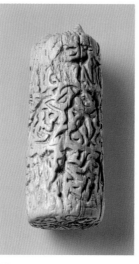

177

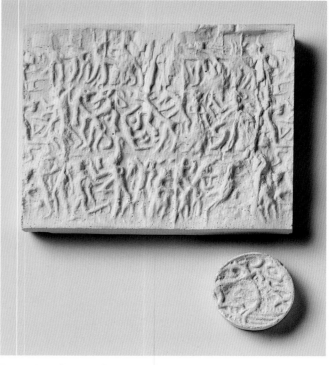

Impressions from catalogue number 177.

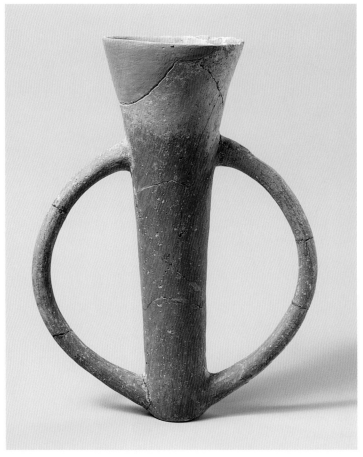

178a

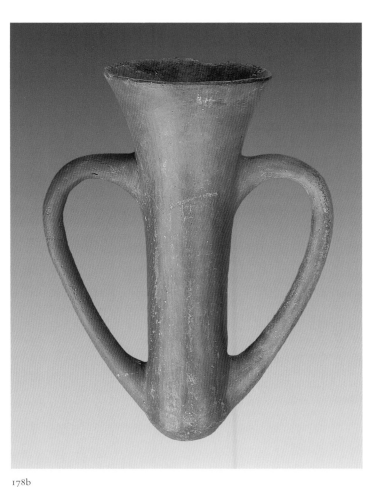

178b

178a–c

Cups with two handles *(depata amphikypella)*

Clay

a. H. 22.5 cm (8⅞ in.); Diam. 8.2 cm (3¼ in.)
Aegean, Limnos, Poliochni, Megaron 317
Early Bronze Age, Yellow Period, ca. 2450–2200 B.C.
National Archaeological Museum, Athens 7127

b. H. 19.5 cm (7⅝ in.); Diam. 8 cm (3⅛ in.)
Anatolia, Troy, Levels II–IV
Early Bronze Age, second half of the 3rd millennium B.C.
Staatliche Museen zu Berlin, Museum für Vor- und Frühgeschichte MVF 2023

c. H. 23.8 cm (9⅜ in.); Diam. 11.5 cm (4½ in.)
Syria, Tell Selenkahiye, SLK 67.1190
Early Bronze Age, late 3rd millennium B.C.
National Museum, Aleppo, Syria 9084

Depas (plural, *depata*) is the ancient Greek term used by archaeologists for a vase with a funnel-shaped body and two vertical, amply curved handles.[1] The type retains the name originally assigned by Heinrich Schliemann, who used a Homeric term from the *Iliad* without chronological or typological relevance. The shape was common in the northeastern Aegean during Early Bronze Age II—mainly found in Poliochni period V (cat. no. 178a) and periods II–V at Troy, where the *depas* form is supposed to have been created (see cat. no. 178b). It has a wide distribution throughout the Aegean world (Cyclades, Skyros, Peukakia, Orchomenos, Lerna, Samos), and Caria and Lycia. The use of vessels of this particular shape remains unknown.

Tall cylindrical cups with two vertical loop-handles (*depata amphikypella*) and often with rounded bases were introduced during the Early Bronze Age and became very popular. They are usually wheel-made, although a few examples were shaped by hand.[2] The cups vary in handle and body form as well as in color.

Troy was the first site where these highly distinctive vessels were excavated. Examples from other sites, such as those here from Poliochni and Tell Selenkahiye (cat. no. 178c), demonstrate the *depata*'s wide range and provide evidence of Troy's trading relations with central Anatolia and the Aegean; they also offer chronological clues and perhaps indicate the existence of similar drinking habits in different regions.[3] New excavations may extend the known limits of the *depata*'s distribution farther to the west, as did the recent

ET

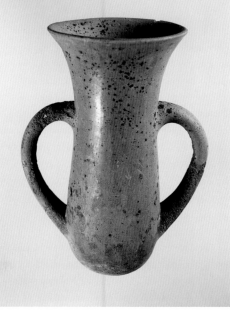

178c

discovery of a single *depas* at the Early Bronze
III settlement of Helike on the southwest
shore of the Gulf of Corinth, in the northern
Peloponnese.[4] The current excavator of Troy,
Manfred Korfmann, interprets the widespread
occurrence of the *depas amphikypellon* as a
demonstration of how luxury goods and fash-
ions connected distant regions in the third
millennium B.C.[5]

A double-handled vessel of Anatolian style
is depicted on an Akkadian stele fragment
(fig. 61), although the shape of its body is
quite different from those shown here.[6] The
scene on the stele depicts prisoners and soldiers;
the vessel, probably part of the spoils of an
Akkadian campaign, was likely to have been
made of gold or silver.   NC

1. Bernabò-Brea 1976, pl. 191a; cf. Podzuweit 1979,
pp. 151–53, pl. 6.1.
2. Orthmann 1963, p. 104, no. 1/08, pl. 1.
3. Latacz et al. 2001, p. 357, fig. 385, p. 363, fig. 398.
4. Katsonopoulou, forthcoming.
5. Korfmann 2001, p. 218.
6. Börker-Klähn 1982, nos. 22a, 22b.

179

Anthropomorphic jar with facial features in relief

Clay, originally burnished
H. 13 cm (5⅛ in.); Diam. of body 8.3 cm (3¼ in.);
Diam. of rim 6.7 cm (2⅝ in.)
Anatolia, Troy, Levels II–V
Early Bronze Age, second half of the 3rd
millennium B.C.
National Archaeological Museum, Athens 4437

This vessel has a spherical body, a high neck
with an everted rim, and a flat base. The pro-
trusions on the body denote breasts and the
navel, while the vertical, wing-shaped handles
give the impression of raised arms. The neck
of the vessel bears two spherical projections
representing eyes below two horizontal lines
indicating eyebrows. A sharp conical protuber-
ance suggests the nose, and the ears are spiral
shaped. The lid is missing, but in this class of
anthropomorphic vases, it is usually discoid or
curved, with a small horn-shaped projection
at the top.

The vase is a typical example of the anthropomorphic pottery from Troy datable to Early
Bronze Age II–III (Troy II–V). Pottery with
moulded, incised, or painted renderings of

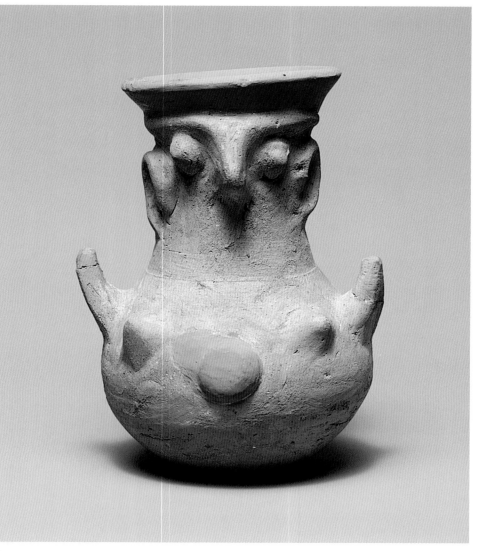

179

human features or full figures—for the most
part female—constitutes a special category of
Early Bronze Age pottery (phases II and III)
throughout the Aegean and western Anatolian
world, with a particular significance, probably
symbolic, and a special use, possibly ritual.[1]

ET

1. Demakopoulou 1990, p. 154, no. 13. For the shape,
see Podzuweit 1979, pp. 193–94, pl. 15.2; and for two
very similar vases, see Schliemann 1885, p. 390, no. 182,
p. 392, no. 186.

180

Disk-shaped female figure

Alabaster
H. 20.2 cm (8 in.); W. 14.1 cm (5½ in.)
Anatolia, Kültepe (ancient Kanesh)
Early Bronze Age, late 3rd millennium B.C.
Kayseri Archaeological Museum, Turkey 535

In Anatolia the sculptural tradition of making
voluptuous and naturalistically executed
female figurines dates back to the Ceramic
Neolithic period (ca. 7000–4000 B.C.).
Examples are found at such celebrated sites as
Çatal Höyük and Hacilar, among others.[1]
Production continued in the region throughout the succeeding millennia, but during the
Early Bronze Age more naturalistically formed
human representations were made alongside
highly stylized schematic figurines often
referred to by scholars as "idols."[2] This type,
peculiar to western and central Anatolia, comprises flat figurines of various sizes, round or
violin-shaped in outline, with modeled or triangular heads. A number are carved with multiple heads and necks, continuing a tradition
first encountered at the early site of Çatal
Höyük.[3] Some of the figurines may represent
men. The majority, however, are female.

One example of this schematic type is the
present figure.[4] The modeled head on the

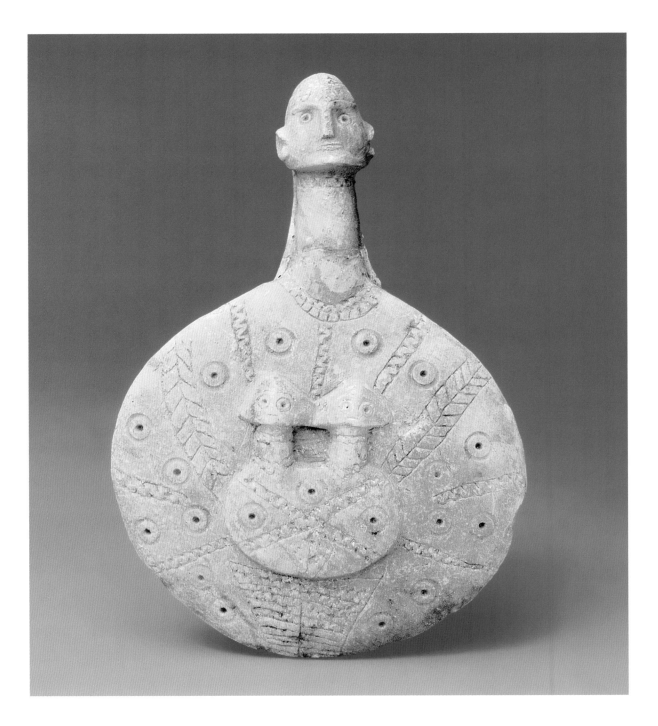

elongated neck is intricately carved, bringing a touch of naturalism to the otherwise geometric figure. There are circular eyes, distinctive joined eyebrows emphasizing a long straight nose, crescent-shaped ears, and full lips.[5] A thick braid encircles the forehead and falls at the back of the head in multiple plaits. Apart from this detail there are no other markings on the back. A smaller single figure with two triangular heads is carved in relief on the lower abdomen of the main figure. Only the eyes and joined eyebrows are detailed on the smaller figure.

Carving and drilling produced the details on both figures. Large dotted circles spaced randomly are interrupted by bands of zigzag and herringboned lines, which may represent jewelry, organs, or appendages. The two larger herringboned bands, perhaps representing arms, emerge from the shoulder area of the main figure and appear to hold the smaller figurine by its shoulders. The pubic area on both figures is emphasized by triangles decorated with parallel lines and stippling, suggesting that these "idols" are female.

At Kültepe disk-shaped figurines were excavated alongside more naturalistic representations in the same kinds of buildings and at the same levels, suggesting that these two strikingly different artistic and perhaps religious types of artifact were contemporary.[6] Because some of these structures were undoubtedly religious in purpose, these circular figurines may be fertility, cult, or votive objects. Thus, the present figurine may represent a mother goddess with her two female children.[7] At the same time, the overall shape is extremely phallic, giving the statuette an almost androgynous quality, which may be associated with fertility.   SG

1. Kohlmeyer 1995, pp. 2639–42, and Kulaçoğlu 1992, nos. 7–61.

2. For a variety of disk-shaped figures, see H. Müller-Karpe 1974, pl. 296.

3. Two-headed figurines are known from Çatal Höyük; see Kulaçoğlu 1992, fig. 9. Stone figures with multiple heads, dating to the end of the fourth millennium B.C., were excavated at Tell Brak in Syria; see Mallowan 1947, p. 34, pl. 51. Although the cultural connections between northern Syria and Anatolia were strong during the third millennium B.C., the fact remains that Syrian figurines of this period are naturalistic while those of central Anatolia remain more schematized, suggesting that the latter are a local artistic phenomenon without any links to neighboring regions. For a discussion of the relationship between northern Syria and Anatolia during the Bronze Age, see T. Özgüç 1986, pp. 31–47.

4. Similar figures have been excavated in cult buildings and graves at Kültepe, a site in central Anatolia, as well as at the nearby sites of Zencidere and Acemhöyük. For a complete bibliography on the figures from Kültepe and other sites, see T. Özgüç 1993.

5. These facial features are reminiscent of the "face urns" from Troy II (ca. 2500 B.C.). For examples, see Alkim 1969, pls. 52, 53, and, in this catalogue, number 179.

6. T. Özgüç 1993, pp. 511–14.

7. Bossert 1942, p. 40.

THE CENTRAL ANATOLIAN PLATEAU: THE TOMBS OF ALACA HÖYÜK

OSCAR WHITE MUSCARELLA

In the nineteenth century Western scholars began to visit eastern Turkey, primarily to see the vast site at Boğazköy—ancient Hattusha, capital of the Hittites—discovered in 1834 by Charles Texier. A year later M. G. Hamilton was the first non-Turk to visit the ruins of Höyük (Mound), as Alaca Höyük was then known, thirty kilometers to the northwest, where the Sphinx Gate and some reliefs were still above ground and visible. Others followed, among them G. Perrot, who in the 1860s cleared the Sphinx Gate and part of the reliefs. Other brief excavations were undertaken: in 1881 by W. M. Ramsey, in 1893 by E. Chantre, and in 1906 by H. Winckler and T. Makridy.[1] But the first systematic and concentrated excavations were conducted by the Turkish archaeologist Hamit Zübeyr Koşay from 1935 to 1948.[2]

The site yielded cultural remains from the Early Bronze Age (third millennium B.C.), the later Middle Bronze Age, and also the Hittite, Phrygian, Roman, and Byzantine periods, revealing evidence of some four thousand years of human occupation. What makes the site a major one in cultural history and of great modern interest are the preserved Hittite walls with their figural reliefs and monumental Sphinx Gate, and the earlier extraordinary group of thirteen intact tombs, unique in the Anatolian Early Bronze Age in their structure and contents. The tombs all contained to varying degrees quantities of symbolic and elite sumptuous objects made of gold, silver, copper alloy, lapis lazuli, and various other stones, related to both the secular and the religious concerns of the people at the site.[3]

In the first year of excavation three tombs were recovered, B, R, and T; the next year produced A, A' (lying directly over, and thus later than, A), and C; in the next three years seven more were uncovered, D, E, F, H, K, L, and S. The tombs were recovered at slightly different levels close together in a cemetery area and below the Hittite level.[4] All were shallow, rectangular earth pits of different sizes, lined at the top with rubble stones and cut about seventy-five centimeters to one meter into the earth. Perhaps each was covered by a roof of logs and wood beams, on top of which in some cases were the remains of animal sacrifices, including paired bovine heads (fig. 77). In each tomb was a single occupant laid out in a contracted position, with grave goods such as bracelets, diadems, and anklets placed on

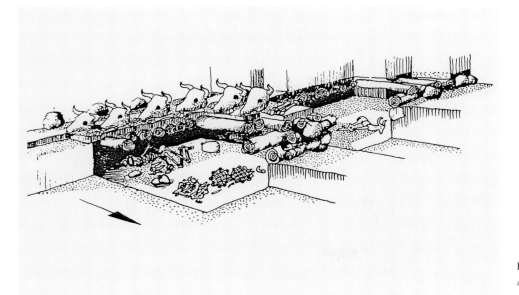

Fig. 77. Drawing of reconstructed Tomb L, Alaca Höyük. Early Bronze Age, late 3rd millennium B.C.

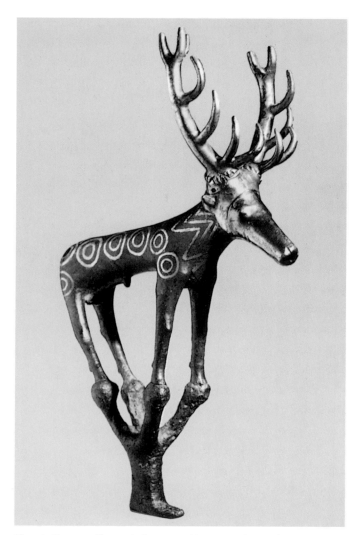

Fig. 78. Copper-alloy and silver stag. Alaca Höyük, Tomb B, Early Bronze Age, ca. 2500–2200 B.C. Museum of Anatolian Civilizations, Ankara, 11878.

or many more years. It is certain that the tombs are to be dated within the last two or three centuries of the third millennium B.C., in the late Early Bronze Age II or III periods of Anatolian archaeology. This makes them approximately contemporary with several other Early Bronze Age sites known in the area, such as Horoztepe (see cat. no. 190) and Mahmatlar (see fig. 79), for example, both apparently centers of local authority.[6]

The significance of the Alaca Höyük tombs is that they document the presence of a major polity, a state whose authority, no doubt a king, commanded the wealth and power to obtain precious imported materials, to control quality craftsmen who could transform these into sumptuous elite and religiously charged artifacts, and to organize the labor-intensive activity to construct the tombs.

1. For bibliography, see Koşay n.d., pp. 17–18, and Koşay 1937, pp. 1–2.
2. Koşay was a member of the first generation of Turkish archaeologists, all of whom were encouraged by Kemal Atatürk to study abroad and to create a Turkish discipline of archaeology. Exemplary was the promptness with which the Alaca excavation reports were published—in 1937, 1944, and 1951—and for their time they presented much important information. Where problems exist they are in the description of stratigraphic information, a common difficulty in archaeology until the second half of the twentieth century, and of the specific locations of the material in the tombs.
3. The primary publications on the tombs are Koşay 1937, Koşay 1944, Koşay 1951, and Koşay n.d. But see also Özyar 1988 for a good summary of tomb groups with appropriate line drawings of the tombs and their contents.
4. Özyar (1988, pp. 5–6) plausibly suggests that the tombs were dug into a sloped part of the mound.
5. Excavation techniques and skills improved over the years, and the best views of the tombs and their construction are to be seen in Koşay 1944, pp. 79, 81, and Koşay 1951, p. 53, fig. 32, pls. 157 (Tomb E), 167 (Tomb F), 189, 191 (Tomb L).
6. See Koşay 1951, pp. 154–56, for the excavator's views on the nature of the tombs and their chronology. For summaries and a bibliography of the different opinions regarding tomb sequences and chronological problems, see Muscarella 1988a, pp. 396–98, and notes; and Özyar 1988, pp. 3–7. Horoztepe had some of the same types of artifacts that were found at Alaca (see entry for cat. no. 190).

the skeleton, adjacent to it, or along a wall.[5] These burial goods were of different materials: gold, silver, copper alloy, iron, bone, clay, and stone. They included several diadems (see cat. no. 183), various vessels (see cat. no. 187), jewelry and decorative objects (see cat. nos. 182–185), standards of stags and bulls (see cat. no. 188; fig. 78) and stylized nude females (see cat. no. 181), and copper-alloy standards in geometric open-worked and other forms (see cat. no. 189; fig. 80). In only one burial, Tomb A, was an attempt made to sex the skeleton. It was determined to be female, apparently based on an interpretation of the artifacts, that is, the quantity of jewelry. This is not an unreasonable interpretation, but the issue remains to be studied further.

Continuously under review are questions concerning whether the tombs were extramural or intramural, what precisely are the deposition sequence and relative age of the thirteen tombs, and whether they were built over a few generations

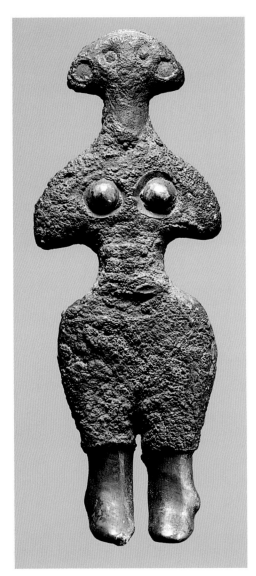

has added gold breasts and boots, and the legs are separated. The copper-alloy figurine has one gold disk, at the ear position—perhaps it is an earring, the other one having been lost. The ungilt breasts are fully modeled, the legs are held close together, and the pubic area is prominently depicted.

A striking, plain silver figurine of the same form but with arms extended and with no sexual details exhibited comes from Tomb A' at the site, while three copper-alloy statuettes—two nude women who hold objects in their hands and a small figure (a child?) of more conventional and more naturalistic form—derive from Tomb H. All five were also placed next to the chest of the deceased.[2] Why occupants of only three of the thirteen tombs at Alaca were buried with female figurines is unknown to us.

At least two statuettes excavated at other sites in Anatolia, both close in date to the ones found at Alaca, are reminiscent of them, while at the same time exhibiting local characteristics. A copper-alloy nude female figurine from Horoztepe is rendered more naturalistically, with prominent buttocks and large ears and nose. She nurses a child. And from Hasanoğlan was recovered a nude female statuette made of silver and with gold leaf placed over the head, neck, and breasts, and with the arms folded across the body (fig. 75).[3]

Beginning in Neolithic times sculptures of nude females were made in Anatolia and elsewhere in the Near East, and these Early Bronze Age figurines continue that tradition. That most of them—surely the present example—represent a female charged with power, perhaps a deity, seems to be the most plausible interpretation.   OWM

1. Koşay 1951, pp. 168–69, pls. 190, 195; Kulaçoğlu 1992, nos. 98, 99.
2. Koşay 1938, pl. 89; Koşay 1951, pls. 118, 123, 124, 139; Kulaçoğlu 1992, nos. 97, 100–103.
3. Kulaçoğlu 1992, nos. 103, 104.

182

Appliqué of paired nude female figures

Gold
H. 4 cm (1⅝ in.); W. 4 cm (1⅝ in.)
Anatolia, Alaca Höyük, Tomb H
Early Bronze Age, late 3rd millennium B.C.
Ankara Museum of Anatolian Civilizations, Turkey 6042

Five plaque figures, including this one—all exactly the same—were found in Tomb H at Alaca Höyük next to the deceased at chin level. Associated with them in the same area in front of the body were a good number of other objects, including three copper-alloy human figurines and several gold artifacts.[1] Each plaque consists of two stylized female forms joined at their downward-curving arms and

181

Standing nude female figure wearing boots

Silver and gold
H. 10.6 cm (4⅛ in.)
Anatolia, Alaca Höyük, Tomb L
Early Bronze Age, late 3rd millennium B.C.
Ankara Museum of Anatolian Civilizations, Turkey 8801

Two anthropomorphic figurines, the present example and one of copper alloy, were recovered from Tomb L at Alaca Höyük lying on their backs adjacent to the chest of the deceased.[1] Both figurines are female and essentially have the same form: a semicircular head on a prominent neck, a pinched waist, the suggestion of arms bent across and held close to the body, and round eyes. There are some differences in detail. The present example

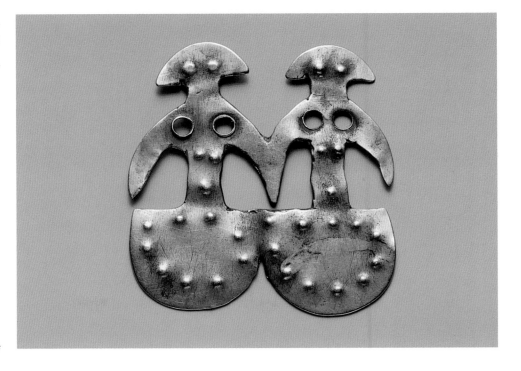

lower bodies. Their body parts are represented schematically: the eyes are raised dots on a semicircular head atop a thick neck; the breasts and navel are also raised dots; and the border of the paddle-shaped lower body is decorated with raised bumps, apparently to represent pubic hair. There are no legs. Two holes above the breasts allowed the idols to be sewn to fabric, whether clothing or something else remains unknown. The basic shape and the pairing produce an aesthetically pleasing form.

No other tomb contained such paired figures, but the semicircular head on a thick neck, as well as dangling arms, is also found on a silver statue in the round from Tomb A', while the head shape alone is duplicated on a silver and gold figure (cat. no. 181) and a copper-alloy statuette from Tomb L.[2]

Figures of this contour are sometimes called violin-shaped, for obvious reasons. The form is not restricted to Alaca. It occurs in several other areas of Anatolia throughout the third millennium B.C. At Ahlatlibel, Karaoğlan, and Etiyokusu, for example, southwest of Alaca, a number of single-figure terracotta examples have been recovered. And a flat copper-alloy single-figure example in the Ankara Museum is very close in its stylized body form to the Alaca gold pairs.[3] Stone examples of more schematized violin-shaped figures, without face or body markings, are known from Beycesultan and Karataş farther west.[4]

OWM

1. Koşay 1951, p. 157, pl. 129; for the figurines, see pls. 124, 129, 139.
2. Koşay 1938, p. 115, pl. 89; Koşay 1951, pp. 168–69, pl. 195. See also Kulaçoğlu 1992, nos. 97–99.
3. Kulaçoğlu 1992, nos. 79–83, 85–90, 93, 94. For modern productions of these objects, see Schuster collection sale, Sotheby's, London, July 10, 1989, no. 65.
4. Kulaçoğlu 1992, nos. 105–14.

183

Diadem with an elaborate open-worked pattern

Gold
H. 5.4 cm (2⅛ in.); Diam. 19.2 cm (7½ in.)
Anatolia, Alaca Höyük, Tomb A
Early Bronze Age, late 3rd millennium B.C.
Ankara Museum of Anatolian Civilizations, Turkey
11857

One of five examples from Alaca, this diadem is formed in a simple but compelling open-worked pattern of four rows of Xs. It was uncovered on the head of the skeleton, precisely as were three gold diadems from Tombs E, H, and L, whereas one from K was recovered directly in front of the face. The diadem from Tomb H is similar to, but much smaller than, the present example, while the others are simple, plain bands.[1] Tomb A's diadem may actually be a crown, inasmuch as it is the most elaborate of all those recovered at the site. Furthermore, the burial is one of the richest at Alaca, containing, aside from pottery, four open-worked "solar" disks (see also cat. no. 189), a stag standard (see also fig. 78), and a quantity

of gold jewelry, including brooches, pins, necklaces, and bracelets (see also cat. nos. 184, 185).

The diadem-crown, distinguished not only by its large size from the others recovered in Tomb A but also by its precious material, suggests that an elite, very high or highest ranking royal individual was buried in Tomb A. The nature of the jewelry in the burial may indicate that this individual was female, but we do not have enough information about jewelry gendering in Early Bronze Age Anatolia to make a firm decision.[2]

OWM

1. For Tomb A, see Koşay 1938, pl. 82 (pl. 92 is the same photo but captioned, in error, here as Tomb A'). For other diadems, see Koşay 1951, pls. 167 (Tomb E), 185 (Tomb K), 141 (in color), 129 (Tomb H), 198 (Tomb L). See also Özyar 1988, pls. 21–26.
2. If Mellink (1956, p. 52) is correct in assuming that the round, handled, copper-alloy, panlike object from this tomb is in fact a mirror (see pls. 4, 5; and also pl. 6, from Tomb A'), it would be an argument for a female occupant, princess or queen, of Tomb A. Koşay (1944, p. 80) claimed the skeleton was that of a woman; see also Özyar 1988, p. 26.

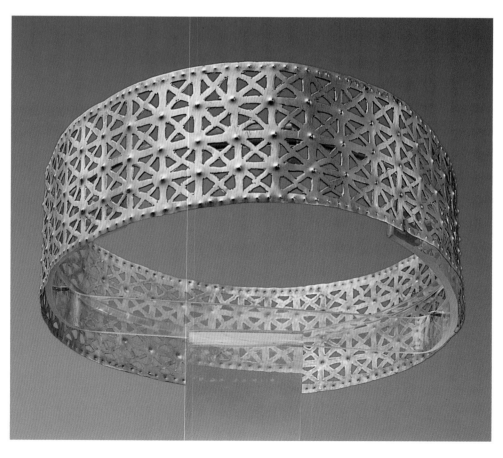

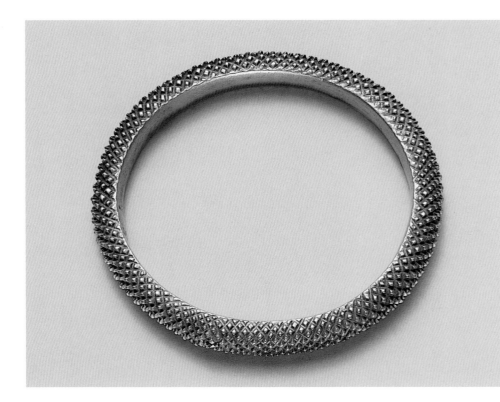

Pin with flanged head

Gold
L. 18.5 cm (7¼ in.)
Anatolia, Alaca Höyük, Tomb B, Al.240
Early Bronze Age, late 3rd millennium B.C.
Ankara Museum of Anatolian Civilizations, Turkey
11660

This pin is made in two units, the pin itself
and the six-flanged top. It appears to be the
longest straight pin recovered at Alaca. It and a
silver pin with pyriform head were found just
behind the skeleton; they no doubt fastened
the garment, or shroud, of the deceased. Only
one other tomb at the cemetery contained
similar flange-headed gold or gold-headed
pins, two or three from Tomb A, where they
were recovered in situ as the holding pins of
figure-eight-shaped brooches.[1] Pins with the
same distinctive flanged head have been

184

Bracelet

Gold
Diam. 6.5 cm (2½ in.)
Anatolia, Alaca Höyük, Tomb A', Al.35a
Early Bronze Age, late 3rd millennium B.C.
Ankara Museum of Anatolian Civilizations, Turkey
11720

This is the slightly smaller bracelet from a
pair excavated from Tomb A' at Alaca Höyük
in central Anatolia.[1] The outer surface is
decorated with small knobs that rise from
diamond-shaped fields formed by intersecting
diagonal lines. A sparkling effect is achieved
by the pattern's many light-scattering facets.
The inner wall is smooth.

As with other metal objects recovered from
the richly appointed burials at this site, the
elegantly bold design of the bracelet seems to
reflect an advanced aesthetic sensibility. A certain degree of technical sophistication is also
suggested by the apparent presence of a metallurgical join where the two ends are sleeved
together. It appears that this bracelet and its
companion were worked around a core of pliable material that was later removed through a
hole in the inner wall.[2]   J-FL

1. Koşay 1944, p. 115, pl. 92.
2. See the description in Bingöl 1999, p. 173.

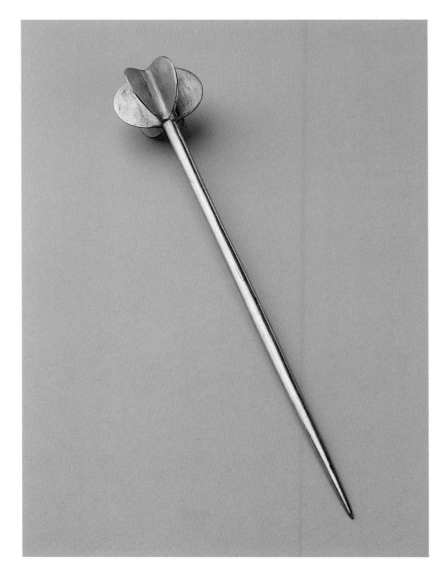

excavated at sites to the south of Alaca, along an old north-south trade route. Some 150 kilometers directly to the south, at the site of Kültepe, were recovered gold and silver pins with the same head form. These occur in tombs of early-second-millennium date.[2] And at Alishar Höyük, midway between Alaca and Kültepe, several copper-alloy examples were recovered.[3]

Straight pins made of precious metals were recovered from only three other Alaca tombs, H, K, and L, and these also find parallels at other sites, including Troy in northwestern Anatolia.[4]

OWM

1. For Tomb B, see Arik 1937, pls. 166, 167, 182; note also the flanged beads from this tomb, pl. 181, top. In Koşay n.d., there is a photograph of Tomb B's contents that shows two pins, one the example discussed here. For Tomb A, see Koşay 1944, pp. 101, 111, nos. 28–30; see also Mellink 1956, pl. 2:12.
2. T. Özgüç 1986, p. 33, fig. 30, pl. 70, nos. 12, 13, 15, 16, pl. H.
3. Schmidt 1932, pp. 159, 161, upper left.
4. Mellink 1956, pp. 50–51, pl. 2:14a,b.

186

Long-stemmed goblet

Gold
H. 12.5 cm (4⅞ in.); Diam. 8.6 cm (3⅜ in.)
Anatolia, Alaca Höyük, Tomb K, Al. K4
Early Bronze Age, late 3rd millennium B.C.
Ankara Museum of Anatolian Civilizations, Turkey 8776

Three gold goblets—shallow cups set on a high, cylindrical foot or stand—were recovered from the Alaca Höyük cemetery, two from Tomb B and one from K. The bases are either flat or slightly cone-shaped.[1] The stands are decorated in a fairly deep grooved design, on the example from Tomb B with an alternating swirl, on this one from K with horizontal rows of chevrons. In addition, Tomb K contained a silver goblet inlaid with gold strips on the otherwise plain cup and stand.[2] Furthermore, Tombs B and K each contained a gold pitcher (see cat. no. 187a). It is of cultural interest to note that in a tomb at Mahmatlar, some one hundred kilometers east of Alaca, both a gold goblet, completely plain, and a gold pitcher were also recovered together (see fig. 79).[3]

That goblets and pitchers made of precious metals occur together in the same tombs

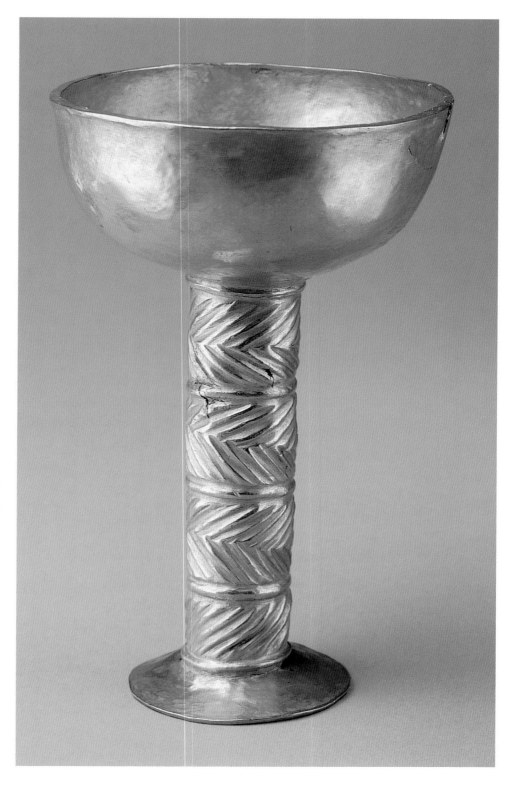

suggests that they functioned together in some purposeful social or ritual role, perhaps connected to the funeral ceremony.

OWM

1. For Tomb B, see Arik 1937, pls. 168, 169: the goblet shape is described as a champagne cup *(coupe à champagne)*; for Tomb K, see Koşay 1951, p. 166, pl. 177, top. See also Akurgal 1962, pl. 17, and Toker 1992, pp. 41–45, 185–86, nos. 11, 12, 15. Note that in Arik 1937 I cannot find number 15, a foot for a goblet now missing its cup, listed as from Tomb B, but I include it here as one of the three.
2. Koşay 1951, p. 166, pl. 177, bottom; Toker 1992, pp. 44, 186, no. 14.
3. Koşay and Akok 1950, pls. 37–39, nos. 8, 9, 11, 12; Toker 1992, pp. 33, 43, 183, 186, nos. 3, 13; see Mellaart 1966, p. 157, fig. 48, for all the gold and silver vessels from Alaca and Mahmatlar.

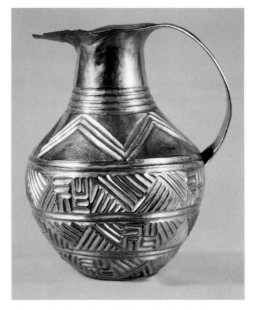

Fig. 79. Gold pitcher. Mahmatlar, Early Bronze Age, ca. 2500–2200 B.C. Museum of Anatolian Civilizations, Ankara, 15076.

187a, b

Gold ewers

a. H. 14.3 cm (15⅝ in.); Diam. 8.8 cm (3½ in.)
Anatolia, Alaca Höyük, Tomb B, Al.242
Early Bronze Age, late 3rd millennium B.C.
Ankara Museum of Anatolian Civilizations,
Turkey 11722

b. H. 17.8 cm (7 in.); Diam. 12.1 cm (4¾ in.)
Central Anatolia
Early Bronze Age, late 3rd millennium B.C.
The Metropolitan Museum of Art, New York; Harris
Brisbane Dick Fund, 1957 57.67

Tomb B was one of three discovered at Alaca Höyük in 1935, the first year of systematic excavation at the site. Among its contents was a gold pitcher, or ewer, two gold goblets, a gold flange-headed pin (cat. no. 185), gold earrings and beads, and a number of copper-alloy open-worked and animal-topped standards.[1]

The ewer (cat. no. 187a) has an ovoid body sloping gently up to a relatively thin vertical neck that terminates in a short upward-pointing spout; three thin grooves are incised in the neck. A single sheet of flattened gold was

raised to create the vessel and its flat handle; the latter extends from the mouth to the body, where its end is soldered in place. Before the ewer was raised, a low-relief design of chevrons was hammered on the gold sheet, covering the whole body of the vessel; at the base is a starlike configuration produced by the converging chevrons. Another gold pitcher of similar form and manufacture but with a smaller neck, a longer spout, and a decorative pattern raised higher than that on this example from Tomb B was also recovered in the Alaca cemetery, in Tomb K (which also contained a gold goblet [cat. no. 186]). Asymmetrical, oblique crescents or swirls and an irregular pattern of chevrons make up its design; at the base is a swastika encased in swirls.[2]

A third gold pitcher of the same form was excavated in a tomb at Mahmatlar, near Amasya, more than one hundred kilometers east of Alaca (see fig. 79).[3] This vessel differs from its Alaca counterparts only in its tectonic

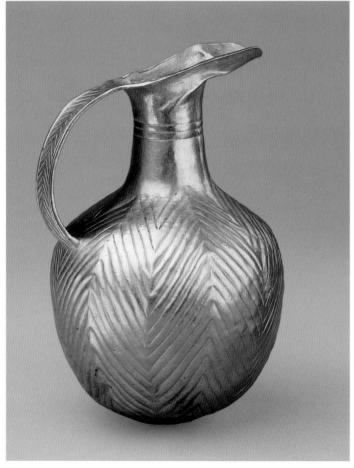

187a

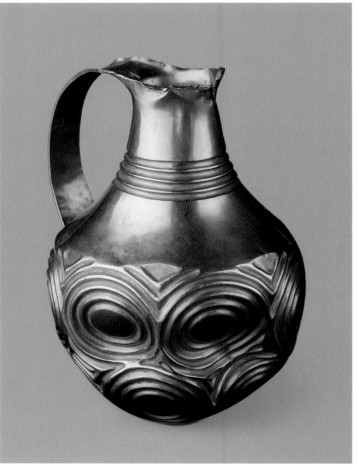

187b

decoration strategy. There is a repoussé decoration of lozenges and swastikas on the lower half of the vessel, a chevron pattern above, and four grooves on the base of the neck; at the bottom is a seemingly random pattern. Its form, neck pattern, and general body decoration relate the vessel to the Alaca examples.

Demonstrating both the extensive use of precious metals to make prestige vessels and the importance of the ewer shape at Alaca Höyük, seven silver examples, either decorated with grooved designs or plain, were present in five tombs, A, E, H, K, and L.[4] Thus, six of the thirteen tombs at the site contained ewers made of precious metals: two tombs, B and K, contained gold ewers, and K also had two silver ewers; and four other tombs, A, E, H, and L, contained only silver ewers. It is relevant to note that several copper-alloy ewers were recovered at Alaca, but none from the above-mentioned tombs.[5] Copper-alloy ewers occurred in at least two other Anatolian sites—Polatli, west of Ankara, and a burial at Horoztepe, east of Mahmatlar.[6] Perhaps the best explanation for the presence of ewers in so many tombs is that they were used in a ritual for pouring libations, perhaps related to the funeral ceremonies.

Two other gold ewers have been published. Both are known from the antiquities market. One was acquired in 1957 by the Metropolitan Museum (cat. no. 187b).[7] Its body decoration, which differs from that on the excavated examples just discussed, consists of patterns of contiguous concentric circles framed by chevrons, set below the handle-base position. This design is one found in the glyptic of Anatolia, the Levant, and the Aegean during the second half of the third millennium B.C.[8] Like the Mahmatlar vessel, the ewer has four grooves at the base of its neck, and there is a swastika at the base. The other stray gold ewer at one time belonged to the same dealer who owned the Metropolitan Museum's vessel. It was offered for sale at an auction in Switzerland in 1960.[9] Fairly deeply grooved zigzags and lozenges below a zone of regular zigzags decorate its lower body; the upper zone is plain. Its handle seems to be correctly formed.

The deep-grooved and original design on the Metropolitan Museum's ewer, which sets it apart from the others, could reflect either a geographic or a chronological distance—or indeed both—between workshops. But it is best to avoid speculation, for archaeologists have insufficient information to settle such questions about the manufacture of these gold vessels. Nevertheless, it is clear that ewers of the very same form and essential body decoration have been excavated at sites more than one hundred kilometers apart (Alaca and Mahmatlar) and, moreover, have been recovered alongside footed goblets (see cat. no. 186).[10] These occurrences manifestly demonstrate some cultural communication and perhaps also political relationships between polities of power and authority. Whether these communications occurred over a relatively short or a long time remains to be resolved.

OWM

1. Arik 1937, pp. 54–57, pl. 171 and colorpl. 7, for the present gold ewer; see also Akurgal 1962, pl. 14, and Toker 1992, pp. 30–31, 183, no. 1.
2. Koşay 1951, p. 166, pls. 170, 176, top; see also Akurgal 1962, pl. 15, and Toker 1992, pp. 32, 183, no. 2.
3. Koşay and Akok 1950, p. 483, pl. 38:8,9; Toker 1992, pp. 33, 183, no. 3. The finds were either confiscated from or donated to the authorities by the local people who first recovered the material; see Mellaart 1966, p. 184. Probably intact when excavated, the spout was damaged after recovery. It has since been restored in a horizontal position—perhaps incorrectly. See Muscarella 1988a, p. 399, for a map of Anatolia that includes the sites mentioned in this report.
4. Koşay 1938, pp. 104, 117; Koşay 1951, pp. 160, 165, 168, 169, pls. 132, 165, 179, 196. The grooved decoration also occurs on ceramic vessels and shards; see Arik 1937, pls. 121, 123, 127, and Koşay 1944, p. 115. See also Akurgal 1962, pl. 12, for the one from Tomb A.
5. Koşay 1951, pp. 161 pl. 147 (from Tomb D), 170 pl. 204 (from Tomb S); Arik 1937, pl. 235 (from Tomb R); see also Toker 1992, pp. 34, 35, 37, 184, nos. 4, 5, 7. Although measurements are not available for all the ewers, the gold vessels are between two and six or seven centimeters shorter than the silver and copper-alloy examples.
6. The best photographs are in Toker 1992, pp. 38–40, 185, nos. 8, 9, 10; the last two, from Polatli, are smaller than all the other pitchers known. See also Özgüç and Akok 1958, pp. 10, 43, fig. 4, pl. 4:3. Toker 1992, no. 6, is another example, said to be of lead; its origin is not known, but it is assumed to derive from a named site.
7. *Bulletin of The Metropolitan Museum of Art* 18 (April 1960), p. 254, fig. 12; *Bulletin of The Metropolitan Museum of Art* 26 (January 1968), p. 194; Akurgal 1962, fig. 16. Tezcan (1960, pp. 30–31, pls. 15, 16) relates it to the Mahmatlar vessel. Although a general geographic provenience—the Kizil Irmak (Halys River)–Black Sea region—may be safely posited for the vessel, published references to a findspot "near" or "in" Amasya have no manifest archaeological value.
8. Aruz 1998a, p. 307.
9. See Ars Antiqua, Lucerne, *Antike Kunstwerke*, sale cat., May 14, 1960, pl. 71 (the height is given as eighteen centimeters). A photograph made in 1958 shows

damage to the mouth—where a bent-back but extant spout seems to be present—and to the handle top and body; in the catalogue photograph all has been repaired. The grooved decoration on this vessel is atypical and deserves more study.
10. See Mellaart 1966, p. 157, fig. 14, for a convenient drawing of the ewers and goblets.

188

Bull standard

Copper alloy and electrum
H. 48 cm (18⅞ in.)
Anatolia, Alaca Höyük, Tomb C
Early Bronze Age, late 3rd millennium B.C.
Ankara Museum of Anatolian Civilizations, Turkey
11850

The bull or stag on a pedestal is one of the most common depositions in the Alaca Höyük burials. Ten in all were deposited, seven representing bulls, and three, stags; they derive from ten tombs, one figure from each. The animals are large but relatively slim, with a thin muzzle and long, prominent horns; each was placed away from but facing in the direction of the deceased.[1] They all are represented upright and as either walking or resting, set on a base of one or more elements above a tang for attachment to a now-missing, perhaps wood, support or staff. The present bull is set on a four-pronged base that supports its feet, set at an angle to the tang. Inlaid on one shoulder is an electrum band, a decoration found in more elaborate form on two other bulls and one stag from Tombs B, H, and L (fig. 78).

Excavated from a tomb at Horoztepe (see cat. no. 190), about sixty kilometers east of Alaca, were a bull on a pedestal and an open-worked disk, both formally the same as those from Alaca (see cat. no. 189).[2]

The bull represented in an awe-inspiring and powerful pose has a long history in Anatolia, continuing through the millennia among different peoples and polities. Here it surely represents the thunderstorm deity, invoked in many depictions and in later second-millennium-B.C. texts. The stag is often described as a protective deity in later Hittite texts. Why some Alaca tombs (the majority) contained a bull image and others a stag eludes us.[3]

OWM

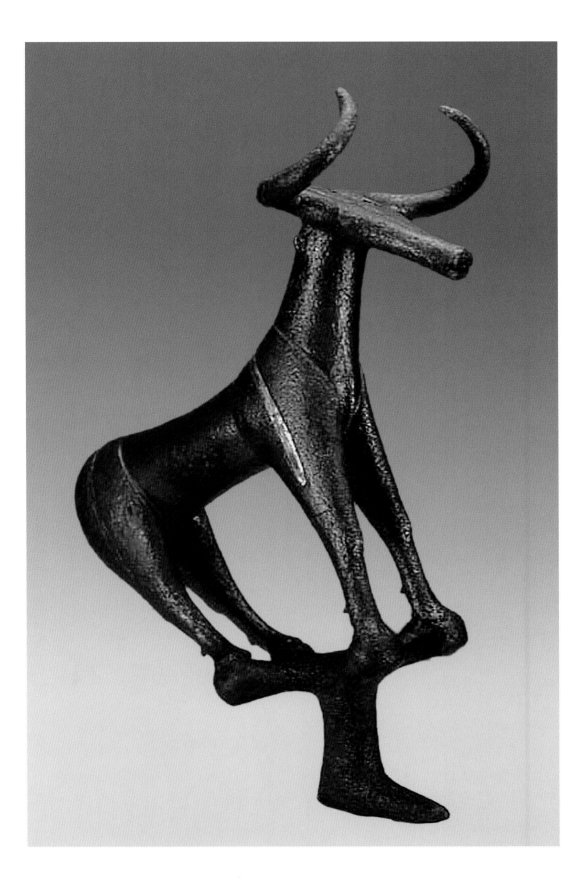

1. Bulls derive from Tombs C, D, E, H, K, L, and T: Koşay 1944, pls. 62, 96, 97 (the present example); Koşay 1951, pls. 150, 162, 122, 130, 173, 190, 192; Koşay 1937, p. 85, fig. 116, pl. 271. Stags were recovered in Tombs A, A', and B: Koşay 1938, pls. 84, 89; Koşay 1937, pls. 202–5. See Orthmann 1967, p. 36. See also Özyar 1988, pls. 19–23, 24–26, and the plates in Koşay n.d. for some tomb groups mentioned here; also Özyar 1988, pp. 72–77, for discussions of the animal pedestals.

2. Özgüç and Akok 1958, pp. 44–45, 47–48, pls. 7:2, 11:1a–c. Note that a small statuette of a stag was also found in the tomb, p. 48, pl. 14:1.

3. Orthmann (1967, p. 53) believed that these animal images were placed on the body of a wagon. See also Özyar 1988, pp. 65–70, for various interpretations of and views of them.

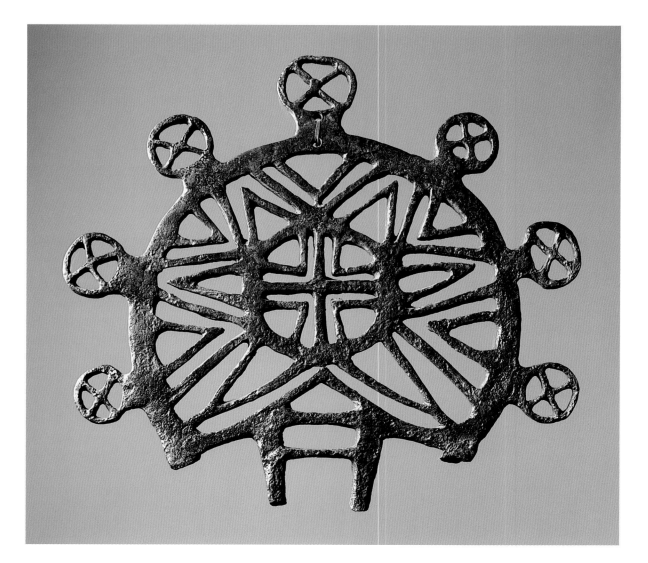

189

Open-worked standard

Copper alloy
H. 27.5 cm (10⅞ in.)
Anatolia, Alaca Höyük, Tomb E
Early Bronze Age, late 3rd millennium B.C.
Ankara Museum of Anatolian Civilizations,
Turkey 7128

The flat disk formed as an open-worked geometric grill pattern is a characteristic artifact from the Alaca Höyük tombs (see also the pattern on cat. no. 183), for about twenty examples were recovered there from ten burials.[1] This disk's pattern consists of a central cross surrounded by a band of zigzags. To the perimeter, or frame, are attached seven small open-worked disks. The two prongs firmly anchored the standard to a base. A similar but semicircular open-worked disk was recovered close to this example.[2] Other disks of this form from the tombs are rounded, or half-circular,

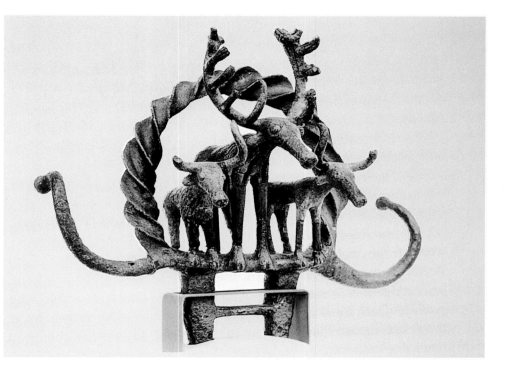

Fig. 80. Copper-alloy standard with two bulls and a stag. Alaca Höyük, Tomb B, Early Bronze Age, late 3rd millennium B.C. Museum of Anatolian Civilizations, Ankara, 18728.

or lozenge-shaped, and within the frame they all have similar geometric openwork. Eleven have small fixed disks on the outer perimeter; a few have hanging, free-swinging disks that perhaps were so devised to make a sound when shaken.

All the standards seem to be of copper or bronze. From Tombs A, A', C, and D, along with open-worked disks of geometric design were recovered four related, open-worked standards, each with the figure of an animal in the round within the disk and with horns at the base (fig. 80).

Like the bull and stag standards, the disks surely also had a religious purpose; perhaps the types express related but distinct spiritual values. Indeed, many scholars, including R. O. Arik, the first excavator, have assumed that the disks represent the sun, a possible but unprovable interpretation.[3]

One other site in Anatolia, Horoztepe, about sixty kilometers east of Alaca, yielded grave goods that included an open-worked disk and a bull on a pedestal that are formally the same as those from Alaca.[4]

OWM

1. Tombs A, A', B, C, D, E, H, L, S, and T; see Koşay 1937, pls. 190–95, 262–65; Koşay 1938, pls. 64, 84; Koşay 1944, pl. 91; Koşay 1951, pls. 91, 153, 154, 164, 193, 194; for convenience, see the plates in Koşay n.d., where the tomb groups and groups of disks are shown. See also Orthmann 1967, pp. 37–40. Very useful is Özyar 1988: see pls. 5–17, for the disks, and pls. 19–27, for the Tombs. Three small examples were also recovered in tombs C and T.
2. Koşay 1951, pls. 157, 164.
3. Arik (1937, p. 119) said they were not used as rein rings; however, Orthmann (1967, pp. 52–53) believed the disks functioned primarily as rein rings for the yoke of a wagon. For a summary of opinions regarding the function of the disks, see Orthmann 1967, pp. 34–35, and Özyar 1988, pp. 65–70.
4. Özgüç and Akok 1958, pp. 44–45, 47–48, pls. 7:2, 11:1a–c.
\

190

Sistrum with horned animals

Copper alloy
H. 24.5 cm (9⅝ in.)
Anatolia, Horoztepe
Early Bronze Age, late 3rd millennium B.C.
Ankara Museum of Anatolian Civilizations, Turkey 18519

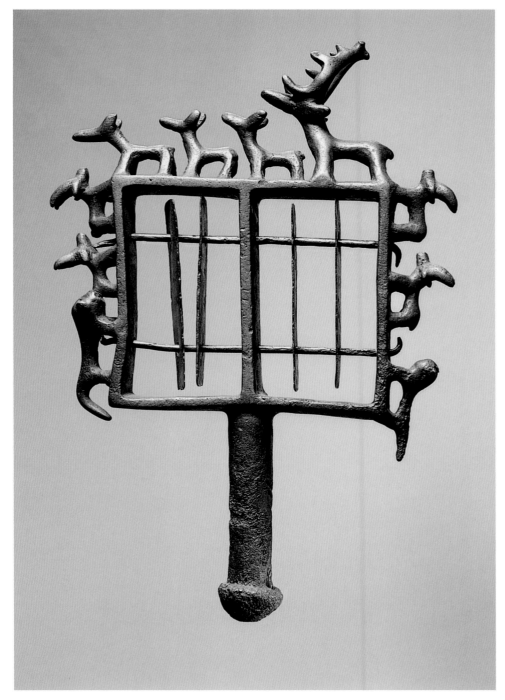

In 1957 Turkish archaeologists excavated at Horoztepe, east of Mahmatlar and Alaca Höyük, following up on reports that a collection of ancient and important copper-alloy objects acquired three years earlier by the Museum of Anatolian Civilizations, Ankara, had derived from a modern cemetery at that site. There, in an intact ancient tomb under the cemetery, T. Özgüç and M. Akok recovered a good number of copper-alloy artifacts.[1] Several were the same types of objects recovered from burials at Alaca Höyük: castanets, a mirror, an open-worked disk (see cat. no. 189), a bull on a pedestal (see cat. no. 188), and a statuette of a woman, this one nursing a baby.

The evidence linking the material acquired by the Ankara museum in 1954 to the site of Horoztepe is circumstantial but not improbable, given the fact that authorities in the nearest town, Tokat, were the first to acquire it and that there were indications at the site of pillaged ancient tombs next to the place where Özgüç and Akok excavated. Among the objects acquired by the Ankara museum was this sistrum, or rattle, formed as an open square internally divided by a central rod; from two horizontal rods hang four loosely attached, thin metal sheets. Below the frame is a solid cylindrical handle, which when shaken allows the metal sheets to create an appropriate sound. Distinguishing this sistrum are a row of does and one stag that "walk" along the top rim and, at each side of the frame, two groups of caprids being attacked by a feline.

Two sistra from a collection acquired by the Metropolitan Museum in 1955 are clearly connected functionally and culturally to the example perhaps from Horoztepe.[2] The parallels are not so much in basic form, for the Metropolitan's rattles are U-shaped and have round, not rectangular, metal sound-sheets, but in basic function and also because they, too, have animals placed along the frame. We can readily accept the interpretation that the sistrum was probably used in charged, sacred performances, perhaps along with the accompanying castanets. The sistrum was deposited in the Horoztepe tomb along with other nonsecular objects, such as the female statuette, disk, and stag pedestal.

OWM

1. For a report on the nature of the 1954 and 1955 museum acquisitions and on the excavation at Horoztepe, see Özgüç and Akok 1957, pp. 211–19; Özgüç and Akok 1958, pp. 37–61; and Muscarella 1988a, pp. 394–96, and nn. 1–3.
2. Muscarella 1988a, pp. 400–401.

THE NORTH CAUCASUS

ELENA IZBITSER

The North Caucasus, separated from Trans-Caucasia by the main range of the Caucasus Mountains, stretches from the shores of the Black Sea and the Sea of Azov in the west to the Caspian Sea in the east. In this region a number of important archaeological cultures developed in the Early Bronze Age, among them that of Maikop. The Maikop culture occupied most areas of the North Caucasus, with a concentration of sites in the Kuban Valley and in the central part of the region, where, at present, about a dozen settlements and several hundred burials from kurgans (burial mounds) are known.

At the end of the nineteenth century Nikolai Ivanovich Veselovsky excavated a kurgan in the town of Maikop (now the capital of the Republic of Adygeya, Russian Federation) and two others near the village of Novosvobodnaya (also in Adygeya),[1] in which a wealth of precious artifacts were found. These early discoveries played an essential role in the development of archaeology in the North Caucasus. They also formed a basis for the cultural attribution of ordinary graves with similar burial rites. The spectacular finds from the graves at these sites remain an issue of continuous discussion. All scholars agree that the silver vessels, gold appliqués, beads, metal implements, and animal figurines from the Maikop burial, as well as related objects from the Staromyshastovskaya hoard, have parallels in the Near East. Some categories of artifacts, such as beads made of carnelian, turquoise, lapis lazuli, and meerschaum, undoubtedly were imported to the area, since those materials are not found in the North Caucasus but are known in Iran, Anatolia, and Central Asia. As for metal implements and vessels, the opinion prevails that they were produced locally, after Near Eastern models.[2]

When the study of the prehistoric sites in the North Caucasus began, the burials in the Maikop and Novosvobodnaya kurgans were considered to be contemporary on the basis of the contracted position in which all of the skeletons were interred; the presence of a red substance, reported to be cinnabar; the burial architecture (although the graves at Novosvobodnaya are built of stone slabs, and in the Maikop kurgan wood was used); and the similarity in the types of beads that were found. Later, however, the Novosvobodnaya burials were interpreted as representing the last stage of the Maikop culture. Some scholars have also suggested that Novosvobodnaya not only is later but represents a separate culture, with Central European roots.[3]

The date of the Maikop culture has been significantly revised during the last decades. To a great degree it depends on the chronology of the Near Eastern finds that seem to parallel objects from the North Caucasus. In the 1920s M. I. Rostovtzeff, having very limited material at hand, compared images on the Maikop silver vessels and gold appliqués (see cat. nos. 192, 194) to glyptic representations, as well as to bone and ivory articles from Egypt, Nubia, and Elam, which might point to a date in the fourth millennium B.C.[4] Close parallels between early Maikop pottery and metal implements and objects from Mesopotamia, Syria, and eastern Anatolia (specifically from Amuq F and Gawra XII–IX) support the early date. The presence in the North Caucasus of Near Eastern pottery types, similar in shape and surface appearance, has led some scholars to suggest a Near Eastern migration to the North Caucasus in the Late Uruk period.[5]

Radiocarbon analysis conducted in recent years has established an even earlier chronology for the Maikop culture, beginning in the early centuries of the fourth millennium B.C. According to this chronology the Maikop kurgan, representing a late phase of the culture, should be dated to the middle of the fourth millennium.[6] Nevertheless, according to our present knowledge, an analysis of materials cannot fully support such an early date. Comparisons with the Near East provide a range of dates from the late fourth through the third millennium B.C. Faceted, double-conoid, and ribbed, ball-shaped, gold beads found in Maikop-culture graves are comparable to beads from the Royal Cemetery at Ur. At the same time, burial finds in a Novosvobodnaya grave included a ribbed, ball-shaped bead and a copper-alloy spearhead similar to examples discovered in an

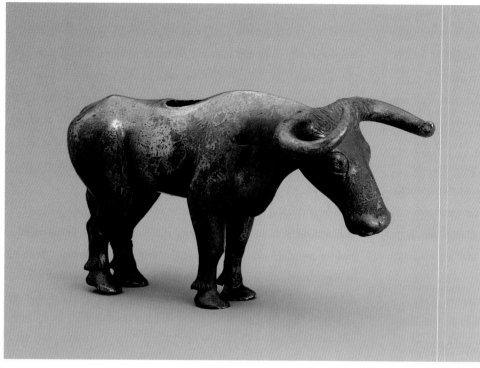

191b

eastern side of the main burial, between the remains of the skeleton and a collection of luxury vessels (see cat. nos. 192, 193) and parallel to one another, lay hollow gold and silver rods with the bull statuettes affixed to them. There were four bulls in all: two of gold and two of silver. All were cast from wax models with a secondary working of details over the casting. Their size and individual details demonstrate that they form two pairs, each of which includes one example in gold and one in silver.

According to the description by the excavator, Nikolai Ivanovich Veselovsky, all the bulls were threaded on the rods: the two gold on the half-silver, half-gold ones; the two silver on the silver ones. There were six of these rods in all. In addition to the four with bulls, there were also two rods, each half-gold and half-silver, that had nothing on them. Veselovsky believed that these objects "could be recognized as staffs, standards, or symbols of authority (scepters)." The upper parts of the rods end in a cap "with a spiral incision and slits." [2] A single intact rod with a cap and "threaded gold bull" has been preserved; its height is 112 centimeters.

It is difficult to determine precisely how many rods there were, but the number seems to have been about eight or ten. B.V. Farmakovsky, agreeing with the excavator, asserted that there were six and that they belonged to a single object; most likely "the six sticks made up the frame for a canopy." [3]   YP

1. They were previously published in *Otchet Imperatorskoi Arkheologicheskoi Kommissii* 1897, p. 5; Farmakovsky 1914, pl. 21; *From the Land of the Scythians* 1975, p. 97, no. 2; Barkova et al. 1984, p. 28, no. 1; and Karabelnik et al. 1993, pp. 34–35, nos. 5, 6.
2. Veselovsky 1897, pp. 51–52.
3. Farmakovsky 1914, pp. 53–56.

192

Vessel with incised decoration

Silver
H. 10.2 cm (4 in.); Weight 75 g
Late 4th–early 3rd millennium B.C.
North Caucasus, Maikop kurgan
The State Hermitage Museum, St. Petersburg, Russia 34-95

A sharp indentation separates the high conical neck of this vessel from its hemispherical body. The base is circular. The vessel was made by hammering. Encircling the body is a depiction of a procession of animals that, according to N. K. Vereshchagin, can be identified as possibly west Caucasian goats, aurochs, and, more than likely, cheetahs. [1] At the base of the neck is a band with a geometric pattern. On the bottom is an intricate, twelve-petaled rosette.

The vessel was found near the eastern wall of the Maikop kurgan's main chamber, among a group of silver and gold vases, the most

distinctive of which (see fig. 82) has the representation of a landscape on the neck. Depicted are three mountain ridges with two double peaks, trees, and a feeding bear; two rivers flow down the mountains and fall into a lake shown on the base of the vessel. On the body are two circles of animals, including a lion, a boar, a tarpan (?), west Caucasian goats, aurochs, and (in Vereshchagin's opinion) perhaps a saiga antelope. [2] Despite the stylistic similarity of the depictions on the two pictorial vessels, they appear to have been made by different artists, both working with a pointed tool.

Identifying parallels for the animal images has been a complicated task. Scholars have related them to creatures in Egyptian, Anatolian, and Mesopotamian art. [3] Also in dispute is whether the landscapes indicate a specific locale or a symbolic setting. B.V. Farmakovsky interpreted the composition here as "the symbolic depiction of a kingdom" in which "all life seems concentrated." [4] Despite this, he insisted that the artist had in mind the mountains and rivers of the Caucasian range. He identified the double-peaked mountains as the Elbrus and Kazbek, and the rivers as the Kuban and the Terek. Quite recently these ideas were revived by D. A. Machinsky, [5] who identifies the mountain peaks as the Elbrus, but as seen from two different sides, the north and the south. The two rivers—according to him, the Kuban and the Inguri—have their sources on different sides of the Caucasian ridge and fall into the same body of water, the Black Sea.

YP

1. Vereshchagin 1959, pp. 271, 281, 382.
2. Ibid., pp. 271, 329, 330, 358, 382. Some researchers believe that the animals are not intended to be "seen" in a single landscape zone (Korenevsky 1988, pp. 90–91), whereas others believe that the animals depicted together may have shared the same West Asian habitat at the same time (Baryshnikov). Piotrovsky 1994, pp. 88–89.
3. Farmakovsky (1914, pp. 61, 62) believed that the animals are similar to examples in Hittite art; however, he noted several parallels on monuments from Predynastic Egypt. In the opinion of Andreeva (1979, p. 34) the depictions are much closer to Egyptian and eastern Mediterranean renderings.
4. Farmakovsky 1914, pp. 73–75.
5. Machinsky 2000.

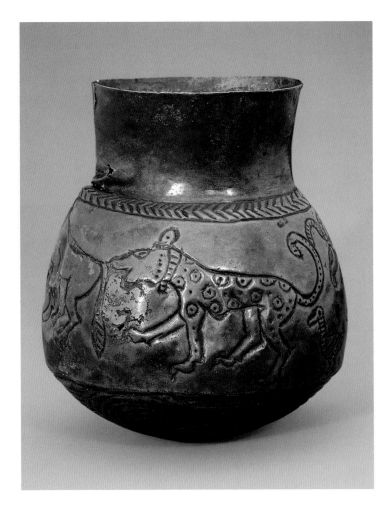

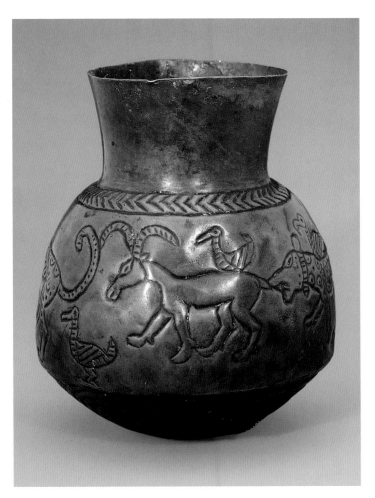

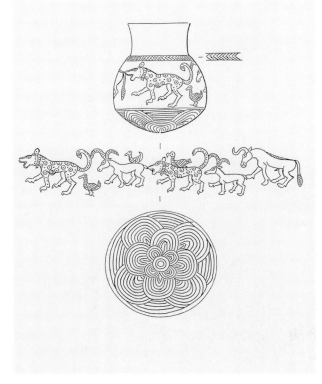

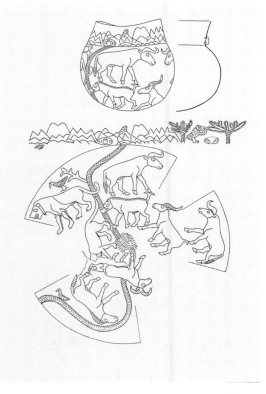

Fig. 81. Drawing of catalogue number 192 showing incised decoration.

Fig. 82. Drawing of a silver vessel with incised landscape and animal files. Maikop, late 4th–early 3rd millennium B.C. The State Hermitage Museum, St. Petersburg, 34-94.

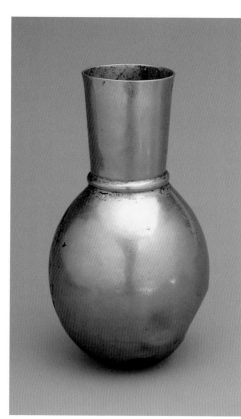

194a–d

Appliqués of lions, bulls, and rings

Gold and cinnabar
a. Large lions: L. 6 cm (2⅜ in.)
b. Small lions: L. 4.8 cm (1⅞ in.)
c. Bulls: L. 3.1 cm (1¼ in.)
d. Rings: Diam. 3.4 cm (1⅜ in.)
North Caucasus, Maikop kurgan
Late 4th–early 3rd millennium B.C.
The State Hermitage Museum, St. Petersburg,
Russia 34-30, 34-31, 34-32, 34-33

Gold appliqués in the form of lions and bulls, as well as rings, rosettes, and diadems (see cat. no. 195), were found in the Maikop kurgan along with gold, silver, carnelian, and turquoise beads (cat. no. 196).[1] All the animal-shaped appliqués were stamped and pierced along the edges for attachment to fabric. Thirty-seven are in the form of striding lions, facing either left or right. Some are well executed, and some are not. Other appliqués, also of poorer quality, are in the form of bulls facing right. Forty stamped gold appliqués are in the shape of rings, with openings made along the edges.

All the appliqués were found with the body in the main burial and, in the opinion of the excavator, Nikolai Ivanovich Veselovsky, must once have covered the attire of the deceased.[2] B.V. Farmakovsky, however, believed that the "folding sticks" of the canopy frame (see entry for cat. no. 191) and the "threaded-on gold figures that were found on the deceased probably represented adornments not of the clothing but rather of the light fabric of the canopy with which the deceased was evidently covered."[3]

YP

1. Some of these objects were previously published in *From the Land of the Scythians* 1975, p. 97, no. 1, pl. 2; Mohen and Piotrovsky 1979, pp. 128–29, nos. 106–8; and Barkova et al. 1984, pp. 28–29, nos. 2–4.
2. Veselovsky 1897, p. 51.
3. Farmakovsky 1914, pp. 53–54.

193

Vessel

Gold
H. 13.6 cm (5⅜ in.)
North Caucasus, Maikop kurgan
Late 4th–early 3rd millennium B.C.
The State Hermitage Museum, St. Petersburg,
Russia 34-89

This is one of two gold vessels found near the eastern wall of the main chamber of the Maikop kurgan, among formal metal cookware made of gold and silver.[1] It is of slender proportions, with an ovoid body and a high cylindrical neck that widens slightly and is separated from the body by a raised rib. The bottom is small in diameter and concave. The object, which the excavator called a pitcher, was shaped by hammering. The second vessel, which is small and shallow, Veselovsky described as a low vessel in the shape of a saltcellar.[2]

YP

1. The vessels were previously published in *From the Land of the Scythians* 1975, p. 97, no. 3, and Mohen and Piotrovsky 1979, pp. 128–29, no. 110.
2. *Otchet Imperatorskoi Arkheologicheskoi Kommissii* 1897, p. 6; Veselovsky 1897, p. 52.

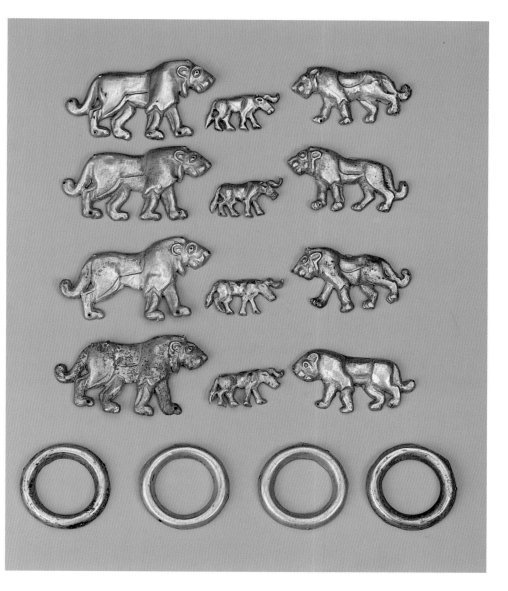

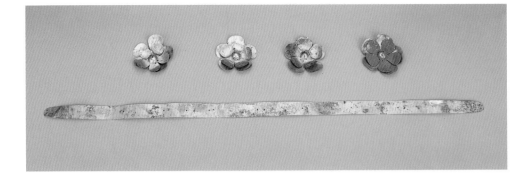

North Caucasus, Maikop kurgan
Late 4th–early 3rd millennium B.C.

a. Carnelian
L. 1.8–2.6 cm (¹¹⁄₁₆–1 in.); Diam. 0.5–1 cm (³⁄₁₆–³⁄₈ in.)
The State Hermitage Museum, St. Petersburg,
Russia 34-72

b. Turquoise
L. 0.4–1 cm (³⁄₁₆–³⁄₈ in.)
The State Hermitage Museum, St. Petersburg,
Russia 34-66

195a, b

Diadem and rosettes

Gold
a. Ribbon fillet: L. 34 cm (13³⁄₈ in.); W. 1.2 cm (½ in.)
b. Rosettes: H. 3.2–3.9 cm (1¼–1½ in.)
North Caucasus, Maikop kurgan
Late 4th–early 3rd millennium B.C.
The State Hermitage Museum, St. Petersburg,
Russia 34-35, 34-34

Ten gold rosettes were found in the Maikop burial, cut from gold leaf and each consisting of two layers of petals. The petals are not completely uniform in size and proportions. These ornaments have no direct parallels but may be related to multipetaled rosettes discovered in Uruk-period burials at Tepe Gawra, in northern Mesopotamia.

According to the excavator, Nikolai Ivanovich Veselovsky, the ten rosettes were found on the remains of the body buried in the southern part of the main grave, along with appliqués in the form of lions, bulls, and rings (see cat. no. 194) and numerous beads (see cat. no. 196). Two ribbonlike gold diadems were also found; these are pierced with pairs of openings at the ends as well as horizontally along the width. Veselovsky said that the bands were found with their wide side "on the back of the head, directly on the ground."[1] B.V. Farmakovsky associated the rosettes with the diadems.[2] He suggested that the small holes on the gold bands were used for attaching the rosettes, with five on each diadem. The diadems would have been sewn to a fabric headdress that narrowed at the top, analogous in form to the crowns worn by later Hittite and Assyrian kings.   YP

1. Veselovsky 1897, p. 51.
2. Farmakovsky 1914, p. 52.

The carnelian beads found in the Maikop kurgan include 5 large cylindrical examples and 2 that are barrel-shaped and elongated, 114 biconical beads, and 74 that are ring shaped. According to the excavator's description, gold, silver, carnelian, and turquoise beads were found along with the gold appliqués (cat. no. 194) in the main burial in the kurgan.[1] While other explanations have been offered, it is possible that all of these ornaments may have formed a complex, multipart chest adornment. Similar broad collars made of beads—known as *wesekh*—were widespread in Egypt. Scribes, officials, and priests who conducted funeral services were given them in recognition of special services.

The turquoise collection consists of both beads and pendants of various shapes and sizes. They include one flat oval with openings

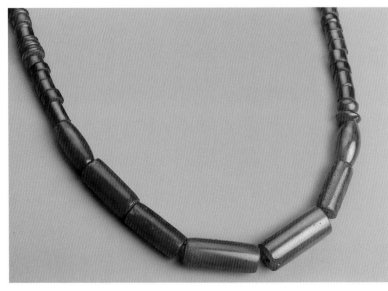

196a

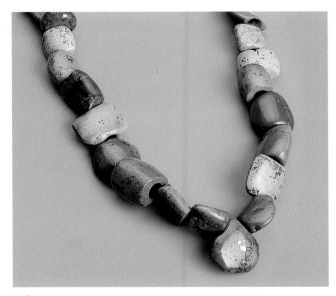

196b

lengthwise and crosswise; five flattened cylindrical beads; two three-sided examples, one in the form of a button; and twenty-four flat beads of irregular shape.   YP

1. Veselovsky 1897, p. 51.

197

String of beads

Gold
Each tube: L. 2 cm (¾ in.); Diam. 0.25 cm (⅛ in.)
Each flat disk bead: L. 1.7 cm (¹¹⁄₁₆ in.)
Twisted rod: L. 7.5 cm (3 in.)
Large ring: Diam. 2.8 cm (1⅛ in.)
North Caucasus, Novosvobodnaya, Kurgan 2, Burial 1
Mid-3rd millennium B.C.
National Museum of the Republic of Adygeya,
Maikop, Russia

These gold beads were discovered with a single body in a grave covered by a large mound some 6.5–8 meters in diameter.[1] They have been reconstructed into the necklace that consists of a twisted gold rod, six tubes formed from small rings, two large rings, and ten flat disk beads with a raised midrib. The latter were probably made by hammering two pieces of gold on either side of a central rod that was subsequently removed. Such beads have been widely recovered at sites from the Aegean to the Indus (see cat. nos. 120, 159, 280), and these examples demonstrate that the Caucasus region was part of the extensive trade network responsible for the spread of this bead form (see "Art and Interconnections in the Third Millennium B.C.," by Joan Aruz, in this catalogue). These flat beads, however, have a rounded, heart shape, which differs from the more widely distributed oval variety and may reflect local style.   PC

1. Rezepkin 2000, p. 52, pl. 22.

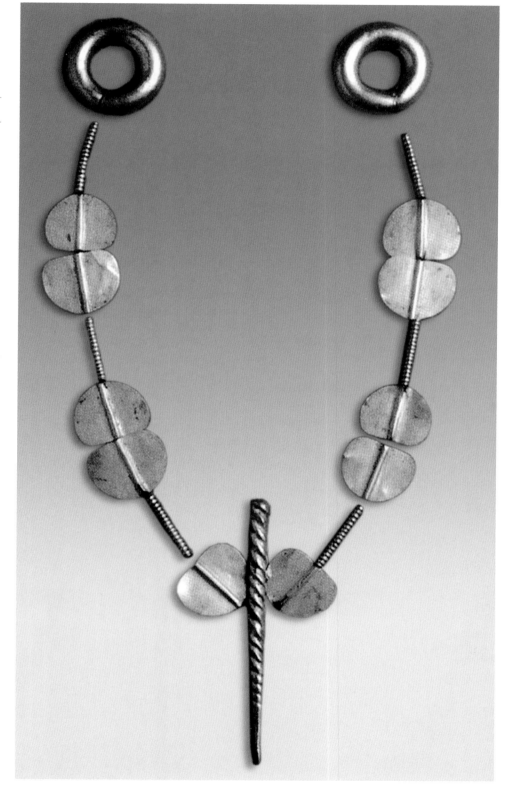

Novosvobodnaya

In 1898 Nikolai Ivanovich Veselovsky excavated two kurgans with megalithic tombs at the village of Tsarskaya (now Novosvobodnaya in the Republic of Adygeya).[1] The material from these tombs occupies the next chronological position after the cultural remains found in the Maikop kurgan.

Nearly a century later the Kuban Expedition of the Institute of Archaeology, Leningrad Branch, began excavating a group of kurgans situated four kilometers northwest of the village. Unearthed in 1979–80, Kurgan 31 occupies the northernmost position in a chain of eight large mounds extending from north to south (Kurgan 31 is 67 meters in diameter and 4.1 meters high).[2] When the mound was being formed, a circle of stones was laid down around Burial 5, a megalithic, two-chambered tomb covered with two stone slabs.

The first chamber toward the north measures 1.15 meters along the eastern and western walls and 1.18 and 1.26 meters, respectively, in width. The length of the second chamber is 1.96 meters, and the width at the front wall is 1.27 meters; the height of the chamber is 0.76–0.81 meters. Cut in the center of the front slab is a round hole with a diameter between 0.42 and 0.43 meters. There were two skeletons in Burial 5—a child under the age of seven and an adult. Dozens of objects, lying in two and three layers, filled the chamber.

YP

1. Otchet Imperatorskoi Arkheologicheskoi Kommissi 1898, pp. 33–35; Popova 1963.
2. Rezepkin 1991, pp. 167–97; Rezepkin 2000, pp. 62–67.

198a, b

Two-pronged hooks

Arsenical copper
a. H. 10.5 cm (4⅛ in.); W. 10.3 cm (4 in.); L. of socket 5 cm (2 in.); Diam. of socket 2 cm (¾ in.)
b. H. 8.4 cm (3¼ in.); W. 10.6 cm (4⅛ in.); L. of socket 4.6 cm (1¾ in.); Diam. of socket 1.6 cm (⅝ in.)
North Caucasus, Novosvobodnaya, Kurgan 31, Burial 5
Mid-3rd millennium B.C.
The State Hermitage Museum, St. Petersburg, Russia 2785/1, 2

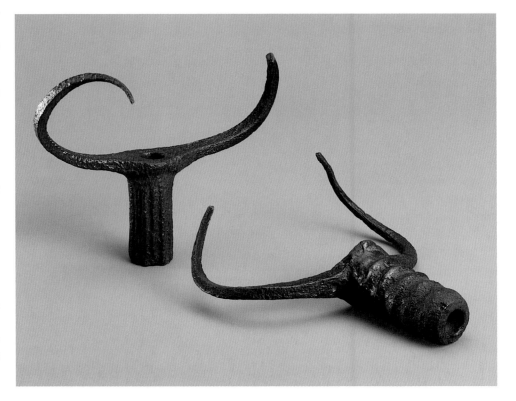

These enigmatic objects, which almost suggest a bucranial form, may be two-pronged hooks. They are solid-cast, and their central sockets, found in section, have horizontal and vertical scoring. The "hooks" were found in close proximity to a plate made of arsenical copper, probably household cookware, under which were placed animal bones. They may thus have been used in connection with food preparation. They were buried along with other functional items such as woodworking instruments and metalworking tools, as well as weapons and prestige items—precious metal vessels, jewelry, and ritual objects. Such an array of goods is typical of royal burials and probably symbolized the magnitude and power of the important personage who was entombed.

YP

Susa: Beyond the Zagros Mountains

The Zagros Mountains, which stretch from west of the Caspian Sea to the Gulf, divided the lowlands of Mesopotamia from the Iranian plateau but were not an insurmountable barrier to trade and communications. Passes, such as the one formed by the valley of the Diyala River, led through the mountains, giving dwellers in Mesopotamia access to resources and civilizations farther east. A very important site, where overland and sea routes converged, was Susa, at the southern end of the mountain chain. Lying on an eastern extension of the Mesopotamian plain, this city was often within the cultural and political orbit of Mesopotamian states. Akkadian and Ur III royal inscriptions emphasize Susa's importance as a starting point for both military and trading expeditions. The city acted as a gateway through the mountains to regions both east and north, but it also had southward connections to the waterway of the Gulf. Indeed, objects excavated at Susa reveal artistic traditions linking it with the Gulf, the Indus Valley, and western Central Asia.

PC

199

Standing male figure with clasped hands

Alabaster
H. 14.5 cm (5¾ in.); W. 5.8 cm (2¼ in.); Thickness 4 cm (1⅝ in.)
Iran, Susa, Acropole
Early Dynastic III, ca. 2550–2250 B.C.
Musée du Louvre, Département des Antiquités Orientales, Paris Sb 77

This statuette of an orant, or votive figure, is evidence that Susa was within the Sumerian sphere of influence during the Early Dynastic period, indicating that worshipers there observed the Mesopotamian custom of placing their images in the temple to perpetuate their prayers.[1] The figure has his hands joined in a devout attitude and wears a tufted garment, rendered in a stylized manner by two rows of thin strips. After 2500 B.C. a garment that left the right shoulder uncovered usually characterized men of princely or royal status (see cat. no. 88);[2] however, the quality of this statuette does not suggest a member of the elite. The combination of the geometrically stylized face, plaited hair, and clothing has been called "cubist" by Pierre Amiet and also appears in an earlier orant from Susa dating to the Late Uruk period.[3] The inlays of different materials for the eyes and eyebrows, so typical of Early Dynastic sculpture in Mesopotamia (see cat. no. 24), are absent here.

AB

1. For further reference, see Mecquenem 1911, p. 45, fig. 9; Le Breton 1957, p. 121, fig. 44(5); Amiet 1966, no. 132; Bahrani 1992, no. 50.
2. This can be observed on representations of king Ishqi-Mari and of king Enannatum on the Stele of the Vultures (fig. 52) as well as on two large statues from Susa; see Amiet 1966, nos. 141, 142.
3. The figure, from the first Archaic deposit, is dated to the Susa II period; see ibid., fig. 48.

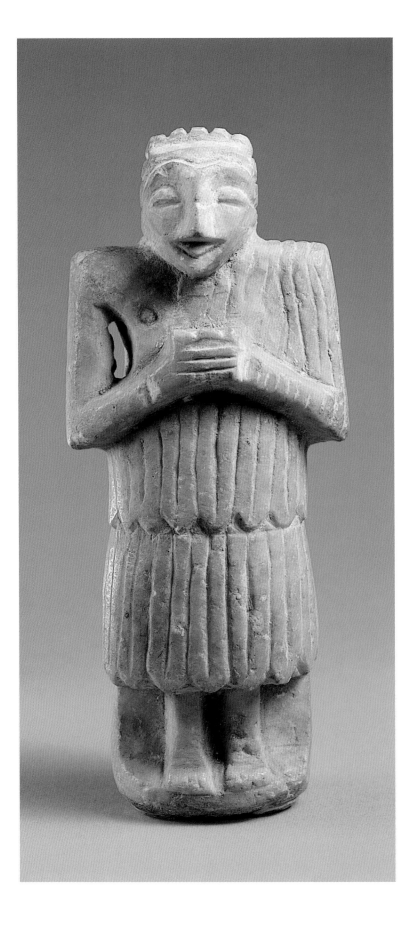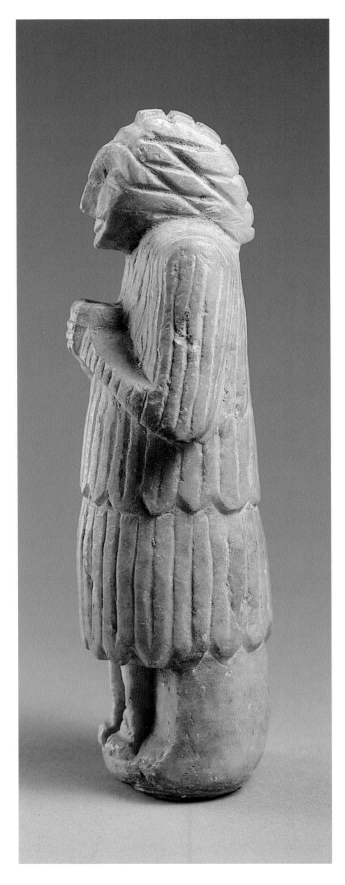

Wall plaque with banquet and animal attack scene

Alabaster
H. 17.6 cm (6⅞ in.); W. 16 cm (6¼ in.)
Iran, Susa, Acropole, Ninhursanga temple
Early Dynastic II, ca. 2650–2550 B.C.
Musée du Louvre, Département des Antiquités
Orientales, Paris Sb 41

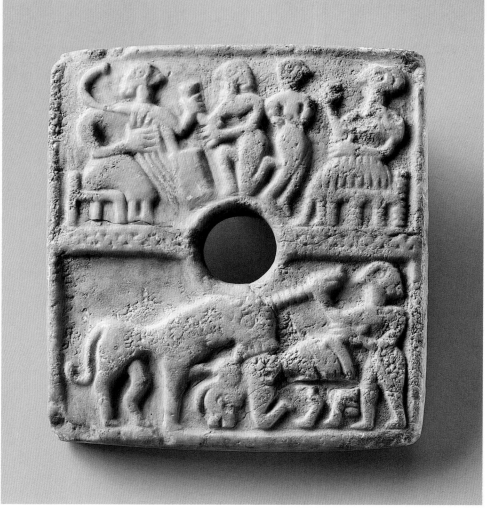

This plaque has a round central perforation and two registers sculpted in low relief.[1] The upper register depicts a banquet scene in which a man and a woman on low-backed seats both hold goblets. With her other hand the woman grasps the strings of a harp, which, oddly, is turned toward her.[2] Two nude attendants stand between the seated figures. On the lower register, a nude hero is stabbing the head of a lion with a weapon, possibly a dagger, as the lion attacks a bull kneeling in front of it.[3]

The banquet scene is a common motif on perforated plaques from Early Dynastic Mesopotamia (see cat. no. 32). The woman on this relief wears a long smooth robe; the man is dressed in a tufted garment, suggesting that the plaque dates to the Early Dynastic II period.[4] However, the resemblance between this plaque, found in Susa, and contemporaneous Mesopotamian plaques is only formal. A wealth of details in this example expresses a local style, especially the association of a banquet scene with one of animal combat (which are more common on seals than on perforated plaques) and the lack of symmetry in the composition. The animals, for example, would normally appear in a heraldic position, or at least opposite one another (see cat. no 55). In addition, the woman would hold a branch or an ear of grain, not a musical instrument, which is usually played by a servant (see cat. nos. 60b, c). The imbalance between the central figures above the perforation reveals the clumsiness of an artisan largely unfamiliar with this type of manufacture.[5] Conversely, the apparent equality between the sexes is a trait common to all perforated plaques, which, it is believed, were fasteners used to secure temple doors.[6]

AB

1. For further reference, see Mecquenem 1911, p. 47, fig. 12; Le Breton 1957, p. 121, fig. 45(10); Amiet 1966, no. 178; Boese 1971, pp. 47–50, no. 58, 193, pl. 24; Bahrani 1992, no. 51.
2. Usually the sound box, not the lyre, is turned toward the musician.

3. Bulls and lions were frequently paired in mythology beginning in the Late Uruk–Jamdat Nasr period, not only in relief on limestone vases but also on Proto-Elamite tablets. A bull submitting to a lion appears on one of the perforated plaques found in the Inanna temple in Nippur; see Hansen 1963, pl. 3.
4. The large pair of orants found with the repository of statues in the Abu temple in Eshnunna (modern Tell Asmar) exhibits the same distinction between masculine and feminine clothing; see Frankfort 1943, pp. 13–16, pls. 1–6. The same distinction is seen on banquet scenes on perforated reliefs; see Boese 1971, pls. 1, 3, 5, 9, 17.
5. Perforated plaques found at Susa are often incised; see Amiet 1966, figs. 125–27, 129.
6. Hansen 1963, pp. 145–66.

String of beads

Carnelian, lapis lazuli, zonate agate, rock crystal, calcite, glazed baked steatite, chlorite, faience, gold, copper alloy, and silver
Iran, Susa
Akkadian (?), ca. 2300–2159 B.C.
Musée du Louvre, Département des Antiquités
Orientales, Paris Sb 13099

Nothing is known about the context or discovery of this necklace,[1] which is a modern reconstruction. Roland de Mecquenem, the excavator of Susa, dated it on a label as being from the "twenty-fifth century B.C.," but it is more likely a later work, from the Akkadian period or even the Third Dynasty of Ur.

The necklace consists of eighty-seven beads made of diverse materials, primarily carnelian and lapis lazuli.[2] The combination of those two materials, common in the third millennium, is magnificently illustrated in the royal tombs

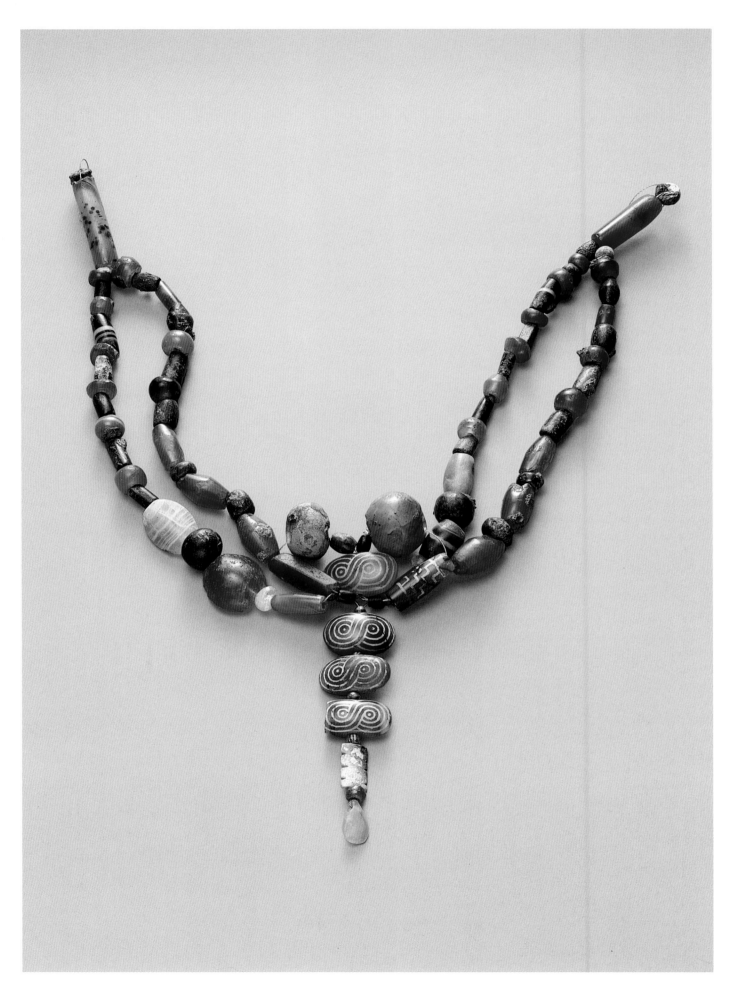

at Ur (see cat. nos. 62, 72–74). The carnelian, its beautiful translucent orange color attesting to the high quality of the stone, probably comes exclusively from the Indus region (see cat. no. 283). Five of the carnelian beads are engraved with a white alkali—four oval-shaped decorated with a guilloche pattern and one cylindrical bead decorated with a stepped motif. These belong to the well-known category of etched beads. The other carnelian beads are biconical, globular, and cylindrical. The lapis lazuli beads are generally cylindrical and globular. In addition to these two types of stone beads are three dark-colored and two light-colored beads in banded agate; two small rock crystal beads; one translucent blue-green calcite bead; a poorly preserved chlorite bead; and two glazed baked steatite beads, one a flattened globular bead that still bears traces of green glaze, the other rectangular and decorated with grooves on the long sides.[3] The latter steatite bead is identical to those on a necklace in the Louvre presumed to come from Central Asia.[4] Two minuscule round faience beads, produced using a related technique, are beside the two large cylindrical carnelian beads.

There are a few metal beads, including four small gold ones containing a high percentage of silver (almost 30 percent by mass) and copper (2 percent). We do not know whether these are intentionally manufactured alloys or electrum. The "copper" bead is now too corroded to determine which type of copper alloy it contains. Notably, coagulated silver chloride adheres to the surface of most of the stone or metal beads, indicating that silver beads were once present. These are now lost because the silver deteriorated in the soil, leaving the silver chloride as a by-product. It has not been possible to identify a few of the brown beads because of surface contamination by copper and silver.

In a study on the precious beads of the ancient Near East,[5] Françoise Tallon remarks that during the Akkadian period they became smaller, agate was used more frequently, and a bulkier bead hung from the center of necklaces. Here, the group of engraved oval carnelian beads takes the place of the heavy agate bead in the center. Although "the necklace found in Susa is a *testis unus* from which it is difficult to draw conclusions," we may nevertheless note the originality of this collection of beads in its great variety of materials and color.[6]   AB

1. Amiet 1986, pp. 144, 148, fig. 92b; Tallon 1995, no. 23.
2. This unconfirmed analysis of the materials was conducted by Benoît Mille and Anne Bouquillon

of the C2RMF using the particle accelerator (PIXE method); unpublished report of the C2RMF, no. R 3122 of September 18, 2002.
3. For the technique used to produce the steatite beads, see cat. no. 248.
4. SB 9373; see Amiet 1986, fig. 100.
5. Tallon 1995, p. 58.
6. Amiet 1986, p. 144.

202a–h

Vase à la cachette

Iran, Susa, Acropole
Early Dynastic IIIB, ca. 2400–2250 B.C.

a. Jar and lid
Fired clay and paint
Jar: H. 51 cm (20⅛ in.); Diam. 26 cm (10¼ in.)
Musée du Louvre, Département des Antiquités Orientales, Paris   Sb 2723, Sb 2723 bis

b. Open bracelet, spiral, and twisted rings
Copper alloy, gold, and silver
1. Bracelet: Diam. 4.6–6.8 cm (1¾–2⅝ in.)
2. Twisted ring: Diam. 2–2.3 cm (¾–⅞ in.)
3. Spiral: Diam. 4.6 cm (1¾ in.)
4. Ring: Diam. 1.9–2 cm (¾ in.)

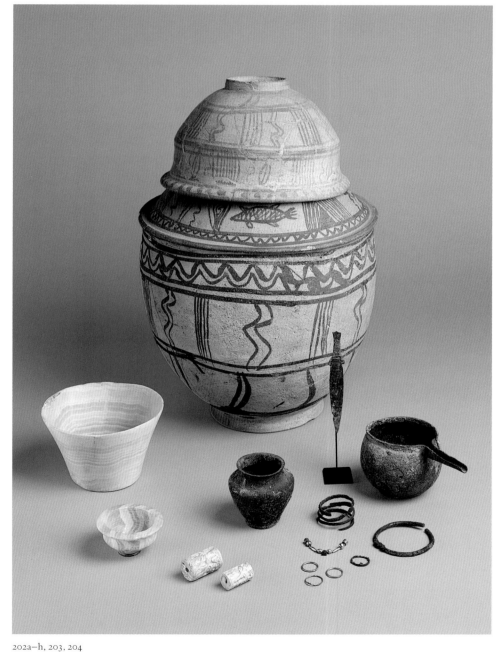

202a–h, 203, 204

Musée du Louvre, Département des Antiquités Orientales, Paris Sb 2723/61, Sb 2723/42, Sb 2723/40

c. Beads and connectors with a frog amulet
Gold, silver, and lapis lazuli
Beads: L. 0.3–1.3 cm (⅛–½ in.)
Frog amulet: L. 0.7 cm (¼ in.)
Musée du Louvre, Département des Antiquités Orientales, Paris Sb 2723/61-63

d. Cup
Alabaster
H. 4.1 cm (1⅝ in.); Diam. 7.5 cm (3 in.)
Musée du Louvre, Département des Antiquités Orientales, Paris Sb 2723/49

e. Truncated vessel
Alabaster
H. 9.7 cm (3⅞ in.); Diam. 15 cm (5⅞ in.)
Musée du Louvre, Département des Antiquités Orientales, Paris Sb 2723/47

f. Carinated vessel with ring base
Copper alloy
H. 7.5 cm (3 in.); Diam. 7.5 cm (3 in.)
Musée du Louvre, Département des Antiquités Orientales, Paris Sb 2723/26

g. Globular vessel with open spout
Copper alloy
H. 8.1 cm (3¼ in.); Diam. 9.4 cm (3¾ in.)
Musée du Louvre, Département des Antiquités Orientales, Paris Sb 2723/25

h. Dagger
Arsenical copper
L. 13.2 cm (5¼ in.)
Musée du Louvre, Département des Antiquités Orientales, Paris Sb 2723/12

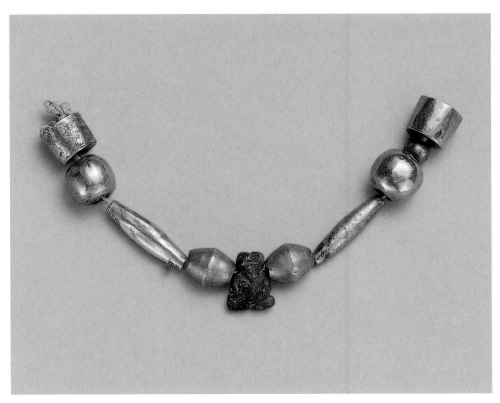

202c

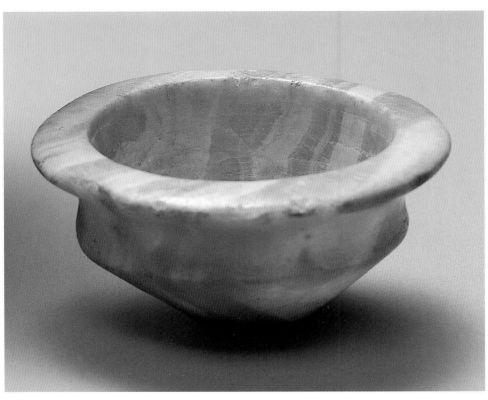

202d

During the period when Sumerian civilization flourished, the region of Susiana fell into decline. The discovery at Susa of a treasure known as the *vase à la cachette* is thus all the more important.[1] The objects presented here were initially assembled within two ceramic vases: the first, which has disappeared, was undecorated and, in accordance with an Indus Valley tradition, was covered with a round copper plate. The second vessel, seen here, is accompanied by a ceramic cover and constitutes a corrupted version of Susian second-style ceramic.[2] Its principal painted motif is a large spread-winged bird protecting its nestlings.[3] The vessel contained a variety of items, including forty-eight manufactured copper or bronze objects; five large plano-convex copper ingots containing small percentages of arsenic and nickel; three gold rings; a ring composed of three twisted circles of gold, silver, and copper; seven gold beads and two gold connectors; one minuscule lapis lazuli frog; eleven veined alabaster vases; one glazed shard; thirteen small stones; and six cylinder seals.[4]

The typology of the metal objects in the *vase à la cachette* varies widely. Although inspired in part by forms from Mesopotamia and Luristan, the goods are less rich than those from the royal tombs at Ur and less exuberant than those from Luristan. The homogeneous composition of

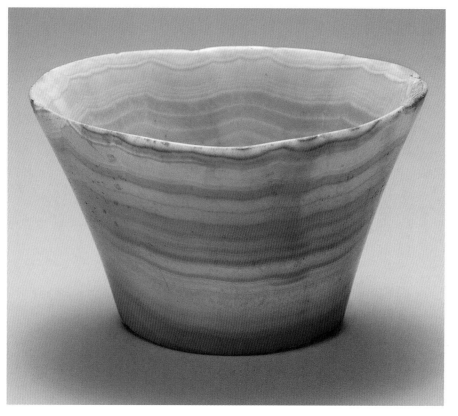

202e

the copper in all of the objects, including the ingots, indicates that they were a coherent set from a single era.[5] The copper, naturally alloyed with arsenic, is from Oman (ancient Magan) and reflects a climate of exchange with the Gulf that existed in the third millennium B.C. The tools, containers, ornaments, and weapons in the find were commonly made of copper.[6] The shapes of the two metal vessels displayed here (cat. nos. 202f, g) are an earlier type. The carinated vase and four other objects are made of copper combined with tin, a technological innovation that was a rarity at the time.[7] The bracelet is in the form of a simple ring. The spiral is unique at Susa, but several are known to have existed at Tepe Hissar.[8] The dagger is of a type specific to Iran.

The dearth of precious materials in the *vase à la cachette* is surprising considering the large quantities of gold and lapis lazuli in

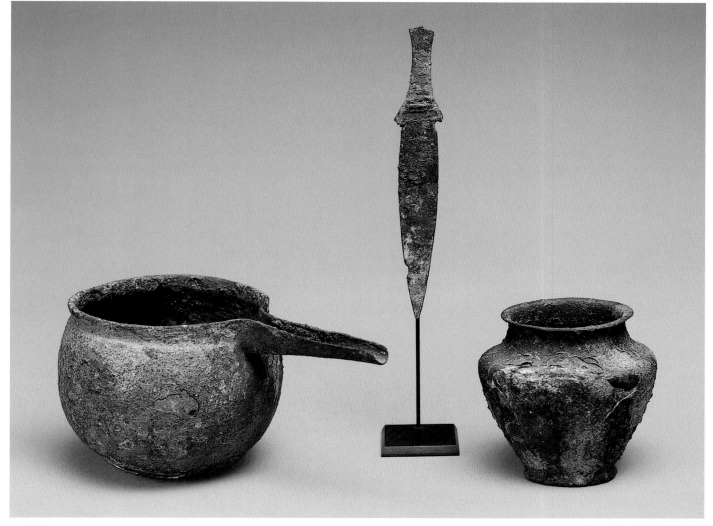

202g,h,f

southern Mesopotamia, which was fairly close by. We have only a minuscule lapis lazuli frog and a few spherical, tapered, and biconical rings and beads made from gold alloyed with a large percentage of silver. The two gold connectors anticipate a fashion that would develop in the following period.

The alabaster vases in the hoard were not manufactured locally. They are made of a high-quality, almost transparent material rich in yellow and white veins, which the sculptor skillfully used to excellent effect. Susian artisans, in contrast, used a fairly crude material, found in abundance in funerary contexts. Two centers of eastern Iran specialized in such luxury goods: Shahr-i Sokhta in Seistan, and Shahdad in the Dasht-i Lut.[9] Vessels similar in form were also found at Ur. Indeed, Susa seems to have acted as an intermediary between Mesopotamia and the trans-Elamite world for the production of alabaster objects.[10]

The primary importance of the small faience shard is that its original glaze is preserved almost intact. Its intense blue-green color makes it possible to imagine the original color of the glazed steatite beads (see cat. no. 248).

The heterogeneous content of the *vase à la cachette* points to Susa's relations with distant regions, particularly the Indus Valley, eastern Iran, and the Gulf. The large quantity of metal and the recast objects, such as the ingots and the adze fragments, suggest the original owner of the vase was an itinerant merchant and metallurgist. For some unknown reason, he must have hidden his treasure and never reclaimed it. According to Pierre Amiet, the find could also represent "a tribute paid by vassals" or a collection assigned a monetary value.[11] The thirteen stones could be late accounting tokens derived from the *calculi* system of the Uruk period (see "Uruk and the Formation of the City," by Hans J. Nissen, in this catalogue). AB

1. For further reference on the *vase à la cachette*, see Mecquenem 1912, p. 144, no. 287; Morgan 1912, fig. 117; Mecquenem 1934, pp. 189–90, fig. 21; Le Breton 1959, pp. 117–20; Amiet 1986, pp. 125–27; Tallon 1987, vol. 1, pp. 328–33, vol. 2, nos. 1075, 1086, 1107–10, 1165–69, 103, 781, 794; and Benoit 2003, p. 36. For the seals, see Delaporte 1920, pls. 30(5). S.410, 31(7); and Amiet 1980, nos. 1018, 114.
2. This name is given to painted ceramic from third-millennium Susa to distinguish it from the style of Susa I.
3. This motif was also transposed onto bitumen vases; see cat. no. 241b.
4. A milking scene on one of these is also found contemporaneously on inlaid friezes from Kish (see cat. no. 51b) and in the temple of Tell al Ubaid (fig. 14).
5. Tallon 1987, vol. 1, p. 330.
6. These include a mortise, chisel, saw, pruning knife, strainer, pan of scales, rod, adzes, and a unique spade; cups, bowls, and carinated vases; a mirror with a handle, bracelets, rings, and beads; and flat or curved axes and daggers.
7. Only four objects contain more than 7 percent tin: the strainer, two vases, and a flat adze.
8. Schmidt 1937, pl. 28B.
9. Ciarla 1979, pp. 319–35. The author insists the artisans of Shahr-i Sokhta preferred a polychromatic to a monochromatic material.
10. See Casanova 1991, p. 90.
11. Amiet 1986, p. 126.

203

Cylinder seal with a contest scene, from the *vase à la cachette*

Alabaster
H. 4 cm (1⅝ in.); Diam. 2.5 cm (1 in.)
Iran, Susa, Acropole
Early Dynastic IIIA, ca. 2550–2400 B.C.
Musée du Louvre, Département des Antiquités
Orientales, Paris   Sb 2723/60

This finely carved seal depicts an antelope with ringed horns being attacked by a rearing lion. A second lion crosses behind the first and attacks a bovine that turns its head back. Beside this group, a nude hero, with separate locks of hair standing on end, typical of the period, grasps the tail of the antelope with one hand and with the other hand stabs it with a dagger. The small globular elements, such as the eyes and edges of the lions' muzzles, were made with a drill.

Contest scenes between heroes, animals, and mythological creatures remained popular throughout the Early Dynastic III period; however, the composition of the figures changed over time. Originally the scene was a continuous frieze, but later groups were separated to form truncated pyramids. The finest of this later style is well illustrated by seals discovered in the royal graves at Ur (cat. no. 55a). This seal, which was found among the objects in the *vase à la cachette* (see cat. no. 202), is very similar to examples known from Ur, and it may have come originally from southern Mesopotamia.[1]

AB

1. See, for example, Collon 1987, pp. 28–29, no. 83.

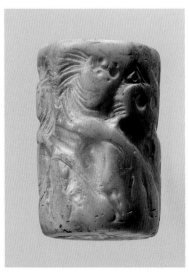

203

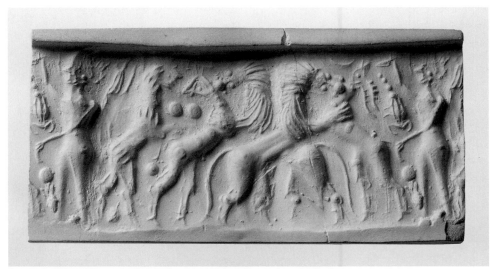

Impression from catalogue number 203.

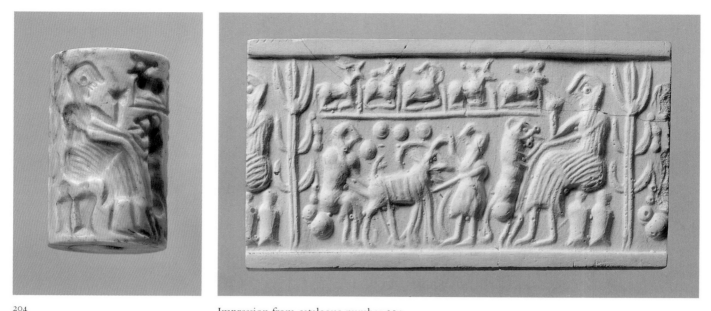

204

Impression from catalogue number 204.

204

Cylinder seal with a milking scene, from the *vase à la cachette*

Shell
H. 3.2 cm (1¼ in.); Diam. 1.9 cm (¾ in.)
Iran, Susa, Acropole
Early Dynastic IIIA, ca. 2550–2400 B.C.
Musée du Louvre, Département des Antiquités
Orientales, Paris Sb 2723/58

The cylinder seals in the hoard from Susa called *vase à la cachette*—with their variety of materials, styles, imagery, and dates of manufacture—further emphasize the importance of this collection of objects as evidence for interconnections. Four of the cylinders look Mesopotamian (see cat. no. 203), while the other two reflect relations with the Gulf and the Indus Valley.[1]

This seal, finely worked in shell, has turned green from contact with the objects in the hoard that were made of copper, a material that is associated in the ancient texts with the land of Magan (identified with the Oman Peninsula). Stylistically the seal is quite unusual, suggesting that it may be a local product. Although carved with a distinctive use of the drill, characteristic of Early Dynastic IIIA glyptic in Mesopotamia, the bold design with

sharply cut figures recalls the style of seals from the Gulf region (see cat. no. 218).[2] On the Susa cylinder, framing a two-register scene (when rolled to show the intended design), is a tall stalk of grain resembling millet or sorghum.[3] The latter has parallels on the lower register of the famous cult vessel from Uruk (figs. 9, 10). The main scenes—of animal husbandry and a very docile lion or a dog before a large seated figure—are represented below a row of recumbent goats. A standing figure wearing a tufted short garment steadies a goat while the animal is milked by a man seated behind it. The large figure, bearded and holding a cup, is seated on two milk jars and wears a long striated (tufted?) garment. The upright attendant animal appears to paw and lick him.

Scenes of milking and dairy production with figures seated behind cows are common in the art of Syria and Mesopotamia during the Early Dynastic period, particularly on the inlaid friezes from Kish and al Ubaid (see cat. no. 51b; fig. 14). The latter frieze is from a temple dedicated to Ninhursanga, the goddess of wild and herd animals and the "birthgiver and nurturer" of humans.

Another seal in the Susa deposit contains iconographic features that derive from a

source farther east. It is engraved with the image of a zebu facing a striding lion.[4] In its posture the zebu resembles the short-horned bulls with heads lowered over troughs found in Harappan glyptic. This is also the most common image on the circular stamp seals, which are thought by some scholars to have been made specifically for Meluhha (probably Indus) trade in the Near East; examples have been found in Mesopotamia, the Gulf, and Susa (see cat. nos. 301d, e).   JA

1. For the Mesopotamian-style cylinder seals, see Delaporte 1920, pls. 14:12 (S.37), 30:5 (S.410, no. 203 in this catalogue), 31:7 (S.434), 32:12 (S.459). For one cylinder that probably reflects connections with the Indus Valley, see ibid., pl. 27:4 (S.348). For the present seal, cat. no. 204, see Aruz 1992, pp. 108–9, no. 40, and Delaporte 1920, pl. 33:2 (S. 464).
2. For other examples also with Mesopotamia-derived imagery, see Amiet 1986, pl. 279:6,7.
3. Victoria John of the Brooklyn Botanic Garden has made this tentative identification of the plant. For the identification of the stalks on the Uruk vase, see Crawford 1991b, p. 44.
4. Delaporte 1920, pl. 27:4 (S.348).

For additional objects from Susa, see catalogue numbers 273, 292.

THE GULF: DILMUN AND MAGAN

D. T. POTTS

Mesopotamian cuneiform inscriptions of the late third and early second millennia B.C., which refer to the Gulf as the "Lower Sea," distinguish between two lands along the Arabian coast. The first, Dilmun, in the central Gulf, encompassed Bahrain and the mainland opposite it; the second, Magan, in the lower Gulf, extended across what are today the United Arab Emirates and the Sultanate of Oman (the region is sometimes called the Oman Peninsula).[1] Modern archaeologists, however, generally refer to the Bronze Age material culture of Bahrain as the Barbar culture, and they divide the third-millennium remains of the Oman Peninsula into two cultures or periods: the Hafit (about 3000–2500 B.C.) and the Umm an-Nar (about 2500–2000 B.C.). The names Barbar, Hafit, and Umm an-Nar are those of important sites in these areas, which were inhabited during the periods in question.

Bahrain has been the subject of archaeological investigation since the late nineteenth century, when the thousands of burial mounds that are such a prominent feature of the landscape in the northern part of the main island first attracted attention.[2] Over the years hundreds of tombs have been excavated on Bahrain by both foreign and local archaeologists.[3] The principal settlement throughout all periods of Bahrain history is the great mound (700 by 400 meters; 8 meters high) situated on the north-central coast of the main island. Known today as Qalat al-Bahrain, the site was established about 2300–2200 B.C.[4] Another important settlement, one with a remarkably regular pattern of houses, is located nearby, at the site of Saar.[5] And a major temple complex, the so-called Barbar temple, lies near the modern village of Barbar.[6] Established in the late third millennium B.C., it consisted originally of a shrine situated atop a trapezoidal platform (23–25 by 15–17 meters; about 2 meters high) erected on a low mound sloping in a southwesterly direction toward one of Bahrain's many natural artesian springs.[7] We know from Mesopotamian cuneiform inscriptions that Enzak was the principal deity of Dilmun; however, no epigraphic evidence has been found either at Barbar or in the slightly later temple at Saar that identifies the deities worshiped at those sites. It has been suggested that the square stone enclosure around the Barbar spring, with steps leading down to the water, is a representation of the mythical *abzu,* or body of freshwater, that the Sumerians believed lay under the earth's surface—an idea based on the purely speculative suggestion that the Barbar temple was sacred to the Sumerian deity Enki.[8]

Although rich in artesian water and noted for its date gardens, the land of Bahrain is not a significant source of exportable goods. Nevertheless, according to Mesopotamian sources Dilmun was able to supply its trading partners with timber, copper, tin, ivory, and other materials that must have come from farther afield. Thus, like the modern port of Dubai, the region grew wealthy by selling goods acquired from the Indus Valley (for example, ivory), Magan (copper), and Afghanistan (tin) to the temples and merchant houses of Sumerian cities such as Lagash and Ur.

During the late third millennium B.C. Mesopotamia imported from Magan much copper, soft stone (steatite and chlorite), and diorite (a hard black stone favored in Lagash by the sculptors of Gudea's statues, for example). The ophiolite of Oman was a rich source of all these materials. Settlement throughout Magan was dispersed, and late-third-millennium-B.C. towns have been found from Ras al-Jins on the southeastern coast of Oman to Umm an-Nar Island off the western coast of the modern emirate Abu Dhabi. Tell Abraq, from which many of the Gulf finds in this exhibition derive, was one of the principal towns of ancient Magan at this time.[9] Located on the arid coast of the emirates Umm al-Qaiwan and Sharjah, it was a settlement of palm-frond houses, or *barastis,* scattered around a circular fortress about forty meters in diameter built of mud brick faced with stone. Excavations at Tell Abraq from 1989 to 1998 showed that the inhabitants of the settlement kept domesticated sheep, goats, and cattle; ate locally available fish and shellfish; and cultivated date gardens, in the shade of which they grew wheat and barley.[10] The sustainability of a settlement in this area was based on the relative abundance of freshwater, tapped at Tell Abraq by at least one well contained within the fortification.

The casting of copper and bronze was practiced extensively at the site, the tin coming in all probability from sources in southern Afghanistan.[11] Links with other parts of the Near East and Central and South Asia are illustrated by a wide array of imported finds, including weights, beads, ivory objects, and pottery from the Indus Valley; ivory combs (cat. no. 212), ceramics, and possibly other precious goods (cat. no. 210) from Bactria (northern Afghanistan and southern Uzbekistan); ceramics from Baluchistan (cat. no. 216), Elam (southwestern Iran), and southern Mesopotamia; and seals from Elam and Dilmun. The high incidence of bronze found at Tell Abraq highlights the movement of tin—one of the most important commodities traded in the late third millennium—and it is possible that many of the other foreign goods found at Tell Abraq accompanied this important metal.

Much of the evidence for foreign contacts at Tell Abraq comes from a collective tomb, six meters in diameter, used at the very end of the third millennium.[12] Collective burial, in which most or all of the members of a community were buried together in one large freestanding stone structure, was the norm in the Oman Peninsula during this period. These so-called Umm an-Nar tombs are named after the island near Abu Dhabi City, where they were first excavated. At least 394 individuals were buried in the tomb at Tell Abraq, and although many such tombs in the other communities that dotted the landscape of ancient Magan were robbed in antiquity, long before archaeologists excavated them, it is likely that comparable burial figures obtained there, too.

It is interesting that burial customs and most probably social organization, as well, differed in Dilmun and Magan. In Dilmun individual burial—in a large mound or within stone chambers clustered in a group (perhaps representing family cemeteries) beneath a single mound—was the norm. In Magan, however, collective burial was universally practiced during the third millennium. Thus, a "collective mentality" may have distinguished the society of Magan from the very mercantile, more literate society of Dilmun, where the individual seems to have played a greater role. This may reflect the difference between a tribal society (Magan) and an urbanized, commercial society (Dilmun).

Both Dilmun and Magan controlled natural resources that were in demand in the cities of southern Mesopotamia. For the most part peaceful trade provided those cities with what they wanted from the lands of the Lower Sea, but we also know that at least two military expeditions were sent out from Akkad against Magan, and that at least one king of Magan sent gold dust as tribute to Ur during the Ur III period. Beyond these few facts, however, our knowledge of political relations between Dilmun and Magan and their northern neighbors is imprecise at best.

1. D. Potts 1990.
2. Rice 1983.
3. See, for example, Ibrahim 1982; Mughal 1983; Srivastava 1991; and Lombard 1999.
4. Højlund and Andersen 1994; Højlund and Andersen 1997.
5. Crawford, Killick, and Moon 1997.
6. Mortensen 1986.
7. Andersen 1986.
8. Ibid.
9. D. Potts 2000.
10. On the inhabitants' fish and shellfish diet, see Stephan 1995; M. Uerpmann 2001. On their cultivation of dates, wheat, and barley, see Willcox and Tengberg 1995.
11. See Weeks 1997 and Weeks 1999.
12. Potts and Weeks 1999.

Handle in the shape of a standing male figure

Copper alloy
H. 13.5 cm (5⅜ in.)
Gulf region, Bahrain, Barbar temple IIA
Late 3rd–early 2nd millennium B.C.
Bahrain National Museum, Manama

This male figure was found with a group of copper-alloy objects deposited within a temple complex excavated on the island of Bahrain. This deposit, which included representations of a long-necked bird and a bull's head (cat. no. 206), was placed in a square pit located in the northeastern corner of a raised courtyard within the center of the sacred site.[1] As suggested by its compact outline and the holes drilled in the splayed section below its feet, this figure served as a handle for another object, such as a mirror, that is now lost. The fact that he is nude and clean shaven, with his hands deferentially clasped against his chest, suggests that this object may have been made for use in a sacred context.

Located off the western shore of the Gulf, the island of Bahrain—known in ancient texts as Dilmun—was an important trading center through which resources were supplied to Mesopotamia from lands to the south and east. The rich interplay of materials and cultures facilitated by this entrepôt is reflected in this figure. Cast in a copper alloy by the lost-wax technique, it may have been produced in Central Asia, where several handled mirrors have been found.[2] The use of the figure as a foundation deposit within a temple complex comparable in design to those found in Sumer also indicates Dilmun's close cultural connections with Mesopotamia.[3]   J-FL

1. See D. Potts 1990, pp. 192ff.
2. For bibliography and comparisons of this object, see ibid., p. 205. See also Pittman 1984, p. 39.
3. See Andersen 1986, pp. 165–77.

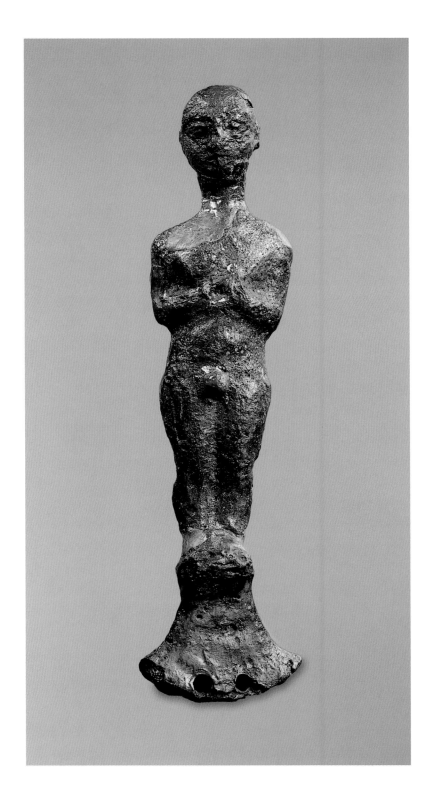

Copper Alloys and Metal Sources

Although copper extraction and refining began well before the third millennium B.C., *it was during this period that copper production greatly increased, as evidenced by numerous textual references to metal procurement, alloying, and classification. This written evidence, along with the examination of objects and industrial debris using modern analytical techniques and the information obtained from geological surveys, has been employed in an attempt to chart the development of copper production, beginning with the location of ore sources. Although these studies have provided few conclusive results, they have demonstrated the extraordinary skill of ancient metalworkers in exploiting available resources and the importance of long-distance trade in disseminating technological discoveries.*[1]

Without the benefit of chemical analysis, ancient copper objects were for many years frequently classified as bronze. Bronze, by its primary definition, is an alloy whose main constituents are copper and tin. It has advantages over pure copper in terms of producing cast objects, including a lower melting point and a greater liquidity when molten because of a decreased oxidation of the copper.[2] *The addition of tin raises the hardness of the final metal, a crucial factor in the manufacture of tools and weapons before the advent of iron alloys. Tin also imparts a golden color to the alloy that may have been desirable for certain types of objects.*[3]

Although the existence of bronze in Mesopotamia is attested both in texts and in objects dated to the beginning of the Early Dynastic period, this alloy did not become consistently used in the Near East until the middle of the second millennium B.C. *(see, however, "The Gulf: Dilmun and Magan," by D. T. Potts, in this catalogue). Prior to that time a significant percentage of metal objects were made using essentially unalloyed copper or arsenical copper alloys. Arsenic is found as a natural impurity in the copper sulfide ores that were mined during that period, and the fairly low arsenic concentrations often found suggest that arsenic formed a natural alloy with copper when the ore was refined. Since arsenic provided some of the same benefits as tin, copper ores containing arsenic may have been purposefully exploited even before the concept of alloying was known. After that time, it is possible that arsenic ores were added intentionally during the smelting process.*[4]

The slow adoption of bronze was at least partly a result of the limited availability of tin.[5] *In comparison with iron and, to a lesser extent, copper, deposits of tin oxides are relatively rare. In addition,*

tin is not associated with copper ore bodies beyond trace amounts. It is generally thought that tin was obtained from alluvial deposits in what is now Afghanistan, a region that also appears to have been the primary source of lapis lazuli and possibly gold. Like these other rare materials, tin may have been traded initially as a precious commodity and used in the production of highly valued objects.[6] *Archaeological evidence of tin mining in Anatolia during the Early Bronze Age indicates that this region may have served as an early—if indirect—source of tin.*[7] *In any case, it is likely that the earliest experimentation with bronze alloys occurred near the source of tin ores rather than in Mesopotamia proper, where the supply of tin remained dependent on long-distance trade.*

The main sources of copper ore were in the mountainous regions surrounding Mesopotamia. Mines in Iran, particularly the Anarak region where the Talmessi mine is located, and in Oman, which has been identified with the land known as Magan in ancient texts, were important suppliers of smelted copper that needed to be further refined prior to use. Mesopotamian texts also indicate that copper was obtained from Meluhha, "land of the east," which may have received partially refined metal from mines in Central Asia. Dilmun—modern Bahrain—was well situated to serve as a mediator in the copper trade, a role that became increasingly important in the late third and early second millennium. There were also numerous copper mines in Anatolia that were crucial to the early development of metalworking in that region.[8]

J-FL

1. For an excellent and comprehensive review of the literature on mining, refining, and fabrication of copper-alloy objects, see Moorey 1994, pp. 240–79.
2. Since lead also lowered the melting point and facilitated casting, it was occasionally added to cast bronze alloys during this period, although usually not in high concentrations. Lead was never added to metal that was to be worked by hammering, as it reduced the malleability of the metal.
3. Bronze alloys may have been prized for their prestige value during the third millennium before their later, more widespread adoption for practical applications. See Stech and Pigott 1986, pp. 39–64.
4. At this time, it is not possible to distinguish between natural and intentional arsenical copper alloys, although high arsenic content would seem to indicate the latter. See Charles 1967, pp. 21–26.
5. The seminal study on the problem of tin is Muhly 1973. See also Franklin, Olin, and Wertime 1978.
6. See Muhly 1985, pp. 275–91, and Stech and Pigott 1986, pp. 45–46.
7. See Yener 1989, pp. 200–203, and a contrasting view in Hall and Steadman 1991, pp. 217–34.
8. See de Jesus 1980. Although it is possible that some Cypriot copper may have entered the Near East via Levantine ports, this source did not become important to the region until much later. See Muhly et al. 1992.

Bull's head

Copper alloy
H. 18 cm (7⅛ in.); Diam. of horns 15 cm (5⅞ in.)
Gulf region, Bahrain, Barbar temple IIA
Late 3rd–early 2nd millennium B.C.
Bahrain National Museum, Manama 517.FJ

This magnificent bull's head is the most celebrated object from the Dilmun culture. The
animal's cranium is strongly modeled, with a
groove and a low ridge highlighting the
depressions that form the nostrils and emphasizing the flat snout. Surrounding the snout,
and further accentuating it, is a double band.
Cutouts indicate the eyes and the earholes,
which are formed from flat pieces of metal
extending from the side of the face to the
horns. A wide band across the top of the head
and between the horns is decorated with
parallel lines that have diagonal incisions slanting down from left to right. The horns of the
bull describe a low curve and, before meeting
over the head, turn back to point almost
straight up.

The head was found beneath the floor of
the temple at Barbar, part of a hoard of objects
including the anthropomorphic mirror handle
discussed in catalogue number 205. Although
Level IIA dates to the Isin-Larsa period
(2017–1763 B.C.), the hoard contained objects
from earlier times. This bull's head has been
compared to the Early Dynastic Mesopotamian
examples from Ur, Khafajah, al Ubaid, and
Tello,[1] and is particularly close in style to the
silver head of a horned animal from the
cemetery at Ur.[2] Peder Mortensen has noted,
however, that the horns closely parallel those
of bulls and bull-men on cylinder seals from
the Late Akkadian (see cat. no. 146) and Ur III
periods.[3] In fact, this bull's head derives from a
long and widespread tradition; similar examples
have been found from Mesopotamia through
the Gulf region to southern Turkmenistan.[4]
It is unclear if it was manufactured locally or
came to Bahrain through the extensive network
of trade routes that converged on the island.

PC

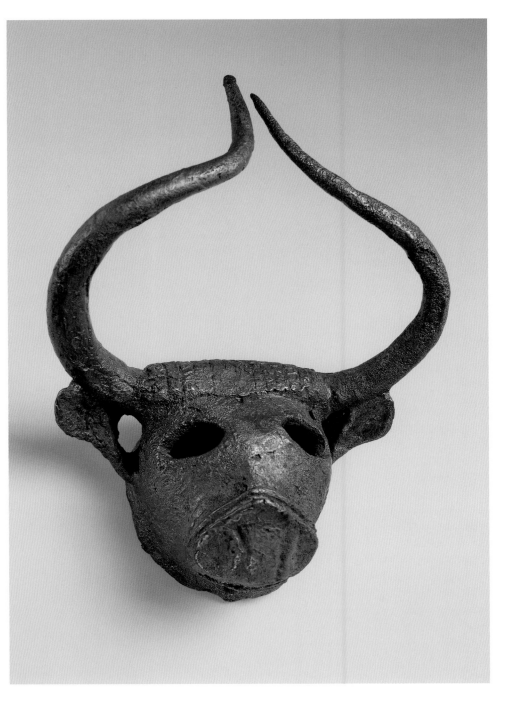

1. During Caspers 1971, pp. 217–24.
2. Zettler and Horne 1998, p. 63, no. 9.
3. Mortensen 1986, p. 184.
4. Masson 1976, pp. 14–19.

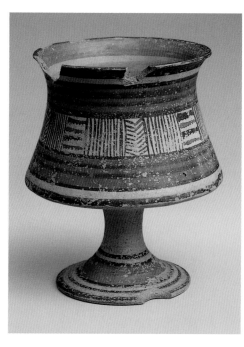

208

String of etched carnelian beads

L. 22 cm (8⅝ in.)
Gulf region, Bahrain, Hamad Town
Late 3rd–early 2nd millennium B.C.
Bahrain National Museum, Manama

Ancient Dilmun—on the maritime route between the Indus Valley and Mesopotamia—acted as an intermediary for the westward transfer of raw and finished materials from the Harappan world, such as carnelian beads with etched (or "bleached") geometric patterns. Coveted by the social elite, such beads have been found in significant quantities in the Royal Cemetery at Ur and in burials at other sites in Mesopotamia as well as in graves on Bahrain and the Oman Peninsula.[1]

Represented on this string are oval lentoid beads etched with a single white ring or "eye" pattern and more elongated elliptical lentoids with tangent circles or "spectacles"—representing some of the simplest and most common designs in the repertoire of motifs etched on carnelian beads. Examples ornamented with the eye design were found in the major cities of the Indus Valley as well as at Mesopotamian sites such as Ur, Kish, and Nippur. Parallels for the tangent-circle design come from Chanhudaro (see cat. no. 284) as well as from Ur, Kish, and Eshnunna.   JA

1. Vogt 1996, p. 113.

207

Footed goblet with geometric patterns

Fired clay
H. 20 cm (7⅞ in.); Diam. 12 cm (4¾ in.)
Gulf region, Bahrain, Saar, Necropolis, Tumulus 140
Late 3rd–early 2nd millennium B.C.
Bahrain National Museum, Manama 1843-2-89

This vessel with concave sides and flaring lip, resting on a well-balanced pedestal, is comparable to undecorated footed cups from Indus Valley, Baluchistan, and Central Asian sites.[1] The body is encircled with black horizontal bands filled in with red paint. Thicker black bands decorate the rim and the base of the vessel and pedestal. Carefully painted geometric patterns of vertical and horizontal lines, intercepted by boxes of chevrons, embellish the central register, where the natural buff color of the clay highlights the design.

Although a number of similarly shaped clay vessels are known from the surrounding region, it is an example in copper, excavated from a grave at the nearby site of Hamad Town, that is closest to this chalice in form.[2]

SG

1. Crawford 2000, p. 85. For south Asian examples, see the text on the Mehrgarh excavations in C. Jarrige et al. 1995, and specifically for Mohenjo-daro, see Baudot 1987, fig. 4:10; for Central Asian examples, see Francfort 1989, p. 355 (Dashly Tepe), fig. 37, Type III, I, and Khlopin 1981, fig. 7 (Parkhai II grave).
2. Vine 1993, p. 30.

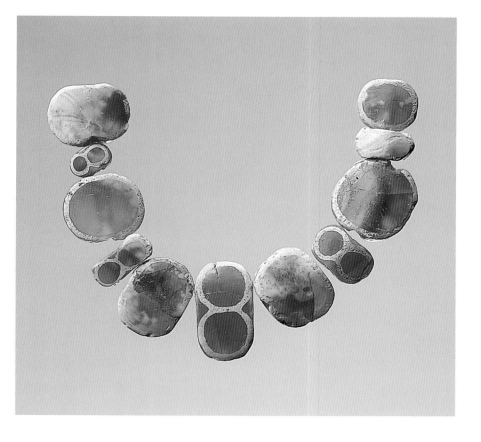

Tell Abraq

The remains of this large settlement almost straddles the border of Umm al-Qaiwain and Sharjah in the United Arab Emirates. Between 1989 and 1998 a team of Australian archaeologists excavated the site, which was continuously occupied from about 2200 to 300 B.C. It is dominated by a large fortification tower forty meters in diameter that dates to the late Umm an-Nar period (ca. 2200–2000 B.C.). Ten meters to the west of the tower is a circular tomb about six meters in diameter in which the remains of nearly 350 individuals have been recovered. Tell Abraq is today located several kilometers south of the shoreline, but it was almost certainly a coastal site in antiquity. Throughout its occupation it was very much in touch with the outside world, as is revealed by artifacts unearthed at Tell Abraq but originating in the Indus Valley, Mesopotamia, Iran, Baluchistan, and Central Asia.

PC

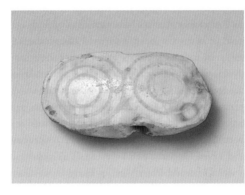

209

Etched carnelian bead

L. 1.8 cm (¹¹⁄₁₆ in.); W. 0.9 cm (³⁄₈ in.)
Gulf region, Sharjah, Tell Abraq, Umm an-Nar–type tomb, TA 2106
Late 3rd millennium B.C.
Sharjah Archaeological Museum, United Arab Emirates

This etched carnelian bead, the only such example found at Tell Abraq, is decorated with two triple circles. A type of material evidence widely used to indicate trade in Indus Valley archaeology, etched carnelian beads have also been discovered in small quantities at other sites on the Oman Peninsula. It is likely that many of the undecorated carnelian and agate beads found in the Gulf region—which are far more numerous there than decorated ones—were also imported from the Indus Valley (see "Art and Interconnections in the Third Millennium B.C.," by Joan Aruz, in this catalogue).

DTP

210a, b

Ram figurine and double-urial pendant

Red gold
Gulf region, Sharjah, Tell Abraq, Umm an-Nar–type tomb
Late 3rd millennium B.C.
Sharjah Archaeological Museum, United Arab Emirates

a. H. 2.03 cm (¹³⁄₁₆ in.); L. 1.98 cm (³⁄₄ in.)
TA 2280

b. H. 2.01 cm (¹³⁄₁₆ in.); L. 3.3 cm (1¼ in.)
TA 2457

The red-gold pendant in the shape of a ram (cat. no. 210a) shows a realistically modeled, muscular animal.[1] The details of curving horn, eye, muzzle, ear, front fleece, belly, legs, and tail are all clearly indicated. It was probably cast in a unifacial mould, for the reverse is smooth. Two small semicircular loops were soldered to the back of the ornament so that when suspended as part of a necklace, the ram would hang perfectly straight. The pendant has no obvious known parallels.

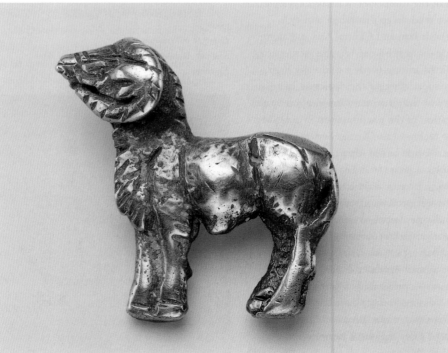

210a

GULF SEALS

217

Cylinder seal with a presentation scene

Grayish brown stone
H. 3.5 cm (1⅜ in.); Diam. at center 1.85 cm (¾ in.);
Diam. at ends 2 cm (¾ in.)
Gulf region, Failaka, Tell Sa'ad, F3 lt
Ur III, ca. 2097–1989 B.C.
National Council for Culture, Arts, and Letters,
Kuwait National Museum 881 AGS

The popularity of the presentation scene on cylinder seals of the Ur III period (see cat. no. 320)[1] remained current well into the succeeding Isin and Larsa dynasties.[2] Typically depicted is a male worshiper, presumably the seal's owner, being led by a goddess before a seated deity or deified king.[3]

This seal was excavated from a settlement comprising small stone houses;[4] the impression reveals a bald, clean-shaven man at the left, wearing the customary robe with fringed vertical edges, and holding the palm of his right hand before his mouth. The goddess at the center, who wears a striated robe and a crown with a single pair of horns, grasps his left wrist. She raises her oversized left hand, rendered here with three fingers and a thumb, as she approaches another goddess, at the

right, who is seated on a throne in the form of a double box. She wears a flounced robe and a crown with a single pair of horns and gestures with her raised right hand to the goddess leading the worshiper. An eight-pointed star within a horizontal crescent moon is situated high up in the area between the goddesses; the field behind the seated goddess was left empty to accommodate an inscription panel.

Several features of this seal suggest that it was the product of a less-skilled, perhaps local, seal-cutter: the overly long neck of the worshiper and the coarseness of the fringes on his garment; the inept positioning of the crown; the obtuse rather than acute angle at the elbow of the right arm of the standing goddess, and her four-fingered hand; and the slightly off vertical positioning of the seated goddess. That aspects of late-third-millennium Mesopotamian culture were sufficiently valued on the island of Failaka to give rise to locally produced imitations of the Mesopotamian presentation scene—originally made for high-ranking members of the royal and temple administrations[5]—is evidenced both by the presence of

likely imported cylinder seals[6] and by the incorporation of iconographic elements derived from presentation as well as banquet scenes on locally manufactured stamp seals (see cat. nos. 220d, e).   RW

1. Collon 1982, p. 129.
2. Collon 1986, p. 59.
3. Winter 1986, p. 253.
4. Kjaerum 1983, p. 8.
5. Winter 1987a, p. 79.
6. Kjaerum 1983, pp. 154–55, no. 368; Pic 1990, p. 139, no. 24.

218

Cylinder seal with confronted figures and a tree

Steatite
H. 2.2 cm (⅞ in.); Diam. 1.15 cm (⁷⁄₁₆ in.)
Gulf region, Failaka, F6 1174
Early Dilmun, ca. 2000–1800 B.C.
National Council for Culture, Arts, and Letters,
Kuwait National Museum 1129 AXJ

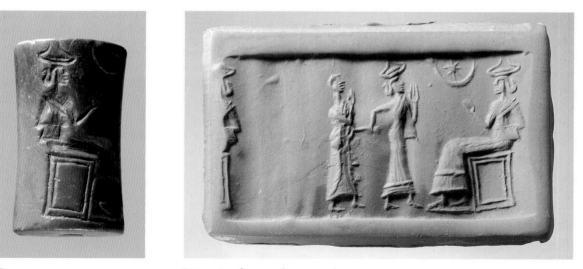

217

Impression from catalogue number 217.

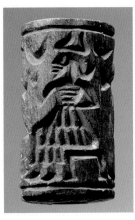

218

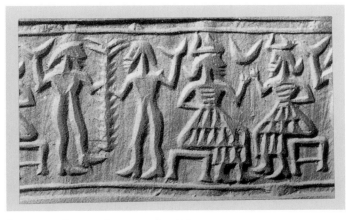

Impression from catalogue number 218.

The cylindrical form and the imagery of the seal exhibited here clearly illustrate how strong was Mesopotamian influence on the glyptic art of the Gulf.[1] The image is a crude imitation of a Mesopotamian banquet scene. Two figures are seated on stools, which have been made to differ slightly by the addition of a second horizontal bar to the one on the right. Horned headdresses identify the figures as deities. They are dressed in garments with tufts, indicated by vertical striations, and their lower bodies appear exaggeratedly triangular. A crescent fills the space above and between them. Two nude worshipers, each of whom holds a crescent, flank a stylized tree, perhaps a date palm.[2] Although the scene may have Mesopotamian roots, the peculiar details of the tree and the manner in which the humans are depicted—with elongated bodies and horizontal facial features—are typical of Gulf seals. This seal has counterparts at Susa, in Iran, where similarly nude worshipers are shown in front of enthroned deities.[3]

SG

1. For more information, the reader should consult Kjaerum 1980.
2. Nude figures are seen in round stamp seals from Failaka, as are trees resembling date palms; see Kjaerum 1983, seals 157, 355.
3. Amiet 1972, seals 1975, 2021. Also see Aruz 1992, p. 120, no. 79.

219

Vessel fragment with a hero, bull-man, and lion

Chlorite (?)
H. 5.2 cm (2 in.); W. 3.8 cm (1½ in.)
Gulf region, Failaka
Early Dilmun, ca. 2000–1800 B.C.
National Council for Culture, Arts, and Letters,
Kuwait National Museum KM 3021

This enigmatic fragment of a chlorite (?) vessel stands in contrast to other chlorite objects from the Gulf region that can be associated with the "Intercultural Style."[1] The piece appears to relate more closely to local stone-vessel and seal production. Here the partly preserved figures are grounded on a baseline indicated by a rope pattern. This decorative

scheme is known from "local" vessels excavated at Failaka in which, as here, the scene is divided into two registers.[2]

In the partially preserved upper register a lion is depicted, head lowered, with liquid streaming from its gaping mouth. To the right the lower portion of an upright bull, possibly a bull-man with a long tail, and a nude hero are modeled in high relief. Only faint traces of parallel lines are visible on the lower register.[3] The linear body of the nude figure with high-arched feet and one arm dangling to the side, and the large size of the bull-man relative to the other figures, also find stylistic counterparts in the local Gulf glyptic.[4]

While these local stylistic links are strong, the vomiting lion and a stafflike object, possibly a gatepost, are foreign decorative elements with Mesopotamian parallels.[5] Vomiting animals occur on Akkadian and Old Babylonian seals (see cat. no. 142), where fantastic animals are carved with linear bodies and clawed feet and are associated with water deities.[6] In the Failaka fragment the animal is clearly a lion, whose mane and haunch are carved with patterned fur; counterparts for this exist on steatite vessel fragments recovered during uncontrolled excavation on the nearby island of Tarut (see cat. no. 224b).[7]

Although there are clearly recognizable iconographic connections between the decoration on this shard and the Mesopotamian cultural sphere, the fragment is formally closer to the local Gulf style, even though the combination of figures has no known parallels in

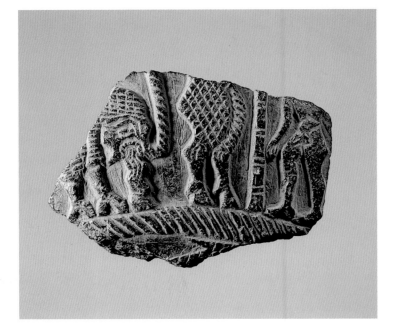

the Gulf region. It seems safe to suggest that either the vessel was of foreign manufacture, which would account for the peculiar subject and some aspects of its rendering, or it was produced locally based on a misunderstood Mesopotamian model. SG

1. For a discussion of chlorite and steatite vessels from the Gulf, see Burkholder 1971; Zarins 1978; and Howard-Carter n.d.. For a discussion of the "Intercultural Style," see also "Art and Interconnections in the Third Millennium B.C.," by Joan Aruz, in this catalogue; see also the entries for catalogue numbers 224, 225a, 239, 240.
2. See Failaka 1966, figs. 49 and 50. The rope pattern on the present vessel tilts to the left, whereas on other Failaka examples it tilts to the right.
3. The "tail" may also be interpreted as a leash for the lion held by the bull-man; however, tails that look like this are known from Failaka seals; for examples, see Kjaerum 1980.
4. Ibid., nos. 140–44, 187, 188.
5. Scenes with nude heroes and water deities, bull-man with staff, and gateposts are well illustrated in the Mesopotamian glyptic arts; for examples, see Collon 1986, p. 90, nos. 144–47, 150–53. Howard-Carter (n.d.) suggests the gatepost on this vessel may be a reed bundle symbolizing Inanna (museum description label, Kuwait National Museum, Al-Kuwait).
6. In these seals the deities are shown standing on lion-griffins from whose mouths liquid streams; see Porada 1948, no. 220, and Buchanan 1966, no. 335.
7. The paws of the present lion may also be clawlike, but the lack of any detailing makes this uncertain.

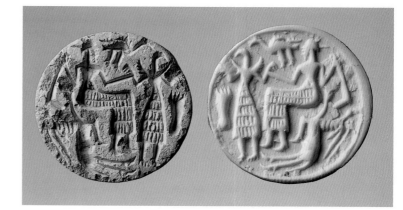

220a

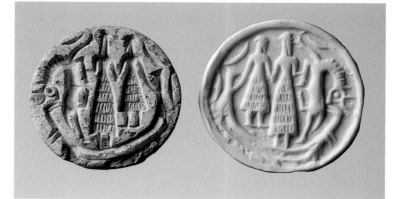

220b

220a–g

Stamp seals with figures and animals

Steatite
Early Dilmun, ca. 2000–1800 B.C.

a. *Diam. 2.9 cm (1⅛ in.); Thickness 1.25 cm (½ in.)*
Gulf region, Bahrain, Karrana
Bahrain National Museum, Manama 4061

b. *Diam. 2.4 cm (1 in.); Thickness 1.15 cm (⁷⁄₁₆ in.)*
Gulf region, Bahrain, Hamad Town
Bahrain National Museum, Manama 4054

c. *Diam. 3 cm (1⅛ in.); Thickness 1.3 cm (½ in.)*
Gulf region, Failaka, Tell Sa'ad, F3, trench I, nu
National Council for Culture, Arts, and Letters,
Kuwait National Museum 881 AIT

d. *Diam. 6.5 cm (2½ in.); Thickness 3 cm (1⅛ in.)*
Gulf region, Failaka, Tell Sa'id, F5, trench Q, ALL
National Council for Culture, Arts, and Letters,
Kuwait National Museum

e. *Diam. 2.8 cm (1⅛ in.); Thickness 1.3 cm (½ in.)*
Gulf region, Failaka, Tell Sa'id, F5 ADO
National Council for Culture, Arts, and Letters,
Kuwait National Museum

f. *Diam. 2.5 cm (1 in.); Thickness 1.3 cm (½ in.)*
Gulf region, Failaka, Tell Sa'ad, F3, trench B, u
National Council for Culture, Arts, and Letters,
Kuwait National Museum 881 UK

g. *Diam. 3.5 cm (1⅜ in.); Thickness 1.25 cm (½ in.)*
Gulf region, Failaka, F6, trench SN, F6 98
National Council for Culture, Arts, and Letters,
Kuwait National Museum 1129 CE

A number of decorative elements on the seals excavated at Bahrain and Failaka—two islands in the Gulf, which have been identified with the legendary kingdom of Dilmun—can be traced to Mesopotamia, Iran, the Indus Valley, Anatolia, and Central Asia.[1] The cultural influences that these foreign motifs reflect stemmed from the maritime trade that connected the far-flung cities of the region beginning about 2500 B.C. and lasting until about 1500 B.C.

Epigraphic evidence from dated seal impressions and tablets found at Susa and Ur suggests that the Dilmun stamp seals, with their distinctive circular shape, were made between the end of the third millennium B.C. and the early second millennium B.C.[2] They are characterized by a flat obverse and a hemispherical reverse. Their backs are pierced for suspension and scored with multiple grooves at right angles to the piercing. Pairs of concentric circles are placed symmetrically on either side of the grooves. Other characteristic features of the Dilmun glyptic include the manner in which animals and human figures are depicted. Deep cavities mark the eyes of animals, and there is no indication of a pupil; human figures, seen in profile, have linear bodies and stylized facial features rendered with horizontal lines.[3]

Foreign decorative elements on Dilmun seals include typical third-millennium-B.C. Mesopotamian imagery centered on male figures engaged in a rich repertoire of activities, including presentations in which local gods are occasionally adorned with the Mesopotamian horned crown (see cat. no. 218); as protectors of the flock; in contests with animals (see cat. no. 220b); and in drinking or banquet scenes (see cat. nos. 220d, e). In these scenes the adaptation of Mesopotamian dress, horned crown, bull-men (see cat. no. 220c), standards, and lyres with taurine sound boxes (see cat. no. 220f) indicates a close contact

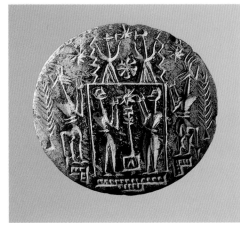

220c

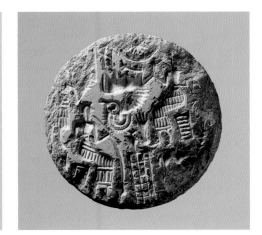

220d

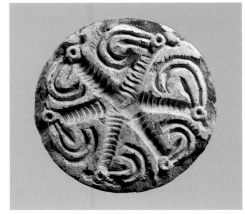

220e

between the two regions and may signify a spiritual affinity.[4]

In catalogue number 220a a seated figure holds an axelike tool in one hand and reaches for the hand of a standing winged creature, possibly a deity, with the other.[5] Similar winged figures on seals dating to the third millennium B.C. are known from both Mesopotamia and Central Asia. The northern connection is underscored in this image by a solitary foot (here with four toes), a motif known from Central Asia and Syria and Iran.[6] Two more seemingly unrelated elements—a bird and a gazelle—complete the composition.

Ships and boats are a common theme.[7] In catalogue number 220b the image can be interpreted as a variation of the Mesopotamian contest scene. Here, the central figure dressed in a tufted garment stands in a boat. He grasps an animal's foreleg with one hand, while the other is extended toward a companion figure. The craft resembles the modern-day *mashhuf*—a small boat with a rather shallow draft, ideal for marsh travel. The boat with its upturned stern is reminiscent of vessels depicted in the earlier seals of Ur, a motif rarely occurring in the second-millennium-B.C. Mesopotamian glyptic.[8]

The Mesopotamian pictorial repertoire is again reflected on a Dilmun seal showing two figures in an architectural setting (cat. no. 220c). The motif may best be compared with that of an early Old Babylonian seal in the Yale Babylonian Collection, New Haven, where suppliant deities and worshipers face an altar within a temple.[9] Here, two nude, belted men stand in profile within a structure that may be a temple. They raise their hands in a gesture of respect toward a star standard on a podium.[10] On the roof are two winged creatures and two

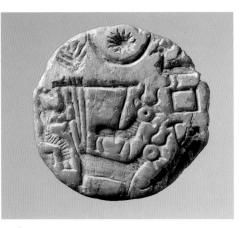

220f

220g

vertical snakes that they may be grasping.[11] Two nude, double-belted fantastic beings with what seem to be three horns flank the structure and repeat the central worshipers' gestures.[12] Local decorative motifs such as a rosette, three stars, and two tree branches complete the harmonious, almost symmetrical composition that is so typical of later Dilmun seals.[13]

Mesopotamian banquet imagery occurs on three seals. In catalogue number 220e a high podium on which a small jar is placed separates two seated figures who confront each other. One of them is drinking through a long straw from a jar comparable in size to the one on the podium. This drinking scene closely parallels the image on a sealing dated to the reign of Gungunum of Larsa.[14] Such drinking scenes must have had propitious significance for local Dilmunite seal owners.[15]

On a second seal with banquet imagery—by far the largest of the seven seals discussed here—two men dressed in tiered, flounced skirts face each other (cat. no. 220d). Seated on rectangular stools, they are flanked by a ladder

and a bird; between them are four vessels beneath a crescent and a star. Below, occupying most of the seal's surface, are two vertical rows of bovids and recumbent antelopes. Two human figures, one nude, the other clothed, each raise one hand.

On the third seal a seated man plays a three-stringed lyre (cat. no. 220f). The sound box is similar to Mesopotamian examples, such as those excavated from the royal tombs of Ur (see cat. no. 58) and those depicted on the Standard of Ur (cat. no. 52) and in glyptic art (see cat. no. 60c). On preserved Mesopotamian lyres, bulls' heads decorate the boxes, but in the present example the artist has created the music box out of the body of a bull so that its back acts as a strut—a detail paralleled on a stele from Tello, where the sound box of a lyre is formed by two superimposed bulls, one in profile.[16]

Seals with a radial composition form a distinct group. An example in this exhibition (cat. no. 220g) displays six antelope heads radiating like a six-pointed star from a central point. This decoration closely resembles that on sealings excavated at the early-second-millennium-B.C. site of Acemhöyük, in central Anatolia.[17] Similar compositions are recorded earlier, however, at the site of Mohenjo-daro in the Indus Valley.[18]

SG

1. Kjaerum 1986 and Kjaerum 1994. For further reference, the reader should consult the following works, which the author used in preparing this entry: Gadd 1932; Porada 1965; N. Özgüç 1966; During Caspers 1970–71; Kjaerum 1980; Mitchell 1986; D. Potts 1990; Harper, Aruz, and Tallon 1992; Nayeem 1992; Eidem 1994; Lamberg-Karlovsky and Sabloff 1995; Zettler and Horne 1998; Lombard 1999; and Crawford and Rice 2000.
2. At Failaka early Dilmun seals were found in association with post-Akkadian Ur III seals; see Kjaerum 1986, pp. 269–70. An Ur tablet is dated to the tenth year of the reign of Gungunum of Larsa, about 1908 B.C.; see Hallo and Buchanan 1965.
3. The practice of cutting hollow cavities for eyes characterizes some Early Dynastic seals from Mesopotamia; see Buchanan 1966, pls. 1, 2a.
4. Kjaerum 1999, p. 116.
5. In his recent study of Dilmun seals Al-Sindi (1999, p. 33) identifies the winged figure as the god of the underworld. He describes the implement as a weapon (ibid., p. 326), but its appearance on other seals in a different composition makes this interpretation improbable; see Kjaerum 1983, p. 113, no. 264.
6. The bird-man on a Metropolitan Museum seal also has outstretched wings but is accompanied by two antithetical birds; see MMA 1984.4 in Baghestani 1997, pp. 307–8, pl. 1. For deities with birds, see Aruz 1998b, pp. 16–17. For winged figures in Mesopotamia, see Legrain 1951, no. 103, pl. 8. The foot motif on a seal from Qalat al-Bahrain is rendered in a single undifferentiated form with thin lines and four prong-like toes; see Kjaerum 1994, p. 324, fig. 1731, p. 328, no. 12. On the foot motif, see also Porada 1971b, p. 332. Square seals discovered at Tell Brak in the Jamdat Nasr levels show feet separated by a snake; however, the feet are much more stylized than the foot in the Qalat al-Bahrain example. Human feet are also shown on a third-millennium-B.C. Iranian seal from Tepe Yahya and a redware pottery impression of the same era from Shahr-i Sokhta, also in Iran. The Tepe Yahya seal shows two feet, like the Tell Brak seals; see Pittman 2001a, p. 265, and Hakemi 1997, p. 660.
7. Model boats have also been excavated at Failaka; see Kjaerum 1983, pp. 113–15, 139, nos. 262–66, 343.
8. Legrain 1936, pl. 37. For the boats in the Indus Valley glyptic, see cat. no. 299.
9. Buchanan 1981, p. 277.
10. This motif is well represented on other seals from Failaka; see Kjaerum 1983, pp. 133, 145.
11. This scene is reminiscent of the eagle-and-snake motif from the Iranian and Mesopotamian chlorite vessels in the "Intercultural Style" (see "Art and Interconnections in the Third Millennium B.C.," by Joan Aruz, in this catalogue).
12. An attempt on the seal engraver's part to distinguish between two spaces—indoors, where the ritual

takes place, and the area near the outer walls of the temple—is suggested by the relative higher position of these figures.

13. Tree branches (possibly palm fronds) in association with a podium are also seen on seals from Qalat al-Bahrain; see Kjaerum 1994, pp. 342, 347.
14. Hallo and Buchanan 1965, pp. 199–203.
15. Porada 1971b, p. 335.
16. In a dedicatory inscription to the god Nanna, Gudea of Lagash says that a harp (or lyre) bellows like a bull; Woolley 1934, p. 258. In the upper register of the stele from Tello, a figure carrying a hoe resembles the figure on this Failaka seal; see Suter 2000, pp. 184, 353, and Parpola 1996, p. 230. On the Stele of Ur-Namma (cat. no. 317) the king is shown bearing a similar hoe.
17. In the Anatolian example griffin heads on long necks radiate from the center of a dot-in-circle motif. See N. Özgüç 1966, pl. 26:6; Porada 1971a, pp. 331–36; N. Özgüç 1980, pp. 61–87; and Boehmer 1986, p. 294.
18. Marshall 1931, pl. 112:383.

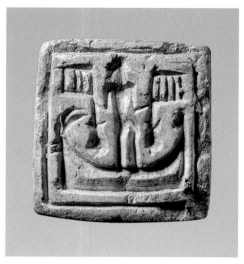

221

Stamp seal with a boat scene

Steatite
L. 2 cm (⅞ in.); W. 1.9 cm (¾ in.)
Gulf region, Failaka, F6 758
Early Dilmun, ca. 2000–1800 B.C.
National Council for Culture, Arts, and Letters, Kuwait National Museum 1129 ADY

This seal from Failaka Island, at the head of the Gulf, is unusual in shape, as it is square rather than circular possibly alluding to the most common form of Harappan seals. The subject is a nude male figure standing in the middle of a flat-bottomed boat, facing right.[1] The man's arms are bent at the elbow, perpendicular to his torso. Beside him two jars stand on the deck of the boat, each containing a long pole to which is attached a hatched square that perhaps represents a banner.[2]

Flat-bottomed vessels with a single sail were used to transport cargoes in shallow tidal waters, but the one illustrated on this seal lacks a sail.[3] If the two vertical posts on the stern are interpreted as steering paddles, then it resembles a model found in India at Lothal, which appears to have had square sails.[4]

Although the seal's shape is atypical, all the decorative elements, including the boat and the two jars, find parallels on other seals from Dilmun, indicating that this one was made in the region where it was found.[5]

SG

1. Six square stamp seals from Failaka have been published. Some are two-sided, and none of the six shows the same image. See Kjaerum 1983, seal nos. 197, 234, 254, 266, 335, 367.
2. The jars are similar to the drinking jars depicted on another seal from Failaka (cat. no. 220e).
3. It is unlikely that the hatched squares represent sails, since the poles to which they are attached emerge from vases. The two diagonal lines on the body of the boat may represent the reed bundles from which these craft were built. A second type of boat depicted on a Failaka seal has a curved bottom with sharply upturned bow and stern, similar to the boat depicted on a Mohenjo-daro tablet (see cat. no. 299). For a discussion of the types of vessels in use during the third millennium B.C. and their different functions, see Ratnagar 1981, pp. 157–82.
4. On the Lothal boat model, three blind holes used as sockets may have held the masts of square-shaped sails. See Tripathi and Srivastava 1994, pl. 58.
5. For further reference, the reader should consult the following works, which the author used in preparing this entry: Gadd 1932; Porada 1965; N. Özgüç 1966; During Caspers 1970–71; Kjaerum 1980; Mitchell 1986; D. Potts 1990; Harper, Aruz, and Tallon 1992; Nayeem 1992; Eidem 1994; Lamberg-Karlovsky and Sabloff 1995; Zettler and Horne 1998; Lombard 1999; and Crawford and Rice 2000.

The Island of Tarut

From the middle of the third millennium B.C., extensive trade linked the Gulf with surrounding regions and civilizations. At that time a number of settlements were established on and near the Arabian mainland. The most important such site discovered is located on the small island of Tarut, very close to the shore of Arabia and north of the islands of Bahrain. It may have served as a point of access to the mainland. Large quantities of worked chlorite in the "Intercultural Style" (see "'Intercultural Style' Carved Chlorite Objects," by Joan Aruz, in this catalogue) have been found on Tarut. The stone was perhaps obtained from a source near Jabrin, in what is now Saudi Arabia. Tarut's international connections are spectacularly demonstrated by the discovery there of a large statue of a man, nude but wearing a belt, that is stylistically related to similar figures found in Mesopotamia.

PC

222

Standing nude belted male figure

Limestone
H. 94 cm (37 in.)
Gulf region, Tarut Island
Mid-to-late 3rd millennium B.C.
National Museum, Riyadh, Saudi Arabia

This unique and impressive sculpture has strong connections with Mesopotamian religious imagery. The male figure is bald. He has prominent ears with the folds of the pinna clearly indicated. The eyebrows form a continuous ridge and appear to have joined at the top of the damaged nose. His eyes are sunk into his face and outlined by a ridge. The damaged mouth is modeled above a heavy chin. There is a break in the neck that apparently occurred when the sculpture was recovered. A V-shaped depression below the chin between broad shoulders suggests the collarbones. His hands are held together high on his chest, with the right hand over the left, as on Mesopotamian votive sculpture (see cat. no. 24). The left thumb rests over the right and the fingernails are indicated. Sharp elbows are held free of the upper body, which is flat in comparison with the lower half. He is nude apart from a three-strand belt, where a break has occurred, also apparently during recovery. The broad, blocklike hips are reminiscent of the forms of Late Uruk sculpture (see cat. no. 8), although the legs are more strongly modeled here than in those earlier works. His genitals are clearly

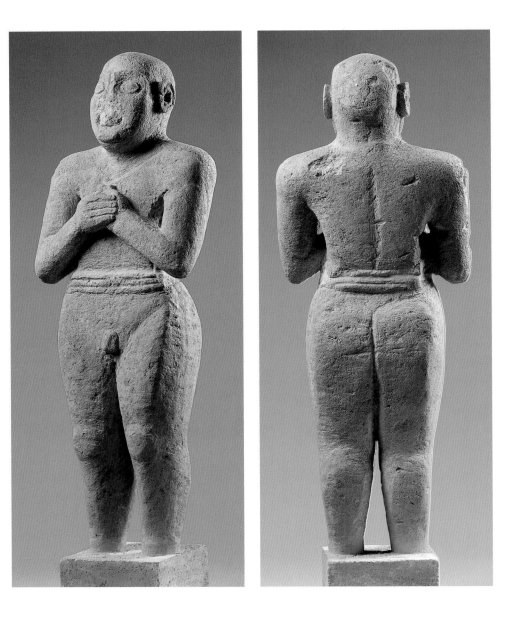

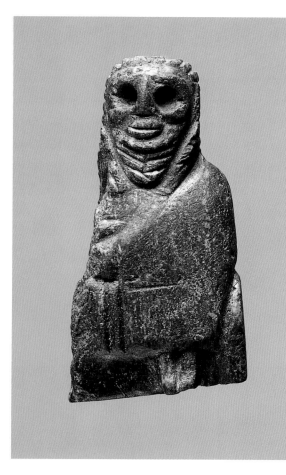
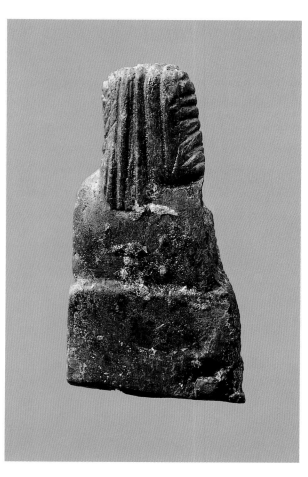

indicated, and a groove marks the division of the legs, both front and rear, down to the modeled knees. The lower legs are carved separately. His feet are missing.

The figure, along with a number of other pieces from different periods (see cat. no. 223), was unearthed at Tarut in 1965 during ground leveling.[1] As a result the original context was lost. The statue has been dated to Early Dynastic II because it recalls the nude, triple-belted figures of cast copper on offering stands from Khafajah in eastern Mesopotamia and other similar images of that time (see cat. nos. 18, 38).[2] Although it has also been placed in the Jamdat Nasr period,[3] the limited contact between Mesopotamia and the Gulf at this time suggests that a date sometime in the Early Dynastic period is more likely.

PC

1. Rashid 1970, p. 160.
2. Ibid., pp. 159–66, pls. 2–6; D. Potts 1990, pp. 67–68; Rice 1994, pp. 219–21, fig. 8.4.
3. Ippolitoni-Strika 1986.

223

Cloaked figure

Lapis lazuli
H. 5 cm (2 in.)
Gulf region, Tarut Island
Mid-to-late 3rd millennium B.C.
National Museum, Riyadh, Saudi Arabia

This unique and tiny but powerfully expressive figurine was discovered during quarrying for the construction of a road, together with a number of objects, many of which can be dated to the third millennium B.C. (see cat. no. 222).[1] The scale of the object makes it impossible to determine if a man or woman is depicted, but the modeling is very fine. The face is enclosed in a hood or possibly is framed by hair worn in pigtails, as is the case on metal and stone sculpture of the Early Dynastic period from sites in the Diyala region of Mesopotamia.[2] The facial features are very distinctive, with the eyes and small straight nose, as well as the very full lips and modeled cheeks, clearly indicated. The neck consists of three parallel lines

that may signify either a beard or folds of cloth. A cloak, the left side of which is drawn across the front of the figure, hides the arms and hands. It is possible that the figure is seated and that the projections at the sides of the sculpture represent the arms of a chair. The lower half of the body is not shown. The lapis lazuli from which the figure is carved would have reached Tarut from Afghanistan but, without comparative material, it is not known whether the figure was carved at the source or at its ultimate destination.

PC

1. Rashid 1970, p. 160; D. Potts 1990, pp. 66–67; Rice 1994, p. 221, fig. 8.6.
2. D. Potts 1990, p. 67; Frankfort 1943, pls. 55–57.

"Intercultural Style" Carved Chlorite Objects

In the mid-to-late third millennium B.C., one phenomenon provides highly graphic evidence for cultural interpenetration across the vast region that stretches west to east between the Euphrates and Indus Rivers and north to south between the Oxus and the Gulf. That is the production and distribution of chlorite vessels and handled "weights" carved in low relief with elaborately patterned or inlaid surfaces. These objects share a distinctive repertoire of figural and geometric imagery and a characteristic manner of representing human figures that can be related to the art of eastern Iran. They integrate iconographic elements derived from both Near Eastern and Harappan traditions. The most elaborately carved and intact examples derive from Mesopotamian temples and tombs or have no archaeological provenance. Their contexts or inscriptions point to dates in the Early Dynastic and Akkadian periods.

Important decorated fragments exhibiting the full range and characteristics of the "Intercultural Style" were found, along with unfinished pieces, in two widely separated areas beyond Mesopotamia: Tepe Yahya in southeastern Iran (possibly the ancient "land of Marhashi"), and Tarut, an island in the Gulf close to the Arabian coast. Archaeological excavations at Tepe Yahya have revealed a production center of the late third millennium B.C. in a region rich in chlorite. On Tarut, construction work and digging for gardens have uncovered about six hundred complete and fragmentary vessels and weights, which are thought to derive from the numerous stone-lined cist graves on the island. Because some objects from Tarut were partially formed or appear to have been recut and because unworked chunks of chlorite were also found, it has been suggested that the raw material was available locally and that the island acted as a center for production, completion, and transshipment of the carved objects. *JA*

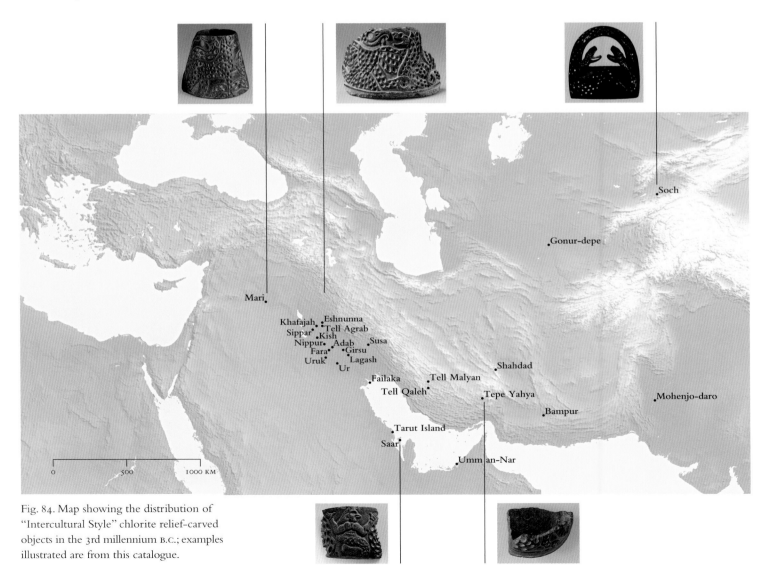

Fig. 84. Map showing the distribution of "Intercultural Style" chlorite relief-carved objects in the 3rd millennium B.C.; examples illustrated are from this catalogue.

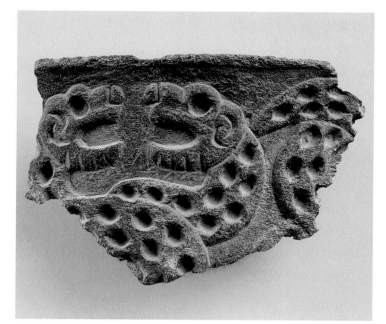

224a

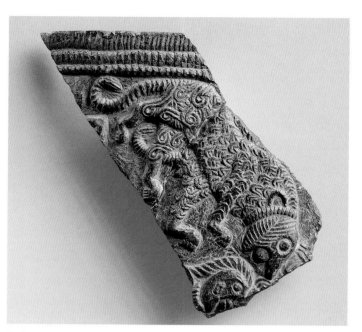

224b

224a–h

Vessel fragments with figural and geometric designs

Chlorite
Gulf region, Tarut Island
Mid-to-late 3rd millennium B.C.

a. H. 6 cm (2⅜ in.); W. 9 cm (3½ in.)
National Museum, Riyadh, Saudi Arabia 2662

b. H. 9 cm (3½ in.); W. 4.8 cm (1⅞ in.)
National Museum, Riyadh, Saudi Arabia 2652

c. 1, 2. total, H. 15 cm (5⅞ in.)
National Museum, Riyadh, Saudi Arabia 2663, 2664

d. H. 7.5 cm (3 in.); W. 10.8 cm (4¼ in.)
National Museum, Riyadh, Saudi Arabia 2632

e. H. 4.5 cm (1¾ in.); W. 15 cm (5⅞ in.)
National Museum, Riyadh, Saudi Arabia 2660

f. H. 7.7 cm (3 in.)
National Museum, Riyadh, Saudi Arabia 2633

g. H. 7 cm (2¾ in.); W. 12.6 cm (5 in.)
National Museum, Riyadh, Saudi Arabia 2648

h. H. 9 cm (3½ in.); W. 18.6 cm (7⅜ in.)
National Museum, Riyadh, Saudi Arabia 2639

These nine fragments offer a good sampling of the typical known "Intercultural Style" motifs. The confronting snakes on the first example (cat. no. 224a), identified as such by

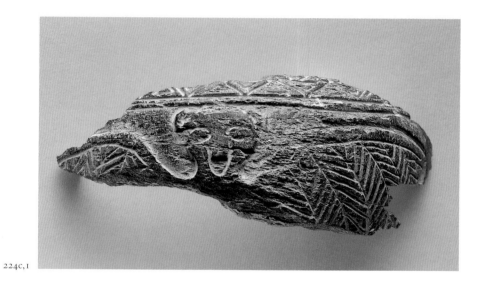

224c,1

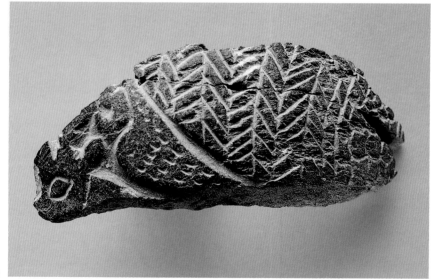

224c,2

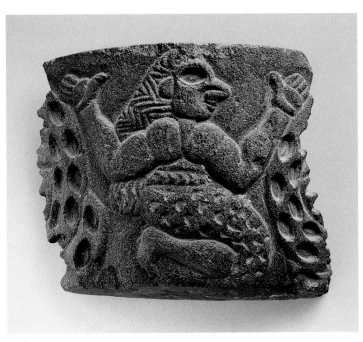

224d

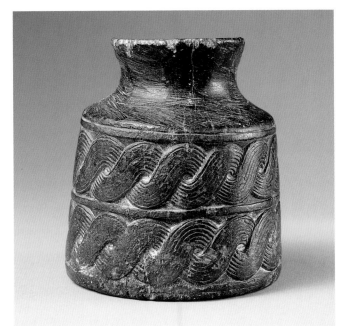

224f

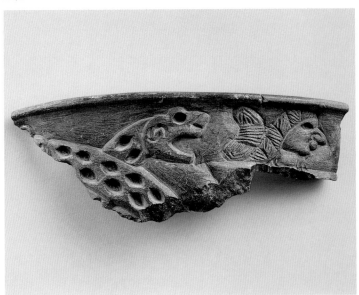

224e

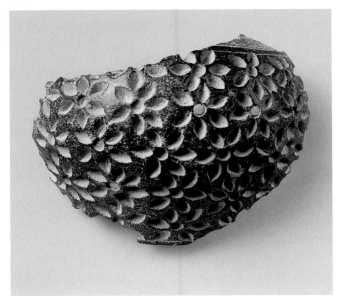

224g

oval inlays that represent scales, are from Tarut,
in the Gulf, an island where many other similarly decorated vessels were recovered.[1] The
same scene also occurs on vessel fragments at
Tepe Yahya in southeastern Iran and at Susa in
southwestern Iran.[2] Two fragments here depict
men in combat with or controlling snakes
(cat. nos. 224d, e) characterized by oval inlays;
both men are typically Early Dynastic in
physiognomy and hairstyle (see entry for cat.
no. 227)—an apparently similar scene occurs
on a chlorite vessel from Uruk.[3]

The bird of prey Imdugud, shown on two
fragments from one vessel (cat. nos. 224c,1,2),
was a common image in the Early Dynastic
period, as evidence from silver vessels found at
Tello and Mari demonstrates.[4] An odd piece

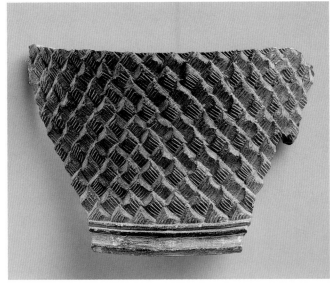

224h

(cat. no. 224b) depicts a feline at an oblique angle over what seems to be the head of a bearded, long-haired man. Both the scene and the feline's body patterning remain unparalleled on "Intercultural Style" artifacts.[5]

The other vessel fragments are all geometrically decorated, the rosette-inlaid vessel (cat. no. 224g) alone being unique in design.[6] The palm tree motif and guilloche pattern seen in catalogue numbers 225a and 224f are well documented across the region where the "Intercultural Style" is found (see entry for cat. no. 225b), as is equally the mat-weave pattern (cat. no. 224h).[7]   OWM

1. Catalogue number 224a was previously published in Burkholder 1971, no. 20, and Zarins 1978, no. 58, pl. 67. See also Zarins 1978, nos. 157, 545, pls. 67, 68. For valuable information concerning how the National Museum, Riyadh, acquired the Tarut material, see Zarins 1978, p. 67. G. Burkholder of ARAMCO was a major—and personally generous—source; see also Burkholder 1971, note on p. 306.
2. Lamberg-Karlovsky 1988, pp. 78–79, E; Miroschedji 1973, p. 12, pl. 1:f,g.
3. Catalogue number 224d was previously published in Zarins 1978, no. 546, pl. 70. For another master of snakes, compare Amiet 1986, p. 271, no. 73 (Boston), which is questionable (see Muscarella 2000, pp. 169–70, no. 8). Catalogue number 224e was published in Burkholder 1971, no. 21, pl. 7, and Zarins 1978, no. 49, pl. 70. For the scene on the Uruk vessel, see Lindemeyer and Martin 1993, no. 690, pl. 61; what creature exists behind the man with hair in a braided bun is unclear because, although snakelike, it has round, not oval, inlays.
4. Catalogue number 224c was previously published in Burkholder 1971, no. 13, fig. 2, pl. 5, and Zarins 1978, no. 69, pl. 68. For the vessels from Tello and Mari, see Durrani 1964, pls. 6, and 7, 8, respectively. For other forms where the bird's head is in profile and other creatures may be juxtaposed, compare Durrani 1964, pl. 5:2,3; Muscarella 1993, fig. 5; see also the example from Nippur (cat. no. 234).
5. Catalogue number 224b was previously published in Burkholder 1971, no. 15, pl. 6, and Zarins 1978, no. 47, pl. 70. One wonders whether this fragment is correctly included in the "Intercultural Style."
6. Catalogue number 224g was previously published in Burkholder 1971, no. 10, fig. 1, pl. 4, and Zarins 1978, no. 54, pl. 69.
7. See Burkholder 1971, no. 1, pl. 3 (possibly a fragment from the same vessel); Miroschedji 1973, figs. 5, 9, pls. 2:j, 5:c; Lamberg-Karlovsky 1988, figs. 1:E, 4:L, pl. 9. Note that the one certain example of the "Intercultural Style" known from farther east, at Mohenjo-daro, is a fragment with a mat-weave pattern; see Durrani 1964, pl. 1:2.

225a

Vessel fragment with a palm tree

Chlorite
H. 9.9 cm (3⅞ in.); W. 12 cm (4¾ in.)
Gulf region, Tarut Island
Mid-to-late 3rd millennium B.C.
National Museum, Riyadh, Saudi Arabia 2655

225b

Handled weight with palm trees

Chlorite schist
H. 22.9 cm (9 in.); W. 25.1 cm (9⅞ in.); Thickness 4.6 cm (1¾ in.)
Gulf region or eastern Iran
Mid-to-late 3rd millennium B.C.
The Metropolitan Museum of Art, New York; Gift of Norbert Schimmel Trust, 1989 1989.281.40

Some "Intercultural Style" objects show the characteristic Near Eastern motif of the date palm. These objects include vessel fragments—discovered both on the Gulf island of Tarut (see cat. no. 225a) and at Kish, in Mesopotamia—as well as "handled weights," an unexcavated example of which is in the Metropolitan Museum's collection (cat. no. 225b). At least five such "weights" have been excavated, two

of which show the palm tree motif—one in southeastern Iran, at Tepe Yahya, and another at Nippur, in Mesopotamia[1]—and about fifteen unprovenienced examples, including fragments, are known.[2] On one face of the Museum's "weight" (we do not know if an obverse and reverse were intended) are depictions of three date-bearing palm trees, their bases seemingly connected but probably sharing a water canal; on the other face is an exquisitely carved row of guilloches (the "weight" from Nippur also has the date-palm motif on one side and a guilloche on the other). There are excavated objects and those without provenience that bear the same basic palm-tree motif. These objects, a "weight" and seven vessels,[3] include a conical vase with everted rim in the Metropolitan Museum.[4]

OWM

1. Muscarella 1993, pp. 143–45, figs. 1, 3.
2. See Muscarella 1993 for all the examples; for number 225b in this catalogue, see p. 149, no. 6, fig. 10; note 2 lists other possible weights excavated at or near Tepe Yahya. Five additional decorated "weights" have come to my attention: Bonham's, Knightsbridge, London, sale, April 13, 2000, no. 300, same as Bonham's, Knightsbridge, London, sale, November 8, 2001, no. 201; Hôtel Drouot, Paris, sale, February 13, 14, 2002, no. 393; Barakat Gallery, Beverly Hills, sale, vol. 32, n.d.,

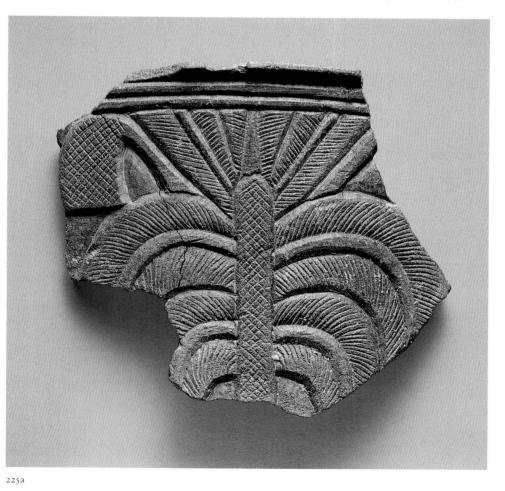

225a

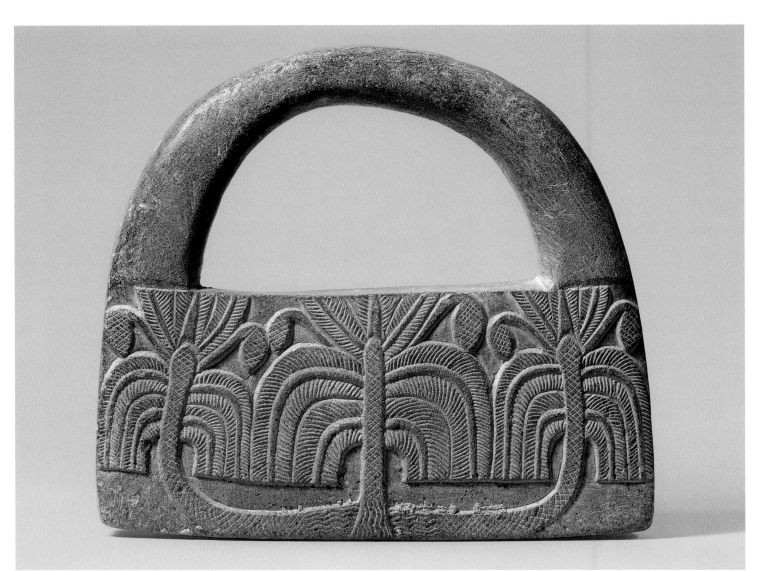

225b

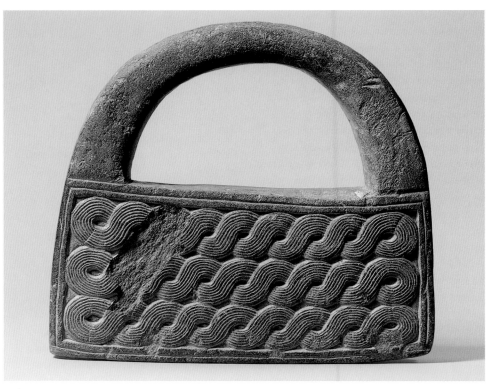

PE.6179; and two unpublished examples belonging to
dealers. All five are to my mind questionable.
3. Burkholder 1971, p. 309, no. 9, pl. 4; Zarins 1978,
no. 51, also nos. 39, 122, 139, 581; Muscarella 1993,
pp. 144–47, no. 2, fig. 6 (said to be but not from
Palmyra); Durrani 1964, p. 68, fig. 9 (said to be but
not from Susa). The others are questionable: Christie's,
New York, sale, June 8, 2001, nos. 332 (a vase), 333,
334 (both chalices); and Hôtel Drouot, Paris, sale,
October 22, 2001, nos. 398, 399 (a vase and a cup).
4. Acc. no. 17.190.106. See Pittman 1984, pp. 12, 22,
fig. 1.

225b

226

Conical vessel with a zebu

Chlorite and calcite
H. 11.4 cm (4½ in.)
Probably Gulf region, Tarut Island
Mid-to-late 3rd millennium B.C.
The Metropolitan Museum of Art, New York; Lent by
Mrs. Constantine Sidamon-Eristoff L.1978.31

This vessel is of particular interest for two reasons. First, it enlarges the corpus of "Intercultural Style" chlorite vessels bearing imagery derived from the Indus Valley. Second, it is attributed to Al-Rafiah, on the east coast of the island of Tarut.[1] Here a considerable number of fragmentary examples with elaborate figural motifs have been found (see cat. no. 224), perhaps originally intended for shipment to the temple repositories of Mesopotamia.[2]

Depicted in a carved and inlaid technique are two zebus striding one behind the other in a rich landscape. The modeled bodies of the animals are starkly outlined, emerging from a flat background in a manner characteristic of "Intercultural Style" vessels. Their eyes, muzzles, horns, and humps are sharply differentiated by deep incisions and sweeping curves. The humps are not patterned as in other examples (see cat. no. 227) but are embellished with circular areas of inlay, like those used on other vessels to indicate the spots on leopards' coats (see cat. nos. 232, 233). Here a few white stone insets survive. Inlays were also used to accentuate the animals' curved beards and floral elements in the background.

Of great interest is the treatment of the background, which is covered with geometric patterning to suggest mountains, water, and perhaps land in a "conceptual" perspective, where depth of field corresponds to height. The mountains are depicted as a series of overlapping, nested scallops, forming a pattern similar to the imbrications that sometime cover large areas of vessels of this type.[3] Below are horizontal streams of wavy lines ending in a spiral hook, which seem to emerge behind the animals' heads from curving parallel lines that probably indicate a river. The flowers between the legs of the animals are perhaps meant to indicate the riverbank along which they walk.

Water is treated in a similar fashion on a cylindrical cup in the British Museum (cat. no. 227). Additionally, on the finely modeled Akkadian seal of Ibni-sharrum, a scribe

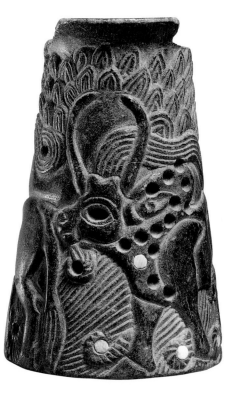

of Shar-kali-sharri (cat. no. 135), two water buffaloes stand on a horizontal band of parallel wavy lines over a scalloped background that indicates a mountain river.

JA

1. Kohl 1975, p. 27, fig. 8; Burkholder 1984, pls. 10, 11; Pittman 1984, pp. 20, 22–23; Zarins 1989, p. 101, fig. 15.
2. For vessels with similar imagery, see Frankfort 1936a, p. 431, fig. 10.
3. See Pittman 1984, fig. 1, opp. p. 13, where imbricate patterning and bands of palms are juxtaposed.

227

Cylindrical vessel with heroes and animals

Chlorite
H. 11.4 cm (4½ in.); Diam. 17.8 cm (7 in.)
Mesopotamia
Mid-3rd millennium B.C.
Trustees of The British Museum, London BM 128887

This elaborately carved "Intercultural Style" chlorite vessel combines stylistic elements that are paralleled in eastern Iran and western Central Asia with iconography that mingles Mesopotamian, Iranian, and Harappan

imagery (see "Art and Interconnections in the Third Millennium B.C.," by Joan Aruz, in this catalogue). Although not from a controlled excavation, it is often said to come from Khafajah, in the Diyala region of Mesopotamia, based on an article written by Henri Frankfort in 1932.[1] As with most of the elaborately carved chlorite vessels from Mesopotamia, this piece is likely to have originally been deposited in a temple. The site of Khafajah in fact yielded a conical chlorite vase in the same style with equally complex imagery; it was discovered in the temple of the moon god Sin.[2]

On one side of the British Museum vessel the composition is dominated by a master of animals controlling two menacing snakes with bared fangs above two addorsed felines. To the left, another figure with a developed nude torso kneels over two addorsed standing zebus; he holds streams of water over their heads, and there are palm fronds in the background. The two heroes have a similar physiognomy, hairstyle, and a belted "net skirt" of the type worn by "priest-kings" in the preceding Late Uruk period (see "Art of the Early City-States," by Donald P. Hansen, in this catalogue). They resemble depictions on other chlorite vessels from both Mesopotamia and the Gulf island of Tarut, where a production center appears to have been located. Fragments of chlorite vessels from the Shara temple at Tell Agrab, not far from Khafajah, show a very similar kneeling figure as well as a scorpion and a zebu with patterned hump.[3] A piece from Tarut depicts a kneeling figure with patterned skirt and arms outstretched between two snakes (cat. no. 224d; see also cat. no. 224e). The style of these figures can be traced to eastern Iran, the source of metalwork and seals with similar images (cat. no. 228).[4] In this region as well as in western Central Asia, domination over serpents is a very prominent theme.[5]

To the right of the master of snakes on the British Museum vessel, a lion and vulture tear at the belly of a fallen and probably dead short-horned bull, perhaps of the type so commonly represented on Harappan-looking circular stamp seals found at Ur and other Mesopotamian sites (see "Art and Interconnections in the Third Millennium B.C.," by Joan Aruz, in this catalogue). According to Dominique Collon, the wild beasts represent chaos and are in contrast with the humans, who express control over the destructive forces of nature and bear the promise of fertility in the form of life-giving water.[6]

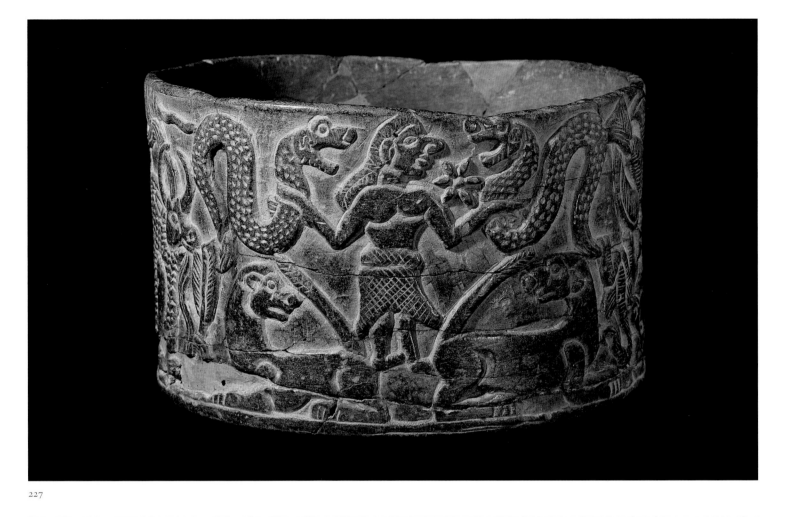

227

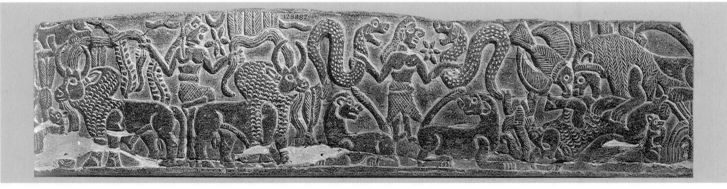

Fig. 85. Rolled-out photograph of a cylindrical vessel with heroes and animals (cat. no. 227).

The figures are executed in rather flat, low relief, with an emphasis on their outlines and patterned surfaces, particularly garments and body fur. Close parallels for the animals can be discovered on the numerous fragments of other carved chlorite objects found in Mesopotamia and Syria, eastern Iran, and Central Asia, and on the Arabian island of Tarut. These include the serpents with their distinctive broken-S-curve ears and undulating bodies (see cat. nos. 224a, 234, 236; fig. 87);

scorpions with striated bodies; zebus with patterned (or inlaid) humps and frontal horns, recalling depictions on numerous Harappan square seals (see cat. no. 296); and the swooping vulture with herringbone and hatched designs that indicate feathers.[7] The palm tree below the attacking lion can be closely related to one on a fragment from Tarut (see cat. no. 225a) and to another on a "handled weight" in the Metropolitan Museum (see cat. no. 225b). Only the little bears that stand to pluck the

date fruits seem to be out of place in this visual world. In fact, their closest iconographic parallel is on a silver vessel from Maikop, in the distant Caucasus region, where a bear is depicted feeding from a more northern-looking tree against a background of mountains and rivers (see fig. 82).[8] Bears were probably brought to Mesopotamia, as they were to Egypt, as gifts from Syria and perhaps from regions farther to the north as well. They are also included in the musical scene showing a bull lyre held by a bear and played by a don-key on the sound box of an actual lyre from the Royal Cemetery at Ur (cat. no. 58).[9]

JA

1. Herz (1966) reviews the problem; see also Frankfort 1932, p. 12.
2. Hansen 1975b, pl. 77.
3. Frankfort 1936b, p. 134, figs. 10, 12.
4. Porada 1993a, pp. 48ff.; see also "Art and Inter-connections in the Third Millennium B.C.," by Joan Aruz, in this catalogue.
5. Aruz 1998b, pp. 17–19.
6. Collon 1998, pp. 36–37; Collon 1995, p. 69.
7. For examples of scorpions with striated bodies from Nippur, see Herz 1966, p. 167, no. 12, pl. 7:12; from Bismaya, see ibid., pl. 7:13, and Banks 1912, p. 267; from Ur, see Woolley 1955, pl. 35, and Herz 1966, pl. 7:15. For the zebus, see Frankfort 1936b, p. 134, figs. 10, 12. For the vulture, see Burkholder 1971, p. 310, pl. 4, no. 12; Parrot 1956, pl. 50:660; Herz 1966, p. 166, no. 9, pl. 7:7.
8. Piotrovsky 1994, pp. 78–79, pl. 37.
9. Pittman (2002) includes bears among the animals traditionally shown in human postures in Proto-Elamite art. Pittman further notes that these creatures may have become familiar in urban centers of the third millennium B.C., like the trained bears that are often seen in the modern cities of the Middle East.

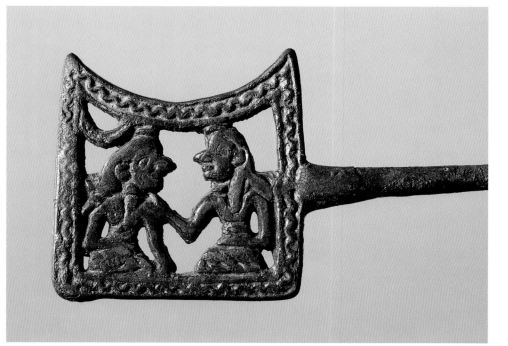

228

228

Open-worked pin with two seated figures

Copper alloy
L. 24.8 cm (9¾ in.); L. of head 5.3 cm (2⅛ in.);
H. of head 5.1 cm (2 in.)
Eastern Iran or Central Asia
Late 3rd–early 2nd millennium B.C.
Musée du Louvre, Département des Antiquités
Orientales, Paris; Gift of M. Foroughi 1975 AO 26068

The perforated head of this large pin is archi-tectural in form.[1] The top is a curved lintel[2] that suggests the scene unfolds inside a house, even though a crescent moon appears on the left. Two figures with long hair[3] and bare tor-sos face each other; both crouch in garments made perhaps of tufted wool. The figure on the right places his hand on the shoulder of his female companion. Although the sex of the two figures is almost indistinguishable, it is possible to identify them as a man and a woman on the basis of comparison with simi-lar scenes. For example, the Musée du Louvre possesses a small disk in lapis lazuli on which the same couple, in opposite positions, can be found on each face.[4] A compartmented seal

from Bactria-Margiana also bears the figures of a man and a woman facing each other.[5] Indeed, there are a number of examples of this type,[6] some with one of the figures holding a goblet. Pierre Amiet believes the figures are engaged in a flirtatious conversation; however, Victor Sarianidi suggests that the conversation has a mythical meaning: the transmission of a "revelation" from one individual to another.[7]

The representation of the figures—the large hooked nose, thick and protruding lips, double braid of hair, almond eyes, and promi-nent pectorals shown frontally—belongs to the iconography of the trans-Elamite world. The placement of the decoration suggests this pin was worn horizontally.

AB

1. For further reference, see Amiet 1974a, pp. 104–5, fig. 8, and Amiet 1986, p. 169, fig. 127.
2. Lintel construction is represented frequently on chlorite vases and on the gray ceramics of Bampur IV and V, or as a clay model or copper support.
3. The hair of male figures is often divided into two thick locks, one falling down the back, the other alongside the face; see Amiet 1986, figs. 73, 128.
4. AO26073; see ibid., fig. 128.
5. Sarianidi 1998b, no. 48-1, 2.
6. See, for example, the Standard of Shahdad, in Amiet 1986, fig. 126; see also catalogue number 229.
7. Sarianidi 1998b, p. 34.

229

Stamp seal with a seated figure, animals, and landscape

Lapis lazuli
W. 4 cm (1⅝ in.); L. 3.1 cm (1¼ in.); Thickness
2.5 cm (1 in.)
Eastern Iran
Mid-to-late 3rd millennium B.C.
Trustees of The British Museum, London
BM 1992-10-7, 1

This stamp seal with a wide, perforated handle at the back was originally almost square, but because of damage, the bottom corners are missing. Formerly, two figures faced each other. Only the face, one shoulder, and one arm of the figure on the left (in the impression) survive; the arm is raised and holds a tall cup. On the right, a man is shown frontally but with his head in profile; he has a prominent nose and long hair hanging down his back, with one lock falling beside his face. His legs are folded beneath him, covered by a skirt. His forearms are parallel to his legs, and his hands, with palms together, are held below his chest. Between the figures is a large drill hole, above which is a horizontal line with short vertical strokes extending from it and four rows of semicircular notches; this may represent a fenced enclosure or clouds and rain. To the right is a tadpolelike creature. At the right side of the seal is a goat facing left, with long horns, a triple zigzag beard, and a short tail. Below and facing right is a zebu with horns

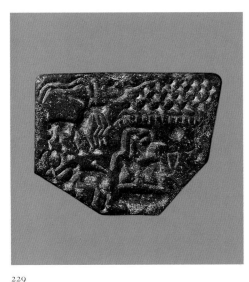

229

The main fragment of this vessel (Oriental Institute A195A) is well known from numerous publications. Less well known is the smaller piece (Oriental Institute A195B), published by Edgar Banks in 1912.[1] The two are joined by a third fragment, now in the Istanbul Archaeological Museum, a neglected fact that was first noted by Otto Weber in 1917.[2] A drawing (fig. 86) illustrates how the three pieces were once joined together.

The design is executed in a combination of low relief and inlay. Only one piece of the latter, the white skirt of one figure (Oriental Institute A195C), remains. Banks notes, however, that a bit of lapis lazuli inlay in one of the branches was still in place when the piece was discovered. At the bottom of the vessel are seven male figures. All have long hair and large noses and wear knee-length skirts and flat caps decorated with a series of vertical incisions. Each has a circular drilled depression at the top of his breastbone that seems to have been intended for an inlay, perhaps representing a large bead on a necklace. The two figures on the left, both with three "feathers" and a long "ribbon" protruding from their caps, appear to be leaving or standing in front of an elaborately decorated facade with objects projecting from the roof.[3] The first carries a sprig of vegetation in his left hand; similar sprigs

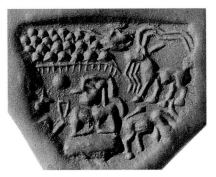

Impression from catalogue number 229.

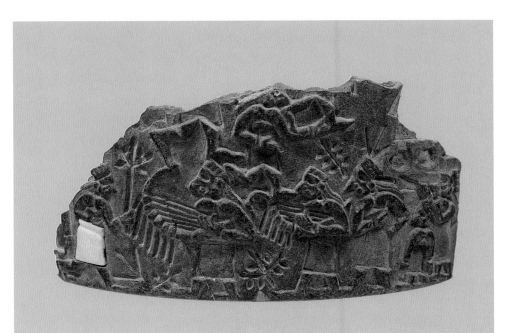

230

shown frontally, its tail raised over its back. The scene can be related to imagery found on the copper standard from Shahdad in southeastern Iran, on "Intercultural Style" vessels (cat. no. 227), as well as on seals from the Harappan civilization (see cat. no. 296). Comparisons with this material suggest that the figure on the left may be female and that the large drill hole in front of her represents a rosette,[1] which implies that the seal originated from within the culture of southeastern Iran.

PC

1. Collon 1998, pp. 31–39.

230

Vessel fragment with a procession of musicians

Chlorite and limestone or marble
H. 10.8 cm (4¼ in.); W. 20 cm (7⅞ in.)
Mesopotamia, Adab (modern Bismaya)
Early Dynastic I, ca. 2900–2650 B.C.
The Oriental Institute of the University of Chicago
A195A, B, C

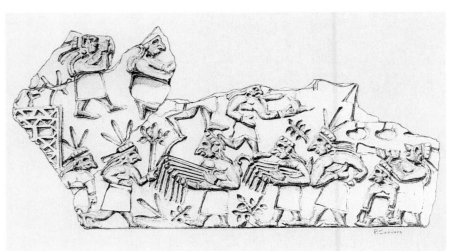

Fig. 86. Drawing of vessel fragments, including catalogue number 230.

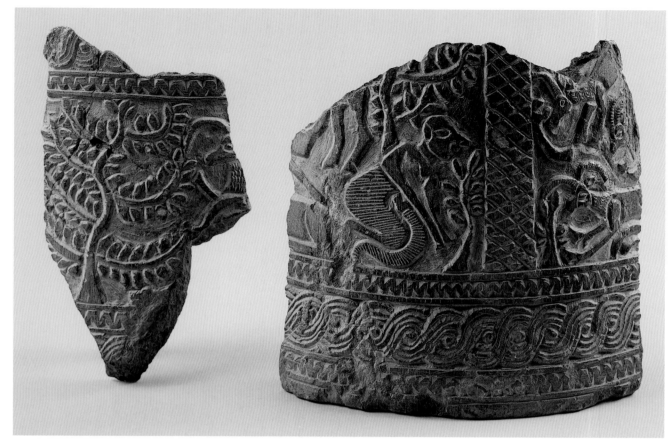

231b,a

sprout from the ground and appear scattered in the field. Approaching him are five musicians: two carrying harps or lutes, followed by a drummer with his instrument under his left arm, and succeeded by a smaller figure and a trumpeter. Above these men are remains of five additional, similarly represented, men facing right; one is kneeling while the others stride or run along. The lowest of these men appears to grasp the foot of the man running before him, which may be intended to suggest involvement in some kind of wrestling match. On the right are the remains of a figure; only the bottom of an ankle-length garment and settings for boots with upturned toes, originally inlaid, are preserved.

KLW

1. Banks 1912, pp. 266–69.
2. O. Weber 1917, pp. 391–92.
3. A similar facade occurs on a vessel from the Shara temple at Tell Agrab, now in the Iraq Museum, Baghdad, published in the *Illustrated London News,* September 12, 1936, p. 131.

231a, b

Vessel fragments with a figure and a tree

Chlorite
a. H. 20 cm (7⅞ in.); W. 20 cm (7⅞ in.); Thickness 2–3.4 cm (¾–1⅜ in.)
b. H. 19.7 cm (7¾ in.)
Syria, Mari, Shamash temple, M.2226, M.2227, M.2151–53, M.2182, M.2625
Early Dynastic III, ca. 2550–2250 B.C.
National Museum, Damascus, Syria 2058

These two fragments originally belonged to one of a number of tall, elaborately carved, conical vessels dedicated in the temples of the ancient Near East. Several such votives were found in the temples at Mari. In contrast, however, to the bold, inlaid depictions of lions and snakes or finely patterned carvings on conical, cylindrical, and pyriform containers found in the Ishtar temple, here we see the image of a man kneeling before a plant and a large palm-tree trunk, facing three goats with widely curving horns. A second fragment continues the scene, showing a similar creature standing on its (missing) hind legs to feed from a branching tree. The scene is framed by horizontal borders above and below, each with a guilloche pattern between wavy bands. The guilloche pattern is found on "Intercultural Style" chlorite "weights" and vessels, one in this catalogue from the Gulf island of Tarut (cat. no. 224f); it became a characteristic feature of Syrian glyptic art in the early second millennium B.C.

The man is distinguished by a bald head, a long prominent nose, a nude torso, and a curving, striated garment tapering into a single visible leg, with a second striated curved element below it. The treatment of the lower body has caused some scholars to interpret this figure as a scorpion-man, based on representations of scorpions on "Intercultural Style" vessels.

Elements of the imagery on this piece, which was dedicated in the temple of the sun god, can be related to a vessel of similar form from the temple of the moon god at the site of Khafajah in the Diyala region of Mesopotamia.[1] Here we also find scenes of horned animals executed in a similarly stark style, with a geometric (architectural) pattern as the lower border.

JA

1. Hansen 1975b, pl. 77.

Conical vessel with a leopard and snake

Chlorite
H. 14.5 cm (5¾ in.); Diam. 13 cm (5⅛ in.)
Syria, Mari, Ishtar temple
Early Dynastic III, ca. 2550–2250 B.C.
National Museum, Aleppo, Syria 7829

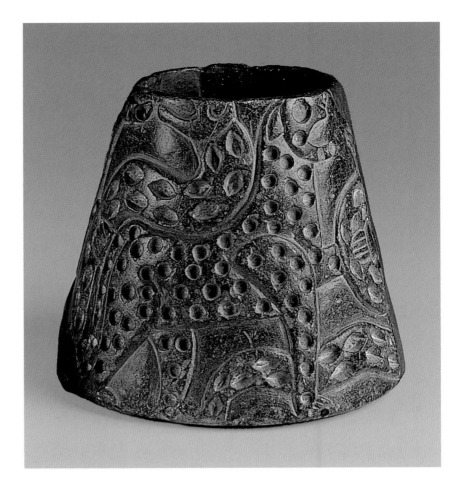

Among the sculptures and other votive objects discovered during excavations of the Ishtar temple at Mari were many complete and fragmentary chlorite vessels in the distinctive "Intercultural Style" that has its closest parallels in the art of eastern Iran. These vessels enjoyed wide distribution along the trade routes that brought lapis lazuli and other precious materials as far west as Mari. "Intercultural Style" vessels have not been found at other Syrian sites, and the extensive international connections of Mari are further emphasized by the discovery of a Central Asian compartmented stamp seal in the pillared room of the Early Dynastic palace.[1]

One of the most important themes expressed in the Mari corpus of chlorite vessels is the struggle between two powerful creatures, the leopard and the snake. On this conical vessel, a leopard with circular depressions that once held inlays to indicate spots strides to the right with one forepaw raised, grasping a snake in its paw. The body of the serpent is coiled beneath the leopard's other foreleg, and its scales were indicated by elliptical inlays. A second snake curls into the curve of the leopard's back. A similar scene showing a leopard confronting and coiled in a serpent's body is depicted on a fragment now in Berlin, bearing a dedicatory inscription of the Akkadian ruler Rimush (cat. no. 233). Another scene, this one on a conical vessel from the Ishtar temple at Nippur, also shows a feline, eye-to-eye with a serpent. Their faces are very similar in form, except for the distinctive snake ear in the form of a broken S-curve (fig. 87). This feature is shared by a number of snake images from different locations in the Gulf region, Mesopotamia, Central Asia, and Iran (see cat. nos. 224a, 227, 236).[2] A large intact jar from the Ishtar temple at Mari is carved with guilloche chains originally embellished with elliptical inlays. Certainly symbolic of serpents, they resemble the reverse side of the vessel from the Ishtar temple at Nippur, where the ophidian bodies coil into a guilloche pattern.   JA

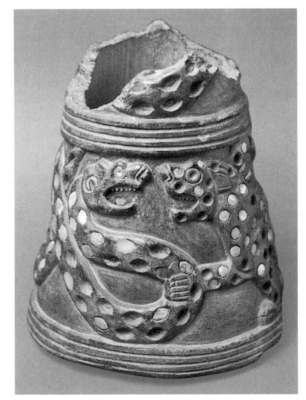

Fig. 87. Chlorite relief-carved vessel with a snake and a leopard. Nippur, Early Dynastic IIIA, ca. 2550–2400 B.C. Iraq Museum, Baghdad, IM 66071.

1. Beyer 1989, pp. 111ff.
2. For an example from Shahdad, in Iran, see Hakemi 1997, p. 20 (two snakes).

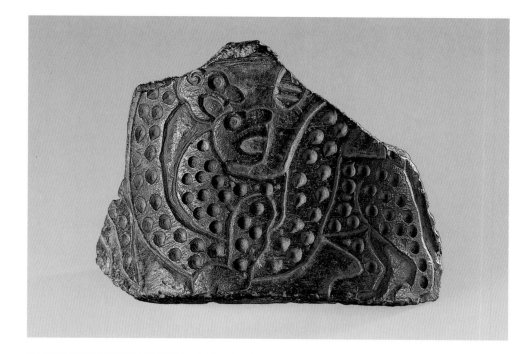

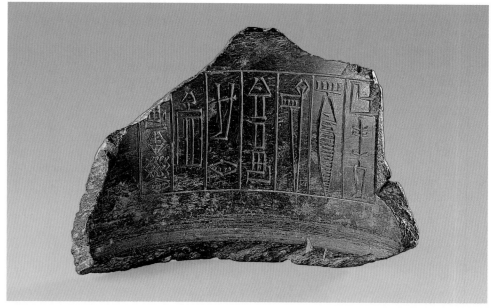

233

Vessel fragment with a leopard (?) and snake

Cuneiform inscription
Chlorite
H. 12.5 cm (4⅞ in.); W. 16.5 cm (6½ in.); Diam.
21 cm (8¼ in.)
Mesopotamia (?)
Early Dynastic III–Akkadian, ca. 2550–2236 B.C.
Staatliche Museen zu Berlin, Vorderasiatisches
Museum VA 5298

This fragment is from the side and part of the bottom of a goblet that was decorated on the outside with relief and inlay work. A leopard (?)

is depicted locked in combat with a serpent. The motif was first carved into the soft stone in low relief, then drilled with holes to hold inlays. The depressions in the feline figure are round; those in the serpent are oval. Similar vessels have been found that have small pieces of shell in the depressions, greatly enhancing the object's visual appeal. No inlays remain in the fragment shown here.

A seven-line inscription appears on the inside. It was probably added some time after the piece was made and thus provides only a

terminus ante quem for the date of the vessel itself. It reads, "Rimush, king of Kish, who crushes Elam and Parahshum."

Chlorite vessel fragments of this kind are known from various sites in the Gulf region, Syria, and Mesopotamia (see cat. nos. 224a, 232, 234). The techniques and motifs they display suggest that they were all made in the same production center. One well-researched site in that area presenting evidence of chlorite and steatite work is at Tepe Yahya, Iran (see cat. no. 242).   LM

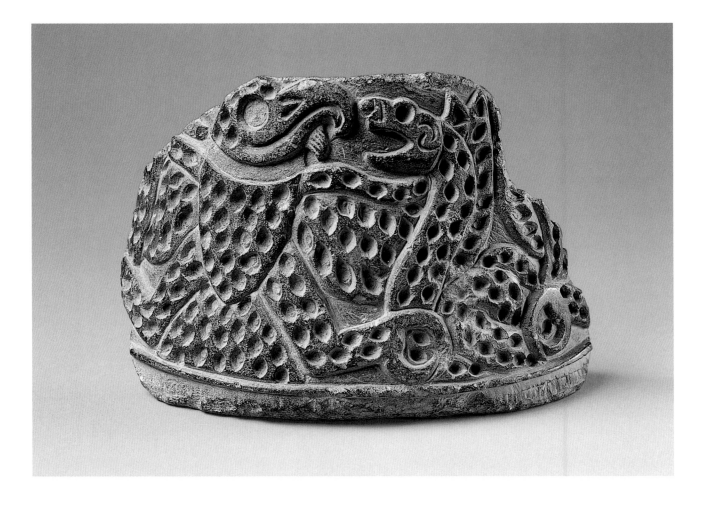

234

Vessel fragment with a snake and eagle

Chlorite
H. 15 cm (5 ⅞ in.)
Mesopotamia, Nippur
Early Dynastic III, ca. 2550–2250 B.C.
Eski Şark Museum, Istanbul

This is one of four vessel fragments in the "Intercultural Style" found at Nippur.[1] They were executed in a similar style and technique and are related iconographically. Depicted here is an eagle, its profile head with a prominent round eye and downward-curving beak facing a coiled snake. The serpent, with a smaller circular eye and characteristic broken-S-curved ear, rears up, ready to strike the eagle with its menacing gaping jaws. The bird's preserved left talon is placed over the first horizontal coil of the snake's body. Its chest, tail, wings, and legs are frontally displayed. One expects that it originally formed the central element of an antithetical composition, with a second snake clutched in its right talon.

The bodies of both creatures are executed in rather flat relief embellished with elliptical cutouts for inlays. The head of the eagle was also inlaid, and the eyes of both creatures would have received inlays of colored stone. Like a second, more complete fragment from Nippur, this one has parallel horizontal incisions on the base, and it may have been of similar conical form.

The second fragment (fig. 87) was found in the Inanna temple at the site, in Level VIIB, which has been dated to Early Dynastic IIIA (ca. 2550–2400 B.C.). It also depicts a snake coiling in an attack posture, but in this case confronting a leopard. Both creatures have cells for inlay on the heads as well as the bodies, and their gaping jaws display teeth or fangs.[2]

Snakes confront lions and eagles on a number of "Intercultural Style" inlaid relief vessels discovered in Mesopotamian and Syrian temple contexts (see cat. no. 232). Perhaps the closest parallel for the composition of catalogue number 234 is on a vessel from

Early Dynastic building levels in the E-anna Precinct at Uruk; on that fragment the wings and talons of eagles are superposed on the bodies of coiling serpents.[3] Two unprovenanced objects bear similar imagery. One is a conical vessel in the Miho Museum, Japan (see entry for cat. no. 235, for the possible significance of eagle and snake). The other is a "handled weight" in the Tehran Museum, Iran, with bird and serpent on one face and with architectural decoration typical of "Intercultural Style" objects on the reverse.[4]   JA

1. Peters (1897, pls. opp. pp. 140, 146) reports its discovery at Nippur with material dating from the time of Amar-Su'ena. For the other three fragments, see Herz 1966, p. 165, no. 6, pl. 4:9; p. 174, no. 32, pl. 10:5–6, p. 167, no. 12, pl. 7:3. See Herz (ibid., p. 176, no. 35), who mentions that E. Unger says it comes from Adab.
2. Herz 1966, p. 174.
3. For a reconstruction of the designs, see ibid., pls. B (no. 38), C (no. 35).
4. Muscarella 1993, no. 1.

235

Conical vessel with deities, snakes, bulls, and a bird of prey

Chlorite
H. 23.5 cm (9¼ in.); Diam. of mouth 8.6 cm (3⅜ in.);
Diam. of base 12.9 cm (5⅛ in.)
Iran
Mid-to-late 3rd millennium B.C.
The Shinji Shumeikai, Japan SS 1498

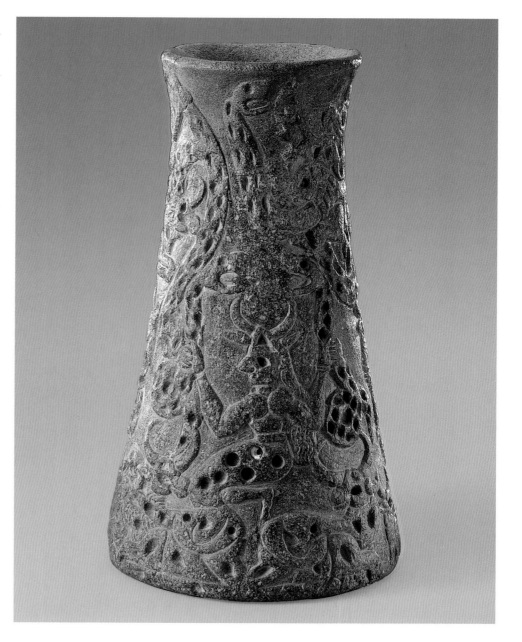

This extraordinary vase carved and inlaid in the "Intercultural Style" lacks archaeological provenance but was probably originally dedicated as a votive offering in a Mesopotamian temple. The figural scene presents a synthesis of many of the motifs on other "Intercultural Style" chlorite vessels, weights, and fragments. It extends all over the field of this conical vessel with a slightly everted rim, a form used for carvings of human and animal figures as well as of geometric designs that suggest plants and basketry.[1]

The theme conveyed is the control of fierce and dangerous forces, represented by serpents, as well as of beneficent powers, in the form of bulls—a contrast also evident on another carved chlorite vessel in this catalogue (cat. no. 227). Horned divinities, loosely arranged in one register, kneel above addorsed bulls and leopards, holding alternately snakes and bulls with large crescent-shaped horns. The more constricted space afforded the upper row of figures shows two other similarly displayed deities, one very small, grasping the necks of two snakes, above merged bovine forequarters. They share the upper register with a bird of prey that grasps serpents in its talons. The coils of the various snakes extend horizontally and vertically over the field in a composition similar to that on a vessel fragment from Uruk, where serpents are also caught up in an eagle's claws.[2] Another fragment from Nippur has the same theme (cat. no. 234).[3] The eagle and the serpent were long ago recognized by Rudolf Wittkower as quintessential symbols of heavenly light and underworld darkness.[4] In the myth of Etana, the eagle, liberated from the snake, carries Etana to the sky (cat. nos. 148, 340).

Some stylistic features of the human and animal figures on the vase find parallels on

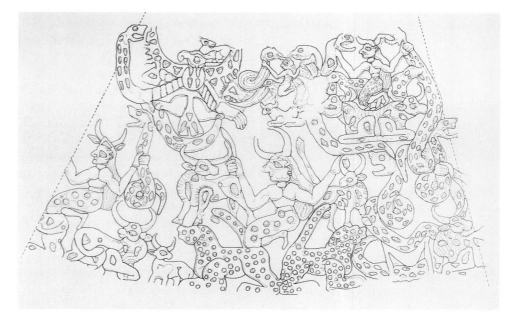

Fig. 88. Drawing of a conical vessel with deities, snakes, bulls, and a bird of prey (cat. no. 235).

objects of the "Intercultural Style" found in or thought to come from Mesopotamia, Iran, and the Gulf. The figures are carved in a familiar, starkly modeled, and highly patterned manner. The divinities, in a kneeling posture, display the long bulbous noses and full cheeks, long hair, and muscular torsos typical of the style. The snakes, with menacing open mouths, are rather crudely executed, lacking details of fangs and ears in the manner of some of the simpler and bolder compositions on "Intercultural Style" vessels without human figures (see cat. no. 232). There are areas of confused renderings on this vessel as well, particularly where creatures emerge from the crowd of figures in the upper register. It is also difficult to distinguish the individual serpents among the coiling mass that covers the background. This is a rare example of a composition (see also cat. no. 224d) in which the details of anthropomorphic figures were possibly filled with inlays (none of which have been preserved). The garments of the divinities, like the pelts of the leopards, are patterned with circular depressions to hold colorful stones, while the serpents have the usual elliptically shaped depressions. The bulls' bodies have cutouts of various shapes; the circular forms are paralleled on the dewlap of a zebu on a conical vessel that has been attributed to the island of Tarut in the Gulf (cat. no. 226).

JA

1. Pittman 1984, fig. 1 opp. p. 13, p. 14, fig. 2.
2. Lindemeyer and Martin 1993, pl. 68.
3. Contenau 1927–31, vol. 2, p. 694, fig. 484, discussed by Herz 1966, no. 35.
4. Wittkower 1970, pp. 294ff.

236

Handled weight with confronted snakes

Chlorite or steatite
Central Asia, Soch
Mid-to-late 3rd millennium B.C.
Historical Museum of Uzbekistan, Tashkent

According to Tashkent Museum records, at the end of the nineteenth century workers at a building site on the outskirts of the town of Soch recovered this stone object from the ground at a depth of ten meters. What became of the piece immediately after its discovery was not recorded, but six years later it was

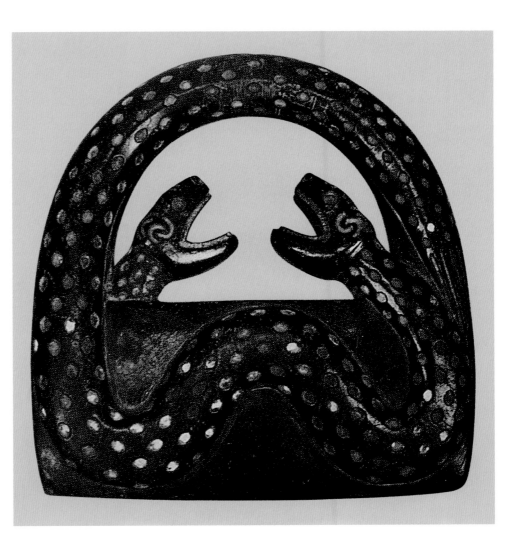

listed in the museum's collection. Thus, aside from its putative provenience, nothing is known of its cultural context or of the presence of any juxtaposed material at the site where it was found.[1] Its shape and decoration are in the "Intercultural Style" (see "Art and Interconnections in the Third Millennium B.C.," by Joan Aruz, in this catalogue), but its use is unknown. Perhaps it was a weight (see entry for cat. no. 225b).

The "weight" is sculpted from a single piece of stone in a clever manner. Both faces show a snake whose body curves up to form a "handle," while its open-mouthed head projects freely in the central space between the handle and the body. The snakes' jaws are threateningly open—whether apotropaically or in mutual warning is not clear—and teeth are visible, some apparently inserted separately. The nostrils are articulated. As is typical of snakes represented in the "Intercultural Style" (see cat. nos. 224a, e, 232–235), the bodies here

have oval cutouts for inlays, and the ears are formed as reversed, U-shaped loops. The stone was polished for use.[2]

OWM

1. Sarianidi 1986, p. 151, fig. 43. If Soch or a neighboring site was indeed its provenience, the findspot is the northernmost locus for such an object and also for "Intercultural Style" material in general. See also Muscarella 1993, pp. 144–45, no. 5, fig. 5.
2. For the inlays and ear pattern, see, for example, Durrani 1964, pl. 6; Burkholder 1971, figs. 17–21; Miroschedji 1973, pl. 1; Zarins 1978, pls. 67, 68; Kohl 1979, p. 64, fig. 5; Lamberg-Karlovsky 1988, p. 78, fig. 3, E.; and Muscarella 1993, p. 144, no. 5.

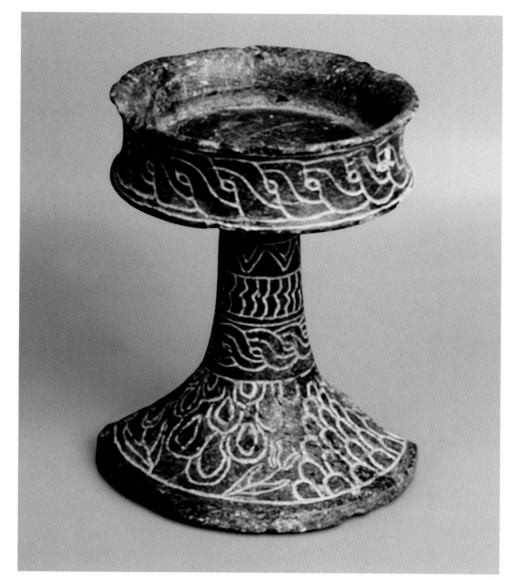

237a

to the Gulf (see cat. nos. 224f, 231). On the base, delicate tulip or poppy flowers emerge in between scalloped patterns and pendant drop clusters that may suggest a mountain landscape with water or land. This scene seems to be related to the theme of flowing liquid, rendered on the stem of the cup as vertical waves. If the flower is identified as a poppy, this could allude to the hallucinatory drink that Victor Sarianidi thinks was used for ritual purposes. This flower representation is also found on a steatite miniature bottle from Gonur as well as on seals and amulets in black chlorite.[1]

In contrast to the stemmed cup, the cosmetic box (cat. no. 237b) is decorated with purely geometric patterns that are engraved in two registers. Its zigzag motifs are reminiscent of carved chlorite vessels imitating basketry. The box was found in a hoard in a tomb with male and female skeletons, in front of whom a dog was also buried. The tomb's rich furnishings consisted of about thirty objects made of precious materials, including a copper-alloy mirror in a wood case inlaid with shells, carnelian necklaces, silver and alabaster vessels, and fragments of gold leaf.   EVF

1. Sarianidi 1968, pp. 23, 304–5, nos. 1663, 1665; Sarianidi 2002, p. 126 above right: steatite miniature vessel.

237a, b

Vessels with guilloche and zigzags

Steatite
Western Central Asia, Gonur-depe, necropolis
Late 3rd–early 2nd millennium B.C.
The National Museum of Turkmenistan Named After
Saparmurat Turkmenbashi, Ashgabat
a. Tomb 1750
b. H. 9.4 cm (3¾ in.); Diam. 13.3 cm (5 1/4 in.)
Tomb 1999

The variety of material culture at the site of Gonur-depe reflects long-distance trade marked by strong international features. The exceptional cup on a tall stem (cat. no. 237a) is almost completely covered with decorative patterns, most prominently the guilloche. The same motif appears on chlorite vessels of the "Intercultural Style" found at sites from Syria

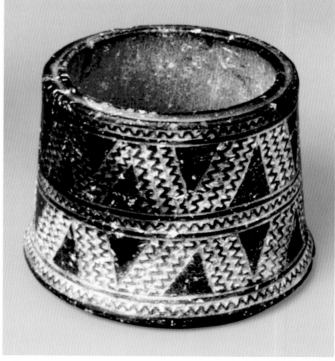

237b

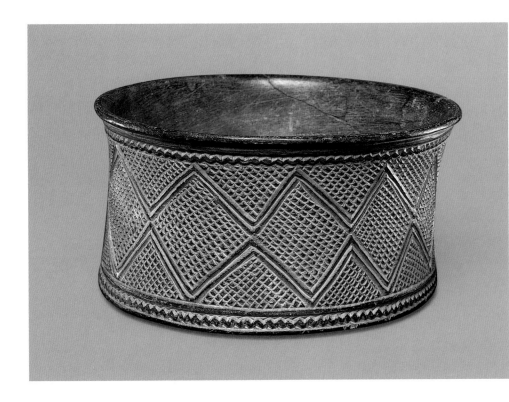

Cylindrical vessel with a hut motif and zigzag bands

Chlorite
H. 7.7 cm (3 in.); Diam. 12.2 cm (4¾ in.)
Gulf region, Bahrain, Saar
Mid–late 3rd millennium B.C.
Bahrain National Museum, Manama 358-2-88

This completely preserved bowl was excavated at Saar, on Bahrain. It bears a classic "Intercultural Style" motif, which is called the hut design because the vertical structures with incurved tops are generally interpreted to be architectural units, perhaps doors.[1] Above the hut is a band of triangles that is probably not related. The hut motif's distribution is widespread, occurring across the full geographic range where the style exists, at sites in Mesopotamia, Syria, Iran (see cat. no. 242b), and the Gulf, fully justifying the label "Intercultural."[2]

OWM

1. See Durrani 1964, pp. 75–76. Miroschedji (1973, pp. 15–19) discusses the identification of the motif.
2. For Mesopotamia (for example, Khafajah, Tello, Sippar, Bismaya, Kish, Ur, and Uruk), see Durrani 1964, pls. 3, 4; Lamberg-Karlovsky 1988, nos. 19–26, 59, 503; and Lindemeyer and Martin 1993, nos. 774, 797, 1105. For Syria (Mari), see Durrani 1964, pl. 4,

238

Cylindrical vessel with rows of zigzags

Dark gray steatite
H. 10.2 cm (4 in.); Diam. 18.5 cm (7¼ in.)
Mesopotamia, Ur, PG 800, Puabi's Tomb, U. 10523
Early Dynastic IIIA, ca. 2550–2400 B.C.
University of Pennsylvania Museum of Archaeology and Anthropology, Philadelphia B17168

This cylindrical bowl has slightly concave sides. The exterior rim is decorated with a wave pattern beneath a straight line; at the bottom this wave pattern is framed by straight lines. In between, the main decoration consists of an imbricate pattern enclosed within triangles or diamonds formed by two zigzag lines. These lines, carved in relief and shown in mirror image, encircle the vessel. The bowl was found, along with a lapis lazuli cup, near the northwestern corner of a large box in the center of the death pit of Puabi's grave. Such vessels, which belong to the "Intercultural Style" (see "Art and Interconnections in the Third Millennium B.C.," by Joan Aruz, in this catalogue), have been found from Syria to Central Asia and the Indus Valley and date to the mid- to late third millennium B.C. The discovery of "Intercultural Style" vessels on islands in the Gulf suggests that some examples reached Mesopotamia by sea. Indeed, the decoration on this bowl closely resembles

chlorite vessels from Bahrain and Tarut in the Gulf, as well as from Susa.[2]

PC

1. Zarins 1978, pl. 70, no. 106.
2. Miroschedji 1973, fig. 5.11, pl. 3h.

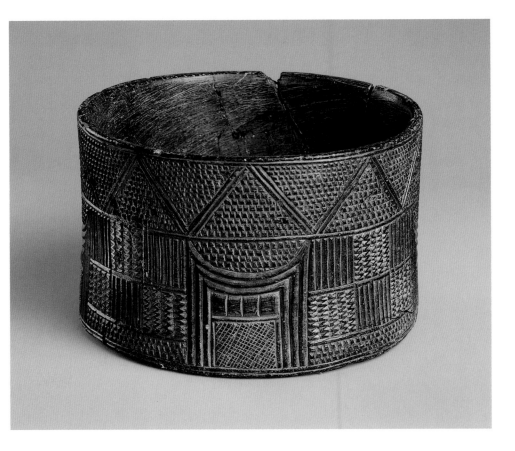

and Lamberg-Karlovsky 1988, nos. 80–85. For Iran (Susa and Tepe Yahya), see Durrani 1964, pl. 3; Miroschedji 1973, pl. 5:c,d; and Lamberg-Karlovsky 1988, p. 81, fig. 4, pls. 6, 8, 9. The example in the Tehran Museum, Iran, often published as deriving from Azerbaijan, has no provenience; see Muscarella 1993, p. 144, fig. 5. For examples from the Gulf, see Zarins 1978, pl. 66, and Lamberg-Karlovsky 1988, nos. 34–37, 270–79, 281–83.

240

Vessel fragment with a woven pattern

Steatite
H. 6.5 cm (2½ in.); Thickness 1.7 cm (¹¹⁄₁₆ in.)
Gulf region, Failaka
Late 3rd millennium B.C.
National Council on Culture, Arts, and Letters, Kuwait National Museum KM 367

The allover surface decoration of this fragmentary cylindrical, flat-bottomed vessel consists of oblique rows of diamond-shaped, crosshatched planes. The carefully executed design resembles the weave of a basket or mat.[1] Two pairs of horizontal grooves encircle the vessel at the lip and base, cutting the diamond motif in half and forming two rows of truncated lozenges. The simple, repetitive design is enriched by many individual variations in the curved and straight lines of the hatching. Common on carved steatite and chlorite vessels of the "Intercultural Style," the pattern,

which may or may not imitate weaving, is known from a number of third-millennium B.C. sites in Mesopotamia, Iran, the Gulf region (see cat. no. 224h), and the Indus Valley.[2] The device of deeply carved diamonds in high relief closely resembles the motif on fragmentary Iranian examples from Tepe Yahya (cat. no. 242c) and Susa.[3]   SG

1. Kohl 1974, p. 187.
2. See Baudot 1987; Durrani 1964; Kohl 1974; and Burkholder 1971.
3. See Miroschedji 1973, pl. 5:c.

241a, b

Vessel fragments

Bitumen compound
a. H. 6 cm (2⅜ in.); Diam. 10.6 cm (4⅛ in.)
b. H. 5 cm (2 in.); L. 8 cm (3⅛ in.)
Iran, Susa
Mid-to-late 3rd millennium B.C.
Musée du Louvre, Département des Antiquités Orientales, Paris Sb 9416, Sb 364

Sculpture in bitumen, a black hydrocarbon, was a Susian tradition that first appeared during the Uruk period with a striking representation of a bird of prey.[1] In about the middle of the third millennium B.C. statues, supports for offerings, bas-reliefs, and door fittings were also made of bitumen.[2] In addition, local

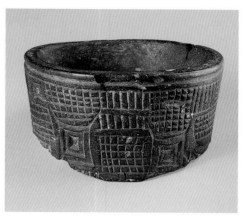

241a

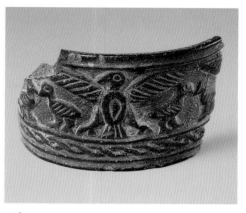

241b

artisans seeking to imitate exotic luxury goods from southeastern Iran,[3] perhaps from the ancient country of Marhashi, used it as a substitute for chlorite. The vase fragments displayed here are examples of this practice; indeed, the architectural theme of catalogue number 241a is borrowed from such luxury goods. It has motifs of small bricks and squares with concave sides that form houses with curved lintels, as if seen from above (for example, cat. no. 239).[4] The second fragment (cat. no. 241b), with the motif of a spread-winged bird-of-prey protecting its nestlings, is inspired by chlorite vessels depicting eagles (see cat. no. 234) as well as by what is known as the "second style" of Early Dynastic period painted ceramics.[5] The bird-of-prey theme also derives from glyptic, in which an eagle, depicted in a position intended to connote protection more than constraint, may exert a symbolic dominion over peacefully grazing herds.[6]

Until 1997 the substance used in these fragments was considered to be a bitumen compound artificially composed of a viscous element (hydrocarbon) and of mineral scouring agents such as crushed calcite. To make it suitable for carving, the mixture was supposedly heated to slightly under 250 degrees Celsius, which gave it the required homogeneity and

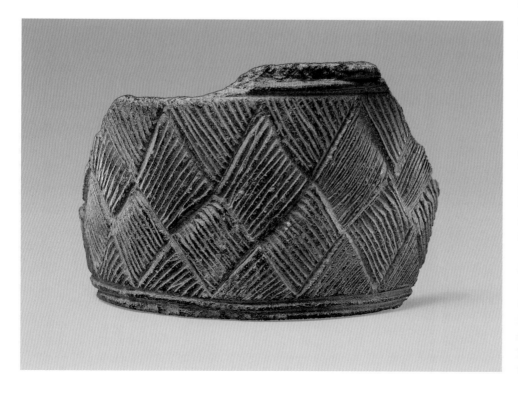

hardness. However, the discovery of bitumen in a natural solid state in a geologic fault in Luristan now leads us to consider it a natural substance that was worked like stone.[7]

AB

1. See Amiet 1966, fig. 86.
2. Ibid., figs. 117, 119–24, 133.
3. The best-known center of this trade, Tepe Yahya, was a major supplier of *marhushum,* an ancient term that probably designated chlorite. See Amiet 1986, p. 138.
4. For further reference, see Amiet 1979, p. 200, pl. 20b; Amiet 1986, pp. 124, 137, fig. 64; Connan and Deschesne 1996, pp. 162–63, no. 74.
5. For further reference, see Amiet 1966, no. 118; Connan and Deschesne 1996, p. 165, no. 79.
6. Amiet 1980, pl. 94:1227.
7. Connan and Deschesne 1998, pp. 13–16. A natural vein of bituminous rock approximately one hundred kilometers long and a maximum of one meter thick is located one hundred kilometers northwest of Susa. According to Deschesne, bitumen and crystalline rocks rose from the deeper strata during a tectonic shift, and rock crushed during the tremor combined intimately with the viscous bitumen; the mixture was then trapped in a fault, where it was compressed. Nature itself thus did the work that was long attributed to human hands.

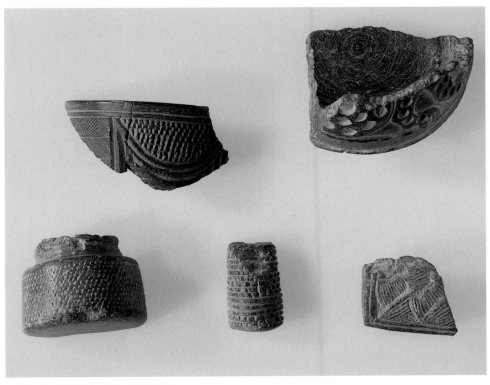

242b, 242a, top; 242d, 242e, 242c, bottom

242a–e

Vessel fragments

Chlorite
Iran, Tepe Yahya
Tepe Yahya IVB, ca. 2400–2100 B.C.
Peabody Museum, Harvard University, Cambridge, Massachusetts

a. H. 9.4 cm (3¾ in.)
XA TT1 #68

b. H. 5 cm (2 in.)
BW TT5-5

c. H. 3 cm (1⅛ in.)
B TT5A-1-1

d. H. 8 cm (3⅛ in.)
BW 6 sur 7'69

e. H. 4 cm (1⅝ in.)
BWTT5 '69

Among the many cultural remains dating to the third millennium B.C. discovered in the imposing mound of Tepe Yahya, on the edge of the desert in southeastern Iran, is a group of elaborately carved chlorite vessels decorated with figural and geometric designs in the "Intercultural Style" (see "Art and Interconnections in the Third Millennium B.C.," by Joan Aruz, in this catalogue).[1] Similar finds have been made at twenty-eight other sites, on the Iranian Plateau and in the Gulf region, Mesopotamia, the Indus Valley, and Bactria-Margiana.[2] Workplace debris and unfinished pieces found at Tepe Yahya identify the site as a center of production for these vessels. Although the ways in which they were exchanged and traded are still debated, the similarity of their carved decoration suggests the existence of cultural as well as economic ties throughout a very wide geographic region.[3]

One fragment of a chlorite vessel from Tepe Yahya (cat. no. 242a) bears the classic "Intercultural Style" motif of fighting animals, one a feline and the other a serpent. The feline's pelt is indicated by a pattern of circles, while ovals suggest the scales of the snake. These animal types are differentiated in the same way on stone vessel fragments from Mari and Nippur (see cat. no. 232; fig. 87).

Other fragments from the site have geometric designs, some of which may derive from basketry, plant, and architectural elements (see cat. nos. 242b–e). One prominent pattern is the hut motif (see cat. no. 242b), characterized by a bent lintel, often doubled or tripled, over a wall or a doorway. This motif has been found carved on stone vessels recovered in Mesopotamia at Khafajah, Bismaya, Mari, and Nippur.[4] In addition to the Mesopotamian examples, comparable hut designs on stone vessels are known from sites in Iran at Susa and Shahdad, and, in the Gulf region, at Saar (cat. no. 239). Imitations in ceramic gray ware of this design have also been found at Shahr-i Sokhta and Bampur.[5] The discovery of these "Intercultural Style" chlorite vessels in temples and burials in Mesopotamia suggests that they were valued not only for the high quality of their craftsmanship but also for their iconography. The meaning of their decoration, however, remains a mystery.

SG

1. This readily available stone was used throughout the occupation of the site, from the Neolithic until the Iron Age; see Kohl 2001, p. 210.
2. Kohl 2001; Lamberg-Karlovsky 1988. For examples from the Indus Valley (Mohenjo-daro), see Mackay 1932, pp. 356–57; for Gulf examples, see Burkholder 1971; and for Mesopotamian pieces, see Durrani 1964. Of the large corpus of "Intercultural Style" vessels excavated at Tepe Yahya, 75 percent were found in Level IVB (ca. 2400–2100 B.C.); the remaining 25 percent, found in later levels, may or may not have been heirlooms. See Kohl 2001, p. 214.
3. Baudot 1987, pp. 1–36.
4. See Kohl 1974, p. 177; Durrani 1964; and Baudot 1987.
5. Kohl 1974, p. 182; Miroschedji 1973; Baudot 1987, p. 8, pl. 4.

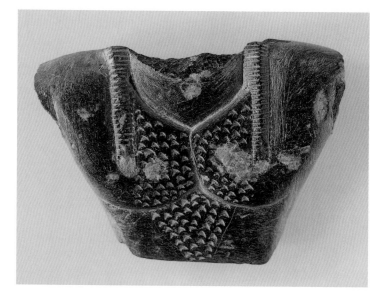

243

Fragment of a male torso

Chlorite
H. 12 cm (4¾ in.); W. 7 cm (2¼ in.)
Iran, Tepe Yahya, #70 BWTT5 '69 Reg. #164
Tepe Yahya IVB, ca. 2400–2100 B.C.
Peabody Museum, Harvard University, Cambridge,
Massachusetts

Only two pieces carved with figural images were found among the many chlorite objects excavated from Level IVB at Tepe Yahya.[1] One is a shaft-hole axe with incised-eagle decoration.[2] The other is this fragmentary torso, which may have been part of a frieze on a plaque or a bowl. What remains is the carved image of a broad-shouldered man with strong pectoral muscles. A vertical line and two semi-circular incisions delineate his breasts.[3] The patch of arrow-shaped indentations may indicate hair. Two parallel braids rest on either side of his chest. His strong and well-defined neck is heavily articulated.

Some characteristics of the Tepe Yahya torso, such as the broad shoulders and the linear outlining of the breasts, suggest the well-known images of scarred men (see cat. no. 244).[4] On those enigmatic sculptures, however, the bodies are far more rigid; moreover, the pectoral muscles on this sculpture from Tepe Yahya are strongly emphasized and naturally rendered, whereas they are merely suggested on the scarred men. Comparison with certain figures on "Intercultural Style" chlorite vessels from Mesopotamia proves more fruitful.[5] The braids suggested by parallel horizontal incisions are almost identical to the plaits of kneeling

figures on an "Intercultural Style" vessel in the British Museum (cat. no. 227).[6] Similar details in an engraving on a pin from Shahdad, Iran, however, suggest that the present sculptural fragment reflects a tradition of carving that may have originated in the eastern highlands of Iran.[7]

SG

1. For background on the subject of this entry, the reader should consult Strommenger 1964; Orthmann 1975; and Amiet 1986.
2. For the axe, see Lamberg-Karlovsky 1970, p. 43; Kohl 1974; and Kohl 2001, pp. 216–17.
3. Similar lines exist on seated female statuettes from Central Asia.
4. The breasts on the scarred men are similarly demarcated, with a vertical line and two semicircular lines that emphasize the breasts' fullness. See Porada 1971a, pp. 328–29, and Porada 1975, pp. 364–65.
5. As is noted in Kohl 1974, p. 67, and Lamberg-Karlovsky 1970, p. 43. For the reliefs on chlorite vessels from Mesopotamia, see Strommenger 1964, pl. 38. The third-millennium Mesopotamian sculptures are depicted with similar braids; see Frankfort 1939, pls. 43–46. The braids are also seen on an Elamite rock relief at Kurangun, where the Elamite god Napirisha is depicted enthroned on a serpent chair. See Harper, Aruz, and Tallon 1992, p. 8.
6. Lamberg-Karlovsky 1970, p. 43. The figures on the chlorite vessels, however, are two-dimensional and always seen in profile. Because the Tepe Yahya torso has two braids, it is possible that it was a portion of a three-dimensional sculpture rather than part of a frieze.
7. In 1970 Lamberg-Karlovsky (ibid.) suggested that the Tepe Yahya torso belongs to such a tradition. The subsequent excavations at the site and the parallel with the Shahdad pin further support this theory. For the Shahdad example, see Hakemi 1997, p. 715.

244

Standing male with a scarred face

Chlorite, calcite, meteoric iron, and shell (?)
H. 11.7 cm (4⅝ in.); W. 5 cm (2 in.)
Eastern Iran
Late 3rd–early 2nd millennium B.C.
Musée du Louvre, Département des Antiquités
Orientales, Paris AO 21104

This statuette is composed of three separately made units—an upper body, a short skirt, and legs—and is made from two distinctly colored stones, chlorite and calcite.[1] It is said to have been found along with several similar objects in the region of Fars, in southern Iran. The solid body is covered with scales, which may indicate an ophidian character. Scholars call this anthropomorphic serpent-dragon the scarred man, or *Narbenmann*, because of the characteristic deep gash across the right side of the face, which may originally have been inlaid. One eye and the lower lip of this example are still encrusted with calcium carbonate, perhaps indicating the use of shell. The head is encircled by a band of meteoric iron, and there is a small hole on the forehead that was perhaps intended to accommodate horns.[2] Two minuscule holes on each lip could have sealed the mouth, according to Roman Ghirshman, rendering the figure mute.[3]

Four complete scarred men and other, more fragmentary examples are known, one of them on loan to the Ancient Near East permanent galleries at The Metropolitan Museum of Art.[4] All hold an object under one arm that may be a vessel, perhaps containing beneficent waters.[5] Henri-Paul Francfort has claimed that this figure is connected with a type of female statuette, also made of contrasting light and dark stone, known in Bactria-Margiana (see cat. no. 259).[6] The female is sometimes called a princess, but she more likely represents a goddess of the highest rank. A high-ranking female is also depicted on some compartmented seals (see cat. no. 261). One of her roles may be to control the dragon, the guardian of subterranean waters. In assisting with the spread of spring floods, she transforms the evil powers of the monster into a beneficial force.[7] However, any geographical or mythological connection between the seated female and the scarred man awaits archaeological confirmation.[8]

AB

1. For further reference, see Parrot 1962, pp. 93–94, no. 2; Musée du Louvre 1963, pp. 231–36, pl. 14; Nagel 1968, pp. 110–11, and, more generally, pp. 104–19; Spycket 1981, pp. 115–17; Benoit 2003.

2. The analyses of the material used nondestructive processes—X-ray diffraction, which makes a mineralogical analysis possible, and the PIXE (Particle-Induced X-ray Emission) protocol using the AGLAE particle accelerator, which allows for a detailed chemical analysis. They were carried out by Anne Bouquillon at C2RMF (formerly Laboratoire des Musées de France), unpublished analysis report no. 2831, April 4, 2000, pp. 1–3.

3. Ghirshman 1963, p. 154.

4. Anonymous Loan, 1999, L. 1999.70.

5. Francfort 1994, p. 414.

6. The use of contrasting materials is reversed in the princesses: the body parts are light in color and the clothing, made of steatite, chlorite, or serpentine, all related materials, is dark. See Francfort 1994, pp. 406–18.

7. It is for this reason that the scarred man is covered with the scales of a snake, the chthonic animal par excellence.

8. In particular, it awaits the excavation in Bactria-Margiana of statuettes of scarred men.

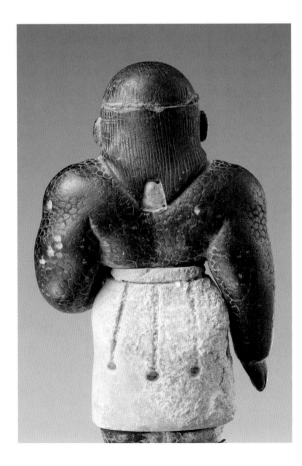

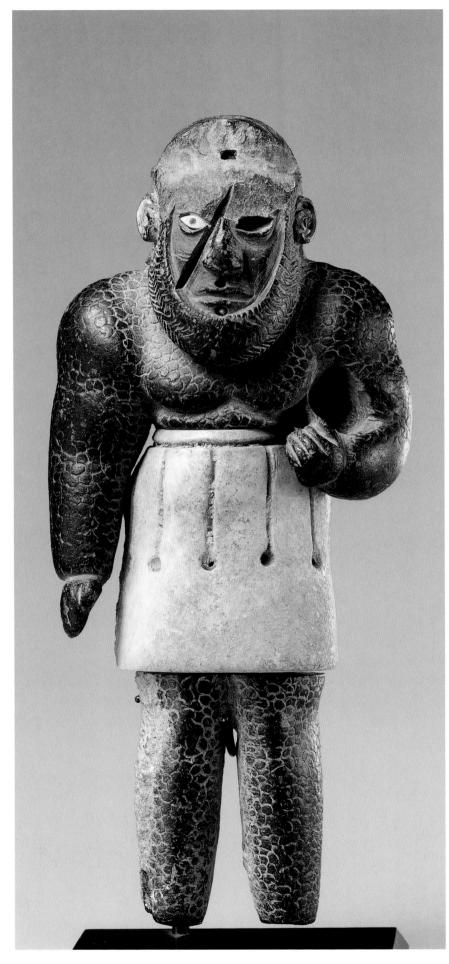

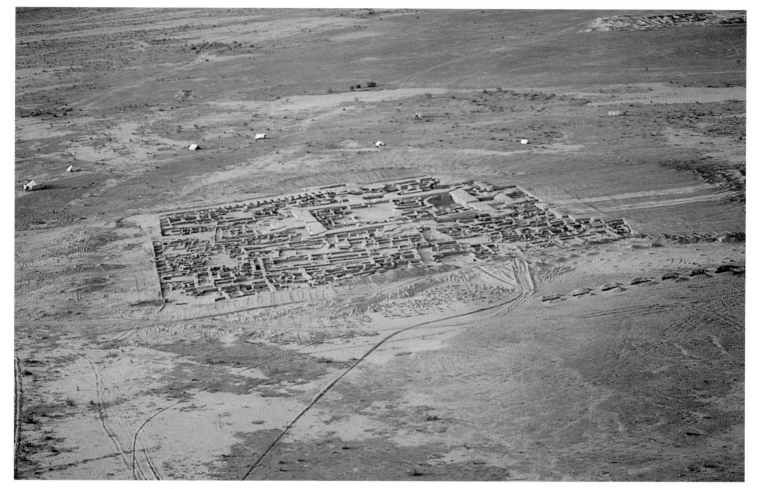
The excavated settlement of Gonur-depe in Turkmenistan.

PATHWAYS ACROSS EURASIA

MAURIZIO TOSI AND C. C. LAMBERG-KARLOVSKY

More than twenty thousand beads and other objects of lapis lazuli were buried in the royal graves at Ur to adorn rulers and courtiers on their path to heaven. All the raw blue stone originated within a single mountain chain, Sar-i Sang, almost three thousand kilometers east of Ur; indeed, almost all the lapis lazuli in the ancient Near East came from this mountain range deep within the Hindu Kush, the main Central Asian divide, almost on the border of modern China. To carry it all the way to Mesopotamia and beyond—for it was also highly fashionable in Egypt—a long chain of oasis settlements and towns grew up, along the same route taken in historical times by silk traders, which we call the Silk Road. We know from Mesopotamian texts and archaeological excavations that throughout the Bronze Age other goods traveled the same way: metals such as gold, tin, and copper; exotic woods; precious stones like turquoise and agates; fine textiles; furniture; and exotic animals and plants. Surprisingly, the cuneiform tablets make little mention of those who provided the goods. The Mesopotamians during the third millennium B.C. appear to have known very little of the lands and people beyond the Iranian Plateau, despite their role in supplying the gold and lapis lazuli that were indispensable for the representation of the power of Sumerian kingship. The place-names that recur most frequently—Aratta, Tukrish, Harali—are all of uncertain location. To reach Aratta, the ambassador sent by Enmerkar, first king of Uruk, had to cross "seven mountains," a canonical expression, then as now, for any faraway place, outside the geographic boundaries of one's own world (see entry for cat. no. 336). Many cultures flourished beyond the Great Iranian Desert in the second half of the third millennium. Thanks to the work of Piotr Steinkeller the land of Marhashi is known to us as a kingdom that ruled the archipelago of oasis farm communities scattered among copper-bearing mountains and salty deserts east of Anshan, the Elamite heartland in the highlands of Fars.[1]

But if only a few places east of Elam are mentioned in the Mesopotamian records, the archaeological evidence for them is plentiful; sites are dotted across the alluvial farmland from the Iranian Plateau to the borders of India and China. During the fourth and third millennia B.C., civilization appears to have left no vacuum in the space between the great cities of Mesopotamia and those of the Indus Valley. By 4000 B.C. incipient forms of urban life were developing across eastern Iran and Central Asia—modern Turkmenistan, Uzbekistan, and Afghanistan—as far as the Chinese province of Xinjiang, the homeland of nomads. Rich and distinctive cultures flourished across these rugged parts of the continental landmass, and like stepping-stones, they connected the Near East with the heartland of Asia. The precious stones and metals that arrived at Ur about 2400 B.C. for its elaborate rituals of death and power were carried along circuits of exchange that had already been active for two millennia.

Unlike the cradles of Bronze Age civilization—in Egypt, Mesopotamia, and the Indus Valley, and on the North China Plain—the Central Asian one had no dominant river to integrate peoples and resources along a trunk corridor of communication that transected all ecosystems between mountains and ocean. No navel, no name. Nevertheless, between 4500 and 2500 B.C., alluvial enclaves across eastern Iran and Central Asia, from the smallest piedmont oases to vast landlocked basins like the Hilmand or the Zeravshan, were intensively exploited by communities of farmers and herders, whose arts and crafts were often as advanced as those of the Near East. These enclaves encompassed a vast and diversified tapestry of peoples, apparently organized as independent polities but culturally unified, probably as a result of directing a considerable part of their resources to an exchange economy. In those isolated lands of scarcity and climatic extremes, trade became a subsistence strategy and ultimately an expression of political ingenuity, a prefiguration of commerce along the Silk Road or the Spice Seaways around the Indian Ocean rim in later, historical times.[2]

FERTILE ISLANDS BETWEEN MOUNTAIN AND DESERT

In order to understand the Bronze Age civilizations in eastern Iran and Central Asia we need to consider their geographic setting and the development of their cultural achievements. The region is characterized by the arid extremes of a continental climate and the tectonic corrugations resulting from the Indian tectonic plate's ancient collision with Eurasia. Its southern border begins in western Iran with the gapless folding of the Zagros Mountains and continues east to the regions of Makran and Baluchistan in a sequence of parallel crests that separate the inland Asian basins from the sea and its mitigating influence. To the north the Elburz Mountains and Kopet Dagh form another continuous wall stretching eastward from the Anatolian Plateau to the Central Asian highlands in the Pamirs and the Hindu Kush.

North of the Kopet Dagh we reach the high plateau of Central Asia with its unique riverine system. Here all major streams, the Zeravshan, Murghab, Tedzhen, and Amu Darya (the Oxus), debouch into the desert called Karakum. Along these rivers, and particularly in their deltaic fans of meandering channels, major settlements formed patches of fertility. These green oases bordered the desert margins like lush islands in a sea of emptiness. The higher the escarpment, the longer were the rivers and the wider the silt deposits where tillage was possible. Where the catchment's basins lie three thousand meters above sea level, the drainage from many streams may combine to form vast alluvial plains.

Agriculture depends on these fertile enclaves that cut across different ecological zones, from the high mountains to the desert lowlands, giving access to a broad spectrum of resources. Metals and other minerals, game, and wood were found in the mountain zones, and pasture for sheep and goats was available all year round if the flocks were moved between hills and steppes. Additional subsistence could be generated by fishing and by foraging wild species of plants and animals living between swamps, desert, and mountains.

Although small by comparison with Bronze Age Egypt and Mesopotamia, the concentration of resources and settlements in the region was large enough to permit the growth of complex polities during the fourth and third millennia B.C. While neither draft vehicles nor camels came into use until the end of the third millennium, goods and raw materials moved consistently throughout the region, ensuring a high level of economic and cultural integration, with shared technologies, material culture, burial rituals, and settlement patterns.

Exchange networks covered a vast area from the Nile to the Oxus and the Indus, and goods traveled both overland and by sea. As early as the fourth millennium, local circuits of exchange became integrated, allowing rare and precious commodities such as lapis lazuli to travel great distances. These networks laid the foundation for the long-distance trade routes that characterized the Bronze Age and brought the cultures of Mesopotamia, the Gulf, the Indus Valley, Iran, and Central Asia into a single zone of commercial interaction.

RECORD KEEPING AND THE CONTROL OF STOCKS: INNOVATION ON THE EVE OF URBANIZATION

A traveler in the first half of the fourth millennium B.C. moving from the Mediterranean Levant to either of the eastern extremes of the Chalcolithic world along the Zeravshan or the Indus would have passed through hundreds of towns and thousands of villages with similar cultural characteristics that offset their ethnic and linguistic differences. These settlements were rather evenly distributed in small aggregations of independent polities.

After 3500 B.C. the emergence of early state structures in Greater Mesopotamia completely altered the symmetry of the political landscape. A traveler would now meet with wholly new conditions in a far less peaceful social environment. The cultural and political transformation that occurred during the fourth millennium B.C. in Mesopotamia advanced the Near East beyond every other region in the world. This was not just another destabilization of the old order, but a true revolution. Like other great transformations in human history, it produced radical material and ideological changes in all expressions of culture. The ultimate outcome of an increasing centralization of labor and wealth was the foundation of cities and a complete reorganization of population and resources in the new man-made landscape. Powerful means of production and management were established, not only in Greater Mesopotamia, including Proto-Elamite Iran, but also far beyond, in the Anatolian and Iranian highlands. Within approximately three hundred years state structures developed from the Nile to the Indus.

The principal archaeological indicators of the new organization are cylinder seals and their impressions on clay. These tools for keeping records of transactions, especially the administration and distribution of rations to pay for labor, were used to control all kinds of containers, from storerooms to pots and bags, clay counters, and standardized vessels, such as beveled-rim bowls. The critical innovation was the creation of a recording system that could be detached from household control and expanded to cover all kinds of transactions. The invention, in the late fourth millennium B.C., of writing on tablets marked a turning point in human history.

In eastern Iran and Central Asia the emergence of early state structures appears to have been a more gradual process. Not until the very end of the fourth millennium can significant changes be detected in the archaeological record. These include an expansion in the size of the central towns within each settlement system, an increasing social differentiation in the size and function of architecture, and the spread of more elaborate and diversified burial types. All the basic elements of the material culture, from architecture to pottery types, developed out of local Chalcolithic traditions. Writing and the other new instruments of administration, however, were directly imported from the Proto-Elamite world of southwest Iran. Record keeping, standardization of rations, and control of stocks spread across the whole of the Iranian Plateau and beyond.

A DISCONTINUOUS URBANIZATION

Urbanization was possible in the larger Chalcolithic settlement systems, such as Xabis on the edge of the Dasht-i Lut, or in the regions of Kandahar, Seistan, and Gorgan, where the alluvial floodplains encompassed more than three thousand square kilometers. During the first half of the third millennium B.C. central sites in these areas—Shahdad, Shahr-i Sokhta, Mundigak, and Tureng-tepe—expanded at growth rates closely matching those in predynastic Mesopotamia and the Indus Valley. By 2500 B.C. each of the four sites extended over two hundred hectares, with about fifteen to twenty thousand people living in the core of the city and its suburbs. Large ceremonial compounds overlooked by high, stepped-pyramid-like structures have been identified at Tureng-tepe, Mundigak, and Shahr-i Sokhta. The one at Tureng-tepe is a true ziggurat, twenty-five meters in height and eighty meters along each side of the base—the same size as the one built half a millennium later by Ur-Namma at Ur (figs. 104, 105). The precinct wall at Mundigak enclosed a two-hectare area. The Shahr-i Sokhta complex, probably smaller in size, located from aerial photographs, also extends for two hectares, and the high terrace has a central staircase three meters wide. These large sites, as well as the smaller communities on the Iranian Plateau, such as Tepe Yahya, Tell Malyan, Bampur, Godin, and Tepe Hissar, indicate that throughout the third millennium there was a dynamic regional exchange as well as long-distance trade with Mesopotamia.

COLLAPSE AND TRANSFORMATION

Throughout Central Asia the growth of urban societies was seriously challenged after 2400 B.C. Within less than three hundred years, none of the major centers that developed during the first half of the third millennium was still functioning as such. The causes for this "urban collapse" remain a mystery that only future research can resolve. Looking toward the end of the third millennium, however, we witness the unfolding of momentous events in the Central Asian world of southern Turkmenistan, Uzbekistan, and northern Afghanistan. At this time, in place of the Chalcolithic towns and villages that had dotted the foothills of the Kopet Dagh, there appeared a cultural constellation that was to have a major impact upon distant Mesopotamia, the Eurasian steppes, the Iranian Plateau, and the Indus Valley.

BACTRIA AND MARGIANA IN THE BRONZE AGE

It is not often that archaeologists discover what some might call a cultural complex and others might term a state but that all would agree, at the very least, was a complex chiefdom. In the early 1970s Victor Sarianidi of Moscow's Institute of Archaeology, in collaboration with colleagues affiliated with the Turkmen Academy of Sciences, discovered in the ancient deltaic fan of the Murghab River numerous archaeological sites sharing a distinctive material culture. They called their discovery the Bactria-Margiana Archaeological Complex (BMAC). Bactria was the name given by the Greeks to northern Afghanistan and the territories surrounding the Amu Darya, while Margiana (ancient Margush) was a province of the Persian Empire whose regional capital was Merv in Turkmenistan.

The origins of the culture represented by the BMAC is much debated. Sarianidi placed them in Anatolia and northern Syria, boldly hypothesizing migration by way of southeastern Iran to western Central Asia. An alternative view, accepted by most archaeologists, is that the complex reflects cultural continuity with earlier sites along the foothills of the Kopet Dagh, such as Altyn-depe, that were abandoned in favor of the oases in the Murghab River delta in Bactria-Margiana.

To date, more than a dozen BMAC sites have been excavated in northern Afghanistan, southern Uzbekistan, and Turkmenistan. They range in size from ten to fifty hectares, and their chronological span is between 2100 and 1800 B.C. Gonur-depe, excavated over a ten-year period under the direction of Sarianidi, has contributed the most to our understanding of the BMAC communities. One of the settlement's most impressive features is a highly distinctive and exceptionally large architectural footprint. In the Russian literature it is referred to as a temple. Whatever its function, this monumental structure is as large as, if not larger than, the great buildings of the third millennium B.C. in Mesopotamia and the Indus Valley. At Gonurdepe, the outer wall of the square "temple" measures 125 meters on each side and is embellished by rectangular and semicircular bastions. The interior contains dozens of rooms, many offering evidence that metal, ceramic, and decorative craft objects were made there. At Togolok 21, the "temple" measures approximately 50 by 60 meters; it is surrounded by a wall measuring 110 meters on the short sides and 120 on the long and is studded with semicircular bastions. All known BMAC sites contain monumental structures heavily fortified by walls and bastions. They are located approximately thirty to fifty kilometers from each other, roughly a day's march. Rather than "temples," these buildings may be forerunners of the *qala,* one of Central Asia's most enduring architectural types. The *qala* is an extremely large, fortified complex, which in the Iron Age and in the medieval period served as the residence of the territorial ruler, or khan, and his retinue.

The material culture of the BMAC is equally distinctive both in its style and in the quality of its production. Cylinder seals feature anthropomorphic deities, heroes in combat with dragons, griffin demons, and winged lions. The very rich metallurgical inventory includes some exceptional silver and gold vessels (see cat. nos. 253, 254, 257); shaft-hole axes richly adorned with the figures of animals in combat (see cat. no. 264); trumpets of faience, silver, and gold (see cat. no. 256); silver and gold pins often ornamented with heads of animals; and compartmented seals with figural and geometric motifs (cat. nos. 260–263). Alabaster, calcite, and steatite vessels abound in a variety of shapes and with a wealth of incised and appliquéd designs. Female statuettes have also been found, the bodies carved from two pieces of chlorite or steatite, the heads and hands of white stone, ivory, or bone, and the hair of lapis lazuli or steatite (see cat. no. 259). The only complete excavated example to date comes from the necropolis of Gonur, where Sarianidi has discovered more than 2,500 burials. Figurine fragments have also been recovered from Togolok 21 and from Harappa in Pakistan.

Recent archaeological surveys and excavations indicate that the BMAC settlements were in close proximity to the pastoral nomads of the Andronovo culture, who inhabited the vast North Eurasian steppes. The territory of the Andronovo culture extended as far as the western borders of China, where the nomads acted as the intermediaries of BMAC influence. This influence can be seen in both the metallurgy and the architecture of Xinjiang. Numerous BMAC artifacts found at the major cities of the Indus civilization, such as Mohenjo-daro and Harappa, provide testimony for BMAC interaction with its southern neighbors. Similarly, artifacts characteristic of the culture have been found at sites throughout the Iranian Plateau. At Tepe Hissar, in northeastern Iran, compartmented copper-alloy seals, beads, and personal ornaments found in the numerous burials at the site are evidence of cultural links with the BMAC (see cat. no. 247). One building at Tepe Hissar, which contained many BMAC artifacts, offers direct evidence for the presence of BMAC residents. BMAC remains have also been recovered farther south, at Shahdad, Tepe Yahya, and, particularly, Susa (see entry for cat. no. 273). Even more distant from the BMAC heartland are the materials recovered from graves at Sibri and Nausharo (cat. no. 302a), in Baluchistan, and from Tell Abraq, in the Gulf region (see entry for cat. no. 210).

Who were the people whose material culture we call BMAC? Above all, they were farmers dependent upon extensive irrigation for their harvest of cereals, fruits, and vegetables. Among their domesticated animals they relied principally upon sheep, goats, cattle, and, as draft animals donkeys, asses, and onagers. Sarianidi believes that they were Indo-Aryans, whose religious beliefs provided the foundation for Zoroastrianism. Within the BMAC "temples" Sarianidi identifies fire altars and sacrificial areas, as well as specific objects and architectural features described in passages of the *Rig-Veda* and the *Avesta,* the holy texts of the Indo-Aryans and Zoroastrians. Sarianidi readily admits, in his most recent book, that few have embraced his controversial hypotheses.[3] Nevertheless, for some thirty years his indefatigable labor has placed before us a culture that had a broad impact on the Bronze Age of Asia.

What happened to the BMAC? It was followed by the Takirbai culture, which displays continuities in material culture with the BMAC, yet profound differences as well. The remarkable unity of the BMAC, with its concentration of wealth in large settlements focused upon "temples," gave way to a multiplicity of heterogeneous towns and villages. Every cultural transformation is unique: there are no general laws directing the processes of change. The mutation of a culture, no less than the rise and fall of a civilization, remains an enduring puzzle with multiple solutions.

1. Steinkeller 1982, pp. 237–65.
2. Di Cosmo 2000, pp. 392–407.
3. Sarianidi 2002.

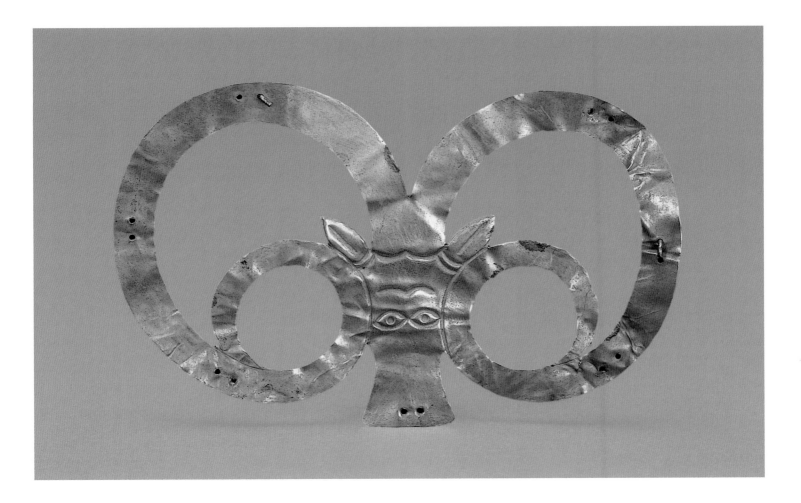

245

Mouflon head appliqué

Gold
H. 8.5 cm (3⅜ in.) ; W. 14 cm (5½ in.)
Iran, Tepe Hissar, Treasure Hill Hoard I, H3210
Hissar III, ca. 2500–2000 B.C.
American Museum of Natural History, New York
73-3278

This is one of five almost identical ornaments discovered in the Treasure Hill Hoard I at Tepe Hissar, Iran.[1] Made of gold, the stylized head is a flat cutout, with raised ears, incised, elliptical eyes, and a pair of large horns. The staring eyes suggest the image may have had a special significance, now forgotten.[2] The horns spring from a scalloped line between the ears and curve magnificently outward to rest on the cheeks. Seven pairs of perforations pierce the horns and the beard of the animal, and one set forms the nostrils. The mouflon with exaggerated horns is a popular motif on pottery dating to the earliest levels of Tepe Hissar and Tepe Sialk, a site somewhat farther to the south.[3] The curvature of the horns, the squared-off muzzle, and the ears of this specimen find close parallels on copper pins discovered in fourth-millennium-B.C. graves at Susa.[4]

Among the personal ornaments recovered from the Treasure Hill Hoard I and in Period III graves of Tepe Hissar are a number of gold and silver diadems, some of which are embellished with repoussé decorations and stippled with either zigzags or groups of parallel lines. A silver diadem apparently encircling a skeleton's head, found along with a fan in a grave of Hissar III date, is decorated with a delicate repoussé stag, mouflon, and ibex, as well as other decorative elements such as concentric circles separated by stippled lines.[5] The spiraling horn of the mouflon on that diadem closely resembles those on the present gold mouflon head.

The high quality of the goods discovered in the graves and on Treasure Hill is a clear indication that some individuals had an elevated social status and considerable wealth. This conclusion is reinforced by the high standard of craftsmanship and sophistication of the gold mouflons and other personal ornaments, which may have been worn as appliqués on clothing by the most privileged members of society.[6]

The manner in which horned animals are depicted at Tepe Hissar connects the site iconographically to earlier Chalcolithic-period pottery decorations of northeastern and southwestern Iran.[7] The identifiable features, especially the exaggerated horns, suggest a style of decoration that is peculiar to the Iranian Plateau, where it may have originated. The persistence of this type of decoration in the archaeological record throughout later millennia and its spread east into western Central Asia suggest the significant role that Tepe Hissar may have played in the transfer of motifs and styles across a vast region during the great era of trade and cultural contact in the third millennium B.C.[8]   SG

1. The curvature of the horns suggests this mouflon is, in fact, a trans-Caspian urial, whose natural habitat is the mountainous ranges, valleys, and desert plateau of the Aral-Caspian watershed. This subspecies of the mountainous argali lives only in southwestern Kazakhstan, northwestern Turkmenistan, western

Uzbekistan, and northeastern Iran, suggesting that the subject of this ornament may reflect the local fauna of Tepe Hissar.

2. Porada 1965, p. 44.

3. A silver diadem from Hissar Level III, first reported in Schmidt 1933, pl. 122:a, is decorated with an ibex and a mouflon, the latter shown frontally. For mouflon and ibex representations on pottery from Tepe Sialk, see Ghirshman 1938–39, pls. 70 (S119), (S155), 71 (S1800).

4. For a discussion of the copper pins at Susa, see Tallon 1987, p. 296, nos. 978, 979.

5. Schmidt 1933, p. 401. These objects were discovered in Grave DF08 X-1; oddly enough, however, the diadem is not mentioned in the final excavation report (Schmidt 1937).

6. Textile samples from Tepe Hissar suggest that the appliqués may have been sewn on cloth; see Ellis 1989. It is also possible that these mouflon heads may have been attached to a diadem in a manner similar to that in which animals and floral ornaments of gold are attached to a gold and lapis lazuli diadem found in queen Puabi's tomb chamber at Ur; see Zettler and Horne 1998, pp. 92–94.

7. Some of the finest ceramic vessels in the large corpus discovered by Jacques de Morgan in the cemetery of Susa are decorated with a variety of animals including ibex with horns that curve back to cover the whole body; see Harper, Aruz, and Tallon 1992, nos. 1, 4, 9.

8. Representations of animals reduced to their most characteristic features, such as the large, curving tail, big ears, and squared-off muzzle of this mouflon, date to as early as the fourth millennium B.C. on the Iranian Plateau, and they continued to be made during the Proto-Elamite period, which lasted until about 2800 B.C. See Amiet 1966, p. 69, fig. 30, and Harper, Aruz, and Tallon 1992, pp. 72–78. For Central Asian examples, see Masson and Kiiatkina 1981, pp. 107–34, fig. 14, and Masson 1988, p. 68, pl. 23.

246

Double-spiral pendant

Copper alloy
H. 4.4 cm (1¾ in.); W. 4.4 cm (1¾ in.)
Iran, Tepe Hissar, CG10 X-10, H4333
Hissar III, ca. 2500–2000 B.C.
American Museum of Natural History, New York
73-3239

Spiral pins and wands were some of the most common products of Anatolian and Iranian metallurgy in the third and second millennia B.C.[1] Spiral-headed pins have also been recovered in third-millennium contexts in Central Asia at Anau, Mundigak, and Parkhai II, and in the Indus Valley at Chanhudaro and Mohenjo-daro.[2] Analysis of finds from these and other sites has made it possible to group the pins with a double-spiral head into different types

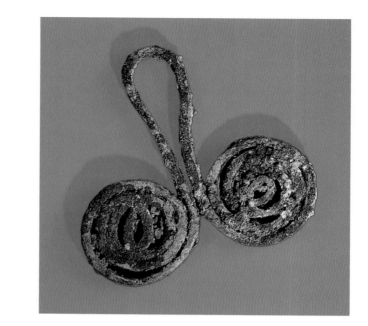

according to the number of loops in the spirals and the thickness of the ends.

At Tepe Hissar, a site in north-central Iran just south of the Caspian Sea, sharply pointed pins and wands, both with a double-spiral motif, occur as early as Hissar II (ca. 3000–2500 B.C.) but are more frequent in Hissar III (ca. 2500–2000 B.C.). Pendants such as the present example are made from wire that is rectangular in cross section. Pins with similarly decorated double-spiral heads have been recovered at Shahr-i Sokhta and at Tepe Giyan in southeastern and southwestern Iran, respectively.[3] Double-spiral silver pins and copper pendants have also been found in a Hissar III context.[4] Double-spiral pendants are common at the Early Bronze Age site of Eskiyapar in central Anatolia, where in one grave a necklace of 24 gold double-spiral beads and 152 cylindrical beads of various sizes was discovered.[5] A gold bracelet from Troy is also similarly embellished with more than 50 double spirals that are attached to the band (fig. 76).[6] It would be tempting to connect the spread of the double-spiral motif with the movement of goods and ideas during the Early Bronze Age along the well-traveled route of the lapis lazuli trade, which includes the strategically placed site of Tepe Hissar. The pervasive similarities of this design, however, across this vast region make it impossible to pinpoint its place of origin. It is also possible that each region and culture interpreted the double-spiral design differently. An early study by Henri Frankfort suggested that the looped bands—which are similar to the Tepe Hissar and Ur examples of the double spiral—discovered in reliefs on

terracotta plaques now in the Iraq Museum, Baghdad, may have symbolized the goddess Ninhursanga, one of whose functions was to preside over childbirth.[7] Although the use of these pendants is not clear, a female terracotta figurine from Altyn-depe, in southern Turkmenistan, is embellished with double-spiral objects around the neck and chest, suggesting that the Tepe Hissar example may have been worn in a similar fashion.[8]   SG

1. Gold pins with a double-spiral motif dating to about 2300 B.C. have been recovered at Troy; see Smithsonian Institution 1966, nos. 35–38. For similar pins from Iran, see Tosi 1983, p. 166.

2. For Mundigak, see Casal 1961; for Parkhai II, see Khlopin 1981, pp. 3–34; for Chanhudaro, see Mackay 1943.

3. Herzfeld 1941, p. 148, pl. 30.

4. The archaeological field number for these is H3609. Copper spiral pendants at Tepe Hissar closely parallel the gold examples discovered at Ur. See Woolley 1934, pl. 134 (U.9656), and Maxwell-Hyslop 1971, p. 79.

5. For the double-spiral pendants from Eskiyapar, see Özgüç and Temizer 1993, p. 616, pl. 111.

6. For the Troy bracelet, see Chūkinto Bunka Sentā 1985, no. 67, and Schliemann 1881, p. 552, fig. 874. For double-spiral pendants found at Ur, see Woolley 1934, p. 372, fig. 79. Double-spiral pendants in silver were also found at Tureng-tepe, in Iran; see Deshayes 1966, pl. 3, fig 8.

7. Frankfort 1944, pp. 198–200. It is intriguing to note that the pregnant women among the fellahin in Upper Egypt wear padlocks with a double-spiral motif that function as apotropaic pendants; see Blackman and Blackman 1935, p. 32, pl. 1. It is feasible to suggest a similar function for the Tepe Hissar double-spiral pendants.

8. For the Altyn-depe figurine, see Masson and Kiiatkina 1981, p. 126, fig. 15a.

247a–e

Beads

Turquoise, lapis lazuli, and silver
Iran, Tepe Hissar, "dancer's grave," CF55 X-1, H2388
Hissar III, ca. 2500–2000 B.C.

a. Turquoise bead: L. 2.5 cm (1 in.); W. 2.3 cm (⅞ in.)
b. Lapis lazuli tube: L. 1.7 cm (¹¹⁄₁₆ in.)
c. Double horn: H. 1.7 cm (¹¹⁄₁₆ in.)
d. Silver tubes: L. 1.5–2.9 cm (⁹⁄₁₆–1⅛ in.)
University of Pennsylvania Museum of Archaeology
and Anthropology, Philadelphia 33-21-1017

e. Ram's head: H. 1.5 cm (⁹⁄₁₆ in.)
American Museum of Natural History, New York
73-3236

Great quantities of beads were found in the graves at Tepe Hissar, in a variety of shapes and materials. Beads from Hissar I (ca. 3500–3000 B.C.), the earliest level of this site in northern Iran, were fashioned of gypsum in white and gray shades, of red jasper, and, less frequently, of black bitumen, frit, and alabaster; occasionally, copper was used to make disks, tubes, and rectangular and oblong beads. In the later Hissar II and III levels (ca. 3000–2000 B.C.), the types of beads remain the same but new materials, such as lapis lazuli, turquoise, brown-red carnelian, serpentine, mother-of-pearl, and the more precious silver and gold, are in evidence.[1]

Among the most interesting groups of beads at the site are those recovered among the burial goods in Level III. The variety of form and raw material yielded an attractive array, with amber and banded chalcedony evidently the most important new materials. Also encountered in Level III, though more rarely, are tubular and spherical carnelian beads etched with an elliptical eye design encrusted with white pigment—evidence that the people of Tepe Hissar were in contact with the cultures of the Indus Valley.[2] Perhaps the most distinctive and interesting examples in the corpus are the beads found in the "dancer's grave," so named after the dancing position in which the deceased woman was buried.[3] Her skeleton was found interred with a number of objects, including silver and copper earrings, copper boxes, and a silver jar, as well as lapis, turquoise, silver, and copper beads.

The necklace reconstructed from the loose beads found in the "dancer's grave" is composed of a turquoise crenellated bead, five tubes—one of lapis and four of silver (such

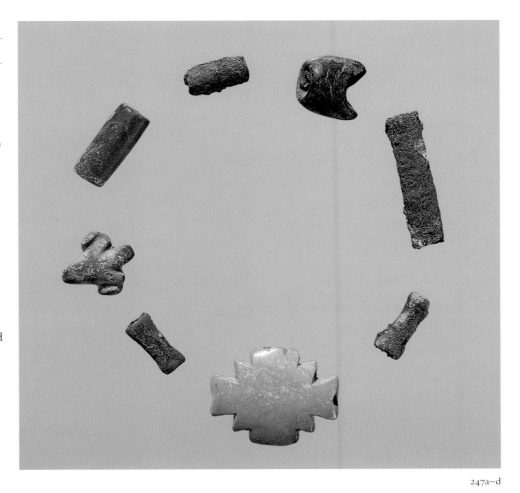

247a–d

tubes were also made in gold)—a lapis lazuli double horn, and a lapis lazuli ram's head. The crenellated bead is distinctive in both its shape and its material.[4] Although turquoise objects are found elsewhere in Hissar III levels, the closest parallel at this site is a comparably shaped bead in silver.[5] The pattern is also known from shell inlays at Harappan sites and pottery decoration, metalwork (cat. nos. 252, 253), stamp seals, and inlays from Central Asia.[6] The motif is especially prominent at the southern Turkmenistan site of Altyn-depe, where it reverberates in architectural details, such as the stepped niches cut in walls (fig. 89), pottery decorations, and carved terracotta boxes (called "reliquaries" by the excavators; see cat. no. 251; fig. 90).[7]

Most of the stone from which the beads found at Tepe Hissar were made were locally available. Turquoise comes from important sources between Kerman and Yazd, in Iran, and evidence of early workings in this stone are known from the third-millennium site of Shahr-i Sokhta in Iranian Seistan.[8] Silver was also readily available both in Iran, located in the southeast at Kuh-i Nugre and between Fasa and Zahedan, close to Tepe Hissar and in neighboring Afghanistan.[9] The lapis lazuli,

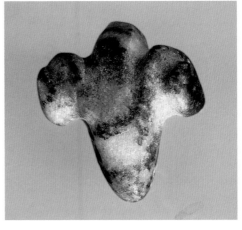

247e

however, is probably from the Kerano Munjan district of Badakhshan province in Afghanistan.[10] Most of the bead shapes from Tepe Hissar find parallels in examples from the southern Mesopotamian sites of Ur and Kish. This is especially true of oval, tubular, lozenge-shaped, and concave beads. Most intriguing are the banded chalcedony beads from Treasure Hill at Tepe Hissar, which are reminiscent of the V-shaped, flattened agate beads from the royal graves of Ur.[11]

SG

1. As in Mesopotamia, the most probable source for mother-of-pearl at Tepe Hissar was the Gulf region, where the black lip, a pearl oyster *(Pinctada margaritifera)* was widespread; Moorey 1994, p. 139.

2. The process of making etched carnelian beads is discussed by Beck (1933, pp. 384–90) and more recently by Kenoyer (1998, p. 143). Woolley (1934, p. 373) considered these etched carnelian beads an Indus Valley invention. For a discussion of the different types of carnelian beads from the Indus Valley, see Kenoyer 1998, pp. 142–43, 205.

3. Schmidt 1937, p. 234, figs. 141, 142, and schema on p. 244.

4. The crenellated motif has been found in pottery decoration and on copper-alloy stamp seals from the site of Mundigak, in Afghanistan, Period IV; see Casal 1961, pl. 45, fig. 91.

5. The rectangular, cross-shaped, and crenellated beads dating to Hissar III were almost always produced from precious materials such as lapis lazuli, turquoise, and silver (field number H2365); cf. Schmidt 1937, pl. 55, fig. 133 (field number H2386).

6. For the Harappan shell inlays, see Marshall 1931, pl. 155 (31,32) and p. 566, and Vats 1940, pl. 132. Also of interest is a stepped inlay from Ur and, from Kish, an etched carnelian bead with a crenellated or stepped motif; see Beck 1933, pl. 71:A.18.

7. The vertical walls of monumental buildings at Altyn-depe are embellished with stepped pilasters. See Masson 1988, p. 112, pls. 1, 18.

8. Piperno 1977, p. 145.

9. Marshall 1931, pp. 675–77.

10. Herrmann 1968, pp. 21–57.

11. On the chalcedony beads from Treasure Hill, see Schmidt 1937, pls. 35, 66 (field number H3216). On the agate bead from Ur, see Woolley 1934.

248

String of crenellated beads

Fired and glazed steatite
H. of central bead 3.7 cm (1½ in.); L. of small beads
1–1.9 cm (⅜–¾ in.)
Western Central Asia
Late 3rd–early 2nd millennium B.C.
Musée du Louvre, Département des Antiquités
Orientales, Paris AO 26126

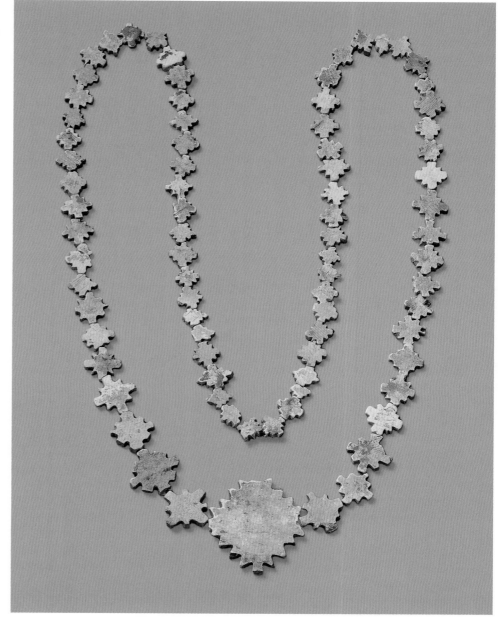

The beads of this necklace offer an excellent illustration of the different ways steatite was treated in the third millennium B.C.[1] The block of steatite, which is soft to work, was first formed into a parallelepiped and perforated at each end. (To limit the risk of breakage, it was preferable to form the holes at the beginning of the manufacturing process rather than at the end, when the object was more brittle.) When still soft, this standardized piece was cut up into fine slabs of variable thickness, as indicated by the saw marks still clearly visible on both faces of the beads. Each slab was then cut into the form of a staggered cross. Finally, the pieces were heated and glazed. The steatite recrystallized during that phase, making the material harder and more resistant and helping the glaze adhere better to the stone.[2]

Analyses by X-ray diffraction reveal that the beads were fired at temperatures between eight hundred and one thousand degrees Celsius[3] and that the coloring agent in the glaze contained copper combined with iron, nickel, and arsenic, but no trace of tin. This glaze composition was totally unknown in the civilization of the Indus Valley, where glazed steatite objects were of high quality;[4] however, it is perfectly consistent with the composition of copper ore from Oman, which was rich in metallic impurities and commonly used in Iran and Mesopotamia in the third millennium B.C.[5] Because of their copper content, the beads would originally have had a beautiful blue-green color, which now appears only in a few spots.

Beads of this type are found in the culture of Zamanbaba, in Uzbekistan, east of the Amu Darya, or Oxus, River.[6] In addition, the crenellated-cross motif appears on cylindrical steatite vases;[7] on ceramics from Quetta, in Baluchistan, which are in turn derived from those of Geoksyur, Turkmenistan; and on Indus pottery (for related examples, see cat. nos. 252, 269). In Iran some compartmented seals from Shahr-i Sokhta[8] and Shahdad[9] as well as silver and turquoise beads from Tepe Hissar[10] (see cat. no. 247) adopt the same form. A necklace from Susa made of glazed steatite and enstatite (completely fired steatite) beads is further evidence of a vast cultural community that Pierre Amiet calls "trans-Elamite."[11] The transformation of steatite into enstatite and the manufacture of objects from kaolin offer proof that trans-Elamite artisans could control temperatures as high as thirteen hundred degrees Celsius.[12]   AB

1. Amiet 1977a, p. 101, fig. 12.
2. Steatite in its natural state has a hardness level on the Mohs' scale of 1, whereas fired steatite (or enstatite) is at level 6 to 7; see Vandiver 1983, p. A67.
3. At eight hundred degrees Celsius, steatite recrystallizes into a mixture of enstatite and cristobalite. The analyses were performed by Anne Bouquillon at C2RMF (formerly Laboratoire des Musées de France), unpublished analysis report no. 3082, June 20, 2002, pp. 1–5. My warm thanks to the author of this report, who performed the analyses on short notice and clarified the sequence of operations for me.

4. Barthélémy de Saizieu 2001, pp. 93–111.
5. See catalogue number 202.
6. Masson and Sarianidi 1972, p. 127, fig. 32, right.
7. See especially a small vase in the Louvre (AO 29456), in Amiet 1988b, p. 365, fig. 11.
8. Tucci 1977, p. 257, no. 7; Amiet 1986, fig. 147(5).
9. For an impression of this seal, see Hakemi 1997, p. 672, no. 16.
10. Schmidt 1937, pl. 55H.2365.
11. Amiet 1986, fig. 100.
12. Ibid; the hanging ring on the Susa necklace is made from kaolin.

Altyn-depe

The settlement of Altyn-depe is one of the largest and best studied from the Eneolithic period through the Bronze Age in Central Asia. Located in southern Turkmenistan, it lies five to six kilometers east of the first line of foothills of the Kopet Dagh, in the Tejen River valley.

All the stages of cultural evolution can be traced at Altyn-depe, from a settlement of early farmers to one of the early urban type. Although the site was surrounded by massive mud-brick walls (1–1.7 meters thick) at the turn of the fourth to third millennium B.C., their defensive nature is dubious; more likely, they were the retaining walls reinforcing the perimeter of the settlement. For the period of Namazga V, three strata have been exposed, revealing an enclosed elite district. At this time, Altyn-depe was an urban settlement with a complex internal structure.

At the site itself, full continuity has been established for a number of cultural phenomena beginning with the late Eneolithic, represented by the Geoksyur variant of the Anau culture. The painted ceramics of the Early Bronze Age represent a development of Geoksyur traditions. These connections can be traced even more clearly in the terracotta sculpture. Judging from the settlement's materials, the transition from the Early Bronze Age to the Namazga V complex occurred without any particular cataclysms. The continuity in the material record is linked to the direct continuity in the composition of the population, based on the evidence of skeletons.

Altyn-depe had close ties to and interactions with populations residing in Iran, Bactria, and the Indus Valley. An overland trade route went northwest from the civilization of Harappa all the way to the settled oases on the southern outskirts of the Karakum Desert and continued into Iran (see "Pathways across Eurasia," by Maurizio Tosi and C. C. Lamberg-Karlovsky, in this catalogue).

The demise of this early urban Bronze Age center is the result of a gradual decline connected with resettlement to other territories. The residents abandoned their homes, taking their property with them. Some of the settlers of the lowlands went east to the Murghab River delta. Similar events occurred in neighboring territories. It was at this time that several centers in Iran and the Indus Valley were deserted.   YP

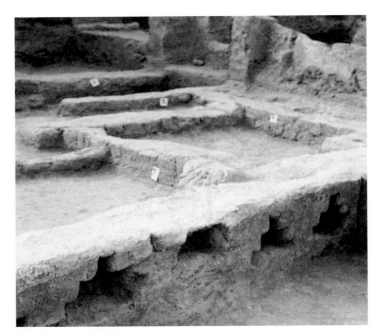

Fig. 89. Room with niches in a stepped motif, Altyn-depe. Namazga V, late 3rd millennium B.C.

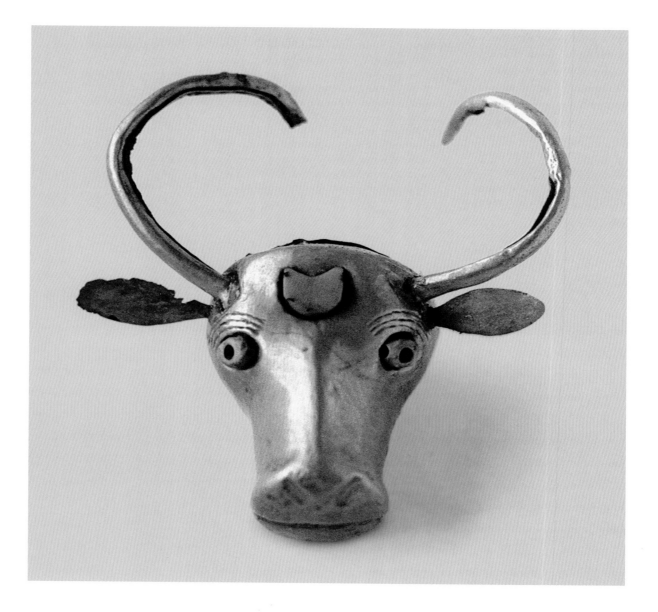

249

Bull's head

Gold, silver, and turquoise
H. 7.5 cm (3 in.)
Western Central Asia, Altyn-depe, Excavation 7, room 7
Namazga V, late 3rd millennium B.C.
The National Museum of Turkmenistan Named After
Saparmurat Turkmenbashi, Ashgabat

The bull's head was a powerful symbol not only in the arts of the ancient Near East but also—as is demonstrated by this unique example, which may have been an amulet—of ancient western Central Asia. Cast from solid gold, the bull's head has separate gold ears and horns, the latter made of silver wire covered with gold foil. The muzzle is flat and round at the end, where the mouth and nostrils are indicated by depressions; along each side are three holes, perhaps to allow for attachment to an unknown object. Turquoise beads are inlaid in the bull's eyes, above which three curved lines are punched into the gold to indicate eyebrows. Depictions of bull's heads with geometric inlay in the forehead have been found at Ur, Khafajah, Mari (see cat. no. 95), and Bahrain (see cat. no. 206), but the choice of turquoise for the inlay here and its kidney shape are distinctive characteristics of the art of western Central Asia. The shape, for example, finds parallels in the decorations on a stone shoe from a burial at Gonur-depe (see cat. no. 266) and on objects found in the Indus Valley (see cat. no. 288).

The bull's head was discovered in one of five connected rectangular rooms that were part of an extensive, elite funerary complex, close to the remains of a massive stepped platform.[1] It was among a number of precious objects, including a gold wolf's head, scattered along the floor, to the west of a rectangular mud-brick emplacement that originally had been covered with wood planking. The room also contained human and animal bones and a variety of vessels.   PC

1. Masson 1988, pp. 68, 74–78.

250a, b

Seated female figurines

Terracotta
Western Central Asia, Altyn-depe, settlement,
Excavation 9
Namazga V, late 3rd millennium B.C.

a. H. 13.7 cm (5⅜ in.)
Building 10(a)
The State Hermitage Museum, St. Petersburg,
Russia 2851-56

b. H. 16.2 cm (6⅜ in.)
Building 11, crypt
The State Hermitage Museum, St. Petersburg,
Russia 2851-62

These solid, schematic figurines of seated women have protuberances at neck level suggesting outstretched arms.[1] In each example a narrow waist merges smoothly into broad hips. The lower part of each figurine is bent at a seventy- to ninety-degree angle, creating the impression of a seated pose. Set on a long neck is a head with a hooked nose jutting forward, indicated by a simple tuck, and almond-shaped, applied eyes with narrow slits, above which eyebrows have been scratched in with tiny pinpricks. Neither figure has a mouth. The high headdresses (or coiffures) are decorated in front with radiating lines. Appliquéd clay attached to the back indicates a fall of hair, on which slanted, crisscrossing lines suggest a tightly woven braid. Each figure also has two tresses in front, long enough to reach the applied conical breasts. On the taller figure (cat. no. 250b) the tresses are snakelike; on the smaller (cat. no. 250a) they form spiral coils, and three horizontal lines on the neck indicate a multistranded necklace. On the lower hip area of both figures three horizontal bands seem to suggest a loincloth or belt, but the incised lines appear only on the front. On the part of the body that is bent forward the pubic triangle is depicted with dots. Scratched on the center of each torso in front is a depiction of a plant or tree—a straight trunk and branches spreading upward. On the arm-protuberances are markings—a triangle with cilia; the reverse of each figurine exhibits the same pattern.

The figurines are made of high-quality clay with a light-colored coating and are superbly fired. In all likelihood, they were intended for long-term use. The smaller example was found in Building 10, on the floor of a corridor, a part of which was evidently used for funeral rites.

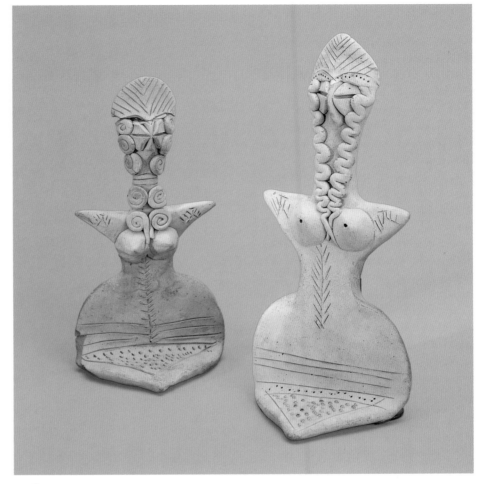
250a,b

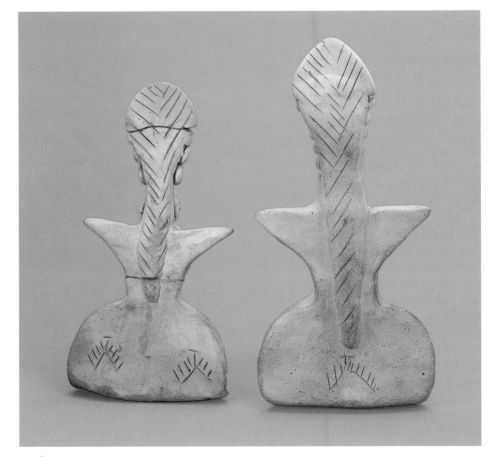
250a,b

Here, too, stood two other female figurines and three miniature ceramic vessels. The taller example was found in Building 11, in an oblong crypt measuring 2.2 by 2.6 meters. Inside the crypt were found the remains of eleven buried bodies. Two figurines lay in the southeastern corner of the chamber. Also found here were twenty-eight vessels, silver and copper-alloy rings, a copper-alloy seal, and 417 beads.

Clay figurines are characteristic of the Altyn-depe Archaeological Complex. Appliquéd and scratched details and marks wholly replace the painting of the Eneolithic period at the site. The signs and details were made on the wet clay with a sharp metal tool.

Figurines of this type suggest the idea of fertility. In these depictions, one can in all likelihood see the protectress of the clan and city, who, according to I. E. Berezkin, was connected with the heavenly sphere or, according to E. V. Antonova, was the goddess personifying the earth.[2]   YP

1. On the site of Altyn-depe, see Masson 1981a, table 8:3. The present figurines were previously published in Mohen and Piotrovsky 1979, pp. 94–95, nos. 65, 66.
2. Berezkin 1981, pp. 21–22; Antonova 1984, pp. 144–45.

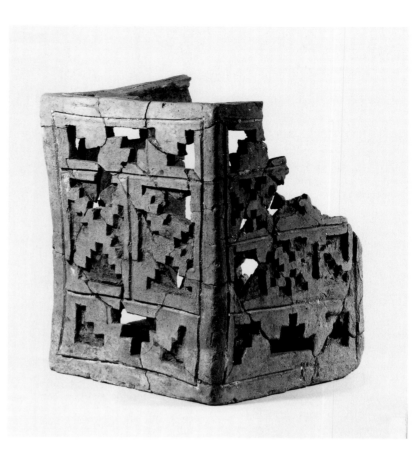

251

Open-worked carved box with crenellated decoration

Fired clay
H. 8.5 cm (3⅜ in.); W. 5 cm (2 in.)
Western Central Asia, Altyn-depe, Excavation 9, room 118
Namazga V, late 3rd millennium B.C.
Institute of the History of Material Culture of the Russian Academy of Sciences, St. Petersburg

This box-shaped object was found in the elite quarters of Altyn-depe, in modern Turkmenistan, where large houses with many rooms and open courtyards often were associated with elaborate burials and specialized buildings believed to be sanctuaries. Close by there were often storerooms, where cult objects and other valuable items, sometimes including terracotta boxes, were kept. This terracotta box, the original use of which is unknown, comes from one of a group of aligned rooms to the north of a courtyard, which, because of its size, may have been a

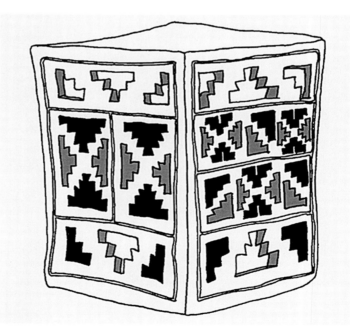

Fig. 90. Drawing of the reconstructed open-worked carved box with crenellated decoration (cat. no. 251) indicating the areas that were originally painted.

place where the public assembled. Most of one side of the box is missing, and it once may have had a lid. In some examples patterns of shallow depressions in the shape of stepped diamonds and triangles were cut into the clay. Here the sides are divided into four rectangles by shallow grooves with recessed stepped triangles. Within the top rectangle the triangles have been cut through the clay walls, as has the central triangle of the bottom register. The cut surfaces are covered with red paint, and the recessed areas have either black or red paint.[1] Such crenellated designs are widespread in the art of western Central Asia and appear on architecture, compartmented stamp seals, jewelry, inlays, and pottery.[2] The extensive trade network that linked Central Asia to the west and the south is revealed by the existence of objects with these stepped designs, examples of which were found in Iran, Baluchistan, and the Gulf region (see cat. nos. 247, 269).

PC

1. The information about the paint was kindly supplied by Yuri Piotrovsky.
2. For examples of crenellated decoration, see Masson 1988, pls. 1 (on architecture), 22:4 (on jewelry), and Kircho 1981 (on pottery). For various forms of the stepped triangle on compartmented stamp seals, see Sarianidi 1998, pp. 110–25.

252

Vessel with crenellated pattern

Fired clay
H. 20.2 cm (8 in.); Diam. 14 cm (5½ in.)
Western Central Asia, Kara-depe, settlement at Aztyk, Kara-depe IB
Namazga III, early 3rd millennium B.C.
The State Hermitage Museum, St. Petersburg, Russia 2847-14

This vessel comes from a grave (Burial 20) edged with mud bricks in the mound at Kara-depe, one of the largest settlements of early farmers in the southern part of Turkmenistan.[1] Found in the burial were the remains of an elderly woman, at whose left wrist the object was discovered. The vessel is tall, nearly cylindrical, with walls tapering toward the mouth. Two-thirds of the light-toned slip surface is covered with a pattern painted in a dark umber. The pattern consists of four panels divided by double vertical lines and a zigzag line between them. Diagonal lines divide each panel into four triangles, or single lines form triangles. In the triangles is a pattern comprising steplike elements. The shape of the vessel is rare for the Namazga III period.

Very characteristic of the late Eneolithic period of the western cultural region of southern Turkmenistan (the Namazga III complex) are painted ceramics with organic admixtures in the paste and complicated monochromatic geometric and zoomorphic patterns. Early (Kara-depe IB) and more advanced (Kara-depe IA) stages of development of the Namazga III complex have been delineated on the basis of an analysis of the ceramics and stratigraphy of the Kara-depe burial sites.

The vessels of Kara-depe IB have a fairly substantial organic admixture in the grayish, poorly fired paste; their glazed surfaces are decorated with monochromatic, primarily geometric, patterns consisting of large motifs similar to the motifs of ceramics in the Geoksyur style.

YP

1. The most useful reference on the site remains the excavation publication, Masson 1960, tables 30:10, 35:7.

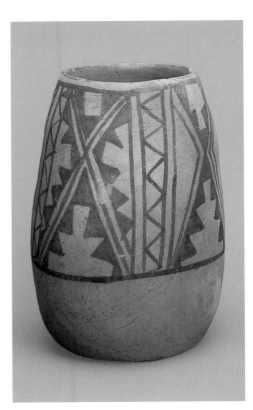

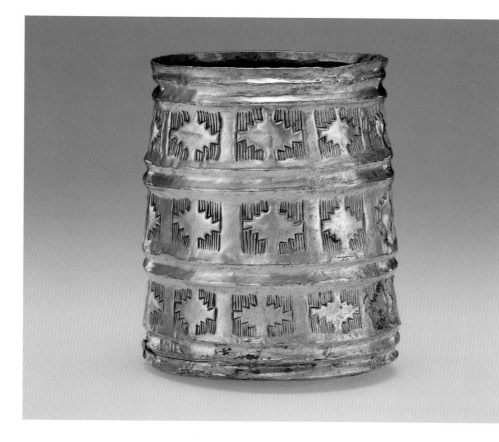

253

Cylindrical cup with crenellated decoration

Silver
H. 12.4 cm (4⅞ in.); Diam. of rim 11.7 cm (4⅝ in.);
Diam. of bottom 11.7 cm (4⅝ in.); H. of foot 0.2 cm
(¹/₁₆ in.); Diam. of foot 6.7 cm (2⅝ in.); Weight 105.8 g
Western Central Asia
Late 3rd–early 2nd millennium B.C.
Miho Museum, Japan SF 3.142

This is one of many cylindrical silver vessels that are thought to have originated in western Central Asia on the basis of their form and decoration.[1] The cup is hammered from one piece of nearly pure silver and has repoussé decoration with chased and engraved lines.[2] Raised horizontal bands protrude from the surface to define three registers, each of which is divided into ten rectangular panels. These panels, which contain a central crenellated cross surrounded by vertical hatching, alternate with plain, narrow vertical bands. Since the vessel is wider at the base than at the rim, the crosses increase in size from higher to lower registers, so that the rows of panels do not align from top to bottom. The vessel has a dropped circular foot, similar to that on other cups attributed to the

Bactria-Margiana culture (see cat. no. 257).

The crenellated-cross pattern was widespread in both Iran and western Central Asia during the third millennium B.C. Perhaps the largest renderings of the motif survive in Proto-Elamite-period wall painting at the Iranian site of Tell Malyan and in the architecture and so-called reliquaries found at Altyndepe, Turkmenistan (see cat. no. 251; fig. 90).[3] Stepped patterns were also used on pottery (see cat. no. 252), and crenellated-cross-shaped beads (see cat. nos. 247, 248) and seals (see fig. 101) were produced in these regions as well.[4] The motif is also found on Central Asian gold and silver vessels (see cat. no. 254)—some from the so-called Fullol Hoard—as well as on a cylindrical "Intercultural Style" chlorite vessel now in the Musée du Louvre, Paris.[5]

JA

1. See Amiet 1986, pp. 201, 326, fig. 200.
2. Technical notes on this cup were provided by Pieter Meyers; see Meyers 1996b, p. 173, no. 6; see also Aruz in Arnold et al. 1996, pp. 18–19.
3. Amiet 1986, p. 262, fig. 52; Masson 1988, pls. 1, 18.
4. For pottery with this motif, see Masson 1988, pls. 4, 25, 27, 42.
5. Maxwell-Hyslop 1982, p. 28, figs. 5–7; Amiet 1988b, p. 365, fig. 11.

254

Cylindrical box and lid with lions, bulls, and wolves in relief

Silver
H. 23.1 cm (9⅛ in.); Diam. 20 cm (7⅞ in.)
Western Central Asia
Late 3rd–early 2nd millennium B.C.
The Metropolitan Museum of Art, New York; Lent by Shelby White and Leon Levy L.1999.74.1

A number of distinctive cylindrical silver vessels, many bearing the images of important personages engaged in ceremonial and hunting activities (see cat. no. 257), are thought on stylistic grounds to have been produced in the region of Bactria-Margiana in Central Asia. Perhaps the most unusual example is this extraordinary box with a cylindrical neck and lid now corroded closed. The vessel bears scenes of animal combat between the usual adversaries in Mesopotamian art, lions and bulls. The lid shows two wolves lying on the foreparts and hind leg of an antelope, a depiction very much like one on a Bactrian silver seal.[1] The images are executed in both high and low relief, bordered by finely incised crenellated patterns, which have parallels in the designs on a number of objects attributed to the Oxus region (see cat. no. 253).[2]

The main scene comprises two registers. In the upper row, four lions stride to the right, one of them biting the belly of a dead bull, its hind legs in the air. Below, four lions stride to the left, and one bites the neck of a collapsing bull in front of it.[3] The sculptural quality of the figures, combined with very distinctive linear patterning used to define the musculature of the front and hind legs, as well as the intricate patterning for body fur, recalls generally the earlier art of Proto-Elamite Iran and the imagery on some "Intercultural Style" chlorite vessels (see "Art and Interconnections in the Third Millennium B.C.," by Joan Aruz, in this catalogue). The closest parallels, however—both for the rather wooden stances of the animals and for the patterning on the bulls' bodies—can be found on similar cylindrical vessels that formed part of the Fullol Hoard, which is reported to have come from northern Afghanistan.[4] A cylindrical silver vessel in the Miho Museum, Japan (cat. no. 257), with a Central Asian ceremonial scene based on Mesopotamian banquet imagery, also depicts oxen that exhibit similar body patterning. On both vessels, the interest in portraying

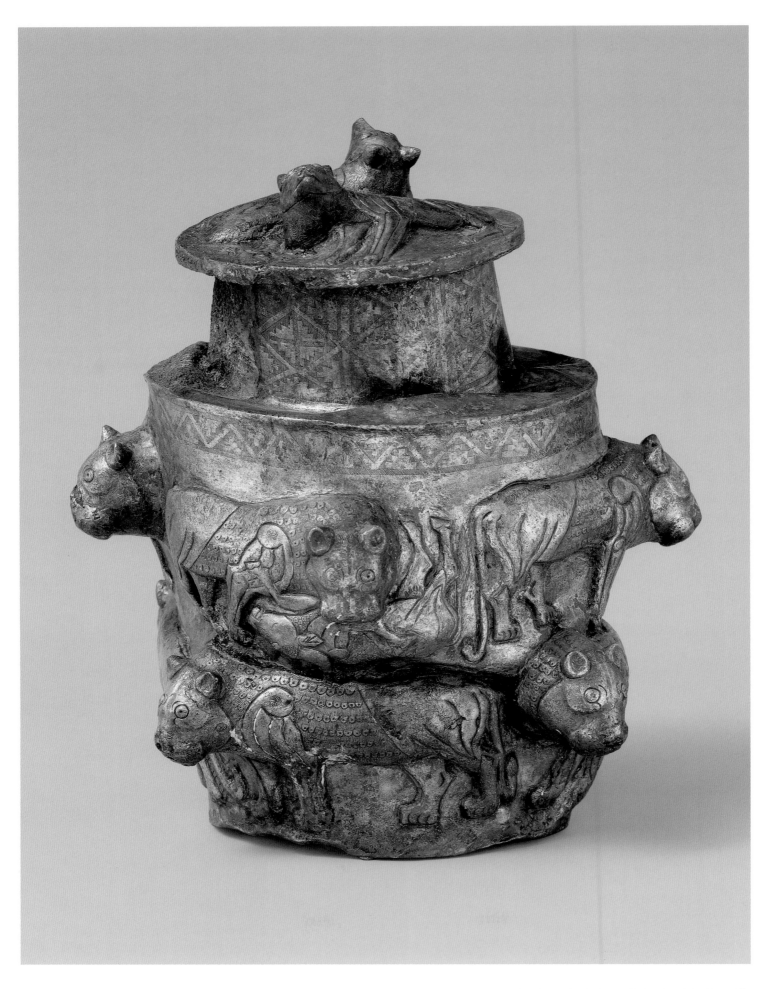

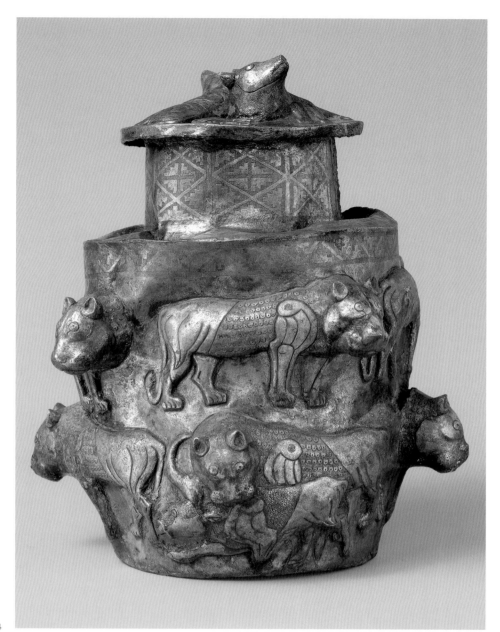

254

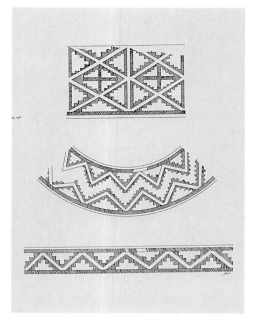

Fig. 91b. Drawing of the crenellated patterns incised on catalogue number 254.

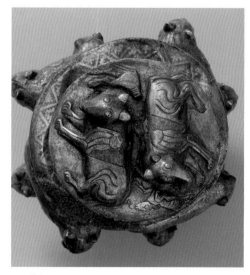

254, lid

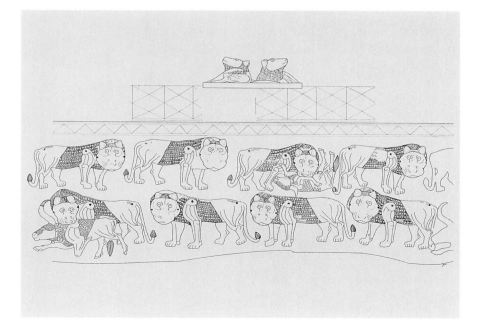

Fig. 91a. Rolled-out drawing of a cylindrical box and lid with lions, bulls, and wolves depicted in relief (cat. no. 254).

depth of field is clearly manifested in the use of varying levels of relief and incision and, on the vase in Japan, by shading.

JA

Technical remarks

This box is a tour de force of ancient silver-smithing in which the malleable nature of the metal has been fully exploited to dramatic effect. After the general shape of the container and its lid was achieved by hammering, the high-relief figures were created by repoussé. Frequent annealing was necessary in order to relieve the internal stresses caused by working the metal. Support on the inside of the vessel and lid during the final shaping and chasing of the exterior may have been provided by applying a backing of bitumen that was later removed. Such support would have been particularly necessary in the areas of high relief, where the metal was stretched thin and susceptible to deformation. The silver chloride layer of corrosion that formed on the surface during burial has been removed except for a small patch on the shoulder and neck.

J-FL

1. Sarianidi 1998b, pp. 70–71, figs. 107.1,2.
2. See Amiet 1986, pp. 201, 322, figs. 193 (Fullol Hoard), 262:52 (Tell Malyan wall painting). See also catalogue number 251, a "reliquary" from Altyn-depe, and figure 101, a Bactria-Margiana seal from the Indus. Many compartmented seals also exhibit this motif.
3. For a Bactria-Margiana stamp seal depicting a lion attacking a bull from above, see Sarianidi 1998b, p. 183, no. 965.2.
4. Amiet (1988a, pp. 136, 161) describes this hoard as a collection put together from clandestine excavations in northern Afghanistan. See also Tosi and Wardak 1972, pp. 9–17.

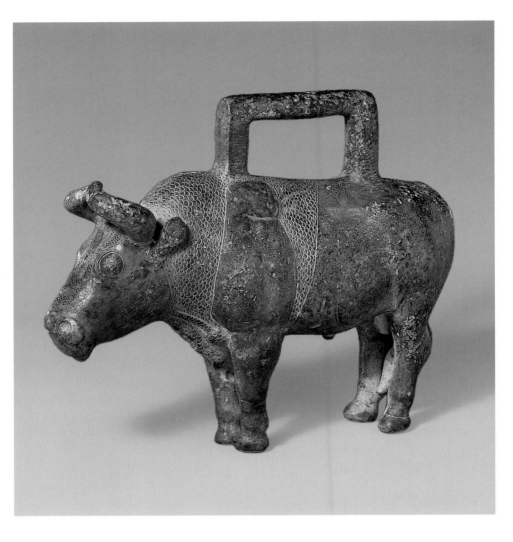

255

Handled weight in the form of a standing bull

Lead
H. 26 cm (10¼ in.); L. 32.4 cm (12¾ in.)
Western Central Asia
Late 3rd–early 2nd millennium B.C.
Miho Museum, Japan SF 4.005

Both the large handle and the unusual use of lead as the casting metal suggest that this statuette of a bull functioned as a weight.[1] The handle also evinces a typological connection

with decorated chlorite objects of the "Intercultural Style" that are assumed to have been used as weights but that may have had another, now-unknown significance or function (see cat. no. 225b).[2] Given the care lavished in its execution, it is conceivable that the figure was invested with symbolic significance and may have been used on important occasions or for other special purposes.

The massive body of this bull is articulated by chased lines and fields of scalloped patterning that surround the shoulders and cover the head between the eyes. This patterning indicates that a longhaired bovine genus of the highlands is represented. The depiction of this type of bull in a ploughing scene on a silver cup attributed to Bactria-Margiana indicates the animal was domesticated for agricultural work in the region (see cat. no. 257).[3]

The weight-to-volume ratio suggests that at least the main section of the bull's body was cast over a ceramic core. Circular plugs found on both sides of the body may fill holes left

by the removal of copper-alloy core supports. The object is in surprisingly good condition, but some pitting has occurred around the horns, and there is extensive cracking in all four legs. In addition, the wear found at the base of the legs is indicative of use before burial. Although the source of the lead used is not known, the high purity of the metal suggests that it may have been recovered as a by-product of the extraction of silver, which appears to have been used extensively in Bactria-Margiana, from argentiferous lead ores.[4]

J-FL

1. For a full description of this object, see the catalogue entry by Aruz in Arnold et al. 1996, pp. 24–25.
2. See Muscarella 1993, pp. 143–54.
3. See catalogue entry by Aruz in Arnold et al. 1996, pp. 14–17.
4. EDS analysis of a sample was performed by Mark Wypyski at the Metropolitan Museum in 1996. Whether the silver used in Bactria was extracted from lead and/or smelted from silver ores is an unresolved question. See Moorey 1994, pp. 232–35.

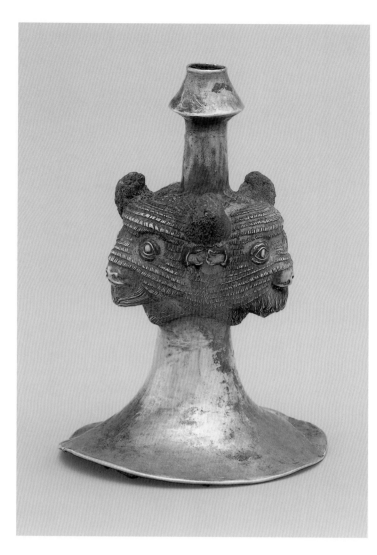
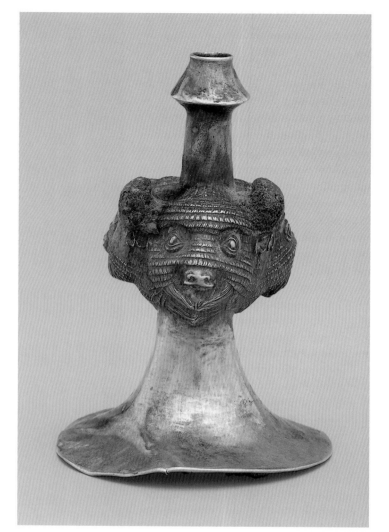

256

"Trumpet" with three bison heads

Gold, silver alloy, copper alloy, and bitumen
H. 9.2 cm (3⁵⁄₈ in.); Diam. 6.2 cm (2½ in.)
Western Central Asia
Late 3rd–early 2nd millennium B.C.
The Metropolitan Museum of Art, New York; Lent by
Shelby White and Leon Levy L.2001.65.1

Encircling the cylindrical shaft of this trumpet-shaped object are three bison heads, modeled from gold sheet over a bitumen core and with hair patterning produced by chasing. Three silver-alloy horns are inserted into holes cut through the gold; a single horn separates each head from the one adjacent to it, giving the impression that each bison has a pair of horns. The heads can be compared stylistically with the heads of horned men on compartmented stamp seals from western Central Asia.[1] A mineralized copper-alloy liner was inserted into the "trumpet" and secured at the wide,

flared end by folding back the thin gold and crimping it around the copper. At the other end of the shaft, the gold is formed into a tip with a recessed lip. This end was strengthened by folding the gold sheet over the lip into the hollow shaft.

This remarkable object may have been blown to produce a sound during the hunt or ritual ceremonies. Alternatively, it may be a miniature version of a musical instrument, designed as a mortuary gift. It may also have served as a symbol of status for members of the ruling elite. It is one of two gold and two copper-alloy "trumpets" first recorded in 1978–79 in Kabul, Afghanistan, and alleged to have come from burials in the region of Bactria-Margiana.[2] Two comparable gold "trumpets" were part of the so-called Astrabad Treasure,[3] and three further examples were

discovered in Iran, at Tepe Hissar.[4] Recent excavations in Turkmenistan, at the Gonur necropolis, have revealed a rich burial containing a similar "trumpet" of copper alloy with a human face on the shaft as well as an example in faience.[5]   PC

1. Sarianidi 1998b, nos. 26, 32.
2. Pottier 1984, p. 72.
3. Rostovtzeff 1920b, pl. 3.
4. Schmidt 1937, p. 210, fig. 121.
5. Sarianidi 2002, pp. 235–36, 239.

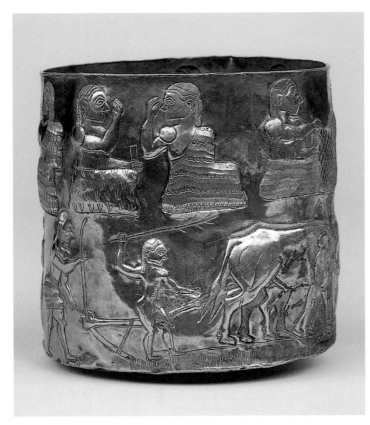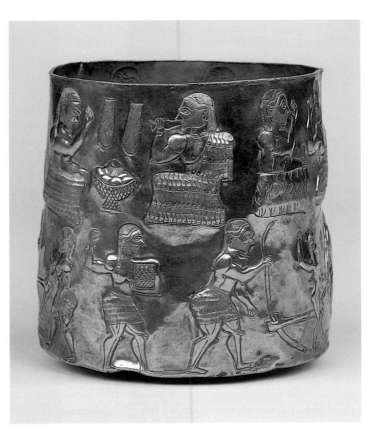

257

Cylindrical cup with agricultural and ceremonial scenes

Silver
H. 12.2–12.6 cm (4¼–5 in.)
Western Central Asia
Late 3rd–early 2nd millennium B.C.
Miho Museum, Japan SF 3.055

A tradition of fine metalworking appears to have developed in western Central Asia in the late third millennium and early second millennium B.C. Based on comparisons with excavated pottery and with finds in the so-called Fullol Hoard of objects from northern Afghanistan, a number of unprovenanced gold and silver vessels have been attributed to Bronze Age Bactria-Margiana.[1] Perhaps the most exceptional pieces are cylindrical silver vessels with elaborate figural scenes executed in low relief with incised details, all of which may have come from a single workshop.

On the present example, which was hammered from a single piece of silver, an elaborate depiction was executed in repoussé, sometimes so deep that the tool cut through the surface of the metal.[2] Bearded and mustached male banqueters wearing fillets in their long, bound hair are seated in a row above a scene of men and boys ploughing a field. The main personage in this upper row, who faces to our left, is distinguished by an elliptically shaped bead on his fillet. He also wears a necklace and bracelet with similar beads, all bearing hatched patterns that may be intended to suggest a veined stone, such as agate. A robe with very clearly rendered tiers of individual tufts covers one arm entirely and envelops the rectangular form of his lower body. The man's exposed

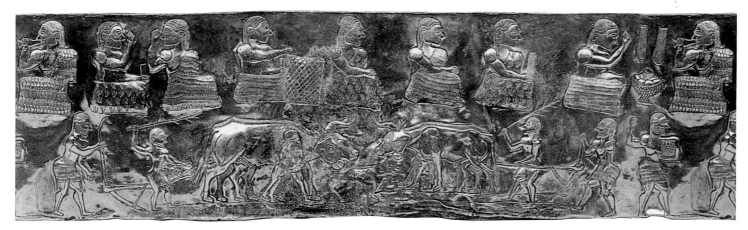

257, rolled out

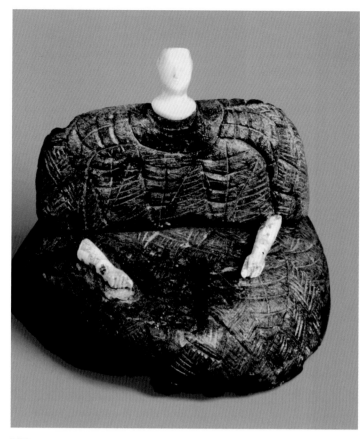

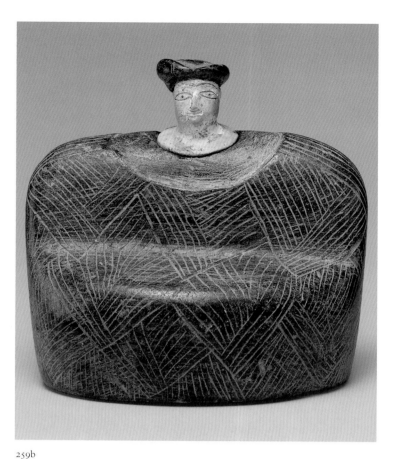

259a

259b

the course of excavations, is a group of chlorite and steatite female statuettes characterized by a massive and dignified body. They are depicted clothed from neck to feet in a sheepskin garment, the tufts either carved in relief or incised. When the first unprovenienced examples were published, some scholars believed they came from Fars, in southwestern Iran, but in fact they derive from Turkmenistan (in ancient times called Margiana) and Pakistan, where they have been found in both tombs and nonfunerary contexts.[1] At least thirty-eight examples, complete or fragmentary, are known at present. Of these, about eleven have been excavated, nine in southeastern Turkmenistan, and two in Pakistan.[2] The only complete example is from Tomb 1799 at Gonur-depe (cat. no. 259a). The figure is composed of two separately made body-garment parts and a separately made light-colored stone head (with no hair or covering preserved); the hands, also separate, rest on the lap.[3] Two complete but headless examples may also derive from Gonur (at least one from a burial).[4] The other examples include, from Gonur, an isolated arm, two feet, head(s), and a garment fragment; from nearby Togolok a garment fragment and an isolated foot;[5] from Quetta, in Baluchistan, the bottom section of a two-part statuette; and from

Harappa, in the Indus Valley, a steatite wig.[6] The twenty-seven unexcavated examples, including the Metropolitan piece (cat. no. 259b), are housed in museums and private collections.[7]

Nearly all examples depict the subject either seated or squatting, with her lap extended forward; on four a backless chair is visible.[8] The majority of the bodies were carved in one piece, but at least ten were made in two neatly joining parts. In all preserved examples the neck and head, made of a light-colored stone and in some cases strikingly beautiful and powerful, were separately carved and placed in a concave shoulder cavity; separately made steatite wigs or hats were also fitted on the head. Disconnected arms, also made of light-colored stone, are sometimes preserved; the upper arm area is sometimes articulated in the body. The arms are simply placed on the lap, as demonstrated by the excavated example from Gonur-depe. In a very few examples, one excavated and three unexcavated, there is a small rectangular cutout at the base of the garment, which probably originally held an added foot or feet; indeed, this is perhaps verified by one unexcavated example that is exhibited with a foot protruding from its cavity. In these four examples the women are manifestly squatting.[9] Based on the incomplete data of

those with preserved heads, the figures vary in height from 7.8 to 20.6 centimeters and in width from at least 5 to 16 centimeters.

Attempts have been made to interpret these figures as deities or prominent humans, but insufficient information exists to permit a satisfactory conclusion.[10] There is no doubt, however, that they are charged beings, physically massive but projecting a calm power and authority.[11] Their chronology is also debated, although recent carbon-14 results suggest a date in the early second millennium B.C.[12]

OWM

1. Among those who believed they came from Fars were Ghirshman (1968, pp. 244–45), Porada (1975, p. 375), and Spycket (1981, p. 213). Most scholars consistently write as if the statuettes derive only from burials: Spycket 1981, p. 215; Pottier 1984, p. 46; Amiet 1986, p. 200; Amiet 1988a, p. 177; Francfort 1994, p. 407; Hiebert 1994, p. 378.
2. To date none derive from Afghanistan.
3. *Ligabue Magazine* 20, no. 39 (2001), pp. 155, 172.
4. Sarianidi 2002, p. 142, top and bottom. No excavation information on these examples exists at present.
5. Specifically, Togolok 21. Hiebert 1994, pp. 377–78, fig. 3A; Sarianidi 1998a, pp. 49, 50, figs. 17:1,12,13, 18:8. Hiebert (1994, fig. 3A) gives a locus for one garment fragment as Togolok, whereas Sarianidi (1998a, fig. 18:11) describes it as coming from Gonur-depe.

6. Jarrige and Hassan 1989, pp. 156, 160, fig. 10; the wig is published in Meadow 2002, pp. 189–97.

7. Ghirshman 1968, figs. 1–5, 6–8; Amiet 1977a, pl. 3, fig. 13; Sotheby's, London, sale, July 12, 1983, no. 61; Pottier 1984, nos. 295–300; Sarianidi 1985, fig. 3:1; Amiet 1988a, fig. 20b; Hôtel Drouot, Paris, Montague collection sale, October 10, 1988, nos. A, B; Salvatori 1988, figs. 108, 109, 111–13; Aruz 1999b, p. 42, no. 7; Sotheby's, New York, sale, June 14, 2000, no. 123; Sotheby's, New York, sale, June 12, 2001, no. 111; Christie's, New York, sale, June 12, 2002, no. 313 dealer, London; dealer, New York; Bonham's, sale, November 7, 2002, no. 198; J.-P. Carbonnel collection (at least two fragments: Amiet [1977b] and Pottier [1984] published examples in this collection without notifying the reader—see Amiet 1986, pp. 194f., n. 1. One of these pieces was sold to N. Schimmel, who donated it to The Metropolitan Museum of Art). Some examples with "crudely" incised garments raise concern about authenticity—but excavated comparative evidence is lacking. The example from Christie's has a low-positioned, narrow lap, a triangular zone at the neck, and ruled incisions—all unusual; the examples from Bonham's, the London dealer, and Hôtel Drouot (no. A) raise questions regarding their age. Isolated heads on the market are not included in this inventory.

8. Ghirshman (1968, p. 237, figs. 1–5) says an example in the Musée du Louvre, Paris, is standing, but note its extended lap; an example in the Foroughi collection (ibid., figs. 6–8) appears to be standing. Three of those seated on chairs may be seen in Sotheby's, London, sale, July 11, 1983, no. 61, and Pottier 1984, nos. 295, 296; the fourth was included in a sale at Sotheby's, New York, June 14, 2000, no. 213.

9. The four examples with a cutout are: the complete statuette from Tomb 1799 at Gonur-depe (see note 3 above; on the left side); Aruz 1999b, p. 42, no. 7 (on the right side); Salvatori 1988, figs. 112, 113. Aruz (1999b) and Jean M. Evans (personal communication) noted that the cutout space was probably for added feet. A silver vase from Iran (Hinz 1969, pp. 11–12, pl. 5) depicting a squatting woman shows two feet protruding from the right side of her garment. The tufted garment, the pose, and the position of the feet manifestly relate this vessel and its narrative iconographically and ideologically to the steatite and chlorite statuettes; see Ghirshman 1968, p. 244.

10. As deities in Ghirshman 1968, pp. 243–44; Pottier 1984, p. 75; and Francfort 1994, p. 410; as queens in Amiet 1986, p. 200, and Amiet 1988a, p. 177. According to Pittman (1984, p. 51), the evidence suggests that both humans and deities could be shown squatting and wearing a tufted robe. Many writers, for example, Spycket 1981, p. 215; Pottier 1984, p. 86; Amiet 1986, p. 200; Amiet 1988a, p. 177; Francfort 1994, p. 407; and Hiebert 1994, p. 328, write as if the statuettes derive only from burials.

11. A group of six unprovenienced chlorite statuettes of men with prominently scarred faces has been associated by some scholars with the seated ladies (an example in this catalogue is number 244). They were first published in Ghirshman 1961, no. 12, and in Ghirshman 1963a, figs. 1–3. Their alleged cultural relationship to the female statuettes is not manifest.

12. About 1750 B.C.; see Hiebert 1994, charts, pp. 374–75. Meadow (2002, p. 193) suggests an earlier date.

260

Compartmented stamp seal with winged goddess on a dragon

Silver
Western Central Asia, Gonur-depe, Tomb 570
Late 3rd–early 2nd millennium B.C.
The National Museum of Turkmenistan Named After Saparmurat Turkmenbashi, Ashgabat

Beginning in the mid-third millennium B.C. a tradition of metal compartmented stamp seals decorated with geometric, floral, or figural designs emerged in western Central Asia. These seals were cast, probably by the lost-wax method, most commonly in a copper alloy, although examples in silver, like the present piece, and gold are known. Incisions in the metal provide the details of the decoration, and the background space is cut away.

This seal depicts a female figure wearing a tufted full-length robe. The image is a well-known type in the art of western Central Asia (see cat. nos. 258, 259). Here the female is shown with wings, suggesting that she is a deity.

Perhaps she is related to the Mesopotamian goddess Ishtar, who is shown with similarly outstretched wings from the Akkadian period onward (see cat. no. 139). On a seal in the Musée du Louvre, Paris (cat. no. 261), the wings are replaced by animals emerging from the figure's shoulders, a detail that again indicates her divine nature. The females on both seals are shown in identical poses: their faces are in profile looking to the right, and each sits sidesaddle on a scaly dragon facing backward with its tail curling up toward the rider. The monsters' tails and front paws cross the frames of the seals, and their mouths are open in a snarl. However, not only the wings and animals on the shoulders but also other variations in the details of the two seals suggest that two distinct deities are represented. The hair of the figure on the present seal falls behind her shoulders with a sidelock hanging in front of the ear, whereas on the

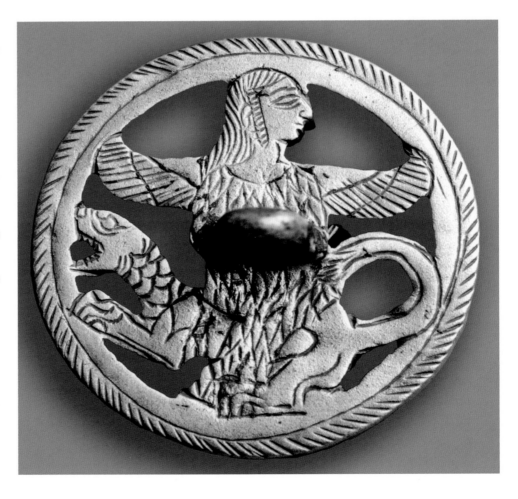

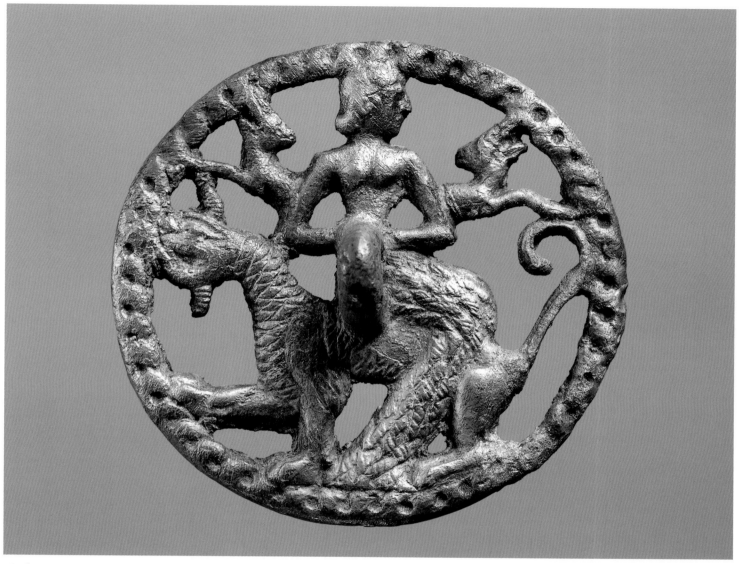

261 obverse

Louvre seal the hair is shorter and perhaps curled at the ends. Here the deity wears a full-length tufted robe, but the breasts of the woman on the Louvre example appear to be uncovered. The dragons are also distinguished from each other, with the Louvre monster displaying a single horn on its head and a beard hanging from its jaw while the present beast has neither. The knob on this seal was presumably used for holding the object while making impressions.   PC

261

Compartmented stamp seal with a goddess seated on a dragon

Silver
Diam. 6.7 cm (2⅝ in.); Diam. of ring 2.2 cm (⅞ in.)
Western Central Asia
Late 3rd–early 2nd millennium B.C.
Musée du Louvre, Département des Antiquités
Orientales, Paris; Acquisition 1992 AO 30226

The most beautiful compartmented seals come from Bactria-Margiana. They are equipped with a loop handle on the back, by which they were held to make an impression in clay, and are made of arsenical copper or, more rarely, silver or gold. The designs on such seals often make reference to local Oxus mythology. On the back of this silver seal, which has a guilloche border, is a goddess of the highest rank.[1] She is always depicted with

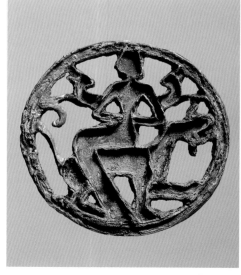

261 reverse

anthropomorphic features and is associated with water and the cycle of nature. She appears to reign over the animal and plant worlds as well as over hybrid beings such as dragons or winged demons, who are often endowed with the heads of birds of prey.[2]

Here the goddess is dressed in a long tufted garment that leaves her breasts uncovered. The foreparts of caprids burst forth from her arms, and her hands are joined at her waist. She sits sidesaddle on a bearded, one-horned Bactrian dragon that combines the body, tail, and feet of a lion with the slender neck and scales of a snake.[3] The dragon is familiar in Bactrian iconography; one serves as the seat for a goddess holding a goblet on a copper-alloy compartmented seal in the Louvre.[4] Her general attitude, which is fairly static, as in other depictions of the goddess, may express a beneficent character.[5]

This representation appears to borrow certain elements from Mesopotamia, specifically the image of the dragon, the garment worn by the goddess, and the emergence of animal attributes from the deity's shoulders.[6] This last detail, moreover, suggests that the seal dates from the late third millennium B.C. because the motif first appears on an impression of the seal of Gudea, governor of Lagash (fig. 107).[7] The absence of a horned crown, found on the goddesses of both Mesopotamia and of the Elamite and trans-Elamite world, the representation of the figure with the upper body frontal but the head in profile, and the seated posture on a dragon appear to be local traditions.[8]

The reverse of the seal has compartments that roughly follow the outline of the obverse design. Although imprints of compartmented seals were made on pottery from eastern Iran, no impressions have been found in Bactria-Margiana. This has led Pierre Amiet to conclude that in Central Asia they may have been used as amulets.[9] The presence of a small bead pierced by a hole on the ring of the seal does seem to indicate that the object was worn.

AB

1. The mythological hierarchy of Bactria-Margiana, modeled on that of the contemporary society, is organized into an order of three ranks. For further reference on this seal, see Pottier 1980, pp. 167–74, pl. 1; Pottier 1984, p. 76, no. 332; Amiet 1986, pp. 147, 198, fig. 184; Sarianidi 1998b, p. 26, no. 16-1.
2. Dragons belong to the old mythological font of the Eastern world, from Mesopotamia to East Asia. For dragons with the heads of birds of prey, see Amiet 1986, fig. 186.

3. Lion-dragons, snake-dragons, and, more rarely, anthropomorphic dragons (see cat. no. 244) are mythological entities common in the Oxus civilization.
4. That seal, AO 26067, is on the cover of Amiet 1986.
5. She appears in the same attitude on other seals; see Sarianidi 1998b, nos. 19, 24, 37, 38–40.
6. The attribute animal of the personal god of Gudea, Ningishzida, is the bashmum snake-dragon. This winged animal has horns, a snake's body with scales represented by dots, the back paws of a lion, the talons of a bird of prey in front, and an upright tail that ends in a scorpion's stinger. It seems to play a role of magical protection.
7. On that example the heads of horned snakes burst forth from the shoulders of Ningishzida, who leads the king before the god of the state of Lagash; these heads correspond to the personality of Ningishzida's attribute animal, the bashmum; see Collon 1987, no. 531.
8. Elamite deities appear for the first time on an impression of a goldsmith's seal; see Amiet 1966, fig. 156.
9. Amiet 1988a, p. 169.

262

Stamp seal with a winged deity and lions

Gold
Diam. 3.4 cm (1 3/8 in.)
Western Central Asia
Late 3rd–early 2nd millennium B.C.
Museum zu Allerheiligen, Schaffhausen, Sammlung Ebnöther, Switzerland Eb 33345

In the art of Bactria-Margiana the most pervasive mark of divinity—known mainly from depictions on seals—is a pair of wings emanating from the shoulders of an otherwise human form. Scholars have recognized in a number of representations of a top-ranking, probably male, deity certain other divine features as well: short or long hair but no beard; a nude torso—and on the present seal a necklace

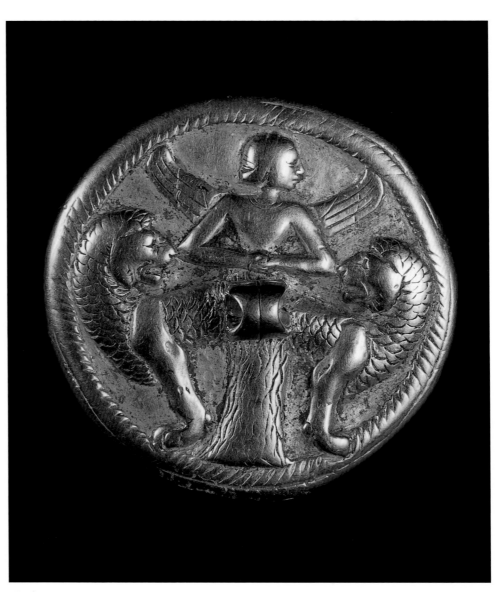

262 obverse

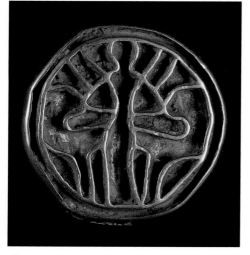

262 reverse

(or diaphanous garment defined only by a neckline); a tapered waist and indication of pectorals; arms bent at the elbow and hands held toward the body at the waist; a long garment that may be textured with either a scalloped or a hatched pattern; and an association with powerful animals and mythical beasts—felines, snakes, and dragons—that either serve as the deity's vehicle or attribute or come under his or her domination. While the garments appear to be generally related to those worn by Mesopotamian gods, these figures lack the obligatory Mesopotamian horned headdress, a feature that was certainly transmitted as far as eastern Iran and possibly even to the Indus Valley (see cat. no. 293).[1] Wings are also attributes of the Mesopotamian goddess Ishtar (see cat. no. 139), and they emerge from the shoulders of both horned and bareheaded deities depicted on eastern Iranian seals.[2] One cylinder-seal depiction from the southeast Iranian site of Tepe Yahya, which is very similar to images on Bactria-Margiana compartmented seals, includes a standing figure flanked by a snake and a quadruped.[3]

Some seals with representations of these important figures are made of precious metals, cast by the lost-wax technique.[4] The present rare gold example is a disk with the figures decorated in relief and by incision; on the reverse the disk acts as the base for attached strips of gold that form compartments and roughly echo the design on the obverse. The god's lower body merges with the foreparts of two addorsed lions, at the point where the loop handle protrudes. The lions look inward, and the composition is encircled in a ropelike border. A very similar silver seal, also without provenance, depicts the same scene, and a

copper-alloy open-worked example shows the deity (with birds rather than wings) standing between two lions facing outward.[5]

A cylindrical vessel in the so-called Astrabad Treasure from Iran, probably of Bactrian manufacture, depicts a related scene: a standing, bare-chested figure extending his arms above a lion and a snake.[6] On that vessel, however, the man wears the textured garment but lacks other features that would define him as a god.

JA

1. Amiet 1986, pp. 298–99, fig. 132:2–6, 8–10 (a bucranium).
2. Ibid., pp. 298–99, fig. 132:5, 6, 9.
3. Ibid., p. 299, fig. 132:7.
4. Aruz 1998b, pp. 14ff.; Amiet 1986, fig. 319:185.
5. Baghestani 1997, p. 292, fig. 399, p. 296, fig. 405.
6. Amiet 1986, pp. 186, 204, 307, fig. 149; Amiet 1988a, pp. 136, 161. Amiet considers the Astrabad Treasure to be a contrived collection of objects from clandestine excavations, like the Fullol Hoard from Afghanistan.

263

Compartmented stamp seal with an eagle and snakes

Silver
Western Central Asia, Gonur-depe, Tomb 555
Late 3rd–early 2nd millennium B.C.
The National Museum of Turkmenistan Named After Saparmurat Turkmenbashi, Ashgabat

This compartmented stamp seal depicts an eagle facing right. Its outstretched wings showing one set of feathers curl at the tips. Against the upper part of each wing rests the head of a serpent, perhaps intended to be viewed as biting the bird. Each snake's scaly body hangs behind a wing and curls back on itself. The eagle's talons grasp the curled tails. In the center of the seal, above the eagle's long tail, is a raised knob. The edge of the seal is decorated with hatching.

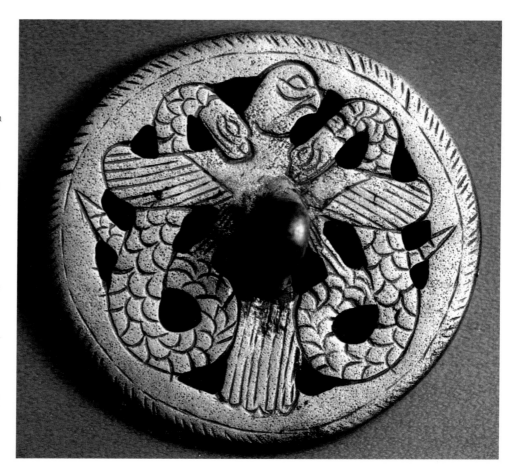

263

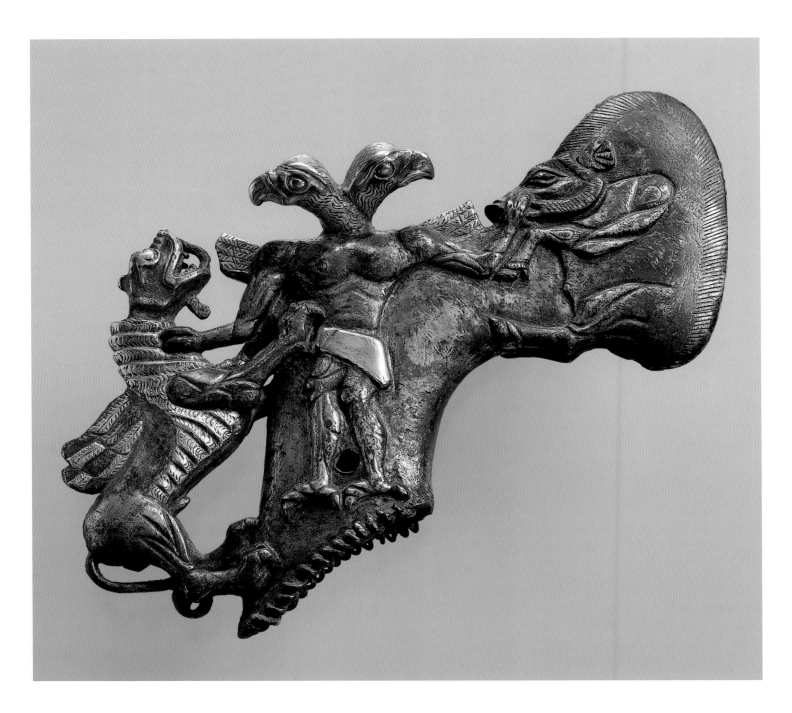

The meaning of the combat of the snake and eagle is unknown. Similar imagery is found on "Intercultural Style" vessels (see cat. no. 234). Double snakes are frequently represented on compartmented seals, and one example is known in which the eagle is reduced to outstretched wings that seem to emerge from the two snakes.[1] However, snakes on seals are more often shown being dominated by male or female anthropomorphic figures, some of which are winged, suggesting that they may be deities.[2] Eagles also appear on numerous compartmented seals but are usually depicted without accompanying figures. Examples of seals with double-headed eagles or representations of kneeling humans with eagle's

heads—comparable to the bird-demon on a shaft-hole axe from Bactria-Margiana (cat. no. 264)—suggest the eagle had an important role in religion or mythology in western Central Asia.[3]   PC

1. Sarianidi 1998b, p. 75, no. 125.
2. For examples, see ibid., nos. 25–31. The tradition of human figures grasping snakes is known as early as the Ubaid period (fifth millennium B.C.); see Boehmer 1999, p. 145, pl. 130.
3. For examples of eagles shown alone, see Sarianidi 1998b, nos. 126–91. The double-headed eagle appears on ibid., p. 75, nos. 126–28. For the kneeling bird-man, see ibid., p. 63, nos. 58, 59.

264

Shaft-hole axe with a bird-demon, boar, and winged dragon

Silver and gold foil
H. to top of bird-demon heads: 10.8 cm (4¼ in.);
L. 15 cm (5⅞ in.); Weight 581 g
Shaft hole: L. 5.1 cm (2 in.); W. 1.59 cm (⅝ in.)
Western Central Asia
Late 3rd–early 2nd millennium B.C.
The Metropolitan Museum of Art, New York; Purchase, Harris Brisbane Dick Fund, and James N. Spear and Schimmel Foundation Inc. Gifts, 1982   1982.5

This spectacularly animated weapon exemplifies the superb quality of Central

Asian metalwork. It was cast in a single piece, with the exception of the bird heads on the central figure—which were inserted into a recess along the top edge of the blade—the dragon's tail, and the small silver rings inserted into holes around the lower edge of the shaft hole. The bird heads, now bent out of plane, may have been fashioned entirely of gold.[1] Other areas, such as the kilt and wings of the central figure and the body and wings of the dragon, were gilt with foil burnished down over the silver. In addition to gilding, the bodies of the figures were enriched by extensive chasing. While the materials used indicate that this axe head served a ceremonial function, the remains of wood preserved inside the shaft hole show that it was mounted on a haft when buried. In form it recalls axes of a type attributed to Central Asia; examples have been found in Iran and are depicted on Elamite glyptic of the twentieth century B.C.[2]

Domination over dangerous forces is expressed in the imagery on the axe. The griffin demon, the only part-human, part-animal upright creature in the art of western Central Asia, is depicted on both sides of the blade, in each case having the protruding head, wings, and talons of a bird of prey, appended to the muscular body of a human male wearing a kilt. This apparently heroic and beneficent creature is portrayed in a human standing posture, with broad shoulders and a tapering waist, its human arms outstretched to grab the snout of a contorted boar and the neck of an aggressive Bactrian dragon. The latter is a distinctive creature with a feline body, wings and claws, and the head and gaping mouth of an attacking snake. The back of the boar forms the edge of the axe blade.

Dominant winged griffin demons are depicted on both the cylinder seals and the stamp seals of the Bactria-Margiana region. One example holds up reversed horned animals, while others may sit on snakes.[3] Perhaps the closest foreign parallel for this creature is found on a door sealing from Susa, in Iran; there a figure with a human body and a bird head, outspread wings, and claws for feet stands upright between a scorpion and a monkey.[4] The site of Susa is also the source of a number of axes formed in the shapes of animals; some of these objects were probably imported from western Central Asia.[5]

A bronze axe-shaped object in the British Museum, sculpted with the forms of an attacking tiger with inlaid silver stripes and ibex prey, also has a boar-shaped blade.[6] The boar also appears occasionally on the stamp and cylinder seals of Bactria-Margiana. On cushion-shaped seals with images on both faces it may be paired with a bird of prey or a dragon.[7] The dragon is a more popular image in the glyptic of this region, paired not only with eagles or griffin demons but also with heroes holding snakes.[8]

JA

1. Technical comments in this paragraph have been provided by Jean-François de Lapérouse, Associate Conservator, Objects Conservation, Metropolitan Museum. X-radiographs indicate that these heads may be hollow. In addition, the bottom edge of the birds' neck appears to be gold across its thickness.
2. Pittman 1984, p. 73; Amiet 1998a, p. 134, fig. 7, p. 130, fig. 1.
3. Sarianidi 1998b, pp. 53:13, 173:917.1, 175:923.1, 63:61.
4. Aruz 1998b, pp. 20ff.; this sealing has most recently been discussed in Pittman 2002.
5. See T. Potts 1994, pp. 168ff.
6. Collon 1995, p. 87, no. 68; Maxwell-Hyslop 1987.
7. Pittman 1984, p. 60, fig. 29b. Sarianidi 1998b, p. 265:1453, shows a cylinder seal with a lion attacking a boar; p. 297:1636 illustrates a seal or amulet shaped like a boar; see also p. 185:981, 982.
8. Sarianidi 1998b, pp. 171:904, 173:917, 177:938–40 are some characteristic examples.

265

Camel-shaped stamp seal with a bull-leaping scene

Chlorite
H. 3.2 cm (1¼ in.)
Western Central Asia, Togolok 21, southern court
Late 3rd–early 2nd millennium B.C.
The National Museum of Turkmenistan Named After Saparmurat Turkmenbashi, Ashgabat 831-1212

Stone stamp seals, which are usually made of chlorite, are a well-known class of Bactria-Margiana glyptic. Many of them share similar iconography with copper-alloy compartmented seals from the Oxus region. Their geometric shapes vary, but all are pierced and decorated on both faces with a design obtained by combining drilling and engraving techniques.

This extraordinary amulet is unique in both composition and style. Its upper face portrays a Bactrian camel with a prominent mouth biting its left hind leg. The rendering of the hair tuft on the forehead, the long fur

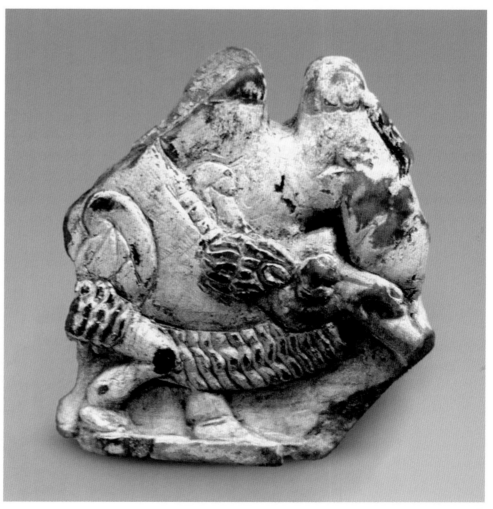

265

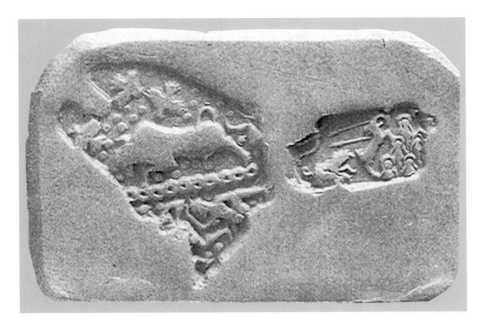

Impression from catalogue number 265.

on the neck and humps, the elongated snout, and the torsion of the body, with its emphasis on the musculature of the shoulder, attains compactness as well as dynamism. This powerful image antedates the "animal style" of the sixth to fourth century B.C. in the southern Urals, Siberia, and the Altai region and can be considered an astonishing forerunner of what became one of the most common scenes of animal attack in nomadic art.[1]

The iconography engraved on the other two faces of the seal is also quite exceptional. On the flat reverse, two registers are separated by a guilloche chain. Above, a zebu is depicted in a "flying gallop" with a leaping man, whose legs alone are preserved; below are a running and a sitting man, probably from the same contest scene (see entry for cat. no. 301). The third scene, carved on the side of the amulet, depicts hunters attacking a pair of rampant ibexes on a mountain represented by a scalloped pattern. The portrayal of humans in narrative scenes is unusual in Bactria-Margiana glyptic. However, the extraordinary silver vessels produced in western Central Asia during the late third to the early second millennium B.C., feature complex figural scenes of ceremony and hunt (see cat. no. 257).   EVF

1. For striking similarities with this amulet, see a bronze phalera from Filippovka, kurgan 1 (fourth century B.C.) in Aruz et al. 2000, p. 84, no. 13.

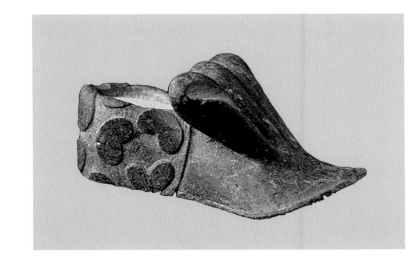

266

Stone shoe

Steatite
Western Central Asia, Gonur-depe, necropolis
Late 3rd–early 2nd millennium B.C.
The National Museum of Turkmenistan Named After
Saparmurat Turkmenbashi, Ashgabat

This extraordinary and unique object is in the form of a soft, heelless shoe, with a slightly upturned and pointed toe. From the top of the slipper protrudes a wide decorative tongue that consists of a frill of three parallel rounded and bulbous forms, the tops of which are free of the vamp. The back is less deeply carved than the front and has kidney-shaped decorations on the exterior; these bear a distinctive, perhaps symbolic, significance in the art of ancient western Central Asia. An inlay in this form also decorates the head of a gold bull from Altyn-depe (see cat. no. 249). Kidney-shaped inlays are known as well from the Indus Valley (see cat. no. 288). Only the elite (or the gods) may have worn such elaborate shoes, and thus this stone version may represent authority imbued with magical symbolism.   PC

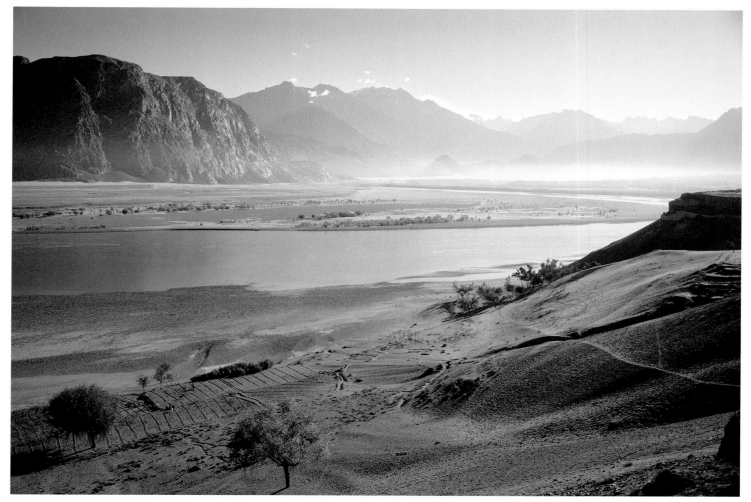

The Indus River with mountains beyond.

THE INDUS CIVILIZATION

JONATHAN MARK KENOYER

South Asia's first cities were established about 2600 B.C. in what are now Pakistan and western India. The peoples who built and ruled these cities belong to the Indus civilization or Harappan culture. This civilization developed at approximately the same time as the early city-states of Egypt and Mesopotamia. Although there were economic and cultural contacts between these early urban societies, significant differences are seen in their respective artistic styles, symbols, technologies, and social organization. These differences can be attributed to the fact that each civilization evolved from local cultures that had roots extending back to the earliest Neolithic farming and pastoral communities. The unique character of the Indus civilization is revealed by its architecture and city planning, its various arts, and the technologies used to produce them.

This urban civilization spread over a vast geographic region, from the mountains of Baluchistan and Afghanistan to the coastal regions of Makran, Sindh, and Gujarat. Through economic interaction as well as social and political alliances, the local farming communities became more integrated, and the various regional styles of arts, symbols, tools, and technologies became more similar. Large cities and smaller towns grew up along the major trade routes as administrative and ritual centers. During the full urban phase of this civilization, there is evidence for trade contact with the surrounding cultures in the Gulf, West and Central Asia, and peninsular India. The urban expansion and increasing stratification of social classes in the Indus cities required the development of new forms of symbolic expression and new mechanisms for reinforcing social organization. The most characteristic of these expressive and unifying forms were elaborate ornaments, seals, writing, decorated pottery, and new forms of ritual objects. Although there is a general unity in style and symbol over this vast area, there are specific regional variations. Also, the manufacture of symbols was slightly different in each region.

The unified character of this culture continued for almost seven hundred years, after which there is evidence for a gradual trend toward regionalization. Through the processes of overexpansion and changes in important river patterns, the Harappan urban centers began to decline about 1900 B.C., and the unifying cultural forms of the cities were no longer useful. However, the regional cultures that began to take shape did retain some of the characteristic forms and technologies of the Harappan culture. These continuities provide an important thread connecting the developments of the first urban civilization to later cultures that became dominant in the regions of northern Pakistan and India. Some of the technologies, architecture, artistic symbols, and aspects of social organization that characterized the first urban centers of the Indus civilization have continued up to the present in the urban setting of traditional South Asian cities.

Research on the Indus Valley tradition has been going on since the first discovery of inscribed seals at Harappa in the late 1800s, and scholars from all of the major countries of the world have been involved. Important excavations were begun at the larger sites in the 1920s, and numerous excavations at smaller sites have broadened our understanding of this unique culture; however, many misconceptions rooted in the theoretical and cultural biases of the earliest excavators persist. One of them is that the Indus urban society was the result of colonization from Mesopotamia. Another is that it appeared suddenly and then disappeared, having no influence on later cultural developments. Yet another is that it was a strictly uniform culture ruled by a "priest-king" from two major capitals. These misconceptions are gradually being replaced with more informed interpretations.

NEOLITHIC MEHRGARH

The site of Mehrgarh, Pakistan, provides evidence of the earliest agricultural and pastoral communities in South Asia. Located at the foot of the Bolan Pass, the site was first inhabited about 7000 B.C. by farmers and herders of cattle, sheep, and goats. These early settlers lived in mud-brick houses, wove baskets, and adorned themselves with elaborate beaded ornaments made

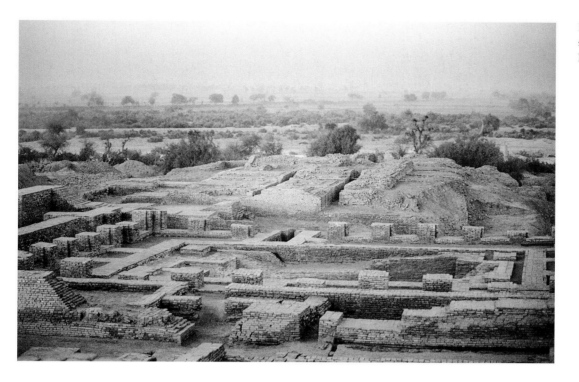

Fig. 93. View of Mohenjo-daro, showing the large water tank and hall. Harappan, ca. 2600–1900 B.C.

of seashells and colored stones either traded from distant areas or collected during pastoral migrations.

The earliest terracotta figurines and pottery were produced about 4500 B.C., and many of the designs on the vessels may replicate woven motifs on the earlier baskets. By 3500 to 2600 B.C. numerous regional cultures had emerged throughout the Indus Valley, distinguished by specific styles of painted pottery, figurines, and ornament. Mehrgarh and the somewhat later, nearby settlement at Nausharo were major centers for the manufacture of distinctive pottery and figurines. The gradual expansion,

interaction, and eventual synthesis of these regional cultures set the stage for the integration of the entire Indus Valley during the Harappan period, about 2600 B.C.

URBAN INDUS

During the Harappan period, large cities and towns emerged at major crossroads in rich agricultural regions (see fig. 70a). The ruling communities of these cities developed a distinctive form of writing and appear to have controlled a vast geographic area—some 650,000 square kilometers—twice as large as that

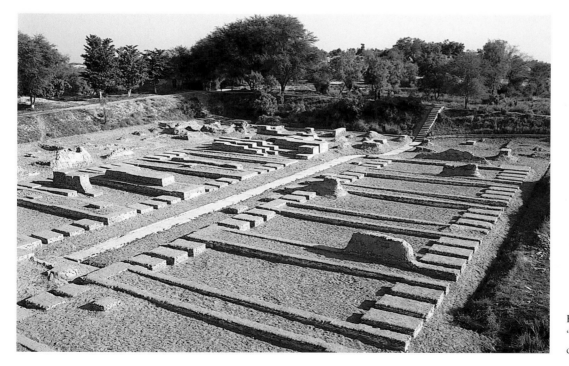

Fig. 94. Large hall (called the "granary"), Harappa. Harappan, ca. 2600–1900 B.C.

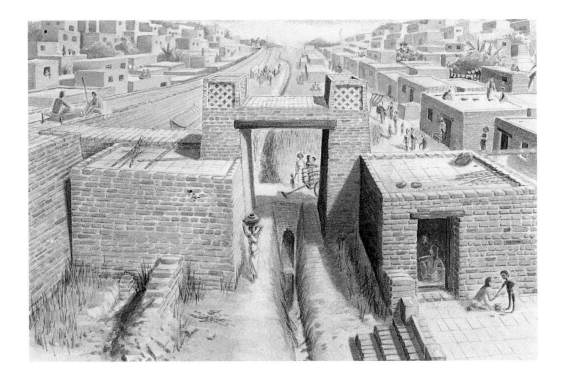

Fig. 95. Reconstruction of the gateway, Harappa. Harappan, ca. 2600–1900 B.C.

controlled by Mesopotamian or Egyptian cultures at this same time in history.

More than fifteen hundred Indus settlements have been discovered, but archaeologists have been able to excavate only a handful of different types of sites in each of the major regions. The earliest excavations focused on large cities located along the Indus River and its tributaries: Mohenjo-daro, on the Indus in Sindh, southern Pakistan (see fig. 93), and Harappa, on the Ravi River in Punjab, northern Pakistan (see fig. 94). Other equally large cities have been found along the dried-up Hakra-Nara River to the east, including two unexcavated sites that are almost as large as Mohenjo-daro: Ganweriwala in Cholistan, Pakistan, and Rakhigarhi, in Haryana, India. Dholavira, a fifth major town, which has been excavated, is located on a small island that controlled trade through the Greater Rann of Kutch (Gujarat, India). Several smaller towns, rural villages, and mining, trading, and coastal settlements of the Harappan period have also been excavated in both Pakistan and western India.

Excavations at Harappa and Mohenjo-daro and smaller sites revealed well-planned cities and towns built on massive mud-brick platforms that protected the inhabitants against seasonal floods (see fig. 95). In the larger cities the houses were built of baked brick, while at smaller towns most houses were built of sun-dried mud brick. The settlements had major streets running north-south and east-west, with smaller streets and alleys connecting neighborhoods to the main thoroughfares (see fig. 96). The houses were often two-storied and usually had a bathing area supplied with water from a neighborhood well.

All of the houses were connected to an elaborate citywide drainage system that reflects a well-organized civic authority. At Mohenjo-daro there is a large water tank that may have served as a public or ritual bathing area (see fig. 97). Other important structures include large halls (often mistakenly called granaries) and industrial complexes that suggest some level of state control of economic resources and production.

UTILITARIAN AND DECORATIVE OBJECTS

The unique character of this civilization is revealed through the artistry and technology that produced sculpture, figurines, seals, ornaments, painted pottery, tools, and utensils. Specific objects such as bangles, seals, and figurines are thought to reflect or represent key elements of social organization, ritual beliefs, and technological advancement. On the basis of comparisons with contemporaneous cultures in Mesopotamia and Central Asia, as well as through the study of historical continuities in South Asia itself, it is possible to understand how these objects may have been used and what they may have meant to the people who used them.

Indus artisans produced a wide range of utilitarian and decorative objects using specialized techniques of stone working, pottery production, and metallurgy. Copper and bronze were used to make ornaments, tools, mirrors, pots, and pans. Bone, shell, and ivory were crafted into tools, ornaments, gaming pieces, and, especially, inlay for furniture. Silver and gold utensils and ornaments and fine ceramic objects, such as stoneware bangles

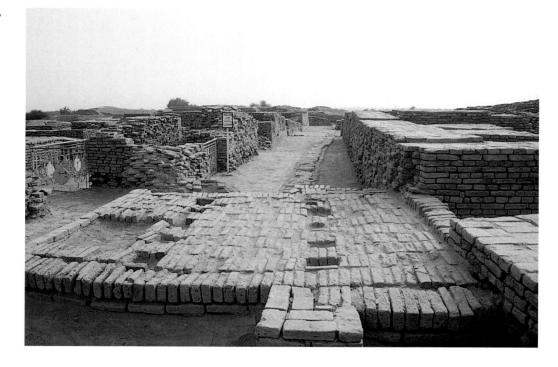

Fig. 96. Street, Mohenjo-daro. Harappan, ca. 2600–1900 B.C.

and faience ornaments, were also produced. We guess that many of these objects were made for the wealthy merchants and the ruling classes, because identical utensils and ornaments were turned out in terracotta, presumably for ordinary people.

SEALS AND WRITING

The most unusual and intriguing artifacts of Harappan culture are square seals made of stone and engraved with symbols and animal motifs. The most common beast carved on the seals is a mythical unicorn; also represented are the bull, elephant, water buffalo, zebu, antelope, tiger, and rhinoceros. Abstract or pictographic symbols engraved above the animals represent the Indus form of writing. The presence of writing on seals, as well as on pottery and other objects, indicates that the Indus people had developed a system for recording the names of deities, or people, or materials. On the average, the inscriptions are very short, consisting of about seven symbols, and the direction of writing is usually from right to left. Scholars have not yet been able to decipher these short inscriptions and will not be able to do so until some longer texts or bilingual inscriptions are discovered.

RELIGION AND BELIEF SYSTEMS

Without the aid of written texts it is difficult to reconstruct the Indus religion. Some of the excavated clay figurines of animals, men, and women were probably used in special rituals. Soft limestone was used to carve small sculptures of deities or important people.

Many of the seals have narrative scenes that appear to include deities and ceremonies. The Indus people buried their dead in wood coffins accompanied by many pottery vessels that were probably filled with food for the use of the deceased in the afterlife. Most individuals, both male and female, were buried with some simple ornaments, such as shell or copper bangles and agate beads. Elaborate ornaments of gold, silver, and precious stones were never included in the burials and must have been inherited by living relatives. No distinctly royal burials have been found.

TRADE AND EXCHANGE

The Indus cities were connected through well-developed trade systems with rural agricultural communities, mining areas, and locations where important resources could be obtained. They used pack animals, riverboats, and bullock carts for transport. This trade is reflected in the widespread distribution of exquisite beads, ornaments, metal tools, and pottery, all of which were produced by specialized artisans in the major towns and cities. Livestock, cotton, lumber, grain, and other foodstuffs were probably the major commodities of this internal trade. There was also external trade with Central Asia, the Gulf region, and the distant Mesopotamian cities, such as Susa and Ur.

DECLINE AND LEGACY

Earlier scholars thought that the Indus civilization disappeared about 1900 B.C., but recent excavations in Pakistan and western India indicate that it gradually became fragmented into smaller

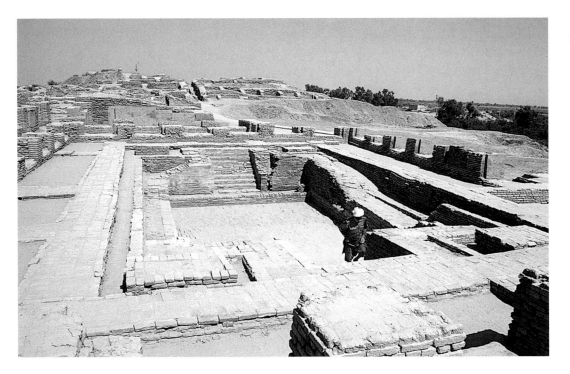

Fig. 97. Large water tank, possibly a public or ritual bathing area, Mohenjo-daro. Harappan, ca. 2600–1900 B.C.

regional cultures, now referred to as Late Harappan or post-Harappan. The ruling classes and merchants of the major urban centers were no longer able to control the trade networks that had served to integrate such a vast geographic area, and the use of standardized weights, writing, and seals gradually became unnecessary.

The decline of the major urban centers and the fragmentation of the Indus culture can be attributed in part to natural changes in the rivers, which disrupted the agricultural and economic system. About 1900 B.C. the tributaries of the Hakra-Nara River became diverted to the Indus in the west and the Yamuna in the east. As the river dried up, people migrated to the central Indus Valley, the Ganga-Yamuna valley, or the fertile plains of Gujarat, in western India. The Indus River itself began to change its course, bringing destructive floods.

Although certain distinguishing aspects of the Indus civilization such as writing and weights disappeared, many other aspects of Indus technology, art, agriculture, and possibly social organization persisted among the Late and post-Harappan cultures. These traditions eventually became incorporated in the new urban civilization that arose during what is termed the Early Historical period, about 600 B.C.

Baluchistan

The cities that emerged in the vast alluvial plain of the Indus River and its tributaries in about 2600 B.C. had origins and a continued history that were closely connected with developments to the west, in the rugged but highly differentiated environment of Baluchistan. Excavations there in the Kachhi plain, at Mehrgarh, Nausharo, and Pirak, have revealed a long cultural sequence starting in the Neolithic period. From the beginning of settled life in the seventh millennium B.C. through the mid-third millennium, the number of settlements in the region continued to increase, reflecting the successful production of food through farming and pastoralism. It is clear that trade connections extended from the highlands into the Indus plains and south to the coast. New technologies that were developed included the making of highly fired ceramics, glazed steatite, and decorated carnelian and metalworking. Many of the area's technological and artistic traditions became essential components of the Harappan civilization that developed later. These advances are also reflected in objects manufactured in Baluchistan but found at sites along the Gulf and at centers such as Susa. They underscore the role the region played in creating many of the artistic traditions of the Indus Valley and disseminating them to the wider world. PC

Seated nude female figure with an elaborate hairdressing

Terracotta
H. 9.3 cm (3⅝ in.); W. 3 cm (1⅛ in.)
Baluchistan, Mehrgarh
Mehrgarh VI, ca. 3000 B.C.
National Museum, Karachi EB 1002/1003
Courtesy of the Department of Archaeology and
Museums, Ministry of Minorities, Culture, Sports,
Tourism, and Youth Affairs, Government of Pakistan

Among the most distinctive female figures from Baluchistan are the seated women with hair piled on both sides of the head.[1] This example has hair spiraling in two massive buns, but others have layers of curled hair.[2] The eyes are punched in, and the ornaments and hair are all appliquéd. The neck and chest are covered with layers of necklaces, and along the topmost layer are punctate designs, possibly indicating beads or designed metal. No traces of pigment remain on this example, but the hair of similar figures is colored black or red (perhaps to indicate henna) and the ornaments often are painted red and yellow, possibly to represent carnelian and gold or polished copper, respectively. The arms are tucked beneath the breasts, and the legs are bent at the knees.

JMK

1. On these figures, see C. Jarrige 1988.
2. Jarrige and Lechevallier 1979, p. 508, fig. 25.

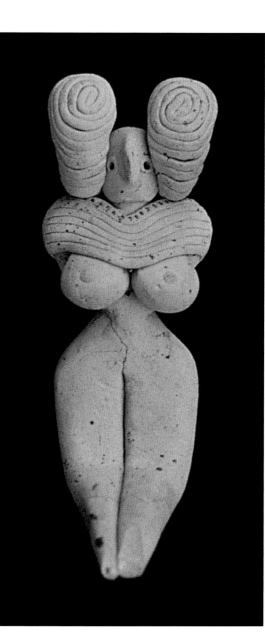

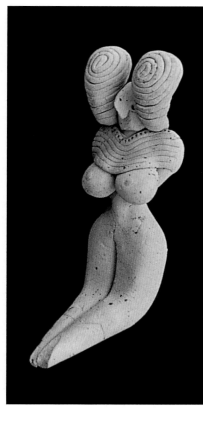

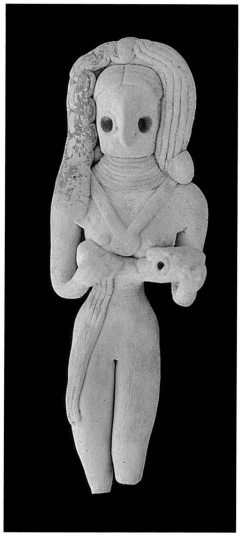

268a

268a, b

Standing figures holding infants

Terracotta

a. H. 12.2 cm (4¾ in.); W. 4 cm (1⅝ in.)
Baluchistan, Mehrgarh
Mehrgarh VII, ca. 2800–2600 B.C.
National Museum, Karachi 145
Courtesy of the Department of Archaeology and
Museums, Ministry of Minorities, Culture, Sports,
Tourism, and Youth Affairs, Government of Pakistan

b. H. 12.4 cm (4⅞ in.); W. 5.1 cm (2 in.)
Baluchistan, Nausharo, NS 87
Nausharo ID, ca. 2600–2500 B.C.
Islamabad Museum, Islamabad EBK 5784
Courtesy of the Department of Archaeology and
Museums, Ministry of Minorities, Culture, Sports,
Tourism, and Youth Affairs, Government of Pakistan

Female figures from Baluchistan and the Indus Valley are distinguished by their exquisite

The woman is holding the stylized figure of an infant and has four long lengths of what may be fabric hanging from her right hand. The deep, hollow eyes of woman and infant are painted black, and there are traces of yellowish red pigment on the ornaments and the hanging fabric.[1]

While some figures from the region are clearly male or female, others combine characteristics of both sexes. The second example here (cat. no. 268b) was found with seven others in a burned room at Nausharo dating between 2600 and 2500 B.C.[2] All of the others are clearly sexed, but this one may represent a transvestite. The elaborate headdress is typical of female figurines, yet the subject's chest and clothing are similar to those of male figures. Like many female headdresses of the same era, this one is bordered by large disk-shaped ornaments. The headband is painted red; the hair and face are painted red-brown. The long, almond-shaped eyes are lined with black pigment. The chest with small, applied nipples was attached to the core of the body. The figure wears trousers gathered at the calf. This person is carrying an infant wearing a masculine turban. The infant's eyebrows and long, almond-shaped eyes are painted black.   JMK

1. C. Jarrige 1988, pp. 66–67.
2. C. Jarrige in J.-F. Jarrige 1998, pp. 193–95, fig. 24:b1; Samzun 1992, pp. 245–52, fig. 29.5,5.

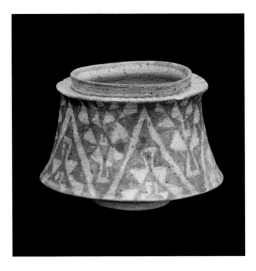

of the Indus Valley to southeastern Iran.[1] Examples of this pottery were also carried by merchants and nomads during their travels within the Indus Valley, and fragments have been found at the site of Harappa dating to about 2800–2600 B.C. and possibly even earlier. The motifs painted on Faiz Mohammad Gray Ware include geometric designs such as are seen on this canister, as well as a wide range of floral and stylized animal motifs.[2] The stepped motif displayed here was popular in Central Asia and Iran (see cat. nos. 247, 248, 251–254). This type of pottery was no longer made after the beginning of the mature Harappan period, about 2600 B.C.   JMK

1. R. Wright 1989.
2. J.-F. Jarrige 1988, pp. 105–7.

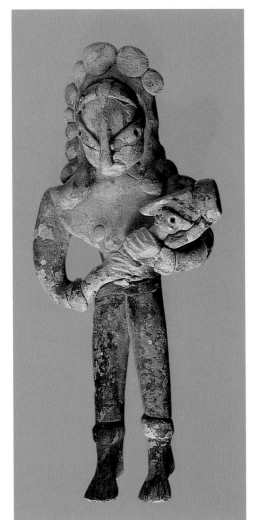

268b

hairdressing and ornaments, often painted with black, yellow, and red pigments. They were probably used in domestic rituals and afterward may have been picked up by children and played with until they were broken and discarded. No special shrines with collections of figures have been discovered, and most examples have been found along with domestic debris. The female figure from Mehrgarh (cat. no. 268a) has a massive fall of hair on both sides of the head, to which an ornament or pendant is attached at the center. A separate band of hair lies on the forehead, carefully combed (or braided) and parted in the middle. On the figure's right the falling hair is curled and painted black, and the wavy lengths extend over the shoulder. On its left the hair is straight and an appliqué ornament is attached at shoulder level. On this side the hair is painted yellow and red, possibly indicating the use of henna. Necklaces of graduated length adorn the neck, and a longer one with a circular pendant falls to the large breasts, which have appliqué nipples.

269

Canister with stepped triangle motifs

Fired clay
H. 6 cm (2⅜ in.); Diam. 7.5 cm (3 in.)
Baluchistan, Mehrgarh, 3704
Mehrgarh VII, ca. 2800–2600 B.C.
National Museum, Karachi
Courtesy of the Department of Archaeology and Museums, Ministry of Minorities, Culture, Sports, Tourism, and Youth Affairs, Government of Pakistan

This distinctive style of gray fired pottery with black painted motifs is referred to as Faiz Mohammad Gray Ware. Although it was first recorded at sites in the Quetta valley of Pakistan, the site of Mehrgarh was one of the major production centers for this type of vessel. From Mehrgarh and other smaller manufactories, it was traded far and wide throughout Baluchistan, from the borders

270a, b

Bull pendants

Gold
a. H. 5.4 cm (2⅛ in.); L. 7.2 cm (2⅞ in.)
b. H. 5.2 cm (2 in.); L. 7 cm (2¾ in.)
Baluchistan, Quetta Valley
Ca. 2000–1900 B.C.
National Museum, Karachi SHQ 01, 02
Courtesy of the Department of Archaeology and Museums, Ministry of Minorities, Culture, Sports, Tourism, and Youth Affairs, Government of Pakistan

These two miniature bull figures were found in a hoard associated with a burial, along with a large collection of gold ornaments, a gold cup or chalice (cat. no. 271), pottery, and carved stone ritual objects, all of which can be dated to about 2000–1900 B.C.[1] The bull

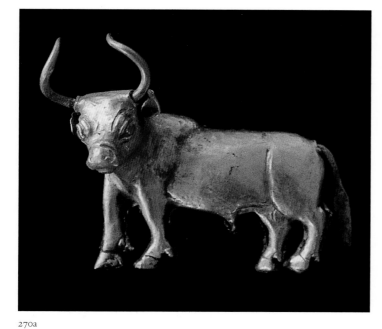

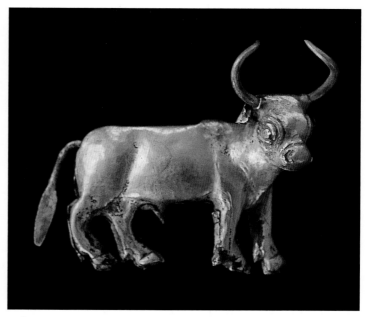

270a   270b

ornaments appear to have been made with a combination of techniques, including raising, chasing, and joining. The hollow body may have been hammered out into a hollow mould to chase the details of the face and body, and then filled with resin. The horns, ears, and tail are all joined to the body without use of a solder. The back of the ornament was attached by crimping the edges over the front, also without solder. Two loops are attached to the back to facilitate attachment to a necklace or head ornament. Hundreds of tiny gold disk beads and fragments of gold foil were found in the same deposit, along with two large agate beads set with gold. All these various components may have been combined into a single elaborate ornament.[2]

JMK

1. J.-F. Jarrige 1988, pp. 115–16; Jarrige and Hassan 1989.
2. J.-F. Jarrige 1988, pp. 115–16.

This cup or chalice is one of only a few examples of repoussé goldworking, a craft that must have been widespread in the Indo-Iranian region about 2000–1900 B.C.[1] The motifs include four lions chasing one another around the body of the vessel and framed by a simple line above and a ribbed border below. The lower part of the cup is decorated with the motif of a double cord loosely twisted into a wavy pattern. The hollow, flaring base may have been filled with resin to add weight, as it is relatively narrow and otherwise would not

have been stable when the vessel was filled with liquid. This cup was part of a hoard that contained two gold bulls (cat. nos. 270a,b) and other ornaments associated with a burial. Although it was found at the borders of the Indus Valley, its shape and style are more closely related to the arts of Central Asia and Iran than to those of the Harappan civilization.

JMK

1. J.-F. Jarrige 1988, pp. 115–16; Jarrige and Hassan 1989.

271

Footed cup with lions and guilloche

Gold
H. 8.8 cm (3½ in.); Diam. 9.5 cm (3¾ in.)
Baluchistan, Quetta Valley
Ca. 2000–1900 B.C.
National Museum, Karachi SHQ 03
Courtesy of the Department of Archaeology and Museums, Ministry of Minorities, Culture, Sports, Tourism, and Youth Affairs, Government of Pakistan

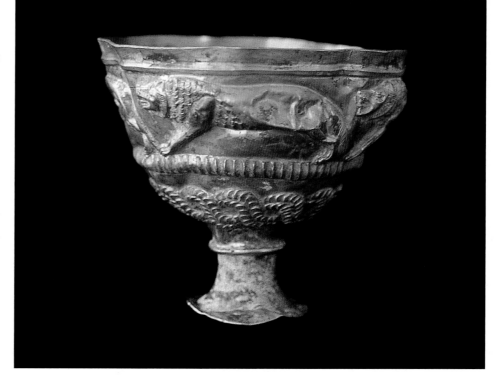

Cities of the Indus Valley

Between 2600 and 1900 B.C., large cities and smaller towns sharing a common culture dominated a thousand-mile region in what is now Pakistan and northwestern India. Like the older urban centers in Mesopotamia, these settlements had developed along trade routes to serve as administrative and ritual centers. Major excavations have been undertaken at four of them, Mohenjo-daro, Harappa, Chanhudaro, and Dholavira. Although the cities of the Indus Valley might seem at first glance to have resembled those of Mesopotamia—mud brick was used in both regions to create houses, imposing city walls, and platforms supporting monumental architecture—there were a number of major differences. The Harappan cities were built of standardized, burnt bricks, whereas sun-dried bricks were the norm in Mesopotamia. While cities beside the Tigris and Euphrates Rivers were dominated by royal and religious architecture, there is little evidence for such structures in the Indus Valley (although buildings like the "granaries" at Mohenjo-daro and Harappa possibly were halls where the elite gathered, and the famous great bath at Mohenjo-daro probably had a special religious function). The Indus sites were laid out on a grid pattern, with distinct walled sectors or mounds oriented in different directions; although there is limited evidence from Mesopotamia and Syria (and early sites like Habuba Kabira do appear to follow a grid pattern), it appears that cities there were generally quite irregular in plan. While many Mesopotamian cities continued to exist for millennia, the cities of the Indus Valley lasted just over seven hundred years, during which time they were home to effective and powerful rulers supported by generations of artisans, traders, and farmers.

PC

272a

Torso of a "priest-king"

Steatite
H. 17.5 cm (6⅞ in.); W. 11 cm (4⅜ in.)
Indus Valley, Mohenjo-daro, DK 1909
Harappan, ca. 2000–1900 B.C.
National Museum, Karachi NMP 50.852
Courtesy of the Department of Archaeology and Museums, Ministry of Minorities, Culture, Sports, Tourism, and Youth Affairs, Government of Pakistan

272b

Seated male figure with a cloak

Yellow limestone
H. 28 cm (11 in.); W. 22 cm (8⅝ in.)
Indus Valley, Mohenjo-daro, L 950
Harappan, ca. 2000–1900 B.C.
Islamabad Museum, Islamabad NMP 50.874
Courtesy of the Department of Archaeology and Museums, Ministry of Minorities, Culture, Sports, Tourism, and Youth Affairs, Government of Pakistan

Small stone sculptures, although not common, were generally present at the largest Indus Valley sites. During the 1920s and 1930s a collection of seated male figurines and some recumbent ram figures (see cat. no. 275) were recovered from Mohenjo-daro, and two miniature male stone sculptures were found at Harappa. More recently a seated male sculpture in stone was found at the site of Dholavira.[1] The seated male sculptures probably do not represent rulers of the Harappan civilization. A more likely explanation is that they are commemorative statues of clan leaders or ancestral figures from communities in the larger cities. None of the stone figurines from Indus sites have been found in undisturbed archaeological contexts, and most were broken in antiquity. Some scholars suggest that the ancient breakage was purposeful, but since the sculptures are made from soft stone it is also possible that they were broken unintentionally and discarded. Their appearance in the uppermost levels of both sites suggests that they were common only toward the end of the mature Harappan period, about 2000–1900 B.C.[2]

The torso of a seated man (cat. no. 272a), commonly referred to as the Priest-King, is one of the most exquisite stone sculptures from the site of Mohenjo-daro.[3] Carved from soft steatite, it was hardened by baking in a kiln at more than one thousand degrees Celsius. The sculptor combined naturalistic detail with stylized forms to create a powerful image that appears much bigger than it actually is. A fillet, or ribbon headband, with a circular inlaid ornament is carved on the forehead, and a similar but smaller ornament adorns the upper right arm. The two ends of the fillet dangle down behind. The hair is carefully combed toward the back. As is common on other seated figures, a separately carved bun may have been attached to the back of the head, which is flat, or there may have been a more elaborate headdress with horns and a central plume. A hole beneath each of the highly stylized ears suggests that a necklace or other head ornament was attached to the sculpture. The figure is wearing an elaborately decorated cloak draped over the left shoulder and across the chest. Designs on the fabric are carved in relief with trefoil, double-circle, and single-circle motifs that were originally filled with red pigment. When the sculpture was first excavated, faint traces of a blackish background color that may have originally been green or blue filled the space around the trefoils. Drill holes in the center of each circle indicate that the trefoils were made with a specialized drill and then touched up with a chisel. The eyes are deeply incised and may have held inlay of shell or colored stone.

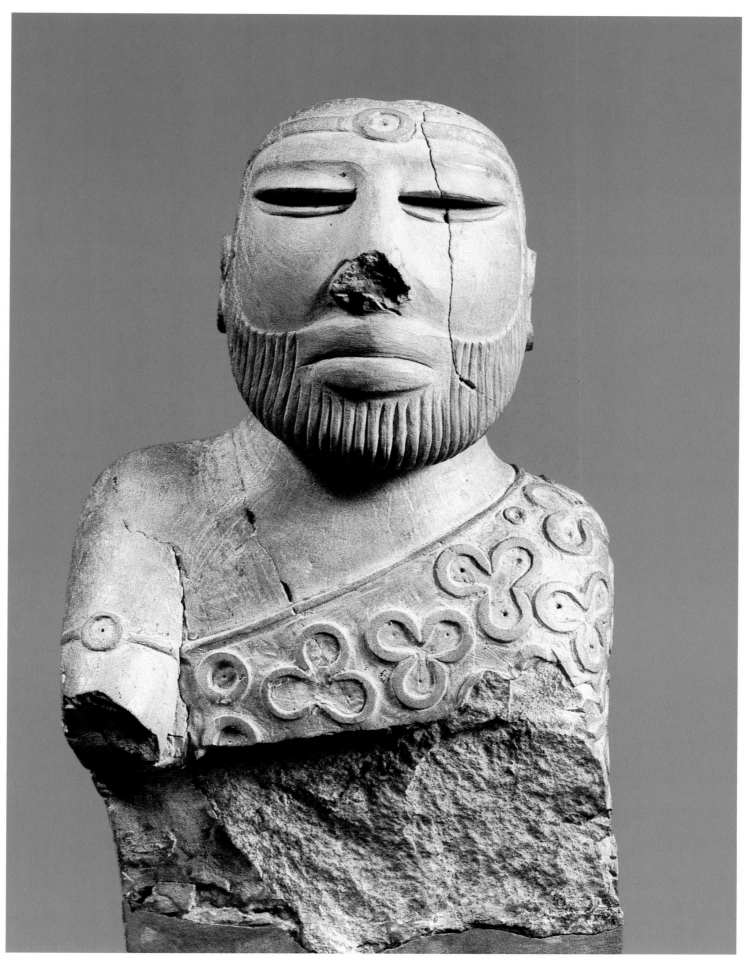

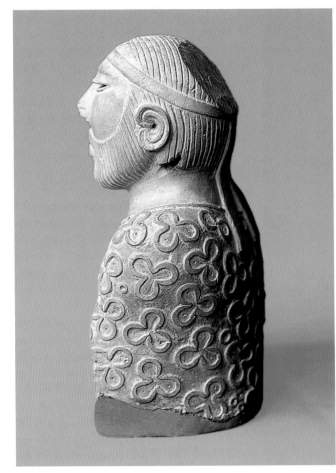

272a

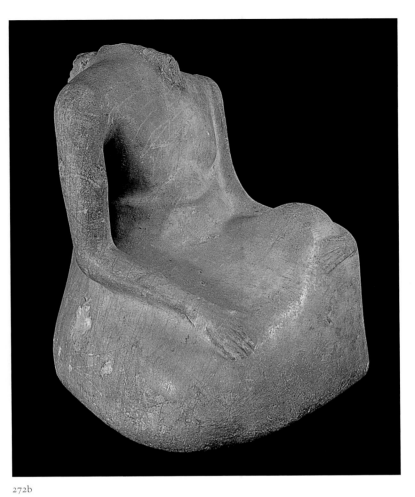

272b

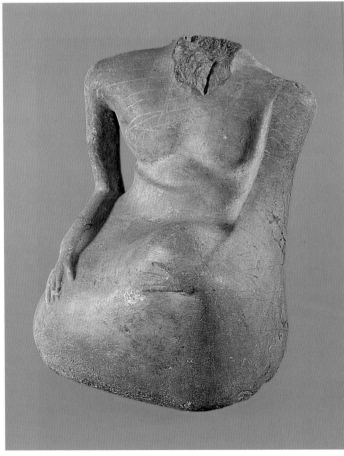

272b

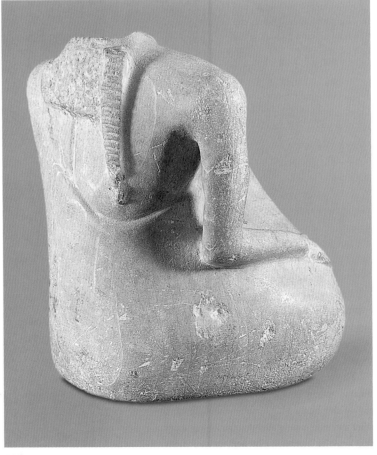

272b

A less unusual ram sculpture, made of stone, shows legs folded underneath the body and ears drooping to the side (cat. no. 275b). The large, curving horns and massive beard hanging over the chest suggest that this may depict the urial *(Ovis vignei),* a form of wild sheep that was common throughout Baluchistan and the Sulaiman Hills. The face was broken in antiquity or possibly during the original excavations in the 1920s and 1930s. In 1981, during surface surveys at the site, the broken portion of the face was discovered; exposure on the surface of the mound for more than fifty years had caused it to weather and change color.[2] A second ram sculpture of this type found at Mohenjo-daro is missing the top part of the head.[3] The curving horn and drooping ear are clearly visible, however, on the right side, and the details of the hairy beard are carved in stylized form. This ram is seated on a pedestal, suggesting that it may have had some special ritual importance in Harappan culture. It is possible that wild rams were tamed and kept for ritual purposes or sacrifice. Some Indus seals show large rams in narrative scenes associated with worship and other ceremonies (see cat. no. 294).

JMK

1. Mackay 1938b, pp. 188, 640, pl. 66:23.
2. Ardeleanu-Jansen 1987, pp. 59–68.
3. Marshall 1931, p. 360, pl. 100:9.

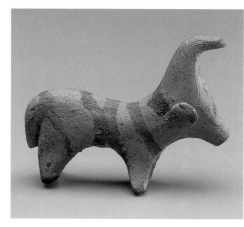

276

ending on the single horn. The horn curves forward, and the snout is long and narrow, as is also the case with the unicorn figures carved on seals. Like many animal figurines from the initial phase of the mature Harappan period (ca. 2600–2450 B.C.), this unicorn's front and back legs are joined together.[3] A hole has been poked in the belly, which may have been used to attach the figurine to a stick for use as a puppet or as a small standard of the kind carried in the processions depicted on some seals.[4]

JMK

1. Mackay 1943, pl. 55:11.
2. Kenoyer 1998, p. 87, fig. 5:15.
3. Kenoyer 1991, pp. 33, 57.
4. Kenoyer 1998, p. 87.

277

Standing female figure holding an offering

Copper alloy
H. 13.2 cm (5¼ in.); W. 4.7 cm (1⅞ in.)
Indus Valley, Mohenjo-daro, DK 12728
Harappan, ca. 2600–1900 B.C.
National Museum, Karachi NMP 50.883
Courtesy of the Department of Archaeology and Museums, Ministry of Minorities, Culture, Sports, Tourism, and Youth Affairs, Government of Pakistan

Copper-alloy figures made by the lost-wax casting technique have been found at many Indus Valley sites. Much of the minute detail of these small sculptures has been obliterated by wear and exposure, but careful observation reveals the dynamic expression and subtle messages in the pose. This elegant female figure from Mohenjo-daro stands with her head held high and hair tied in a horizontal bun low on the back of the neck. Traces of long, almond-shaped eyes are visible, but the

276

Unicorn figurine

Terracotta
L. 4.6 cm (1¾ in.)
Indus Valley, Chanhudaro, 4718
Harappan, ca. 2600–1900 B.C.
Museum of Fine Arts, Boston; Joint Expedition of the American School of Indic and Iranian Studies and the Museum of Fine Arts, 1935–1936 season, MFA 36.2210

The five unicorn figurines found at the site of Chanhudaro offer concrete evidence for the belief in a mythical one-horned animal.[1] They reflect a regionally distinct style of modeling and should be compared with unicorn seals found at all Indus sites (see cat. no. 295b) and the rare examples of clay unicorn figurines found at Mohenjo-daro and at Harappa.[2] This unicorn has a red-painted band spiraling around its body and over the appliquéd eyes,

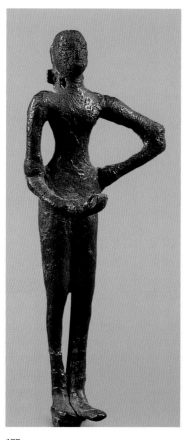

277

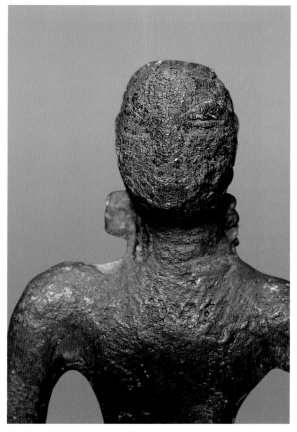

Detail, cat. no. 277

facial expression has been obscured by corrosion. The left hand is placed on the hip with the elbow projecting to the left, while the right hand extends out in front of the waist, holding a small bowl or offering.[1] There is no indication of the necklaces or belt seen on many Harappan terracotta figurines, but many bangles adorn the upper left arm, and a few bangles are indicated above the right elbow.

Another small cast figurine from Mohenjo-daro shows a woman standing in a more dynamic pose, with the right hand on the hip and the left hand holding a bowl resting on the bent left leg (fig. 98). This figure has been referred to as a dancing girl, based on a colonial British perception of Indian dancers, but it more likely represents a woman carrying an offering, as is the case with this sculpture. JMK

1. Mackay 1938b, p. 274, pl. 73:9–11.

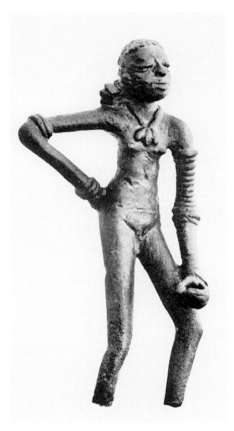

Fig. 98. Copper-alloy female figure wearing bangles and holding a small bowl. Mohenjo-daro, Harappan, ca. 2600–1900 B.C. National Museum, New Delhi, 195.

278a, b

Female figures with headdresses and jewelry

Terracotta
Harappan, ca. 2600–1900 B.C.

a. H. 18.7 cm (7⅜ in.); W. 9.5 cm (3¾ in.)
Indus Valley, Mohenjo-daro, DK 2384
National Museum, Karachi NMP 50.509
Courtesy of the Department of Archaeology and Museums, Ministry of Minorities, Culture, Sports, Tourism, and Youth Affairs, Government of Pakistan

b. H. 13.2 cm (5¼ in.)
Indus Valley, Harappa
National Museum, Karachi HP 1603
Courtesy of the Department of Archaeology and Museums, Ministry of Minorities, Culture, Sports, Tourism, and Youth Affairs, Government of Pakistan

The figure from Mohenjo-daro (cat. no. 278a) represents one of the most common types of small female sculptures made in the Indus Valley region, where they have been found at urban

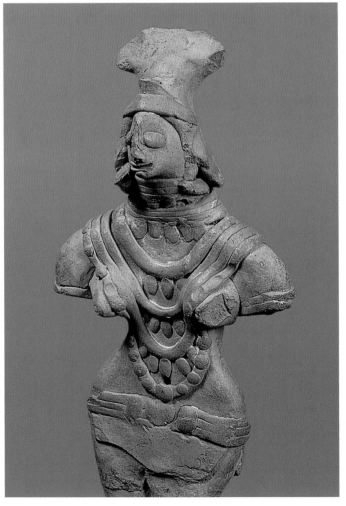

278a

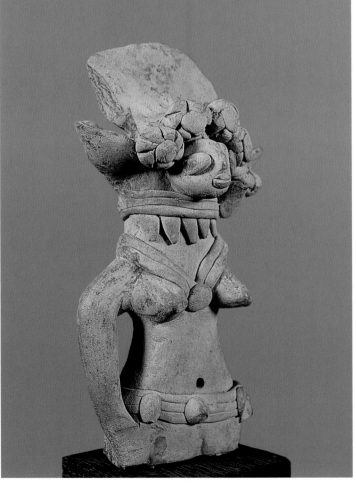

278b

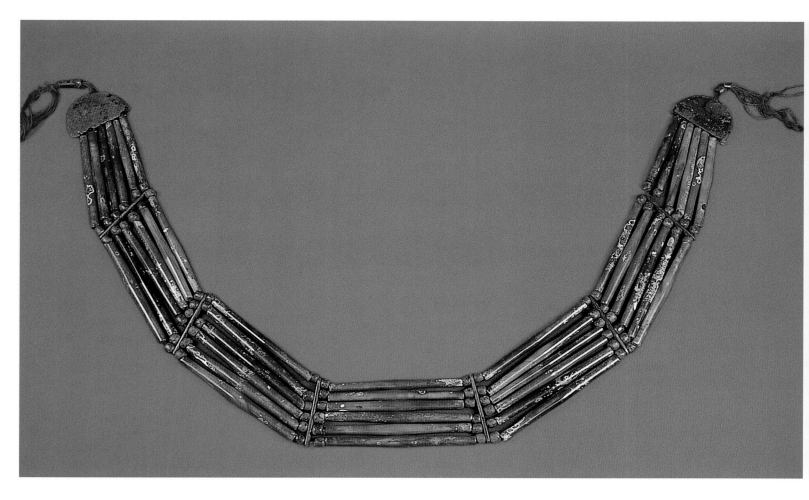

centers as well as in smaller settlements. The fan-shaped headdress originally had wide, cup-shaped extensions on either side of the head, framed by braided tresses. The head and body may actually belong to different figures, but both parts are in the same general style.[1] Numerous strands of chokers and pendant bead necklaces drape over the breasts and extend to the waist. Traces of bangles are visible at the broken ends of the arms, which would have been covered with them. The woman is wearing a short skirt belted with three strands of what were probably beads. The belt is fastened with a large circular buckle and two side pieces that are similar to the copper-alloy terminals seen on the massive carnelian belts found in hoards at Mohenjo-daro and Harappa (see cat. no. 279).

The female figure from the site of Harappa (cat. no. 278b) has four flowers arranged on the front of her fan-shaped headdress, with cups at two sides and braided edging.[2] This style of headdress is found only on figures from Harappa, and it appears to have been most common during the final phases of the mature Harappan period, between about 2200 and 1900 B.C. Recent discoveries of similar figures from the site indicate that this fan-shaped headdress and the side cups were

probably painted black. The other ornaments are very similar to those adorning female figures from Mohenjo-daro. The triple-strand choker has pendant beads, and the double-strand necklace supports a disk-shaped pendant that falls between the breasts. A triple-strand belt ornamented with disks is worn low on the hips and may have been intended to represent the beaded carnelian belts found at Harappa and Mohenjo-daro (see cat. no. 279). Although some scholars have argued that the figures with a floral headdress from Harappa are in a style brought from Mesopotamia to the Indus Valley, there is insufficient evidence to support this theory.[3] It is also possible that the women found in the royal tombs at Ur wearing a gold flower headdress of this type may actually have been serving women from the Indus Valley (see entry for cat. no. 61); it will be possible to test this theory using modern chemical analysis of their bones and teeth.[4]   JMK

1. Marshall 1931, p. 338, pl. 94:14.
2. A similar headdress is seen on a figure illustrated in Vats 1940, p. 297, pl. 77:37.
3. For the theory, see During Caspers 1994b, pp. 187–92.
4. See Kenoyer 1997.

279

Belt

Carnelian and copper alloy
W. 10 cm (4 in.); L. 105 cm (41⅜ in.)
Indus Valley, Mohenjo-daro, Hoard DK IE
Harappan, ca. 2600–1900 B.C.
Mohenjo-daro Museum, Mohenjo-daro   MM 1121
Courtesy of the Department of Archaeology and Museums, Ministry of Minorities, Culture, Sports, Tourism, and Youth Affairs, Government of Pakistan

The massive carnelian belt from Mohenjo-daro is one of the most exquisite ornaments of the Indus Valley. It was found in a hoard of jewelry carefully packed into a copper pot and hidden under the floor of a house.[1] Other items found with the belt include gold ear studs, needlelike pendants, stone beads, and gold settings for the beads. The belt itself is made from forty-two long biconical carnelian beads, seventy-two spherical bronze beads, six copper-alloy spacer beads, two half-moon-shaped copper-alloy terminals, and two hollow, cylindrical copper-alloy terminals. Large numbers of long carnelian beads at sites such as Harappa and Dholavira suggest that other belts were present at the larger urban centers, but only one

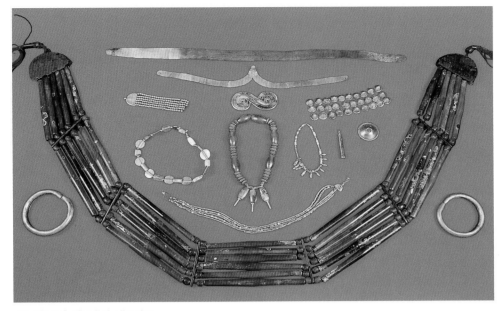

279-282 and other Indus jewelry

additional complete example has been found, at the site of Allahdino.[2] Carnelian beads—single or in short strands—appear to have been traded throughout the Indus Valley and adjacent regions, where they were highly valued. It is important to note that no examples of these beads have been found in Indus burials.

Detailed studies of long carnelian beads from Ur indicate that some of them were made in the Indus Valley, while others were probably made in Mesopotamia by migrant craftsmen from the Indus who used their own style of drills and raw materials (see cat. no. 80).[3] Some of these Indus bead makers may have been members of the so-called Meluhhan minority that is documented in Mesopotamian texts (see cat. no. 303).[4]

Prior to the advent of diamond drilling, the ancient Indus bead makers produced the longest and slenderest carnelian beads in the world. This was accomplished using a special stone drill made from rock that was heated to create a new material composed primarily of quartz, sillimanite, mullite, hematite, and titanium-oxide phases. This extremely hard and durable material is referred to as "Ernestite," in honor of Ernest J. H. Mackay, who was the first to discover and recognize the importance of these drills.[5] Even with this hard-stone drill, experimental studies indicate that it would have taken between three and eight days of drilling to perforate the long beads found on this belt from Mohenjo-daro. The belt may have required two or three years to complete, since it is difficult to obtain long nodules of carnelian and since the manufacture of this stone into beads requires

heating and careful grinding and polishing in addition to the drilling process itself.   JMK

1. Marshall 1931, p. 520, pl. 151:B10.
2. On long carnelian beads at Dholavira, see Bisht 1987 and Bisht 1990. On the belt found at Allahdino, see Kenoyer 1998, p. 138.
3. Kenoyer 1998, pp. 160–61.
4. Parpola, Parpola, and Brunswig 1977.
5. Kenoyer and Vidale 1992.

280

String of beads

Gold and semiprecious stones
W. 1.43 cm (⁹⁄₁₆ in.); L. of gold beads 1.49 cm (⁹⁄₁₆ in.)
Indus Valley, Mohenjo-daro, Hoard 3, HR 4212 a(d)
Harappan, ca. 2600–1900 B.C.
Mohenjo-daro Museum, Mohenjo-daro MM 1369
Courtesy of the Department of Archaeology and Museums, Ministry of Minorities, Culture, Sports, Tourism, and Youth Affairs, Government of Pakistan

This strand represents half of a string of beads that was divided between Pakistan and India when the two countries were partitioned in 1947. Reconstructed by the excavators according to its originally recorded placement, the full string came from one of the hoards or stockpiles of jewelry that were found in the houses of Mohenjo-daro.[1] The beads include a number of flat gold disks with tubular string-holes, perhaps the most widespread form of distinctive precious-metal beads made in the third millennium B.C. The distribution of notable examples found west of the Indus Valley is along sea and land routes from the Aegean through western Asia—extending from Aigina to eastern Iran, and from the North Caucasus to the Gulf (see fig. 72). Other elements of the

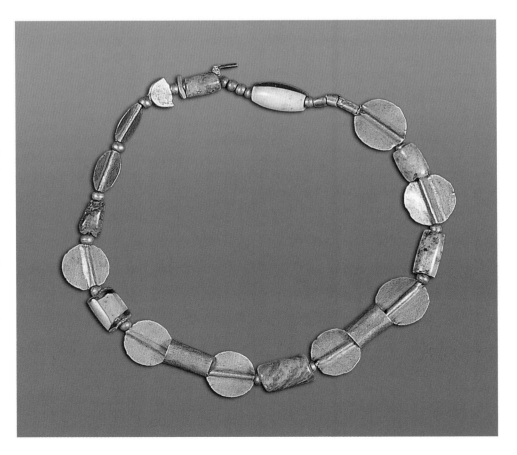

necklace include small gold spheres, which act as spacers between the gold-disk beads and colorful stone beads made of banded agate, amazonite, and turquoise—the latter suggesting connections with Iran and Central Asia.

JA

1. See Kenoyer 1998, p. 140, fig. 7:34, p. 201, no. 56.

281

String of beads

Gold, vesuvianite or grossular garnet, agate, jasper, and steatite
L. 18 cm (7⅛ in.)
Indus Valley, Mohenjo-daro, DK 1541
Harappan, ca. 2600–1900 B.C.
Mohenjo-daro Museum, Mohenjo-daro MM 1367
Courtesy of the Department of Archaeology and Museums, Ministry of Minorities, Culture, Sports, Tourism, and Youth Affairs, Government of Pakistan

This and other important examples of Indus jewelry are part of a major hoard found buried in a silver jar in a room of the DK area of Mohenjo-daro.[1] The distinctive necklace in stone and gold with pendant beads is in a style that has its roots in the early period at Mehrgarh, Baluchistan. Originally it had twice as many beads, but with the partition of India and Pakistan in 1947 the necklace was divided, each country receiving one-half of the original. The hollow gold beads are filled with a sandy matrix that was probably mixed with resin. The stone beads include banded agate, mottled and orbicular jasper, fired steatite, and a green stone (vesuvianite or grossular garnet) that was originally reported as jade. The pendant agate and jasper beads are attached with thick gold wire, and steatite beads with gold caps separate each of the pendant beads.

JMK

1. Marshall 1931, pl. 148:A6.

282

Double-spiral brooch with inlay

Gold and dark glazed steatite
W. 3.2 cm (1¼ in.); L. 6.6 cm (2⅝ in.)
Indus Valley, Harappa, 8060 e
Harappan, ca. 2600–1900 B.C.
Mohenjo-daro Museum, Mohenjo-daro MM 1376, 50.22/2
Courtesy of the Department of Archaeology and Museums, Ministry of Minorities, Culture, Sports, Tourism, and Youth Affairs, Government of Pakistan

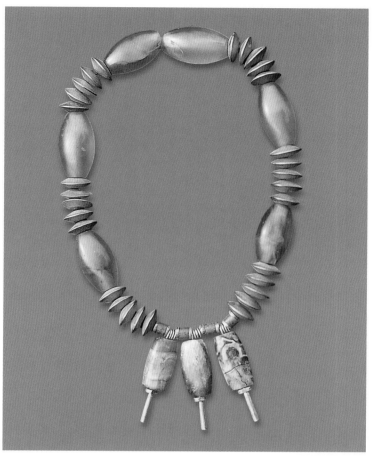

This brooch made of gold and inlaid with tiny steatite beads exemplifies the high level of Indus Valley gold crafting. It was found in a hoard at the site of Harappa, along with another similar brooch, gold bangles, hollow conical beads, and numerous necklaces of pendant beads made of jasper and agate.[1] The back is made of thin, hammered gold that has been burnished to remove all traces of manufacture. Three gold bands have been soldered to the gold backing creating channels into which glazed steatite beads with gold caps have been set, using some form of resin. The beads in one channel were originally glazed a dark blue, perhaps in imitation of lapis lazuli, while the ones in the other channel were a lighter blue or blue green, similar to turquoise. Both lapis lazuli and turquoise were occasionally used by Indus craftsmen, but they turn dark when exposed to body oils and sweat. Indus people appear to have preferred the shiny imitations made from glazed faience. The spiral is seen on some painted pottery, but in general it is not a common motif in Indus art.

JMK

1. Vats 1940, p. 64, pl. 137:15.

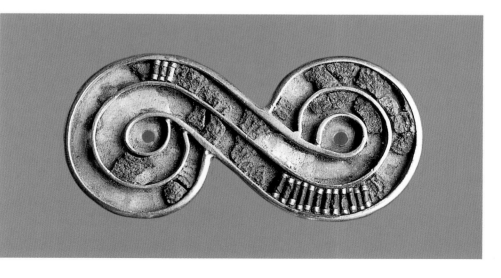

Beads of the Indus Valley

The beads of the Indus Valley or Harappan civilization are an important source of information about patterns of trade and technology as well as the emergence of specialized crafts and hierarchical urban society during the third millennium B.C., both in the Indus Valley and in Mesopotamia. Raw materials of bead making such as carnelian and lapis lazuli were obtained from distant resource areas and imported to the urban centers of the Indus region to be manufactured into exquisite ornaments. In early urban communities such as Mohenjo-daro and Harappa beaded ornaments were used as symbols of economic wealth and status, as well as for ritual purposes.

In some cases common materials were used to replicate shapes and styles of beads made from exotic and precious materials. Long biconical beads of terracotta were painted red to imitate the valuable long carnelian bicones. Steatite was painted red and white or incised and inlaid with different colors to imitate veined stone beads. In faience bead making the colors of the glazes apparently imitated turquoise, lapis lazuli, shell or white steatite, and even carnelian. Even in the production of hard-stone beads the same pattern is seen. Carnelian, for example, was bleached with white lines to imitate natural orbicular jasper with eye designs. And many copper beads with high tin content may have been made to imitate more precious gold beads.

The production of beads that look similar but are made from materials of different quality indicates that beads were used in two different ways within Harappan society. On the one hand, elites distinguished their status and wealth by wearing beads made from exotic materials or produced through complex or arduous manufacturing processes. Examples would be the exotic patterned jasper beads with eye designs, the tiny microbeads (one millimeter in diameter) made from steatite, or the long carnelian beads perforated by means of slender drills made of hard stone (see entry for cat. no. 279). At the same time, the members of other communities would have been wearing imitations of these more valuable ornaments either for their ritual value or in an attempt to emulate the elites. This pattern of sharing styles reflects the vertical integration of hierarchical Indus society, while the variations in raw materials and technology express ritual, economic, or political status.

Since highly prized beads and their imitations were objects of social and ritual value, it was important for the elites as well as the merchants to control their manufacture and distribution. This was done directly by restricting production to supervised workshops or indirectly by controlling access to raw materials and finished goods. The walled and gated cities of the region made it easy to tax goods and materials coming into and out of the urban markets and production areas. Finished beads were used locally or traded regionally and, occasionally, beyond the Indus Valley to Central Asia, the Gulf, Iran, and Mesopotamia. Some of the most valuable Indus beads, such as banded agates and long carnelian beads, were sold at large urban centers in Mesopotamia and Elam. Whereas in the Indus these beads were kept in circulation and passed on from generation to generation, in Mesopotamia they were usually buried with elites as part of their funerary offerings, stimulating the need for more trade and wealth acquisition.

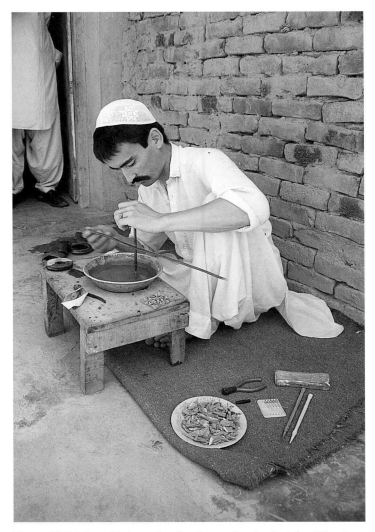

Fig. 99. Haji Ashoor, Turkmen bead maker, perforating lapis lazuli beads using an age-old technique with a bow-and-string and tiny drills.

Studies of modern bead makers in Pakistan and India yield useful insights into ancient bead production. For example, the Afghan craftsmen of today who make lapis lazuli beads often travel far from their hometowns to urban centers where markets are safe and profitable (fig. 99). The production of long carnelian beads similar to those found in the Indus cities and traded to distant Mesopotamia can be observed in the agate-bead workshops of Khambhat, India. Through these studies and experimental reconstructions it is possible to estimate the time and effort needed to produce a single Harappan agate bead (three to eight days of drilling alone) or the large carnelian belts from Mohenjo-daro (two to three years; see cat. no. 279).

JMK

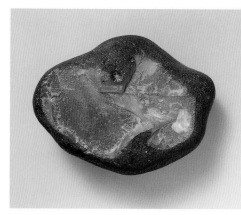

283

Nodule of unworked carnelian

L. 7.6 cm (3 in.); Thickness 2.9 cm (1⅛ in.)
Indus Valley, Chanhudaro
Harappan, ca. 2600–1900 B.C.
Museum of Fine Arts, Boston; Joint Expedition of the American School of Indic and Iranian Studies and the Museum of Fine Arts, 1935–36 season,
MFA 36.1607, on loan to The Metropolitan Museum of Art, New York L.1999.59.10

Obtained from sources in Kutch and Gujarat,[1] carnelian was used extensively in the Harappan civilization for bead making (see "Beads of the Indus Valley," by Jonathan Mark Kenoyer, in this catalogue). Carnelian was imported into Mesopotamia from the Indus Valley as well as from Iran.[2]

PC

1. Kenoyer 1998, p. 92.
2. Moorey 1994, p. 97.

284a–g

Etched carnelian beads

a. L. 1.3 cm (½ in.); W. 1.5 cm (⅝ in.); Thickness 0.4 cm (³⁄₁₆ in.)
b. L. 0.6 cm (¼ in.); W. 1 cm (⅜ in.); Thickness 0.4 cm (³⁄₁₆ in.)
c. L. 1.5 cm (⅝ in.); W. 0.8 cm (⁵⁄₁₆ in.); Thickness 0.4 cm (³⁄₁₆ in.)
d. L. 0.4 cm (³⁄₁₆ in.); W. 1 cm (⅜ in.); Thickness 0.4 cm (³⁄₁₆ in.)
e. L. 0.4 cm (³⁄₁₆ in.); W. 1 cm (⅜ in.); Thickness 0.4 cm (³⁄₁₆ in.)
f. L. 0.8 cm (⁵⁄₁₆ in.); W. 0.9 cm (⅜ in.); Thickness 0.4 cm (³⁄₁₆ in.)
g. L. 0.8 cm (⁵⁄₁₆ in.); W. 0.4 cm (³⁄₁₆ in.)
Indus Valley, Chanhudaro
Harappan, ca. 2600–1900 B.C.
Museum of Fine Arts, Boston; Joint Expedition of the American School of Indic and Iranian Studies and the Museum of Fine Arts, 1935–36 season,
MFA 36.1703, .1082; MFA 36.1075, .1078, .1080,

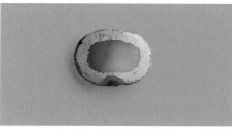

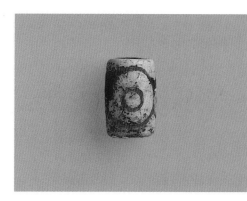

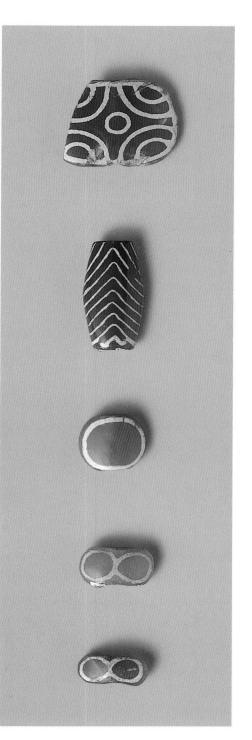

.1081, .1083, on loan to The Metropolitan Museum of Art, New York L.1999.59.11−.13, .18, .19

Chanhudaro, in ancient Sindh, appears to have been a major Harappan center for the production of a large variety of beads, including both etched (bleached) and long biconical types of carved carnelian. Many were carried west along the land and maritime routes and were eventually buried in elite Mesopotamian graves. Small bead workshops have been identified at Chanhudaro, containing both finished and unfinished beads and metal and stone drills. Nodules of the raw material found at the site (see cat. no. 283) had probably been brought to Sindh from the region of present-day Gujarat and the Gulf of Cambay, where the ancient port city of Lothal also had a flourishing bead industry.[1]

A variety of types is represented by this selection of etched carnelian beads. They include lentoids with oval or elliptical faces, bearing either the motif of a single white ring or "eye" or a "spectacle" design of tangent ovals. These very common designs can be found at a number of sites in the Indus Valley as well as in Mesopotamia and the Gulf (see cat. nos. 79a, 209).[2] A flattened lentoid bead with rounded rectangular faces bears a more unusual compartment design consisting of a central circle framed by concentric arcs; it can be closely paralleled at Ur and Kish.[3] The single barrel-shaped bead carved with a nested-chevron pattern may be related to examples from both Mesopotamia and Iran.

JA

1. Mackay 1937 pp. 1ff.; During Caspers 1972, pp. 93ff.
2. See Reade 1979, fig. 1:D1 (found at Ur, Kish, and Nippur), D6 (found at Ur, Eshnunna, and Kish as well as at Mundigak, in Central Asia, and Chanhudaro and Lothal in the Indus). See also ibid., fig. 3.
3. Ibid., fig. 1:D10-11. See also ibid., fig. 2.

285a, b

Bangles

Gold
a. Diam. 5.8−6.1 cm (2¼−2⅜ in.)
b. Diam. 6.1−6.5 cm (2⅜−2½ in.)
Indus Valley, Mohenjo-daro
Harappan, ca. 2600−1900 B.C.
Mohenjo-daro Museum, Mohenjo-daro MM 1382 (50.28/5), MM 1384 (50.40)
Courtesy of the Department of Archaeology and Museums, Ministry of Minorities, Culture, Sports, Tourism, and Youth Affairs, Government of Pakistan

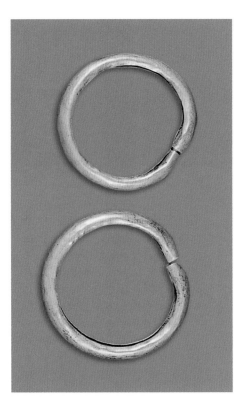

Gold was undoubtedly one of the most valuable materials used for making ornaments in the Indus Valley. However, very few examples in gold are preserved. This pair of hollow sheet-gold bangles was found in a hoard at the site of Mohenjo-daro.[1] They were made by rolling a hammered sheet into a cylinder and joining the long sides in a seam on the interior of the bangle. The ends are not joined, a type of construction that allows the bangle to be twisted apart in order to slip it over the wrist or above the elbow. Bangles were an important form of ornament in the Indus cities. Figurines and depictions on seals indicate that they were worn by men, women, and children (see cat. nos. 277, 293, 294).

JMK

1. Marshall 1931, p. 529, pl. 151:A9, A10.

286

Bangle with ribbed design

Faience
Diam. 7.3−8.5 cm (2⅞−3⅜ in.)
Indus Valley, Harappa, 13041
Harappan, ca. 2000−1900 B.C.
National Museum, Karachi NMP 54.3447
Courtesy of the Department of Archaeology and Museums, Ministry of Minorities, Culture, Sports, Tourism, and Youth Affairs, Government of Pakistan

In the Indus Valley faience was used to make many different styles of bangles, ranging in color from white to deep blue-green. Some faience bangles are plain, but others have incised chevron or spiral designs, and this example has deeply carved cogs or ribbing along the exterior. The interior outline of the bangle is similar to that of shell bangles or the symbolic kidney- or womb-shaped motif (see cat. no. 288). Traces of blue-green glaze are found on the points and edges of the ribbing but not in

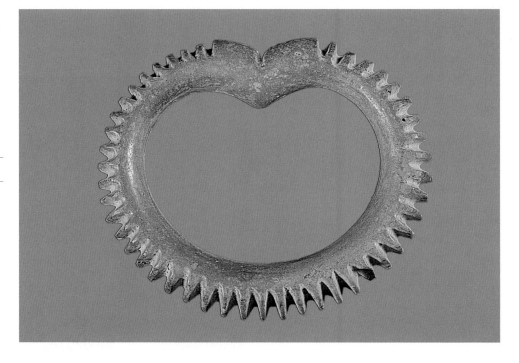

the deeply carved indentations. A matching pair was found with this bangle near the large building (the so-called granary) on Mound F at Harappa.[1]

Indus faience is a vitreous paste produced from finely ground quartz and colored with various minerals. While in some aspects Indus faience technology is broadly similar to Mesopotamian, the Indus artisans took the process further by first using a flux to melt rock quartz in high-temperature kilns (at more than one thousand degrees Celsius) to produce a glassy frit. The frit was then mixed with a colorant. After regrinding on smooth stones, the powder was once again mixed with a flux and formed into ornaments that were then refired to create a strongly fused, glassy material. Although many contemporary cultures produced faience ornaments, only Indus faience was strong enough to produce thin bangles that would not break with normal jostling on the wrist. It may have been the basis of the new glass technology that appeared about 1700 B.C., during the Late Harappan period.[2]

JMK

1. Vats 1940, p. 449.
2. Kenoyer 1997.

287a, b

Shell bangles

a. Diam. 8.9–9.1 cm (3½–3⅝ in.)
Indus Valley, Harappa, B 1578
Harappan, ca. 2600–1900 B.C.
National Museum, Karachi 54.3554, HM 13828
Courtesy of the Department of Archaeology and Museums, Ministry of Minorities, Culture, Sports, Tourism, and Youth Affairs, Government of Pakistan

b. Diam. 9 cm (3½ in.)
Iran, Susa
Late 3rd millennium B.C.
Musée du Louvre, Département des Antiquités Orientales, Paris Sb 14473

Shell bangles are found at all major Indus Valley settlements. They appear to have symbolized an overarching ideological unity as well as expressed gender and possibly ethnic distinctions. Generally speaking, thin shell bangles were not removed from the body after death, for they are found in many of the Indus burials at the sites of Harappa, Kalibangan, and Lothal. All Indus-period shell bangles have been incised with a distinctive chevron design

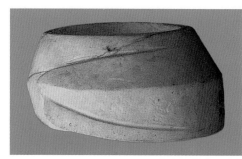

287a

such as is seen in these examples. Wide shell bangles of this type have never been found in Indus burials but have been recovered from burials in Central Asia and at the site of Susa in southwestern Iran (cat. no. 287b). Such wide shell bangles may have been carried there by traders or worn by Harappan women who accompanied the traders. They were usually made from the large gastropod *Turbinella pyrum*—as was catalogue number 287a —but sometimes the shells of other large gastropods, such as *Fasciolaria trapezium,* or bivalves, were used.[1] Bangles from Chanhudaro were made from the large murex *Chicoreus ramosus.* These large gastropods are found along the Makran coast to the west of Karachi or in the Rann of Kutch. Large quantities of waste from bangle manufacturing have been found at sites in both regions as well as at the major urban centers themselves. The gastropods were cut with a large metal saw to make rough circlets that were then ground and smoothed to create the elegant white ornaments seen here.

JMK

1. Kenoyer 1984.

Inlays

Shell
H. 3–6.5 cm (1⅛–2½ in.)
Indus Valley, Mohenjo-daro
Harappan, ca. 2600–1900 B.C.
Mohenjo-daro Museum, Mohenjo-daro MM 903, 904, 905, 907, 912, 5093, 5094, 5095, 5096, 5097, 5098, 8083
Courtesy of the Department of Archaeology and Museums, Ministry of Minorities, Culture, Sports, Tourism, and Youth Affairs, Government of Pakistan

White shell inlay was used to decorate wood furniture as well as stone sculpture. The material does not yellow and is more durable than ivory. Most pieces were made from scraps of shell remaining from the production of shell bangles, but some larger ones were cut from the thick body of the large gastropod *Lambis truncata sebae.* Complex designs were created using large tabular sheets with stepped edges and tabular curved segments incised with the intersecting-circle motif. Smaller, lenticular pieces were used for the eyes on sculptures or could have been combined with concave, square pieces for constructing the common intersecting-circle motif or flower shapes. Other distinctive shapes include the womb-shaped fretted design, intersecting-circle design, stepped cross, fretted petal shape, and stepped-cross component. Many of these pieces were found in a single workshop at the site of Mohenjo-daro, but the craft of inlay was practiced at all of the major Indus settlements.[1] Some examples of Indus shell inlay may have been traded to Mesopotamia, but, generally speaking, the Mesopotamian craftsmen

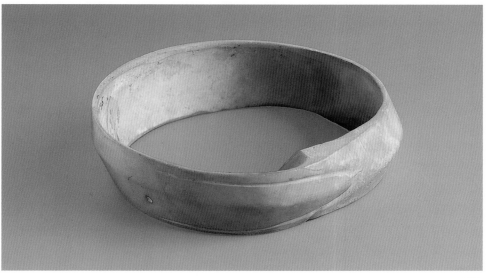

287b

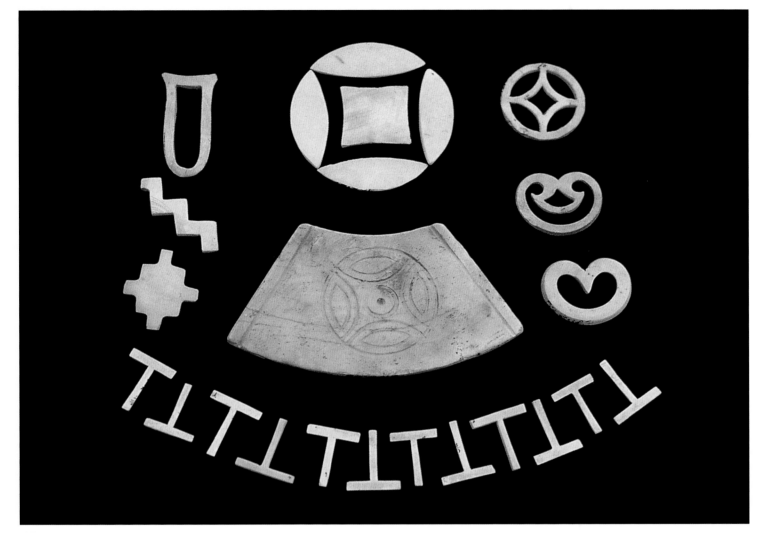

288

preferred to manufacture their own designs
using raw shell obtained from Oman or the
Indus Valley.[2]   JMK

1. On the Mohenjo-daro workshop, see Mackay
1938b, pls. 141:10–13, 142:28, 30, 30a, 34.
2. Gensheimer 1984.

289a, b

Shell ladles

a. L. 3.2 cm (1¼ in.); W. 2.8 cm (1⅛ in.)
Indus Valley, Chanhudaro, 2453
Harappan, ca. 2600–1900 B.C.
Museum of Fine Arts, Boston; Joint Expedition of
the American School of Indic and Iranian Studies
and the Museum of Fine Arts, 1935–36 season
MFA 36.2399

b. L. 11.2 cm (4⅜ in.)
Mesopotamia, Girsu (modern Tello)
Mid-to-late 3rd millennium B.C.

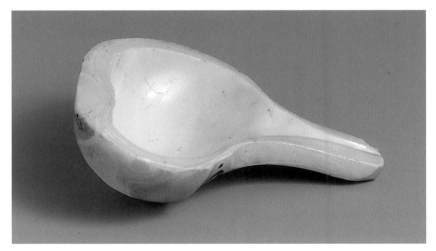

289a

Musée du Louvre, Département des Antiquités
Orientales, Paris AO 15298

Among the most distinctive shell objects produced in the Indus Valley are shell ladles made
from the spiny murex (*Chicoreus ramosus*).

This species is found in the Gulf of Kutch as
well as along the Makran coast west of Karachi.
It is also found along the coast of Oman, but
the primary manufacturing centers for shell
ladles were the larger cities of the Indus Valley
or smaller villages along the coast around

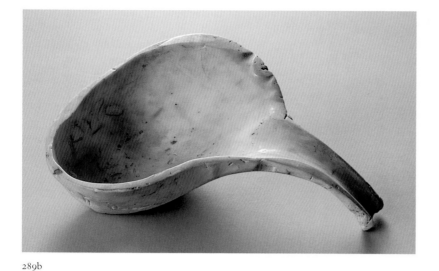

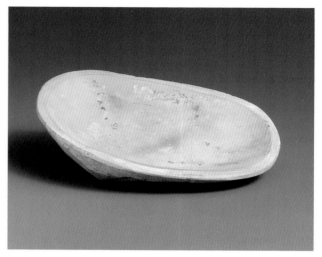

289b

290a

Gujarat. The shell ladle from the site of Tello (cat. no. 289b) may have originated at the site of Nageshwar in the Rann of Kutch, where massive quantities of shell-ladle manufacturing waste have been found.[1] The ladles made there in rough form appear to have been sent on to major urban centers such as Mohenjo-daro, Harappa, or Chanhudaro for finishing.

The miniature ladle from Chanhudaro (cat. no. 289a) is also made from the *Chicoreus ramosus* shell.[2] Its small size may indicate that it was used for administering small doses of medicine or for ladling small quantities of sacred liquids during special rituals. JMK

1. The ladle from Tello was first published in Aynard 1966, p. 31, fig. 5. On its origin at Nageshwar, see Bhan and Kenoyer 1984.
2. Mackay 1943, pl. 90:13.

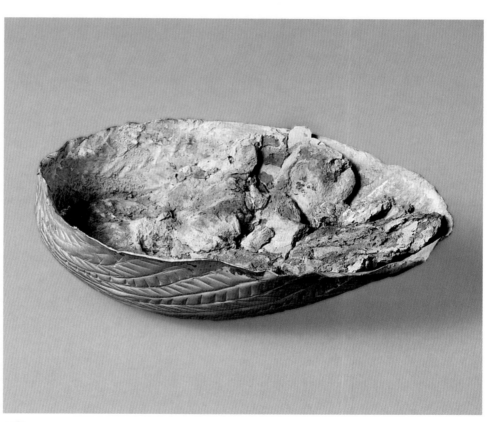

290b

290a

Shell container

L. 7.4 cm (2⅞ in.)
Indus Valley, Chanhudaro
Harappan, ca. 2600–1900 B.C.
Museum of Fine Arts, Boston; Joint Expedition of the American School of Indic and Iranian Studies and the Museum of Fine Arts, 1935–36 season, MFA 36.2384

290b

Container in the shape of a shell

Gold
L. 8 cm (3⅛ in.); W. 6.2 cm (2½ in.)
Mesopotamia, Ur, U. 10932

Early Dynastic IIIA, ca. 2550–2400 B.C.
University of Pennsylvania Museum of Archaeology and Anthropology, Philadelphia B16710

Numerous real shells filled with pigments were found in the royal burials at Ur, but this cosmetic container from Ur (cat. no. 290b) is made of gold in the shape of the humble *Cardium* shell. Found throughout the estuarine areas of the Gulf, this species of shell was used for containers in both the Indus Valley and Mesopotamia.

One artifact from the Indus Valley site of Chanhudaro (cat. no. 290a) was made from the body whorl of a large marine shell, either *Chicoreus ramosus* or *Lambis truncata sebae*. While its original function may have been to hold pigments, the depressions on the interior indicate that it was held in the hand as a pivot, or drill back, for bow drilling. JMK

291a, b

Pouring vessels in shell form

Early Dynastic IIIA, ca. 2550–2400 B.C.

a. Shell
L. 18 cm (7⅛ in.); W. 18 cm (7⅛ in.)
Mesopotamia, Ur, PG 143, U.8191
University of Pennsylvania Museum of Archaeology
and Anthropology, Philadelphia B17194

b. Silver
L. 27.8 cm (11 in.); W. 13.3 cm (5¼ in.)
Mesopotamia, Ur, U.10886
University of Pennsylvania Museum of Archaeology
and Anthropology, Philadelphia B17081

During the Early Dynastic period in Mesopotamia, shell containers such as the one shown
here (cat. no. 291a) were made from the
marine species *Fasciolaria trapezium.* The central
columella was removed and the internal septa
were ground smooth to create a distinctive
container. The exterior was often carved with
geometric or avian designs. One silver ladle
from the royal burials at Ur was made in the
shape of a shell and given an extended spout
to facilitate pouring (cat. no. 291b). The form
is similar to that of containers made from the
shell *Fasciolaria trapezium* or *Lambis truncata sebae.*

JMK

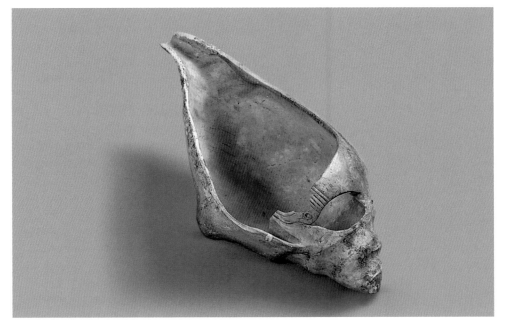

291a

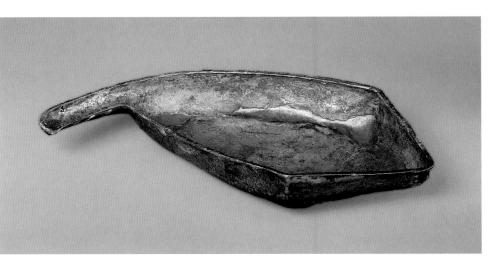

291b

292a, b

Cubical weights

Harappan, ca. 2600–1900 B.C.

a. Chert and agate
H. 0.7–8.6 cm (¼–3⅜ in.)
Indus Valley, Chanhudaro
Museum of Fine Arts, Boston; Joint Expedition of
the American School of Indic and Iranian Studies
and the Museum of Fine Arts, 1935–36 season,
MFA 36.2274, .2297, .2299; 36.2305, .2308, .2316,
.2322, .2325, .2328

b. Veined jasper
H. 2.8 cm (1⅛ in.); W. 1.9 cm (¾ in.)
Iran, Susa, Acropole, foundation deposit at the
Inshushinak temple
Musée du Louvre, Département des Antiquités
Orientales, Paris Sb 17774

The weight system of the Indus Valley civilization was standardized, and nearly identical
weights were used in all of the settlements for

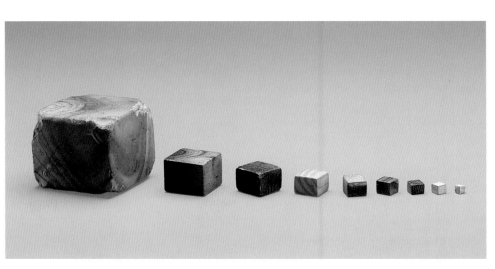

292a

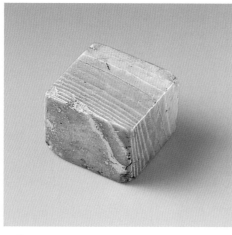

292b

this exhibition (cat. no. 292b) was found in a prince's funerary repository from the twelfth century B.C., long after the period when it was used in the Indus region. Given that it was deposited in a prestigious context, it must have been preserved as a rarity and perceived as a precious object.

The Indus weight system was binary, with two seeds of barley or one seed of the red and black gunja *(Abrus precatorius)* representing the smallest unit, 0.109 grams. Eight of the gunja seeds or sixteen grains of barley are equal to the smallest known Indus weights, which average 0.871 grams. In this group of cubes found in various archaeological contexts at Chanhudaro the smallest weighs 0.856 grams.[1] The most common Indus weight is approximately 13.7 grams, which is sixteen times heavier than that. With the larger weights the system shifts to a decimal increase, according to which the largest weight is one hundred times heavier than the sixteenth multiple in

the binary system. The largest cube in the group from Chanhudaro weighs 1,330.68 grams, which is 40 grams short of the official standard. Obviously someone was losing out when using this weight.

In addition to the more common cubical weights, truncated spherical weights have been found at many of the larger Indus Valley sites. These weights conform to the same system as the cubical forms and may represent a regional style preferred by some merchants. Although some of the Indus weight categories are similar to those found in Egypt and Mesopotamia, the similarities appear to be coincidental and not the result of intentional correlation for trade or taxation purposes.

JMK

1. For more information on the Chanhudaro weights in this exhibition, see Mackay 1943, pp. 239–46, pl. 91:29–32.

the valuation of precious commodities such as gold, gems, spices, and perfumes, and for taxation purposes. Indus weights were also found at sites along the Gulf and most notably at Susa in southwestern Iran. The Susa weight in

INDUS SEALS

293

Stamp seal with a seated male figure

Indus inscription
Steatite
L. 2.7 cm (1⅛ in.); W. 2.7 cm (1⅛ in.)
Indus Valley, Mohenjo-daro, DK 12050
Harappan, ca. 2000–1900 B.C.
Islamabad Museum, Islamabad NMP 50.296
Courtesy of the Department of Archaeology and Museums, Ministry of Minorities, Culture, Sports, Tourism, and Youth Affairs, Government of Pakistan

This type of seal, with the horned deity shown wearing bangles on both arms and seated in yogic position on a throne, appeared at the larger Indus Valley sites during the final phase of the Harappan period.[1] The nude image, which appears to have three faces and is bearded, wears a headdress of wide, spreading zebu bull or water-buffalo horns, two upward-projecting points, and a branch with three pipal leaves sprouting from the center. The beard could represent the short beard of the tiger.[2] This combination of motifs may

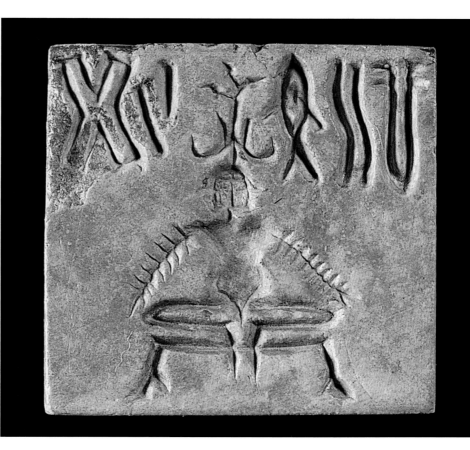

represent the synthesis of various beliefs. For example, the horned headdress probably represents some form of deity or sacred power, while the plant motifs most likely relate to fertility or procreation. Scholars have differing opinions as to the sex of this figure. Some argue that it is male and others female. Five signs in the undeciphered Indus script appear on either side of the headdress. The figure wears seven bangles on the right arm and six on the left, and the hands rest on the knees. The heels are pressed together under the groin, and the feet project beyond the edge of the throne. The legs of the throne are carved with the hoof of a bovine, as on bull and unicorn seals. The seal may not have been fired, but the stone is very hard. There is a grooved and perforated boss on the back.

The most famous Harappan image of a horned god is found on a seal from Mohenjo-daro that shows a male deity seated in yogic position with erect phallus (fig. 100b). Wearing bangles on both arms and a series of graduated necklaces reaching to his waist, this deity has a massive headdress of wide, spreading water-buffalo horns and a central fan-shaped element, possibly representing feathers or branches. The figure is sitting among ferocious wild animals: a rhinoceros, a water buffalo, an elephant, and a tiger, while two antelopes are seen beneath the dais or throne. Because of similarities in a few iconographic elements, some scholars have suggested that this seated figure represents an early form of the Hindu deity Siva, specifically in his role as the master of animals, Pasupati Nath. While the iconographic elements seen in yogic postures, phallic representations, and narrative scenes may have been borrowed by later religious groups, there is no confirmed connection between the horned figure on the Indus seals and later Hindu deities.   JMK

1. Mackay 1938b, p. 335, pl. 87:222.
2. Kenoyer 1998, pp. 112ff.

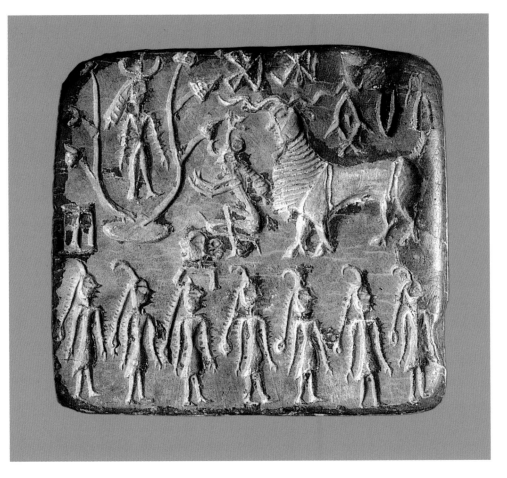

294

Stamp seal with a deity in a tree and a human-headed horned quadruped

Indus inscription
Steatite
L. 4.1 cm (1⅝ in.); W. 3.4 cm (1⅜ in.)
Indus Valley, Mohenjo-daro, DK 6847
Harappan, ca. 2000–1900 B.C.
Islamabad Museum, Islamabad NMP 50.295
Courtesy of the Department of Archaeology and Museums, Ministry of Minorities, Culture, Sports, Tourism, and Youth Affairs, Government of Pakistan

Public rituals and processions were essential for the practice of religion in the early urban centers such as Mohenjo-daro and Harappa. No structures that can be identified as temples have been discovered, and the main place of worship may have been in the open or at the foot of a sacred tree. This seal is one of several that depict a deity associated with the sacred pipal (fig) tree with heart-shaped leaves. In this example the deity is standing in the tree wearing a horned headdress and bangles on both arms and looking down on a kneeling worshiper, who is also wearing a horned and plumed headdress.[1] A human head with hair tied in a bun rests on a small stool in front of the worshiper, and in the background is a giant ram with a human face. Seven figures with bangles on their arms and wearing plumed headdresses stand in a procession, completing the narrative. The processing figures wear long skirts, and their long hair falls in a braid to the waist. Some scholars argue that the skirts indicate female worshipers, but since no distinctive female breasts are indicated, the figures may also be interpreted as male or transvestite priests. Several script signs are interspersed with the figures along the top of the seal, and a single sign is placed at the base of the tree. This scene may represent a special ritual sacrifice to a deity. The seal is made from low-fired tan steatite, and traces of whitened surface are still present in the deeply carved areas. It has a grooved and perforated boss, and the edges are worn and rounded from repeated use.

JMK

1. Mackay 1938b, pls. 94:430, 99:686a.

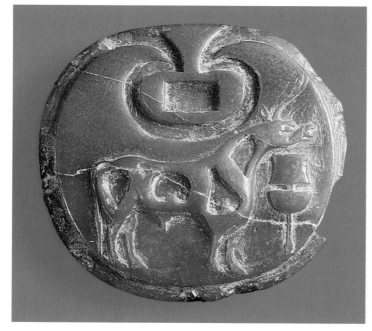

295a

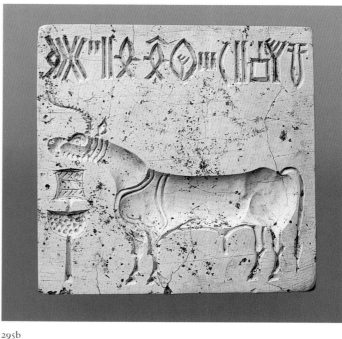

295b

295a, b

Pendant and stamp seal with unicorns and ritual offering stands

Steatite
Harappan, ca. 2000–1900 B.C.

a. L. 6.3 cm (2½ in.); W. 6.8 cm (2⅝ in.)
Indus Valley, Mohenjo-daro, DK 8063
National Museum, Karachi 50.125
Courtesy of the Department of Archaeology and
Museums, Ministry of Minorities, Culture, Sports,
Tourism, and Youth Affairs, Government of Pakistan

b. Indus inscription
L. 5.2 cm (2 in.); W. 5.2 cm (2 in.)
Indus Valley, Harappa, 8796-01
Harappa Museum, Harappa H99-4064
Courtesy of the Department of Archaeology and
Museums, Ministry of Minorities, Culture, Sports,
Tourism, and Youth Affairs, Government of Pakistan

The mythical unicorn motif dates back to the Harappan period in the Indus Valley. This unique pendant (cat. no. 295a) combines the unicorn with other important symbols that appear to have had sacred meaning for the Indus people.[1] The body of the animal has a kidney- or womb-shaped symbol on its belly; the same motif—which is also a common design in shell inlay (see cat. no. 288)—is adapted to form the frame for the pendant. Two leaf shapes of the sacred fig, or pipal tree, are depicted at the animal's shoulder and rump, and a ritual offering stand is placed in

front of the beast. The deeply incised frame and the symbols on the unicorn were probably filled with pigment or set with inlay. The tan steatite is unfired.

The unicorn is the most common image found on Harappan stone stamp seals. This extremely large seal from Harappa (cat. no. 295b) includes one of the most spectacular carvings of the unicorn accompanied by a relatively long undeciphered inscription across the top of the seal. As on a terracotta figurine from Chanhudaro (cat. no. 276), the small head of the animal is tilted up and the gracefully curving horn projects forward. Carved lines on the arching neck and the shoulders may represent a collar and decorative covering. The sex of the unicorn is not clear, since a long drooping flap of skin, or dibble, below the belly is common on both male and female bovids and thus does not necessarily represent male genitalia here. No examples of the unicorn are depicted with testicles, which are occasionally carved on bull images (see cat. no. 296). A ritual offering stand, which has been interpreted variously as an incense burner or a sacred filter for making an intoxicating drink called soma, is placed in front of the unicorn. Large seals such as this one would have been used by powerful officials, merchants, or landowners to seal goods and documents.

No unicorn symbol has been found from the period prior to the rise of the Indus cities or after their fall. It probably represents a major clan or merchant community that dominated the Indus economic, political, and ritual system. Some unicorn seals have been found as far away

as Mesopotamia, but after the decline of the Indus civilization, this motif disappears from South Asian art and iconography. The legend of the unicorn from the Indus Valley appears to have been kept alive in West Asia, however, whence it is thought to have spread to Europe during Roman times.   JMK

1. Mackay 1938b, p. 546, pl. 91:59.

296

Stamp seal with a zebu and script

Indus inscription
Steatite
L. 3.8 cm (1½ in.); W. 3.9 cm (1½ in.)
Indus Valley, Mohenjo-daro, B 588
Harappan, ca. 2600–1900 B.C.
Islamabad Museum, Islamabad NMP 50.236
Courtesy of the Department of Archaeology and
Museums, Ministry of Minorities, Culture, Sports,
Tourism, and Youth Affairs, Government of Pakistan

In addition to the mythical unicorn, various powerful wild and domestic animals, such as the zebu (humped bull), elephant, water buffalo, and antelope, are depicted on Indus seals. With the exception of the unicorn, all of these animal motifs persisted after the end of the Indus cities in South Asian iconography, where they represent certain deities or moral qualities. In the context of the Indus civilization these animal symbols may have reflected a hierarchy among the elites or identified hereditary

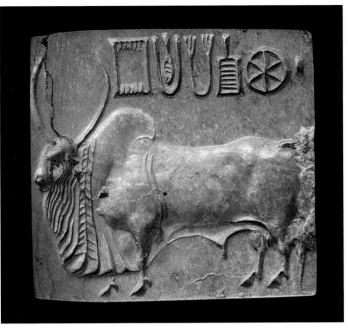

296

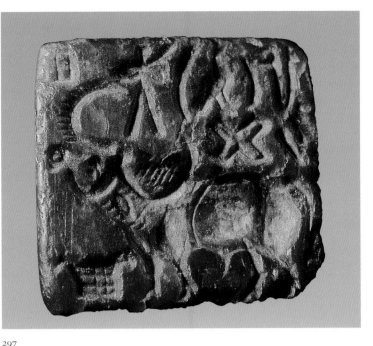

297

merchant communities, sodalities, clans, or even different classes of administrative officials. This large square seal has one of the most detailed carvings known of the humped-bull motif.[1] Six signs in the Indus script appear along the top of the seal, but no ritual offering stand is depicted (see entry for cat. nos. 295a,b). The curving horns rise majestically above the head, and a carefully braided collar falls along the heavy dewlap. On this figure the details of male genitalia are intentionally distinguished.

The curve in the left edge of the seal may have been designed to accommodate stamping on the concave neck of large storage jars. It is also possible that the seal carver made a mistake and recarved the head of the bull after scraping away the edge of the seal. This seal has not been fully fired or hardened and may represent an unfinished object. The boss on the back is broken.   JMK

1. Marshall 1931, p. 337, pl. 111.

297

Stamp seal with a water buffalo

Indus inscription
Steatite
L. 2.8 cm (1⅛ in.); W. 2.8 cm (1⅛ in.)
Indus Valley, Mohenjo-daro, SD 2697
Harappan, ca. 2600–1900 B.C.
National Museum, Karachi MM 50.279
Courtesy of the Department of Archaeology and
Museums, Ministry of Minorities, Culture, Sports,
Tourism, and Youth Affairs, Government of Pakistan

As is usual on Indus Valley seals that show a water buffalo, this animal is standing with upraised head and both horns clearly visible.[1] A feeding trough is placed in front of it, and a double row of undecipherable script fills the entire space above. The horns are incised to show the natural growth lines. During the Akkadian period, cylinder seals in Mesopotamia depict water buffaloes in a similar pose that may have been copied from Indus seals (see cat. no. 135).[2]   JMK

1. Mackay 1938b, p. 391.
2. For a Mesopotamian seal with water buffalo, see Parpola 1994, p. 252, and Collon 1987, no. 529.

298

Stamp seal with an elephant

Indus inscription
Steatite
L. 3.1 cm (1⅛ in.); W. 3.1 cm (1⅛ in.)
Indus Valley, Mohenjo-daro, DK 353
Harappan, ca. 2600–1900 B.C.
Lahore Museum, Pakistan MN L.P-902
Courtesy of the Department of Archaeology and
Museums, Ministry of Minorities, Culture, Sports,
Tourism, and Youth Affairs, Government of Pakistan

The elephant was the most powerful animal of the Indus Valley region and appears as one of the earliest animal motifs on Early Indus seals,

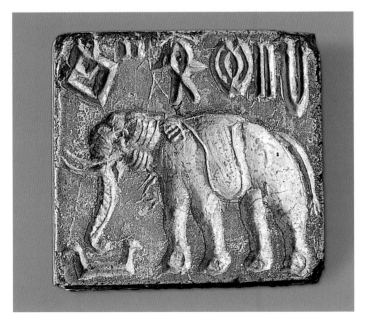

298

about 2800 B.C.[1] This example dates to about 2600–1900 B.C. and includes the undeciphered Indus script. Wild animals on seals are usually depicted with an offering trough. The stone from which the object is made is low-fired steatite, and there is a perforated boss on the back.   JMK

1. Meadow and Kenoyer 2001, pp. 19–30.

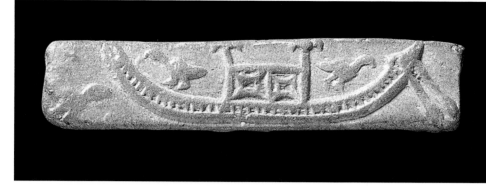

299

Three-sided moulded tablet with a boat and gharial

Indus inscription
Fired clay
L. 4.6 cm (1¾ in.); W. 1.2 cm (⁷⁄₁₆ in.)
Indus Valley, Mohenjo-daro, MD 602
Harappan, ca. 2600–1900 B.C.
Islamabad Museum, Islamabad NMP 1384
Courtesy of the Department of Archaeology and Museums, Ministry of Minorities, Culture, Sports, Tourism, and Youth Affairs, Government of Pakistan

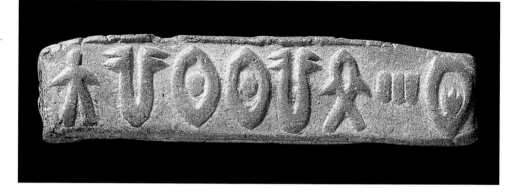

Moulded tablets such as this one may have been made for special ritual purposes or for documenting trading events. On one side is a flat-bottomed boat with a central hut that has leafy fronds at the top of two poles. Such boats would have been essential for travel along the sandy and shallow rivers of the Indus Valley. Two birds perch on the deck, and a large double rudder extends from the stern. Other craft are represented in the glyptic of the third millennium B.C. A boat on a steatite seal from the Gulf may have had a sail (see cat. no. 221). Deep-keeled seagoing vessels with sails were necessary for travel across the Gulf, connecting the Indus cities with Failaka Island and Mesopotamia.

On the other side of the tablet is a snout-nosed gharial with a fish in its mouth. This type of crocodile was common along the Indus River and must have had some special ritual significance, since it is found on many narrative seals and incised steatite tablets. The third side has eight signs of the undeciphered Indus script.[1]   JMK

1. Dales 1965, p. 147; Dales 1968, p. 39.

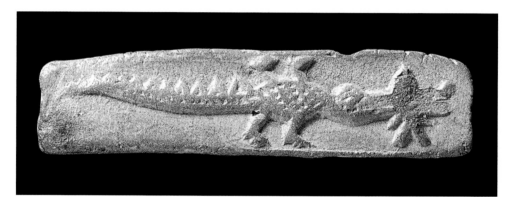

SEALS AND
INTERCONNECTIONS

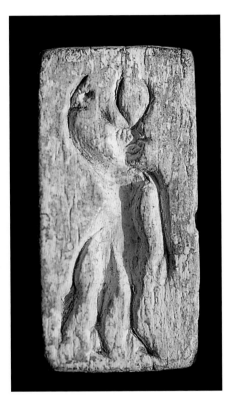

300a

300a

Stamp seal with a bull-man

Indus inscription
Fired steatite
H. 2.3 cm (7/8 in.); W. 1.9 cm (3/4 in.)
Indus Valley, Mohenjo-daro
Harappan, ca. 2600–1900 B.C.
National Museum, Karachi NMP 50.214
Courtesy of the Department of Archaeology and
Museums, Ministry of Minorities, Culture, Sports,
Tourism, and Youth Affairs, Government of Pakistan

300b

Moulded tablet with a hero, tigers, and a bull hunt scene

Fired clay
L. 3.9 cm (1½ in.); W. 1.5–1.6 cm (5/8 in.)
Indus Valley, Harappa, Lot 4651-01, Mound ET
Harappan, ca. 2600–1900 B.C.
Harappa Museum, Harappa H95-2486
Courtesy of the Department of Archaeology and
Museums, Ministry of Minorities, Culture, Sports,
Tourism, and Youth Affairs, Government of Pakistan

300c

Stamp seal with a hero and tigers

Fired steatite
L. 1.2 cm (¼ in.); W. 1.2 cm (¼ in.); Thickness
0.4 cm (3/16 in.)
Indus Valley, Mohenjo-daro
Harappan, ca. 2600–1900 B.C.
Mohenjo-daro Museum, Mohenjo-daro NMK 50.283
Courtesy of the Department of Archaeology and
Museums, Ministry of Minorities, Culture, Sports,
Tourism, and Youth Affairs, Government of Pakistan

300d

Stamp seal with a human-headed horned quadruped

Indus inscription
Fired steatite
L. 1.3 cm (½ in.); W. 1.3 cm (½ in.); Thickness
1.4 cm (½ in.)
Indus Valley, Mohenjo-daro, DK6658
Harappan, ca. 2600–1900 B.C.
Lahore Museum, Lahore L.P.-1727
Courtesy of the Department of Archaeology and
Museums, Ministry of Minorities, Culture, Sports,
Tourism, and Youth Affairs, Government of Pakistan

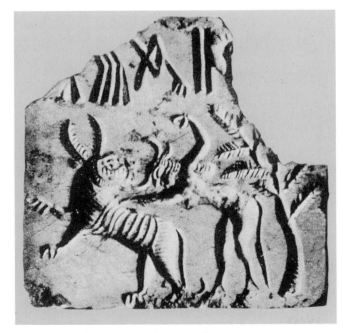

Fig. 100a. Steatite stamp seal depicting a bovine-human attacking a horned tiger. Mohenjo-daro, Harappan, ca. 2600–1900 B.C. National Museum, New Delhi, DK 5075/123.

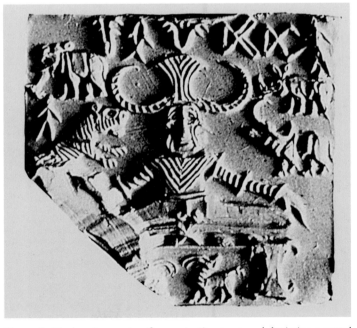

Fig. 100b. Modern impression from a steatite stamp seal depicting a seated horned male figure. Seal: Mohenjo-daro, Harappan, ca. 2600–1900 B.C. National Museum, New Delhi, DK 5075/144.

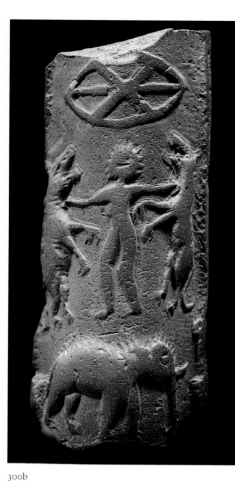

300b

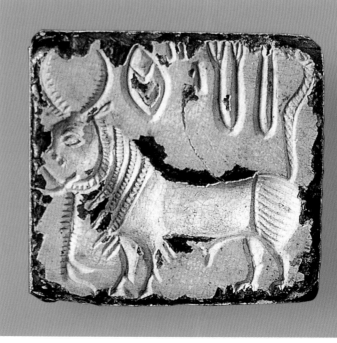

300b

The glyptic traditions of the Harappan and Mesopotamian worlds are very different in essential respects, including the forms of seals and methods of impressing them, as well as their corpus of imagery. Because of the easily recognizable characteristics of each tradition, one is able to notice unusual features that may have been introduced as a result of cultural exchange across Asia. Although no imported Mesopotamian seals have been identified in the Indus Valley, certain Indus motifs may not necessarily have been independently invented. These include figures known as masters of animals dominating felines, supernatural creatures composed of human and animal elements, and depictions of bovine vaulting.[1]

Perhaps the most convincing parallels between Near Eastern and Harappan seal imagery are the scenes of nude heroes holding powerful felines at bay. In Mesopotamia this expression of human domination over the powerful forces of nature took two main forms: an antithetical three-figure composition (see cat. no. 58) and a contest scene that might include nude heroes, bull-men (bison-men), lions, and bulls in either continuous compositions or, later, in groups of two and three combatants (cat. nos. 55, 146).[2] In Iran and Central Asia the theme is expressed in balanced three-figure antithetical compositions that show a human in control of felines and bulls as well as fearsome creatures such as snakes (see cat. no. 227). Tigers are overpowered by nude figures in comparable scenes on Indus Valley glyptic (see cat. nos. 300b, 300c).[3]

On one extraordinary Harappan seal, however, the supernatural character of such imagery is emphasized by the use of mythical

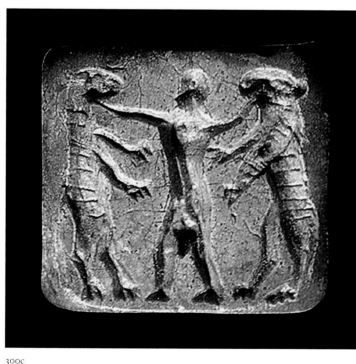

300c

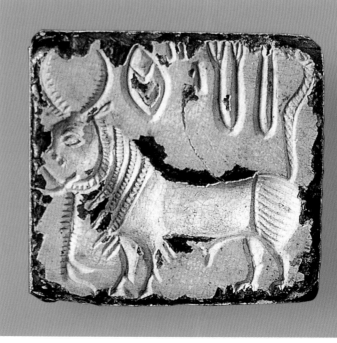

300d

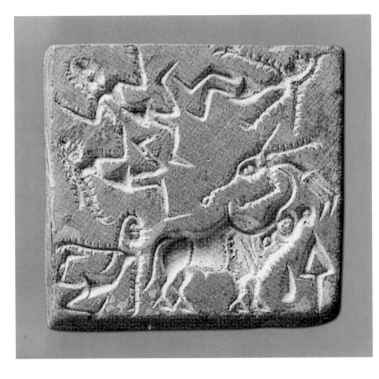

Fig. 100c. Steatite stamp seal with a water buffalo and leapers. Seal: Mohenjo-daro, Harappan, ca. 2600–1900 B.C. National Museum, New Dehli, 147.

creatures, including the anthropomorphic bull-man so typical of Mesopotamian art (but lacking the usual beard). One such composite with the body of a human female (?) and the horns, hooves, and tail of a bull stands on two legs but is bent over in quasi-animal posture, overpowering a tiger with bovine horns (fig. 100a). Other Harappan seals depict the bull-man standing upright, in one case engraved on the two narrow sides or edges of a rectangular seal with unicorn images on the main faces (cat. no. 300a).[4] A highly significant anthropomorphic figure in Harappan art seated in what resembles a yogic position—and in one instance surrounded by animals (cat. no. 293; fig. 100b)—has been interpreted by some scholars as a divine bull-man. He displays impressive bovine horns like those of the water buffalo and bangled human arms with hooves for hands.[5] The association of this figure with other Harappan mythic or ritual motifs that are expressed in ways familiar from other cultures is seen in one of the antithetical scenes discussed above (cat. no. 300b). On one side of this tablet—a type of object that has been likened in its visual effect to Near Eastern cylinder-seal impressions—a hero (possibly female) controls felines below a wheel-shaped sign and above an elephant. The reverse shows the "yogic" figure seated next to a scene of a man attacking a bovine, beneath a gharial.

Scenes in a natural setting, involving humans treading on the heads of or vaulting over the

horns of water buffaloes as well as spearing the beasts, occur also on Harappan stamp seals (see fig. 100c).[6] Asko Parpola has associated such scenes with an archaic Vedic myth in which a water buffalo was sacrificed during rites of seasonal renewal.[7] Noting the appearance of water buffaloes on seals of important personages in the late Akkadian period in Mesopotamia, Parpola explains the Near Eastern motif of a hero placing a foot on the head of the animal and holding its horns to be the result of contact with the Indus Valley, as is documented in the cuneiform literature.[8] It is possible that Harappan art also inspired the depiction of bull leaping in the art of Central Asia. A very interesting stamp seal found in Turkmenistan is engraved with a charging zebu in a flying gallop with a vaulter falling behind it and other hunters below (see cat. no. 265). The dynamic posture of the zebu, however, with head down and hind legs extended, recalls depictions on Syrian seals of the early second millennium B.C.[9]

The body parts of tiger, elephant, bovine, and goat or ram are also recognizable in the supernatural quadrupeds on Harappan glyptic, all of which display human heads.[10] One characteristic example from Mohenjo-daro (cat. no. 300d) is in the form of a powerful human-headed bull with curving horns, the pronounced dewlap and fold of skin below the belly of the Indus zebu (see cat. no. 296), an elephant's trunk, and a serpentine tail.[11]

Like the human-headed bulls or bisons in Mesopotamian art (see cat. no. 157), horned human-headed quadrupeds appear to have played an important role in Harappan ritual: a human-headed horned creature is depicted in one very elaborate scene of worship on a seal from Mohenjo-daro (see cat. no. 294). One can only note that during the third millennium B.C. in Mesopotamia and the Indus Valley—two distant regions—very similar devices were utilized to evoke the divine world.

JA

1. For discussions of iconographic parallels, see Parpola 1984, pp. 176ff.; During Caspers 1970–71, pp. 107ff.
2. On the antithetical three-figure composition in Mesopotamia, see Parpola 1984, pp. 177–78, figs. 23:3,4.
3. Joshi and Parpola 1987, pl. 76: M-306–8.
4. Marshall 1931, vol. 2, pp. 372, 373, 389, vol. 3, pls. 111:356, 109:227, 230; Vats 1940, vol. 2, pl. 93:305.
5. See Franke-Vogt 1991, pp. 78ff., pl. 32:220–22; Srinivason 1975–76, pp. 47f., 56.
6. Franke-Vogt 1991, pp. 91ff., pl. 35:250–54.
7. Parpola 1984, pp. 184–85.
8. Ibid., pp. 182ff.
9. Aruz 1995c, pp. 36ff.
10. A composite creature with horns and the full body of a human attached to the hindquarters of a tiger is found both on a cylinder seal from Kalibangan (see fig. 71b) and on stamp seals from Mohenjo-daro; see Joshi and Parpola 1987, pl. 311:K-65, pl. 77:M-311.
11. Shah and Parpola 1991, pls. 137–39; Joshi and Parpola 1987, pls. 73, 74; Franke-Vogt 1991, pp. 76ff., pl. 31:211–15.

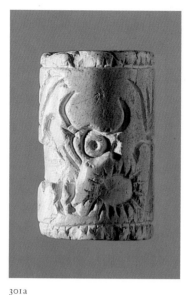

301a

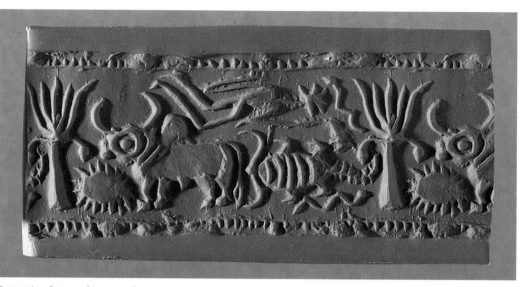

Impression from catalogue number 301a.

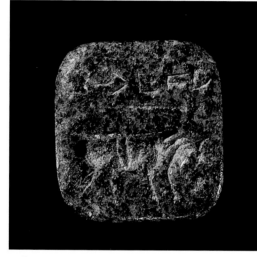

301b

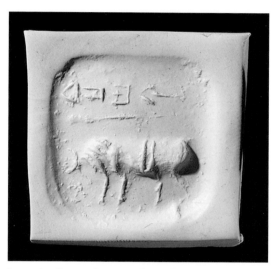

Impression from catalogue number 301b.

301a

Cylinder seal with a zebu, scorpion, man, snake, and tree

Enstatite
H. 2.6 cm (1 in.); Diam. 1.55 cm (⅝ in.)
Mesopotamia, Ur, U.16220
Late 3rd millennium B.C.
Trustees of The British Museum, London BM 122947

301b

Stamp seal with a bull and cuneiform signs

Cuneiform inscription
Gray steatite
H. 1.1 cm (⁷⁄₁₆ in.); L. 2.7 cm (1⅛ in.); W. 2.4 cm (1 in.)
Mesopotamia, Ur, surface soil beyond Diqdiqqah
Late 3rd millennium B.C.
Trustees of The British Museum, London BM 120573

301c

Cylinder seal with zebus and signs

Fired steatite
H. 2.3 cm (⅞ in.); Diam. 1.6 cm (⅝ in.)
Iran, Susa
Late 3rd millennium B.C.
Musée du Louvre, Département des Antiquités Orientales, Paris Sb 2425

301d

Stamp seal with a bull and signs

Green serpentine
H. 1.2 cm (⁷⁄₁₆ in.); W. 2.2 cm (⅞ in.)
Iran, Susa
Late 3rd millennium B.C.
Musée du Louvre, Département des Antiquités Orientales, Paris Sb 5614

301e

Stamp seal with a bull and signs

Green steatite
H. 1.45 cm (⁹⁄₁₆ in.); W. 2.9 cm (1⅛ in.)
Gulf region, Qalat al-Bahrain, Period IIa, Trench D, Level 19
Late 3rd millennium B.C.
Bahrain National Museum, Manama 3011-11-90

Cylinder and stamp seals—essential tools of the long-distance traders—may provide visual evidence for cultural interaction in their combination of images and forms. The Mesopotamian seal shape—a cylinder—was utilized only occasionally in the Indus Valley, for images that may bear some western features.¹ At Near Eastern sites, however, the impact of Harappan glyptic is much more readily identifiable. One cylinder seal from Ur (cat. no. 301a) bears the image of a zebu, with wide-set horns curving

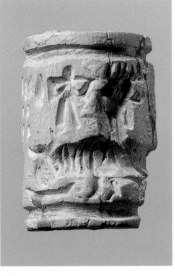

301c

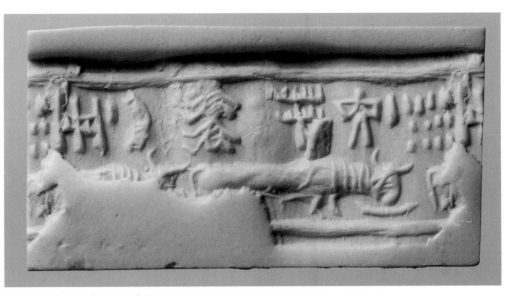

Impression from catalogue number 301c.

inward and with stylistic characteristics that
relate it to bovine images on pottery from
Kulli, in Baluchistan, and animal depictions on
seals from the Gulf.[2] In this rendering, the
majesty of the powerful Harappan zebu (see
cat. no. 296), expressed in its large, frontally
displayed horns, strong musculature, heavy
dewlap, and emphasized potency, is truly lost.[3]

The zebu on the Ur cylinder is not displayed
alone, but rather in a scene with snakes, a
scorpion, a rayed oval device that has been
identified as a bale of fodder, and a Near
Eastern date palm. Above is a very stylized
human figure with a starlike head, one arm
down and the other bent, both very elongated;
it has been interpreted as a variation on an
Indus sign, or as a performer of bull acrobatics
engaged in bull capture. The latter theme was
represented in the art of the Indus Valley and
of Central Asia in the late third and early second
millennium B.C. (see cat. no. 265; fig. 100c).
The Ur cylinder was found in a vaulted burial
of the Larsa period cut into an Ur III royal
tomb of the late third millennium B.C., perhaps Shulgi's mausoleum.[4]

A cylinder seal from Susa (cat. no. 301c)
depicts two short-horned bulls (only one of
which is fully preserved) with their heads bent
over a trough. This Harappan motif is very
common on circular stamp seals with Harappan
boss handles from Mesopotamia, Iran, and the
Gulf. In contrast, however, to the bull on a
stamp seal from Susa (cat. no. 301d), which
retains some of the original proportions of
Harappan bulls,[5] the animals on this Susa
cylinder seal are elongated like depictions of
the animals on pottery from Kulli. Despite
Asko Parpola's opinion that the signs above

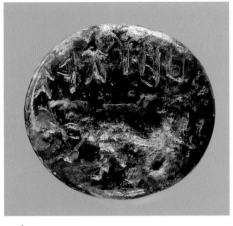

301d

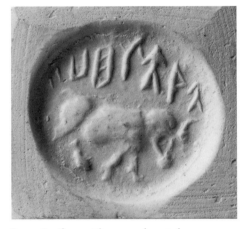

Impression from catalogue number 301d.

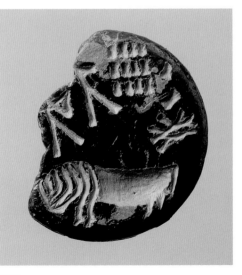

301e

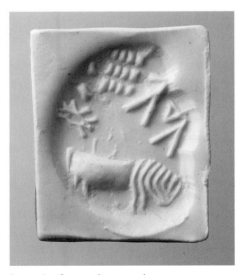

Impression from catalogue number 301e.

the images are probably "native Harappan," it
is difficult to believe this piece was made by a
Harappan craftsman.[6]

It has been proposed that the fired steatite
circular stamp seals with boss handles and

images of short-horned bulls found in
Mesopotamia may have been produced by or
for Harappan merchants working abroad.[7]
Other such seals with Mesopotamian motifs
or adapted foreign imagery were certainly

local products.[8] One stamp seal with bull imagery is of particular interest in this regard (cat. no. 301b). Although rectangular like a Harappan seal, it has a typically Near Eastern ridge handle and is made of steatite that was not fired white. Furthermore, in place of the usual Harappan signs above the animal but also displayed horizontally, there is a cuneiform inscription consisting of three or four signs. The seal was presumably produced by a Mesopotamian, but no satisfactory reading in a known language has yet been suggested.[9] The bull's body lacks the usual modeling and definition that we find in the Harappan style. Similarly a green steatite circular seal found at Qalat al-Bahrain (cat. no. 301e), along with a tablet dated to the Isin-Larsa period, is probably of local manufacture.[10] Here the original Harappan motif is reinterpreted to show a very stylized bull with a pattern of curving lines covering the head and neck, perhaps alluding to the dewlap.

JA

1. A cylinder seal from Mohenjo-daro with a series of animals can be compared to a Proto-Elamite cylinder seal with similar creatures; for the former, see Mode 1959, pl. 71, and for the latter, see Amiet 1980, no. 548. A cylinder seal from Kalibangan (see fig. 71b) includes a Harappan supernatural creature with horns that closely resemble those of deities on cylinder seals from eastern Iran; see Joshi and Parpola 1987, pl. 311:K-65, and Amiet 1986, p. 299:8; see also Chakrabarti 1978, pp. 106–7, and During Caspers 1994a, pp. 93ff.
2. See "Art and Interconnections in the Third Millennium B.C.," by Joan Aruz, in this catalogue; see also Gadd 1932, p. 8, no. 6.
3. A similar phenomenon is evident in the representation of the elephant and rhinoceros on a cylinder seal from Tell Asmar (fig. 71a), where the sagging back and bent legs of the elephant do not capture the essence of the animal's form and the rendering of the head is confused. The usual vertical line marking the transition from the profile face to the ear becomes a network of designs and creates a nearly frontal appearance for the head, especially since the eye is inconspicuously placed above the tusks. For the Tell Asmar seal, see Frankfort 1933, p. 50, As. 31–32.
4. Gadd 1932, p. 8, no. 6; Mitchell 1986, p. 282, no. 17, p. 283, fig. 118. See also During Caspers 1993–95, p. 13.
5. See "Art and Interconnections in the Third Millennium B.C.," by Joan Aruz, in this catalogue.
6. This is also the opinion of During Caspers (1993–95, p. 13, fig. 10), who disputes Parpola's interpretation that the piece was made by a Harappan craftsman unfamiliar with cylinder seals; see Parpola 1994, p. 313.
7. See "Art and Interconnections in the Third Millennium B.C.," by Joan Aruz, in this catalogue.
8. See, for instance, Gadd 1932, pl. 18.
9. Ibid., pp. 5–6, no. 1; Mitchell 1986, p. 280, no. 7, p. 281, fig. 111.
10. On the seal and tablet, see D. Potts 1990, p. 218; Eidem 1994, pp. 301–3; Al-Sindi 1999, p. 357; and

Brunswig, Parpola, and Potts 1983, p. 104, no. 8, p. 106, no. 8, where the language is also determined to be non-Harappan.

302a

Compartmented stamp seal with a zebu

Copper alloy
L. 4.3 cm (1¾ in.); W. 3.8 cm (1½ in.); Thickness 0.5 cm (³⁄₁₆ in.)
Baluchistan, Nausharo, Sector G, phase IB
Nausharo, ca. 2400 B.C.
Exploration Branch, Karachi EXB 5639
Courtesy of the Department of Archaeology and Museums, Ministry of Minorities, Culture, Sports, Tourism, and Youth Affairs, Government of Pakistan

302b

Bulla with an eagle and elephant

Fired clay
Diam. 2.8 cm (1⅛ in.); Thickness 0.65 cm (¼ in.)
Indus Valley, Mohenjo-daro, DK 8489
Harappan, ca. 2000–1900 B.C.
Courtesy of the Department of Archaeology and Museums, Ministry of Minorities, Culture, Sports, Tourism, and Youth Affairs, Government of Pakistan NMP 50.402

Two main types of stamp seal are characteristic of the ancient cultures in the Oxus region: stone seals in cushion form and other shapes, and seals of gold, silver, or copper alloy in circular, animal, and geometric forms. The metal seals often bear an image on one face and strips of metal on the reverse raised to form compartments that follow the outline of the primary design. When stamped, these compartmented seals cut into the clay to create a distinctively sharp image. The presence of Oxus seals in the Indus Valley suggests both trade and cultural interaction between Central and South Asia. This connection is also documented by the discovery of Harappan seals at Altyn-depe, and the presence of a Harappan trading establishment at Shortugai, on the Oxus River.

The glyptic evidence, though limited to a few examples, is varied in form and geographic distribution. Perhaps the most widespread type of Oxus seal is the copper-alloy compartmented version, which has been found at sites in Syria, Iran, and Baluchistan, as well as at Mohenjo-daro. The depiction of the

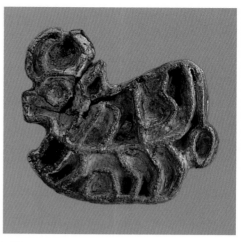

302a

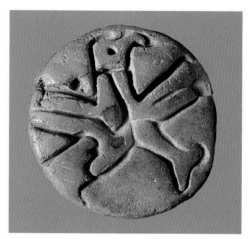

302b

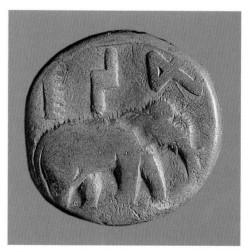

302b

typically Harappan zebu on such seals from both Mohenjo-daro and Nausharo, and their impressions on pottery from Shahr-i Sokhta, in southeastern Iran, may indicate some special significance for this image in the context of interregional exchange.[1] The Nausharo seal (cat. no. 302a), found in a phase at the site that appears to predate a mature Harappan

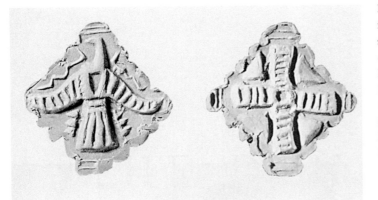

Fig. 101. Modern impressions from a steatite stamp seal with eagle, imported from Bactria-Margiana. Harappan, ca. 2600–1900 B.C. Archaeological Survey of India, Purana Qila, New Delhi, AS 80.2.60.

presence, depicts the animal striding, with characteristic inward-curving horns, a circular eye, and geometric patterns to divide and define areas of the body, such as the forequarters, legs, belly, hindquarters, and tail.[2] It recalls a compartment seal from Altyn-depe, where the patterning is simpler.[3]

Both Nausharo and Mohenjo-daro have produced two Central Asian compartmented seals. A third remarkable object from Mohenjo-daro is an (intentionally) fired circular piece of clay, bearing the impression of a different type of seal on each face (cat. no. 302b).[4] This object has been interpreted either as a bulla or token used in the transfer of goods or as an amulet.[5] Depicted on one face is the impression of a Harappan stone seal with an elephant and Indus signs. On the reverse, however, is the sharp outline made by a Central Asian compartmented metal seal of an eagle with profile head and frontally displayed wings. A second fragment from Mohenjo-daro bears a similar impression (presumably from the same original).[6] Unlike the bull motif on the Nausharo copper-alloy seal, the eagle image is one unfamiliar in the art of the Indus Valley. It is found, however, on another Central Asian import to the site of Harappa (fig. 101), a lozenge-shaped stone seal with stepped outline. With a frontal eagle displaying linear patterning on one face and a hatched cross pattern on the other, this seal made of white steatite, a material also used to create Harappan seals, finds close parallels in its form and imagery with the glyptic of Bactria-Margiana.[7]   JA

1. Baghestani 1997, p. 184, fig. 27.
2. It is one of two compartmented seals found at Nausharo. For the second, with a cross pattern, from the mature Harappan level, see Baghestani 1997, p. 57, and J-F. Jarrige 1974–86, pl. 39B.
3. Baghestani 1997, p. 184, fig. 27:68. The bull's triangular hump on the Nausharo seal reminds one of

later images of so-called bull gods on Anatolian seals, one found in the twentieth-century-B.C. grave of an Assyrian merchant with Indus connections; see Aruz 1995a, p. 60, no. 41.
4. Franke-Vogt 1995, pp. 150ff., 153, 159:5,6; Franke-Vogt 1991, pl. 10:26,27.
5. Kenoyer 1998, p. 88 (as a bulla or token); Mackay 1938b, p. 349 (as an amulet).
6. For parallels, see Franke-Vogt 1991, p. 73, and Baghestani 1997, p. 170.
7. Sarianidi 1998b, pp. 300–301, no. 1648.1.

303

Cylinder seal of Shu-ilishu, interpreter for Meluhha

Cuneiform inscription in Old Akkadian
Serpentine
H. 2.9 cm (1⅛ in.); Diam. 1.8 cm (¾ in.)
Mesopotamia
Akkadian, ca. 2220–2159 B.C.
Musée du Louvre, Département des Antiquités Orientales, Paris AO 22310

This seal is engraved with a scene of worship.[1] Two votive figures dressed in long fringed robes pay tribute to a mother goddess, seated on a cube-shaped stool. The first brings a deer as an offering, and the second holds a situla. Behind the goddess, a small human figure

attends a kettle placed on a trivet; above her are two jars on a shelf. The goddess holds a small bearded figure on her knees. On some seals of this type she is shown holding a leafy branch instead of the small figure. This scene, therefore, may evoke the birth of a young god personifying vegetation.

The design is engraved in a rudimentary style; however, the interest of this seal lies less in its decoration than in the position held by its owner, Shu-ilishu, who was an interpreter for the region of Meluhha. The relations between Akkad and that distant region of the Indus Valley are referenced in various documents. An inscription dating from the reign of Sargon, known through an Old Babylonian–period copy, indicates that boats from Meluhha came to moor alongside the quays of Akkad;[2] other Sargonic texts mention men from Meluhha. Seals, beads, a weight, and shell-shaped objects from the Indus Valley, where the Harappan civilization flourished from about 2600 to 1900 B.C., have been found at various sites in Mesopotamia (see cat. nos. 287b, 289b, 292b). Similarly, the presence on Mesopotamian soil of exotic animals such as the water buffalo (see cat. no. 135) confirms the existence of exchanges between the two regions. The seal of Shu-ilishu is thus a valuable document that reinforces this evidence, emphasizing the fact that commercial or diplomatic relations with the region of Meluhha were regular enough to justify the existence of a professional interpreter. Unfortunately, nothing more is known about Shu-ilishu, who possessed a typically Mesopotamian name and seal.   FD

1. For further reference, see De Clercq and Ménant 1888, no. 83; Frankfort 1939, pl. 22c; Boehmer 1965, no. 1299, fig. 557; and Collon 1987, no. 637. This seal was also exhibited in *Bas-reliefs imaginaires* (Amiet 1973, no. 259).
2. Sollberger and Kupper 1971, 2A1b.

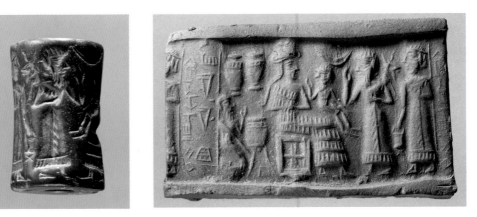

303   Impression from catalogue number 303.

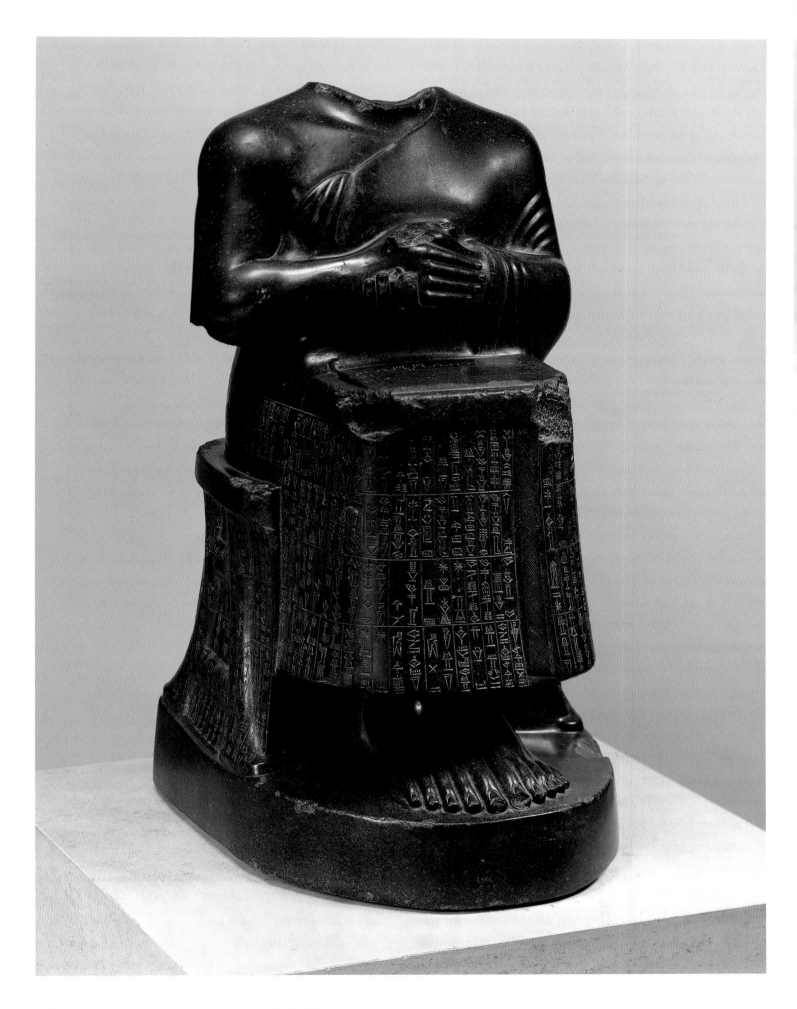

Seated statue of Gudea: Architect with Plan

Cuneiform inscription in Sumerian
Diorite
H. 93 cm (36⅝ in.); W. 46.5 cm (18¼ in.); Thickness
61.5 cm (24¼ in.)
Plan: L. 28.5 cm (11¼ in.); W. 16.5 cm (6½ in.)
Mesopotamia, Girsu (modern Tello), Court A of the
Palace of Adad-nadin-ahi
Second Dynasty of Lagash, reign of Gudea,
ca. 2090 B.C.
Musée du Louvre, Département des Antiquités
Orientales, Paris AO 2

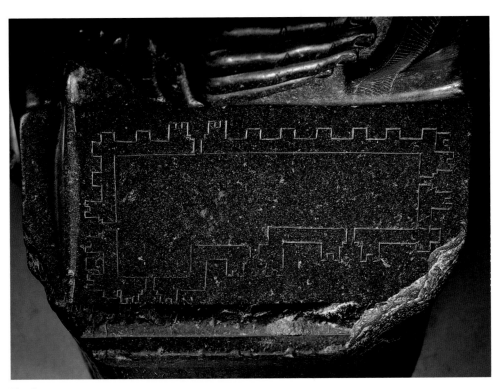

Detail, cat. no. 304.

Among the many statues dedicated by Gudea that represent him standing or seated before the deities whose temples he built or restored, Statue B, known as the Architect with Plan, is remarkable.[1] The quality of both its stone and carving; the tablet on Gudea's knees bearing an engraved architectural plan, a stylus, and a graduated rule; and the inscription—unique in its length and content—that covers almost the entire statue, makes this lifesize statue a monument of exceptional interest. It depicts the ruler conventionally seated on a stool with its legs set wide apart, connected by two crosspieces that support the seat. He is barefoot, and his hands are joined, a gesture acknowledging the deity. He wears a long royal mantle with a fringed edge; one section covers his left arm, and the other is pulled under his right arm and tucked into the front, forming folds.[2]

The statue is dedicated to Ningirsu, the major god of the Lagash pantheon. It personifies Gudea as the architect of Ningirsu's temple, the E-ninnu, the principal building project of Gudea's reign. The plan, which probably depicts the enclosure of Ningirsu's sanctuary,[3] is an orthogonal projection, and it follows the conventions for Mesopotamian architecture made of unbaked and baked bricks: a thick wall is reinforced by external buttresses and, along its length, by fortified doors (six in this case) equipped with redans and flanked by towers. The wall thus delimits an elongated, irregular interior space devoid of structures. On each of the wall's short sides and on the outside, a small structure—one of them may be an altar surmounted by horns, a divine attribute, or the support for a statue or stele—is placed in a recess. The graduated rule is not well preserved, but sixteen sections of it—with divisions

numbered 1 to 6, separated by empty spaces—can be reconstituted.[4]

The text on the back of the statue begins with a list of regular offerings, as for a cult statue: "for the statue of Gudea, *ensi* of Lagash, (the statue of) the man who built the E-ninnu." The statue, continues the inscription, "must remain at the site of the libations" (col. 7:55), where the deceased rulers received sacrifices.[5] That dictate follows from the statue's function, which is to replace Gudea in front of his god and to transmit the ruler's words to him (col. 7:47–48), in particular, the message that the E-ninnu was built according to divine rules and the laws of society.

Ensi, the official title of Gudea that was given after the enumeration of offerings, reveals that the gods in the pantheon had conferred on him rulership along with the qualities necessary to rule. The account of the temple's construction lists materials from the rest of the known world, an indication of the power of Lagash: "The day he built the temple of Ningirsu, his beloved lord opened the way to him from the Lower Sea to the Upper Sea" (col. 5:22–6:69), meaning from the Mediterranean to the Gulf. The statue was then created and a name given to it, which brought it to life: "From the foreign

country of Magan, he brought diorite [and] sculpted it into the form of a stone statue. He named it: 'For my lord, I built his house, life is my reward,' and he brought it to him in the E-ninnu. Gudea gave word to the statue" (col. 7:10–21).

A reference to diorite in a literary composition written during Gudea's lifetime or shortly thereafter may mention this statue: "When the king who established your renown in perpetuity has sculpted his statue for eternity, and has placed it in the place of libations in my E-ninnu, the temple full of splendor, may you be there in the place that belongs to you" (*Lugale* XI: 475–77). The text engraved on the statue affirms that exaltation of diorite as a noble material, more precious even than metals or precious stones: "For this statue nobody was supposed to use silver or lapis lazuli, neither should copper or tin or bronze be a working (material). It is (exclusively) of diorite" (col. 7:47–54). The connotation is that diorite is more durable than the other materials and is thus more worthy of representing the sovereign and perpetuating his memory before the god. The inscription ends with a long malediction against potential profaners. It seems that later rulers heeded these words,

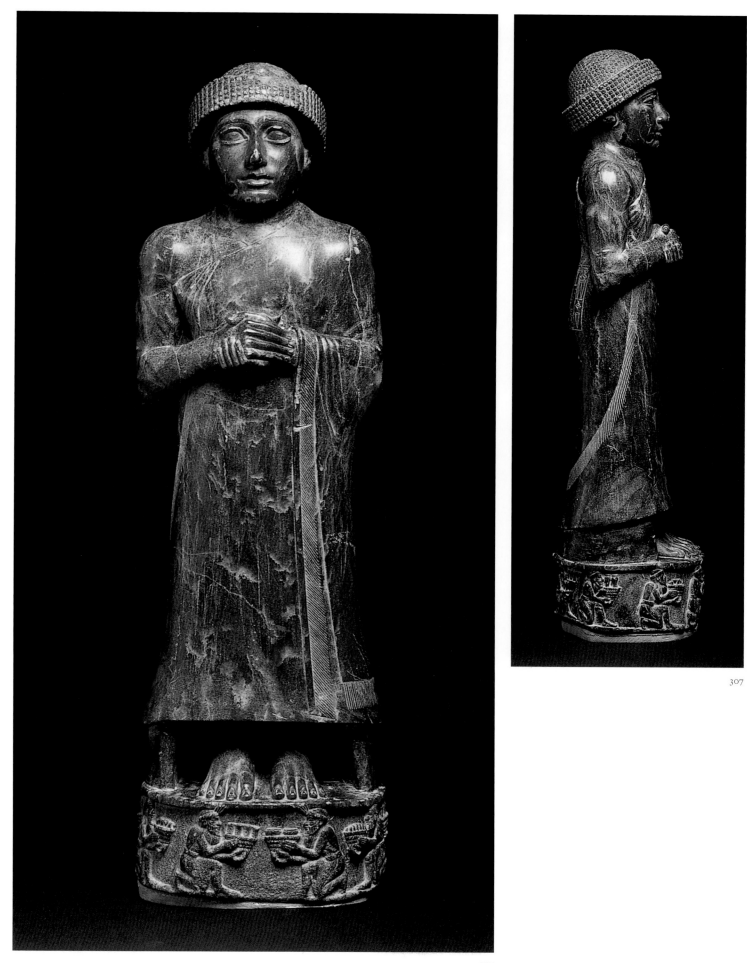

307

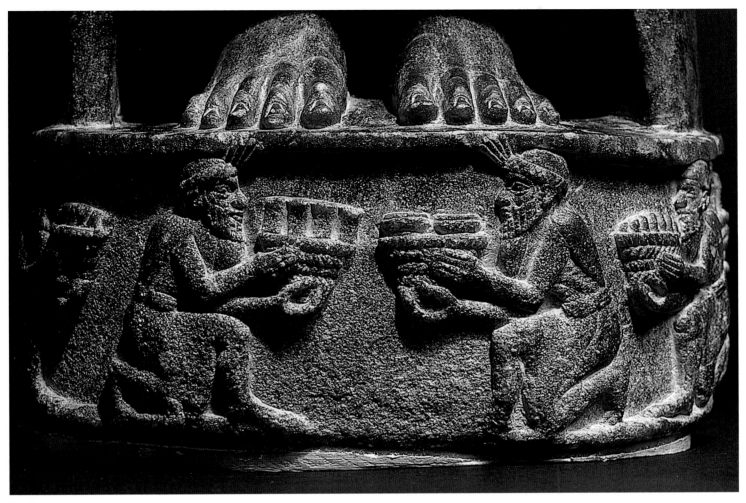

Detail, cat. no. 307.

and lips to manifest a unique psychological naturalism, and another thought the head disproportionate to the body—both opinions reflecting perhaps subtle differences with the Gudea examples.[3] Beneath the feet is a high base with an unusual scene depicting in relief kneeling men carrying objects, perhaps as tribute bearers.

The Louvre acquired its headless statue in 1925, the Metropolitan Museum acquired its head in 1947, and since 1974 the ensemble has been on exhibit alternately in New York City and Paris. We remain ignorant as to whether the head was broken from the statue in antiquity or shortly before 1925. According to the French excavators, local Arabs showed them the exact spot at Tello where statues—including this one of Ur-Ningirsu, minus its head—had been found.[4] The fact that the Louvre's and Metropolitan Museum's two sections join is very rare.[5] Equally rare is the stone, which is in the chlorite family.

As with other Gudea-period statues (see cat. nos. 305, 306), the present statue has its

detractors and defenders. Some accept the body as ancient but are not at ease with the head or the join, maintaining either that the head is ancient but does not in fact join the body or that the head is not ancient.[6] Several scholars accept the ensemble as ancient.[7] At least one condemns both body and head as modern.[8] The present author finds no problem with the ensemble, assuming that the head and body fit together naturally.   OWM

1. Steinkeller (1988, p. 51) allots Ur-Ningirsu and his successor together a total of at least five years of governance.
2. Parrot 1948, pp. 208–9, 170, 209, pl. 19:d; Hansen 1988, p. 12, figs. 11, 12; Schlossman 1978–79, p. 64, figs. 15–17. On the authenticity of the Berlin bearded torso (VA 8790), see Strommenger 1960, p. 67; Strommenger 1964, pl. 137; Orthmann 1975, p. 179, no. 64; Braun-Holzinger 1991, pp. 269–70, ST 137; and Suter 2000, p. 185. Concerning the small lamb bearer in Berlin (VA 8788), see Meissner 1928–29, pp. 5–6, pl. 4:1; Strommenger 1960, p. 67; Spycket 1981, p. 197, pl. 133; Braun-Holzinger 1991, pp. 269–70, ST 138; and Edzard 1997, p. 187.

3. Schlossman 1978–79, pp. 65–67; Amiet 1974, pp. 245–46.
4. Parrot 1948, pp. 158–59; Suter 2000, p. 36.
5. Among the many Gudea-type heads known (that is, of Gudea and Ur-Ningirsu), six were excavated: two at Tello, one of which wears a headdress or "turban," one from Nippur, and three from Ur; see Johansen 1978, p. 13, pls. 44–46, and Woolley 1955, pp. 51, 189, pl. 42. This modest corpus of provenienced works contrasts with the large number, about fourteen heads (not including the one under review here), known to me from the antiquities market. Several of the latter have been termed forgeries (Johansen 1978, p. 40, pls. 92, 93; Muscarella 2000, p. 174, nos. 1, 2). The head in Cleveland is probably modern (see Shepherd 1963, p. 246; contrast Johansen 1978, p. 23, pls. 80–83, 97–98), and the Leiden, Madrid, and Harvard heads are suspicious (Johansen 1978, pp. 27–28). Of the Gudea statues excavated at Tello, only one (Louvre Statue I) was recovered complete with its head (see entry for cat. no. 305). None of the other eleven joins with any known excavated or unexcavated head of Gudea.
6. Strommenger 1960, p. 67; Strommenger 1964, pl. 139; Opificius 1957–71, p. 397.
7. Parrot 1948, p. 208; Orthmann 1975, p. 178, pl. 62:a,b; Schlossman 1978–79, pp. 64–67; Spycket 1981, p. 195; Hansen 1988, p. 12; Suter 2000, p. 185.
8. Johansen 1978, p. 39.

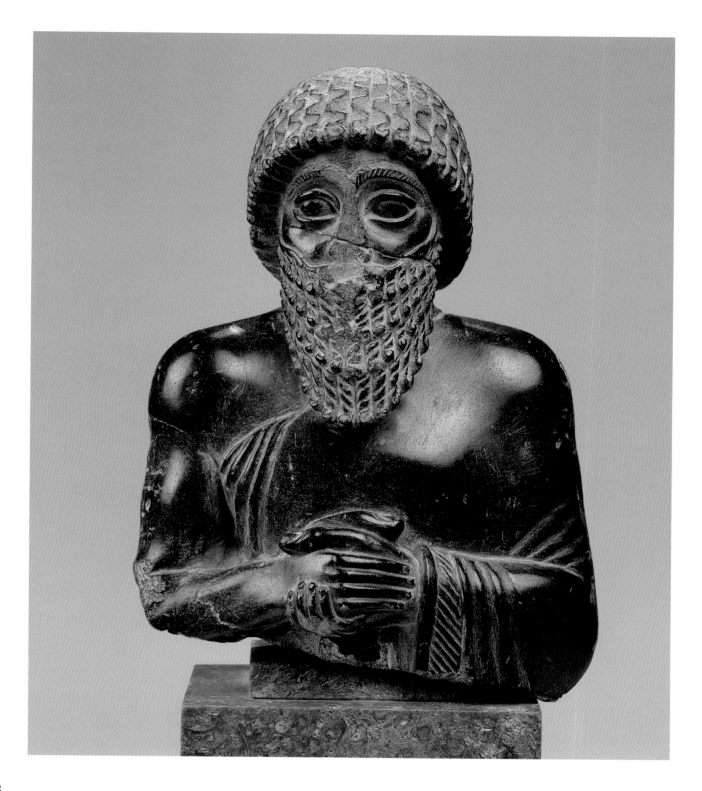

308

Fragment of a statue of Ur-Ningirsu

Cuneiform inscription in Sumerian
Diorite
H. 18 cm (7⅛ in.)
Mesopotamia, probably Girsu (modern Tello)
Second Dynasty of Lagash, reign of Ur-Ningirsu,
ca. 2080 B.C.
Staatliche Museen zu Berlin, Vorderasiatisches
Museum VA 8790

The few fragmentary statues of Ur-Ningirsu that have come down to us reveal iconographical contrasts with representations of his father and predecessor, Gudea.[1]

While Gudea presented himself as bald or with a highly stylized headgear and always beardless (see cat. nos. 305, 306), this image of Ur-Ningirsu recalls Akkadian traditions by displaying an exuberant beard and coiffure. His hairstyle consists of individual wavy

strands of hair, each ending in a curl. Together they cover the head like a wig or a fur cap, nearly obscuring the forehead, extending down to the nape of the neck and hiding the ears. Equally unusual for the period is the tapering beard, which consists of four tiers of carefully arranged locks that completely cover the lower half of the face. This way of representing hair and beard is reminiscent of earlier Akkadian sculpture, in which the rendering is quite similar. The upper part of the face is dominated by large eyes, with pronounced upper and lower lids and eyebrows that meet in the center. The nose and mouth are damaged.

Ur-Ningirsu's hands are folded in front of his chest in a gesture of prayer. His garment leaves his right shoulder bare and is secured above the right breast by a tucked-in corner of the fabric. The garment is obviously of finely woven cloth, for the modeling of the body, particularly of the upper left arm and the back, is visible beneath it. This simple garment, its sole decoration a fringed border, is typical of the late third millennium B.C.

The inscription on the back, a dedication from Ur-Ningirsu to his god Ningishzida, also states his relationship to Gudea: "For Ningishzida, his (personal) god, Ur-Ningirsu, ruler of Lagash, son of Gudea, ruler of Lagash." Comparison with a longer inscription on a different statue of Ur-Ningirsu has led a number of scholars to hypothesize that the present inscription originally included a second column, now missing because of the statue's fragmentary condition.   RH

1. See Spycket 1981, pp. 185ff; Marzahn 1987, pp. 29ff.; Braun-Holzinger 1991, pp. 269ff.; and Edzard 1997, p. 186.

309

Head of a ruler

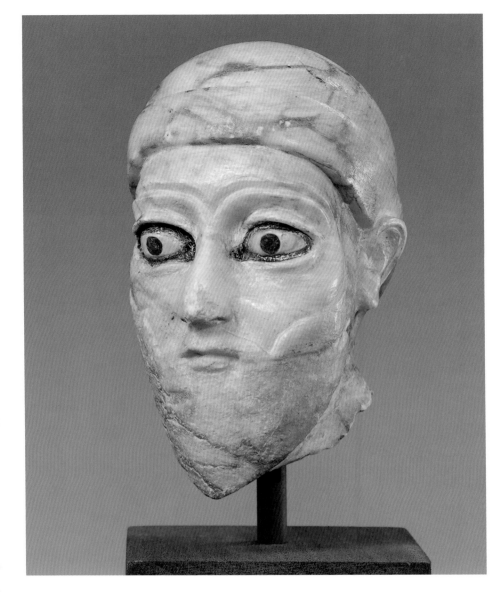

Gypsum, ivory, and bitumen; modern blue fill
H. 10.2 cm (4 in.); W. 6.4 cm (2½ in.)
Mesopotamia, Adab (modern Bismaya)
Ur III, ca. 2097–1989 B.C.
The Oriental Institute of the University of Chicago OIM A 173

This gypsum head is one of the most famous sculptures from the ancient Near East, partly because of the early date of its discovery and partly because of its delicate and naturalistic carving. It represents a man who is identified as a king by his rounded turban, which has a broad brim and leaves his ears exposed. The modeling of the face shows a striking sensitivity to the underlying skeletal structure, with high cheekbones, sunken temples, and a delicately arching nose, the tip of which has been damaged. The eyebrows, which meet over the bridge of the nose, were once inlaid in another material. The eyes still retain their original inlay of ivory set in bitumen; the blue paste pupils are a twentieth-century addition. The smoothness of the skin and turban contrasts with the rough surface of the mustache and pointed beard, which undoubtedly were added in a different material modeled to show the richly curled beard befitting a Mesopotamian monarch. A narrow strip of the forehead just below the turban is also rough, suggesting that the waves of hair protruding from under the brim—as, for example, on the figure of Ur-Namma on his famous stele (cat. no. 317; figs. 109, 110)[1]—were similarly added.

The Bismaya head has traditionally been dated to the Akkadian period. Henri Frankfort compared it to a famous copper-alloy head from Nineveh (fig. 57), now in Baghdad, commenting that they were so closely related "in style and type that the two cannot be separated."[2] He especially noted the similarities in the line of the beard on the cheek and the profile of the nose. However, the plain turban worn by this ruler is at home in the succeeding Ur III period, a date supported by the circumstances of its discovery. The head was found seventy centimeters below the surface, in a small chamber eight meters from the west corner of the temple terrace at Bismaya, along with a fragment of an inscribed stone vessel dedicated by Ur-Ashgi, governor of Adab, for the life of Shulgi.[3] If dated to the Ur III period, the head is one more bit of evidence that the attention to and success in depicting anatomical detail that were characteristic of Akkadian art did not end with that dynasty, as Jeanny Vorys Canby has already noted in her work on the Ur-Namma stele.[4]   KLW

1. See, for example, Canby 2001, pls. 3b, 31.
2. Frankfort 1943, p. 19.
3. Banks 1912, pp. 256–57; Wilson 2002, pp. 285–86.
4. Canby 2001, p. 10.

Female figure with clasped hands

Chlorite
H. 17.8 cm (7 in.); W. 11.8 cm (4⅝ in.); Thickness
6.7 cm (2⅝ in.)
Mesopotamia, Girsu (modern Tello)
Ur III, ca. 2097–1989 B.C.
Musée du Louvre, Département des Antiquités
Orientales, Paris AO 295

The statuette, whose lower part is lost, perhaps depriving us of an inscription that would identify its subject, is most likely an idealized votive portrait of a royal princess of Lagash.[1] A dozen incomplete statuettes of ladies of high rank were found on the site of Tello (ancient Girsu, capital of the state of Lagash). All are carved in a soft stone, such as chlorite or limestone; hard and precious diorite seems to have been reserved for representation of the sovereign. The female effigies are generally small, but this one, which when whole probably measured more than thirty centimeters in height, is an exception.

The details of the statuette are all characteristic of the period. The hair, wavy on the temples and pulled into a chignon on top of the head, is covered with a veil held by a headband around the forehead. A necklace composed of five rigid hoops encircles the neck. The clothing, made of a fringed material with scalloped edges, follows the contours of the body. The material lies flat against the chest, passes under the arms, and then crosses in the back to form a low **V** before covering both shoulders and falling in two symmetrical sections in front.[2]

The remarkably high quality of the sculpture and the articulation of the face lead us to believe this may be one of Gudea's wives, Ninalla—daughter of Ur-Ba'u, Gudea's predecessor on the throne of Lagash—or Geme-Shulpae. Women played an important role in the court of Lagash. The three daughters of Ur-Ba'u married three princes who each reigned subsequently, thus assuring the continuity of the Second Dynasty of Lagash and the legitimacy of its sovereigns.   BA–S

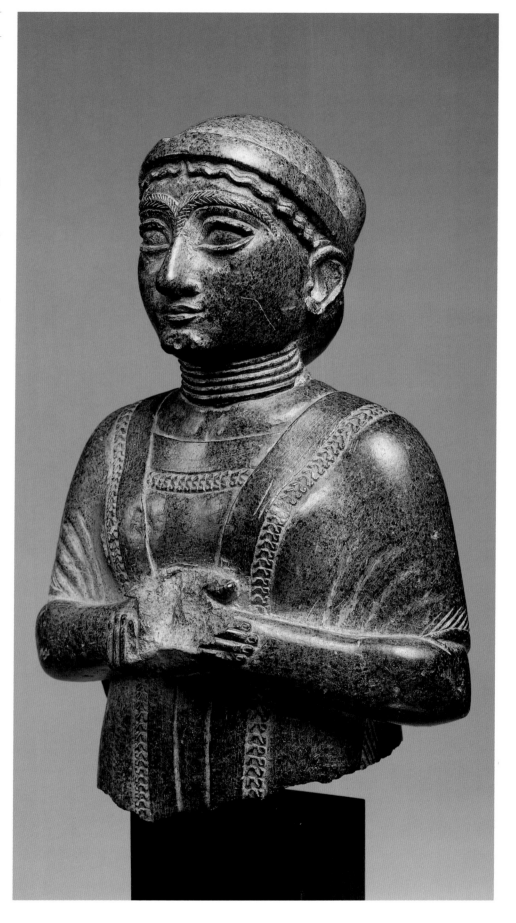

1. For further reference, see Sarzec and Heuzey 1884–1912, vol. 1, pp. 344–45, vol. 2, pl. 24bis, fig. 2a–d; Heuzey 1902, pp. 246–50, no. 105; Parrot 1948, pp. 190–91, fig. 41a; Spycket 1981, pp. 199ff., pl. 136a,b.
2. For sketches, see Heuzey and Heuzey (1935), pls. 42, 42bis.

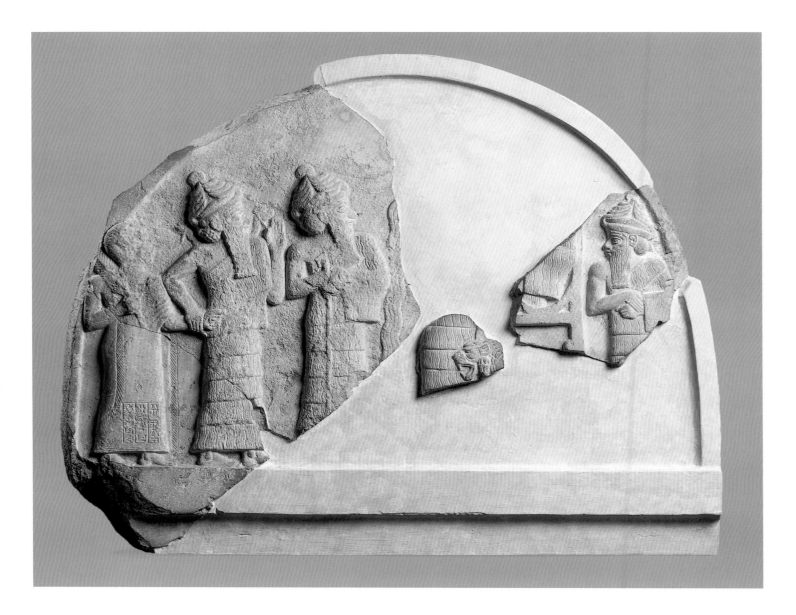

311

Fragments of a stele of Gudea

Cuneiform inscription in Sumerian
Limestone
H. 70.5 cm (27¼ in.); W. 65 cm (25⅝ in.)
Mesopotamia, Girsu (modern Tello)
Second Dynasty of Lagash, reign of Gudea,
ca. 2090 B.C.
Staatliche Museen zu Berlin, Vorderasiatisches
Museum; Gift of Julius Isaak 1892/93 VA 2796,
VA 2909

These relief fragments, combined to form a
stele, were bought on the art market, and
therefore we cannot know where they came
from or whether they were in fact part of a
single object. A number of fragments of similar
steles were discovered during archaeological

excavations at Tello. The relief presents a typical
motif from this period, a so-called presentation
scene, in which a lesser deity leads a supplicant
into the presence of a higher god, who is usually
enthroned. Here the supplicant is identified by
the brief inscription on his robe: "Gudea, ruler
of Lagash."

Gudea is bald, wears a long robe with
fringed edges, and carries a palm branch in his
right hand. The god Ningishzida, recognizable
from the dragon's heads emerging from his
shoulders, strides before him. He has grasped
Gudea's left wrist as he leads him—we know
this from comparable depictions on seals—
toward an enthroned deity. He is wearing a
horned crown shown en face and a flounced
robe that reaches down to his feet. His hair
is artfully tied up in back, and his beard falls

over his chest. His left hand is raised in greeting.
The god standing in front of him has not
been identified.

Since the scene is preserved only in fragments, the source of the streams of water in
front of this last figure can only be guessed at.
Often we see gods holding vessels from which
life-giving water pours forth (see cat. nos. 135,
139). In a less common variant "angel-like"
beings hovering in the sky are seen pouring
liquid out of a vessel (see fig. 109b).

The curved back of a throne and yet
another, somewhat smaller, deity are preserved
on the fragment at right. This piece and the
fragment at left were clearly the outer sections,
as we see from their rounded edges, and they
provide a good indication of the stele's original shape.

The enthroned deity has not survived but can be reconstructed through comparison with other monuments. Assuming that the position of this fragment is correct, and that the fragment with the lion (center) does not belong to the stele (see "Technical note," below), the streams of water suggest that he is Enki, the god of subterranean freshwater (see entry for cat. no. 141). A seal impression from Tello shows Gudea being led by Ningishzida into the presence of Enki, who is seated on a throne composed of vessels pouring forth water (fig. 107).[1]   RH

Technical note

According to Gudea Cylinder A, Gudea erected at least seven steles in the temple of Ningirsu, patron god of Girsu.[2] Excavations turned up no intact monuments but did uncover widely strewn fragments.[3] While only a few of these bear inscriptions, the majority of them have been ascribed to Gudea on the basis of the circumstances of their discovery or their style.[4]

Attempts to reconstruct the Gudea steles have drawn heavily on Cylinders A and B, in which Gudea's building activities and the rituals associated with them are described in detail. However, the only agreed-upon feature is the basic form of this stele, which is understood to have had a curved top and to have been divided into friezelike registers.[5]

The fragments of the curved top section shown here were presented to the Königliche Museen in Berlin by Julius Isaak in 1892 or 1893. All the other Gudea relief fragments in the Berlin collection were purchased in Baghdad in 1897.[6] However, the newly calculated radius of the curved section, clearly smaller than previously assumed, does not leave much room for additional figures in the reconstruction.[7]

In order to verify that the fragments in question are in fact related, an analysis of the limestone was undertaken.[8] This showed that two fragments, one with a god's head, once believed to belong to the seated deity,[9] and the other with a lion throne, differ significantly in chemical composition from the main stele fragments and from each other. Thus, earlier interpretations relating to the enthroned deity are rendered obsolete.[10] Since it is not known whether the backs as well as the fronts of Neo-Sumerian steles were carved, even the relative position of the two rim fragments is not certain. Proposals for the arrangement of

all Gudea stele fragments therefore can only be hypothetical, except when the fragments clearly fit together (compare cat. no. 317).

NC

1. Information in this entry is based on Braun-Holzinger 1991, pp. 269f., and Edzard 1997, p. 186.
2. Edzard 1997, pp. 83–84.
3. Suter 2000, pp. 161–64.
4. Börker-Klähn 1982, p. 141; Suter 2000, p. 161.
5. Suter 2000, pp. 277–80, 293–94; also Börker-Klähn 1982, pp. 20–21.
6. For want of documentation, it can only be assumed that the arrangement of the fragments was based on the thinking of the director in the early 1890s of the Vorderasiatische Abteilung, Friedrich Delitzsch, and his colleague Leopold Messerschmidt.
7. According to Börker-Klähn 1982, p. 23, the width was about 110 centimeters; according to a recent calculation by L. Martin, Vorderasiatisches Museum, Berlin, the width was 88 centimeters.
8. Two samples were taken from different spots on each fragment. They were tested by Gerwulf Schneider of the Arbeitgruppe Archäometrie at the Freie Universität, Berlin.
9. Börker-Klähn 1982, p. 142, no. 38.
10. E. Meyer 1906, pp. 49–51; G. Meyer 1965, p. 13; Boehmer 1967, pp. 290–91; Börker-Klähn 1982, p. 24; Suter 2000, p. 198.

312a, b

Foundation pegs naming Gudea

Cuneiform inscription in Sumerian
Copper alloy
Mesopotamia, Girsu (modern Tello)
Second Dynasty of Lagash, reign of Gudea,
ca. 2090 B.C.

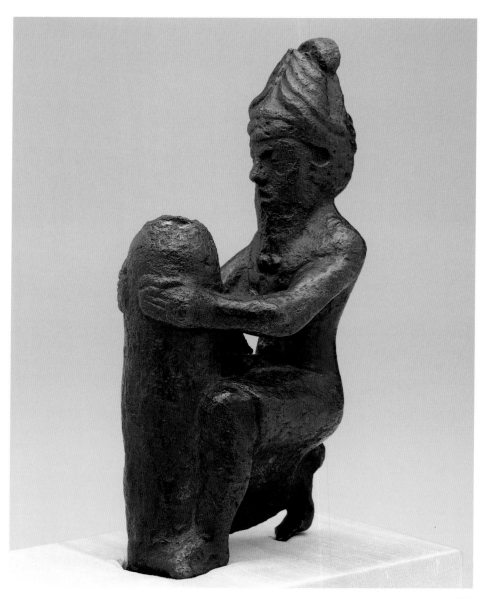

312a

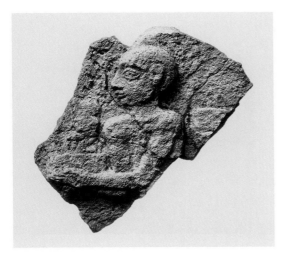

Fig. 108. Limestone stele fragment attributed to the reign of Gudea showing a foundation peg similar to catalogue numbers 312a,b. Girsu, ca. 2090 B.C. Musée du Louvre, Paris, AO 4581bis.

a. H. 20.3 cm (8 in.)
The Nelson-Atkins Museum of Art, Kansas City, Missouri; Purchase, Nelson Trust 30-1/50

b. H. 33.5 cm (13¼ in.)
The Metropolitan Museum of Art, New York; Lent by The Pierpont Morgan Library L.1995.61

Among the foundation figures recovered from the site of Tello, ancient Girsu, are examples in the form of a kneeling male deity wearing a horned headdress and holding a thick peg in his hands.[1] The figures date solely to the reign of Ur-Ba'u and his successor Gudea as *ensi* over the state of Lagash, of which Girsu was a principal city. Approximately twenty examples were excavated at Lagash and are divided among three museums: the Musée du Louvre in Paris, the Eski Şark Museum in Istanbul, and the Nelson-Atkins Museum of Art in Kansas City (cat. no. 312a).[2] At least fourteen examples have surfaced on the art market, whence derives the Pierpont Morgan Library example (cat. no. 312b); it is possible that all the purchased examples came from Tello, since this style of figure has not been found at other sites.[3] The deity kneels while also sitting astride a projecting ledge. He wears a short skirt and is apparently bare-chested, and his headdress is that of a deity bearing four pairs of horns. The peg he grasps in both hands projects below his legs so that when inserted into a brick the deity's body would be resting flush with the surface. Some of these figures, including the Morgan Library example (cat. no. 312b), bear an inscription on the peg and right thigh, mentioning various deities. A number of them were recovered at corners or doorways of a major building, set in pairs or in threes, and often placed in brick boxes, with inscribed tablets and sometimes along with another figure form.[4] This kneeling deity with a peg also appears in two-dimensional works of art from Gudea's time (fig. 108).[5] The identity of the deity remains unknown, though he might represent the personal god of Ur-Ba'u and Gudea. Perhaps he was a foundation for the dynasty as well as its temples and, as a peg incorporated into the building, may have been intended to bestow blessings on the kings for all time.   OWM

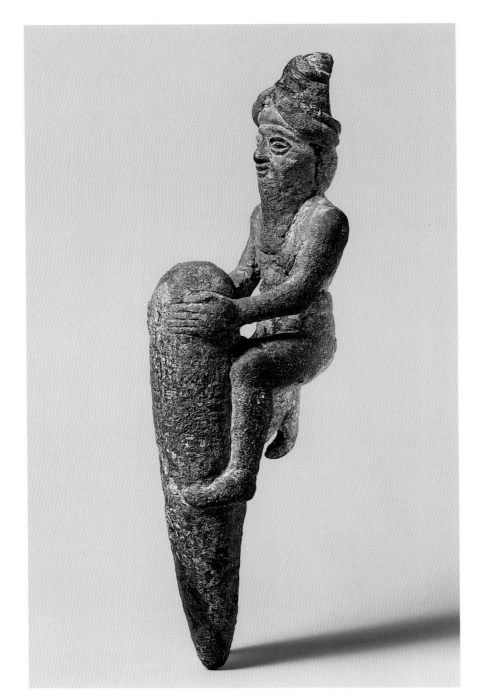

1. See Parrot 1948, pp. 202–5; Ellis 1968, pp. 60–62, figs. 17–19; Rashid 1983, pl. 39; and Suter 2000, pp. 53, 61–62, 313–20, figs. 6, 7.
2. For a list of excavated examples, see Ellis 1968, p. 61, n. 105; Schlossman 1976, pp. 9–10, n. 2; Strommenger 1957–71, pp. 683f.; Rashid 1983,

312b

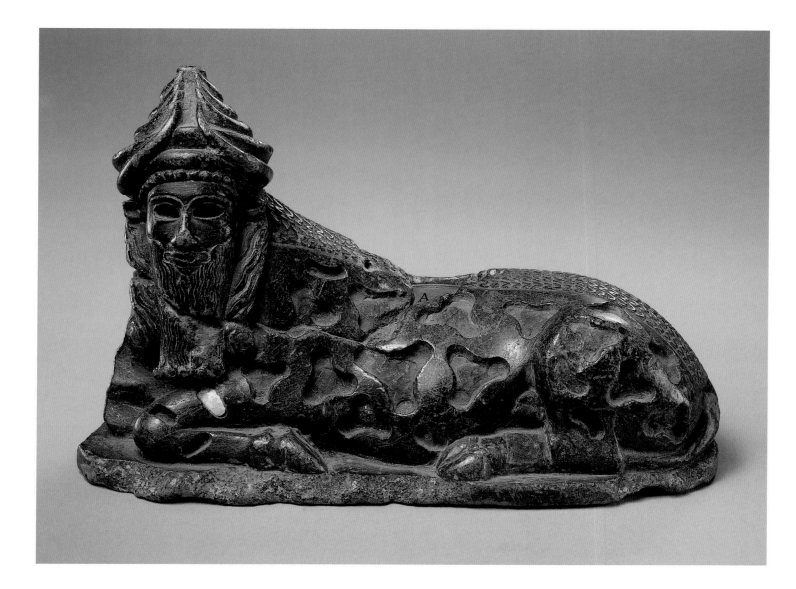

pp. 19–21; and Suter 2000, pp. 313–17. In addition, there are two in the Nelson-Atkins Museum of Art excavated at Tello, one example published here; see Taggart, McKenna, and Wilson 1973, vol. 2, pp. 10–11.
3. For twelve examples without provenience in museums, see Rashid 1983, pp. 21–22. In addition, there is one in the Cleveland Museum of Art and one in Japan, probably in the Hirayama collection in Kamakura; Hori 1983, no. 18; see also Muscarella 1988a, p. 312, n. 6.
4. Also, there may be tablets referring to different buildings and to different deities, a feature that has confused scholars: Ellis 1968, p. 62; Schlossman 1976, pp. 10–11.
5. Ellis 1968, figs. 15, 16; Schlossman 1976, pp. 13f.; Suter 2000, pp. 61, 368 st 55.

313

Recumbent human-headed bull or bison

Steatite and shell
H. 12 cm (4¾ in.); L. 19 cm (7½ in.)
Cavity: L. 4 cm (1⅝ in.)
Mesopotamia
Ur III, ca. 2097–1989 B.C.
Musée du Louvre, Département des Antiquités Orientales, Paris   AO 3146

Representations of bovines with human heads are found throughout the history of Mesopotamia. The creature is a *lama* deity: a beneficent, protective spirit—the bison—generally associated with the sun god, Shamash. Several statuettes dating to the late third millennium B.C. depict the god as bearded, with bovine ears

and a horned tiara, and in a recumbent position with its head turned. Such statuettes come from various Sumerian sites, with the majority from Tello,[1] although examples are also known from Syria (see cat. nos. 111, 157a).

This example displays particularly careful work;[2] the eyes and body have trilobate or, as in the paws, lozenge-shaped cavities that would have received inlay; a single shell element survives. An irregularly shaped elongated cavity located in the middle of the back, and also found on other examples, may have accommodated a removable offering bowl, in keeping with a usage attested in Mesopotamian iconography.[3] Two narrower horizontal perforations in front of that cavity, however, might lead one to think a small lid was meant to be attached to it.

BA–S

1. For a general study, see Huot 1978, pp. 104–10.
2. For further reference, see Heuzey 1900–1901, pp. 7–11 and pl. 1; Parrot 1948, p. 146 and pl. 12a; Huot 1978, pp. 106, 108; Spycket 1981, p. 220.
3. See especially the dog statuette from Tello, inscribed in the name of king Sumu-ilum of Larsa (nineteenth century B.C.), which bears on its back a mortise into which an unpolished tenon was inserted, supporting a small oval-shaped bowl (Parrot 1948, pl. 31). That example may be a reuse. Glyptic iconography also depicts a seated deity—most often Shamash—placing his foot on the back of similar hybrid creatures (see, for example, Huot 1978, n. 1, fig. 4e), which may lead one to believe they served as supports for divine statuettes, but that is less likely.

that period symbolized vigor and fecundity more than any particular deity.

The statuette rests on a rectangular plinth; underneath it, part of a strong tenon attached to the initial section of the two horizontal shanks is still visible. These might be the remnants of two rings of a terret, and the animal may have been part of the decoration of a rein ring, such as those found in the cemeteries at Ur or Kish (see cat. no. 66).[3] The immobility of this figure may indicate a date later than that of those examples, in which the animal figure is represented in motion.   FD

1. For further reference, see Heuzey 1902, no. 173, and Caubet and Bernus-Taylor 1991, p. 24.
2. A copper alloy comprising the following percentages of metals: Copper, 88.070; arsenic, 11.258; cobalt, 0.8; nickel, 0.135; silver, 0.188; tin, 0.026; gold, 0.015; lead, 0.074; bismuth, 0.007. Analysis by the Centre de Recherche et de Restauration des Musées de France, Paris.
3. Calmeyer 1964, pp. 68–84.

314

Inlaid bull statuette

Arsenical copper and silver
H. 11.2 cm (4⅜ in.); L. 9.7 cm (3⅞ in.); W. 3.7 cm (1½ in.)
Mesopotamia
End of the 3rd millennium B.C.
Musée du Louvre, Département des Antiquités Orientales, Paris AO 2151

This bull statuette attests not only to the great technical mastery achieved by the metallurgists of the third millennium B.C. but also to their remarkable talent in depicting animals.[1] It was cast using the lost-wax technique in a metal composed of copper and arsenic[2] and was inlaid with fine strips of silver that realistically evoke the fur of the animal. Very few examples are known of this delicate inlay technique. Statuettes of stags and bulls crowning standards discovered at Alaca Höyük and dating from the second half of the third millennium B.C. were, it seems, decorated using the same process (see cat. no. 188; fig. 78).[3]

The young bull depicted here stands firmly on his slender, sinewy legs, and the hoofs are carefully detailed. The muscular mass of the shoulders and hindquarters is stylized with restraint; the subtle modeling is accentuated by the silver inlays. The muzzle is short, with an emphasis placed on the long, curved horns characteristic of representations of bulls in the Early Dynastic period (see cat. no. 42). The eyes have lost their inlay, as has the small triangular cavity on the forehead. This cavity is found on many depictions of bovine heads, such as those that adorned the lyres discovered at Ur (see cat. no. 58). It probably denoted the sacred character of the animal, which during

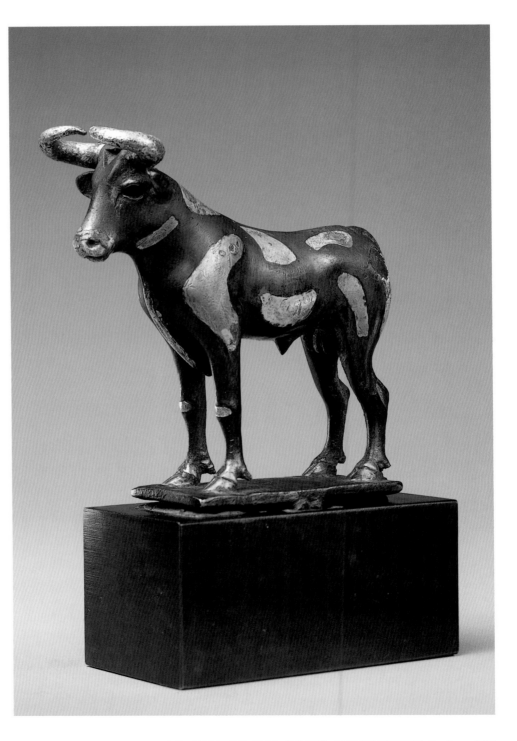

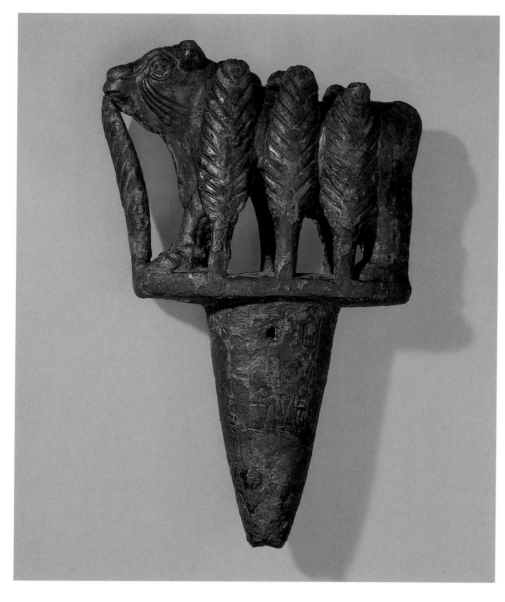

Shulgi.[2] The bull calf, therefore, appears to have had an established relationship with goddesses. However, the palm fronds here may relate to ideas of kingship. Three stele fragments are known that depict Gudea carrying—in his right hand—a palm frond shaped exactly like those surrounding the bull. Claudia Suter suggests that the palm may have been identified with the royal insignium, the word for which in texts is usually translated as "scepter."[3] Since texts compare Gudea to a bull raising his horns on entering a temple,[4] it is possible that this image relates to the ruler's association with the goddess.   PC

1. Edzard 1997, pp. 125–26.
2. All three pegs are in the Musée du Louvre, Paris; see Suter 2000, p. 64.
3. Ibid., pp. 291–92.
4. Gudea Cylinder B, lines 1238–40, The Electronic Text Corpus of Sumerian Literature, http://www-etcsl.orient.ox.ac.uk/section2/tr217.htm, accessed June 17, 2002.

316

Lid decorated with intertwined snakes

Steatite
L. 11.3 cm (4½ in.); W. 7.5 cm (3 in.)
Mesopotamia, Girsu (modern Tello), Ningishzida temple
Ur III, ca. 2097–1989 B.C.
Musée du Louvre, Département des Antiquités Orientales, Paris AO 12843

This lid fit onto the lower part of a box or lamp.[1] The inside face has a flat edge about 0.5 centimeters wide, which is slightly recessed in relation to the central surface to assure a tight fit. A circular perforation (diam. 0.35 cm) through the center of the protruding section formed by two snake heads indicates that a peg held the two parts of the object together, creating a pivoting lid. The top is sculpted in relief with an ornamental motif of two complete, interlacing snakes, their heads close together. The body of a third snake constricts, harmonizing the entanglement.

The lid, exhumed from the ruins of the temple of Ningishzida in Tello, was part of the cultic implements of the god. Henri de Genouillac said he had found "nearly everywhere on this site fragments of terracotta boxes and lids with reliefs of snakes."[2]

315

Foundation peg with a bull and palm fronds

Cuneiform inscription in Sumerian
Copper alloy
H. 19.4 cm (7⅝ in.); L. 12 cm (4¾ in.)
Mesopotamia
Second Dynasty of Lagash, reign of Gudea, ca. 2090 B.C.
Trustees of The British Museum, London BM 135993

This foundation peg is outstanding in both subject and quality of execution; its rectangular plinth is surmounted by a standing bull surrounded by tall reeds or palm fronds. On either side of the animal are three stalks, while a seventh frond, in front of the bull, touches its mouth. The bull is very carefully modeled, with its head shown facing forward; the small horns suggest that the animal is a calf. The eyelids are thick, and several folds of skin seem to stretch from the nostrils to the nape of the neck. The tail reaches the ground. The cuneiform inscription on the peg records the rebuilding of the temple of the goddess Nanshe in her city of Nina (modern Zurghul) by Gudea.[1] Nanshe belongs to the local pantheon of the city-state of Lagash, but there is no textual evidence connecting the goddess with a bull. The closest parallels are three foundation pegs from Tello, all depicting a bull calf lying down on a plinth surmounting the peg. Two record Gudea's construction of Inanna's temple E-anna, and a third is dedicated to Nanshe by the ruler

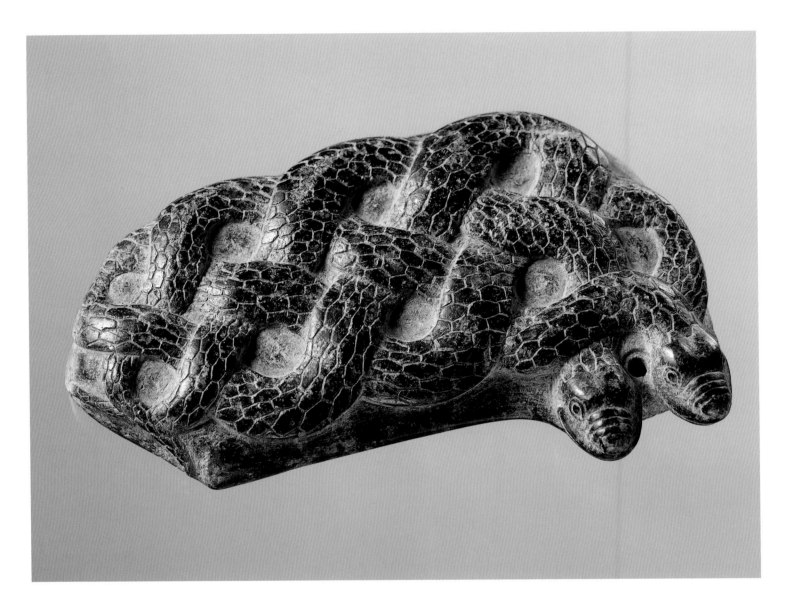

Ningishzida, the personal god of Gudea whose name may mean "lord of the true wood," is a chthonic deity; he disappears underground, into the underworld, on a seasonal basis. He is connected to vegetation, perhaps to the growth of the date palm—the only tree in the land of Sumer—which has sinuous roots and a trunk that is scaly like a snake. He is also associated with the horned snake dragon.

BA–S

1. For further reference, see Genouillac 1930, pp. 169–86; Genouillac 1934–36, vol. 2, p. 36, pl. C and 85; Parrot 1948, pp. 197, 199, fig. 42g; Spycket 1981, pl. 136:a, b. Genouillac (1930, p. 178) considered the object a "lamp cover," a hypothesis adopted by Parrot (1948, p. 199) and accepted ever since. The form favors that hypothesis, but the pivot hole leads us to believe it is a box.
2. Genouillac 1930, p. 178.

317

Fragment of "Ur-Namma" stele

Pink-buff limestone
H. 105 cm (39⅝ in.); W. 71.8 cm (28¼ in.); Thickness 11 cm (4⅜ in.)
Mesopotamia, Ur
Ur III, reign of Ur-Namma, ca. 2097–2080 B.C.
University of Pennsylvania Museum of Archaeology and Anthropology, Philadelphia   CBS 16676.14

In the 1920s the University of Pennsylvania and British Museum expedition to Ur, led by Sir Leonard Woolley, discovered hundreds of pieces belonging to a tall royal stele that had stood in a courtyard just below the ziggurat terrace and seemed to honor Ur-Namma, the founder of Ur's Third Dynasty. The stele was once more than ten feet high and had five registers of relief scenes on each side (see figs. 109a,b). In 1927

the best pieces were assembled into a reconstructed stele by Paul Casci, a restorer from the Galleria degli Uffizi in Florence; the project was supervised by the Sumerologist Leon Legrain, who was the curator of the Babylonian Collection at the University of Pennsylvania Museum and a member of the Ur expedition. In the same year Legrain published a description of the work, "The Stela of the Flying Angels."[1] Woolley's description appeared in 1974.[2]

However, this original analysis of the scenes and the stele's reconstruction and publication were somewhat hasty and in some cases inaccurate. In 1986 a careful reexamination of the reconstruction and of the many other pieces conscientiously saved by Woolley and stored in the University of Pennsylvania Museum's basement led to the discovery of new details that enlarged and clarified the

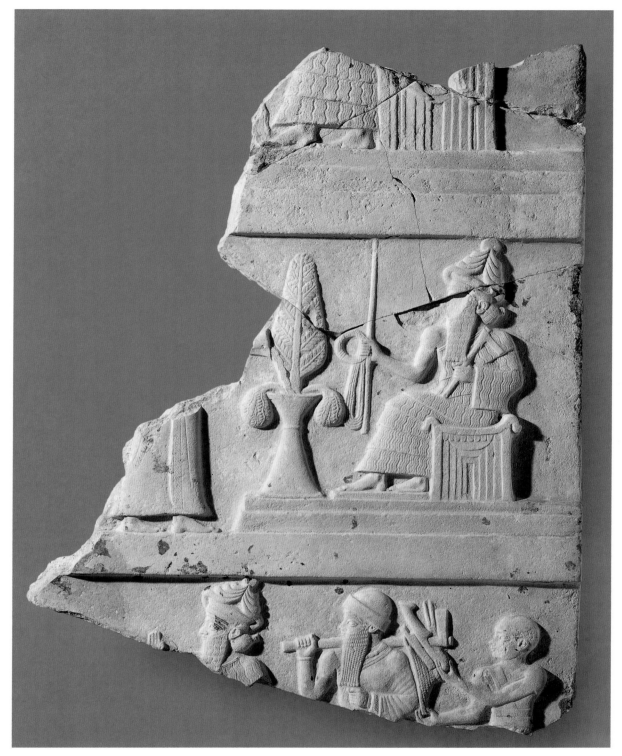

317

stele's famous scenes. As a result the monument was dismantled, the pieces cleaned and reconsolidated, and the correct reconstruction established. In addition, since no photograph could illustrate every detail, carefully measured, tonal drawings were made of the more than one hundred separate pieces carrying recognizable relief. The reconstruction on paper (figs. 109a,b) contains only those elements where the placement is certain and some fairly obvious restorations. Each fragment is numbered; some fragments are made up of joining pieces. The two faces are now labeled "good" and "poor," reflecting the condition of the surface and replacing the old designations "obverse" and "reverse," for which there is as yet no evidence. The project was recently published.[3] The relief's elegance and consistently delicate carving, now visible, will astonish those who know the monument only from old photographs.

Enough of the stele is preserved to confirm the sequence of registers on both sides. Various aspects of kingship are illustrated, part metaphorically, part literally. Some scenes are unique; others are striking variations on older compositions. Recently the

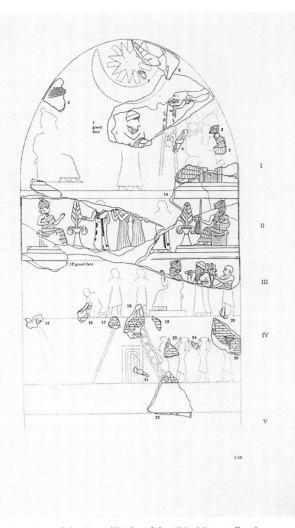

Fig. 109a. Drawing of the "good" side of the "Ur-Namma" stele (cat. no. 317).

Fig. 109b. Drawing of the "poor" side of the "Ur-Namma" stele (cat. no. 317).

piece bearing the name Ur-Namma was found to be carved of a different stone from the other pieces. Still, both its subject matter and its style suggest that the monument belongs to Ur-Namma's era. Like works of the preceding Akkadian Dynasty, it displays an interest in anatomical detail and remarkable skill in depicting it, vigorous poses, and scenes that break through the register system.

Displayed in the current exhibition is fragment 14, which includes parts of registers I, II, and III. Register II is the only one preserved in its full (five-foot) width. The right-hand section (fragment 14) is in almost mint condition, even though the six pieces that make it up were separated for more than three and a half millennia. Two had been reused as sockets for door poles. On this fragment can be seen the extraordinary sensitivity of the carving, not just of the face but also of the elegant feet and the muscular structure of the arms,

chest, and shoulder, even when hidden under heavy clothing.

On the left side of the scene (fragment 12), a goddess, wearing a heavy crown with four horns and the typical deity's robe made of rows of tufts, is seated on a dais. She holds out her left hand in greeting toward a king wrapped in a plain long robe, who is followed by a minor goddess in a clinging pleated gown. The heads of both are missing, but the figures are easily identified from their costumes. The king pours a libation into a small tree standing in a vessel set before the goddess. At the right, on the fragment exhibited, another, plumper figure of a king, facing the opposite way, repeats this ritual before a male deity. The god holds in his extended right hand a short staff and a coil made of five strands of rope, its dangling ends looped up. This is not the familiar rod-and-ring symbol—perhaps the ropes are those the king used to bind enemies, through a nose ring.[4]

At the right above this scene is a corner of the stele's curved top register. It shows the lower part of a seated divinity who holds a figure on its lap. The scene was identified by Woolley and others as a goddess holding an infant. Recently, fragments of the upper part of the seated figure showing a male hairdo under which a large, adult hand encircles the shoulders were found among those stored in the University of Pennsylvania Museum. These suggest, on the contrary, that the deity was a god with a goddess seated on his lap. The king stands before them, hand raised in greeting; too little is preserved of this upper section for further identification.

Below the main scene on fragment 14 is the right upper corner of register III. A bald servant, at far right, helps a king carry building tools hung over an axe on his shoulder—a basket for making clay mortar and a collapsed plough for digging the earth to make mud bricks. That a ceremony existed for making the first brick of a building is known from texts. The king and servant stand behind a seated god who raises his hand in awe as he gazes at a building under construction beneath him that is preserved on a group of small fragments. These depict workmen carrying baskets of clay, one climbing a ladder up to where the king sits, another leaning over the roof. The god who sits in front of the king makes a gesture of greeting to the structure, an act that mirrors the praise addressed to personified temples in Sumerian hymns. This scene, like the wrestling scene on the opposite side, occupies two registers.

Register I of the opposite, "poor," face shows two kings back-to-back. One pours a libation into a tree. The scene below that, in register II, involves butchering and a chariot in front of a row of standards. Registers III and IV depict various aspects of a wrestling match, observed by a king and a deity seated on elevated platforms. Below two drummers with an enormous round drum are the remains of a two-line cuneiform Sumerian inscription; they mention several canals dug by the king and enumerate curses directed at any who would "do evil against" the monument. Register V shows the worship of a king.

JVC

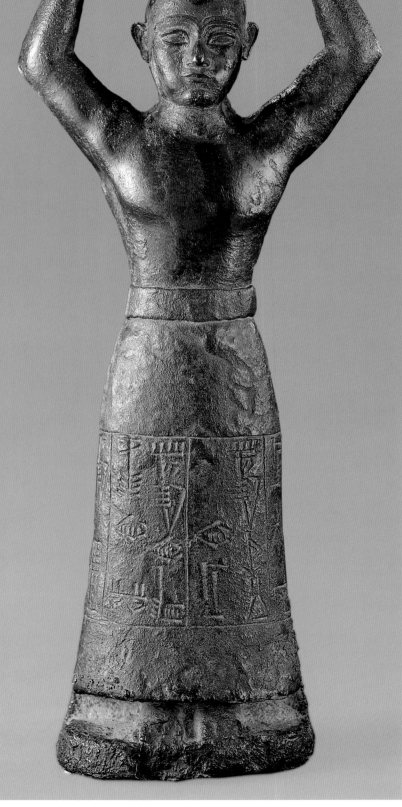

318a

1. Legrain 1927, pp. 75–98.
2. Woolley 1974, pp. 75–81.
3. Canby 2001.
4. As they were at Sar-i Pul, Iran, at the end of the third millennium B.C. (see Börker-Klähn 1982, no. 31), or by Esarhaddon in the seventh century B.C. (ibid., no. 219).

318a, b

Foundation figures of Ur-Namma holding a basket

Cuneiform inscription in Sumerian
Copper alloy
Mesopotamia
Ur III, reign of Ur-Namma, ca. 2097–2080 B.C.

a. H. 33.5 cm (13¼ in.); W. 13 cm (5⅛ in.)
The Pierpont Morgan Library, New York; MLC2

b. H. 27.3 cm (10¾ in.)
The Metropolitan Museum of Art, New York; Gift of Mrs. William H. Moore, 1947 47.49

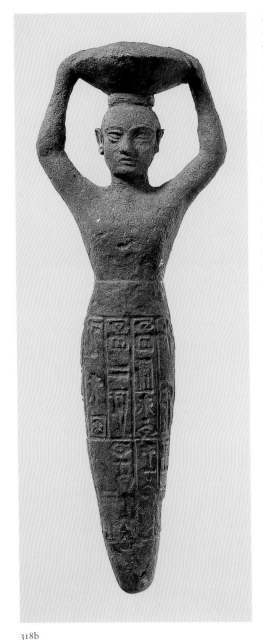

318b

Anthropomorphic figures were deposited in the foundation of Mesopotamian buildings beginning no later than the Early Dynastic II or III periods (see entry for cat. no. 39). During the reign of Ur-Namma (ca. 2097–2080 B.C.) there came into use two new varieties of metal foundation peg, both in the form of a human figure with a basket. The first form (cat. no. 318a) depicts a man with a bare torso wearing a long skirt extending to the feet, which stand on a narrow, flat base.[1] The second (cat. no. 318b) essentially continues the typical earlier form of a clean-shaven man with bare torso tapering into a peg, now blunt and rounded. The head is bald, however, and the face is serene, with calm eyes and proportionally rendered nose and mouth.

Inscriptions on the peg or on any accompanying tablet confirm that both types functioned to record the king's building works. Excavated Ur III pegs are known from Ur, Nippur, Tello, Uruk, and Susa, and many examples without provenience are also known.[2] The other Ur III ruler whose foundation pegs survive is Ur-Namma's successor, Shulgi.[3] Under this king only the traditional peg form was deposited.[4] There are noticeable differences in the form of the face and arms of figures from the two reigns.[5] The last examples of foundation pegs appear in the reign of Rim-Sin, king of Larsa (ca. 1807–1748 B.C.).[6] The full number of all foundation pegs known, excavated or otherwise, is about 180.[7]

OWM

1. This long-skirted form is basically related to the full-bodied, short-skirted form, introduced by Gudea of Lagash, that stands on a short peg; see Ellis 1968, p. 61, figs. 19 (of Gudea), 22 (of Ur-Namma). The Pierpont Morgan Library figure (cat. no. 318a) was acquired in the early 1900s; see Schlossman 1976, p. 16, n. 27.

2. V. Crawford 1959, pp. 78, 81–82; Ellis 1968, pp. 63–69; Rashid 1957–71, pp. 658–59; Rashid 1983, pp. 24–35; and Muscarella 1988a, pp. 305–13.

3. Ellis 1968, p. 65. Rashid (1957–71, p. 658, and table 1, cols. 12, 13) places two dealer-derived figurines as "wohl aus Ur stammen" (probably from Ur) and "wohl aus Girsu" (probably from Girsu), but with no evidence. Rashid (1983, p. 35, nos. 170, 171) lists both examples correctly as "Kunsthandel" (art market).

4. See Zettler 1987a, pp. 29ff., figs. 3, 4, 6–9, for an example of a Shulgi foundation peg in its deposit box excavated at Ur.

5. Muscarella 1988a, pp. 305–13, nos. 435, 436.

6. Rashid 1983, pp. 37–40; Zettler 1987a, p. 34, fig. 13:a,b.

7. Muscarella 1988a, p. 312, n. 6; Rashid (1983) lists 178, but others periodically turn up in dealers' shops or auction houses.

319

Cylinder seal of Hashamer with a presentation scene

Cuneiform inscription in Sumerian
Greenstone
H. 5.3 cm (2⅛ in.); Diam. 3 cm (1⅛ in.)
Mesopotamia
Ur III, reign of Ur-Namma, ca. 2097–2080 B.C.
Trustees of The British Museum, London BM 89126

This seal, the only example with an inscription mentioning king Ur-Namma, is of very high quality. It is carved with one of the best-known themes in the large corpus of third-millennium glyptic, the presentation scene, in which a goddess leads a male figure by the hand toward a seated god or king.[1] During the Ur III period, the presentation scene was

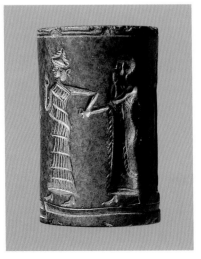

319

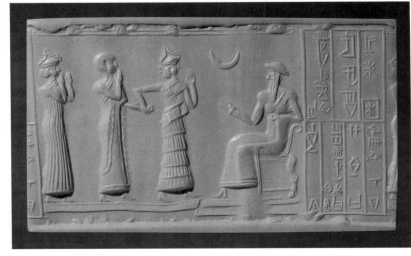

Impression from catalogue number 319.

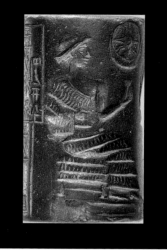

320

Impression from catalogue number 320.

ubiquitous on seals, and it has been suggested that the seal owners and rulers were depicted with specific features.[2] At the right (as seen in the modern impression) is a seated male figure extending his right hand toward a goddess wearing a frontally depicted multiple-horned crown and a flounced robe. She, in turn, is leading a man by the hand who is dressed in a long, fringed garment, and whose right arm is bent in the gesture of worship. Behind him stands another goddess, with both hands raised, wearing a striated robe and a multiple-horned headdress. The seated figure, who is bearded, wears a plain robe, a bracelet on his right wrist, and a brimmed hat typical of a Mesopotamian ruler. The chair on which he sits, whose rear leg is shaped like a bull's, is raised on a two-stepped altar beneath a crescent moon. Unlike the figures on most seals of this genre, the seated man here does not hold a cup in his raised hand. A seven-line inscription identifies the ruler as Ur-Namma and the seal owner as Hashamer, administrator of Ishkun-Sin on behalf of the king.[3]   PC

1. Franke 1977, pp. 61–66.
2. Winter 1987a, pp. 69–93.
3. Frayne 1997, pp. 88–89.

320

Cylinder seal with a presentation scene

Cuneiform inscription in Sumerian
Hematite
H. 2.8 cm (1⅛ in.); Diam. 1.7 cm (¹¹/₁₆ in.)
Mesopotamia
Ur III, reign of Ibbi-Sin, ca. 2013–1989 B.C.
The Metropolitan Museum of Art, New York, Gift of Martin and Sarah Cherkasky, 1988   1988.380.2

A presentation scene before a seated deity, which became an increasingly popular subject in Akkadian-period glyptic (see cat. no. 143), was the most common motif on cylinder seals of the Ur III period.[1] In this impression,[2] the bald, clean-shaven worshiper at the left, wearing a long, fringed robe and holding the palm of his right hand before his mouth, presumably is the seal's owner, Ilum-bani, identifiable from the framed, eight-line text panel:[3]

> Ibbi-Sin, the mighty king, king of Ur, king of the world (literally, four corners)— Ilum-bani, the overseer, son of Ili-ukin, (is) your servant.

He is led by a goddess wearing a flounced robe that drapes over her left shoulder and a cap with four pairs of horns. She grasps his left wrist in her right hand, raises her left hand in a salute, and presents the worshiper to the seated figure of a deified king,[4] apparently a young Ibbi-Sin, who, in the inscription, is identified with the divine determinative.[5] He, too, wears a flounced garment draped over his left shoulder and a brimmed cap. Seated on a padded stool set on a low platform, he holds forth a cup perched on his pursed fingertips.[6] A star disk within a crescent moon occupies the upper field in front of the king.

These seals, highly standardized in both their iconography and their inscription formulas, were apparently "restricted to a class of high public officials ranking just below the king in the administrative hierarchy."[7]

RW

1. Collon 1982, p. 129.
2. See Pittman 1987, pp. 56, 79, no. 23.
3. Winter 1986, p. 253.
4. For the general characteristics of this motif, see Collon 1982, p. 161.
5. Winter 1987a, p. 74.
6. For oil as the possible content of this vessel, see Winter 1986, pp. 260–62.
7. Winter 1987a, p. 70.

LITERATURE
AND LEGACY

This speech was long and difficult to understand. . . . Because the messenger's mouth was too heavy and he could not repeat it, the king of Kulaba formed some clay and put words on it as if on a tablet. Before that time the inscribing of words on clay (tablets) did not exist; but now, in the sun of that day, it was indeed so!

Enmerkar and the Lord of Aratta

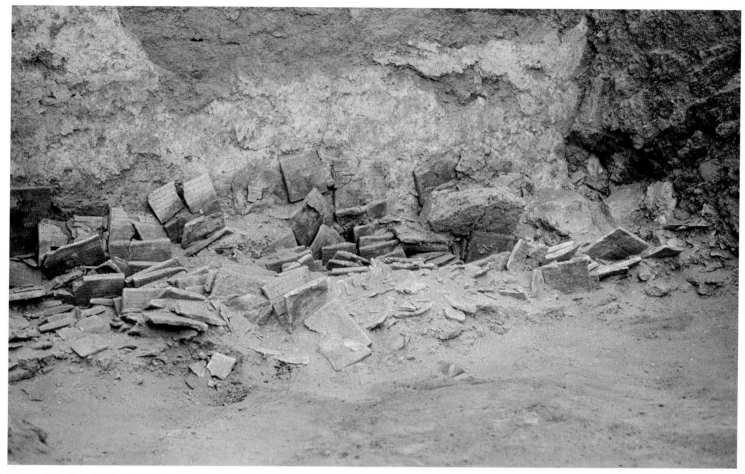

Tablets of the Great Archive (L.2769) in situ, Palace G, Ebla.

THE EARLIEST
SCHOLASTIC TRADITION

PIOTR MICHALOWSKI

THE BEGINNINGS OF WRITING

Sometime about 3200 B.C. people living far apart, in Egypt and in southern Mesopotamia (Sumer), discovered ways of systematically preserving complex information about the world outside human memory, independently inventing the first writing systems.[1] Sumerian writing was executed by means of a reed stylus on clay tablets. At first, signs were drawn in the clay, but the process soon changed to impressing strokes. The slanted tip of the stylus gave rise to the modern name *cuneiform,* which means "wedge-shaped" in Latin. Some think that this writing method developed from earlier forms of counting, but there are good reasons to think that it was an entirely new technology, invented as a system.

The earliest known cuneiform writing was clearly designed for complex accounting and bookkeeping. It consisted of approximately sixty different number signs and more than nine hundred ideograms; if we include various combinations and modifications, the number rises to more than nineteen hundred. Its discrete symbols stood for nouns, primarily names of commodities, as well as a few basic adjectives and perhaps some administrative actions, but with no grammatical elements. In theory, such a system could be read in any language, and some have speculated that it may represent a hitherto unattested pre-Sumerian language; but most scholars still insist that the underlying language was Sumerian.

We might also well speculate that others, in Mesopotamia and elsewhere, had developed complex private accounting methods that disappeared together with their inventors.[2] Cuneiform was different, however; it not only was practical and efficient but also carried with it the means of its own reproduction both in space and in time. We have more than five thousand early texts from the southern Sumerian city of Uruk,

representing several phases of the earliest writing: 85 percent of these tablets are administrative accounts; the remaining 15 percent are multiple duplicates of thematic lists of words.[3] These lists, mundane though they may seem, are the visible marks of the educational system that was used to train new scribes and reproduce the writing system for succeeding generations. No doubt much of the instruction was oral, if the later analogies are of any use, but the copying of such lists constituted the primary manner of learning actual writing. Although few such study tablets that correspond to the earliest forms of Uruk writing have been found, the very fact that they exist at all is enough to suggest that these lists were meant to be part of the system from the very beginning. And as soon as writing spread beyond southern Mesopotamia to the north, the school texts were exported as well. The site of Jamdat Nasr, not far from the northern Babylonian city of Kish, has offered up a sizable number of tablets roughly contemporary with the last stages of the Uruk archives, including duplicates of two archaic word lists.

More than fourteen such thematic lists have survived from Uruk, and five of them are attested among the earliest tablets. The two most common among them are a list of official titles and professional names, which is documented by 185 examples, and a list of containers known from ninety-one exercises. By contrast, a text enumerating various plant names is only attested in five exemplars, while a list of names of pigs is known merely from two tablets. Other compositions include names of grains, metals, wood, cattle, and fish, as well as geographic names. These texts all share the same structure: they consist of entries made up of the numerical sign "one," which means simply "item," followed by a noun. One enigmatic text, known as the Tribute List, has vexed scholars, and on the basis of later versions it has even been suggested that it is the earliest known literary text, but this remains very doubtful. Among the unique features of this composition is the repetition of signs in various groupings, testifying to its didactic function.

Two characteristics of these early scholastic exercises stand out: the long life and the rigid nature of this textual tradition. Lexical texts, albeit often in very different forms, retained their central place in scribal education for thousands of years, perhaps as late as the second or even third century A.D.[4] A few of the earliest such texts, including the well-documented professions list, remained virtually unchanged until the beginning of the second millennium B.C., when they were finally abandoned in favor of less anachronistic compositions. This is all the more remarkable since the writing system underwent many changes in the intervening periods, and most of the words and many of the signs had long gone out of use. Indeed, only a handful of new lists appears in the Early Dynastic period, and it is possible that some of them existed earlier but remain to be found. The ones that are new demonstrate a need to modernize the lexical tradition in the light of current language use. Already in the Uruk period there is a remarkable homogeneity in the tradition—there are very few variants; this makes one suspect that students learned by copying clay examples rather than by memorization and dictation, which was often the norm later.

The history of cuneiform is marked by discontinuities in the archaeological record: periods of bounty are often followed by stretches with little or no documentation. This in no way reflects ancient writing practices; rather, it is a function of the way texts were stored and of the vagaries of archaeological discovery. Cuneiform tablets were not kept indefinitely, and most archives cover no more than two or, at the most, three generations. School texts were also kept only for short periods of time, and therefore we find concentrations of such texts in archaeological levels immediately preceding destruction or abandonment of buildings as well as in secondary and even tertiary contexts, often discarded far from their original place of storage. And so it was in the case of the earliest phases of the history of writing.

EARLY DYNASTIC DEVELOPMENTS

Although the art of writing was undoubtedly widely employed in the Late Uruk period, we have absolutely no documentation for its use in the immediate aftermath of the Uruk collapse. Texts from the city of Ur, dated approximately a century after the last archaic ones, demonstrate subtle changes in the use of cuneiform and amply document the underlying Sumerian language, primarily, although not exclusively, by means of the notation of Sumerian personal names. Similar to the earlier situation, these are almost all accounts, but some thirty scribal exercises, including the ubiquitous professional names list, provide a small glimpse of instructional practices.

The tablets from Ur give us but a glance into a period when Mesopotamians experimented with writing, expanding its scope and application, its relationship with natural language, and its social setting. When documentation resumes in the later part of the Early Dynastic (ED) period, we encounter a completely new inscriptional universe. Cuneiform writing, which had hitherto been limited to the registration of administrative accounts and school word lists, had been turned into a flexible tool that could also register the transitory flow of linguistic narrative in the permanence of clay, and the scribes of Sumer used this new freedom to compose written poetry. This sudden explosion of literary creativity seems to have affected most of southern Mesopotamia and soon spread to other areas of the Near East, so that various politically independent city-states shared a highly uniform written culture; many literary tablets have been recovered from Fara (ancient Shuruppak) and Abu Salabikh, but smaller numbers have also been discovered at Nippur, Adab, and elsewhere.[5]

Fascinating as these texts may be, we still cannot read them with ease. The lexical texts provide a direct link with earlier practices, although new thematic lists were added to the curriculum to keep up with changing linguistic and administrative practice, and new types of exercises were also developed.[6] But the new ED narratives were written in a skeletal system that makes it very difficult for anyone who does not know the texts by heart to understand them fully. Signs were arranged in cases in a manner driven more by aesthetics than by linguistic order, and most grammatical elements were not written at all. To make things even more complicated, some of the ED cuneiforms signs were no longer in use in later times and are therefore difficult to interpret. More problematic are a substantial number of narratives written with the same signs, which, however, have completely different meanings and syllabic readings. As a result, it is virtually impossible to translate in full the Sumerian texts from this period. Nevertheless, we can read a sentence here or a section there, and a few texts can be interpreted rather well on the basis of later, more complete versions. Thus, seen through the murky lens of our imperfect understanding, the earliest known written poetry emerges in fragments.

Perhaps the most striking characteristic of this new literature is that it is almost exclusively mythological, with no obvious connections with contemporary social or political events, which may explain why it was so easily adapted by people in different cities.[7] The few exceptions—a hymn to the temple of the mother goddess in the city of Kesh, the wise instructions of a legendary antediluvian king of Shuruppak (cat. no. 335)—are obviously of more than local interest, and a short tale about the sexual liaison between an ancient king of Uruk named Lugalbanda and the goddess Ninsumuna obviously mixes myth with legend. A series of short hymns to the divinities and temples of the land shows an interest in the common religious traditions of Mesopotamia, and a collection of proverbs provides more earthly topics. There are also texts concerning the goddesses Inanna and Sud (the patron deity of the city of Shuruppak) and the god Ushumgal. Some of the myths begin in primeval times, marking mythical time and space:

> In those remote days it was,
> In those remote nights it was,
> In those remote years it was. . . .[8]

One poem describes some of the events of that time:

> Powerful Heaven stood there in (his) manliness,
> Heaven and Earth screamed at one another,
> For at that time the Enki and Ninki (ancestor gods)
> existed not,
> The god Enlil did not yet exist,
> The goddess Ninlil did not exist. . . .[9]

This euphemism for cosmic sexual union is echoed in another Early Dynastic poem that states that "Heaven conversed with Earth, and Earth conversed with Heaven."[10]

CUNEIFORM LITERACY BEYOND SOUTHERN MESOPOTAMIA

From the fragmentary evidence at our disposal it seems that the scholastic tradition was uniformly stable throughout Sumer and neighboring areas; indeed, the lexical texts from cities such as Fara, Abu Salabikh, Uruk, Nippur, and Ur show hardly any variations at all. Lexical tablets from the city of Susa provide evidence of the spread of Mesopotamian learning eastward into Iran. In 1978 an Italian team discovered well-preserved Early Dynastic–period archives (cat. nos. 322–328) in the Syrian city of Ebla, modern Tell Mardikh, and it immediately became clear that cuneiform writing had traveled to the west as well. Other cities in the region have since yielded similar materials. The major Ebla archive, found right next to the throne room of a majestic palace, contained a broad range of archival tablets written in at least three languages (Sumerian, Akkadian, and Eblaite), including short- and long-term accounts, letters, treaties, incantations, and rituals, as well as literary materials such as divine hymns and myths, lexical lists, and various school exercises. Among the school texts we find duplicates of thematic lists from Abu Salabikh in addition to similar local compositions that were designed to help scribes master the application of Sumerian cuneiform to the Semitic Eblaite language that was used for letters, rituals, magical charms, and everyday administrative accounts. The Mesopotamian scholastic tradition was represented at Ebla not only by the lexical texts and by Sumerian poems and exercises but also by the Semitic Akkadian-language poetry that must have come from north of Sumer.[11] Because the Ebla archives survived intact, they provide us with unique information, but scattered accounts recovered from the town of Tell Beydar (ancient Nabada) and from the major cities of Mari and Tell Brak (ancient Nagar), as well as isolated school texts from Mari and Brak, abundantly demonstrate that Mesopotamian cuneiform was used throughout Syria at the time.

THE SARGONIC AND UR III PERIODS

Sometime about 2300–2245 B.C. a king by the name of Sargon managed to bring together the lands of Sumer and Akkad, as well as many surrounding areas, under a strong centralized authority. His empire survived for more than two centuries, but although there are many administrative records from the time, for some reason school texts from this period are rare. When the Sargonic state disintegrated, some cities returned to local rule, while others fell under various levels of domination from Iran. After perhaps no more than one generation, a new king by the name of Ur-Namma (ca. 2097–2080 B.C.) came to power in Ur and quickly united the lands of Sumer and Akkad, driving out the foreign Gutians from the south and Elamites from the north. His military successes were matched by administrative and organizational achievements: he rapidly reestablished a centralized bureaucracy and instigated massive public building projects throughout the realm. His works were abruptly brought to an end when he was killed on the battlefield in the eighteenth year of his reign. This tragic event threw a cloud over the whole land, since the martial death of a king could only mean that the gods had withdrawn their support for the realm. His son and successor Shulgi (ca. 2079–2032 B.C.) somehow managed to hold the kingdom together and to weather the ideological crisis precipitated by the death of his father. Shulgi initiated many administrative, legal, and organizational reforms, but his most profound and long-lasting ones lay in the changes that he or his administration imposed on the school curriculum.

In hymns to the king, Shulgi was portrayed as a learned man who had mastered the scribal and musical arts, who could converse in many languages, and who established schools in the cities of Nippur and Ur. It is difficult to know what to make of these claims, but there are some clues that support the words of his poets. Although we cannot properly evaluate the full range of literary creativity under the kings of Ur because few such texts from the period have survived and most of these remain unpublished, it seems fairly certain that radical changes took place during the reign of king Shulgi. It appears that his scribes completely restructured the world of scholarship and teaching: the old lexical texts that had their roots in the very beginning of writing were preserved and revised, but the abundant repertoire of early myths seems to have been discarded and to have disappeared forever.

In its place a new literature was formulated that was wholeheartedly geared toward the veneration of the new dynasty and its kings. The gods and goddesses of the land were celebrated with elaborate hymns, or odes, as were their temples, and the rulers of the land were counted in their number after Shulgi proclaimed himself to be a god. Other new texts were composed to fulfill the didactic needs of the new schools, which were clearly organized with the training of loyal bureaucrats in mind; even the temples were brought under royal control and the worship of divine kings helped integrate the elites and the religious establishments of various cities into the centralized structure of power. The heroic self-representation of royalty, directed at current and future officials as well as to the kings themselves, was manifest in architecture, urban renewal, and the plastic arts, in public ceremony, and in the overhaul of the written tradition. The family of Ur-Namma came from Uruk, and epics glorifying the legendary ancient kings of that city, including Enmerkar and Gilgamesh, provided much of the foundational myth of the dynasty. Some of these texts survived in Ur III manuscripts, but for the most part this literature is known to us in revised and updated Old Babylonian versions that are almost two hundred years later.

THE OLD BABYLONIAN SCHOOLS

Sumerian literature has become synonymous with Old Babylonian–period literature (ca. 2000–1500 B.C.). There are good reasons for this: although literary tablets from this time have been found in almost every excavated city, the largest numbers by far have been discovered at Nippur and Ur.[12] Thousands of school texts were uncovered at Nippur toward the end of the nineteenth century, but there is little indication of just where these tablets were found. When archaeologists returned to the site after World War II, they found smaller numbers of school texts in residential areas, some discarded on the floors of abandoned houses, others used as fill to prop up a clay bench. Of the two houses from Ur that contained large collections of scholastic texts only one might have been a place of learning; the tablets in the other house clearly came from somewhere else and were reused as fill. It is evident from all of this that there were no large central schools in Old Babylonian times. Rather, education took place in the home, where priests or bureaucrats taught young boys, mostly their own children, how to read and write. A few female literati are known, but these are exceptions; they either were royal daughters or worked in the exclusively female quarter in the city of Sippar that was the home of sequestered elite women who were devotees of the wife of the sun god. The picture of domestic education is confirmed by discoveries in smaller regional centers, where literary tablets were excavated in elite private houses. If larger organized schools of the kind depicted in literary texts about education existed, we have not found them. Thus, Old Babylonian literature is simply school literature, and the surviving tablets are probably all the exercises of schoolboys.

Ancient descriptions of the schools (Sumerian, *eduba'a*) provide us with a picture of children sitting on the ground in the courtyard with their teacher, listening to his explanations, repeating his dictated words, and drawing cuneiform signs in the sand. We must stress again that there was a complex oral component to this learning process, one that, for obvious reasons, is completely inaccessible to us. The logical and well-thought-out curriculum of nineteenth- and eighteenth-century-B.C. Babylonia can only be briefly summarized here. We can follow the first steps through simple exercises that teachers wrote for students to imitate. Some of these examples were round pieces of clay with a few lines on one side, copied by the young adept on the reverse; others were rectangular with one exercise rendered from memory on the obverse, and a new one on the left side of the reverse that was copied repeatedly on the right. At Nippur pupils began their study with a simple list of repeated syllables that began with the sequence *a a / a a a / a ku / a ku ku / me me,* and so forth; a similar list used in some other cities began *me me / pa pa / a a / a a a / ku ku / lu lu / maš/ maš maš,* and so on. These simple signs were arranged by graphic similarity, and repetition provided the combination of motor and mental skills.

Next came another list of syllables, whose opening lines read *tu ta ti / nu na ni,* which reinforced the study of signs and syllables, supported by assonance as a mnemonic device. After the basic signs and their associated syllabic pronunciations came an introduction to the lexical values of signs and to the nouns of the Sumerian language. The vehicles for this level of instruction were thematic lexical texts, the Old Babylonian descendants of the first archaic lists, now arranged into a series that covered the names of various materials and objects made from these materials, beginning with wood, reeds, clay, leather, and metals and then moving to domestic and wild animals, stones, plants, fish, birds, garments, and terrestrial and celestial geography and ending with foodstuffs. We should note that sometime after the end of Ur III the old lexicographic corpus was largely discarded and replaced with new thematic lists and with newly developed pronunciation guides, or syllabaries. It is not clear if the pupil had to learn all of this or only selected parts in the process of study. This thematic enumeration was followed by another text that had replaced an out-of-date ancestor from the archaic period: a list of professional names. Students also had to learn complex syllabaries that provided the multiple syllabic values of cuneiform signs, their Sumerian word values, and the Akkadian translations of these words, although for the most part the translations remained part of the oral side of learning and were only written down in exceptional circumstances when the teachers demanded it. Other lists and exercises were also studied, including series consisting of compound signs, grammatical paradigms, mathematical problems and examples, as well as short excerpts from poems and proverbs.

When the pupil knew enough signs to proceed beyond this stage, he studied a series of four short elementary poems, three basic royal odes, and a hymn to Nidaba, the goddess of writing. These texts had been chosen for their relative simplicity, for their basic vocabulary, and for the repetition of signs, words, and phrases, all geared to pedagogical purposes. Once again it is important to stress that the students were not simply learning the technique of calligraphy but were also studying Sumerian, a language that had long ceased to be spoken and that bore no resemblance to the Akkadian they spoke at home. Having mastered these four texts, they moved on to a sequence of ten more complex literary compositions of various types that explored more diverse vocabulary, grammar, and style. This decade began with hymns to kings Shulgi and Lipit-Eshtar, the Hymn to the Hoe (cat. no. 339), and hymns to the goddess Inanna and the god Enlil, as well as to the temple of the mother goddess at Kesh, proceeded to a poem describing a visit to Nippur by the god Enki, a mythological tale about Inanna, and a hymn to the goddess Nungal, and ended with the epic tale that described how the legendary hero Gilgamesh and his companion Enkidu went on an expedition to cut wood in the Cedar Forest and in the process murdered Huwawa, the guardian of the trees.[13]

It is not clear if all students graduated to higher levels of the curriculum, where more literary materials were the subjects of study. The full range of literary texts from Nippur and elsewhere is fairly well known, even if some of the compositions remain incomplete. There is quite a bit of textual variation from place to place, and even within the same city. It seems that unlike their Early Dynastic ancestors, the Old Babylonian schoolmasters had much redactional leeway and were free to create their own versions of texts. Through a cumulative system of sifting and modernization of the tradition, the Ur III literary core had been edited and added to with accretions from later times, including numerous hymns from the reigns of the kings of the First Dynasty of Isin (ca. 2002–1777 B.C.) and to a lesser extent from the Dynasty of Larsa (ca. 2010–1748 B.C.). Only two Early Dynastic poems that survived the Ur III literary purge remained in the curriculum: the hymn to the temple at Kesh and The Instructions of Shuruppak (cat. no. 335). The course of study included myths, epics, debate poems, proverbs, letters, numerous royal and divine hymns, prayers, city laments, various historiographic texts, short humorous tales, and meditations on the world order. There are some hints that the situation may have been different in areas outside Nippur and southern Mesopotamia, where there seems to have been an accent on ritual texts such as cultic laments and prayers as well as magical charms. Some of these more practical texts may actually have belonged to priestly or even temple libraries. The relative paucity of such compositions at Nippur may be misleading, however, as it is perhaps due more to limitations of our samples than to the situation as it existed in antiquity.

The schools were the preliminary training ground for the next generation of scribes, administrators, and priests, but Sumerian literature was not studied with such practical goals in mind. After all, the language was long dead and was a typical "nonmother tongue," taught by old men to young boys who would hardly ever get to use it outside the school environment. To be sure, as priests they would have to use Sumerian liturgical texts, but other than that the language of everyday life and of scribal administration would be a high dialect of their native tongue, which was mostly Akkadian. Yet much like schoolchildren in other cultures before the advent of mass literacy, their education had broader aims and they would learn practical applications on the job after graduation. They had to master the basics of reading and writing, but they were also immersed in an ancient common Mesopotamian literary tradition, they learned how to bond with the literate classes, and they were indoctrinated into a worldview that supported the current structure of society and the state.[14] But like much of what had gone before, this was not destined to last. The Nippur houses were abandoned in the middle of the eighteenth century, and while some school texts remain from the next few centuries, relatively little is known of the changes that took place in education at this time. During the middle of the second millennium B.C. the educational system continued to be revised and was increasingly geared to the teaching of Akkadian, although Sumerian was studied until cuneiform writing was abandoned in the first centuries of our era. Only a few of the old poems survived, but they were joined by many new ones as Mesopotamian literature continued to change and evolve.

1. On the origins of cuneiform, see Michalowski 1996; for an overview of its history and structure, see Cooper 1996.

2. We should note here the existence of the still-undeciphered Proto-Elamite script that was widely used in Iran toward the end of the fourth millennium and at the beginning of the third millennium B.C. (Englund 1996). Like cuneiform, Proto-Elamite was written on clay tablets and was apparently used only for accounts.

3. For detailed surveys of the Uruk-period tablets, see Nissen, Damerow, and Englund 1993, as well as Englund 1998.

4. The Mesopotamian lexical tradition has been described by Civil 1975, Civil 1995, and Veldhuis 1999.

5. The texts from Fara and Abu Salabikh are catalogued and surveyed in Krebernik 1998. On ED lexicography, see Civil 1984a and Civil 1987. On ED literature in general, see Rubio Pardo 1996.

6. On some interesting school texts from the period, see Civil 1983 and Marchesi 1999.

7. For an overview of Sumerian literature, see Michalowski 1995.

8. Biggs 1974, no. 283, i:1–3; see also ibid., nos. 290, 389, and Jestin 1937, no. 79.

9. Thureau-Dangin in Cros 1910–14, vol. 2 (1911), p. 180 (AO 4153), ii:1–6.

10. Barton 1918, no. 1, i:12–14.

11. The two Semitic hymns, one to the sun deity (cat. no. 328) and another to the goddess Nidaba, have been treated by Krebernik 1992.

12. On Old Babylonian schooling and the school curriculum, see Vanstiphout 1995b and Tinney 1998b.

13. See Tinney 1999.

14. See Michalowski 1991.

EARLY DYNASTIC PERIOD

321

Cuneiform tablet with an administrative document

Cuneiform inscription in Sumerian
Clay
H. 7.5 cm (3 in.); W. 7.5 cm (3 in.)
Mesopotamia, Shuruppak (modern Fara)
Early Dynastic IIIA, ca. 2550–2400 B.C.
Staatliche Museen zu Berlin, Vorderasiatisches
Museum VA 12736

The documents from Fara provide a glimpse of a differentiated and well-organized administration concerned not only with the territory of ancient Shuruppak itself but also regions well beyond it, since there is mention in some accounting texts of inhabitants from other places in Sumer. The personal names in some of the Fara tablets also indicate the presence of a non-Sumerian element in the population. They reflect the background of the bilingual written tradition of Sumerian and Akkadian, known to us from later documents, that created a distinctive Mesopotamian culture.

This little square tablet with rounded corners is inscribed in the typical form, indicating semantic units without representing the correct spoken grammatical sequence; for example, the second line is actually written "Uruk. People. Contracted." The signs are clearly derived from the pictographic signs of the preceding Uruk period.

Translation:

140 laborers
contracted people from Uruk
215 from Adab
74 from Nippur
110 from Lagash
66 from Shuruppak
128 from Umma.

In all:
660 minus 10 laborers[1]
contracted laborers from Sumer.

JM

1. The numbers are written in the sexagesimal system, which explains the subtraction in the statement of the sum.

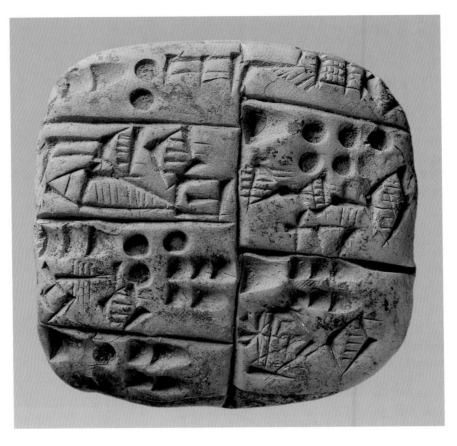

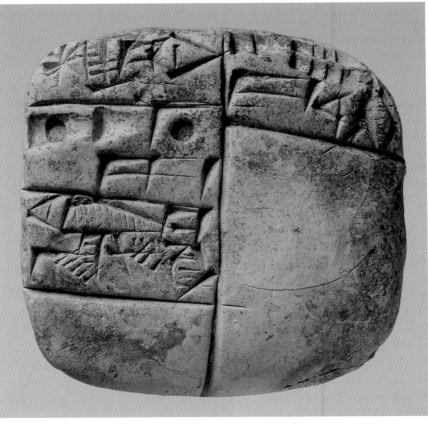

323a

Cuneiform tablet with a consignment of cloth

Cuneiform inscription in Eblaite
Clay
H. 14.5 cm (5¾ in.); W. 13.5 cm (5⅜ in.); Thickness
2 cm (¾ in.)
Syria, Ebla (modern Tell Mardikh), Palace G,
TM.75.G.1319
Early Bronze Age, Mardikh IIb 1, ca. 2350–2250 B.C.
Idlib Museum, Syria 105/104

323b

Cuneiform tablet with a list of equids

Cuneiform inscription in Eblaite
Clay
H. 9.3 cm (3⅝ in.); W. 8.8 cm (3½ in.); Thickness
2.8 cm (1⅛ in.)
Syria, Ebla (modern Tell Mardikh), Ninni-zaza
temple, TM.75.G.2032
Early Bronze Age, Mardikh IIb 1, ca. 2350–2250 B.C.
Idlib Museum, Syria 817

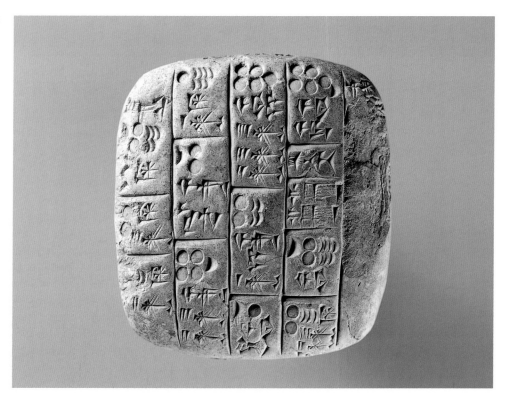

The most common type of administrative document found in the archives at Ebla consists of monthly accounts regarding the consignment of cloth. These accounts record consignments of woolen garments and, in a few cases, those of linen. The garments, of greater or lesser value according to the social status of the consignee, were sometimes embellished with jewelry or ceremonial weapons. Recorded also are certain amounts of unwoven spun wool that were paid as a salary to female personnel of low rank. The texts end with partial sums for the cloth, followed by an overall sum and the name of the month for which the information was recorded. In calculating amounts of spun wool, the Ebla texts document the use of an autonomous system of weights. The first tablet seen here (cat. no. 323a) is among those that have permitted the reconstruction of this system. It consisted of three units of weight. The base unit was simply called a "stone" (that is, a "weighing stone"), whereas the other two units had the value of two "stones" and four "stones," respectively. In Mesopotamian documents units of weight different from those customarily adopted (talent, mina, shekel) were sometimes used as well for calculating amounts of wool.

The text of the second tablet (cat. no. 323b), which was left unfinished, belongs to a type that listed team and pack animals present in Ebla or in villages under its rule. This text distinguishes, according to their functions, 185 pairs of mules, certainly to be used to pull carts, and 80 donkeys, perhaps to be used as pack animals in the caravans of trade merchants. Other mules and donkeys are listed and differentiated by sex and age.[1]

PF

1. Information in this entry is based, for (a), on Zaccagnini 1984, pp. 189–204; and for (b), on Edzard 1981, p. 61, and Mander 1990, p. 200.

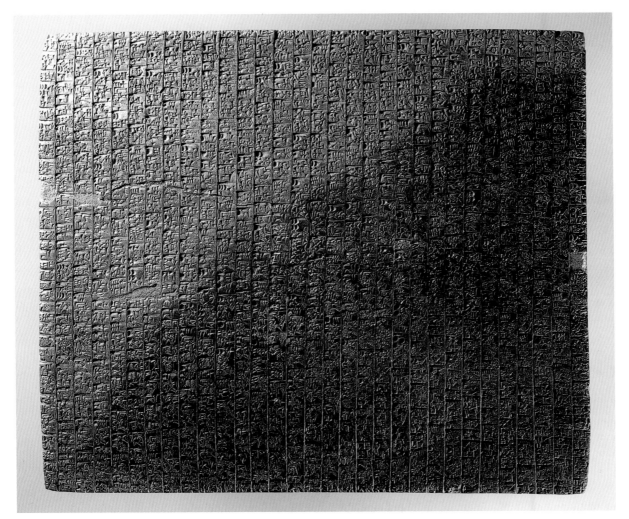

324a

Cuneiform tablet with a yearly account of metals

Cuneiform inscription in Eblaite
Clay
H. 37 cm (14⅝ in.); W. 31.5 cm (12⅜ in.); Thickness
2.5 cm (1 in.)
Syria, Ebla (modern Tell Mardikh), Palace G,
TM.75.G.2429
Early Bronze Age, Mardikh IIb 1, ca. 2350–2250 B.C.
Idlib Museum, Syria 1213

324b

Cuneiform tablet with a record of gold and silver tributes paid to Mari

Cuneiform inscription in Eblaite
Clay
H. 12 cm (4¾ in.); W. 10.5 cm (4⅛ in.); Thickness
1.5 cm (⅝ in.)
Syria, Ebla (modern Tell Mardikh), Palace G,
TM.75.G.1271
Early Bronze Age, Mardikh IIb 1, ca. 2350–2250 B.C.
Idlib Museum, Syria 56

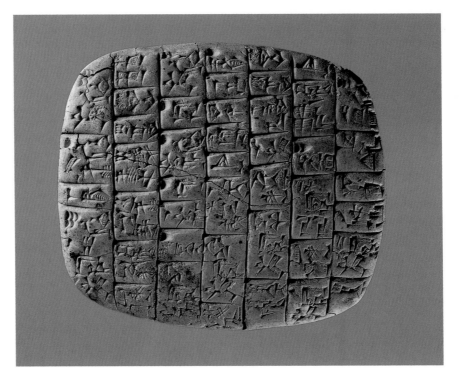

The yearly accounts of silver and gold constitute an administrative typology introduced by the minister Ibrium and used throughout the following period of the minister Ibbi-Zikir. The accounts were drawn up on large tablets that grew in size as Ebla's economic power increased and that reached the dimensions of the larger one exhibited here. All the yearly accounts of precious metals begin with an entry that records the spending of "one mina of silver for the silver head of the god Kura," evidence of the annual rite by which the statue of the god, protector of the royal family, was refurbished. Next in the list come entries that in some cases correspond to accounts for cloth of the same year. In each entry of expenditures, gold is quantified by an equivalent in silver. The accounts close with a final sum indicating total expenditures and the residual amount available in the treasury. In the first text shown here (cat. no. 324a) total expenditures come to 369 minas of silver (173.43 kg) with a residual amount of 1,109 minas of silver (521.23 kg). Only occasionally does a chronological reference appear with the final sum as it does in our text: "Year (in which the king) conquered Niliga'u."

Reports of Enna-Dagan's letter regarding the tribute Ebla had to pay to Mari (see cat. no. 326a) are confirmed in numerous Ebla administrative texts that can be dated to the reign of Igrish-Khalab and to the early period of the reign of his successor, Irkab-Damu. The second text shown here (cat. no. 324b) records the payment of 34 minas and 37 shekels of silver (16.25 kg) and 2 minas of gold (0.94 kg) to be given to the king of Mari and to other people of high rank in his court in the year in which Enna-Dagan became king. Higher amounts are recorded during the reign of Iplul-Il; the king alone is indicated as having received a total of 547.23 kilograms of silver and 42.06 kilograms of gold.[1]   PF

1. Information in this entry is based, for (a), on Archi 1996, pp. 73–99, and Waetzoldt 2001, pp. 407–76; and for (b), on Archi 1985, pp. 63–83, and Archi 1988, pp. 47–49.

325

Cuneiform tablet with a list of personnel

Cuneiform inscription in Eblaite
Clay
H. 8.8 cm (3½ in.); W. 9 cm (3½ in.); Thickness 2 cm
(¾ in.)
Syria, Ebla (modern Tell Mardikh), Palace G,
TM.75.G.1655
Early Bronze Age, Mardikh IIb 1, ca. 2350–2250 B.C.
Idlib Museum, Syria 440

The only example of its kind, this list of personnel shows the contingents of men, totaling 11,700, to be found in the city of Tin at the moment the text was drawn up. In the first fourteen contingents, the number of men belonging to each group is given (in decreasing order, from 800 to 300), together with the "lord" to whom they are subordinated. Next come the 4,700 men employed directly in the palace. The term used on this tablet to indicate the personnel *(gurush-gurush)* refers, in Ebla texts, to men working for the administration, employed in production or in military activity. The fact that so many men were stationed in a provincial center, probably located northeast of Ebla, suggests that this military activity may have been connected with events that led to the treaty with Abarsal (see entry for cat. no. 326c). In support of this hypothesis, it should be noted that the first "lord" on the list is Tir, a person who had an important position in the administration at the time the treaty was drafted.[1]   PF

1. Information in this entry is based on D'Agostino 1996, pp. 71–73.

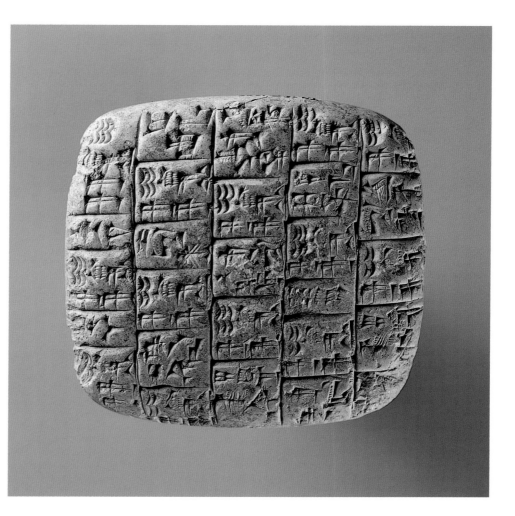

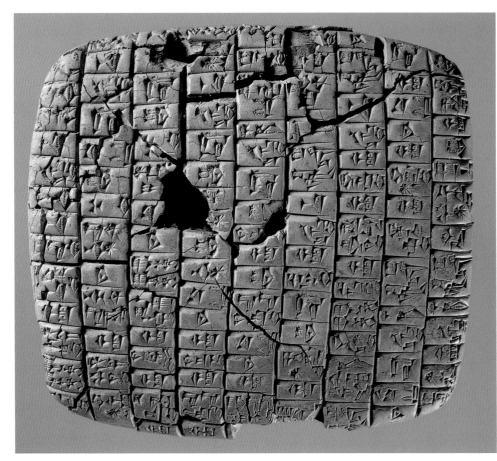

326a

326a

Cuneiform tablet with a letter from Enna-Dagan, king of Mari, to the king of Ebla

Cuneiform inscription in Eblaite
Clay
H. 13.7 cm (5⅜ in.); W. 14 cm (5½ in.); Thickness
3.8 cm (1½ in.)
Syria, Ebla (modern Tell Mardikh), Palace G,
TM.75.G.2367
Early Bronze Age, Mardikh IIb 1, ca. 2350–2250 B.C.
National Museum, Aleppo, Syria 11300

326b

Cuneiform tablet with a letter concerning Kish and Nagar

Cuneiform inscription in Eblaite
Clay
H. 7.8 cm (3⅛ in.); W. 8.2 cm (3¼ in.); Thickness
1.5 cm (⅝ in.)
Syria, Ebla (modern Tell Mardikh), Palace G,
TM.75.G.1391
Early Bronze Age, Mardikh IIb 1, ca. 2350–2250 B.C.
Idlib Museum, Syria 176

326c

Cuneiform tablet with a treaty with Abarsal

Cuneiform inscription in Eblaite
Clay
H. 22.1 cm (8¾ in.); W. 23.9 cm (9⅜ in.); Thickness
5 cm (2 in.)
Syria, Ebla (modern Tell Mardikh), Palace G,
TM.75.G.2420
Early Bronze Age, Mardikh IIb 1, ca. 2350–2250 B.C.
Idlib Museum, Syria 1204

In the earliest period documented in the Central Archives, Ebla was faced with the political and military activity of Mari. When the enemy army posed a real threat, Ebla decided it would be wise to accept the imposition of a tribute. The letter from Enna-Dagan (cat. no. 326a) refers to the victorious military campaigns that had progressively extended the influence of Mari in northern Syria. These campaigns are listed, beginning with the earliest: "Yanup, king of Mari, defeated Aburu and Ilgi, in the territory of Ba'lan: on the mountain of Labanan he left a mound (of corpses)." The same model of text is repeated for succeeding kings, with very few variations. Enna-Dagan mentions, further-more, that Ebla had been forced by Iplul-Il to pay a tribute, and he confirms the dominion

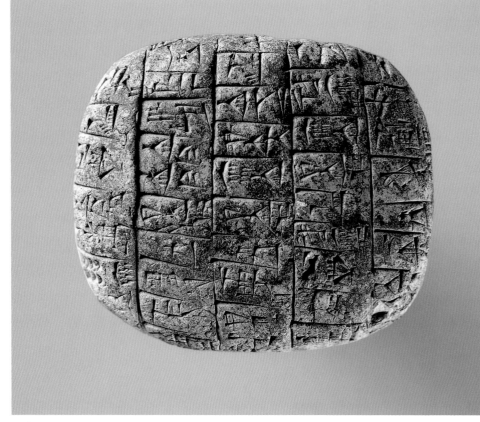

326b

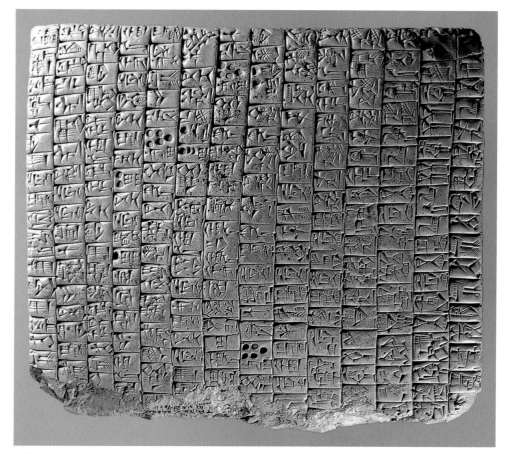

326c

of Mari over the two countries (the Lower Country and the Upper Country). The letter closes with an imprecation reminiscent of the maledictions with which alliance treaties end. Despite the poor state of preservation, the last paragraph of the letter can be interpreted as follows: "If they pull out from under this yoke, may the lance of Iplul-Il, king of Mari, strike their heads." The punishment for rebels was to come from the spear of Iplul-Il himself, in the hands, evidently, of the equally valorous Enna-Dagan.

Most of the letters found in the archives are addressed from the king or high officials to their subordinates. Whereas the officials are cited by name, the king, according to the Eblaite protocol, is never mentioned. This convention is observed in the text of the tablet concerning Kish and Nagar (cat. no. 326b), which starts with the formula "Thus (says) the king to Tubkhu-Hadda." The mention of this person places the letter in the records of the final phase of the archives: Tubkhu-Hadda, son of the minister Ibbi-Zikir, is mentioned along with his father in reference to official functions only in the texts of the last period. Thus, the king referred to as the author of this document

is certainly the last ruler of Ebla, Ish'ar-Damu. In the letter the king gives instructions and asks for information about amounts of silver, either allotted or received, the highest recorded figure being 800 minas (376 kg). The letter is interesting from a historical point of view since it mentions the king of Kish (called *lugal,* the Mesopotamian title) and the ruler of Nagar (the main center now identified with Tell Brak, in the Khabur area): "And then, as to the rest of the king of Kish and of the king of Nagar, when he was present, how much did they give?" The latter sovereign is explicitly mentioned with reference to a recent stay at Ebla, which offers a further hint of relative chronology. We know from an administrative document that the king of Nagar went to Ebla to arrange the conditions for the dynastic marriage of his son to Ish'ar-Damu's daughter, Tagrish-Damu.

The tablet with the treaty with Abarsal (cat. no. 326c) records the most ancient political treaty ever found entirely preserved. The city of Abarsal (so named according to the conventional transcription of the writing) is supposed to be found in the region to the east of the Euphrates River and to have had influence

spreading to the river, as shown by some clauses of the treaty. The document, consisting of 632 cases, starts with a statement of the Eblaite sphere of influence. Both paragraphs of the tablet end with the same formula: "The walled places (and) all places which (are) under the control of the king of Ebla, belong to the king of Ebla; the walled places (and) all places which (are) under the control of the king of Abarsal, belong to the king of Abarsal." The treaty clauses, often introduced by the conjunction "if," are formulated with an accurate syntax. Some of them define equal obligations; others clearly favor Ebla. Among the former clauses it is worth noticing those fixing the punishment for manslaughter or willful murder: "If in (the festival of) the month of Ishi someone from Abarsal will kill an Eblaite in a riot, he will give as blood-money 50 rams." The clauses of political and commercial content clearly show that Ebla fixed the conditions of the treaty. The king of Abarsal will not allow anyone to travel to Ebla without permission from the king of Ebla: "Thus (says) the king of Ebla to Abarsal: 'Without my permission you will let nobody travel toward (my) country; (if) you let him travel, you will have broken the oath. (When) I will order (it) they will travel.'" The king of Abarsal is compelled to inform Ebla at once of anything plotted against it: "As to any evil plan you may hear of, you will send a messenger as quick as possible. If you are on a long journey [you are not compelled to send a messenger]; (but if while) you are present you hear of an evil plan (and) do not send any messenger, you will have broken the oath." The treaty promises the curse of the gods against all those who act with bad intentions and ends with a last warning not to undertake any military expedition against Ebla.[1]

PF

1. Information in this entry is based, for (a), on Pettinato 1980, pp. 231–45; Edzard 1981, pp. 89–97; and Fronzaroli 2002, pp. 35–42; for (b), on Archi 1981, p. 78, and Biga 1987, p. 46; and for (c), on Sollberger 1980, pp. 129–60; W. Lambert 1987, pp. 353–64; Edzard 1992, pp. 187–217; and Fronzaroli 2002, pp. 43–76.

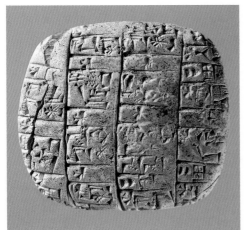

327

Cuneiform tablet with offerings to dead kings

Cuneiform inscription in Eblaite
Clay
H. 7.4 cm (2⅞ in.); W. 7 cm (2¼ in.); Thickness
1.5 cm (⅝ in.)
Syria, Ebla (modern Tell Mardikh), Palace G,
TM.75.G.2628
Early Bronze Age, Mardikh IIb 1, ca. 2350–2250 B.C.
Idlib Museum, Syria   10820

The importance of the cult of dead ancestors is documented in two long texts on royal wedding rites and confirmed by the existence of administrative texts that record the sheep offered on such occasions. The tablet exhibited here lists sacrificial offerings of sheep for ten sovereigns and for four pairs of divinities. The rites take place at Darib, which can probably be identified as modern-day Atareb, located about thirty kilometers north of Ebla. The ten deceased sovereigns are listed in inverse chronological order, starting with Irkab-Damu, father of the last king of Ebla. These same names, listed in the same order, are also to be found in the work of a scribe, beginning with the name Ish'ar-Damu (the last king). This second list gives the names of earlier kings as well, including those mentioned in the two texts on royal wedding rites. Amana, to whom sacrifices were offered in the royal rituals at Uduhudu, is twenty-second in the list; Shagish, Ibbit-Li'm, and Ishrut-Damu, to whom sacrifices were offered in the mausoleum of Nenash, are nineteenth, seventeenth, and sixteenth, respectively, in the list.[1]   PF

1. Information in this entry is based on Archi 1988, pp. 165–66, and Archi 2001, pp. 1–13.

328

Cuneiform tablet with a hymn to Shamash

Cuneiform inscription in Akkadian
Clay
H. 18 cm (7⅛ in.); W. 16.5 cm (6½ in.); Thickness
2.5 cm (1 in.)
Syria, Ebla (modern Tell Mardikh), Palace G,
TM.75.G.2421
Early Bronze Age, Mardikh IIb 1, ca. 2350–2250 B.C.
Idlib Museum, Syria   1205

The hymn to the sun god Shamash, composed in a language classifiable as an archaic Akkadian dialect, is the longest literary text of the third millennium B.C. written in a Semitic language. Its Mesopotamian provenance is proven by the existence of a duplicate found at Tell Abu Salabikh. Interpretation of the text is possible only in part, because of the complexity of the writing system. The hymn begins with a list of attributes in praise of the god: "The bolt of (venerable) heaven, the exalted one of the gods, in whom heaven trusts, Shamash, who holds the life of the land. . . ." The god guarantees a safe journey to merchants bringing precious goods from distant lands: ". . . to the merchants he gave goods. The foreign lands yielded lapis lazuli and silver, the cedar forest yielded (pure) wood, boxwood and cypress, exquisite emblems. . . . Aromatic oil, vegetable oil and honey, the goods of the merchants and the smoke of the gods, juniper, almond and . . . , products of the foreign land, he caused to be brought by his boats." Further on, the text mentions the sun god riding the human-faced bull or bison (*kusarikkum;* see entry for cat. no. 111), traveling to the opposite shore of the sea. The hymn ends affirming the lordship of Shamash over Sippar, the city in which this text must have been composed.[1]

PF

1. Information in this entry is based on Edzard 1984, pp. 28–31; Lambert 1989, pp. 1–32; and Krebernik 1992, pp. 63–149. The translation of the excerpts from the hymn are from Krebernik 1992.

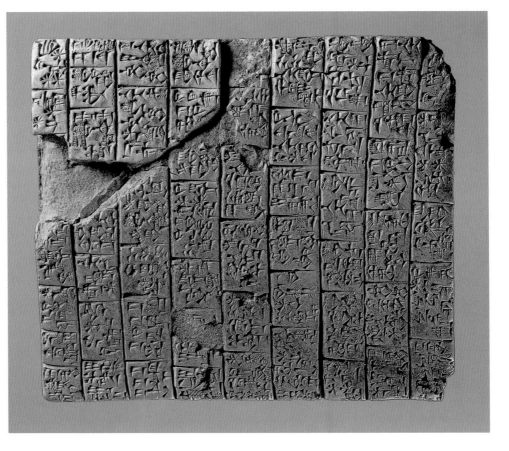

329

Cuneiform tablet with a Sumerian medical text

Cuneiform inscription in Sumerian
Clay
H. 10.2 cm (4 in.); W. 16.5 cm (6½ in.); Thickness
1.9 cm (¾ in.)
Mesopotamia, Nippur
Ur III, ca. 2097–1989 B.C.
University of Pennsylvania Museum of Archaeology
and Anthropology, Philadelphia CBS 14221

This tablet contains some of the earliest medical prescriptions at present known.[1] Although there are a few other early texts of this type, none is as extensive as this four-column Ur III tablet from Nippur. Mesopotamian medical lore is well known from numerous first-millennium tablets, but second- and third-millennium information is much more sparse. It is therefore of interest that the present text in many ways anticipates the Akkadian-language prescriptions known from later times. This is of some help in the analysis of the Sumerian text, but many uncertainties remain and we cannot identify all the ingredients that are enumerated here.

The first twenty or so lines are damaged and difficult to reconstruct. The remainder of the tablet contains fifteen prescriptions grouped in three sections containing ingredients for compresses, potions, and salves. The compresses, or poultices, were an important part of Mesopotamian medical lore. This text contains eight such prescriptions that instruct the reader to crush various ingredients, mix them with beer or water, and then, after rubbing the afflicted place with oil, to fasten them in a compress on the body. The three therapeutic drinks that follow also consist of crushed ingredients; these are supposed to be infused in beer and then given to the patient to drink. The final four prescriptions contain complex instructions for rubbing the patient with various mixtures and anointing him or her with oil. Unfortunately, the nature of the affliction that is so treated is not clear from the preserved passages.   PM

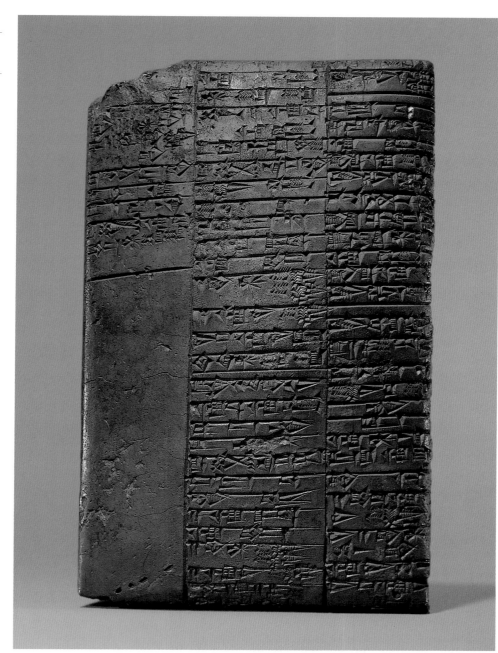

1. First published by Legrain 1940; Kramer presented his interpretation of the text in many popular articles, including Kramer 1959. A full edition was presented by Civil 1960.

OLD BABYLONIAN PERIOD

330

Cuneiform prism with the Sumerian King List

Cuneiform inscription in Sumerian
Clay
H. 20 cm (7⅞ in.); W. 9.1 cm (3⅝ in.)
Mesopotamia
Old Babylonian period, ca. 1740 B.C.
Visitors of the Ashmolean Museum, Oxford
AN 1923.444

The cycle of hegemonic cities in early Mesopotamian history is described in this text.[1] The
repetitive listing of cities, "dynasties," and
kings was designed to bolster the fiction that
only one urban power center ruled the land at
any one time. The composition, until recently
known only from Old Babylonian copies, was
undoubtedly created as part of the complex
legitimization project of the kings of the Third
Dynasty of Ur, which managed to unify
southern Mesopotamia for about a century
(ca. 2097–1989 B.C.). There is an unpublished
early version from the time of Shulgi, the second king of the dynasty, which differs in some
respects from the more elaborate, later versions.

The full composition has been reconstructed
from numerous Old Babylonian school copies.
Although this beautiful prism is the only
complete version, it is not necessarily the best
exemplar. No two versions of the King List
are the same. The text has many variants: some
recensions begin after the Flood; dynasties
are listed in different orders; and certain
expressions differ, as do the lengths of reign
of individual kings.

The opening lines of the prism read:

> After kingship had descended from the
> heavens, (the seat of) kingship was in
> (the city of) Eridu. In Eridu, Alulim
> became king and reigned for 28,800 years.
> Alalgar reigned for 36,000 years. (In sum)
> 2 kings reigned for 64,800 years. Eridu
> was abandoned and (the seat of) kingship
> was taken to (the city of) Badtibira.

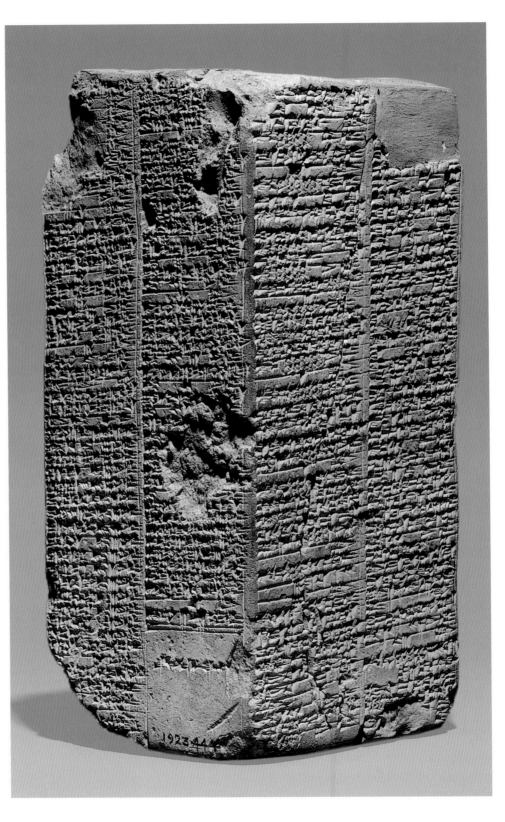

In Badtibira, Enmenluana reigned for 43,200 years; Enmengalana reigned for 28,800 years, Dumuzi, the shepherd, reigned for 36,000 years. (In sum) 3 kings reigned for 108,000 years.

Then Badtibira was abandoned and (the seat of) kingship was taken to (the city of) Larak. In Larak, Ensipaziana reigned for 28,800 years. (In sum) 1 king reigned for 28,800 years.

Then Larak was abandoned and (the seat of) kingship was taken to Sippar. In Sippar Enmendurana became king and reigned for 21,000 years. (In sum) 1 king reigned for 21,000 years.

Then Sippar was abandoned and (the seat of) kingship was taken to (the city of) Shuruppak. In Shuruppak Ubar-Tutu became king and reigned for 18,600 years. (In sum) 1 king reigned for 18,600 years.

In 5 cities 8 kings reigned for 241,200 years. Then the flood swept over (the land).

After the flood had swept over (the land and) kingship had (once again) descended from the heavens, (the seat of) kingship was in (the city of) Kish. In Kish, Gushur became king and reigned for 1,200 years. . . .

PM

1. The classic edition is by Jacobsen (1939), who used the Ashmolean prism as the basic text. Many new pieces have been published since then, most recently by Vincente 1995. The most recent translation, Glassner 1993, pp. 137–42, is also based on this source.

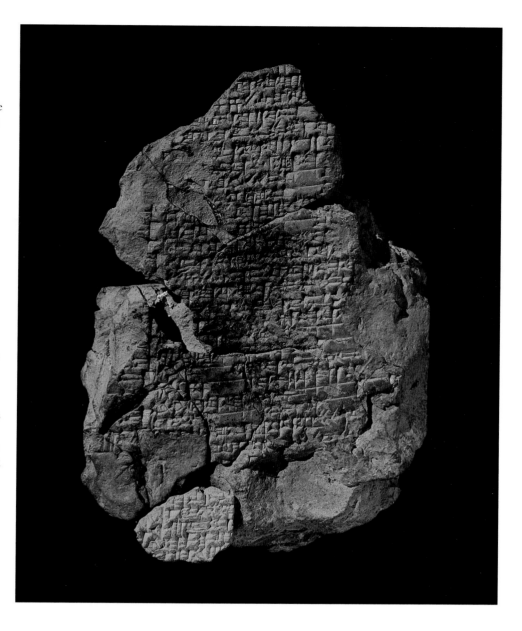

331

Cuneiform tablet with a Shulgi hymn

Cuneiform inscription in Sumerian
Clay
H. 12.7 cm (5 in.); W. 8.9 cm (3½ in.); Thickness
3.8 cm (1½ in.)
Mesopotamia
Old Babylonian period, ca. 1740 B.C.
University of Pennsylvania Museum of Archaeology and Anthropology, Philadelphia UM 29-13-556, N 4264, N 6717, N 7040, N 7107

When the kings of Ur unified southern Babylonia, they instituted many reforms, including revisions of the writing system, of schooling, and of the use of literature for social integration as well as glorification of the Crown. Many hymns extolling the deeds and divine qualities of kings were composed at the time, although we know most of them by means of later copies. This is one of the many hymns proclaiming the might of the divine Shulgi (ca. 2079–2032), the second king of the dynasty.[1]

As the poem opens, the king is traveling from the capital of Ur to the city of Uruk, home of Inanna, goddess of war and carnal love. Dressed in all his finery, he attracts the attention of the goddess, who promises to make love to him. Shulgi takes the place of Inanna's lover Dumuzi. She then announces the king's fate:

In battle I shall be your vanguard,
In combat, like a page, I shall carry your weapons,
In the assembly I shall be your wise advisor,
On campaign I shall be your inspiration!

Shulgi then proceeds to the city of Larsa, where he visits the sun god Utu, Inanna's brother; to Ennigi, where he is blessed by Ninazu; and finally back to Ur, where he enters the temple of the moon god Nanna. Seated on his throne in Ur, king Shulgi dispenses justice for his land.   PM

1. Edition: Klein 1981b, pp. 124–66. It is now generally recognized that this hymn, X, constitutes the missing end of another poem known as Shulgi O (ibid., pp. 50–123). The full text, which numbered almost six hundred lines, is the longest known Shulgi hymn.

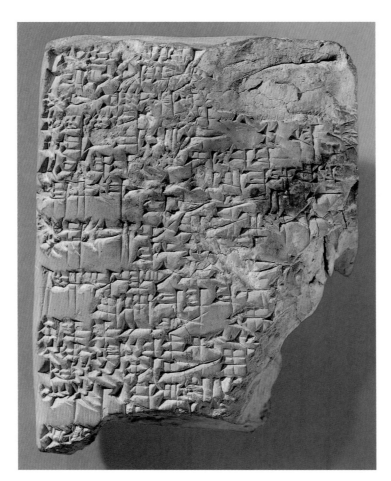

332

Cuneiform tablet with a letter from Ishbi-Erra to Ibbi-Sin, ruler of Ur

Cuneiform inscription in Sumerian
Clay
H. 6.4 cm (2½ in.); W. 8.3 cm (3¼ in.); Thickness
2.5 cm (1 in.)
Mesopotamia, Nippur
Old Babylonian period, ca. 1740 B.C.
University of Pennsylvania Museum of Archaeology
and Anthropology, Philadelphia CBS 2272

Sumerian epistolary literature was an important part of second-millennium schooling in Mesopotamia, although after graduation scribes never composed letters in the ancient language, as all contemporary correspondence was carried out in the Old Babylonian dialect of Akkadian. The letters of the kings of the Third Dynasty of Ur, some real, some fictitious, are particularly well documented. Four letters concerning events that led up to the fall of the kingdom in the time of king Ibbi-Sin (ca. 2013–1989 B.C.) have a special place in this correspondence, since they were often grouped in what we would today describe as an epistolary novella. The authenticity of the events described in these letters is open to doubt, but in essence they describe

the complex historical situation that allowed a high official by the name of Ishbi-Erra to take over the cities of Isin and Nippur. Once in power there, he was able to proclaim independence from Ur and found a new dynasty that would rule Sumer after the fall of his former master Ibbi-Sin. Ishbi-Erra came from the Syrian city of Mari, which was strongly bound to Ur through one or more dynastic marriages. When the southern parts of the Ur kingdom abandoned the Crown and provisions became scarce in the capital, the king dispatched Ishbi-Erra to the north to purchase grain. The officer complied, but then blackmailed his master into giving him the cities of Nippur and Isin and paying double the original price of the grain he had managed to buy. In this disingenuous letter Ishbi-Erra writes:[1]

To Ibbi-Sin, my lord, speak: Thus says Ishbi-Erra, your servant:
"You instructed me to (undertake an) expedition from Isin to Kazallu, to purchase grain. The market price of grain having reached one shekel per bushel, twenty talents of silver were invested in the purchase of grain. Word having reached me that the hostile Amorites had entered your land, I brought all the grain—seventy-two

thousand bushels—into (the city of) Isin. But now all the Amorites have entered Sumer and have captured all the great storehouses, one by one. Because of (these) Amorites I cannot hand over the grain for threshing; they are too strong for me and I am stuck (here). Your majesty should caulk six hundred one hundred and twenty bushel boats . . . and let . . . all of the boats . . . so that they be transferred upriver, up the Idkura and the Palishtum canals to a safe threshing floor, and I shall go (upstream) ahead of them. Put me in charge of the place where the boat(s) moor. Should you be short on grain, I will deliver you grain. Your majesty, the Elamite is distressed by (this) war (and) his (own) grain rations are quickly coming to an end. . . . Do not rush to become his servant (and) do not follow him! I have (enough) grain to provision your palace and the whole city for fifteen years, so appoint me to guard Isin and Nippur! May my king know (all of this)!"

PM

1. Editions: Michalowski 1976, pp. 243–51; Michalowski forthcoming. Translations: Kramer 1963, p. 333; Kramer in Barnett and Kramer 1963, pp. 21–22; Römer 1985, pp. 344–46.

333

Cuneiform tablet with the Lamentation over the Destruction of Sumer and Ur

Cuneiform inscription in Sumerian
Clay
H. 12.7 cm (5 in.); W. 12.7 cm (5 in.); Thickness
3.8 cm (1½ in.)
Mesopotamia
Old Babylonian period, ca. 1740 B.C.
University of Pennsylvania Museum of Archaeology
and Anthropology, Philadelphia N 1735, N 1764,
N 1783, N 6287, Ni 4414

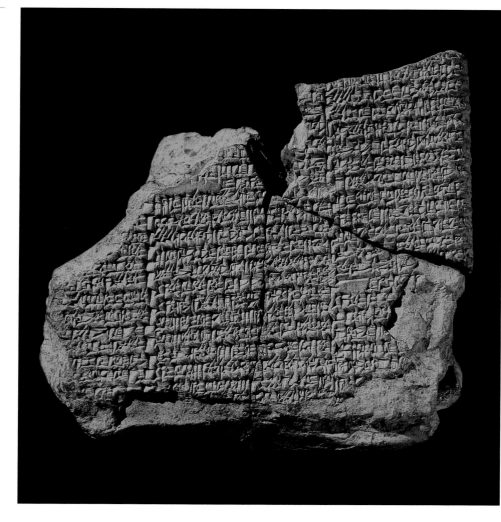

When the fifth king of the Third Dynasty of Ur, Ibbi-Sin, mounted the throne about 2013 B.C., his kingdom covered most of Babylonia and various border principalities in Iran. After fewer than four years, many central as well as outlying provinces split off, creating independent states. Two decades later Iranian armies from areas that had only recently been under the thumb of Ur sacked what was left of the realm, including the capital. We know very little about the historical processes that led to the decline and fall of Ur; to describe these events scholars have relied on later literary texts that mix fact with fiction. The main sources are a set of literary letters, including the one described above (see entry for cat. no. 332), and this long poem that describes the calamity that took place about 1989 B.C.[1]

The Lamentation opens with a long section describing the divine decision to end the rule of Ur and

That (king) Ibbi-Sin be taken to the land of Elam in fetters,
That from the mountain Zabu, which is on the edge of the sea land, up to the borders of Anshan
Like a bird that has flown its nest, he shall never return to his city.

Furthermore,

To quickly subdue (Ur) like a yoked ox, to bow its neck to the ground,
(The gods) An, Enlil, Enki, and Ninmah decided its fate.
Its fate, which cannot be changed, who can overturn it—
Who can oppose the commands of An and Enlil?

An frightened the (very) dwelling of Sumer, the people were afraid,
Enlil blew an evil storm; silence lay upon the city,
Nintu bolted the door of the storehouses of the land,
Enki blocked the water in the Tigris and Euphrates,
Utu took away the pronouncement of equity and justice,
Inanna handed over (victory in) strife and battle to a rebellious land,
Ningirsu wasted Sumer like milk poured to the dogs.
Revolt descended upon the land, something that no one had ever known,
Something unseen, which had no name, something that could not be fathomed.

The god of that city turned away, its shepherd vanished.
The people, in fear, could barely breathe,
The storm immobilizes them; the storm does not let them return,
For them there is no return; the time of captivity does not pass.

Thereupon the various deities abandon their cities, which are taken one by one by enemy forces. After the fall of Ur itself, the gods relent, and the storm—that is, the Iranian armies—is lifted. Calm returns to Ur, but its king has been led off in shackles, never to return.   PM

1. Edition: Michalowski 1989.

334

Cuneiform tablet with the "law code" of Lipit-Eshtar

Cuneiform inscription in Sumerian
Clay
H. 15.2 cm (6 in.); W. 14.6 cm (5¾ in.); Thickness
3.8 cm (1½ in.)
Mesopotamia, Nippur
Old Babylonian period, ca. 1740 B.C.
University of Pennsylvania Museum of Archaeology
and Anthropology, Philadelphia UM 29-16-55,
UM 29-16-249, N 1791

This royal inscription of king Lipit-Eshtar of Isin (ca. 1919–1909 B.C.) contains a collection of ideal legal decisions that were intended to demonstrate the Crown's concern for, and control of, justice in the land.[1] At least one earlier king, Ur-Namma of Ur, had commissioned a similar monument, and later rulers, including the famous Hammurabi of Babylon, would follow suit. Although popularly described as "law codes," these are nothing of the kind, as they had no statutory legal value. The text was originally inscribed on stone steles that were erected in public places, but aside from a few stone fragments it is known today only from school copies on clay tablets. Although the text is still incomplete, the general outlines can be reconstructed with assurance. It opens with a first-person prologue that resembles a royal hymn, which leads into the legal examples, of which approximately fifty are preserved, and is followed by an epilogue that includes a standard curse on anyone who might want to erase or alter the inscription.

The composition begins with the words:

When great An, father of the gods, and
Enlil, king of all the lands, the master who
determines destinies, bestowed a beneficent
reign unto (the goddess) Ninisina (of the
city of Isin) . . . I, Lipit-Eshtar, who am the
pious shepherd of (the city of) Nippur,
the effective farmer of (the city of) Ur,
who never neglects (the city of) Eridu,
the ruler proper for the (city of) Uruk,
king of (the city of) Isin, king of Sumer
and Akkad, chosen by the heart of (the
goddess) Inanna—By the command of (the
god) Enlil I established justice in Sumer
and Akkad.

After describing how he released debts and imposed social order, the king lists examples of just decisions.   PM

1. Most recent edition: Roth 1995, pp. 23–35.

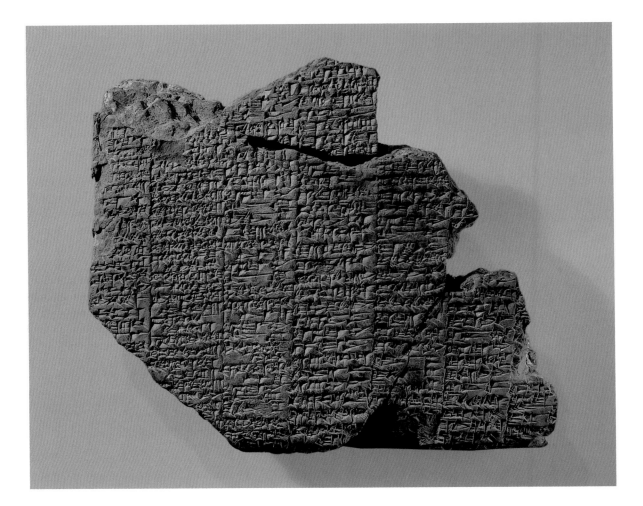

335

Cuneiform tablet with the Instructions of Shuruppak

Cuneiform inscription in Sumerian
Clay
H. 8.9 cm (3½ in.); W. 10.2 cm (4 in.); Thickness
3.8 cm (1½ in.)
Mesopotamia
Old Babylonian period, ca. 1740 B.C.
University of Pennsylvania Museum of Archaeology
and Anthropology, Philadelphia   UM 29-13-326,
UM 29-16-240

This four-column tablet originally contained
the second half of a composition recounting
the wise advice given to the legendary
Ziusudra, survivor of the Great Flood (see cat.
no. 341), by his father, Shuruppak, son of
Ubar-Tutu.[1] According to the Sumerian King
List (see entry for cat. no. 330), the latter was
the king of the southern Mesopotamian city
of Shuruppak who ruled just before the Great
Flood. The poem begins with traditional lines
that place the action in remote antiquity:

In those days, in those distant days it was,
In those nights, in those remote nights it
was,

In those years, in those distant years it was—;
At that time, one who had wisdom, who
possessed knowledge and intelligence and
wisdom was living in Sumer:
Shuruppak, the one who had wisdom, who
possessed knowledge and intelligence, was
living in Sumer.
(This) Shuruppak gave his son instructions,
Shuruppak, son of Ubar-Tutu, gave instruc-
tions to his son Ziusudra:
"O my son, I want to give you instructions,
so pay attention,
Do not neglect my instructions
Do not go against my words
For an elder's instructions are precious and
you must submit to them!"

The body of the text consists of proverbial
sayings as well as detailed admonitions. The
wise one tells his son: "Don't drive away a
debtor, for he may turn into your enemy!"
The tablet illustrated here begins with the
line: "Don't beat a farmer's son, for he might
then destroy your irrigation ditch!"
The Instructions had the longest history
of any piece of Mesopotamian literature. The
text is mainly known in this eighteenth-century

Sumerian version, but there is also a redac-
tion from nine hundred years earlier and an
eleventh-century-B.C. Akkadian translation
from the city of Ashur.   PM

1. Editions: Alster 1974, with additions by Civil
1984b, pp. 281–98; Alster 1987, pp. 199–206; Alster
1990, pp. 15–19. Translations: Wilcke 1978; Römer 1990,
pp. 48–67.

336

Cuneiform tablet with the legend of Enmerkar and the Lord of Aratta

Cuneiform inscription in Sumerian
Clay
H. 7.6 cm (3 in.); W. 5.6 cm (2¼ in.); Thickness 3 cm
(1⅛ in.)
Mesopotamia, Nippur
Old Babylonian period, ca. 1740 B.C.
University of Pennsylvania Museum of Archaeology
and Anthropology, Philadelphia   CBS 2150

This composition is part of a set of four poems
centered on the matter of Aratta.[1] Aratta, a
mythical city in Iran, was a symbolic source of

precious metals and stones for Sumer. The poems were set in Early Dynastic times, during the reign of the legendary king Enmerkar of Uruk, although they were probably composed much later, in the Ur III period. This particular poem describes the rivalry between Enmerkar of Uruk-Kulaba and an unnamed ruler of Aratta, who vie for the attentions of the goddess Inanna; the true focus of the text, however, is the cultural superiority of Sumerian civilization over the lands that provided its luxury goods by means of tribute and trade. The poem begins with a hymn to the city of Uruk, quickly zeroing in on the main topic:

(At that time) the foreign land of Dilmun did not exist . . . ,
But the E-anna (temple) of Uruk-Kulaba was grounded,

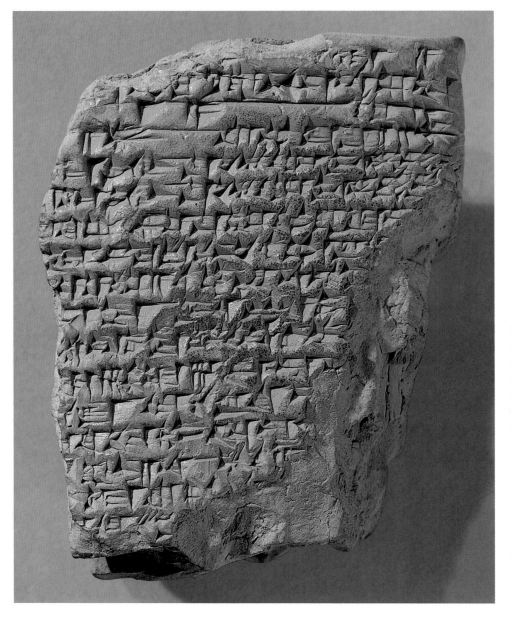

And the dwelling of Pure Inanna
Sparkled midst Brickwork Kulaba like silver in the lode.
[*Goods*] were not yet delivered, and there was no exchange,
[*Tribute*] was not yet delivered and there was no foreign trade
Neither [gold], silver, copper, tin, blocks of lapis lazuli,
[Nor mountain stones] were yet brought down voluntarily from the mountain lands.

And so Enmerkar makes a plea to his goddess Inanna:

"O sister mine, make Aratta, for Uruk's sake,
Skillfully work gold and silver for me!
[Make them cut for me] translucent lapis lazuli in blocks,

[Make them *prepare* for me] *electrum* and translucent lapis!"

The rivalry between Uruk and Aratta is settled, not by force, but by wit. The kings send a messenger across the vast mountain ranges that separate the two cities with demands of submission and with riddles to solve. After two such exchanges, in which Uruk took the upper hand, Enmerkar once again dictated his message to the envoy, but:

This speech was long and difficult to understand;
The messenger's mouth was too heavy and he could not repeat it.
Because the messenger's mouth was too heavy and he could not repeat it,
The king of Kulaba formed some clay and put words on it as if on a tablet.
Before that time the inscribing of words on clay (tablets) did not exist;
But now, in the sun of that day, it was indeed so (established)—
The king of Kulaba had inscribed words as if on a tablet, it was indeed so (established)!

After the messenger arrived in Aratta,

The king of Aratta set a clay lamp
Before the messenger.
(In its light) the king of Aratta looked at the clay (tablet).
The spoken words were but nails, and his brow darkened.
The king of Aratta kept staring into the clay lump.

This remarkable story—the only ancient Sumerian tale about the origins of writing—demonstrates in what respects the Mesopotamians viewed themselves superior to their neighbors. The metaphor "nails" for cuneiform anticipates by millennia the modern term, which is derived from Latin ("wedge-shaped"). The unfortunate ruler of Aratta immediately recognized the power of the newly literate king of Uruk and had to submit to his rule.

PM

1. See, in general, Vanstiphout 1995a. Edition: Cohen 1973. Translation: Jacobsen 1987a, pp. 275–319. A new English translation by Vanstiphout will be published soon in the Society of Biblical Literature, Writings from the Ancient World Series.

Cuneiform tablet with the Myth of Enki and Ninhursanga

Cuneiform inscription in Sumerian
Clay
H. 12.7 cm (5 in.); W. 19.1 cm (7½ in.); Thickness
2.5 cm (1 in.)
Mesopotamia, Nippur
Old Babylonian period, ca. 1740 B.C.
University of Pennsylvania Museum of Archaeology
and Anthropology, Philadelphia CBS 4561

This tablet forms part of a narrative that may be the most complex and enigmatic of all Sumerian myths, a story of fertility, incest, and even cannibalism.[1] It begins in the sacred land of Dilmun, usually identified with the Gulf island of Bahrain, at a time when nothing existed there. The goddess of the place complains to her father, Enki, about the island's barrenness. He blesses it, endows it with freshwater, and transforms it into a center of shipping commerce.

In Sumerian times the island of Dilmun was a thriving trade emporium, where sailors, commercial agents, and entrepreneurs from Mesopotamia, Iran, Oman (Magan), and even perhaps India (Meluhha) exchanged goods and ideas. For the Mesopotamians, Iran was the source of most precious woods, metals, and stones, some mined there, others from as far east as India and Afghanistan, while their own land exported wool, cloth, grain, and other agricultural products. In one version of the poem, found in the city of Ur, Enki's blessing describes this trade in detail, listing the various eastern sources of luxury goods (an echo of this can be found in Enmerkar and the Lord of Aratta, cat. no. 336):

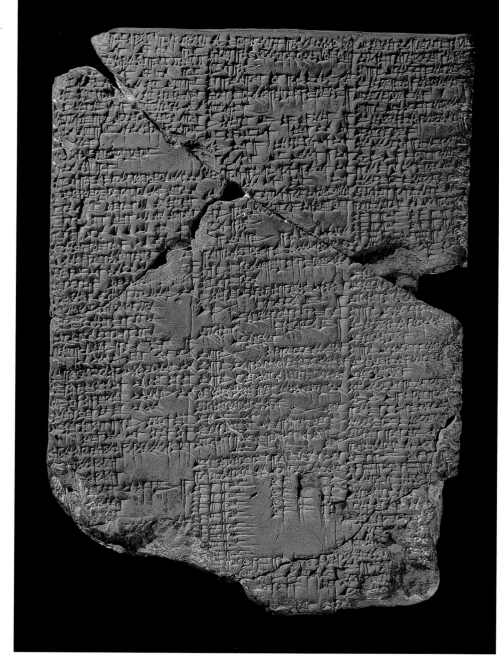

Your city shall (be established as?) the center of all water commerce in the land,
Dilmun shall (be established as) the center of all water commerce in the land,
The foreign land of Tukrish shall trade with you precious metals from Harali
And precious stones from . . .
The foreign land of Meluhha shall bring you prized and desirable carnelian
Mes wood of Magan and lovely *aba* wood In great boats.
The foreign land of Marhashi
Will *shower* you with prized stones, with topaz,
The foreign land of Magan shall [*bring*] you

Strong resilient copper, dolerite, *u* and *shumin* stone,
The Sealand shall [*bring*] you dolerite *fit for a king*,
The (nomads of) the Tent-Land shall [*bring*] you lovely multicolored wool,
The foreign land of Elam will offer you first-grade wool as tribute,
The shrine Ur, seat of royal power, city [of . . .]
Shall [*bring*] you boatloads of grain, oils, carpets, and fine cloth,

And the teeming ocean shall [offer] you its riches!

In this new abundant land Enki mates with the mother goddess Ninhursanga and as a result their daughter Ninmu is born. Enki then makes love to his daughter, and also to the offspring of that union, again producing a daughter, the spider goddess of weaving named Uttu. Enki once again lusts after the little girl, in the guise of a gardener woos her with gifts, and impregnates her with his seed.

Uttu, filled with the divine seed, cries out in pain. The mother goddess comes to her aid and plucks out the seeds, from which seven plants grow. The ever-voracious Enki immediately devours these plants, whereupon he is cursed by Ninhursanga. The text is broken at this point, but it appears that Enki becomes ill and that a fox offers to reconcile him with the mother goddess. Ninhursanga then places the sick Enki next to her vagina, lays her hands on him, and says:

"O, my brother, what is it that pains you?"
—"The top of my head *(ugudili)* pains me!"
And she gave birth to Ab'u.
"O my brother, what is it that pains you?"
"The hair on my head *(pasiki)* pains me!"
And she gave birth to Ninsikila.
"O my brother, what is it that pains you?"
—"My feet *(ngiri)* pain me!"
And she gave birth to Ninngiriutu.
"O my brother, what is it that pains you?"
—"My mouth *(ka)* pains me!"
And she gave birth to Ninkasi.
"O my brother, what is it that pains you?"
—"My throat *(zi)* pains me!"
And she gave birth to Nazi.
"O my brother, what is it that pains you?"
—"My arms *(a)* pain me!"
And she gave birth to Azimua.
"O my brother, what is it that pains you?"
—"My ribs *(ti)* pain me!"
And she gave birth to Ninti.
"O my brother, what is it that pains you?"
—"My side *(zag)* pains me!"
And she gave birth to Enzag.
(Enki then announced:) "The children that have been born shall not lack presents:
Ab'u shall be the master of plants *(u)*,
Ninsikila shall be the lord of (the land of) Magan,
Ninngiriutu shall marry Ninazu,
Ninkasi (the goddess of brewing) shall be the one who fills the heart (with joy),
Nazi shall marry Nindara,
Azimua shall marry Ningishzida,
Ninti shall be the mistress of the month,
And Enzag shall be the master of Dilmun!"
To Enki be praise!

PM

1. Editions: Kramer 1945; Attinger 1984. Translations: Jacobsen 1987a, pp. 181–204; Bottéro and Kramer 1989, pp. 151–64; Römer 1993, pp. 363–86.

338

Cuneiform tablet with the Myth of Enlil and Ninlil

Cuneiform inscription in Sumerian
Clay
H. 7.6 cm (3 in.); W. 9.5 cm (3¾ in.); Thickness 3.8 cm (1½ in.)
Mesopotamia, Nippur
Old Babylonian period, ca. 1740 B.C.
University of Pennsylvania Museum of Archaeology and Anthropology, Philadelphia   CBS 8176, 8215, 13853, Ni 2707

This is one of two very different Sumerian poems that explain how the Nippur god Enlil, the effective head of the Sumerian pantheon, found a wife named Ninlil.[1] The myth begins in Nippur, where the young lady's mother tells her not to walk along the riverbank because she will attract the attention of Enlil, who will want her. Predictably, the girl disobeys her mother and is approached by Enlil, who propositions her but is rejected. The lovelorn god finds a way of making love to her, nevertheless, and from their union is born the moon god Nanna, also known as Sin. Enlil retreats into the netherworld, but the great gods capture him and banish him from Nippur for his crime. He leaves, followed by Ninlil, and disguises himself as a gatekeeper, as guardian of the river that borders the netherworld, and as the master of the boat that crosses these waters. In the form of each character he makes love to Ninlil, and after each encounter she gives birth: first to the twin deities of the netherworld, Nergal and Meslamtaea, then to the chthonic god Ninazu, and finally to the divine canal inspector Enbilulu. Unexpectedly, and without any explanation, Enlil's crimes are forgiven, and the poem ends with glorious praise for the god of Nippur:

Enlil is god, Enlil is king!
He is the lord whose orders cannot be altered,
Whose foremost commands cannot be changed!
Because of his praiseworthy care of Mother Ninlil,
Praise be to Father Enlil!

PM

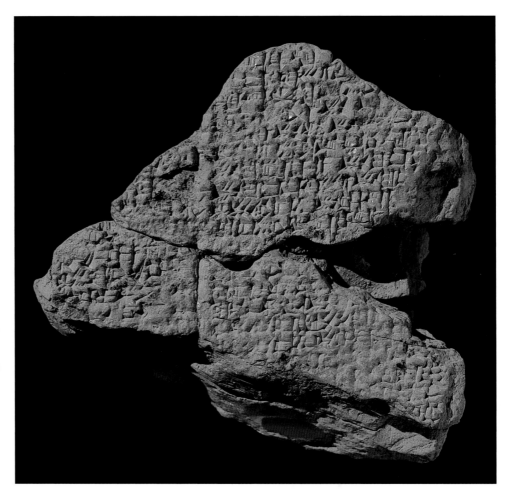

1. Edited by Behrens 1978. For discussion and an English translation, see Cooper 1980. Other translations: Jacobsen 1987a, pp. 167–80; Bottéro and Kramer 1989, pp. 105–15; Römer 1993, pp. 421–34.

339

Cuneiform tablet with the Hymn to the Hoe

Cuneiform inscription in Sumerian
Clay
H. 8.3 cm (3¼ in.); W. 14 cm (5½ in.); Thickness
3.2 cm (1¼ in.)
Mesopotamia, Nippur
Old Babylonian period, ca. 1740 B.C.
University of Pennsylvania Museum of Archaeology
and Anthropology, Philadelphia CBS 13877

A short composition of 109 lines, this text glorifies the ubiquitous garden hoe.[1] It was apparently widely studied, as we have more than sixty copies of the poem from schools in Nippur, Ur, and elsewhere. The Sumerian word for "hoe" wa*s al;* the text cleverly plays on the syllables */al/* and */ar/* in all possible forms. The author searched out words that contained these syllables and also used the verbal prefix *al-* on many of the verbs, achieving a didactic and perhaps even humorous "study in *al.*" The narrative, such as it is, begins with the Creation. The god Enlil, with the help of his hoe, forms the city of Nippur, the axis of the heavens and the earth, and apportions the workloads (Sumerian *altar*), and then:

> Enlil praised his hoe *(al),*
> His hoe *(al)* made of gold, with a lapis lazuli tip
> His hoe, whose tied-on blade *(al sala)* was made with silver and gold,
> His hoe, the side of whose shaft was like a lapis lazuli plough,
> Whose blade was like a battering ram *(gud si dili)* that attacks great *(gal)* walls.

Various other divine shrines are then constructed throughout Sumer with the help of the hoe, and the poem ends with a short hymn of praise to Enlil's magnificent tool.

PM

1. There is no edition of the composition. English translation: Farber 1997.

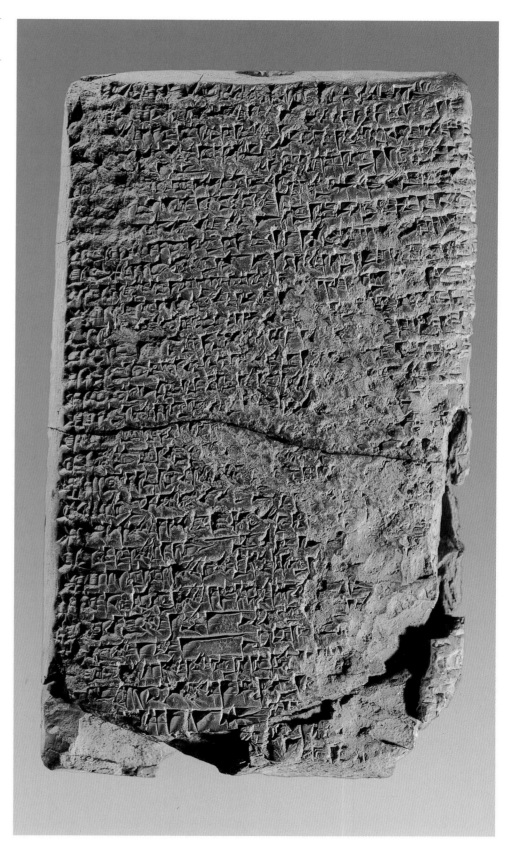

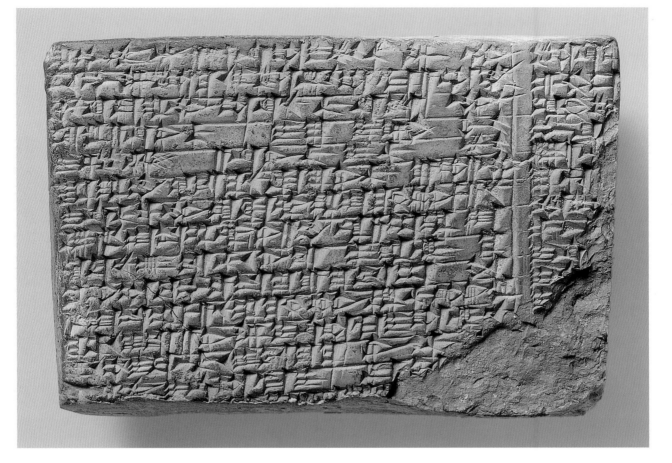

340

Cuneiform tablet with the Myth of Etana

Cuneiform inscription in Akkadian
Clay
H. 7 cm (2¾ in.); W. 10.5 cm (4⅛ in.)
Mesopotamia, Larsa (?)
Old Babylonian period, ca. 1740
The Pierpont Morgan Library, New York MLC 1363

In the Sumerian literary tradition Etana was a legendary king of the northern city of Kish. According to the Old Babylonian version of the Sumerian King List (cat. no. 330), he was "a shepherd who ascended to the heavens, who made fast all the lands." After his death he became an officer in the netherworld, alongside the other great legendary ruler from primeval days, Gilgamesh of the southern city of Uruk. To date no Sumerian stories about Etana have come to light, but he was the hero of a fascinating Akkadian-language myth known in still-incomplete versions that originated in various times and various places, from Old Babylonian Susa in Iran to Neo-Assyrian

Nineveh.[1] Although the various versions differ considerably and some details are missing, including the all-important conclusion, the broad outlines of the story can be reconstructed in part.

The narrative begins when the gods establish the office of kingship and bestow it on Etana of Kish. The king builds temples, including one for the storm god that contains a tree with a snake living in its root and an eagle in its crown. Although these creatures had sworn friendship, the eagle eats the snake's offspring. For his offense, the eagle is thrown in a pit; eventually his cries touch the heart of Shamash, the sun god, who controls justice. But Shamash cannot directly aid the evildoer, and so he sets in motion a plan to help the eagle. Because he is without heir, king Etana has been praying to the sun god for help. Shamash instructs him to save the eagle, who will help him find the plant of birth, which will provide him with children. Etana comes to the aid of the eagle and gets him out of the

pit. Spurred on by a dream, he grabs the eagle by the wings and the two fly in search of the plant, an amazing flight that is described in detail. When they lose sight of the earth, the king loses his nerve and begs the eagle to set him down so he can return to his city. The bird complies, and there the story breaks off. Thus it is impossible to know if Etana failed in his quest or if he obtained the plant by some other means.

A number of Old Akkadian seals depict a bearded man mounted on an eagle (see cat. no. 148), and some have suggested that this is an illustration of the Etana story. There are, however, many reasons to question this interpretation.[2]   PM

1. The latest edition, with full discussion of the interpretive and textual problems of the Etana Myth, is Haul 2000. Recent English translations can be found in Dalley 1991, pp. 189–202, and Foster 1995, pp. 102–14.
2. For a summary of this discussion, see Haul 2000, pp. 40–44.

Cuneiform tablet with the Sumerian Flood story

Cuneiform inscription in Sumerian
Clay
H. 10.2 cm (4 in.); W. 13.3 cm (5¼ in.); Thickness
4.5 cm (1¾ in.)
Mesopotamia, Nippur
Old Babylonian period, ca. 1740 B.C.
University of Pennsylvania Museum of Archaeology
and Anthropology, Philadelphia CBS 10673, 10867

How the god Enlil attempted to wipe out humanity by means of a Great Flood is recounted in this fragmentary poem.[1] After the creation of the world all was well; humanity was established, animals multiplied everywhere, kingship was lowered from the heavens, and the main cities of Sumer were apportioned to the major divinities. The text breaks at this point, but from parallel Babylonian stories we can surmise that the noise of teeming humanity proved to be too much for Enlil, who decided to put an end to it. The other gods and goddesses lamented this decision, but only the crafty Enki took action, revealing the future to a king by the name of Ziusudra. The text breaks once again, but it undoubtedly continued with a description of the construction of a large boat that would withstand the coming deluge. And so Ziusudra survived the Flood:

> All the destructive winds (and) gales were present,
> The storm swept over the capitals.
> After the storm had swept the country for seven days and seven nights. . . .
> And the destructive wind had rocked the huge boat in the high water,
> The Sun came out, illuminating the earth and the sky.

> Ziusudra made an opening in the huge boat,
> And the Sun with its rays entered the huge boat.
> The king Ziusudra
> Prostrated himself before the sun god;
> The king slaughtered a large number of bulls and sheep.

Thus Ziusudra saved the seed of humanity. In return he was made immortal and was settled in far-off Dilmun, the Sumerian name equated by scholars with the Gulf island of Bahrain.

PM

1. Edited by Civil 1969. Translations: Jacobsen 1981, pp. 513–29; Kramer 1983a, pp. 115–21; Jacobsen 1987a, pp. 145–50; Römer 1993, pp. 448–58.

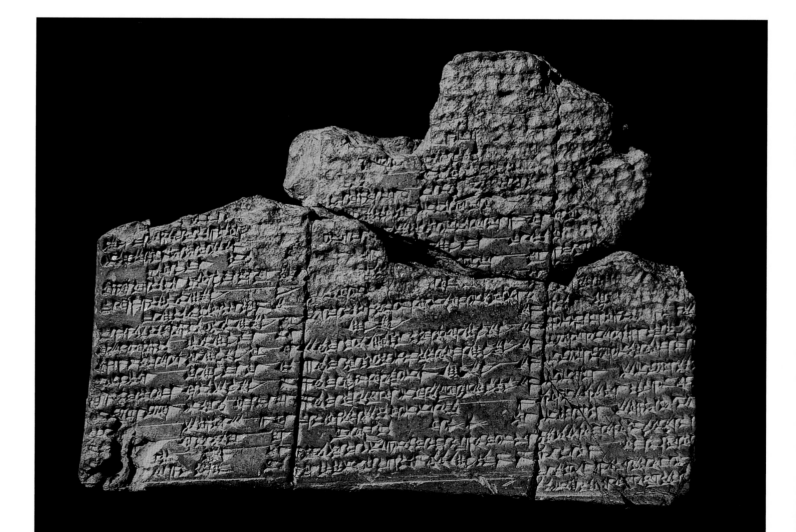

URUK AND THE WORLD OF GILGAMESH

BEATE SALJE

In royal hymns of the Third Dynasty of Ur, the kings of Ur traced their descent back to the rulers of the Early Dynastic city of Uruk and thus were able to claim legitimacy as its political successor. Ur-Namma, the first king of the Third Dynasty of Ur, claimed to be the older brother of Gilgamesh (in Sumerian, Bilgames), the legendary king of Uruk; Ur-Namma's family may have come from Uruk. King Shulgi, who succeeded Ur-Namma, also claimed to be the brother and friend of Gilgamesh, whom he glorified for bringing about the political ascendancy of Uruk. It was probably during the reign of Shulgi that a group of epics about the First Dynasty of Uruk was composed and orally transmitted stories of the heroic exploits of Gilgamesh were recorded on cuneiform tablets. Five independent Gilgamesh stories may first have appeared in written form during the Ur III dynasty but are primarily known today from eighteenth-century-B.C. copies made in the Old Babylonian period for use in the school curriculum (see "The Earliest Scholastic Tradition," by Piotr Michalowski, in this catalogue).

The Gilgamesh myths were independent Sumerian compositions, not parts of an epic cycle or pieces of a continuous heroic narrative. Gilgamesh and Akka presents a tale in which Gilgamesh, the king of Uruk, triumphs over his foe Akka, ruler of the city of Kish. Gilgamesh and Huwawa, known in two versions, called A and B, describes an expedition to the Cedar Forest, where Gilgamesh subdues Huwawa, guardian of the forest, who is then slain by Enkidu, Gilgamesh's servant. In Gilgamesh and the Netherworld, Enkidu descends into the Netherworld, where he is taken captive; on his return to the world of the living he tells Gilgamesh about the terrible conditions that beset the dead. In The Death of Gilgamesh, Gilgamesh lies on his deathbed and dreams that the gods are meeting to review his life and discuss his destiny. The fifth myth, Gilgamesh and the Bull of Heaven, deals with the antagonistic relationship between Gilgamesh and Inanna, the queen of heaven.

During the Old Babylonian period, a time of significant literary creativity, a new Babylonian work with origins in oral literature, Surpassing All Other Kings, was composed in Akkadian. This epic incorporated Akkadian translations of parts of the older Sumerian versions of Gilgamesh and the Bull of Heaven and Gilgamesh and Huwawa. Unfortunately, its text survives today only in fragmentary form. During the late second millennium the epic was revised and expanded; later tradition attributed the revised narrative poem to Sin-liqe-uninni, a learned scholar of the Kassite period from Uruk. By that time the poem had been renamed and was called He Who Saw the Deep. We know it today as the Epic of Gilgamesh. A nearly complete edition of this masterwork, called the Standard Version, exists on twelve tablets of the seventh century B.C. discovered at Nineveh, in the library of king Ashurbanipal of Assyria.[1]

By the fourteenth century B.C. the Gilgamesh story was already widely distributed. Since Akkadian was used as a lingua franca in international correspondence by the major powers of the day—the Egyptians, Hittites, Assyrians, and Babylonians—it is hardly surprising that the Epic of Gilgamesh found its way into the Levant and to the Hittite capital Hattusha in central Anatolia.

THE GILGAMESH STORY

In the Standard Version of the poem, Gilgamesh, who is two parts god and one part man, lives in the southern Mesopotamian city of Uruk. The poem tells of his heroic deeds and his efforts to attain fame and eternal life. Mad with power and glorying in his semidivine status, Gilgamesh tyrannizes the people of Uruk. According to one interpretation of the text he claims the *jus primae noctis,* or right to the first night with a vassal's bride, and forces enormous numbers of young men to labor building the city wall. The people's complaints about their unhappy condition and the king's neglect of his duties reach the ears of the gods, who determine to confront Gilgamesh with a man of strength equal to his. For that purpose the goddess Aruru forms the wild man Enkidu out of clay. At first Enkidu lives with the beasts, but Shamhat, a prostitute, lures him away from his natural surroundings, and in his first introduction to civilization he shares bread and drinks beer with shepherds outside the city. When he arrives at Uruk, Enkidu challenges the tyrannical Gilgamesh; however, after a fierce battle he is forced to acknowledge the king's superiority. Gilgamesh is delighted to find an equal partner, and the two become friends. In search of glory, they determine to test their strength against Humbaba (the Sumerian Huwawa), guardian of the Cedar Forest in Lebanon. The leaders of Uruk attempt to hold them back, but to no avail, and with the help of Gilgamesh's mother, the goddess Ninsun, the pair win the support of the sun god Shamash. Although plagued by nightmares during their journey, they reach the forest of cedars and kill Humbaba. They then fell the cedars and take the wood back to Uruk for building material.

Dazzled by Gilgamesh's heroic exploits, the goddess Ishtar (the Sumerian Inanna) demonstrates her desire for him, but he rejects her, saying that he has no wish to share the fate of her rejected lovers. Ishtar is enraged and calls on her father, Anu, to send her the Bull of Heaven to kill the king. However, Gilgamesh and Enkidu slay the bull. Enkidu is plagued by nightmares, foretelling his death; he rages against his fate, falls ill, and dies. Gilgamesh, inconsolable in his grief and forced to confront the finite nature of earthly existence, goes off in search of eternal life. Wandering toward the end of the world, he crosses high mountains, encounters men in the form of scorpions, and discovers a garden made of precious jewels. With the assistance of the tavern keeper Shiduri he tracks down the ferryman Urshanabi, who, in a voyage fraught with dangers, takes him across the river of death to Uta-napishti, survivor of the Deluge. The latter assures Gilgamesh that immortality is reserved for the gods alone, and that only because he himself survived the Deluge has it been granted to him as well. Uta-napishti does, however, tell the king where to find a rejuvenating plant. Gilgamesh finds the plant and sets out with it toward Uruk, but along the way a serpent steals it and promptly is rejuvenated

instead of the king. Gilgamesh finally returns to Uruk with the ferryman and there realizes that although he has failed to attain immortality, he has grown in wisdom.

THE WORLD OF GILGAMESH

In the Sumerian King List, Gilgamesh appears as the fifth ruler in the first Uruk dynasty, which means that he ruled about 2750 B.C. Although the written versions of the Gilgamesh poems date to later epochs, they still preserve remnants of the world of Uruk that are not recorded in any contemporaneous documents, remnants that help conjure a vivid picture of this oldest city and bring to life the world of Gilgamesh.

According to the Standard Version of the epic, it was Gilgamesh who built the vast wall around Uruk. (The extant wall system encompasses an area of more than two square miles.) An Uruk-period seal impression from the site depicts a crenellated city wall, suggesting that the wall known from Early Dynastic I was probably already there in the Late Uruk period.[2] Some clues about building practices in Early Uruk can be gleaned from Sumerian cylinder seals. A number of seals contain picture-signs of bundles of reeds twisted at the top to form a loop, symbols of both the goddess Inanna and the city of Uruk. On other seals bundles of reeds represent simple shelters for sheep (see cat. no. 10c). The bundles can also symbolize a temple, as they do on the great cult vessel in Uruk (figs. 9, 10). In addition, reed bundles appear as a three-dimensional ornament on buildings.

Gilgamesh, offspring of the goddess Ninsun and holy Lugalbanda, is described in Gilgamesh and the Bull of Heaven as a wild bull, a man of battle, athletic in strength, with well-proportioned limbs and a very black beard. In Gilgamesh and Akka he has bison eyes, a lapis lazuli beard, and elegant fingers. References to the ruler's dark eyes and lapis beard (compare the lapis beard of the god Ninurta in the Sumerian myth Lugale) are thought to signify that he is a mature, well-developed male.[3]

It is possible to think of Gilgamesh as a king who also functioned as a high priest (or "priest-king"), like the figure often seen on cylinder seals. The priest-king seems to be dressed in a kind of net robe during cult rituals and is often shown feeding the sacred herd of the goddess Inanna. On one seal (fig. 110), the herd, symbolized by two rams, is fed rosette-shaped flowers, another symbol of the goddess Inanna. This seal image, with depictions of reed bundles and two large cult vases topped by a lamb, is very similar to the scene in the uppermost frieze of the great cult vase from Uruk (figs. 9, 10),[4] which also shows reed

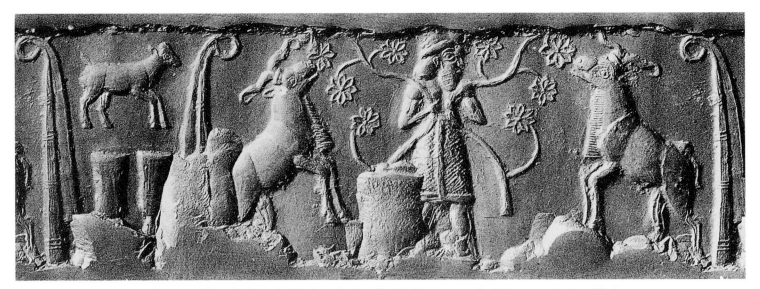

Fig. 110. Modern impression from a marble cylinder seal depicting a "priest-king" with two rams. Seal: Mesopotamia, Late Uruk, ca. 3300–3000 B.C. Vorderasiatisches Museum, Berlin, VA 10537.

bundles, two containers, and other similar elements. On another seal from the Early Uruk period, the man in the net robe appears in a boat, flanked by a shrine on one side and a stepped altar atop a bull, with reed-bundle symbols of the goddess, on the other (fig. 111). This scene too bears some resemblance to the top register of the Uruk Vase. Both of these seals are made of materials not found in Mesopotamia; one is of marble, with a copper mount in the form of a recumbent sheep, and the second is of lapis lazuli, with the mount a recumbent calf in silver. Beads from Uruk of lapis lazuli, rock crystal, and carnelian (see cat. no. 3) are contemporary with these seals. Lapis lazuli had to be brought from its source in the mountains of Afghanistan, and texts of the third millennium B.C. associate copper with the Gulf region. Cylinder seals and beads of precious materials may have had apotropaic or amuletic value. Perhaps for this reason, raw

materials such as gold, silver, lapis lazuli, and carnelian are in the ancient Near East traditionally associated with burials and the foundation deposits of religious edifices.

A number of images of animals, apparently used in cult rituals, were discovered in the temple precinct of the goddess Inanna in Uruk. They are the same animals we see on the Uruk Vase: rams and sheep. One example is a recumbent ram with close-set, snail-shaped horns, which must have been affixed to a base and have supported some sort of ornament atop a silver rod emerging from its back (cat. no. 2a). A particularly beautiful example in this exhibition is a recumbent calf made of marble whose spots are suggested by trefoil-shaped inlays of lapis lazuli (cat. no. 2b). The nearly lifesize head of a sheep (cat. no. 1) probably came from a cult precinct in E-anna ("House of Heaven"), a temple in Uruk dedicated to the goddess Inanna. Cattle appear

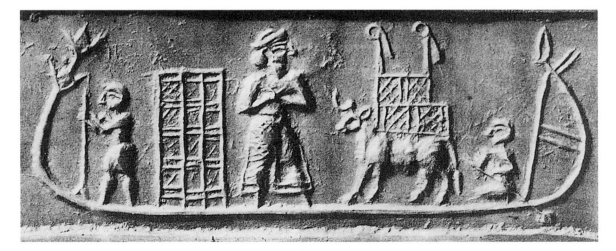

Fig. 111. Modern impression from a lapis lazuli cylinder seal depicting a "priest-king" in a boat. Seal: Mesopotamia, Late Uruk, ca. 3300–3000 B.C. Vorderasiatisches Museum, Berlin, VA 11040.

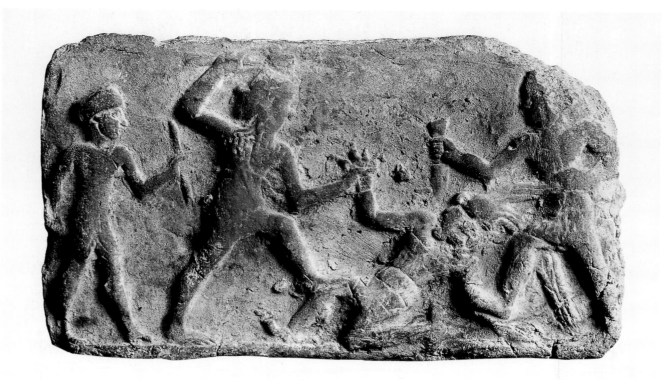

Fig. 112. Terracotta plaque depicting the death of Huwawa. Mesopotamia, early 2nd millennium B.C. Vorderasiatisches Museum, Berlin, VA 7246.

to be associated particularly closely with the priest-king, as they are on the seal where he is shown feeding a flock (cat. no. 10b). A chlorite bowl dated to the Late Uruk period is carved with four cows circling the vessel, their heads turned outward in full relief so that they gaze at the viewer (cat. no. 12).

Enkidu is the companion of Gilgamesh in the Standard Version of the epic and his servant in the Sumerian myths. Enkidu's life among the wild animals is described in Tablet II; accustomed to eating grass with the gazelles, he does not eat bread or drink ale. In his initiation to civilization, however, he learns to eat as humans do and to drink beer—seven pitchers at one time.[5] Beer drinking is equated with civilized life, and as an animal-man Enkidu initially does not understand the intoxicating nature of the drink. In fact, among the earliest written documents are recipes for beer making, complete with specified quantities of the various ingredients.[6] And a brewery seems to have existed in the Early Dynastic period at Lagash (present-day Al-Hiba), where a building belonging to the Kitchen (or Bagara) Temple of Ningirsu contained a large tank for liquids, a series of storage vats, and a huge oven. A tablet mentions the brewery and a brewer. In this earliest brewery known, beer was probably prepared for Ningirsu.

GILGAMESH IN ART

It is difficult to identify depictions of Gilgamesh on sculpture or cylinder seals. Scenes on Akkadian cylinder seals of heroes involved in combat have often been associated with Gilgamesh and Enkidu, but facile comparisons of the images with the myth are often in error. Any linkage of text and image needs to be based on close reading of an edition of the myth that is contemporary with its purported iconography.

The death of Huwawa, who tried to prevent Gilgamesh and Enkidu from felling the cedars of Lebanon, is often associated with a terracotta plaque from the beginning of the second millennium B.C. (fig. 112). The bearded hero places his foot on the ogre's leg, grasps him by the wrist, and is about to strike him with a club, while the beardless figure uses his foot to hold down the opponent's arm, grasps him by his long hair, and drives a knife into his neck. A bystander, staff in hand, observes the encounter. The image conforms most closely to the Sumerian Gilgamesh and Huwawa myth, in which Enkidu is said to sever the head of Huwawa at the neck. The smaller figure to the left of the hero may be one of the fifty men of Uruk said to accompany Gilgamesh and Enkidu to the Cedar Forest.

Charles, J. A.

1967 "Early Arsenical Bronzes—A Metal-lurgical View." *American Journal of Archaeology* 71, pp. 21–26.

Charpin, Dominique

1987 "Tablettes présargoniques de Mari." *MARI* 5, pp. 65–128.

Christian, Viktor

1940 *Altertumskunde des Zweistromlandes von der Vorzeit bis zum Ende der Achaemeniden-herrschaft.* Leipzig.

Chūkintō Bunka Sentā (Middle Eastern Culture Center)

1985 *Toruko bunmei ten / Uygarliklar ülkesi Türkiye / Land of Civilizations: Turkey.* Tokyo: Idemitsu Museum of Arts.

Ciarla, R.

1979 "The Manufacture of Alabaster Vessels at Shahr i-Sokhta and Mundigak in the 3rd Millennium B.C.: A Problem of Cultural Identity." In *Iranica,* edited by Gherardo Gnoli and A.V. Rossi, pp. 319-35. Series Minor X. Naples.

Civil, Miguel

1960 "Prescriptions médicales sumériennes." *Revue d'assyriologie et d'archéologie orientale* 54, pp. 57–72.

1969 "The Sumerian Flood Story." In *Atra-Hasīs: The Babylonian Story of the Flood,* by W. G. Lambert and A. R. Millard, pp. 138–45. Oxford.

1975 "Lexicography." In *Sumerological Studies in Honor of Thorkild Jacobsen on His Seventieth Birthday,* edited by S. J. Lieberman, pp. 123–57. Chicago.

1980 "Les limites de l'information textuelle." In *L'archéologie de l'Iraq du début de l'époque néolithique à 333 avant notre ère.* Colloques Internationaux de C.N.R.S., no. 580. Paris.

1983 "An Early Dynastic School Exercise from Lagaš (Al-Hiba 29)." *Bibliotheca Orientalis* 40, pp. 559–66.

1984a "Bilingualism in Logographically Written Languages: Sumerian in Ebla." In *Il bilinguismo a Ebla,* edited by Luigi Cagni, pp. 75–97. Naples.

1984b "Notes on the 'Instructions of Šurup-pak.'" *Journal of Near Eastern Studies* 43, pp. 281–98.

1985 "Ur III Bureaucracy: Quantitative Aspects." In *The Organization of Power: Aspects of Bureaucracy in the Ancient Near East,* edited by McG. Gibson and R. D. Biggs, pp. 35–44. Chicago.

1987 "The Early History of HAR-ra: The Ebla Link." In *Ebla, 1975–1985,* edited by Luigi Cagni, pp. 131–58. Naples.

1989 "The Statue of Šulgi-ki-ur$_5$-sag$_9$-kalam-ma, Part One: The Inscription." In *Dumu-e$_2$-dub-ba-a: Studies in Honor of Åke W. Sjöberg,* edited by Hermann Behrens et al., pp. 49–64. Occasional Publications of the Samuel Noah Kramer Fund, 11. Philadelphia.

1995 "Ancient Mesopotamian Lexicography." In *Civilizations of the Ancient Near East,*

edited by Jack Sasson et al., pp. 2305–14. New York.

de Clercq, Louis, and Joachim Ménant

1888 *Collection de Clercq: Catalogue méthodique et raisonné. . . .* 7 vols. Vols. 3, 4 by André de Ridder. Paris.

Cleuziou, Serge

1989 "The Early Dilmun Period (Third and Early Second Millennium B.C.)." In *Bahrain National Museum Archaeological Collection, Vol. 1: A Selection of Pre-Islamic Antiquities from Excavations 1954–1975,* edited by P. Lombard and M. Kervran, pp. 11–36. Bahrain: Ministry of Information.

Cleuziou, Serge, and Maurizio Tosi

1986 as editors. *The Joint Hadd Project: Summary Report on the First Season.* Rome.

1987 as editors. *The Joint Hadd Project: Summary Report on the Second Season, November 1986–January 1987.* N.p.

2000 "Ra's al-Jinz and the Prehistoric Coastal Cultures of the Ja'alan." *Journal of Oman Studies* 11, pp. 19–73.

Cohen, Sol

1973 "Enmerkar and the Lord of Aratta." Ph.D. dissertation, University of Pennsylvania, Philadelphia.

Cohn, Norman R. C.

1996 *Noah's Flood: The Genesis Story in Western Thought.* New Haven.

Colbow, Gudrun

1987 *Zur Rundplastik des Gudea von Lagaš.* Münchener vorderasiatische Studien, vol. 5. Munich.

Collon, Dominique

1982 *Catalogue of the Western Asiatic Seals in the British Museum: Cylinder Seals.* Vol. 2, *Akkadian–Post Akkadian–Ur III Periods.* London.

1986 *Catalogue of the Western Asiatic Seals in the British Museum: Cylinder Seals.* Vol. 3, *Isin-Larsa and Old Babylonian Periods.* Contributions by Margaret Sax and C. B. F. Walker. London.

1987 *First Impressions: Cylinder Seals in the Ancient Near East.* London: British Museum.

1995 *Ancient Near Eastern Art.* London: British Museum.

1996 "Mesopotamia and the Indus: The Evidence of the Seals." In *The Indian Ocean in Antiquity,* edited by J. Reade, pp. 209–25. London: British Museum.

1998 "Lapis Lazuli from the East: A Stamp Seal in the British Museum." *Ancient Civilizations from Scythia to Siberia* 5, pp. 31–39.

2001 *Cylinder Seals.* Vol. 5, *Neo-Assyrian and Neo-Babylonian Periods.* Contributions by Margaret Sax and C. B. F. Walker. London: British Museum.

Connan, Jacques, and Odile Deschesne

1996 *Le bitume à Suse: Collection du Musée du Louvre.* Paris.

1998 "Un matériau énigmatique: Le mastic du bitume de Suse." *Techné,* no. 7, pp. 13–16.

Contenau, Georges

1927–31 *Manuel d'archéologie orientale depuis les origines jusqu'à l'époque d'Alexandre.* Vols. 1, 2. Paris.

Conti, Giovanni

1990 *Miscellanea Eblaitica, 3: Il sillabario della quarta fonte della lista lessicale bilingue eblaita.* Quaderni di semitistica, 17. Florence.

Cooper, Jerrold S.

1980 Review of Behrens 1978. *Journal of Cuneiform Studies* 32, pp. 175–88.

1983a *The Curse of Agade.* Baltimore.

1983b *Reconstructing History from Ancient Inscriptions: The Lagash-Umma Border Conflict.* Sources from the Ancient Near East, vol. 2, fasc. 1. Malibu.

1986 *Presargonic Inscriptions.* Sumerian and Akkadian Royal Inscription, vol. 1; American Oriental Society, Translations Series, vol. 1. New Haven.

1993 "Sacred Marriage and Popular Cult in Early Mesopotamia." In *Official Cult and Popular Religion in the Ancient Near East,* edited by E. Matsushima, pp. 81–96. Heidelberg.

1996 "Sumerian and Akkadian." In *The World's Writing Systems,* edited by Peter T. Daniels and William Bright, pp. 37–56. Oxford.

Corpus der minoischen und mykenischen Siegel

1964 *Corpus der minoischen und mykenischen Siegel.* Vol. 1. Edited by Friedrich Matz. Berlin.

Crawford, Harriet

1991a "Seals from the First Season's Excavation at Saar, Bahrain." *Cambridge Archaeological Journal* 1, no. 2, pp. 255–62.

1991b *Sumer and the Sumerians.* Cambridge.

2000 "Bahrain: Warehouse of the Gulf." In *Traces of Paradise: The Archaeology of Bahrain, 2500 BC–300 AD.* Exh. cat. London: Brunei Gallery.

2002 "'Nearer My God to Thee?' The Relationship between Man and His Gods in Third-Millennium BC Mesopotamia." In *Of Pots and Plans: Papers on the Archaeology and History of Mesopotamia and Syria Presented to David Oates in Honour of His 75th Birthday,* edited by Lamia al-Gailani Werr et al. London.

Crawford, Harriet, Robert Killick, and Jane Moon, eds.

1997 *The Dilmun Temple at Saar: Bahrain and Its Archaeological Inheritance.* London-Bahrain Archaeological Expedition, Saar Excavation Reports, vol. 1. London and New York.

Crawford, Harriet, and Michael Rice, eds.

2000 *Traces of Paradise: The Archaeology of Bahrain, 2500 BC–300 AD.* Exh. cat. London: Brunei Gallery; Dilmun Committee.

Crawford, Vaughn

1959 "Nippur, the Holy City." *Archaeology* 12, no. 2, pp. 74–83.

Cros, Gaston

1910–14 *Nouvelles fouilles de Tello.* 3 vols. Paris.

Cultraro, Massimo

1999   "Non e tutt' oro quel che luce." In *Epì pónton plazomenói: Simposio italiano di Studi Egei dedicato a Luigi Bernabò Brea e Giovanni Pugliese Carratelli,* edited by V. La Rosa, D. Palermo, and L. Vagnetti, pp. 41–52. Rome.

Curtis, John

1984   *Nush-i Jan III: The Small Finds.* London: British Institute of Persian Studies.

Curvers, Hans, and Glenn M. Schwartz

1997   "Umm el-Marra: A Bronze Age Urban Center on the Jabbul Plain, Western Syria." *American Journal of Archaeology* 101, pp. 201–27.

D'Agostino, Franco

1996   *Testi amministrativi di Ebla: Archivio L.2769.* 2 vols. Materiali per il vocabolario sumerico, vol. 3; Materiali epigrafici di Ebla, vol. 7. Rome: Università degli Studi di Roma "La Sapienza."

Dales, George F.

1960   "Mesopotamian and Related Female Figurines: Their Chronology, Diffusion, and Cultural Function." Ph.D. dissertation, University of Pennsylvania, Philadelphia.

1965   "New Investigations at Mohenjo-daro." *Archaeology* 18, no. 2, pp. 145–50.

1968   "Of Dice and Men." *Journal of the American Oriental Society* 88, pp. 14–23.

Dalley, Stephanie

1991   *Myths from Mesopotamia: Creation, the Flood, Gilgamesh and Others.* Oxford.

David, Hélène

1996   "Styles and Evolution: Soft Stone Vessels During the Bronze Age in the Oman Peninsula." *Proceedings of the Seminar for Arabian Studies* 26, pp. 31–46.

De Cardi, Beatrice

1970   *Excavations at Bampur, a Third Millennium Settlement in Persian Baluchistan, 1966.* Anthropological Papers of the American Museum of Natural History, vol. 51, part 3. New York.

Deimel, Anton

1923   *Die Inschriften von Fara.* Vol. 2, *Schultexte aus Fara.* Leipzig.

de Jesus, Prentiss S.

1980   *The Development of Prehistoric Mining and Metallurgy in Anatolia.* British Archaeological Reports International Series, vol. 74. Oxford.

Delaporte, Louis

1920   *Catalogue des cylindres, cachets, et pierres gravées de style oriental.* Vol. 1, *Fouilles et missions.* Paris.

Delougaz, Pinhas

1933   *I. Plano-Convex Bricks and the Methods of Their Employment; II. The Treatment of Clay Tablets in the Field.* Oriental Institute of the University of Chicago, Studies in Ancient Oriental Civilization, no. 7. Chicago.

1940   *The Temple Oval at Khafajah.* Contribution by Thorkild Jacobsen. University of Chicago, Oriental Institute Publications, vol. 53. Chicago.

1952   *Pottery from the Diyala Region.* University of Chicago, Oriental Institute Publications, vol. 63. Chicago.

Delougaz, Pinhas, Harold D. Hill, and Seton Lloyd

1967   *Private Houses and Graves in the Diyala Region.* University of Chicago, Oriental Institute Publications, vol. 88. Chicago.

Delougaz, Pinhas, and Seton Lloyd

1942   *Pre-Sargonid Temples in the Diyala Region.* Contributions by Henri Frankfort and Thorkild Jacobsen. University of Chicago, Oriental Institute Publications, vol. 58. Chicago.

Demakopoulou, Katie, ed.

1990   *Troy, Mycenae, Tiryns, Orchomenos: Heinrich Schliemann, the 100th Anniversary of His Death.* Exh. cat. Athens: National Archaeological Museum.

1998   *The Aidonia Treasure: Seals and Jewellery of the Aegean Late Bronze Age.* Exh. cat. Melbourne: Hellenic Antiquities; Athens: Ministry of Culture.

Demisch, Heinz

1977   *Die Sphinx: Geschichte ihrer Darst. von d. Anfängen bis zur Gegenwart.* Stuttgart.

Depuydt, Leo

1995   "'More Valuable than All Gold': Ptolemy's Royal Canon and Babylonian Chronology." *Journal of Cuneiform Studies* 47, pp. 97–119.

Deshayes, J.

1966   "Rapport préliminaire sur la sixième campagne de fouille à Tureng Tépé (1965)." *Iranica Antiqua* 6, pp. 1–5.

Diakonoff, Igor M.

1947   "On an Ancient Oriental Sculpture" (in Russian). *Travaux du Département oriental* 4 (Leningrad, Ermitazh, Otdel Vostoka), pp. 107–18.

Di Cosmo, Nicola

2000   "The Ancient City-States of the Tarim Basin." In *A Comparative Study of Thirty City-State Cultures,* edited by Mogens Herman Hansen. Copenhagen.

Dolce, Rita

1978   *Gli intarsi mesopotamici dell'epoca protodinastica.* 2 vols. Serie archeologica, 23. Rome.

1996   "Gudea di Lagash e il suo regno: Stato di grazio o stato di immunità?" *Studi Micenei ed Egeo-Anatolici,* fasc. 38, pp. 7–38.

1998   "The Palatial Ebla Culture in the Context of North Mesopotamia and North Syrian Main Powers." In *About Subartu: Studies Devoted to Upper Mesopotamia,* vol. 4, part. 2, *Culture, Society, Image,* edited by Marc Lebeau, pp. 67–81. Turnhout.

Dörpfeld, Wilhelm

1902   *Troja und Ilion: Ergebnisse der Ausgrabungen in den vorhistorischen und historischen Schichten von Ilion, 1870–1894.* Contributions by Alfred Brückner, Hans von Fritze, Alfred Götze, Hubert Schmidt, Wilhelm Wilberg, and Hermann Winnefeld. Athens.

Dossin, Georges

1968   "L'inscription de Mesannepada." In *Le "trésor" d'Ur,* by André Parrot, pp. 53–59. Paris.

Doumas, Christos, and Vincenzo La Rosa, eds.

1997   *He Poliochne kai he proime epoche tou Chalkou sto Voreio Aigaio: Diethnes synedrio Athena, 22–25 Apriliou 1996 / Poliochni e l'antica età del bronzo nell'Egeo settentrionale: Convegno internazionale Atene, 22–25 Aprile 1996.* Athens.

Dundees, Alan

1988   *The Flood Myth.* Berkeley.

Dunham, Sally

1986   "Sumerian Words for Foundation." *Revue d'assyriologie et d'archéologie orientale* 80, pp. 31–64.

During Caspers, Elisabeth C. L.

1970–71   "Some Motifs as Evidence for Maritime Contact between Sumer and the Indus Valley." *Persica* 5, pp. 107–18.

1971   "The Bull's Head from Barbar Temple II, Bahrain: A Contact with Early Dynastic Sumer." *East and West* 21, pp. 217–24.

1972   "Etched Cornelian Beads." *Bulletin of the Institute of Archaeology* 10, pp. 83–98.

1982   "Sumerian Traders and Businessmen Residing in the Indus Valley Cities: A Critical Assessment of the Archaeological Evidence." *ANNALI* 42, pp. 337–80.

1984   "Sumerian Trading Communities Residing in Harappan Society." In *Frontiers of the Indus Civilization,* edited by B. B. Lal et al., pp. 363–70. New Delhi.

1986   "Animal Designs and Gulf Chronology." In *Bahrain through the Ages,* edited by H. A. Al-Khalifa and M. Rice, pp. 286–304. London.

1993–95   "The Meluhhan Cultural Heritage: Indianesque Stamp and Cylinder Seals, and Their Relevance for the Acculturation Process of the Harappans Abroad." *Persica* 15, pp. 7–27.

1994a   "Non-Indus Glyptics in a Harappan Context." *Iranica Antiqua* 29, pp. 83–106.

1994b   "Vanity Portrayed in Clay: The Female Terracotta Figurines from Harappa." In *South Asian Archaeology 1993,* edited by A. Parpola and P. Koskikallio, pp. 183–92. Helsinki.

1996   "Local MBAC Materials in the Arabian Gulf and Their Manufacturers." *Proceedings of the Seminar for Arabian Studies* 26, pp. 47–64.

1998   "The MBAC and the Harappan Script." *Ancient Civilizations from Scythia to Siberia* 5, pp. 40–58.

Durrani, F. A.

1964   "Stone Vases as Evidence of Connection between Mesopotamia and the Indus Valley." *Ancient Pakistan* 1, pp. 51–96.

1981   "Rehman Dheri and the Birth of Civilization in Pakistan." *Bulletin of the Institute of Archaeology, London University* 18, pp. 191–207.

Easton, D. F.

1984   "Priam's Treasure." *Anatolian Studies* 34, pp. 141–69.

Eaton-Krauss, Marianne

1985   "Fragment of Egyptian Jar Lid." In *Ebla to Damascus: Art and Archaeology of Ancient Syria,* edited Harvey Weiss, p. 170, no. 79. Exh. cat. Washington, D.C.: Smithsonian Institution.

Ebeling, Erich

1915–23   *Keilschrifttexte aus Assur religiösen Inhalts.* 2 vols. Wissenschaftliche Veröffentlichungen der Deutschen Orient-Gesellschaft, 28, 34. Leipzig.

Edens, Christopher

1993   "Indus-Arabian Interaction during the Bronze Age: A Review." In *Harappan Civilization: A Recent Perspective,* edited by G. Possehl, pp. 335–63. Delhi.

Edzard, Dietz Otto

1959   "Enmebaragesi von Kiš." *Zeitschrift für Assyriologie und vorderasiatische Archäologie* 53, pp. 9–26.

1972   "Ḥamṭu, marû und freie Reduplikation beim sumerischen Verbum (Fortsetzung)." *Zeitschrift für Assyriologie und vorderasiatische Archäologie* 62, pp. 1–34.

1980–83   "Königslisten und Chroniken, A. Sumerisch." In *Reallexikon der Assyriologie und vorderasiatischen Archäologie,* edited by D. O. Edzard, vol. 6, pp. 77–86. Berlin and New York.

1981   *Verwaltungstexte verschiedenen Inhalts: Aus dem Archiv L. 2769.* Archivi Reali di Ebla, Testi, 2. Rome.

1984   *Hymnen, Beschwörungen und Verwandtes aus dem Archiv L. 2769.* Archivi Reali di Ebla, Testi 5. Rome.

1992   "Der Vertrag von Ebla mit *A-bar-QA.*" In *Literature and Literary Language at Ebla,* edited by Pelio Fronzaroli, pp. 187–217. Quaderni di semitistica, no. 18. Florence.

1997   *Gudea and His Dynasty.* The Royal Inscriptions of Mesopotamia. Early Periods, vol. 3, part 1. Toronto.

Ehrenberg, Erica, ed.

2002   *Leaving No Stones Unturned: Essays on the Ancient Near East and Egypt in Honor of Donald P. Hansen.* Winona Lake, Ind.

Ehrich, Robert W., ed.

1992   *Chronologies in Old World Archaeology.* 3rd ed. 2 vols. Chicago.

Eidem, Jesper

1994   "Cuneiform Inscriptions." In *Qala'at al-Bahrain,* by F. A. Højlund and H. Andersen. Aarhus.

Electronic Text Corpus of Sumerian Literature

1998–   J. A. Black, G. Cunningham, E. Fluckiger-Hawker, E. Robson, and G. Zólyomi, trans. *The Electronic Text Corpus of Sumerian Literature* (http://www-etcsl.orient.ox.ac.uk/). Oxford.

Ellis, Richard S.

1968   *Foundation Deposits in Ancient Mesopotamia.* Yale Near Eastern Researches, 2. New Haven.

1989   "Note on a Textile Sample from the Main Mound at Tappeh Hesar, 1976."

In *Tappeh Hesar,* edited by Robert H. Dyson and Susan M. Howard, pp. 119–20. Florence.

1995   "The Trouble with 'Hairies.'" *Iraq* 57, pp. 159–65.

Emre, Kutlu

1971   *Anadolu kurşun figürinleri ve taş kaliplari / Anatolain Lead Figurines and Their Stone Moulds.* Ankara.

Englund, Robert K.

1994   *Archaic Administrative Texts from Uruk: The Early Campaigns.* Contribution by Rainer M. Boehmer. Ausgrabungen der Deutschen Forschungsgemeinschaft in Uruk-Warka, vol. 15; Archaische Texte aus Uruk, vol. 5. Berlin.

1996   "The Proto-Elamite Script." In *The World's Writing Systems,* edited by Peter T. Daniels and William Bright, pp. 160–64. Oxford.

1998   "Texts from the Late Uruk Period." In *Mesopotamien: Späturuk-Zeit und Frühdynastische Zeit,* edited by Josef Bauer, Robert K. Englund, and Manfred Krebernik, pp. 15–233. Göttingen.

Evans, Arthur

1895   *Cretan Pictographs and Pre-Phoenician Script; with an Account of a Sepulchral Deposit at Hagios Onuphrios near Phaestos in Its Relation to Primitive Cretan and Aegean Culture.* London.

Failaka

1966   *Archaeological Investigations in the Island of Failaka* (in Arabic). Kuwait.

Fairservis, Walter A.

1956   *Excavations in the Quetta Valley, West Pakistan.* Anthropological Papers of the American Museum of Natural History, vol. 45, part 2. New York.

1961   *Archaeological Studies in the Seistan Basin of Southwestern Afghanistan and Eastern Iran.* Anthropological Papers of the American Museum of Natural History, vol. 48, part 1. New York.

Falkenstein, Adam

1958   "Enheduana, die Tochter Sargons von Akkade." *Revue d'assyriologie et d'archéologie orientale* 52, pp. 129–31.

Falkenstein, Adam, and Ruth Opificius

1957–71   "Girsu." In *Reallexikon der Assyriologie und vorderasiatischen Archäologie,* edited by E. Weidner and W. von Soden, vol. 3, pp. 385–401. Berlin and New York.

Farber, Gertrud

1997   "Sumerian Canonical Compositions. A. Divine Focus. 1. Myths: The Song of the Hoe (1.157)." In *The Context of Scripture, I: Canonical Compositions from the Biblical World,* edited by William W. Hallo, pp. 511–13. Leiden.

Farmakovsky, B. V.

1914   "Arkhaichesky Period v Rossii" (The Archaic Period in Russia). *Materialy po arkheologii Rossii* (Materials on the Archaeology of Russia), no. 34, pp. 15–78.

Felli, Candida

2001   "Some Notes on the Akkadian Glyptic

from Tell Brak." In *Excavations at Tell Brak, Volume 2: Nagar in the Third Millennium B.C.,* edited by David Oates, Joan Oates, and Helen McDonald, pp. 141–50. Cambridge.

Finkel, I. L.

1992   "Les plus anciens jeux de table: La tablette des règles du jeu royal d'Ur." *Musées 1992,* pp. 154–55.

Finkelstein, Jacob J.

1963   "The Antediluvian Kings: A University of California Tablet." *Journal of Cuneiform Studies* 17, pp. 39–51.

1974   "The West, the Bible, and the Ancient Near East: Apperceptions and Categorizations." *Man,* n.s., 9, pp. 591–608.

Firth, Cecil M., and Battiscombe Gunn

1926   *Excavations at Saqqara: Teti Pyramid Cemeteries.* 2 vols. Service des Antiquités de l'Égypte. Cairo.

Fischer, Claudia

1996   "Gudea zwischen Tradition und Moderne." *Baghdader Mitteilungen* 27, pp. 215–28.

Fortin, Michel, ed.

1999   *Syria: Land of Civilizations.* Exh. cat. Translation by Jane Macauly. Montreal: Musée de la Civilisation de Québec.

Foster, Benjamin R.

1985   "The Sargonic Victory Stele from Telloh." *Iraq* 47, pp. 15–30.

1993   *Before the Muses: An Anthology of Akkadian Literature.* 2 vols. Bethesda.

1995   *From Distant Days: Myths, Tales and Poetry of Ancient Mesopotamia.* Bethesda.

Foster, Benjamin, Douglas Frayne, and Gary Beckman

2001   *The Epic of Gilgamesh: A New Translation, Analogues, Criticism.* New York and London.

Foxvog, Daniel A.

1980   "Funerary Furnishings in an Early Sumerian Text from Adab." In *Death in Mesopotamia: XXVIe Rencontre Assyriologique Internationale,* edited by Bendt Alster, pp. 67–75. Mesopotamia 8. Copenhagen.

Francfort, Henri-Paul

1989   *Fouilles de Shortughaï: Recherches sur l'Asie centrale protohistorique.* Contributions by Ch. Boisset et al. 2 vols. Mémoires de la Mission archéologique française en Asie centrale, vol. 2. Paris.

1994   "The Central Asian Dimension of the Symbolic System in Bactria and Margiana." *Antiquity* 68, no. 259, pp. 406–18.

Frangipane, Marcella

2000   "The Late Chalcolithic / EB I sequence at Arslantepe: Chronological and Cultural Remarks from a Frontier Site." In *Chronologies des pays du Caucase et de l'Euphrate aux IVe–IIIe millénaires,* edited by Catherine Marro and Harald Hauptmann, pp. 439–71. Paris.

Franke, Judith A.

1977   "Presentation Seals of the Ur III / Isin

Larsa Period." In *Seals and Sealing in the Ancient Near East,* edited by McGuire Gibson and Robert D. Biggs, pp. 61–66. Bibliotheca Mesopotamica, vol. 6. Malibu.

Franke-Vogt, Ute

1991   *Die Glyptik aus Mohenjo-Daro: Uniformität und Variabilität in der Induskultur. Untersuchungen zur Typologie, Ikonographie und räumlichen Verteilung.* 2 vols. Mainz am Rhein.

1995   "Vom Oxus zum Indus: Zwei Kompartmentsiegel aus Mohenjo-daro (Pakistan)." In *Beiträge zur Kulturgeschichte Vorderasiens: Festschrift für Rainer Michael Boehmer,* edited by U. Finkbeiner, R. Dittmann, and H. Hauptmann, pp. 145–65. Mainz am Rhein.

Frankfort, Henri

1932   *Archeology and the Sumerian Problem.* Oriental Institute of the University of Chicago, Studies in Ancient Oriental Civilization, no. 4. Chicago.

1933   *Tell Asmar, Khafaje, and Khorsabad: Second Preliminary Report of the Iraq Expedition.* Oriental Institute of the University of Chicago, Oriental Institute Communications, no. 16. Chicago.

1934a   *Iraq Excavations of the Oriental Institute, 1932/33: Third Preliminary Report of the Iraq Expedition.* Oriental Institute of the University of Chicago, Oriental Institute Communications, no. 17. Chicago.

1934b   "Mari et Opis. Essai de Chronologie." *Revue d'assyriologie et d'archéologie orientale* 31, pp. 173–79.

1935a   "Early Dynastic Sculptured Maceheads." In "Miscellanea Orientalia Dedicata Antonio Deimel," *Analecta Orientalia* 12, pp. 105–21.

1935b   *Oriental Institute Discoveries in Iraq, 1933/34: Fourth Preliminary Report of the Iraq Expedition.* Oriental Institute of the University of Chicago, Oriental Institute Communications, no. 19. Chicago.

1936a   "A New Site in Mesopotamia: Tell Agrab." *Illustrated London News,* September 12, p. 432.

1936b   *Progress of the Work of the Oriental Institute in Iraq, 1934/35: Fifth Preliminary Report of the Iraq Expedition.* Oriental Institute of the University of Chicago, Oriental Institute Communications, no. 20. Chicago.

1939   *Sculpture of the Third Millennium B.C. from Tell Asmar and Khafajah.* Oriental Institute of the University of Chicago, Oriental Institute Communications, no. 44. Chicago.

1943   *More Sculpture from the Diyala Region.* University of Chicago Oriental Institute Publications, vol. 60. Chicago.

1944   "A Note on the Lady of Birth." *Journal of Near Eastern Studies* 3, pp. 198–200.

1954   *The Art and Architecture of the Ancient Orient.* Pelican History of Art. Baltimore and Harmondsworth.

1955a   *The Art and Architecture of the Ancient Orient.* Pelican History of Art. Baltimore.

1955b   *Stratified Cylinder Seals from the Diyala Region.* University of Chicago Oriental Institute Publications, vol. 72. Chicago.

1956   *The Birth of Civilization in the Near East.* Garden City, N.Y.

1970   *The Art and Architecture of the Ancient Orient.* 4th ed. Pelican History of Art. Harmondsworth.

1996   *The Art and Architecture of the Ancient Orient.* Reprint. Yale University Press Pelican History of Art. New Haven.

Frankfort, Henri, Thorkild Jacobsen, and Conrad Preusser

1932   *Tell Asmar and Khafaje: The First Season's Work in Eshnunna, 1930–31.* Oriental Institute of the University of Chicago, Oriental Institute Communications, no. 13. Chicago.

Frankfort, Henri, Seton Lloyd, and Thorkild Jacobsen

1940   *The Gimilsin Temple and the Palace of the Rulers at Tell Asmar.* University of Chicago Oriental Institute Publications, vol. 43. Chicago.

Franklin, Alan D., Jacqueline S. Olin, and Theodore A. Wertime, eds.

1978   *The Search for Ancient Tin.* A Seminar Held at the Smithsonian Institution and the National Bureau of Standards, Washington, D.C., March 14–15, 1977. Washington, D.C.

Frayne, Douglas R.

1993   *The Royal Inscriptions of Mesopotamia. Early Periods.* Vol. 2, *Sargonic and Gutian Periods, 2334–2113 B.C.* Toronto.

1997   *The Royal Inscriptions of Mesopotamia. Early Periods.* Vol. 3, part 2, *Ur III Period, 2112–2004 B.C.* Toronto.

1999   "The Zagros Campaigns of Šulgi and Amar-Suena." In *Nuzi at Seventy-Five,* edited by D. I. Owen and G. Wilhelm, pp. 141–99. Bethesda.

Friberg, Jöran

1986   "The Early Roots of Babylonian Mathematics, III: Three Remarkable Texts from Ancient Ebla." *VO* 6, pp. 3–25.

Frifelt, Karen

1991   *The Island of Umm an-Nar.* Vol. 1, *Third Millennium Graves.* Højberg and Aarhus.

From the Land of the Scythians

1975   *From the Land of the Scythians: Ancient Treasures from the Museums of the U.S.S.R., 3000 B.C.–100 B.C.* Exh. cat. New York: The Metropolitan Museum of Art.

Fronzaroli, Pelio

1992   as editor. *Literature and Literary Language at Ebla.* Quaderni di semitistica, no. 18. Florence.

1993   *Testi rituali della regalità (Archivio L. 2769).* Contribution by Amalia Catagnoti. Archivi Reali di Ebla, Testi 11. Rome.

2002   *Testi di cancelleria: I rapporti con le città.* Rome.

Frymer-Kensky, Tikva

1977   "The Atrahasis Epic and Its Significance for Our Understanding of Genesis 1–9," *Biblical Archaeologist* 40, pp. 147–55.

Fuhr-Jaeppelt, Ilse

1972   *Materialien zur Ikonographie des Löwenadlers Anzu-Imdugud.* Munich.

Gadd, Cyril John

1932   "Seals of Ancient Indian Style Found at Ur." *Proceedings of the British Academy* 18, pp. 3–22.

Gadd, Cyril John, and Leon Legrain

1928   *Ur Excavations; Texts.* Vol. 1, *Royal Inscriptions.* London.

Garstang, John

1906   "Excavations at Hierakonpolis, at Esna and in Nubia." *Annales du Service des antiquités de l'Égypte* 7, p. 135.

Gasche, Hermann, J. A. Armstrong, S. W. Cole, and V. G. Gurzadyan

1998   *Dating the Fall of Babylon: A Reappraisal of Second-Millennium Chronology.* Mesopotamian History and Environment, Series 2, Memoirs, vol. 4. Chicago.

2000   "The New Chronology." In *Just in Time; Akkadica* 119–20.

Gates, Marie-Henriette

2000   "Kinet Höyük (Hatay, Turkey) and MB Levantine Chronology." In *Just in Time; Akkadica* 119–20, pp. 77–101.

Gelb, Ignace J.

1992   "Mari and the Kish Civilization." In *Mari in Retrospect: Fifty Years of Mari and Mari Studies,* edited by Gordon D. Young, pp. 121–202. Winona Lake, Ind.

Gelb, Ignace J., Piotr Steinkeller, and Robert M. Whiting Jr.

1991   *Earliest Land Tenure Systems in the Near East: Ancient Kudurrus.* 2 vols. University of Chicago Oriental Institute Publications, vol. 104. Chicago.

Genouillac, Henri de

1930   "Rapport sur les travaux de la mission de Tello. IIᵉ campagne: 1929–30." *Revue d'assyriologie et d'archéologie orientale* 27, pp. 169–86.

1934–36   as editor. *Fouilles de Telloh.* Contributions by André Parrot et al. 2 vols. Paris: Mission Archéologique de Musée du Louvre.

Gensheimer, Thomas R.

1984   "The Role of Shell in Mesopotamia; Evidence for Trade Exchange with Oman and the Indus Valley." *Paléorient* 10, pp. 65–73.

George, Andrew R., trans.

1999   *The Epic of Gilgamesh: The Babylonian Epic Poem and Other Texts in Akkadian and Sumerian.* New York.

Ghirshman, Roman

1938–39   *Fouilles de Sialk près de Kashan, 1933, 1934, 1937.* 2 vols. Musée du Louvre, Département des antiquités orientales, Série archéologique, vol. 4. Paris.

1961   *Sept mille ans d'art en Iran.* Exh. cat. Paris: Musée du Petit Palais.

1963   *Perse: Proto-Iraniens, Mèdes, Achéménides.* L'univers des formes, vol. 5. Paris.

1963a   "Statuettes archaïques du Fars (Iran)." *Artibus Asiae* 26, pp. 151–60.

1968   "Deux statuettes élamites du plateau iranien." *Artibus Asiae* 30, pp. 237–48.

Gibson, McGuire, D. P. Hansen, and R. L. Zettler

2001   "Nippur. B." In *Reallexikon der Assyriologie und Vorderasiatischen Archäologie,* edited by D. O. Edzard, vol. 9, pp. 546–65. Berlin and New York.

Gibson, McGuire, and Augusta McMahon

1995   "Investigation of the Early Dynastic-Akkadian Transition: Report of the 18th and 19th Seasons of Excavation in Area WF, Nippur." *Iraq* 57, pp. 1–39.

1997   "The Early Dynastic-Akkadian Transition, Part 2: The Authors' Response." *Iraq* 59, pp. 9–14.

Gilbert, Allan

1995   "The Flora and Fauna of the Ancient Near East." In *Civilizations of the Ancient Near East,* edited by Jack Sasson et al., vol. 1, pp. 153–74. New York.

Glassner, Jean-Jacques, trans.

1993   *Chroniques mésopotamiennes.* Paris.

1994   "La fin d'Akkadé: Approche chronologique." *Nouvelles assyriologiques brèves et utilitaires,* 1994, pp. 8–9, no. 9.

Grayson, Albert K.

1975   *Assyrian and Babylonian Chronicles.* Texts from Cuneiform Sources, vol. 5. Locust Valley, N.Y.

Haas, Volkert

1995   "Death and the Afterlife in Hittite Thoughts." In *Civilizations of the Ancient Near East,* edited by Jack Sasson et al., vol. 3, pp. 2012–30. New York.

Hakemi, Ali

1997   *Shahdad: Archaeological Excavations of a Bronze Age Center in Iran.* Translated and edited by S. M. S. Sajjadi. Istituto Italiano per il Medio ed Estremo Oriente, Centro Scavi e Ricerche Archeologiche, Reports and Memoirs, vol. 27. Rome.

Hall, H. R.

1919   "Excavations at El-Mukayyar, Abu Shahrain and El-'Obeid." *Proceedings of the Society of Antiquaries,* December, pp. 22–44.

1923   "Ur and Eridu: The British Museum Excavations of 1919." *Journal of Egyptian Archaeology* 9, pp. 177–95.

1927–28   "Sumerian Stone Sculptured Vases." *British Museum Quarterly* 2, pp. 12–15.

1928   *Babylonian and Assyrian Sculpture in the British Museum.* Paris.

Hall, H. R., and Sir Leonard Woolley

1927   *Ur Excavations.* Vol. 1, *Al-'Ubaid: A Report on the Work Carried Out at al-'Ubaid for the British Museum in 1919 and for the Joint Expedition in 1922–3.* Contributions by C. J. Gadd and Sir Arthur Keith. London.

Hall, M. E., and S. R. Steadman

1991   "Tin and Anatolia: Another Look." *Journal of Mediterranean Archaeology* 4, pp. 217–34.

Hallo, William W.

1957   *Early Mesopotamian Royal Titles: A Philologic and Historical Analysis.* American Oriental Series, vol. 43. New Haven.

1957–71   "Gutium." In *Reallexikon der Assyriologie und vorderasiatischen Archäologie,* edited by E. Weidner and W. von Soden, vol. 3, pp. 708–20. Berlin and New York.

1963   "Royal Hymns and Mesopotamian Unity." *Journal of Cuneiform Studies* 17, pp. 112–18.

1966   "The Coronation of Ur-Nammu." *Journal of Cuneiform Studies* 20, pp. 133–41.

1971   "Antediluvian Cities." *Journal of Cuneiform Studies* 23, pp. 57–67.

1976   "Women of Sumer." In *The Legacy of Sumer,* edited by D. Schmandt-Besserat, pp. 23–40. Bibliotheca Mesopotamica 4. Malibu.

1996   *Origins: The Ancient Near Eastern Background of Some Modern Western Institutions.* Studies in the History and Culture of the Ancient Near East, vol. 6. Leiden.

Hallo, William W., and Briggs Buchanan

1965   "A Persian Gulf Seal on an Old Babylonian Mercantile Agreement." In *Studies in Honor of Benno Landsberger on His Seventy-fifth Birthday,* vol. 1, pp. 199–203. Chicago.

Hallo, William W., and J. J. A. van Dijk

1968   *The Exaltation of Inanna.* Yale Near Eastern Researches, vol. 3. New Haven.

Hallo, William W., and W. K. Simpson

1971   *The Ancient Near East: A History.* New York.

1998   *The Ancient Near East: A History.* 2nd ed. New York.

Hansen, Donald P.

1963   "New Votive Plaques from Nippur." *Journal of Near Eastern Studies* 22, pp. 145–66.

1970a   "Al Hiba, 1968–1969: A Preliminary Report." *Artibus Asiae* 32, pp. 247–48.

1970b   "A Proto-Elamite Silver Figurine in The Metropolitan Museum of Art." *Metropolitan Museum Journal* 3, pp. 5–14.

1971   "Some Early Dynastic I Sealings from Nippur." In *Studies Presented to George M. A. Hanfmann,* edited by D. G. Mitten et al., pp. 47–54. Cambridge, Mass.

1975a   "Frühsumerische und Frühdynastische Rundplastik." In *Der alte Orient,* edited by Winfried Orthmann, pp. 158–70. Propyläen Kunstgeschichte, vol. 14. Berlin.

1975b   "Frühsumerische und Frühdynastische Flachbildkunst." In *Der alte Orient,* edited by Winfried Orthmann, pp. 179–93. Propyläen Kunstgeschichte, vol. 14. Berlin.

1978   "Al-Hiba: A Summary of Four Seasons of Excavation, 1968–1976." *Sumer* 34, pp. 72–85.

1980–83   "Lagaš." In *Reallexikon der Assyriologie und vorderasiatischen Archäologie,* edited by D. O. Edzard, vol. 6, p. 425. Berlin and New York.

1988   "A Sculpture of Gudea, Governor of Lagash." *Bulletin of the Detroit Institute of Arts* 64, no. 1, pp. 4–19.

1992   "Royal Building Activity at Sumerian Lagash in the Early Dynastic Period." *Biblical Archaeologist,* December, pp. 206–11.

1998   "Art of the Royal Tombs of Ur: A Brief Interpretation." In *Treasures from the Royal Tombs of Ur,* edited by Richard L. Zettler and Lee Horne, pp. 43–72. Philadelphia.

2001   "The Reclining Human-Faced Bison Sculpture from Area SS." In *Excavations at Tell Brak, Volume 2: Nagar in the Third Millennium BC,* by David Oates, Joan Oates, and Helen McDonald, pp. 257–63. Cambridge.

2002   "Through the Love of Ishtar." In *Of Pots and Pans: Papers on the Archaeology and History of Mesopotamia and Syria Presented to David Oates in Honour of His 75th Birthday,* edited by Lamia al-Gailani Werr et al., pp. 91–112. London.

Hansen, Donald P., and George F. Dales

1962   "The Temple of Inanna, Queen of Heaven at Nippur." *Archaeology* 15 (June), pp. 75–84.

Harper, Prudence O., Joan Aruz, and Françoise Tallon, eds.

1992   *The Royal City of Susa: Ancient Near Eastern Treasures in the Louvre.* Exh. cat. New York: The Metropolitan Museum of Art.

Harper, Prudence O., et al.

1995   *Assyrian Origins: Discoveries at Ashur on the Tigris. Antiquities in the Vorderasiatisches Museum, Berlin.* Exh. cat. New York: The Metropolitan Museum of Art.

Haul, Michael

2000   *Das Etana-Epos: Ein Mythos von der Himmelfahrt des Königs von Kiš.* Göttinger Arbeitshefte zur altorientalischen Literatur, no. 1. Göttingen.

Heath Wiencke, Martha

1989   "Change in Early Helladic II." *American Journal of Archaeology* 93, pp. 495–509.

Heimpel, Wolfgang

1987   "Das Untere Meer." *Zeitschrift für Assyriologie und vorderasiatische Archäologie* 77, pp. 22–91.

1991   "Some Observations on Trade and Myth in Early Babylonia." In *Ancient Economy in Mythology: East and West,* edited by M. Silver, pp. 187–92. Savage, Md.

1998   "A Circumambulation Rite." *Acta Sumerologica* 20, pp. 13–16.

Heinrich, Ernst

1931   *Fara: Ergebnisse der Ausgrabungen der Deutschen Orient-Gesellschaft in Fara und Abu Hatab, 1902–03.* Edited by Walter Andrae. Berlin: Staatliche Museen zu Berlin, Vorderasiatische Abteilung.

1936   *Kleinfunde aus den archaischen Tempelschichten in Uruk.* Contribution by Max Hilzheimer. Ausgrabungen der Deutschen Forschungsgemeinschaft in Uruk-Warka, vol. 1. Berlin.

1937   *Achter vorläufiger Bericht über die von der Forschungsgemeinschaft in Uruk-Warka unternommenen Ausgrabungen.* Berlin.

1982   *Die Tempel und Heiligtümer im alten Mesopotamien: Typologie, Morphologie und Geschichte.* 2 vols. Berlin.

Helck, Wolfgang

1971   *Die Beziehungen Ägyptens zu Vorderasien im 3. und 2. Jahrtausend v. Chr.* 2nd ed. Ägyptologische Abhandlungen, vol. 5. Wiesbaden.

Helms, Mary W.

1993   *Craft and the Kingly Ideal: Art, Trade, and Power.* Austin.

Herodotus

1996   *The Histories.* Translated by Aubrey de Sélincourt; revised with notes by John Marincola. New ed. London.

Herrmann, Georgina

1968   "Lapis Lazuli: the Early Phases of Its Trade." *Iraq* 30, pp. 21–57.

Herz, Alexandra

1966   "A Study of Steatite Vases of the Early Dynastic Period in Mesopotamia." M.A. thesis, New York University, Institute of Fine Arts.

Herzfeld, Ernst E.

1941   *Iran in the Ancient East: Archaeological Studies Presented in the Lowell Lectures at Boston.* London.

Heuzey, Léon A.

1900–1901 "Le taureau chaldéen androcéphale et la sculpture à incrustations." *Monuments Piot* 7, pp. 7–11 and pl. 1.

1902   *Catalogue des antiquités chaldéennes: Sculpture et gravure à la pointe.* Paris: Musée National du Louvre.

Heuzey, Léon A., and Jacques Heuzey

1935   *Histoire du costume dans l'Antiquité classique. L'Orient: Égypte—Mésopotamie—Syrie—Phénicie.* Paris.

Hiebert, F.

1994   "Production Evidence for the Origins of the Oxus Civilization." *Antiquity* 68, pp. 372–87.

Hill, Harold D., Thorkild Jacobsen, and Pinhas Delougaz

1990   *Old Babylonian Public Buildings in the Diyala Region.* Contributions by Thomas A. Holland and Augusta McMahon. University of Chicago Oriental Institute Publications, vol. 98. Chicago.

Hilprecht, Hermann V.

1903   *Die Ausgrabungen der Universität von Pennsylvania im Bêl-Tempel zu Nippur: Ein Vortrag.* Leipzig.

Hinz, W.

1969   *Altiranische Funde und Forschungen.* Berlin.

Hiroyuki 1991. *See* Ii 1991.

Höckman, O.

1976   "Die Kykladen und ihre ostlichen Nachbarn." In *Kunst und Kultur der Kykladeninseln im 3. Jahrtausend v. Chr.,* edited by Jürgen Thimme. Karlsruhe.

Højlund, Flemming, and Helmut Andersen

1994   *Qala'at al-Bahrain.* Vol. 1, *The Northern City Wall and the Islamic Fortress.* Contributions by Olivier Callot et al. Jutland Archaeological Society Publications, vol. 30, no. 1. Aarhus.

1997   *Qala'at al-Bahrain.* Vol. 2, *The Central Monument Buildings.* Contributions by Olivier Callot et al. Jutland Archaeological Society Publications, vol. 30, no. 2. Aarhus.

Hori, Akira

1983   *Oriento no fubo ten / Faces in Ancient Near East.* Exh. cat. Tokyo: Kodai Oriento Hakubutsukan.

Howard-Carter, Theresa

n.d.   Accession notes, Kuwait National Museum, al-Kuwait, [1989?]. Copy of catalogue card in the files of the Department of Ancient Near Eastern Art, The Metropolitan Museum of Art, New York.

Hrouda, B.

1979   Review of Johansen 1978. *Zeitschrift für Assyriologie und vorderasiatische Archäologie* 69, pp. 149–51.

Hruška, Blahoslav

1975   *Der Mythenadler Anzu in Literatur und Vorstellung des alten Mesopotamien.* Budapest.

Huber, Peter J.

2000   "Astronomy and Ancient Chronology." *Just in Time; Akkadica* 119–20, pp. 159–76.

Hunger, Hermann

2000   "Uses of Enūma Anu Enlil for Chronology." *Just in Time; Akkadica* 119–20, pp. 155–58.

Huot, Jean-Louis

1978   "The Man-Faced Bull L. 76.17 of Larsa." *Sumer* 34, pp. 104–10.

1983   *Larsa et 'Oueili, travaux de 1978–1981.* Paris.

Huot, J. L., V. Pardo, and A. Rougeulle

1980   "À propos de la perle L.76.5 de Larsa: Les perles à quatre spirales." *Iraq* 42, no. 2, pp. 121–29.

Hurowitz, Victor

1992   *I Have Built You an Exalted House: Temple Building in the Bible in the Light of Mesopotamian and Northwest Semitic Writings.* Sheffield.

Ibrahim, Moawiyah

1982   *Excavations of the Arab Expedition at Sar el-Jisr, Bahrain.* In English and Arabic. Manamah.

Ii Hiroyuki

1991   "'Potters Tool' in Mesopotamia during the Fifth to Third Millenium B.C." (in Japanese). *Al-Rafidan* 12, pp. 1–57.

Indus Civilization

2000   *Sekai yondai bunmei Indasu bunmei ten / Indus Civilization.* Exh. cat. Tokyo: Tokyo Bijutsukan; NHK Puromoshon.

Ingholt, Harald

1940   *Rapport préliminaire sur sept campagnes de fouilles a Hama en Syrie (1932–1938).* Copenhagen.

Inizan, Marie-Louise

1993   "At the Dawn of Trade, Cornelian from India to Mesopotamia in the Third Millennium: The Example of Tello." In *South Asian Archaeology 1991,* edited by A. J. Gail and G. J. R. Mevissen, pp. 123–31. Stuttgart.

Invernizzi, Antonio

1992–   *Dal Tigri all'Eufrate.* 2 vols. to date. Studi e materiali di archeologia, Università degli studi di Torino, Fondo di studi Parini-Chirio, 5, 6. Florence.

Ippolitoni-Strika, Fiorella

1986   "The Tarut Statue as a Peripheral Contribution to the Knowledge of Early Mesopotamian Plastic Art." In *Bahrain*

through the Ages, edited by H. A. Al-Khalifa and M. Rice, pp. 311–24. London.

Jacobsen, Thorkild

1939   *The Sumerian King List.* Oriental Institute of the University of Chicago, Assyriological Studies, no. 11. Chicago.

1953   "The Reign of Ibbi-Suen." *Journal of Cuneiform Studies* 7, pp. 36–47.

1957   "Early Political Development in Mesopotamia." *Zeitschrift für Assyriologie und vorderasiatische Archäologie* 52, pp. 91–140.

1976   *The Treasures of Darkness: A History of Mesopotamian Religion.* New Haven.

1981   "The Eridu Genesis." *Journal of Biblical Literature* 100, pp. 513–29. Reprinted in *"I Studied Inscriptions before the Flood": Ancient Near Eastern, Literary, and Linguistic Approaches to Genesis 1–11,* edited by R. S. Hess and D. T. Tsumura, pp. 129–42. Winona Lake, Ind., 1994.

1984   "The Harab Myth." *Sources for the Ancient Near East* 2, no. 3, pp. 99–120.

1987a   as translator and editor. *The Harps That Once . . . : Sumerian Poetry in Translation.* New Haven.

1987b   "Pictures and Pictorial Language (The Burney Relief)." In *Figurative Language in the Ancient Near East,* edited by D. Mindlin, M. J. Geller, and J. E. Wansbrough, pp. 1–11. London.

1989   "God or Worshiper." In *Essays in Ancient Civilization Presented to Helene J. Kantor,* edited by A. Leonard Jr. and B. B. Williams, pp. 125–30. Chicago.

Jakob-Rost, Liane

1992a   "Gründungsfigur in Form einer Statuette mit Inschrift." *Das Vorderasiatische Museum* (Staatliche Museen zu Berlin), p. 84.

1992b   "Teil der Stiftmosaikfassade von einem Innenhof des Eanna-Tempels." *Das Vorderasiatische Museum* (Staatliche Museen zu Berlin), p. 54.

1992c   "Zwei Statuetten von liegenden Tieren." *Das Vorderasiatische Museum* (Staatliche Museen zu Berlin), p. 66.

Jans, Greta, and Joachim Bretschneider

1998   "Wagon and Chariot Representations in the Early Dynastic Glyptic." In *About Subartu: Studies Devoted to Upper Mesopotamia,* vol. 4, part 2, *Culture, Society, Image,* edited by Marc Lebeau. Turnhout.

Jarrige, Catherine

1988   "Les figurines humaines au Baluchistan." In *Les cités oubliées de l'Indus: Archéologie du Pakistan,* edited by J.-F. Jarrige, pp. 65–70. Exh. cat. Paris: Musée Naitonal des Arts Asiatiques Guimet.

Jarrige, Catherine, et al., eds.

1995   *Mehrgarh. Field Reports, 1974–1985, from Neolithic Times to the Indus Civilization.* Karachi.

Jarrige, Jean-François

1974–86 "Excavations at Mehrgarh-Nausharo." *Pakistan Archaeology* 10–22, pp. 63–131.

1988   as editor. *Les cités oubliées de l'Indus: Archéologie du Pakistan.* Exh. cat. Paris:

Musée National des Arts Asiatiques Guimet.

Jarrige, Jean-François, and M. U. Hassan
1989 "Funerary Complexes in Baluchistan at the End of the Third Millennium in the Light of Recent Discoveries at Mehrgarh and Quetta." In *South Asian Archaeology 1985,* edited by Karen Frifelt and Per Sørensen, pp. 150–66. London.

Jarrige, Jean-François, and M. Lechevallier
1979 "Excavations at Mehrgarh, Baluchistan: Their Significance in the Prehistorical Context of the Indo-Pakistani Borderlands." In *South Asian Archaeology 1977,* edited by M. Taddei, pp. 463–535. Naples.

Jaspers, Karl
1953 *The Origin and Goal of History.* Translated from German by Michael Bullock. New Haven.

Jéquier, Gustave
1905 "Fouilles de Suse de 1899 à 1902." *Mémoires de la Délégation en Perse* 7, pp. 9–41.

Jestin, Raymond
1937 *Tablettes sumériennes de Suruppak conservées au Musée de Stamboul.* Paris.
1955 "Übungen in Edubba." *Zeitschrift für Assyriologie und vorderasiatische Archäologie* 51, pp. 37–44.

Johansen, Flemming
1978 *Statues of Gudea, Ancient and Modern.* Contribution by Bendt Alster; translated by Janet Manzello and Marianne Christensen. Mesopotamia, vol. 6. Copenhagen.

Joshi, Jagat Pati, and Asko Parpola
1987 *Corpus of Indus Seals and Inscriptions.* Vol. 1, *Collections in India.* Helsinki: Suomalainen Tiedeakatemia.

Just in Time
2000 *Just in Time; Proceedings of the International Colloquium on Ancient Near Eastern Chronology, 2nd Millenium BC; Ghent, 7–9 July 2000.* Akkadica 119–20. Brussels.

Kantor, Helene
1966 "Landscape in Akkadian Art." *Journal of Near Eastern Studies* 25, pp. 145–52.

Karabelnik, Marianne, et al.
1993 *Aus den Schatzkammern Eurasiens: Meisterwerke antiker Kunst.* Exh. cat. Zürich: Kunsthaus.

Katsonopoulou, Dora
forthcoming "A Depas Amphikypellon from Helike, Achaia, Greece." In *Ancient Helike and Aigialeia; Archaeological Sites in Geologically Active Regions: Proceedings of the Third International Conference.*

Kelly-Buccellati, Marilyn
1986 as editor. *Insight through Images: Studies in Honor of Edith Porada.* Bibliotheca Mesopotamica, vol. 21. Malibu.
1998 "The Workshop of Urkesh." In *Mozan III. Urkesh and the Hurrians,* edited by G. Buccellati and M. Kelly-Buccellati, pp. 41–50. Malibu.
2001 "Überlegungen zur funktionellen und historischen Bestimmung des Königspalastes AP in Urkesh: Bericht über die 13. Kampagne in Tell Mozan / Urkesh. Ausgrabungen im Gebiet AA, Juni–August 2000." *Mitteilungen der Deutschen Orient-Gesellschaft zu Berlin* 133, pp. 59–96.

Kenoyer, Jonathan M.
1984 "Shell Working Industries of the Indus Civilization: A Summary." *Paléorient* 10, pp. 49–63.
1991 "Urban Process in the Indus Tradition: A Preliminary Model from Harappa." In *Harappa Excavations, 1986–1990,* edited by R. H. Meadow, pp. 29–60. Madison.
1994 "Faience Ornaments of Harappa and the Indus Civilization." *Ornament* 17, no. 3, pp. 35–39, 95.
1997 "Trade and Technology of the Indus Valley: New Insights from Harappa, Pakistan." *World Archaeology* 29, pp. 262–80.
1998 *Ancient Cities of the Indus Valley Civilization.* Karachi and Islamabad.

Kenoyer, Jonathan M., and R. H. Meadow
2001 "The Ravi Phase Craft Traditions at Harappa, Pakistan." In *South Asian Archaeology 1997,* edited by M. Taddei and G. De Marco. Rome and Naples.

Kenoyer, Jonathan M., and M. Vidale
1992 "A New Look at Stone Drills of the Indus Valley Tradition." In *Materials Issues in Art and Archaeology, III,* edited by Pamela Vandiver et al., pp. 495–518. Pittsburgh.

Kenoyer, Jonathan M., M. Vidale, and K. K. Bhan
1994 "Carnelian Bead Production in Khambhat India: An Ethnoarchaeological Study" In *Living Traditions: Studies in the Ethnoarchaeology of South Asia,* edited by B. Allchin. New Delhi and Oxford.

Khlopin, I. N.
1981 "The Early Bronze Age Cemetery in Parkhai II: The First Two Seasons of Excavations, 1977–78." In *The Bronze Age Civilization of Central Asia: Recent Soviet Discoveries,* edited by Philip L. Kohl, pp. 3–34. Armonk, N.Y.

King, Leonard W.
1910 *A History of Babylonia and Assyria from Prehistoric Times to the Persian Conquest.* 2 vols. London.

Kircho, L. B.
1981 "The Problem of the Origin of the Early Bronze Age Culture of Southern Turkmenia." In *The Bronze Age Civilization of Central Asia: Recent Soviet Discoveries,* edited by Philip L. Kohl. Armonk, N.Y.

Kjaerum, Poul
1980 "Seals of 'Dilmun-Type' from Failaka, Kuwait." *Proceedings of the Seminar for Arabian Studies* 10, pp. 45–53.
1983 *Failaka/Dilmun, the Second Millennium Settlements.* Vol. 1, no. 1, *The Stamp and Cylinder Seals.* Jutland Archaeological Society Publications, vol. 17, no. 1. Aarhus.
1986 "The Dilmun Seals as Evidence of Long Distance Relations in the Early Second Millennium B.C." In *Bahrain through the Ages,* edited by H. A. Al-Khalifa and M. Rice, pp. 269–77. London.
1994 "Stamp-Seals, Seal Impressions, and Seal Blanks." In *Qala'at al-Bahrain.* Moesgård, Aarhus.
1999 "The Hidden Art of Dilmun: The Stamp-Seals." In *Bahrain: The Civilisation of the Two Seas from Dilmun to Tylos,* pp. 115–20. Paris.

Klein, Jacob
1981a *The Royal Hymns of Shulgi, King of Ur: Man's Quest for Immortal Fame.* Transactions of the American Philosophical Society, 71, part 7. Philadelphia.
1981b *Three Šulgi Hymns. Sumerian Royal Hymns Glorifying King Šulgi of Ur.* Ramat-Gan, Israel.
1989a "Building and Dedication Hymns in Sumerian Literature." *Acta Sumerologica* 11, pp. 27–67.
1989b "From Gudea to Shulgi: Continuity and Change in Sumerian Literary Tradition." In *Dumu-e$_2$-dub-ba-a: Studies in Honor of Åke W. Sjöberg,* edited by Hermann Behrens et al., pp. 289–302. Occasional Publications of the Samuel Noah Kramer Fund, 11. Philadelphia.
1990 "The 'Bane' of Humanity: A Lifespan of One Hundred Twenty Years." *Acta Sumerologica* 12, pp. 57–70.
1997 "Enki and Ninmah (1.159)." In *The Context of Scripture I: Canonical Compositions from the Biblical World,* edited by William W. Hallo, pp. 516–18. Leiden.

Klengel, E., and H. Klengel
1980 "Zum Fragment eines Steatitgefäßes mit einer Inschrift des Rimush von Akkad." *Rocznik Orientalistyczny* 41, pp. 45–51.

Klengel-Brandt, E.
1992 "Drei Tierfigürchen." *Das Vorderasiatische Museum* (Staatliche Museen zu Berlin), p. 61.

Kobayashi, Toshiko
1988 "A Study of the Peg Figurine with the Inscription of Enannatum I." *Orient* 24.

Kohl, Philip L.
1974 "Seeds of Upheaval: The Production of Chlorite at Tepe Yahya and an Analysis of Commodity Production and Trade in Southwest Asia in the Mid-Third Millennium." 2 vols. Ph.D. dissertation, Harvard University, Cambridge, Mass.
1975 "Carved Chlorite Vessels: A Trade in Finished Commodities in the Mid-Third Millennium." *Expedition* 18, no. 1, pp. 18–31.
1979 "The 'World Economy' of West Asia in the Third Millennium B.C." In *South Asian Archaeology 1977,* edited by M. Taddei, pp. 55–85. Naples.
2001 "Reflections on the Production of Chlorite at Tepe Yahya: 25 Years Later." In *Excavations at Tepe Yahya, Iran, 1967–1975: The Third Millennium,* by D. Potts, pp. 209–30. American School of Prehistoric Research Bulletin 45. Cambridge, Mass.:

Peabody Museum of Archaeology and Ethnology.

Kohl, Philip L., G. Harbottle, and E. V. Sayre

1979   "Physical and Chemical Analyses of Soft Stone Vessels from Southwest Asia." *Archaeometry* 21, pp. 131–59.

Kohlmeyer, Kay

1985   "Mari (Tell Hariri)." In *Ebla to Damascus: Art and Archaeology of Ancient Syria,* edited by Harvey Weiss, pp. 130–33. Exh. cat. Washington, D.C.: Smithsonian Institution.

1995   "Anatolian Architectural Decorations, Statuary, and Stelae." In *Civilizations of the Ancient Near East,* edited by Jack Sasson et al., pp. 2639–60. New York.

Korenevsky, S. N.

1988   "K voprosu o meste proizvodstva metal-licheskikh veshchei Maikopskogo kur-gana" (On the Question of the Place of Production of the Metallic Objects from the Maikop Barrow). In *Voprosy arkhe-ologii Adygei, Maikop* (Problems in the Archaeology of Adygei and Maikop), pp. 86–104. Maikop.

Korfmann, Manfred

2001   "Der 'Schatz A' und seine Fundsituation. Bemerkungen zum historischen und chronologischen Umfeld des 'Schatzfund-horizontes' in Troia." In *Beiträge zur vorderasiatischen Archäologie. Winfried Orthmann gewidmet,* edited by J.-W. Meyer, M. Novák, and A. Pruss, pp. 212–35. Frankfurt am Main.

Koşay, Hâmit Zübeyr

n.d.   *Alacahöyük.* N.p.: Turkish Press, Broadcasting, and Tourist Department.

1937   *Elamca-Türkçe dilakrabiligi / Elamisch-Türkische Sprachverwandts[c]haft.* Ankara.

1938   *Türk Tarih Kurumu tarafindan vapilan Alaca Höyük Hafriyatı: 1936 daki çalismalara ve kesiflere ait ilk rapor.* Türk Tarih Kurumu Yayinlarindan, ser. 5, no. 2. Ankara.

1944   *Ausgrabungen von Alaca Höyük: Ein Vorbericht über die im Auftrage der Türkischen Geschichtskommission im Sommer 1936 durchgeführten Forschungen und Entdeckungen.* Veröffentlichungen der Türkischen Geschichtskommission, ser. 5, no. 2a. Ankara.

1951   *Türk Tarih Kurumu tarafindan yapilan Alaca Höyük Kazisi, 1937–1939 / Les fouilles d'Alaca Höyük entreprises par la Société d'Histoire Turque, Rapport préliminaire sur les travaux en 1937–1939.* Türk Tarih Kurumu Yayinlarindan, ser. 5, no. 5. Ankara.

Koşay, Hâmit Zübeyr, and M. Akok

1950   "Amasya Mahmatlar Köyü Definesi." *Belleten: Türk Tarih Kurumu* 14, pp. 481–85.

Kramer, Samuel Noah

1945   as editor and translator. *Enki and Ninhursag: A Sumerian Paradise Myth.* Bulletin of the American Schools of Oriental Research, Supplementary Studies 1. New Haven.

1959   "The World's Oldest Known Prescrip-tions." *CIBA Journal* 12, pp. 2–7.

1963   *The Sumerians: Their History, Culture, and Character.* Chicago.

1967   "The Death of Ur-Nammu." *Journal of Cuneiform Studies* 21, pp. 104–22.

1983a   "The Sumerian Deluge Myth Reviewed and Revised." *Anatolian Studies* 33, pp. 115–21.

1983b   "The Ur-Nammu Law Code: Who Was Its Author?" *Orientalia* 52, pp. 453–56.

Krebernik, Manfred

1984   *Die Beschwörungen aus Fara und Ebla: Untersuchungen zur ältesten keilschriftlichen Beschwörungsliteratur.* Texte und Studien zur Orientalistik, vol. 2. Hildesheim.

1992   "Mesopotamian Myths at Ebla: ARET 5, 6 and ARET 5, 7." In *Literature and Literary Language at Ebla,* edited by Pelio Fronzaroli, pp. 63–150. Quaderni di semitistica, no. 18. Florence.

1998   "Die Texte aus Fara und Tell Abū Ṣalābīh." In *Mesopotamien: Späturuk-Zeit und Frühdynastische Zeit,* edited by Josef Bauer, Robert K. Englund, and Manfred Krebernik, pp. 237–430. Göttingen.

Kuhrt, Amelie

1995   *The Ancient Near East, c. 3000–330 BC.* 2 vols. London and New York.

Kulaçoğlu, Belma

1992   *Gods and Goddesses.* Translated by Jean Öztürk. Ankara: Museum of Anatolian Civilizations.

Kuniholm, P. I., B. Kromer, S. W. Manning, M. Newton, C. E. Latini, and M. J. Bruce

1996   "Anatolian Tree Rings and the Absolute Chronology of the Eastern Mediterranean, 2220–718 BC." *Nature* 381 (June 27), pp. 780–83.

Kutscher, Rafael

1974   "An Offering to the Statue of Shulgi." *Tel Aviv* 1, pp. 55–59.

Lafont, Bertrand

1983   "Deux notes sur les règnes de Shu-Sin et Ibbi-Sin." *Revue d'assyriologie et d'archéologie orientale* 77, pp. 69–71.

Lamberg-Karlovsky, C. C.

1970   *Excavations at Tepe Yahya, Iran, 1967–1969.* American School of Prehistoric Research, Harvard University, Bulletin, no. 27. Cambridge, Mass.

1988   "The 'Intercultural Style' Carved Vessels." *Iranica Antiqua* 23, pp. 45–95.

1993   "The Biography of an Object: The Intercultural Style Vessels of the Third Millennium B.C." In *History from Things: Essays on Material Culture,* edited by Steven Lubar and W. David Kingery, pp. 270–92. Washington, D.C.

1997   "Our Past Matters: Materials and Industries of the Ancient Near East." *Journal of the American Oriental Society* 117, pp. 87–102.

2001   "Afterword: Excavations at Tepe Yahya: Reconstructing the Past." In *Excavations at Tepe Yahya, Iran, 1967–1975,* edited by D. Potts, pp. 269–80. Cambridge, Mass.

Lamberg-Karlovsky, C. C., and Jeremy A. Sabloff

1995   *Ancient Civilizations: The Near East and Mesoamerica.* 2nd ed. Prospect Heights, Ill.

Lamberg-Karlovsky, C. C., and M. Tosi

1973   "Shahr-i Sokhta and Tepe Yahya: Tracks on the Earliest History of the Iranian Plateau." *East and West* 23, pp. 21–57.

Lambert, Maurice

1953   "Deux textes de Gudea." *Revue d'assyriolo-gie et d'archéologie orientale* 47, pp. 83–86.

Lambert, Maurice, and J.-R. Tournay

1951   "La statue B de Gudea." *Revue d'assyriolo-gie et d'archéologie orientale* 45, pp. 49–66.

Lambert, W. G.

1985   "The Pantheon of Mari." *MARI* 4, pp. 525–39.

1987   "The Treaty of Ebla." In *Ebla, 1975–1985,* edited by Luigi Cagni, pp. 353–64. Naples.

1989   "Notes on a Work of the Most Ancient Semitic Literature." *Journal of Cuneiform Studies* 41, pp. 1–32.

1992   "The Relationship of Sumerian and Babylonian Myth as Seen in Accounts of Creation." In *La circulation des biens, des personnes et des idées dans le Proche-Orient ancien. Actes de la 38e Rencontre Assyriologique Internationale (Paris, 8–10 juillet 1991),* edited by Dominique Charpin and Francis Joannès. Paris.

1998   "Technical Terminology for Creation in the Ancient Near East." In *Intellectual Life of the Ancient Near East: Papers Presented at the 43rd Rencontre Assyriologique Internationale, Prague, July 1–5, 1996,* edited by Jiří Prosecký, pp. 189–93. Prague.

Lambert, W. G., and Alan R. Millard

1969   *Atra-hasīs: The Babylonian Story of the Flood.* Oxford.

Lambert, W. G., and Simon Parker

1966   *Enuma Eliš: The Babylonian Epic of Creation.* Oxford.

La Niece, S.

1995   "Depletion Gilding from Third Millennium BC Ur." *Iraq* 57, pp. 41–47.

La Rosa, Vincenzo

1997   In *Poliochne Lemno en amichthaloesse: Hena kentro tes proimes epoches tou Chalkou sto Voreio Aigaio / Poliochni nella Lemno fumosa: Un centro dell'antica età del Bronzo nell'Egeo settentrionale / Poliochni on Smoke-Shroud[ed] Lemnos: An Early Bronze Age Centre in the North Aegean,* pp. 86–127. Exh. cat. Athens: Scuola Archeologica Italiana di Atene.

Latacz, Joachim, et al.

2001   *Troia. Traum und Wirklichkeit.* Stuttgart.

Lebeau, Marc

1990   "La céramique du tombeau 300 de Mari (Temple d'Ishtar)." *Mari, Annales de Recherches Interdisciplinaires* (Paris) 6, pp. 349–74.

2000   "Stratified Archaeological Evidence and Compared Periodizations in the Syrian Jezirah during the Third Millennium B.C." In *Chronologies des pays du Caucase et de l'Euphrate aux IVe–IIIe millénaires,* edited by Catherine Marro and Harald Hauptmann, pp. 167–92. Paris.

Le Breton, Louis
1957   "The Early Periods at Susa, Mesopotamian Relations." *Iraq* 19, pp. 79–124.
1959   "The Early Periods at Susa." *Iraq* 19, pp. 117–20.

Legrain, Léon
1927   "The Stela of the Flying Angels." *Museum Journal* 18, pp. 75–98.
1936   *Archaic Seal-Impressions.* Publications of the Joint Expedition of the British Museum and of the Museum of the University of Pennsylvania, to Mesopotamia: Ur Excavations, vol. 3. London.
1940   "Nippur Old Drugstore." *University Museum Bulletin* 8 (January), pp. 25–27.
1951   *Seal Cylinders.* Publications of the Joint Expedition of the British Museum and of the University Museum, University of Pennsylvania, Philadelphia, to Mesopotamia: Ur Excavations, vol. 10. London.

Leiden
1986   *Schatten uit Turkije / Türkiye'nin tarihi zenginlikleri / Treasures from Turkey.* Exh. cat. Leiden: Rijksmuseum van Oudheden.

Leinwand, Nancy
1984   "A Study of Anatolian Weathergods of the Old Assyrian Colony Period." Ph.D. dissertation, Bryn Mawr College, Bryn Mawr, Pa.

Lenzen, Heinrich
1965   *XXI. vorläufiger Bericht über die von dem Deutschen archäologischen Institut und der Deutschen Orient-Gesellschaft aus Mitteln der Deutschen Forschungsgemeinschaft unternommenen Ausgrabungen in Uruk-Warka: Winter 1962/63.* Contributions by Hansjörg Schmid, Mark A. Brandes, Gerlind Wülker. Abhandlungen der Deutschen Orient-Gesellschaft, no. 10. Berlin.

Ligabue, Giancarlo, and Sandro Salvatori, eds.
1988   *Bactria: An Ancient Oasis Civilization from the Sands of Afghanistan.* Centro Studi Ricerche Ligabue, Studies and Documents, vol. 3. Venice.

Lilyquist, Christine
1993   "Granulation and Glass: Chronological and Stylistic Investigations at Selected Sites, ca. 2500–1400 B.C.E.," *Bulletin of the American Schools of Oriental Research,* nos. 290–91, p. 33.

Limper, Klaudia
1988   *Uruk. Perlen—Ketten—Anhänger; Grabungen, 1912–1985.* Ausgrabungen in Uruk-Warka, Endberichte, vol. 2. Mainz am Rhein.

Lindemeyer, Elke, and Lutz Martin
1993   *Uruk. Kleinfunde III. Kleinfunde im Vorderasiatischen Museum zu Berlin: Steingefässe und Asphalt, Farbreste, Fritte, Glas, Holz, Knochen/Elfenbein, Muschel/Perlmutt/Schnecke.* Contributions by Marlies Heinz, Rudolf Kilias, Hans Neumann, and Josef Riederer. Ausgrabungen in Uruk-Warka, Endberichte, vol. 9. Mainz am Rhein.

Littauer, Mary Aiken, and Joost Crouwel
1973   "The Vulture Stela and an Early Type of Two-Wheeled Vehicle." *Journal of Near Eastern Studies* 32, pp. 324–29.
1979   *Wheeled Vehicles and Ridden Animals in the Ancient Near East.* Handbuch der Orientalistik, Abt. 7, Kunst und Archäologie, vol. 1. Leiden.

Liverani, Mario, ed.
1993   *Akkad, the First World Empire: Structure, Ideology, Traditions.* Papers from the conference held at the University of Rome "La Sapienza," 1990. Padua.

Lloyd, Seton
1946   "Some Recent Additions to the Iraq Museum." *Sumer* 2, pp. 1–5.
1962   *Beycesultan.* British Institute of Archaeology at Ankara, Occasional Publications, no. 11. London.
1967   *Early Highland Peoples of Anatolia.* New York.

Lloyd, Seton, and Fuad Safar
1943   "Tell Uqair Excavations by the Iraq Government's Directorate of Antiquities in 1940 and 1941." *Journal of Near Eastern Studies,* pp. 131–58.

Lombard, Pierre
1999   *Bahrain: The Civilisation of the Two Seas from Dilmun to Tylos.* Exh. cat. Paris: Institut du Monde Arabe.

van Loon, Maurits N.
1973   "First Results of the 1972 Excavations at Tell Selenkahiye." *Les annales archéologiques arabes syriennes* 23, pp. 145–58.

Machinsky, D. A.
2000   "Ob obraznom stroe serebrianykh i zolotykh khudozhestvennykh izdelii iz Maikopskogo kurgana" (On the Figurative System on the Gold and Silver Decorative Items from the Maikop Kurgan). In *Sussitia: Sbornik statei pamiati Iuriia Viktorovicha Andreeva* (Collection of Essays in Memory of Iurii Viktorovich Andreev), pp. 45–70. Saint Petersburg.

Mackay, Ernest J. H.
1925   "Sumerian Connections with Ancient India." *Journal of the Royal Asiatic Society,* pp. 697–701.
1928–29   "Excavations at Mohenjo-daro." *Annual Report of the Archaeological Survey of India,* pp. 67–75.
1929   *A Sumerian Palace and the "A" Cemetery at Kish, Mesopotamia. Part II.* Field Museum of Natural History, Anthropology Memoirs vol. 1, no. 2. Chicago.
1932   "An Important Link between Ancient India and Elam." *Antiquity* 6, pp. 356–57.
1937   "Bead Making in Ancient Sind." *Journal of the American Oriental Society* 57, pp. 1–15.
1938a   "Excavations at Chanhu-daro by the American School of Indic and Iranian Studies and the Museum of Fine Arts, Boston." *Smithsonian Report for 1937,* pp. 469–78.
1938b   *Further Excavations at Mohenjo-daro; Being an Official Account of Archaeological Excavations at Mohenjo-daro Carried out by the Government of India between the Years 1927 and 1931.* 2 vols. New Delhi.
1943   *Chanhu-Daro Excavations, 1935–36.* American Oriental Series, vol. 20. New Haven.

Maeda, Tohru
1988   "Two Rulers by the Name of Ur-Ningirsu in Pre-Ur III Lagash." *Acta Sumerologica* 10, pp. 19–32.

Mallowan, Max E. L.
1936   "The Bronze Head of the Akkadian Period from Nineveh." *Iraq* 3, pp. 104–10.
1947   "Excavations at Brak and Chagar Bazar." *Iraq* 9, pp. 1–259.
1964   "A Cylinder Seal in the Uruk–Jamdat Nasr Style." *Baghdader Mitteilungen* 3, pp. 65–67.
1965   *Early Mesopotamia and Iran.* London and New York.
1966   "Tell Chuēra in Nordost-Syrien." *Iraq* 28, pp. 89–95.

Mander, Pietro
1990   *Administrative Texts of the Archive L.2769.* Materiali epigrafici di Ebla, 10. Rome.

Manning, Sturt W.
1999   *A Test of Time: The Volcano of Thera and the Chronology and History of the Aegean and East Mediterranean in the Mid Second Millennium BC.* Oxford.

Manning, S. W., B. Kromer, P. I. Kuniholm, and M. W. Newton
2001   "Anatolian Tree Rings and a New Chronology for the East Mediterranean Bronze Ages." *Science* 294 (December 21), pp. 2532–35.

Marchesi, Gianni
1999   "Notes on Two Alleged Literary Texts from al-Hiba/Lagaš." *Studi epigrafici e linguistici sul Vicino Oriente antico* 16, pp. 3–17.

Marchetti, N., and L. Nigro
1995–96   "Handicraft Production, Secondary Food Transformation and Storage in the Public Building P4 at EB IVA Ebla." *Berytus* 42, pp. 9–36.

Margueron, Jean-Claude
1976   "Maquettes architecturales de Meskeneh-Emar." *Syria* 53, pp. 193–232.
1985   "Quelques remarques sur les temples de Mari." *Mari: Annales de recherche interdisciplinaires* 4, pp. 487–507.

Marshall, Sir John, ed.
1931   *Mohenjo-daro and the Indus Civilization; Being an Official Account of Archaeological Excavations at Mohenjo-daro Carried Out by the Government of India between the Years 1922 and 1927.* 3 vols. London.

Martin, Harriet P.
1988   *Fara: A Reconstruction of the Ancient Mesopotamian City of Shuruppak.* Birmingham.

Martin, L.
1993   "Steingefäße." In *Uruk, Kleinfunde III, Ausgrabungen in Uruk-Warka, Endberichte 9,* by E. Lindemeyer and L. Martin, pp. 73–74, 82–83, 112, 159–61. Mainz am Rhein.

Marylou, Jean-Marie

1999   *Tombes et nécropoles de Mari*. Mission Archéologique de Mari, vol. 5. Beirut.

Marzahn, J.

1987   "Sumerische Inschriften des Vorderasiatischen Museums zu Berlin." *Altorientalische Forschungen* 14, pp. 29ff.

1992   "Kopf eines Stieres" and "Fragment eines reliefierten Steingefäßes." In *Das Vorderasiatische Museum*, pp. 74, 80. Berlin: Staatliche Museen.

Masson, V. M.

1960   *Kara-depe u Artyka: Trudy Yuzhno-Turkmenistanskoi arkheologischeskoi kompleksnoi ekpeditsii* [Kara-Depe at Artyk: Works of the Southern Turkmenistan Archaeological Complex Expedition], vol. 10. Ashgabat.

1976   "Altin-Depe and the Bull Cult." *Antiquity* 50 (March), pp. 14–19.

1981a   *Altyn-depe*. Leningrad.

1981b   "Seals of a Proto-Indian Type from Altyn-depe." In *The Bronze Age Civilization of Central Asia: Recent Soviet Discoveries*, edited by Philip L. Kohl. Armonk, N.Y.

1988   *Altyn-Depe*. Translated by Henry N. Michael. University Museum Monograph, vol. 55. Philadelphia: University Museum.

Masson, V. M., and T. P. Kiiatkina

1981   "Man at the Dawn of Civilization." In *The Bronze Age Civilization of Central Asia: Recent Soviet Discoveries*, edited by Philip L. Kohl. Armonk, N.Y.

Masson, V. M., and V. I. Sarianidi

1972   *Central Asia: Turkmenia before the Achaemenids*. Ancient People and Places, 79. London.

Matney, T., G. Algaze, and Holly Pittman

1997   "Excavations at Titris Höyük in Southeastern Turkey: A Preliminary Report of the 1996 Season." *Anatolica* 23, pp. 61–84.

Matthews, Donald M.

1991   "Tell Brak 1990: The Glyptic." *Iraq* 53, pp. 147–57.

1997   *The Early Glyptic of Tell Brak*. Orbis biblicus et orientalis; series archaeologica, vol. 15. Fribourg.

1997a   "The Early Dynastic-Akkadian Transition, Part I: When Did the Akkadian Period Begin?" *Iraq* 59, pp. 1–7.

Matthews, Roger J.

1993   *Cities, Seals and Writing: Archaic Seal Impressions from Jemdet Nasr and Ur*. Materialien zu den frühen Schriftzeugnissen des Vorderen Orients, vol. 2. Berlin.

1994   "Imperial Catastrophe or Local Incident? An Akkadian Hoard from Tell Brak, Syria." *Cambridge Archaeological Journal* 4, pp. 290–302.

2000   "Fourth and Third Millennia Chronologies: The View from Tell Brak, North-east Syria." In *Chronologies des pays du Caucase et de l'Euphrate aux IVe–IIIe millénaires*, edited by Catherine

Marro and Harald Hauptmann, pp. 66–72. Paris.

Matthews, Roger, W. Matthews, and H. McDonald

1994   "Excavations at Tell Brak, 1994." *Iraq* 56, pp. 177–94.

Matthiae, Paolo

1977   *Ebla: An Empire Rediscovered*. Translated by Christopher Holme. London.

1979a   "Appunti di iconografia eblaita." *Studi Eblaiti* 1, pp. 17–31.

1979b   "DU.UB^ki di Mardikh IIB1=TU.BA^ki di Alalakh VII." *Studi Eblaiti* 1, pp. 115ff.

1980a   *Ebla: An Empire Rediscovered*. Translated by Christopher Holme. London.

1980b   "Fouilles à Tell Mardikh-Ebla, 1978: Le Batiment Q et la Necropole Princière du Bronze Moyen II." *Akkadica* 17, pp. 1–38.

1980c   "Some Fragments of Early Syrian Sculpture from Royal Palace G of Tell Mardikh-Ebla." *Journal of Near Eastern Studies* 39, pp. 249–73.

1984   *I Tesori di Ebla*. Rome.

1986   "The Archives of the Royal Palace G of Ebla. Distribution and Arrangement of the Tablets According to the Archaeological Evidence, in Archives and Libraries." In *Cuneiform Archives and Libraries: Papers Read at the 30e Rencontre Assyriologique Internationale, Leiden, 4–8 July 1983*, edited by Klaas R. Veenhof, pp. 53–71. Istanbul.

1987   "The Destruction of Ebla Royal Palace: Interconnections between Syria, Mesopotamia and Egypt in the Late EB IVA." In *High, Middle, or Low?: Acts of an International Colloquium on Absolute Chronology Held at the University of Gothenburg 20th–22nd August 1987*, part 3, edited by Paul Åström, pp. 163–69. Gothenburg.

1989a   *Ebla: Un impero ritrovato. Dai primi scavi alle ultime scoperte*. Turin.

1989b   "Masterpieces of Early and Old Syrian Art: Discoveries of the 1988 Ebla Excavations in a Historical Perspective." *Proceedings of the British Academy* 75, pp. 25–56.

1993   "L'Aire Sacrée d'Ishtar à Ebla: Résultats des fouilles de 1990–1992." *Comptes rendus de l'Académie des Inscriptions et Belles-Lettres*, pp. 613–62.

1995   *Ebla: Un impero ritrovato. Dai primi scavi alle ultime scoperte*. 3rd ed., rev. Turin.

1998   "Les fortifications d'Ebla paléo-syrienne: Fouilles à Tell Mardikh-Ebla (1995–1997)." *Comptes rendus de l'Académie des Inscriptions et Belles-Lettres*, pp. 557–88.

2000   "Nouvelles fouilles à Ebla (1998–1999): Forts et palais de l'enceinte urbaine." *Comptes rendus de l'Académie des Inscriptions et Belles-Lettres*, pp. 567–610.

2002   "About the Formation of the Old Syrian Architectural Tradition." In *Of Pots and Plans: Papers on the Archaeology and History of Mesopotamia and Syria Presented to David Oates in Honour of His 75th Birthday*, edited by Lamia al-Gailani Werr et al., pp. 191–209. London.

forthcoming   "Assedi divini e ostaggi umani da Ebla a Troia. Sulla tradizione epica prima dell'Iliade." *Rendiconti dell'Accademia Nazionale dei Lincei*.

Matthiae, P., F. Pinnock, and G. Scandone Matthiae, eds.

1995   *Ebla, alle origini della civiltà urbana: Trent'anni di scavi in Siria dell'Università di Roma "La Sapienza."* Exh. cat. Rome: Palazzo Venezia.

Maul, Stefan M.

2002   "Neue Textvertreter der elften Tafel des Gilgamesch-Epos aus Assur." *Mitteilungen der Deutschen Orientgesellschaft zu Berlin* 13, pp. 33–50.

Maxwell-Hyslop, K. Rachel

1960   "The Ur Jewellery." *Iraq* 22, pp. 105–16.

1971   *Western Asiatic Jewellery, c. 3000–612 B.C.* London.

1982   "The Kosh-Tapa Fullol Hoard." *Afghan Studies*, no. 1–4, pp. 25–37.

1987   "British Museum 'Axe' No. 123268: A Bactrian Bronze." *Bulletin of the Asia Institute*, n.s., 1, pp. 17–26.

1989   "An Early Group of Quadruple Spirals." In *Anatolia and the Ancient Near East: Studies in Honor of Tahsin Özgüç*, edited by K. Emre et al., pp. 215–23. Ankara: Türk Tarih Kurumu Basimevi.

1992   "The Goddess Nanše." *Iraq* 54, pp. 79–82.

Mayer-Opificius, Ruth

1986   "Schmuck als Schutz: Amulette in Vorderasien." *Antike Welt* 17, pp. 27–30.

1988   "Gedanken zur Bedeutung frühdynastischer Rundbilder." In *Ad bene et fideliter seminandum: Festgabe für Karlheinz Deller zum 21. Februar 1987*, edited by Gerlinde Mauer and Ursula Magen, pp. 247–68. Kevelaer.

McCown, Donald E.

1942   *The Comparative Stratigraphy of Early Iran*. Oriental Institute of the University of Chicago, Studies in Ancient Oriental Civilization, no. 23. Chicago.

McDonald, Helen

2001   "Third Millennium Beads and Pendants." In *Excavations at Tell Brak*, vol. 2, edited by David Oates, Joan Oates, and Helen McDonald, pp. 225–32. Cambridge.

McGeehan-Liritzis, V.

1996   *The Role and Development of Metallurgy in the Late Neolithic and Early Bronze Age of Greece*. Jonsered.

McHale-Moore, R.

2000   "The Mystery of Enheduanna's Disk." *Journal of the Ancient Near Eastern Society* 27, pp. 69–74.

McKeon, J. F.

1970   "An Akkadian Victory Stele." *Bulletin of the Museum of Fine Arts, Boston* 68, p. 226–43.

Meadow, Richard H.

2002   "The Chronological and Cultural Significance of a Steatite Wig from Harappa." *Iranica Antiqua* 37, pp. 189–200.

Meadow, Richard H., and J. M. Kenoyer

2001   "Recent Discoveries and Highlights from Excavations at Harappa, 1998–2000."

Indo-Koko-Kenkyu: Indian Archaeological Studies 22, pp. 19–30.

2002   "Harappa Excavations, 1998–1999: New Evidence for the Development and Manifestation of the Harappan Phenomenon." In *South Asian Archaeology 1999,* edited by R. van Kooij and E. M. Raven. Leiden.

2003   "Excavations at Harappa 2000–2001: New Insights on Chronology and City Organization." In *South Asian Archaeology 2001,* edited by C. Jarrige and V. Lefèvre. Paris. In press.

Mecquenem, Roland de

1911   "Vestiges de constructions élamites." *Recueil de travaux relatifs à la philologie et à l'archéologie égyptiennes et assyriennes* 33, pp. 38–55.

1925   "Inventaire de cachets et de cylindres (Suse 1923–1924)." *Revue d'assyriologie et d'archéologie orientale* 22, pp. 1–15.

1934   "Fouilles de Suse, 1929–1933." *Mémoires de la Mission archéologique de Perse, Mission de Susiane* 25, pp. 177–237.

Meissner, Bruno

1920   *Babylonien und Assyrien.* Vol. 1. Heidelberg.

1928–29   "Sumerer und Semiten in Babylonien." *Archiv für Orientforschung* 5, pp. 1–10.

Mellaart, J.

1966   *The Chalcolithic and Early Bronze Ages in the Near East and Anatolia.* Beirut.

Mellink, Machteld J.

1956   "The Royal Tombs at Alaca Hüyük and the Aegean World." In *The Aegean and the Near East: Studies Presented to Hetty Goldman on Her Seventy-fifth Birthday,* edited by Saul S. Weinberg, pp. 39–59. Locust Valley, N.Y.

1969   "Excavations at Karataş-Semayük in Lycia, 1968." *American Journal of Archaeology* 73, pp. 319–31.

Mendone, Lina, ed.

1997   *Poliochne Lemno en amichthaloesse: Hena kentro tes proimes epoches tou Chalkou sto Voreio Aigaio / Poliochni nella Lemno fumosa: Un centro dell'antica età del Bronzo nell'Egeo settentrionale / Poliochni on Smoke-Shroud[ed] Lemnos: An Early Bronze Age Centre in the North Aegean.* Exh. cat. Athens: Scuola Archeologica Italiana di Atene.

Méry, Sophie

2000   *Les céramiques d'Oman et l'Asie moyenne: Une archéologie des échanges à l'âge du Bronze.* Centre National de la Recherche Scientifique, Centre d'Études Préhistoire, Antiquité, Moyen Âge, monographies, no. 23. Paris.

Meyer, Eduard

1906   *Sumerier und Semiten in Babylonien.* Berlin.

Meyer, Gerhard Rudolf

1965   *Altorientalische Denkmäler im Vorderasiatischen Museum zu Berlin.* Leipzig.

Meyerhoff, Hans, ed.

1959   *The Philosophy of History in Our Time: An Anthology.* Garden City, N.Y.

Meyers, Pieter

1996a   "Cylindrical Cup with Agricultural and Ceremonial Scenes." In *Ancient Art from the Shumei Family Collection,* p. 173, no. 5. Exh. cat. New York: The Metropolitan Museum of Art.

1996b   "Cylindrical Cup with Crenellated Decoration." In *Ancient Art from the Shumei Family Collection,* p. 173, no. 6. Exh. cat. New York: The Metropolitan Museum of Art.

Michalowski, Piotr

1976   "The Royal Correspondence of Ur." Ph.D. dissertation, Yale University, New Haven.

1977   "The Death of Šulgi." *Orientalia,* n.s., 46, pp. 220–25.

1985   "Third Millennium Contacts: Observations on the Relationships between Mari and Ebla." *Journal of the American Oriental Society* 105, pp. 293–302.

1986   "Mental Maps and Ideology: Observations on Subartu." In *The Origins of Cities in Dry-Farming Syria and Mesopotamia in the Third Millennium B.C.,* edited by H. Weiss, pp. 129–56. Guilford, Conn.

1987   "Charisma and Control: On Continuity and Change in Early Mesopotamian Bureaucratic Systems." In *The Organization of Power: Aspects of Bureaucracy in the Ancient Near East,* edited by McGuire Gibson and Robert D. Biggs, pp. 45–57. Chicago.

1988a   "Divine Heroes and Historical Self-Representation: From Gilgamesh to Shulgi." *Bulletin of the Society of Mesopotamian Studies* 16, pp. 19–23.

1988b   "Magan and Meluhha Once Again." *Journal of Cuneiform Studies* 40, pp. 156–64.

1989   *The Lamentation over the Destruction of Sumer and Ur.* Mesopotamian Civilizations, 1. Winona Lake, Ind.

1991   "Charisma and Control: On Continuity and Change in Early Mesopotamian Bureaucratic Systems." In *The Organization of Power: Aspects of Bureaucracy in the Ancient Near East,* edited by McGuire Gibson and Robert D. Biggs, pp. 45–58. 2nd ed., rev. Chicago.

1993   "Memory and Deed: The Historiography of the Political Expansion of the Akkad State." In *Akkad: The First World Empire. Structure, Ideology, Traditions,* edited by Mario Liverani, pp. 69–90. Padua.

1995   "Sumerian Literature: An Overview." In *Civilizations of the Ancient Near East,* edited by Jack Sasson et al., pp. 2277–91. New York.

1996   "Mesopotamian Cuneiform. Origin." In *The World's Writing Systems,* edited by Peter T. Daniels and William Bright, pp. 33–36. Oxford.

1997   "Sumerians." In *The Oxford Encyclopedia of Archaeology in the Near East,* edited by Eric M. Meyers, vol. 5, pp. 95–101. New York.

1998   "The Unbearable Lightness of Enlil." In *Intellectual Life of the Ancient Near East: Papers Presented at the 43rd Rencontre Assyriologique International, Prague, July 1–5, 1996,* edited by Jiří Prosecký, pp. 237–47. Prague.

2003   "The Life and Death of the Sumerian Language in Comparative Perspective." *Acta Sumerologica.* Forthcoming.

forthcoming   *The Royal Correspondence of Ur.* Mesopotamian Civilizations. Winona Lake, Ind.

Michalowski, Piotr, and C. B. F. Walker

1989   "A New Sumerian 'Law Code.'" In *Dumu-e₂-dub-ba-a: Studies in Honor of Åke W. Sjöberg,* edited by Hermann Behrens et al., pp. 383–96. Occasional Publications of the Samuel Noah Kramer Fund, 11. Philadelphia.

Michel, Cécile

2002   "Nouvelles données pour la chronologie du IIe millénaire." *Nouvelles assyriologiques brèves et utilitaires,* no. 1, pp. 17–18, no. 20.

Michel, Cécile, and P. Rocher

2000   "La chronologie du IIe millénaire revue à l'ombre d'une éclipse de soleil." *Jaarbericht "Ex Oriente Lux"* 35–36, pp. 111–26.

Millard, Alan R.

1984   "The Etymology of Eden." *Vestus Testamentum* 34, pp. 103–6.

Miller, Naomi F.

2000   "Plant Forms in Jewellery from the Royal Cemetery at Ur." *Iraq* 62, pp. 149–55.

Miroschedji, Pierre de

1973   "Vases et objets en stéatite susiens du Musée du Louvre." *Cahiers de la Délégation Archéologique française en Iran* 3, no. 3, pp. 9–79.

Mitchell, T. C.

1986   "Indus and Gulf Type Seals from Ur." In *Bahrain through the Ages,* edited by H. A. Al-Khalifa and M. Rice, pp. 278–85. London.

Mode, Heinz A.

1959   *Das frühe Indien.* Stuttgart.

Mohen, Jean-Pierre, and Boris Borisovich Piotrovsky

1979   *Avant les Scythes: Préhistoire de l'art en U.R.S.S.* Exh. cat. Paris: Grand Palais.

Møller, Eva

1980   "On the Gudea Statue in the NY Carlsberg Glyptotek." *Assyriological Miscellanies* 1, pp. 51–56.

Moorey, P. R. S.

1977   "What Do We Know about the People Buried in the Royal Cemetery?" *Expedition* 20 (fall), pp. 24–40.

1982   "The Archaeological Evidence for Metallurgy and Related Technologies in Mesopotamia, c. 5500–2100 B.C." *Iraq* 44, pp. 13–38.

1985   *Materials and Manufacture in Ancient Mesopotamia: The Evidence of Archaeology and Art; Metals and Metalwork, Glazed Materials and Glass.* British Archaeological Reports, International Series, no. 237. Oxford.

1993 "Iran: A Sumerian El-Dorado?" In *Early Mesopotamia and Iran: Contact and Conflict 3500–1600 B.C.*, edited by J. Curtis, pp. 31–43. London: British Museum.

1994 *Ancient Mesopotamian Materials and Industries: The Archaeological Evidence.* Oxford and New York.

1996 "A Stone Replica of an Early Dynastic III Royal Hairstyle?" *Collectanea Orientalia,* CPOA 3, pp. 227–38.

1999 "Blue Stones in the Ancient Near East: Turquoise and Lapis Lazuli." In *Cornaline et pierres précieuses: La Méditerranée de l'antiquité à l'Islam,* edited by A. Caubet, pp. 175–88. Paris: Musée du Louvre.

Moortgat, Anton

1965 *Tell Chuera in Nordost-Syrien: Bericht über die vierte Grabungskampagne, 1963.* Wissenschaftliche Abhandlungen der Arbeitsgemeinschaft für Forschung des Landes Nordrhein-Westfalen, vol. 31. Cologne.

1967a *Die Kunst des Alten Mesopotamien: Die klassische Kunst Vorderasiens.* Cologne.

1967b *Tell Chuera in Nordost-Syrien: Vorläufiger Bericht über die fünfte Grabungskampagne 1964.* Schriften der Max Freiherr von Oppenheim-Stiftung, no. 6. Wiesbaden.

1968 "Frühe kanaanäische-sumerische Berührungen in Mari." *Baghdader Mitteilungen* 4, pp. 221–31.

1969 *The Art of Ancient Mesopotamia: The Classical Art of the Near East.* Translated by Judith Wilson. London and New York.

1988 *Vorderasiatische Rollsiegel: Ein Beitrag zur Geschichte der Steinschneidekunst.* Berlin.

Moortgat, Anton, and Ursula Moortgat-Correns

1974 "Archäologische Bemerkungen zu einem Schatzfund im vorsargonischen Palast in Mari mit einer Tabelle der wichtigsten Vergleichsstücke." *Iraq* 36, pp. 155–67.

Mortensen, Peder

1986 "The Barbar Temple: Its Chronology and Foreign Relations Reconsidered." In *Bahrain through the Ages,* edited by H. A. Al-Khalifa and M. Rice, pp. 178–85. London.

Mughal, M. Rafique

1983 *The Dilmun Burial Complex at Sar: The 1980–82 Excavations in Bahrain.* [Manama, Bahrain.]

Muhly, J. D.

1973 *Copper and Tin: The Distribution of Mineral Resources and the Nature of the Metals Trade in the Bronze Age.* New Haven.

1985 "Sources of Tin and the Beginnings of Bronze Metallurgy." *American Journal of Archaeology* 89, pp. 275–91.

Muhly, J. D., et al.

1992 *Early Metallurgy in Cyprus 4000–500 B.C.* Nicosia.

Müller, Maya

1976 *Frühgeschichtlicher Fürst aus dem Iraq.* Züricher archäologische Hefte, vol. 1. Zürich.

Müller-Karpe, Hermann

1974 *Handbuch der Vorgeschichte.* Vol. 3, *Kupferzeit.* Berlin.

Müller-Karpe, Michael

1993 *Metallgefässe im Iraq I: Von den Anfangen bis zur Akkad-Zeit.* Contributions by Emmerich Pászthory and Ernst Pernicka. Prähistorische Bronzefunde, Abteilung 2, vol. 14. Stuttgart.

Munchaev, R. M.

1994 "Maikopskaya kultura" (Maikop Culture). In *Epokha bronzy Kavkaza i Sredney Azii: Ranniaia i sredniaia bronza Kavkaza* (The Bronze Age in the Caucasus and Central Asia: The Early and Middle Bronze in the Caucasus), edited by K. Kh. Kushnareva and V. I. Markovin, pp. 158–224. Moscow.

2001 "Maikop I Mesopotamiia: Itogi izucheniia I perspektivy" (Maikop and Mesopotamia: Study Results and Prospects). In *Severnyy Kavkaz: Istoriko-arkheologicheskie ocherki I zameiki: Sbornik statei. Materialy I issledovaniia po arkheologii Rossii* (Northern Caucasus: Historical-Archaeological Sketches and Notes. Collection of Essays: Materials and Research on the Archaeology of Russia), vol. 3, pp. 33–35. Moscow.

Mundy, Jennifer, ed.

2001 *Surrealism: Desire Unbound.* Exh. cat. London: Tate Modern.

Muscarella, Oscar White

1988a *Bronze and Iron: Ancient Near Eastern Artifacts in the Metropolitan Museum of Art.* New York.

1988b "Comments on the Urkish Lion Pegs." In *Mozan I: The Soundings of the First Two Seasons,* edited by G. Buccellati and M. Kelly-Buccellati, pp. 93–99. Bibliotheca Mesopotamica 20. Malibu.

1993 "Intercultural Style 'Weights.'" *Bulletin of the Asia Institute: Iranian Studies in Honor of A. D. H. Bivar,* n.s., 7, pp. 143–53.

2000 *The Lie Became Great: The Forgery of Ancient Near Eastern Cultures.* Studies in the Art and Archaeology of Antiquity, vol. 1. Groningen.

Musche, Brigitte

1992 *Vorderasiatischer Schmuck von den Anfängen bis zur Zeit der Achaemeniden.* Handbuch der Orientalistik, Abteilung 7, Kunst und Archäologie, vol. 1, part 2, B, Lfg. 7. Leiden.

Musée du Louvre

1963 "Acquisitions et inédits du Musée du Louvre." *Syria* 40, pp. 231–36.

Nagel, Wolfram

1968 "Westmakkanische Rundplastik." *Berliner Jahrbuch für Vor- und Frühgeschichte* 8, pp. 104–19.

Nagel, Wolfram, and Eva Strommenger

1995 "Sechzig Jahre Forschung zur frühdynastischen Bildkunst und ein neues Denkmal des Urdynastikums." In *Beiträge zur Kulturgeschichte Vorderasiens: Festschrift für Rainer Michael Boehmer,* edited by U. Finkbeiner, R. Dittmann, and H. Hauptmann, pp. 455–68. Mainz am Rhein.

Nayeem, Muhammed Abdul

1992 *Bahrain. Prehistory and Protohistory of the Arabian Peninsula,* vol. 2. Hyderabad, India.

Nekhaev, A. A.

1986 "Pogrebenie maikopskoi kultury iz kurgana y sela Krasnogvardeiskoe." *Sovetskaia arkheologiia* 1, pp. 244–48.

Neu, Erich

1996 *Das hurritische Epos der Freilassung.* Vol. 1, *Untersuchungen zu einem hurritisch-hethitischen Textensemble aus Hattuša.* Studien zu den Bogazköy-Texten, no. 32. Wiesbaden.

Neumann, H.

1981 "Eine Inschrift des Königs Lugalkisalsi." *Altorientalische Forschungen* 8, pp. 75–82.

Nigro, L.

1998a "The Two Steles of Sargon: Iconology and Visual Propaganda at the Beginning of Royal Akkadian Relief." *Iraq* 60, pp. 1–18.

1998b "Visual Role and Ideological Meaning of the Enemies in the Royal Akkadian Relief." In *Intellectual Life in the Ancient Near East,* edited by Jiří Prosecký, pp. 283–97. Prague.

Nissen, Hans Jörg

1966 *Zur Datierung des Königsfridhofes von Ur: Unter besonderer Berücksichtigung der Stratigraphie der Privatgräber.* Beiträge zur Ur- und frühgeschichtlichen Archäologie des Mittelmeer-Kulturraumes, vol. 3. Bonn.

1986 "The Archaic Texts from Uruk." *World Archaeology* 17, pp. 317–34.

1988 *The Early History of the Ancient Near East, 9000–2000 B.C.* Chicago and London.

Nissen, Hans Jörg, Peter Damerow, and Robert K. Englund

1991 *Frühe Schrift und Techniken der Wirtschaftsverwaltung im alten Vorderen Orient: Informationsspeicherung und verarbeitung vor 5000 Jahren.* Exh. cat. Berlin/Charlottenburg: Museum für Vor- und Frühgeschichte.

1993 *Archaic Bookkeeping: Early Writing and Techniques of Economic Administration in the Ancient Near East.* Translated by Paul Larsen. Chicago.

Nylander, C.

1980 "Earless in Nineveh: Who Mutilated Sargon's Head?" *American Journal of Archaeology* 84, pp. 329–33.

Oates, David

1973 "Form and Function in Mesopotamian Temple Architecture." Paper given at the XXe Rencontre Assyriologique, Internationale. Leiden. Summarized in *Archaeology* 26 (1973), pp. 141–42.

Oates, David, and Joan Oates

1993 "Excavations at Tell Brak 1992–93." *Iraq* 55, pp. 155–99.

1994 "Tell Brak: A Stratigraphic Summary, 1976–1993." *Iraq* 56, pp. 167–76.

Oates, David, Joan Oates, and Helen McDonald, eds.

2001   *Excavations at Tell Brak.* Vol 2: *Nagar in the Third Millennium BC.* Cambridge.

Oates, Joan

1979   *Babylon.* Ancient Peoples and Places, vol. 94. London.

Opificius, Ruth

1957–71   "Girsu." In *Reallexikon der Assyriologie und vorderasiatischen Archäologie,* edited by E. Weidner and W. von Soden, vol. 3, pp. 385–401. Berlin and New York.

Oppenheim, A. Leo

1954   "The Seafaring Merchants of Ur." *Journal of the American Oriental Society* 74, pp. 6–17.

Orthmann, Winfried

1963   *Die Keramik der frühen Bronzezeit aus Inneranatolien.* Istanbuler Forschungen, vol. 24. Berlin.

1967   "Zu den 'Standarten' aus Alaca Hüyük." *Istanbuler Mitteilungen* 17, pp. 34–54.

1975   *Der alte Orient.* Propyläen Kunstgeschichte, vol. 14. Berlin.

1985   *Der alte Orient.* Propyläen Kunstgeschichte, vol. 18. Berlin.

1990a   "L'architecture religieuse de Tell Chuera." *Akkadica* 69, pp. 1–18.

1990b   *Tell Chuera: Ausgrabungen der Max Freiherr von Oppenheim-Stiftung in Nordost-Syrien / Tall Khuerah: Hafriyat Mu'asasah Maks Fraiher fun 'Obnhaim fi shahal sharq Suriya.* Damascus and Tartū.

Ortiz, George

1996   *In Pursuit of the Absolute: Art of the Ancient World. The George Ortiz Collection.* Rev. hardcover ed. Benteli Verlag, Berne.

Otchet Imperatorskoi Arkheologicheskoi Kommissii

1897   *Otchet Imperatorskoi Arkheologicheskoi Kommissii za 1897 g.* (Report of the Imperial Archaeological Commission for 1897), pp. 2–11. Saint Petersburg, pub. 1900.

1898   *Otchet Imperatorskoi Arkheologicheskoi Kommissii za 1898 g.* (Report of the Imperial Archaeological Commission for 1897), pp. 33–35. Saint Petersburg, pub. 1901.

Özgüç, Nimet

1965   *Kültepe mühür baskilarinda Anadolu grubu / The Anatolian Group of Cylinder Seal Impressions from Kültepe.* Türk Tarih Kurumu Yayinlari, ser. 5, no. 22. Ankara.

1966   "Excavations at Acemhöyük." *Anatolia* 6.

1968   *Kanis Karumu Ib Kati Mühürleri ve Mühür Baskilari / Seals and Seal Impressions of Level 1b from Karum Kanish.* Türk Tarih Kurumu Yayinlari, ser. 5, no. 25. Ankara.

1980   "Seal Impressions from the Palaces at Acemhöyük." In *Ancient Art in Seals,* edited by Edith Porada, pp. 61–87. Princeton.

Özgüç, Tahsin

1986   "New Observations on the Relationship of Kültepe with Southeast Anatolia and North Syria during the Third Millennium B.C." In *Ancient Anatolia: Aspects of Change and Cultural Development: Essays in Honor of Machteld J. Mellink,* edited by J.V. Canby et al., pp. 31–47. Madison.

1993   "Alabaster Idols and Statuettes from Kültepe." In *Between the Rivers and over the Mountains: Archaeologica Anatolica et Mesopotamica Alba Palmieri Dedicat,* edited by M. Frangipane et al. Rome.

Özgüç, Tahsin, and M. Akok

1957   "Objects from Horoztepe." *Belleten* 21, pp. 211–19.

1958   *Horoztepe eski tunç devri mezarliği ve iskân yeri / An Early Bronze Age Settlement and Cemetery.* Ankara.

Özgüç, Tahsin, and R. Temizer

1993   "The Eskiyapar Treasure." In *Aspects of Art and Iconography: Anatolia and Its Neighbors. Studies in Honor of Nimet Özgüç,* pp. 613–28. Ankara.

Özyar, Aslı

1988   "The Tombs of Alaca Höyük: A New Evaluation of Selected Topics." M.A. thesis, Bryn Mawr College, Bryn Mawr, Pa.

Palmieri, Alberto M.

1981   "Excavations at Arslantepe." *Anatolian Studies* 31, pp. 101–19.

Palmieri, Alberto M., and Gian Maria Di Nocera

2000   "The Metal Objects from the 'Royal' Tomb at Arslantepe (Malatya-Turkey)." In *Landscapes: Territories, Frontiers and Horizons in the Ancient Near East. Papers Presented to the XLIVe Rencontre Assyriologique Internationale, Venezia, 7–11 July 1997. Part III. Landscape in Ideology, Religion, Literature, and Art,* edited by L. Milano et al., pp. 179–90. Padua.

Parpola, Asko

1984   "New Correspondences between Harrapan and Near Eastern Glyptic Art." In *South Asian Archaeology 1981,* edited by B. Allchin, pp. 176–96. Cambridge.

1994   *Deciphering the Indus Script.* Cambridge and New York.

1996   "A Sumerian Motif in Late Indus Seals." In *The Indian Ocean in Antiquity,* by Julian Reade, pp. 227–33. London.

Parpola, S., Asko Parpola, and Robert H. Brunswig Jr.

1977   "The Meluhha Village: Evidence of Acculturation of Harappan Traders in Late Third Millennium Mesopotamia?" *Journal of the Economic and Social History of the Orient* 20, pp. 129–65.

Parrot, André

1935   "Les fouilles de Mari: Première campagne (hiver, 1933–34). Rapport préliminaire." *Syria* 16, pp. 1–28.

1937   "Les fouilles de Mari: Troisième campagne (hiver, 1935–36)." *Syria* 18, pp. 54–84.

1948   *Tello: Vingt campagnes de fouilles (1877–1933).* Paris.

1952   "Les fouilles de Mari: Septième campagne (hiver, 1951–1952)." *Syria* 29, pp. 183–203.

1954   "Les fouilles de Mari: Neuvième campagne (automne 1953)." *Syria* 31, pp. 152–71.

1956   *Mission archéologique de Mari.* Vol. 1, *Le temple d'Ishtar.* 3 vols. Institut français d'Archéologie de Beyrouth, Bibliothèque archéologique et historique, vol. 65. Paris.

1959   *Mission archéologique de Mari.* Vol. 2, *Le palais.* 3 vols. Institut français d'Archéologie de Beyrouth, Bibliothèque archéologique et historique, vols. 68–70. Paris.

1962   "Les fouilles de Mari: Douzième campagne (automne 1961)." *Syria* 39, pp. 151–79.

1962a   "Nouvelles acquisitions: Département des Antiquités orientales." *La revue du Louvre et des Musées de France,* no. 2, pp. 93–94.

1964   "Les fouilles de Mari: Treizième campagne (printemps 1964)." *Syria* 41, pp. 3–20.

1967   *Mission archéologique de Mari.* Vol. 3, *Les Temples d'Ishtarat et de Ninni-zaza.* Institut français d'Archéologie de Beyrouth, Bibliothèque archéologique et historique, vol. 86. Paris.

1968   *Mission archéologique de Mari.* Vol. 4, *Le "trésor" d'Ur.* Institut français d'Archéologie de Beyrouth, Bibliothèque archéologique et historique, vol. 87. Contribution by Georges Dossin. Paris.

1969   "Les fouilles de Mari: Dix-septième campagne (automne 1968)." *Syria* 46, pp. 191–208.

1971   "Les fouilles de Mari: Dix-neuvième campagne (printemps 1971)." *Syria* 48, pp. 253–70.

Parrot, André, and Jean Nougayrol

1948   "Un document de fondation hourrite." *Revue d'assyriologie et d'archéologie orientale* 42, pp. 1–20.

Peltenburg, Edgar

1999   "The Living and the Ancestors: Early Bronze Age Mortuary Practices at Jerablus Tahtani." In *Archaeology of the Upper Syrian Euphrates, the Tishrin Dam Area: Proceedings of the International Symposium Held at Barcelona, January 28th–30th, 1998,* edited by Gregorio del Olmo Lete and Jean-Luis Monero Fenollós, pp. 427–42. Aula Orientalis Supplementa 15. Barcelona.

Pelzel, Suzanne Meek

1973   "Perforated Sumerian Votive Plaques." Ph.D. dissertation, New York University.

Pereiro, Carmen Valdés

1999   "Tell Qara Quzaq: A Summary of the First Results." In *Archaeology of the Upper Syrian Euphrates, the Tishrin Dam Area: Proceedings of the International Symposium Held at Barcelona, January 28th–30th, 1998,* edited by Gregorio del Olmo Lete and Jean-Luis Monero Fenollós, pp. 117–27. Aula Orientalis Supplementa 15. Barcelona.

Perlov, B.

1980   "The Families of the Ensis Urbau and Gudea and Their Funerary Cult." In *Death in Mesopotamia,* edited by B. Alster, pp. 77–81. Copenhagen.

Peters, John P.

1897   *Nippur; or, Explorations and Adventures on the Euphrates. The Narrative of the University of Pennsylvania Expedition to Babylonia in the Years 1888–1890.* 2 vols. New York.

Pettinato, Giovanni

1971   *Das altorientalische Menschenbild und die sumerischen und akkadischen Schöpfungs-smythen.* Abhandlungen der Heidelberger Akademie der Wissenschaften, Philosophisch-historische Klasse, Jahrg. 1971, 1. Abh. Heidelberg.

1980   "Bollettino militare della campagna di Ebla conto la città di Mari." *Oriens Antiquus* 19, pp. 231–45.

1981   *Testi lessicali monolingui della Biblioteca L.2769.* Contributions by Robert Biggs et al. Series maior, Istituto Universitario Orientale di Napoli, Seminario di Studi Asiatici, vol. 3. Naples.

1982   *Testi lessicali bilingui della Biblioteca L.2769.* Contributions by E. Arcari, A. Magi-Spinetti, and G. Visicato. Series maior, Istituto Universitario Orientale di Napoli, Seminario di Studi Asiatici, vol. 4. Naples.

1986   *Ebla: Nuovi orizzonti della storia.* Milan.

Pfälzner, Peter

2002   "Modes of Storage and the Development of Economic Systems in the Early Jezireh Period." In *Of Pots and Plans: Papers on the Archaeology and History of Mesopotamia and Syria Presented to David Oates in Honour of His 75th Birthday,* edited by Lamia al-Gailani Werr et al., pp. 259–86. London.

Philip, Graham

1989   *Metal Weapons of the Early and Middle Bronze Ages in Syria-Palestine.* 2 vols. British Archaeological Reports, International Series, no. 526. Oxford.

Pic, Marielle

1990   "Quelques eléments de glyptiques." In *Failaka: Fouilles françaises, 1986–1988,* edited by Yves Calvet and Jacqueline Gachet, pp. 125–40. Travaux de la Maison de l'Orient, 18. Lyon.

Pinnock, Frances

1986   "The Lapis Lazuli Trade in the Third Millennium B.C. and the Evidence of the Royal Palace at Ebla." In *Insight through Images,* edited by M. Kelly-Buccellati, pp. 221–28. Malibu.

1988   "Observations on the Trade of Lapis Lazuli in the IIIrd Millennium B.C." In *Wirtschaft und Gesellschaft von Ebla: Akten der Internationalen Tagung Heidelberg 1986,* edited by H. Hauptmann and Hartmut Waetzoldt, pp. 107–10. Heidelberg.

1990   "Patterns of Trade at Ebla in the Third Millennium B.C." *Les annales archéologiques arabes syriennes* 40, pp. 39–49.

1992   "Le turban royal éblaïte." *Nouvelles assyriologiques brèves et utilitaires,* pp. 15–16.

Piotrovsky, Yuri

1991   "Datirovka arkheologicheskogo kompleksa Maikopskogo kurgana (Oshad) i problemy khronologii maikopskoi kul'tury" (Dating of the Archaeological Complex of the Maikop Barrow [Oshad] and Problems in the Chronology of Maikop Culture). In *Maikopskii fenomen v drevnei istorii Kavkaza i Vostochnoi Evropy* (The Maikop Phenomenon in the Ancient History of the Caucasus and Eastern Europe), pp. 15–20. Leningrad.

1993   "'Maikop' i Drevniy Vostok" (Maikop and the Ancient East). In *Ermitazhnye chteniia: pamiati B.B. Piotrovskogo (14.II. 1908–15.X.1990); kratkoe soderzhanie dokladov* (Hermitage Readings in Memory of B. B. Piotrovsky), edited by E.V. Zeimal, pp. 48–50. Saint Petersburg.

1994   "Vessel Decorated with a Landscape." In *Great Art Treasures in the Hermitage Museum, St. Petersburg,* edited by V. Suslov, vol. 1, p. 79, no. 37. New York.

1994a   "Zametki o sosudakh s izobrazheniiami iz Maikopskogo kurgana (Oshad)" (Remarks on Vessels with Images from the Maikop Barrow [Oshad]). In *Pamiatniki drevnego i srednevekogo iskusstva: Problemy arkheologii* (Monuments of Ancient and Medieval Art: Problems of Archaeology), vol. 3, pp. 85–92. Saint Petersburg.

1998   "Periodizatsiia iuvelirnykh izdelii v Tsirkumpontiiskoii provintsii (eneolit-ranniaia bronza)." In *Shliman, Peterburg, Troia,* pp. 82–92. Saint Petersburg.

Piperno, Marcello

1977   "The Graveyard." In *La città bruciata del deserto salato,* edited by P. Basaglia et al., pp. 115–55. Venice.

Pittman, Holly

1984   *Art of the Bronze Age: Southeastern Iran, Western Central Asia, and the Indus Valley.* Contributions by Edith Porada. New York: The Metropolitan Museum of Art.

1987   *Ancient Art in Miniature: Near Eastern Seals from the Collection of Martin and Sarah Cherkasky.* Contributions by Joan Aruz. Exh. cat. New York: The Metropolitan Museum of Art.

1990   "Silver Cylindrical Cup." In *Glories of the Past: Ancient Art from the Shelby White and Leon Levy Collection,* edited by Dietrich von Bothmer, pp. 43–44, no. 30. Exh. cat. New York: The Metropolitan Museum of Art.

1998   "Jewelry." In *Treasures from the Royal Tombs of Ur,* edited by Richard L. Zettler and Lee Horne, pp. 87–122. Philadelphia.

2000   "Administrative Evidence from Hacinebi Tepe: An Essay on the Local and the Colonial." *Paléorient* 25, no. 1, pp. 43–50.

2001a   "Glyptic Art of Period IV." In *Excavations at Tepe Yahya, Iran, 1967–1975,* edited by D. Potts, pp. 231–68. Cambridge, Mass.

2001b   "Mesopotamian Intraregional Relations Reflected through Glyptic Evidence in the Late Chalcolithic 1–5 Periods." In *Uruk, Mesopotamia, and Its Neighbors,* edited by Mitchell S. Rothman, pp. 403–43. Santa Fe.

2002   "The 'Jeweler's' Seal from Susa and Art of Awan." In *Leaving No Stones Unturned,*

edited by Erica Ehrenberg, pp. 211–35. Winona Lake, Ind.

Plenderleith, H. J.

1934   "Metals and Metal Technique." In *The Royal Cemetery,* by Sir Leonard Woolley, vol. 2, pp. 284–98.

Podzuweit, Christian

1979   *Trojanische Gefässformen der Frühbronzezeit in Anatolien, der Ägäis und angrenzenden Gebieten: Ein Beitrag zur vergleichenden Stratigraphie.* Mainz am Rhein.

Pollock, Susan

1985   "Chronology of the Royal Cemetery of Ur." *Iraq* 47, pp. 129–47.

1999   *Ancient Mesopotamia: The Eden That Never Was.* Cambridge.

Pomponio, Francesco, and Paolo Xella

1997   *Les dieux d'Ebla: Étude analytique des divinités éblaïtes à l'époque des archives royales du IIIe millénaire.* Alter Orient und Altes Testament, vol. 245. Münster.

Popova, T. B.

1963   *Dol'meny stanitsy Novosvobodnoi: Trudy Gosudarstvennogo Istoricheskogo muzeia. Pamiatniki kul'tury* (Kurgans from Novosvobodnaia Village: Works of the State Historical Museum. Monuments of Culture). No. 34. Moscow.

Porada, Edith

1948   *Corpus of Ancient Near Eastern Seals in American Collections.* Vol. 1, *The Collection of the Pierpont Morgan Library.* Edited for the Committee of Ancient Near Eastern Seals, a project of the Iranian Institute, the Oriental Institute of the University of Chicago, and the Yale Babylonian Collection; contributions by Briggs Buchanan. Bollingen Series, vol. 14. New York.

1950   "A Leonine Figure of the Protoliterate Period of Mesopotamia." *Journal of the American Oriental Society* 70, pp. 223–26.

1960   "Notes on the Sargonid Cylinder Seal Ur 364." *Iraq* 22, pp. 116–23.

1961   Review of André Parrot, *Temple d'Ishtar. Bibliotheca Orientalis* 18 (May–July), pp. 160–63.

1965   *The Art of Ancient Iran: Pre-Islamic Cultures.* Contributions by R. H. Dyson and C. K. Wilkinson. New York. Also published as *Ancient Iran: The Art of Pre-Islamic Times,* London.

1971a   "Excursus: Comments on Steatite Carvings from Saudi Arabia and Other Parts of the Ancient Near East." *Artibus Asiae* 33, pp. 323–31.

1971b   "Remarks on Seals Found in the Gulf States." *Artibus Asiae* 33, pp. 331–37.

1975   "Iranische Kunst." In *Der alte Orient,* edited by Winfried Orthmann, pp. 363–98. Berlin.

1976   Section on seals in "L'ivorio et l'osso." In *Poliochni: Città preistorica nell'isola di Lemnos,* vol. 2, pp. 300ff. Rome.

1980   "A Lapis Lazuli Figurine from Hierakonpolis in Egypt." *Iranica Antiqua* 15, pp. 175–80.

1983 Review of *Siegelabrollungen aus den archaischen Bauschicten in Uruk-Warka,* by M. A. Brandes. *Journal of the American Oriental Society* 103, p. 476.

1987 "On the Origins of 'Aquarius.'" In *Language, Literature, and History: Philological Papers Presented to Erica Reiner,* edited by F. Rochberg-Halton. New Haven: American Oriental Society.

1992 "A Man with Serpents." In *Von Uruk nach Tuttul: Eine Festschrift für Eva Strommenger,* pp. 171–79. Munich and Vienna.

1993a "Seals and Related Objects from Early Mesopotamia and Iran." In *Early Mesopotamia and Iran: Contact and Conflict, 3500–1600 B.C.,* edited by J. Curtis, pp. 44–53. London: British Museum.

1993b "Why Cylinder Seals?: Engraved Cylindrical Seal Stones of the Ancient Near East, Fourth to First Millennium B.C." *Art Bulletin* 75, pp. 563–82.

Porada, Edith, Donald P. Hansen, Sally Dunham, and Sidney H. Babcock

1992 "The Chronology of Mesopotamia, ca. 7000–1600 B.C." In *Chronologies in Old World Archaeology,* edited by Robert W. Ehrich, vol. 1, pp. 77–121. 3rd ed. Chicago.

Porter, Anne

2002 "The Dynamics of Death: Ancestors, Pastoralism and the Origins of a Third-Millennium City in Syria." *Bulletin of the American Schools of Oriental Research* 325, pp. 1–36.

Possehl, Gregory L.

1996 "Meluhha." In *The Indian Ocean in Antiquity,* edited by Julian Reade, pp. 133–208. London: British Museum.

Postgate, J. N.

1992 *Early Mesopotamia: Society and Economy at the Dawn of History.* London and New York.

Pottier, Edmond, Jacques de Morgan, and Roland de Mecquenem

1912 *Céramique peinte de Suse et petits monuments de l'époque archaïque.* Mémoires de la Mission archéologique en Iran, vol. 13. Paris.

Pottier, Marie-Hélène

1980 "Un cachet en argent de Bactriane." *Iranica Antiqua* 15, pp. 167–74.

1984 *Matériel funéraire de la Bactriane Méridionale de l'Âge du Bronze.* Paris.

Potts, Daniel T.

1981 "Echoes of Mesopotamian Divinity on a Cylinder Seal from South-Eastern Iran." *Revue d'assyriologie et d'archéologie orientale* 75, pp. 135–42.

1990 *The Arabian Gulf in Antiquity.* Vol. 1, *From Prehistory to the Fall of the Achaemenid Empire.* Oxford.

1993 "A New Bactrian Find from Southeastern Arabia." *Antiquity* 67, pp. 591–96.

1994 "South and Central Asian Elements at Tell Abraq (Emirate of Umm al-Qaiwain, United Arab Emirates), ca. 2200 B.C.–A.D. 400." In *South Asian Archaeology*

1993, edited by Asko Parpola and Petteri Koskikallio, vol. 2, pp. 615–28. Helsinki.

1997 *Mesopotamian Civilization: The Material Foundations.* Ithaca, N.Y.

2000 *Ancient Magan: The Secrets of Tell Abraq.* London.

2001a "Before the Emirates: An Archaeological and Historical Account of Developments in the Region, ca. 5000 B.C. to 676 A.D." In *United Arab Emirates: A New Perspective,* edited by Ibrahim Al Abed and Peter Hellyer, pp. 28–69. London.

2001b *Excavations at Tepe Yahya, Iran, 1967–1975: The Third Millennium.* Contributions by Holly Pittman and Philip L. Kohl. American School of Prehistoric Research Bulletin 45. Cambridge, Mass.: Peabody Museum of Archaeology and Ethnology.

2003 "Tepe Yahya, Tell Abraq, and the Chronology of the Bampur Sequence." *Iranica antiqua* 38. In press.

Potts, Daniel T., and Lloyd R. Weeks

1999 "An AMS Radiocarbon Chronology for the Umm al-Nar Type Tomb at Tell Abraq." *Tribulus* 9, no. 1, pp. 9–10.

Potts, Timothy F.

1989 "Foreign Stone Vessels of the Late Third Millennium B.C. from Southern Mesopotamia: Their Origins and Mechanisms of Exchange." *Iraq* 51, pp. 123–64.

1994 *Mesopotamia and the East: An Archaeological and Historical Study of Foreign Relations, 3400–2000 B.C.* Oxford University Committee for Archaeology, Monograph, no. 37. Oxford.

Powell, M. A.

1989 "Masse und Gewichte." In *Reallexikon der Assyriologie und vorderasiatischen Archäologie,* edited by D. O. Edzard, vol. 7, p. 462. Berlin and New York.

Pritchard, James B.

1943 *Palestinian Figurines in Relation to Certain Goddesses Known through Literature.* American Oriental Series, vol. 24. New Haven.

Quarantelli, E., ed.

1985 *The Land Between Two Rivers: Twenty Years of Italian Archaeology in the Middle East; The Treasures of Mesopotamia.* Turin.

Quibell, James E., and Frederick W. Green

1902 *Hierakonpolis.* Part 2. Egyptian Research Account, 5th Memoir. London.

Rao, S. R.

1973 *Lothal and the Indus Civilization.* Bombay and New York.

1985 *Lothal, a Harappan Port Town, 1955–62.* Vol. 2. Contributions by S. S. Sarkar et al. Memoirs of the Archaeological Survey of India, no. 78. New Delhi.

Rashid, Subhi Anwar

1957–71 "Gründungsbeigaben." In *Reallexikon der Assyriologie und vorderasiatischen Archäologie,* edited by E. Weidner and W. won Soden, vol. 3, pp. 655–61. Berlin and New York.

1970 "Eine frühdynastische Statue von der Insel Tarut im Persischen Golf." In *Gesellschaften im Alten Zweistromland und*

in den angrenzenden Gebieten—XVIII. Rencontre Assyriologique Internationale, München, 29. Juni bis 3. Juli, edited by Dietz O. Edzard, pp. 159–66. Munich.

1983 *Gründungsfiguren im Iraq.* Prähistorische Bronzefunde, Abt. 1, vol. 2. Munich.

1984 *Musikgeschichte in Bildern. Mesopotamien.* Leipzig.

Ratnagar, Shereen

1981 *Encounters: The Westerly Trade of the Harappa Civilization.* Delhi and New York.

Ravn, Otto E.

1960 *A Catalogue of Oriental Cylinder Seals and Seal Impressions in the Danish National Museum.* Nationalmuseets skrifter; Arkaeologisk-historisk raekke, vol. 8. Copenhagen: Nationalmuseet.

Reade, Julian E.

1979 *Early Etched Beads and the Indus-Mesopotamia Trade.* British Museum Occasional Paper, no. 2. London.

1981 "Akkadian Sculpture Fragments from Eridu." *Baghdader Mitteilungen* 12, pp. 9–11.

1996 as editor. *The Indian Ocean in Antiquity.* London: British Museum.

1997 "Sumerian Origins." In *Sumerian Gods and Their Representations,* edited by Irving L. Finkel and Markham J. Geller, pp. 221–27. Cuneiform Monographs 7. Groningen.

2000 "Absolute Dates and Assyrian Calendars." *Just in Time; Akkadica* 119–20, pp. 151–53.

2001 "Assyrian King-Lists, the Royal Tombs of Ur, and Indus Origins." *Journal of Near Eastern Studies* 60, pp. 1–29.

Redford, Donald B.

1986 "Egypt and Western Asia in the Old Kingdom." *Journal of the American Research Center in Egypt* 23, pp. 125–43.

Reiner, Erica

1961 "The Aetiological Myth of the Seven Sages." *Orientalia* 30, pp. 1–11.

Reinholdt, C.

1993 "Der Thyreatis-Hortfund in Berlin: Untersuchungen zum vormykenischen Edelmetallschmuck in Griechenland." *Jahrbuch des Deutschen Archäologischen Instituts* 108, pp. 1–41.

Renger, Johannes

1967 "Untersuchungen zum Priestertum in der altbabylonischen Zeit." *Zeitschrift für Assyriologie und vorderasiatische Archäologie* 58, pp. 110–88.

Rezepkin, Alexei D.

1991 "Kurgan 31 mogil'nika Klady: Problemy genezisa i khronologii maikopskoi kul'-tury" (Barrow 31 from the Klada Burial Ground: Problems in the Genesis and Chronology of Maikop Culture). In *Drevnie kul'tury Prikuban'ia (po materialam arkheologicheskikh rabot v zone melioratsii Krasnodarskogo kraia)* (Ancient Cultures of the Kuban Region [Based on Materials from Archeological Work in the Land Improvement Zone of Krasnodar Territory]), pp. 167–97. Leningrad.

2000 *Das frühbronzezeitliche Gräberfeld von Klady und die Maikop-Kultur in*

Nordwestkaukasien. Translated by Ida Nagler. Archäologie in Eurasien, vol. 10. Deutsches Archäologisches Institut Eurasien-Abteilung. Rahden/Westf.

Rice, Michael

1983   *Dilmun Discovered: The Early Years of Archaeology in Bahrain.* Bahrain and London.

1986   *See* Al-Khalifa and Rice 1986.

1994   *The Archaeology of the Arabian Gulf, c. 5000–323 BC.* London.

Robins, Gay

1999   "Hair and the Construction of Identity in Ancient Egypt, c. 1480–1350 B.C." *Journal of the American Research Center in Egypt* 36, pp. 55–69.

Römer, Willem H. Ph.

1985   "Literarische Königsbriefe historischen Inhalts." In *Rechts- und Wirtschaftsurkunden, Historisch-chronologische Texte,* edited by Otto Kaiser, pp. 343–53. Texte aus der Umwelt des Alten Testaments 1, no. 4. Gütersloh.

1990   "'Weisheitstexte' und Texte m.B.a. den Schulbetrieb in sumerischer Sprache." In *Weisheitstexte, 1,* edited by Otto Kaiser, pp. 17–109. Texte aus der Umwelt des Alten Testaments 3, no. 1. Gütersloh.

1993   *Mythen und Epen in sumerischer Sprache.* Texte aus der Umwelt des Alten Testaments, 3, no. 3. Contribution by Dietz O. Edzard. Gütersloh.

Rossi-Osmida, Gabriele

2002   "Considerations on the Necropolis at Gonur-Depe." In *Margiana: Gonur Depe Necropolis; Ten Years of Excavations by Ligabue Study and Research Center,* pp. 69–120.

Rostovtzeff, Michael Ivanovitch

1920a   "La stèle d'Untaš-GAL." *Revue d'assyriologie et d'archéologie orientale* 17, pp. 113–16.

1920b   "The Sumerian Treasure of Astrabad." *Journal of Egyptian Archaeology* 6, pp. 4–27.

1922   *Iranian and Greeks in South Russia.* Oxford.

Roth, Martha T.

1995   *Law Collections from Mesopotamia and Asia Minor.* Edited by Piotr Michalowski; contribution by Harry A. Hoffner Jr. Writings from the Ancient World, no. 6. Atlanta.

Rubio Pardo, José Gonzalo

1996   "Los albores de la literatura Sirio-Mesopotámica en el III milenio: Ebla, Fara y Abu Ṣalābīḥ." In *Literatura e historia en el próximo Oriente antiguo,* edited by E. Martínez Borobio, pp. 31–46. Toledo.

Rudolph, Wolf

1995   *A Golden Legacy: Ancient Jewelry from the Burton Y. Berry Collection at the Indiana University Art Museum.* Edited by Linda Baden; contribution by Barbara Deppert. Exh. cat. Bloomington: Indiana University Art Museum.

Rutter, Jeremy B.

1995   *The Pottery of Lerna IV.* Foreword by Martha Heath Wiencke, contributions by M. Attas et al. Princeton.

Safar, Fuad, Mohammad Ali Mustafa, and Seton Lloyd

1981   *Eridu.* Baghdad: State Organisation of Antiquities and Heritage.

Sakellarakis, Ioannis

1972   with Ephe Sapouna-Sakellaraki. "Apothetes kerameikes tes teleutaias phaseos ton proanaktorikon chronon eis Archanes." *Archiologiki Ephermeris Chronika,* pp. 1–11.

1977   "Ta kykladika stoixeia ton Archanon." *Archaiologika Analekta ex Athēnōn* 10, pp. 93–115. **need to fill in accents**

1997   with Ephe Sapouna-Sakellaraki. *Archanes: Minoan Crete in a New Light.* 2 vols. Athens.

Sallaberger, Walther

1999   "Ur III-Zeit." In *Mesopotamien. Akkade-Zeit und Ur III Zeit,* edited by P. Attinger and M. Wäfler, pp. 121–414. Göttingen.

Salvatori, Sandro

1988   "Early Bactrian Objects in Private Collections." In *Bactria: An Ancient Oasis Civilization from the Sands of Afghanistan,* edited by Giancarlo Ligabue and Sandro Salvatori, pp. 181–87. Venice.

Salvini, Mirjo

1998   "The Earliest Evidence of the Hurrians before the Formation of the Reign of Mittanni." In *Mozan III. Urkesh and the Hurrians,* edited by G. Buccellati and M. Kelly-Buccellati, pp. 99–115. Malibu.

Samzun, A.

1992   "Observations on the Characteristics of the Pre-Harappan Remains, Pottery, and Artifacts at Nausharo, Pakistan (2700–2500 B.C.)." In *South Asian Archaeology 1989,* edited by C. Jarrige, pp. 245–52. Madison, Wisc.

Sarianidi, Victor Ivanovich

1968   *Myths of Ancient Bactria and Margiana on Its Seals and Amulets.* Moscow.

1985   *L'archéologie de la Bactriane ancienne.* Paris.

1986   *Die Kunst des alten Afghanistan.* Leipzig.

1998a   *Margiana and Protozoroastrianism.* Athens.

1998b   *Myths of Ancient Bactria and Margiana on Its Seals and Amulets.* Moscow.

2002   *Margus: Ancient Oriental Kingdom in the Old Delta of the Murghab.* Ashkhabad.

Sarzec, Ernest de, and Léon Heuzey

1884–1912   *Découvertes en Chaldée.* Edited by Léon Heuzey. 2 vols. in 3 parts. Paris.

Scandone Matthiae, Gabriella

1979   "Vasi iscritti di Chefren e Pepi I dal Palazzo Reale G di Ebla." *Studia Eblaiti* 1, no. 3–4, pp. 33–44.

1982   "Inscriptions royales égyptiennes de l'Ancien Empire à Ebla." In *Mesopotamien und seine Nachbarn: XXVe Rencontre Assyriologique Internationale, Berlin 1978,* pp. 125–30. Berlin.

1991   "Gli intarsi egittizzanti del palazzo settentrionale di Ebla." *Scienza all'antichita* 5, pp. 423–59.

Scheil, Vincent

1925a   "Un nouveau sceau hindou pseudo-sumérien." *Revue d'assyriologie et d'archéologie orientale* 22, pp. 55–56.

1925b   "Une nouvelle statue de Gudéa." *Revue d'assyriologie et d'archéologie orientale* 22, pp. 41–43.

Schliemann, Heinrich

1874   *Trojanische Alterthümer: Bericht über die Ausgrabungen in Troja.* Leipzig.

1881   *Ilios: The City and Country of the Trojans. The Results of Researches and Discoveries on the Site of Troy and throughout the Troad in the Years 1871, 72, 73, 78, 79; Including an Autobiography of the Author.* New York.

1885   *Ilios: Ville et pays des Troyens résultat des fouilles sur l'emplacement de Troi et des explorations faites en Troade de 1871 à 1882.* Translated by E. Egger. Paris.

Schlossman, Betty L.

1976   "Two Foundation Figurines." In *Ancient Mesopotamian Art and Selected Texts: The Pierpont Morgan Library,* pp. 9–25. New York.

1978–79   "Portraiture in Mesopotamia in the Late Third and Early Second Millennium B.C." *Archiv für Orientforschung* 26, pp. 56–77.

Schmandt-Besserat, Denise

1993   "Images of Enship." In *Between the Rivers and over the Mountains: Archaeologica Anatolica et Mesopotamica Alba Palmieri dedicata,* edited by M. Frangipane et al., pp. 201–20. Rome.

Schmidt, Erich

1932   *The Alishar Hüyük, Seasons of 1928 and 1929.* Chicago.

1933   "Tepe Hissar Excavations 1931." *The Museum Journal* 23, no. 4, pp. 323–487.

1937   *Excavations at Tepe Hissar, Damghan.* Contribution by Fiske Kimball. Philadelphia: University Museum.

Schmidt, Hubert

1902   *Heinrich Schliemann's Sammlung trojanischer Altertümer.* Berlin: Königliche Museen zu Berlin.

Schwartz, Glenn M., and Harvey Weiss

1992   "Syria." In *Chronologies in Old World Archaeology,* edited by Robert W. Ehrich, vol. 1, pp. 221–43; vol. 2, pp. 185–202. 3rd ed. Chicago.

Schwartz, Glenn M., Hans H. Curvers, and Barbara Stuart

2000   "A Third-Millennium Élite Tomb from Tell Umm el-Marra, Syria." *Antiquity* 74, pp. 771–72.

Schwartz, Glenn M., Hans H. Curvers, Fokke A. Gerritsen, Jennifer A. MacCormack, Naomi F. Miller, and Jill A. Weber

2000   "Excavation and Survey in the Jabbul Plain, Western Syria: The Umm el-Marra Project 1996–7." *American Journal of Archaeology* 104, pp. 419–62.

Selz, Gudrun

1983   *Die Bankettszene: Entwicklung eines "überzeitlichen" Bildmotivs in Mesopotamien: von der frühdynastischen bis zur Akkad-Zeit.* Wiesbaden.

Shaffer, Aaron

1963   "Sumerian Sources of Tablet XII of the Epic of Gilgameš." Ph.D. dissertation, University of Pennsylvania. Philadelphia.

Shah, Sayyid Ghulam Mustafa, and Asko Parpola, eds.

1991   *Corpus of Indus Seals and Inscriptions.* Vol. 2, *Collections in Pakistan.* Contributions by Ahmad Nabi Khan et al. Helsinki.

Shepherd, Dorothy

1963   "Gudea, Patesi of Lagash." *Bulletin of the Cleveland Museum of Art* 50, no. 9, pp. 243–48.

Shliman, Peterburg, Troia

1998   *Shliman, Peterburg, Troia* (Schliemann. Petersburg. Troy). Exh. cat. Saint Petersburg.

Sigrist, Marcel

1992   *Drehem.* Sumerian Archival Texts, vol. 1. Bethesda.

Sjöberg, Åke W.

1976   "in-nin šà-gur₄-ra. A Hymn to the Goddess Inanna by the en-Priestess Enheduanna." *Zeitschrift für Assyriologie und vorderasiatische Archäologie* 65, pp. 161–253.

2002   "In the Beginning." In *Riches Hidden in Secret Places: Ancient Near Eastern Studies in Memory of Thorkild Jacobsen,* edited by Tzvi Abush, pp. 229–47. Winona Lake, Ind.

Sjöberg, Åke W., and Eugen Bergmann

1969   *The Collection of the Sumerian Temple Hymns.* Contribution by Gene B. Gragg. Texts from Cuneiform Sources, vol. 3. Locust Valley, N.Y.

Smithsonian Institution

1966   *Art Treasures of Turkey.* [Exh. cat.]. Washington, D.C.: Smithsonian Institution.

von Soden, Wolfram

1971   "Review of André Parrot, *Le trésor d'Ur,* MAM IV, Paris." *Orientalistische Literaturzeitung* 66 (March–April), cols. 141–44.

Soldt, Wilfred van

2000   "Syrian Chronology in the Old and Early Middle Babylonian Periods." *Just in Time; Akkadica* 119–20, pp. 103–16.

Sollberger, Edmond

1954–55   "Sur la chronologie des rois d'Ur et quelques problèmes connexes." *Archiv für Orientforschung* 17, pp. 10–48.

1956   "Selected Texts from American Collections." *Journal of Cuneiform Studies* 11, pp. 11–31.

1960   "Notes on the Early Inscriptions from Ur and El-'Obēd." *Iraq* 22, pp. 69–89.

1967   "The Rulers of Lagaš." *Journal of Cuneiform Studies* 21, pp. 279–91.

1980   "The So-Called Treaty between Ebla and 'Ashur.'" *Studia Eblaiti* 3, pp. 129–60.

1983   "A Statue for Shu-Sin." *Anatolian Studies* 33, pp. 73–74.

Sollberger, Edmond, and Jean Robert Kupper

1971   *Inscriptions royales sumériennes et akkadiennes.* Littératures anciennes du Proche-Orient, vol. 3. Paris.

Soucek, Priscilla

1976   "The Temple of Solomon in Islamic Legend and Art." In *The Temple of Solomon,* edited by J. Gutmann. Missoula, Mont.

Spycket, Agnès

1954   "La coiffure féminine en Mésopotamie,"

parts 1, 2. *Revue d'assyriologie et d'archéologie orientale* 48, pp. 113–29, 169–77.

1955   "La coiffure féminine en Mésopotamie," part 3. *Revue d'assyriologie et d'archéologie orientale* 49, pp. 113–28.

1968   *Les statues de culte dans les textes mésopotamiens: Des origines à la Ire dynastie de Babylone.* Paris.

1981   *La statuaire du Proche-Orient Ancien.* Handbuch der Orientalistik, Abt. 7, Kunst und Archäologie, Der alte vordere Orient, vol. 1, 2. Abschnitt, Die Denkmaler, B, Vorderasien, Lieferung 2. Leiden and Cologne.

Srinivasan, Doris

1975–76   "The So-Called Proto-Śiva Seal from Mohenjo-Daro: An Iconological Assessment." *Archives of Asian Art* 29, pp. 47–58.

Srivastava, K. M.

1991   *Madinat Hamad: Burial Mounds, 1984–85.* Manama, Bahrain.

Stech, T., and V. C. Pigott

1986   "The Metals Trade in Southwest Asia in the Third Millennium B.C." *Iraq* 48, pp. 39–64.

Steible, Horst

1982   *Die altsumerischen Bau- und Weihinschriften.* 2 vols. Contributions by Hermann Behrens. Freiburger altorientalische Studien, vol. 5. Wiesbaden.

1991   *Die neusumerischen Bau- und Weihinschriften.* Vol. 1, *Inschriften der II. Dynastie von 'Lagaš.'* Freiburger altorientalische Studien, vol. 9. Stuttgart.

1994   "Versuch einer Chronologie der Statuen des Gudea von Lagash." *Mitteilungen der Deutschen Orient-Gesellschaft* 126, pp. 81–104.

Stein, Sir Aurel

1937   *Archaeological Reconnaissances in Northwestern India and South-eastern Iran.* Contributions by Fred H. Andrews and R. L. Hobson. London.

Steinkeller, Piotr

1982   "The Question of Marhaši: A Contribution to the Historical Geography of Iran in the Third Millennium B.C." *Zeitschrift für Assyriologie und vorderasiatische Archäologie* 72, pp. 237–65.

1984   "Communications I." *Revue d'assyriologie et d'archéologie orientale* 78, pp. 83–84.

1987   "The Administrative and Economic Organisation of the Ur III State: The Core and the Periphery." In *The Organization of Power: Aspects of Bureaucracy in the Ancient Near East,* edited by McGuire Gibson and Robert D. Biggs, pp. 19–42. Chicago.

1988   "The Date of Gudea and His Dynasty." *Journal of Cuneiform Studies* 40, pp. 47–53.

1992a   "Early Semitic Literature and Third Millennium Seals with Mythological Motifs." In *Literature and Literary Language at Ebla,* edited by Pelio Fronzaroli, pp. 243–75. Florence.

1992b   "Mesopotamia in the Third Millennium B.C." In *Anchor Bible Dictionary,* edited by

D. N. Freedman, vol. 4, pp. 724–32. New York.

1993   "Early Political Development in Mesopotamia and the Origins of the Sargonic Empire." In *Akkad, the First World Empire: Structure, Ideology, Traditions,* edited by Mario Liverani, pp. 107–29. Padua.

1998   "The Historical Background of Urkesh and the Hurrian Beginnings in Northern Mesopotamia." In *Mozen III, Urkesh and the Hurrians,* edited by G. Buccellati and M. Kelly-Buccellati, 23, pp. 75–98. Malibu.

1999   "On Rulers, Priests and Sacred Marriage: Tracing the Evolution of Early Sumerian Kingship." In *Priests and Officials in the Ancient Near East: The City and Its LIfe Held at the Middle Eastern Culture Center in Japan (Mitaka, Tokyo), March 22–24, 1996,* edited by Kazuko Watanabe, pp. 103–37. Heidelberg.

2000   "Archaic City Seals and the Question of Early Babylonian Unity." In *Riches Hidden in Secret Places: Ancient Near Eastern Studies in Memory of Thorkild Jacobsen,* edited by T. Abusch, pp. 249–57. Winona Lake, Ind.

2002   "More on the Archaic City Seals." *Nouvelles assyriologiques brèves et utilitaires,* no. 2, p. 29.

Stephan, Elisabeth

1995   "Preliminary Report on the Faunal Remains of the First Two Seasons of Tell Abraq/Umm al Quwain/United Arab Emirates." In *Archaeozoology of the Near East II: Proceedings of the Second International Symposium on the Archaeozoology of Southwestern Asia and Adjacent Areas,* edited by H. Buitenhuis and H.-P. Uerpmann, pp. 53–63. Leiden.

Stos-Gale, Z. A., N. Gale, and G. Gilmore

1984   "Early Bronze Age Trojan Metal Sources and Anatolians in the Cyclades." *Oxford Journal of Archaeology* 3, pp. 23–43.

Strommenger, Eva

1957–71   "Gudea." In *Reallexikon der Assyriologie und vorderasiatischen Archäologie,* edited by E. Weidner and W. von Soden, vol. 3, pp. 680–87. Berlin and New York.

1960   "Das Menschenbild in der altmesopamischen Rundplastik von Mesilim bis Hammurapi." *Baghdader Mitteilungen* 1, pp. 1–103.

1964   *5000 Years of the Art of Mesopotamia.* Translated by Christina Haglund. New York.

1967   *Gefässe aus Uruk von der neubabylonischen Zeit bis zu den Sasaniden.* Ausgrabungen der Deutschen Forschungsgemeinschaft in Uruk-Warka, vol. 7. Contribution by Rudolf Macuch. Berlin.

1971   "Mesopotamische Gewandtypen von der Frühsumerischen bis zur Larsa-Zeit." *Acta Praehistorica et Archaeologica* 2, pp. 37–55.

1980   "The Chronological Division of the Archaic Levels of Uruk-Eanna VI to

III/II: Past and Present." *American Journal of Archaeology* 84, pp. 479–87.

1986   "Early Metal Figures from Assur and the Technology of Metal Casting." *Sumer* 42, pp. 114–15.

Sürenhagen, Dietrich

2002   "Death in Mesopotamia: The 'Royal Tombs' of Ur Revisited." In *Of Pots and Plans: Papers on the Archaeology and History of Mesopotamia and Syria Presented to David Oates in Honour of His 75th Birthday,* edited by Lamia al-Gailani Werr et al., pp. 324–38. London.

Suter, Claudia E.

1991–93   "A Shulgi Statuette from Tello." *Journal of Cuneiform Studies* 43–45, pp. 63–70.

2000   *Gudea's Temple Building: The Representation of an Early Mesopotamian Ruler in Text and Image.* Cuneiform Monographs, vol. 17. Groningen.

Taggart, Ross E., George L. McKenna, and M. F. Wilson, eds.

1973   *Handbook of the Collections in the William Rockhill Nelson Gallery of Art and Mary Atkins Museum of Fine Arts, Kansas City, Missouri.* 2 vols. 5th ed. Kansas City.

Tallon, Françoise

1987   *Métallurgie susienne I: De la fondation de Suse au XVIIIe avant J.-C.* 2 vols. Contributions by Jean-Michel Malfoy and Michel Menu. Notes et documents des musées de France, vol. 15. Paris.

1992a   "Art and the Ruler: Gudea of Lagash." *Asian Art* 5 (winter), pp. 31–51.

1992b   "The 'Trouvaille de la statuette d'or' from the Inshushinak Temple Precinct." In "The 'Trouvaille de la statuette d'or' from the Inshushinak Temple Precinct." In *The Royal City of Susa,* edited by Prudence O. Harper, Joan Aruz, and Françoise Tallon, pp. 145–53. Exh. cat. New York: The Metropolitan Museum of Art.

1995   as editor. *Les pierres précieuses de l'Orient ancien: Des Sumériens aux Sassanides.* Les dossiers du Musée du Louvre; Exposition-dossier du Département des antiquités orientales, no. 49. Exh. cat. Paris: Musée du Louvre.

Taylor, John, Paul Craddock, and Fleur Shearman

1998   "Egyptian Hollow-Cast Bronze Statues of the Early First Millennium BC: The Development of a New Technology." *Apollo,* n.s., 148 (July), pp. 9–19.

Tefnin, R.

1981–82   "Tall Umm al-Marra." *Archiv für Orient-forschung* 28, pp. 235–39.

Tezcan, Burhan

1960   "New Finds from Horoztepe." *Anatolia* 5, pp. 29–46.

Thapar, B. K.

1979   "Kalibangan: A Harappan Metropolis beyond the Indus Valley." In *Ancient Cities of the Indus,* edited by Gregory L. Possehl, pp. 196–202. New Delhi.

Thimme, Jürgen, ed.

1976   *Kunst und Kultur der Kykladeninseln im 3.*

Jahrtausend v. Chr. Exh. cat. Karlsruhe: Karlsruher Schloss, sponsored by the International Council of Museums.

Thureau-Dangin, François

1905   *Les inscriptions de Sumer et d'Akkad: Transcription et tradition.* Paris.

1924   "Statuettes de Tello." *Monuments et mémoires publiés par l'Académie des inscriptions et belles-lettres* (Fondation Eugène Piot) 27, pp. 97–111.

1934   "Inscriptions votives sur des statuettes de Ma'eri." *Revue d'assyriologie et d'archéologie orientale* 31, pp. 137–44.

1937   "Une tablette en or provenant d'Umma." *Revue d'assyriologie et d'archéologie orientale* 34, pp. 177–82.

Tigay, Jeffrey H.

1993   "On Evaluating Claims of Literary Borrowing." In *The Tablet and the Scroll: Essays in Honor of William W. Hallo,* edited by Mark E. Cohn, Daniel C. Snell, and David B. Weisberg. Bethesda.

Tinney, Steve

1998a   "Death and Burial in Early Mesopotamia: The View from the Texts." In *Treasures from the Royal Tombs of Ur,* edited by Richard L. Zettler and Lee Horne, pp. 26–28. Philadelphia.

1998b   "Texts, Tablets, and Teaching. Scribal Education in Nippur and Ur." *Expedition* 40, no. 2, pp. 40–50.

1999   "On the Curricular Setting of Sumerian Literature." *Iraq* 61, pp. 159–72.

Toker, Ayşe

1992   *Metal Vessels.* Revised and edited by Jean Öztürk. Ankara: Museum of Ancient Civilizations.

Tokyo

1991   *Portraits du Louvre: Choix d'oeuvres dans les collections du Louvre.* Exh. cat. Tokyo: Kokusitsu Seiyo Bijutsukan (Museum of Western Art).

Tolstikov, Vladimir P., and Michail Yu Treister

1996   *The Gold of Troy: Searching for Homer's Fabled City.* Exh. cat. New York: Abrams, in association with A. S. Pushkin State Museum of Fine Arts.

Tonietti, Maria Vittoria

1998   "The Mobility of the NAR and the Sumerian Personal Names in Pre-Sargonic Mari Onomasticon." In *About Subartu: Studies Devoted to Upper Mesopotamia,* edited by Marc Lebeau, vol. 2, pp. 83–101. Turnhout.

Tosi, Maurizio, ed.

1983   *Prehistoric Sīstān.* Istituto Italiano per il Medio ed Estremo Oriente, Centro Studi e Scavi Archeologici in Asia; Istituto Universitario Orientale di Napoli, Seminario di Studi Asiatici, Reports and memoirs, vol. 19, no. 1. Rome.

Tosi, Maurizio, and Rauf Wardak

1972   "The Fullol Hoard: A New Find from Bronze-Age Afghanistan." *East and West* 22, pp. 9–17.

Trifonov, V. A.

1996   "Popravki k absoliutnoi khronologii kul'tur

epokhi eneolita-bronzy Severnogo Kavkaza" (Corrections to the Absolute Chronology of the Cultures of the Bronze Age in the Northern Caucasus). In *Mezhdu Aziei i Evropoi: Kavkaz v IV-I tys. do n. e.: Materialy konferentsii, posviashchennoi 100-letiiu so dnia razhdeniia A. A. Iessena* (Between Asia and Europe: The Caucasus from the Fourth to the First Millennium B.C. Materials from a Conference Devoted to the Hundredth Anniversary of the Birth of A. A. Iessen), pp. 43–49. Saint Petersburg.

2001   "Popravki k absoliutnoi khronologii kultur epokhi eneolita-srednei bronzy Kavkaza, stepnoi i lesostepnoi zon Evropy (po dannym radiouglerodnogo analiza)" (Corrections to the Absolute Chronology of the Cultures of the Middle Bronze Age of the Caucasus, the Steppe, and Forest-Steppe Zones of Europe [Based on Data from Radiocarbon Analysis]). In *Bronzovyi vek Vostochnoi Evropy: Kharakteristika kul'tur, khronologiia i periodizatsiia. Materialy mezhdunarodnoi konferentsii K stoletiiu periodizatsii. V. A. Gorodtsova bronzovogo veka iuzhnoi poloviny Vostochnoi Evropy* (The Bronze Age of Eastern Europe: Characteristics of the Cultures, Chronology, and Periodization. Materials from the International Conference. On the Hundredth Anniversary of V. A. Gorodtsov's Periodization of the Bronze Age in the Southern Half of Eastern Europe), pp. 71–82. Samara.

Tripathi, Vibha, and Ajeet K. Srivastava

1994   *The Indus Terracottas.* Delhi.

Tucci, Giuseppe, ed.

1977   *La città bruciata del deserto salato.* Contributions by Piero Basaglia et al. Rome.

Tunça, Önhan

1984   *L'architecture religieuse protodynastique en Mesopotamie.* 2 vols. Akkadica, Supplementum, vol. 2. Louvain.

Tzedakis, Yannis, and Holley Martlew

1999   *Minoans and Mycenaeans: Flavours of Their Time.* Exh. cat. Athens: National Archaeological Museum.

Uerpmann, Hans-Peter

1987   *The Ancient Distribution of Ungulate Mammals in the Middle East: Fauna and Archaeological Sites in Southwest Asia and Northeast Africa.* Beiheft zum Tübinger Atlas des vorderen Orients, Reihe A, Naturwissenschaften, no. 27. Wiesbaden.

Uerpmann, Margarethe

2001   "Remarks on the Animal Economy of Tell Abraq (Emirates of Sharjah and Umm al-Qaywayn, UAE)." *Proceedings of the Seminar for Arabian Studies* 31, pp. 227–33.

Valdez, Raul, C. F. Nadler, and T. D. Bunch

1978   "Evolution of Wild Sheep in Iran." *Evolution* 32, pp. 56–72.

Vallat, François

1997   "La date du règne de Gudea." *Nouvelles assyriologiques brèves et utilitaires,* no. 1, pp. 35–36, no. 37.

2000 "L'Élam du IIe millénaire et la chronologie courte." *Just in Time; Akkadica* 119–20,
pp. 7–17.

Van Buren, Elizabeth Douglas

1939 *The Fauna of Ancient Mesopotamia as
Represented in Art.* Analecta Orientalia,
vol. 18. Rome.

1945 *Symbols of the Gods in Mesopotamian Art.*
Analecta Orientalia, vol. 23. Rome.

Van de Mieroop, Marc

1997 *The Ancient Mesopotamian City.* Oxford.

2002 "In Search of Prestige: Foreign Contacts
and the Rise of an Elite in Early Dynastic
Babylonia." In *Leaving No Stones Unturned,*
edited by Erica Ehrenberg, pp. 125–37.
Winona Lake, Ind.

Vandiver, Pamela

1983 "Paleolithic Pigments and Processing."
M.S. thesis, Massachusetts Institute of
Technology, Cambridge, Mass.

Van Driel, G.

1973 Review of Ellis 1968. *Journal of the
American Oriental Society* 93, pp. 67–74.

Vanstiphout, Herman L. J.

1995a "The Matter of Aratta: An Overview."
Orientalia Lovaniensia Periodica 26,
pp. 5–20.

1995b "On the Old Babylonian Eduba Curriculum." In *Centres of Learning: Learning
and Location in Pre-Modern Europe and the
Near East,* edited by J. M. Drijvers and
A. A. MacDonald, pp. 3–16. Leiden.

1997 "Why Did Enki Organize the World?"
In *Sumerian Gods and Their Representations,*
edited by Irving L. Finkel and Markham
J. Geller, pp. 117–34. Groningen.

Vats, Madho Sarup

1940 *Excavations at Harappa; Being an Account
of Archaeological Excavations at Harappa
Carried out between the Years 1920–21 and
1933–34.* 2 vols. Delhi.

Veenhof, Klaas R.

2000 "Old Assyrian Chronology." *Just in Time;
Akkadica* 119–20, pp. 137–50.

Veldhuis, Niek

1999 "Continuity and Change in Mesopo-
tamian Lexical Tradition." In *Aspects of
Genre and Type in Pre-Modern Literary
Cultures,* edited by Bert Roest and
Herman Vanstiphout, pp. 101–18.
Groningen.

Vereshchagin, N. K.

1959 *Mlekopitaiushchie Kavkaza: Istoriia
formirovaniia fauny* (Mammals of the
Caucasus: History of Fauna Formation).
Moscow and Leningrad.

Veselovsky, Nikolai Ivanovich

1897 "Rukopisnyi Arkhiv IIMK RAN, fond
1, 1896, d.204" (Institute of the History
of Material Culture, Russian Academy of
Sciences, Manuscript Archive, Archive 1,
1896, file 204), pp. 51–52v.

Vincente, Claudine-Adrienne

1995 "The Tall Leilān Recension of the
Sumerian King List." *Zeitschrift für
Assyriologie und vorderasiatische Archäologie*
85, pp. 234–70.

Vine, Peter, ed.

1993 *Bahrain National Museum.* London.

Vogel, Helga

2000 "Statuen, die sichtbar machen zur
ästhetischen, religiösen und politischen
Bedeutung der Statuen des Gudea."
Baghdader Mitteilungen 31, pp. 65–86.

Vogt, B.

1996 "Bronze Age Maritime Trade in the
Indian Ocean: Harappan Traits on the
Oman Peninsula." In *The Indian Ocean in
Antiquity,* edited by Julian Reade, pp. 107–
32. London: British Museum.

Voigt, Mary

1983 *Hajji Firuz Tepe, Iran: The Neolithic
Settlement.* Contributions by Richard H.
Meadow, Jean Turnquist, John Winter,
and Eric Parkinson. Hasanlu Excavation
Reports, vol. 1; University Museum
Monograph, vol. 50. Philadelphia.

Voigt, Mary, and Robert H. Dyson Jr.

1992 "Iran." In *Chronologies in Old World
Archaeology,* edited by Robert W. Ehrich,
vol. 1, pp. 122–78. 3rd ed. Chicago.

Waetzoldt, Hartmut

2001 *Wirtschafts- und Verwaltungstexte aus Ebla:
Archiv L. 2769.* Materiali per il vocabolario sumerico, vol. 7; Materiali epigrafici
de Ebla, vol. 12. Rome.

**Walker, Christopher B. F., and Dominique
Collon**

1980 "Hormuzd Rassam's Excavations for the
British Museum at Sippar in 1881–1882."
In *Tell ed-Der,* edited by Léon De Meyer,
vol. 3, pp. 93–112. Louvain.

Walter, Hans, and Florens Felten

1981 *Alt-Ägina.* Vol. 3, no. 1, *Die vorgeschichtliche
Stadt: Befestigungen, Häuser, Funde.* 2 vols.
Mainz am Rhein.

Ward, W. H.

1886 "Two Babylonian Seal-Cylinders."
American Journal of Archaeology 2, pp. 46–48.

1888 "Two Stone Tablets with Hieroglyphic
Babylonian Writing." *American Journal of
Archaeology* 4, pp. 39–41.

Wartke, Ralf-B.

1992a "Libationsgefäss mit Einlagen." *Das
Vorderasiatische Museum* (Staatliche
Museen zu Berlin), p. 59.

1992b "Teil einer Stiftmosaikverkleidung von
einem Podest an einem Innenhof des
Eanna-Tempels." *Das Vorderasiatische
Museum* (Staatliche Museen zu Berlin),
p. 52.

1995 Catalogue entries. In *Assyrian Origins:
Discoveries at Ashur on the Tigris. Antiquities
in the Vorderasiatisches Museum, Berlin,*
edited by Prudence O. Harper et al.
Exh. cat. New York: The Metropolitan
Museum of Art

Watelin, Louis Charles, and Stephen Langdon

1934 *Excavations at Kish: The Herbert Weld (for
the University of Oxford) and Field Museum
of Natural History (Chicago) Expedition to
Mesopotamia.* Vol. 4, *1925–1930.* Paris.

Weadock, Penelope N.

1975 "The *Giparu* at Ur." *Iraq* 37, pp. 101–28.

Weber, Jill, and Richard L. Zettler

1998 "Tools and Weapons." In *Treasures from
the Royal Tombs of Ur,* edited by Richard
L. Zettler and Lee Horne. Philadelphia.

Weber, Otto

1917 "Altorientalische Kultgeräte." *Mitteilungen der Vorderasiatischen Gesellschaft*
22, pp. 391–92.

Weeks, Lloyd R.

1997 "Prehistoric Metallurgy at Tell Abraq,
U.A.E." *Arabian Archaeology and Epigraphy*
8, pp. 11–85.

1999 "Lead Isotope Analyses from Tell Abraq,
United Arab Emirates: New Data
Regarding the 'Tin Problem' in Western
Asia." *Antiquity* 73, pp. 49–64.

Weiss, Harvey, ed.

1985 *Ebla to Damascus: Art and Archaeology of
Ancient Syria. An Exhibition from the
Directorate-General of Antiquities and
Museums, Syrian Arab Republic.* Exh. cat.
Washington, D.C.: Smithsonian Institution.

1986 *The Origins of Cities in Dry-Farming Syria
and Mesopotamia in the Third Millennium
B.C.* Guilford, Conn.

Weiss, Harvey, and M.-A. Courty

1993 "The Genesis and Collapse of the
Akkadian Empire: The Accidental
Refraction of Historical Law." *Studies in
the History of the Ancient Near East* 5,
pp. 131–56.

Westenholz, Joan Goodnick

1989 "Enheduanna, En-Priestess, Hen of
Nanna, Spouse of Nanna." In *Dumu-e₂-
dub-ba-a: Studies in Honor of Åke W.
Sjöberg,* edited by Hermann Behrens et
al., pp. 539–56. Occasional Publications
of the Samuel Noah Kramer Fund, 11.
Philadelphia.

1997 *Legends of the Kings of Akkade.* Winona
Lake, Ind.

Wheeler, Sir Mortimer

1968 *The Indus Civilization; Supplementary
Volume to the Cambridge History of India.*
3rd ed. Cambridge.

Whiting, Robert

1976 "Tiš-Atal of Niniveh and Babati, Uncle
of Šu-Sin." *Journal of Cuneiform Studies*
28, pp. 173–82.

von Wickede, Alwo

1990 *Prähistorische Stempelglyptik in Vorderasien.*
Munich.

Wiener, Malcolm

forthcoming "Time Out: The Current Impasse in
Bronze Age Archaeological Dating." In
*Aegaeum 23: Metron. Measuring the Aegean
Bronze Age.* Proceedings of the 9th
International Aegean Conference
Organized by the University of Liege
and Yale University, April 18–21, 2002.

Wiggermann, F. A. M.

1985–86 "The Staff of Ninšubura, Studies in
Babylonian Demonology, II." *Jaarbericht
Ex Oriente Lux* 29, pp. 3–34.

1992 *Mesopotamian Protective Spirits: The Ritual
Texts.* Cuneiform Monographs, vol. 1.
Groningen.

1995 "Extensions of and Contradictions to Dr. Porada's Lecture." In *Man and Images in the Ancient Near East,* edited by Edith Porada, pp. 77–154. Anshen Transdisciplinary Lectures in Art, Science, and the Philosophy of Culture, monograph 4. Wakefield, R.I., and Emeryville, Calif.

Wilcke, Claus

1978 "Philologische Bemerkungen zum 'Rat des Šuruppag' und Versuch einer neuen Übersetzung." *Zeitschrift für Assyriologie und vorderasiatischen Archäologie* 68, pp. 196–232.

Wilhelm, Gernot

1998 "Die Inschrift des Tišatal von Urkeš." In *Mozan III. Urkesh and the Hurrians,* edited by G. Buccellati and M. Kelly-Buccellati, pp. 117–43. Malibu.

Willcox, George, and Margareta Tengberg

1995 "Preliminary Report on the Archaeobotanical Investigations at Tell Abraq with Special Attention to Chaff Impressions in Mud Brick." *Arabian Archaeology and Epigraphy* 6 (August), pp. 129–38.

Wilson, Karen

1986 "Nippur: The Definition of a Mesopotamian Jamdat Nasr Assemblage." In *Ǧamdat Naṣr. Period or Regional Style?,* edited by U. Finkbeiner and W. Rölig, pp. 57–89. Tübinger Atlas der Vorderen Orients, Beinheft B 62. Wiesbaden.

2002 "The Temple Mound at Bismaya." In *Leaving No Stones Unturned,* edited by Erica Ehrenberg, pp. 285–86. Winona Lake, Ind.

Winkelmann, Sylvia

1993 "Elam, Baktrien, Belutschistan: Wo liegen die Vorläufer der Hockerplastiken der Induskultur? Erste Gedanken." *Iranica Antiqua* 28, pp. 57–96.

1995 "Nordwest-indische Bezüge auf baktrischen Siegeln." *Altorientalische Forschungen* 22, pp. 165–82.

2001 "Ein neuer baktrischer Stempelzylinder." In *Beiträge zur Vorderasiatischen Archäologie. Winfried Orthmann gewidmet,* pp. 484–93. Frankfurt am Main.

Winstone, H. V. F.

1990 *Woolley of Ur: The Life of Sir Leonard Woolley.* London.

Winter, Irene J.

1984 "Review of Spycket, *La statuaire du proche-orient ancien.*" *Journal of Cuneiform Studies* 36, pp. 102–14.

1985 "After the Battle Is Over: The *Stele of the Vultures* and the Beginning of Historical Narrative in the Art of the Ancient Near East." In *Pictorial Narrative in Antiquity and the Middle Ages,* edited by Herbert L. Kessler and Mariana Shreve Simpson, pp. 11–26. Studies in the History of Art, vol. 16. Washington, D.C.

1986 "The King and the Cup: Iconography of the Royal Presentation Scene on Ur III Seals." In *Insight through Images: Studies in Honor of Edith Porada,* edited by Marilyn Kelly-Buccellati, pp. 253–68. Malibu.

1987a "The Legitimation of Authority through Image and Legend: Seals Belonging to Officials in the Administrative Bureaucracy of the Ur III State." In *The Organization of Power: Aspects of Bureaucracy in the Ancient Near East,* edited by McGuire Gibson and Robert D. Biggs, pp. 69–93. Chicago.

1987b "Women in Public: The Disk of Enheduanna, the Beginning of the Office of EN-Priestess and the Weight of Visual Evidence." In *La femme dans le Proche-Orient antique: Compte rendu de la XXXIIIe Rencontre Assyriologique Internationale (Paris, 7–10 juillet 1986),* edited by Jean-Marie Durand, pp. 189–201. Paris.

1989 "The Body of the Able Ruler: Toward an Understanding of the Statues of Gudea." In *Dumu-e₂-dub-ba-a: Studies in Honor of Åke W. Sjöberg,* edited by Hermann Behrens et al., pp. 573–84. Occasional Publications of the Samuel Noah Kramer Fund, 11. Philadelphia.

1991 "Legitimation of Authority through Images and Legend: Seals Belonging to Officials in the Administrative Bureaucracy of the Ur III State." In *The Organization of Power: Aspects of Bureaucracy in the Ancient Near East,* edited by McGuire Gibson and Robert D. Biggs, pp. 59–99. 2nd ed., rev. Chicago.

1992 "'Idols of the King': Royal Images as Recipients of Ritual Action in Ancient Mesopotamia." *Journal of Ritual Studies* 6, no. 1, pp. 13–42.

1999a "The Aesthetic Value of Lapis Lazuli in Mesopotamia." In *Cornaline et pierres précieuses: La Méditerranée de l'antiquité à l'Islam,* edited by A. Caubet, pp. 43–58. Paris: Musée du Louvre.

1999b "Reading Ritual in the Archaeological Record." In *Fluchtpunkt Uruk: Archäologische Einheit aus methodischer Vielfalt. Schriften für Hans Jörg Nissen,* edited by H. Kühne, R. Bernbeck, and K. Bartl, pp. 229–56. Rahden.

1999c "Tree(s) on the Mountain: Landscape and Territory on the Victory Stele of Naram-Sin of Agade." In *Landscapes: Territories, Frontiers, and Horizons in the Ancient Near East: Papers Presented to the XLIVe Rencontre Assyriologique Internationale, Venezia, 7–11 July 1997,* edited by Lucio Milano, pp. 63–72. Padua.

Wiseman, D. J.

1960 "The Goddess Lama at Ur." *Iraq* 22, pp. 166–71.

Wittkower

1970 "Eagle and Serpent. A Study in the Migration of Symbols." *Journal of the Warburg and Courtauld Institutes* 2, pp. 293–325. Reprint.

Woolley, Sir Leonard

1914 "Hittite Burial Customs." *Liverpool Annals of Art and Archaeology* 6, pp. 87–98.

1926 "Excavations at Ur." *Antiquaries Journal* 6, pp. 365–401.

1934 *The Royal Cemetery: A Report on the Predynastic and Sargonid Graves Excavated between 1926 and 1931.* 2 vols. Contributions by E. R. Burrows et al. Publications of the Joint Expedition of the British Museum and of the Museum of the University of Pennsylvania to Mesopotamia: Ur Excavations, vol. 2. London.

1939 *The Ziggurat and Its Surroundings.* Publications of the Joint Expedition of the British Museum and of the Museum of the University of Pennsylvania to Mesopotamia: Ur Excavations, vol. 5. London.

1955 *The Early Periods: A Report on the Sites and Objects Prior in Date to the Third Dynasty of Ur Discovered in the Course of the Excavations.* Publications of the Joint Expedition of the British Museum and of the Museum of the University of Pennsylvania to Mesopotamia: Ur Excavations, vol. 4. London.

1974 "The Stela of Ur-Nammu." In *Ur Excavations,* vol. 6, *The Buildings of the Third Dynasty,* pp. 75–81. London.

Woolley, Sir Leonard, and Max E. L. Mallowan

1976 *The Old Babylonian Period.* Publications of the Joint Expedition of the British Museum and of the Museum of the University of Pennsylvania to Mesopotamia: Ur Excavations, vol. 7. London.

Woolley, Sir Leonard, and P. R. S. Moorey

1982 *Ur 'of the Chaldees': A Revised and Updated Edition of Sir Leonard Woolley's Excavations at Ur.* Ithaca, N.Y.

Wright, Henry T.

1980 "Problems of Absolute Chronology in Protohistoric Mesopotamia." *Paléorient* 6, pp. 93–98.

Wright, Henry T., and Gregory Johnson

1975 "Population, Exchange, and Early State Formation in Southwestern Iran." *American Anthropologist* 77, pp. 267–89.

Wright, Henry T., and E. S. A. Rupley

2001 "Calibrated Radiocarbon Age Determinations of Uruk-Related Assemblages." In *Uruk Mesopotamia and Its Neighbors: Cross-Cultural Interactions in the Era of State Formation,* edited by Mitchell S. Rothman. Santa Fe.

Wright, Rita P.

1989 "New Perspectives on Third Millennium Painted Grey Wares." In *South Asian Archaeology 1985,* edited by Karen Frifelt and Per Sørensen, pp. 137–49. London.

Xella, Paolo

1995 "Death and Afterlife in Canaanite and Hebrew Thought." In *Civilizations of the Ancient Near East,* edited by Jack Sasson et al., vol. 3, pp. 2059–70. New York.

Yener, A.

1989 "Kestel: An Early Bronze Age Source of Tin Ore in the Taurus Mountains, Turkey." *Science* 224, pp. 200–203.

Yildiz, F.

1981 "A Tablet of Codex Ur-Nammu from Sippar." *Orientalia,* n.s., 50, pp. 87–97.

Yoffee, Norman

1981   *Explaining Trade in Ancient Western Asia.* Monographs on the Ancient Near East, vol. 2, fasc. 2. Malibu.

Zaccagnini, C.

1984   "The Terminology of Weight Measures for Wool at Ebla." In *Studies on the Language of Ebla,* edited by P. Fronzaroli, pp. 189–204. Florence.

1986   "The Dilmun Standard and Its Relationship with Indus and Near Eastern Weight Systems." *Iraq* 40, pp. 19–23.

Zarins, Juris

1978   "Steatite Vessels in the Riyadh Museum." *Atlal: Journal of Saudi Arabian Archaeology* 2, pp. 65–93.

1989   "Eastern Saudi Arabia and External Relations: Selected Ceramic, Steatite, and Textual Evidence, 3500–1900 B.C." In *South Asian Archaeology 1985,* edited by Karen Frifelt and Per Sørensen. London.

Zettler, Richard L.

1977   "The Sargonic Royal Seal: A Consideration of Sealing in Mesopotamia." In *Seals and Sealing in the Ancient Near East,* edited by McGuire Gibson and Robert D. Biggs, pp. 33–39. Bibliotheca Mesopotamica, vol. 6. Malibu.

1987a   "From Beneath the Temple." *Expedition* 28, no. 3, pp. 29–38.

1987b   "Sealings as Artifacts of Institutional Administration in Ancient Mesopotamia." *Journal of Cuneiform Studies* 39, pp. 210–14.

1989   "Pottery Profiles Reconstructed from Jar Sealings in the Lower Seal Impression Strata (SIS 8-4) at Ur: New Evidence for Dating." In *Essays in Ancient Civilization Presented to Helene J. Kantor,* edited by A. Leonard Jr. and B. B. Williams. Chicago.

1989a   "The Statue of Šulgi-ki-ur$_5$-sag$_9$-kalam-ma, Part Two: The Statue." In *Dumu-e$_2$-dub-ba-a: Studies in Honor of Åke W. Sjöberg,* edited by Hermann Behrens et al. Occasional Papers of the Samuel Noah Kramer Fund, 11. Philadelphia.

1998a   "The Royal Cemetery of Ur." In Zettler and Horne 1998, pp. 21–25.

1998b   "Stone Vessels." In Zettler and Horne 1998, pp. 149–60.

Zettler, Richard L., and Lee Horne, eds.

1998   *Treasures from the Royal Tombs of Ur.* Exh. cat. University of Pennsylvania Museum of Archaeology and Anthropology, Philadelphia.

INDEX

Page references to illustrations and their captions are in *italics*

a (arm), 475

A'ali, 244

A'anepada (king of Ur), 28, 84, 85, 96

Abarsal, 462–64, *464*

Abbas I (shah of Persia), *489*

Ab'u (god), 475

Abu Dhabi, 307, 308

Abu Kemal, 136

Abu Salabikh, 452

Abu Shahrein. *See* Eridu

Abu temple (Tell Asmar), 59, *60*, 61, 300n3

Abydos, 251

abzu (Sumerian; primeval ocean), 307, 486

Abzubandu, 31

accounting systems, 13, 305, 451

Acemhöyük. *See* Purushkanda

Adab (Bismaya), 54, 63–64, *63–64*, 80, 81n5, 149n2, 333, 420, 435, *435*

    literary tablets of, 452

Adad-nadin-ahi (Babylonian prince), 424, 425, 429

Adad-nirari II (king of Assyria), 5

Adam and Eve, *488*

Adda (scribe), 214

Administrative tablet with seal impressions (cat. no. 11), 40–41, *41*

Adu, 133

Adygeya, 289, 296

Aegean islands, 8, 163, 184, 243–44, *254*, 255–56, 270, 274, 284

    map of, *234*

    seals of, 247–48

    See also Aigina; Poliochni

Afghanistan, 18, 42, 111, 117, 129, 131, 324, 347, 349, 377

    Fullol Hoard and, 360, 363n4, 365

    mining in

        lapis lazuli, 18, 117, 129, 131, 166, 178, 252, 324, 353, 396, 481

        silver, 353

        tin, 307, 308, 310

Agade, 4–5, 187, 189, 192, 193, 195, 197, 198

agate, beads of, 33, 112, *112*, 300–302, *301*, 394, *394*, 395

Ahlatlibel, 280

Aigina (island), 8, 243, 255, 260–61, *261*

A'Imdugud (king of Ur), 96

Akalamdug (king of Ur), 96

Akitu festival, 487

Akka (king of Kish), 479, 480

Akkad, 21, 118, 136–38, *137*

    art of, 189–223

        cylinder seals of, 197–98, 208–9, *209*, 213–21, *213–21*, 226, *226*, 227, *227*, 230–31, *231*, 247, 311, 405

empire of, 4–5, 423n1

    maps of, *10, 188*

    military expeditions to Magan (Oman) by, 308

    sculpture of, 434–35

    See also Naram-Sin; Sargon of Akkad

Akkadian language, 5

    archaic dialect of, *465, 465*

    as lingua franca, 479

    See also cuneiform inscriptions—in Akkadian language; Old Akkadian (dialect)

Akok, M., 287

Akshak, 21

Akurgal (son of king of Lagash), 71, *71*

alabaster

    cylinder seal of, 305, *305*

    in foundation peg, 80–81, *80*

    plaque of, 300, *300*

    sculpture of, 52, *52*

        Anatolia, 274–75, *275*

        Gonur-depe, 367–68, *368*

        Susa, 298, *299*

        Tell Chuera, 62–63, *62*

        Umma, 51–52, *51*

        Uruk, 25–26, *25*

    steles of, 204–5, *204–5*

        abstract female figure on, 163, *163*

    vessel of, 303, *304*

    votive disk of, 200, *200*

Alaca Höyük, 156, 181, 183, 185, 244, 255, 258, 262, 270, 277–88, *277–88*, 441

Alalakh, 231

Alalgar (king of Eridu), 467

Albright-Knox Art Gallery, Buffalo, 46

Aleppo, 168, 179

Al-Hiba. *See* Lagash

Alishar Höyük, 272

Allahdino, 393

Allen, James P., "Egypt and the Near East in the Third Millennium B.C.," 251

Al-Mutawakkil (caliph), *492*

Al-Rafiah, 330

Altyn-depe, 243, 247, 349, 352, 353, 355–59, *355–58*, 375, 413

Al Ubaid. *See* Tell al Ubaid

Alulim (king of Eridu), 467

Amana (king of Ebla), 465

amazonite, 394

amber, 353

American Museum of Natural History, New York, 351–53

American School of Indic and Iranian Studies, 396, 399–401

American Schools of Oriental Research, Boston, 58

Amiet, Pierre, 298, 305, 332, 355, 371, 388

Amorgos, 248

Amorite language, 5

Amorites, 138, 423n1, 469

Amu Darya (Oxus River), 4, 242, 247, 348, 360, 370, 371n3, 412

amulets (or possible amulets), 112, *112*, 129, *129*, 140, 258, 303, *303*, 356, *356*, 371, 374–75, *374–75*, 389, *389, 412*, 413

Amuq region, 267, 272, 289

An (god), 12, 32, 65, 143, 470, 471, 486, 489

Anarak region, 310

Anatolia (Turkey), 4, 8, 47, 117, 129, 135, 163, 183, 184, 203, 243–44, 274

    Aegean islands and, 255–56

    bull imagery in, 246

    gold pins of, 265, *265*

    map of, *234*

    mining in, 310

    moulds of, 257

    North Caucasus and, 289

    seals of, 247, 249n59, 272

    See also Alaca Höyük

Anau, 352, 355

ancestor veneration, 180, *465, 465*

Andrae, Walter, 56

Andronovo culture, 350

Anita (cupbearer), 71, *71*

Ankara Museum of Anatolian Civilizations, 268, 278–87

Anshan (Tepe Malyan), 26, 42, 347

Antaki Collection, London, 159

antelopes, 380, 404

Anthropomorphic jar with facial features in relief (cat. no. 179), 274, *274*

Antikensammlung, Berlin, 261

Antonova, E.V., 358

Anu (god), 483

Anu ziggurat (Uruk), 24

Anzu (mythical bird), 140

Apameia Kibotos, *490*

apkallu (sage), 488

Appliqué of paired nude female figures (cat. no. 182), 279–80, *279*

appliqués

    Harappan, 382, *382*

    mouflon head (cat. no. 245), 351–52, *351*

Appliqués of lions, bulls, and rings (cat. no. 194), 289, 294, *294*

apsu (Akkadian; primeval ocean), 214, 487

Arabia, 4, 7

Arabian Nights, The, 248n16

Arad, 251

Aramaic language, 424

Aratta, 3, 117, 239, 347

    Lord of, 18, 245, 472–73, *473*

Archaeological Museum, Heraklion, 256

Archaeological Museum of Aigina, 261

Archaeological Survey of India, *240, 413*

Archaic Level IV (Uruk), 11, 13, 14

Archanes, 248, 256, 272

Architect with Plan statue (cat. no. 304), 29, 69, 418–21, 425, 427–28, 427
Armanum, 168
arsenic. See copper and copper alloy—arsenical
Arslantepe, 267, 290
Aruru (goddess), 480
Aruz, Joan
    "Art and Interconnections in the Third Millennium B.C.," 239–50
    "Art of the First Cities," 3–8
Ashmolean Museum, Oxford, 90–92, 252, 467
Ashoor, Haji, 395
Ashur, 142, 221, 233, 244, 472
Ashurbanipal (king of Assyria), 479
Ashusikildingir (queen of Ur), 96
Astrabad Treasure, 364, 366n1, 372
Athens, 264, 267
Atra-hasis, Epic of, 487, 489–93
Attika (Attica), 255, 256n2
aurochs, 292, 293
Avesta, 350
axe, shaft-hole, 373–73, 373
Azimua (goddess), 475
Azov, Sea of, 289
Aztyk, 359

Babylon (Babylonia), 168
    Akitu festival in, 487
    chronology of, 5
    fertility of, 4
    Marduk's temple (E-sagila) in, 487
    meaning of word, 493
    See also Hammurabi; Old Babylonian period
Bactria-Margiana, 7, 245, 247, 308, 315, 332, 343, 360, 363, 364, 365, 370, 374, 375, 388, 413
    winged deities of, 371–72, 371
Bactria-Margiana Archaeological Complex (BMAC), 349–50
Bactrian dragons, 247, 370, 371, 373–74, 373
Badakhshan, 111, 117, 129, 131, 242, 353
Badtibira, 69, 467–68
Bagara temple, Lagash, 482
Baghdad, 5, 58
Baghouz, 136
Bahar (god), 486
Bahrain, 244. See also Dilmun
Bahrain National Museum, 309, 311, 312, 410, 341
Ba'lan, 463
Baluchistan, 111, 243, 247, 308, 312, 315, 317, 348, 350, 354, 368, 377, 381–84, 382–84, 390, 412–13, 412
Balu-ili (cupbearer), 219
Bampur, 317, 343, 349
bangles
    Indus design, 398
    shell, 398, 398
Bangles (cat. no. 285), 397, 397
Bangle with ribbed design (cat. no. 286), 397–98, 397
Banks, Edgar, 333
banquet scenes, 30–31, 73, 73, 97, 106, 106, 109–10, 109, 146–47, 146, 300, 300, 319, 321, 321, 365–66, 365
Bara'irnum (queen of Umma), 78
Barakisumun, 75, 76
Barasagnudi, 71, 71
barastis (palm-frond house), 307

Barbar temple (Bahrain), 307, 309, 309, 311, 311
basalt, 22, 203, 203
Bassetki, 80, 187, 195, 195, 217
battle scenes, 158–59, 158, 189–90, 190, 196–97, 196, 201–2, 201–2
Ba'u (goddess), temple of (Tello), 69, 425
Bead (cat. no. 124), 185, 185
Bead with filigree and cloisons (cat. no. 75), 128, 128
Bead with flanges (cat. no. 119), 181–82, 182
Bead naming Mesanepada (cat. no. 84), 35, 139, 143, 143
beads
    agate, 33, 112, 112, 300–302, 301, 394, 394, 395
    of Aigina, 260, 261, 261
    Akkadian, 231, 232, 300–302, 301
    carnelian. See carnelian—beads of
    copper, 395
    crenellated, 353–55, 353, 354
    etched, 130–31, 130–31, 261, 261
    faience, 300–302, 301, 395
    flat, with tubular midrib, 182–83, 182, 240, 243, 263, 263, 296, 296, 393–94, 393
    gold. See gold—beads of
    Harappan, 392–94, 393–94, 396, 396
        production of, 395–96, 395
    of Kish, 243, 312, 397
    maps of findspots, by type, 240–42
    of Mari, in Treasure of Ur, 139–40, 143–45, 143–45
    multiple-flanged, 144, 181–82, 182
    of North Caucasus, 289, 296, 296
    of Puabi in Ur cemetery, 33, 112–13, 112–13
    quadruple-spiral, 129, 129, 185, 185, 241, 243–44, 266–67, 266
    silver, 33, 182, 182, 233, 233, 243–44, 353, 353
    of Susa, 243, 201–3, 202, 300–302, 301
    of Tell Abraq, 314, 314
    of Tell Brak, 231–33, 232, 233, 244
    of Tell Umm el-Marra, 181–82, 181, 182
    of Tepe Hissar, 353–54, 353
    of Ur. See Ur—beads of
    of Uruk, 17–18, 17
Beads (cat. no. 247), 350, 353–54, 353, 359
Beads and pendants (cat. no. 123), 185, 185
bears, 331–32, 331, 332n9
Belt (cat. no. 279), 132, 261, 392–93, 392
Berezkin, I. E., 358
Berlin. See Antikensammlung; Museum für Vor- und Frühgeschichte; Vorderasiatisches Museum
Berossos (priest), 487, 494n18
Beycesultan, 280
Bible, Book of Genesis in, 485–87, 490, 493–94
Bilgames, 479, 489. See also Gilgamesh
bird-demon, 373, 373
birds, 48, 49, 87, 87, 163, 163, 185, 185, 330–31, 331, 338, 339, 342, 342. See also eagles
Bismaya. See Adab
bison-men. See bull-men
Bit Resh temple (Uruk), 15
bitumen, 28, 32, 85, 100, 118, 121, 140, 142, 230, 353, 364, 435, 435
    technique of using, 342–43, 343n7
    vessel fragments of, 342–43, 342
Black-on-gray ware vessels (cat. no. 216), 317, 317
Black Sea, 289
"Blau" monuments (cat. no. 9), 39, 39
boars, 41, 41, 373–74, 373

Boğazköy. See Hattusha
Boiotia, 255, 270
bone, 83, 83, 256, 256
    Harappan use of, 379
Boston. See American Schools of Oriental Research; Museum of Fine Arts
Bowl with bulls in relief (cat. no. 12), 40, 42, 42, 482
Bowl with triangle cutouts for inlays (cat. no. 122), 184, 184
bowls, 128, 341, 341
boxes
    cosmetic, 114, 114, 340, 340
    with lions, bulls, and wolves in relief, 360–63, 361–62
    open-worked carved, 358–59, 358
Bracelet (cat. no. 184), 281, 281
bracelets, 143–45, 144, 302, 303, 304. See also beads
breccia, pink, 151, 151
brick construction, 21, 26, 385
    ruler carrying basket for, 31, 31, 420, 446–47, 446
British Museum, London, 23, 32, 48, 70, 74, 85, 85, 93, 97, 101, 103, 109, 116, 121, 122, 125, 126, 128, 197, 205, 213, 215, 218, 219, 220, 257, 330, 332, 374, 410, 442, 447, 483
bronze
    definition of, 310
    Harappan, 379
    Tell Abraq casting of, 308–9
Bronze Age. See Early Bronze Age; Late Bronze Age; Middle Bronze Age
Brooklyn Museum of Art, 45, 46
Bulla with an eagle and an elephant (cat. no. 392b), 412–13, 412
Bull fitting (cat. no. 95), 156, 156, 356
Bull of Heaven, 479, 480, 483–84, 483
bull leaping, 374–75, 375, 409, 409, 411
Bull-man (cat. no. 18), 51–52, 51
bull-men (bison-men)
    bent-leg tradition of, 230–31, 230
    inlays of, 175, 176
    on lyre, 106, 106
    on plaque, 88, 88
    sculpture of, 27 51–52, 51
    on seals, 146, 146, 217–18, 218, 230–31, 230–31, 407, 409
    on vessels, 118, 118, 319–20, 320
Bull pendants (cat. no. 270), 383–84, 384
Bull standard (cat. no. 188), 284–85, 285, 441
Bull standards (cat. no. 191), 291–92, 291–92
bulls
    appliqués of, 294, 294
    on clay tablet, 56–57, 57
    on foundation peg, 442, 442
    Harappan, 246
    humped. See zebus
    on lyre, 105–6, 105–6
    pendants of, 383–84, 384
    sculpture of, 26, 27, 27, 43, 43, 83, 83, 85, 85, 115, 115, 156, 156, 174, 174, 311, 311, 356, 356, 441, 441
    on seals, 40, 40, 374–75, 374–75
    on standard, 284–85, 285
    on "Standard of Ur," 100
    two-headed, 258
    vessels with, 42, 42, 48, 49, 330, 331, 338–39, 338, 360–62, 361–62
    as weight, 363, 363

Bull's head (cat. no. 206), 311, *311,* 356
Bull's head (cat. no. 249), 356, *356,* 375
Byblos, 241, 248, 251, 253, 272

Cain, *488,* 494n23
calcite, 18, *18,* 118, *118,* 128, 214, 253, *253,* 300–302,
    301, 330, 331, 344, *345*
    production of, 62
Cambay, Gulf of, 243, 397
Camel-shaped stamp seal with a bull-leaping scene
    (cat. no. 265), 374–75, *374–75,* 409
Canby, Jeanny Vorys, 258, 435
Canister with stepped triangle motifs (cat. no. 269),
    359, 383, *383*
Cardi, Beatrice de, 317
Cardium shells, 400, *400*
carnelian, 110–13, *110–12,* 122, *123,* 125, *125,* 126,
    127–30, 128, 130–32, *132,* 143, *144,* 231–32, *231*
    beads of, 8, 33, 79–80, *79–80,* 130–31, *130–31,*
        185, 243, 260, 261, *261,* 295, *295,* 300–302,
        301, 312, *312,* 313, *313,* 353
        map, *242*
        production, 395–96, *395*
    belt of, 392–93, *392–93*
    sources of, 129, 145, 302, 396
    unworked, 396, *396*
Casci, Paul, 443
Caspian Sea, 289
casting
    of bronze at Tell Abraq, 308–9
    of gold dagger, 102, *102*
    See also lost-wax casting
Çatal Höyük, 274
cattle. *See* bulls; cows and calves
Caucasus, 292. *See also* North Caucasus
cedars of Lebanon, 251, 455, 480, 482
cemeteries
    of Gonur-depe, 364, 366–68
    of Kish, 89, 91
    of Ur. *See* Ur—cemetery of
Central Asia, 4, 347–75
    horses from, 159
    interconnections of, 7, 117, 129, 241, 261
    "Intercultural Style" and, 244, 245
    lost-wax technique in, 309
    map of, *235*
    seals of, 247, 348–49, *350*
    seated female figures of, 159, 172, 367–69, *367–68*
    turquoise of, 243, 356, *356*
    See also Amu Darya (Oxus River); Altyn-depe;
        Bactria-Margiana; Gonur-depe; Kara-depe;
        Tepe Hissar; Turkmenistan; urials;
        Uzbekistan
ceramic tile wall panel, Safavid, *489*
Chagai Hills (Baluchistan), 111, 248n17
chalcedony, 218, *218,* 353, *483*
Chalcolithic age, 261, 348, 349, 351
chalices. *See* cups
Chanhudaro, 312, 315, 352, 385, 390, *390,* 398–402,
    399–401
Chantre, E., 277
chariots, 72, *72,* 95, 97, *98,* 159–60, *159, 160,* 189,
    215, *215*
cheetahs, 292, *293*
chert, 219, *219*
Chicago. *See* University of Chicago
Chicoreus ramosus, 398–400

Child's diadem with roundels (cat. no. 76), 128, *128*
Chios, 270
chlorite
    "Intercultural Style" objects of, 247, 325–45,
        326–45, 360
    sculpture of, 367–68, *368,* 388, *388,* 431–33,
        432–33, 436, *436*
    sources and carving of, 244, 325, 336, 343, 343n
    in string of beads, 300–302, *301*
    vessels of, 42, *42,* 78n4, 247, 319–20, *319,* 330–39,
        330, 331, 333–38
    compartmented, 316, *316*
chokers, 112, *112,* 205, *205,* 391, 392
Cholistan, 379
Christie, Agatha, 224
chronology, 5, 8n11
Cincinnati Art Museum, 52
cinnabar, 294
circles, incised concentric, 315–16, *315, 316*
city-states, 11, 21
    official ideologies of, 6
clay, 18–20, *19, 20,* 227, *227*
    anthropomorphic jar of, 274, *274*
    black-on-gray ware vessels of, 317, *317*
    cups of, 273–74, *273*
    mankind formed from, 486
    open-worked carved box of, 358–59, *358*
    rosettes of, 86–87, *86*
    vessels of, 20, *20,* 207–8, *208,* 359–60, *359,* 383,
        383
    See also terracotta
clay tablets
    administrative, Mesopotamian, 40–41, *41*
    of Ebla, 166–67, *167, 168,* 458–65
    of Fara, 56–57, *57,* 457, *457*
    moulded Indus, 406, *406,* 407, *408,* 409
    poem on origin of, 472–73, *473*
    Proto-Elamite, *27*
    of Ur Third Dynasty, 418
    of Uruk, 13, *14*
Cloaked figure (cat. no. 223), 324, *324*
Cochin, India, 101
collars, 122, 123, *123,* 126, 127, *127*
Collon, Dominique, 330
Comb (cat. no. 61a), 110–11, *110–11*
Combs with incised concentric circles (cat. no.
    212), 315, *315*
Compartment stamp seal with an eagle and
    snakes (cat. no. 263), 372–73, *372*
Compartment stamp seal with a goddess seated
    on a dragon (cat. no. 261), 370–71, *370*
Compartment stamp seal with winged goddess
    on a dragon (cat. no. 260), 369–70, *369*
Compartment stamp seal with a zebu (cat. no.
    302a), 412, *412*
compartmented stamp seals, 247, 369–71, *369, 370*
Compartmented vessel with incised concentric
    circles (cat. no. 214), 316, *316*
Composite figure of a seated veiled woman (cat. no.
    108), 169, *169*
Composite seated female figures (cat. no. 259), 169,
    367–68, *368*
Cone mosaic panel (cat. no. 5), 18–19, *19,* 86
Conical vessel with deities, snakes, bulls, and a bird
    of prey (cat. no. 235), 245, 338–39, *338*
Conical vessel with a leopard and snake (cat. no.
    232), 245, 335, *335*

Conical vessel with a zebu (cat. no. 226), 330, *330*
Container in the shape of a shell (cat. no. 290b),
    118, 400, *400*
contest scenes, 48–50, *49,* 103, *103,* 106, *106,* 207–8,
    208, 305, *305,* 330–32, *331,* 408, *408,* 409
copper and copper alloy
    arsenical, 46–48, *46–48,* 79, 80, 81, *81,* 82n3, 223,
        267, 297, *297,* 303–4, 304, *310,* 370, *441,* 441
    beads of, 353, 395
    in belt, 392–93, *392–93*
    bracelet of, 302, *303*
    chisels of, 62
    foundation pegs of, 80–81, *80,* 220–21, *221,* 441,
        441, 446–47, *447*
    in friezes, *28,* 87–88, *88*
    in Greece and Anatolia, 255, 256n2
    Harappan, 379
    helmet of, 103, *103*
    hooks of, 297, *297*
    in lost-wax casting, 210, 441
    for mounts on cylinder seals, 39–40, *40,* 220–21,
        221
    in pendants, 140, *141,* 352–53, *352*
    pins of, 185, *185,* 332, *332*
    plaque of, 104, *104*
    relief of, 85, *85*
    sculpture of, 46–48, *46–48,* 79–83, *79, 81–83,* 85,
        85, 121, *121,* 142, *142,* 187, 194–95, *194, 195,*
        210–12, *211,* 217, *278,* 279, 280, *286,* 309,
        309, 389–91, *390–91,* 446–47, *446*
    sistrum of, 190, 287–88, *287*
    sources of, 251, 307, 308, 310, 310n8
    spear or spearhead of, 68, 289–90
    standards of, 284–87, *285, 286*
    tin first combined with, 304, 305n7
    "trumpets" of, 364, *364*
    vessels of, 284, 303, *304*
    See also bronze
corridor houses, 255–56, 256n5
Cosmetic box lid inlaid with a lion attacking a
    caprid (cat. no. 63), 114, *114*
cosmetic box with zigzag pattern (cat. no. 237b),
    340, *340*
cows and calves, 17, *17,* 28, *28,* 87, *87,* 92, *92,* 174,
    174, 306
Creation, in Sumerian literature, 485–87, 494n17
    Hymn to the Hoe, 455, 476, *476,* 486
Creation Epic, 217, 486–87
crenellated motif, 353–55, *353, 354,* 358–60, *358–60,*
    362
Crete
    goddess with poppies from, 272
    interconnections with, 8, 247–48, 256–57, *256,*
        258n7
crocodile, 406, *406*
Cruyl, Lievin, *492*
cuffs, 112, *112,* 122, 123, *124*
cuneiform inscriptions, 5, 336, *336*
    in Akkadian language, 5, 207–8, *208,* 216, 219–
        20, *219,* 227, *227,* 229–30, *229,* 477, *477*
    derivation of word, 451
    description of, 451, *452*
    in an early Semitic dialect, 148, *149*
    Ebla discovery of, 166–67, *168*
    in Eblaite language, 453
    in Hurrian language, 222, 226, *226*
    proto-, 11, 39, *39,* 40–41, *41,* 53, *53*

in Sumerian language, 64–65, 65, 71, 71, 75–78, 76–78, 80, 80, 103, 103, 109, 109, 143, 143, 200, 201, 202, 243, 315, 427, 427, 428, 428, 430, 431, 434, 437–39, 442, 446–47, 446–47, 457–59, 457–59, 466–76, 466–76, 478, 478

    changes after Uruk period, 452–53

    original development, 451

    undecipherable, on stamp seal, 410, 410, 412

Cuneiform prism with the Sumerian King List (cat. no. 330), 467–68, 467

Cuneiform tablet with an administrative document (cat. no. 321), 457, 457

Cuneiform tablet with a bilingual lexical list (cat. no. 322b), 458–59, 458

Cuneiform tablet with a consignment of cloth (cat. no. 323a), 36, 460, 460

Cuneiform tablet with the Hymn to the Hoe (cat. no. 339), 455, 476, 476, 486

Cuneiform tablet with a hymn to Shamash (cat. no. 328), 36, 167, 245, 465, 465

Cuneiform tablet with the Instructions of Shuruppak (cat. no. 335), 455, 472, 472

Cuneiform tablet with the Lamentation over the Destruction of Sumer and Ur (cat. no. 333), 470, 470

Cuneiform tablet with the "law code" of Lipit-Eshtar (cat. no. 334), 471, 471

Cuneiform tablet with the legend of Enmerkar and the Lord of Aratta (cat. no. 336), 245, 472–73, 473

Cuneiform tablet with a letter concerning Kish and Nagar (cat. no. 326b), 36, 167, 463–64, 463

Cuneiform tablet with a letter from Enna-Dagan, king of Mari, to the king of Ebla (cat. no. 326a), 36, 167, 463–64, 463

Cuneiform tablet with a letter from Ishbi-Erra to Ibbi-Sin, ruler of Ur (cat. no. 332), 469, 469

Cuneiform tablet with a list of equids (cat. no. 323b), 36, 460, 460

Cuneiform tablet with a list of personnel (cat. no. 325), 36, 462, 462

Cuneiform tablet with a mathematical text (cat. no. 322c), 458–49, 459

Cuneiform tablet with a monolingual Sumerian text (cat. no. 322), 36, 167, 458–59, 458

Cuneiform tablet with the Myth of Enki and Ninhursanga (cat. no. 337), 474–75, 474, 487

Cuneiform tablet with the Myth of Enlil and Ninlil (cat. no. 338), 475–76, 475

Cuneiform tablet with the Myth of Etana (cat. no. 340), 198, 219, 477, 477

Cuneiform tablet with offerings to dead kings (cat. no. 327), 36, 465, 465

Cuneiform tablet with a record of gold and silver tributes paid to Mari (cat. no. 324b), 36, 461–62, 461

Cuneiform tablet with a Shulgi hymn (cat. no. 331), 468, 468

Cuneiform tablet with the Sumerian Flood story (cat. no. 341), 478, 478

Cuneiform tablet with a Sumerian medical text (cat. no. 329), 466, 466

Cuneiform tablet with a treaty with Abarsal (cat. no. 326c), 36, 167, 463–64, 464

Cuneiform tablet with a word list and an incised bull (cat. no. 23), 56–57, 57

Cuneiform tablet with a yearly account of metals (cat. no. 324a), 36, 461–62, 461

Cup on a stand (cat. no. 215), 316–17, 316

cups

    with crenellated decoration, 360, 360

    with guilloches, 340, 340, 384, 384

    with scenes, 365–66, 365

    spouted, 116–17, 116–17

    of Susa, 302, 303

    two-handled. See: depas amphikypellon

Cyclades, 7, 244, 248, 255–57, 262, 265, 270, 272, 273

Cylinders A and B, 140, 415, 418, 424n33, 428n3, 438

Cylinder seal with battle of the gods (cat. no. 144), 202, 216–17, 216

Cylinder seal with a chariot scene (cat. no. 101), 159–60, 160

Cylinder seal with confronted figures and a tree (cat. no. 218), 318–19, 319

Cylinder seal with a contest scene (cat. no. 203), 139, 305, 305

Cylinder seal of Hashamer with a presentation scene (cat. no. 319), 447–48, 447

Cylinder seal with a hero combating a buffalo and a bull-man combating a lion (cat. no. 146), 52, 197, 217–18, 218

Cylinder seal with a hero combating a lion (cat. no. 147), 218, 218

Cylinder seal with hunters (cat. no. 150), 220, 220

Cylinder seal with ibex in a landscape (cat. no. 149), 219–20, 219

Cylinder seal of Ibni-sharrum, a scribe of Shar-kali-sharri (cat. no. 135), 208–9, 209, 330

Cylinder seal with kneeling nude heroes (cat. no. 145), 217, 217

Cylinder seal with Mesopotamian deities (cat. no. 139), 213–14, 213

Cylinder seal with a milking scene, from the vase à la cachette (cat. no. 204), 139, 306, 306

Cylinder seal with the myth of Etana (?) (cat. no. 148), 219, 219, 477

Cylinder seal with a presentation scene (cat. no. 217), 318, 318

Cylinder seal with a presentation scene (cat. no. 320), 448, 448

Cylinder seal with a seated deity and vegetation deities (cat. no. 151), 220–21, 221

Cylinder seal of Shu-ilishu, interpreter for Meluhha (cat. no. 303), 246, 413, 413

Cylinder seal with storm god in a chariot pulled by a lion-griffin (cat. no. 142), 140, 215, 215

Cylinder seal with the sun god (cat. no. 140), 214, 214, 231

Cylinder seal with a sun god and a human-headed bull or bison (cat. no. 157b), 230–31, 231

Cylinder seal with vegetation deities (cat. no. 143), 215–16, 216

Cylinder seal with water god seated in enclosure (cat. no. 141), 214–15, 215

Cylinder seal with a zebu, scorpion, man, snake, and tree (cat. no. 301a), 410–11, 410

Cylinder seal with zebus and signs (cat. no. 301c), 410, 411, 411

cylinder seals, 55, 55, 121–22, 122

    Akkadian, 197–98, 208–9, 209, 213–21, 213–21, 226, 226, 227, 227, 230–31, 231, 247, 311, 405

    of Central Asia, 247, 348–49, 350

    with Gilgamesh and Ishtar (Inanna), 483, 483

    griffin demons on, 374

    of Gulf region, 318–19, 318–19

    Harappan, 240

    history of, 13, 14, 39–40, 348–49

    of Mari, 80, 161, 161

    Middle Assyrian, 492

    found at Poliochni, 272, 272

    "priest-king" on, 480–81, 481

    Proto-Elamite, 26–27, 27, 43, 45

    of Susa, 305, 305, 306, 306

    of Tell Asmar, 239

    of Ur, 34, 54, 54, 91, 103, 103, 217, 311, 410–11, 410

    of Uruk, 13, 14, 23, 23, 24, 39–41, 40, 52, 87

Cylinder seals with banquet scenes (cat. no. 60), 33, 109–10, 109

Cylinder seals with humans and animals (cat. no. 10), 24, 39–40, 40

Cylinder seals with ritual and ceremonial scenes (cat. no. 87), 35, 80, 146–47, 146, 201

Cylinder seals with royal names (cat. no. 55), 103, 103, 109, 115

Cylindrical box and lid with lions, bulls, and wolves in relief (cat. no. 254), 360–63, 361–62

Cylindrical cup with agricultural and ceremonial scenes (cat. no. 257), 360, 365–66, 365

Cylindrical cup with crenellated decoration (cat. no. 253), 360, 360

Cylindrical vessel with heroes and animals (cat. no. 227), 245, 330–32, 331

Cylindrical vessel with a hut motif and zigzag bands (cat. no. 239), 341–42, 341

Cylindrical vessel with rows of zigzags (cat. no. 238), 341, 341

Dagan temple, Mari, 154, 154n4, 155n5, 161, 183n2

daggers, 102, 102, 103, 106, 181, 303, 304

Damin, 317

"dancer's grave" (Tepe Hissar), 353–54, 353

Dardanelles, 270

Darib (probably Atareb), 465

Dasht-i Lut, 305, 317, 349

Death of Bilgames (myth), 489

Death of Gilgamesh (epic), 93, 148, 479

Decker, C., 492

dedicatory figures. See votive figures

deer, 146, 146, 287

Deir ez-Zor, Museum of, 152, 158, 163, 221, 226, 227, 231, 233, 257

Delougaz, Pinhas, 84

Dendera, 253

Dentalium, 260

depatas amphikypellon, 255, 256n3, 262, 273–74, 273

depletion gilding, 79, 120

Detroit Institute of Arts, 430, 431

Deutsche Orient Gesellschaft Expedition, 11, 56

Dholavira, 379, 385

diabase, 77, 77

Diadem and rosettes (cat. no. 195), 295, 295

diadems, 291, 351, 352n6

Diadem with an elaborate open-worked pattern (cat. no. 183), 280, 280

Dilmun, 3, 424n2, 473, 478

    bowl from, 341, 341

    cylinder seals of, 318–19, 319

    description of, 307–8

    Enki-Ninhursanga myth and, 474

as Garden of Eden, 474, 487–88, *488*

  handle figure from, 309, *309*

  stamp seals of, 320–21, *320–21*

  trade with, 68–69, 71, 239

diorite, 156, *156*, 220, *220*

  Egyptian bowls and goblets of, 166

  royal use of, 29–30, *30*, 62, 69, 191, *192, 193*, 195,
    212, 213, 307, *420*, 434–35, *434*

    Gudea's preference, 419–20, *426–28, 427–31,
      430, 431*

Disk of Enheduanna, daughter of Sargon (cat. no.
  128), 74, 200–201, *200*

Disk ornament and triangular pendant with a star
  motif (cat. no. 121), 183, *183*

Disk pendant with a horizontal string tube (cat. no.
  165), 261, *261*

Disk-shaped female figure (cat. no. 180), 163, 274–
  76, *275*

Disputation between Ewe and Wheat, 486

Diyala River and region, 5, 27, 29, 45, 48, 51, 58–61,
  59–61, 80, 161, 245, 298

Diyarbakir region, 203

dogs, 219, *219*, 441n3

donkeys, 159, 228

Dossin, Georges, 139, 143

Double-spiral brooch with inlay (cat. no. 282), 394,
  394

double-spiral motif, 129–30, *129*, 352–53, *352*, 394,
  394

Double-spiral pendant (cat. no. 77), 129, *129*

Double-spiral pendant (cat. no. 246), 352, *352*

dragons

  Bactrian, 247, *370, 371*, 373–74, *373*

  horned snake, 371nn6, *7, 423, 423*, 437, *437*, 442,
    442

  winged goddess on, 369–70, *369*

Drehem. *See* Puzrish-Dagan

Dubai, 307

dub-sar (scribe), 229

Dumuzi (god), 24, 122, 468

Dumuzi (king of Badtibira), 468

Duram, 218

Ea (god), 203, *213*, 214–15, *215*, 217, 493

eagles

  on bulla, 412–13, *412*

  on cylinder seals, 146, *147*

  double-headed, 373

  in Etana myth, 477

  lion-headed (Imdugud), 68, 75–76, *76*, 85, *85,
    88, 88*, 140, *141*, 175, *175*, 190, *191*, 231–32,
    232, 245, *326*, 327

  on stamp seal, 372–73, *372*

  on vessels, 337, *337*, 342

E-anna Precinct (Uruk), 12, *12*, 16–18, 337, 481–82

Early Bronze Age, 5, 7–8, 163–86, *169–86*, 244,
  247–48, 251, 255–88, 352, 355, 458–65

Early Dynastic period

  archaeological establishment of, 58

  brick in, 21

  cuneiform of, 452–53

  I, 5, 15, 26–27, 34, 50–55, 59, 61, 68

  II, 5, 27, 29, 52, 59, 68, 72, 79–81, 90–92, 136,
    300, 323–24, *323*

  III, 5, 27, 62, 63, 68, 69, 74, 78, 80–84, 94, 136–38,
    145, 149, 151–62, *192, 193*, 218, 298, 334,
    335, 337

IIIA, 31, 56, 66, 70, 71, 97–132, 158, 306, *335, 341*,
  457

IIIB, 31, 39, 64, 75, 77, 80, 85–88, 140–49, 189,
  336

  map of Near East during, *10*

  poetry of, 455

  royal statues of, 429

  "second style" of ceramics in, 342

  votive figures in, 29–30, *30*, 59–64, *59–64*, 66–
    67, *67*

"Early Gold Age," 260, *261*

Early Helladic Age, 260

earrings

  basket, 268, *269*, 271, *271*

  crescent, 271, *271*

  lobed crescent, 221–22, *221*, 267–68, *267*

  with poppy pendants, 271–72, *272*

  shell type, 271, *271*

  of Ur, 122–23, *123*, 126, 127, *127*

    Puabi's, *110–11, 111*

Ebih-Il (superintendent), 137

Ebla (Tell Mardikh), 7, 21, 133, 136, 165–78, *165*, 194

  archives of, 153, 167, *450*, 453, 458, 459, 463

  cuneiform tablets of, 458–65, *458–65*

  destructions of, 168

  Egyptian objects found at, 36, 173, 241–42, 251,
    253, *253*

  inlays of, 88, 174–77, *174–77*

  lexical lists in, 167

  palace of, 166, *166*

  sculpture of, 36, 169–74, *169–74*

  unworked lapis lazuli at, 178, *178*

Eblaite language, 5, 167, 453

  cuneiform tablets in, 458–65, *458–65*

  dictionary of Sumerian in, 167, 458–49, *458*

eduba'a (school), 454

education. *See* schools; school texts

Egypt

  interconnections with, 7, 36, 104, 151, 166, 173,
    240–41, 251

  raptor-ruler association in, 46

Elam, 4, 308, 474

  seated female figure of, 367, *367*

  Shutruk-Nahhunte of, 140n6, 189, 193, 195

  wars of, 69, 469, 470

  See also Proto-Elamite period; Susa

Elamite language, 5, 42

Elbrus Mountain, 292

Elburz Mountains, 348

electrum, 116, *116, 117*, 258, 265n1, 302

elephants, *239*, 246, 380, 405–6, *405*, 412n3, 412–13,
  412

  Syrian, 143

  See also ivory

Emar, 136

Emir Gray Ware, 317

Emporio, 270

Enakale (king of Umma), 78

Enannatum I (king of Lagash), 69, 75–76, 80–81

Enannatum II (king of Lagash), 75

Enbilulu (god), 475

Enceinte Sacrée (Mari), 137

endan (ruler), 222, 224, 227

Enheduanna (daughter of Sargon), 74–75, *74*, 200–
  201, *200*

Enhegal (king of Lagash), 68

E-ninnu, Girsu. *See* Ningirsu (god), temple of

Enki (god), 4, 9, 31, 214, 217, 244, 307, 428n3, 438,
  453, 455, 470

  humanity saved by, 478, *478*

  poem on myth of Ninhursanga and, 474–75, *474*,
    487–88

  world organized by, 486

Enkidu (companion or servant of Gilgamesh), 455,
  479, 480, 482–84, 493

Enlil (god), 29, 34, 52, 58, 148–49, 453, 455, 470, 471,
  485–86, 489

  Great Flood caused by, 478, *478*

  myth of Ninlil and, 475–76, *475*

  temple of (Tello), 66, 69

Enmendurana (king of Sippar), 468

Enmenluana (king of Badtibira), 468

Enmerkar (king of Uruk), 18, 239, 245, 347, 454,
  472–73, *473*

Enmerkar and the Lord of Aratta, 449

Enmetena (king of Lagash), 29–30, *30*, 33, 58, 64,
  69, 88n2, 149n2, 194

Enna-Dagan (king of Mari), 462–64, *463*

Ennigi, 468

ensi (ruler), 29, 31, 148–49, 427, 439

Ensipaziana (king of Larak), 468

enstatite, 355, 355n2, 410, *410*

entu-priestess, 74, 200–201, 201n4

Enuma elish, 486

Enzak (god), 307, 475

Epic of Atra-hasis, 487, 489–93

Epic of Creation, 217, 486–87

Epic of Gilgamesh, 13, 15, 33, 56, 248n16, 479–82,
  487

  Great Flood in, 485, 493

Eridu (Abu Shahrein), 205, 467, 471

  cone mosaics of, 19, 86

Ernestite, 393

E-sagila, Babylon, 487

Eshnunna (Tell Asmar), 45, 58, 140, 145, 147, 246,
  312, 412n3

Eski Şark Museum, Istanbul, 56n, 63, 80, 203, 337, 439

Eskiyapar, 233, 243, 244, 255, 262, 267, 268, 270, 271,
  352

Etana (mythical king-shepherd), 198, 219, *219*, 338,
  477, *477*

etched beads, 130–31, *130–31*, 261, *261*, 301, 302,
  312, *312*, 313, *313*, 396–97, *396*

Etched carnelian beads (cat. no. 284), 396–97, *396*

Etiyokusu, 280

Euboia, 255, 256n2

Euphrates River, 4, 15, 68, 89, 93, *134, 135, 416*, 423

Evans, Jean M., "Approaching the Divine," 417–24

Exploration Branch, Karachi, 388, 412

Eye Temple (Tell Brak), 18–19, *19–20*, 87

faience, 389, 394

  bangle of, 397–98, *398*

  beads of, 300–302, *301, 395*

  in Indus Valley, 389, 394, 398

  shard of in *vase à la cachette*, 305

  "trumpet" of, 364

Failaka, 318–22, *318–22*, 342, 406

Fairservis, Walter A., 317

Faiz Mohammad Gray Ware, 317, 383, *383*

Fara (Shuruppak), 26, 32, 54, 56–57, *57*, 489, 493

  administrative tablet of, 457, *457*

  literary tablets of, 452, 453

  in Sumerian King List, 468

Farmakovsky, B.V., 292, 294, 295

Fars, 344, 347, 367, 368

Fasa, 353

Fasciolaria trapezium, 398, 401

Female figure with clasped hands (cat. no. 310), 436, *436*

Female figures with headdresses and jewelry (cat. no. 278), 391–92, *391*

Female figures wearing tall headdresses (cat. no. 92), 29, 35, 153–55, *153–54*, 169

Figure aux Plumes, 68, *68*, 424n20

filigree, 181, *181*, 271

Finds associated with Body 51 (cat. no. 72), 122–24, *123–24*, 144

Finds associated with Body 54 (cat. no. 73), 125–26, *125–26*

Finds associated with Body 55 (cat. no. 74), 126–27, *127*

finger rings, 112, *112*, 124

First Intermediate Period (Egypt, ca. 2250–2050 B.C.), 251

Flat beads with a tubular midrib (cat. no. 120), 182, *182*

Flat beads with raised midribs (cat. no. 211), 314, *314*

Flood. *See* Great Flood

Footed goblet with geometric patterns (cat. no. 207), 312, *312*

Foster, Benjamin R., 202

Foundation figure of Lugalkisalsi (cat. no. 27), 30, 64–65, *65*

Foundation figures of Ur-Namma holding a basket (cat. no. 318), 446–47, *446–47*

Foundation peg with a bull and palm fronds (cat. no. 315), 81, 442, *442*

Foundation peg with tablet of Enmetena (cat. no. 39), 80–81, *80*

Foundation pegs (cat. no. 153), 222–23, *222–23*

Foundation pegs naming Gudea (cat. no. 312), 81, 438–39, *438–39*

Fragment of an Egyptian jar lid naming Pepi I (cat. no. 161), 36, 166, 241, 253, *253*

Fragment of a head of a ruler (cat. no. 137), 195, 212–13, *212*

Fragment of a male torso (cat. no. 243), 344, *344*

Fragment of a Mesopotamian victory stele (cat. no. 127), 199, *199*

Fragment of a statue of Ur-Ningirsu (cat. no. 308), 29, 434–35, *434*

Fragment of "Ur-Namma" stele (cat. no. 317), 322n16, 417–18, 435, 443–46, *444–45*

Fragment of a wall plaque with a chariot scene (cat. no. 31), 30, 72, *72*

Fragments of a head of a ruler (?) (cat. no. 138), 213, *213*

Francfort, Henri-Paul, 344

Frankfort, Henri, 5, 50, 330, 352, 435

Frieze with inlays of warriors (cat. no. 48), 90, *90*, 161

Frieze from a temple altar (cat. no. 6), 19–20, *19*

Friezes with inlays of cows and birds (cat. no. 46), 87–88, *87*

frit, 231, 353, 398

frontality, meaning of, 74–75, *74*

Fullol Hoard, 360, 365, 366n1

furniture inlays, Harappan, 398, *399*

furniture plaques and panels, of Ebla, 170, *171*, 174, *174*

Game board and fourteen gaming pieces (cat. no. 53), 101, *101*

Ganweriwala, 379

Garden of Eden, *489*, 494n20
  as Dilmun, 474, 487–88, *488*

garnet, 394, *394*

garter, 112, *112*

Gatumdug (goddess), 425

Gawra (Tepe Gawra), 289, 295

gazelles, 228

Gelb, I. J., 167

Geme-Shulpae (wife of Gudea), 436

Genesis, Book of, 485–87, *490*, 492, 493–94

Genouillac, Henri de, 68, 69n

Geoksyur, 354, 355, 359

Geshtinanna (goddess), 431

gharial, *239*, 246, 406, *406*

Ghirshman, Roman, 344

Gilgamesh (king of Uruk), 95, 96, 454, 455, 477, 479–84, 486
  in art, 482–84, *482–83*
  See also Bilgames; Death of Gilgamesh; Epic of Gilgamesh

gipar (residence), 74, 75n3, 200, 201n8

Girsu (Tello), 83, 189, 195, 321, 440
  as capital of Lagash, 68–69
  carnelian beads in, 243
  East Tell at, 68
  Geshtinanna temple at, 431
  Ningirsu temple (E-ninnu) at, 69, 71, 190, 415, 418, 420, 424–25, 427, 442–43, *443*
  plaques or reliefs from, 31, 71, *71*, 76
  second century B.C. revival of, 424
  shell ladle of, 399–400, *400*
  stamp seal of, 246
  steles from, 193, 201–2, *201–2*, 437–38, *437*
  Tell A at, 68, 69
  Tell B at, 68
  See also Lagash

Gishakidu (king of Umma), 78

goats, 38n29, 73, *73*, 121–22, *122*, 146–47, *146*, 219, *219*, 245, 292, *293*, 306, *306*, 334, *334*
  head of markhor goat (cat. no. 41), 32, 82, *82*
  pendant of wild goat (cat. no. 117), 180, *180*, 180–81n

goblets, 282, *282*

Godin, 349

gods and goddesses
  on Akkadian cylinder seals, 198, 213–17, 219–21
  artistic representation of, 6, 30
  battle of, 216–17, *216*, 229, *229*
  Enki's original organization of, 486
  horns of, 6, 30, *77*, 78, 142, *142*, 206–7, *206*, 216, *216*, 221–22, *222*, 318, *318*, 371, 372, 389, 402–3, *402*, 409, 438–39, *439*, 445, *445*
  hymns to, 453–55, 465, *465*
  on "Intercultural Style" vessel, 338–39, *338*
  lama, 440, *440*
  rebellion of, 486, 493
  rulers as, 197, 206–7, *206–7*, 419
  sexual union of, 453
  winged, 213–14, *213*, 247, 369–72, *369*, *371*, 373

gold
  appliqués of, 279–80, *279*, 294, *294*, 351–52, *351*
  bangle of, 397, *397*
  beads of, 143–45, *144*, 181–82, *182*, 185, *185*, 233, *233*, 243–44, 263, *263*, 264, *264*, 266–67, *266*, 289, 296, *296*, 300–302, *301*, 314, *314*, 352, 393–94, *393*, *394*
  bracelets of, 281, *281*, 352
  brooch of, 394, *394*
  cup of, 384, *384*
  daggers of, 102, *102*, 181
  diadems of, 280, *280*, 291, 295, *295*
  earrings of, 110–11, *111*, 122–23, *123*, 126, 127, *127*, 221–22, *221*, 271–72, *271–72*
  granulation technique of working, 268, 268n1, 271
  in Great Death Pit, 120–27, *121*, *123–27*
  in "Great Lyre," 105, *105*
  Harappan use of, 379, 383–84, *384*
  helmet of, 34–35, *35*
  pendants of, 181, *181*, 185, *185*, 186, *186*, 231, *232*, 261, *261*, 313–14, *313–14*, 383–84, *384*
  perforated bars of, 185, *185*
  pins of, 111, *112*, 265, *265*
  plaques of, 78, *78*
  red, 313–14, *313–14*
  rosettes of, 295, *295*
  in royal tombs, 94, 128–30, *119*, *128–31*
    Puabi's tomb, 110–13, *110–13*, 116–18, *116*
  sculpture of, 256, *257*, 279, *279*, 356, *356*
  sources of, 117, 131, 243–44
  stamp seal of, 371–72, *371–72*
  standards of, 291–92, *291–92*
  in Treasure of Ur, 140, *141–45*, *142–45*
  "trumpet" of, 364, *364*
  vessels of, 282–84, *282*, *283*, 294, *294*

gold alloy, 79

Gold ewers (cat. no. 187), 258, 283–84, *283*

gold foil, *18–19*, *19*, 120, 162, *162*, 172–73, *173*, 373–74

gold or electrum, earrings of, 268, *269*

Gonur-depe, 340, *346*, 349–50, 356, 364, 366–75, *367–75*, 372–73, *372*, 375, *375*

Gorgan (region), 349

granulation technique of working gold, 268, 268n1, 271

Great Archive (Ebla), 167, *168*, 450

Great Death Pit (Ur), 32, 94–95, 109, 110, 120–27, *120–27*

Greater Mesopotamia
  meaning of term, 4
  Sumerian influence on art of, 34

Great Flood, 4, 89, 468
  in Christian tradition, 490–91
  on cuneiform tablet, 478, *478*
  in Epic of Gilgamesh, 485, 493
  Sumerian Flood Story, 9
  survivor of, 472, 480

"Great Lyre" with bull's head and inlaid front panel (cat. no. 58), 33, 83, 105–7, *105–6*, 117, 118, 356, 441

Greece
  interconnections with, 7–8, 243–44, 255–56, 265, 270
  Mycenaean, 271–72

greenstone, 162, *162*, 213, *213*, 215, *216*, 248, 447–48, *447*

griffin, 215, *215*

griffin demons, 374

Gudea (king of Lagash), 69, 81, 322n16
  construction by, 248, 418, 442
  Cylinders A and B of, 140, 415, 418, 424n33, 428n3, 438

foundation pegs naming, 438–39, *438–39*
personal god of, 371nn6, 7, 423, *423,* 431
statues of, 418–20, 422, *426–28, 427–31,* 429n4,
    430–31
    Hellenistic rediscovery, 424–25
steles of, 422, *422,* 423, 437–38, *437*
guilloche pattern, 181, *181,* 243, *301,* 302, *327,* 328, 334,
    334, 335, 340, *340,* 370, *370,* 375, *375,* 384, *384*
Gujarat, 261, 377, 379, 381, 396, 397, 400
Gula (goddess), 71, *71*
Gulf region, 307–45
    seals of, 306, 318–22, *318–22*
    See also Dilmun; Oman
Gungunum (king of Larsa), 321, 322n2
Gushur (king of Kish), 468
Guti peoples (Gutians), 5, 15, 69, 417
Guzana, 231
gypsum
    beads of, 17, *17,* 353
    mosaics of, 19
    production of, 62
    sculpture of, 50–51, *50,* 152–53, *152–53,* 59–61,
        59–61, 148–55, *148–55,* 435, *435*
        Mari portrait of Ur-Nanshe, 152–53, *152–53*
    stele of, 53, *53*
    vessels of, 48–50, *49*

Habuba Kabira (Tell Qannas), vessel from, 20, *20*
Hacilar, 274
Hairpin with incised concentric circles (cat. no.
    213), 315–16, *316*
hair ribbons, *110–11,* 111, 122, *123,* 125–27, *125–27*
hair rings, 110–11, *110–11,* 124, 271, *271*
Hajar Mountains, 316
Hakemi, Ali, 317
Hakra-Nara River, 379, 381
Hall, H. R., 84
Ham, *491*
Hama, 246, 272
Hamad Town, 312, 320
Hamilton, M. G., 277
Hammam, 183
Hammurabi (king of Babylon), 138, 168, 471
Handled weight with confronted snakes (cat. no.
    236), 339, *339*
Handled weight in the form of a standing bull (cat.
    no. 255), 363, *363*
Handled weight with palm trees (cat. no. 225b), 244,
    328–29, *329*
Handle in the shape of a standing male figure (cat.
    no. 205), 309, *309*
Hansen, Donald P., 431
    "Art of Akkadian Dynasty," 189–98
    "Art of the Early City-States," 21–37
Harali, 347, 474
Harallu, 117
Harappa, *378–79,* 379, 385, 395
    bangles of, 397–98, *397*
    brooch from, 394, *394*
    clay unicorn figurines of, 390
    pendant from, 404, *404*
    sculpture from, 391–92, *391*
    seal from, 407, *408,* 409
Harappa Museum, 404, 407
Harappan civilization (Indus Valley cities), 4, 8n5,
    145, 377–409, *378, 379*
    carnelian of, 242, *243, 301,* 302, 396, *396*

combs of, 315
cylinder seals of, *240,* 247
etched beads of, 130–31, *130–31,* 261, *261, 301,*
    302, 312, *312,* 313, *313,* 396–97, *396*
in Mesopotamia, 246
Mesopotamian culture compared to that of, 385,
    408, 409
stamp seals of, 380, 402–13, *402–13*
utilitarian and decorative objects in, 379–80
weights system of, 401–2, *401–2*
worship in, 403, *403*
See also Chanhudaro; Harappa; Indus River and
    Valley; Mohenjo-daro
Harappan language, 5, 246, 380, *402,* 403–7, *404–7,* 411
harps. *See under* musical instruments
Haryana, 379
Hasanoğlan, *256,* 257, *258,* 279
Hashamer (administrator), 447–48, *447*
Hathor (goddess), 253
Hattusha (Boğazköy), 168, 277, 479
Head of a bull (cat. no. 42), 83, *83,* 441
Head of a bull (cat. no. 65), 83, 115, *115*
headdresses, 75n2, 110–11, *110–11,* 122–28, *123,* 127,
    142, *142*
    Harappan, 391–92, *392*
    Mari women with, 153–55, *153–54,* 161, *161,* 164,
        164
Headdresses for composite statues (cat. no. 109), 36,
    169–72, *170–71*
Head of a lion (cat. no. 64), 32, 114–15, *114*
Head of a markhor goat (cat. no. 41), 32, 82, *82*
Head of a ruler (cat. no. 136), 195, 210–12, *211*
Head of a ruler (cat. no. 309), 435, *435*
Head of a sheep (cat. no. 1), 16–17, *17,* 26, 481
Heinrich, Ernst, 56
Helike, 274
Hellenistic rediscovery of Gudea statuary, 424–25
Helmet on a crushed skull (cat. no. 56), 103, *103*
helmet, gold, of Meskalamdug, 34–35, *35*
Helms, Mary, 239
hematite, 393, 448, *448*
Hephaistos (god), 270
Heraion, 270
Hermitage Museum. *See* State Hermitage Museum
Herodotos, 4
heroes. *See* contest scenes
"He Who Saw the Deep," 479
Hierakonpolis, 252
Hilmand, 347
Hinduism, 403
Hindu Kush, 348
Historical Museum of Uzbekistan, Tashkent, 339
Hittite language, 168
Hittites, 168, 179, 271, 277, 292n3
Hoard (cat. no. 158), 140, 231–32, *232,* 258
hollow casting, lifesize, 210, *211*
Homer's *Iliad,* 168
Horoztepe, *258, 278,* 284, 287–88
horses, 159, 231–32, *232*
houses
    brick construction of, 21, 26, 385
    corridor, 255–56
    Harappan, 379
    palm-frond, 307
    reed, 2, 28, *28*
Human face for a composite figure (cat. no. 105),
    162, *162*

human-headed bulls or bisons. *See* bull-men
human-headed horned quadrupeds, 403, *403,* 407,
    408, 409
Humbaba, 480. *See also* Huwawa
hunting, *22–23,* 23, 37n5, 41, 150, *150,* 375. *See also*
    animals
Hurrian language, 5, 168, 222, 224
    cuneiform in, 222, 226, *226*
Hurrians, 168, 222, 432n1
hut motif, 341, *341,* 343, *343*
Huwawa (guardian of the trees), 455, 479, 482, *482.*
    See also Humbaba
hyena, 106, *106*
Hymn to the Hoe (cat. no. 339), 455, 476, *476,* 486
hymns, 453–55, 465, *465*

Iahdun-Li'm (king of Mari), 138
Ibbi-Sin (king of Ur; ca. 2013–1989 B.C.), 419, 448,
    469, *469,* 470, *470*
Ibbit-Li'm (king of Ebla), 465
Ibbi-Zikir (Eblaite minister), 253, 462, 464
ibex, 81–82, *81,* 163, *163,* 180n, 219–20, *219,* 351
Ibni-sharrum (scribe), 197, 208, 330
Ibrium (Eblaite minister), 462
Idkura canal, 469
Idlib Museum, 169, 172, 175, 458, 460–63, 465
idol pendants, 185, 261, 268
Igrish-Khalab (king of Ebla), 462
Ikiztepe, 267
Iku-Shamagan (king of Mari), 155–56, *155*
Il (king of Umma), 78
Ilum-bani (overseer), 448
Imdugud. *See* eagle—lion-headed
Inanna (goddess), 12, 15, 16, 22–25, 28, 30, 32, 54, 81,
    104, 148, 242, 425, 453, 455, 471, 480
    Enmerkar's plea to, 473
    Gilgamesh and, 479, 480, 483–84, *483*
    rosette-shaped flowers as symbol of, 480, *481*
    in Shulgi hymn, 468
    song about, 18
    symbol of, 55, 122
    See also Ishtar
Inanna temple, Nippur, 22, 32, 50–51, 66–67, *66–67,*
    118, 300n3, 337
Inanna temple, Uruk. *See* E-anna
Incised plaque with a battle scene (cat. no. 99), 35,
    157, 158–59, *159*
Incised slab with an abstract female figure and ani-
    mals (cat. no. 106), 163, *163*
India, 101, 240
    Harappan civilization and, 377, 379
Indus River and Valley, 4, 111, 129, 143, 209, 312,
    343, *376,* 377–409
    interconnections with, 243, 308, 350, 353, 355,
        366, 380, 388
    map of, *235*
    Meluhha as, 239
    See also Harappa; Harappan civilization;
        Mohenjo-daro
Inlaid bull statuette (cat. no. 314), 441, *441*
Inlaid frieze of a soldier and a prisoner (cat. no. 97),
    35, 90, 157–58, *157*
Inlaid open-work furniture panel (cat. no. 114), 174,
    174
Inlaid panel from front of a lyre (cat. no. 59), 107, *107*
Inlaid panel with an animal sacrifice scene (cat. no.
    96), 35, 156–57, *157*

Inlaid vessel in the form of an ostrich egg (cat. no. 70a), 118, *119*

Inlay of a bound prisoner (cat. no. 49), 90–91, *91*

Inlay of a female musician (cat. no. 50), 91, *91*

Inlay of a musician with a bull's-head lyre (cat. no. 102), 160, *160*

Inlay of onager heads in a reconstructed chariot scene (cat. no. 100), 35, 159, *159*

Inlay of a soldier (cat. no. 98), 158, *158*

Inlay of a woman's head (cat. no. 104b), 161–62, *161*, *182*

Inlay of a woman wearing a cylinder seal (cat. no. 104a), 161, *161*

Inlays (cat. no. 288), 356, 375, 398–99, *399*

Inlays from a milking scene (cat. no. 51), 92, *92*

Inlays of men holding walking sticks (cat. no. 103), 160–61, *160–61*

Inlays of warriors, a lion-headed bird, and human-headed bulls or bisons (cat. no. 115), 36, 175–77, *175–77*

Inshushinak temple, Susa, 401–2

Institute of Archaeology, Russia, 297, 349

Instructions of Shuruppak (cat. no. 335), 455, 472, *472*

interconnections, 239–50, 474

"Intercultural Style," 170, 244–48, 319, 323, 325–32, *326–31*, 334, *334–45*, 335–45, 360, 373

    map of, *325*

intersecting-circle motif, 398, *399*

Iplul-Il (king of Mari), 462–64

Ipum-Sar (scribe), 149, *150*

Iran, 4, 7, 34, 42, 47, 107, 117, 129, 135, 145, 242–47, 330, 332

    emergence of state in, 349

    "Intercultural Style" and, 244

    mining in

        copper, 310

        diorite, 62

    as source of goods, 474

    See also Proto-Elamite period; Susa

Iraq Museum, Baghdad, *22*, 24, *25*, *27*, 28, 30, 35, 50, 52, 73, 102, *162*, *194*, *195*, 335, 352

Irkab-Damu (king of Ebla), 462, 465

iron, meteoric, 344, *345*

Isaak, Julius, 438

Isfahan, *489*

Ish'ar-Damu (king of Ebla), 464, 465

Ishbi-Erra (king of Isin), 469, *469*

Ishchali, 58

Ishkun-Sin, 448

Ishqi-Mari (king of Mari), 34, 64, 137, 148–49, *148*, 170, 176, 189, 194

Ishrut-Damu (king of Ebla), 465

Ishtar (goddess), 34, 187, 192, 197, 204, 206–7, *206*, *213*, *214*, 242, 247, 369, 372, 480

    See also Inanna

Ishtarat (goddess), 156

Ishtarat temple, Mari, 118, 137, 151n1, 155, 164

Ishtar temple, Ashur, 142, 257

Ishtar temple, Mari, 137, 148, 153–55, 334, 335

Ishtar temple, Nippur, 335

Isin, 455, 469

    "law code" of, 471, *471*

Isin-Larsa period (2017–1763 B.C.), 311, 318, 412

Islam

    burial of Qu'rans in, 29

    Noah and the Ark in art of, *491*

    paradise in, *489*

Islamabad Museum, 382, 385, 402–4, 406

Israel, Mesopotamian tradition in, 493–94

Istanbul Archaeological Museum, 262, 263, 265, 268

ivory, 142, *142*, 156, *157*, 248, 256, *256*, 272, *272*, 307, *315*, 315–16, 435, *435*

    Harappan, 379

Izbitser, Elena, "The North Caucasus," 289–90

Jabbul plain, 179

Jabrin, 323

Jacobsen, Thorkild, 54, 423, 494n3

Jamdat Nasr

    City Seal impression of, 54

    clay tablets from, 451

Jamdat Nasr period (ca. 3000 B.C.), 21, 68, 89, 251, 261

    art of, 16–19, *16–18*, 26–28, 156, 174, 324

    cylinder seals of, 39–40, *40*, 161

    definition of, 15

    vessels of, 48–50, *49*

Japheth, *491*

Jar sealing with a contest scene and an inscription of Naram-Sin (cat. no. 134), 207–8, *208*

jasper, 169, *169*, 394, *394*, 395

    red, 217, *217*, 231–32, *232*, 353

Jaspers, Karl, 3

Jaxartes River. *See* Syr Darya

Jazira plateau, 4, 47, 223

Jokha. *See* Umma

Kachhi plain, 381

Kalibangan, *240*, 246, 315, 398

Kalki (scribe), 220

Kandahar, 349

Kanesh. *See* Kültepe

KAR 4 (text), 487, 494n18

Karakum Desert, 348, 355

Karaoğlan, 280

Karataş, 264, *264*, 280

Karrana, 320

Kastri, 270

Kastri/Lefkandi I group, 255, 256n3, 262, 273–74, *273*

Kayseri Archaeological Museum, 274

Kazallu, 469

Kazbek Mountain, 292

Kengir League, 54

Kenoyer, Jonathan Mark, 243

    "The Indus Civilization," 377–81

Kerano Munjan, 353

Kerman, 353

Kesh, 54, 453, 455

Khabur River and region, 135, 136, 228

Khafajah, 29, 30, 58, 72, 73, *73*, 81, 155, 183, 245, 324, 330

    sculpture of, 59–61, *60–61*, 356

Khafre (pharaoh), 166, 241

Khalili Collection of Islamic Art, *491*

Khasekhemui (pharaoh), 251

Khurab, 317

Khuzistan, 42

kidney-shaped (womb-shaped) motif, 397, *397*, 398, *399*, 404, *404*

Kircher, Athanasius

    Garden of Eden of, *488*

    Tower of Babel of, *492*

Kish (Tell Ingharra), 21, 118, 328, 459

    Akka as king of, 479

    beads of, 243, 312, 397

description of, 89

Eblaite cuneiform tablet on, *463*, *464*

filigree work in, 181

inlays of, 90–92, *90–92*, 161, 306

interconnections of, 136

knowledge of kings of, 21

Mesalim, king of, 68, 69

possible school of sculpture in, 192

Rimush, king of, 183, 195, 201–2, 335, 336

Sargon of Akkad and, 189

seals of, 147, 216–17, *216*, 246

in Sumerian King List, 468

use of title of king of, 143

Kitchen Temple, Lagash, 482

Kleiner Antentempel, Tell Chuera, 62, 63

Kneeling bull holding a vessel (cat. no. 13), 26, 43, *43*, 107

Kneeling man holding a vessel (cat. no. 17), 27, 50–51, *50*

Kneeling nude man with serpents (cat. no. 19), 52, *52*

Kolonna. *See* Aigina

Königliche Museen, Berlin, 438

Kopet Dagh, 348, 349, 355

Korfmann, Manfred, 274

Koşay, Hamit Zübeyr, 277, 278n2

Koukonisi, 270

Kuban Expedition, 297

Kuban River and Valley, 289, 292

Kuh-i Nugre, 353

Kulaba, 15, 449, 473

Kulli, 411

Kültepe, 181, 221, 255, 272, 275, 282

Kura (god), 462

kurgans, 289–90

Kurigalzu (Kassite king), 139, 140n6

kusarikkum (bison-man), 36, 88, 172–73, 217, 231, 465. *See also* bull-men

Kutch, 379, 396, 398–400

Kuwait National Museum, Al-Kuwait, 318–22, 342

Labanan mountain, 463

ladles, shell, 399–400, *399–400*

Lagash

    administration of, 418, 419

    brewery at, 482

    cylinder seals of, 423

    in Early Dynastic period, 21, 68, 149, 419

    foundation peg of, 80–81, *80*

    god of. *See* Ningirsu

    interconnections of, 307, 424n27

    sculpture of, 70, 212–13, *212*, 418–20, 422, 424n28, *426–28*, 427–36, 429n4, *430–36*

        female figures, 436, *436*

        Hellenistic rediscovery, 424–25

    Second Dynasty of, 417, 429

    See also Enannatum; Enmetena; Gudea; Ur-Nanshe

lahmum (hairy), 48, 52

Lahore Museum, 405, 407

lama (deity), 440, *440*

Lamberg-Karlovsky, C. C., "Pathways across Eurasia" (with Maurizio Tosi), 347–50

Lambert, W. G., 487

Lambis truncata sebae shell, 398, 400, 401

Lamentation over the Destruction of Sumer and Ur, 470, *470*

Lamgi-Mari. *See* Ishqi-Mari
language
    originally same in whole world, 493
    See also specific languages
Lapérouse, Jean François, 374
lapis lazuli
    Afghan and other sources of, 18, 117, 129, 131,
        166, 178, 248n17, 252, 324
    amulet of, 303, *303*
    availability of, 180
    beads of, 112, *112–13*, 143–45, *143–44*, 185, *185*,
        300–302, *301*, 353, *353*
    cylinder seals of, 103, *103*, 109–10, *109–10*, 216–
        17, *216*, 481, *481*
    disk of, 332
    Ebla pieces of, 178, *178*, 242
    on game board, 101, *101*
    in Indus Valley, 145, 242
    jewelry and headdresses of, 110–14, *110–14*, 122–
        28, *123–32*, 140–42, *141*, 145, *145*, 180, *180*,
        231–32, *232*
    in lyres, 105–7, *105–7*
    Mari bead of (cat. no. 84), 35
    ram's head in, 353, *353*
    sculpture of, 16–17, *17*, 144–15, *114–15*, 121, *121*,
        142, *142*, 162, *162*, 324, *324*
        Egyptian, 252, *252*
    sources of, 241–43, 347, 348
    stamp seal of, 332–33, *333*
    on "Standard of Ur," 97, *97–100*
    vessels of, 117, *117*, 118, *119*
Larak, 468
Larsa, 54, 69, 244, 447, 455, 468
Late Bronze Age, 179
Late Harappan culture, 381
Late Uruk period (ca. 3300–3000 B.C.)
    description of, 14–16
    map of the Near East during, *10*
    See also Jamdat Nasr period; Uruk
"law codes," 471, *471*
lead
    casting facilitated by, 310
    handled bull weight of, 363, *363*
    moulded nude female figures in, 257–58, *257*
Lebanon, 251, 455, 480, 482
Legrain, Leon, 443
Leningrad. *See* St. Petersburg
leopards, 173, *173*, 245, 335, *335*, 336, *336*, 338–39,
    338
leopard skins, 72, 72n, 157–58, *157–58*, 176, *176*
Lerna, 255, 273
Lesbos, 270
Leukas, 256n2, 270
Levant, the, 247–48, 251, 253, 272, 284, 493
lexical lists, 13–14, 451–53, 458–59, *458*
    in Ebla, 167
libation plaques, 74–75, *74–75*
Lid decorated with intertwined snakes (cat. no. 316),
    442–43, *443*
Limantepe, 255
limestone
    cylinder seals of, 23, *23*
    foundation pegs in, 222, *222*
    in Harappan civilization, 380, 385, *387*, 388
    inlays of, 90–91, *90–91*, 166, 175–77, *175–77*
    mould of (cat. no. 133), 197, 206–7, *206–7*
    plaques of, *31*, 68, *68*, 88, *88*, 158, *158*

production of, 62
sculpture of, 16, *17*, 63–66, *63–65*, *67*, 169, *169*,
    172–74, *172–74*, 323–24, *323*, 385, *387*,
    388
steles of, 201–2, *201–2*, 422, 437–38, *437*, 443–46,
    444–45
type of
    bituminous, 16–17, *17*, *18*, *18*
    black, 59–61, *59*
    blue, *18–19*, *19*
    crystalline, 44–45, *45*
    pink, 85, *85*
    pink-buff, 443, *444–45*
    red, 97, *97–100*, 101, 118, *119*, 121, *121*, 156, *157*
    white, 90–91, *90*, *91*
    yellow, 385, *387*, 388
vessels of, 48–50, *49*, 128
Limnos. *See* Poliochni
lion-griffin, 215, *215*
Lion-headed eagle pendant (cat. no. 81), 35, 140, *141*
lion-headed eagles (Imdugud). *See* eagles—lion-
    headed
lions, 41, *41*, 68, 104, *104*, 292, *293*, 300, *300*
    appliqués of, 294, *294*
    cup with, 384, *384*
    on cylinder seals, 41, *41*, 103, *103*, 146–47, *147*,
        197, 214, *214*, 217–19, *218*, *219*, 227, *227*,
        272, *272*, 305, *305*
    foundation pegs of, 222–23, *222–23*
    as guardian animals, 222
    on "Intercultural Style" vessel, 330–31, *331*
    lion-hunt stele (Uruk), 22, *23*
    pendant with, 231–32, *232*
    sculpture of, 114–15, *114*, 174, *174*
    on stamp seal, 371–72, *371*
    vomiting, 319–20, *319*
Lipit-Eshtar (king of Isin), 455, 471, *471*
Lloyd, Seton, 84
Lobed crescent earrings (cat. no. 152), 221–22, *221*
Long-stemmed goblet (cat. no. 186), 282, *282*
Loop-handled stamp cylinder seal with humans and
    animals (cat. no. 177), 248, 272, *272*
lost-wax casting, 79–80, *79*, *81–83*, 82, 83, 115, *115*,
    210–12, *211–12*, 309, *309*, 369, 372, 390, 441
Lothal, 243, 322, 322n4, 397, 398
Lubadag (god), 222, 223
lugal (king), 464
Lugalbanda (king of Uruk), 453, 480
Lugaldalu (king of Adab), 63–64, *63–64*, 149n2
Lugale myth, 480
Lugalezen (son of king of Lagash), 71, *71*
Lugalkisalsi (king of Uruk and Ur), 31–32, 64–65,
    65, 149
Lugalsha-engur (king of Lagash), 68
Lugalzagezi (king of Umma), 69
Lullubi people, 195
Luristan, 47
Lycia, 264, *264*, 273
lyres, 33, 105–7, *105–7*, 160, *160*, 321, *321*, 332, 422.
    See also "Great Lyre"

mace-head, 68
Mace-head dedicated for the life of Enannatum
    (cat. no. 35), 75–76, *76*, 88, 157
Machinsky, D. A., 292
Mackay, Ernest J. H., 91, 393
Magan. *See* Oman

magnesite, 44–45, *45*
magnetite, 39, *40*
Magritte, René, 163
Mahmatlar, 278, 283–84, *283*
Maikop, 270, 289–96, *291–95*
Maison des Fruits, 69
Makran, 348, 377, 398, 399
Makridy, T., 277
Mallowan, Max, 224
Manishtushu (king of Akkad), 193–94, *193*, 230, 420
mankind created, 486
maps and plans
    of Akkadian empire, *188*
    of distribution of "Intercultural Style" chlorite
        objects, *325*
    of Ebla palace, *166*
    of findspots of beads by type, *240–42*
    of Late Uruk and Early Dynastic sites, *10*
    of Mari palace and temples, *137–39*
    of Nippur, Inanna temple, *66*
    of Umm el-Marra Tomb 1, *179*
    of Ur III state, *414*
    Ur
        Great Death Pit, *120*
        Puabi's tomb, *108*
        Royal Cemetery, *93*
    Urkesh palace, *225*
marble, 39, *40*, 122, 481, *481*
    white, *18–19*, *19*, 87, 162, *162*
Marduk (god), 486–87
Margueron, Jean-Claude, "Mari and the Syro-
    Mesopotamian World," 135–38
Marhashi, 244, 249nn22, *24*, 325, 342, 347, 474
Mari, 6–7, 21, 34–36, 69, 90, 133, 135–64
    beads of. *See* beads—of Mari
    costume of rulers of, 148–49, *148*
    cuneiform in, 453
    cylinder seals of, 146–47, *146*, 220–21, *221*
    earrings of, 221–22, *221*
    Ebla's tribute to, 36, 461–64, *461*, *463*
    headdresses of, 153–55, *153–54*, 161, *161*, 164, *164*
    history and environment of, 135–38
    inlays of, 88, 245
    mosaics of, 138, 182
    pendants of, 140, *141*, 145, *145*, 180
    plans and reconstruction of, 135, *137–39*
    sculpture of, 35–36, 142–43, *142*, 148–56, *148–46*,
        164, *164*, 169–74, *170–74*, 175, 356
    Treasure of Ur from, 139–47, *140–46*, 180, 181
    vessels of, 335, *335*, 343
    votive figures of, 35, 148–55, *148–55*
    ziggurat of, *146*, 147
    See also Dagan temple; Ishqi-Mari; Ishtar temple;
        Ishtarat temple; Ninni-zaza temple;
        Shamash temple
mashhuf (boat), 321
Mask of a horned figure (cat. no. 274), 388–89, *388*
massif rouge, Mari, 137, 162
mathematical text, cuneiform tablet with a (cat. no.
    332c), 458–49, *459*
Matthiae, Paolo, 241
    "Ebla and the Early Urbanization of Syria,"
        165–68
Mature Early Syrian period, 165
mat-weave pattern, *327*, 328, 328n7, 342, *342*
Maxwell-Hyslop, Rachel, 244
Mecquenem, Roland de, 300

medical text, cuneiform tablet with a Sumerian (cat. no. 329), 466, *466*

megaron, 255, 262

Megiddo, 493

Mehrgarh, 377–78, 381, 382, *382,* 394

Meluhha, 209, 239, 242, 243, 246, 248, 310, 393, 413, 474

Mesalim (king of Kish), 68, 69

Mesanepada (king of Ur), 35, 84, 189, 96, 139, 140, 143, *143*

Meskalamdug (king of Ur), 33–35, 96, 102, 103, 143, 194

    gold helmet of, 34–35, *35*

Meskiagnuna (king of Ur), 96

Meslamtaea (deity), 475

Mesopotamia

    Book of Genesis and myths of, 485–87, *490,* 493–94

    Central Asian trade with, 349

    first union of, 136

    geography and extent of, 4

    Harappan immigrants in, 246, 398, 411

    Indus culture compared to that of, 385, 408, 409

    Kircher's Garden of Eden located in, *488*

    map of, *10*

    North Caucasus and, 289–90

    peoples of, 4–5

mes (wood), 474

metal-covered wood, 85, *85,* 105, *105,* 172–73, *173*

metalworking techniques, 79

meteoric iron, 344, *345*

Metropolian Museum of Art, New York, 43, 53, 59, 66, 79, 81, 195, 210, 216, 217, 219, 222, 283, 284, 328, 330, 344, 360, 364, 367, 396–97, 428–29, 431, 433, 439, 446, 448, *489*

Michalowski, Piotr, 54

    "The Earliest Scholastic Tradition," 451–56

microbeads, 395

Middle Bronze Age, 36, 165, 179, 277

Middle Kingdom (Egypt), 251

Miho Museum, Japan, 337, 360, 363, 365

Miri Qalat, 315

Miroschedji, Pierre de, 316, 317

Mitannian Empire, 179

Mochlos, 248, 255, 262

Mohenjo-daro, 4, *378,* 379, 395

    bangles of, 397, *397*

    beads from, 393–94, *393, 394*

    belt from, 132, 392–93, *393*

    BMAC artifacts at, 350

    combs of, 315

    "Intercultural Style" in, 328n7

    mask from, 388–89, *388*

    pendant from, 404, *404*

    sculpture of, 395–92, *386–87, 389–91*

    shell inlays of, 398–99, *399*

    spiral-headed pins at, 352

    stamp seals of, 322, *403,* 405, *405,* 407–9, *407, 409,* 412–13, *412*

    yogic figure with erect phallus, 403, *407*

Mohenjo-daro Museum, 389, 392–94, 397, 398, 407

Moorey, Roger, 96, 239, 244

Morgan Library, New York, 197, 208, 214, 215, 217, 416, 477, 439

Mortensen, Peter, 311

Mosaic columns (cat. no., 44), 85–86, *86*

mosaics

    in Mari, 138, 182

    in Uruk, 18–19, *19*

    See also "Standard of Ur"

mother-of-pearl, 353, 354n1

Mouflon head appliqué (cat. no. 245), 351–52, *351*

Moulded tablet with a hero, tigers, and a bull hunt scene (cat. no. 300b), 407, *408*

Mould fragment with a deified ruler and the goddess Ishtar (cat. no. 133), 197, 206–7, *206–7*

Moulds for jewelry, seals, and amulets (cat. nos. 163b, 163c, 164), 257–58, *257, 259*

Mount Ararat, *488*

Mount Nimush, 493

Mozan. *See* Urkesh

mullite, 393

mu-na-ru (consecrated), 143

Mundigak, 349, 352

Murghab River, 348, 349, 355

Mursilis I (Old Hittite king), 168

Muscarella, Oscar White, "The Central Anatolian Plateau," 277–78

Musée du Louvre, Paris, *24, 27, 31, 38, 45,* 68, 71, 78, 81, *190, 191, 192, 193,* 197, 199, *201–2,* 208, 212, 222, 258, 298, 300–305, 332, 342, 344, 354, 360, 366n4, 369–71, 399, 401, 410, 413, 420, *423,* 427, 429, 431, 433, 439, 440, 441

Musées Royaux d'Art et d'Histoire, Brussels, *220*

Museum zu Allerheiligen, Schaffhausen, 371

Museum of Fine Arts, Boston, 204, 396, 399–401

Museum für Vor- und Frühgeschichte, Berlin, 273

musical instruments and musicians

    animals as decorative elements of, 83

    on Lagash stele, *422*

    Plaque with addorsed lions trampling enemies (cat. no. 57), 104–5, *104*

    on shell inlay, 91, *91,* 160, *160*

    "trumpet," 364, *364*

    in Ur cemetery, 33–34, 95, 107, *107,* 311

        Great Death Pit, 120

        "Great Lyre" with bull's head and inlaid front panel (cat. no. 58), 33, 83, 105–7, *105–6,* 117, 118, 356, 441

    Ur-Nanshe sculpture portrait, 138, 152–53, *152–53,* 170

    on vessel fragment, 333–34, *333*

    on wall plaque, 73, *73*

    See also lyres

Myrina, 270

mythology in cuneiform literature, 452–53

Nabada. *See* Tell Beydar

Nagar. *See* Tell Brak

Nageshwar, 400

Namazga period, 355–59, *355–59*

Namma (goddess), 31–32, 65

Nanna (god), 22, 32, 74, 75n3, 200, 468, 475

Nanshe (goddess), 244

    temple of (Nina), 442

Naram-Sin (king of Akkad), 6, 136, 137, 168, 194, 200, 206–8, *206,* 213

    daughters of, 201n5, 225, 227

    divinity of, 195–97, *196*

    steles of, 195–96, *196,* 203–4, *203,* 420

Narbenmann, 344, *345. See also* scarred men

Nasiriya Stele (cat. no. 131), 204, *204,* 205

National Archaeological Museum, Athens, 264, 267, 271–74

National Museum, Aleppo, 20, 148, 149, 155–57, 164, 169, 172–74, 178, 180–86, 253, 273, 335

National Museum, Damascus, 62, 140, 143, 145, 146, 149, 151, 153, 155, 159–63, *171,* 220, 334

National Museum, Karachi, 382–85, 389–91, 397, 398, 404, 405, 407

National Museum, New Delhi, 407

National Museum, Riyadh, 323, 324, 326, 328

National Museum of the Republic of Adygeya, Maikop, 296

National Museum of Turkmenistan Named After Saparmurat Turkmenbashi, Ashgabat, 340, 356, 367, 369, 372, 375

Nausharo, 247, 350, 378, 381–83, *383,* 412–13, *412*

Nazi (goddess), 475

necklaces, 126–27, *126,* 143–45, *144. See also* beads

Nelson-Atkins Museum of Art, Kansas City, 439

Neolithic period, 261, 270, 377–78, 381

    ceramic, 274

    sculpture of, 279

Neo-Sumerian, use of term, 5, 417

Nergal (god), 222, 223, 475

New York Public Library, *488, 492*

ngiri (foot), 475

Nidaba (goddess), 455

Niliga'u, 462

nimrum (leopard), 173

nin (queen), 110, 111

Nina (Zurghul), 68, 442

Ninalla (queen of Lagash), 436

Ninazu (god), 468, 475

Ninbanda (queen of Ur), 96, 103

Nindara (god), 420, 475

Nineveh, 477, 479

    Akkadian copper-alloy head from, 194–95, *194,* 210–12, 435

Ningal (goddess), 200

Ningirsu (god), 22, 31, 68, 75–76, 105, 190–92, *191,* 248, 423, 425

    Kitchen (Bagara) Temple of, 482

    temple of (E-ninnu, Girsu), 69, 71, 190, 415, 418, 420, 424–25, 427

Ningishzida (personal god of Lagash kings), 371n6, 423, *423, 423,* 431, 435, 437, *437,* 475

    temple of (Girsu), 442–43, *443*

Ninhursanga (goddess), 28, 87, 163, 352, 425

    poem on myth of Enki and, 474–75, *474,* 487–88

Ninhursanga temple (Mari), 137

Ninhursanga temple (Tell al Ubaid), 85–88, *85–88,* 306

Ninisina (goddess), 471

Ninkasi (goddess), 475

Ninki (god), 453

Ninlil (goddess), 453, 485

    Myth of Enlil and, 475–76, *475*

Ninmah (goddess), 470, 486, 487

Ninmu (goddess), 474–75

Ninngiriutu (goddess), 475

Ninni-zaza (deity), 34, 156

    temple of, Mari, 137, *138,* 149, *149–51,* 151, 151n1, 152, 153, 159, 160

Ninsikila (god), 475

Ninsumuna (goddess), 453

Ninsun (goddess), 480

Ninti (goddess), 475
  temple of, Khafajah, 29, 59, 60–61, 61
Ninurta (god), 480
Nippur
  abandonment of, 456
  clay tablets of, 57, 469, 469
    Flood story, 478, 478
    literary tablets, 452, 454, 455
    medical text, 466, 466
  friezes of, 90
  god of, 475, 476
  "Intercultural Style" at, 335, 337, 337
  schools at, 454
  sculpture of, 162, 162
  vessels of, 27, 245, 343
  votive figures of, 66–67, 67, 161
  weight of, 328
  "Where Flesh Came Forth," site in, 486
  See also Inanna temple; Ishtar temple
Nisaba (goddess), 30, 78
Nissen, Hans J., "Uruk and the Formation of the
    City," 11–20
Noah and the Ark, 490–91
Nodule of unworked carnelian (cat. no. 283), 396,
    396
North Caucasus, 267, 270, 289–97, 291–97
Northern Fort (Ebla), 166
Novosvobodnaya, 289, 290, 296–97, 296–97
Nubadig (god), 223
nudity
  as motif, 23, 38
  of religious personnel, 79–80
  as sign of purification, 75, 75
Nungal (goddess), 455
Nuska (god), 213, 214

Old Akkadian (dialect), 167, 203, 207, 207, 208, 220,
    227, 227, 413, 413. See also Akkadian language
Old Babylonian period
  cuneiform prism of, 467–68, 467
  schools of, 454–56
olivine-gabbro, 199, 199
Oman (Magan), 239, 248, 248n8, 304, 474
  description of, 307–8
  mining in, 306, 307, 354
    diorite, 29, 62, 191, 307, 420, 427
  shell from, 399
onagers, 72, 72, 97, 98, 116, 116, 159, 159
Open-worked carved box with crenellated decora-
    tion (cat. no. 251), 353, 358–59, 358
Open-worked pin with two seated figures (cat. no.
    228), 245, 332, 332
Open-worked standard (cat. no.189), 286–87, 286
ophiolite, 307
orants. See votive figures
Orchomenos, 270, 273
Oriental Institute. See University of Chicago
Oshad (Maikop) kurgan, 290–96, 291–95
Ostrich egg with inlaid attachments (cat. no. 70b),
    118, 119
ostrich-eggshell vessels, 32
Oxus River. See Amu Darya
Özgüç, T., 287

Pabilgagi (king of Umma), 52
Pair of basket earrings with dangling pendants (cat.
    no. 174), 185, 271, 271

Pair of crescent earrings (cat. no. 175), 271, 271
Pair of earrings with poppy pendants (cat. no. 176),
    271–72, 272
Pairs of basket earrings (cat. no. 173), 268, 269
Pairs of lobed crescent earrings (cat. nos. 171, 172),
    267–68, 267, 291
Pakistan, 111, 248n17, 368, 377, 379. See also
    Baluchistan; Harappan civilization
palace, 89–92
Palamari, 270
Palishtum canal, 469
palm-tree motif, 328–29, 328–29
Pamir Mountains, 348
paragonite, 430–31, 430–31, 431n2
Parkhai II, 352
Parpola, Asko, 409, 411
Parrot, André, 69n, 146, 429
Pasupati Nath (god), 403
Peabody Museum, Harvard University, Cambridge,
    Massachusetts, 343, 344
pearls, 295, 295. See also mother-of-pearl
Pendant with an applied lozenge (cat. no. 126), 186,
    186
Pendant with a filigree guilloche pattern (cat. no.
    118), 181, 181
Pendant and stamp seal with unicorns and ritual
    offering stands (cat. no. 295), 404, 404
Pendant with two roundels (cat. no. 86), 35, 145, 145,
    258
pendants, 180, 180, 183, 183, 290
  Anatolian, 258
  double-spiral, 129–30, 129, 352–53, 352
  gold, 181, 181, 185, 185, 186, 186, 231, 232, 261,
    261, 313–14, 313–14, 383–84, 384
  Harappan, 404, 404
  idol, 185, 261, 268
  of Mari, 140, 141, 145, 145, 180
  mould for, 258
Pepi I (pharaoh), 36, 241, 253, 166
Perrot, G., 277
Pfälzner, Peter, 224
phallic image, 403, 407
phyllite, 39, 39
Pieces of unworked lapis lazuli (cat. no. 116), 178,
    178
Pin with a bird head (cat. no. 125), 185, 185
Pin with flanged head (cat. no. 185), 181, 281–82, 281
Pin with seated female figure (cat. no. 258), 367, 367
pins, 111, 112, 181, 182, 265, 265
  open-worked, with figures, 332, 332
  of Susa, 351
  See also toggle pins
pipal, 402–4, 402–4
Pirak, 381
Pir Hussein, 203
plano-convex bricks, 21, 26
Plano-Convex Building, Kish, 89
Plaque with addorsed lions trampling enemies (cat.
    no. 57), 104–5, 104
Plaque dedicated by a queen of Umma (cat. no. 37),
    78, 78
Plaque with a libation scene (cat. no. 34), 75, 75
Plaque with a lion-headed eagle and human-
    headed bull or bison (cat. no. 47), 88, 88
plaques
  of Mari, with battle scene, 35
  quadruple-spiral, 266–67, 266

of slaying of the Bull of Heaven, 483, 483
  See also relief plaques
poetry, 452–55
  Disputation between Ewe and Wheat, 486
  on Enmerkar and Lord of Aratta, 472–73, 473
  Flood story, 478, 478
  Hymn to the Hoe, 476, 476, 486
  Lamentation over the Destruction of Sumer and
    Ur, 470, 470
  Myth of Enki and Ninhursanga, 474–75, 474
  Myth of Enlil and Ninlil, 475–76, 475
  See also Death of Gilgamesh; Epic of Gilgamesh
Polatli, 284
Poliochni (Limnos), 185, 244, 248, 255, 262, 264–68,
    270–72, 271–73
polos, 154, 154n3, 155n5–6
poppy images, 271–72, 272
Porada, Edith, 245, 272
post-Harappan culture, 381
Potts, D. T., "The Gulf," 307–8
Pouring vessel with human-headed bull or bison in
    relief (cat. no. 69), 106, 118, 118
Pouring vessels in shell form (cat. no. 291), 118, 401, 401
pregnant women, amulets used by, 129, 129
presentation scenes, 215–16, 216, 318, 318, 423, 423,
    437, 437, 447–48, 447, 448
"Priam's Treasure," 262, 267
priestesses
  of Ebla, 169
  of Sippar, 454
  of Ur, 75–75, 74, 200–201, 200, 201n4
"priest-king"
  on cylinder seals, 40–41, 40, 41, 480–81, 481
  Gilgamesh as, 480
  on "Intercultural Style" vessel, 330–31, 331
  as intermediary, 23–24
  torso of, Indus Valley, 385–88, 386–87
  Uruk sculptures of, 25, 26, 38, 38, 194
  as warrior, 23, 23, 24
priests, Sumerian liturgy of, 455
prisoners, 23, 33, 90–91, 91, 97, 98–99, 157, 157, 160,
    160, 176–77, 176–77, 191, 197, 199, 199, 201–2,
    202, 445, 446n4
Proto-Elamite period, 26, 27, 34, 42–48, 43–48, 107,
    245, 348, 349, 360
Proto-Elamite script, 456n2
Protoliterate period, 28, 30, 90
Ptolemy, Royal Canon, 5
Puabi (queen of Ur), 32, 79, 96, 103, 106, 108–17,
    108–17, 341
  headdresses of servants of, 392
  plan of tomb of, 108
Puabi's beaded cape and jewelry (cat. no. 62), 33,
    111–13, 112–13, 243
Puabi's headdress (cat. no. 61), 33, 110–11, 110–11
Punjab, 379
Purana Qila, New Delhi, 240
Purushkanda (Acemhöyük), 239, 322
Pushkin State Museum of Fine Arts, Moscow, 268
Puzrish-Dagan (Drehem), 418
Puzur-Inshushinak (king of Elam), 367, 367, 422
Puzur-Shullat (priest), 218

Qalat al-Bahrain, 307, 322nn6, 13, 410
Quadruple-spiral beads (cat. no. 170a), 233, 244,
    266–67, 266
Quadruple-spiral plaques (cat. no. 170b), 266–67, 266

quartz, 393

Quetta, 354, 368, 383, 384

Qu'ran, 29, 491

Rakhigarh, 379

Ram figurine and double-urial pendant (cat. no. 210), 313–14, *313–14*

rams, 17, *17*, 122, 353, *353*, 389–90, *389*

Ramsey, W. M., 277

Ras al-Jins, 307, 315

Rashid al-Din, *491*

Rassam, Hormuzd, 258

Ravi River, 379

Reade, Julian, 131

    "The Royal Tombs of Ur," 93–96

Rearing goat with a flowering plant (cat. no. 71), 32, 121–22, *121*

Recumbent animals (cat. no. 2), 16–17, *17*, 481

Recumbent calf (cat. no. 113), 36, 174, *174*

Recumbent human-headed bull or bison (cat. no. 111), 36, 172–73, *173*, 231

Recumbent human-headed bull or bison (cat. no. 157a), 230–31, *230*

Recumbent human-headed bull or bison (cat. no. 313), 440–41, *440*

reed bundles, 480–81, *481*

reed houses, *2*, 28, *28*

Reinholdt, Claus, "The Aegean and Western Anatolia," 255–58

Rein ring with an onager (cat. no. 66), 33, 116, *116*

relief plaques, 30–31, *31*, 68, *68*, 71–75, *71–75*, 78, 85, *85*, 88, *88*, 300, *300*

"reliquaries," 353, 360

repoussé decoration, *283*, 284, 351, 360, *360*, 365

rhinoceros, *239*, 246, 380, 412n3

Rig-Veda, 350

Rim-Sin (king of Larsa; ca. 1807–1748 B.C.), 447

Rimush (king of Akkad), 193, 195, 201–2, 335, 336

rock crystal, 300–2, *301*

rod-and-ring symbol, 445, *445*

rosettes, 55, *55*, 86–87, *87*, 112, *112*, 121, 122, 128, *128*, 140, *141*

Rostovtzeff, M. I., 289

Royal Canon (Ptolemy), 5

Russian Academy of Sciences, St. Petersburg, 358

Saar, 307, 341, 343

sacrifice

    of animals, 156–57, *157*

    human, 94–96, *94*

St. Petersburg (Leningrad), 297

Sajur River, 183

Salje, Beate, "Uruk and the World of Gilgamesh," 479–84

Samarra, Great Mosque, *492*

Sammelfund, 16–18

Samos, 248, 270, 273

Samsi-Addu (Shamshi-Adad; king of Assyria), 138

Samsun Museum, Turkey, 266

sandstone, *16*, 26, 389–90, *389*

Saqqara, 253

Sargon of Akkad (ca. 2300–2245 B.C.), 4, 58, 89, 149, 189, 213, 241, 453

    daughter of, 74–75, *74*, 200–201, *200*

    stele of, 191

    trade routes opened by, 239

    Upper Syrian conquest of, 36, 168

Sarianidi, Victor, 332, 340, 349, 350, 366

Sar-i-Pul, 446n4

Sar-i Sang, 242, 347

Saronic Gulf, 260

Sarzec, Ernest de, 68, 69, 69n, 202, 424–25, 429n1

Saza (building), 166

scarred men, 344, *345*, 369n11

scepter, 128

Schaeffer, Claude, 168

schist, 39, *39*, 156, 157, *157*

Schliemann, Heinrich, 8, 184, 262, 263, 265n1, 267, 268, 273

Schmandt-Besserat, Denise, 41

schools

    Old Babylonian, 454–56

    Shulgi's, 454

school texts for writing, 56–57, *57*, 451, 452, 454

scorpion-men, 106, *106*, 334, *334*, 480

scorpions, 245, 246, 330, 331, 410–11, *410*

sculpture, 27

    Aegean, 256, *256*

    of Akkad, 193–95, *193–95*, 210–13, *211–13*

    of Altyn-depe, 356–58, *356*, *357*

    Anatolian, 256, 257, 258, 259, 274–75, *275*

    of eastern Iran, 344, *345*

    of Ebla, 36, 169–74, *169–74*

    Egyptian, 252, *252*

    of Eshnunna (Tell Asmar), 59–61, *59*

    females with folded arms, 256–57, *256*

    of Girsu, 70

    Harappan, 382–83, *382*, *383*, 385–88, *386–87*, 389–92, *389–91*

    of Khafajah, 59–61, *60–61*, 356

    of Mari, 35–36, 142–43, *142*, 148–56, *148–46*, 164, *164*, 169–74, *170–74*, 175, 356

    of Nippur, *162*, *162*

    Proto-Elamite, 46–48, *46–48*

    of Susa, 298, *299*

    of Tell Agrab, 50–51, *50*

    of Tell Selenkahiye, 164, *164*

    of Tepe Yahya, 344, *344*

    of Umma, 51–52, *51*

    of unknown sites, 52, *52*, 70

    of Uruk, 16–17, *16–17*, 25–26, *25*, 38, *38*

    See also two seated figures; votive figures

Seal Impression Strata (SIS), 27, 34, 54, *54*

Sealing with a cylinder seal impression depicting a battle of the gods (cat. no. 156), 229–30, *229*

Sealing with a cylinder seal impression depicting a hero and bull-man combating a lion and water buffalo (cat. no. 155), 227, *227*

Sealing with a cylinder seal impression depicting royal family (cat. no. 154), 226, *226*

Sealing with impression of City Seal (cat. no. 21), 27, 54, *54*

Sealing with impressions of men, snakes, and rosettes (cat. no. 22), 27, 55, *55*

sealing of a jar, 207–8, *208*

seals, 245–48

    of Kish, 147, 216–17, *216*, 246

    See also cylinder seals; stamp seals

Seated couple (cat. no. 93), 29, 35, 155, *155*

Seated female figures, 357–58, *357*, 367–69, *367–68*

Seated figure and torso fragment of the singer Ur-Nanshe (cat. no. 91), 29, 33, 35, 138, 152–53, *152–53*, 170

Seated male figure with a cloak (cat. no. 272b), 385, *387*, 388

Seated nude female figure with an elaborate hairdressing (cat. no. 267), 382, *382*

Seated ram figurines (cat. no. 275), 389–90, *389*

Seated statue of Gudea: Architect with Plan (cat. no. 304), 29, 69, 418–21, 425, 427–28, *427*

Seated statue of Gudea (cat. no. 305), 29, 69, 428–30, *428*

Seistan, 317, 349

Seleucid dynasty, 15

Semitic languages, 4–5, 152, 155, 167

    cuneiform in, 148, 149

serpentine, 219, *219*, 220, 258, 259, 353, 413, *413*

    black, 214, *214*

    dark, 230, *230*

    green, 410, *411*

    green-black, 217, *218*

serpents (snakes)

    in Etana myth, 477

    in "Intercultural Style," 245, 326–27, *326*, *327*, 330, *331*, 335–39, *335–39*, 343, *343*

    of Ningishzida, 371nn6, 7, 423, *423*, 437, *437*, 442, *442*

    sculpture of man with, 52, *52*

    on seals, 55, *55*, 410–11, *410*, 411

    on stamp seal, 372–73, *372*

Shaft-hole axe with a bird-demon, boar, and winged dragon (cat. no. 264), 373–73, *373*

Shagish (king of Ebla), 465

Shahdad, 305, 317, 333, 343, 344, 349, 350, 355

Shahr-i Sokhta, 242, 247, 305, 343, 349, 352, 353, 355, 412

Shakkan (god), 228

Shakkanakku dynasty, 138, 221

Shakullum (scribe), 197, 218

shale

    black, 85, *85*, 87, *87*, 101, *101*

    green, *18–19*, 19

shamanism, 48

Shamash (god), 88, 167, 213, 214, *214*, 217, 231, *231*, 237, 440

    in Etana myth, 477

    cuneiform tablet with hymn to, 465, *465*

    Gilgamesh and, 480

    temple of (Mari), 137, 156, 334

Shamshi-Adad. *See* Samsi-Addu

Shara (god), 78

    temple of (Tell Agrab), 27, 48, 50, 81, 330, 334n3

Sharjah, 307, 313–17

Sharjah Archaeological Museum, 313–17

Shar-kali-sharri (king of Akkad), 194, 197, 208, 330, 417

Shatpum (owner of cylinder seal), 217

Shatt el Hai, 68

sheep, 219, *219*

    on Gulf gold pendant, 313–14, *314*

    head of (cat. no. 1), 16–17, *17*, 26

shell

    beads of, 17, *17*

    cylinder seals of, 103, *103*, 146, *146*, 215, *215*

    disk of, 183, *183*

    earrings of, 271, *271*

    Harappan, 379

    inlays of, 91–92, *91–92*, 118, 119, 160–62, *160–61*, 398–99, *399*

    friezes, 87, *87*, 156–59, *156–59*

mosaic, 85–86, *86*, 97, *97–101*, 107, *107*
    sculptures, 59–62, *59–61*, 81–82, *81–82*, 105,
        105, 114, *114*, 115, *115*, 142, *142*, 156, *156*,
        171, 440, *440*
    necklace of, 124
    plaque of, 75, *75*
    pouring vessels in form of, 401, *401*
    uses of, 147
Shell bangles (cat. no. 287), 398, *398*
Shell container (cat. no. 290a), 400, *400*
Shell ladles (cat. no. 289), 399–400, *399–400*
Shem, *491*
Shiduri (tavern keeper), 480
Shimiga (god), 222
Shinji Shumeikai, Japan, 338
ships and boats, *320*, 321, 322n7, 406, *406*
    Noah's Ark, *491*
Shortugai, 242
Shu-ilishu (interpreter), 413, *413*
Shulgi (king of Ur; ca. 2079–2032 B.C.), 417, 467
    dedication to Ningal by, 243
    foundation pegs and, 81, 424n38, 442, 447
    on future of Sumerian literature, 8n16
    Gilgamesh glorified by, 479
    hymns to, 454, 455, 468, *469*
    as linguist, 5, 454
    processions of statues of, 419
    reforms of, 417, 453–54
Shulutul (deity), 80
Shuruppak (city). *See* Fara
Shuruppak, Instructions of (cat. no. 335), 455, 472,
    472
Shu-Sin (king of Ur), 419
Shutruk-Nahhunte (king of Elam; ca. 1190–1155
    B.C.), 140n6, 189, 193, 195
Shuweda (cup-bearer), 155–56
Sibri, 350
Silk Road, 4, 7, 347
sillimanite, 393
silver, 16–17, *17–19*, 19, 142, *142*, 145, *145*
    beads of, 33, 182, *182*, 233, *233*, 243–44, 353, *353*
    Harappan, 379
    pendants of, 145, *145*, 231–32, *232*
    pin of, 367, *367*
    in royal tombs, 94, 105, *105*, 112, *112*, 114–15, *114*,
        116, *116*, 121, *121*, 122, 124, *124*, 126, *126*,
        128
    in sculpture
        Alaca Höyük, *278*, 279, *279*
        Altyn-depe, 356, *356*
        Hasanoğlan, *256*, 257, 279
        inlay of bull statuette, 441, *441*
        Mari, 142, *142*
        Proto-Elamite, 43, *43*
        Uruk, 16, 17, *17*, 27
    shaft-hole axe of, 373–73, *373*
    stamp seal of, 369–70, *369*
    standards of, 291–92, *291–92*
    in temple frieze, *18–19*, 19–20
    "trumpet" with, 364, *364*
    vessels of, 284, 290, 292, *293*, 360, *360*, 365–66,
        365
    pouring vessel in form of shell, 400, *400*
Sin (god). *See* Nanna
Sinai Peninsula, 251
Sindh, 377, 379, 397
Sin-liqe-uninni (scholar), 479

Sin temple, Khafajah, 73, 330
Sippar, 195, 257–58, 420
    female literati in, 454
    hymn to god of, 465, *465*
    in Sumerian King List, 468
Sistrum with horned animals (cat. no., 190), 287–
    88, *287*
Siva (god), 403
Skirt fragment for a composite figure (cat. no. 110),
    172, *172*
Skyros, 270, 273
slate, 90, *90*
Small Archive (Ebla), 167
snake-dragons, 371nn3, *6, 7*
snakes. *See* serpents
Soch, 339
Soden, Wolfram von, 139
soldiers (warriors)
    in battle scenes, 158–59, *158*, 189–90, *190*, 196–
        97, *196*, 201–2, *201–2*
    inlays of, 158, *158*, 175–77, *176*
    leopard skins of, 72n2, 157–58, *157–58*, 176, *176*
    with prisoners, 23, *23*, 90–91, *91*, 157, *157*, 199,
        199, 201–2, 202, 204, *204*
    in Ur tombs, 33, 94, *94*
    See also chariots
Song of Liberation (Hurrian epic), 168
Spar, Ira, "The Mesopotamian Legacy," 485–94
Sphinx Gate, Alaca Höyük, 277
spirals, 302, *302*, 304. *See also* double-spiral motif
Spouted cup (cat. no. 67a), 116–17, *116*
Spouted cup (cat. no. 68), 117, *117*
Spouted ring-shaped vessel (cat. no. 7), 20, *20*
Spouted vessel with inlaid bands (cat. no. 4), 18, *18*
Staatliche Museen zu Berlin. *See* Museum für Vor-
    und Frühgeschichte; Vorderasiatisches
    Museum
stags, 85, *85*, 120, 284, *286*, 287, *287*, 351
Stamp seal with a boat scene (cat. no. 221), 322, *322*
Stamp seal with a bull and cuneiform signs (cat. no.
    301b), 410–12, *410*
Stamp seal with a bull-man (cat. no. 300a), 407, *407*,
    409
Stamp seal with a bull and signs (cat. no. 301d), 410–
    11, *411*
Stamp seal with a bull and signs (cat. no. 301e), 410,
    411,*412*
Stamp seal with a deity in a tree and a human-
    headed horned quadruped (cat. no. 294), 403,
    403, 409
Stamp seal with an elephant (cat. no. 298), 405–6,
    406
Stamp seal with a hero and tigers (cat. no. 300c),
    407, *407*, 408
Stamp seal with a seated figure, animals, and land-
    scape (cat. no. 229), 245, 332–33, *333*
Stamp seal with a seated male figure (cat. no. 293),
    402–3, *402*, 409
Stamp seal with a winged deity and lions (cat. no.
    262), 371–72, *371–72*
Stamp seal with a zebu and script (cat. no. 296), 245,
    404–5, *405*, 411
stamp seals
    camel-shaped, 374–75, *374–75*, 409
    compartmented, 247, 369–71, *369*, *370*, 372–73,
        372, 412–13, *412*
    geographic distribution of, 246, 247

griffin demons on, 374
    Harappan, 380, 402–13, *402–13*
        yogic figure with erect phallus, 403, *407*
    with radial composition, 321–22, *321*
Standard Professions List, 458
"Standard of Ur" (cat. no. 52), 33, 72, 76, 88, 90, *97–
    100*, *97–100*, 103, 110, 159, 160, 173n1
standards. *See* Bull standards; Open-worked stan-
    dard; "Standard of Ur"
Standing bull (cat. no. 43), 79, 85, *85*
Standing female figure with clasped hands (cat. no.
    28), 29, 66–67, *67*
Standing female figure with clasped hands (cat. no.
    29), 29, 70, *70*
Standing female figure holding an offering (cat.
    no. 277), 390–91, *390–91*
Standing figure of Ishqi-Mari (cat. no. 88), 29, 35,
    137, 148–49, *148*, 170, 176, 189, 194, 298
Standing figure of Lugaldalu (cat. no. 26), 63–64,
    63–64
Standing figures holding infants (cat. no. 268), 382,
    383, *382–83*
Standing lioness demon (cat. no. 14), 26, *44–45*, 45
Standing male figure (cat. no. 90), 29, 35, 151, *151*
Standing male figure with clasped hands (cat. no. 25),
    29, 62–63, *63*
Standing male figure with clasped hands (cat. no.
    199), 298, *299*
Standing male figures with clasped hands (cat. no. 24),
    29, 59–61, *59–61*, 90
Standing male figures with clasped hands (cat. no.
    89), 29, 35, 149–51, *149–50*
Standing male with a scarred face (cat. no. 244),
    344, *345*
Standing nude female figure (cat. no. 83), 35, 142–
    43, *142*
Standing nude female figure wearing boots (cat. no.
    181), 279, *279*
Standing nude female figure with folded arms (cat.
    no. 160), 252, *252*
Standing nude female figure with folded arms
    (cat. no. 162), 256–57, *256*
Standing nude female figure with folded arms (cat.
    no. 163a), 257–58, *257*
Standing nude female figures (cat. no. 107), 164, *164*
Standing nude goddess with horned headdress
    (cat. no. 82), 35–36, 142, *142*
Standing nude "priest-king" (cat. no. 8), 35, 38, *38*,
    194
Standing statue of Gudea (cat. no. 306), 26, 69, 430–
    31, *430*
Standing statue of Ur-Ningirsu (cat. no. 307), 29,
    419, 431–33, *432–33*
Staromyshastovskaya, 289
State Hermitage Museum, St. Petersburg, 290–96, 359
states
    Central Asian development of, 348–49
    See also city-states
Statue of a seated man (cat. no. 273), 388, *388*
steatite, 62
    beads of, 300–302, *301*, 305, 354–55, *354*
        imitations of veined beads, 395
        microbeads, 395
    in brooch, 394, *394*
    completely fired (enstatite), 355, 355n2, 410, *410*
    glazed, *239*, 300–2, *301*, 305, 354–55, *354*, 381,
        394, *394*

gray and dark gray, 340, *340,* 410, *410*
green, 410, *411*
Indus "priest-king" torso of, 385–88, *386–87*
lid of, 442–43, *443*
moulds of, 257–58, *257*
sculpture of, 367–68, *368,* 440–41, *440*
seals of, *239,* 246, 318–22, *319–21,* 402–12, *402–11*
shoe of, 375, *375*
vessels of, 155–56, *155,* 316–17, *316,* 340, *340,*
342–43, *342*
weight of, 339, *339*
wigs of, 169, 170, *171,* 368
Stein, Sir Marc Aurel, 317
Steinkeller, Piotr, 54, 347
Stele fragment naming Naram-Sin (cat. no. 130),
203–4, *203*
Stele fragment with a warrior (cat. no. 131), 204,
204, 205
Stele fragments with combat scenes and inscriptions
attributed to Rimush (cat. no. 129), 193, 201–
2, *201–2*
Stele fragments with male and female figures (cat.
no. 132), 205, *205*
Stele of Ur-Namma (cat. no. 317), 322n16, 417–18,
435, 443–46, *444–45*
Stele of Ushumgal (cat. no. 20), 53, *53,* 90, 91
Stele of the Vultures (of Eannatum of Lagash), 35,
69, 175, 189–92, *190–91,* 298n2
steles
with abstract female figure and animals, 163, *163*
Akkadian, 191–92, *192,* 195–97, *197,* 199, *199,*
201–6, *201–6*
of Naram-Sin at Sippar, 195–96, *195*
at Tello (Girsu), 193
stepped cross, 398, *399*
stepped patterns, *355,* 359–60, *359,* 383, *383*
Stocklet, Phillippe R., 431
stone, 159, 160, *160–61,* 184, *184*
bituminous, 28
black, 185
grayish brown, 318, *318*
moulds made of, 257–58, *257*
red, 82, *82*
stone drill, 393, 395
Stone shoe (cat. no. 266), 356, 375, *375*
storm god, 215, *215*
Striding horned demons (cat. no. 15), 46–48, *46–48*
Striding male figure with a box on his head (cat.
no. 38), 79–80, *79*
String of beads (cat. no. 3), 17–18, *17*
String of beads (cat. no. 159), 233, *233, 244*
String of beads (cat. no. 197), 296, *296*
String of beads (cat. no. 201), 300–302, *301*
String of beads (cat. no. 280), 393–94, *393*
String of beads (cat. no. 281), 394, *394*
String of beads with quadruple-spiral pendant (cat.
no. 78), 129–30, *129*
String of crenellated beads (cat. no. 248), 354–55, *354*
String of etched carnelian beads (cat. no. 208), 312,
312
Strings of beads (cat. no. 80), 132, *132*
Strings of beads (cat. no. 85), 35, 143–45, *144,* 181
Strings of beads (cat. no. 167), 263, *263*
Strings of beads (cat. no. 168), 264, *264*
Strings of beads (cat. no. 196), 294, 295–96, *295*
Strings of etched carnelian and other beads (cat. no.
79), 79–80, *79–80*

Subartu, 222
Subir, 222
Sud (goddess), 453
sukkal (minister), 75, 76
Sulaiman Hills, 390
Sumer, 4, 21–36, 93, 189, 470
as center of civilization, 8, 8n16
graves with rulers and attendants in, 32
map of, *10*
Sumerian Flood Story, 9
Sumerian King List, 21, 35, 89, 143, 189, 417, 472,
477
cuneiform prism with, 467–68, *467*
Gilgamesh in, 480
Great Flood in, 488
variant texts of, 467
Sumerian language, 4
cuneiform. *See* cuneiform inscriptions—in
Sumerian language
Eblaite dictionary of, 167, 458–49, *458*
Old Babylonian schools and, 454–56
overview of literature in, 485
as predominant in Ur III period, 417
taught later as dead language, 455
See also poetry
"Sumerian Renaissance," 417
Sumerograms, 459
Sumu-ilum (king of Larsa), 441n3
Surpassing All Other Kings (epic), 479
Susa, 42, 352n7
Akkadian booty found at, 189, 191–97, *192, 193,*
196, 199, 205
beads of, 243, 201–3, *202,* 300–302, *301*
bird-demon of, 374
copper pins of, 351
Etana myth from, 477
Harappan cubical weights from, 401–2, *402*
interconnections with, 251, 350
lexical tablets of, 453
relief boulder at, 422
sculpture of, 298, *299,* 342–43, *342,* 388, *388*
seals of, 23, *24, 45,* 54, *319,* 246, 410–11, *410, 411*
shell bangle from, 398, *398*
temple of, 401–2
Treasure of Ur and, 139, 140n6
vessels of, 327, 341–43, 352n7
Suter, Claudia, 429, 442
Syr Darya (Jaxartes River), 4
Syria, 4, 7, 8, 19, 34, 95, 135, 136, 184, 244, 331
Anatolia and, 276n3
cuneiform in, 453
maps of, *234, 236, 414*
North Caucasus and, 289
Sargon of Akkad's conquests in, 36, 168
urbanization of, 164
Syrian style, 231
Syro-Cilicia, 272
Syros, 270

tabletop or tray, 121–22, *122*
Tagrish-Damu (princess of Ebla), 464
Takirbai culture, 350
Talmessi mine, 310
tankard, one-handled, 255
Tar'am-Agade (daughter of Naram-Sin), 225, 227
Tarut, 244, 245, 316, 325–28, 330, 331, 334, 339, 341
Tashkent, 339

Taurus Mountains, 135, 136, *238*
Tedzhen River, 348, 355
Tehran Museum, 337
Tell Abraq, 307–8, 313–17, *313–17,* 350
Tell Abu Salabikh, 465
Tell Agrab, 58, 59, 80, 83, 210. *See also* Shara—
temple of
Tell al Ubaid, 20, 26, 68, 83–88, *84–88,* 306
temple frieze of, 28, *28*
Tell Asmar. *See* Eshnunna
Tell Banat, 169, 170, 172, 184–86, *184–86*
Tell Beydar (Nabada), 159, 453
Tell Brak (Nagar), 159, 228
in Akkadian period, 140, 173, 183, 221
beads of, 231–33, *232, 233,* 244
cuneiform in, 453
Eblaite cuneiform tablet regarding, *463,* 464
Eye Temple at, *18–19,* 19–20, 87
moulded nude female figure from, 257–58, *257*
pendants of, 180, 181, 231–32, *232,* 261, 290
sculpture of, 230–31, *231*
seals of, 229–30, *229,* 267, 322n6
Tell Chuera, 62
Tell el 'Oueili, 47
Tell Halaf. *See* Guzanna
Tell Hariri. *See* Mari
Tell Ingharra. *See* Kish
Tell Malyan, 349, 360
Tell Mardikh. *See* Ebla
Tell Mozan. *See* Urkesh
Tell Munbaqa, 218
Tello. *See* Girsu
Tell Qannas. *See* Habuba Kabira
Tell Qara Quzak, 183
Tell Sa'ad, 318, 320
Tell Selenkahiye, 164, 233, 273, *273*
Tell Umm el-Marra, 179–86, *179–86. See also* Tuba
temenos (Gonur-depe), 366
Temple Oval (Khafajah), 81
temples, 6, 55–88
architectural description of, 427
conventional depiction of, 74, *74*
dedicated stone vessels in, 155–56, *155*
foundations for, 80
Late Uruk conventional depiction of, 74, *74*
palacelike structure of, 419
reconstructed facade of, *84*
ruler and building of, 31, *31,* 418, 420, *444, 445–*
47, *446*
votive figures in. *See* votive figures
Tepe Gawra. *See* Gawra
Tepe Giyan, 352
Tepe Hissar, 243, 304, 349–54, *351–53,* 364
Tepe Malyan. *See* Anshan
Tepe Nush-i Jan, 244
Tepe Sialk, 351
Tepe Yahya, 244, 317, 322n6, 325, 328, 336, 343n3,
349, 350, 372
chlorite fragments from, 343, *343,* 344, *344*
Terek River, 292
terracotta, 280, 352, 353, 357, *357,* 483, *483*
Harappan, 378, 380, 382–83, *382, 383,* 389–92,
388–91, 395
Texier, Charles, 277
Thebes, 270
Thermi, 270
Thessaly, 255

Three-sided moulded tablet with a boat and gharial (cat. no. 299), 406, *406*
Thyreatis, 255, 260, 270
ti (rib), 475
Tiamat (deity), 217, 487
tiger-men, *209*, 246, 409n10
tigers, 247, 374, 380, 402, 403, 407, *407*, *408*, 409
Tigris River, 4, 5, 68, 423
tin, 307, 308
    bronze as alloy of copper and, 310
    copper combined with, 304, 305n7
    sources of, 310
Tin (city), 462
Tinney, Steve, 183
Tir (administrator), 462
Tishatal (king of Urkesh), 81, 222, 224
titanium oxide, 393
Titris Höyük, 257
toggle pins, 122, *124*, 125–27, *126*, *127*, 182
Togolok 21, 350, 368
Torso of a "priest-king" (cat. no. 272a), 385–88, *386–87*
Tosi, Maurizio, 7
    "Pathways across Eurasia" (with C. C. Lamberg-Karlovsky), 347–50
Tower of Babel, *492*, 493–94
trade, 239–50. *See also* interconnections
trans-Elamite culture, 7, 355, 388, *388*
Trapezoidal Archive, Ebla, 167
Treasure of Ur, Mari, 139–47, *140–46*, 180, 181
Tribute List, 451
Troad, 260, 270
Troy, 8
    anthropomorphic jar from, 274, *274*
    beads of, 182, 185, 233, 243, 263–67, *263–66*
    bracelets from, *262*, 352
    depas amphikypellon of, 273
    destruction of Ebla compared to siege of, 168
    earrings of, 266–67, *267*, *269*, 271
    freestanding houses at, 255, 262
    gold pins from, 265, *265*, 352n1
    moulded nude female figures from, 258
    "wooden chest" of, 184
"Trumpet" with three bison heads (cat. no. 256), 364, *364*
Tsarskaya. *See* Novosvobodnaya
Tuba, 179
Tubkhu-Hadda (son of minister), 464
Tukrish, 347, 474
Tuli (kitchen head), 226
Tumbler (cat. no. 67b), 116, 117, *117*
Tupkish (king of Urkesh), 224–26
Turbinella pyrum, 398
Tureng-tepe, 349
Turkmen Academy of Sciences, Ashkhabad, 349
Turkmenistan, 311, 340, 347, 351n1, 354, 359, *359*, *395*. *See also* Altyn-depe; Gonur-depe; National Museum
turquoise, 243, 249n22, 295–96, *295*, 353, 394
    kidney-shaped inlays of, 356, *356*
    sources of, 251, 353
Tutub. *See* Khafajah
Two-pronged hooks (cat. no. 198), 297, *297*
two seated figures, 332, *332*

Ubaid. *See* Tell al Ubaid
Ubar-Tutu (father of Gilgamesh), 468, 489, 472, 493

Ubil-Eshtar (brother of king of Akkad), 220
Uduhudu, 465
Ugarit, 167, 168, 223
Ukin-Ulmash (son of Naram-Sin), 227
Ulmash temple (Agade), 197
Umma (Jokha), 21, 51, 62, 68–69, 189, 246
    gold plaque of queen of, 78, *78*
Umm al-Qaiwan, 307, 313, 315
Umm an-Nar Island, 307, 308, 313–17, *313–16*
Unicorn figurine (cat. no. 276), 390, *390*
unicorns, 246, 380, 404, *404*
Universität Zürich, Archäologische Sammlung, 38
University of Chicago, Oriental Institute of the, 48, 50, 58, 73, 80, 333, 435
University of Pennsylvania Museum of Archaeology and Anthropology, 32, 55, 56, 58, 59, 72, 82, 85–87, 93, 102–5, 107, 109–11, 114–18, 121, 129, 130, 132, 200, 265, 268, 341, 353, 400, 401, 443, 466, 468–72, 474–76, 478
Upright leopard (cat. no. 112), 173, *173*
Uqnitum (queen of Urkesh), 224–26, *226*
Ur
    beads of, 33, 112, *112*, 122–28, *124*, 126–32, 129–32, 181, 182, 289–44, 263, *263*, 264, 266, *266–67*, 266, *289*, 397
    as capital of southern Mesopotamia, 15
    cemetery of, 32–35, 91, 180, 243
        Great Death Pit, 32, 94–95, 109, 110, 120–27, *120–27*
        Royal Cemetery, 93–117, *93–117*, 156, 217, 221, 243, 244, 266, 268n1, 289, 290, 305, 312
    City Seal impression of, 54, *54*
    cone mosaics in, 19
    cuneiform of, 452
    cylinder seals of, *34*, 54, *54*, 91, 103, *103*, 217, 311, 410–11, *410*
    dagger from, 102, *102*
    entu-priestess of, 74–75, *74*, 200–201, *200*
    game board from, 101, *101*
    goddess of. *See* Nanna
    human sacrifice at, 94–96, *94*
    inlays of, 90, 175
    interconnections with, 136, 255, 307, 312, 315
    jewelry and headdresses from, 33, 110–14, *110–14*, 122–33, *123–33*, 180, 221, 243, 266, 392
    knowledge of kings of, 21
    lion plaque of, 104–5, *104*
    Lipit-Eshtar and, 471
    literary tablets of, 454
    Magan (Oman) tribute to, 308
    pendants of, 145, 180
    sculpture of, 32, 83, 114–16, *114–16*, 121–22, *121*, 213, *213*
    stamp seals of, 246, 410, *410*, 412, 413, *413*
    Third Dynasty of (Ur III), *414*, 417–19, 443, 453–54, 467, 479, 488
        fall of, 469–70, *469–70*
    Treasure of (Mari), 139–47, *140–46*, 180, 181
    vessels of, 116–18, *116–19*, 400, *400*
    ziggurat of, *421*
    See also "Great Lyre"; Shulgi; "Standard of Ur"
Urab (scribe), 208
Ur-Ashgi (governor of Adab), 435
Ur-Ba'u (king of Lagash), 81, 417, 420, *420*, 422, 436, 439
Urfa Museum (Turkey), 257

urials, 313–14, *314*, 351n1, 390
Urkesh (Tell Mozan), 81, 222–27, *224*, *225–27*
Ur-Namma (king of Ur; 2097–2080 B.C.), 15, 349, 417, 454, 479
    architecture of, *421*, 422
    battlefield death of, 453
    cylinder seal with mention of, 447–48, *447*
    "law code" of, 471
    statue of, 446–47, *446*
    Stele of, 417–18, 435, *417–18*, *435*, 443–46, *444–45*
Ur-Nanshe (king of Lagash; ca. 2450 B.C.), 31, *31*, 68–69, 71, *71*, 80, 420
Ur-Nanshe (singer), 138, 152–53, *152–53*, 170
Ur-Ningirsu (king of Lagash), statues of, 29, 419, 422, 431–35, *432–34*
Ur-Pabilsag (king of Ur), 96
Urshanabi (ferryman), 480
Uruk (Warka), 11–23, 42, 54, 69, 80, 86, 145, 215, 306, 327, 454, 471
    accounting system of, 13, 305
    cylinder seals of, 13, 14, 23, *23*, *24*, 39–41, *40*, 52, 87
    E-anna Precinct in, 12, *12*, 16–18, 337, 481–82
    Egyptian interconnections with, 251
    Gilgamesh as legendary king of, 15, 479
    goddess of. *See* Inanna
    knowledge of kings of, 21
    lion-hunt stele from, *22*, 23
    natural world in art of, 423
    North Caucasus and, 289
    poem on rivalry between Aratta and, 472–73, *473*
    sculpture of, 16–17, *16–17*, 25–26, *25*, 38, *38*, 170
    temples of, 12, 14, 15, 74, *74*
    written texts of, 451, 457
    ziggurat of, 24
    See also Enmerkar; Lugalkisalsi
Urukagina (king of Lagash), 69
Uruk Vase, 14, 16n, 24, *24–25*, 75n8, 80, 423, 480–81
Ushumgal (god), 53, 453
Ushumgal (priest), 53, *53*
Usmu (Ea's vizier), *213*, 214
Uta-napishti (survivor of Great Flood), 56, 480, 493
Uttu (spider goddess of weaving), 474–75, 487
Utu (god), 147, 214, 468, 470
Utuhengal (king of Uruk), 15
Uzbekistan, 245, 308, 339, 347, 349, 352n, 354

Van de Mieroop, Marc, 239
Vase à la cachette (cat. no. 202), 302–5, *302–4*, 306, *306*
vegetation deities, 215–16, *216*, 413, *413*, 443
Vereshchagin, N. K., 292
Veselovsky, Nikolai Ivanovich, 289, 290, 292, 294, 295, 297
Vessel (cat. no. 193), 291, 294, *294*
Vessel with crenellated pattern (cat. no. 252), 359, *359*
Vessel dedicated for Iku-Shamagan (cat. no. 94), 30, 155–56, *155*
Vessel fragment with a hero, bull-man, and lion (cat. no. 219), 319–20, *320*
Vessel fragment with an image of a goddess (cat. no. 36), 77–78, *77*
Vessel fragment with a leopard (?) and snake (cat. no. 233), 336, *336*
Vessel fragment with a palm tree (cat. no. 225a), 328, *328*

Vessel fragment with a procession of musicians (cat. no. 230), 245, 333–34, *333*

Vessel fragment with a snake and eagle (cat. no. 234), 337, *337*, 342, 373

Vessel fragment with a woven pattern (cat. no. 240), 342, *342*

Vessel fragments (cat. no. 241), 342–43, *342*

Vessel fragments (cat. no. 242), 343, *343*

Vessel fragments with figural and geometric designs (cat. no. 224), 326–28, *326–27*

Vessel fragments with a figure and a tree (cat. no. 231), 30, 334, *334*

Vessel stand with ibex support (cat. no. 40), 81–82, *81*

Vessel with incised decoration (cat. no. 192), 289, 291, 282, *293*

Vessels with guilloche and zigzags (cat. no. 237), 340, *340*

Vessels with nude heroes and animals in relief (cat. no. 16), 48–50, *49*

vesuvianite, 394, *394*

Vorderasiatisches Museum, Berlin, 16–19, 23, 42, 56, 64, 77, 81, 83, 122, 434, 437, 457, *481–83*, 492

votive figures, 70, *70*
   of Adab, 63–64, *63–64*
   Akkadian, 193–94, *193*, 413, *413*
   of Diyala region, 59–61, *59–61*
   of Lagash, 29–30, *30*
   of Mari, 35, 148–55, *148–55*
   of Nippur, 66–67, *67*
   seated couples as, 155, *155*
   of Susa, 298, *299*
   of Tell Chuera, 62–63, *62*
   of Uruk, 16–17, *17*

vulture, 330–31, *331*

walking sticks, Inlays of men holding (cat. no. 103), 160–61, *160–61*

Wallenfels, Ronald, 140

Wall nails inlaid with rosettes (cat. no. 45), 86–87, *86*

Wall plaque with banquet and animal attack scene (cat. no. 200), 30, 300, *300*

Wall plaque with banqueters and musicians (cat. no. 32), 30, 33, 73, *73*, 109

Wall plaque with libation scenes (cat. no. 33), 30, 74–75, *74*, 76, 78

Wall plaque of Ur-Nanshe and family (cat. no. 30), 30, 31, 71, *71*

Warka. *See* Uruk

warriors. *See* soldiers

water buffaloes, 197, 208–9, *209*, 217, 227, *227*, 231, *231*, 247, 330, 380, 405, *405*, 407, *408*
   ancient sacrifice of, 409

Weber, Otto, 333

weights, 244–45, 325, 328, *329*, 334, 339, *339*, 363, *363*
   Eblaite system of, 460
   Harappan cubical, 401–2, *401–2*

"When on High," 486–87

"Where Flesh Came Forth," 486

White Temple, Uruk, 12, 14, 15

wigs. *See* headdresses

wild asses. *See* onagers

Wild goat pendant (cat. no. 117), 180, *180*

Winckler, H., 277

Wittkower, Rudolf, 338

wolves, 360–62, *361, 362*

womb-shaped (kidney-shaped) motif, 397, *397*, 398, *399*, 404, *404*

women
   literate, 454
   See also priestesses

wood, metal-covered, 85, *85*, 105, *105*, 172–73, *173*

wood and shell furniture plaque and panels, 170, *171*, 174, *174*

wood coffins, 184

wood sculpture, 36, 85, *85*, 171

Woolley, Sir Leonard, 32–34, 75, 84–87, 93–97, 101, 103, 108, 111, 113–16, 118, 120, 122–24, 128, 132, 144, 180, 243, 443, 445

Worcester Art Museum, Massachusetts, 59

woven pattern. *See* mat-weave pattern

wreaths (cat. no. 61c), 110–11, *110–11*

writing
   beginnings of, 451–52
   goddess of, 455
   poem on origin of, 472–73, *473*
   See also clay tablets; cuneiform inscriptions; cylinder seals; stamp seals

Xabis, 317, 349

Xinjiang, 347, 350

X-ray diffraction, 345n2, 354

Yale Babylonian Collection, New Haven, 24, 39, 202, 321

Yamhad kingdom, 179

Yamuna River, 381

Yanup (king of Mari), 463

Yarim-Lim I (of Aleppo), 168

Yarmuti, 168

Yazd, 353

Yellow Period (at Poliochni, ca. 2450–2200 B.C.), 270–73

Zagros Mountains, 15, 48, 195, 298, 348

Zahedan, 353

Zamanbaba, 354

Zamena (wet nurse), 226

zebus, 245–47, 306, 330–31, *330, 331*, 375, *375*, 380, 404, 405, *405*, 410–11, *410, 411*

Zeravshan River, 347, 348

ziggurats, *492*
   building of, at Mari, *146*, 147
   Tower of Babel compared to, *492*
   of Tureng-tepe, 349
   of Ur, *421*
   of Uruk, 24

zigzag pattern, 340, *340*, 341, *341*

Ziusudra (survivor of Great Flood), 472, 478, 489

Zoroastrianism, 350

Zurghul. *See* Nina

PHOTOGRAPH CREDITS

Photographs were in most cases provided by the owners of the works and are reproduced by their permission; their courtesy is gratefully acknowledged. Additional credits follow.

Maurice Aeschimann, Geneva © George Ortiz
    cat. no. 18 (rear view)
From Akurgal 2001   figs. 78, 80
Guillermo Algaze   cat. no. 163b
Alinari, Florence   fig. 115
From Alkim 1983   cat. no. 170
From Amiet 1966   fig. 8
From Amiet 1977a   figs. 11b, 106
From Amiet 1980   figs. 21, 28
© Friends of the Ashmolean Museum, Oxford
    cat. nos. 10c, 48–51, 160, 330
From Borker-Klahn 1982   fig. 61
Bernard Von Bothmer   fig. 13
From Brandes 1979   fig. 7
© The Trustees of the British Museum, London
    cover, cat. nos. 9, 16a, 29, 33–35, 44a, 52, 53, 55a,
    56, 60a, 66, 67a, 70b, 72–76, 132, 138, 139, 143,
    147, 148, 150, 163c, 164, 227, 229 (seal), 301a, b,
    315, 319, fig. 85
Dean Brown (2000), courtesy the Brooklyn
    Museum of Art   cat. nos. 14, 15a
Giorgio Buccellati   fig. 65
Hillel Burger   cat. nos. 242, 243
From Canby 2001   fig. 109
Paul Collins   fig. 43
From Collon 1987   figs. 64, 114
From Collon 1995   fig. 30
Corbis   pp. 238, 254, 376, 416
From Delaporte 1920   fig. 108
Jean M. Evans   pp. 134, 228
Giorgos Fafalis   cat. nos. 162, 165, 166, 168, 171,
    172, 174–78a, 179
From Fortin 1999, Deir ez-Zor Museum, Syria
    Jacques Lessard, photographer   cat. nos. 99,
    106, 157a
From Fortin 1999, Idlib Museum, Syria
    Jacques Lessard, photographer   cat. nos. 115e, 322c
From Fortin 1999, National Museum, Aleppo
    Mohamad Al-roumi, photographer   cat. no. 232
From Fortin 1999, National Museum, Aleppo
    Jacques Lessard, photographer   cat. nos. 88, 93,
    96, 97, 107b
From Fortin 1999, National Museum, Damascus
    Jacques Lessard, photographer   cat. nos. 25, 81,
    84, 85a, b, 89a, 92a
From Frankfort 1955   figs. 25, 71a
From Gelb, Steinkeller, and Whiting 1991   fig. 22
Anwar Abdel Ghafour   cat. nos. 6, 7, 82, 83, 85c,
    86, 87a–c (seals), 89b, c, 90, 91b, 92b, 94, 95, 98,

100a, b, 102–5, 107a, 108–26, 151, 152, 154–156,
    158, 159, 161, 163a, 231, 322a, b, 323–28
From Hall and Woolley 1927   fig. 29
Donald P. Hansen   fig. 42
Robert Harding Picture Library   p. 2
From Harper, Aruz, and Tallon 1992   figs. 12, 55,
    56, 59
Fredrik T. Hiebert   p. 356
From Heinrich 1936   fig. 10
From Hinz 1969   fig. 92
Hirmer Verlag photo archive   figs. 5, 9, 11a, 14, 18,
    54
From Indus Civilization 2000   figs. 100c, 299
From Invernizzi 1992   figs. 58, 87
Catherine Jarrige   cat. nos. 268a, 269, 270a, b, 271,
    302a
From Joshi and Parpola 1987   figs. 71b, 100a, 101
Jonathan Mark Kenoyer   figs. 93–99
Jonathan Mark Kenoyer © HARP, courtesy the
    Department of Archaeology and Museums,
    Ministry of Minorities, Culture, Sports, Tourism,
    and Youth Affairs, Government of Pakistan
    cat. nos. 267, 268b, 272, 274, 275, 277–82, 285–
    87a, 288, 293–98, 300a, c, d, 302b
Kjaerum 1983   cat. no. 218 (impression)
Paul Lachenauer, Photo Studio, The Metropolitan
    Museum of Art, New York   cat. nos. 28, 101
    (impression), 144, 145, 225b, 226, 254, 256, 318b,
    320
Paul Lachenauer, Photo Studio, The Metropolitan
    Museum of Art, New York © The Pierpont
    Morgan Library, New York   cat. nos. 141, 283,
    289a, 290a, 292a
From Legrain 1936   figs. 17, 24
Yoram Lehmann, Jerusalem © George Ortiz
    cat. no. 18 (front view)
From Leiden 1986   cat. no. 180
From Lloyd 1967   fig. 77
Musée du Louvre, Paris, photo archive   fig. 52, 53
From Mallowan 1964   fig. 6
Jean-Claude Margueron   figs. 38–40
From Masson 1988   fig. 90
From Matthews 1993   fig. 23
From Matthiae 1980a   figs. 44, 46
Paolo Matthiae   fig. 45, p. 450
R. H. Meadow © HARP, courtesy the Department
    of Archaeology and Museums, Ministry of
    Minorities, Culture, Sports, Tourism, and Youth
    Affairs, Government of Pakistan   cat. no. 300b
From Mode 1959   fig. 100b
From Moortgat 1969   fig. 4
From Moortgat 1988   figs. 110, 111, 120
© The Pierpont Morgan Library, New York
    cat. nos. 140, 142, 146, 318a, 340

© Museum of Fine Arts, Boston   cat. nos. 131, 276,
    283, 284, 289a, 290a, 292a
From Oates, Oates, and McDonald 2001   fig. 69
From Orthmann 1975   figs. 15, 16, 27, 47, 104, 108
From Parrot 1968   cat. nos. 87a–c (impressions),
    fig. 41
From Postgate 1992   fig. 3
D. T. Potts   fig. 83
Anandroop Roy   figs. 1, 2, 51, 70a, b, 72–74, 84,
    102
From Sarianidi 1998b   cat. no. 258
Scala/Art Resource, New York   figs. 117, 122
From Schatten uit Turkije, no. 67   fig. 76
Glenn Schwartz   figs. 48, 50
From Sekai bijutsu daizenshu 2000   figs. 37, 57
From Shliman, Peterburg, and Troia 1998
    cat. no. 197
From Tallon 1992   fig. 103
From Treasures of Ancient Bactria 2002   cat. no. 257
    (rolled out)
The University of Pennsylvania Museum of
    Archaeology and Anthropology, by which all
    rights are reserved   cat. nos. 21, 22, 24c, d, 31,
    41, 43, 44b, 45–47, 54, 55b, 57–59, 60b, c, 61–65,
    67b, 68–70a, 71, 77–80, 128, 169a, 173b, 238,
    247a–d, 290b, 291, 317, 329, 331–39, 341
From Weiss 1985, National Museum, Damascus
    cat. no. 91a
Bruce White   cat. nos. 26, 39, 130, 167, 169b, 181–
    87a, 188–90, 205–18 (seal), 219–25a, 234, 239,
    240, 301e
Bruce White, courtesy Musée du Louvre, Paris
    cat. nos. 30, 37, 127, 129, 135, 137, 153a, 164, 199–
    204, 228, 241, 244, 248, 261, 273, 287b, 289b,
    292b, 301c, d, 303, 304, 307, 310, 313, 314, 316,
From Woolley 1934   figs. 31, 32, 34–36
From Woolley 1939   fig. 105
From Woolley 1955   fig. 60
Joseph Zehari, courtesy The Pierpont Morgan
    Library, New York   cat. nos. 10a, b (impressions),
    133, 134, 157b
From Zettler and Horne 1998   fig. 33

Additional credits for drawings:

Pnina Arad, courtesy The Israel Museum, Jerusalem
    fig. 116
Joan Aruz   figs. 19a, b
Giorgio Buccellati   fig. 66
Pietro Pozzi   figs. 67, 68
Barbara Stuart   fig. 49
Simon Sullivan   figs. 62, 63, 88
Jo Wood-Brown   figs. 91a, b